追寻经贸足迹 扬起伟业风帆

中国对外经济贸易年鉴

中国对外经济贸易年鉴编辑委员会

（总第十七期）

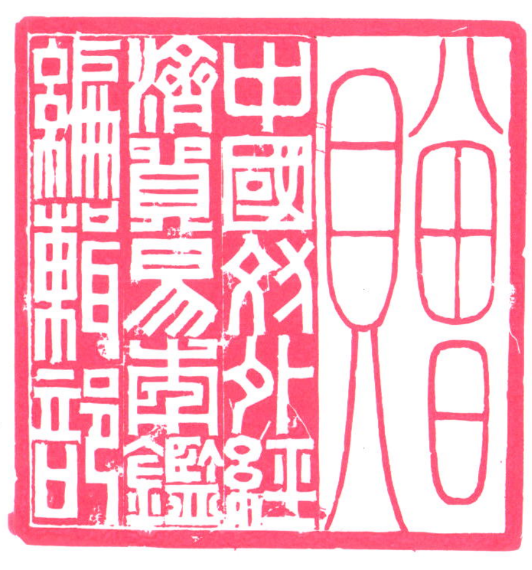

2000

中国对外经济贸易出版社

京工商广临字2000116号

图书在版编目（CIP）数据

中国对外经济贸易年鉴．2000／中国对外经济贸易年鉴编辑委员会编．－北京：中国对外经济贸易出版社，2000.9

ISBN 7-80004-825-X

Ⅰ．中…　Ⅱ．中…　Ⅲ．对外贸易－中国－2000－年鉴　Ⅳ．F752-54

中国版本图书馆CIP数据核字（2000）第39113号

责任编辑　钟边武
版式设计　张瑞文
责任校对　李可钦

中国对外经济贸易年鉴2000
中国对外经济贸易年鉴编辑委员会
中国对外经济贸易出版社　出版发行
北京安定门外大街东后巷28号　邮政编码100710
新华书店北京发行所　发行
兵器工业出版社印刷厂　印刷
787×1092毫米　16开本　58.5印张　84插页　1756千字
2000年9月第1版　2000年9月第1次印刷
印数：5000

ISBN-7-80004-825-X
Z·89

定价：360.00元

2000年5月19日，国家主席江泽民在北京中南海会见前来与中方举行中欧关于中国加入世界贸易组织谈判的欧盟委员会贸易委员帕斯卡尔·拉米。

2000 年 2 月 17 日，国务院总理朱镕基在北京中南海会见世界贸易组织总干事穆尔。

2000年5月10日，中国和比利时港务研讨会在北京召开。国务委员吴仪和比利时王储菲利普出席会议并致辞。这是在研讨会上，菲利普王储和吴仪为欧中商务合作中心新建的专业商务网站——“欧中在线”开通而共同按动电钮。

1999年11月15日，中美在北京签署关于中国加入世贸组织的双边协议。这是中国外经贸部部长石广生和美国贸易代表巴尔舍夫斯基在签署协议。

中国对外开放格局图示

1981年7月，国家决定在深圳、珠海、汕头和厦门设立经济特区；1984年5月，国家决定进一步开放14个沿海港口城市；1985年2月，国家决定将长江三角洲、珠江三角洲和闽南厦漳泉三角地区开放为沿海经济开发区；1988年3月，国家决定将沿海经济开放区扩展到辽东半岛、山东半岛以及其他沿海地区的城市，批准设立海南经济特区；1990年国家决定开发和开放上海浦东新区；1992年，国家进一步开放6个沿江港口城市、13个内陆边境城市和18个内陆省会城市，批准设立保税区；1994年，国家决定设立苏州工业园区。

一、经济特区：5个（23个市、县）

二、沿海开放城市：15个

三、沿海经济开放区

辽宁省：（23个市、县） 河北省：（14个市、县）

天津市：（5个县） 山东省：（31个市、县）

江苏省：（47个市、县） 浙江省：（34个市、县）

福建省：（37个市、县） 广东省：（57个市、县）

广西壮族自治区：（6个市、县） 上海市：（6个县）

四、沿江开放城市：9个

五、省会（首府）开放城市：18个

六、沿边开放城镇：13个市、县、镇

七、国家级经济技术开发区：32个

八、保税区：15个

九、边境经济合作区：14个

十、高新技术产业开发区：53个

十一、国家旅游度假区：11个

十二、三峡经济开放区：17个县、市

一、经济特区

二、沿海开放城市

三、沿海经济开放区

四、沿江开放城市

五、省会开放城市

同中国签有经济贸易协定、投资保护协议和避免双重征税协定的国家和地区简表

截止 1999 年 12 月 31 日

“●”表示同我国签有贸易协定或议定书及经济合作协定的国家和组织（21 个）

“▲”表示同我国签有双边投资保护协定的国家和地区（93 个）

“◆”表示同我国签定避免双重征税协定的国家（65 个）

亚洲			
蒙古	● ▲ ◆	塔吉克斯坦	● ▲
朝鲜	●	乌兹别克斯坦	● ▲ ◆
韩国	● ▲ ◆	土库曼斯坦	● ▲
日本	● ▲ ◆	格鲁吉亚	● ▲
越南	● ▲ ◆	阿塞拜疆	● ▲
老挝	● ▲ ◆	亚美尼亚	● ▲ ◆
柬埔寨	● ▲	巴基斯坦	● ▲ ◆
缅甸	●	伊朗	● ▲
泰国	● ▲ ◆	科威特	▲ ◆
马来西亚	● ▲ ◆	沙特阿拉伯	▲
新加坡	▲ ◆	巴林	▲
菲律宾	● ▲ ◆	卡塔尔	▲
印度尼西亚	● ▲	阿拉伯联合酋长国	▲ ◆
尼泊尔	●	阿曼	▲
孟加拉国	● ▲ ◆	也门	▲
印度	● ◆	叙利亚	▲
斯里兰卡	● ▲	塞浦路斯	● ◆
哈萨克斯坦	● ▲	土耳其	● ▲ ◆
吉尔吉斯斯坦	● ▲	以色列	▲ ◆
黎巴嫩	▲		

非洲			
埃及	● ▲ ◆	吉布提	●
利比亚	●	肯尼亚	●
突尼斯	●	坦桑尼亚	●
阿尔及利亚	● ▲	卢旺达	●
摩洛哥	● ▲	布隆迪	●
毛里塔里亚	●	刚果	● ▲
马里	● ▲	加蓬	● ▲
佛得角	● ▲	安哥拉	●
几内亚	●	赞比亚	● ▲
科特迪瓦	●	莫桑比克	●
加纳	● ▲	毛里求斯	▲ ◆
多哥	●	津巴布韦	● ▲
贝宁	●	博茨瓦纳	●
尼日尔	●	纳米比亚	●
尼日利亚	● ▲	南非	● ▲
喀麦隆	● ▲	厄立特里亚	●
赤道内内亚	●	塞拉利昂	●
中非	●	索马里	●
埃塞俄比亚	● ▲	马达加斯加	●
苏丹	◆	塞舌尔	◆

欧洲			
冰岛	● ▲ ◆	瑞士	● ▲ ◆
丹麦	● ▲ ◆	荷兰	● ▲ ◆
挪威	● ▲ ◆	比利时	● ▲ ◆
瑞典	● ▲ ◆	卢森堡	● ▲ ◆
芬兰	● ▲ ◆	英国	● ▲ ◆
爱沙尼亚	● ▲ ◆	爱尔兰	● ◆
拉脱维亚	● ◆	法国	● ▲ ◆
立陶宛	● ▲ ◆	西班牙	● ▲ ◆
俄罗斯	● ▲ ◆	葡萄牙	● ▲ ◆
白俄罗斯	● ▲ ◆	意大利	● ▲ ◆
乌克兰	● ▲ ◆	马耳他	● ◆
摩尔多瓦	● ▲	南斯拉夫联盟	● ▲ ◆
波兰	● ▲ ◆	斯洛文尼亚	● ▲ ◆
捷克	● ◆	克罗地亚	● ▲ ◆
斯洛伐克	● ▲	马其顿	▲ ◆
匈牙利	● ▲ ◆	罗马尼亚	● ▲ ◆
德国	● ◆	保加利亚	● ▲ ◆
奥地利	● ▲ ◆	阿尔巴尼亚	▲ ◆
列支敦士登	瑞士托管	希腊	▲ ◆

大洋洲			
澳大利亚	● ▲ ◆	密克罗尼西亚联邦	●
新西兰	● ▲ ◆	萨摩亚	●
巴布亚新几内亚	● ▲ ◆	库克群岛	●
瓦努阿图	●	斐济	●
基里巴斯	●		

北美洲			
美国	● ◆	古巴	▲
墨西哥	●	牙买加	▲ ◆
特立尼达和多巴哥	●	加拿大	◆

南美洲			
哥伦比亚	●	巴西	● ◆
委内瑞拉	●	玻利维亚	● ▲
苏里南	●	智利	● ▲
厄瓜多尔	● ▲	阿根廷	● ▲
秘鲁	● ▲	乌拉圭	● ▲
巴巴多斯	▲		

序

对外贸易经济合作部部长
《中国对外经济贸易年鉴》编委会主任委员 石廣生

1999年是我国外经贸发展史上重要的一年。在这一年里，世界经济发展速度逐渐加快，由于中央继续采取了扩大内需等一系列政策，我国国民经济保持了较快的增长，为外经贸事业发展创造了良好的发展环境。党中央、国务院还制定了一系列支持外经贸发展的政策措施，成为外经贸发展的重要保障。在此基础上，经过各部门、各地方，尤其是外经贸行业广大干部职工的共同努力，我国外经贸事业在遭受亚洲金融危机的影响历经两年多的困难和徘徊局面后，终于重新步入了稳定增长的轨道。

对外贸易出现转折，出口转降为升，进口增长较快。全国进出口总额3607亿美元，增长11.3%，其中：出口1949亿美元，增长6.1%，进口1658亿美元，增长18.2%，贸易顺差291亿美元。出口的主要特点是：对主要市场出口仍保持较快的增长；出口商品结构进一步优化；由于国际市场商品价格普遍走低，我国出口商品价格也比上年同期有一定下降，但我们依靠增加出口数量实现了出口增长。进口是继1991年至1993年高速增长后的又一次高速增长，主要特点是：全年保持较高增长速度，并高于出口增长速度；一般贸易进口增长迅猛。

利用外资稳步发展。实际利用外资金额有所下降，但继续保持相当规模。全年合同外资金额412.38亿美元，下降20.90%；实际使用外资金额403.98亿美元，下降11.37%。中西部地区合同外资金额16.8亿美元，占全国合同外资总额的比重比去年同期略有增长。

对外承包工程和劳务合作取得新的进展,经营主体结构和市场结构有所优化。对外援助稳步发展，利用援外资金带动境外加工贸易和对外承包工程取得一定进展。

境外加工贸易初见成效,对外投资继续发展。经国家批准的境外加工贸易项目151个,中方投资额3.3亿美元。中方投资主体多为国内知名企业,承建的项目大多属于我国具有较强优势的行业,主要分布在亚洲、非洲、拉美、东欧和独联体等发展中国家和地区。

实施科技兴贸战略,成绩突出。与有关部门合作,出台了《外经贸部、科技部关于推动高新技术产品出口的指导性意见》,制订了《科技兴贸行动计划》和《高新技术产品出口目录》，积极推动高新技术产品出口，全年高新技术产品出口达247亿美元,比上年增长23%。

外经贸体制改革继续深化。建立了“审批从宽、管理从严”的新机制,积极推动生产企业进出口经营权由审批制向登记制转变；继续减少了出口许可证管理的商品种类,对配额许可证商品实行动态管理,初步建立对商品配额执行情况的核查反馈机制;完善了进出口配额分配、招标办法;改革了中国出口商品交易会,优化参展企业结构,优化展品结构。

“入世”谈判取得重大突破,多双边经贸关系进一步发展。我国先后同印尼、日本、澳大利亚、智利、美国和加拿大就我国加入世贸组织达成双边协议,都取得了“双赢”的结果。特别是与美国达成协议,是我国“入世”谈判的重大突破,大大加快了我国加入世贸组织的进程。我国积极参加亚太经合组织奥克兰会议和第三届亚欧会议,增进了亚太地区的经济技术合作,加强了亚欧经贸关系。我国与美、日、欧等主要经贸伙伴、周边国家和广大发展中国家的经贸关系快速发展、不断加强。

2000年版《中国对外经济贸易年鉴》较为全面、翔实地展示了1999年我国对外贸易、利用外资、对外经济技术合作等方面的改革与发展情况及其相关政策，是海内外各界人士了解和研究中国对外经济贸易发展的权威性工具书和史料性参考书。值此2000年版《中国对外经济贸易年鉴》出版之际,我谨代表外经贸部和《年鉴》编委会,向关心、支持我国外经贸发展,以及关心、支持和参与《年鉴》的编辑、出版工作的各地、各界朋友表示诚挚的谢意。

2000年是世纪交替之年,也是我国“九五”计划的最后一年。机遇与挑战并存。让我们共同携手,为促进新世纪中国外经贸的持续、健康发展做出新的贡献!

2000年7月

编　辑　说　明

一、《中国对外经济贸易年鉴》由中华人民共和国对外贸易经济合作部年鉴编辑委员会编纂，编委会主任、副主任分别由对外贸易经济合作部部长和海关总署领导担任。

二、本《年鉴》是一部详细记述中国对外经济贸易发展情况的政府年度出版物，是中国对外经济贸易领域仅有的一部专业性年鉴，创刊于1984年，每年出版一期，每期用中、英两种文字分册出版，本期为第17期。

三、本《年鉴》内容全面、系统，资料翔实，是海内外经济、贸易、工商、金融等各界人士了解、研究中国贸易、投资和对外经济合作的权威性工具书和史料性参考书。

四、本《年鉴》保持连续性和完整性，但上期刊登过的内容，下期不再重复。读者欲了解1998年或以前的中国对外经济贸易情况，请参阅前16期《年鉴》。

五、本期《年鉴》共设9个栏目，全面、系统地记述了1999年中国对外经济贸易发展情况；

（一）“文献”栏目。精选党和国家领导人关于中国经济形势、改革开放方针政策的论述等重要文件3篇；收录对外贸易经济合作部有关领导关于中国对外经济贸易政策和情况的文章或发言6篇，共9篇。

（二）“专文”栏目。约请对外贸易经济合作部部分职能司负责人和海关总署、国家进出口商品检验局、国家旅游局等部门有关负责人撰写我国对外经济贸易有关情况的文章，共13篇。

（三）“法规”栏目。收录1999年我国公布的涉外经济贸易法律、条例、规定、办法等，共67篇。

（四）“地方经贸”栏目。刊载包括台湾省在内的全国各省、自治区、直辖市、计划单列市、沿海开放城市、经济特区、香港和澳门特别行政区1999年对外经济贸易基本情况和统计数字，共57篇。

（五）“国别（地区）经贸”栏目。刊载13篇介绍1999年我国同有关国家和地区双边经济贸易关系的文章。

（六）“统计”栏目。包括对外贸易、利用外资和对外经济合作3个部分。

（七）“大事记”栏目。主要记载1999年全国对外经贸工作中的重要事件。

（八）“机构”栏目。刊登对外贸易经济合作部机关，各事业单位、各商会、协会、学会、各外贸中心、各特派员办事处、各省市、自治区外经贸厅（委）通讯录。

（九）“附录”栏目。分为两部分，第一部分刊有中国国民经济基本情况统计和中国对外经济贸易方面的大量信息资料；第二部分刊载有关世界黄金储备、外汇储备、进出口贸易、引进外资、经济援助和经济合作方面的统计数字，以及对外贸易经济合作部主要出版物介绍等。

六、“地方经贸”等栏目里的有关数字，由于统计口径、方法不一致，有些与“统计”栏目中的数字不完全一致，以“统计”栏目中的数字为准。

七、各省、自治区、直辖市的排列顺序，按照国务院行政区划统一规定的先后排列，计划单列市、沿海开放城市和经济特区等均排在其所属的省、自治区后面。

八、多年以来，本《年鉴》承蒙各部门、各地方、各公司和作者、译（审）者的积极支持协助，受到国内外广大读者的欢迎和鼓励，在此谨表示衷心谢意，并祈望继续给予关心和支持。对本《年鉴》存在的不足之处，诚请提出批评和改进意见，以使本《年鉴》日臻完善。来信请寄：北京市安定门外东后巷28号外经贸部《年鉴》编辑部，电话：010－64246856。

《中国对外经济贸易年鉴》编辑部

2000年7月于北京

《中国对外经济贸易年鉴》编辑委员会

《中国对外经济贸易年鉴》编辑人员

《中国对外经济贸易年鉴》特约撰稿人

尹　刚　对外贸易经济合作部亚洲司
许七一　对外贸易经济合作部亚洲司
赵刘庆　对外贸易经济合作部西亚非洲司
林　培　对外贸易经济合作部西亚非洲司
鲍　程　对外贸易经济合作部欧洲司
刘雪松　对外贸易经济合作部欧洲司
刘成军　对外贸易经济合作部美洲大洋洲司
程　蓉　对外贸易经济合作部美洲大洋洲司
杨石翟　对外贸易经济合作部美洲大洋洲司
李家鹏　对外贸易经济合作部美洲大洋洲司
邢玉芬　对外贸易经济合作部条约法律司
付　强　国际贸易经济合作研究院
刘雪琴　国际贸易经济合作研究院
邢厚媛　国际贸易经济合作研究院
薛　宏　国际贸易经济合作研究院
石宝祥　国家出入境检验检疫局
万中心　海关总署
李小维　国家统计局
黄洪博　国家外汇管理局
高顺礼　国家旅游局
张学群　北京市对外经济贸易委员会
穆　群　天津市对外经济贸易委员会
王密科　河北省对外贸易经济合作厅
吕美荣　秦皇岛市对外贸易经济合作局
刘付云　山西省对外贸易经济合作厅
李春生　内蒙古自治区对外贸易经济合作厅
王　迪　辽宁省对外贸易经济合作厅
徐　森　辽宁省对外贸易经济合作厅
苑宝清　沈阳市对外经济贸易委员会
姜中科　大连市对外经济贸易委员会
王海涛　吉林省对外贸易经济合作厅
孟繁军　长春市对外贸易经济合作局
朱丽华　黑龙江省对外贸易经济合作厅
徐　涛　哈尔滨市对外贸易经济合作局
乐淑君　上海市对外经济贸易委员会
宋义军　江苏省对外经济贸易委员会
黄建新　南京市对外经济贸易委员会
王百奇　连云港市对外经济贸易委员会
成昌宏　南通市对外经济贸易委员会
陈志成　浙江省对外贸易经济合作厅
沈洁玉　宁波市对外贸易经济合作委员会
汪丐罗　温州市对外贸易经济合作局
王凤鸣　安徽省对外经济贸易委员会
吴文华　福建省对外经济贸易委员会
黄寿荣　厦门市贸易发展委员会
朱光华　福州市对外经济贸易委员会
杨宝根　江西省国际经济贸易学会
蔡玉祥　山东省对外经济贸易委员会
窦　民　青岛市对外经济贸易委员会
姜英松　烟台市对外经济贸易委员会
卢凤英　河南省对外贸易经济合作厅
曹文铸　湖北省对外贸易经济合作厅
韩　菁　武汉市对外经济贸易委员会
张永青　湖南省对外经济贸易委员会
周树德　广东省对外贸易经济合作厅
曹卫红　广州市对外经济贸易委员会
赵铁成　深圳市贸易发展局
张晓君　珠海市对外经济贸易委员会
邱长奕　汕头市对外经济贸易委员会
孙海峰　湛江市对外经济贸易委员会
李亦之　广西壮族自治区对外贸易经济合作厅
蒋维明　北海市对外贸易经济合作局
杨照耀　海南省商贸经济合作厅
何德麟　重庆市对外贸易经济合作委员会
孙跃华　四川省对外贸易经济合作委员会
矫　晖　成都市对外贸易经济合作委员会
曾　韵　贵州省对外贸易经济合作厅
刘可杰　云南省对外贸易经济合作厅
冯林国　西藏自治区对外贸易经济合作厅
张　洁　陕西省对外贸易经济合作厅
苏福祥　西安市对外贸易经济合作局
李忠义　甘肃省对外贸易经济合作厅
公　保　青海省对外贸易经济合作厅
刘进国　宁夏回族自治区对外贸易经济合作厅
关　群　新疆维吾尔自治区对外贸易经济合作厅

目　　录

文　　献

第一部分

第二部分

专　　文

目录

法　　规

综　　合

对外贸易

目录

目录

利用外资

对外经济合作

海关、税收

金融、外汇

检验、检疫

地 方 经 贸

目录

国别（地区）经贸

统　　计

对外贸易

目录

附　　录

第一部分

第二部分

SUMEC

中设江苏机械设备进出口集团公司

CHINA JIANGSU MACHINERY & EQUIPMENT I/E GROUP CORP.

中设江苏机械设备进出口集团公司(SUMEC)，主要从事机电产品及轻纺产品的进出口业务。目前集团公司下属全资、控股及参股联营企业共20多家，业务范围包括进出口贸易、国内贸易、工业生产、实业投资、高新技术开发、房地产开发、商品展览等。进出口贸易是集团公司的主营业务，目前从事进出口贸易主要有六大子公司：江苏苏美达船舶工程有限公司、江苏苏美达成套设备工程有限公司、江苏苏美达机电国际贸易有限公司、江苏苏美达五金工具国际贸易有限公司、江苏苏美达轻纺国际贸易有限公司、江苏苏美达国际贸易有限公司。

公司始创于1978年。20年来，SUMEC本着“平等互利，服务至上”的宗旨，坚持以市场为导向，不断进行适应性调整，使公司业务保持了持续、快速、健康发展的良好势头，累计实现进出口额近30亿美元，曾多次被外经贸部、机电部、国务院机电办授予机电产品出口先进企业称号。1997年，SUMEC在全国进出口总额最大的500家企业中名列51位；1998年，完成进出口总额4.86亿美元，在全国进出口总额最大的500家企业中名列35位，集团公司因此荣获国务院、外经贸部及江苏省人民政府的表彰。

1999年，集团公司在保证进出口规模和经济效益继续取得较好成绩的同时，进一步加强管理，提高服务质量，全面通过ISO9002国际质量体系认证，顺利获得中国进出口商品质量认证中心(CQC)颁发的《质量体系认证证书》，并被外经贸部确定为首批重点联系企业。

世纪之交，SUMEC通过组建苏美达集团(SUMEC GROUP)，充分发挥集团的综合优势，在继续巩固发展商品经营的同时，积极发展资本、资产经营及高新技术产业，努力实现以商品经营为基础，商品经营与资本、资产经营协调发展，创造跨世纪发展新优势。

法人代表：

地　　址：南京市长江路198号
邮　　编：210018
电　　话：86-25-4511888(总机)
传　　真：86-25-4411772,4525966
互联网址：http://www.sumec.com
电子信箱：sumec@public1.ptt.js.cn

江苏春兰电器有限公司

Jiangsu Chunlan Electrical Appliance Co., Ltd.

春兰电器是春兰集团旗下五大产业集团之一，下辖八家制造工厂和一个研究所。产品主要有空调、冰箱、洗衣机、压缩机及彩电，年生产能力：空调200万台，冰箱100万台，洗衣机50万台，压缩机100万台，彩电100万台。并通过ISO9001标准认证；产品已获得BSI，HKQAA，T ü V，S，CE等国际认证，畅销世界82个国家和地区，并在中国香港、日本、新加坡、澳大利亚、意大利、法国、阿联酋、美国设立分公司，出口贸易额逐年成倍高速增长。

The company is the biggest one of five industrial groups subordinate to Chunlan Group, administers eight factories and one research institute. The products of the company are: Air Conditioner, boasts an annual productivity of two million and a half; Refrigerator, one million; Washing Machine, half a million; Compressor, one a million Color TV Set, one million. Chunlan won ISO9001 certificate at a very early time in China. The products have been awarded certificates by various prestigious international agencies, like the BSI in Britain, HKQAA in HongKong, T ü V in Germany, S in Argentina and CE in the European Economic Community. Chunlan air-conditioners, refrigerators and other products sell well in 82 countries and regions in the world, and had set up overseas offices in HongKong, Japan, Singapore, Australia, Italy, France, UAE and USA. The exportation of Chunlan products has been increasing rapidly in successive years.

地址：江苏省泰州市扬州路170号　邮编（P.C）：225300

Add：170 Yangzhou Road, Taizhou, Jiangsu, China

法人代表：李家成　联系人：蔡先生、李先生、王先生

President：Mr. Li Jiacheng　Contact：Mr. Cai, Mr. Lee, Mr. Wang

电话（Tel）：86-523-6601287/6601289　传真（Fax）：86-523-6560043

网址（Web Site）：http：//www.chunlan.com

E-mail：cleie.tz@public.tz.js.cn

伴随着时间的跨越，我们步入了一个崭新的时代。在中国电信事业飞速发展的今天，BISC公司的全体同仁经过艰苦的努力，走过了辉煌和不平凡的一年。回首1999年，北京国际交换系统有限公司在各方面取得了令人瞩目的业绩。在我们共同的努力下，我们的产品EWSD程控数字交换设备在国内销售总量达到3000万端口，同时，EWSD在世界的拥有量达到2亿端口。这是BISC公司自1998年EWSD在中国的销售总量突破2000万线之后的又一个历史性的突破。我们为迎来这一重要历史时刻而感到高兴和自豪。

BISC公司自1990年11月16日成立以来，在中国邮电通信事业迅猛发展的推动下，公司也得到了迅速的成长和壮大。从年产量30万线，到今天的年生产量700万线和年销售量达到600线，产品遍布全国29个省市自治区和直辖市的业绩，我们感到公司能够迅速成长的关键在于广大客户对我们的支持与信任，对BISC的产品的充分肯定和信赖。

展望新千年，我们更加充满信心：这是因为，EWSD产品自诞生以来，在技术和性能上从未停止不前它始终跟踪世界通信技术的发展和新通信业务的需要。BISC公司最新推出的SURPASS网络无限，并提供语音和数据相融合的业务，充分体现了BISC公司为用户提供先进技术愿望和实力。BISC公司已在全国设立了12个办事处和众多联络处，为广大客户提供优质的服务。BISC公司将以不断创新的精神，努力实现产品的市场占有率不断提高，提升产品质量和服务质量，成为用户信赖的朋友。BISC公司将和广大用户一道，在新的千年，共同开创我国电信事业美好的未来。

We stepped into a new era in accordance with the time crossing the century. At the circumstance of the speedy development of China Telecommunications Industry, BISC has also passed a brilliant and unordinary year 1999 by means of the efforts from all staff. Glance back at the past year, BISC has got great achievement from all aspects. Total Sales volume of our EWSD switching system has tooped 30 million ports in China and 200 million ports worldwide as well. It is a new historic breakthrough since its sales volume reached 20 million ports in China. We are highly proud of meeting this important historic moment.

Since its establishment of November 16, 1990. BISC has grown and developed fast with the blooming of China Telecommunications Industry. Its production capacity jumped to 7 million lines from 300 thousand lines and sales volume has reached 6 million lines per year. Our product EWSD has covered 29 provinces, municipalities and automatic regions. We realized that the key reason of great development is the big support and trust from our customers.

Looking ahead, we are full of confidence. It is attributed to our EWSD never stopping catching the new demand and technology of world telecommunications on its technology and performance, BISC has launched "SURPASS - Networking Beyond Limits°±, to provides the voice/date convergence service. BISC has set up 12 Regional Offices and Liaisons all over China in order to offer the best service to the customers. BISC will make good effort to improve its market-share, products quality and service with its constant creative spirit, and be the friends customers trust most as well. BISC will together with our customers to expand our brilliant future on Telecommunications Industry in New Millennium.

北京国际交换系统有限公司(BISC)

Beijing International Switching System Gorp.Ltd(BISC)

北京酒仙桥路14号　邮编：100016
电话：010-64346688　用户热线：010-64381234
传真：010-64363123
网址：http://www bisc.com.cn

Add.No.14 Jiu Xianqiao Road, Chaoyang District.
Beijing. P.R.China.　Post No:100016
Tel: 010-64346688　Hot Line: 010-64381234
Fax: 010-64363123　http: //www.bisc.com.cn

浙江中大集团控股有限公司

浙江中大集团控股有限公司是经省政府批准成立的实行国有资产授权经营的大型企业集团。公司现有浙江中大集团股份有限公司（上市公司）、浙江中大技术进出口集团有限公司、浙江省对外贸易公司、浙江中大商贸有限公司等4家直属企业，48家三级企业（其中外贸企业11家、内贸企业13家、工业企业9家、投资企业3家、海外企业或办事处12家）。公司总资产32.63亿元，净资产10.06亿元。

中大控股公司主要从事服装、纺织品、机电产品、成套设备、食品等进出口及国内贸易、工业生产、房地产开发、投资等业务，已形成外贸、内贸、工业、服务贸易同步发展的产业格局。1999年，公司实现利润1.55亿元，同比增长13.97%。

外贸是中大集团的经营主业，99年进出口总额8.46亿美元，其中出口创汇3.95亿美元，同比增长9.45%；收汇3.83亿美元，同比增长16.06%；内贸以品牌经营为手段，初步形成购物、娱乐、配货三大中心；中大房产以开发中高档精品楼盘为主，成为省内知名房产公司；工业以高科技为导向，以镍氢电池产业化基地、信息软件产业为重点的高科技产业体系正在形成中；以投资为主的服务贸易是企业新的利润增长点，发展势头良好。

中大控股公司将进一步解放思想、更新观念、抓住机遇、大胆实践、开拓创新，力争在三至五年内，成为以外贸为主业，集外贸、内贸、工业、服务贸易于一体的中大式综合商社型大企业。

Zhejiang Zhongda Group holding Co., Ltd. is a large enterprise group directly under the Zhejiang province grovernment. Currently it consists of 4 direct subsidiaries, namely Zhongda group Co., Ltd. (public listed), zhejiang zhongda technical imp. & exp. Co., Ltd. zhejiang foreign trade company, zhejiang zhongda commerce & trading Co., Ltd. 48 extention subsidiaries (11 in foreign trade, 13 in domestic trade, 9 in manufacturing, 3 in investment, 12 overseas). Total assets Yn3263m, net assets Yn 1006m.

Zhongda engages in 4 major business sectors: import & export of textiles, electro-mechnical products, complete plants and foods; domestic trade and real estate development; manufacturing; investment. It has formed an industrial pattern with synchronized development. In 1999, it earn profit of Yn 155m, up 29.2% over 1998.

Foreign trade is zhongda's mainstream business. In 1999, it's import and export turn-over of us$84.6m, of which export accounted 39.5m and up 9.45% over 1998; In the domestic trade sector, zhongda insisit in brand management, it consists of shopping, recveation and distribution centers; zhongda's real-estate devotes to high-quality bulidings, it's becoming famous company in province; zhongda is high-tech oriented, focusing on Ni-MH battery, software industry. Service trade is zhongda's new profit contributor, it has strong growth potential.

Zhongda is resolute to grow into, within 3-5 years, a comprehensive firm focusing in foreign trade, domestic trade, manufactuing and service trade.

地址：中国 · 杭州 · 中大广场A座
邮编：310003
电话：0086-0571-5777388
传真：0086-0571-5777008

Add：Tower A, Zhongda Plaza, Hangzhou, China
Post Code：310003
Tel：0086-0571-5777388
Fax：0086-0571-5777008

河北圣仑进出口集团公司
河北圣仑进出口股份有限公司

BRIEF OF HEBEI SHENGLUN IMP.&EXP.(GROUP)CORP. & HEBEI SHENG LUN I/E CORD.,LTD.

总经理：陈振国
General Manager:Chen Zhenguo

河北圣仑进出口集团公司是由原河北省服装进出口公司和原河北省针棉织品进出口公司全部产权合并，按照现代企业制度要求。进行公司制改造组建而成的国有外贸企业，现有职工588人，下辖7个综合部室和26家控股，参股公司，在美国、日本、韩国、中国香港、沙特、英国、德国、波兰、捷克等国家和地区设有9家海外企业及7家合资企业，总资产4.05亿元人民币，年进出口额2亿美元。

集团公司主要经营服装、针棉织品、毛织品、棉织品、粮油食品、土畜产品、非金属矿产品、黑色金属、有色金属、化工类产品(不含化学危险品)建筑材料、日用百货、轻工业品、纺织品、医药保健品、机械设备、仪器仪表、工农具、五金制品、机电产品、电子计算机配件、日用陶瓷、厚胎瓷、炻瓷美术陶瓷、抽纱制品、草柳制品、塑料雨衣、尼龙雨衣及塑料制品、鞋帽、丝毯、地毯、丝毛合织毯、皮件玻璃制品、工艺美术品(不含金银首饰)、人造花、玩具、圣诞礼品等商品及技术的进出口业务；开展“三来一补”进料加工业务；经营对销贸易和转口贸易。公司与370多家外商保持密切联系，产品行销世界五大洲99个国家和地区，1999年通过ISO9002国际标准质量体系认证及英国UKAS皇冠标志质量体系认证。“晚香玉”牌床上用品，“莲花池”牌阿袍、服装，“瑞香”牌毛衫，“足球”牌文化衫等商品享誉海内外。新注册的“圣仑”牌商标已与广大客户、商家见面。

我公司在进出口贸易中采取灵活的贸易方式，大力开展合资经营、合作经营、易货贸易、进料、来料加工等项业务，使我集团公司的进出口贸易建立在更广泛、更坚实的基础上，逐步向国际化多功能，综合经营方向发展。

河北圣仑进出口集团公司、河北圣仑进出口股份有限公司将一如既往的本着“平等互利”和“重合同守信用”的原则，与所有新老客商建立和发展良好的贸易关系，竭诚欢迎海内外贸易界人士来函、来电、来人洽谈业务，增进贸易往来。

Hebei Shenglun Imp.& Exp.(Group) Corp.is a state-owned foreign trade enterprise,incorporated with former Hebei Garments Imp.& Exp. Corp and Hebei Knitwear and Home textiles I/E Corp.with their whole property right on the basis of modern enterprise system and carrying on the corporate reconstruction.There are 588 staffs here. We have set up 7 administrative divisions and 26 holding co. Ltd.or hold the shares of them.There are 9 overseas enterprises in U.S.A.,South Korea,Hong Kong,saudi Arabia,Britain,Germany, Poland and Czech.We also have 7 joint Ventures. Our total assets is Renminbi 405 million and total imp & exp. Volume is USD200 million.

The group corp.mainly deals in import and export of commodity and technology as follows: garments,knitwears and home textiles. woollen knitwears, cereals, oils and foodstaffs, native produce and animal-by products,non-metallic minerals, ferrous,non-ferrous metals, chemicals (not including chemical dangerous articles), building materials, light industrial products, textiles, medicines & health products, machinery & equipment, instruments tools, agricultural implements, hardwares, mechanical and electronic products, electronic computer devices, castings, daily-use ceramics,thick padding ceramics, stonewares,artistic ceramics, drawnwork, straw & willow wares,plastic raincoats,nylon raincoats and other plastic products,shoes & hats,silk carpets. rugs.silk-wool carpets, leather products,glasswares, arts and crafts (not including gold or silver ornaments), artificial flowers, toys, christmas gifts and so on. We adopt processing trade on supplied material, supplied samples or designs, compensation trade, barter trade and entrepot trade. We keep good business relations, with more than 370 customers in 99 countries and regions. In 1999, the quality system of our corporation passed the registration of ISO9002 and UKAS quality management. "Tuberose"brand bedclothes. " Lotos Pond"brand arabian robes and grments, "Dapane" brand woollen kntwear and " Football" brand T-shirts enjoy great fame at home and abroad. New registered "Shenglun" brand has been started using and will meet customers soon.

Hebei Shenglun Imp. & Exp. (Group) Corp. adopt flexible trading means to develop business,such as joint venture. cooperation, barter trade,compensation trade, processing with imported and supplied materials, to build our import and export business on more solid and steady basis,to make it develop in the direction of internationalization, mulitfunction and comprehensive management.

Hebei Shenglun Imp. & Exp. (Group) Corp. will always establish or develop good business relations with new or old customers on the basis of "Equality and Mutual Benefits" and " Honor Contracts and Maintain Commercial Integrity" We warmly welcome figures of business at home or abroad to contact with us and promote the business relations between us.

地址：中国河北石家庄和平西路499号圣仑大厦
Add: Shenglun Building No.499 West Heping Rd., Shijiazhuang, Hebei, China. Postcode: 050061
Tel: 86-311-7043789,7046313 Fax: 86-311-7042790,7057354
E-mail: knit@public.sj.he.cn hebg@public.sj.he.cn.

奥林巴斯（深圳）工业有限公司

OLYMPOS (SHENZHEN) INDUSTRIAL LTD.

奥林巴斯（深圳）工业有限公司成立于1991年12月，生产照相机、微型录音机及零部件。公司位于深圳市高新技术产业园区，占地面积10万平方米，建筑面积1万平方米。公司投资总额8，080万美元，员工3，400人。年产相机180万台，是集团内最大的相机生产基地。

我公司已发展成为初具规模、管理先进的现代化企业。连年被评为全国先进外商投资企业、海关A类企业、深圳市出口大户、深圳市重点扶持出口型企业、1998年作为全国100家先进外商投资企业受到外经贸部的表彰，并于1996年12月通过ISO9002质量体系认证、1999年9月ISO14001环境管理体系认证。总经理大石诚于1998年10月当选深圳市荣誉市民。

Olympus(Shenzhen) Industrial Co.,Ltd.,established in December 1991,specializes in producing cameras, micro-recorders and spare parts.Located in the High & New Industry Park in Shenzhen,the Olympus occupies an area of 100,000m^2 and floorage of 10,000m^2. It is the biggest camera producing base of the Olympus Group,with total investment of 80.80 million USD, 3,400 stuffs and 1.80 million annual output of cameras.

Olympus has developed to be a modernized company with large scale and advanced management experience. Year after year, it is conferred the title of National Advanced Foreign Investment Company, elected A Class Company by the Chinese Customs, and classified major exporter and mainly supported exporter by Shenzhen government. In 1998, the Chinese Ministry of Foreign Trade and Economic Cooperation praied Olympus as one of the National 100 Advanced Foreign Investment Companies. Olympus was also awarded certifications of ISO9002 in December 1996 and ISO14001 in September 1999. 大石诚, president of the company, was elected Shenzhen's Honorable Resident in October 1998.

地址：广东省深圳市南山南头第五工业区
邮编：518056
TEL：6631118　FAX：6631084

ADD: NAN TOO STH INDUSTRIAL DISTRICT NANSHAN.
SHENZHEN GUANGTONG PROVINCE.PROF CHINA
TEL:6631118　FAX:6631084

浙江东方集团股份有限公司

Zhejiang Orient Holdings Co. Ltd.

浙江东方集团股份有限公司是一家外贸行业的上市公司（证券名称：浙江东方，证券代码：600120）。

公司主要从事进出口贸易。在海内外有着良好的信誉和稳固的市场渠道，已与美加、欧洲、日本、澳大利亚、中国香港等80多个国家和地区建立了贸易关系，客户达500多家。主要经营的棉、毛、丝、麻各类面料的针织、梭织服装和家用纺织品等出口商品，品种已达3000多种，其中"福星"、"玉泉"、"天使"等品牌，在国际上享有较高声誉。还在拓展出口业务，以及各类纺织品原辅料、染化料与所需机械设备等进口业务的同时；承包境外工程和境内国际招标工程，对外派遣生产及服务行业的劳务人员；开发进出口商品的国内销售，以及仓储、运输、实业投资开发、经济技术咨询、旅游服务、信息技术开发应用等多种经营。经营方式采用自营、委托代理、合资、合作、联营、进料加工、来料加工、转口贸易、招标、投标等。

1999年，公司完成主营业务收入26亿元，比上年增长42%；出口创汇22095万美元，增长26%；进口6627万美元，增长62%；进出口总额28722万美元，增长33%；利润总额8514万元，增长57%；被浙江省人民政府评为浙江省模范集体。

目前，集团公司拥有全资直属国内外企业22家，投资联营企业10家，比较固定的产销联营企业150余家，净资产达3.6亿元，初步形 成了以贸易为龙头，实业为基础，贸易、医药、化工、信息产业、金融、房地产、国际运输等有机结合的企业集团，逐步向实业化、多元化、国际化、大集团模式发展。

Zhejiang Orient Group Com. Ltd. is a public foreign trade company. Its stock name: Zhejiang Orient. Its stock code: 600120.

The company specializes in import and export business. With its good credit and stale market channels, it has established trade relationship with over 500 clients in more than 80 countries and territories such as USA, Canada, Europe, Japan, Australia and Hong Kong. Its main export products cover knit clothes, shuttle clothes and household textile made from various materials such as cotton, wool, silk and linen. It also has many brands with high reputation in the world such as "Fu Xing", "YuQuan" and "Tian Shi". The company keeps on developing its export business, imports all sorts of textile's raw material, relative machine and equipment. At the same time, it develops a diversified economy such as overseas contracts, international bids, sending labors of manufacturing industry and service abroad, civil distribution of import and export goods, warehousing, transport, industrial investment and development, economic and technical consultation, tourism service, information technology development and application, etc. The methods of business operation include trading as principals, agents, joint ventures, cooperative business operation, processing with imported material and provided material, entrepot trade, tendering, and submitting tenders.

In 1999, the company's main business revenue was 2.6 billion RMB, increased 42% year on year, its export value increased 26%, to 287.22 million USD, its import and export value increased 33%, to 85.14 million BMB. It was awarded a model group by Zhejiang government.

Today, with total assets of 360 million RMB, the company has owned 22 Chinese and foreign companies, invested 10 joint ventures, and established 150 manufacturing and distributing joint ventures. Taking trade as the mainstay, industries as the basis, combining trade organically with medicine, chemistry, finance, real estate, international and transportation, it is becoming an industrialized and internationalized enterprise group and a diversified economy step by step.

地址： 杭州市庆春路199号 **邮编** (Post Code)：310006
Add : No. 199 Qingchun Road, Hangzhou, China
电话 (Tel)：0571-7215678 转
传真 (Fax)：0571-7215000
网址 (Web site)：http ://www.chinaorient.com
董事长： 刘宁生 **总经理：** 吴建华

中国化工建设总公司

China National Chemical Construction Corporation

CNCCC 天津化工研究设计院科研楼
CNCCC Tianjin Chemical Research & Design Institute

中国化工建设总公司(简称CNCCC)，是隶属于中央企业工委直接管理的以化工技术、设备及产品进出口贸易、承包海内外工程业务为主业，集化工科研、生产、投资、仓储服务于一体的综合性集团公司。

CNCCC先后为国内引进大型化工、石油化工、轮胎等成套生产装置百余套和关键技术设备千余项，总金额近百亿美元；在化工产品进出口、成套技术设备出口和海内外工程承包方面均有雄厚实力，出口经营额多年保持在3亿美元以上。业务范围涵盖化工、轮胎、橡胶制品、化肥、农药和医药等10多个门类；CNCCC是财政部、外经贸部批准，被世界银行等国际金融组织认可的具有国际招标采购资格的中国最早的四大招标公司之一，先后完成了大批世行、亚洲开发银行和外国政府贷款项目的国际招标和设备采购业务，项目涉及环保、农业、交通、能源、化工、石油化工、扶贫等众多领域。CNCCC拥有自己的化工研究院、工程设计院；拥有规模、技术一流的DSD酸生产企业、若干个精细化工产品出口生产基地和液体化工仓储公司；控股大型的复合化肥生产企业；在国内外主要地区、港口和货源集散地设有子公司和办事机构。

CNCCC是外经贸部出口重点联系企业之一，在在经贸部发表的中国进出口额最大的500家企业中99年列第62位，在国内外市场上享有较高的知名度、良好的信誉和较为丰富的市场资源。CNCCC愿在经贸、科研、生产等各个领域与国内外企业建立和发展多种形式的合作关系。

中阿化肥有限公司复合肥生产装置
NPK Production Line of sino-Arab Chemical Fertilize Co., Ltd.

CNCCC总承包的中国云南大黄磷工程项目
Yellow phosphate project in Yunnan contracted by CNCCC

CNCCC出口到伊朗的三聚氰胺生产装置
Melamine Plant exported to Iran by CNCCC

China National Chemical Construction Corporation(abbreviated as CNCCC) is an export-oriented enterprise group directly under the central government, engaged in industry, R&d, engineering and service with trade taking the lead,and committed to foreign trade and international cooperation for Chinese chemical industry.

Over 100 complete plants and 1000 technologies and critical equipment have been imported by CNCCC for chemical, petrochemical and rubber industry with a total value of nearly 10 billion US dollars. CNCCC is also competitive in import and export of chemical products, export of technologies and equipment,overseas engineering contraction. The annual export volume of CNCCC has been more than 300 million US dollars for many years.Its business scope contains more than 10 profession kinds,such as chemical, tyre, rubber products, fertilizers, pesticide and pharmaceutical. As one of the four earliest tendering companies in China, granted by MOF and MOFTEC, approved by World Bank and other international financial organization, CNCCC has undertaken large numbers of international tendering and equipment purchasing for projects financed by World Bank, Asia Development Bank and foreign governments.The tendering business covers such industries of national economy as environmental protection, agriculture, communication, energy saving,chemical and petrochemical.CNCCC has its own R&D and engineering company, the largest DSD acid producing factory in Asia,several fine chemical production bases,and liquid chemical warehousing company. CNCCC is the holding company of Sino-Arab Chemical Fertilizers Company Ltd, which is the largest compound fertilizer producer in China, and established domestic subsidiaries at the main ports and distributing centers and overseas branches and representative offices in the countries and regions who are the main trading partners with China.

CNCCC has been ranked within firsh forth companies for succession years on the list of top 500 Chinese companies in terms of import and export volume.It is the

155th among the top 225 international engineering contractors worldwide. CNCCC enjoys high reputation and rich market resource at home and abroad.

CNCCC is willing to build and develop extensive cooperation with domestic and fo

reign enterprises in the line of trade,science,and production.

地址：北京和平里7区16号楼 邮编：100013
电话：64214043 64213697
传真：64215982 64215527
网址：http: //www.cnccc.com.cn
电子信箱：cnccc@cnccc.com.cn

Add: Beijing No.16 Qiqu, Hepingli, (Zpi Code:100013)
Tel: 64214043, 64213697
Fax: 64215982, 64215527
Web: http: //www.cnccc.com.cn
E-mail: cnccc@cnccc.com.cn

中国中原对外工程公司

China Zhongyuan Engineering Corporation

巴基斯坦核电站全景:
A panorama view of Chashma 300M We Nuclear Power Plant in Pakistan

中国中原对外工程公司(中原公司)是国家授权的唯一的国际核工程承包公司和政府认定的高新技术企业。自1983年成立以来，承建了阿尔及利亚核研究中心，巴基斯坦核电站等大型核工程。其间，还承建了污水处理厂、化工厂、常规电站、民用建筑、体育场、机场停机坪等大量的工业设施及民用工程。1993年经有关部门批准，中原公司获得了进出口贸易经营权和代理权，地域遍及30多个国家与地区。公司现有专业技术人员近200人，其中拥有高级技术职称人员90名，中国工程院院士1名。

大型工程机械(650吨吊车):
Large construction machinery (650t crawling crane)

阿尔及利亚核研究中心全景:
A panorama view of Nuclear Research Center Project in Algeria

China Zhongyuan Engineering Corporation(CZEC), is designated by the national competent administration for exclusively executing the international nuclear projects and officially attributed the status as Hi-Tech Enterprise. Since its founding in 1983,CZEC has completed some important nuclear projects such as Nuclear Research Center Project in Algeria and Chashma 300MWe Nuclear Power Plant in Pakistan.CZEC has also undertaken many industrial installations and civil engineering projects like sewage treatment plants, chemical plants, conventional power plants, stadiums, airports, etc. Thanks to the approval of the national competent administration in 1993, CZEC has extended its business scope to import and export trade and developed its business links with over thirty countries and regions so far.Among its 200 technical and professional employees, over ninety of them have senior technical titles including one crowned with Member of the Chinese Academy of Engineering(CAE).

热室和机械手:
Hot cell equipped with tele-manipulators

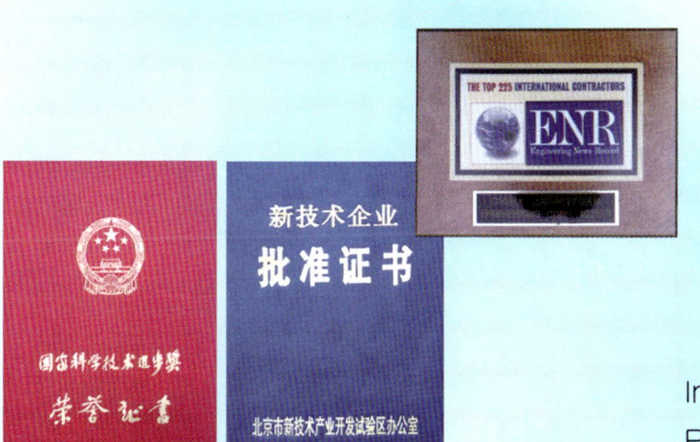

荣誉及资质照一组:
Qualification certificates and awards

中原公司互联网网址为: http://www.czec.com.cn
电话: 8610-62355635　传真: 8610-62355640
邮编: 100083　地址: 北京8320信箱
E-mail:czec@mail.netchina.com.cn

Internet address: http: //www.czec.com.cn
Phone number:8610-62355635 Fax number:8610-62355640
Post code:100083 Postal address: P.O.Box 8320, Beijing
E-mail: czec@mail.netchina.com.cn

中国土木工程集团公司简介

COMPANY PROFILE

中国土木工程集团公司（简称中土集团公司）是中国实行改革开放后率先进入国际工程承包市场的大型国有企业之一。中土集团公司的前身是铁道部援外办公室，具有丰富的土木工程经验，特别是在铁路建设方面，独具特色，实力雄厚，早在七十年代就在非洲修建了著名的坦赞铁路。经过20多年在国际工程承包市场上的竞争，中土集团公司已跻身于世界大型国际承包商的行列，在中国国内同行业中一直居领先地位。

目前中土集团公司以国际土木工程承包为主业，同时经营设计咨询、房地产开发、进出口贸易、实业投资、劳务合作和酒店服务等多种业务，在25个国家和地区设有子公司或常驻机构，在中国境内拥有13家全资子公司。中土集团公司已通过ISO 9001质量体系认证并获得世界银行、亚洲开发银行和联合国开发计划署的有关工程设计咨询的资格认可。

随着新世纪的来临，中土集团公司将一如既往，信守合同，保证工程和服务质量，灵活经营，讲求实效，在平等互利的基础上继续同海内外各界朋友真诚合作。

As a large state-owned enterprise, China Civil Engineering Construction Corporation (CCECC) was one of the earliest established Chinese companies engaged in business of international economic cooperation in 1978 when China adopted the policy of reform and opening-up. In the early 1970s, CCECC, in its former name as Foreign-Aid Bureau of the Ministry of Railways, undertook the survey, design and construction of Tanzania-Zambia railway in Africa. With strenuous efforts in the past twenty-odd years, CCECC has been listed among the world's top 225 international contractors and has always been holding the lead in the industry of engineering construction at home.

With international construction contracting as its main business and railway construction as the speciality, CCECC has now developed a wide scope of its business covering design & consultancy, real estate development, import & export trading, industrial investment, manpower supply as well as hotel management, etc.. The business operations of CCECC have spread over 40 countries and regions where 25 overseas offices or subsidiaries have been established in addition to 13 domestic subsidiaries. In addition to the Certificate of ISO 9001, the consulting qualification of CCECC has been approved respectively by the World Bank, Asia Development Bank (ADB) and the United Nations Development Program (UNDP).

With the advent of the New Millennium, CCECC shall, as always, honor its contracts, guarantee the quality of its construction and services, achieve more flexible, diversified and effective business operations and cooperate with its friends both at home and abroad on the basis of equality and mutual benefit.

中国大连国际合作(集团)股份有限公司

China Dalian International Cooperation(Group) Holdings.Ltd.

董事长：朱明义

总经理：王新民

The China Dalian International Cooperation(Group) Holdings.Ltd. (CDIG) is an enterprise with the qualification of legal person and the authority to do international business.Internatioal economic and technical cooperation is the major activity of this corporation,including international project contracting,international labor service,ocean shipping,ocean fishery,import/export,real estate,and the undertaking of contracts for foreign aid etc.and has had the honor of winning many awards,such as "Excellence in management of the international economic and trading enterprises" and "AAA Credit Corporation".CDIG is also recognized as one of the 100 best national companies and one of the 20 largest international economic corporations in China.In 1998,the corporation came into the Shenzhen A stock exchange market and we are the first one of Dalian's international economic and trading corporations coming into the market,CDIG was rewarded Quality System Certificate Issued by CQC in June,1999.

中国大连国际合作(集团)股份有限公司是具有法人资格和对外经营权的企业。公司以对外经济技术合作为主导产业，主营业务包括国际工程承包、国际劳务合作、远洋运输、远洋渔业、进出口贸易、房地产、国内外投资以及承担国家经援项目等。公司先后荣获全国外经贸系统先进单位，“AAA”级信誉单位。1998年，公司以优良的经营业绩成为大连市外经贸行业首家上市公司。

地址：中国大连市西岗区黄河路219号
No.219, Huanghe Road, Xigang District, Dalian, China
电话 Tel: 86-411-3780366, 86-411-3780386
传真 Fax: 86-411-3780186, 86-411-3780286
网址 Http: //www.china-gdig. com
电子信箱： E -mail: pao@china-cdig. com
邮编 Zpi Code: 116011

公司获得ISO9002质量体系认证证书
CDIG Quality System Certificate Issued By CQC

MCC 中国冶金建设集团公司

China Metallurgical Construction (Group) Corporation

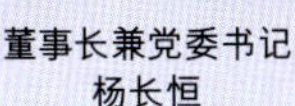

董事长兼党委书记
杨长恒

副董事长、总经理
马延利

副董事长、常务副总经理
李书臣

中国冶金建设集团公司(简称中冶集团)是中央管理的国家大型企业集团，所属28家成员单位，包括12个国家一级施工企业，9个国家甲级设计研究院，3个国家甲级勘察研究院，4个大型科研院所和科研中心。

公司企业法人代表、董事长杨长恒，总经理马延利。

1999年度，中冶集团总资产207.1亿元人民币，从业人员近14万人。1999年营业收入130.1亿元，其中：施工产值99.6亿元，设计及科研收入8.5亿元。实现利税4.3亿元。中冶集团1999年实现对外经贸合同额34833万美元，完成外经贸收入10274万美元。

中冶集团多次获得国家建设工程鲁班金像奖、质量金奖、国家科技进步特等奖，具有良好的质量信誉。

近年来，中冶集团在承接国内外钢铁工业新建、扩建和重大技术改造项目的同时，还充分发挥各成员单位在建设项目的投资咨询、设计、勘察、设备、材料、施工、科研等方面所具有的技术、管理、装备、资信、信息优势，在国内外有色冶金、交通、能源、市政基础设施、机械、化工、建材、矿山、水利、民用商业建筑等领域承担了大量建设项目。

中冶集团成功承建了巴基斯坦山达克铜金矿、新加坡PSA集装箱钢结构库房、墨西哥纺织厂、约旦哈桑体育城、中国香港大屿山住宅、学校、泰国高速公路、柬埔寨泰文隆水泥厂、越南海防供水等大型工程项目；国内的济青公路、首都机场改扩建工程、中央电视台广州太平天国影视基地和中央影视基地、北京太运大厦等工程项目。

中冶集团的成员单位分布在北京、上海、天津、重庆、辽宁、河北、山西、湖北、安徽、内蒙、四川等十二个省市自治区，经营机构遍布全国，相对集中在东部经济中心城市、沿海经济特区、西部重要工业城市。并在海外设有30家经营机构。

中冶集团在重庆、上海等成功运做了大型房地产开发项目，在北京、广州、上海、江苏、河北、四川、辽宁等地投资于钢结构制作、新型建筑材料生产等实业项目，均取得了显著效益。

中冶集团成功实施的国内有色冶金矿山生产承包和国外大型钢铁厂生产劳务承包，得到了业主的肯定，显示了中冶集团技术、管理的实力。

中冶集团与世界上著名的承包商、设计商、冶金机电设备厂商保持着良好的合资、合营、合作关系。

中冶集团开展对外工程总承包，带动机电设备、技术、劳务出口的业务，得到了国家主管部门的大力扶持，并以其经营业绩获得了国家银行的资信支持。

中冶集团是新中国钢铁工业建设的主力军，伴随着国家改革、开放的进程发展、壮大，现已跻身于全球大型国家承包商和大型工程设计公司之列。

中冶集团满怀信心迎接国际承包市场的挑战，胜利跨入新世纪。

Administered by the State, China Metallurgical Construction (Group) Corporation (MCC Group in short) is a large national multi-business enterprise group with 28 members. The group members include 12 construction enterprises with national Grade A qualifications, 9 design and research institutes with national Grade A qualifications, 3 geotechnical research institutes with national Grade A qualifications, and other 4 large scientific study and research centers.

For the year of 1999, the total assets of MMC Group is RMB 20.76 billion yuan, and the number of employees is totaled about 140,000. MCC Group has reached a turnover of RMB 13.01 billion yuan in 1999, out of which RMB 9.96 billion yuan was made in term of construction value, and RMB 850 million yuan made through design and scientific research work. The Group has realized a profit tax of RMB 430 million yuan for the year. Also in 1999, MCC Group has fulfilled a total contract value of US$ 348.33 million and revenue of US$102.74 million through foreign trade and economic activities.

MCC Group has been awarded on several occasions with Lu-Ban Gold Medal, Quality Gold Medal, and National Special Medal for Scientific Progress for its performance of the national construction projects, and has established a sound reputation for its quality performance.

Since the beginning of this year, while contracting the construction, expansion and technical renovation in steel sectors both at home and abroad, MCC Group has managed to make the most of the technical and managerial skills as well as such other advantages of the Group members in respect of investment consultancy, design, survey and prospection, equipment, materials, construction and scientific research, as a result, MCC Group has undertaken plentiful projects in the field of nonferrous industry, transportation, energy, urban infrastructure services, machinery, petrochemical industry, building materials, mining, water irrigation, and construction for civil as well as commercial purposes.

The projects completed by MCC Group include: Saindak Copper Gold Minerals Development in Pakistan, Keppel Distripart Container Freight Station in Singapore, Prince Hassan Sports City in Jordan, Rural Drainage Rehabilitation Scheme in Hong Kong, High-Way Construction in Thailand, Cement Plant in Cambodia, Hai-Phong Water Supply in Vietnam, Jinan-Qingdao Expressway in Shandong Province, Capital Airport Renovation and Expansion in Beijing, CCTV Movie City in Guangzhou, and Taiyun Mansion in Beijing.

The members of MCC Group are located in Beijing, Shanghai, Tianjin, Chongqing, Liaoning, Hebei, Shanxi, Hubei, Anhui, Inner Mongolia, and Sichuan, with business branches covering all over the country, mainly in the eastern and coastal developed areas and the strategic industrial cities of the western part of China. Further, MCC Group has established 30 offshore business branches.

MCC Group has successfully developed big real estate projects in Chongqing and Shanghai, and has achieved sound economic results through investment in steel fabrication and new building materials manufacturing in Beijing, Guangzhou, Shanghai, Jiangsu, Hebei, Sichuan and Liaoning.

The contractual performance by MCC Group for nonferrous mining and production projects in China, and production management and technical supervision for large steel complexes in abroad have been highly regarded by the clients and have demonstrated the technical competence and managerial skills of MCC Group.

MCC Group has maintained very good relations with the world famous contractors, designers and metallurgical equipment manufacturers by means of joint venture, partnership and cooperation.

The competent departments of the State have been tremendously supportive to MCC Group for its general contraction business conducted in abroad which has substantially promoted the export of electromechanical equipment, and provision of technical and labor services. The business achievements made by MCC Group have helped to secure strong financial backup from Chinese banks.

A main force for the construction of steel industry of a brand new China, MCC Group has grown and developed with implementation of the policy of reform and opening up by the State. For 12 years consecutively, MCC Group has been admitted as one of the 225 top contracting companies in the world, and has been listed for several times as one of the 200 world famous engineering design institutions.

In face of the challenges in the international contracting market, MCC Group is filled with full confidence of victory, striding into a new era.

地址：北京市朝阳区安贞里三区二十三号　Add：No. 23, Block 3, Anzhenli, Beijing
电话 (Tel)：64411166　传真 (Fax)：64419166　邮编 (Post Code)：100029

上海新联纺进出口有限公司

SHANGHAI NEW UNION TEXTRA I/E CO., LTD

上海新联纺进出口有限公司创建于1985年2月，是一家工贸结合的外贸公司，公司资产总额达十五亿元，注册资本一亿五千七百多万元。主要生产和出口色织布、漂色花布、各类服装、床上用品、厨房用品、针织品等纺织产品，并经营高新电子、化工、轻工、重工、工艺品等产品。1999年的出口总额达1.42亿美元，在经贸部发表的中国进出口总额最大的500家企业中，98年名列第171位。在今年五月，我司通过了ISO9002的质量认证。目前公司拥有六个分公司、八个子公司和一批核心工厂，一九八八年起公司分别在中国香港、美国、日本和中东等地设立海外机构。公司在对外贸易中充分发挥工贸结合的优势，积极采用国际贸易惯例开展各种贸易。

Established in February 1985, the Shanghai New United Textile Import and Export Co., Ltd. (SHNUTEX) is an integrating industry and foreign trade company with total assets of 1.5 billion RMB and registered assets of 157 million RMB. SHNUTEX mainly produces and exports such textile as yarn-dyed fabric, bleached and dyed colour fabric, clothes, bedding, kitchen utensils, knit goods, etc. It also engages in high and new electronics, chemical products, light industrial products, heavy industrial products and handicrafts. In 1999, the total export of SHNUTEX was 142 million USD, coming out in front of the national 500 biggest import and export corporations. In may 2000, We are Committed to the ISO9002 series of quality standards, to the principles and practices of total quality management. SHNUTEX has established overseas offices in Hong Kong, USA, Japan and the Middle East. It makes the most of its superiority of integrating industry and trade in trading process and develops all kinds of trade according to international trade practice.

董事长：顾关林　　Chairman：Gu Guan-lin

地址：中国 · 上海市交通路1565号

邮编（Post Code）：200065

Add：1565, Jiao Tong Lu, Shanghai, China

电话（Tel）：0086-21-56098899

传真（Fax）：0086-21-56098877

网址（Web site）：http：//www.sh-nutex.com

E-mail：nutex@public.sta.net.cn

东莞市建筑材料进出口公司

本公司是广东省东莞市外经贸资产经营有限公司辖属的外贸公司。1998年，公司在经贸部发表的中国进出口总额最大的500家企业中列第61位，并于1999年跨入中国外经贸部100家重点联系企业之列。

公司经营五金矿产、建筑材料、轻工业品、化工类、工艺品、食品、医药保健品、服装、纺织品、钢材、装饰材料、木制品、运输工具、机械设备、仪器仪表等，承办“三来一补”、“三资”企业的加工贸易、易货贸易、代购、代销、代运、销售、代理进出口业务。公司设有废品收购站、保税仓、出口监管仓、中转仓、报关部、货运服务公司，为客户提供一条龙的配套服务。

公司竭诚为海内外客商提供最优质的产品和服务，热忱欢迎各界人士前来洽谈业务，共同发展！

Dongguan City Building Materials Imp. & Exp. Corporation is a subordinate foreign trade corporation of Guangdong Dongguan Foreign Economy and Trade Capital Management Corporation. In 1998, our company ranked No. 61 among China's 500 leading enterprises that handle the business of import and export and became one of 100 Key Contact Companies of China Foreign Economy and Trade Department in 1999.

The company deals in hardware products, building materials, light industrial products, chemical products, handicraft articles, foods, medical and health-care products, clothes, textile, steel, ornament materials, wooden products, transportation tools, machinery, equipment and apparatus, etc. We also handle processing trade with processing plants and foreign-invest enterprises, barter trade, acting as an agent for purchasing, marketing, transportation, import and export. The company has waste purchasing station, bounded area, export supervision warehouse, transit warehouse, customs clearing dep., and freight transportation service company.

We attentively offer the best products and service to customers all over the world. Warmly welcome all home-aboard traders to hold a business talk and create a prosperous cause together with us.

DONGGUAN BUILDING MATERIALS IMP. & EXP. CO.

法人代表：王佛禧
地　　址：广东省东莞市建设路1号口岸大楼3楼
联系电话：(0769) 2816022 2816818
邮　　编：523072
电子邮箱：Dgbm@dg.163mail.net

Legitive Person: Wang Fuxi
Add: 3 Floor, International Port Building, No. 1, Jianshe Road, Dongguan City, Guangdong, PRC. Postal Code: 523072
Tel: (0769)2816022 2816818 Fax: (0769)2816533
E-mail: Dgbm@dg.163mail.net

广东省丝绸（集团）公司
广东省丝绸进出口（集团）公司

广东是全国蚕桑主产区之一，广东丝绸业对外贸易有悠久历史，早在公元前的汉代就开辟了经马来半岛、缅甸沿岸、印度、斯里兰卡的“海上丝绸之路”。

广东省丝绸（集团）公司是集农、工、商、贸、科研、教育为一体的大型外贸企业，广东省授权经营和重点扶持的大型企业集团，1999年全省丝绸系统进出口总值达5.37亿美元，居全国同行业前茅，在经贸部发表的中国进出口总额最大的500家企业中，历年榜上有名。

广东省丝绸（集团）公司成立40多年来，与世界上80多个国家和地区的客商长期有着良好的贸易伙伴关系，近十年来进出口业务迅速发展，主营业务有：丝绸纺织、轻工机电、五金化工、土畜产、陶瓷工艺、文体用品、医药保健等商品的进出口。集团公司致力于创名牌“SILIQUE”产品，以优质服务和良好信誉塑造企业形象。

诚挚欢迎世界各地工商界人士与我们建立和扩大贸易往来和经济技术交流与合作。

GuangDong is one of the major sericultural bases in China, enjoying a long history in silk foreign trade. The famous Silk Road on Sea originated in GuangDong in as early as Han Dynasty, BC and extended through Malaysia Peninsula, Burma coast, India and Sri Lanka to the world.

GuangDong Silk Imp. & Exp. Corp. (Group) is a large-scale foreign trade enterprise. It integrates agriculture, industry, commerce, trade, scientific research and education. The corporation is one of the key large-scale enterprises officially approved and supported by the government of GuangDong Province. In 1999, the corporation achieved a total import and export volume of 537 million U.S.dollars, accounting for the 2nd place in the national silk industry and one of the 500 biggest import and export enterprises, the 500 biggest service-oriented enterprises and the 100 biggest industrial and commercial enterprises in China.

GuangDong Silk Imp. & Exp. Corp. (Group) has maintained friendly and long-term business partnership with clients from over 60 countries and regions for more than 40 years since its establishment. The corporation has achieved a rapid development in its business in recent ten years. The corporation has been engaged in the import and export of various products including silk and textiles, light industrial products, machinery and electronic appliances and equipment, metals and chemical products, native and animal by-products, ceramics, arts and crafts, stationary and sports goods and medicine and health products. The corporation has also dedicated itself in launching its own brand "SILIQUE" and establishing an international image of good quality, good service and good creditability.

We hereby sincerely welcome all personages from domestic and international industrial and commercial circles to establish and extend business co-operation and technological exchanges with us.

地址：中国 · 广东省广州市东风西路198号
Add : No. 198, Dong Feng Road West, Guangzhou, China
邮编（Post Code）: 510180
电话总机（Tel）: 83337448转
传真（Fax）: 83332995
网址（Web）: silique.com
E-mail : gdsilk@public.guangzhou.gd.cn

中国联合石油有限责任公司

CHINA NATIONAL UNITED OIL CORPORATION

中国联合石油有限责任公司（简称中联油）成立于1993年1月8日，由中国石油天然气股份有限公司（简称中国石油）持股70%，中国化工进出口总公司持股30%。1999年底，中联油成为中国石油的国际贸易专业公司，主要从事中国石油的原油、成品油、天然气、石化产品进出口及技术引进等国际业务并进行归口管理。截止1999年底，累计进出口额70多亿美元，境外国际贸易额6.6亿美元。中联油将继续发扬“诚信、进取”的企业精神，为股东创造优异的回报，为社会做出更大的贡献。

China National United Oil Corporation (known as Chinaoil) was established on January 8, 1993, whose capital stock is 70% owned by PetroChina Company Limited (known as PetroChina), and 30% owned by China National Chemicals Import and Export Corporation (known as Sinochem). Since the end of 1999, Chinaoil has become the specialised international trading company of PetroChina, mainly in the international business areas of import and export of curde, oil products, natural gas, chemical products and technical importation, etc. By the end of 1999, the total revenue for import and export is more than 7 billion U.S. dollars, together with 660 million U.S. dollars from international trading overseas. Chinaoil will carry forward the entrepreneurial spirit of "sincerity, credibility and initiative", maximize the return for the shareholders and make more contributions for the society.

地址：北京市西城区阜成门外大街2号万通新世界广场A座22层

Add：22/F, Bldg. A Vantone New World Plaza, No. 2 Fuwai Street, Beijing, China

邮编 (Post Code)：100037

电话 (Tel)：68041188

传真 (Fax)：68587091/2

中国武汉国际经济技术合作公司

总经理易海螺先生
General Manager: Mr. Yi Hailuo

中国武汉国际经济技术合作公司（CWIC）是1984年经国务院批准成立的一家综合性外经贸国有企业。

主要经营范围：承包国外工程；境内外资工程；承担我国政府对外经济援助项目；承包工程所需的设备、材料出口；对外派遣各类劳务人员（含海员）并提供服务；在海外举办各类非贸易性企业；培训各类劳务人员（含研修生）及进出口业务。

公司拥有11家分公司。十余年来，先后承担了伊拉克高级俱乐部、巴格达立交桥 、塞拉利昂农技站、佛得角国家图书馆等二十余个建设和经济技术合作项目。劳务合作遍及新加坡、日本、沙特、中国澳门等54个国家和地区。进出口贸易年创汇2000多万美元，2000年成功履行了8200万美元的船舶出口。

公司出口瑞典“芬马斯特”号8050DWT滚装船
8050DWT Ro — Ro Vessel "FLNNMASTER" exported to Sweden

我公司承建的佛得角国家图书馆
Our corporation's project of Cape Verde Country Library

塞拉利昂政府官员视察我公司援塞农技站水稻试验田
Officials of SIERRA Leone inspected rice probation planted by our company's agricultural technical assistance station

Since with 1984 the approval of State Council of the People's Republic of China, China Wuhan Corporation for International Economic and Technical Cooperation (CWIC) has grown into a powerful state — owned synthetically foreign economic cooperation and trade unit.

The corporation now includes eleven branches. Its scope of business stretches to contract foreign projects, domestic foreign-funded projects and foreign programs mandated by the Chinese government. It is also involved in import and export business as well as to supply various labor services (including sailors) and set up various service enterprises to foreign countries. Moreover, the corporation could train labors (including research fellows) and export equipment or materials demanded in constructed engineering projects.

In these years, we have taken part in the constructions of over 20 large engineering and economic technical cooperation projects abroad. The achievements include an advanced club in Iraq, a pedestrian overpass at in Baghdad, several agricultural stations in Sierra Leone, and the national library in Cape Verde. Furthermore, we have been exporting labor services from Singapore, Macao, Japan, Saudi Arabia to 50 other countries and regions. As to our foreign trade, the import and export can make a profit of more than $20,000,000 each year. Especially in 2000, we succeed to complete a series of vessel export contracts of $ 82,000,000.

地址：中国武汉市汉口台北1路38号
Add: No. 38, Taibei Yi Road, Hankou, Wuhan, P.R.C.
邮编 (Post Code): 430015
电话 (Tel): 0086-27-85803128
传真 (Fax): 0086-27-85777496
E-mail: Cwicty@public.wh..hb.cn..

我公司承接的摩洛哥首都体育馆钢结构维修工程
The repairing project of Morocco Captial stadium's steel structure by our corporation

SCIHC 深圳市建设投资控股公司

深圳市建设投资控股公司成立于1996年12月，是深圳市三家市级国有资产经营公司之一。建设控股公司现在直属企业21家，其中，集团公司15家，上市公司7家（深房、物业、长城、振业、天地、天健、万山）。截止1999年底，公司总资产329.4亿元，净资产103.08亿元。

建设控股公司经营范围广泛，主业为建筑、房地产业。1999年，全控股公司企业总产值为59.10亿元，建筑业产值48.30亿元，从事境外工程承包收入2932万美元，劳务输出2371万美元，创汇2897万美元。公司自93年取得对外经济技术合作经营权以来，在中国香港成功地接揽了地铁516、501工程及赤腊角新机场停机坪304工程等项目。1998年，公司制订了具有建设性的组建国际化工程总承包公司的计划，于1999年成功地收购了一家中国香港建筑公司，并开始在中国香港参与西铁和东铁支线项目的工程联合投标，取得了不俗的成绩。

展望未来，建设控股将按照公司的总体发展战略，生产经营和资本经营有机结合，国内市场与国外市场双向开拓，努力建设成为以建筑、房地产为主体、多元化经营协调配套发展的跨行业、跨地区、跨国 家的国有控股公司。

中国企业联合会理事长张彦宁一行考察我司，并为我司题词“奋力开拓国内外市场，实现集约化、规模化、国际化经营”。

Shenzhen Construction Investment Holding Corporation (referred as SCIHC) was one of the three Shenzhen municipal capital management companies, established in December 1996. SCIHC has 21 key subsidiary companies including 15 group companies, 7 stock public companies. By the end of 1999, SCIHC's total asset is RMB 32.94 billion, net asset is RMB 10.308 billion.

SCIHC is mainly engaged in construction and real estate field, it also has great varieties of business. In 1999, it had enterprise output 5910 million Yuan and construction output 4830 million Yuan, overseas construction contracting income USD 29.32 million, and labor export income USD 23.71 million. It has successfully finished several construction projects in Hong Kong. Under the company's plan of developing into an international general-contracting company, SCIHC purchased a Hong Kong construction company in 1999, starts to tender for HK west rail and east rail extensions projects and achieves satisfactory result.

Looking forward to the future, SCIHC will strive to diversify, multinationize its business and become an international state-owned consortium.

地址：深圳市红岭中路2118号
电话：0755-5595595
传真：0755-5569201
邮编：518008
电子信箱：szclhc@public.szptt.net.cn

Add：No.2118 Hongling M. Road Shenzhen China
Tel：0755-5595595
Fax：0755-5569201
P.C.：518008
E-mail：szclhc@public.szptt.net.cn

江西省粮油食品进出口公司

EVERGREEN

Jiangxi Cereals, Oils & Foodstuffs Import & Export (Group) Corp.

江西省粮油食品进出口公司创建于1963年，是江西省经营进出口贸易较早的专业外贸公司。经过30多年的发展，现已拥有10个子公司，6个中外合资企业，5个参股联营企业，并在美国设有分支机构。公司系统现有职工1200余人，拥有总资产4.47亿元，净资产1.97亿元。1999年进出口贸易额为16249万美元。其中出口16231万美元。在经贸部发表的中国进出口总额最大的500家企业中，99年名列第293位，多次受到外经贸部的表彰。1995年荣获外经贸部“全国对外经贸优秀企业”称号；1996年荣获外经贸部企协“全国外经贸质量效益型先进企业”称号；1997年荣获外经贸部“全国外经贸系统先进集体”称号；连续9年荣获省外经贸厅“全省经贸行业先进单位”称号，并多次受到省人民政府和上级有关部门的表彰和奖励。

公司主要经营粮油食品进出口业务，承担以粮油食品为主的进料加工、来料加工、补偿贸易、转口贸易和代理业务等。30多年来，通过不断拓展，公司先后与欧盟、美国、加拿大、日本和东南亚等世界上50多个国家和地区建立了贸易关系。公司的“长青牌”商标在国内外享有良好声誉，长青牌系列产品品种齐全、质量上乘，深受国内外用户欢迎。

经理、高级经济师：王中阳
General Manager and Senior Economist: Wang Zhong Yang

Founded in 1963, Jiangxi Cereals Oil & Foodstuff Import & Export (Group) Corp. is the earliest foreign trade company in Jiangxi. After 30 years' development, it now has 10 subsidiaries, 6 joint ventures, 5 jointly run businesses and has set up branches in the US. The company now has more than 1,200 staffs and total assets of RMB 4.47 million and net asset of RMB 1.97 million. In 1999, its import and export volume was USD 16249 million, among which export reached USD 16231 million. It has ranked among the top 500 largest import and export companies for 9 successive years since 1991 and has won favorable comments for several times from the Ministry of Foreign Trade & Economic Cooperation. It was awarded the title "Excellent National Foreign Trade & Economic Enterprise" by MOFTEC in 1995 and "National Foreign Trade & Economic Quality and Profit Advanced Enterprise" in 1996; "Advanced Collective in the State Foreign Trade and Economic Systems" in 1997, and "Advanced Unit in Provincial Economic and Trade Systems" for 9 successive years. The company mainly deals in the import and export business of cereals and foodstuffs, and conducted business in processing with supplied materials and samples, compensation trade, entrepot trade, etc. The company has established trading relations with more than 50 countries and regions like the EU, America, Canada, Japan and Southeastern Asia. Its "Ever-green" brand enjoys favorable comments at home and abroad.

地址：江西省南昌市站前路200号外贸大厦5楼　邮编 (Post Code)：330002
Add：5th Floor Foreign Trade Builidng No. 200 Zhan Qian Road Nanchang City Jiangxi Province
电话 (Tel)：(0791) 6223237 6225210 6224256 6223603 6225054 6216434 6262324 6216094
传真 (Fax)：(0791) 6223843　电报挂号 (Cable)：7350（南昌）CEROILFOOD
网址 (Web site)：http://www.jxcof.com　E-mail：jxcof@public.nc.jx.cn

重庆对外建设总公司

The Briefing of Chongqing International Construction Corporation

重庆对外建设总公司是经中华人民共和国对外经济贸易部批准，拥有对外工程承包，对外劳务输出和进出口贸易经营权，经国家建设部批准具有一级工程施工总承包资质的国有企业，具有独立法人地位。公司注册资金为1亿6千万人民币，在国外拥有1200万美元的机械设备及房地产业。

公司自1985年成立以来，先后在埃及、苏丹、索马里、乌干达、坦桑尼亚、肯尼亚、南非、尼泊尔、蒙古、越南、柬埔寨、斐济、瑞士等国家承建多项国际承包工程及劳务合作项目，签约金额达2.6亿美元，十多年来为国家创汇3千多万美元。在索马里的哈－博公路，阿－巴公路，莫迪尔水渠，乌干达的3号公路，埃及的WB3工程，苏丹的乌－霍公路，尼泊尔库勒卡里二号防灾项目上，都以质量好，速度快受到业主，监理工程师、世界银行代表及我国驻外使馆经济商务代表处的好评和高度赞扬，曾在多个国家获许不经资审直接投标的认可；公司于1994年被四川省建委授予建筑业对外开拓先进企业奖，获重庆市外经贸委颁发的一九九八年度对外承包工程新市场开拓企业奖。公司九十年代中期开始积极参加国内的工程建设及开发，已完工的江北国际机场联检大楼、内江至宜宾高速公路及长江宾江路照明工程等项目均被评为省市优质工程。

公司为技术密集型管理公司，专业技术力量雄厚，高中级工程技术、经济、财会、翻译人员占员工总数的82%，其中教授级高级工程师5人。公司具有独立承揽国内外各类道路、桥梁、机场、码头、给排水、工业与民用建筑、安装工程的能力。在国外的坦桑尼亚非洲公司、乌干达有限公司、苏丹有限公司，匈牙利富渝商贸公司、尼泊尔有限公司，在国内的昆明、广东、广西、海南分公司及物业管理公司，设备物质公司，劳务合作公司、工程监理公司，分别从事国际国内工程承包，进出口贸易，劳务输出、设备租凭及咨询服务等业务。公司直属企业与紧密层企业形成集团优势，以国际国内工程总承包为主业，开展国内外的各种经营活动。

公司在国际国内工程承包市场中，本着“质量第一、信誉第一”的宗旨，长期坚持“保质、守信、薄利、重义”的经营方针，热忱提供优质服务。公司业务范围广泛，经营方式灵活，在平等互利的基础上与各界同仁合作，开拓市场，共谋发展。

Chongqing International Construction Corporation (abbreviated as CICO) was approved by the Ministry of Construction of the People's Republic of China to be a first-grade contractor of construction, with the qualification of a sole legal person, and authorized by the Ministry of Foreign Trade and Economic Cooperation of the People's Republic of China to undertake contract projects, provide labor service abroad and do import ane export business. CICO'S registered capital is up to RMB160 million yuan and the machinery equipment and real estate possessed by CICO abroad come to USD12 million.

CICO has completed quite a number of construction works and labor service items with total contract amount of USD260 million in Egypt, Sudan, Somalia, Uganda, Tanzania, Kenya, South Africa, Nepal, Mongolia, Vietnam, Cambodia, Figi and Switzerland since its founding in 1985. In the past ten years and more, CICO has earned foreign exchanges amounting to more than USD30 million for the country. A number of works completed by CICO, such as the Afgoi-Baido Road, the Hargeisa-Borama Road and the Mordile Canal in Somalia, the Third Highway Project in Uganda, the West Beheira Settlement Project in Egypt, the Kulekhani Disaster Prevention Project (II) in Nepal and the E1 OBEID-EN HUNOUD Road in Sudan won favourable comments and high commendations of the Employers, the consultants, the representatives of the world Bank and the Commercial Counsellors' offices of Chinese embassies for high quality and completion on schedule. In some countries, CICO is exempted from pre-qualifying procedures in bidding process. CICO was awarded the Prize of Advanced Enterprise in Overseas Development of Construction Industry by the Sichuan Provincial Urban and Rural Construction Commission in 1994 and the Prize for New Market Development in Undertaking Overseas Works by the Chongqing Municipal Foreign Trade and Economic Cooperation Commission in 1998. From mid-1990s, CICO began to con tract and develop domestic construction works actively. The completed joint inspection building of Chongqing Jiangbei International Airport, the Neijiang- Yibin Expressway, the Changjiang Bound Road Lighting Project and so on were appraised as high quality projects.

CICO is of a technology-intensive managerial organization, 82% of whose staff members are engineers, economists, accountants and translators holding senior or intermediate professional titles including five professors of engineering, capable of independently undertaking various works of civil engineering construction such as road, bridge, airport, port, drainage system, industrial and civil buidlings and facility installation. CICO's subsidiaries and branches at home and aborad such as CICO Africa Co ltd in Tanzania, CICO Uganda Co ltd, CICO Sudan Co ltd, CICO Hungary Fuyu International KFT, CICO Nepal Co ltd, CICO Kunming Branhc, CICO Guangdong Branch, CICO Guangxi Branch, CICO Hainan Branch, CICO Property Management Co ltd, CICO Equipment & Material Co ltd, CICO labour Service Cooperation Co ltd and Chengzheng Construction Consulting Co ltd engage in international and domestic works undertaking, import, export, labour service supply abroad, equipment leasing and technical consultation separately. With the advantage of the group corporation consisting of the subsidiaries and associated corporations, CICO does diverse businesses at home and abroad, taking international works undertaking as its main line.

In domestic and overseas contracting markets, CICO, persisting in the "principle of putting quality and reputation top priority" and the operation policy of "securing high quality, standing by the deed, seeking for small profit and stressing on good faith", has been sincerely providing superior services for customers. With diverse ways of doing business and a wide range of business scope, CICO. is anticipates cooperating with friends of all circles in developing new markets and making great progress together on the basis of equality and mutual benefit.

青岛中大（集团）股份有限公司

Qingdao Zhongda (Group) Stock Co., Ltd.

青岛中大集团是由青岛中大（集团）股份有限公司为核心企业，中日合资青岛大吉制衣有限公司，中美合资青岛中大康贝尔电池有限公司、与台湾合资青岛中大运动器械有限公司为紧密层企业组建的大型企业集团。

青岛中大（集团）股份有限公司主要生产各类中、高档棉针织内衣，是大型针织内衣出口企业，拥有自营进出口权。"金牛"牌棉针织内衣在日本、东南亚及中东地区享有很高声誉，并荣获"国优"和青岛名牌产品称号。

青岛大吉制衣有限公司主要生产"BVD"牌棉针织内衣，产品全部出口日本。

青岛中大康贝尔电池有限公司主要生产"猎豹"牌系列免维护蓄电池，质量可靠，性能一流，是当今蓄电池的换代产品，填补国内空白。全套自动化生产设备国内首次由美国引进，是当代生产免维护蓄电池先进的设备，产品出口美国。

青岛中大运动器械有限公司主要生产猎豹牌系列健身器械和钢家具，产品出口美国、日本及东南亚等地区。

QINGDAO ZHONGDA GROUP is one large-size corporation, composed of the coring enterprise-Qingdao ZhongDa (Group) Stock Co., Ltd. and the member enterprises including Sino-Japanese joint venture Qingdao DaJi Clothing Co., Ltd. Sino-American joint venture Qingdzo Zhongda-Kangbeier Battery Co., Ltd., Mainland-Taiwan joint venture Qingdao Zhongda Sports Apparatus Co., Ltd.

QINGDAO ZHONGDA (GROUP) STOCK CO. LTD. is one large-scale underwears export enterprise which enjoys import and export right. Its main products are varies of moderate-and high-level cotton knitting underwears. "Golden Ox" Brand products are awarded "National High Quality Product" Title and "Qingdao Famous Brand Product" Title. In Japan, Southeast Asia and Middle East, the products enjoy high reputation.

QINGDAO DAJI CLOTHING CO., LTD. mainly produces world famous brand-"BVD" Brand cotton knitting underwears, its products are all exported to Japan.

QINGDAO ZHONGDA-KANGBEIER BATTERY CO., LTD. mainly produces series of "CHEETAH" Brand free maintenance batteries. Quality is liable, properties are first-rate. The product which is nowadays generation-renewed battery fills the blank of national battery field. A complete set of production equipment, the most advanced in the world, is introduced from U.S.A.

QINGDAO ZHONGDA SPORTS APPARATUS CO., LTD. mainly produces series of "CHEETAH" Brand sports apparatus and plastic steel furnitures. Its products have a good-ready market in U.S.A., Japan and Southeast Asia etc.

地址：中国青岛嘉宾路 5 号
Add : No. 5 Jiabin Road, Qingdao, China
邮编 (Post Code) : 266031
电话 (Tel) : 0086-0532-3757008
传真 (Fax) : 0086-0532-3717112

浙江省土产畜产进出口公司

ZHEJIANG NATIVE PRODUCE & ANIMAL BY-PRODUCTS I/E CORP.

浙江省土产畜产进出口公司成立于1975年2月，经过二十多年的发展，已成为中国外经贸系统大型企业之一，拥有员工270人，下设三个子公司，共有18个业务部、6个职能管理部门、3个直属工厂、2个自有仓库、1个海外分支机构。经营品种达20个门类、200余种，远销世界80多个国家和地区。90年代起，实施了“安全、规模、效益”经营方针后，企业获得了长足的发展，到1999年实现进出口33656万美元，其中出口30292万美元，在经贸部发表的中国进出口总额最大的500家企业中，99年名列第89位，出口额最大的200家企业中，名列第44位，并连续三年人均年创汇达百万美元，居全国外贸之前列。

本公司注册资金为7418万人民币，资金可靠，实力雄厚，享誉国内外，与世界五大洲2000家客商建立了稳定的贸易关系，并始终坚持“质量第一，信誉至上，服务上乘，互惠互利”的宗旨，竭诚欢迎世界各地的商界朋友来华以各种贸易方式与我洽谈生意，我方将根据客户需求不断开发新的经营项目和品种。

Zhejiang Native Produce & Animal By-Products Imp. & Exp. Corp. was established in Feb. 1975. Through over twenty years development, It has become one of the large-scale enterprises in China's foreign economic and trade circle. It employs 270 stuff members, consists of 3 subsidiary companies and possesses 18 business depts, 6 management (functional) depts, 3 affiliated factories, 2 wholly owned warehouses, 1 overseas branch office. The corp. deals with 20 categories, more than 200 varieties of products, selling well over 80 countries and regions in the world. Since the 1990s, the corp. has achieved great development through carring out the management principle: "Safety, Large scale, Efficiency". In 1999, its import and export volume amounted to USD 336.56 millions, ranking 89th among the top 500 import and export enterprises in China; the export volume reached USD 302.92 millions, ranking 44th among the top 200 export enterprises in China. The annual foreign exchange earning has reached USD1 million per capita for three consecutive years, ranking first in China's foreign trade circle.

Registered capital of the corp. is RMB74.18 millions. With good credibility and sound financial capabilities, the corp. enjoys high reputation at home and abroad, and has established steady trade relations with 2000 customers in the world. Adhering to the principle of "quality first, reputation first, excellent service, mutual benefit", we cordially welcome business friends from all parts of the world to our corp, for business negotiation through various trade methods. We will also devote to the development and improvement of new products or items in accordance with customer's requirements.

公司总经理：龚荣祥先生
地址：中国杭州中山北路308号　　邮编：310003
电话：0086-571-5773808/5773705
传真：0086-571-5773780/5773706
网址：http://www.zjnac.com
电子邮件：znac@mail.hz.zj.cn

GENERAL MANAGER：MR. GONG RONGXIANG
Add：308 North Zhongshan Road, Hangzhou, China 310003
Tel：0086-571-5773808/5773705
Fax：0086-571-5773780/5773706
Web Site：http://www.zjnac.com
E-mail：znac@mail.hz.zj.cn

中国石油天然气管道局

CHINA PETROLEUM PIPELINE BUREAU

中国石油天然气管道局，是中国专门从事管道勘察设计、施工建设、科技开发和技术服务的特大型国有企业。截止1999年底，拥有管道科技、勘察、设计、施工、管理等专业人才4000余人，获国家专利81项，局级以上科技进步奖287项；资产净值44亿元，拥有大型专业设备5000余台（套）；年管道施工能力3000公里，能承担2000米宽河流穿越工程。30年来，在国内外共建设长输管道21000多公里，储油罐370余座计788万立方米；穿越黄河、尼罗河等大中河流400多处；先后承揽了伊朗、伊拉克、突尼斯、马来西亚、苏丹等国际管道工程。

陕京输气管道黄河跨越

China Petroleum Bureau is the largest state-owned enterprise specialized in survey, engineering, construction and technical service for pipeline industry in China. By the end of 1999, the staffs of various professions nearly reach up to 4000 persons, awarded with 81 National patents and honored with 287 Science and Technology progress rewards and the net asset is valued RMB 4.4 billion yuan; It owns 5,000 units (sets) of large special equipment, and capable of constructing 3000 km pipeline per year and of undertaking the river crossing projects with the width 2,000 ms. In the last 30 years, more than 21,000km pipeline, and about 370 units of storage tanks with total volume of 7.88 million m^3 have been completed both at home and abroad; and 400 of the large and medium-sized river crossings such as the Yellow River and the Nile have been carried out successfully; and some overseas pipeline projects have been contracted and completed in Iraq, Kuwait, Tunis, Malaysia and Sudan.

突尼斯国输气管道下沟施工现场

塔克拉玛干沙漠输油、输气、通讯光缆三条管道同时铺设

春战涩宁兰输气管道

法人代表：苏士峰
地址：河北省廊坊市金光道46号
Add：No. 46, Jinguang Road, Langfang, Hebei
邮编（Post Code）：065000
电话（Tel）：0086-316-2075229
传真（Fax）：0086-316-2075921
网址（Web）：http://www.china-petropipe.com
E-mail：gdjcnpc@public.lfptt.he.cn

福建省林业进出口公司

Fujian Forestry Import and Export Corporation

原竹及竹地板

福建省林业进出口公司是福建林业的对外窗口，是经中华人民共和国对外贸易经济合作部核准的专业外贸公司，经营进出口及代理进出口业务。现已开拓林产化工产品、香料油、木材及其制品、竹材及其制品、鞋、帽、服装、电机、食用菌等三十多个品种，贸易涉及美国、日本、新加坡、中国香港、东南亚等二十多个国家和地区。

公司坚持“平等互利、重合同、守信用”的宗旨，竭诚欢迎国内外经贸人士前来洽谈。

Fujian Forestry Import and Export Corporation serves as a window open to the outside world for the Province's forestry industry. Approved by the Ministry of Foreign Trade and Economic Cooperation of People's Republic of China, the Corporation is professionally engaged in foreign trade and relevant agent businesses. The Corporation covers more than 30 trading commodities which include forest chemicals, spice oil, timber and its products, bamboo and its products, footwear, hats, garments, electrical machinery and edible funguses. Our trade partners are from over 20 foreign countries and regions such as United States, Japan, Singapore, Hongkong and South-east Asian Economies.

The Corporation runs on the principle of "Equality and Mutual Benefit, Credit and Contract First". We are willing to establish business relations with friends all over the world.

各种香料及香料油

Add : 7/F Sun Plaza, Hudong Road, Fuzhou, Fujian, China

Fax : 0591-7855962

http : //www.ffiec.com

E-mail : ffiec@public.fz.fj.cn

木制品

美国旭电公司
旭电（苏州）科技有限公司

Solectron Corporation & Solectron (Suzhou) Technology Co., Ltd.

美国旭电公司位于加州硅谷，是全球大型的高科技电子制造服务公司。

旭电（苏州）科技有限公司是美国旭电公司为适应客户在亚太区业务的扩展而设立的一个子公司。公司成立于1996年3月，厂址设于苏州新加坡工业园区内。公司本着成为世界一流高科技电子制造与研发公司及未来总公司亚洲区发展中心之宗旨，一直致力于电脑及周边设备及通讯与网络系统等印刷线路板组装测试及整机组装测试和销售等业务，并不断投入资金用于厂房建设，高科技生产设备购置及新员工培训等。

Solectron Corporation, located in Silicon Valley, is the world's largest electronic manufacturing services (EMS) company. The company has twice been granted Malcolm Baldrige National Quality Award in the US.

Solectron (Suzhou) Technology Co., Ltd. is a wholly owned subsidiary of Solectron Corporation founded in China-Singapore Suzhou Industrial Park in March 1996. Since its opening, the company has been engaged in addressing the increasing customer demand in the Asia Pacific Region and offering printed circuit board assembly, system integration, and box build services to its OEM (Original Electronic Equipment) customers.

地址：中国江苏省苏州市中新苏州工业园区苏茜路9号　邮编：215021
Add : No.9, Suqian Road, China-Singapore Suzhou Industrial Park, Suzhou, Jiangsu, China 215021
电话 (Tel) : 86-512-7612300
传真 (Fax) : 86-512-7618430
网址 (Web Site) : www.solectron.com

张家港浦项不锈钢有限公司

The Brief Introduction of Zhangjiagang Pohang Stainless Steel Co., Ltd.

张家港浦项不锈钢有限公司是由韩国浦项综合制铁株式会社与中国江苏沙钢集团共建的中外合资冷轧不锈钢生产企业。投资额2.16亿美元，投资比例：韩国浦项80%；沙钢占20%。年生产能力14万吨，是国内目前大型的不锈钢冷轧薄板生产厂家之一。

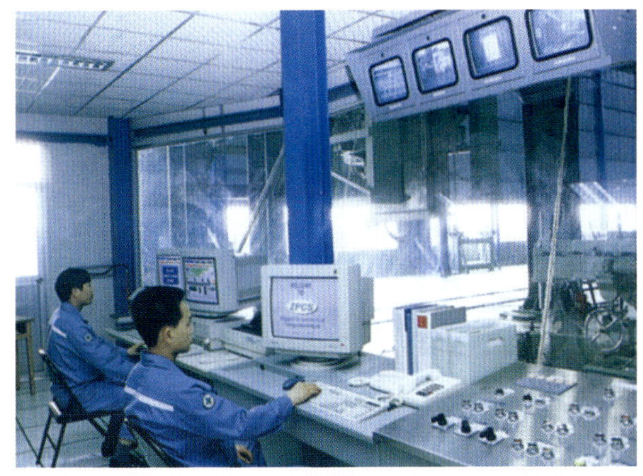

本公司采用美国等国家的先进设备，整个工艺流程实行计算机控制，生产各种规格、表面质量的冷轧不锈钢薄板，产品质量与韩国浦项相比毫不逊色。本公司另有一热镀锌板生产线，年生产能力10万吨，产品质量上乘，广泛应用于各行业。

公司全体员工本着“资源有限，创意无限”的浦项精神，全力拼搏，与广大客户携手共进。

地址：江苏省张家港市锦丰镇沿江开发区
电话（Tel）：0520-8553660
传真（Fax）：0520-8553680

Zhangjiagang Pohang Stainless Steel Co., Ltd. (ZPSS)---the biggest joint venture enterprise in China specialized in cold rolling STS, which is invested by Pohang Iron & Steel Co., Ltd., Korea (POSCO) and Jiangsu Shangang Group (Shagang) together. The total investment is US$216 million, ratio of investment is: POSCO 80%; Shangang 20%. The annual output is 140,000 tons. At present, it is one of the biggest manufacturers which produce cold rolling STS sheet in China.

The company adopt the advanced equipment from America and other countries, the whole technology flow is controlled by the computer. The cold rolling STS sheet products are in range of all specification and surface quality, and the quality of ZPSS' products is as excellent as that of POSCO.

Besides the STS, the company also has another production line of hot-dip galvanized steel, the annual output is 100,000 tons, the quality is good, and the product is used for all kinds of trade extensively.

The staff of the company will try every best to go forward with all clients together depending on the POSCO sprit of "limited resource, boundless creation".

顺达电脑厂有限公司外貌

外国客人在车间参观

先进的 BOOK ST 生产组装线

广东省顺达电脑厂有限公司

顺达电脑厂有限公司是台湾神达电脑股份有限公司于一九九三年在伦教镇投资合办的省高新技术企业。工厂占地面积30万平方米，现有员工4000多人，其中大专以上文化占三成，主要生产液晶显示屏彩显、书本电脑、个人电脑系统、机箱本体及周边配套组件。一九九九年实际出口创汇1.7亿美元，公司持有ISO9002和ISO14001国际品质与环保体系认证证书，除生产自有MITAC商标的产品外，还不断获得全球一流信息大公司认可给予大量之订单，进行OEM和ODM之生产。

地址：广东省顺德市伦教镇顺达路1号

董事长：蔡丰赐　　总经理：李祖哲

电话：(0765) 7753168　　传真：(0765) 7759246

网址：http://www.mitac.com.cn

MITAC computer (SHUN DE) Co. Ltd. is a high-technological company in LUNJIAO town of SHUNDE GUANGDONG CHINA, established in 1993. Invested by MITAC international Co. in TAIWAN. The area of firm is about 300000sq m, with more than 4000 employees including 30% junior college or above.

Our products include:

LDC MTR, Notebook, PC system, and others peripheral of computer. The export sale was US$1.7 billion in 1999. Awarded ISO9002 and ISO14001 certification. Cooperate with the globe leading computer company and processing OEM and ODM manufacture, besides "MITAC" brand production.

浙江省工艺品进出口公司

ZHEJIANG ARTS AND CRAFTS IMPORT & EXPORT CORP.

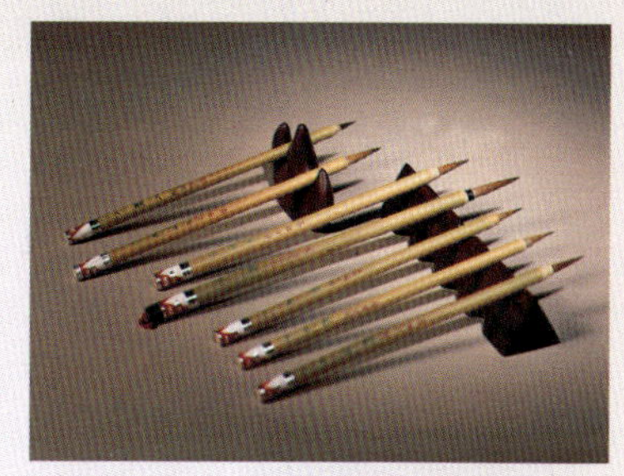

本公司自1981年成立以来，业务不断发展，1999年度出口创汇达1.3亿多美元，进出口总值达1.5亿多美元，成为中国工艺品进出口系统和浙江省外系统的骨干公司之一，在经贸部发表的中国进出口总额最大的500家企业中，96年名列第196位。

公司主要出口品种有抽纱品、礼品、服装、床上用品、特艺品、手套、鞋帽、蔺草制品、草麻制品、箱包玩具、家具、竹柳制品、伞类等十四个大类，已与世界五大洲60多个国家和地区的1500余家客户、国内1000多家生产企业建立起长期的友合作关系，拥有控股直属企业25家，并在美、日、德建立了贸易公司和代表处。

ZHEJIANG ARTS AND CRAFTS IMPORT & EXPORT CORP. was established in 1981. Since then our company has been developing very fast and the business grows constantly. By 1999 our export sales have reached over 1.3 billion US Dollars and total value of import and export sales was over 1.5 billion US Dollars. Now it becomes one of the main companies among the nation-wide arts and crafts import and export companies and provincial foreign trading enterprises. It is ranked number 200 among the top 500 import and export enterprises in the county.

The company manufactures and exports mainly 14 categories of products such as drawn-work and embroidery, gifts and toys, garments, home textiles, native handcrafts, gloves and scarves, footwear and headwear, straw and sisal products, handbags and lug-gages, furniture, bamboo and willow products, umbrellas, etc.. We have business relations with more than 1500 customers from 60 countries and areas all over 5 continents. We have established long term relationship with over 1000 manufacturers in the country and have 25 share-hold subsidiary manufacturers. We established overseas companies and offices in USA, Japan, and Germany.

We will continue to offer our customers and friends along with our best quality products and good service and cooperate with our friends from all parts of the world to create a bright future together.

公司总经理：孟庆武　General Manager : Mr. Meng Qingwu

地址：中国杭州中山北路12号　邮编 (Post Code) : 310003

Add : 12 N Zhongshan Road, Hangzhou, China

电话 (Tel) : 571-7068888

传真 (Fax) : 571-7063838/7065533/7068811/7063030

E-mail : zjarts@zjart.com

Web : www. zjart.com

东方国际（集团）有限公司

Orient International (Holding) Co., LTD.

东方国际（集团）有限公司（以下称东方国际集团）是由上海市丝绸进出口公司、上海市服装进出口公司、上海市纺织品进出口公司、上海市针织品进出口公司、上海市家用纺织品进出口公司等五家专业外贸公司，在中央有关部委的关心、支持和上海市委、市政府的指导、推动下，自愿联合组建的大型外贸企业集团。组建集团的这五家外贸公司历史悠久，经营规模较大，经营效益较好，出口业绩历年来在上海名列前茅，曾为上海口岸的外贸出口作出重大贡献。

集团组建时，上海市国有资产管理委员会授权东方国际（集团）有限公司依据产权关系，统一管理经营集团内各成员企业的国有资产。

一九九四年十一月，集团组建以来，始终坚持以改革为动力，以增强国际市场的开拓能力和竞争能力，不断推进企业结构调整和优化组合，实施产品结构、市场结构、客户结构和贸易方式结构的“四大结构调整”，依靠科技进步，产品创新，扩大出口规模，并在突出与加强主业的同时，努力拓展综合功能，加快集团成长和发展的步伐。目前，集团共有全资控股子公司20家，投资的生产、服务企业逾300家，另有各类海外企业和机构41家；与世界120多个国家和地区有着广泛的贸易往来，出口商品达5000多个大类品种；出口产品从纺织品、服装逐步扩展到轻工、机电、化工、生物医药等；集团经营业务已涉及对外贸易、对外经济技术合作、金融、物流、商业、房地产、旅游、广告展览和实业投资等各种领域。截止1998年，集团的总资产、净资产分别达到91亿元和19亿元，比集团组建时的1994年增长46%与76%；进出口总额按可比业务统计为30.5亿美元，其中出口总额为20.3亿美元，进口总额为10.2亿美元，与集团组建时相比，分别增长61%、36%和156%。在经贸部发表的中国进出口总额最大的500家企业中，99年名列第5位；出口额最大的200家企业中，99年名列第1位。

东方国际集团成立揭牌仪式（1994年11月18日）
The opening ceremony of OIH on Nov. 18, 1994

前排中：董事长、党委书记 王祖康
前排左一：副董事长、总裁、党委副书记 汪阳
前排右一：党委副书记 陈苏明
后排中：常务董事、副总裁 王龙坤
中排左二：常委董事、副总裁 许耀光
中排左一：常务董事、副总裁 钟伟民
中排右一：常务董事、副总裁 加静仪（女）
后排左一：常务董事、副总裁 张士翔
后排右一：纪委书记 陆朴鸣

根据新世纪发展蓝图，东方国际集团的发展战略目标是，基本形成与社会主义市场经济相适应的组织体制和运行机制，基本形成与大集团加速成长相适应的发展格局和经营规模；力争在新世纪，把东方国际集团建设成为与市场经济发展相适应，以贸易为导向，以实业为基础，多功能有机结合，产业结构合理，经营规模领先，在国际、国内市场有一定开拓能力和竞争能力的大型跨国企业集团，争取跻身世界大集团行列。

新世纪我们将面临新的挑战和困难，然而集团组建和发展的历程使我们更加充满信心，坚定地带领集团全体员工改革创新、锐意进取，面对新世纪，抓住新机遇，拓展新空间，寻求新发展，用我们的辛勤耕耘，迎接东方国际集团加速发展的美好春天！

OIH is a consortium consisting of Shanghai Silk I/E Co., Ltd., Shanghai Garments I/E Co., Ltd., Shanghai Textile I/E Co., Ltd., Shanghai Knitwear I/E Co., Ltd. and Shanghai Home Textiles I/E Co., Ltd. OIH was created on voluntary basis and has been endorsed by the governing ministries of the state, CPC Shanghai Municipal Committee and the municipal government of Shanghai. Before the merger, the above-mentioned companies were all successful players in the trade and stood out for profitability and export volume.

After establishment of the company in November of 1994, OIH was entrusted by Shanghai State Assets Administration to manage the assets of its member companies.

Since November 1994, OIH has positioned to enhance its marketing and competitiveness in international market. While committing itself to structural adjustment, particular in product, market, customer and means of trading, OIH has conducted R&D and product innonvation to drive export. Apart from efforts in consolidating the group's overall competitiveness, OIH never ceases to develop the capability of its members. So far, OIH has 20 wholly owned and holding subsidiaries, over 300 manufacturing and service enterprises and 41 overseas enterprises and organizations. OIH is now exporting over 5000 categories of products to some 120 countries and regions with the products ranging from textile and garments to light industrial products, machinery and electronics, petrochemicals and bio-pharmaceutical products, etc. The business of OIH now encompasses foreign trade, foreign economic and technological cooperation, financing, logistics, commerce, real estate, tourism, advertising & exhibition and investment, etc. In 1998, the group's total asset and net asset stood at 9.1 billion and 1.9 billion renminbi, an increase of 46% and 76% over 1994 respectively. The total import and export was US$3.05 billion by comparable business statistics, including uS$2.03 billion of export and US$1.02 billiion of import, an increase of 61%, 36% and 156% over 1994 respectively. OIH now ranks fifith by total import and export and thrid by export in top 500 export and import enterprises in China.

The strategy of OIH is to create a truly marker-oriented corporate structure and operation mechanism and to reach economy of scale. Also, OIH is aiming to diversify its business to become a competitive multinatinal business group.

The new century comes with new challenges, yet we have drawn confidence from the considerable growth of the group in past years, and we will continue to innovate and look for new growth opportunities. Through joined efforts we will create a beautiful future for the company.

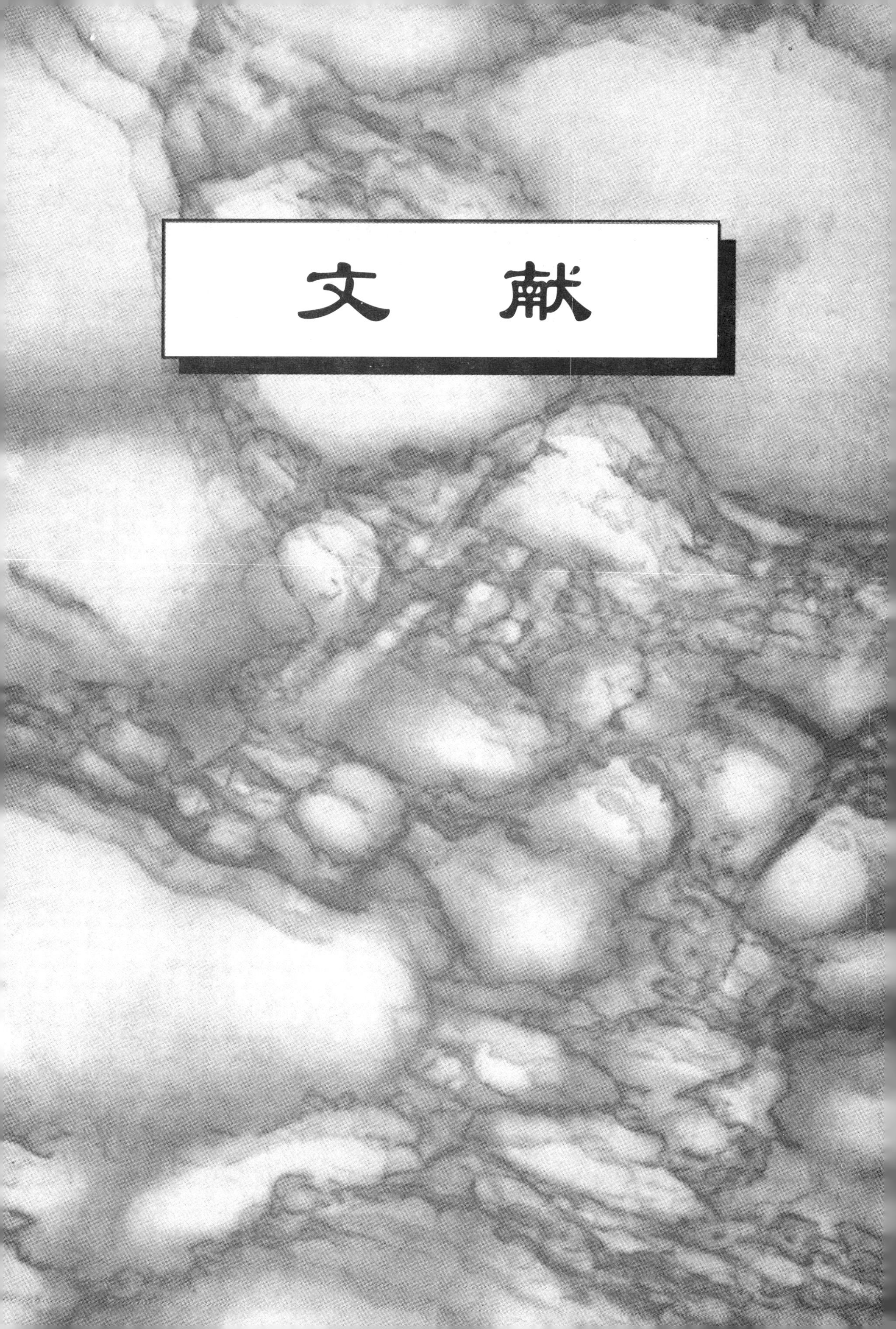

文献

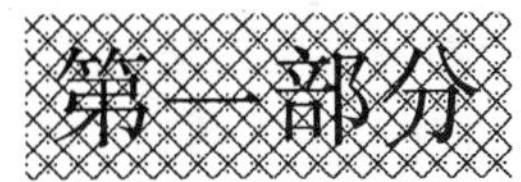

国家主席江泽民在亚太经合组织第七次领导人非正式会议上的讲话（节录）

1999 年 9 月 13 日　新西兰　奥克兰

今年是亚太经合组织成立十周年。十年来，亚太经合组织坚持推进经济合作，实现共同繁荣的宗旨，在各成员的共同努力下，不断发展壮大，已经成为亚太地区乃至世界上最重要的经济合作组织之一，总结亚太经合组织的发展历程，我认为有五条成功的经验可以记取。

一是坚持亚太经合组织的经济论坛性质，集中精力开展区域经济合作。这是亚太经合组织发挥积极作用、保持旺盛生命力的根本前提条件。

二是亚太经合组织逐步形成了自己独特的合作方式，即大家公认的“APEC 方式”。这一合作方式承认多样性，强调自主自愿、协商一致、灵活渐进等原则。实践证明，这些原则对保证各成员的经济合作沿着正确的方向发展，发挥了重要的作用。

三是按照多样性特点的要求，在实施贸易投资自由化的同时，照顾各成员的经济发展水平和承受能力，规定两个时间表，不强求一致。

四是重视经济技术合作，努力推动科技交流、技术合作和技术转让，以及在基础设施建设、人力资源开发等领域的合作，使经济技术合作与贸易投资自由化这两个轮子一起转，共同承载亚太经合组织前进。

五是根据形势的发展变化，加强对金融问题的研究和探讨，并对维护正常金融秩序、共同防范金融风险采取相应的措施。

20 世纪即将过去，新世纪的曙光已经出现。亚太经合组织向何处去，这是我们各成员的领导人都在认真思考的问题。亚太的发展离不开世界。当前，国际形势总体上仍然趋向缓和，但天下并不太平。和平与发展这两大问题至今一个也没有解决，而且面临新的挑战。世界上不稳定和不确定的因素明显增加。人们普遍感到这个世界还很不安全。在这样复杂的形势下，我们这些领导人，更需要从本国人民和世界人民的根本利益出发，顺应历史的潮流，坚持不懈地推进和平与发展的崇高事业，努力使我们生活的亚太地区，在 21 世纪成为一个和平、稳定、发展、繁荣的地区。摆在亚太经合组织面前的任务有两个，一是坚定不移地维护亚太地区和平稳定的局面，二是进一步促进亚太地区经济的增长。在这两个方面，亚太经合组织都可以也必须发挥应有的作用。我认为，要使亚太经合组织保持生命力，为地区和世界经济繁荣作出更大的贡献，应该做好六个方面的工作。

第一，积极促进亚太地区经济的共同繁荣。亚太经合组织各成员都在不同程度上受到亚洲金融危机的影响，有的受到巨大损失。克服这些影响，促进各成员经济的普遍发展，这是我们共同面临的任务，也是当务之急。各成员特别是发展中成员，要继续加强自身经济结构的调整和改革。同时发达成员要积极提供有利条件，包括实施积极负责的财政和货币政策，保持主要货币汇率的稳定，为促进地区经济的全面发展与繁荣创造良好的环境。亚太经合组织要在加强各成员，特别是加强发达成员与发展中成员之间宏观经济政策的协调与对话，缩小经济全球化趋势带来的负面影响等方面，进一步发挥自己的作用。

第二，积极深化区域经济技术合作，为亚太地区的中长期发展打下良好的基础。各成员在发展经济的同时，应着眼长远，更加注重自身能力的建设，并致力于解决影响区域经济长远发展的一些深层次问题。要推动经济技术合作取得实质性进展，特别是要加强在科技交流、人力资源开发、基础设施建设等方面的合作，进一步改善投资和贸易环境，以保证亚太经济的稳定持续发展。

第三，积极稳妥地推动贸易投资自由化进程，促进多边贸易体制的健康发展。亚太经合组织的贸易投资自由化已取得了长足的进展，特别是发展中成员为参加这一进程，克服了许多困难，作出了很大的努力。但令人遗憾的是，亚洲金融危机发生后，针对发展中成员的形形色色的贸易保护主义有所滋长。这不利于受到危机严重损害的成员的经济恢复，也不利于多边贸易体制的发展，对发达成员自身也没有好处。各成员特别是发达成员应从区域经济合作的大局出发，采取切实有效的措施，抑制贸易保护主义，进一步向发展中成员开放市场，扩大区域贸易。世界贸易组织对促进全球贸易增长发挥了重要作用。但它还缺乏完整性和代表性。亚太经合组织作为在国际经济事务中有重要影响的组织，应该为维护各成员的利益，完善多边贸易体制作出应有的贡献。

第四，积极加强国际金融领域的合作，推动建立公正合理的国际金融新秩序。金融是现代经济的核心。国际金融的稳定，关系到亚太经合组织各成员的切身利益，关系到地区经济的稳定和发展。抵御金融风险，防止金融危机的再度发生，是各成员的重要任务。为此，要改革和完善国际金融体制，促进国际金融市场安全有序地运行。特别是发达成员，要加强对国际金融流动的监管，遏制国际游资的过度投机，帮助发展中成员提高预测和防范能力。同时，要尊重有关国家和地区为克服金融危机的影响所作出的自主选择，不要将自己的制度和模式强加于人。

第五，积极维护亚太经合组织发展的正确方向，保持亚太经合组织的生机与活力。亚太经合组织有着与其他组织不同的独特的“APEC 方式”。坚持这个合作方式，亚太经合组织就能发展；试图修改或放弃这个合作方式，亚太经合组织的发展就必然会遇到困难和挫折。不论何时，都要坚持亚太经合组织的基本原则，以利为促进亚太地区的稳定和繁荣作出更大的贡献。

第六，积极推进亚太经合组织发展中成员间的互利合作。第二次世界大战以后，广大第三世界国家迅速崛起，特别是东亚发展中国家和地区创造了举世瞩目的经济成就。发展中国家尽管还面临不少困难，但始终是国际舞台上一支重要力量。它们地大物博，人口众多，具有巨大的发展潜力。加强南南合作，是所有发展中国家的共同愿望，也是当今国际关系中一个重要问题，它标志着历史发展和世界进步的方向。亚太经合组织的发展中成员应发挥各自的特长，积极进行优势互补，广泛开展南南经济合作，促进共同发展和共同繁荣。

我们高兴地看到，经过两年的艰苦奋斗，亚太地区一些国家的经济已从金融危机的影响中走出了低谷，逐步恢复增长，正在朝着好的方向发展。这是令人鼓舞的。让我们各成员共同把握机遇，从各自的实际情况出发，加强相互协调与合作，为促进亚太地区经济的合面发展与繁荣而作出不懈的努力！

政府工作报告（节录）

国务院总理朱镕基2000年3月5日在第九届全国人民代表大会第三次会议上的报告

一、1999年国内工作回顾

1999年，全国各族人民在中国共产党领导下，奋发图强，努力推进改革开放和现代化建设事业，各方面工作都取得了新的成绩。

国民经济发展质量提高。国内生产总值增长率达到预期目标，经济结构有所调整，经济效益明显改善。农业生产获得好收成，种植结构开始进行调整。工业生产在结构调整中持续增长，淘汰了一批落后生产能力，减少了市场滞销产品的生产，产品销售率稳定上升。全年工业企业实现利润2202亿元，比上年增长52%；其中国有和国有控股工业企业实现利润967亿元，增长77.7%，都创造了近五年来的最高水平。大多数行业经济效益明显回升，全国有27个省、自治区、直辖市工业效益好于上年。国家财政收入比上年增加1501亿元，总额首次突破万亿元，达到11377亿元。金融平稳运行，货币供应和信贷总量继续增长。外贸出口从7月份开始大幅度回升，全年达到1949亿美元，比上年增长6.1%。实际利用外商直接投资比上年略有减少，但保持了相当规模。人民币汇率稳定，国家外汇储备年底达到1547亿美元。整个国民经济继续朝着好的方向发展。

国有企业改革和脱困取得重要进展。政企分开步伐加快，中央党政机关与所办经济实体和管理的直属企业脱钩的工作基本完成，军队、武警部队和政法机关不再从事经商活动。重点国有企业的改组继续推进，组建了一批大型企业集团。企业内部改革和转换经营机制的工作进一步加强。通过兼并破产、改组联合、债转股和加强管理等措施，国有及国有控股大中型工业企业中的亏损户，有了显著减少。纺织行业提前一年实现三年脱困目标，其他行业也出现了增盈或减亏的好势头。东北三省等老工业基地国有企业改革和脱困有了重大转机，扭亏增盈成效显著。这些进展鼓舞了广大干部群众战胜困难的勇气和信心，说明中央确定的国有企业改革和脱困三年目标是能够实现的。

科技教育和社会事业全面发展。技术创新和科技成果转化的步伐加快，基础科学研究和高技术研究得到加强，科技体制改革进一步深化。基本普及九年义务教育和基本扫除青壮年文盲的工作取得重要进展。普通高等学校招生规模比上年扩大47.4%，增幅之大是多年来没有的。教育改革迈出新的步伐，素质教育逐步推进。环境保护和生态建设明显加强，社会科学进一步发展。文学艺术、新闻出版、广播影视、计划生育、卫生、体育等各项事业，都取得新成绩。社会主义精神文明和民主法制建设继续加强，基层民主政治建设有新的进展。深入开展严厉打击各种犯罪活动的斗争，强化社会治安综合治理，维护了社会稳定。廉政建设和反腐败斗争取得新的成果。国防现代化建设进一步加强。

城乡人民生活继续改善。从去年7月1日起，国家较大幅度增加了城镇中低收入者的收入。包括将国有企业下岗职工基本生活费水平、失业保险金水平、城镇居民最低生活保障金水平提高30%；增加机关事业单位在职职工工资和离退休人员的离退休费；提高国有企业离退休人员养老金标准；补发拖欠的国有企业离退休人员统筹项目内的养老金；提高部分优抚对象抚恤标准等。落实这些措施，国家财政共增加支出540多亿元，全国有8400多万人受益。城镇居民人均可支配收入，考虑价格下降因素比上年实际增长9.3%；农村居民人均纯收入实际增长3.8%。贫困人口减少800万人。国家增加了法定节假日天数，既促进了消费，又提高了人民的生活质量。

去年，我们隆重庆祝了新中国成立50周年，顺利实现了澳门回归祖国。这两件大事，极大地激发了全国各族人民振兴中华的热情，增强了民族凝聚力。

这些成绩的取得，是以江泽民同志为核心的党中央统揽全局、正确领导的结果。去年我们坚决反对以美国为首的北约袭击我国驻南联盟使馆的野蛮行径，沉重打击以李登辉为代表的台湾分裂势力的嚣张气焰，果断处理"法轮功"邪教问题，这些斗争取得的重大胜利，具有极其深远的政治意义，为我们从事经济建设创造了良好的社会环境。根据党中央的决定，在县级以上党政领导班子和领导干部中开展"讲学习、讲政治、讲正气"的教育，明显提高了各级领导干部的思想政治素质，保证了改革开放和社会主义现代化建设的顺利进行。与此同时，中央正确把握经济走势，在去年二季度经济出现下滑的关键时刻，果断作出了增发国债、增加居民收入等进一步扩大内需的重要决策，综合运用各种宏观调控手段，鼓励投资、消费、出口，对拉动经济增长和效益回升发挥了重大作用。经过这几年的实践和探索，我们既积累了治理通货膨胀的丰富经验，又取得了遏制通货紧缩趋势的初步经验。

这些成绩的取得，也是全国上下努力奋斗的结果。广大干部群众面对各种困难，坚定信心，知难而进，认真贯彻执行中央的方针政策，发挥了主动精神，付出了辛勤劳动。这里，我代表国务院，向奋斗在全国各条战线的广大工人、农民、知识分子、干部、人民解放军和武警部队官兵、公安干警以及各界人士，表示崇高的敬意！向关心与支持祖国建设和统一的香港特别行政区、澳门特别行政区同胞和台湾同胞以及海外侨胞，表示衷心的感谢！

我们清醒地看到，前进中还有不少困难和问题。经济生活中的主要问题仍然是有效需求不足，经济结构不合理的矛盾仍很突出，劳动就业压力增大，农民收入增长减缓。许多领域和单位管理松懈，效率低下，损失浪费惊人，重大安全事故时有发生。有些政府工作人员漠视群众疾苦，官僚主义、形式主义和虚报浮夸等问题比较突出。有的政策在一些基层没有得到认真落实。一些消极腐败现象滋生蔓延的势头还没有得到遏制。有的地方社会治安状况不好。对于这些问题，我们要继续采取有力措施，切实加以解决。

各位代表！

2000年是世纪交替之年，是全面实现我国社会主义现代化建设第二步战略目标的最后一年，做好今年政府工作具有承前启后的重要意义。各级政府要按照党中央关于今年工作的总要求，以邓小平理论和党的基本路线为指导，认真贯彻党的十五大和十五届三中、四中全会精神，继续执行中央关于推动改革开放和经济发展的一系列政策措施，正确处理改革、发展、稳定的关系，保持国民经济持续快速健康发展，切实加强社会主义精神文明建设和民主法制建设，促进社会全面进步，以优异的成绩迎接新世纪。

二、坚持实行扩大内需的方针

发展是硬道理，是解决我们面临问题的关键。只有在提高效益的前提下保持经济较快增长，才有利于缓解企业生产经营困难，减轻就业压力，促进结构调整和深化改革，也才能增加财政收入，防范金融风险，保持社会稳定。为此，我们必须坚定不移地贯彻执行扩大内需的方针，以及相应的宏观经济政策。

继续实施积极的财政政策。这是当前扩大内需最直接和有效的手段。两年来，中央坚持实施积极的财政政策，同时努力发挥货币政策的作用，综合运用多种手段调节经济运行，并不断充实和完善这些政策措施。既向银行增发国债用以扩大投资，又增加居民收入以促进消费；既加强基础设施建设，又支持企业技术改造；既努力扩大国内需求，又积极鼓励增加出口。实践证明，实行积极财政政策是完全正确的，取得的成效是明显的。从国债投资的效果看，两年来通过财政向银行发行 2100 亿元长期国债，带动 4200 多亿元银行贷款和自筹资金，用于增加基础设施投资，共建设 5100 多个项目。已建成的主要有：加固大江大河大湖堤防近 6100 公里；新增公路通车里程 1.2 万公里，其中高速公路 3358 公里；增加铁路新线 1423 公里、复线 643 公里；城市基础设施建设和环境保护整治明显加快，许多城市面貌发生了较大变化；加快了企业技术改造和高新技术产业化进程；新建和改造农村电网高低压线路 90 万公里；建成仓容 250 亿公斤的国家粮食储备库。所有这些，不仅有力地促进了当前经济增长，而且为经济的长远发展打下了更好基础。

今年继续实行积极财政政策的主要内容，包括以下几个方面。一是发行 1000 亿元长期国债，重点投向水利、交通、通信等基础投施建设，科技和教育设施建设，环境整治与生态建设和企业技术改造，并向中西部地区倾斜。新增国债投资首先用于在建项目，确保这些项目按时竣工投产。努力提高投资效益，严防“钓鱼”项目和“胡子”工程。强化工程质量管理，加强稽察和审计监督，杜绝劣质工程和挪用项目资金。二是继续贯彻落实去年出台的调整收入分配的各项政策措施，保障城镇中低收入居民的收入稳定增长。企业也应在提高经济效益的基础上适当增加职工工资。各级财政要调整支出结构，确保国有企业下岗职工基本生活费、离退休人员基本养老金、城镇居民最低生活保障金和公务员工资的按时足额发放。三是进一步运用税收、价格等手段，并继续清理某些限制消费的政策和法规，鼓励投资、促进消费、增加出口。

近年来财政赤字和债务有所增加，这是确保改革、发展、稳定大局的需要。今年把支付国债利息列入财政预算支出，赤字比按原口径计算多一些，但当年财政赤字和发债规模大体保持去年水平，仍控制在可以承受的范围内。从较长时期看，只要经济保持较快增长，经济效益不断提高，财政偿还债务的能力是有保障的。同时，我们也要积极采取措施，认真警惕和防范财政风险。

进一步发挥货币政策的作用。金融系统要正确处理支持经济增长与防范金融风险的关系，在坚持稳健经营的原则下，从多方面加大对经济发展的支持力度。中国人民银行要运用多种货币政策工具，及时调控货币供应总量。要切实改进金融服务。国有银行应加强内部资金调度，合理划分贷款审批权限，及时发放与国债投资项目配套的固定资产贷款，保证有市场、有效益、守信用企业的流动资金贷款需要。切实增加对各种所有制中小企业特别是科技型企业的贷款。努力解决农民贷款难问题。对重复建设、产品积压和需要压缩生产能力的企业，应当停止或压缩贷款。要大力发展住房、助学和大件商品的消费信贷，改进办法，简化手续，提高审贷效率。进一步规范和发展证券市场，增加企业直接融资比重。完善股票发行上市制度，支持国有大型企业和高新技术企业上市融资。依法严格审批保险企业，积极拓展保险业务。

继续按照1997年中央召开的全国金融工作会议的要求，深化金融改革，整顿金融秩序，强化金融监管和法治，防范和化解金融风险，努力提高经营效益，为进一步发挥货币政策的作用创造良好条件。

今年，除继续保持国债投资规模外，相应增加银行固定资产投资贷款和鼓励企业自筹投资，还要引导集体、私营、个体经济增加投资，并改善投资环境，吸引更多的外商直接投资。同时，要综合运用经济、法律手段和必要的行政手段，严格制止重复建设，努力提高投资效益。

要提高改革措施的透明度、改善居民心理预期，鼓励居民增加即期消费。现在，一些与群众利益密切相关的重大改革措施都已经出台，各地在落实改革措施过程中要充分考虑群众的承受能力，原来由国家和社会负担的费用不能转嫁到群众身上。要积极培育住房等新的消费热点，使住房建设真正成为重要产业。积极发展电信、旅游、文化、娱乐、保健、体育等服务性消费。特别要千方百计增加农民收入，开拓农村市场。继续严格执行减轻农民负担的有关政策。积极推进农村税费改革，从根本上减轻农民负担，今年将在安徽省进行试点，总结经验后再行展开。加大扶贫工作力度，努力实现“八七”扶贫攻坚计划的目标。

三、大力推进经济结构的战略性调整

加快经济结构的战略性调整，是当前扩大内需、促进经济增长的迫切要求，也是适应我国经济发展阶段性变化、应对日趋激烈的国际竞争的根本性措施。这种调整既要解决当前的突出问题，更要着眼于长远发展，提高国民经济的整体素质，促进经济再上新台阶。调整和优化经济结构，要坚持以市场为导向，依靠科技进步，采取适应社会主义市场经济发展的新机制、新办法。今年要着重抓好以下工作。

进一步稳定和加强农业的基础地位。在农业连年丰收、农产品相对过剩的情况下，尤其要防止忽视、放松农业的倾向。当前我国农业进入了一个新的发展阶段，对农业结构进行战略性调整是这个阶段的重要任务。要积极引导农民调整农业产业结构，发展畜牧业、林业和水产业，发展粮食和其他农产品的深加工。努力调整种植业、畜牧业品种和品质结构，积极推广应用农业科技成果，面向市场发展优质农产品。同时，发挥资源优势和区域比较优势，调整农业区域生产结构。要因地制宜，大力发展高效农业、生态农业、出口农业。在调整农业结构中，要充分尊重农民生产经营自主权，不能搞强迫命令。

发展专业合作经济组织和公司加农户等产业化经营，把分散经营的农户同大市场连接起来，带动农业结构调整。引导和支持乡镇企业面向市场调整结构，提高管理水平和技术水平。统筹规划，采取有力的政策措施，加快小城镇发展。切实保护耕地。进一步加强以水利为重点的农业基础设施建设，改善农村生产和生活条件。

加大工业结构调整力度。要围绕优化结构、提高质量和效益、增强国际竞争力，着重抓好四个环节。一是遵循市场经济规律，综合运用多种手段，限制没有市场销路的产品生产。进一步关闭技术落后、质量低劣、浪费资源、污染严重的小厂小矿；淘汰落后的设备、技术和工艺，压缩一些行业的过剩生产能力。二是采取有力措施加快企业技术改造，并向老工业基地倾斜。坚持质量第一，采用先进标准，更新和优化产品结构。努力开发有市场需求的新技术、新工艺和新产品；鼓励增产适销对路产品，特别是名优产品。三是积极发展新兴产业和高技术产业，特别是发展信息、生物工程、新能源、新材料和环保等产业。同时，注意发展劳动密集型产业。四是继续推进行业改组，促进重点行业提高规模效益，优化布局。努力提高重大装备工业和基础材料工业的生产技术水平。国务院有关部门要抓紧制定规划和相应的配套措施，促进工业结构调整和优化升级。

发展第三产业，对于优化经济结构、广开就业门路和扩大消费，有着重要作用。在继续发展运输、商贸等产业的同时，要大力发展信息、金融、旅游、社区服务和中介服务等产业，逐步提高第三产业在国民经济中的比重。

实施西部地区大开发战略，加快中西部地区的发展，是党中央贯彻邓小平关于我国现代化建设“两个大局”战略思想，面向新世纪所作出的重大决策。这对于扩大内需、推动国民经济持续增长，对于促进各地区经济协调发展，最终实现共同富裕，对于加强民族团结、维护社会稳定和巩固边防，都具有十分重要的意义。实施这个重大决策，是一项系统工程和长期任务，既要有紧迫感，又必须统筹规划，突出重点，分步实施，防止一哄而起。

当前和今后一段时期，要集中力量抓好以下几个方面。一是加快基础设施建设。以公路建设为重点，加强铁路、机场、天然气管道干线的建设。加强电网、通信、广播电视以及大中城市基础设施建设。尤其要把水资源的合理开发和节水工作放在突出位置。要抓紧做好若干重大骨干工程的研究论证和前期准备工作，争取早日开工建设。二是切实搞好生态环境保护和建设。大力开展植树种草，治理水土流失，防治荒漠化。加大长江上游、黄河上中游天然林保护工程的实施力度。陡坡耕地要有计划、有步骤地退耕还林还草。抓住当前粮食等农产品相对充裕的有利时机，采取“退耕还林（草）、封山绿化、以粮代赈、个体承包”的综合性措施，以粮换林换草。这项工作要加强规划和政策引导，尊重农民意愿，搞好试点，逐步推行。要坚决制止新的毁林毁草开荒。三是根据当地的地理、气候和资源等条件，着力发展有自己特色的优势产业，有条件的地方要发展高新技术产业。四是大力发展科技和教育。加快科技成果转化，积极培养各级各类人才，全面提高劳动者素质。五是进一步扩大对外开放。改善投资环境，积极引进境外资金、技术和管理经验。

东部地区要继续发挥优势，不断提高经济素质和竞争力，更好地发展和壮大自己，有条件的地方要率先实现现代化。同时，继续采取联合开发、互利合作、对口支援、干部交流等多种形式，加大对中西部地区的支持力度。中西部地区要抓住机遇，加快改革开放步伐，发扬自力更生、艰苦创业的精神，注重实效，扎实工作，努力搞好各项建设。

四、继续推进改革，全面加强管理

要按照党中央确定的建立和完善社会主义市场经济体制的要求，继续推进各项改革，为促进结构调整、提高经济效益和实现国民经济持续快速健康发展提供强大的动力。

国有企业改革是深化经济体制改革的中心环节。贯彻落实党的十五届四中全会决定，实现国有企业改革和脱困三年目标，使大多数国有大中型亏损企业摆脱困境，在大多数国有大中型骨干企业初步建立现代企业制度。这是今年政府工作的重中之重。要抓紧制定符合我国国情的现代企业制度的基本规范，使企业有所遵循。突出抓好企业管理体制改革、转换企业经营机制和完善法人治理结构。加强和改善对国有大中型企业的稽察和监管，逐步健全和规范监事会制度。依法向国有企业派出监事会，检查企业财务，对董事、经理的职务行为进行监督，维护国有资产所有者权益。加强国有重点企业领导班子的管理和建设。进一步完善企业集团对所属子公司的管理，构建符合现代企业制度要求的母子公司体制。深化企业劳动、人事、分配等各项制度改革，建立企业激励机制、约束机制。在部分好的企业试行经理（厂长）年薪制、持有股权等分配方式。认真落实增加银行核销呆坏账准备金的规模、对符合条件的企业实行债转股、提高企业直接融资比重等措施，改善国有企业资产负债结构，促进企业扭亏脱困。稳步推进国有经济的战略性调整。积极探索公有制的多种有效实现形式。宜于实行股份制的国有大中型企业，要利用股票市场，抓紧进行股份制改革。努力培育具有国际竞争力的大型企业集团，同时，从实际出发，采取多种形式放开搞活国有中小企业。加快中小企业服务体系建设。坚持公有制经济为主体，鼓励和引导个体、私营等非公有制经济健康发展。

继续贯彻执行中央关于粮食流通体制改革的方针政策。坚持按保护价敞开收购农民余粮。

认真执行粮食优质优价政策，促进粮食品种结构调整。根据市场供需情况和调整粮食品种结构的需要，国务院已确定部分粮食品种退出保护价收购范围，要做好相应的政策调整工作。继续抓好国有粮食购销企业改革，推进政企分开，转换经营机制，努力降低成本。要总结实践经验，进一步完善粮食流通体制改革的政策和措施。

财税、金融、投融资、分配、流通等方面的体制改革，要继续有序推进。城镇住房和医疗保险、医药卫生体制的改革，中央已经制定了指导性意见，各省、自治区、直辖市要因地制宜作出决策，组织实施。

现在，中央关于改革和发展的大政方针已经明确，一些重要的法律、法规也已颁布。要保证中央的政策措施和国家的法律法规真正得以贯彻落实，当务之急是“严”字当头，强化管理。当前，生产、建设、流通等各个领域普遍存在管理松懈、纪律松弛、秩序混乱的现象，有些地方和单位有法不依、有令不行、有禁不止，严重影响中央方针政策的贯彻落实和各项改革的推进，已经到了非解决不可的时候。今年，国务院各部门和地方各级政府都要以改革的精神，突出抓好管理。工业、农业、财税、金融、贸易和科技、教育、文化、卫生等各行各业，也都要在加强管理上下大功夫。这里讲的管理，包括加强监督和整顿。

切实加强企业科学管理。所有企业都要从严治企，苦练内功，着力抓好成本管理、资金管理和质量管理等薄弱环节。要根据国内外市场变化，正确制定企业发展战略、技术创新战略和市场营销战略。充分依靠和发挥职工群众积极性，健全企业民主管理制度，实行厂务公开。特别要加强企业基础管理工作，改变部分企业账目不清、数字不实、信息失真的状况，严禁弄虚作假。高度重视和切实加强安全生产，及时消除事故隐患。建立和完善各项规章制度，严格实行各个环节的岗位责任制。国有企业领导班子要认真执行廉洁自律的有关规定，坚决抵制和反对各种腐败现象。

严肃财经纪律，严格财经管理。增强预算的透明度和约束力。加强预算执行的监督和审计。切实贯彻《会计法》，提高会计信息质量。依法治税，严禁越权减免税收行为，依法清理和收缴欠税，加大打击偷税、逃税、骗税、抗税的力度，维护税法的统一性和严肃性。进一步加强各种财政性资金的“收支两条线”管理和监督检查，将预算外资金管理纳入法制化轨道。大力清理和取消各种乱收费。切实加强对金融机构的监管，特别要采取有效措施，加强对金融机构各级主要领导干部和重要业务人员的监督和管理。继续清理和整顿非法的和有严重问题的金融机构。加强和改进外汇管理。整顿社会信用，严格结算纪律。依法收贷收息，清还企业间相互拖欠。清理和规范经济鉴证类社会中介机构。加强行政监察和审计监督，充分发挥监察和审计部门的作用。

进一步整顿市场秩序。依法严厉惩处制售假冒伪劣商品、侵犯消费者权益和各种商业欺诈行为。继续严厉打击走私贩私活动。坚决制止各 种分割、封锁市场的地方保护和不正当竞争行为。取缔非法药品市场，严肃查处医药购销中的违法行为。严格执行《建筑法》、《招标投标法》，建立健全和严格执行项目法人责任制、招标投标制、工程监理制和合同管理制，严肃查处建设单位规避招标或搞假招标的行为，禁止勘察、设计、施工、监理等单位转包和违法分包的做法。

全面加强管理，从根本上说是要依法规范和维护社会主义市场经济秩序，形成和健全各方面的科学管理制度和机制。各行各业和各单位都要坚持高标准、严要求，找准自己在管理方面存在的问题，立即从规章制度建设和转换机制等方面采取措施，强化管理和监督。各级领导干部都要坚持原则，不怕得罪人，敢于抓管理；同时，也要适应改革开放的新情况，采取有效的方法和手段，善于抓管理。

五、加快科技、教育发展，加强精神文明建设

积极实施科教兴国战略和可持续发展战略，促进经济结构调整，提高经济整体素质，推动经济和社会协调发展。

大力开发和推广对传统产业升级起关键作用、有共性的高新技术。推动优势科技力量，参与企业技术改造和重大引进项目的消化吸收与创新工作。加快高新技术产业化进程，重点培育一批竞争力强的高新技术产品和企业。继续办好国家高新技术产业开发区。加强国家创新体系建设。重视和加强基础研究和高技术研究，支持一支精干的高水平科研队伍，在这些领域进行开拓性的工作。继续推进科技管理体制改革，使应用型科研机构和其他有面向市场能力的科研机构转制为企业，或进入企业加强技术开发工作；同时进行社会公益类科研机构的改革试点。积极发展多种形式的产学研结合。加强知识产权的保护和管理。加大对科技、

教育的投人，提高资金使用效益。积极发展哲学社会科学。哲学社会科学工作者要深入研究改革开放和现代化建设中的重大理论和实践问题，更好地为建设有中国特色社会主义的事业服务。

深化教育改革，全面推进素质教育。各级各类学校都要加强德育工作，努力培养学生的创新精神和实践能力，切实减轻中小学生过重的课业负担，促进学生德、智、体、美全面发展。要加大工作力度，如期实现基本普及九年义务教育和基本扫除青壮年文盲工作的目标。进一步发展高中阶段教育、高等教育和各类职业教育。继续扩大普通高等学校招生，通过后勤服务社会化等措施，解决学生宿舍、食堂、教学设施等实际问题。大力推行个人助学信贷。广开渠道，为高校毕业生就业创造条件。积极发展民办教育。运用现代信息技术，发展远程教育。继续推进教育管理体制改革，今后除教育部和少数特殊部门外，国务院其他部门不再直接管理学校，形成中央和省两级政府办学、以地方政府管理为主的新体制。深化学校内部管理体制改革，高度重视学校思想政治工作。加强教师队伍建设，全面提高教师素质。加大各方面对贫困地区教育对口支援的力度。

改革和完善优秀人才的收入分配制度，形成激励机制。对在国家关键领域和岗位工作的科技人员，要采取特殊措施改善他们的工作和生活条件。同时，实行有效的政策，鼓励和吸引留学人员以及在国外的优秀人才回国工作。

坚持走可持续发展道路。继续加强计划生育工作，努力稳定低生育水平，搞好优生优育，重点抓好农村和流动人口计划生育管理与服务。加强老龄人口的工作。关心和支持残疾人事业。认真贯彻实施中国妇女、儿童发展纲要。要加大城市环境污染治理力度，突出抓好重点城市、流域、区域、海域污染防治工程，全面实现既定的环境保护和治理目标。搞好城乡规划工作。加强自然资源管理，依法保护和合理利用土地、森林、草原、矿产、海洋和水资源。进一步做好卫生、体育工作，重视疾病预防和控制，加强城市社区卫生服务和农村初级卫生保健，提高人民群众的健康水平。

各级政府要坚持“两手抓、两手都要硬”的方针，高度重视和加强社会主义精神文明建设。既要重视提高科学文化水平，又要切实抓好思想道德建设。继续进行爱国主义、集体主义、社会主义教育，引导广大人民群众特别是青少年树立正确的世界观、人生观、价值观，坚定建设有中国特色社会主义的理想信念。深入扎实地开展群众性精神文明创建活动。要在全社会弘扬科学精神，普及科学知识，传播科学方法，反对愚昧迷信。繁荣文学艺术、新闻出版、广播影视等事业，坚持正确的舆论导向，多出思想性和艺术性相统一的优秀精神产品。搞好文物保护和档案工作。加强文化设施建设。整顿娱乐、音像和书报刊市场，加强文化市场管理，继续开展“扫黄打非”斗争，严厉打击盗版活动。倡导文明健康的生活方式，开展丰富多彩的群众性文化、体育活动。

六、进一步扩大对外开放

当前，世界经济贸易形势总体趋好，我国加入世贸组织的进程加快。我们必须抓住新的机遇，迎接新的挑战，采取更加有力的措施，以更为积极的姿态扩大对外开放，力争对外贸易和利用外资有新的增长。

继续实行以质取胜和市场多元化战略，贯彻落实各项鼓励出口的政策，努力扩大出口。一是积极调整出口商品结构，进一步扩大机电产品出口，加快纺织、服装、轻工等传统出口商品的升级换代，提高高新技术产品的出口比重。扩大农产品出口。二是积极开拓国际市场，特别要大力拓展非洲、拉美、东欧、独联体等新兴市场，积极发展与周边国家及发展中国家的经贸关系。鼓励国内有比较优势的企业到境外投资办厂，开展加工贸易，或者合作开发资源。继续发展对外承包工程和劳务合作。三是深化外贸体制改革。外贸企业要形成积极开拓国际市场的经营机制，强化内部管理。进一步扩大生产企业的自营出口权。减少出口商品主动配额的品种，改革配额管理和招标办法。优化进口商品结构，增加国内急需的关键设备、技术和重要原材料的进口。抓紧研究和推进电子商务。

积极有效地利用外资。进一步扩大对外开放的领域和地域。逐步推进商业、外贸、金融、保险、证券、电信、旅游和中介服务等领域的对外开放。放宽外商投资在技术转让、内销比例和一些行业持股比例的限制，鼓励外商投资农业、基础设施、环保产业和高新技术产业。积极吸引跨国公司来华投资，特别是鼓励他们投资研究开发和参与国有企业的改组、改造。

适应我国加入世贸组织步伐加快的形势，抓紧做好各项准备工作。各行各业和广大企业都要加快改革，强化管理，提高技术水平，增强竞争能力和抗御风险能力。同时，抓紧调整和完善有关的法律法规。大力培训各类专门人才。(以下略)

吴仪国务委员在全国外经贸工作会议上的讲话（节录）

1999年12月22日

一、今年外经贸工作取得了比较好的成绩，应该充分肯定

关于今年外经贸工作的成绩，石广生同志还将做全面总结，我认为以下几个方面比较突出：

第一，外贸出口比预计的要好，不仅转降为升，而且近几个月增长幅度还比较大。考虑到去年外贸出口只增长了0.5%，亚洲金融危机的阴影还比较重，我们面临的困难比较多，因此年初提出的目标是力争实现一定程度的增长。一定程度是多少？一般都认为是1%左右的样子。实际情况是上半年还是负增长。从7月份开始，外贸出口扭转了近一年连续下降的局面，出现了增长的势头，增长幅度逐月上升。1至11月，增长了6.6%。这里边不排除一些地方存在虚报出口、骗取退税的问题，但总的看，出口呈逐步上升的趋势。考虑到去年12月份基数比较大，预计全年可以增长5%左右。这样的成绩确实是比预计的要好，可以看出，我国的外贸出口已经基本摆脱了亚洲金融危机的阴影，重新步入增长轨道。

第二，利用外资保持了较大规模，完成了预定的目标。年初我们考虑受亚洲金融危机的影响，全年实际利用外资可能会在350亿美元左右。现在统计，1至11月份，实际利用外资370.9亿美元，已经实现了预定的目标，到年底还会再增加一些。

上述两项成果对于拉动经济增长、实现全年经济工作目标具有不可忽视的重要作用。如今年我们的外贸出口增长5%，就比去年净增92亿美元，这就等于增加了760多亿元人民币的市场需求，还可以增加大量人员就业。

第三，对外承包工程和劳务合作取得了新的发展。据统计，对外承包工程和劳务合作营业额预计全年将达到105亿美元以上，这也是历年来最高的水平。

第四，与美国就中国加入世贸组织达成了双边协议，排除了我加入世贸组织的主要障碍。这一重大胜利，是以江泽民同志为核心的党中央高瞻远瞩，审时度势，从战略高度处理中美关系的结果。在党中央、国务院的领导下，外经贸部做了大量工作，包括全面研究我加入世贸组织问题，与有关部门、地方和企业沟通情况，广泛征求意见，深入调查研究；谈判中坚持原则，维护我国尊严，夜以继日开展工作等，这些也应该充分肯定。

总之，今年外经贸工作成绩比较好。全国所有从事外经贸工作的同志为此作出了积极的努力，付出了辛勤的劳动。我代表国务院向所有从事外经贸工作的同志和支持外经贸工作的国务院有关部门、各级地方政府表示衷心的感谢和诚挚的慰问。

总结今年的外经贸工作，我们可以得出两点重要启示。一是要充分发挥政策的整体集成效应。用发展的方法解决前进中的问题，适应形势变化适时调整宏观经济政策，在关键时刻

及时采取措施解决突出问题，是中央总结近年来领导经济工作的三条基本经验之一。今年上半年外经贸面临出口下降、利用外资减少的困难，国家果断地采取一系列积极措施，鼓励扩大出口，特别是鼓励扩大机电产品出口，鼓励扩大利用外资，鼓励企业开展境外带料加工，完善加工贸易管理。不少地方也结合自己的实际情况，制定了相应的政策措施，调动了企业的积极性，扭转了出口下降的局面。事实证明，制定符合实际的政策，结合实际执行政策，是我们做好工作的重要保证。二是在困难的时候要保持良好的精神状态，坚定信心，努力工作。今年所有从事外经贸工作的同志在困难面前没有丧失信心，没有退缩。外经贸部连续召开会议，千方百计，广开思路，狠抓各项扩大外贸出口和利用外资政策的落实。国务院各有关部门通力协作，密切配合，地方外经贸部门和各类外贸企业广大干部职工想方设法克服困难，才使外贸出口有了这样显著的成绩。这样的成绩来之不易。今后我们的外经贸工作还可能遇到这样那样的困难，希望同志们永远保持这样一种精神状态。

在这里，我也请同志们注意，今年我国外经贸工作，特别是外贸出口转降为升的轨迹与世界经济的变化是大体一致的。亚洲经济今年基本上走出了困境，经济增长从第一季度到第三季度，，韩国由 4.5% 上升到 12.3%，香港由 -3.2% 跃升到 4.5%，日本由 -0.4% 回升到 0.9%，其他一些国家、地区都有不同程度的增长。欧洲经济有起色，美国经济持续增长。这说明，随着我国对外联系日益密切，世界经济的波动对我国外经贸工作的影响也越来越直接。

二、当前国际经济形势及对我外经贸工作的影响

明年世界经济形势，总的看仍然趋好。国际货币基金组织等一些国际机构都对当前世界经济增长率做出了比较乐观的估计。12 月 7 日世界银行发表的报告，把对今年世界经济增长率的预计从原先估计的 1.8% 提高到 2.6%，对明年增长率的预计也从 2.4% 提高到了 2.9%。在国际上颇有权威的美林证券公司日前也发表预测报告指出，今年全球经济增长可能为 2.7%，明年可望达到 3.3%，在美国、日本和欧洲经济增长的同时，亚洲和拉丁美洲的新兴市场也将出现经济强劲复苏的局面，其增长率可望分别达到 6% 和 3.3%。预测的数字尽管不同，但都认为明年全球经济的增长速度将会加快。世贸组织还预计，国际商品价格将有所回升，国际贸易将出现新的增长态势，明年世界贸易增长率将超过今年，达到 6% - 7%。

当然也要看到，世界经济增长的基础并不牢固，风险和隐患仍然不同程度地存在。美国股市和美元汇率有可能发生波动，欧洲失业率居高不下，成为困扰欧元区经济的一大难题。日本长期积累的结构性问题短期内难于克服。受金融危机冲击的国家经济复苏的基础还很薄弱，不能排除局部地区突发动荡和反复的可能性。就国际贸易来看，保护主义盛行，一些国家经常利用技术壁垒、严格的商检等手段对进口设限。

在分析国际经济形势时，有三个动向值得我们高度关注。这就是江总书记在中央经济工作会议上对今后一个时期世界经济形势发展趋势所作出的基本判断：世界范围内正在进行经济结构调整，科技进步突飞猛进，跨国公司的影响力日益增大。根据这个判断，我认为世界经济形势的主要特点以及对我国外经贸工作的影响还表现在以下几个方面：

第一，科技进步和知识创新，推动世界范围内的经济结构加快调整。高新技术的发展和广泛运用，使社会生产方式和生活方式发生了重大变化，知识或智力资源的占有、配置、生产和应用已成为经济发展的主要依托。世界各国尤其是发达国家的产业结构、产品结构、企业结构发生了重大变化。新兴产业特别是信息产业的发展，正在改变和取代传统产业。伴随着全球范围经济结构的调整，国际贸易正在进入结构调整期，高科技产品、信息产品等新兴产品的国际需求增多，初级产品、低附加值产品的国际需求相对减少，国际市场竞争更加激烈。为了抢占21世纪国际竞争的制高点，世界各国纷纷重视科技进步和产品创新，加大科技投入，提高自身竞争能力。科技进步和知识创新日益成为国际经济竞争的主导力量。而在我国出口商品中，利润低的初级产品所占比重大，高技术产品特别是拥有自主知识产权的高技术产品出口少，出口商品结构不够优化的矛盾将更加突出。

第二，跨国公司的迅速扩张，加速了生产、投资、贸易、金融的全球化。经济全球化促使世界经济从国际贸易时代向国际生产时代转变，资源在全球范围内的配置有利于生产力的发展和世界经济的增长，但又使世界各国贫富差距扩大，造成国际力量对比失衡，南北矛盾加剧。它使金融风险增大，风险转嫁问题更加突出。经济全球化凸现了我国在市场规模和劳动力成本等方面的优势，有利于产业结构的调整和优化。但我国经济发展水平还不高，利用机遇和防范风险能力相对较弱，对我国经济安全造成潜在威胁。我国国有外经贸企业普遍债务负担沉重，一些企业体制僵化、管理混乱、融资困难。这些长期以来存在的老问题仍然是制约我国外经贸发展的重要因素。

第三，世纪之交，国际资本流动出现若干新的特征：国际资本流动的速度、流动的规模不断扩大，国际资本市场融资和外国直接投资总额由1986年的2.8万亿美元增加到1998年的13.8万亿美元；国际资本结构由传统的银行资金为主转为外国直接投资、银行信贷和债权市场三分天下的基本格局；越来越多的国际直接投资开始采取并购的形式，发达国家之间的资本流动成为国际资本流动的主流，目前，全球直接投资的一半以上是以跨国企业并购形式进行的，并且90%以上发生在发达国家之间。我国虽然连续6年成为吸引外资最多的发展中国家，但由于我们跨国公司的数量和规模远落后于发达国家，吸收外资方式还难以适应当前国际资本流动的变化趋势。

总之，从当前国际国内经济形势总体发展趋势看，随着国际经济形势的好转和我国国民经济持续稳定增长，明年我国外经贸发展的环境可能稍好于今年。我们要抓住这一有利时机，推动我国外经贸取得新的发展。但我们也要看到，由于国际市场竞争日益激烈和我国经济结构存在的深层次矛盾，我国外经贸发展仍然面临着许多不确定因素，外贸出口和利用外资的形势仍很严峻，因此，我们要保持清醒的头脑，不能盲目乐观，要充分估计各种可能遇到的挑战和困难，做好应对各种困难的准备。

三、认真落实中央经济工作会议精神，做好明年的外经贸工作

明年是世纪交替之年，也是完成“九五”计划的最后一年。中央对做好明年的经济工作非常重视。关于外经贸的具体工作，石广生同志还要部署，我只强调几个问题：

（一）要坚持从大局出发，为国民经济总体发展目标服务

外经贸是我国国民经济的重要组成部分，外经贸工作要始终从国民经济发展大局出发，充分发挥自身的应有作用，为实现中央经济工作会议提出的各项任务服务。

大力调整经济结构，促进产业优化升级，是当前和今后一个时期我国经济工作的主要着力点。外经贸工作要主动加快外经贸政策和产业政策的相互融合，及时为国内生产企业提供国际市场信息；优化进口结构，增加进口国内产业升级和结构调整所需的技术、设备和商品；优化外商投资的产业结构，引导外商投资鼓励类产业。

贯彻党的十五届四中全会精神，加快国有企业改革，是明年我国经济工作的重中之重。目前，我国所有大中型国有工业企业已基本取得对外经营权，要加强引导国有工业企业发挥自身比较优势开拓国际市场；充分利用多双边经贸交流的机会，更多地向国外推出我国的优势企业和产品；要按照党的十五届四中全会精神，加大国有外经贸企业改革力度，努力使国有外经贸企业重新焕发生机与活力。

不失时机地实施西部大开发战略，加快中西部地区经济发展，是党中央总揽全局，面向新世纪作出的重大决策。我认为，进一步加大中西部地区对外开放力度，大力发展对外经济贸易，以开放促发展，是加快中西部发展的重要途径。外经贸战线的同志们，要把支持西部大开发当作己任。要抓紧落实国家已出台的鼓励中西部地区发展的各项政策，并针对实际情况，加大政策扶持力度，进一步提出有利于中西部对外开放的优惠政策。在对外招商中，要把中西部地区放到突出的地位，吸引更多的外资投向中西部地区；要鼓励和支持沿海地区的外商投资企业到中西部地区开展再投资，实现产业梯度转移。要按照国家的政策导向，因势利导，吸引更多的外商投资于国家鼓励的交通、能源等基础设施建设项目和生态农业、水资源综合利用等环境保护项目以及高新技术项目；允许中外合资合作，开发中西部地区的旅游资源。大胆鼓励外资参与中西部地区国有工业企业的改组改造。要打通中西部地区通江达海、连接周边国家的运输通道；认真落实边境贸易的各项优惠政策，鼓励中西部地区大力发展边境贸易。

（二）力争出口较快增长，尽可能多地吸收外资，为国民经济发展多做贡献

千方百计扩大出口，积极有效利用外资，是中央经济工作会议对外经贸工作提出的重要任务，明年外经贸工作一定要为完成这一任务下大功夫。今年我们加大对外贸出口的扶持力度，出台多项鼓励措施，这些措施将在明年继续发挥有效作用。要保持政策的稳定性，并及时予以完善。加工贸易目前在我国外资中占的比重很大，加工贸易出口已接近50%。对加工贸易要坚持优化存量、控制增量、规范经营、提高水平的方针，关键是要加强监管。今年出台并根据外商、加工贸易企业和地方的意见调整了一些政策措施，出发点就是贯彻好这个方针。希望各地、各部门在执行新的加工贸易政策中作好完善工作，及时了解执行中的问题，并认真、及时加以解决。

外贸出口步入增长轨道后，研究鼓励出口政策一定要立足长远，要从研究制定应对亚洲金融危机的短期措施为主，向建立健全长期稳定的出口促进体系为主转变，推动出口融资担保基金、中小企业开拓国际市场专项基金、出口保函基金的建立，完善出口信用保险。外经贸部和国务院有关部门从现在起就要着手这方面的工作。

利用外资工作要着重做好商业、金融、保险、电信、旅游等领域的对外开放，提高我国

服务业的发展水平，推动我国服务贸易逐步走向国际市场；推动吸收外资从依靠政策优势向综合环境优势转变，改进各级政府部门的工作，改善对外资企业服务，妥善解决外商投资中的经济纠纷；要积极探索在国有企业改革中利用外资的有效途径，完善相关立法，允许外资进入企业拍卖市场或通过购并参与国有企业的改组改制，有重点地推动国有大中型企业与跨国公司的联合。

（三）依靠科技进步，努力提高我国出口商品竞争力

依靠科技创新和技术进步，是提高我国出口商品竞争力的首要途径。在去年全国外经贸工作会议上，外经贸部提出了科技兴贸战略。一年来，外经贸部和科技部等部门一起做了很多工作，制定并组织实施了《科技兴贸行动计划》，取得了初步成效。实践证明，科技兴贸是我国从贸易大国走向贸易强国的必由之路，是科教兴国战略在外经贸领域的具体体现。从长远和发展的眼光来看，通过实施科技兴贸战略，能尽快实现我国出口商品结构调整，从而大大提高我国出口商品的国际竞争力。在当前及今后一个时期，优化出口商品结构，提高国际竞争力要重点抓好以下几项工作。一是努力扩大高技术含量、高附加值机电产品的出口。机电产品是近年来我国最具竞争力和发展潜力的出口商品，是我国外贸出口的新增长点。今年1－11月，全国机电产品出口增长16.4%，远高于同期外贸出口的增长速度。要把它作为出口商品的龙头，紧紧抓住，下大力气挖掘潜力。要采取有效措施，鼓励机电企业跟踪行业技术发展的前沿，大胆进行技术创新，在国际市场上形成中国机电产品的技术特色和科技优势。二是大力发展高新技术产品出口，要加速推动科研院所和生产企业的结合、生产企业和外经贸企业的结合，实现科工贸一体化，促进高科技产业化，推动更多的高新技术产品走向国际市场。三是加快纺织、服装等传统出口商品的升级换代。针对当前纺织行业存在的后整理技术落后，面料品质不高、缺少知名品牌等问题，加强技术攻关，提高产品质量和档次，扩大国际市场份额。四是面向国际市场，大力提高技术水平和管理水平，结合农业产业化经营，促进农产品加工转化、增值，使更多的农产品走向国际市场。五是从各方面着手，多管齐下，通过争创名牌、更新营销观念和方式、强化售后服务等手段，变长期以来我国出口商品单一的价格优势，为科技、品牌、营销、服务和价格的综合优势。

（四）加强部际协调和部门协作，创造外经贸发展的有利环境

在今年的外经贸工作中，各项鼓励扩大出口、利用外资政策的制定出台、贯彻落实都离不开计委、经贸委、财政、金融、海关、税务、外汇、商检等部门的密切配合。我希望各有关部门，继续坚持这种好的做法，及时相互沟通情况，协调政策。外经贸主管部门要和其他有关部门建立必要的协商合作机制。每一个部门都要跳出本部门的小圈圈，站在全局的高度来看待外贸出口和吸收外资工作，多搞优势互补，少搞磨擦，要形成发展对外经贸的合力，共同为我国外经贸发展创造良好的政策环境，促进国民经济的发展。

我还要讲一讲关于各地机电办机构改革和国家级经济技术开发区的管理问题。目前，各地正在进行政府机构改革。关于各地机电办的改革问题，国务院已经明确要按照上下对口的原则进行改革。各地经贸部门要按照这一原则，和当地外经贸委做好衔接，将机电办的机构、职能、人员成建制地划转外经贸主管部门，保持机电产品进出口管理队伍的稳定。

前不久，国务院决定，国家级经济技术开发区的有关具体业务工作，由外经贸部综合协

调和指导。国家级经济技术开发区是我国对外开放的排头兵，在我国外贸出口和吸收外资等各项外经贸工作中发挥着重要作用。国家级经济技术开发区一开始建立就确定了“三为主一致力”的方针，即以吸收外资为主、工业项目为主、出口创汇为主，致力于发展高新技术的方针，实践证明这个方针是完全正确的，要坚持下去。外经贸主管部门要研究加强对国家级经济技术开发区工作的宏观指导，采取措施促进开发区做好出口和引资工作，更好地发挥开发区在对外开放中的窗口、示范、辐射和带动作用，尽可能多地吸收外资。要支持区内企业进入跨国公司的国际销售网络，积极引进为跨国公司产品配套的面向全球生产供应零部件的外商投资项目，使一些企业进入跨国公司国际一体化的生产销售体系，扩大我产品在国际市场的份额。

我在这里还要强调一点，当前国家在财政并不宽裕的情况下，出台了一系列支持外经贸发展的政策，是很不容易的。一定要非常珍惜它。我们一定要继续严厉打击走私贩私和骗退税等各种违法犯罪行为，特别是最近一些地方虚报出口、骗取退税的现象又有所抬头，外经贸、海关、税务等部门一定要狠狠打击，决不能允许这些违法犯罪活动干扰国家政策的正常实施，危害广大守法企业的正常生产经营。

（五）进一步推动境外加工贸易发展，促进与发展中国家的经贸合作

推动境外加工贸易的发展是我们的一项重要工作。目前我国在海外已经办起了135家企业，分布在48个国家，主要是家电、轻工、制药、机电、服装加工等行业。其中，今年新批34个项目，中方协议投资额近6400万美元，项目投产后可带动出口3亿美元以上。总的来说，这项工作还处在起步阶段，有的地方、有的企业充分利用政策，已经取得了明显的成效。

最近，江总书记多次强调要从战略高度重视做好发展中国家的工作。大力开展同发展中国家的经贸合作，是加强我国对这些国家工作的重要内容。我认为开展境外加工贸易，不仅有利于发挥我国的比较优势，带动我国设备和原材料出口，而且也是加强与发展中国家经贸合作的一个重要方式，是大有可为的。因此，要继续鼓励我国企业到发展中国家投资办厂，特别是合作开发森林等我国需要的资源。加强同发展中国家的经济技术合作，尤其是进行资源开发方面的合作，具有十分重要的意义。

开展境外加工贸易，要充分发挥驻外经商参处在国外第一线的作用，加强信息收集，抓紧建立和完善境外投资环境信息库，及时向国内企业提供翔实的境外市场需求、招商项目、企业资信、法律法规等实用信息。国内要落实好信贷、保险、外汇等各项鼓励政策，为企业提供便利，做好服务。要加快制定区域实施方案，避免我们的企业到国外盲目设点，重复建设，无序竞争，自相残杀。要从严管理境外加工贸易企业，杜绝国有资产流失。

（六）以澳门回归为契机，加强对港澳台的经贸工作

为了确保澳门回归后的长期稳定和发展，我们要深刻领会“一国两制”方针的精神，认真贯彻中央对澳门的各项方针政策，了解和熟悉澳门基本法的有关规定，推动内地与澳门的经贸合作。要以澳门回归为契机，进一步做好对港澳的经贸工作。今年8月，中央专门召开了中央港澳工作会议，提出要“充分利用优势，积极支持配合，增进互利合作，实现共同发展”。这是我们加强对港澳经贸合作的基本指导方针。祖国内地与港澳地区之间的经贸关系

是国家主体与单独关税区的关系，一方面要遵循国际经贸活动的惯例，另一方面也要按照“同等优先、适当放宽”的原则，对港澳商人来内地开展贸易、投资、科技合作，给予必要的支持，推动港澳经济的健康发展。

港澳地区是祖国内地重要的经贸合作伙伴。当前内地与港澳的经贸关系由于受亚洲金融危机冲击，出现一定波动。今后，我们要进一步发挥港澳自由港和转口港的优势，努力扩大对港澳出口和经港澳的转口；加大吸引港澳企业家来内地投资的力度，推动港澳经济向内延伸发展；把内地与港澳科技合作作为经贸合作新的增长点。讲求实效，把单纯的科技合作发展到经济、贸易、技术一体化的全面合作，从“三来一补”、“前店后厂”的低层次合作发展到促进产业升级、开发新产品，特别是信息技术、生物技术和新材料技术等新兴技术领域的合作，为内地与港澳的经贸合作增添新的活力，实现新的发展。

今年 11 月初，内地与香港特别行政区成功举行了第一次商贸联委会，正式启动了内地与香港特别行政区经贸部门高层次的交流与联络机制。这对促进内地与香港经贸关系的平稳发展产生了良好的作用。澳门回归后，外经贸部也要积极推动建立与澳门经贸合作的官方协商机制。

当前对台经贸工作虽然受到李登辉“两国论”的干扰，但也有新的发展机遇。港澳与台湾的经贸关系已成为两岸关系中重要的特殊组成部分。我们要充分利用港澳的各种有利条件，推动两岸“三通”，加强对台经贸工作，为最终实现祖国和平统一创造条件。

四、关于我国加入 WTO 问题

大家都很关心我国加入 WTO 问题。经过 13 年的艰辛历程，今年 11 月 15 日，中美最终签署了关于我国加入 WTO 的双边协议，大大加快了我国加入 WTO 谈判的进程。

这次中美 WTO 谈判是在党中央、国务院的正确领导下进行的。中美最终达成协议，符合我国的根本利益，体现了以江泽民同志为核心的党的第三代领导集体深化体制改革、扩大对外开放的巨大勇气和坚定决心，得到了全国人民的广泛拥护，受到了世界舆论的一致好评。

加入 WTO 是我国改革开放历史进程中的一件大事，对我国经济在下个世纪的发展具有深远影响，对近期的经济增长也有积极意义。

为了加强领导，做好我国加入 WTO 的各项工作，根据党中央、国务院领导同志指示，成立了 WTO 工作小组，国务院各有关部门也都成立了本部门的 WTO 工作小组。当前，我们要抓紧时间，充实、调整和完善现行的涉外经济法律、法规，建立起适应 WTO 规则要求的经济贸易法律体系；要在全社会范围内加快普及 WTO 的基本知识。目前中央已经决定，由中组部负责各部门、各省（区、市）党政一把手的培训，由国家经贸委负责大型企业一把手的培训，由外经贸部负责 WTO 专门人才的培训。各级外经贸主管部门的领导干部要带头学习，认真参加培训；各产业部门要针对本行业的特点，及早研究提出可操作的应对措施，并组织实施；各级地方政府特别是外经贸主管部门要积极推动当地各类企业熟悉 WTO 的规则，趋利避害，尽快适应新的市场竞争环境。加入 WTO 是当前我国经济工作中的一件大事，是一项系统工程，头绪繁杂，需要做的工作还很多，各部门要在中央的统一领导和部署下，密切配合，共同做好对内对外工作。

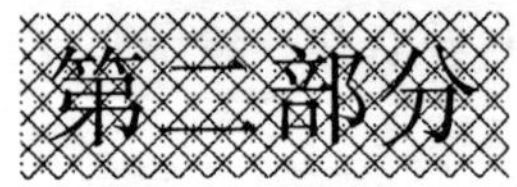

抓住新机遇　迎接新挑战 开创2000年全国外经贸工作新局面

外经贸部石广生部长

在2000年全国外经贸工作会议上的报告

1999年12月22日

这次全国外经贸工作会议是一次面向新世纪的重要会议。会议的主要任务是：以邓小平理论和党的十五大精神为指导，贯彻落实中央经济工作会议精神，总结1999年全国外经贸工作，分析当前形势，部署2000年全国外经贸工作，统一思想，明确任务，坚定信心，全面完成2000年各项外经贸任务，为国民经济持续快速健康发展作出新的贡献。

一、1999年全国外经贸工作在困难的形势下取得了可喜成绩

1999年是不平凡的一年。我国国民经济继续保持快速增长；澳门顺利回归祖国；开展了对邪教“法轮功”和李登辉“两国论”的有力批判。1999年也是我国外经贸发展重要的一年。面对国际国内复杂多变的政治经济形势，在党中央、国务院的正确领导下，我国外经贸经过两年多的困难时期，出现了稳定增长的好形势，外贸出口转降为升，吸收外资保持相当规模，“入世”谈判取得重大突破，各项工作都取得新的成绩。

出口转降为升，进口增长较快。据海关统计，今年1－11月，全国进出口总额3230亿美元，比去年同期增长12.7%。其中，出口1747亿美元，增长6.6%；进口1483亿美元，增长20.9%。贸易顺差264亿美元。预计全年外贸出口将增长6%左右，高于去年的水平，也高于今年世界贸易的平均增长速度。

今年前11个月我国进出口贸易的主要特点是：

出口在经历上半年的持续下降后，从7月份开始转降为升，增速加快。7、8、9、10、11月当月出口分别增长7.5%、17.8%、20.2%、23.8%和28.8%。进口持续增长，主要表现为一般贸易进口大幅增长，前11个月，一般贸易进口596.8亿美元，增长65.8%。

出口商品结构进一步优化，1－11月，全国高新技术产品出口220亿美元，增长24.8%。机电产品出口689.4亿美元，增长16.4%，占全国出口总额的比重由去年同期的36.1%升至39.5%。同时，服装、纺织面料等大宗商品出口继续回升，11月份当月，服装、纺织面料和鞋类出口增速分别达57%、26%和47%。

前11个月，一般贸易出口706亿美元，增长6%；加工贸易出口998亿美元，增长

7.6%。加工贸易进口658.8亿美元，增长6.6%。国有企业仍然是我国外贸出口的主体力量，出口882.1亿美元，增长1.8%；外商投资企业出口796.1亿美元，增长10.9%。国有企业进口666.4亿美元，增长30.1%；外商投资企业进口766亿美元，增长12.1%。

1－11月，全国十大出口省市为：广东、上海、江苏、浙江、山东、福建、北京、辽宁、天津和河北。我国的十大贸易伙伴为日本、美国、香港、韩国、台湾省、德国、新加坡、英国、法国、荷兰。

实际吸收外资继续保持相当规模。1－11月，全国合同外资金额356.4亿美元，下降18.9%；实际使用外资金额370.9亿美元，下降9.7%。预计全年我国实际吸收外资将达到或超过400亿美元，虽然略低于去年，但仍保持相当规模。截至11月底，全国累计合同外资金额6081.6亿美元，实际使用外资金额3045.4亿美元。

前11个月，我国吸收外资的主要特点是：亚洲十国/地区、欧盟十五国、美国、部分自由港对华投资合同额均有所下降，但美国对华实际投资38.9亿美元，增长9.6%。1－11月，亚洲十国/地区对华投资合同额213.5亿美元，下降10.3%；欧盟十五国对华投资合同额36.1亿美元，下降33.4%；美国对华投资合同额51.3亿美元，下降10.2%；部分自由港对华投资合同额34.4亿美元，下降48.8%。新批外商投资企业平均单项吸收外资金额233.6万美元，中西部地区合同外资金额16.8亿美元，占全国合同外资总额的比重比去年同期略有增长。

对外承包和劳务合作取得新的进展。1－11月，全国新签对外承包工程和劳务合作合同额102.7亿美元，增长2.1%；完成营业额87.9亿美元，增长6.7%；带动国产设备材料出口5.1亿美元；11月末在外劳务人数36.6万人。预计全年对外承包工程和劳务合作营业额将达105亿美元，增长5%。对外承包和劳务合作改革取得新的进展，制订了对外承包工程和劳务合作改革方案并组织实施。经营主体结构和市场结构有所优化，赋予300多家专业工程公司和大型企业开展对外承包工程业务；对香港、美国等10多个有潜力的市场和50多个2000万美元以上的大项目进行了重点推动。

对外援助稳步发展，援外任务执行情况良好。1－11月，我国同12个国家新签13笔对外优惠贷款协议；在24个国家实施了39个援外合资合作项目；同71个国家和国际组织新签了78笔对外援款协议。对外援助配合外交工作发挥了重要作用，利用援外资金带动境外加工贸易和对外承包工程取得良好进展。

境外加工贸易初见成效，对外投资继续发展。向100多家企业颁发了《境外加工贸易企业批准证书》。承建了135个境外加工贸易项目，中方投资约1.4亿美元。已承建的项目大多属于我国具有较强优势的行业，主要分布在亚洲、非洲、拉美、东欧和独联体等发展中国家和地区。中方投资主体多为国内知名企业，经营情况良好。

前三季度，经外经贸部批准或在外经贸部备案的境外企业231家，中方投资约3.3亿美元，增长72.8%。投资重点从原来的贸易型企业为主，逐步转向生产型企业为主，生产具有我国比较优势的产品；单个项目投资规模逐步扩大，投资分布日益广泛，遍布世界160多个国家和地区。

科技兴贸战略正在实施，成绩突出。与有关部门合作，制订了《科技兴贸行动计划》和

《高新技术产品出口目录》；组织推动北京、上海、深圳等15个城市和53个国家级高新技术产业开发区发展高新技术产品出口；确定166家高新技术产品出口企业和92种高 技术出口产品，给予重点支持；选择信息、生物医药、新材料等五大领域作为重点突破；与有关部门和地方联合举办了首届中国（深圳）国际高新技术成果交易会和第二届北京高新技术产业国际周，取得了良好社会影响。

外经贸体制改革继续深化。建立“审批从宽、管理从严”的新机制，积极推动生产企业和上市公司进出口经营权由审批制向登记制转变。对配额许可证商品实行动态管理，将实行出口许可证管理的商品由去年的115种减少为59种，初步建立了对商品配额执行情况核查反馈机制。完善进出口配额分配、招标办法，配额分配进一步向生产企业倾斜，修订了《机电产品进口配额管理办法》。制定了《国际招标机构资格审定办法》，规范我国机电产品国际招标工作。改革中国出口商品交易会，优化参展企业结构，扩大生产企业、外商投资企业的参展规模，放宽高新技术产品生产企业的参展资格；优化展品结构，支持和鼓励名优特新产品参展。

“入世”谈判取得重大突破，多双边经贸关系进一步发展。在党中央、国务院的正确决策和直接领导下，今年我国先后同印尼、日本、澳大利亚、智利、美国和加拿大就我国加入世贸组织达成双边协议，都取得了“双赢”的结果。特别是与美国达成协议，是我国“入世”谈判的重大突破，解决了我国加入世贸组织的关键，大大加快了我国加入世贸组织的进程。我国积极参加亚太经合组织奥克兰会议和第三届亚欧会议，在其中发挥重要作用，促进了亚太地区贸易投资自由化和便利化进程，增进了亚太地区的经济技术合作，加强了亚欧经贸关系。我国与周边国家和广大发展中国家的经贸关系快速发展，主办了三期中非高级经济官员研修班，有来自35个国家的69名学员参加研修；与美、日、欧等主要经贸伙伴的双边经贸关系不断加强；与港澳台地区的经贸关系日益密切，同香港特区政府有关部门召开了商贸联委会，同澳门地区的经贸关系稳步推进，同台湾省的经贸关系取得新的发展，颁布了《台湾同胞投资保护法实施细则》。

在今年困难的形势下，特别是亚洲金融危机的影响依然存在的情况下，我国外经贸发展取得这些成绩，是十分可喜的，超过了年初的预料。这些成绩的取得，首先是党中央、国务院正确领导的结果。每当外经贸发展处于关键时刻，党中央、国务院总是及时地为我们指明方向，给予我们坚定的支持；每当我们取得成绩，党中央、国务院又总是不断地鼓励我们，给予我们充分的肯定。这极大地增强了我们克服困难、做好工作的信心。同时，这些成绩也是国务院各部委大力支持和协作的结果，许多重大外经贸政策的出台和外经贸环境的改善，都离不开各部门的支持与合作。这些成绩还是各地区党政部门关心和支持的结果，是全国所有外经贸工作干部职工齐心协力、共同奋斗的结果。

二、当前我国外经贸发展面临的形势

2000年是世纪交替之年，也是我国“九五”计划的最后一年。在世纪之交的重要时刻，立足当前，面向未来，认真做好明年的外经贸工作，不断提高外经贸发展的质量和水平，对促进新世纪我国外经贸和国民经济的持续发展具有重要意义。

党中央、国务院始终高度重视外经贸工作。在中央经济工作会议上，江泽民总书记再次强调："千方百计扩大出口，积极有效地利用外资，对于拉动经济增长具有不可忽视 的重要作用。"朱镕基总理也指出：积极扩大出口和利用外资"对于实现明年经济增长目标、保持国际收支平衡，至关重要。"并要求我们认识到"明年扩大出口和利用外资的难度仍然很大。我们必须知难而进，以更大的努力，千方百计地扩大出口和吸收外资。"

按照党中央、国务院的要求做好外经贸工作，我们首先要正确地分析和判断国际国内经济贸易发展的新形势，制定相应的政策措施，振奋精神，开拓进取，全面完成2000年的各项外经贸工作任务。

当前，世界经济贸易正在发生积极的变化，我国国民经济继续保持快速增长。总体上看，明年我国外经贸发展面临的国内外形势有可能会好于今年。但是，影响和制约我国外经贸发展的许多国内外因素依然存在，明年的困难仍然很大，机遇与挑战并存。对此，我们必须有清醒的认识。

明年我国外经贸发展的主要有利因素有：

第一，世界经济贸易继续保持增长，国际市场需求增加，我国外经贸发展的空间增大。随着世界经济贸易形势的好转，目前，各主要国际经济组织都对今年和明年的世界经济贸易发展作出比较乐观的预测。国际货币基金组织10月份预测，今年世界经济和国际贸易将分别增长3%和3.9%，而2000年将分别提高到3.5%和6.2%。世界银行最新预测，今年和明年的世界经济将增长2.6%和2.9%，比3月份的预测分别调高0.8和0.5个百分点。世界贸易组织预计今年世界贸易将增长4%，明年将扩张到6%－7%的水平。从国别和地区情况看，美国经济将继续有所增长；日本经济正在恢复；欧洲经济平稳发展；东亚地区特别是韩国、泰国等经济复苏加快，亚洲金融危机的影响进一步减弱；大多数发展中国家的经济增长也将加快。随着世界经济贸易形势的好转，国际市场商品价格有所回升，石油价格上扬，一些原料类初级产品价格回升10%以上。

第二，经济全球化加速发展，为我国外经贸发展带来新的机遇。经济全球化使得世界各国经济的相互依存和相互影响更加明显。为了适应新形势的发展，许多国家纷纷放宽一些贸易和投资限制，为发展对外贸易和促进外资流入提供多种优惠措施，推动国际贸易进一步发展，加速了国际资本流动，促使国际贸易的增长速度高于世界经济的增长速度、资本跨国流动的增长速度高于国际贸易的增长速度。世贸组织等多边贸易机构，也积极推动有关国家和地区落实乌拉圭回合协议，进一步开放市场；世贸组织新一轮谈判即将启动，这都将推动贸易投资自由化和便利化的进一步发展。

第三，我国即将加入世贸组织，将对国民经济的改革与发展产生深远影响，为外经贸带来新的发展契机。加入世贸组织，将进一步改善我国外经贸发展的国际经贸环境，我国将可以在世贸组织确定的多边、稳定、无条件最惠国待遇原则下，享受WTO各成员贸易投资自由化的便利，促进我国经济融入世界经济体系，发展对外贸易、吸收外资和参与国际经济合作，更好地适应经济全球化的发展趋势。我国加入世贸组织后，在享受相应权利同时，也要承担相应的义务，履行我国的对外承诺，这可能给我国的一些产业带来挑战和压力。这些挑战和压力，可以通过改革变压力为动力。经过二十多年改革开放的实践，我们既积累了改革开放的经验，又有了一定的承受能力，我们有信心迎接这个挑战。

第四，国民经济持续快速增长，为我国外经贸持续发展提供了坚实基础。近两年，我国国民经济成功地抵御了亚洲金融危机的影响，保持持续快速发展。今年前三季度，我国国内生产总值增长7.4%，预计全年增长将达到或超过7%。明年，国家将继续扩大内需，实施积极的财政政策，加强基础设施建设，稳步推进各项改革，推进实施西部大开发战略，保持国民经济的发展势头，预计国内生产总值仍将增长7%左右，这是我国外经贸发展的重要保障。

第五，我国加快经济结构调整和国有企业改革，制定出台了一系列促进外经贸发展的政策，增强了我国企业和产品的国际竞争能力。近年来，特别是今年以来，国家制定一系列政策措施，加大了对扩大出口和吸收外资的信贷、税收、保险等支持，这些政策明年将继续发挥重要作用，产生更为明显的效应。今年，党中央、国务院召开全国技术创新大会，通过了《关于加强技术创新，发展高科技，实现产业化的决定》，将有力推动高新技术产业发展和传统产业的升级换代，提高我国出口商品的质量、档次和附加值。党的十五届四中全会通过了《关于国有企业改革和发展若干重大问题的决定》，将大大加快国有企业包括国有外经贸企业的改革进程，有利于国有企业增强活力、提高效益，强化我国外经贸发展的微观基础。同时，我国各类外经贸企业经过近两年严峻形势的考验，积累了迎接挑战、克服困难的经验，提高了开拓国际市场的能力。

明年我国外经贸发展的主要不利因素有：

第一，世界经济贸易发展存在不确定性。经济全球化在促进世界经济贸易发展的同时，也拉大了国家间的贫富差距，世界经济贸易发展不平衡的矛盾更加突出，增长的基础并不牢固，引发局部波动的可能性增加。美国经济连续9年增长，不稳定因素有所显现；日本经济尚未完全走出低谷，恢复正常尚需时日；欧洲失业率居高不下，困扰着欧元区的经济发展；受金融危机冲击的东南亚国家经济复苏的基础依然脆弱，局部地区可能出现反复；国际市场竞争更加激烈，商品价格波动不定，这些都将增加我国外经贸发展的不确定性。

第二，世界经济结构调整加快，跨国购并成为全球直接投资的主要形式，给我国外经贸发展带来严峻挑战。世界范围内的经济结构调整是经济全球化加速发展和科学技术突飞猛进的必然结果。在跨国公司和跨国投资的推动下，世界经济结构加速调整，带动国际贸易商品结构发生重大变化。高科技产品、信息产品等新兴产品的国际需求增多，在国际贸易中比重增加；初级产品、低附加值产品的国际需求相应减少，竞争加剧，价格下降。跨国购并成为全球直接投资的主要形式，占全球直接投资的60%以上，其中90%的跨国购并发生在美欧等发达国家之间。由于我国技术创新能力不足、产品结构不能完全适应国际竞争，实行跨国购并的条件尚不具备，不利于我国扩大出口和吸收外资。

第三，国际贸易保护主义手段不断翻新。目前，发达国家之间的贸易战不断升级，贸易保护主义日趋明显；发达国家往往通过滥用反倾销、或以设限、技术壁垒、环保壁垒等新的贸易保护措施，限制发展中国家商品进入本国市场；一些国家拒不承认我国的市场经济国家地位，频频对我滥用反倾销措施。据统计，近年来外国对我出口商品滥用反倾销和保障措施案件大幅上升，今年1－11月又立案39起，涉案金额达5亿美元，对我国出口的影响加大。

第四，国内仍然存在一些制约外经贸发展的因素。我国出口商品结构不够优化，国际竞争力不强；国有外经贸企业债务负担沉重，市场开拓能力和国际竞争能力亟待提高；外经贸管理不够完善，不能很好地适应新形势发展的需要；亚洲金融危机后一些国家实施更加开放的政策，增加对外商投资的优惠，我国投资环境的相对优势有所减弱。我国加入世贸组织后也将有一个磨合期，短期内可能还有一些负面影响，不能期望一旦“入世”，外贸出口和吸收外资等就能立即取得突破性发展等。

总之，我们一定要全面地分析和把握形势。既要看到形势有利的一面，努力抓住机遇，推动外经贸取得新的发展，也要坚持马克思主义的“两点论”，充分估计工作中可能出现的各种挑战和困难，宁可把挑战估计得充分一些，把困难想得多一些，及早研究制定对策，争取工作主动。

三、2000年我国外经贸发展的主要任务和工作

按照中央经济工作会议的要求，根据当前我国外经贸发展面临的国际国内形势。明年，我国外经贸工作的指导思想是：以邓小平理论和党的十五大精神为指导，认真贯彻中央经济工作会议精神，适应我国即将加入世贸组织的新形势，突出抓好扩大开放、以质取胜、体制改革和市场开拓，从总体上提高我国对外经济贸易的国际竞争能力，促进国民经济持续快速健康发展。

根据这一指导思想，明年，我们要重点做好以下工作：继续千方百计扩大出口，做好进口工作，保持进出口贸易的稳定增长；进一步扩大对外开放，积极有效利用外资，提高吸收外资的质量和水平；加快实施“科技兴贸”战略，优化进出口商品结构，扩大机电产品和高新技术产品出口；深化外经贸体制改革，加强对国有外经贸企业改革的宏观指导；大力发展对外承包工程和劳务合作，不断扩大国际市场的占有份额；做好援外工作；大力发展和促进与发展中国家及周边国家的经贸合作；鼓励有条件的企业对外投资，积极发展境外加工贸易；贯彻“西部大开发”战略，加强对中西部地区外经贸发展的支持和指导；做好加入世界贸易组织的各项工作，大力发展多双边经贸关系，创造有利的国际经贸环境；加强外经贸法制建设，全面推进依法行政；建立外经贸信息服务体系，做好外经贸政策和发展战略研究等。

为了完成明年的各项外经贸任务，要做好以下主要工作：

（一）继续千方百计扩大出口，做好进口工作

千方百计扩大出口是我国外经贸工作的重中之重。我们要始终准确把握形势，及时研究对策；始终坚持以改革促发展，正确处理外经贸改革与发展中的各种关系；始终不断培育外贸出口新的增长点，大力开拓国际市场。

要继续落实国家各项鼓励扩大出口的政策措施，充分发挥政策效应；继续加强税贸、银贸、关贸和汇贸协作，形成各部门共同支持扩大出口的合力。

按照世贸组织规则和国际通行做法，完善出口促进政策，改革出口管理体制，实现出口工作由近两年研究制定短期的反危机措施为主，转向研究保障外贸出口稳定发展的促进和服务体系为主。积极推动建立新形势下支持扩大出口的金融、保险、税收等服务体系。

大力扶持和推动一般贸易出口，促进加工贸易健康有序发展。继续贯彻国办发 35 号文件精神，对加工贸易企业实行分类管理，鼓励企业使用国产原材料和设备。加强出口收汇考核，增加出口收汇，提高出口效益。

继续推动有条件的企业开展境外加工贸易。落实国办发 17 号文件精神，办好已建成的加工贸易项目，支持企业扩大加工装配规模，鼓励与国外企业合作开发我国有需求的资源性、战略性项目。同时，加强协调和监督管理，避免盲目布点、无序竞争。

做好出口工作要突出重点，广东、上海、江苏等全国十大出口省市首先要确保出口任务的完成；各级外经贸主管部门都要抓好所联系的重点出口企业的出口工作，积极引导中小企业包括乡镇企业扩大出口；要重点抓好大宗商品的出口工作，提高产品质量和档次；要努力增加对亚洲市场的出口，巩固传统市场，开拓新兴市场。

抓好出口商品的国际安全认证、质量认证、环保认证等基础性工作，突破国外相关技术壁垒，增强出口后劲。引导和扶持出口企业实施品牌战略，在国际市场上争创中国名牌。

根据国民经济发展的需要，积极增加进口，调整进口商品结构，重点进口国内产业结构升级急需的关键设备、技术和原材料；推动进出结合。

维护正常的对外贸易经营秩序，防止低价出口和恶性竞争；继续严厉打击走私、骗汇、逃套汇、骗退税等违法犯罪活动。

（二）进一步扩大对外开放，积极有效利用外资

根据国民经济发展的需要和我国加入 WTO 所作出的对外承诺，继续扩大对外开放领域，有步骤地开放金融、保险、电信、外贸、商业、旅游以及会计师事务所、律师事务所等，允许在这些领域根据我国的有关规定设立中外合资、合作或外商独资企业，扩大开放地域、数量和经营范围。

继续落实国办发 73 号文件，完善配套措施。抓紧清理和调整不利于吸收外资的有关规定，简化外商投资项目及企业设立的审批程序，提高办事效率。

修订《外商投资产业指导目录》。继续坚持以市场换技术的方针，加强对美日欧等发达国家招商引资，鼓励跨国公司来华投资，推动与世界各国和地区中小企业的合资合作。引导外商投资农业、高新技术产业、基础工业和基础设施、环保产业和出口创汇产业，鼓励外商在华设立研发中心，扩大国内采购。推进国有企业吸收外资进行改组改造，促进国有大型企业与跨国公司的联合。

加强对全国投资促进工作的协调和指导，继续办好中国投资贸易洽谈会，完善中国投资贸易洽谈会现有的投资促进网络。加强对国家级经济技术开发区工作的宏观指导，促进开发区做好吸收外资工作。依法加强对外商投资企业的管理，进一步提高吸收外资的质量、水平和效益。

大力改善外商投资环境，强化对外商投资企业的服务；坚决制止对外商投资企业的乱收费、乱检查和乱摊派；完善联合年检制度，加强对外商投资企业的管理，依法保护外商投资企业的合法权益。

（三）加快实施“科技兴贸”战略，努力扩大高新技术产品出口

贯彻“科教兴国”战略和全国技术创新大会精神，按照《科技兴贸行动计划》，加快落实促进高新技术产品出口的“五定”（定产品、定企业、定市场、定目标、定时间）任务，以信息、生物制药等五大领域为突破，大力促进科技成果转化为商品，推动计算机软件等各种高新技术产品出口。争取明年高新技术产品出口300亿美元，占出口总额的比重达到15%。

加快运用高新技术改造传统出口产业，选择出口潜力大的机电、纺织和农产品加工等行业，与有关部门协作进行重点攻关，把高新技术出口企业的技术改造投资纳入国家技改投资规划，加大支持力度。

在北京、上海、深圳等地建立高新技术产品出口工业园的试点，借鉴国外成功经验，在风险投资、财政税务、货币兑换等方面，制订鼓励技术创新、扶持高新产业、培育出口基地的相关政策。办好中国国际高新技术成果交易会和北京国际高新技术产业周。

（四）完善机电产品进出口管理体制，大力促进机电产品出口

加强机电产品生产企业技术改造、质量认证等基础性工作，完善机电产品出口生产体系；发挥我国机电产品的比较优势，提高国际营销能力，完善售后服务体系，大力开拓国际市场，推动机电产品和成套设备特别是计算机及零部件、高档家用电器、通信设备、船舶、飞机及航空器、汽车及零部件等产品扩大出口，提高出口的质量和效益；努力实现国务院确定的明年机电产品出口800亿美元的目标。力争通过3-5年的努力，使机电产品在出口总额中所占比重由目前的近40%提高到50%。

各地机电办要继续抓好“2115”工程，促进机电产品出口较快增长。下大力气强化机电产品出口的物质基础，抓好机电产品生产建设体系；切实抓好重点高新技术机电产品的出口，提高出口产品的技术含量和附加值，培育新的出口增长点。

改革和完善机电产品进口管理体制，推动和规范国际招标采购业务，通过登记、技术标准、电子商务等手段，建立完善的宏观监控体系。

（五）深化外经贸体制改革，加强对国有外经贸企业改革的宏观指导

按照我国《“九五”计划和2010年远景目标纲要》和世贸组织规则，加快建立统一、规范的外经贸管理体制。扩大进出口经营权登记备案制的范围，由目前的部分大中型国有企业，扩大到所有国有生产企业和集体生产企业；逐步放宽非公有制生产企业经营进出口的条件，降低对其注册资金和销售收入等方面的要求；减少出口商品主动配额品种，改进配额管理和招标办法；对配额许可证管理的商品实行动态管理，加强配额许可证使用情况的核查反馈；理顺进出口经营体制，逐步减少限定企业经营的商品品种；扩大中外合资外贸公司的试点区域，由目前的深圳特区和浦东新区，扩大到所有直辖市、省会城市及经济特区。

按照“政事分开”的原则，加快推进外经贸中介服务体系改革，强化进出口商会的服务职能，更好地为各类外经贸企业服务。

根据十五届四中全会精神，深化国有外经贸企业改革。针对当前国有外经贸企业存在的突出问题，会同有关部门加快研究出台《国有外经贸企业改革指导意见》。明年上半年，组织召开全国外经贸企业改革经验交流会，推动企业深化改革。

加强对境外中资企业的管理和指导。按照国务院总理办公会议精神，会同国家计委共同牵头制订境外中资企业审批登记、行业指导、统计等管理办法，规范境外企业经营行为。

（六）加快对外承包工程与劳务合作工作改革，做好援外工作

进一步优化对外承包经营主体结构，培育一批能与国际大承包商竞争与合作的大型对外承包工程企业；巩固和深度开发亚洲、非洲、拉美等市场，积极开拓欧美等发达国家市场；推动设计咨询带动工程总承包，重点抓大型工程承包项目，特别是技术含量高，能带动国产设备、材料、技术和劳务出口的项目；认真落实中俄森林资源采伐及其他互利合作项目。

逐步完善以金融服务为主的对外承包工程服务体系，推动设立对外承包工程保函风险基金，推动金融部门扩大大型承包工程企业的授信额度，允许有条件的企业境外融资或境外上市，以BOT合同、租赁合同等有价合同进行质押和贴现。整顿经营秩序，建立有效规范的监管体系。

加快对外劳务合作改革，坚持组织派遣和中介服务并存，团体劳务和零星劳务并重，实行不同形式的对外劳务合作，维护外派劳务人员合法权益。

继续深化援外方式改革，积极推动优惠贷款方式，加快落实优惠贷款项目，加强贷后管理。进一步规范援外项目的管理，继续坚持援外项目招、投标制度，进一步扩大实体企业参与投标的比例，对有条件的援外项目推行ISO9000质量体系标准。

（七）大力加强与发展中国家及周边国家的经贸合作

加强与发展中国家和周边国家的经贸合作，是一项重要的长期工作，党中央、国务院十分重视。我国与广大发展中国家有着相似的历史遭遇和发展本国经济的共同任务，加强经贸合作具有坚实的基础；维护世界和平，建立多极世界，需要广大发展中国家的团结协作；我国与广大发展中国家长期友好，经济互补性强，经贸合作的潜力巨大；广大发展中国家市场广阔，加强与发展中国家的经贸合作，既有利于发展中国家发展经济，也有利于我国外经贸实现市场多元化。我国与周边国家地理位置相近，经济联系密切，具有发展经贸关系良好条件。

加强与发展中国家和周边国家的经贸合作，重点要做好以下工作：扩大同发展中国家和周边国家的进出口贸易，努力解决贸易不平衡问题；积极推动有比较优势的企业到发展中国家和周边国家进行投资、开展境外加工贸易；改善同发展中国家和周边国家发展经贸关系的环境和条件；办好在发展中国家和周边国家设立的投资贸易中心及商品分拨中心；加强与发展中国家和周边国家经贸人员的交流、培训，增进了解，发展友谊，促进友好，扩大共识；做好对发展中国家的援助工作。

（八）贯彻“西部大开发战略”，加强对中西部地区外经贸工作的支持和指导

贯彻落实中央领导和中央经济工作会议提出的“西部大开发”战略，积极宣传中西部地区自然资源、劳动力资源优势以及潜在市场优势，引导外商向中西部地区投资。

具体落实国务院确定的支持中西部地区外经贸发展的各项政策措施，推动中西部地区尽快制定外商投资优势产业和优势项目目录；会同国家有关部门制定放宽中西部地区吸收外资领域、设立外商投资企业的具体办法；引导和鼓励沿海地区外商投资企业到中西部地区开展再投资、承包经营和管理内资企业等。

鼓励中西部地区运用区位优势发展边境贸易，落实边境贸易的各项优惠政策。引导和推动外国政府和国际组织的对华无偿援助重点投向中西部地区，推动拓展援助合作新领域，支持扶贫开发。

中西部地区要发挥自身地区优势、资源优势和劳动力优势等各种优势，积极发展有地区特色的对外经济贸易，促进经济发展。

（九）做好加入世贸组织的各项工作，积极发展多双边经贸关系

加紧“入世”谈判，尽快完成与欧盟等22个世贸组织成员的双边谈判，完成总议定书和工作组报告的起草审核工作。按照中央的统一部署，加强宣传，普及世贸组织基础知识，引导国内企业趋利避害，适应新形势下的国际竞争。协助有关主管部门落实我国“入世”协议的有关内容。

积极参与世贸组织新一轮谈判和新规则的制定，维护我国和广大发展中国家的利益。积极参加亚太经合组织和亚欧会议的各项活动，进一步推动亚太地区的贸易与投资自由化进程，促进亚太、亚欧地区的经济技术合作。

抓住我国加入世贸组织的有利契机，加强与有关发达国家和主要经贸伙伴的双边经贸关系。反对各种形式的国际贸易保护主义，维护我国的经济权益。

加强内地与香港的经贸合作，保持香港的繁荣稳定；做好对澳门的经贸工作，促进澳门社会稳定和经济发展；推动海峡两岸经贸交往，促使两岸早日实现“三通”，促进祖国统一。

（十）加强外经贸法制建设，全面推进依法行政

按照我国社会主义市场经济发展和加入世贸组织的要求，建议修改完善我国《对外贸易法》和《中外合资经营企业法》、《中外合作经营企业法》、《外资企业法》三部外商投资的基本法律；在国务院法制办的统一安排下，清理现有涉外经济法规和规章；加快涉外经济法规的立法工作，尽快制订有关商品进出口、外贸代理、边境贸易、加工贸易、技术进出口、原产地管理、劳务合作、海外投资、对外援助、电子商务及反倾销、反补贴、保障措施等方面的法律法规。当前要重点抓好与WTO规则不一致，不利于我国深化改革、扩大开放的有关法规和部门规章的清理、修订工作。

贯彻国务院《关于全面推进依法行政的决定》，严格依法行政，进一步加强运用法律手段和经济手段管理外经贸活动；建立和完善外经贸行政监督检查制度；加强外经贸法律队伍建设，培养新形势下保障外经贸发展的法律人才；根据加入世贸组织后的新情况，积极组织力量，做好反倾销的应诉工作以及其他涉外法律纠纷的处理工作。

（十一）建立外经贸信息服务体系，抓好外经贸政策和发展战略研究

加快建立外经贸信息服务体系，帮助企业特别是中小企业了解国际市场动态，拓展海外市场。按照政府资助、市场化运作、开放式管理的模式，研究设立有关的专门机构，承担国际、国内贸易信息的收集、加工、发布的职能。加强国家重点建设项目“金关工程——外经贸专用网”的建设，充分发挥其信息、管理和服务的作用；及时为驻外机构提供信息和对外宣传材料；强化驻外经商机构的调研、信息服务和对外宣传工作；加快驻外经商机构与EDI中心的联网步伐，建立和完善驻外机构报送政务及商务信息的网络系统，为国内提供更多的驻在国的经济贸易信息；积极推进企业运用国际电子商务。

加强外经贸 政策研究，重点做好外经贸改革与发展中难点、热点问题及中长期发展战略的研究；加强外经贸政策研究队伍建设，充分发挥有关研究机构和社会力量的积极性，为外经贸发展提供及时有效的理论和政策服务；做好外经贸“十五”规划的编制工作。

（十二）以讲学习、讲政治、讲正气为主要内容，加强和改进思想政治工作

2000年，我国外经贸工作的任务十分繁重。各级外经贸主管部门在狠抓业务工作的同时，要坚持“两手抓、两手都要硬”，以开展讲学习、讲政治、讲正气为主要内容，加强和改进思想政治工作。

从事外经贸工作的各级领导干部要认真学习马列主义、毛泽东思想、邓小平理论和党的十五大精神，努力掌握指导外经贸工作的思想武器，在对外开放和外经贸发展中坚持正确方向。要大力弘扬理论联系实际的学风，深入实际，调查研究，善于总结实践经验，解决实际问题。要提高政治敏锐性和政治鉴别力，增强全局意识和责任感，善于从讲政治的高度观察和分析问题，想大事，议大事，抓大事，不断解决外经贸改革和发展中出现的新情况、新问题。

要坚持不懈地开展反腐败斗争，加强廉政建设。要通过开展“三讲”教育，切实从源头上、制度上防止腐败，一旦发现问题，严厉打击，坚决查处个别害群之马。

要加强各级外经贸主管部门的机关建设，切实转变政府职能，转变工作方式，转变工作作风，提高工作效率，不断增强全心全意为人民服务的自觉性。要坚持走群众路线，虚心听取群众意见，切实解决企业和群众关心的问题。要主动加强部门协作，从国家利益的大局出发，妥善处理好同各方面的关系，形成支持外经贸发展的合力，共同促进外经贸发展。

做好明年的外经贸工作，任务艰巨，意义深远。让我们高举邓小平理论伟大旗帜，紧密团结在以江泽民同志为核心的党中央周围，同心同德，奋力开拓，努力创造新的业绩，全面完成各项外经贸工作任务，豪迈地跨向新世纪。

迈向新千年的中美经贸关系

对外贸易经济合作部副部长　孙振宇

2000 年 1 月 10 日

怀着喜悦的心情，带着美好的憧憬，人类刚刚告别了 20 世纪，迎来了又一个千年。当新千年到来的钟声在世界各地次第响起的时候，每个人，无论他驻足在北京中华世纪坛的近旁，还是徜徉在纽约时代广场的街头，都会期盼并祝愿一个更加美好的明天。21 世纪人类的福祉来自何方？来自科学的进步，来自文明的发展，当然，古老的经济学原理早就告诉我们，这种福祉也来自互利的贸易与合作。

一

中美互利通商的历史源远流长。从 1784 年 8 月，美国商船“中国皇后号”满载西洋参、毛皮、胡椒等商品驶达广州开始，到中国改革开放的 1978 年间，中美贸易曾经有过短暂的辉煌，但总的来说，双边贸易规模不大，经贸合作领域有限，而且由于历史的原因，还曾一度中断。

1979 年元旦，中华人民共和国和美利坚合众国正式建立外交关系，7 月，《中美贸易关系协定》在京签订，中美经贸关系健康发展的基石由此奠定。20 多年来，随着中国改革开放的前进步伐，中美贸易迅速发展，与此同时，越来越多的美国企业来华投资并取得了成功。

根据中国海关统计，1979 年至 1998 年间，双边贸易额累计达 3645 亿美元。1998 年，中美双边贸易额近 550 亿美元，相当于 1979 年中美建交之初的 22 倍多。最新统计显示，1999 年 1 到 11 月，中美贸易总额已逾 555 亿美元。今天，美国已成为中国的第二大贸易伙伴，中国则是美国的第四大贸易伙伴。中国是美国飞机、化肥、电站、电子、化工和机械设备等产品不可多得的市场；美国则吸收了中国制造的大量价廉物美的商品。

80 年代初，以汽车行业为代表的第一批美国企业开始在中国投资。随着中国改革开放的不断深入和经济建设速度的加快，美国企业在华直接投资的规模逐年扩大，领域不断拓宽。截止 1999 年 10 月底，美国投资项目累计逾 2.8 万个，合同金额约 509 亿美元，实际投入约 246 亿美元。无论是以合同金额还是以实际投入金额排序，美国在华直接投资额都名列各国对华投资额之首。全美 500 家大企业中，已有 200 多家在中国投资，其中不乏通用汽车、摩托罗拉、宝洁等世界级跨国公司。目前，美国直接投资已遍及机械、冶金、石油、电子、通讯、化工、纺织、轻工、食品、农业、医药、环保、金融、保险等中国国民经济的各主要行业。美国企业最早投资中国的汽车、计算机和人寿保险领域并在中国的日用化学品、通讯设备、饮料、快餐等市场上占有巨大竞争优势。根据1998年中国工业经济统计年鉴，在电子及通讯设备、电力行业，美资企业1997年利润总额分别占中国该行业利润总额的85.8%和13.6%。美国企业在中国投资获利的同时，也为中国带来了先进的技术和管理经验并吸纳了一部分中国的劳动力。

刚刚过去的20世纪最后一年目睹了中美两国签署关于中国加入世界贸易组织的协议。由于中美双方共同的勇气和努力，遗憾留给了过去，希望留给了未来。以此为契机，中美经贸关系将有望进入一个健康、持续和稳定发展的新时期。在这种新形势下，互利合作将成为中美经贸关系的主旋律，矛盾冲突虽然难以避免，但将在多边的框架中，依据法治精神，得以公平解决。

二

中美两国何以建立如此密切的经贸关系？经济的高度互补、企业的积极参与和两国领导人富有战略眼光的政治关怀是三大关键因素。

中美两国分处经济发展的不同阶段，资源条件、技术条件、产业结构以及消费水平存在巨大差异，两国经济因此呈现高度互补的特点。中国是最大的发展中国家，12亿5千万人口、连续16年年均7%的经济增长率、相对落后的科技、难以满足经济增长需要的基础设施、短缺的资金，这些都意味着庞大的市场、庞大的需求。富有商业头脑和开拓精神的美国企业家不会允许自己失去这样的机会。美国是最大的发达国家，人口众多、资本充足、科技发达，中国看重美国的市场，同时也需要美国的资金、技术和先进的管理经验。中美两国经济的互补性构成了双方发展经贸合作的现实基础。

企业界的大力推动是中美经贸关系蓬勃发展和显示活力的重要源泉。企业是市场经济的主体，也是经济全球化条件下发展国际贸易和经济合作的主导力量。中美两国企业在中美经贸关系发展过程中始终扮演着主要角色。美国的大企业通过开展对华直接投资实现了资源的合理配置，而众多的中小企业则以贸易、投资、经济技术合作等灵活多样的方式发挥自身的特长。中国企业实力虽然不及美国同行，但对发展中美经贸合作倾注了同样的热情。经过二十几年的探索和实践，双方企业不仅获得良好经济效益，而且积累了丰富的经验，为今后的发展打下了坚实的基础。

两国最高领导人关于建立面向21世纪中美建设性战略伙伴关系的伟大构想是中美经贸关系健康稳定发展的根本保障。进入90年代以来，中美高层进行了史无前例的、频繁的交流。1997年11月，中国国家主席江泽民成功地对美国进行了国事访问；1998年6月，美国总统克林顿应邀回访。与克林顿总统访华相隔不到一年，1999年4月，中国国务院总理朱镕基又应邀赴美访问。中美两国高层互访对双方加深了解、增进友谊、扩大共识、发展合作产生了积极的影响，同时也为中美经贸关系的发展注入了新的活力。

在人类迈入新千年的时候，中美经贸合作业已成为中美关系这一世界上最重要的双边关系的主要支柱之一，它不仅促进了两国经济的繁荣，增加了就业机会，改善了人民生活，而且也为彼此增进了解、加强友谊做出了巨大贡献。

三

我们高兴地看到，中美经贸关系的大道正越走越宽，与此同时，我们双方也都切实关注一些问题。在此，我想就中国加入世界贸易组织、美国给予中国永久正常贸易关系地位、美国对华出口管制和中美贸易不平衡问题谈一些看法。

中国的发展离不开世界，世界的繁荣需要中国，这是中国坚持加入世界贸易组织的根本考虑。随着改革开放的深入发展，中国市场将进一步向世界开放。加入世贸组织不仅将使我们的开放获得新的动力，而且将使我们的权利得到有效的保障。如我们的承诺，在过去九次下调进口关税的基础上，2000 年我们将把工业品平均进口关税降至 15%，并进一步在 2005 年之前降至 10%。我们将逐步拓展利用外资的领域，继续健全外商投资的法律法规体系，依法严格保护外资企业的正当权益，保护知识产权，改善对外商投资企业的服务，为外商来华拓展商机创造更好的环境。

随着经济和社会发展的不断推进，中国市场的潜力将进一步展现。目前中国每年的进口额在 1500 亿美元左右，据测算，未来 7 年，中国的进口总额将达到 1.5 万亿美元。今后一个时期，中国将重点发展水利、能源、交通、通讯、原材料、环保、重大装备等基础产业。根据世界银行的估算，10 年内中国在基础设施方面的需求将达到 7440 亿美元。我们欢迎美国企业来华投资或参与市场开发。

作为中国加入世界贸易组织努力的一部分，中国将进一步开放农产品市场，更多的美国小麦、柑橘、肉类将进入中国市场，走上普通中国人的餐桌。

根据中美两国关于中国加入世贸组织的双边协议，加入世贸组织以后，我们将进一步开放服务业，为外商投资金融、保险、旅游、商业零售、外贸、法律咨询等服务业领域提供更多的机会。中国的服务业发展水平相对较低，逐步开放服务业市场，引入外来竞争，既符合中国的利益，也符合外国投资者的利益。

中国将继续鼓励外商投资高新技术产业。中国政府新近出台了一系列税收和金融方面的优惠政策，支持外国高科技投资者。此外，中国还将在总结现有经验的基础上，继续探索利用外国风险投资发展中国高科技产业的可能性。

中国还将加强中西部地区的开发和开放。这是一片幅员辽阔、资源丰富的地区，发展潜力巨大，但是长期以来发展滞后。落后的原因是交通闭塞，信息不畅。近年来，随着国家增加对中西部地区的基础设施投入，昔日的落后局面已经发生了很大的改观。沉睡多年的中国中西部已经做好了张开双臂，欢迎来自四面八方的企业家前往投资的充分准备。

有人可能担心中国不遵守承诺？我可以告诉大家，这种担心是多余的。如果中国只图享受加入世贸组织的好处，而不愿承担义务，就不会历时 13 年同美方开展一轮又一轮的艰苦谈判。事实上，中国已经开始采取实际行动，执行中美双边协议。为使中国国内法同世贸组织的国际法相一致，我们正着手修改现行外贸法和外资企业法。就在这个月，我们将派出农产品检疫小组赴美检疫，以利于美国的柑橘等农产品对华出口。中国将严肃认真地履行协议。中国加入 WTO 有利于世界，有利于中美两国。

相互给予正常贸易关系地位是中美经贸关系的基石。美国方面承诺在中美达成关于中国加入世贸组织双边协议后，将解决给予中国永久正常贸易关系地位问题。希望美国国会顺应时势，促成这一问题的早日圆满解决。在座各位都是在美国各界有影响的知名人士，希望继续发挥积极作用，尽快解决这一问题。

另一个是歧视性的对华高技术出口管制问题。21 世纪既然是合作的世纪，中美两国的战略利益既然是一致的，美国为何还坚持冷战思维，视中国为假想敌，在高技术出口问题上不惜牺牲自身经济利益，处处对华设限？我们呼吁美国政府摒弃这种政策，以更开放的心态推动中美经贸交流的发展。

当然，从美方的角度，你们可能会关心美国对华贸易逆差问题。作为主管对外贸易的中国政府高级官员，我对这个问题有一些认识，而且我的认识也为包括克林顿总统前经济顾问劳拉·泰森女士和知名专家伯格斯腾先生在内的众多美国学者的观点所印证。在经济全球化条件下，对贸易不平衡问题应该有全新的认识。暂且不论中美双方统计方法不同导致的统计差异，仅跨国公司投资对传统贸易的影响、地区产业结构调整引发的加工贸易的地区转移和转口贸易三方面，就足以造成如今规模的美国对华贸易逆差。这是一个复杂的问题，是一个发展过程中的问题，有它的历史背景和地缘背景，责备中国不开放市场是没有依据的，也是不负责任的。

回顾历史，我们为 20 年中美经贸合作的丰硕成果感到欣喜；展望未来，我们为 21 世纪中美经贸交流的广阔前景感到鼓舞。

拓展中美经贸合作是中国的真诚愿望，也是美国的利益所在。正常健康的中美经贸关系不仅有助于两国经济的繁荣，而且有助于亚太乃至世界经济的稳定与发展。浩瀚的太平洋虽然从地理上把我们两个伟大的国家隔开，但是中美经贸合作却在两国之间、两国人民心灵之间架起了一座理解与友谊的桥梁。为了 21 世纪的共同繁荣，让我们携起手来，为这座桥梁的长久巩固与持续通畅不断作出新的贡献！

（本文根据孙振宇副部长 2000 年 1 月 10 日与中美知名人士会晤时的演讲稿编辑整理）

迎接我国加入世贸组织的机遇和挑战

对外贸易经济合作部副部长　龙永图

WTO 是世界上最大的多边贸易组织，已经有 135 个国家和地区参加，我国作为目前世界第十大贸易大国，加入 WTO 是我国深化改革、扩大开放和建立社会主义市场经济体制的内在要求，是我国经济发展的需要，也是世界经济发展的需要。

WTO 的前身是关贸总协定。我国是 1948 年开始实施的关贸总协定的 23 个创始缔约国之一。由于历史原因，新中国成立以后的一段时间里没有参加关贸总协定的活动。

1978 年起我国实行改革开放政策，根据对外开放的需要，我国政府于 1986 年 7 月正式向关贸总协定提出恢复我缔约方地位的申请，开始中国的“复关”谈判。

我国加入 WTO 的基本原则是一贯的，自江泽民主席 1993 年在西雅图与美国总统克林顿首次会晤以来，江泽民主席及我国政府多次阐明了我“复关”和加入 WTO 的三条原则：第一，关贸总协定/WTO 是一个国际性组织，如果没有中国的参加是不完整的；第二，中国要参加毫无疑问是作为发展中国家参加；第三，中国的参加是以权利与义务的平衡为原则的。我国在复关和加入 WTO 的谈判中，始终坚持了这些原则。

我国复关和加入 WTO 谈判已进行了两个阶段，即对中国贸易体制的审议阶段（1986 年—1992 年）和市场准入谈判阶段（1992 年至今）。目前仍在进行的市场准入谈判是整个加入谈判的核心阶段，谈判主要解决开放市场的速度、范围、条件等问题。WTO 成员中，要求与我国进行双边市场准入谈判的有 37 个。目前我国已经与 29 个 WTO 成员结束了双边谈判。

按照 WTO 的加入程序，我国需要结束所有的双边谈判，并完成加入 WTO 的多边谈判程序，包括起草确定我国权利义务法律关系的加入议定书。然后经 WTO 总理事会审议批准，我国提交国内的批准文件，就可以正式成为 WTO 成员了。随着谈判进程的加快，应当说，我国加入 WTO 的日子已经为期不远了。

邓小平同志指出，“现在的世界是开放的世界。”“关起门来搞建设是不能成功的，中国的发展离不开世界。”随着科学技术的飞速进步和经济全球化趋势的加速发展，国际间的经济技术交流与合作，对世界各国经济的发展起着越来越重要的作用。改革开放 20 年的经验告诉我们，只有积极参与国际经济合作与竞争，有效利用国际经贸规则，趋利避害，才能充分发挥我国的优势，保持经济的稳定和发展。

加入 WTO，对我国经济发展有利有弊，但总的看来是利大于弊，符合我国根本利益。

（一）加入 WTO 为我国改革开放和经济建设营造一个有利的国际环境

第一，我国加入 WTO 后，按照国际通行规则办事，遵守多边贸易规则，增加贸易政策和管理的透明度，保证经贸政策的统一实施，逐步实行国民待遇等，将会有助于在国际上进一步树立我国改革开放和负责任的经济大国的形象，有助于消除所谓“中国威胁论”，增强我国市场对外国投资者的吸引力，使我国扩大吸引外资工作和质量更上一层楼。

第二，能够使我国在所有WTO成员提供的一个多边、稳定、无条件的最惠国待遇原则下进行国际贸易，可以享受其他国家和地区开放市场的好处，主要贸易大国对我的歧视性贸易限制将逐步取消。这对我扩大出口，发展我国具有比较优势（如纺织品、家电等）的产业，都有很大的促进作用。以纺织品为例，目前我国100多亿美元的纺织品出口受制于美、欧等国实行的配额限制，占我国纺织品总出口的25%。在我国成为WTO成员后，发达国家必须按照WTO《纺织品与服装协议》的规定逐步放松限制，在2005年最终取消所有配额管理。在2005年配额取消前，根据WTO协议规定的配额增长率测算，我国纺织品出口每年至少可增长5000万美元的出口机会。2005年配额取消后，我国纺织业将获得更多的出口和就业机会。对于其他行业，加入WTO也会带来不同程度的新的进入国际市场的机会。

第三，加入WTO将使中国有可能利用多边争端解决机制，有利于经济贸易的非政治化，有利于创造稳定的外部环境和赢得更多的海外市场，使我国除了双边渠道外，获得一个解决贸易纠纷的多边途径和手段，增加我国在处理对外经贸关系方面的回旋余地。

（二）有利于加快国内产业结构调整，增强我国企业的竞争力

加入WTO有助于我国社会主义市场经济体制的建立和完善，推进我国的改革开放进程，促进经济结构调整和产业升级，提高有关产业和服务业的国际竞争力，增强我国的经济实力。与此同时，还将推进我国现代企业制度的建立，更好的利用外国资金、技术和管理经验，提高我国企业的管理水平。

以农业为例，加入WTO有利于我国适量进口那些以土地资源为主要生产要素、国内比较优势不够的大宗产品，出口劳动密集型农产品，包括水果、蔬菜、畜产品、水产品等具有比较优势的农产品，进而调整农业产业结构。

以保险业的开放为例，美国友邦保险公司1992年进入我国市场后，引进了国际通行的保险营销制度，提高了中资保险公司的服务意识，促进了中国个人寿险业务的迅速发展，其中上海的总保费收入以每年30%以上的速度递增。

以汽车产业为例，由于国际竞争的加强，国内大的汽车企业将会进一步走向联合，实现规模经济，增强竞争能力，改变目前我国汽车工业散、乱、差的局面，从而带来更大的发展机遇。

（三）提高我国的国际地位，参与国际贸易新规则的制定

我国作为联合国常任理事国、世界银行和国际货币基金组织的成员，加入WTO，参与多边经贸规则的制订，将大大地提高中国的国际地位，充分发挥我国在国际经济事务中的作用，反映和维护我国和发展中国家的正当权益。

（四）有利于我国参与经济全球化

为了适应经济全球化、贸易自由化的形势，我国需要寻求稳定、透明、可预见的多边贸易机制的保障，在参与经济全球化过程中更好地趋利避害，发展自己。按国际规则办事，降低关税和非关税壁垒，有利于我国全面参与全球性生产和国际分工。

同时，加入WTO还有利于加强我国与跨国公司的合作。跨国公司是经济全球化的主要动力，我承诺按照国际规则办事，有利于提高跨国公司与中国合作的信心；有利于加强中国企业与跨国公司的合作，引进跨国公司的资金、技术和管理经验，利用跨国公司的销售渠道和网络，扩大出口。

WTO作为国际贸易组织，每个成员都必须遵循权利与义务平衡的原则，在享受一定权利的同时，履行相应的义务，承担开放市场所面临的风险与压力。

我国加入WTO后，我国对外经贸管理将一定程度地受到加入WTO规则的制约。加入WTO后，需要对我国有关的涉外经济法律、法规和政策进行清理、修改，对一些不符合WTO规则的做法进行调整。我们要履行WTO义务，对经济贸易不能再完全按原有方式进行管理，这无论是在观念上还是在体制上都要有新的变化，政府机关和企业管理人员的工作方式也需要适应新的形势。

同时，开放市场会使国内一些产业面临更为激烈的竞争。过去在市场开放方面，我国根据经济发展要求和经济体制改革的进程，主要采取自主开放的方式。加入WTO后，我国需要遵守WTO各项协议关于市场开放的规定，这在我们开放市场的速度和步骤上都会形成一定的压力。随着更多的外国产品和服务进入我国市场，我国的企业将面临更激烈的竞争，特别是那些成本高、技术水平低和管理落后的企业，将面临更加严峻的挑战。

总之，我国在获得加入WTO的益处的同时，也会面临一些挑战。如果处理不好，也有可能给经济发展带来一些弊端。为此，我们要积极迎接WTO带来的机遇和挑战，未雨绸缪，做好各方面的充分准备。

第一，全国上下要统一思想，提高认识。要把加入WTO与我国建设社会主义市场经济体制结合起来，通盘考虑，统一部署。各级领导干部要对加入WTO的长远战略意义有充分认识，对可能带来的风险，面临的挑战也要有足够的思想准备。

第二，各地、各部门要根据WTO协议的要求和我国所作出的承诺，认真研究和提出有针对性的、可操作的应对措施，以迎接加入WTO和21世纪经济全球化对我国的挑战。

1. 加强对农业的保护和支持。综合利用WTO《农业协议》的规定，防范或减轻进口农产品的冲击；为保障粮食安全，继续实行国家保护价的收购；加大农业投入，加快农业科技进步，调整农业结构，改良品种，提高质量；千方百计扩大我国优势农产品和高附加值农产品的生产和出口。加快建立完整的农产品质量标准体系，完善动植物检疫标准，加强国外疫情的监测和检疫。生产、贸易、检疫等各部门要密切配合，综合运用各种手段，特别是检疫和标准手段，做到按市场需要进口。要大力拓展农民就业和增收的渠道。

2. 尽快提高工业企业的国际竞争力，深化企业改革，建立适应社会主义市场经济要求的现代企业制度和经营机制；加快企业战略性改组，发展专业化和社会化生产协作体系；形成合理的经济规模发展一批实力雄厚的大企业和大集团；大力改造传统产业，发展高新技术产业，建立技术创新体系，提高企业开发创新能力。同时，根据WTO有关幼稚产业保护等条款，通过运用合理的关税和非关税措施，包括紧急进口保障措施和反倾销措施，确保关系我经济安全和重大经济利益的产业持续健康稳定发展。

3. 有步骤地开放服务贸易市场。区别不同情况，有选择地、以稳健、稳妥的方式逐步扩大电信、银行、证券、保险、商业、外贸、旅游、音像等服务领域的对外开放，严格审批程序，加强行业监督管理。要确保国家信息安全，防范金融风险和不良文化的侵入。积极推进服务行业管理体制的改革，加强管理，改善服务，提高竞争能力。

第三，以加入WTO为契机，加强立法和执法工作，尽快建立健全我国经济贸易法律体系，进一步推动我国的法制建设，充分运用法律手段保护和促进我经济与社会的发展。对现行的涉外经济法律、法规和政策要进行充实、调整和完善，提高监管水平，以保证对外开放过程中的主动权，提高自我保护、自我发展的能力。

第四，培养WTO专门人材，掌握国际规则。加快培养一大批熟悉我国国情，具有很好的外语水平、丰富的专业知识的WTO专门人材，加强对经济全球化的研究，掌握和运用有关WTO的基本知识和规则，以使我国能有效地参与国际规则的制定，并充分利用多边规则和国际通行的手段发展我国经济贸易，保护我国的经济权益和经济安全。

加入WTO是我国改革开放过程中的一件大事，对中国经济在21世纪的发展具有深远影响，对近期经济增长也有积极意义。改革开放特别是90年代以来，我国综合国力和经济实力显著增强，已经具备了一定的承受能力。只要我们提高认识，统一思想、未雨绸缪，充分准备，通过改革，变压力为动力，就一定能够充分抓住我国加入世界贸易组织的机遇，促进我国经济的发展，并把市场开放的风险降低到最小的程度。

周可仁副部长在外经贸部促进重点联系企业扩大出口工作会议上的讲话

1999 年 5 月 11 日

这次促进重点联系企业扩大出口工作会议，是根据石广生部长的提议决定召开的。这是外经贸部今年推动企业扩大出口的一项重要举措。利用今天这个机会，我代表外经贸部向参加今天会议的代表表示热烈欢迎，对各企业多年来在出口工作中做出的努力表示衷心感谢。

目前，外经贸部已经在全国范围内、从各类从事外经贸业务的企业中确定了 50 家重点联系企业。根据海关统计，这 50 家重点联系企业 1998 年出口额排在全国的前 50 名。参加今天会议的是 31 家国有企业，另外 19 家三资企业将另外开会。从这次会议开始，外经贸部将与这些企业建立经常性的联系制度，从企业层面及时了解在出口贸易中的各种问题，尽早采取相应的对策和措施，推动这些企业进一步扩大出口，促进全国出口贸易的发展。

下面，我代表外经贸部讲三个问题。

一、当前我国的外经贸形势

由于亚洲金融危机的影响，我国外贸出口与利用外资工作均受到相当大的不利影响。据估计，1998 年我国出口损失在 200 亿美元以上。从今年 1—4 月份外贸出口与利用外资情况看，目前亚洲金融危机的影响还在持续加深。

今年 1—4 月，全国进出口总额 988.47 亿美元，比去年同期增长 1.2%。其中，出口 520.25 亿美元，下降 7.8%；进口 468.21 亿美元，增长 13.6%。今年 1—4 月我国进出口有以下特点：

1. 出口每个月都是负增长。1、2、3、4 月份降幅分别为 10.8%、10.2%、3.6%、7.3%。

2. 外商投资企业出口小幅增长。外商投资企业出口 246.75 亿美元，增长 2.9%，3 月、4 月已连续两个月保持增长，但远低于去年同期的增长幅度。

3. 国有企业和一般贸易出口降幅较大。国有企业出口 255.3 亿美元，下降 16.5%；一般贸易出口 201.97 亿美元，下降 15.4%。

4. 加工贸易出口下降。加工贸易出口 305.5 亿美元，下降 0.7%。其中，进料加工出口（占加工贸易出口的 70%）下降幅度较大。

5. 对香港出口大幅下降，降幅达 34.4%；对日本出口增长 0.5%；对韩国、印尼、泰国、马来西亚出口分别增长 9.5%、29.6%、1.5% 和 0.2%；对美国出口增长 7.9%；对欧盟出口下降 2.1%。

6. 机电产品出口继续保持增长，增幅为 5.6%；服装、纺织纱线、织物及制品、鞋类、玩具、塑料制品、箱包等传统劳动密集型产品降幅依然较大，降幅都在 10% 左右。

从利用外资的情况看，今年以来，亚洲金融危机对我国吸收外资的直接冲击并没有减弱。据外经贸部统计，1—4 月，我国累计新签合同外资额 114.18 亿美元，下降 15.78%；实际使用外资额 102.4 亿美元，下降 12.6%。

我国出口贸易和吸收外资年初以来下降的根本原因在于外部环境依然严峻，对扩大出口和吸收外资的制约影响持续加深。这主要表现在：第一，发生金融危机的部分国家（地区）出口由降转增，在欧美市场上与我展开激烈竞争，我外贸出口不仅要面对巨大的价格压力，还要面对数量上的直接竞争压力。第二，世界经济增长放缓，市场需求萎缩。据估计，今年世界经济增长将由去年的 1.8% 下降为 1.7%；欧盟最近已将其经济增长预测由 2.4% 调至 2.1%；日本经济依然低迷，预测全年仅增长 0.5%。第三，国际市场价格受全球性生产过剩与出口竞争加剧的交互影响继续走低。第四，吸收外商直接投资来源减少。亚洲金融危机以来，国际投资商对发展中国家投资更加谨慎。我国主要的外资来源地受亚洲金融危机影响，对外投资能力被削弱，短期内难以恢复过去的增长势头。部分危机国家（地区）经济开始恢复，加上其制定了更加优惠的外资政策，也对我国吸收外商投资形成新的挑战。因此，今年我国出口贸易和吸收外资的总体形势仍不容乐观。

当然，我国出口和吸收外资也有不少有利因素，只要妥善应对，政策措施得力，今年也有一定发展空间。目前经济全球化的进程并没有中断；欧美和其他多数国家经济保持增长；国内经济继续保持“高增长、低通胀”的良好局面；我国商品出口规模和外资来源多样化程度高于大多数发展中国家；我国政治稳定、社会稳定、货币稳定、市场潜力大，对外商仍有较强的吸引力。关键是我们上上下下、方方面面要密切协作，按照全国外经贸工作会议、全国外贸出口电视电话会的精神，进一步狠抓落实。外经贸部对今年的工作抓得很紧，已经成立了进出口工作领导小组、吸收外资领导小组、外经改革领导小组、科技兴贸领导小组以及企业改革指导小组，分别由部领导牵头，具体抓落实。4 月中旬，外经贸部和海关总署联合召开了关贸协作会议，研究并制订了支持外贸出口和合作打击走私的有关措施。5 月初，又召开了全国吸收外资工作经验交流电视电话会。今年下半年还要召开银贸、税贸、汇贸等协作会以及全国推动高新技术产品出口会议等。我们就是要通过这些会议和各项实实在在的工作，为我国出口贸易和吸收外资创造一个更加良好的环境，实现今年外贸出口一定程度增长和保持吸收外资相当规模的预定目标。

二、建立外经贸部与重点企业经常性的联系制度，是推动扩大出口的一项重要工作

以千方百计扩大出口，力争一定程度增长，更多更好吸收外资，不断提高利用外资水平为重点，全面做好各项外经贸工作，是国家今年交给我们的外经贸工作任务。为此，石广生部长今年年初就提出了“抓大”、“抓重”、“抓急”的要求。从推动企业扩大出口的角度讲，“抓大、抓重、抓急”就是要抓住大企业，抓住重点企业，为企业提供优质服务，为千方百计扩大出口排忧解难。抓住了出口额大的重点企业，就抓住了影响出口贸易全局的关键。根据这个要求，我们把海关统计 1998 年出口排在前 50 位的企业确定为经常性联系的企业。这 50 家企业 1998 年共出口 181 亿美元，占全国当年出口总额的 9.8%，相当于我国中西部地

区 19 个省、自治区、直辖市的出口额。可见，这 50 家企业在我国出口贸易中占有举足轻重的地位。

为了落实好促进重点联系企业扩大出口的工作，外经贸部已经拟定了促进重点联系企业扩大出口的工作方案。根据这个方案，外经贸部将建立与这 50 家重点企业经常性的联系制度，由发展司和外资司作为牵头单位，其中 31 家国有企业由发展司负责牵头联系，19 家外商投资企业由外资司负责牵头联系。这两个司都制订了具体的联系工作制度和落实措施。在今天会议上，发展司将向 31 家重点联系企业介绍外经贸部的联系工作制度。

建立这种经常性联系制度，处理好外经贸部和重点联系企业的关系至关重要。外经贸部和重点联系企业之间是服务与被服务的关系，外经贸部机关要从政策上、业务上、信息上为重点联系企业及时提供服务。从政策上为重点联系企业服务，就是在研究制订或修订调整有关出口方面政策的时候，要更多地征求这些重点联系企业的意见；政策出台后，要及时向这些企业通报；还要从这些企业了解政策落实执行情况，分析政策效应。从业务上为重点联系企业服务，就是外经贸部要经常地、主动地与这些企业联系，了解企业在扩大出口等各项工作中遇到的困难和问题，在外经贸部职权范围内能够解决的及时予以解决，为企业排忧解难，创造良好的环境，同时外经贸部也要从宏观上对这些企业在发展外贸出口和其他外经贸业务方面作必要的指导。从信息上为重点联系企业服务，就是外经贸部要主动地将国际市场信息、国别和地区的市场需求信息、国际国内有关外经贸方面的政策性信息等及时通报给这些企业。

总之，在外经贸部促进重点联系企业扩大出口的工作中，要体现出在市场经济条件下政府与企业的新型关系。当然，服务也包括指导。外经贸部与重点企业建立经常性联系制度的目的只有一个，就是推动和促进外贸出口，实现今年全国外贸出口保持一定程度增长的目标。

从这次会议开始，外经贸部与重点企业正式建立起经常性联系制度。外经贸部机关同这项工作有关的司局和 31 家重点企业今天也都见了面。从外经贸部的角度讲，这项联系制度将长期坚持，并不断总结加以完善，联系的工作内容应当不断充实，但联系的对象不能一成不变，要定期进行动态调整，调整的依据是海关统计的企业年度出口实绩。如果哪家企业下一年度的出口额下来了，没有进入全国前 50 名，那就自然从重点联系企业的名单中退出了。因此，对企业来说，这个联系对象不是固定不变的，不是终身制的。如果企业想成为外经贸部重点联系的对象，那就要不断作出努力，使本企业的出口额不断扩大。从这个意义上讲，企业被外经贸部列为重点联系企业，既是对这些企业出口工作的一个肯定，是企业的一笔无形资产，又会给这些企业进一步扩大出口、加快发展带来压力，产生动力。

三、共同努力，建立起有效的经常性联系制度，推动我国出口贸易发展

经常性联系制度是适应社会主义市场经济发展的要求，在外经贸部机关和重点出口企业之间建立的双向交流和联系制度，需要外经贸部和重点企业两个方面大胆探索，共同努力，并在实践中不断充实和完善。在这里，我提出以下几点希望和要求：

（一）外经贸部有关司局要把与重点企业的联系列入日常工作日程。作为全国外经贸工

作业务主管部门，外经贸部机关要彻底从传统计划经济的思维定式中解脱出来，牢固树立“大经贸”观念和为企业服务、为基层服务的思想，加快转变机关工作作风。外经贸部有关司局要按照各自的职能，以发展的眼光把联系制度建立起来，充实起来，坚持下去，务求成效。既要为各类企业特别是重点联系企业及时提供服务，又要善于从这些重点联系企业中发现问题，制订政策，提炼经验，用以指导全国出口工作。

（二）希望重点联系企业要千方百计扩大出口，力争今年出口实现更大程度增长。国务院要求今年全国出口要力争一定程度增长，有条件的地区和企业要力争更大程度增长。参加这次会议的企业，在实业基础、贸易渠道、企业管理、人才和资金等各方面都有比较好的基础，有条件力争今年出口实现更大程度增长。千方百计扩大出口不仅是我国国民经济发展全局的迫切要求，也是企业自身生存和发展的客观要求。企业被外经贸部列为重点联系的对象，无论是扩大出口还是企业发展，也都存在机遇，起码在获得政策信息和市场信息方面占了先机。因此，希望你们充分运用好这个条件，进一步做好出口工作，努力使出口的规模与效益不断迈上新台阶，壮大本企业的实力，并带动其他企业千方百计扩大出口，为我国对外经济贸易事业的发展作出积极贡献。

（三）希望重点联系企业积极配合外经贸部有关司局工作，使联系制度发挥应有的作用。为及时了解和掌握出口工作中带有普遍性的问题，我们非常欢迎各个企业通过联系制度积极主动地向外经贸部反映企业的意见和要求，与此同时，外经贸部确定的牵头联系司将会不定期地组织有关司局到重点联系企业进行实地调研，也会不定期地向企业要一些材料和数据，请大家积极给予配合，在提供有关材料、数据和反映问题时，一定要坚持实事求是，讲真话、讲实话，只有这样，我们对存在的问题而采取的解决措施才会得当。这个制度是为企业服务的，外经贸部派人到企业了解情况，不会增加企业的负担。请大家放心。

（四）希望重点联系企业彻底转变观念，依靠自身力量，在扩大出口和企业发展上不断取得进步。在计划经济条件下，企业是政府机构的附属物；而在社会主义市场经济条件下，企业是自主经营、自负盈亏、自我发展、自我约束的法人实体。作为外经贸业务主管部门，外经贸部要适应社会主义市场经济发展的要求，尽心尽力为企业服务，竭尽全力为扩大出口创造相对宽松的外部环境。而企业出口贸易的发展，经济实力的增强，还要依靠企业自身不断加强管理，改善经营，不断深化改革，“等靠要”的思想是根本要不得的。在建立重点企业联系制度的时候，我要特别强调这一点。

对外开放 新时期最鲜明的特征

对外贸易经济合作部党组成员、中纪委驻部纪检组长 刘向东

1999年12月30日

一

党的十一届三中全会以来在邓小平理论的指导下制定的一系列政策，概括起来就是改革开放，这是我们新时期最鲜明的特征。邓小平同志是我国改革开放和现代化建设的总设计师，在我国历史发展的关键时刻，以其非凡的政治敏锐和判断力，精辟地总结了我国发展的历史经验教训以及世界各国发展的经验，分析了和平和发展成为时代主题，阐明了争取长时间和平环境进行国内建设的必要性和可能性，准确及时地把握时代发展的脉搏和契机，提出了当今世界是开放的世界，任何国家的发展都离不开世界这个时代的趋势，果断地作出实行对外开放的重大决策。这是邓小平同志作为我们党第二代领导核心对马克思主义和毛泽东思想的继承和发展。开辟了我国走向富强的广阔道路。

二十多年来，党中央高举邓小平理论的旗帜，忠实贯彻执行邓小平对外开放思想，实现了我国历史上的一次大飞跃，社会主义在中国显示的蓬勃生机和活力，为全世界所瞩目。我国对外开放形成了由沿海到内地、由一般加工业到服务业的全方位、多层次的对外开放格局，国民经济由封闭和半封闭状态走向开放型经济。外经贸管理体制改革朝着“统一政策、放开经营、平等竞争、自负盈亏、工贸结合、推行代理制”的方向不断深化。对外开放口岸由原来的广州、大连、上海、青岛、天津等少数几个，已增加到今天的海陆空一类口岸240多个；关税平均总水平由40%以上降低到17%，非关税措施也大幅度减少；人民币实现了经常项目下的可兑换。对外经济贸易合作破除许多旧的思想框框束缚，开辟了利用外资、对外承包工程和劳务合作、技术出口、对外投资、接受援助等新领域；对外贸易渠道拓宽，方式更加灵活；援外方式不断改进，正向互利合作发展；技术贸易实现引进和输出的双向发展，整个对外经济贸易形成了商品、资金、技术、劳务紧密结合，相互促进的局面。外经贸经营主体多元化，正由经营许可制向自主登记制转变，初步形成了覆盖全社会、各物质生产部门共同参与的空前活跃的大经贸格局。对外经贸关系迅速拓展，目前，我国已同世界上220多个国家和地区有贸易关系，170多个国家和地区有资金合作，130多个国家和地区开展承包工程和劳务合作，对136个国家提供经济技术援助，同绝大多数国际经济组织特别是联合国发展系统发展了广泛的合作关系，参与了许多区域性经济组织及单项商品国际组织的合作，形成了双边、多边经贸关系相互促进、共同发展的生动局面。我国在对外经贸合作中，重合同、守信用坚持以质取胜，国际信誉和合作水平大为提高。对外开放使我国经济发展的回旋余地扩大，避免了以往的大起大落，1979年到1998年，年均保持了9%以上的持续、快速、健康发展。对外贸易进出口额由1978年的206亿美元增加到1998年的3239亿

美元，增长14.7倍，年均增长近15%，远远高于同期世界贸易增长速度，在世界贸易中的位次由1978年的第32位上升到1997年的第10位。国家外汇储备由十几亿美元增加到1450亿美元。这是远远超出人们预料的，充分显示出邓小平对外开放思想的巨大威力。1980年在制定国民经济发展规划时提出到2000年进出口总额达到1600亿美元，有的人还认为做不到，没有想到1998年已经超过这个目标的一倍，广东一个省的进出口额就能达到1600亿美元。利用外资从无到有，实际投入资金累计达到4200多亿美元，其中直接投资2674亿美元，兴办外商投资项目32万多个，1993年以来年吸收直接投资额仅次于美国，居世界第二位，发展中国家第一位。对外承包工程和劳务合作异军突起，累计完成营业额583.7亿美元，派出劳务人员177万人。其他各项对外经济合作都得到长足的全面发展。

二

对外开放、对外经济贸易的发展，在国民经济发展中发挥了不可替代的重要作用。概括起来是：

一是扩大了资源的配置范围，拓宽了经济发展的回旋余地。随着生产技术的发展，对资源的需求更为广泛，世界上没有一个国家能够拥有其经济现代化所需的全部资源和技术，必须通过国际间的交换，利用两种资源（国内资源和国际资源）、两个市场（国内市场和国际市场），互通有无，取长补短。我国虽然地大物博，但是人口众多，人均资源占有量少；资源储量很不平衡，有的资源探明储量很少，不能满足经济发展的需要；有的由于资金技术等问题不能解决，难以充分供应。这些都需要通过对外经济贸易活动来解决。比如钢铁工业，我国富铁矿储量少，开采投资大，周期长；钢铁工业的技术比较落后。我们通过进口外国的铁矿砂，引进先进技术设备，使我国的钢产量达到1亿多吨，成为世界产钢大国，钢材除供应国内需要，还可出口。农业是国民经济的基础，而农作物生长需要的钾肥，我国储量很少；生产技术又比较复杂，也是通过国际间的交换合作解决的，还有木材、铜等。我国出口已占当年国民生产总值的20%以上，利用外资“八五”计划期间年均占社会固定资产总投资的11%，1997年上升到14.9%，成为支持国民经济发展的重要因素。如果不发展国际交换与合作，利用两个市场、两种资源，我国经济是很难有今天这样局面的。

二是发挥比较优势，促进经济结构和产业结构的调整，提高国民经济运行的整体效益。每个国家，不论大小、贫富，都有自己的比较优势，也有自己的相对劣势。我国的相对优势是人口众多，劳动力丰富，且勤奋智慧；市场广阔，具有潜力；某些资源丰富，某些产业和科研力量有一定基础。但是，我国发展起步晚，底子薄，基础设施和技术比较落后，资金严重不足。我们利用优势条件吸引外来投资，引进先进适用技术，加快了我国的水利、能源、交通、通讯等基础设施建设，加快企业的技术改造；促进机械、电子、石化、汽车和建筑业等支柱产业的发展。特别是利用两种资源、两个市场，使我国生产能力和劳动力丰富的优势得到发挥，真正成为国家的宝贵财富。实行对外开放后，我国大力发展加工贸易，利用外资、对外承包工程和劳务合作，开辟了发挥我国劳动力优势的广阔天地。1998年，加工贸易占我国进出口总额的54%，占出口总额的56%，提供了3000多万个就业岗位；在已开业的15万家“三资”企业就业的人员达1800万人；在外执行承包劳务合同的人员达33万多人；从事一般外贸出口商品生产和经营的人员还要多。这不仅为国家的现代化建设做出了贡献，也使一些地方和人员先富起来。

三是吸取人类创造的文明成果，在较高的起点上发展，形成后发优势。按照我国现代化建设三步走的战略，我们要用 100 年时间，达到西方发达国家用了 300 多年时间达到的经济发展水平。这是因为我们社会主义制度比资本主义有比较优势，可以调动全社会成员的劳动积极性和创造性，善于采取对外开放政策，通过国际经济技术交流和合作，吸取和借鉴人类共同创造的一切文明成果，特别是先进技术和管理经验，在更高的起点上开发、创新，赶上世界经济技术的发展水平。我国航天、造船、石化、家电、汽车以及纺织、轻工等行业的发展就可充分说明，这是我国发挥社会主义优越性，实现现代化建设目标的必由之路。

四是提高了我国的国际地位，有利于维护国家的安全。对外经济贸易是国家经济实力的综合反映，是联系各国间利益关系的纽带。我国经济实力和与各国、各地区的利害关系是通过对外经济贸易体现出来的。对外经济贸易的发展使别的国家、地区对我国依赖加大，又使我国的实力明显反映出来，其他国家对我采取不友好措施，首先要考虑对自身的损害；在冷战结束，各国转向以综合国力竞争为主的今天，经济合作关系日益成为巩固外交关系的重要因素；对外经济贸易发展有利于我国加强同世界各国的了解和友好关系，创造建设社会主义现代化的良好外部环境，制约别国对我国采取敌视损害行动，有利于国家的安全。

五是推动祖国和平统一进程。祖国大陆和香港、澳门间的经济贸易发展，为香港、澳门的平稳过渡，主权顺利回归创造了条件。台湾省与祖国大陆之间经济贸易合作的发展，加深了台胞对祖国大陆的了解，也使越来越多的人认识到台湾省经济发展离不开祖国大陆，有利于促进祖国的和平统一；我国同世界各国经贸关系的发展，实施市场多元化战略，也有利于遏制台湾当局的“弹性外交”，促使其放弃台独幻想，回到祖国和平统一的道路上来。

实践充分证明，邓小平对外开放理论和党的十一届三中全会以来一系列对外开放政策是无比正确的。

三

邓小平同志指出：“根据我们自己的经验，讲社会主义，首先就是要使生产力发展，这是主要的。只有这样，才能表明社会主义的优越性。”（《邓小平文选》第 2 卷，314 页，人民出版社，1994 年 10 月第 2 版。）在邓小平同志的主持下，制定了我国实现社会主义现代化“三步走”的发展战略，要用西方发达国家 1/3 的时间，达到西方发达国家的经济发展水平，充分反映了社会主义制度的本质和我国坚持社会主义道路的坚定信念，反映了全国人民的迫切愿望，是巩固社会主义制度的根本保证。邓小平同志还一再提醒我们：“中国能不能顶住霸权主义，强权政治的压力，坚持我们的社会主义制度，关键就看能不能争得较快的增长速度，实现我们的发展战略。”（《邓小平文选》第 3 卷，356 页，人民出版社，1993 年 10 月第 1 版。）

当今的世界是开放的世界，随着新技术革命的蓬勃发展，经济全球化和国际贸易、投资自由化在迅速推进，已成为世界发展的主旋律。世界各国和地区都在制定各自的发展战略，顺应潮流，扩大对外开放，以便抓住机遇，更广泛地参与国际分工和合作，发挥比较优势，取获更多利益，促进经济发展。以江泽民同志为核心的党中央充分估计到这种形势，高瞻远瞩地指出："面对经济科技全球化趋势，我们要以更加积极的姿态走向世界，完善全方位、多层次、宽领域的对外开放格局，发展开放型经济，增强国际竞争力，促进经济结构优化和国民经济素质提高。"江泽民同志同时强调指出："能否抓住机遇，历来是关系革命和建设兴衰成败的大问题。"

四

在改革开放和现代化建设的过程中，邓小平同志总是强调要解放思想，实事求是。

国民经济对国际市场的依存度提高，会不会损害我国经济的健康发展？总的来说，经济全球化是现代经济发展的客观要求，每个国家自觉不自觉地都会融入这个潮流中。既然是这样，受国际经济波动的影响是难免的，但是影响的大小因各国的不同情况而异。应当指出的是，各国特别是发达国家都在根据情况的变化，进行经济结构调整，加强国内的宏观调控和国际间的协调，可以缓和或平抑世界经济的大动荡和危机，本世纪 30 年代初那样的世界经济大危机很难再度发生。1997 年下半年发生的亚洲金融危机，尽管对世界经济贸易带来一定不利影响，但仍未改变世界经济贸易发展的总体趋势。当今，以主要经济大国高层次会议为主要形式，辅之以全球经济机构的国际经济协调机制已形成，有利于维护世界经济稳定运行，并促进其发展。我国国内市场广阔，潜力很大，可以利用国内市场的蓄积力和调节力，减缓来自外部的经济冲击。总之，对这个问题不必过多的担心。

扩大对外开放、吸收外商直接投资，会不会冲击"民族经济"发展，动摇社会主义经济基础？对此，邓小平同志在 1991 年视察上海时就指出："开放不坚决不行，现在还有好多障碍阻挡着我们。说'三资'企业不是民族经济，害怕它的发展，这不好嘛。发展经济，不开放是很难搞起来的，世界各国的发展都要搞开放，西方国家在资金和技术上就是互相融合、交流的。"(《邓小平文选》第 3 卷，367 页，人民出版社，1993 年 10 月第 1 版。) 我们要坚持社会主义道路，社会主义的一个重要特征就是以公有制为主体，共同富裕。他在 1992 年南方谈话中明确提出：判断改革和各方面的工作是非得失，归根到底，要以是否有利于发展社会主义社会的生产力，是否有利于增强社会主义国家综合国力，是否有利于提高人民的生活水平为标准。那么利用外资是否影响了社会主义公有制的主体地位？根本没有。目前，外商投资企业工业总产值约占全国的 18%，其中内销产值约占同期全国工业企业内销值的 9% 左右，如果只计算外方股权对应的部分，内销比例大约仅 5%。外商投资企业市场占有率提高的领域主要集中在轻工、饮料等竞争性行业，有些产品是替代进口的。改革开放以来，利用外资弥补了建设资金不足，建设起一批急需发展的项目，并开辟了新的财税来源；引进了先进技术和管理经验，推动了相关工业的技术进步；扩大就业门路，培养了一大批现代管理人才；促进了进出口贸易发展，改善了国际收支平衡；加强了祖国大陆与港澳台地区的经贸联系，对香港、澳门主权的顺利回归和祖国和平统一大业实现发挥重要作用；还促进了经济体制改革的不断深化。可以说，外商投资企业在各种经济成分的企业中是发展最快的，成为支撑我国经济快速增长的重要力量。

党的十五大指出：公有资产占优势，要有量的优势，更要注重质量的提高。国有经济起主导作用，主要体现在控制力上。对关系国民经济命脉的重要行业和关键领域，国有经济必须占支配地位。在其他领域，可以通过资产重组和结构调整，以加强重点，提高国有资产的整体质量。对公有制经济要维护，最根本的是促进其发展。在当今世界科学技术日新月异的情况下，在社会主义市场经济条件下，不发展就会被淘汰，是不以人的意志为转移的。我们要搞活公有资产存量，把国家积累的宝贵资金投向国民经济最重要的行业和项目，使其在国民经济发展中发挥主导作用。同时要大胆利用外资，促进国有企业和集体所有制企业的发展。实践证明，吸收外商直接投资，对现有企业进行嫁接改造，有利于壮大公有制的实力。保持公有制的主体地位，不是限制外商投资，而应是如何利用外资使其发展壮大。

对外开放的扩大是否会影响国家的安全？不可否认，某些国家是企图通过经济贸易推行其对我国分化、西化的阴谋。我们必须提高警惕。但决不可因此影响扩大对外开放，发展同各国的对外经济贸易。对外开放有利于增强国家的经济实力，国家强大才有安全可言，我们不能忘记受侵略、屈辱的历史教训。正如邓小平同志所说：“四人帮”的所作所为从反面使我们更加深刻地认识到，在无产阶级专政的条件下，不搞现代化，科学技术水平不提高，社会生产力不发达，国家的实力得不到加强，人民的物质文化生活得不到改善，那么我们的社会主义政治制度就不能充分巩固，我们国家的安全就没有可靠的保障。对外经济贸易发展，我国对国际市场的依赖增加，外国对我国的依赖也增加，成为安全的重要保障。反对外国利用台湾、西藏、人权等干涉我国内政的斗争胜利，对一些国家双边谈判成功，加入世界贸易组织谈判取得进展，等等，都是很好的例证。

尊重国际惯例，按照国际惯例办事，是对外开放的一个重要方面。如果不尊重国际惯例，不按国际惯例办事，我们的对外开放将寸步难行。当前应当总结经验，进一步克服思想上的障碍，认真学习有关知识，更好地按照国际惯例办事。有人把按国际惯例办事看作是按资本主义原则办事，这是极大的误解。所谓国际惯例，是指国际交往中被多数国家和地区接受的习惯性做法。国际惯例是经过长期实践所形成的行为规则，有的虽不成文，却具有法律约束力。国际惯例是适应国际交往而形成的，同发展市场经济的许多手段一样，资本主义可以利用，社会主义也可以利用。可以说，按照国际惯例办事不仅是我们有自信心、有力量的表现，也是自力更生的重要方面。

对外开放在我国还是一个崭新的事物，需要破除我们长期以来形成的一些旧的思想、观念、理论。所以，必须坚持解放思想、实事求是的思想路线，像邓小平同志教导的那样：“不争论，大胆地试，大胆地闯。”（《邓小平文选》第3卷，374页，人民出版社，1993年10月第1版）这样，我们才能走出一条好路，走出一条新路，干出一番新的事业。

（本文根据刘向东同志为《邓小平对外开放理论与我国的对外开放政策》一书所作序言摘编。）

科技兴贸战略：外贸跨世纪发展的必然选择

对外贸易经济合作部副部长　张　祥

科学技术是第一生产力，科技进步是经济发展的决定性因素。党的十五大明确提出，要实施科教兴国战略，把加速科技进步放在经济社会发展的关键地位，使经济建设真正转到依靠科技进步和提高劳动者素质的轨道上来。1999年初，外经贸部提出并实施科技兴贸战略，这是贯彻科教兴国战略在对外经济贸易领域的具体体现，对提高我国对外贸易的质量和水平，促进国民经济发展具有重大意义。

一、实施科技兴贸战略适应了当前世界经济贸易发展的潮流

科技革命和知识经济兴起给世界经济带来的一个显著变化是，全球产业结构发生了重大而深刻的变化，高新技术产业蓬勃发展，知识密集度不断提高，知识正在成为最具创造力和能动作用的生产要素。美国经济连续8年持续增长，就是依靠科技突破和增量性的创新，从而能够源源不断地推出具有竞争力的新技术、新产品。1998年的统计数字表明，美国高技术产业对GDP增长的贡献率已达到55%，而传统的汽车产业的贡献率只有4%。由于知识与技术在经济发展中具有日益重要的支配作用，国际投资更加重视知识、技术、人才等投资环境，国际产业转移也表现出日益增强的跨越式转移特征，传统的雁形分工模式和梯度转移已部分被打破，一些新兴工业化经济体已经成为全球高新技术产业日益重要的制造基地。目前，新加坡、韩国高新技术产业发展在新兴工业化经济体中已处于领先地位。印度大力发展软件产业，成为仅次于美国的第二大软件出口国。

世界产业结构的重大调整已导致国际市场格局的重大变化。信息产品和其他高新技术产品在国际贸易中所占比重不断上升，需求增长较快；而传统产品的市场容量虽然也在增长，但相对份额却在缩小。亚洲金融危机让人们看到，原料性产品和传统产品的国际贸易受到的冲击最大，普遍出现贸易量萎缩、价格大跌，而高科技产品受到的冲击极小。

随着世界产业结构的飞速变化，我国产业结构和出口商品结构相对落后的矛盾日益突出。1997年我国高新技术产业在制造业中所占比重仅为8.1%，远低于世界平均水平，与发达国家和新兴工业化经济体相比差距更大。我国出口由改革开放前的第32位上升到1998年的世界排名第9位，已成为贸易大国，但还远不是世界贸易强国，抵御风险的能力还不强。据世界贸易组织提供的资料，1998年，世界十大贸易国的高新技术产品出口占本国总出口的比重均在40%左右，而我国仅为11%。我国出口商品结构相对于其他世界贸易大国处于明显劣势，这已成为制约我国对外贸易进一步发展的重要因素。因此，实施科技兴贸战略，适应了世界产业结构调整的趋势，是实现我国出口商品结构战略性调整的需要，是加快我国由贸易大国向贸易强国转变的必然要求。

二、实施科技兴贸战略符合我国国民经济发展和产业结构调整的现实需要

近年来，我国国民经济从总体上保持了“高增长、低通胀”的良好局面，特别是1997年以来成功地抵御了亚洲金融危机的冲击，国民经济保持较快增长，买方市场格局初步形成。但是，我国经济发展也遇到了许多新情况、新问题，特别是消费和投资需求持续不振，出口和利用外资下降，有效需求不足已成为当前较为突出的矛盾。

我国宏观经济出现上述突出矛盾的原因很多，其中最突出的两个问题是：第一，投资、消费和净出口三驾马车对经济增长的拉动作用都在减弱；第二，通货紧缩虽是一种宏观经济现象和货币现象，但也与产业结构不合理密切相关。大量重复建设造成生产能力严重过剩，加剧了企业经营困难，供给结构不合理和技术创新滞后又加剧了供求结构性矛盾。亚洲金融危机以来，全球性生产过剩矛盾充分暴露，进一步加大了我国出口和生产企业的困难。

实施科技兴贸战略可以从以下四方面为当前经济发展和产业结构调整作出积极的贡献：第一，有利于培植新的出口和吸收外商投资增长点。实施科技兴贸战略可以扩大高新技术产品出口，促进外商投资于高新技术产业，扭转出口和吸收外资下降的局面，增强发展后劲，从而更好地拉动经济增长。据统计，1999年上半年高新技术产品出口达107亿美元，比1998年同期增长19%，而同期全国出口总额下降4.6%，这说明高新技术产品出口在逐步扭转出口滑坡方面发挥了积极作用。第二，有利于促进国际收支平衡，保持人民币汇率的稳定。第三，有利于配合我国产业结构调整，使出口结构优化与产业结构调整相互结合、相互促进。第四，有利于促进科技成果商品化、产业化、国际化，提高科技对国民经济的贡献率。

三、实施科技兴贸战略是我国对外贸易跨世纪发展的现实选择

1998年，我国外贸发展遇到了前所未有的困难，全年出口实现了来之不易的0.5%的增长。1999年上半年出口继续滑坡，下半年才开始有所减缓。出口出现这么大的困难不是偶然的，其原因有以下几方面：一是国际市场原料性商品价格持续下降，相当部分劳动密集型产品价格近两年也有一定幅度下降；二是我国现行出口商品结构以低附加值、低技术含量产品为主，有40%左右的产品与东南亚有关国家、地区雷同，在国际市场面临日益激烈的竞争；三是世界经济区域集团化的不利影响加大，贸易保护主义抬头，加剧了出口困难；第四，由于出口竞争力相对削弱，外贸企业出口成本高，出口效益明显下滑，出口缺乏后劲；第五，我国加工贸易出口已占将近60%，其中相当一部分商品档次不高、技术含量和附加值较低。

上述困难和问题使我们深刻认识到，我国外贸发展已经进入了结构调整时期，如何创造新的市场空间，在新形势下走出一条外贸发展的新路，实现外贸出口的可持续发展，已成为摆在我们面前的重要课题。机遇与挑战并存。知识经济的发展是跳跃式的、非线性的。由于信息、知识革命来得如此迅猛，我们完全有可能跨越传统工业化的某些阶段，直接进入信息经济或知识经济阶段。外贸结构的调整也是如此。只有实施科技兴贸战略，才能使外贸从单纯传统产品出口和大批量、低效益产品出口转移到高技术含量、高附加值产品出口这个轨道

上来，才能使我国真正实现由贸易大国向贸易强国的跨越式转变，增强抗御各种外部风险的能力。

四、实施科技兴贸战略的基本思路

科技兴贸战略包括两方面内容：一是大力推动高新技术产品出口；二是运用高新技术成果改造传统出口产业，提高出口产品的技术含量和附加值。根据我国高新技术产业和产品出口现状以及国际市场的变化趋势，高新技术产品出口近期的努力目标是，力争2000年高新技术产品出口达到300亿美元，占我国出口总额的比重由目前的11%提高到15%；长期目标是，到2010年力争高新技术产品出口在全国出口总额中达到30%，初步完成我国出口商品结构由以低附加值、低技术含量产品为主向以高新技术产品为主的转变，并力争再通过3年～5年的努力，在利用高新技术改造若干重点传统出口产业及其关键薄弱环节方面取得突破，使具有较高技术含量和附加值的出口商品的比重提高到50%左右，加工贸易使用国产原材料的比重由目前的20%提高到50%。

根据上述目标，我们确立了实施科技兴贸战略的基本思路：

1．完善规划，纵横结合，立体发展，改善服务

在调查研究的基础上，明确科技兴贸的初步规划和步骤、制定科技兴贸行动计划。这个计划的目标是在我国优势技术领域培育一批有国际竞争能力、附加值高、出口规模大的高新技术出口产品，使我国高新技术产品出口额在今后几年内有较大幅度的增长。目前，已初步选定信息、生物医药、新材料、家电和消费类电子等5个领域作为重点发展行业，并从中选择166个企业的92个产品作为第一批重点扶持对象，给予重点支持，促使出口尽快上规模。

采取纵横立体发展和点、面结合的方式推动科技兴贸战略。目前，全国53个高新技术产业开发区是科技兴贸的主要基地，而北京、上海、武汉等15个城市的高新技术产品出口约占全国的80%以上，成为推进科技兴贸的重点区域。应通过规划、指导、协调和动员，抓好这些区域的科技兴贸工作，以重点带全面。同时，加强全局性规划和政策的研究制定工作，坚持服务优先原则，重视建立健全国际市场信息网络，组织好各类国际市场的开拓活动，促进科技兴贸战略的实施。

2．进一步建立和完善市场体系，推动高新技术产品出口

推动高新技术产品出口是科技兴贸战略的关键内容。应按照高新技术发展“有所为、有所不为”的指导思想，确定“有限目标、突出重点、面向市场、发挥优势”的总体思路，进一步细化高新技术产品出口发展规划。

重点培育一批高新技术出口产品和企业骨干，允许少数具备监管条件的高新技术产业开发区率先进行规范的出口加工区试验，并为创办有中国特色的高科技园区创造条件；适应高新技术产业全球化生产经营的特点，进一步完善高新技术产业发展及产品出口的政策法律体系，促进我国高新技术产业国际竞争力的整体提高；将高新技术产品出口纳入国家出口信贷和外贸发展基金的重点支持对象，给予优先安排；扩大国家出口信用保险规模，完善出口信用保险体制与政策，为高新技术产品出口提供更为便捷、高效的出口信用保险服务；积极推动建立面向出口的风险投资基金，对于出口规模大、前景好的高新技术企业给予重点支持。

此外，还应进一步完善知识产权保护的法律体系，逐步建立国家创新体系，提高我国的总体创新能力，为增强我国高新技术产品出口能力、培植有自主知识产权的国际品牌打下坚实基础。

3．加大政府扶持力度，加强服务职能，搞好国际市场营销服务

按照建设社会主义市场经济的要求，加大政府对科技兴贸战略的支持，从资金、人才、科研投入、海外市场开拓、财税政策以及宏观规划指导、国家间科技合作等方面制定配套措施，加快高新技术产品出口和传统出口商品升级换代步伐。要在制度创新和高科技人才培养方面采取积极措施，如允许科技人员持有技术股、创新股等，为高新技术产品扩大出口创造制度和人才条件。

大力改善政府部门的服务。如：对科研院所和科技型企业进出口经营权实行自动登记制；改进海外投资管理，简化人员进出境手续，为高新技术企业开展国际化经营和对外经济技术交流提供便利条件；协助做好外贸人才培训、参加国内外招商展览等方面的协调服务工作；办好高新技术产品交易会，增强在全国开展科技兴贸的示范效应；加强国际技术交流，及时跟 踪国际先进技术潮流，促进我国出口产业技术水平的提高。

针对高新技术产品国际营销的不同特点，搞好国际市场营销服务。加强对国际市场的调查研究，制定开拓重点市场的计划，做好高新技术产品出口的信息服务工作。应当加强外经贸部门与科技部门、各有关产业部门的联系，并发挥驻外使领馆、经商机构、科技机构的作用，共同做好高新技术产品全球市场信息搜集整理和服务工作，帮助高科技企业寻找市场和合作伙伴。

（本文选自《求是》杂志 2000 年第三期）

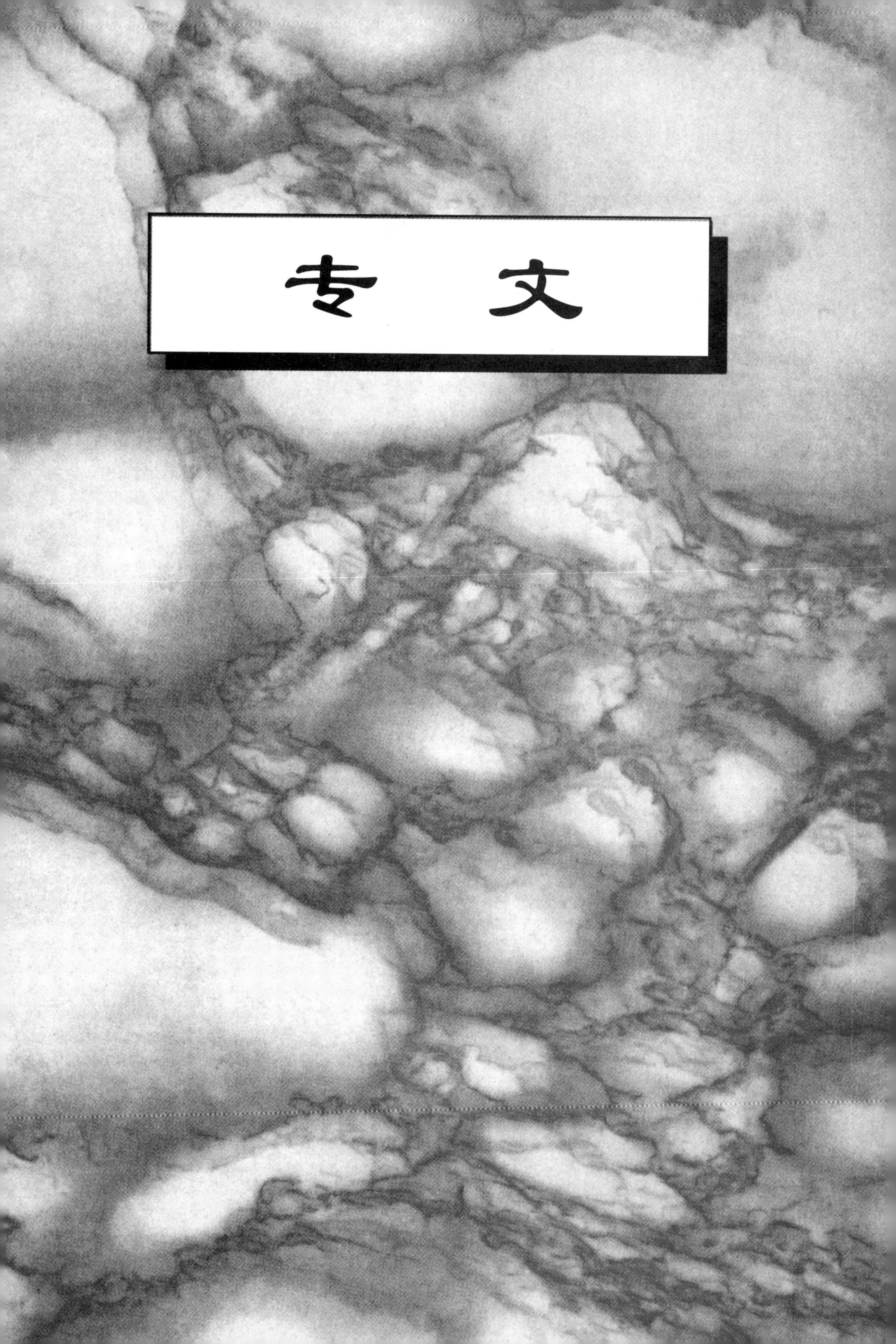

专　文

以境外加工贸易为新起点发展我国的对外投资

对外贸易经济合作部发展司副司长　赵闯

对外投资，是我国实行对外开放政策的具体内容之一。国家鼓励有能力的企业发展对外投资业务。截至 1999 年底，我国企业在 160 多个国家和地区设立了 5900 多家境外企业，中方协议投资额近 70 亿美元。投资的领域也从初期集中在贸易方面，发展到资源开发、生产加工、交通运输、工程承包、旅游餐饮等众多领域。

90 年代初以来，我国企业积极探索以设备、技术等实物资本为主到境外投资办厂、开展境外加工贸易，取得了明显的成效。如一汽、金城、洛拖、海尔、康佳、春兰、上广电、鹿王等一批国内知名企业到境外投资办厂，组装与生产自己的产品，建立自己的销售网络，培育自己的名牌，收到了良好效果。我国的对外投资便以境外加工贸易为新起点，有了进一步的发展。截至 1999 年 12 月 31 日，我国共有境外加工贸易项目 151 个，中方总投资 3.3 亿美元左右。这些项目具有以下特点：

一、轻工、纺织、家用电器等机械电子类加工和服装加工等是境外加工贸易的重点。从上述 151 个境外加工贸易项目的行业分布来看，主要涉及机电、轻工、服装加工、烟草等行业。其中，机电类项目 64 个，占总数 42.4%；轻工类项目 35 个，占总数 23.2%；服装加工类项目 31 个，占总数 20.5%。

二、投资主体多为实力强、管理科学、有一定信誉的国内生产企业，在外经贸部公布的第一批 33 个名牌出口商品企业名单中，有 11 家企业已经获准从事境外加工贸易，其中较为典型的是青岛海尔集团在 11 个国家设立了 15 个家用电器组装厂，中方总投资 4268 万美元，初步形成了全球网络。

三、投资方式以我国企业现有设备及成熟技术和原材料、零部件等实物投资为主，实物投资占中方投资额的 70%以上。

四、项目多集中在政局稳定、投资环境较好，且与我国关系友好、双方有相当经贸合作基础的国家和地区，尤其是亚洲、非洲等发展中国家和地区。亚洲有 64 个项目，占总数的 42.4%；非洲 47 个，占总数 31.1%。

境外加工贸易的健康发展，为发展我国与项目所在国的经贸合作、促进我国产业结构调整、加快我国企业国际化经营步伐等方面发挥了重要作用。主要表现在：

一、有利于我国企业利用国外资源和国外市场，拓宽了企业生存与发展的空间。

上述 151 个项目全部投产后，不仅可以盘活我国企业的存量资产、提高现有设备的使用效率，带动设备和技术出口，而且可使企业有效地利用所在国的土地、劳动力、资金、市场等资源，扩大我国企业生产与经营的空间，从而获得新的发展机遇和相应的效益。

二、加强了与发展中国家的关系，在促进发展中国家经济发展的同时，为我国经济发展创造良好的国际环境。

我国境外加工贸易项目目前主要分布在发展中国家。境外加工贸易的开展为我国与广大发展中国家经济贸易合作注入了新的内容，拓宽了合作的领域，不仅能为当地解决劳动就业、增加税收、满足了当地市场需求、扩大所在国的出口，同时也扩大了我国企业在项目所在国的影响。如：山东笙歌公司在博茨瓦纳设立的服装加工企业为所在国带来了 500 个就业机会，成为中博两国企业合作的典范。我在南非投资设立的 23 个项目涉及彩电、冰箱、洗衣机、音响、服装、灯泡、电焊条、铝制品、搪瓷制品、食品等众多产品的加工生产，已成为中南两国经济贸易合作的重要内容。海尔、康佳集团在印度投资开办冰箱、彩电生产厂，使我国与印度的双边经贸合作有了突破性的进展。

三、促进国内产业结构调整。

通过开展境外加工贸易，为我国企业运用现有技术、设备扩大生产、加快积累、实现结构调整创造了有利的条件，可使企业在更广阔的空间里进行资源的优化配置，加快企业技术更新和产品结构升级，不断增强我国经济发展的动力和后劲。

四、使国内企业加快跨国经营的步伐和内部机制的转换，有利于中国的跨国公司早日形成。

国内优势企业以国内市场为基础，通过境外投资办厂，逐步建立海外生产体系、研发中心、销售网络和融资渠道，进行专业化、集约化和规模化的跨国经营，在全球化浪潮中占据有利位置，进而培育出中国的跨国公司，初步探索了路子，有利于增强国家的经济实力和综合国力。海尔、科龙、春兰等企业通过开展境外加工贸易加快了跨国经营的步伐，并在更大范围的跨国经营中感觉到调整企业内部机制的重要，从而加紧构造科学、合理的符合现代企业制度要求的内部机制，初步显露出未来中国跨国公司的雏形。

随着经济全球化进程日益加快、国际市场竞争日趋激烈，境外加工贸易作为境外投资的一种重要形式，在我国的对外经贸合作中将发挥越来越重要的作用。我国政府和企业将以发展境外加工贸易为起点，为探索中国企业“走出去”的道路不断努力。

抓管理 促发展

对外贸易经济合作部管理司司长　刘国胜

1999年是我国对外贸易克服亚洲金融危机的严重影响，取得新的重大进展的一年。在这一年里，我们努力搞好对外贸易管理，积极扩大出口，取得了一定的成效。

一、完善外贸管理制度

（一）完善出口商品管理体制

进一步减少出口配额与许可证管理的商品范围，完善出口许可证管理制度。制订下发了《2000年出口许可证管理商品目录》，取消了部分商品的出口配额许可证管理，如废棉、羊绒、无毛绒、稀土永磁体、新闻纸、大闸蟹、抽纱、单缸柴油机、黑白电视机等；修订了《出口许可证管理规定》。

完善配额管理办法。制订了《供港鲜活冷冻商品管理暂行办法》，改革供港鲜活冷冻商品的管理、经营和代理体制；发布了《白银出口管理暂行办法》，取消白银出口禁令，对白银出口实行配额许可证管理，保证白银的有序出口。

完善出口商品经营体制。取消了坯绸出口统一联合经营、抽纱出口核定公司经营；制订了《蚕丝类出口经营管理暂行办法》，重新核定蚕丝类出口企业经营资格；下发了《关于进一步改革茶叶出口经营体制的通知》，为企业扩大出口创造较为宽松的政策环境。

完善出口商品配额招标办法。对招标政策及时作了调整：将矾土、红小豆、大蒜、甘草和蜂蜜（非美国市场）等主动配额招标商品调整为有偿使用；适当增加协议招标比例，先协议后公开。这些措施在一定程度上抑制了投标价格的非理性攀升。

（二）完善纺织品配额分配制度

研究制定了《欧洲工业家配额分配管理办法》，下发了《鼓励企业用好纺织品被动配额若干事项的通知》，建立奖优罚劣的动态调整机制，鼓励企业用好用足配额；提高出口高档次、高附加值纺织品的积极性；规范纺织品被动配额分配，减少微观审批事务。

（三）完善加工贸易管理

会同有关部门联合下发了《关于进一步完善加工贸易银行保证金台账制度的意见》（国办发35号文件），对加工贸易企业和商品实行分类管理，对少数敏感商品和违规企业实行加工贸易银行保证金台账“实转”；围绕35号文件，相继出台了《加工贸易审批管理暂行办法》、《加工贸易保税料件内销审批管理办法》、《关于加工贸易企业以多种形式缴纳税款保证金实施办法》等配套办法，推动加工贸易按照“优化存量，控制总量，规范经营，提高水平”的方向健康持续发展。

（四）探索进口体制改革，做好进口管理工作

加强进口经营管理，做好核定公司经营商品的管理工作；与有关部委共同努力，理顺进口管理渠道；根据我国加入世界贸易组织的进程，研究改革

现行货物进口管理体制。

（五）加快外贸管理现代化步伐

制订《进出口商品配额执行情况核查反馈办法》，并在电子商务网上建立了"进出口商品配额执行情况反馈系统"；开发"纺织品被动配额管理系统"、"中标企业配额使用情况查询系统"、"各口岸中标配额签证查询系统"、"自主申领类别配额使用情况查询系统"等计算机程序，提高管理水平；开发"加工贸易计算机审批管理系统"，规范加工贸易审批管理，实现审批自动化和规范化；推动与海关的联网建设。

二、千方百计抓出口

（一）抓大商品出口

密切跟踪粮食、棉花、煤炭、原油、成品油等关系国计民生的大宗商品的出口动态，及时分析研究，提出对策，对扩大出口起到了促进作用。

针对钨、锑、锡、锌等资源性商品生产和出口中存在的问题，加大出口调控力度，对我国有色金属产品出口产生了积极影响。

（二）抓纺织品出口

认真贯彻"大经贸"战略，继续支持国家纺织行业深化改革、扭亏解困和结构调整。

密切跟踪纺织品被动配额的使用情况，采取措施提高配额使用率。1999 年我对美国纺织品配额使用率为 87.4%，比 1998 年增长 6.3 个百分点；对欧盟纺织品配额使用率为 84.5%，比 1998 年增长 6.8 个百分点。

（三）与产业部门协作，共同促进非配额商品出口

在搞好配额许可证商品管理的同时，注重非配额商品的出口与发展。与农业部、国家纺织工业局、国家轻工业局、国家中医药管理局、国家建材局等部门，分别商讨了促进农副产品（蔬菜、水果、花卉等）、纺织品、轻工产品（玩具、陶瓷、鞋等）、中医药产品、建材和非金属矿产品等商品出口的措施。

三、努力营造有利于出口的外部环境

为了排除出口障碍，针对我某些出口商品受到的不公正待遇，与有关国家进行了积极交涉与磋商。

四、充分发挥进出口商会作用

加强对进出口商会工作的指导，加快商会分会建设，提高行业代表性，以服务为中心，推动行业自律，促进商会工作的全面发展。

1999 年中国吸收外商投资回顾与 2000 年展望

对外贸易经济合作部外资司副司长　胡景岩

一、1999 年中国吸收外商投资回顾

1999 年全国吸收外商直接投资取得较好成绩，实际吸收外商投资虽然有所下降，但超过年初的预期值，继续保持较大规模，居全球各国/地区吸收外商直接投资第三位，仅次于美国、英国。1999 年全国新批外商投资企业 16918 家，同比下降 14.55%；合同外贸金额 412.23 亿美元，同比下降 20.88%，实际使用外资金额 403.19 亿美元，同比下降 11.31%。与 1998 年相比，新批合同外资金额净减少 108.79 亿美元，实际使用外资金额净减少 51.44 亿美元。全年月均新批合同外资金额 34.35 亿美元，与去年相比月均净减少 9.06 亿美元。1999 年全国新批合同外资额仅高出实际使用外资额 9.04 亿美元（见表 1）。

1997—1999 年外商直接投资情况

表 1　　　　金额单位：亿美元

	1997 年	1998 年	同比增幅%	1999 年	同比增幅%
项目数	21001	19799	-5.72	16918	-14.55
合同外资金额	510.03	521.02	2.15	412.23	-20.88
实际使用外资金额	452.57	454.63	0.46	403.19	-11.31

数据来源：外经贸部外资统计。

截至 1999 年底，全国累计批准设立外商投资企业 341538 家，合同外资金额 6137.17 亿美元，实际使用外资 3076.31 亿美元。主要特点：

（一）亚洲十国/地区对华投资继续下降，美国、欧盟对华投资合同外资额呈下降趋势，实际投入资金有所增长

亚洲十国/地区（香港、澳门、台湾省、日本、菲律宾、泰国、马来西亚、新加坡、印尼、韩国）1999 年对华投资合同外资金额 242.57 亿美元，同比下降 16.72%；实际投入外资金额 267.93 亿美元，同比下降 14.25%。

欧盟十五国对华投资合同外资金额 40.96 亿美元，同比下降 31.04%，实际投资金额 44.79 亿美元，同比增长 12.58%。

北美地区对华投资合同外资金额 67.15 亿美元，同比下降 9.63%；实际投资额 45.30 亿美元，同比增长 7.48%（见表 2)。

1999 年部分国家/地区对华直接投资情况

表 2　　　　金额单位：万美元

国别/地区	项目数	增幅%	比重%	合同外资	增幅%	比重%	实际使用	增幅%	比重%
总计	16918	14.55	-100.00	4122302	-20.88	100.00	4031871	-11.31	100.00
亚洲十国/地区合计	12277	15.45	-72.57	2425684	-16.72	58.84	2679317	-14.25	66.45
欧盟合计	894	10.78	-5.28	409566	-31.04	9.94	447906	12.58	11.11
北美合计	2395	-9.76	14.16	671526	-9.63	16.29	453028	7.48	11.24
部分自由港合计	601	17.33	-3.55	423453	-42.24	10.27	323820	-27.75	8.03

数据来源：外经贸部外资统计。

（二）外商投资结构进一步优化

外商投资产业结构有所改善。第一产业、第二产业在总量中的比重有所增加。1999 年，外商投资工业项目合同外资金额所占比重为 66.2%，比上年同期上升 1.6 个百分点；外商投资房地产项目合同外资金额所占比重 10.1%，比上年下降 2.7 个百分点。中小项目比上年增多，新批外商投资企业的平均单项合同外资金额 243.7 万美元，比上年下降 7.4%。

1999 年全国新批外商直接投资合同外资金额 412.23 亿美元，其中第一产业 14.72 亿美元，比上年增长 22.2%；第二产业 272.89 亿美元，比上年下降 18.9%；第三产业 124.62 亿美元，比上年下降 27.8%。第一、第二及第三产业所占比重分别为 3.57%、66.20% 及 30.23%，与上年相比，第一、第二产业比重分别增长了 1.26 和 1.62 个百分点，第三产业比重则下降了 2.88 个百分点。实际使用外资的产业结构与合同外资产业结构呈现相同的变化趋势，1999 年实际使用外资金额 403.19 亿美元，其中第一、第二、第三产业比重分别为 1.76%、

66.63%和31.61%（见表3）。

1999年外商直接投资产业结构

表3　　金额单位：亿美元

行业名称	项目数	比重%	同比增减%	合同外资金额	比重%	同比增减%	实际使用外资金额	比重%	同比增减%
总计	16918	100.00	-14.55	412.23	100.00	-20.88	403.19	100.00	-11.31
第一产业	762	4.50	-13.01	14.72	3.57	22.21	7.10	1.76	13.85
第二产业	12288	72.63	-10.87	272.89	66.20	-18.90	268.63	66.63	-8.20
第三产业	3868	22.86	-24.69	124.62	30.23	-27.76	127.45	31.61	-18.17

（三）外商投资方式仍以中外合资、中外合作为主

中外合资和中外合作经营企业仍是我国吸收外商直接投资的主要方式。在1999年新批外商投资企业中，中外合资、合作企业8706家，合同外资金额203.18亿美元，实际使用外资金额240.61亿美元，分别占总量的51.45%、49.29%和59.68%。值得注意的是外商独资企业的合同外资金额207.06亿美元，占总量的50.22%，首次超过中外合资、合作企业合同外资金额的总和（见表4）。

1997—1999年外商直接投资分方式情况

表4　　金额单位：亿美元

方式	项目数			合同外资金额			实际使用外资金额		
	1997年	1998年	1999年	1997年	1998年	1999年	1997年	1998年	1999年
总计	21001	19799	16918	510.03	521.02	412.23	452.57	454.63	403.19
合资经营企业	9001	8107	7050	207.26	172.86	135.15	194.95	183.88	158.27
合作经营企业	2373	2003	1656	120.66	116.56	68.03	89.30	97.19	82.34
外资企业	9602	9673	8201	176.58	217.53	207.06	161.88	164.70	155.45
外商投资股份制	6	9	3	1.51	13.30	1.03	2.88	7.07	2.92
合作开发	1	7	5	4.02	0.78	0.59	3.56	1.79	3.84

数据来源：外经贸部外资统计。

（四）中西部地区合同外资所占比重略有增长

1999年中国吸收外商直接投资区域分布结构趋向改善，中部地区吸收外资下降幅度小于东部地区，在全国吸收外资总量中所占比重有所上升，西部地区所占比重与上年基本持平，东部地区在全国吸收外资总量中所占比重略有下降。

1999年，中西部地区合同外资金额61.58亿美元，所占比重为14.94%，比上年13.06%略有增长；实际使用外资金额49.87亿美元，所占比重为12.11%，比上年12.74%有所下降（见表5）。

1999年东部、中部、西部地区利用外商直接投资情况

表5　　　　金额单位：亿美元

地方名称	项目数	比重%	合同外资	比重%	实际使用	比重%
总计	16918	100.00	412.23	100.00	403.19	100.00
东部	13953	82.47	350.65	85.06	354.34	87.88
中部	2100	12.41	41.18	9.99	37.47	9.29
西部	865	5.11	20.40	4.95	11.38	2.82

东部地区：北京、天津、河北、辽宁、上海、江苏、浙江、福建、山东、广东、海南、广西。

中部地区：山西、内蒙古、吉林、黑龙江、安徽、江西、河南、湖北、湖南。

西部地区：四川、重庆、贵州、云南、陕西、甘肃、青海、宁夏、新疆、西藏。

数据来源：外经贸部外资统计。

（五）外商投资企业继续取得良好的经济效益

目前，来华投资的国家和地区达180多个，外商投资企业已开业近15万家，就业人数超过1800多万人。世界前500家大型跨国公司中已有近400家来华投资。作为中国企业的组成部分，外商投资企业在促进中国经济发展中发挥着重要作用。已投产外商投资企业大部分经营良好。1999年，外商投资企业进出口额达1745.11亿美元，同比增长10.67%；外商投资企业工业增加值4201亿元，同比增长12.9%；工业产值增加值占全国工业产值增量的20.69%；外商投资企业的涉外税收同比增长33.78%，其增加值占全国税收增加值的比重达23.66%。外商投资对国民经济发展的促进作用明显加强。

二、2000年中国吸收外商投资展望

2000年中国吸收外商投资机遇与挑战并存。加入WTO对中国的改革开放、吸收外商投资工作将产生重大影响。我们将以此为契机，紧密围绕鼓励外商投资的各项政策，充分发挥政策效应，努力寻找新的增长点，尽可能多地吸收外商投资。

目前，中国政治稳定，社会安定，国民经济持续增长，人民币币值稳定，外汇储备充实，投资的综合成本较低，中国仍对国际资本具有强大的吸引力，普遍被国际投资者看好。

中国继续实施积极的财政政策和货币政策，扩大国内需求，为外商提供了广阔的投资空间。中国政府决定，2000年继续增发国债，适度增加货币供应。在投资方向上，继续以基础设施建设和企业技术改造为重点，更加注意使其与经济结构调整紧密配合，带动社会投资，启动城乡消费，预计2000年中国经济将增长7%以上。从今后中长期发展看，中国经济能够保持较高的增长速度，水利、能源、交通、通信、原材料、环保、高技术、重大装备等基础设施和产业将是发展重点。预计未来十年，中国仅电力装机将新增2亿千瓦，程控电话2亿线，其中基础设施的投资需万亿美元以上。这都需要更多更好地引进国外资金、先进技术和管理经验。同时，也是中国开放市场，积极参与经济全球化的重要体现。

2000年国内外经济形势的发展趋好和中国加入WTO进程的加快使中国吸收外资出现一个新的局面成为可能，但吸收外资工作依然任重而道远。

今年我们力争在拓展外商投资新领域、完善法律体系、改善政策环境、理顺管理机制、加强依法行政、转变政府职能等方面有所突破，努力将吸收外商投资提高到一个新的水平。

（一）进一步扩大服务贸易领域的对外开放

我们将在商业、外贸、运输、医疗、教育、金融、保险、电信及各类中介机构等服务贸易领域进一步放宽对外商投资的限制，使外商投资在更广阔的层面对促进中国经济发展发挥作用。

（二）努力完善符合国际惯例的外商投资法律体系

中国“入世”后，在享受作为发展中国家权利的同时，也将认真承担相应义务，恪守世贸组织规则，履行中国的对外承诺。中国的对外开放将会有新的发展，中国的整体投资环境将进一步得到改善。

改革开放20年来，中国政府陆续颁布了500多部涉及外商投资的法律法规。遵照WTO的规则，我们正在进行外商投资企业三大法律的修改工作，

对现有的外商投资法规与部门规章有步骤、有计划地进行修订、增补和废止，努力完善符合国际惯例的外商投资法律体系。例如，根据 TRIMS 的原则，我们将对外商投资三法、《外商投资产业指导目录》以及汽车、机电产品等行业的有关法规、规定进行删除和修改。

（三）引导外商向中西部地区投资

中国正在实施的西部大开发战略，为进一步改善外商投资的区域结构奠定了良好的基础，给外商提供了新的投资机会。为外商参与我国中西部地区的合作开发提供了有利条件。中国将公布中西部地区优势产业和项目目录，并帮助中西部地区培训人才，加强基础设施建设，改善投资环境。中国中西部地区正在致力于发展有市场前景的特色经济和优势产业，外商只要能充分利用中国中西部地区现有的工业基础和技术力量，把自身优势和中国中西部地区丰富的自然资源和劳动力资源优势相结合，就一定会变资源优势为经济优势、市场优势，取得丰硕收获。

（四）推动国有企业吸收外商投资和拓展新的投资方式

抓住发达国家新一轮产业结构调整和国际兼并浪潮的时机，推动国有企业吸收外商投资和拓展新的投资方式。

中国鼓励外商以多种形式投资参与国有企业的改组改造。中国正在进行国有经济的战略性调整和国有企业战略性的改组改造。为了实现到本世纪末初步建立现代企业制度的目标，国有企业正在积极探索和发展能够极大促进生产力发展的新形式，吸收外商投资进行改组改造是其中的重要措施之一。目前，由外经贸部牵头制定的有关合并与分立的政策措施已经出台；向外商转让国有资产产权管理办法正在研究之中。

我们将努力拓展新的投资方式，积极协调有关部门制定外商收购、兼并国有企业，进行资产重组的可操作性政策规定及扶持措施。推动 BOT 投资方式、外国公司设立分公司、外商投资企业发行股票、设立中外合资产业基金、扩大投资性公司经营范围、特许权转让等各项规定的制定与完善。

（五）鼓励外商投资企业引进、开发和创新技术

中国的高新技术产业具有广阔的市场前景。中国高度重视强化企业技术创新能力，鼓励跨国公司来华设立研究开发中心，投资于高新技术产业、技术研究开发项目，欢迎外商参与高技术产业化以及传统产业的技术改造，我们也正在探讨风险投资等新的投资方式。

（六）积极吸引跨国公司来华投资

跨国公司一直是中国吸收外商投资的重点。中国鼓励跨国公司来华投资设立研究开发中心；促进已来华投资的跨国公司扩大产品领域，提高产品档次，加深与国内企业的多层次合作，鼓励跨国公司来华投资发展符合我国产业政策的其核心产品及配套产品；逐步放宽对投资性公司在销售方面的限制；吸引跨国公司在华设立地区总部。

（七）不断改善投资环境

中国的整体投资环境将继续得到改善。为改善外商投资企业的经营环境，去年以来，中国政府制定出台了一系列政策措施，加大对外商投资企业的金融支持，支持外商投资企业技术开发和创新，鼓励外商向中西部地区投资，简化外商投资项目及企业设立的审批手续，加快审批进度，坚决制止对外商投资企业的乱收费、乱检查和各种摊派等，进一步改善对外商投资企业的管理和服务。外经贸部还正在会同中央政府其他部门，抓紧清理对外商投资企业的政策规定，尽快调整不利于吸收外资的有关政策规定，健全外商投资的法律法规体系。

2000 年中国吸收外商投资将呈现一个崭新的局面，将会有更多的外商进入中国市场。外商投资企业在国民经济中将起到更大的作用。

实施科技兴贸战略　加快我国由贸易大国向贸易强国的转变

对外贸易经济合作部科技司司长　许复兴

为落实科教兴国战略，顺应经济科技全球化和知识经济蓬勃兴起的潮流，加快我国由贸易大国向贸易强国的转变，1999年初，外经贸部党组提出了科技兴贸战略，并将其作为外经贸工作的一项重要发展战略予以高度重视。在国务院领导的关心支持下，外经贸部同科技部、信息产业部、国家经贸委等部门共同努力，全国各地认真贯彻科技兴贸战略，落实国家出台的一系列扶持鼓励措施，科技兴贸初见成效，为实现出口商品结构调整和全年外贸出口增长作出贡献。

一、科技兴贸战略的内容

通过对国内外广泛调研，外经贸部会同有关部门确定了科技兴贸的主要内容，即：促进我国高新技术产品出口和用高新技术改造传统出口产业，提高出口产品的技术含量和附加值。

根据我国高新技术产品出口现状以及国际市场的变化趋势，确定了科技兴贸的奋斗目标：一方面在我国优势领域培育一批国际竞争力强、附加值高、出口规模较大的高新技术出口产品和企业，使我国高新技术产品出口每年增长20%以上，力争2000年高新技术产品出口300亿美元，占外贸出口的比重由1998年的11%提高到15%；到2010年达到1200亿美元，在全国出口总额中达到30%，初步完成我国出口商品结构由以低附加值、低技术含量产品为主向以高新技术产品为主的转变。另一方面选择出口额最大的机电产品和纺织品作为高新技术改造传统产业重点，力争通过3—5年的努力，使具有较高技术含量和附加值的出口产品的比重提高到50%左右，加工贸易使用国内原材料的比重由目前的20%提高到50%。

根据上述目标，按照高新技术发展“有所为、有所不为”的指导思想，以“有限目标、突出重点、面向市场、发挥优势”为原则，逐步完善科技兴贸战略的基本思路。外经贸部与科技部、信息产业部等部门建立了联合工作机制，制定了《科技兴贸行动计划》。《行动计划》包括宗旨与目标、行动主体、支撑条件和措施、组织与管理等内容。《行动计划》确定对信息、生物医药、新材料、消费类电子及家用电器等五个领域的166家高新技术产品出口企业和92种高新技术出口产品给予重点支持，并积极推动北京、天津、上海、重庆、武汉、沈阳、深圳、南京、成都、西安、广州、厦门、大连、青岛、苏州等15个重点城市和53个国家级高新技术产业开发区发展高新技术产品出口。形成了纵横发展、点面结合的立体发展格局。外经贸部还和国家经贸委等有关部门密切合作，重点抓好出口机电产品和纺织品提高技术含量的工作。在国家技改投资规划中，以出口创汇的重点企业和重点项目为主，加大支持力度。国家经贸委在用于技术改造的财政债券中，先后安排了288个项目用于支持出口企业的技术改造。外经贸部还与海关、税务、外管、银行等部门加强为企业的服务，共同推动科技兴贸工作的开展。

二、1999年实施科技兴贸战略的工作进展

1999年，外经贸部会同有关部门在大量调查研究的基础上，提出了一系列扶持、鼓励高新技术产品出口的政策措施，先后下发了《外经贸部、科技部关于推动高新技术产品出口的指导性意见》、《科技部、外经贸部关于国家高新技术产业开发区高新技术产品出口基地认定暂行办法》、《外经贸部关于对国有、集体所有制的科研院所和高新技术企业实行自营进出口权登记制的通知》等许多文件。这些文件对高新技术产品出口的鼓励政策包括：对高新技术产品出口实行零税率；进出口银行给予优惠贷款；保险公司给予配套保险服务；国家支持高新技术产品出口企业开拓市场；对科研院所经营权实行登记备案制；将高新技术出口产品列入国家产业政策鼓励支持的重点等。

外经贸部和科技部会同海关总署组织百余名技术和贸易专家，参考OECD和北美的高技术产品分类编制了与国际通行海关HS代码相对应的《中国高新技术产品出口目录》。《目录》共确定电子信息、软件、航空航天、光机电一体化、生物医药和医疗器械、新材料、新能源和节能产品以及环境保护等八个高新技术领域，产品条目约1900项。

为推动科技兴贸工作的全面展开，外经贸部会同有关部门先后召开了15个重点城市座谈会、全国技术引进工作研讨会、53个国家级高新技术产业开发区高新技术产品出口工作会议、电子产品出口百强企业工作会议等一系列会议，逐项落实各项工作。10月召开“全国促进高新技术产品出口工作会议”，石广生部长、科技部朱丽兰部长在会上分别作了报告。尤其是7月22日，吴仪国务委员在听取外经贸部、科技部、信息产业部关于科技兴贸的工作汇报时，对这项工作给予充分的肯定，对工作安排作了具体指示，极大地推动了科技兴贸。

为充分发挥市场对资源配置的基础性作用，利用高新技术成果造就市场，利用市场的力量推动高新技术成果的产业化、商品化，1999年外经贸部会同有关部门组织了一年一度的深圳中国国际高新技术成果交易会、北京高新技术产业国际周，形成了我国一北一南、一春一秋、各具特色的国际高科技盛会。10月5日至10日在深圳举办的首届高交会，朱镕基总理和吴仪国务委员参加了开幕式并参观了展览会。高交会成交项目1459项，成交金额为64.94亿美元，这是至今在我国举办的高新技术交易会中成交量最大的。5月举行的国际周，正式签约的高新技术产业合作项目27个、协议总金额达6.8亿美元，比上届增长10%。

此外还组织了企业开拓国际市场活动；编辑出版了国家鼓励高新技术产品出口的政策汇编；并成功举办第一期科技兴贸培训班等。

三、1999年科技兴贸工作取得突出成绩

据海关统计，1999年我国高新技术产品出口247亿美元，比上年增长46亿美元，增幅为23%，高于全国出口增幅约17个百分点。高新技术产品出口占外贸出口的比重达到13%，比上年提高了两个百分点。其中，《科技兴贸行动计划》确定的15个重点城市高新技术产品出口154亿美元，占全国高新技术产品出口总额的62%。与国家经贸委密切合作，利用高新技术改造传统产业可新增出口50亿美元。

我国高新技术产品进出口的变化

表1

指标名称	1991年	1992年	1993年	1994年	1995年	1996年	1997年	1998年	1999年
出口额（亿美元）	28.8	40.0	46.76	63.42	100.91	76.81	96.88	202.5	247.04
年增长速度（%）	/	38.9	17.3	35.6	59.1	-23.9	26.1	109	23
占出口总额%	4.0	4.7	5.1	5.2	6.8	5.08	5.3	11.0	13.0
占工业制成品出口%	5.2	5.9	6.2	6.3	7.9	5.95	6.1	12.4	14.1
进口额（亿美元）	94.4	107.1	159.1	206.0	218.3	188.7	197.8	292.0	375.98
进出口差额（亿美元）	-65.6	-67.1	-112.3	-142.6	-117.4	-111.9	-100.9	-89.5	-128.94
贸易竞争指数	-0.53	-0.46	-0.55	-0.53	-0.37	-0.42	-0.34	-0.18	-0.21

注：1998年高新技术产品进出口统计口径有一定调整。

我国高新技术产品占外贸出口的比重已从1991年的4%提高到1999年的13%，平均每年增加1.12个百分点。1999年，计算机与通信技术类、电子技术类高新技术产品出口分别为172.5亿美元和42亿美元，分别占全部高新技术产品出口额的70%和17%。三资企业在我国高新技术产品出口中仍占据主导地位。1999年三资企业高新技术产品出口额从上年同期的149亿美元增加到187亿美元，占出口总额的比重从74%上升到76%。国有企业高新技术产品出口56亿美元，比上年同期增加6亿美元。我国高新技术产品出口的主要市场为美国、香港特别行政区、日本等发达国家和地区。其中对美国出口60亿美元、香港地区49亿美元、日本24亿美元。此外，对菲律宾、印度、墨西哥、印尼、匈牙利等新兴工业化国家的出口均超过1亿美元，呈上升趋势。高新技术产品贸易竞争指数1991年为-0.53，1993年为-0.55，以后逐年改善，1998年为-0.18，1999年稳定在-0.21，已接近成为有比较优势的出口商品。

实施科技兴贸战略在扩大高新技术产品出口的同时，也使我国对外技术贸易的发展进入到一个新的历史时期。据外经贸部业务统计，1999年全国签订的技术出口合同总金额75.46亿美元，同比增长12.85%。全国对外签订技术引进合同6678项，同比增长6.78%，合同总金额171.62亿美元，同比增长4.8%。

我国技术出口的变化

表2　　金额单位：亿美元

	1997年	1998年	1999年	同比增长%
技术出口总计	55.21	66.87	75.46	12.85
其中：高新技术产品（自主产权）	12.23	23.48	28.9	23.1
技术及成套设备	20.73	22.61	23.84	5.44
大型设备	20.45	18.83	20.58	9.3
技术服务和技术咨询	1.80	1.95	2.14	9.75

注：1998年高新技术产品进出口统计口径有一定调整。

技术出口市场集中在传统市场，主要是东南亚、西亚、南亚等地区的发展中国家。

我国技术引进的变化

表3

年　份	1997年	1998年	1999年	同比增长%
合同数	5984	6254	6678	6.78
总金额（亿美元）	159.23	163.75	171.62	4.81

技术引进的国别日趋多样化，技术引进和设备进口共涉及45个国家和地区。技术引进合同金额超过1亿美元的国家共有18个。技术引进主要集中于美国、日本、欧盟、俄罗斯等国家，居前10位的国家合同金额总计为147.67亿美元，占总金额的86.04%。技术引进和设备进口主要涉及的行业领域为机械、电子、能源、交通、通讯、化工等。技术引进方式日趋合理，技术许可、技术服务、技术咨询等已成为主要的引进方式。合同金额中技术费所占的比例不断增加，1999年技术引进和设备进口中技术费为53.88亿美元，占合同总金额的31.39%。

四、迎接“入世”挑战，做好科技兴贸工作

随着我国加入世界贸易组织步伐的加快，我国产业界面临越来越严峻的挑战。要在竞争中立于不败之地，就要加强我国产品在国内外市场的竞争力，重要途径之一就是实施科技兴贸。要加快技术进步，提高自主创新能力，同时，作为发展中国家，我们要抓住入世的机遇，加强技术的引进、消化、吸收和再创新，充分利用全人类共同创造的成果，尽快缩小同发达国家的差距。2000年我们要进一步做好科技兴贸工作。一方面要落实好《科技兴贸行动计划》的各项任务，加快设立高新技术产业开发区出口示范基地的试点，继续大力开拓国际市场，为企业提供全方位服务，促进高新技术产品出口；另一方面，加强利用高新技术改造传统产业，扩大出口的工作，尽快实现我国由贸易大国向贸易强国的转变。

1999年我国国外经济合作增长迅速成效显著

对外贸易经济合作部国外经济合作司副司长　崔明谟

一、1999年我国国外经济合作业务发展的基本情况

1999年，我国国外经济合作业务继续保持迅速增长势头。新签合同额、完成营业额和年末在外人数均创历史最好成绩：新签合同额130亿美元，比上年同期（下同）增长10.4%（其中，对外承包工程合同额首次突破100亿美元，达101.99亿美元；对外劳务合作26.32亿美元；对外设计咨询1.7亿美元）；完成营业额112.3亿美元，增长10.9%（其中，对外承包工程85.22亿美元；对外劳务合作26.23亿美元；对外设计咨询0.9亿美元）；年末在外人数38.2万人，增加3万人。对外承包工程带动国产设备材料出口6.53亿元。

1999年国外经济合作业务情况表

业务种类	合同额（万美元）	同比增长（%）	营业额（万美元）	同比增长（%）
承包工程	1019897	10.3	852232	9.7
劳务合作	263224	10.2	262268	15.2
设计咨询	17057	21.4	8958	0.7
总　计	1300198	10.4	1123458	10.9

二、1999年我国国外经济合作业务的主要特点

（一）合同额、营业额增长迅速，发展势头良好

1999年对外承包工程和劳务合作新签合同额、完成营业额增长率均超过10%，是近年来业务发展情况较好的一年。由于受东南亚金融危机的滞后影响，上半年业务曾出现波动。随着世界经济形势明显好转，项目机会增多，同时我国经营主体迅速增加，特别是越来越多有实力的大企业走向国际工程承包市场，我国企业在亚、欧、美市场开拓较为顺利，5月份合同额开始增长，到年底实现较大增幅。1999年营业额连续12个月稳定增长。

（二）市场开拓取得良好成效

由于亚洲部分国家（地区）经济逐渐走出低谷，投资力度加大，工程发包项目较多，我国企业在亚洲市场取得良好业绩，1999年新签合同额达75.36亿美元，占总额的58%，增长9.2%。其中香港合同额达29.3亿美元，占总额的22.5%，增长45.1%，此外，新加坡、韩国、台湾、伊拉克等国家和地区增长也较快，增幅分别达27.2%、70.9%、27.3%和20.3倍。在亚洲市场新签合同额超过1亿美元的项目有3个，即香港蓝湾半岛上期项目住宅大楼（2.76亿美元）、泰国科隆泰单压混凝土坝项目（1.84亿美元）和香港将军澳地铁C602标段（1.28亿美元）。

欧洲、美洲市场的开拓取得实质性进展，合同额分别达8.25亿美元和7.98亿美元，增长68.4%和68.2%。我国企业首次在美国承揽到合同额约1.5亿美元的大型总承包项目，并在秘鲁首次通过公开竞标的方式获得合同额近千万美元的国际工程承包项目。此外，我国企业及时抓住巴尔干重建的商机，在南斯拉夫承揽了一个合同额达7500万美元的通讯项目。

因受非洲局部政治动荡的影响，1999年我国企业在非洲市场合同额为18.64亿美元，减少7.7%；但在部分国别市场获得了较大增长，如在尼日利亚和埃塞俄比亚等国均有5000万美元以上的大项目夺标，尼日利亚、埃塞俄比亚、阿尔及利亚合同额分别达2.07亿美元、1.68亿美元、1.35亿等，增长56.7%、91.6%和62.3%。

1999年洲别及主要国别市场情况表

洲别/国别	合同额（万美元）	合同额增幅（%）	营业额（万美元）	营业额增幅（%）	外派劳务人次	年末在外人数
亚洲	753601	9.2	624719	3	166064	280062
香港	292683	45.1	219212	2.3	13648	20915
新加坡	117560	27.2	101864	11.4	31729	73249
日本	36115	8.9	28768	23.3	19460	33028
非洲	186432	7.7	203629	21.3	22994	40113
尼日利亚	20670	56.7	10881	-55.1	507	1157
埃塞俄比亚	16763	91.6	3811	84.7	645	559
欧洲	82451	68.4	30616	-7	18789	22613
俄罗斯联邦	36002	68.4	9095	-25.8	13108	13694
美洲	79832	68.2	33088	20.5	16540	26500
美国	48523	58.7	32316	9.6	8977	17746
委内瑞拉	5811	306.4	963	14.4	106	111
秘鲁	3387	1771.3	873	859.3	59	220
大洋洲及太平洋岛屿	12357	-17.4	18221	-9.3	833	9150

（三）大型工程企业的作用逐步增强，发挥了骨干作用

1999年，合同额前50名企业合同总额为81.04亿美元，占总额的62.3%（其中前10名企业合同额为44.3亿美元，占总额的34.1%），合同额超过1亿美元的企业有21家，其中中国建筑总公司名列首位，总额达19.23亿美元，比上年增长20.4%。新签的大项目多是大型专业工程公司承揽的，这类企业的优势和骨干作用日益显著。30家中国企业进入1999年由美国《工程新闻纪录》评选的全球最大225家国际承包商行列，比上年增加4家，中国建筑总公司的名次由1994年首次参加该评选时的第42名提前到第24名；3家中国企业进入国际工程设计商200强，进一步显示了中国企业的实力。

（四）大项目明显增多，技术含量日益提高

1999年，新签合同额超过1000万美元的工程项目近200个，比上年增加60多个，累计合同额61.3亿美元，占全国对外承包工程合同总额的60%，其中5000万美元以上的工程项目27个，同比增加8个。这些项目大多为总承包和交钥匙工程，有较高的技术含量，如美国MMI冷轧钢厂项目（1.47亿美元）、伊拉克燃机项目（7500万美元）、南斯拉夫90万线GSM项目（7500万美元）等。大项目的增多进一步带动了国内相关设备材料、劳务和技术的出口。

（五）开展多种形式的国际经济合作初见成效

1999年中俄森林资源开发和利用取得实质性进展，签订合同额逾3亿美元（合同期限为10—20年），总采伐量825万立方米，6家中国公司在俄远东地区开始实施森林采伐项目，当年完成采伐量25万立方米，带动设备材料出口约5000万元人民币和带出相关劳务人员1600余人。中俄森林资源开发和利用合作开辟了我国国外经济合作形式多样化的一条新路。

三、2000年我国国外经济合作工作举措

2000年我国国外经济合作总的工作思路为：根据党的十五届四中全会及中央经济工作会议的精神，贯彻落实中央提出的“走出去”开放战略，落实对外承包工程和劳务合作改革工作，大力发展对外承包工程和劳务合作，逐步建立起以金融服务为主的社会服务体系，抓大市场、促大项目，更加有效地带动国产设备材料，特别是成套技术和设备的出口；改革对外劳务合作经营体制，完善劳务人员合法权益的保障机制。

（一）从地区、行业及政策等方面对对外承包工程进行实质性推动

继续实施市场多元化战略，巩固和深度开发香港、泰国、菲律宾、印尼等传统市场，重点开拓印度等南亚市场，沙特、土耳其等中东市场，大力推动我企业进入拉美市场。

结合我国产业结构情况，努力将我国在国际上具有较强竞争优势以及生产能力富余的行业（如电站、纺织、铁路、石油、森工等）推向国际市场。

进一步优化经营主体结构，加快赋予大型企业特别是大型专业工程企业对外承包工程经营权；根据“扶大、扶优、扶强”的原则，对有实力有条件的大型企业在政策上予以支持；采取各种经济手段支持对外承包工程的发展，研究设立“对外承包工程保函风险专项资金”，研究制订对外承包工程项目贷款贴息政策。

（二）进一步规范管理，完善监管措施

2000年要加快立法步伐，尽快出台《中华人民共和国对外承包工程管理条例》。为维护良好的经营秩序，研究制订对外承包工程企业分级管理办法，建立对外承包工程项目许可制度，加强我驻外经商机构对国别市场的一线监管，完善对外承包工程项下设备材料、物资出口的管理办法和对外承包工程的金融和外汇管理制度。同时加强行政监管，根据有关规定对违法违规企业加大处罚力度，达到“处罚一家，教育一片”的目的。

（三）全面推动对外劳务合作改革

结合国际通行做法和我国实际，以扩大劳务合作规模为目标、以保障外派劳务人员合法权益为中心，改革现行管理体制，通过试点，逐步推行对外劳务合作代理制，发挥我国劳动力资源优势，加强和规范管理，实现我国对外劳务合作业务健康、有序发展以及规模和效益的较大增长。

（四）深入研究多种形式的国际经济合作

国际经济合作是涵盖面广、内容十分丰富的业务，对外承包工程、劳务合作和设计咨询是其发展较为成熟、已初具规模的形式。此外，2000年要继续深入探讨森工合作、技术合作、管理合作等多种国际经济合作形式，尤其要在进一步推动中俄森林开发和利用合作的基础上总结和推广经验。

（五）认真研究加入世界贸易组织对我国国外经济合作的影响

随着我国加入世界贸易组织谈判的顺利推进，中国“入世”进程大大加快。“入世”将为我国国外经济合作创造更加优越的外部环境，对我国企业进入国际承包劳务市场产生积极的影响。为此，2000年要加强“入世”对国外经济合作影响的研究，及时调整对策和宏观发展战略，促进国外经济合作的更快发展。

1999年中国对外援助

对外贸易经济合作部对外援助司司长　李国庆

1999年，中国政府一如既往地向广大友好的发展中国家提供了力所能及的援助，积极推进优惠贷款援助方式和援外项目合资合作，推动中国有实力的优秀企业到发展中国家开展企业间的合资合作，

加强援外项目的管理，援外工作管理逐步规范化、科学化，各项援外工作稳步推进并取得新的进展。

一、继续推进优惠贷款援助方式和援外项目合资合作

1999年，中国同13个国家签订14笔优惠贷款协议。中国企业在21个国家实施了28个援外合资合作项目。我部向中国进出口银行推荐了27个优惠贷款项目；中国进出口银行对19个项目进行了可行性评估和经济效益分析，认可通过后签署了借贷协议。

自1995年下半年以来，中国已同47个国家签署了优惠贷款协议，我部向中国进出口银行累计推荐了109个优惠贷款项目，接受优惠贷款的国家从非洲逐步扩展到亚洲、拉美、南太平洋岛国和欧洲，优惠贷款方式已受到广大发展中国家的普遍欢迎。中国企业和受援国企业积极探讨落实当地有资源、有需要、有市场、有效益的各类项目，如合资开采石油、开发森林资源、海洋资源、土地资源等；共同投资兴建工业生产性和机电产品加工组装项目；投资基础设施项目，如更新铁路、建设水电站等；还有社会福利性项目，如开发住房等，既帮助受援国发展民族经济、又培养受援国管理和技术人才，促进共同发展。中国企业在发展中国家开展援外项目合资合作也取得了长足进展，自1992年以来，中国企业已在33个国家启动实施了67个援外合资合作项目，这类项目主要有制衣、制药、农业种植、建材加工、食品加工等。

1999年在积极推进优惠贷款援助方式和援外项目合资合作方面主要做了如下几项工作：

1. 继续做好对外宣传解释工作。我部举办了第三期中国援外方式改革国际研讨会，向来自中亚和蒙古国的经济官员全面介绍中国现行援外方式及其具体做法、中国的对外经贸政策等并与其座谈；在外经贸部和外交部共同举办的中——非经贸官员研修班上，向来华官员介绍中国优惠贷款援助方式及援外工作的操作程序。

2. 规范项目管理操作程序，简化项目审批手续。为进一步推动我国企业与受援国企业积极探讨落实项目，开展企业间的合资合作，我部会同有关部门协商一致，规范优惠贷款和援外项目合资合作的管理操作程序，明确各部门的职责分工，同时简化项目的审批手续，加快了这类项目的实施进度。

3. 加强调查研究，及时解决项目执行中问题。为了解优惠贷款项目执行情况，及时总结经验和教训，我部对部分在实施的优惠贷款项目进行了跟踪调查，了解项目进展情况、存在问题和困难，听取企业要求，并提出建议。

二、加强援外项目的质量管理，援外管理工作日趋规范和科学

1999年，中国同98个国家签订援款协议，在31个国家新承担43个成套项目，主要有蒙古、南非住宅，肯尼亚、喀麦隆、玻利维亚打井，突尼斯水坝，马达加斯加公路，还有向老挝提供水泵，向孟加拉提供牵引车等。在24个国家承担了30个技术合作项目。当年新开工项目30个，如尼日尔社会住宅、安哥拉经济住房、也门立交桥、斐济农村供电、柬埔寨参议院改造等，这些项目都不同程度地满足了受援国的迫切需要。竣工项目32个，如多哥体育场、科特迪瓦剧场、加蓬议会大厦、毛里求斯老年人活动中心、尼泊尔综合体育设施、古巴牌楼等。援外项目的工程质量有了显著提高。

中国还向54个国家提供了67批物资援助，主要包括向朝鲜提供大豆、粮食和柴油，向纳米比亚、多哥、吉布提、巴基斯坦、孟加拉、厄瓜多尔、安提瓜和巴布达、特立尼达和多巴哥、立陶宛提供电脑，向塞拉里昂、布隆迪、土库曼斯坦、阿富汗、南斯拉夫、土耳其提供药品，向中非、莫桑比克、津巴布韦提供吉普车等等。。我国对外物资援助均为受援国所急需，尤其一些救灾物资，为受援国“雪中送炭”，受到受援国政府和人民的普遍欢迎。

在多边援助项下，中国还向亚、非、拉美及东欧地区的62个国家提供了多边培训援助，举办各类技术培训班15个，培训学员327名。涉及现代农业管理、太阳能应用技术、杂交水稻种植技术、长期天气预报等领域。

为加强援外工程的质量管理，规范援外管理工作，我部主要做了以下几项工作：

1. 完善、修订和出台了一系列援外项目管理规章，对援外成套项目的考察、设计、施工和质量检验等做出了明确的规定，使援外工作管理更加规范和科学；

2. 援外工程管理全面引入和贯彻ISO9000国际质量管理和质量保证体系标准。全年，对加纳东当美医院等9个援外成套项目进行了贯标培训，要求这些项目参照ISO9000质量管理办法进行施工、质量监督和管理。保证了援外项目的工程质量；

3. 抓好援外设备、材料和一般物资出境前的检验，援外物资的质量得到有效控制；

4. 加强对援外项目主要负责人的培训。全年，我部对 20 个援外项目的技术组组长、总工程师、总会计师、施工质检员、设计代表和国内部门负责人等 100 多人进行了培训，目的是使承担援外项目的各部门负责人熟悉我国的援外方针和政策，按照援外项目管理规章的要求，分工、协作，共同搞好援外项目。

逆境中发展的两岸经贸关系

对外贸易经济合作部台港澳司司长　王晖

1999 年年初台湾省部分大企业发生了财务危机，7 月份李登辉抛出了“两国论”，9 月份台湾发生了百年罕见的大地震，给台湾经济及两岸经贸交流带来了不利影响。在两岸工商界共同努力下，两岸贸易继续创历史最高水平，合同台资金额仍增长 10%以上，但对台出口增幅较少，实际利用台资金额继续下降。1999 年在两岸关系将可能好于去年及两岸可能先后加入 WTO 的大环境下，预计 2000 年两岸经贸交流形势将好于去年。

一、两岸贸易继续创历史最高纪录，但我对台出口增幅较少

据海关统计，1999 年两岸贸易总额达 234.8 亿美元，在前年首次突破 200 亿美元之后再创新高。台湾仍是我第五大贸易伙伴，仅次于日本、美国、香港、韩国。其中我对台出口 39.5 亿美元，仅增长 2.1%，进口 195.3 亿美元，增长 17.43%，逆差额达 155.8 亿美元，台仍是我最大逆差来源地。台湾“国贸局”统计，1—11 月台对祖国大陆出口 193.41 亿美元，增长 15%，占台出口总额的 17.5%，比去年同期增加 0.9 个百分点，台自祖国大陆进口 40.87 亿美元，增长 8.4%，占台进口总额的 4.1%。从商品结构看（详见附表），我对台出口的主要产品为机电产品、服装及纺织品、煤炭、钢材及集装箱等，其中我机电产品对台出口增长最为显著，但钢铁及钢铁制品、鞋靴半成品等出口下降。我自台进口的主要产品有：塑料原料、纺织原料、机器设备及零部件和钢材等，其中机电产品、钢铁、塑料、人造纤维丝进口增长较快，但纺织品、鞋帽、伞、羽毛制品等自台进口下降。两岸贸易总体走势良好，逐月上升，1—2 月份增长 7.7%，上半年增长 11.6%，全年增长 14.5%。上半年受台湾部分大企业发生财务危机，投资、消费紧缩的不利影响，对台出口出现下降，但降幅逐月减缓，下半年随着我提高出口退税率等政策的推动，我对台出口从 8 月份起缓慢回升。自台进口大幅增长与我实行扩大内需政策、市场需求增大有关。

1999 年对台湾省出口主要商品表

（按最终目的地统计）

金额单位：亿美元

商品名称	单位	数量	金额
自动数据处理设备的零件	吨	23892	1.92
服装及衣着附件	—	—	1.87
自动数据处理设备及其部件	万台	2223	1.40
煤	万吨	551	1.35
钢坯及粗锻件	万吨	74	1.31
集装箱	个	54644	1.31

1999 年对台湾省出口主要商品表（续）

（按最终目的地统计）

金额单位：亿美元

商品名称	单位	数量	金额
静止式变流器	万个	6335	1.02
通断及保护电路装置	—	—	0.95
印刷电路	吨	22376	0.86
纺织纱线、织物及制品	—	—	0.86
二极管及类似半导体件	万个	588522	0.80
电线和电缆	吨	31665	0.74

1999 年从台湾省进口主要商品表

（按原产地统计）

金额单位：亿美元

商品名称	单位	数量	金额
初级形状的塑料	万吨	246	20.65
钢材	万吨	278	14.24
集成电路及微电子组件	万个	417415	11.15
合成纤维长丝机织物	万米	121265	7.57
彩色数据/图形显示管	万只	1028	5.92
未锻造的铜及铜材	吨	242368	5.28
涂覆或浸渍塑料的织物	吨	252714	4.71
自动数据处理设备的零件	吨	20780	4.57
针织或钩编织物	吨	164533	4.26
牛皮革及马皮革	吨	85772	4.20

二、台商仍看好祖国大陆市场的投资前景

据外经贸部统计，1999 年新批准台商投资项目 2523 个，下降 14.1%，实际利用台资金额 26.2 亿美元，下降 13.8%，五年来第一次低于 30 亿美元。这一方面受到祖国大陆整体吸收境外投资形势的影响，另一方面，更主要是受台当局继续实施“戒急用忍”政策、年初台企业出现财务危机影响企业的投资能力、7 月份李登辉抛出“两国论”引起两岸关系紧张等因素的影响，因此台商实际投资大陆金额出现下降。但令人欣慰的是，1999 年新批准合同台资金额仍达 34.2 亿美元，增幅 10.2%，大大好于祖国大陆整体利用外资水平，台商仍看好祖国大陆未来的投资前景。

去年台商投资祖国大陆有以下几个特点：

（一）电子信息产业成为新的投资热点。宏碁、华硕、金像电子等大企业相继落户祖国大陆或扩大在祖国大陆的投资规模。仅 2000 年上半年新投人苏州的台资企业，平均项目规模就达 5000 万美元，主要是电子、信息、化工等高科技项目。宏碁电脑在祖国大陆市场占有率名列第六。台电脑硬体产业大举进驻祖国大陆，有 7 成产品其大陆外移率高达 60% 以上。在台商投资带动下，祖国大陆电脑硬件产品产值近年大幅增长，台“资策会”甚至预测，2000 年祖国大陆将取代台湾省，成为全球第三大电脑硬件产品供应地。此外，包括宏碁电脑、力新国际、凌群电脑、普扬资讯、冈业资讯（英业达集团）智冠科技等 15 家以上台湾省软体业者已在祖国大陆建立庞大的研发基地，运用祖国大陆人力资源开发产品，成为两岸软件业现阶段最主要的合作模式。

（二）台商继续抢攻祖国大陆内销市场。根据一项最新权威调查，在祖国大陆方便食品、纸品、自行车市场上，台资品牌康师傅、统一、旺旺、五月花、捷安特等的市场占有率名列前三位。

（三）继前年批准福建福州、漳州设立“海峡两岸农业合作试验区”之后，1999年我们又批准在山东、海南、黑龙江设立“海峡两岸农业合作试验区”，推动两岸合作上了一个新台阶。

三、协调解决渔工劳务纠纷、维护我渔工合法权益，促进两岸劳务合作的发展

据统计，1999年，祖国大陆共签订对台渔工劳务合同近1707份，合同金额1.45亿美元，增长34%。截至1999年底，累计签订对台渔工劳务合同金额9.96亿美元，累计派出14.4万人次。1999年以来接连发生几起我输台渔工被殴打导致伤亡的严重事故，特别是发生了“金庆十二号”台湾船长杀害我渔工事件和开普敦海域台湾省“威信号”船长殴打渔工事件，引起国务院领导高度关注。我有关部门采取了一系列整治措施，对台渔工劳务秩序和我渔工权益保障在得到逐步改善。

四、2000年两岸经贸关系展望

总体看，发展两岸经贸关系的有利因素是：

（一）两岸加入WTO后降低关税将促进两岸贸易的发展，台湾省灾后重建及民间多项重大工程的相继开工，预计民间投资率将由1999年增长0.9%升为11.8%，将带动祖国大陆产品对台出口。

（二）国际电子产品市场增长周期还会持续一两年，台湾省电子资讯产业掀起购并风潮提高竞争力，有利于台湾省出口电子资讯产品，也将带动我电子信息产品对台出口。

（三）随着我加入WTO进程加快，在商业、金融、保险、电信、旅游等领域，有步骤地扩大开放领域和经营范围，实施西部大开发战略，加快国企改革步伐等，将进一步改善投资环境，新颁布的《中华人民共和国台湾同胞投资保护法实施细则》，将进一步坚定台商投资祖国大陆的信心。在连续两年合同台资金额连续增长10%的基础上，预计2000年实际利用台资金额将实现恢复增长，合同台资金额将继续保持一定的规模。

（四）台湾省大地震对岛内信息产品的生产带来冲击，为满足分散风险的要求，台商会继续将一部分生产基地转移到祖国大陆。

（五）澳门回归之后，港澳在两岸经贸中的桥梁作用将进一步得到增强。

（六）台湾省3月“大选”后，估计两岸关系将好于1999年，客观上有利于两岸经贸交流继续发展。

但两岸经贸交流也面临一些不利因素：

首先，台当局新领导人上台之后，出于政治、经济等方面的考虑，两岸经贸交流的政治障碍仍无法完全消除。全面实现直接“三通”虽在台加入WTO前后面临巨大压力，但因涉及到很多敏感政治问题，短时间内恐难于实现。其次，祖国大陆吸收台资也将受到来自东南亚各国和地区更激烈的竞争。

积极努力开展多边经贸活动
为改革开放发展经济创造良好的国际环境

对外贸易经济合作部国际经贸关系司司长　易小准

世纪之交，以知识经济为特征的全球经济一体化和区域化趋势得到了进一步发展。同时，随着各项改革措施的逐步落实，受亚洲金融危机打击的各国经济相继走出低谷，使得中国的周边国际贸易环境得到了改善。过去一年，中国继续积极参与多边经贸活动和区域经济合作，努力为发展国民经济创造良好的外部环境。

一、中国加入世界贸易组织（WTO）谈判取得突破性进展

1999年11月15日，中美两国政府在平等协商、互谅互让的基础上达成了《中美关于中国加入世界贸易组织的双边协议》。这是中美两国从战略高度审视两国人民长远利益，克服各种困难和障碍，取得的“双赢”成果。这对中美关系和世界经贸的发展都具有重要意义。

中国正在继续与剩余成员加紧进行谈判，争取早日加入世界贸易组织，充分参与新一轮多边贸易体制谈判。目前，与中国举行双边谈判的WTO成员共有37个。截至1999年底，共有16个成员结束了与中国的双边谈判。

16个结束谈判的WTO成员为：

匈牙利、新西兰、韩国、捷克、斯洛伐克、巴基斯坦、土耳其、新加坡、印度尼西亚、日本、澳大利亚、智利、美国、加拿大、古巴、委内瑞拉。

21个未结束谈判的成员为：

欧盟、瑞士、拉脱维亚、墨西哥、厄瓜多尔、哥斯达黎加、危地马拉、斯里兰卡、巴西、秘鲁、乌拉圭、冰岛、挪威、菲律宾、印度、哥伦比亚、泰国、阿根廷、波兰、吉尔吉斯、马来西亚。

1999年11月30日至12月3日，以外经贸部石广生部长为团长的中国政府代表团出席了在美国西雅图举行的WTO第三届部长级会议。12月2日，石广生部长在全体会议上发言，强调指出，WTO应充分尊重发展中国家的经济发展目标以及与之相适应的渐进的市场开放模式；发达国家应当切实履行在乌拉圭回合协议中承诺的义务，改善发展中国家的市场准入环境；制定新的贸易规则必须有发展中国家的充分参与；加强发展中国家之间的协调，增强参与多边贸易体制的集体谈判能力；新一轮多边贸易谈判应集中讨论与贸易有关的问题，不应当把那些与WTO职能无关的问题，如劳工标准等纳入议题当中。

二、积极参与区域经济合作，努力创造稳定、开放的区域经贸环境

中国重视并积极参与了亚太经济合作组织(APEC)、亚欧会议（ASEM）等区域经济贸易组织和亚洲及太平洋经济和社会委员会发展中成员国关于贸易谈判的第一协定（简称曼谷协定）的活动，为促进中国经济发展，扩大对外贸易，吸引外资，推动亚太、亚欧地区贸易投资自由化与便利化进程和经济技术合作做出了自己的贡献。

1999年，江泽民主席出席了在新西兰奥克兰举行的APEC经济领导人非正式会议，阐述了亚太经济合作的发展前景和具体主张。中国积极参与了APEC在贸易投资自由化与便利化、电子商务等方面的工作，共同制定了《APEC促进竞争和管理制度改革原则》、《APEC政府采购非约束性原则》和《APEC电子电气相互认可安排》等重要文件。努力在亚太地区营造稳定和开放的经贸环境，反对贸易保护主义。同时，中国积极推动APEC在各个领域开展多种形式的经济技术合作活动，以缩小发达成员和发展中成员的差距，实现共同繁荣的目标。

1999年，中国与APEC其他成员的经贸关系有了进一步发展。中国与APEC其他20个成员的贸易总额为2667.89亿美元，占中国当年进出口贸易总额的73.97%。同年，中国实际吸收外商直接投资403.19亿美元，其中316.3亿美元来自APEC成员，占中国当年实际利用外资总额的78.45%。

亚欧经贸合作的目标是促进两地区的双向贸易和投资流动。其主要内容是致力于在基础设施建设、能源与环境、中小企业发展、人力资源开发等方面的合作。1999年，中国积极参加了ASEM的经贸合作活动。外经贸部石广生部长率团出席了第二届亚欧经济部长会议，提出了发展亚欧经济关系的重要主张和建议。中国全面参与了《亚欧贸易便利行动计划》和《亚欧投资促进行动计划》的执行，并积极组织国内工商界参加ASEM的工商活动，以增进相互了解，促进相互合作。中国作为《贸易便利行动计划》动植物检疫领域的亚洲牵头人于1999年11月在中国举办了ASEM第二次动植物检疫程序会议。这些活动对促进亚欧和中国与欧洲之间贸易和投资的双向流动产生了积极的影响。

1999年，中国与《曼谷协定》成员国就加入该贸易协定进行的双边谈判取得了突破性进展。在与斯里兰卡签署双边备忘录后，中国又相继与孟加拉和韩国签署双边备忘录，与印度的谈判也只有少量技术问题尚待澄清。至此，中国已实际获得加入该协定所需的2/3多数票。

三、多双边经贸合作取得积极进展

中国与联合国贸发会议和77国集团的合作继续深入开展。1999年为筹备贸发会议第十届大会作了大量的工作，并与贸发会议共同举办了“普惠制及有关贸易法规研讨会”和“国际投资协定及其对发展的影响区域间研讨会”，探讨了中国如何更好地普及和利用普惠制以及积极应对外国反倾销的措施，总结了世界各国发展投资的经验和教训，对发展中国家如何更好地吸收国际投资等问题进行了研究和讨论。中国积极参加了77国集团贸发十大筹备委员会的各项工作，并派代表团出席了第九届77国集团亚洲组部长级会议和第九届77国集团部长级会议。

1999年，在“平等互利”的基础上，中国与经合组织（OECD）的政策对话合作关系取得了积极的进展。通过与经合组织加强高层互访以及在众多领域进行直接合作，双方加强了相互了解，增加了对全球经济发展政策的共识。

多年来，中国利用国际组织和外国政府对华提供的无偿援助，开展中国与这些组织和国家间的经贸交流，引进技术，培训人力资源，为中国的改革开放和社会经济发展，特别是西部开发提供了有利的支持。虽然多双边援助金额有限，但其交流面广泛。有关专家长期在华与我国各级政府官员、专业人员、社区群众共同工作，建立了相互沟通的良好渠道。这些交流与合作为彼此今后进一步交流打下了良好基础。

大力加强法制建设　促进外经贸业务的健康发展

对外贸易经济合作部条约法律司司长　张玉卿

1999年，外经贸法律工作以邓小平理论和党的基本路线为指导，适应外经贸事业的发展和中国加入世贸组织形势的要求，坚持从实际出发，解放思想，实事求是，较好地完成了各项任务，促进和保障了外经贸业务的健康发展。

一、加快立法步伐，完善外经贸法律体系

（一）对外贸易立法

为进一步完善《对外贸易法》的配套规定，参与了《合同法》、《专利法》、《海关法》、《音像制品进口管理办法》、《国际招标机构资格审定办法》等法律、法规的制订和修改工作。针对出口反倾销工作中企业应诉积极性不高，严重影响应诉结果的情况，在认真调研和总结经验的基础上制定了《关于鼓励和督促企业参加国外反倾销案件应诉的若干规定》，于1999年3月10日颁布施行。制定并颁布了《外经贸企业合同管理指导意见》，对规范企业外贸经营、降低对外签约风险起到了重要作用。

1999年，我们积极参与了有关国际机构制订国际贸易统一法的工作，特别是参加联合国国际贸易法委员会的会议。对于贸法会正在制订的《应收款融资转让公约》、《数字签字统一规则》及《私人融资基础设施项目立法指南》等法律文件提出了意见和建议，反映了我国的实践和要求。

（二）外商投资的法律保护

针对形势发展的要求，进一步完善外商投资的配套性法规，颁布了《外商投资企业合并与分立的规定》和《对外贸易经济合作部〈关于外商投资举办投资性公司的暂行规定〉的补充规定》，对进一步完善投资性公司功能，扩大利用外资及出口起到了推动作用。1999年，我们会同人大财经委经济法室共同筹办了“纪念《中外合资经营企业法》颁布实施20周年座谈会”，对宣传依法利用外资起到良好作用。

积极推进双边投资保护协定的商签，完成了与卡塔尔、巴林双边投资保护协定的草签，与莫桑比克、芬兰、荷兰、文莱、伊朗及加拿大分别进行了投资保护协定的签署或修改的商谈，并取得一定进展。

开展国际间投资立法交流，组团参加了亚太经合组织投资专家组、竞争政策研讨会，对亚太经合组织投资政策选择修改提出了增加“减少技术转让限制”的建议，并已在会上讨论通过；对有关成员国提出的“竞争政策核心原则和行动要点”提出了修改意见；在亚太经合组织内，初步完成了我国在争端解决、竞争政策、放宽管理三个方面的单边行动计划的自我评估和修改补充；完成了《亚太经合组织投资指南》的修订工作。

（三）其他方面立法工作

积极参与全国人大法工委组织的《合同法》起草工作，为我国代理法律制度在立法上取得突破性进展作出了贡献；在技术转让方面，就有关的法律问题赴欧洲进行了调研，在此基础上完成了《中华人民共和国技术进出口条例》的起草工作并已上报国务院；参与起草了《对外工程承包管理条例》，已上报国务院；参与了出口管制方面的法律研讨。此外，还就国家有关立法机关及部内起草的法律、法规草案提出了会签意见。

二、配合中国加入WTO，根据中国经济发展的具体情况，清理、修订外经贸法律法规

1999年，中国加入WTO的进程明显加快。为配合中国加入WTO，履行中国作出的承诺，外经贸部积极组织力量，开展了清理、修订和完善中国的外经贸法律、法规工作。

（一）清理、修订外经贸法律法规的宗旨和原则

根据WTO规则和中国做出的承诺，中国应承担的一项主要义务就是：完善中国外经贸法律法规，在全国实行统一的法律制度，使中国外经贸法律法规透明化。清理、修订、完善中国外经贸法律法规是履行上述义务的实际体现和重要步骤。

外经贸部法律法规修订和完善工作总的设想是：结合中国外经贸体制的改革和中国外经贸发展的需要，按照WTO规则和中国在WTO中承诺的要求，全面充实、调整、完善现行的涉外经济法律、法规和规章，初步建立起适应社会主义市场经济需要、符合WTO规则要求，符合中国国情，统一、完备、透明的对外经济贸易法律体系。

清理和修订中国涉外法律法规工作，是在国务院WTO领导小组的领导下，在国务院法制办公室的统一指导下进行的。外经贸部也专门成立了"WTO法律工作领导小组"，并在条法司设办公室，负责此项工作的领导、组织、协调和督办工作，条法司司长兼任主任。自中美签署关于中国加入WTO的双边协议以来，外经贸部以WTO法律工作领导小组为核心，开展了大规模的法律法规和部门规章的清理和修订工作，并取得了一定进展。

对于这次外经贸法律法规的清理和修订工作，国务院已规定，与外贸、外商投资直接有关的规章，凡外经贸部制定、发布的，由外经贸部清理；其他有关部门制定、发布的，由其他部门会同外经贸部清理。今后凡制定外经贸方面的法律法规和规章，由外经贸部发布或者由其他有关部门征求外经贸部意见后发布，以求中国外经贸法律法规和政策的统一。

（二）中国涉外法律法规清理、修订的基本情况

外经贸部认真、全面地开展了与WTO协议及中国对外作出的承诺相关的外经贸法律、行政法规和部门规章的清理与统计工作，并进行了分类、研究与比较。

我们还提出了修改、新制定法律法规的建议。根据轻重缓急的原则，向国务院提出了修订我国现行外经贸法律法规的具体建议。据初步研究，中国加入WTO有关的，需制定的法律法规12件，需要修订的现行法律法规33件，共计45件。近期需要抓紧制定、修订的法律、行政法规，有《中外合资经营企业法》、《中外合作经营企业法》、《外资企业法》、《反倾销条例》、《反补贴条例》、《保障措施条例》、《专利法》、《外资保险公司管理条例》、《外商投资经营电信业的管理规定》等。根据WTO规则规定的过渡期和中国承诺的期限，我们还计划修订《对外贸易法》、《指导外商投资方向暂行规定》和《货物进口管理条例》等。

三、加强国际间知识产权保护合作与交流

1999年，我们派员参加了亚太经合组织举行的知识产权专家组会议和知识产权培训，就成员之间的知识产权合作问题进行探讨。1999年，中欧知识产权合作项目经长期酝酿正式启动。5月，组团赴欧盟就该项目与各欧方单位交换了意见，并拟定和通过了年度工作计划。各有关单位将依据项目计划的进程有序工作，致力于全面提高中国知识产权保护水平。

1999年2月，中美双方举行了知识产权磋商，磋商涉及中美知识产权协议的执行问题，中国打击CD盗版的问题，知识产权法律修改的问题等。根据1995年中美协议的规定，半年一次的定期磋商已经结束，今后的磋商将根据具体问题和情况举行。此外，还与法国、意大利、白俄罗斯、韩国等国家开展了双边知识产权磋商和交流。

为了配合中国"入世"要求，知识产权法律的修改工作进一步加强。目前专利法的规定已经与TRIPS协议基本一致。协同有关部门积极开展打击知识产权侵权行为。1999年中国有关部门共查处商标侵权假冒案件16938件（包括涉外侵权假冒案件1810件），罚款总额1.06亿元，责令赔偿被侵权人经济损失571.7万元，移送司法机关追究刑事责任21人。1999年海关共查处商标侵权案件178起，价值6198万元。这些工作充分表明了中国保护知识产权的决心。

四、反倾销调查与应诉工作

（一）加大反倾销应诉和复审力度，千方百计确保出口

1999年，由于国际贸易保护主义抬头，以及部分国内企业盲目出口等原因，导致国际上对华反倾销案件数量迅速提高，达到四十余起，产品涉及五矿化工、轻纺、机电、土畜和医保等各类产品，涉案金额超过5亿美元。因此我们将千方百计确保出口作为一项突出任务来抓，加大了反倾销应诉和复审工作的力度。派代表团赴欧盟总部和部分成员国专门就反倾销问题进行了政府交涉，阐明中国的市

场经济体制，要求对方尽快取消其不合理的和歧视性的作法，给予中国出口产品和企业以公正待遇。加强了对商会和有关企业的反倾销应诉工作的指导，并召开了有针对性的反倾销工作会议。在应诉中还注重利用反倾销案件交涉费用聘用律师，收到了较好的效果。

（二）积极开展对进口产品反倾销调查工作，维护我国企业的正当权益

按照国际惯例，正确运用反倾销武器，依法对国外进口产品进行反倾销调查，有利于维护正常的国际贸易秩序和企业公平竞争环境。根据《中华人民共和国反倾销和反补贴条例》，1999年6月3日外经贸部发布终裁公告，决定自终裁公告之日起，对原产于加拿大、韩国和美国的进口新闻纸征收9%至78%不等的反倾销税。这是我国第一次依照国际惯例征收反倾销税，显示了我国反倾销的决心和能力。

继新闻纸案之后，应国内产业的要求，我部又先后开启了三起进口反倾销调查案。分别对来自俄罗斯的涉及8个税则号的冷轧硅钢片、来自韩国的聚酯薄膜进行反倾销调查，对来自日本和韩国的涉及7个税则号的不锈钢冷轧薄板反倾销调查正式立案。目前，上述案件的初步裁定工作正在加紧进行。

五、贯彻依法行政精神，认真做好行政复议和普法工作，做好重大经贸案件的协调工作

认真贯彻《行政复议法》，依法开展行政复议和行政诉讼，保护公民、法人和其他组织的合法权益。1999年，外经贸部先后受理和审结了一批行政复议案，并对地方外经贸委的行政复议工作予以协助指导。同时，我们加大了法律宣传和普及的力度，先后举办了短期法律培训班和长期法律培训班，并出版了中德经济法合作项目的培训教材。组织了境外法律培训班，赴加拿大和澳大利亚学习有关法律知识，对于各地外经贸工作人员提高法律素质发挥了积极的作用。

1999年，我们对大量的外贸纠纷案件提供了咨询意见，并继续协助企业解决法律纠纷，协助处理了涉及我国出口管制方面的案件。对重大利用外资项目、特殊类型的外商投资企业的法律问题提出处理意见，解决了一些外商投资企业的重大纠纷。驻德中资公司中方雇员在当地的社会保险问题是一个多年困扰我们的问题，1999年我们派员赴德国进行了调查及磋商，对促使德国政府同意与我国商签避免双重社会保险协定起到关键作用。

六、电子商务法律工作有了新的进展

1999年，我们积极参与了国际电子商务法律交流与合作，密切追踪电子商务法律发展动态，维护了我国作为发展中国家的权益。参加了联合国贸易法委员会的电子商务工作组会议和联合国贸易发展会议电子商务专家会议工作，对《电子签名统一规则》进行了讨论，该规则今后在电子合同和电子身份认证方面将发挥重要的指导意义。作为中国首届电子商务应用博览会的一部分，9月成功举办了中国电子商务法律研讨会，促进了国内电子商务法律研究的交流与合作，产生了广泛的社会反响。

2000年是世纪之交的一年，外经贸法律工作面临着新的形势和机遇。为此，我们将重点做好以下各项工作：一是进一步加强和改进立法工作，进一步加强运用法律手段管理外经贸活动；二是适应中国加入世界贸易组织的新形势，加强对世界贸易组织法律制度的研究，做好相关法律工作；三是根据新情况，积极组织力量做好我国出口产品的反倾销应诉工作；四是完善进口产品反倾销调查机制，不断提高运用反倾销和其他贸易保护措施的能力和水平；五是深入贯彻国务院《关于全面推进依法行政的决定》，严格依法行政，继续推进外经贸依法行政工作；六是加强外经贸法律队伍建设，大力培养新形势下保障外经贸发展的法律人才。

改革创新　努力建设一支高素质的外经贸干部队伍

对外贸易经济合作部人事教育劳动司司长　魏建国

1999年我部干部人事工作以建设一支面向21世纪的高素质外经贸干部队伍为重点，紧紧围绕我部“出口引资”的中心工作，开拓创新，锐意推进干部人事制度改革，取得了较大的成绩。重点抓了

以下几项工作：

一、抓住重点，改革创新，大力加强干部队伍建设

（一）重点加强司局级领导班子调整配备和后备干部的选拔培养工作，认真做好部机关处级干部任免工作

按照中央关于建设高素质干部队伍的总体要求，结合“三讲”教育，重点加强司局级领导班子的调整配备工作，使司局级领导班子的年龄结构、专业结构进一步改善，增强了活力，整体素质进一步提高。截止1999年底，我部共有司局级干部310人，平均年龄52岁。其中正司81人，平均年龄54.7岁；副司229人，平均年龄51岁。45岁以下的司局级干部66人，占总数的21%。我部司局级干部全部具有大专以上学历和本职岗位要求的相关专业知识。为了体现公开、公正、公平的原则，鼓励人才脱颖而出，积极探索选人、用人的新办法、新机制，我部将选择部机关部分副司级领导岗位进行公开选拔试点工作。

有计划、有目标地选拔和培养德才兼备的后备干部是干部队伍建设的重要任务。年底前，在机关各单位的共同努力下，我部进行了一次自下而上广泛地推荐后备干部工作，在较短的时间内建立起一支数量充足、结构合理、素质比较优良的后备干部队伍，得到了干部群众的拥护和支持。

按照干部管理权限，我司认真对部机关处级干部的任职资格进行审查和管理，进一步做好部机关非领导职务的设置和人员管理工作。为了加强群众在干部提拔任用工作中的监督作用，我部将对部机关新提拔的正、副处级干部实行公示制。

截止1999年底，我部公务员总数1510人，平均年龄为36.7岁。部机关共有司局级干部176人，平均年龄52岁。其中正司级49人，平均年龄54岁，最年轻的正司级干部42岁；副司级127人，平均年龄50岁，最年轻的副司级干部36岁。部机关共有处级干部641人，其中正处263人（国内在职163人，驻外91人，特办9人），最年轻的正处级干部31岁；副处级干部378人（国内在职252人，驻外96人，特办、挂职30人），最年轻的副处级干部29岁。

（二）加强部机关和特办干部日常管理工作

根据工作需要，选派了6名司处级干部到艰苦地区和少数民族地区挂职锻炼，接收了3名少数民族干部到我部挂职，安排了7名领导干部参加各类学习进修。在同各司局共同研究的基础上，我司就做好公务员交流轮岗有关工作提出了具体设想。

为加强我部派驻各地特派员办事处的力量，共派遣了34名干部到特办工作。

（三）推行公务员量化考核

我部在总结1998年成功地进行公务员量化考核试点工作经验的基础上，在1999年公务员年度考核中全面推行了量化考核工作。总结考核结果，我们认为，量化考核基本上能够较客观地反映被考核者的实际情况，有效地弥补了以往定性考核的不足。考核结果既为领导了解干部提供了一定的参考，又便于干部本人了解领导和同事们对自己的评价，有利于发扬成绩，找出差距，明确努力方向。通过量化测评，增强了大家的紧迫感，对提高公务员政治、业务素质起到了促进作用，有利于竞争机制的形成和工作作风的转变。

二、积极落实参赞会议精神，推进驻外干部选派和管理体制的改革，进一步做好驻外干部的日常管理工作

（一）进行公开选拔驻外干部试点，建立秘书以下干部考试制度

进行公开选拔驻外干部是驻外干部人事制度改革的一项重大尝试。在部里统一部署下，我司组织了驻外干部的公开选拔工作。参赞公开选拔通过报名和资格审查、外语考试和业务面试、答辩三个阶段，最后根据考试和答辩结果，经批准，确定五名同志分别任驻孟加拉等国使馆经济商务参赞。同时，在本部直属单位、地方外经贸厅和68家外经贸企业范围内进行秘书以下干部公开选拔，从135名报名人员中，选出了驻外干部33名。公开选拔工作的顺利完成，为下一步驻外人员派遣、管理工作改革奠定了基础。为了把好外派干部的外语、业务质量关，我们还建立了秘书以下干部考试制度，规定只有通过考试的干部，才具备派出的资格。

我们将跟踪考察通过公开选拔的参赞在国外第一线的表现情况，在总结经验的基础上，继续推进参赞公开选拔工作。

（二）改革驻外干部培训班，调整了培训班课程设置、授课内容和讲授形式，突出了实用性和可操作性，提高了授课质量。我们还建立了驻外人员到地区司和有关业务司实习制度。

（三）切实加强对驻外干部的管理力度

针对个别驻外机构和驻外干部中存在的违纪现象，我司先后制定、补充、重申了一系列加强管理的规章制度，使管理工作更加有章可循、细致规范。建立了驻外经商机构领导干部提醒制度，对反映有问题的驻外领导干部及时提出警告。

（四）建立外语人才库

经认真调研、广泛论证和征求意见，我们下发了《关于建立我部“驻外干部外语人才库”的通知》，并得到了各单位的积极响应。“人才库”的建立将对我部外语人才资源的充分利用、合理调配起到积极作用。

（五）建立联席会议制度

为了更好地做好驻外干部管理工作，我们与地区司和有关业务司建立了联席会议制度，就驻外机构的有关问题定期进行磋商。

（六）办好《驻外经济商务机构工作通讯》

为了加强对驻外经济商务机构的工作指导，加强国内外信息沟通，便于驻外工作经验交流，及时指出驻外工作中存在的问题，全面提高管理水平，经批准，我们创办了《驻外经济商务机构工作通讯》，我司努力把它办成为外经贸部与各驻外经商机构相互沟通的桥梁。

三、进一步做好培训工作

（一）抓好 WTO 知识培训工作

为了普及 WTO 知识，为我国入世做好必要的准备，经国务院批准，由我部举办 WTO 知识普及和提高性培训班，培训对象为我部机关副处级以上干部、各部委从事 WTO 相关工作的负责人、地方外经贸厅（委、局）负责人、国家级开发区管委会主任等。接到任务后，我司立即会同有关司局研究制定了详细的培训计划，经批准后已开始组织实施。

（二）全力以赴，做好境外加工贸易培训工作

人才培训是境外加工贸易顺利实施的重要保障。在有关司局的协助和支持下，1999 年，我司共举办了 6 期境外加工贸易培训班，来自全国各地的 467 名学员参加了培训，另外，还举办了一期技术人员强化班，有 32 名学员参加培训。为评估培训效果，我司还对已培训的学员进行了跟踪调研，受到地方单位的好评。通过举办境外加工贸易培训班，使学员们掌握了政策，熟悉了境外重点市场和境外投资管理业务，对境外加工贸易业务的各个环节有了全面了解，受到了广大企业代表和地方政府管理部门的普遍好评，对鼓励企业积极开展境外加工贸易业务起到了很好的推动作用。

（三）加强部机关干部培训工作

1999 年，我部机关干部的培训工作主要围绕提高干部的专业知识及技能开展各项工作。一是组织机关干部参加“全国计算机等级考试”并举办了相应培训；举办了办公自动化和网络知识培训。二是与南开大学联合举办了“世界经济”专业研究生课程进修班。三是改革以往干部出国培训选派办法，实行国外培训项目人员公开招考。

四、直属事业单位改革工作

事业单位改革工作涉及面广，政策性强。为积极稳妥地做好我部直属事业单位的改革，1999 年对直属事业单位进行了深入细致的调研工作，提出了直属事业单位改革的初步意见，起草了直属事业单位改革的工作计划。今后，我们将继续推进直属事业单位和商会人事管理改革工作。

管住自己的人　把好国家的门
1999 年海关工作再创佳绩

海关总署办公厅副主任　黄胜强

1999 年，全国海关坚定不移地以邓小平理论和党的十五大精神为指导，立足服从服务于改革开放和经济建设大局，忠实地执行党中央、国务院关于海关工作的各项决策和指示，及时正确地提出了“依法行政，为国把关”的海关工作方针，克服种种困难，经受严峻考验，各项工作取得了新的成绩。

一、打击走私取得明显成效

1999 年，全国海关按照中央的部署，在“两

江”（珠江、西江）、“两北”（北部湾、北仑河）、东南沿海、环香港水域等走私重点水域和中蒙、中朝边境地区连续组织了打击走私联合行动或专项斗争，并取得了重大战果。开展了打击进出口贸易渠道走私的专项斗争，有力地打击了“三假”（假批文、假单证、假印章）、“三伪”（伪报品名、价格、数量）、“飞料”、集装箱藏匿等走私活动。缉私警察队伍边组建边行动，充分行使刑事执法权力，破大案，挖团伙，抓逃犯，极大地震慑了走私犯罪分子。稽查部门积极开展对重点企业和重点商品的专项稽查。1999年，全国海关共查获走私案件13694起，案值75.6亿元，比1998年分别增长63.4%和减少50.9%，其中走私罪嫌疑案件1350起，案值57.6亿元，缴库罚没收入26.3亿元，对3077名走私犯罪嫌疑人采取强制措施，其中990人已经检察机关批准逮捕。经过1年多的艰苦奋战，大规模走私被基本遏制，内地进口统计与香港出口统计数字对比趋于正常，正常贸易进口明显增加，国有企业改革脱困的条件进一步改善。同时，全国海关坚决打击毒品、文物、濒危动植物等走私活动，查获大量反动、淫秽、散发性宗教物品、盗版音像制品，特别是及时查获“法轮功”反宣品，为配合党的3项政治斗争、维护社会稳定作出了应有的贡献。

二、海关税收超大幅度增长

1999年海关税收历史性地突破了1000亿元大关，全年征收关税和进口环节税净入库1590.6亿元，比年度计划超收770.6亿元，比1998年增收711.6亿元，增长80.9%，为中央实施积极的财政政策提供了有力保证。海关税收超大幅度增长的原因，一是打击走私取得明显成果，非法贸易受到遏制，正常贸易进口大幅增长，国家实施积极财政政策、扩大内需和调整产业结构等，推动了一般贸易进口增长和进口商品结构改善，海关税源和税基扩大；二是国家采取的一系列综合治理措施，包括打击骗汇、骗退税等经济犯罪活动和整顿进出口、国内流通、金融、交通运输等方面的经济秩序取得积极成效，进出口企业特别是一些大型企业的纳税成倍增长，海关执法环境得到切实改善；三是全国海关认真汲取湛江案件教训，进一步从严治关，为海关税收超大幅度增长提供了坚强的组织保证；四是全国海关切实加强查验、归类、审价、稽查、清缴欠税、加工贸易核查核销等各项执法工作，确保应收尽收。

三、进出境货物、物品的实际监管进一步加强

全国海关实际监管意识进一步增强，建立、完善并积极落实一系列加强实际监管的规章制度：恢复建立了珠江口4个海关监管站，对来往港澳小型船舶的监管明显加强；整治、清理了一批二类口岸、保税仓库和各类海关监管场所；逐步恢复船边监管，对重点监控船舶开始实行船边监装、监卸，加强了舱单核销；强化放行环节的监控措施，加强了查验管理，查验率和查获率有所提高；内部挖潜，努力增加现场查验人员的比重，借调3000名武警官兵充实一线查验监控力量；清理整顿报关市场，实施企业分类管理，与有关部门加强联系配合，对通关环节物流监控实行联手共管；认真贯彻落实国务院关于加工贸易保证金台账实转各项措施，进一步规范加工贸易海关监管等。1999年全国海关查获的走私大要案中有36%是通过加强实际监管发现的。行邮物品监管工作进一步加强，积极推广旅检通关改革，规范快件监管，为保障世博会、万国邮联大会、世界体操锦标赛和澳门回归等重大活动的顺利进行作出了成绩。

四、信息化管理发挥了重要作用

海关管理信息化水平大大提高。一是基础建设进一步完善。建成并开通了总署与45个直属海关、院校之间光缆数据主干网和直属海关与基层海关之间的近500条数据专线。二是应用范围不断扩大。现代海关业务信息化管理系统5.0版本及税收、统计、财务、罚没收入等一批应用项目投入使用，“海关风险管理信息网”在6个海关试运行并取得初步成果，为通关作业改革和加强海关管理提供了有力的保障。三是计算机联网管理有效打击了进出境走私违法活动。全国结付汇报关单核查系统全面推广运行，使猖獗一时的骗逃套汇活动得到明显遏制，有效阻断了走私的资金渠道；加工贸易、转关运输实行全国海关计算机联网管理，与有关部门实行进出口许可证、出口退税签证和进口车辆证明的计算机联网核对，有力地打击了“三假”、“飞料”、加工贸易假核销走私和骗退税等经济犯罪活动。

1999年海关其他各项工作也取得了较好的成绩。海关进出口统计受到中央领导和有关部门的高度重视和表扬；《海关法》修订草案经国务院第22次常务会议讨论通过后已正式提交全国人大常委会审议；政务信息全年被中办、国办采用和中央领导批示的数量均创历史纪录；财务工作有力保障了海关改革和装备现代化，资金投入是历史上最多的一年；中央关于行政性收费和罚没收入实行“收支两条线”管理措施得到有效落实，海关系统共取消或降低各种收费89种；海关物资装备采购开始实行公开招标；等等。

回顾近年来特别是1998年全国打击走私工作会议召开以来的海关工作实践，海关总署党组总结了3条经验：

第一，必须坚持“依法行政，为国把关”。“依法行政”是海关贯彻党的路线方针政策和“依法治国”基本方略的具体体现，是国家对海关工作的基本要求；“为国把关”是海关的基本职能，是海关工作对改革开放和社会主义现代化建设的最本质的服务。在建立社会主义市场经济体制的过程中，必然存在利益主体的多元化及其矛盾甚至冲突，国家通过法律和政策来规范各种权利和利益关系。海关作为国家进出境监督管理机关，处在错综复杂的各种权利和利益的矛盾交点中，必须把依法行政作为立关之本和立身之本。只有坚持依法行政，才能维护国家的整体利益，正确处理各种权利和利益关系，获得社会广泛的理解和支持。为了迁就局部利益，离开政策法律讲“服务”，放弃把关职能热衷于“做好事”，就必然会出现海关工作职能上的错位和执法上的偏差，实质上是损害国家和人民的利益，也损害局部的合法利益，甚至导致执法腐败的发生和蔓延。

第二，必须坚持“从严治关”。把关必先治关，治关务必从严。政治路线、指导方针确定之后，干部就是决定的因素，干部出了问题，其他一切无从谈起。湛江、厦门案件表明，严重的走私犯罪活动必然和海关的执法腐败相联系，反走私必须反腐败。海关的执法腐败集中表现在与工作对象的关系问题上，吃喝玩乐，不分彼此，潜移默化，有求必应，不能自拔。“傍大款”，无论出自经济目的还是政治目的，都要为此付出沉重的代价。海关是高风险岗位，只有“管住自己的人”，才能“把好国家的门”。海关各级干部都要有忧患意识，做到廉洁从政，勤政为民，淡泊处世，奋发向上。否则，就不配当一个海关关员，就会失去人民的信任。

第三，必须坚持综合治理。这是在建立社会主义市场经济体制过程中和海关垂直领导体制下有效履行海关职能的正确方法和重要途径。进出境违法犯罪活动，都有复杂的社会背景和多方面的社会联系，必须把对进出境监督管理作为系统工程，把海关执法中深层次的问题放到社会的范围里来加以解决，依靠各级党政领导，动员社会各方面的力量，综合治理进出口秩序，加强各个环节的密切配合，才能推进海关各项改革和建设，在全党、全国工作的大格局中更加有效地发挥海关的职能作用。事实上，如果不是党中央、国务院的巨大权威和英明决策，各级党政和社会各方面力量的积极支持、参与，靠海关一家是不可能在一年多的时间里就取得打击走私、税收征管如此大的成绩的。

以上3条经验，对于做好新世纪海关工作具有重要指导意义。

2000年海关工作的总体要求是：以邓小平理论和党的十五大精神为指导，全面贯彻党的十五届三中、四中全会和中央经济工作会议精神，按照“管住自己的人，把好国家的门”的要求，坚持“依法行政，为国把关”和“从严治关”海关工作方针，全面推进以通关作业改革为中心环节的海关各项改革，进一步完善社会主义市场经济体制和垂直领导体制条件下海关行政管理、科技管理和干部管理的各项机制，加强管理，落实制度，强化监督，全面地高质量地完成党和国家交给的各项任务，把海关改革和建设事业胜利推向21世纪。年内重点抓好5个方面的工作：一是常备不懈，严防猛打，绝不允许走私回潮；二是依法治税，强化征管，努力完成税收计划；三是建立健全物流监控体系，确保实际监管到位；四是认真落实中央各项措施，推动加工贸易健康发展；五是加强海关法制和业务基础建设，努力净化海关执法环境。同时，要全面推行通关作业改革，从体制上入手，在机制上加强，从根本上解决海关业务工作中诸多困难和问题。一是调整业务机构设置，明确合理地划分业务事权；二是加强科技工作管理，深化业务科技一体化；三是创新业务管理方法，提高海关执法水平，开发应用“口岸电子执法系统”；四是优化海关人力资源配置，培养新型专业人才。

总署党组经过认真研究，提出了“从严治关”、加强队伍建设的3年目标，即：坚决贯彻落实党中央、国务院关于反腐倡廉的一系列指示精神，在1998年全国打私会以来海关队伍建设的基础上，从现在起，再用2年左右的时间，通过进一步深化教育、从严执纪、强化监督、落实责任，使海关各级领导班子建设得到切实加强，干部队伍素质有较大提高，作风纪律有明显改革，执法腐败现象得到有效遏制，建设廉洁、勤政、务实、高效海关。

根据国务院确定“管理年”的各项要求，海关系统把2000年作为海关工作的“管理落实年”，坚持高标准、严要求，重振雄风，再创新高，为改革开放和社会主义现代化建设做出更大贡献。

1999年我国出入境检验检疫工作取得重大进展

国家出入境检验检疫局办公室主任　魏传忠

1999年是出入境检验检疫改革和发展取得重大进展的一年。一年间，出入境检验检疫系统广大干部职工坚持以党的十五大、十五届三中、四中全会和中央经济工作会议精神为指导，认真贯彻落实党中央、国务院的各项部署，积极稳妥地推进机构改革，严格依法把关，努力为扩大出口服务，在维护国家利益、经济安全和人民健康等方面取得了明显的成绩。

一、各地机构组建全面完成

各级检验检疫机构坚决执行国务院批准的《全国各地出入境检验检疫机构组建方案》，按照国家检验检疫局批复的“三定”方案和人员定岗分流实施办法，坚持既积极又稳妥的方针，克服时间紧、任务重、难度大的困难，至11月底，35个直属局以及下属的278个分支局、272个办事处和320个事业单位全部组建完毕，人员定岗分流基本完成。在机构组建中，各级检验检疫机构认真贯彻中央关于政府机构改革的精神，加强领导，强化管理，深入开展思想政治工作，确保了思想不散、秩序不乱，人员妥善安排，国有资产不流失，业务工作正常开展。

二、各项业务改革协调发展

各级检验检疫机构按照国家局的要求，积极进行了“六个一”即：一次报检报验、一次采样取样、一次检验检疫、一次卫生除害处理、一次收费、一次发证放行管理模式的试点，探索业务融合的途径。围绕检务改革这一中心环节，国家检验检疫局制定了业务流程管理、口岸与内地业务协作、证单、印章、计收费等改革方案。经努力落实相关措施，实现了从2000年1月1日起，全系统统一着装，以统一的工作流程、统一的单证、统一的标志、统一的标准、统一的收费进行执法的目标。新的检验检疫机制的全面启动，标志着检验检疫系统基本完成了国务院确定的“三检合一”的改革任务，也标志着我国出入境检验检疫事业进入了新的历史发展阶段。

三、检验检疫执法把关力度加强

全国检验检疫机构共对233.5万出入境人员实施了卫生检疫，查出各种流行病患者2.7万人；对223.09亿元动植物及产品实施检疫，查出各种有害生物7940批；检验进出口商品310.8万批，货值1191.8亿美元；查出不合格进口商品货值33.8亿美元，查出不合格出口商品货值2.9亿美元。在组织检验检疫过程中，根据国内外传染病的疫情态势，加强了口岸传染病检疫监测，制定了南方五省（区）登革热联防措施。对口岸卫生监督工作进行了规范化管理，在全国12个口岸开展了创建国际卫生机场活动。加强了对重点出口食品的监管力度，强化了出口动植物检疫和农残检验。针对美国、加拿大等国对我出口货物木质包装实行严格检疫的要求，积极制定了相关处理技术规程和监管办法，使我木质包装产品出口基本上未受影响。为保护国家森林与环境，各地检验检疫机构对从美国、日本进口货物的木质包装实施了紧急检疫措施。圆满完成了’99昆明“世博会”检验检疫，妥善处理了欧盟四国“二恶英”事件、香港禽流感风波、“法国葡萄酒事件”等重大突发事件，有效防止了病害的传入传出。完成了对进口小麦携带TCK病菌处理的技术攻关，实现了对集装箱货物的一次卫生除害处理。对出口机电产品的企业实行了分类检验监管制度和超前把关的预验措施。强化了出口国储棉产地检验和口岸查验，进一步加强了对援外物资和进口废物原料的检验监管。加强了进出口安全质量许可制度管理，对六种进口商品实施了电磁兼容强制检测。加强了进出口食品和动植物产品生产企业的卫生注册和对外推荐工作，采取有效措施打击了假冒UL标志行为。开拓了QS9000汽车行业管理体系认证和

ISO14000环保认证、咨询等新领域，CNAB经国际认可组织IAF批准成为其多边协议成员，获得了国际认可。通过检验检疫执法把关，有效维护了国家的利益。

四、支持外贸扩大出口措施有效

为促进外贸扩大出口，检验检疫系统积极贯彻党中央、国务院的指示精神，先后出台了一系列促进外贸扩大出口、促进引进外资及推进国有企业改革和发展的措施，连续四次降低了检验检疫收费。其中，从5月1日起，主动降低了加工贸易的品质检验费和外商投资财产价值鉴定费；6月份对出口煤炭的检验机制进行了重大调整，将产地和口岸两次检验、分别收费改为产地监管，口岸一次检验、一次收费；10月份对外商独资企业不再进行强制性价值鉴定和收取鉴定费；11月，认真落实国家计委、财政部第二批降费规定，将检验检疫收费再次减少了1/3。全年共减少收费约10亿元。

认真落实“收支两条线”要求，从强化制度管理入手，进一步规范了检验检疫行政事业性收费行为。废止了原“三检”机构地方性收费项目和标准，实行了公开收费标准、公布监督举报电话、凭《收费许可证》收费、收支分离、罚缴分离的做法，加大了对重复收费、不检验检疫就收费等违法行为的处罚力度。

坚持既把关，又服务的方针，突破国外技术壁垒，使我国禽肉进入瑞士市场，为恢复对欧盟禽肉出口和扩大水产品出口创造了条件。促使俄罗斯、新加坡解除了对进口我国肉类的禁令。恢复了我国观赏鱼出口英国、澳大利亚，实现了对加拿大、美国、澳大利亚鸭梨的出口，扩大了对美国、日本的荔枝出口。研究成功了稻草无害化消毒处理方法，使日本政府解除了中国稻草输日禁令。同时，努力改进作风，推行了简化手续、提高效率、方便进出的多项服务措施，受到了外经贸企业的欢迎。此外，国家检验检疫局还成功组织了“中国进出口化妆品精品博览会”和“中国进出口质量认证成果展示会”，也收到了较好效果。

五、国际合作与交流进一步扩大

加强了与北美、欧洲、亚洲等有关国家检验检疫部门和国外重要检验检疫机构的联系。国家检验检疫局成功组织了中荷SPS研讨会和SPS国际研讨会等重要外事活动；与国外政府部门和有关机构签定了一批认证和动植物检疫合作协议、议定书及备忘录；与喀麦隆签定了出口商品装船前检验协议。这些成果，都有效配合了“市场多元化”外经贸战略的实施。

为配合我“入世”谈判，与美国有关部门就美国小麦、柑橘输华植物检疫议定书进行了9轮会谈。在此过程中，积极采取务实措施，为“中美农业合作协议》的签定做出了贡献。

1999年中国旅游业再创历史新高峰

国家旅游局局长　何光暐

1999年，旅游全行业认真贯彻中央经济工作会议精神，大力培育和发展旅游业这个新的经济增长点，旅游业取得了历史最好成绩。

一、1999年旅游业发展概况

1. 入境旅游

入境旅游走出亚洲金融危机的阴影，接待旅游者和旅游外汇收入提前实现了“九五”计划目标。

(1) 入境旅游接待：1999年全国入境旅游接待7279.56万人次，增长14.7%。其中：外国人843.23万人次，增长18.6%；港澳同胞6167.15万人次，增长14.1%；台湾同胞258.46万人次，增长18.9%。过夜旅游者2704.7万人次，增长7.9%，由上年位居世界第6位上升至第5位。其中，外国人671.96万人次，增长20.0%；港澳同胞1796.15万人次，增长3.2%；台湾同胞225.73万人次，增长15.6%。

(2) 旅游外汇收入：全国旅游外汇收入140.99亿美元，增长11.9%，仍居世界第7位，旅游外汇收入相当于当年中国外贸出口创汇的7.2%。

(3) 主要客源市场：1999年外国旅华市场摆脱了亚洲金融危机的影响，洲内市场大幅度反弹，洲际市场持续增长，创造了历史最高水平。亚洲客源市场入境增长23.38%，占入境外国人总数的60.7%，比上年增加2.5个百分点。其中，韩国、印尼、泰国、马来西亚等市场增幅均在24%以上，日本客源增长18.0%。欧洲、美洲、大洋洲客源分别增长15.2%、8.2%、8.4%，其中，俄罗斯、德国、法国增幅分别达20.4%、13.4%、12.7%。港澳台入境人数继续保持了两位数的增长，其中，港澳客源入境增长14.05%，台湾客源入境增长18.9%。

2. 国内旅游

1999年国内旅游持续升温，假日经济的特点突出，表现为旺季提前、热点普遍、高潮迭起，出游爆增。

(1) 出游人数：全年出游人数达7.19亿人次，增长3.6%。其中：城镇居民2.84亿人次，农民4.34亿人次。其中，由旅行社承接的城镇游客2274.72万人次（包括一日游游客），占城镇旅游总数的8.0%。

(2) 旅游收入：全年旅游收入2831.92亿元人民币，比上年增长18.4%。国内旅游占旅游总收入的比重达70.8%，比上年提高1.3个百分点。其中：城镇居民旅游消费1748.23亿元，农民旅游消费1083.69亿元。

(3) 人均花费：国内旅游出游人均花费394.00元，比上年增长14.4%。其中：城镇居民国内旅游出游人均花费614.80元，农村农民国内旅游出游人均花费249.50元。

3. 出境旅游

1999年正式开办了中国公民赴澳大利亚、新西兰的自费出国旅游，扩大了赴香港、澳门地区旅游的规模。全年出境旅游923.24万人次，增长9.6%。其中：因公出境496.63万人次，下降5.1%；因私出境426.61万人次，增长33.7%。由旅行社组织出境的有249.56万人次，增长37.8%，出境旅游目的地依次是：香港、澳门、泰国、缅甸、越南、新加坡、马来西亚、俄罗斯、朝鲜、菲律宾。

4. 旅游业产业规模和从业人员

到1999年末，全国共有各类旅游企事业单位25万个，其中旅游住宿设施23.7万个（包括：旅游涉外饭店0.70万个，社会旅馆7.29万个，个体旅馆15.7万个）；旅行社7326个，增长17.7%；旅游车船公司和主要旅游景点等其他旅游企业4882个，增长14.5%。全行业共拥有固定资产原值5331.43亿元，其中：旅游住宿设施占91.1%（旅游涉外饭店占44.4%，社会旅馆占46.7%），旅行社占1.5%，旅游车船公司和主要旅游景点等其他企事业单位占7.4%。旅游业直接从业人员511.69万人，其中：旅游住宿设施占85.8%（旅游涉外饭店占23.8%，社会旅馆55.6%，个体旅馆6.4%），旅行社占2.1%，旅游车船公司和旅游景点等其他企事业单位占12.1%。

二、1999年主要工作成绩

1999年是全国各地认真贯彻中央经济工作会议精神、大力培育和发展旅游业这个新的经济增长点的第一年。今年旅游工作主要有以下特点：

1. 加快培育新增长点的新措施和新办法不断出台。四川、陕西、广西等省区市的党政主要领导深入进行调研和现场办公，解决了影响旅游业发展的系列问题；广东、江苏率先研究实施国民旅游计划；浙江、北京等省市探索实施旅游信贷制度，福建争取了减轻旅游企业负担的具体措施，安徽对旅游商品开发实行鼓励政策，成都等地制定了旅游创汇奖励办法。国家计委首次把旅游项目列入国债项目，国家经贸委正在制定旅游产业政策，财政部尽力增加对旅游业发展的财政支持，国务院扶贫办同意在宁夏六盘山试办旅游扶贫示范区。上述情况，反映了支持大旅游发展的新局面进一步形成。

2. 入境旅游全面增长。各级旅游局抓住亚洲经济逐渐复苏的契机，针对周边市场、欧美市场和其他市场的特点，组织旅游企业，大力开展对外促销工作，积极参加各类国际性旅游展示会、交易会和博览会，取得了良好效果，使我国入境旅游市场实现了全面增长。1998年一度有所下降的外国旅华市场，1999年突破了800万人次大关，比历史最高年份的1997年还高出13%。

3. 国内旅游进一步升温。在政府部门、旅游企业和消费时尚的引导下，国内旅游市场加快发育，规模迅速扩张，潜力充分显现。春节期间，国内旅游高达1800万人次，旅游花费约140亿元；“五一”期间，全国各大景区景点普遍火爆；暑季期间，国内旅游约1.29亿人次，旅游花费约445亿元；国庆期间，国内旅游为4000万人次，旅游花费约141亿元。这四个“黄金时段”形成的国内旅游高峰，有力地拓展了相关各业的市场，显示了旅游业这个新增长点的旺盛生命力和关联带动作用。

4.’99生态环境游影响深远。昆明世界园艺博览会作为'99中国生态环境游的重头戏，在各有关方面的全力支持配合下，取得了圆满成功，共吸引国际国内游客940万人次，实现了预定目标，开创了我国大型会展旅游的成功范例。西南六省区市以此为契机，推出“世界遗产系列游”、“世界屋脊探秘游”、“云贵高原之旅”、“巴蜀经典之旅”等系列产品，初步树立了“西南生态旅游”的区域形象。广东等地开发了农业旅游、山区旅游、海洋旅游等多个主题的生态旅游产品，黑龙江等地丰富了冰雪旅游、森林旅游的内涵，其它地区也紧扣“人与自然和谐共处”这个主题，推出了一大批生态旅游新产品。

5. 行业管理工作继续强化。创建“中国优秀旅游城市”的工作不断走向深入，首批54个优秀旅游城市普遍开展了“二次创优”，又有127个城市参加了第二批创建活动；创建文明示范景区的工作继续扩大，云南石林、福建武夷山、深圳华侨城等10个景区被中央文明办、国家旅游局和建设部联合评定为第二批全国文明风景旅游区示范点；上海市在建立旅游咨询中心方面的探索，广东省在发展青年旅舍方面的探索，无锡、南京、苏州、桂林、西安等地在加强城市“一日游”管理方面的探索，都取得了良好效果。

6. 旅游法制建设继续推进。全行业以学习贯彻国务院颁布的《导游人员管理条例》和国务院召开的依法行政工作会议精神为契机，大力开展宣贯活动，强化市场管理，依法治旅、依法行政取得了新进展；北京、湖北、安徽、内蒙古、贵州等省（区、市）出台了《旅游业管理条例》，山西、内蒙古作出了《关于加快旅游业发展的决定》，江苏制定了《环太湖地区旅游开发管理暂行办法》，四川出台了《旅游投诉暂行规定》，海南发布了《旅游分级管理办法》，旅游法制建设在各地区得到了普遍重视和加强。

7. 业内创新蔚然成风。国家旅游局首次组团参加了中国投资贸易洽谈会，共签约117个，协议额3.6亿美元；国家旅游局在西北和西南地区分别召开的“十五”规划思路座谈会，集思广益，大体理清了西部各省（区、市）旅游业跨世纪大发展的思路，为编制好全国和各地的旅游规划打下了基础；北京在日本、英国开展的“流动的紫禁城”公众促销，文化特色突出，冲击力强，效果显著；浙江省推行实施的“绿色饭店”行动，适应了环境保护和可持续发展的潮流，具有推广价值；河南省对旅游景区（点）实施旅游业务经营许可证制度，在旅游市场管理方面是个新探索；广西、西安开展的“大篷车”巡回促销，在国内旅游促销方面是个创举；京、沪、穗等地旅游企业积极介入旅游电子商务经营，参与国际专业组织的促销网络，拓展了旅游业现代化经营的手段。

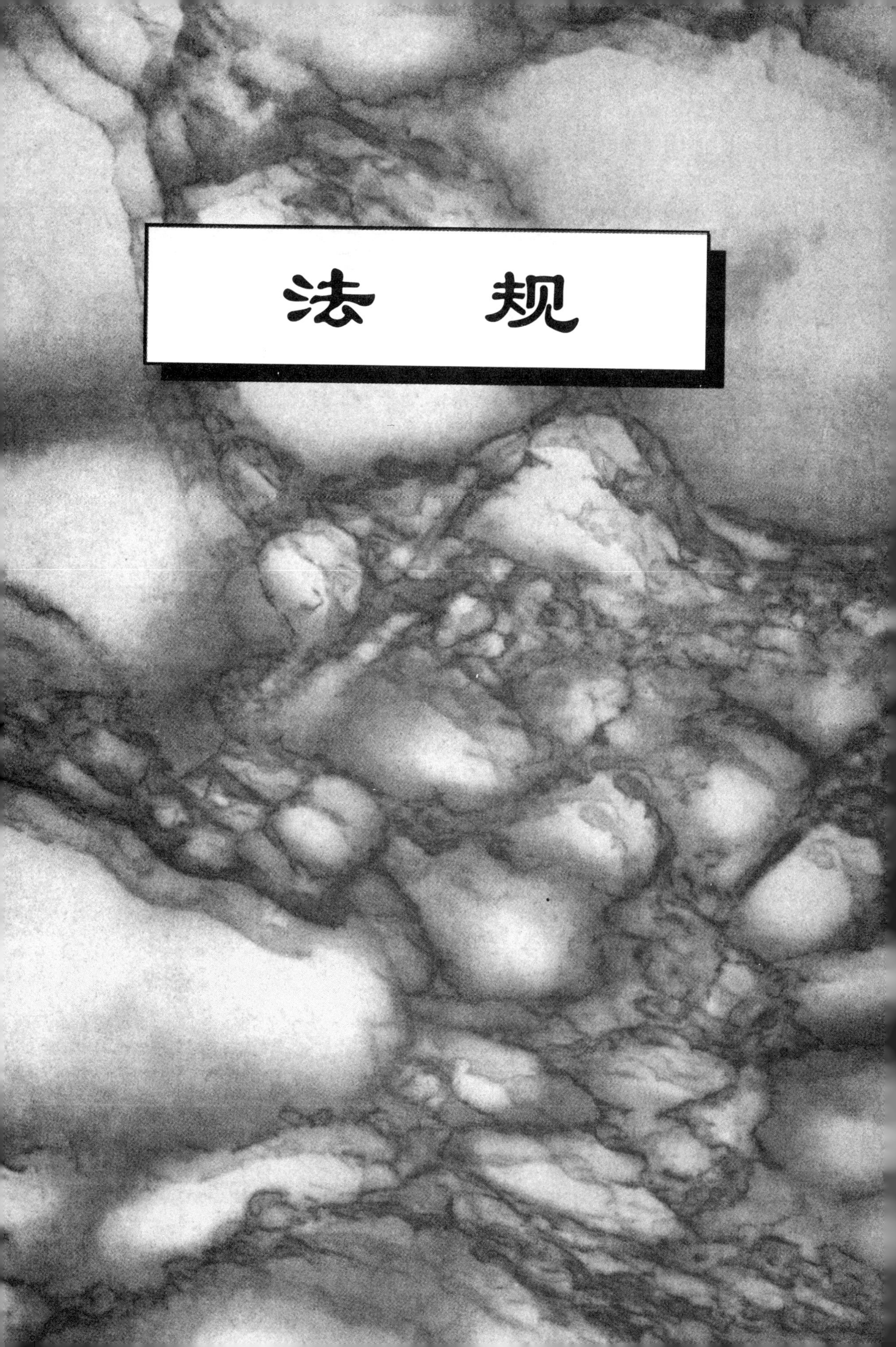

法 规

综　　合

对外贸易经济合作部关于印发《外经贸行业标准化管理办法》的通知

〔1999〕外经贸技发第103号
1999年2月25日

各省、自治区、直辖市及计划单列市外经贸委（厅、局）、本部各直属单位，各商会、协会、学会：

为加强对外经济贸易领域中的标准化工作，根据《中华人民共和国标准化法》及《中华人民共和国标准化法实施条例》的有关规定，结合外经贸行业的实际情况，我部制定了《外经贸行业标准化管理办法》。现将《外经贸行业标准化管理办法》印发给你们，请遵照执行。

附件：如文

附　件

外经贸行业标准化管理办法

第一章　总　　则

第一条　为加强对外经济贸易领域中的标准化工作，根据《中华人民共和国标准化法》和《中华人民共和国标准化法实施条例》，制定本办法。

第二条　本办法适用于外经贸行业标准化工作。

外经贸行业标准化工作包括：建立外经贸行业标准化管理体系；制定、实施国家标准和外经贸行业标准；在外经贸活动中组织采用国际标准；监督外经贸行业中的标准实施情况。

第二章　组织机构和职能

第三条　对外贸易经济合作部（以下简称“外经贸部”）标准化主管部门负责管理全国外经贸行业标准化工作，并具体组织本办法的实施。履行以下职责：

一、贯彻国家有关标准化的法律、法规、方针、政策；

二、制定外经贸标准化工作的中长期规划和年度计划，组织和协调全国外经贸行业的标准化工作；

三、根据国际贸易发展的需要，调整公布《实施检验的进出口商品种类表》等标准化法规；组织制定、修订、审查与外经贸工作有关的国家标准；组织制定、修订、审查和发布外经贸行业标准；

四、在外经贸活动中，组织实施国家标准和行业标准，对标准实施情况进行监督检查，组织国家标准、行业标准的宣传贯彻工作；

五、编制标准化工作人员培训规划并组织实施；

六、组织开展外经贸领域中的国际标准化工作，管理与国际贸易活动相关的国际标准的制定和实施工作；组织参加国内外标准化会议；

七、负责对外经贸专业标准化技术委员会进行管理，并对标准化技术归口单位进行业务指导；

八、监督重大引进项目的标准化审查工作。

第四条 省、自治区、直辖市外经贸主管部门管理其管辖区域内的标准化工作，其职责如下：

一、在外经贸部标准化主管部门的领导下，贯彻执行有关标准化的法律、法规、方针、政策；

二、受外经贸部标准化主管部门的委托，在本地区组织实施标准，并监督检查；

三、受外经贸部标准化主管部门的委托，组织本地区外经贸企、事业单位的标准化人员、内部审核员的培训、管理；

四、指导协调各单位的标准化工作，向外经贸部标准化主管部门汇报标准化工作情况。

第五条 进出口商会、外经贸专业标准化技术委员会和技术归口单位的任务是：

一、协助外经贸部标准化主管部门处理标准审查过程中出现的技术争议问题；

二、承担和组织该专业领域国家标准和行业标准的起草与研究工作；

三、负责和组织该专业领域国际标准和国外标准的分析、研究、验证及采用建议等工作；

四、开展该专业领域的基础标准、标准化理论、标准技术与方法等的研究工作；

五、参与本专业标准体系的编制及标准的复审工作；

六、负责国际标准化组织中对口的技术委员会的联系工作；

七、宣传贯彻该专业领域的标准，了解和掌握标准实施情况，负责该专业领域标准的解释工作。

第六条 外经贸企、事业单位应根据需要设置标准化工作机构，配备专、兼职标准化工作人员，并由主管负责人领导本单位的标准化工作。该机构的任务是：

一、贯彻各级标准，负责本单位标准化的普及工作；

二、负责制定本企业标准，并建立相应的企业标准体系；

三、督促、检查企业实施标准的情况；

四、负责向有关上级标准化主管部门提供标准的实施情况；

五、负责企业实施标准的效果评价；

六、承担上级部门委托的标准化工作任务；

七、参与研制新产品、改进产品、技术改造和技术引进中的标准化工作，提出标准化要求，进行标准化审查；

八、收集与管理同本单位工作有关的标准文献资料，做好标准信息咨询服务工作。

第三章 标准的制定、审批和发布

第七条 在外经贸领域需要统一的下列技术、贸易和管理事项，应当制定国家标准，（含标准样品的制作）：

一、外经贸领域需要统一、协调的通用术语、符号、代号（含代码）、电子数据据传输报文、制图方法等技术语言和格式要求；

二、外经贸活动中，为简化贸易程序，有必要进行统一、规范的各类单证；

三、关于涉及安全卫生、劳动保护、环境保护的出口产品的生产、包装、贮存、运输和使用等事项；

四、国家需要控制的重要产品的技术要求。主要包括国家颁发进出口许可证的商品、对进出口贸易有重大影响的需要统一的、通用的技术要求；

五、外经贸活动中通用的管理技术、工作程序；

六、外经贸标准体系表中的其他标准项目。

第八条 在外经贸活动中，有完全对应的国际标准及国外先进标准，可以制定为国家标准；技术要求达不到国际一般水平的，不得制定为国家标准；对没有相应的国家标准而又需要在全国外经贸行业统一的技术和管理要求，可制定外经贸行业标准。

第九条 涉及安全卫生、劳动保护、环境保护的外经贸标准（包括国家标准和行业标准）属于强制性标准；强制性标准以外的其他标准均属于推荐性标准。

第十条 在企、事业单位内部需要统一的外经贸技术和管理要求，除可采用（或必须采用）国际标准、国家标准和行业标准外，也可由企、事业单位制定符合本单位需要的企业标准。

第十一条 在制定与外经贸活动相关的国家标准、行业标准和企业标准过程中，要积极采用国际标准和国外先进标准，并遵守有关基础标准和通用国家标准的规定。

第十二条 按国家规定，在国家标准的制定、修订过程中，由国务院标准化行政主管部门拨给一定的补助费。

第十三条 国家标准和行业标准的制定，一般由标准起草单位组织起草工作组，根据外经贸部标准制定立项通知的要求，按期完成标准制定任务。涉及面广、意义重大的标准，应由外经贸部标准化主管部门统一组织，并监督完成标准制定任务。

第十四条 国家标准及行业标准制定、修订计划下达后，必须按计划完成。确需调整的项目需要向外经贸部提出书面报告，并填写项目调整申请表，不能完成的项目应予撤销，并扣回补助经费和上交已取得的工作成果。

第十五条 重大国家标准、行业标准的制定、修订，在形成送审稿前，标准起草工作组必须通过多种形式进行调研，并广泛征求意见。

第十六条 凡已满五年标龄的标准，专业标准化技术委员会和归口单位必须按时组织复审并将复审结果报外经贸部。无归口单位的标准由外经贸部组织复审。复审工作不列入年度计划，由各单位参照《国家标准管理办法》的要求自行组织。

第十七条 涉及外经贸活动的国家标准由外经贸部组织制定和申报；行业标准由外经贸部审批、编号、发布；企业标准由企业法人代表和其授权的主管领导审批、编号、发布。

第十八条 国家标准及行业标准出版后，发现个别技术内容存在问题，并必须进行修改时，由标准起草单位提出修改意见，经该专业标准化技术委员会或技术归口单位审核，报外经贸部，按有关规定审批发布。

第四章 标准的实施与监督

第十九条 外经贸标准化管理机构，按照分工管辖范围，依据有关法律、法规，对强制性国家标准、行业标准、以及备案的企业产品标准和已被采用的推荐性标准等实施情况进行监督检查与处理。

第二十条 通过以下方式组织标准的实施与监督工作：

一、企业标准备案；

二、组织、引导企业开展标准体系认可、认证工作；

三、对采用国际标准和国外先进标准的企、事业单位，组织开展验收活动；

四、在研制新产品、改进老产品、技术改造（包括技术引进和设备进口）等工作中，按规定进行适用标准的审查；

五、有计划地对标准实施情况进行监督检查；

六、对标准化管理干部进行培训，提高其组织、协调标准化活动的能力，处理好各方面的关系，以做好各级各类标准的实施工作。

第二十一条 各有关部门和单位在组织外经贸行业标准实施、监督工作中，应就标准的执行情况及时向外经贸部提出建议和意见。

第五章 附　　则

第二十二条 本办法由外经贸部负责解释。

第二十三条 本办法自发布之日起施行。

科学技术部　对外贸易经济合作部
《科技兴贸行动计划》

国科发计字〔1999〕219号

1999年6月

科技兴贸是我国外经贸工作的基本战略。在知识经济迅猛发展、世界经济一体化、亚洲金融危机影响加深、国际经济技术竞争更加激烈的大环境下，制定科技兴贸行动计划，重点促进高技术产品出口，对加快科技成果转化，提高出口商品竞争力，保证出口持续稳定增长，建立我国21世纪的国际竞争优势具有深远的战略意义。

一、计划宗旨与目标

科技兴贸行动计划（简称："兴贸计划"）的宗旨是贯彻落实科教兴国战略，发挥科技及产业优势，扩大我国高技术产品出口，促进我国从外贸大国向外贸强国转变，使外贸出口持续、稳定、快速增长。

计划目标是在我国优势技术领域培育一批国际竞争力强、附加值高、出口规模较大的高技术出口产品和企业，使我国高技术产品出口额在现有基础上以年递增30%的比例增长，力争在2002年高技术产品出口额占外贸出口总额的比重从现在的6%提高到14%。

科技兴贸行动计划是指导性计划，由外经贸部和科技部共同组织实施。

二、计划主体内容

1. 确定和培育高技术出口产品

以国际市场为导向，在我国高技术产品优势技术领域和高技术渗透较好的传统领域选择一批有市场竞争能力、附加值高、对开辟和拓展我国出口市场有重大作用的高技术产品，通过定产品、定企业、定市场、定目标、定时间，创造有利的出口条件，力争在短期内形成较大的出口规模。

1999年先在信息、生物医药、新材料（资源高附加值）、消费类电子和家电等五个行业和领域各优选若干产品作为第一批重点出口产品，给予政策或其他支持。

2. 培育和建立高技术产品出口基地

选择有条件的国家级高新技术产业开发区，培育和建立国家高技术产品出口基地，发挥其高新技术产业集中、信息快、机制活、人才多等有利条件，充分利用国家赋予园区的有关政策，积极引导园区内的企业开拓国际市场，促进高技术产品的出口，加快园区的国际化进程。

选择一批技术开发能力强、出口市场前景良好的高新技术企业、科研院所，培育和建立国家高技术产品出口产业基地，使之成为促进高技术产品出口的中坚力量。具体目标是：

(1) 三年内在信息、生物医药、新材料（资源高附加值）、消费类电子和家电五个行业和领域分批培育和建立一批国家高技术产品出口基地。

(2) 高技术产品出口基地的产品出口有较快增长，在短期内形成有较大出口规模的主导产品，并拥有出口产品的知识产权。

(3) 二至三年内形成相对稳定的出口市场和出口渠道。

(4) 形成高技术出口产品开发能力，推动科技成果转化，带动相关产业的发展。

(5) 组织一批高技术产品出口基地企业通过ISO系列国际标准认证及高技术产品出口必需的其他国际标准认证。

3. 确定一批高技术产品出口重点城市

选择部分高技术产品出口基础较好的城市作为高技术产品出口重点城市。重点城市政府应加强本市的科贸结合，创造支持高技术产品出口的有利条件与环境。优化和调整外贸出口结构，推动区域经济的发展，对全国高技术产品出口工作起引导示范作用。

4. 建立高技术产品出口市场信息服务体系

为开拓高技术产品出口市场，建立适应高技术产品出口特点的市场信息服务体系。

(1) 培育和建立国家技术贸易信息中心，其中设立高技术产品出口咨询服务中介机构。

(2) 发展出口市场信息网络。

国家技术贸易信息中心与外经贸部电子贸易信息网、国家科技信息网等国内外主要信息网以及省市外经贸委、科委、国家高新技术产业开发园区网站联网。高技术产品出口企业和科研院所可享受上网优惠服务。

(3) 发挥我国经贸、科技驻外机构的作用，通过各种形式，向国内外提供国际技术贸易市场需求信息，当前重点向国内外提供高技术产品供求信息。

(4) 积极利用香港、澳门的国际市场渠道，通过中介服务、合资合作等多种合作形式开拓高技术产品出口市场。

5. 建立高技术产品海外生产、加工与销售网络

鼓励有条件的企业和科研院所在国外建立高技术产品生产加工基地、销售网络和售后服务网，并可开展国内高技术产品出口代理业务。

鼓励在重点出口国家和地区建立高技术产品出口代办处和服务中心，为国内企业和科研院所开拓国际市场和代理出口。

建立国外高技术产品生产加工基地、销售网络和售后服务网络，应充分发挥海外华人和留学生的专业知识与信息等优势，利用市场机制，调动他们为我国高技术产品出口服务的积极性，形成包括海外华人和留学生在内的高技术产品出口经纪人队伍。

6. 加强高技术产品出口队伍的建设

加强国际市场开拓队伍的建设，建立一支以企业家为主，具有创业精神的高技术产品国际市场开拓队伍。同时，利用市场机制，吸纳各方力量，充分发挥从事外事、外贸和科技工作的离岗、退休人员的专长和经验，为促进高技术产品市场开拓服务。

举办各种类型的培训班，使有外贸权的科研院所、高技术产品出口基地和出口企业的外贸人员掌握所需的国际技术贸易法律法规、国际惯例、贸易规则、国家有关政策法规知识和电子贸易等先进贸易手段，培养一批懂技术、懂外贸的复合型技贸人才。

建立有效的分配制度，提高市场信息搜集与分析人员、技术开发人员、市场推销人员、售后服务人员等在高技术产品出口收益中的分配比例，以调动各类人员促进高技术产品出口的积极性和创造性。

7. 组织国际高新技术成果交易会

为推动我国高新技术产业的发展，促进高技术产品出口，加强国际间技术贸易和高新技术成果的交流，国家将在国内外组织有关的展览洽谈活动。

(1) 外经贸部、科技部、信息产业部、中国科学院和深圳市政府自 1999 年起每年秋季在深圳举办中国国际高新技术成果交易会。

(2) 外经贸部、科技部和北京市政府每年在北京举办北京高新技术产业国际周。

(3) 外经贸部、科技部和有关部门结合目标市场的开拓工作，组织企业和科研院所到国外举办大型或专业性的中国高技术产品展销会。

三、计划支撑条件和措施

1. 向高技术产品出口科研院所和企业提高出口担保和出口保险

外经贸部、科技部会同有关银行和保险公司共同认定一批资信好的高技术产品出口企业和科研院所，核定一定的授信额度，在授信额度内开具投标保函、履约保函，预付金保函不需资产抵押。人保(集团) 公司为认定企业和科研院所的高技术产品出口提供出口担保和出口保险。

2. 集成现有资源支持高技术产品出口

科技部有关科技计划和科技型中小企业技术创新基金在项目选项、项目目标和资金配置上向高技术出口产品的研究开发倾斜。

外贸发展基金和机电产品出口发展基金在资金配置上向高技术产品出口倾斜。

援外工作和国际科技合作项目要与高技术产品出口相结合。

3. 适时调整和发布《中国高技术产品出口目录》

为配合鼓励高技术产品出口政策的实施，适应我国高技术产品出口发展形势的需要，适时对现行的《中国高技术产品出口目录》进行调整和发布。

4. 编辑出版《技术出口政策法规文件汇编》

组织对国家现行有关技术出口的政策法规进行整理、汇编，进一步促进现行技术出口鼓励政策的贯彻落实。

5. 进一步完善促进高技术产品出口的政策环境

加强促进高技术产品出口的政策研究，根据高技术产品出口发展适时制定相应的政策，对高技术产品出口重点城市和高技术产品出口基地给予相应的政策支持，并鼓励民营企业积极开拓国际市场。

四、计划的组织与管理

1. 建立外经贸部、科技部推动高技术产品出口联席会议制度

外经贸部领导和科技部领导定期召开两部推动高技术产品出口联席会议，确定高技术产品出口的发展战略、工作方针和任务，指导科技兴贸行动计划的编制和实施。

2. 成立科技兴贸行动计划联合办公室

由科技部、外经贸部有关司组成科技兴贸行动计划联合办公室，组织编制和实施科技兴贸行动计划。

3. 外经贸部、科技部分别成立科技兴贸小组

为制定和实施科技兴贸行动计划，外经贸部、科技部分别成立由部内有关单位参加的科技兴贸小组。

对外贸易

对外贸易经济合作部
关于对国家确定的1000家重点企业实行
进出口经营权登记备案制的通知

〔1998〕外经贸政发第829号

国务院各部委、各直属机构、办事机构、直属事业单位，各省、自治区、直辖市及计划单列市外经贸委（厅、局）：

外贸经营权由审批制向依法登记制过渡是我国外贸经营体制改革的一项重要内容。经国务院批准，从1997年开始，对五个经济特区内的生产企业自营进出口权已试行登记制，效果良好。根据中共中央关于"积极推进大中型生产企业实行自营出口"的指示精神，经国务院办公厅批准，对国家确定的1000家重点企业实行进出口经营权登记备案制。现就有关事项通知如下：

一、凡属国家确定的1000家重点企业（以下简称千家企业）均可根据本通知的规定申请登记（国家重点联系企业进出口经营权登记证书的格式详见附件）。

二、千家企业中的国务院各部门所属企业，直接向外经贸部申请登记。

三、千家企业中的地方所属企业，直接向所在省、自治区、直辖市及计划单列市外经贸主管部门申请登记。

四、千家企业申请登记须提交下列文件：

（一）企业的书面申请（包括国家重点联系企业进出口经营权登记证书的有关内容）；

（二）企业法人营业执照（复印件）；

（三）申请的进出口商品目录；

（四）如申请企业为生产性集团公司，需提供集团批准文件、成员企业名单。

五、外经贸部及各省、自治区、直辖市及计划单列市外经贸主管部门须在15个工作日内对千家企业的进出口经营权予以登记，并颁发《国家重点联系企业进出口经营权登记证书》。企业凭该证书到海关、出入境检验检疫、外汇、工商、税务等管理部门办理有关手续后，向外经贸部或所在省、自治区、直辖市及计划单列市外经贸主管部门申领《中华人民共和国进出口企业资格证书》。即可开展进出口业务。

六、千家企业的进出口经营范围：

（一）非生产性企业的进出口经营范围，按照外贸公司的进出口经营范围核定，即：

1. 自营和代理除国家组织统一联合经营的出口商品和国家实行核定公司经营的进口商品以外的其他商品和技术的进出口业务（不另附进出口商品目录）；

2. 经营进料加工和"三来一补"业务；

3. 经营对销贸易和转口贸易。

（二）生产性企业的进出口经营范围，按照自营进出口生产企业的进出口经营范围核定，即：

1. 经营本企业和成员企业自产产品的出口业务（经营国家组织统一联合经营的出口商品需专案上报审批）；

2. 经营本企业和成员企业生产所需的机械设备、零配件、原辅材料的进口业务（经营国家实行核定公司经营的进口商品需专案上报审批）；

3. 加工贸易和补偿贸易业务。

（三）千家企业的进出口经营范围由外经贸部或省、自治区、直辖市及计划单列市外经贸主管部门核准。

七、千家企业经营进出口业务，必须遵守国家的外经贸政策和有关法律、法规，接受当地外经贸主管部门的指导和监督，并服从有关进出口商会的协调。

八、各地外经贸主管部门须及时将登记情况报外经贸部备案。

特此通知。

附件：国家重点联系企业进出口经营权登记证书（略）

对外贸易经济合作部
关于对全国大型工业企业实行自营
进出口权登记备案制的通知

〔1998〕外经贸政发第953号

1999年1月4日

国务院各部委、各直属机构，各省、自治区、直辖市及计划单列市外经贸委（厅、局）：

为扩大生产企业的自营出口，加快进出口经营权从审批制向登记制过渡，我部决定在对国家千户重点企业实行进出口经营权登记备案制的基础上，进一步扩大登记备案制的适用范围，从1999年1月起对全国大型工业企业实行进出口经营权登记备案制。现将有关事项通知如下：

一、本规定所指全国大型工业企业（以下简称大型企业），系指经国家经贸委、国家计委、国家统计局、财政部、劳动部、人事部等六部委审定认证的大型工业企业。

二、凡属上述大型企业均可根据本通知的规定申请进出口经营权登记（全国大型企业进出口经营权登记证书格式详见附件）。

三、国务院各部门直属的大型企业，在与原主管部门脱钩后，凡移交中央管理的，可直接向外经贸部申请登记。移交地方管理的企业，以及地方所属的大型企业，直接向所在省、自治区、直辖市及计划单列市外经贸主管部门申请进出口经营权登记。

四、大型企业申请登记须提交下列文件：

（一）企业的书面申请（包括全国大型企业进出口经营权登记证书的有关内容）；

（二）国务院六部委公布的全国大型工业企业名单或全国大型工业企业证书；

（三）企业法人营业执照（复印件）；

（四）申请的进出口商品目录；

（五）如申请企业为生产性集团公司，需提供集团批准文件、成员企业名单。

五、外经贸部及各省、自治区、直辖市及计划单列市外经贸主管部门须在15个工作日内对大型企业的进出口经营权予以登记，并颁发《全国大型企业进出口经营权登记证书》。企业凭该证书到海关、出入境检验检疫、外汇、工商、税务等管理部门办理有关手续后，向外经贸部或所在省、自治区、直辖市及计划单列市外经贸主管部门申领《中华人民共和国进出口企业资格证书》，即可开展进出口业务。

六、大型企业的进出口经营范围：

（一）经营本企业和成员企业自产产品的出口业务（经营国家组织统一联合经营的出口商品需专案上报审批）；

（二）经营本企业和成员企业生产所需的机械设备、零配件、原辅材料的进口业务（经营国家实行核定公司经营的进口商品需专案上报审批）；

（三）加工贸易和补偿贸易业务。

大型企业的进出口经营范围由外经贸部或省、自治区、直辖市及计划单列市外经贸主管部门核准。

七、大型企业经营进出口业务，必须遵守国家的外经贸政策和有关法律、法规，接受当地外经贸主管部门的指导和监督，并服从有关进出口商会的协调。

八、各地外经贸主管部门须在企业登记进出口经营权后一个月内将登记情况报外经贸部备案。

特此通知。

附件：全国大型企业进出口经营权登记证书格式（略）

对外贸易经济合作部关于授权各省自治区直辖市计划单列市及各经济特区外经贸主管部门办理地方进出口企业更名等事项的通知

〔1998〕外经贸政发第874号

1999年1月5日

各省、自治区、直辖市及计划单列市外经贸委（厅、局），各经济特区外经贸主管部门：

为适应政府机构改革的需要，进一步转变政府职能，提高办事效率，我部决定授权各省、自治区、直辖市、计划单列市及各经济特区外经贸主管部门办理地方进出口企业更名等事项。现就有关问题通知如下：

一、授权本通知附件所列各地方外经贸主管部门办理本地方进出口企业更名等事项，具体为：

（一）办理地方各类进出口企业（包括有进出口经营权的省地（市）县外贸公司、商业物资企业，自营进出口生产企业和科研院所）的更名手续，并核发《中华人民共和国进出口企业资格证书》。

企业申请办理更名手续应报以下材料：外经贸部赋予进出口经营权的批准文件；工商行政管理部门的名称预先核准书或已更名的法人营业执照；如系内部职工持股改制更名的外贸公司，还应提供外经贸部或省级外经贸主管部门的批准文件；企业及其上级主管部门的申请报告；地方外经贸主管部门认为需要申报的其他材料。

（二）审核地方自营进出口生产企业和科研院所的进出口商品目录。

自营进出口生产企业和科研院所进出口商品目录的核定原则为：出口商品：本企业和科研院所自产产品（必须列明具体出口商品）；进口商品：本企业和科研院所生产和科研所需的原辅材料、机械设备、仪器仪表及零部件。

（三）审核自营进出口生产企业集团的成员企业名单。

申报材料应包括：外经贸部赋予该集团公司进出口经营权的批准文件；县级以上政府批准该集团公司成立的批准文件及核定的成员企业名单；成员企业的营业执照；集团公司及其上级主管部门的申请报告；地方外经贸主管部门认为需要申报的其他材料。

二、各地方外经贸主管部门在办理上述授权事项工作中应注意的事项：

（一）原中央各部委企业在地方设立的进出口企业（已脱钩移交地方的企业除外）的更名暂仍在外经贸部办理，其《中华人民共和国进出口企业资格证书》授权各地方外经贸主管部门凭外经贸部批准文件核发。

（二）各类进出口企业申请经营的进出口商品，如属国家统一联合经营的出口商品和国家核定公司经营的进口商品，仍须报外经贸部批准。

（三）企业申请划转进出口经营权（即进出口权从一个企业划转给另外一个企业）仍须报外经贸部批准。

（四）申请更名的各类进出口企业，如涉及企业所有制由国有和集体经济性质改制为私有经济性质或私有经济成分参股，仍须报外经贸部批准。

（五）生产企业申请成立进出口公司仍须报外经贸部批准。

三、各地方外经贸主管部门要严格按照国家有关规定，规范办理地方各类进出口企业的更名、进出口商品目录和集团公司成员企业的审核工作，并每半年将授权办理的情况汇总报外经贸部。各地方外经贸主管部门未按本通知规定而越权办理的事项，外经贸部有权予以制止和撤销，并终止其办理上述事项的授权。

四、本通知未涉及事宜，仍按原规定办理。

五、本通知由外经贸部负责解释。

六、本通知自发布之日起执行。

特此通知。

附件：如文

附　件

外经贸部授权的各地方外经贸主管部门名单

1. 北京市外经贸主管部门
2. 天津市外经贸主管部门
3. 上海市外经贸主管部门
4. 重庆市外经贸主管部门
5. 黑龙江省外经贸主管部门
6. 吉林省外经贸主管部门
7. 辽宁省外经贸主管部门
8. 内蒙古自治区外经贸主管部门
9. 新疆维吾尔自治区外经贸主管部门
10. 新疆生产建设兵团外经贸主管部门
11. 甘肃省外经贸主管部门
12. 宁夏回族自治区外经贸主管部门
13. 陕西省外经贸主管部门
14. 山西省外经贸主管部门
15. 河北省外经贸主管部门
16. 河南省外经贸主管部门
17. 山东省外经贸主管部门
18. 四川省外经贸主管部门
19. 湖北省外经贸主管部门
20. 湖南省外经贸主管部门
21. 安徽省外经贸主管部门
22. 江西省外经贸主管部门
23. 广西壮族自治区外经贸主管部门
24. 贵州省外经贸主管部门
25. 云南省外经贸主管部门
26. 广东省外经贸主管部门
27. 海南省外经贸主管部门
28. 西藏自治区外经贸主管部门
29. 浙江省外经贸主管部门
30. 江苏省外经贸主管部门
31. 福建省外经贸主管部门
32. 青岛市外经贸主管部门
33. 大连市外经贸主管部门
34. 宁波市外经贸主管部门
35. 厦门市外经贸主管部门
36. 珠海市外经贸主管部门
37. 汕头市外经贸主管部门
38. 深圳市外经贸主管部门

对外贸易经济合作部关于两纱两布出口经营权有关事项的通知

〔1999〕外经贸政审函字第178号

1999年1月25日

国务院各部委，各直属机构，各省、自治区、直辖市及计划单列市外经贸委（厅、局）：

根据我部《关于下达1999年对外贸易出口商品配额的通知》（〔1998〕外经贸管出函字第465号），

从1999年起，取消棉纱等商品出口配额许可证管理，两纱两布中仅保留对棉坯布（对日）实行配额管理。现将两纱两布出口经营权有关事项通知如下：

一、凡进出口经营范围为自营和代理除国家组织统一联合经营的出口商品和国家实行核定公司经营的进口商品以外的其他商品及技术的进出口业务的各类外贸公司，自本通知下发之日起，均可经营两纱两布出口业务，我部不再单独办理两纱两布出口经营权的批准手续。

二、凡我部已赋予进出口经营权，并在进出口商品目录中核定有“纺织”商品的商业、物资和供销社企业，自本通知下发之日起，均可经营两纱两布出口业务。

三、自本通知下发之日起，凡我部已赋予自营进出口权的生产企业，均可自营出口本企业自产的两纱两布，我部不再单独办理两纱两布出口经营权的批准手续。

四、根据《关于下达1999年对外贸易出口商品配额的通知》，对日本棉坯布的出口仍实行配额管理。

特此通知。

中华人民共和国对外贸易经济合作部
关于生产企业成立进出口公司有关问题的通知

〔1999〕外经贸政审函字第383号

1999年3月3日

各省、自治区、直辖市及计划单列市外经贸委（厅、局）：

为鼓励自营出口规模较大的生产企业扩大出口，根据现行规定，年自营出口1000万美元以上的大型自营进出口生产企业，经批准，可成立独立的进出口有限责任公司，经营与本企业产品配套的相关或同类商品的进出口业务。此项政策的实施，对扩大自营进出口生产企业的出口发挥了积极作用。现就该政策在实际操作中的有关问题通知如下：

一、符合条件的自营进出口生产企业是否成立进出口公司，由企业根据自营出口经营需要自主决定。生产企业成立进出口公司后，其自营进出口权即划转给新成立的进出口公司，生产企业自身不再享有自营进出口权。

二、生产企业成立的进出口公司（以下简称生产企业进出口公司）必须由该生产企业全资或控股经营并具有独立法人资格。

三、生产企业进出口公司的对外经营范围：

（一）经营本企业或本企业集团成员企业自产产品及相关技术的出口业务；

（二）经营非本企业自产、但与本企业自产产品配套的相关或同类商品的出口业务（以我部核定的商品类别为限）；

（三）经营本企业或本企业集团成员企业生产、科研所需的原辅材料、机械设备、仪器仪表、零配件及相关技术的进口业务；

（四）经营本企业或本企业集团成员企业的进料加工和“三来一补”业务；

（五）在我部核准的出口商品类别范围内代理本企业或本企业集团成员企业自产产品的出口；

（六）不得代理进口业务。

四、生产企业进出口公司出口经我部核准的出口商品类别范围内的非自产产品，享有与出口自产产品同等的政策。

请你委（厅、局）就这一政策与当地海关、税务等部门联系，以取得支持和配合。实际工作中遇到的问题请及时报外经贸部（发展司）。

特此通知。

对外贸易经济合作部
关于公布第一批列为外经贸部重点支持和
发展的名牌出口商品名单的通知

〔1999〕外经贸政发第247号

1999年4月21日

各省、自治区、直辖市及计划单列市外经贸委（厅、局），国际商报社，各外贸中心，中央管理的外经贸企业，各进出口商会，各驻外经济商务机构：

为进一步贯彻实施以质取胜战略，加快培育和创立高质量、高档次、在国际市场有影响和竞争力的系列化名牌出口商品，提高我国出口商品的国际竞争力，外经贸部决定在全国开展创名牌出口商品活动，并确定“重点支持和发展的名牌出口商品”予以推动。

第一批列为外经贸部“重点支持和发展的名牌出口商品”名单的商品类别包括：家用电器、自行车、摩托车、纺织服装、轻工消费品。经会同有关部门共同研究，第一批名单共33个品牌，现予以公布（具体名单附后），并将有关事项通知如下：

一、对列入“重点支持和发展的名牌出口商品”名单的品牌和企业，外经贸部将采取有效措施给予扶持和鼓励，主要包括：

（一）优先支持以品牌为基础组建出口经营、生产、科研开发一体化的经济实体或集团公司；

（二）优先支持企业在海外开展带料加工业务，设立相应的生产、经营和售后服务项目；

（三）优先安排广交会参展，并为其参加国际著名博览会提供条件；

（四）优先安排企业使用中央外贸发展基金，企业开展广告促销、建立国外销售中心也可申请使用中央外贸发展基金；

（五）对出口属于配额管理的商品，在分配数量上给予倾斜；对实行配额招标管理的商品，放宽企业参加投标的资格；

（六）对出口上述名单中机电产品的企业，优先安排国家专项用于机电出口企业的技术改造贴息贷款；对出口空调机、电冰箱、电视机等机电产品的企业，在相应的进口机电产品指标的分配上予以奖励；

（七）对企业到受援国加工、生产、组装上述名单的产品，优先安排使用优惠贷款和援外合资合作项目基金；援外一般物资，优先安排列入上述名单的商品；

（八）对承包工程项下带动列入上述名单的商品出口的项目，优先办理有关手续，并优先安排借用合作基金；

（九）运用出口信用保险的手段，支持列入上述名单的商品出口。

二、外经贸部将建立与企业的联系制度；驻外经济商务机构要加强对“重点支持和发展的名牌出口商品”的宣传，为这些商品开拓市场，包括对建立营销网点、展览、促销等活动给予支持并提供条件；各进出口商会及有关协会要发挥行业组织的优势，积极协助和推动企业开展创名牌出口商品。

三、对列入“重点支持和发展的名牌出口商品”名单的企业，要把在国际市场创立名牌作为一项战略，贯穿于企业的各项经营活动之中，千方百计扩大出口；坚持质量第一，重合同、守信誉，不断创新、不断提高产品质量档次、不断开拓市场；要加大对创立名牌的投入，提高新产品、高技术产品以及系列化产品开发能力，加强在国际市场的广告宣传；要注重保护名牌，包括重视商标在国外的注册，规范授权经营、授权生产等商标使用许可方面的制度。

四、外经贸部对列入“重点支持和发展的名牌出口商品”实行动态管理，并将对其扩大出口和在国际市场创名牌情况进行考核。

各有关单位和企业有何问题和建议，请及时与外经贸部（发展司）联系。

附件：如文

附　件

第一批列为外经贸部“重点支持和发展的名牌出口商品名单”

（共五类33个品牌）

类　别	品牌（商标）	企业（商标所有者）
家用电器	海尔牌	海尔集团公司
	春兰/星威牌	春兰（集团）公司
	美的牌	美的集团股份有限公司
	长虹牌	四川长虹电子集团公司
	TCL牌	TCL集团有限公司
	科龙牌	广东科龙电器股份有限公司
	康佳牌	康佳股份集团有限公司
	海信牌	海信集团公司
	格力牌	珠海格力集团公司
	熊猫牌	南京熊猫电子集团公司
	格兰仕牌	广东格兰仕企业（集团）公司
	小鸭圣吉奥牌	山东小鸭集团有限责任公司
	小天鹅牌	无锡小天鹅股份有限公司
自行车	永久牌	上海永久进出口有限公司
	凤凰牌	凤凰股份有限公司
摩托车	金城牌	金城集团公司
	轻骑牌	中国轻骑集团
	嘉陵牌	中国嘉陵工业股份有限公司（集团）
	建设牌	建设工业（集团）有限责任公司
服　装	鄂尔多斯牌	内蒙古鄂尔多斯羊绒制品股份有限公司
	鹿王牌	内蒙古鹿王羊绒（集团）公司
	圣雪绒牌	圣雪绒国际企业集团有限公司
	黎明牌	沈阳黎明服装集团
	凯喜雅牌	浙江省丝绸进出口公司
	雅戈尔牌	雅戈尔集团股份有限公司
	名瑞牌	广东名瑞（集团）股份有限公司
	苏豪牌	江苏省丝绸进出口集团股份有限公司
	三枪牌	上海三枪集团有限公司
轻工消费品	双星牌（鞋）	青岛双星集团公司
	英雄牌（笔）	英雄金笔厂
	中华牌（笔）	中国第一铅笔股份有限公司
	铃兰牌（办公文教用品）	安徽轻工进出口股份有限公司
	北极星牌（钟表）	烟台北极星钟表（集团）公司

中华人民共和国对外贸易经济合作部关于调整企业申请进出口经营权的资格条件及加强后期管理有关问题的通知

〔1999〕外经贸政审函字第948号

1999年5月31日

各省、自治区、直辖市及计划单列市外经贸委（厅、局）：

为了加快赋予各类企业进出口经营权，积极鼓励和支持有条件的企业走向国际市场，千方百计扩大出口，我部决定调整各类企业申请进出口经营权的资格条件，同时加强对各类进出口企业的后期管理。现就有关事项通知如下：

一、进一步放宽企业申请进出口经营权的资格条件

（一）省属外贸公司

1. 资格条件：

对省属外贸公司实行公司总量与所在省、自治区、直辖市及计划单列市出口额（以海关统计为准）挂钩的动态管理。具体如下：按照1998年出口额沿海省市每1亿美元核定一家公司、中西部省区每3000万美元核定一家公司的原则，核定各省、自治区、直辖市及计划单列市所属外贸公司总量基数；从1999年起按沿海省市出口额每增加3000万美元、中西部省区出口额每增加1000万美元可增加一家有进出口经营权公司的原则，确定各省、自治区、直辖市及计划单列市所属外贸公司的每年增量。申请进出口经营权的省属外贸公司的注册资本沿海地区公司不得少于500万元人民币，中西部地区公司不得少于300万元人民币，并应注册成立两年以上。凡经工商行政管理部门核查，实收资本年审不到位的，不予办理。

2. 申报材料：

（1）省、自治区、直辖市及计划单列市外经贸委（厅、局）的申请文件；

（2）企业的申请报告和经工商行政管理部门年审的法人营业执照（复印件）；

（3）有限责任公司和股份有限公司应提供工商行政管理部门出具的出资比例和出资者所有制性质的证明材料；

（4）其他需要申报的材料。

（二）地（市）、县所属外贸公司

1. 资格条件：

对地（市）、县所属外贸公司实行公司总量与所在地（市）、县经济总量挂钩的动态管理，即：按国内生产总值沿海地区每10亿元人民币核定一家公司、中西部地区每3亿元人民币核定一家公司的原则分别核定地（市）、县外贸公司总量。申请进出口经营权的地（市）、县外贸公司注册资本沿海地区公司不得少于500万元人民币，中西部地区公司不得少于300万元人民币，并应注册成立两年以上。经工商行政管理部门核查，实收资本年审不到位的，不予办理。

2. 申报材料：

（1）省、自治区、直辖市及计划单列市外经贸委（厅、局）的申请文件；

（2）地（市）、县外经贸主管部门的申请文件〔应包括本地（市）或县所属有进出口经营权的外贸公司数量及名单〕；

（3）本地（市）、县的国内生产总值统计资料〔省级或地（市）级统计部门公开出版的《统计年鉴》或公开发表的本级政府的《政府工作报告》〕；

（4）企业的申请报告和经工商行政管理部门年审的法人营业执照（复印件）；

（5）有限责任公司和股份有限公司应提供工商行政管理部门出具的出资比例和出资者所有制性质证明材料；

（6）其他需要申报的材料。

（三）对外承包劳务公司和有外经权的设计院

1. 资格条件：

(1) 对外承包劳务公司近两年年均对外承包工程营业额在500万美元以上，或年均外派劳务在200人次以上，可申请进出口经营权；

(2) 获对外勘测、咨询、设计和监理经营权一年以上且有可供出口的自产产品的设计院可申请自营进出口权；

(3) 获对外勘测、咨询、设计和监理经营权两年以上且近两年年均营业额300万美元以上、外派劳务100人次以上的设计院可申请进出口经营权。

2. 申报材料：

(1) 省、自治区、直辖市及计划单列市外经贸委（厅、局）的申请文件（国家批准的120家大型试点企业集团或中央大型企业工委管理的企业可直接向外经贸部申报，与部委尚未脱钩的企业通过有关部委申报）；

(2) 企业的申请报告和经工商行政管理部门年审的法人营业执照（复印件），外经贸部赋予该企业外经权的批准文件；

(3) 有限责任公司和股份有限公司应提供工商行政管理部门出具的出资比例和出资者所有制性质的证明材料；

(4) 其他需要申报的材料。

(四) 外贸公司子公司

1. 资格条件：

前一年度出口额超过1亿美元的外贸公司，其全资或控股的子公司可申请进出口经营权。注册资本：沿海地区公司不得少于500万元人民币，中西部地区公司不得少于300万元人民币。申请子公司进出口经营权的外贸公司，其所属子公司的出口额每家不得低于1000万美元。

对实行内部职工持股改制的子公司和中西部地区的外贸公司适当放宽申请条件。

2. 申报材料：

(1) 省、自治区、直辖市及计划单列市外经贸委（厅、局）的申请文件（国家批准的120家大型试点企业集团或中央大型企业工委管理的企业可直接向外经贸部申报，与部委尚未脱钩的企业通过有关部委申报）；

(2) 母公司申请报告（须附母公司所属有进出口经营权的子公司名单）、子公司法人营业执照（复印件）；

(3) 子公司为有限责任公司或股份有限公司的，应提供工商行政管理部门出具的子公司出资比例和出资者所有制性质的证明材料；

(4) 其他需要申报的材料。

(五) 实行自营进出口权登记备案制的生产企业

1. 资格条件：

对国家120家大型试点企业集团、国家确定的1000家重点企业、全国大型工业企业以及上述企业所属生产性成员企业申请自营进出口权均实行登记备案制。

2. 申报材料：详见《关于赋予试点企业集团进出口经营权和对外承包劳务经营权有关事项的通知》（〔1998〕外经贸政发第348号）、《关于对国家确定的1000家重点企业实行进出口经营权登记备案制的通知》（〔1998〕外经贸政发第829号）、《关于对全国大型工业企业实行自营进出口权登记备案制的通知》（〔1998〕外经贸政发第953号）、《关于进出口经营权登记备案制有关事项的补充通知》（〔1999〕外经贸政审函字第538号）。

(六) 生产企业申请成立进出口公司

1. 资格条件：

前一年度自营出口500万美元以上的机电生产企业、前一年度自营出口1000万美元以上的非机电生产企业，可申请成立全资或控股的进出口公司，经营本企业自产产品及与自产产品相关或同类的产品（即非自产产品）出口。

2. 申报材料：

(1) 省、自治区、直辖市及计划单列市外经贸委（厅、局）的申请文件；

(2) 企业的申请报告、企业的进出口企业资格证书及法人营业执照、进出口公司的企业名称预先核准通知书（复印件）；

(3) 海关出具的该企业上一年度自营出口额证明和该企业的海关报关号；

(4) 进出口公司为有限责任公司或股份有限公司的，应提供工商行政管理部门出具的公司出资比例和出资者所有制性质的证明材料；

(5) 其他需要申报的材料。

(七) 实行总量控制管理的经济特区非生产性企业

对经济特区非生产性企业申请进出口经营权仍实行总量控制，同时降低总量核定标准，即：经济特区出口额每增加3000万美元可增加核定一家有进出口经营权的非生产性企业。对经济特区年进出口总额达到2000万美元以上或出口额达到1000万美元以上的实行总量控制管理的非生产性企业，取消经营地域限制。

二、进一步加强对各类进出口企业获权后的管理

通过完善对各类进出口企业实行的进出口企业资格证书年审管理，建立进出口企业动态调整、优胜劣汰的管理制度。

（一）对有违规、走私行为的各类进出口企业，按照对外贸易经济合作部和海关总署联合下发的《对违规、走私企业给予警告、暂停或撤销对外贸易、国际货运代理经营许可行政处罚的暂行规定》（〔1998〕外经贸政发第682号）给予外贸经营许可行政处罚。

（二）对有逃、套汇行为的各类进出口企业，按照对外贸易经济合作部下发的《对外贸易经济合作部对逃、套汇外经贸企业给予行政处罚的暂行规定》（〔1998〕外经贸计财发第713号）给予外贸经营许可行政处罚。

（三）对骗取出口退税的各类进出口企业，参照有关规定给予外贸经营许可行政处罚。

（四）对被兼并、原企业法人资格已注销的各类进出口企业，注销其对外贸易经营许可。

（五）对与外商合资的自营进出口生产企业，注销其作为内资企业享有的自营进出口权，其进出口经营活动纳入外商投资企业管理。

（六）对已按法定程序宣布破产的各类进出口企业，注销其对外贸易经营许可。

（七）对未按规定时间申领进出口企业资格证书或不参加进出口企业资格证书年审的企业，视为自动放弃进出口经营权，注销其对外贸易经营许可。

（八）对获得进出口经营权三年以上，但连续三年自营出口额为零和出口供货额低于50万美元的生产企业或科研院所及连续三年年均出口额低于100万美元或进出口额低于200万美元的有进出口经营权的外贸公司（包括有进出口经营权的商业物资企业），撤销其对外贸易经营许可。

（九）对有商标侵权行为的各类进出口企业，给予以下外贸经营许可行政处罚：因商标侵权行为被海关或工商行政管理等部门处罚，但尚未构成犯罪的，给予暂停一年进出口经营权的处罚；对发生严重侵权行为、给商标所有人造成重大经济损失并经司法部门认定或仲裁机构裁定的，给予撤销对外贸易经营许可行政处罚。

（十）对经查实有非法倒卖配额许可证行为的各类进出口企业，视情节轻重给予警告、暂停、取消该商品配额使用权，直至撤销其对外贸易经营许可的行政处罚。

（十一）对本企业出口产品被控倾销而不参加应诉的各类进出口企业，根据外经贸部《关于鼓励和督促企业参加国外反倾销案件应诉的若干规定》（〔1999〕外经贸法字第3号）的有关条款给予相应的对外贸易经营许可行政处罚。

（十二）对经营伪劣商品出口的各类进出口企业，经海关、工商行政管理部门、检验检疫部门或司法部门认定后，视情节轻重，给予对外贸易经营许可行政处罚，其中：首次出口伪劣商品，出口额在50万美元以下的，给予警告行政处罚；出口额在50万美元以上、100万美元以下的，给予暂停出口经营许可一年的处罚；对出口伪劣商品100万美元以上，或受到处罚后两年内仍有出口伪劣商品行为的，给予撤销对外贸易经营许可行政处罚。对经营检验检疫不合格产品出口的，视情节轻重，在检验检疫部门处罚的基础上，给予相应的对外贸易经营许可行政处罚。

（十三）对伪报进出口商品名称，逃避进出口许可证管理的进出口企业，给予撤销对外贸易经营许可行政处罚。

（十四）被撤销对外贸易经营许可的各类进出口企业，在自被撤销之日起两年内不得以任何方式重新申请对外贸易经营许可。

特此函告。

对外贸易经济合作部 关于印发《关于出口商品配额编报、下达和组织实施暂行办法的实施细则》的通知

〔1998〕外经贸管发第980号
1999年1月2日

各省、自治区、直辖市及计划单列市外经贸委（厅、局），各部委直属公司：

为具体实施我部印发的《关于出口商品配额编报、下达和组织实施的暂行办法》(〔1998〕外经贸管发第732号)，建立科学、规范、动态、高效的出口商品配额管理体制，现将《关于出口商品配额编报、下达和组织实施暂行办法的实施细则》印发给你们，请遵照执行。

附件：《关于出口商品配额编报、下达和组织实施暂行办法的实施细则》

附　件

关于出口商品配额编报、下达和组织实施暂行办法的实施细则

第一章　总　　则

第一条　为实施《对外贸易经济合作部关于出口商品配额编报、下达和组织实施的暂行办法》(以下简称《办法》)，进一步推动外经贸领域“两个根本性转变”，建立科学、规范、动态、高效的出口商品配额管理体制，特制定本细则。

第二章　出口配额管理商品的确定

第二条　外经贸部按照国民经济和对外贸易发展战略，根据国内外市场的供需情况，制订、调整实行出口配额管理商品的目录，定期公布。

第三条　出口配额管理商品的范围

(一) 关系国计民生的重要初级农副产品和工业原材料；

(二) 国内供应短缺或不可再生的资源性商品；

(三) 在国际市场或某一市场占主导地位，输出国家或地区的市场容量有限，需要限制出口的重要商品；

(四) 根据我国缔结的双边或多边国际条约、协定、协议，需要限制出口的商品。

第三章　出口商品配额总量的确定和分配

第四条　外经贸部按照《办法》确定的程序和规则，根据出口商品的国内资源、国际市场容量、市场占有率以及国内外市场的供求等情况，本着维护国民经济可持续发展的原则，确定具体商品的年度配额总量。

第五条　外经贸部和各地外经贸主管部门本着“公开、公正、竞争、效益”的原则，从优化出口商品结构、鼓励高附加值、深加工产品出口、规模化经营和提高配额使用率出发，对出口商品配额进行分配。

第六条　配额的分配采取招标（办法另行制

定)、规则化分配等方式进行。

第七条 外经贸部将出口商品配额分配给各省、自治区、直辖市、计划单列市和部委直属公司，具体办法为：

(一) 外经贸部根据国际、国内市场和配额使用情况，参考各地区、各部委直属公司的申请，将商品配额总量按一定比例分成两部分，其中一部分(以下称“A部分”) 分配给有该商品出口实绩的地区和部委直属公司，另一部分 (以下称“B部分”) 分配给没有该商品出口实绩但申请出口的地区和部委直属公司。具体比例视不同商品而定。

(二) 外经贸部根据各地区、各部委直属公司某配额管理商品出口额占全国符合分配标准的地区、部委直属公司该商品出口总额的比例和其申请，将A部分配额按比例切块分配并下达。具体公式如下：

$$\text{各地（部委直属公司）配额量} = \text{A部分配额总量} \times \frac{\text{本地（部委直属公司）该商品出口额}}{\text{全国符合分配标准的地区部委直属公司该商品出口总额}}$$

(三) 对于申请某配额管理商品出口但无该商品出口实绩的地区和部委直属公司，外经贸部按照上一年度该地区、部委直属公司出口总额排序，根据不低于该商品最低分配量的原则，依据其上一年度出口总额占所有无配额但申请出口的地区和部委直属公司上一年度出口总额的比例，将B部分配额切块分配并下达。具体公式如下：

$$\text{地方（部委直属公司）配额量} = \text{B部分配额总量} \times \frac{\text{本地（部委直属公司）出口总额}}{\text{全国申请B部分配额的地方、部委直属公司出口总额}}$$

(四) 单个企业所获得的出口商品配额数量不得低于相应商品出口配额的最低分配标准。

第八条 外经贸部在每年的12月10日前完成配额的年度分配并下达。

第九条 各地外经贸主管部门本着提高配额使用率的原则，确定本地区A、B配额的具体比例，并按照本细则第七条的分配办法，将本地区所得商品配额在20个工作日内分配给本地区各类出口企业(以下简称“二次分配”)。

第十条 有单项管理规定的出口商品仍按照有关管理规定执行。

第四章 经营出口配额管理商品的企业资格

第十一条 经营出口配额管理商品的企业，必须具备以下条件：

(一) 经批准获得进出口经营权。

(二) 严格遵守国家出口管理各项法律、法规和规章制度，参加有关进出口商会并能自觉服从行业协调。

(三) 上一年度已获得出口配额的企业，其配额使用率不低于全国平均水平十个百分点。

(四) 未获得过某商品出口配额而申请经营出口的企业，应具备所申请商品的经营能力 (该公司所有商品的销售额达到一定规模，资产负债情况良好，利润率较高等)。

第五章 出口商品配额调整

第十二条 外经贸部在每年8月31日之前，根据国内资源供应、国际市场需求和商品出口情况，确定配额管理商品调整的种类，对出口配额进行年中调整，其他时间一般不进行配额的调整，但国际、国内市场供求关系发生重大变化、配额使用率低等情况除外。各地外经贸主管部门和各部委直属公司须在7月底之前将配额调整建议上报外经贸部。

第十三条 在年中配额调整时，外经贸部根据各地、各部委直属公司的申请和其出口进度、出口效益，奖优罚劣。

(一) 对于前六个月配额使用率高于全国平均水平的地区和部委直属公司，根据其申请给予追加配额；反之，不予追加配额。

(二) 对于未分得出口商品配额但申请该商品出口的地区和部委直属公司，按照上一年度该地区、部委直属公司出口总额排序，根据不低于该商品最低分配量的原则，将追加配额总量的一定比例分配给前若干名。

(三) 具体分配办法依照本细则第七条执行。

第十四条 各地外经贸主管部门依据本细则第十三条的原则和办法，将追加配额分配给本地区各类出口企业 (以下简称“二次调整”)。

第六章 反馈与核查

第十五条 各地配额二次分配、调整方案应在外经贸部下达出口配额后30个工作日内通过中国国际电子商务网报外经贸部EDI中心备案，同时以书面形式或通过中国国际电子商务网抄送各有关进出口商会和许可证发证机关。

第十六条 外经贸部对各地二次分配、调整方案进行随机抽查。

第十七条 获得出口配额的各类出口企业应于每月10日前将上月的配额管理商品出运情况（出口许可证编号、出口报关单号、出运数量、出口单价）报所属外经贸主管部门，同时抄送有关进出口商会；定期汇总上报配额使用情况，并对外经贸主管部门进行的定向检查和抽查给予积极配合。

第十八条 各地外经贸主管部门和各部委直属公司每月20日前将本地区、本公司配额商品上月及累计出运情况汇总，通过中国国际电子商务网报外经贸部EDI中心。

第十九条 各省级外经贸主管部门和部委直属公司本着提高配额使用率的原则，定期对本地区、本企业出口商品配额执行情况进行自查，对出口商品配额使用率达不到规定要求的企业，要及时收回已分配的配额，进行再分配，并将结果报外经贸部备案。

第二十条 外经贸部定期对各地区、各部委直属公司出口配额使用情况进行定向检查和随机抽查，并作为配额安排和调整的依据。

第七章 罚 则

第二十一条 对违反有关出口管理法律、法规和规章制度的地区和企业，视情节轻重相应扣减、取消其当年出口配额，直至取消其参加相应商品配额分配的资格。

第二十二条 对违反本细则第十七条、第十八条规定的地区和企业，取消其相应商品当年出口配额，同时按其当年配额总量的10%－30%扣减其下一年度的出口配额。

第二十三条 对违反本细则第九条、第十四条有关规定的地方外经贸主管部门，外经贸部有权否决其二次分配、调整方案，并责令其在规定期限内按照第九条、第十四条有关规定重新进行二次分配、调整。

第二十四条 对年配额完成率低于全国平均水平十个百分点的地区和企业，取消其下两年该配额管理商品分配的资格。

第八章 附 则

第二十五条 本细则不适用于三资企业和边境小额贸易。

第二十六条 本细则由外经贸部负责解释。凡以前有关规定与本细则不一致者，以本细则为准。

第二十七条 本细则自1999年1月1日起执行。

对外贸易经济合作部
关于印发《出口商品配额招标办法》及《出口商品配额招标办法实施细则》的通知

〔1998〕外经贸管发第974号

1999年1月2日

各省、自治区、直辖市及计划单列市外经贸委（厅、局），各特派员办事处，配额许可证事务局，各进出口商会，外商投资企业协会，各部委直属总公司：

为了进一步做好出口商品配额招标工作，我部在广泛征求各地和有关部门对招标工作的意见及总结两次纺织品被动配额招标实践经验的基础上，对原《出口商品配额有偿招标办法》和《出口商品配额有偿招标办法实施细则》进行了修改和完善。现将修订后的《出口商品配额招标办法》、《出口商品配额招标办法实施细则》印发给你们，请遵照执行。

附件：一、出口商品配额招标办法

二、出口商品配额招标办法实施细则

附件一

出口商品配额招标办法

第一条 为了完善出口商品配额管理制度，建立公平竞争机制，保障国家的整体利益和出口企业的合法权益，维护对外贸易的正常秩序，根据《中华人民共和国对外贸易法》，制定本办法。

第二条 本办法所规定的出口商品配额招标，系指出口企业通过自主投标竞价，有偿取得和使用国家确定的出口商品配额。

第三条 出口商品配额招标遵循“效益、公正、公开、公平竞争”的原则。

第四条 本办法适用于对全球市场以各种贸易方式出口的招标商品，包括通过一般贸易、进料加工、来料加工、易货贸易、边境贸易、补偿贸易等贸易方式出口以及通过承包工程和劳务输出带出的招标商品，但国务院另有规定者除外。

第五条 对外贸易经济合作部（以下简称外经贸部）统一管理出口商品配额招标工作，并确定招标商品范围，即：国家实行纺织品被动配额管理商品、出口配额管理商品及其他实行出口许可证管理的商品。

第六条 确定招标商品的原则是：

（一）属不可再生的大宗资源性商品；

（二）属在国际市场上占主导地位且价格变化对出口量影响较小的商品；

（三）属供大于求，经营相对分散，易于发生低价竞销，招致国外反倾销诉讼的商品；

（四）属规格、价值等差异不大，便于许可证管理和海关监管的商品。

第七条 外经贸部根据具体商品国内外供求情况及我国与设限国签定的双边协议等因素确定招标商品配额总量。

第八条 外经贸部通过其出口商品配额招标委员会（以下简称招标委员会）负责对招标工作的领导和监督，招标委员会对外经贸部负责。招标委员会由外经贸部有关司局的人员组成。

第九条 招标委员会根据招标商品种类在有关进出口商会设立相应的商品配额招标办公室（以下简称招标办公室）。招标办公室负责招标的具体实施工作，对招标委员会负责。招标办公室由有关进出口商会、中国外商投资企业协会、相关行业协调部门的代表及有关方面的专家组成。

第十条 各省、自治区、直辖市及计划单列市外经贸委、厅、局（以下简称各地外经贸主管部门）负责按招标委员会的要求对本地区投标企业资格进行初审并提供有关材料；在本地区宣传贯彻落实有关招标政策，并负责本地区企业有关招标的联络和组织实施工作。

第十一条 凡由外经贸部批准有外贸经营权的各类出口企业（含外商投资企业），经相应的招标办公室登记，符合规定的条件，可取得投标资格。

第十二条 配额招标采取公开招标、协议招标等方式。对于不同的商品可采取不同的招标方式。

第十三条 在每次招标中，投标企业须按规定发送标书，对于同一商品的同一种招标方式只能投标一次。

第十四条 根据评标规则确定的中标企业须按照有关规定交纳中标保证金和中标金。招标收入纳入国家为发展对外贸易而设立的中央外贸发展基金。

第十五条 中标配额当年有效。企业获得配额后应在配额有效期内到指定的发证机关申领出口许可证。

第十六条 企业无法使用中标配额时，应按照规定程序进行转让或上交。

第十七条 对违反招标法规、扰乱招标工作的个人、团体或企业，外经贸部视情节轻重予以处罚；

对触犯刑律的，移交司法部门追究其刑事责任。

第十八条 对于外经贸部、招标委员会、招标办公室及各地外经贸主管部门因出口配额招标工作本身而发生的开支，按收支两条线的管理原则，每年由外经贸部审核汇总编报预算，由财政部从中央外贸发展基金中核拨，年终清算。

第十九条 外经贸部根据本办法制定具体实施细则。

第二十条 本办法由外经贸部负责解释，自公布之日起施行。原《出口商品配额有偿招标办法》同时废止。

附件二

出口商品配额招标办法实施细则

第一章 总 则

第一条 根据《出口商品配额招标办法》(以下简称《招标办法》)，制定本实施细则。

第二章 组织机构

第二条 对外贸易经济合作部（以下简称外经贸部）出口商品配额招标委员会（以下简称招标委员会）设主任一人、副主任一至二人、委员若干人。

主任由外经贸部主管部领导担任；副主任由外经贸部对外贸易管理司（以下简称贸管司）负责人担任；委员由外经贸部贸管司及有关司局的相关人员担任。

第三条 招标委员会履行下列职责：

(一) 根据不同商品的具体情况在每次招标前确定具体商品每次招标的配额数量以及采取何种招标方式、各招标方式占招标总量的比例；

(二) 审定具体出口商品配额招标方案，指导、监督招标办公室的开标及评标工作，并审定配额招标的中标结果；

(三) 发布配额招标的各类通知、公告、决定等；

(四) 受理招标办公室上报的企业上交配额以及配额转受让签章备案；

(五) 审查中标保证金和中标金的收取及配额使用情况。

外经贸部贸管司负责招标委员会的日常工作。

第四条 招标办公室由主任一人、副主任一人、成员若干人组成。主任由有关进出口商会负责人担任，副主任及成员由有关进出口商会、中国外商投资企业协会、相关行业协调部门的代表及有关方面的专家担任。

招标办公室采取一人一票、少数服从多数的办事规则。

第五条 招标办公室履行下列职责：

(一) 拟订具体出口商品配额招标方案，对方案中有关投标资格标准等重大事项，由招标办公室成员集体讨论、表决确定初步方案后，报招标委员会审定；

(二) 按照投标资格标准确定投标企业名单，并报招标委员会审定；

(三) 负责开标、评标，并将结果报招标委员会审定。

第六条 有关进出口商会负责招标办公室的日常事务，包括：

(一) 拟订有关配额招标的各项通知、公告、决定等并报招标委员会审定；

(二) 按统一格式印制并按规定出具《中标通知书》(见附件一)、《出口商品配额公开招标中标金交款凭证》(见附件二)、《出口商品配额协议招标中标金交款凭证》(见附件三)、《申领配额招标商品出口许可证证明书》(见附件四)、《招标商品配额转受让证明书》(见附件五) 等；

(三) 核查企业交纳中标保证金、中标金等情况，并向招标委员会报告；

(四) 接受企业上交的配额，受理、批准企业配额转受让申请，并报招标委员会签章备案；

(五) 检查、监督企业的配额、许可证使用情况，跟踪核查招标商品出口及市场变化情况，并按季度报招标委员会；

（六）办理招标委员会交办的有关招标的其他事务。

第三章　投标资格、价格、数量及方式

第七条　投标资格

（一）公开招标

凡经外经贸部批准有出口经营权、在工商行政管理部门登记注册，加入有关进出口商会（外商投资企业加入中国外商投资企业协会），注册资本、进出口额达到一定规模的各类出口企业（含外商投资企业），可参加公开招标；经外经贸部核准有边境小额贸易经营权的企业，也可参加投标，其投标商品范围为该边境地区自产产品；但外经贸部另有规定者除外。

（二）协议招标

1. 具有公开招标投标资格，且前2年或前3年该招标商品年平均出口数量或金额之和达到全国年平均出口总量或总金额一定比例的前若干家企业；其他注册资本或生产经营达到一定规模、资产状况及经营效益良好、所产商品附加值高、品牌驰名的出口企业（含外商投资企业）、该招标商品主产地的骨干出口企业及积极参加该商品反倾销应诉并按时足额交纳应诉费用的企业。

2. 纺织品被动配额协议招标投标资格

招标办公室根据招标委员会提供的有关企业在设限国设限前对该国的纺织品出口实绩、我国与设限国家签定的双边协议及其他情况确定协议招标投标资格。

（三）对国务院另有规定的某些商品的投标资格，按国务院规定执行。

第八条　投标企业自主决定投标价格。为防止出现不合理的低标价，招标办公室可视具体情况事先确定并公布最低投标价格，低于最低投标价格的标书视为废标。

为防止出现不合理的高标价，招标委员会有权将明显背离正常价格水平的标书视为废标。

对于协议招标的最低投标价格，可参考年度同一次公开招标中标企业加权平均价确定。也可视情况参考具体商品出口的平均利润、往年配额中标价格及其他因素来确定。

第九条　为了防止中标配额过分集中或分散，招标办公室根据具体情况设定最高投标数量及最低投标数量，并在招标前予以公布。招标办公室可视需要对具体商品根据各类企业出口实绩及经营能力等情况分别设定不同档次的最高投标量。高于最高投标量或低于最低投标量的标书视为废标。

在公开招标中，投标企业可在最高和最低投标量之间自主决定投标数量；其中外商投资企业不得高于外经贸部核定的出口规模减去其协议招标投标量的数量。

在协议招标中，招标办公室按照投标企业前2年或前3年年平均出口实绩、供货及经营能力等情况分别确定其最高投标数量，经招标委员会同意后通知有关企业。

参加纺织品被动配额协议招标的企业，分别在招标办公室确定的各企业最高投标数量内投标，高于其最高投标量的标书视为废标。

第十条　投标企业的出口实绩以海关总署统计数为基准，必要时参考其他经招标委员会认可的证明材料来确定。

第十一条　企业须在规定的时点前以电子标书的方式投标，同时将该电子标书的打印件在规定的时间前寄达招标办公室作为书面备份。投标时以电子数据为准，在招标委员会确认该次电子投标数据无法使用时，方以书面备份标书进行评标。

各类出口企业在规定的截标时间内只能投标一次；企业在发出电子标书后，务必通过电脑接收外经贸部中国国际电子商务中心（以下简称部EDI中心）发出的标书到达反馈信息，在确认标书安全到达后，投标工作方告完成。

第四章　评标规则

第十二条　按照本细则第八条、第九条规定，确认合格标书。

第十三条　电子标书出现下列情况之一者即作为废标处理：

（一）在开标前企业自动向招标办公室申请废标的标书；

（二）超过规定的截标时间送达的标书；

（三）同一企业在规定的时点前成功送达两份（含两份）以上的标书，不论内容相同与否；

（四）其他被招标委员会确认为废标的情况。

第十四条 中标企业的确定

公开招标：将所有合格投标企业的投标价格由高到低进行排列，按照排序先后累计投标企业的投标数量，当累计投标数量与招标总量相等时，计入累计投标总量（即招标总量）的企业，即为中标企业。

如果在最低中标价位的企业投标数量之和超过剩余配额数量时，此价位的企业全部中标。

协议招标：投标价格不低于招标委员会规定的最低投标价格水平的企业均为中标企业。

第十五条 中标价格和中标数量的确定

（一）中标企业的中标价格为其投标价格。

（二）中标数量的确定

1. 在公开招标中，中标企业的中标数量为其投标数量。如果在最低中标价位的企业投标数量之和超过剩余配额数量时，此价位的企业按其投标数量比例分配剩余配额。企业中标数量低于最低投标数量的，按未中标处理；

2. 协议招标中标数量：

(1) 企业中标数量按照下列公式计算：

企业中标数量

＝招标总量

$$\times \frac{\text{该企业投标金额（投标配额价格×投标数量）}}{\text{各中标企业投标金额（投标配额价格×投标数量）总和}}$$

或 (2) 企业的最高中标数量为其投标数量。

第五章　操作程序

第十六条 投标资格审查

招标办公室须在规定时间内对投标企业资格进行复审。并将复审结果及有关材料报招标委员会审定。

第十七条 招标办公室须将招标方案在规定时间内报招标委员会审定。经审定后，在指定新闻媒介上发布招标公告，并公布协议招标企业名单。

第十八条 招标办公室应在评标结束后当天以电子方式公布初步中标结果，投标企业如有疑问，可于公布初步中标结果日起 2 个工作日内向招标办公室提出。招标办公室须在公布日起 3 个工作日内将初步中标结果报招标委员会审定。

第十九条 招标委员会审定中标结果后，须及时通知招标办公室，公布中标企业名单。

第二十条 招标办公室须根据招标委员会通知，及时向中标企业发出《中标通知书》及《出口商品配额公开招标中标金交款凭证》、《出口商品配额协议招标中标金交款凭证》。

第二十一条 中标金的交纳

中标企业须按下列规定交纳配额中标保证金和中标金，且不得由其他企业代交：

（一）中标企业须在规定时间内以支票、汇票、汇款等形式将中标保证金汇到指定银行账户，并出具本企业填写的《出口商品配额公开招标中标金交款凭证》、《出口商品配额协议招标中标金交款凭证》。中标保证金为中标金（金额＝企业中标数量×企业中标价格）的 30％至 80％，具体比例由招标委员会根据具体商品的情况确定。无论中标配额使用情况如何，中标保证金不予退还。

（二）在每次申领出口许可证前，按领证配额数量向指定银行账户交纳相应配额的中标金余额，并出具本企业填写的《出口商品配额公开招标中标金交款凭证》或《出口商品配额协议招标中标金交款凭证》。

第二十二条 在收到企业交纳的中标金后，招标办公室发出《申领配额招标商品出口许可证证明书》。

第二十三条 对于收回的、上交的配额以及其他剩余配额，招标委员会可以根据其数量大小决定实行再次招标，或采取经外经贸部批准的其他方式进行处置。

第六章　配额上交、转让及受让

第二十四条 中标配额使用不完时，企业可在向招标办公室说明理由后，根据自愿原则将其上交或转让。

第二十五条 企业向招标办公室上交配额的时间不得迟于每年的 10 月 31 日。对于季节性强的招标商品，上交配额时间可另行规定。

招标办公室在 10 月 31 日前收到企业上交的配额，其中已交相应中标金的，可予以退还，但不退中标保证金。招标办公室 10 月 31 日以后不受理配额上交事宜。

第二十六条 中标企业须在向指定银行账户交纳拟转让部分配额的相应全额中标金后方可提出转

让。

第二十七条 转受让企业必须将双方同意进行配额转受让的申请报招标办公室审批。受让企业必须具有投标资格。

第二十八条 对于企业上交的配额，招标办公室须在接受上交配额3个工作日内将情况上报招标委员会；对于企业的转受让申请，招标办公室须在受理后3个工作日内按照规定完成审批，并将《招标商品配额转受让证明书》报招标委员会签章备案。招标委员会在3个工作日内完成签章备案，并退招标办公室，同时通知部EDI中心。

第二十九条 招标办公室须及时从上交配额企业或转让企业中标配额数量中扣除其上交或转出的配额数量，在发出《招标商品配额转受让证明书》的同时，向受让企业发出《申领配额招标商品出口许可证证明书》，并分别通知有关发证机关。

第七章 出口许可证

第三十条 配额招标中标企业名单及其中标数量，由外经贸部核准并转发各有关许可证发证机关及各地外经贸主管部门。

第三十一条 核发招标商品出口许可证除依据有关出口许可证管理规定外，还须同时依据：

（一）外经贸部转发的中标企业名单及其中标数量或《招标商品配额转受让证明书》；

（二）《申领配额招标商品出口许可证证明书》。

第八章 罚 则

第三十二条 任何企业或个人都有权利和义务检举、投诉配额招标过程中发生的违反招标办法及本实施细则的作弊作为，对于上述行为，一经查实，外经贸部有权否决该次招标结果，同时对检举、投诉的企业或个人予以奖励。

第三十三条 对于为个人或小团体利益而违反招标办法及本实施细则的招标委员会和招标办公室的成员，外经贸部视情节轻重予以处分，直至移交司法部门追究其刑事责任。

第三十四条 对串标、虚报投标资格条件及以其他手段扰乱配额招标工作的企业，招标委员会将收回其中标配额，并取消其2至4年的该商品配额投标资格。

第三十五条 对已中标而不按规定交纳中标保证金的企业，招标委员会将收回其中标配额，并取消其2年该商品的投标资格。

第三十六条 对于企业未按规定上交、转让，又未在配额有效期截止日前领取的配额以及虽领取但未实际出运的配额，视为被浪费的配额。对浪费全年中标配额小于30%、大于5%的企业，取消其下2年该商品投标资格；对浪费全年中标配额大于或等于30%的企业，取消其3年该商品投标资格。

第三十七条 对于本章以上各条所列举的违规企业，如果其行为构成故意破坏招标工作且情节严重，招标委员会有权取消其单项直至所有招标商品的永久招标资格，并按有关法规交有关部门处理。

第三十八条 中标企业因不可抗力事件而未能按规定交纳中标金（包括中标保证金）的，应在合理的时间内及时提供有关机构出具的证明，经招标办公室决议，由招标委员会批准，可免除其部分或者全部责任。

第三十九条 如因国际市场等原因出现某商品中标配额领证率普遍较低的情况，经招标办公室决议，由招标委员会批准，可免除相关中标企业的部分乃至全部责任。

第九章 附 则

第四十条 招标委员会在指定银行开立专用账户，用于收取中标保证金和中标金。具体事务可委托有关进出口商会办理。

第四十一条 招标办公室须在本细则第二十一条规定的中标保证金收取截止日后5个工作日内向招标委员会报告收取情况。

第四十二条 出口商品配额招标的公告、通知等由招标委员会指定《国际商报》、《国际经贸消息》或其他有关媒介予以发布。

第四十三条 未经外经贸部或招标委员会批准，任何单位、组织或个人均不得发布与配额招标有关的规定、公告或通知等。

第四十四条 本细则由外经贸部负责解释。

第四十五条 本细则自公布之日起实施。原《出口商品配额有偿招标办法实施细则》、《纺织品被动配额部分类别有偿招标和有偿使用实施细则》（试行）、《关于1999年度纺织品被动配额招标若干问题的通知》及其有关规定同时废止。

附件一：《中标通知书》（略）

附件二：《出口商品配额公开招标中标金交款凭证》（略）

附件三：《出口商品配额协议招标中标金交款凭证》（略）

附件四：《申领配额招标商品出口许可证证明书》（略）

附件五：《招标商品配额转受让证明书》（略）

对外贸易经济合作部
关于印发《化肥进口组织实施办法》的通知

〔1999〕外经贸管发第27号

1999年1月29日

各省、自治区、直辖市及计划单列市外经贸委（厅、局），配额许可证事务局：

现将《化肥进口组织实施办法》印发给你们，自发布之日起生效，请遵照执行。

附件：《化肥进口组织实施办法》

附　件

化肥进口组织实施办法

第一章　总　　则

第一条　化肥是关系国计民生的大宗重要商品，为进一步加强和完善对化肥进口的宏观调控，建立公开、公平、公正、效益的进口管理机制，维护化肥正常的进口经营秩序和国内营销秩序，根据《对外贸易法》、《海关法》、《中华人民共和国进口货物许可制度暂行条例》和国务院关于化肥进口管理的有关规定，特制定本办法。

第二条　国家经贸委会同外经贸部负责化肥进口的总量平衡工作。外经贸部负责化肥进口的组织实施工作，并按《国务院关于深化化肥流通体制改革的通知》（国发〔1998〕39号）的精神，加强化肥进口代理企业的业务指导和协调管理。

第三条　外经贸部在不突破化肥进口平衡总量的情况下，负责调整计划。超过进口计划总量的调整，外经贸部在征得国家经贸委同意后下达。

第二章　代理进口企业

第四条　本办法所称代理进口企业，是指依照本办法规定，有资格从事自营或代理化肥进口的外经贸企业。

第五条　外经贸部根据国务院批准的《进口商品经营管理暂行办法》，对化肥进口实行核定公司经营管理。

第六条　列入进口化肥计划的国内用户和代理进口企业是委托与代理关系，代理进口企业受使用进口化肥计划的国内用户委托，代理进口化肥。

进口化肥的国内用户与代理进口企业为同一法人时，可以自行进口化肥。

第七条　其他任何未经核定的公司不得自营或代理进口化肥，进口化肥的国内用户和代理进口企业不得从事“自带客户、自带货源、自带汇票、自行报关和不见进口产品、不见供货货主、不见外商”的进口代理方式（以下简称“四自三不见”），否则发证机关将不予办理进口手续。

第三章　总量的平衡、下达

第八条　国家经贸委负责编制全国化肥进口总量计划，并报国务院批准。

第九条　外经贸部与国家有关部门根据国务院批准的全国进口总量计划，将分省市计划联合下达到各省、自治区、直辖市和计划单列市（以下简称“各地方”）以及国家管理企业。

第十条　为配合国际多、双边谈判需要而进口的化肥，在国务院批准的全国进口总量计划中单列，由外经贸部具体组织实施。

第四章　反馈与调整

第十一条　外经贸部负责对本办法第九条规定的分省市计划的分配和使用情况，进行跟踪核查，各省级主管部门、用户和代理进口企业，有义务及时、如实、详尽地反馈情况。

第十二条　根据国民经济发展的需要、国内外相关市场的情况，和本章第十一条的规定，外经贸部负责对已下达到各地方和国家管理企业的化肥进口计划进行调整。

调整方式包括贸易方式调整、流向调整、品种调整和分配方式调整。

贸易方式调整是指将某一贸易方式项下的进口配额调整为另一贸易方式项下的进口配额。

流向调整是指对国家管理企业之间、地方之间、国家管理企业和地方之间的进口配额进行数量调整。

品种调整是指对各地方和各有关部门进口化肥品种的比例进行调整。

分配方式调整是指对行政分配和通过招标、拍卖等方式分配的进口配额数量进行调整。

第十三条　代理进口企业每年4月、7月、10月和次年1月中旬前向外经贸部上报上一季度的自营和代理进口情况，包括国内用户、销售情况、化肥品种、价格、交货期、国别、代理费等，并附相应的对外合同、代理合同、报关单、提单、国外发票和代理发票等复印件。并于每年2月中旬前将上一年度进口总体情况报外经贸部。

第十四条　地方外经贸主管部门与国家管理企业要在每年4月、7月、10月和次年1月中旬前将上一季度本地方和本企业进口执行情况及相关生产、市场情况报外经贸部，并于每年2月中旬前将上一年度进口总体情况报外经贸部。

第十五条　外经贸部将与海关总署、外汇管理局、银行等有关部门建立计算机联网核查制，及时掌握化肥进口的发证、报关、用汇、进口数量、进口价格情况。

第十六条　外经贸部将与有关部门、产业部门建立日常联系制度，及时掌握化肥国内的生产和市场情况。

第十七条　地方外经贸主管部门与国家管理企业分别在每年4月10日和10月10日之前，向外经贸部上报本地区和本企业需调整的化肥数量、品种的情况，并附必要的证明材料。外经贸部于当年4月底和10月底之前，在总量平衡内负责调整，调整超出全国进口平衡总量，由外经贸部商国家经贸委后联合下达。

第十八条　未经外经贸部同意对进口配额的调整一律无效，发证机关不予签发进口许可证。

第五章　指导和协调进口代理工作

第十九条　各地外经贸主管部门在收到全国化肥进口预订货计划和全年计划以及调整计划后，应立即商地方经贸委了解和汇总本地区化肥的需求，包括所需品种的比例，用户对到货期和进口国别等的要求，并联合地方经贸委下达二次分配计划，经地方省政府批准同意后，报外经贸部备案。

第二十条　各地方使用进口化肥的国内用户，自行委托有进口化肥代理经营权的企业进口，代理进口企业凭国内用户提供的各地方外经贸委（厅、局）、经贸委（经委、计经委）盖章核发的《重要商品进口登记表》（样表附后）签订代理合同。

第二十一条　使用进口化肥的国家管理企业自行委托有进口化肥代理经营权的企业进口，代理进口企业凭国内用户提供的外经贸部核发的《重要商品进口登记表》（样表附后）签订代理合同。

第二十二条　《重要商品进口登记表》一式四联。第一联（绿色）交外经贸部配额许可证事务局；第二联（紫色）外经贸部贸管司存档；第三联（蓝色）代理进口企业存档；第四联（白色）由发放登记表的机关存档。

第二十三条　代理进口企业在签订代理合同时，

须在合同中注明最终确认条款如下：本合同的确认以获得中华人民共和国对外贸易经济合作部签发的进口许可证后最终生效。

第二十四条 地方外经贸主管部门在组织实施化肥进口的过程中，要根据国际市场的变化，结合地方实际情况，协调统一，科学的组织进口，体现动态管理的原则，有序核发《重要商品进口登记表》。

第二十五条 代理进口企业向外经贸部提交《重要商品进口登记表》第一、二联、代理合同等材料，经外经贸部审核后加盖“外经贸部重要商品进口登记专用章”。

代理进口企业凭盖有“外经贸部重要商品进口登记专用章”的《重要商品进口登记表》第一联到配额许可证事务局申领进口许可证。《重要商品进口登记表》为签发进口许可证的惟一凭证。

第二十六条 海关验放货物的惟一凭证为进口许可证。

第二十七条 银行和外汇管理局凭进口许可证和有关单据对外付汇。

第六章 罚 则

第二十八条 对有下列行为之一的国内用户和代理进口企业，外经贸部将依据情节给予警告、减少代理比例、扣减进口配额、暂停或取消代理资格的处罚，触犯刑法的，移交司法机关追究其刑事责任。

（一）代理进口企业未按协议规定的品种、价格、质量、代理费和交货期限交货；

（二）从事“四自三不见”的代理业务；

（三）走私或以加工贸易、转口贸易等名义变相走私进口化肥；

（四）伪造、变造化肥《重要商品进口登记表》；

（五）明知是伪造、变造的《重要商品进口登记表》、进口许可证，而用以进口的；

（六）配额使用率低；

（七）倒卖或非法转让进口配额、进口许可证。

第二十九条 任何单位和企业都有权利和义务检举、投诉有违反本办法的行为。

第七章 附 则

第三十条 边境小额贸易项下，对外经济技术和劳务合作项下的化肥进口管理，按外经贸部制定的有关规定执行。

第三十一条 经济特区企业的化肥进口管理暂按现行有关规定执行。

第三十二条 外商投资企业化肥进口管理暂按现行有关规定执行。

第三十三条 本办法自发布之日起实施，凡过去发布的有关规定与本办法不符的，一律以本办法为准。

第三十四条 本办法由外经贸部负责解释。

附：《重要商品进口登记表》（略）

对外贸易经济合作部
关于印发《原油、成品油进口组织实施办法》的通知

〔1999〕外经贸管发第96号

1999年2月13日

国务院有关部委，各省、自治区、直辖市及计划单列市外经贸委（厅、局），配额许可证事务局，中央管理的外经贸企业：

现将《原油、成品油进口组织实施办法》印发给你们，自发布之日起生效，请遵照执行。

特此通知。

附件：如文

附　件

原油、成品油进口组织实施办法

第一章　总　　则

第一条　为保证原油、成品油（原油、成品油目录详见附件）进口工作的顺利开展，加强和完善对原油、成品油进口的宏观调控，建立公开、公平、公正、效益的进口管理机制，维护原油、成品油正常的进口经营秩序，根据《对外贸易法》、《进口货物许可制度暂行条例》、《进口商品经营管理暂行办法》和国务院对原油、成品油进口管理的有关规定，制定本办法。

第二条　外经贸部负责原油、成品油进口的组织实施工作及对代理进口企业的业务指导和协调管理。

第三条　外经贸部负责对原油、成品油进口计划的调整。调整超过全国进口总量的，外经贸部将征得国家经贸委同意。

第二章　代理进口企业

第四条　本办法所称代理进口企业，是指按照国家法律法规及本办法的有关规定，有资格从事自营或代理原油、成品油进口的企业。

第五条　外经贸部根据国务院批准的《进口商品经营管理暂行办法》对原油、成品油进口实行核定公司经营管理。未经核定的企业一律不得经营原油和成品油的进口业务。

原油、成品油一般贸易代理进口企业由外经贸部审核后报国务院批准。目前原油、成品油一般贸易代理进口企业共有四家，即中国化工进出口总公司、中国国际石化联合公司、中国联合石油公司和珠海振戎公司（均不含其子公司、分公司及分支机构，下同）。

第六条　列入进口原油、成品油计划的用户企业和代理进口企业是委托与代理关系。用户企业在本办法规定的范围内可自行委托有代理进口经营权的企业代理进口。用户企业与代理进口企业为同一法人时，可自行安排生产进口。如出现本办法第七章列明的以及其他违规现象，外经贸部将按有关规定对进口代理比例进行动态管理，优胜劣汰。

第三章　进口计划的下达

第七条　根据国务院批准的原油、成品油进口计划总量，由国家经贸委会同外经贸部联合下达到国务院有关部门（以下简称“各部门”）、各中央管理企业和各省、自治区、直辖市和计划单列市（以下简称“各地方”）。

第八条　各地方外经贸主管部门应及时根据国家经贸委和外经贸部联合下达的原油、成品油进口预订货计划和全年计划、以及本办法第四章外经贸部下达的调整计划，商地方经贸委制定二次分配计划，下达到本地区有关企业，并报外经贸部备案。

国务院有关部门应及时根据国家经贸委和外经贸部联合下达的原油、成品油进口预订货计划和全年计划、以及本办法第四章外经贸部下达的调整计划，制定二次分配计划，下达到本部门有关企业，并报外经贸部备案。

第四章　进口计划的调整

第九条　外经贸部可根据国民经济发展的需要、国内外相关市场的情况及进口执行情况，对原油、成品油的进口计划进行调整。超过进口计划总量的调整，外经贸部将征得国家经贸委同意。

第十条　外经贸部调整原油、成品油进口计划的方式包括：贸易方式调整、流向调整、品种调整和分配方式调整。

贸易方式调整是指将某一贸易方式项下的进口配额或进口登记指标调整为另一贸易方式项下的进口配额。

流向调整是指对各部门、各地方、中央管理企业之间的进口配额或进口登记指标进行数量调整。

品种调整是指对各部门、各地方、中央管理企业进口原油、成品油品种的比例进行调整。

分配方式调整是指对行政分配和通过招标、拍卖等方式分配的进口配额或进口登记指标的数量进行调整。

第十一条 未经外经贸部同意对原油进口登记指标或成品油进口配额进行调整的行为一律无效，发证机关不予签发自动登记进口证明（原油）和进口许可证（成品油）。

第五章 指导和协调进口代理工作

第十二条 各部门所属用户企业和中央管理用户企业进口原油和成品油时，应向外经贸部提出申请，并填写《重要商品进口登记表》，交代理进口企业。代理进口企业将代理合同、进口合同和《重要商品进口登记表》报外经贸部审核加盖“外经贸部重要商品进口登记专用章”后到外经贸部配额许可证事务局申领自动登记进口证明（原油）和进口许可证（成品油）。

第十三条 各地方所属用户企业进口原油和成品油时，应向地方经贸委和外经贸委提出申请，填写《重要商品进口登记表》，经地方经贸委和外经贸委签章后，交代理进口企业。代理进口企业将代理合同、进口合同和《重要商品进口登记表》报外经贸部审核加盖“外经贸部重要商品进口登记专用章”后到外经贸部配额许可证事务局申领自动登记进口证明（原油）和进口许可证（成品油）。

第十四条 《重要商品进口登记表》一式四联。第一联作为办理进口许可证的凭据；第二联外经贸部贸管司存档；第三联代理进口企业存档；第四联登记表发放机关存档。

《重要商品进口登记表》由外经贸部商国家经贸委确定式样，由外经贸部监制。“外经贸部重要商品进口登记专用章”和各地方外经贸委“重要商品进口登记专用章”由外经贸部监制。

第十五条 地方外经贸主管部门在组织实施原油、成品油进口的过程中，要根据国际市场的变化，结合地方实际情况，协调统一，科学地组织进口，体现动态管理的原则，有序核发《重要商品进口登记表》。

第十六条 海关验放的惟一凭证为外经贸部配额许可证事务局签发的自动登记进口证明（原油）和进口许可证（成品油）。

第十七条 银行和外汇管理局凭外经贸部配额许可证事务局签发的自动登记进口证明（原油）和进口许可证（成品油）及有关单据对外付汇。

第六章 反馈与调整

第十八条 外经贸部负责对原油、成品油进口计划的分配和使用情况进行跟踪核查，各部门进口管理机构、各地方外经贸主管部门、用户企业和代理进口企业，有义务将原油、成品油进口情况及时、如实、详尽地反馈给外经贸部。

第十九条 代理进口企业应在每年4月、7月、10月和次年1月中旬前向外经贸部上报上一季度的自营和代理进口情况，包括国内用户、品种、价格、交货期、贸易国别、原产地、代理费，以及报关单、提单、国外发票和代理发票等复印件，并于每年2月中旬前将上一年度进口总体情况报外经贸部。

第二十条 各地方外经贸主管部门、各部门进口管理机构、中央管理企业应在每年4月、7月、10月和次年1月中旬前将上一季度本地方、本部门和本企业进口执行情况及相关生产、市场情况报外经贸部，并于每年2月中旬前将上一年度进口总体情况报外经贸部。

第二十一条 外经贸部将与海关总署、国家外汇管理局、银行等有关部门建立计算机联网核查制，及时掌握原油、成品油进口的发证、报关、用汇、进口数量、进口价格等情况。

第二十二条 外经贸部将与有关部门、产业部门建立日常联系制度，及时掌握原油、成品油国内的生产和市场情况。

第二十三条 各地方、各部门及各中央管理企业应在每年4月10日和10月10日之前，将本地区、本部门和本企业需调整的原油、成品油数量、品种情况报外经贸部，并附必要的证明材料。

第七章 罚 则

第二十四条 对有下列行为之一的用户企业和代理进口企业，外经贸部将根据《对外贸易法》及其他有关规定，依据情节，给予警告、扣减进口配额或进口登记指标直至取消经营资格、限制代理数量、暂停或取消代理资格的处罚。触犯刑法的，移交司法机关追究其刑事责任。

（一）走私或以加工贸易转口等名义变相走私进口原油、成品油的；

（二）伪造或变造《重要商品进口登记表》、自动登记进口证明、进口许可证，或明知是伪造或变造的《重要商品进口登记表》、自动登记进口证明、进口许可证，而用以进口原油、成品油的；

（三）倒卖或非法转让原油进口登记指标、成品油进口配额、《重要商品进口登记表》、自动登记进口证明、进口许可证的；

（四）对外经贸部作出的原油、成品油进口计划调整拒不执行的；

（五）代理进口企业未按委托代理合同规定的品种、价格、质量和交货期限等条件交货的；

（六）代理业务中发生“自带客户、自带货源、自带汇票、自行报关和不见进口产品、不见供货货主、不见外商”（即“四自三不见”）行为的。

第八章　附　　则

第二十五条　边境小额贸易项下、对外经济技术和劳务合作项下的原油、成品油进口管理，按外经贸部制定的有关规定执行。

第二十六条　经济特区企业的原油、成品油进口管理按现行有关规定执行。

第二十七条　外商投资企业进口原油、成品油，由外经贸部审核汇总，报国家经贸委确定总量后，外经贸部按《外商投资企业进口管理实施细则》的有关规定组织实施。

第二十八条　本办法自发布之日起实施，凡过去发布的有关规定与本办法不符的，一律以本办法为准。

第二十九条　本办法由外经贸部负责解释。

附：原油、成品油目录

附

原油、成品油目录

商品类别	商品税则号	商品名称	单位
原　油	27090000	石油原油及从沥青矿物提取的原油	公斤
成品油	27100011	车用汽油及航空汽油	公斤
	27100012	汽油型喷汽燃料	公斤
	27100013	石脑油	公斤
	27100021	煤　油	公斤
	27100031	轻柴油	公斤
	27100032	重柴油	公斤

对外贸易经济合作部　海关总署
关于印发1999年机电产品《配额产品目录》和
《特定产品目录》的通知

〔1999〕外经贸机电发第54号

1999年2月9日

国务院有关部门，各省、自治区、直辖市及计划单列市外经贸委（厅、局）、各地区、各部门机电产品进出口办公室，外经贸部驻各地特派员办事处、配额许可证事务局，广东海关分署、各直属海关：

根据《机电产品进口管理暂行办法》（国家经贸委、外经贸部令1993年第1号），现将1999年机电产品《配额产品目录》和《特定产品目录》印发你们，自1999年3月1日起施行。国家经贸委、外经贸部、海关总署《关于印发1998年机电产品〈配额产品目录〉和〈特定产品目录〉的通知》（国经贸机〔1998〕3号）同时废止。

附件：如文

附　件

一、1999年配额产品目录

配额产品目录		协调制度目录	
序号	商品名称	商品编号	商品名称
1	汽车及其关键件	87012000	半挂车用的公路牵引车
		87021020	装有柴油发动机的机坪客车
		87021091	30座及以上的装有柴油发动机的机动客车
		87021092	20座及以上至29座的装有柴油发动机的机动客车
		87021093	10座及以上至19座的装有柴油发动机的机动客车
		87029010	其他30座及以上的机动客车
		87029020	其他20座及以上至29座的机动客车
		87029030	其他10座及以上至19座的机动客车
		87031000	雪地行走专用机动车；高尔夫球机动车及类似机动车辆
		87032130	排气量不超过1000毫升的汽油型小轿车
		87032190	排气量不超过1000毫升的汽油型其他载人车辆
		87032230	排气量超过1000毫升，但不超过1500毫升的汽油型小轿车
		87032240	排气量超过1000毫升，但不超过1500毫升的汽油型越野车（4轮驱动）
		87032250	排气量超过1000毫升，但不超过1500毫升的汽油型小客车（9座及以下）

续表

配额产品目录		协调制度目录	
序号	商品名称	商品编号	商品名称
	汽车及其关键件	87032290	排气量超过1000毫升，但不超过1500毫升的汽油型其他主要用于载人的机动车
		87032314	排气量超过1500毫升，但不超过2500毫升的汽油型小轿车
		87032315	排气量超过1500毫升，但不超过2500毫升的汽油型越野车（4轮驱动）
		87032316	排气量超过1500毫升，但不超过2500毫升的汽油型小客车（9座及以下）
		87032319	排气量超过1500毫升，但不超过2500毫升的汽油型其他主要用于载人的机动车
		87032334	排气量超过2500毫升，但不超过3000毫升的汽油型小轿车
		87032335	排气量超过2500毫升，但不超过3000毫升的汽油型越野车（4轮驱动）
		87032336	排气量超过2500毫升，但不超过3000毫升的汽油型小客车（9座及以下）
		87032339	排气量超过2500毫升，但不超过3000毫升的汽油型其他主要用于载人的机动车
		87032430	排气量超过3000毫升的汽油型小轿车
		87032440	排气量超过3000毫升的汽油型越野车（4轮驱动）
		87032450	排气量超过3000毫升的汽油型小客车（9座及以下）
		87032490	排气量超过3000毫升的汽油型其他载人车辆
		87033130	排气量不超过1500毫升的柴油型小轿车
		87033140	排气量不超过1500毫升的柴油型越野车（4轮驱动）
		87033150	排气量不超过1500毫升的柴油型小客车（9座及以下）
		87033190	排气量不超过1500毫升的柴油型其他载人车辆
		87033230	排气量超过1500毫升，但不超过2500毫升的柴油型小轿车
		87033240	排气量超过1500毫升，但不超过2500毫升的柴油型越野车（4轮驱动）
		87033250	排气量超过1500毫升，但不超过2500毫升的柴油型小客车
		87033290	排气量超过1500毫升，但不超过2500毫升的柴油型其他主要用于载人的机动车
		87033330	排气量超过2500毫升的柴油型小轿车
		87033340	排气量超过2500毫升的柴油型越野车（4轮驱动）
		87033350	排气量超过2500毫升的柴油型小客车（9座及以下）
		87033390	排气量超过2500毫升的柴油型其他载人机动车
		87039000	未列名主要用于载人的机动车
		87042100	装有柴油发动机，车辆总重量不超过5吨的其他货车
		87042230	装有柴油发动机，车辆总重量超过5吨，但小于14吨的其他货车

续表

配额产品目录		协调制度目录	
序号	商品名称	商品编号	商品名称
	汽车及其关键件	87042240	装有柴油发动机，车辆总重量在14吨及以上，但不超过20吨的其他货车
		87042300	装有柴油发动机，车辆总重量超过20吨的其他货车
		87043100	装有点燃式活塞内燃发动机，车辆总重量不超过5吨的其他货车
		87043230	装有点燃式活塞内燃发动机，车辆总重量超过5吨，但不超过8吨的其他货车
		87043240	装有点燃式活塞内燃发动机，车辆总重量超过8吨的其他货车
		87049000	未列名货运机动车辆
		87052000	机动钻探车
		87053000	机动救火车
		87054000	机动混凝土搅拌车
		87059020	机动放射线检查车
		87059030	机动环境监测车
		87059040	机动医疗车
		87059051	航空电源车（频率为400赫兹）
		87059059	其他电源车
		87059060	飞机加油车、调温车、除冰车
		87059070	道路（包括跑道）扫雪车
		87059080	石油测井车、压裂车、混沙车
		87059090	未列名特殊用途的机动车辆
		84079090	未列名点燃式活塞内燃发动机
		84082010	输出功率在132.39千瓦（180马力）及以上车辆用压燃式活塞内燃发动机
		84082090	其他车辆用压燃式活塞内燃发动机
		87071000	机动小客车的车身（包括驾驶室）
		84143090	非电动机驱动的制冷设备用压缩机
		84152000	机动车辆上供人使用的空气调节器
2	摩托车及其发动机、车架	87111000	装有往复式活塞内燃发动机，排气量不超过50毫升的摩托车及装有辅助发动机的脚踏车
		8711200	装有往复式活塞内燃发动机，排气量超过50毫升，但不超过250毫升的摩托车及装有辅助发动机的脚踏车
		87113000	装有往复式活塞内燃发动机，排气量超过250毫升，但不超过500毫升的摩托车及装有辅助发动机的脚踏车
		87114000	装有往复式活塞内燃发动机，排气量超过500毫升，但不超过800毫升的摩托车及装有辅助发动机的脚踏车
		87115000	装有往复式活塞内燃发动机，排气量超过800毫升的摩托车及装有辅助发动机的脚踏车

续表

配额产品目录		协调制度目录	
序号	商品名称	商品编号	商品名称
	摩托车及其发动机、车架	87119000	未列名摩托车及装有辅助发动机的脚踏车、边车
		84073100	排气量不超过50毫升的车辆用往复式活塞发动机
		84073200	排气量超过50毫升，但不超过250毫升的车辆用往复式活塞发动机
		84073300	排气量超过250毫升，但不超过1000毫升的车辆用往复式活塞发动机
		87141900	其他摩托车零件、附件（车架）
3	彩色电视机及其显像管	85281291	显示屏幕尺寸不超过42厘米的彩色电视接收机
		85281292	显示屏幕尺寸超过42厘米，但不超过52厘米的彩色电视接收机
		85281293	显示屏幕尺寸超过52厘米的彩色电视接收机
		85282100	彩色视频监视器
		85283010	彩色视频投影机
		85401100	彩色阴极射线电视显像管
		85404000	彩色数据/图形显示管，屏幕萤光点间距小于0.4毫米
4	收、录音机及其机芯	85199910	激光唱机
		85203210	数字音频式盒式磁带型装有声音重放装置的其他录音机
		85203290	数字音频式装有声音重放装置的其他磁带录音机
		85203300	未列名盒式磁带型装有声音重放装置的其他录音机
		85203910	开盘式录音机
		85203990	未列名装有声音重放装置的其他磁带录音机
		85271200	袖珍盒式磁带收放机
		85271300	其他不需外接电源的收录（放）音组合机
		85271900	其他不需外接电源的无线电收音机，包括兼可接收无线电话、电报的设备
		85272100	需外接电源的汽车用收录（放）音组合机
		85272900	其他需外接电源的汽车用无线电收音机
		85273100	其他收录（放）音组合机
		85273200	带时钟的收音机
		85273900	未列名无线电收音机
		85229021	盒式磁带录音机或放声机用走带机构（机芯）、不论是否装有磁头
5	电冰箱及其压缩机	84181010	容积超过500升的冷藏－冷冻组合机，各自装在单独外门
		84181020	容积超过200升，但不超过500升的冷藏－冷冻组合机，各自装有单独外门
		84181030	容积不超过200升的冷藏－冷冻组合机，各自装有单独外门
		84182110	容积超过150升的压缩式家用型冷藏箱

续表

配额产品目录		协调制度目录	
序号	商品名称	商品编号	商品名称
	电冰箱及其压缩机	84182120	容积超过50升但不超过150升的压缩式家用型冷藏箱
		84182130	容积不超过50升的压缩式家用型冷藏箱
		84182200	电气吸收式家用型冷藏箱
		84183010	制冷温度在-40℃及以下的柜式冷冻箱，容积不超过800升
		84183021	制冷温度在-40℃以上的柜式冷冻箱，容积超过500升，但不超过800升
		84183029	制冷温度在-40℃以上的柜式冷冻箱，容积不超过500升
		84184010	制冷温度在-40℃及以下的立式冷冻箱，容积不超过900升
		84184021	制冷温度在-40℃以上的立式冷冻箱，容积超过500升，但不超过900升
		84184029	制冷温度在-40℃以上的立式冷冻箱，容积不超过500升
		84185000	其他冷藏或冷冻柜、箱、展示台、陈列箱及类似的冷藏箱或冷冻设备
		84143011	电动机额定功率不超过0.4千瓦的冷藏箱或冷冻箱用压缩机
		84143012	电动机额定功率超过0.4千瓦，但不超过5千瓦的冷藏箱或冷冻箱用压缩机
		84143019	电动机驱动的其他制冷设备用压缩机
6	洗衣机	84501200	干衣量不超过10公斤的非全自动洗衣机，装有离心甩干机
		84501900	干衣量不超过10公斤的其他洗衣机
7	录像设备及其关键件	85211010	磁带型录像机
		85211020	磁带型放像机
		85219010	激光视盘放像机
		8529030	视频信号录制或重放设备的零件、附件（机芯、磁头、磁鼓）
		85253010	特种用途的电视摄像机
		85253090	其他电视摄像机
		85254010	特种用途的静像视频摄像机及其他视频摄录一体机
		85254020	家用型摄录一体机
		85254090	其他静像视频摄像机及其他视频摄录一体机
8	照像机及其机身	90065100	通过镜头取景（单镜头反光式（SLR）），使用胶片宽度不超过35毫米的照相机
		90065200	其他使用胶片宽度小于35毫米的照相机
		90065300	其他使用胶片宽度为35毫米的照相机
		90065900	未列名照相机
9	手表	91011100	原电池或蓄电池驱动仅有机械指示器的手表，表壳用贵金属或包贵金属制成
		91012100	自动上弦的机械手表，表壳用贵金属或包贵金属制成
		91012900	表壳用贵金属或包贵金属制成的其他机械手表

续表

配额产品目录		协调制度目录	
序号	商品名称	商品编号	商品名称
	手表	91021100	其他原电池或蓄电池驱动仅有机械指示器的手表
		91022100	其他自动上弦的手表
		91022900	未列名手表
10	空调器及其压缩机	84151000	独立窗式或壁式空气调节器
		84158110	制冷量不超过4000大卡/时，装有制冷装置及一个冷热循环换向阀的空气调节器
		84158210	其他制冷量不超过4000大卡/时，装有制冷装置的空气调节器
		84143013	电动机额定功率超过0.4千瓦，但不超过5千瓦的空气调节器用压缩机
11	录音录像磁带复制设备	85209000	未列名磁带录音机及其他声音录制设备
		85219090	未列名视频信号录制或重放设备
12	汽车起重机及其底盘	87051010	最大起重重量在100吨及以上的起重车
		87051090	其他机动起重车
		87060040	汽车起重车底盘、装有发动机
13	电子显微镜	90121000	电子显微镜及衍射设备
14	气流纺纱机	84452020	气流纺纱机
15	电子分色机	90061010	电子分色机

二、1999年特定产品目录

特定产品目录		协调制度目录	
序号	商品名称	商品编号	商品名称
01	柴油发动机	84089092	其他输出功率超过14千瓦，但小于132.39千瓦（180马力）的压燃式活塞内燃发动机
02	离心通风机	84145930	离心通风机
03	斗式提升机	84254990	其他提升机
04	装卸船机	84261910	装船机
		84261921	抓斗式卸船机
		84261929	其他卸船机
05	多用途门机	84263000	门座式起重机及座式旋臂起重机
06	轮胎式起重机和	84264110	轮胎式自推进起重机
	集装箱正面吊	84264190	带胶轮的其他自推进起重机械
07	载客电梯	84281010	载客电梯
08	自动扶梯	84284000	自动梯及自动人行道
09	推土机	84291110	发动机输出功率超过235.36千瓦（320马力）的履带式推土

续表

特定产品目录		协调制度目录	
序号	商品名称	商品编号	商品名称
			机及侧铲推土机
10	震动式压路机	84294011	机重18吨及以上的振动压路机
		84294019	其他机动压路机
11	矿用电铲	84305020	矿用电铲
12	糕点生产线	84381000	糕点加工机器及生产通心粉、面条或类似产品的机器
13	造纸制浆设备	84391000	制造纤维素纸浆的机器
		84392000	纸或纸板的抄造机器
		84393000	纸或纸板的整理机器
14	瓦楞纸板(箱)生产设备	84413090	其他制造箱、盒、管、桶及类似容器的机器,但模制成型机器除外
15	纸浆模塑生产设备	84414000	纸浆、纸或纸板制品模制成型机器
16	胶印机	84431910	平张纸进料式胶印机
		84431990	其他胶印机
17	平网印花机	84435912	平网印刷机
18	清梳联合机	84451100	梳理机
19	精梳机	84451200	精梳机
20	自动络筒机	84454010	自动络筒机
21	整经机	84459000	纺织纱线的其他生产及预处理机器
22	剑杆织机	84463020	织物宽度超过30厘米的剑杆织机
23	片梭织机	84463030	织物宽度超过30厘米的片梭织机
24	非家用缝纫机	84522110	非家用型自动平缝机
		84522190	非家用型其他自动缝纫机
25	铝电解多功能联合机组	84542010	炉外精炼设备
26	冷室压铸机	84543010	冷室压铸机
27	数控电加工机床	84563010	数控的用放电处理各种材料的加工机床
28	等离子、火焰切割机	84569910	等离子弧切割机
		84569990	其他用化学法、电子束、离子束或离子束等离子弧处理各种材料的加工机床
29	加工中心	84571010	立式加工中心
		84571020	卧式加工中心
		84571030	龙门式加工中心
		84571090	其他加工中心
30	数控卧式车床	84581100	数控卧式车床
31	热模锻压力机	84621090	其他锻造或冲压机床及锻锤
32	木材削片机	84659600	木材、软木、骨、硬质橡胶、硬质塑料或类似硬质材料剖开、切片或刮削机器
33	长材刨片机	84659600	木材、软木、骨、硬质橡胶、硬质塑料或类似硬质材料剖开、

续表

特定产品目录		协调制度目录	
序号	商品名称	商品编号	商品名称
			切片或刮削机器
34	集散型控制系统	84714991	系统形式的分散型工业过程控制设备
35	水泥生产窑外分解成套设备、立式磨、辊压机	84742010	齿辊式固体矿物质的破碎或磨粉机器
		84742090	其他固体矿物质的破碎或磨粉机器
36	水泥混凝土搅拌站	84743100	混凝土或砂浆混合机器
37	轮胎外胎成型机	84775900	其他模塑或成型机器
38	烟草加工及制作机器	84781000	烟草加工及制作机器
		84789000	烟草加工及制作机器的零件
39	沥青混凝土摊铺机	84791010	沥青混凝土摊铺机
40	模具（汽车、家用电器）	84804100	金属、硬质合金用注模或压模
41	塑料或橡胶用注模或压模	84807100	塑料或橡胶用注模或压模
42	大型减速机	84834020	行星齿轮减速器
43	电力变压器	85042320	额定容量在400兆伏安及以上的液体介质变压器
44	图文传真机	85172100	传真机
45	用户环路载波设备	85175090	未列名有载波通信设备及有线数字通信设备
46	电子音频功率放大器	85184000	音频扩大器
47	数字式卫星通讯地面站	85252019	其他卫星地面站设备
48	无线移动通信系统（含蜂窝、集群、无线寻呼、一点多址）	85173013	数字式移动通信交换机
		85173091	模拟式移动通信交换机
		85252022	手持（包括车载）无线电话机
		85252029	其他移动通讯设备
		85252092	移动通信基地站
		85279010	无线寻呼机
49	黑白摄像机	85253090	其他电视摄像机
50	卫星电视地面接收设备	85252011	电视用卫星地面站设备
		85281210	彩色的卫星电视接收机
		85291020	无线电收音机及其组合机、电视接收机用各种天线或天线反射器及其零件

续表

特定产品目录		协调制度目录	
序号	商品名称	商品编号	商品名称
		85299091	高频调谐器（高频头）
51	电视共用天线及电缆电视分配系统	85291090	品目85.25至85.28所列其他装置或设备用各种天线或天线反射器及其零件
52	消防灭火、报警装置	85311000	防盗或防火报警器及类似装置
53	六氟化硫断路器（含组合电器）	85352900	用于电压不低于72.5千伏线路的自动断路器
54	电缆	85445910	其他电缆，耐压超过80伏，但不超过1000伏
55	光缆	85447000	光缆
56	起拔道捣固车	86040099	铁道及电车道未列名维修或服务车
57	牵引车（除汽车牵引车外）	87019000	未列名牵引车、拖拉机（品目87.09的牵引车除外）
58	电动轮自卸车	87041030	电动轮非公路用货运自卸车
59	油船	89012011	载重量不超过10万吨的成品油船
		89012012	载重量超过10万吨，但不超过30万吨的成品油船
		89012013	载重量超过30万吨的成品油船
		89012021	载重量不超过15万吨的原油船
		89012022	载重量超过15万吨，但不超过30万吨的原油船
		89012023	载重量超过30万吨的原油船
		89012031	容积在2万立方米及以下液化石油气船
		89012032	容积在2万立方米以上液化石油气船
		89012041	容积在2万立方米及以下液化天然气船
		89012042	容积在2万立方米以上液化天然气船
		89012090	其他液货船
60	冷藏船	89013000	冷藏船
61	机动货运船舶及客货兼运船舶	89019021	可载标准箱在6000箱及以下机动集装箱船
		89019022	可载标准箱在6000箱以上机动集装箱船
		89019031	载重量在2万吨及以下机动滚装船
		89019032	载重量在2万吨以上机动滚装船
		89019041	载重量不超过15万吨机动散货船
		89019042	载重量超过15万吨，但不超过30万吨机动散货船
		89019043	载重量超过30万吨的机动散货船
		89019050	机动多用途船
		89019080	其他机动货运船舶及客货兼运船舶
62	机动捕鱼船、加工船及其他加工保藏鱼类产品的	89020010	机动捕鱼船、加工船及其他加工保藏鱼类产品的船舶

续表

特定产品目录		协调制度目录	
序号	商品名称	商品编号	商品名称
	船舶		
63	拖轮及顶推船	89040000	拖轮及顶推船
64	挖泥船	89051000	挖泥船
65	正射投影仪	90083010	正射投影仪
66	海洋重力仪	90158000	其他大地测量、水道测量、海洋、水文、气象或地球物理用仪器及装置
67	医用超声显像诊断仪	90181210	B型超声波诊断仪
68	牙科治疗设备	90184910	装有牙科设备的牙科用椅
69	直线加速器	90189090	其他医疗、外科或兽医用仪器及器具
70	医用X线诊断机组	90221300	其他，牙科用X射线应用设备
		90221400	其他，医疗、外科或兽医用X射线应用设备
71	X射线探伤仪	90221990	未列名X射线的应用设备
72	单光子发射计算机断层扫描装置(ECT)	90222100	医疗、外科、牙科或兽医用α、β、γ射线的应用设备
73	核磁共振波谱仪	90278090	品目90.27所列的未列名仪器及装置
74	X射线衍射仪	90301000	离子射线的测量或检验仪器及装置
75	数字频率计	90304010	测试频率在12.4千兆赫兹以下的数字式频率计
76	动平衡机	90311000	机械零件平衡试验机
77	光纤光缆测试仪(含光时域反射计，光纤熔接机，光功率计，光源)	90318010	光纤通信及光纤性能测试仪

对外贸易经济合作部　海关总署
关于印发《机电产品进口配额管理实施细则》的通知

〔1999〕外经贸机电发第99号

1999年3月11日

各地区、各部门机电产品进出口办公室，广东分署，各直属海关：

根据《中华人民共和国对外贸易法》、《机电产品进口管理暂行办法》（国家经贸委、外经贸部1993年1号令）和对外贸易经济合作部“三定方案”的规定，现将新制定的《机电产品进口配额管理实施细则》下发给你们，请认真贯彻执行。

特此通知。

附　件

对外贸易经济合作部　海关总署
机电产品进口配额管理实施细则

第一章　总　　则

第一条　为适应建立社会主义市场经济体制需要，推动相关工业发展和技术进步，调节国内市场的需求，促进对外贸易健康发展，根据《中华人民共和国对外贸易法》、《机电产品进口管理暂行办法》和对外贸易经济合作部（以下简称外经贸部）“三定方案”，特制定本细则。

第二条　实施进口配额管理的机电产品（以下简称进口配额）是根据国家产业政策、行业发展规划，需适量进口以促进生产、调节市场需求，但过量进口将严重损害国内工业发展和直接影响进口结构、产业结构、产品结构调整，以及危及国家外汇收支地位的机电产品。目前实施进口配额的共有十五种。

第三条　外经贸部负责进口配额管理工作。其主要职责是：负责制定、调整并发布进口配额目录；负责编报、下达和调整年度进口配额计划并组织实施；制定进口配额的分配原则；对各地区（省、自治区、直辖市和计划单列市）、各部门和军队、武警（以下简称各部门）进口配额的使用进行指导、协调、监督和检查；查处有关违规行为。

第四条　进口配额实行两级管理，外经贸部负责管理中央专项和各部门进口配额，各地区机电产品进出口管理机构负责本地区进口配额管理。

第二章　进口配额年度计划的编报

第五条　各地区、各部门机电产品进出口管理机构于每年十月十五日前将本地区、本部门下年度申请进口配额的数量汇总、平衡后报外经贸部（机电产品进出口司）。

第六条　外经贸部根据国民经济及相关产业发展的需要、国家对外贸易发展的总体要求、外汇支付能力和上年度进口配额的执行情况，对各地区、各部门机电产品进出口管理机构上报的进口配额计划进行汇总和综合平衡，编制全国进口配额年度计划，经商有关部门，报国务院批准。

第七条　为保证生产配套，每年一季度，外经贸部可按上年进口配额的1/3进行预安排。每年三季度对进口配额的年度执行情况进行检查和研究，根据国内需求情况，可对进口配额计划进行调整。如需重大调整，须报国务院批准。

第三章　进口配额分配原则和计划的下达

第八条　进口配额的分配原则：

一、重点支持大型骨干企业生产配套的需要，对生产名牌优质产品的企业实行倾斜。

二、根据出口实绩，对出口创汇较多的企业实行进口奖励。

三、优先保障科研、教育、文化、卫生及其他社会公益事业进口配额的需要。

四、对军队、武警和公安等部门的特殊需要予以酌情安排。

五、适当考虑国内市场需求，根据市场供需情况进行安排。

六、对某些进口配额试行招标，具体办法另行制订。

第九条　外经贸部按照国务院批准的进口配额计划，根据各地区、各部门年度生产安排和市场需求，结合上年进口配额实际执行情况，按行政隶属关系将进口配额分批切块下达给各地区机电产品进出口管理机构。

第十条　各地区机电产品进出口管理机构按照外经贸部确定的分配原则及条件，对下达的进口配额进行分配。

第四章　进口配额办理程序

第十一条　进口单位根据需要填写机电产品进口申请表一式二份，提供有关文件和情况说明（包括进口配额用途、引进项目可行性报告等），按行政隶属关系，到主管机电产品进出口管理机构办理进口配额证明。其中属部门自用和国家专项安排进口的，由相应机电产品进出口管理机构转报外经贸部机电产品进出口司申领进口配额证明。属外经贸部下达到各地区的进口配额，进口单位到所在地区机电产品进出口管理机构申领进口配额证明。

第十二条　进口配额证明一式五联。第一联（深红色，有防伪底纹）为申领进口许可证凭证；第二联（白底红色）为外贸公司订货凭证；第三联（蓝色，有防伪底纹）为海关验放凭证；第四联（白底绿色）为办理外汇兑付凭证；第五联（白底黑色）为发证机关存档。

第十三条　进口单位凭外经贸部机电产品进出口司和各地区机电产品进出口管理机构签发的进口配额证明按规定向外经贸部授权发放进口许可证机关申领进口许可证；外贸公司凭进口配额证明对外订货；外汇管理部门和银行凭进口配额证明供汇；海关凭进口许可证验放。

第十四条　进口配额产品的零部件，如每套价格总和达到同型号产品整机价格的60%及以上的，视为构成整机特征，按本细则办理。

第五章　进口配额的调整、管理与检查

第十五条　外经贸部根据进口单位对配额的使用情况做相应调整，实施动态管理。对配额使用率高的可适当增加进口配额，否则予以调减。进口单位如因市场变化或其他原因不能实施进口时，应主动将进口配额交回有关机电产品进出口管理机构，由机电产品进出口管理机构根据实际情况在本地区内进行调剂，或由外经贸部对交回的配额进行再分配。

第十六条　各地区、各部门机电产品进出口管理机构负责对已发放的进口配额进行检查和监督，了解进口配额执行情况并汇总上报外经贸部机电司。进口单位要根据机电产品进出口管理机构的要求，及时反馈进口配额使用情况。

第十七条　外经贸部通过电子网络系统，与海关等有关部门进行电子信息交换、数据核查和反馈，对进口配额的执行情况进行跟踪、检查，必要时调整有关产品的进口配额数量。

第六章　进口配额证明的时效、更改、遗失的处理

第十八条　进口配额证明申领进口许可证有效期为三个月，过期失效。在有效期内没有申领进口许可证的，不再办理延期。

第十九条　进口单位如更改进口配额证明中的内容，须提出更改申请，申明理由，同时重新填报进口申请表。其中申请进口单位、贸易方式、产品用途、产品名称、数量及设备状态不得更改。

第二十条　更改进口配额证明，一律换发新证，原证收回，并在电子网络系统中撤销原发证记录。新换发证件的备注栏中注明“换证”字样。

第二十一条　进口配额证明遗失，必须立即向原进口配额发证机关、原许可证发证机关和报关口岸海关同时挂失。如无不良后果，在进口配额证明失效后可予补发。

第七章　违规与处罚

第二十二条　进口单位有下列情况者，属违反本细则并给予相应处罚：

一、未按本细则办理进口配额证明，而擅自对外签约的，不予补办进口配额证明，其进口产品由海关按有关规定处理。

二、将进口配额产品化整为零、分签合同或分口岸进口，有意逃避进口配额管理的，一经发现，即通知海关注销原分口岸进口凭证，并视情节，给予警告、通报批评，不予重新发证。

三、擅自涂改进口配额证明的，其进口配额证明作废，不予办理更改手续和换发新证。

四、擅自转让和倒卖进口配额证明的，一经发现，即通知海关注销原进口配额证明，并对进口单位停止办理进口配额手续；情节严重触犯法律的，移送司法机关追究刑事责任。

五、伪造进口配额证明的，由司法机关追究刑事责任。

第二十三条 进口管理工作人员玩忽职守、徇私舞弊、滥用职权的，根据情节轻重，由监察部门给予行政处分，触犯法律的，依法追究刑事责任。

第八章 附 则

第二十四条 外商投资企业投资和自用进口配额，根据现行外商投资法律、法规办理。

外商投资企业为生产内销产品所需的进口配额，依照本细则办理。

第二十五条 来料和进料加工生产出口产品所需的进口料件不实行进口配额管理，由海关实行监管。

来料和进料加工项目进口自用和产品内销时，属于进口配额管理的，依照本细则办理。

第二十六条 租赁贸易和补偿贸易所需的进口配额，依照本细则办理。

第二十七条 华侨、港澳台同胞捐赠进口配额，按《国务院关于加强华侨、港澳台同胞捐赠物资管理的若干规定》及有关规定办理。

第二十八条 使用外国政府和国际组织无偿援款的进口配额，依照本细则办理。

第二十九条 凡属经贸往来关系赠送和我国驻外机构及境外施工现场调回的进口配额，依照本细则办理。

第三十条 本细则由外经贸部负责解释，过去有关规定凡与本细则不一致的，以本细则为准。

第三十一条 本细则自1999年4月1日起施行。

中华人民共和国对外贸易经济合作部关于执行《机电产品进口配额管理实施细则》有关问题的通知

〔1999〕外经贸机电函字第223号

1999年3月4日

各地区、各部门机电产品进出口办公室：

外经贸部、海关总署《机电产品进口配额管理实施细则》（以下称《细则》）已颁布实施，现将《细则》执行中的有关问题通知如下：

鉴于今年地方政府机构改革，地方机电产品进出口管理机构的归属尚需明确，电子信息交换、数据核查及反馈的网络系统尚未正式运行，《细则》第四章第十一条关于“属外经贸部下达到各地区的进口配额，进口单位到所在地区机电产品进出口管理机构申领进口配额证明”的条文暂不能实施，由各地区机电产品进出口管理机构根据《细则》确定的进口配额分配原则进行分配，按进口配额申报的程序和条件到外经贸部机电产品进出口司领取《进口配额证明》。

外经贸部将视地方政府机构改革和网络查询的运行情况，积极创造条件，在各地区机电产品进出口管理机构的大力配合下，尽快实现《细则》中提出的分级发证的目标。

中华人民共和国对外贸易经济合作部令

1999年 第1号
1999年3月14日

现将《机电产品国际招标管理办法》予以公布，本办法自1999年5月1日起施行。

部长 石广生

附 件

机电产品国际招标管理办法

第一章 总 则

第一条 为了规范机电产品国际招标行为，建立公开、公平的国际招标竞争机制和公正的评标准则，根据国务院批准发布的《机电产品进口管理暂行办法》、《国务院关于加强利用国外贷款项目进口机电设备管理的通知》特制定本办法。

第二条 本办法所称“国际招标”系指国际公开竞争性招标。

第三条 对外贸易经济合作部（以下简称外经贸部）负责协调、管理和监督全国机电产品的国际招标工作、制定其国际招标规则和管理办法并组织实施、审定机电产品招标机构的资格、承担国家评标委员会的日常工作。

第四条 各地区、各部门机电产品进出口管理机构（以下简称进出口机构）依据本办法，负责本地区、本部门机电产品国际招标过程的监督、协调、管理，承担本地区、本部门评标委员会的日常工作。

第五条 机电产品国际招标机构（以下简称招标机构），承担机电产品国际招标业务。

第六条 本办法所称买方，是指通过国际招标采购机电产品的国家机关、企业、事业单位或其它社会组织。

本办法所称招标机构，是指依照《机电产品国际招标机构资格审定办法》（另行发布，取得招标资格并从事机电产品国际招标业务的法人或社会中介组织。

本办法所称投标人，是指依照招标文件参与投标竞争的法人。

第二章 招标范围

第七条 强制实行国际招标的机电产品：

（一）国家规定通过国际招标采购的机电产品。具体目录由外经贸部负责制定、调整并公布；

（二）使用世界银行、亚洲开发银行、日本海外经济协力基金（OECF）、日本输出入银行（以下简称国外贷款）采购的机电产品；

（三）政府采购项下规定通过国际招标采购的机电产品；

（四）其他贷款机构要求通过国际招标采购的机电产品。

第八条 自愿委托国际招标的机电产品：

（一）对国家管理的进口机电产品（如配额、特定产品等），若采用国际招标方式采购，应由买方经相应进出口机构报外经贸部（申请函见附件一）同意后，向招标机构办理招标委托；

（二）实行进口自动登记的机电产品；

（三）外商投资企业进口自用的机电产品。

第九条 除国外贷款项目，属下列情况之一者可不招标：

（一）使用外国政府贷款或出口信贷；

（二）对外不需支付外汇；

（三）供生产配套用零部件；

（四）旧机电产品；

（五）一次进口金额少于10万美元；

（六）其他不适于通过国际招标采购的机电产品。

第三章 招标文件

第十条 由买方根据采购需要与招标机构或委托咨询服务机构编制招标文件。主要包括下列内容：

（一）招标邀请；

（二）投标人须知；

（三）招标产品的名称、数量、技术规格；

（四）合同条款；

（五）合同格式；

（六）附件：

（1）投标书；

（2）开标一览表；

（3）投标报价表；

（4）货物说明一览表；

（5）规格偏离表；

（6）投标保证金格式；

（7）预付款保函格式；

（8）法人授权书格式；

（9）制造商授权函格式。

第四章 招标程序

第十一条 买方须向具备机电产品招标资格的招标机构签订招标委托协议，并提供招标保证金（使用国外贷款项目除外）。委托招标金额在200万美元及以下的，其保证金为委托招标金额的2%；委托招标金额在200万美元以上的，其超过200万美元部分保证金不得超过委托招标金额的1%。

第十二条 编制招标文件。招标文件应包括技术、商务部分（包括对制造商的业绩要求和评标依据），对其中重要条款要加注“*”号，若其中一条不满足将导致废标。

第十三条 评标依据除构成商务废标条款外，还应包括：技术废标的主要参数与偏差范围；价格评估允许偏离范围及其折价的计算方法。

第十四条 买方将招标文件及设备采购清单、有关项目批复文件按《机电产品进口管理暂行办法》，报相应的进出口机构组织对招标文件进行审核。进出口机构要在二十个工作日内（对于小型单台设备应在十个工作日内）将招标文件审核复函（见格式一）通知买方及有关单位。若因特殊原因不能在规定时间内复函，应及时向买方说明理由和需要延长的时间。

第十五条 未经相应进出口机构同意，不得擅自修改已经审定的招标文件。

第十六条 买方和招标机构在接到招标文件审核复函后，在国家规定的报刊及传媒上刊登招标公告（见格式二）。

第十七条 投标期限自招标文件发售之日起，一般不得少于三十天，对大型成套产品不得少于六十天。

第十八条 按照招标公告发布的时间、地点开标。投标人的投标方案、备选方案、降价声明或价格折扣都要在开标时一并唱出，否则在评标时不予承认。开标时，须有买方、投标方及有关人员参加。

第十九条 招标机构要在开标三日内将开标记录（见格式三）送至或邮寄（以邮戳为准）到相应的进出口机构备案。

第五章 评标规则

第二十条 初评工作由初评委员会负责。初评委员会由买方、招标机构及有关专家等五人以上单数组成，其中专家评标人数不得少于半数。

第二十一条 初评工作应严格按照招标文件、投标书进行评审，分为商务、技术、价格三大部分进行。商务、技术均满足标书要求时，评估价格最低者为中标者。

第二十二条 商务评标要求

下列情况之一者，应予废标：

（一）投标人未提交投标保证金或金额不足、保函有效期不足、投标保证金形式或出证银行不符合招标文件要求的。

（二）超出经营范围投标的。

（三）代理投标人未附有制造商有效委托书的。

（四）投标书无法人代表签字，或签字人无法人代表有效委托书的。

（五）业绩不满足招标文件要求的。

（六）投标有效期不足的。

第二十三条 技术评标要求

（一）投标书不满足技术规格书中主要参数和超出偏差范围的，应予废标。

（二）填写技术比较表时，要按招标文件要求和投标书中的参数如实填写，不得以符号填写。对需要并可以接受澄清的技术问题，经澄清后满足要求的按有效标接受，但要在比较表中注明。

第二十四条 价格评标要求

（一）按招标文件中的评标因素进行评标，计算评标价时对需要加减价的部分要依据招标文件和投标书的内容加以说明。

（二）投标人必须根据招标文件要求和产品技术状况列出质量保证期内必备件的清单和价格，并将该备件价计入投标总价。若所提供的产品不需必备件，应在投标书中说明，否则，评标时将其他有效标中必备件的平均价计入该标评标总价（或按贷款机构要求计入有效标中的最高价）。

（三）利用国外贷款的项目，计算评标总价时，国外产品以 CIF 价、国内产品以出厂价（不含增值税）为计算基础。

（四）除国外贷款的项目，计算评标总价时，以货物到达买方指定安装地点为依据。国外产品为 CIF 价 + 进口环节税 + 国内运输、保险费等；国内产品为出厂价（含增值税）+ 国内运输、保险费等。

（五）在进行价格评标时，如果投标价中有多种货币，以开标当日中国银行卖出汇率统一转换成美元。

第二十五条 评标中其他若干问题处理原则

（一）银行资信证明应提供原件，也可提供银行在开标日前三个月内开具资信证明的复印件。

（二）允许对投标书中不清楚问题进行澄清，不允许对技术、商务、价格等实质性内容进行修改。澄清要通过书面方式进行。

（三）投标人复印招标文件的技术规格作为其投标书中一部分可导致废标。

（四）境内的合资合作企业生产的产品，技术总负责方业绩满足招标文件要求的，视为业绩合格。

第六章 办理进口手续

第二十六条 初评结束十五个工作日内，买方和招标机构要将加盖双方公章并有各评委签名的评标报告（见附件二），按进口管理权限报相应的进出口机构。

第二十七条 进出口机构组织评标委员会在十个工作日内对评标报告进行审核。若无异议，对国外中标产品即按《机电产品进口管理暂行办法》办理有关进口手续。招标机构凭有关进口手续发出中标通知书。其中使用国外贷款项目，在评标报告审核后，还需凭国家评标委员会的《评标结果通知》向贷款方报送评标报告，获其批准后发出中标通知书，并办理有关进口手续。

第二十八条 国外中标产品办理有关进口手续后，方可对外签定供货合同，供货合同签订后五日内向买方退还招标保证金。

第七章 违规与处罚

第二十九条 下列行为之一者，属违规：

（一）相互串通虚假招标的；

（二）评标期间泄漏评标情况的；

（三）以不正当手段干扰招标、评标工作的；

（四）未按本办法评标规则评标的；

（五）评标报告不如实反映招标文件、投标书实际情况的；

（六）评标报告未经审定或未办理进口手续而签订供货合同的；

（七）其他违反本办法的行为。

第三十条 处 罚

（一）属招标机构责任，当次招标无效并给予通报批评，视情节暂停或取消其招标资格。

（二）属投标人责任，当次投标按废标处理，视情节暂停或取消其投标资格。

（三）属买方责任，招标无效并给予通报批评，相应进出口机构不予办理进口手续。

（四）属初评委员会责任，评标报告视为无效。对严重责任人将禁止参加评标工作。

（五）买方未按规定与中标人签订供货合同的，没收其招标保证金，其中 50% 支付给中标人，50% 支付给招标机构。

中标人未按规定与买方签订供货合同的，没收其投标保证金，其中50%支付给买方，50%支付给招标机构。

（六）属违纪的，由监察机关给予行政处分；构成犯罪的，依法追究其法律责任。

第八章　附　　则

第三十一条　如政府（金融组织）间贷款协议另有特殊规定，则按其有关规定执行。

第三十二条　使用国外贷款项目采用当地（区域性）招标或邀请招标方式，须经贷款机构同意，其程序可参照本办法执行。

第三十三条　招标服务费用的收取，按国家有关规定执行。

第三十四条　本办法由外经贸部负责解释。过去有关规定与本办法不符的，均以本办法为准。

（以下附件、表格略）

中华人民共和国对外贸易经济合作部关于边境小额贸易企业出口四种招标机电产品免领出口许可证的通知

〔1999〕外经贸机电函字第256号

1999年6月9日

内蒙古自治区、辽宁省、吉林省、黑龙江省、广西壮族自治区、云南省、西藏自治区、甘肃省、新疆维吾尔自治区、新疆生产建设兵团外经贸委（厅、局），机电产品进出口办公室，海南省商业贸易厅，机电产品进出口办公室：

为贯彻落实关于放宽边境贸易的有关政策，进一步扩大边贸出口，在《关于进一步发展边境贸易的补充规定的通知》（〔1998〕外经贸政发第844号）的基础上，现就边境小额贸易企业出口四种招标机电产品的有关问题通知如下：

边境小额贸易企业通过指定边境口岸出口属招标管理的四种机电产品（黑白电视机、自行车、电风扇、单缸柴油机），可以视同一般机电产品出口，不受机电产品出口招标管理规定的限制，一律免领出口许可证。

中华人民共和国对外贸易经济合作部关于调整生产企业申请成立进出口公司和开展对外经济技术合作业务资格条件有关事项的通知

〔1999〕外经贸政审函字第1772号

1999年9月17日

国务院各部委、各直属机构，各省、自治区、直辖市及计划单列市外经贸委（厅、局）、机电产品进出口办公室：

根据《国务院办公厅转发外经贸部等部门关于进一步采取措施鼓励扩大外贸出口意见的通知》（国办发〔1999〕71号）的精神，为进一步鼓励和支持有实力的生产企业参与国际市场竞争，扩大我国产品出口，我部决定对生产企业成立独立进出口有限公司、机电行业生产企业对外承包劳务经营权的现行审批标准进行适当调整，现将有关事项通知如下：

一、生产企业成立进出口公司的资格条件，由原规定的年自营出口创汇1000万美元以上调整为年自营出口创汇500万美元以上。

二、经我部批准，年自营出口创汇额500万美元以上，具备设计、生产、出口大型成套设备能力的生产企业可承包自产成套设备的境外安装工程（包括境内国际招标工程），并对外派遣实施上述境外工程所需的劳务人员。

三、本通知未涉及内容仍按我部下发的《关于生产企业成立进出口公司有关问题的通知》（〔1999〕外经贸政审函字第383号）和《关于调整企业申请对外承包劳务经营权的资格条件及加强后期管理等问题的通知》（〔1999〕外经贸政审函字第748号）执行。

特此通知。

对外贸易经济合作部关于对国有、集体所有制的科研院所和高新技术企业实行自营进出口权登记制的通知

〔1999〕外经贸政发第595号

1999年10月11日

国务院各部委、各直属机构，各省、自治区、直辖市及计划单列市外经贸委（厅、局）：

为深化外经贸体制改革，进一步鼓励高新技术产品的出口，根据《国务院办公厅转发外经贸部等部门关于进一步采取措施鼓励扩大外贸出口意见的通知》（国办发〔1999〕71号）有关精神，外经贸部决定对全国公有制科研院所和高新技术企业实行自营进出口权登记制。现将具体事项通知如下：

一、本通知所指公有制科研院所和高新技术企业，系指企业法人营业执照上为“国有”或“集体”的科研院所和高新技术企业，及由国有或集体控股的科研院所和高新技术企业；如科研院所为事业单位，尚未改制为企业法人，可授权科研院所直属的一家公有制企业作为其经营进出口业务的窗口企业，办理自营进出口权登记手续。

二、申请自营进出口权登记的公有制科研院所和高新技术企业（以下简称科研院所和高新技术企业）的注册资本应不少于 200 万元人民币，且有本企业自产的科技产品和技术可供出口。

三、科研院所和高新技术企业向工商注册地所在省、自治区、直辖市及计划单列市外经贸主管部门申请登记；在国家工商局注册的科研院所和高新技术企业向营业地所在省、自治区、直辖市及计划单列市外经贸主管部门申请登记。

四、各省、自治区、直辖市及计划单列市外经贸主管部门在收到科研院所和高新技术企业申请后的 10 个工作日内予以登记，并颁发《自营进出口权登记证书》（格式见附件）。科研院所和高新技术企业凭该证书到海关、出入境检验检疫、外汇、工商、税务等管理部门办理有关手续后，向所在省、自治区、直辖市及计划单列市外经贸主管部门申领《中华人民共和国进出口企业资格证书》，即可开展进出口业务。

五、科研院所和高新技术企业申请自营进出口权登记须提交下列材料：

（一）科研院所和高新技术企业的书面申请（须包括自营进出口权登记证书的有关内容）；

（二）企业法人营业执照（复印件）；

（三）申请的进出口商品目录；

（四）如科研院所和高新技术企业为有限责任公司或股份有限公司，须提供由工商行政管理部门或审计部门或会计师事务所出具的有关国有或集体控股的证明（原件）；

（五）登记部门要求的其他材料。

六、经登记获得自营进出口权的科研院所和高新技术企业经营进出口业务，必须遵守国家的外经贸政策和有关法律、法规，接受相关外经贸主管部门的指导和监督，并服从有关进出口商会的协调。

七、外经贸部负责组织实施科研院所和高新技术企业自营进出口权登记制工作，各省、自治区、直辖市及计划单列市外经贸主管部门每半年将登记情况汇总报外经贸部，同时抄送科学技术部和地方科技主管部门。

特此通知。

附件（略）

对外贸易经济合作部
关于对国有、集体生产企业实行自营
进出口权登记制的通知

〔1999〕外经贸政发第 660 号

1999 年 12 月 7 日

国务院各部委、各直属机构，各省、自治区、直辖市及计划单列市外经贸委（厅、局）：

为深化外贸体制改革，积极推动和支持更多有能力的生产企业直接参与国际竞争，根据《国务院办公厅转发外经贸部等部门关于进一步采取措施鼓励扩大外贸出口意见的通知》（国办发〔1999〕71 号）有关精神，外经贸部决定进一步扩大自营进出口权登记制的适用范围，即在对经济特区生产企业、国家千户重点企业和国有大型工业企业实行自营进出口权登记制的基础上，在全国范围内对国有、集体生产企业自营进出口权实行登记制。现将有关事项通知如下：

一、本通知所指国有、集体生产企业（以下简称生产企业），系指企业法人营业执照中注明企业所有制性质是“国有”或“集体”的生产企业，以及经有关部门认定为国有或集体控股的有限责任公司或股份有限公司。

二、申请自营进出口权登记的生产企业需具备以下条件：

（一）生产企业的注册资本应不少于500万元人民币（少数民族地区和中西部地区应不少于300万元人民币），机电行业生产企业的注册资本应不少于200万元人民币；

（二）生产企业必须有固定的生产厂房和开展进出口业务所需的设施、资金和专业人员；

（三）生产企业必须已经开工投产，并有自产的合格产品可供出口；

（四）生产企业的产品必须符合出口质量标准。

三、生产企业向工商注册地所在省、自治区、直辖市及计划单列市外经贸主管部门申请自营进出口权登记；在国家工商局注册的生产企业向营业地所在省、自治区、直辖市及计划单列市外经贸主管部门申请登记。

四、各省、自治区、直辖市及计划单列市外经贸主管部门在收到生产企业申请并征求当地经贸委意见在10个工作日内予以登记，并颁发《生产企业自营进出口权登记证书》（格式详见附件）。生产企业凭该证书到海关、出入境检验检疫、外汇、工商、税务等管理部门办理有关手续后，向所在省、自治区、直辖市及计划单列市外经贸主管部门申领《中华人民共和国进出口企业资格证书》，即可开展进出口业务。

五、生产企业申请自营进出口权登记需提交下列材料：

（一）企业的书面申请（须包括《生产企业自营进出口权登记证书》的有关内容）；

（二）企业法人营业执照（复印件）；

（三）申请的进出口商品目录；

（四）如生产企业为有限责任公司或股份有限公司，须提供由工商行政管理部门或审计部门或会计师事务所出具的有关国有或集体控股的证明（原件）；

（五）登记部门要求的其他材料。

六、自营进出口生产企业的进出口经营范围：

（一）自营本企业（含本企业集团成员企业）自产产品的出口业务；

（二）自营本企业（含本企业集团成员企业）生产、科研所需的机械设备、零配件、原辅材料的进口业务；

（三）经营本企业（含本企业集团成员企业）的进料加工和三来一补贸易业务。

生产企业的进出口经营范围和进出口商品目录由外经贸部及省、自治区、直辖市及计划单列市外经贸主管部门核准。

七、经登记获得自营进出口权的生产企业经营进出口业务，必须遵守国家的有关法律、法规和外经贸政策，接受当地外经贸主管部门的指导和监督，并服从有关进出口商会的协调。生产企业如有违法、违规行为，外经贸部将依据《中华人民共和国对外贸易法》和有关规定，给予相应的行政处罚。

八、外经贸部负责组织实施生产企业自营进出口权登记制工作。各省、自治区、直辖市及计划单列市外经贸主管部门须每半年将登记情况汇总报外经贸部备案，同时抄送国家经贸委和地方经贸委。

特此通知。

附件：（略）

国家药品监督管理局令

第 6 号

《进口药品管理办法》于1999年3月12日经国家药品监督管理局局务会审议通过，现予发布。本办法自1999年5月1日起施行。

局长　郑筱萸

1999年4月22日

进口药品管理办法

第一章 总 则

第一条 为加强进口药品的监督管理，保证进口药品的质量和安全有效，根据《中华人民共和国药品管理法》的规定，制定本办法。

第二条 国家对进口药品实行注册审批制度。进口药品必须取得中华人民共和国国家药品监督管理局核发的《进口药品注册证》，并经国家药品监督管理局授权的口岸药品检验所检验合格。

第三条 国家药品监督管理局主管进口药品的审批和监督管理工作，地方各级药品监督管理部门主管辖区内进口药品的监督管理工作。

第四条 进口药品必须符合《中华人民共和国药品管理法》和中国其他有关法律法规的规定，必须接受国家药品监督管理局对其生产情况的监督检查。

第五条 进口药品必须是临床需要、安全有效、质量可靠的品种。

第二章 申报和注册审批

第六条 申请注册的进口药品必须获得生产国国家药品主管当局注册批准和上市许可。

第七条 进口药品的生产厂必须符合所在国药品生产质量管理规范和中国药品生产质量管理规范（GMP）的要求，必要时须经国家药品监督管理局核查，达到与所生产品种相适应的生产条件和管理水平。

第八条 进口药品注册，须由国外制药厂商驻中国的办事机构或其在中国的注册代理提出申请，填写《进口药品注册证申请表》，连同本办法规定的资料，报国家药品监督管理局审批。

国外制药厂商驻中国的办事机构或其在中国的注册代理必须是在中国工商行政管理部门登记的合法机构。

第九条 申请进口药品注册，须报送以下资料：

（一）药品生产国国家药品主管当局批准药品注册、生产、销售、出口及其生产厂符合药品生产质量管理规范（GMP）的证明文件和公证文件。

（二）国外制药厂商授权中国代理商代理申报的证明文件、中国代理商的工商执照复印件；国外制药厂商常驻中国代表机构登记证复印件。

（三）药品专利证明文件。

（四）药品生产国国家药品主管当局批准的药品说明书。

（五）药品质量标准和检验方法。

（六）药品各项研究结果的综述。

（七）药品处方、生产工艺、药理、毒理及临床研究等详细技术资料。

（八）药品及包装实样和其他资料。

申报资料的具体要求，按照本办法所附《进口药品申报资料细则》（附件一）的规定执行。

第十条 申请注册的进口药品，必须按照本办法所附《进口药品质量复核规则》（附件二）的要求和程序进行质量复核。

第十一条 申请注册的进口药品，必须按照国家药品监督管理局规定的程序和要求在中国进行临床研究（包括生物等效性试验）。其中申请注册的原料药若中国尚未生产，则应用该原料药制成的制剂在中国进行临床研究。临床研究须按照中国《新药审批办法》及《药品临床试验管理规范》（GCP）的规定执行。特殊病种或其他情况需减免临床研究的，需经国家药品监督管理局审查批准。

第十二条 申报品种的质量复核和临床研究结束后，国家药品监督管理局对有关资料进行审查，符合要求的，核发《进口药品注册证》。该品种的质量标准即成为进口药品注册标准，中文说明书为指导进口药品在中国临床使用的法定说明书。

第十三条 对特殊病种的治疗药物，在中国尚没有其他替代药物的情况下，国家药品监督管理局可采取加快审批措施。

第十四条 中国重大灾情、疫情所需药品，临床特需、急需药品，捐赠药品和研究用样品等，在尚未取得《进口药品注册证》的情况下，可经国家药品监督管理局特别批准进口。此类药品仅限在特定药围内用于特定目的。

第十五条 下列情形之一的药品，其进口注册申请将不予批准：

（一）不符合本办法第六条和第七条规定的；

（二）申报资料不符合中国进口药品注册审批要求的；

（三）临床使用中存在严重不良反应的；

（四）临床疗效不确切或所报临床研究资料无法说明药品的确切疗效的；

（五）质量标准及检验方法不完善，质量指标低于中国国家药品标准、中国生物制品规程或国际通用药典以及已注册同类品种的企业标准的；

（六）含有中国禁止进口的成分的；

（七）其他不符合中国有关法律、法规和规定的。

第三章　进口药品注册证

第十六条 《进口药品注册证》是国家药品监督管理局核发的允许国外生产的药品在中国注册、进口和销售使用的批准文件。国家药品监督管理局各口岸药品检验所凭《进口药品注册证》接受报验。

第十七条 《进口药品注册证》分为正本和副本，自发证之日起，有效期三年。

第十八条 《进口药品注册证》按统一格式编号，为注册证号。注册证号由字母 X（Z 或 S）后接八位阿拉伯数字组成，前四位为公元年号，后四位为年内顺序编号；其中 Z 代表中药，S 代表生物制品，X 代表化学药品。

第十九条 《进口药品注册证》规定以下内容：药品通用名称、商品名、主要成分、剂型、规格、包装规格、药品有效期；公司、生产厂名称及地址；注册证有效期、检验、标准、注册证证号、批准时间、发证机关及印鉴等。

批准注册品种的每个不同规格，分别核发《进口药品注册证》；每个《进口药品注册证》最多登载二个包装规格。

第二十条 《进口药品注册证》只对载明的内容有效，其任何内容的改变必须报国家药品监督管理局审核批准。

第二十一条 对部分批准进口注册的原料药、辅料、制剂半成品，国家药品监督管理局将在《进口药品注册证》备注中，限定其使用范围。

第四章　《进口药品注册证》的换发和审批

第二十二条 换发《进口药品注册证》应由国外制药厂商驻中国的办事机构或其在中国的注册代理在注册证期满 6 个月前，向国家药品监督管理局提出申请。超过注册证有效期的按新申请注册品种管理。

第二十三条 申请换发《进口药品注册证》须填写《换发进口药品注册证申请表》，并报送以下资料：

（一）药品生产国国家药品主管当局签发的批准药品注册、生产、销售、出口及符合药品生产质量管理规范（GMP）的证明文件。

（二）国外制药厂商授权中国代理商代理申报的证明文件、中国代理商的工商执照复印件；国外制药厂商常驻中国代表机构登记证复印件。

（三）药品生产国国家药品主管当局批准的药品说明书及其中文译本。

（四）药品处方、生产工艺、质量标准及检验方法。

（五）《进口药品注册证》有效期内在中国进口、销售情况（包括进口批次、数量、进口口岸等）。

（六）进口药品使用及不良反应情况的总结报告。

（七）药品及包装实样和其他资料。

申报资料的具体要求，按《进口药品申报资料细则》的规定执行。

第二十四条 药品处方中辅料、生产工艺、质量标准和说明书等有变化的，须同时报送以下资料：

（一）修改理由及其说明。

（二）生产国国家药品主管当局批准此项修改的证明文件。

（三）此项修改所依据的实验研究资料。

第二十五条 国家药品监督管理局对申请换发《进口药品注册证》的品种进行审查，必要时，可安排质量考核或临床再评价，符合要求的，批准换发《进口药品注册证》，发给新的注册证号。

第二十六条 有下列情形之一的进口药品，其换发《进口药品注册证》申请将不予批准：

（一）发现严重不良反应的；

（二）临床疗效不确切、质量不稳定的；

（三）口岸检验二批不合格的；

（四）已被国家药品监督管理局处罚二次以上的（含二次）；

（五）其他不符合中国有关法律、法规和规定的。

第五章　补充申请

第二十七条　已取得《进口药品注册证》的进口药品，下列情形属补充申请。

（一）《进口药品注册证》注明的通用名称、商品名、公司名称、生产厂名称等改变。

（二）质量标准、生产工艺、有效期等改变。

（三）适应症增加。

（四）说明书内容改变。

（五）包装和标签式样、内容改变。

（六）处方中辅料改变。

（七）产地改换。

（八）药品规格改变或增加。

（九）包装规格改变或增加。

（十）其他与批准注册时申报内容有任何改变的。

第二十八条　补充申请需填写《进口药品补充申请表》，连同《进口药品申报资料细则》规定的补充申请资料，报国家药品监督管理局审查批准。

第二十九条　申请增加适应症，须在中国进行临床试验；药品质量标准改变的，须进行质量标准复核。

第三十条　改换产地、增加药品规格的补充申请，必须在原《进口药品注册证》的有效期满至少12个月前提交；不足12个月的，可按照本办法第四章的规定，申请换发《进口药品注册证》，同时申请改换产地、增加药品规格。

改换产地、增加药品规格的补充申请经国家药品监督管理局审查批准后，核发新产地、新增药品规格的《进口药品注册证》，新注册证号为原注册证号前加字母B构成，注册证有效期以原注册证为准。

第三十一条　《进口药品注册证》规定内容的补充申请，如变更包装规格、通用名称、商品名、公司名称、生产厂名称等，国家药品监督管理局审查批准后，核发新的《进口药品注册证》，原注册证即行作废，并由国家药品监督管理局收回；增加包装规格的补充申请，包括进口分装生产所需大包装规格，国家药品监督管理局审查批准后核发新的《进口药品注册证》，原注册证可继续使用。

新注册证号为原注册证号前加字母B构成，注册证有效期以原注册证为准。

第三十二条　进口药品中文说明书和质量标准的补充申请，经国家药品监督管理局审查批准后，下发修订后的说明书和质量标准，原说明书和质量标准即行废止。

第三十三条　进口药品的包装、标签的式样和内容仅有微小改变的，应向国家药品监督管理局申报备案。

第六章　药品名称、包装、标签和说明书

第三十四条　进口药品必须使用中文药品名称，必须符合中国药品命名原则的规定。

第三十五条　进口药品的包装和标签，必须用中文注明药品名称、主要成分以及注册证号，进口药品必须使用中文说明书。

第三十六条　进口药品的包装、标签和说明书，必须符合中国《药品包装、标签和说明书管理规定》，并经国家药品监督管理局批准后使用。一经批准，其内容不得擅自更改。

第七章　进口检验

第三十七条　国家药品监督管理局根据进口药品管理工作的需要，设立口岸药品检验所，负责已注册品种的口岸检验工作。

第三十八条　中国药品生物制品检定所负责对进口药品检验工作进行组织、协调和指导，对有争议的检验结果进行技术仲裁，其对进口药品的技术仲裁结果为最终结论。

第三十九条　进口药品必须按照《进口药品注册证》载明的质量标准，逐批全项检验。进口药品检验所需标准品、对照品，由中国药品生物制品检定所负责统一制备、标定和分发。《进口药品检验报告书》实行统一格式。

第四十条　进口药品必须从口岸药品检验所所在城市的口岸组织进口。从其他口岸进口的，各口岸药品检验所不得受理检验。

第四十一条 生物制品的进口检验，由中国药品生物制品检定所负责或国家药品监督管理局授权的口岸药品检验所负责。

第四十二条 进口药品到达口岸后，进口单位须填写《进口药品报验单》(附件三)，持《进口药品注册证》(正本或副本)原件，到所在口岸药品检验所报验，并报送以下资料：

(一) 加盖进口单位公章的申报品种《进口药品注册证》复印件。

(二) 加盖进口单位公章的《药品经营企业许可证》复印件。

(三) 申报品种《进口药品注册证》载明的生产国有关部门出具的产地证明原件。

(四) 申报品种的购货合同副本。

(五) 申报品种的装箱单、运单和货运发票。

(六) 申报品种的出厂检验报告书。

(七) 申报品种的中、英文说明书、包装、标签和样品。

(八) 其他有关资料。

预防性生物制品、血液制品，须同时出具国家药品监督管理局核发的《生物制品进口批件》；进口药材应同时出具国家药品监督管理局核发的《进口药材批件》。

第四十三条 口岸药品检验所在收到《进口药品报验单》后，应及时查验进口单位报送的全部资料，核对药品数量，符合要求的，发给《进口药品报验证明》(附件四)。

第四十四条 海关放行后7日内，进口单位应将已交讫的海关税单报所在口岸药品检验所，并联系到存货地点现场抽样。口岸药品检验所应将所有进口货物数量与海关税单核对一致并完成抽样后，签署《进口药品抽样记录单》(附件五)，并将全部货物予以加封。未经检验合格的进口药品不得擅自拆封、调拨和使用。

进口药品抽样，按照国家药品监督管理局《进口药品抽样规定》(附件六)和《进口药材抽样规定》(附件七)执行。

第四十五条 口岸药品检验所抽样后，应及时检验，并在规定时间内出具《进口药品检验报告书》。《进口药品检验报告书》应明确标有“符合规定，准予进口”或“不符合规定，不准进口”的检验结论。需索赔的，应及时出具英文《进口药品检验报告书》。进口检验的样品留存二年。

第四十六条 对检验符合规定的进口药品，口岸药品检验所应及时启封，允许调拨、销售和使用；不符合规定的进口药品就地封存。

第四十七条 进口单位对检验结果有异议时，应在收到《进口药品检验报告书》三十日内向原口岸药品检验所申请复验；如对复验结果仍有异议的，可在收到复验结果三十日内向中国药品生物制品检定所申请仲裁检验。

未申请复验或经仲裁仍不合格的，不合格药品由存货地省级药品监督管理局监督处理。

第四十八条 对检出的不合格进口药品，各口岸药品检验所须在7日内将检验报告书报国家药品监督管理局和中国药品生物制品检定所，同时送其他口岸药品检验所和存货地省级药品监督管理局。中国药品生物制品检定所应在每月第一周将上月不合格进口药品情况统计汇总后报国家药品监督管理局。

第四十九条 下列情形之一的进口药品，其报验申请将不予受理：

(一) 不能提供《进口药品注册证》(正本或副本)、及《生物制品进口批件》或《进口药材批件》原件的；

(二)《进口药品注册证》超过有效期30日的；

(三) 未提供本次申报品种产地证明原件的；

(四) 从事进口业务的单位未取得《药品经营企业许可证》的；

(五) 申报品种的包装、标签等与《进口药品注册证》不一致的；

(六) 无中文说明书或中文说明书与批准的说明书不一致的；

(七) 未在规定口岸进口的；

(八) 报验时，药品制剂距失效期不满六个月，原料药、辅料距失效期不满十二个月的；

(九) 伪造、涂改有关文件和票据的；

(十) 其他不符合进口药品管理有关规定的。

第八章 监督和处罚

第五十条 进口药品必须在《进口药品注册证》载明的生产厂或包装厂完成生产和最终包装。不得在其他国家(或地区)进行生产、改换包装、加贴中文标签和补装中文说明书等。违反上述规定的，口岸药品检验所不予受理其已到岸药品的进口报验。

第五十一条 国内药品生产企业、经营企业以及医疗单位采购进口药品时，供货单位必须提供《进口药品注册证》和《进口药品检验报告书》的复印件，并加盖供货单位的公章。

第五十二条 获得《进口药品注册证》的国外制药厂商，必须按照国家药品监督管理局药品不良反应监察管理的有关规定，及时报告进口药品使用中发生的不良反应，包括在国外发生的不良反应。未按规定报告进口药品的不良反应而造成的一切后果，由国外制药厂商负责。

第五十三条 有下列情形之一的进口药品，禁止销售、使用：

（一）未取得《进口药品注册证》、《生物制品进口批件》或《进口药材批件》进口的；

（二）伪造、假冒《进口药品注册证》、《生物制品进口批件》或《药材进口批件》进口的；

（三）伪造、假冒《进口药品检验报告书》销售的。

第五十四条 有下列情形之一的进口药品，由国家药品监督管理局对国外制药厂商提出警告：

（一）进口检验一批不合格的；

（二）未及时报告药品不良反应情况的；

（三）擅自更改包装和标签的；

（四）包装、标签未注明《进口药品注册证》证号以及未用中文注明药品名称和主要成分的。

第五十五条 有下列情形之一的进口药品，由国家药品监督管理局停止其进口检验：

（一）进口检验二批以上不合格的；

（二）未及时报告药品不良反应，造成严重后果的；

（三）擅自更改国家药品监督管理局批准的中文说明书内容的；

（四）被国家药品监督管理局警告二次以上的（含二次）；

（五）超出《进口药品注册证》限定的使用范围的；

（六）已被国外药品主管当局停止生产、销售和使用的；

（七）其他严重违反中国药品管理的法律、法规和规定的。

第九章 附 则

第五十六条 本办法所称进口药品，除原料药、制剂外，还包括制剂半成品和药用辅料等。

第五十七条 申报单位对我局进口药品注册审批的结论有异议的，可在一月内，迳向国家药品监督管理局申请复审。

第五十八条 麻醉药品、精神药品和放射性药品的进口管理，按照国务院《麻醉药品管理办法》、《精神药品管理办法》和《放射性药品管理办法》的规定执行。

第五十九条 港、澳、台地区生产的药品申请向内地销售、使用的，参照本办法的规定，经国家药品监督管理局批准后，核发《医药产品注册证》。

第六十条 申请进口药品注册须按照国家有关规定缴费。

第六十一条 本办法由国家药品监督管理局负责解释。

第六十二条 本办法自1999年5月1日起实施。有关进口药品的管理规定一律以本办法为准。

附件一：进口药品申报资料细则（略）

附件二：进口药品质量复核规则（略）

附件三：进口药品报验单（略）

附件四：进口药品报验证明（略）

附件五：进口药品抽样记录单（略）

附件六：进口药品抽样规定（略）

附件七：进口药材抽样规定（略）

信息产业部关于加强无线电发射设备管理的通告

信部无〔1999〕363号

1999年4月26日

为维护空中电波秩序，防止有害干扰，确保无线电频率资源的有效利用，保障用户合法权益，严厉打击走私活动，现将进一步加强无线电发射设备管理的有关事项，通告如下：

一、进口和生产无线电通信、导航、定位、测向、雷达、遥控、遥测、广播、电视等各种发射无线电波的设备（不包含可辐射电磁波的工业、科研、医疗设备、电气化运输系统、高压电力线及其他电器装置等），必须严格执行原国家无线电管理委员会（以下简称国家无委）、国家经济贸易委员会、对外贸易经济合作部和海关总署联合发布的《进口无线电发射设备的管理规定》（国无管〔1995〕15号）及原国家无委、国家技术监督局联合发布的《生产无线电发射设备的管理规定》（国无管〔1997〕12号）。

二、自1999年6月1日起，凡在中国境内（不含港澳台地区）生产（以外销为目的除外）的无线电发射设备，各生产厂商须持有信息产业部无线电管理局（以下简称无线电管理局）核发的“无线电发射设备型号核准证”（见附件一）；设备标牌上须标明无线电发射设备型号核准代码（具体格式见附件二），确因设备过小而无法在上面标明其代码，则应在其产品的说明书或使用手册中登载该设备的型号核准代码。

原国家无委核发的“无线电发射设备型号核准证”及其核准代码在其有效期内继续有效。

中华人民共和国对外贸易经济合作部关于公布钢材等5种商品进口核定公司及有关问题的通知

〔1999〕外经贸管进函字第176号

1999年5月22日

各省、自治区、直辖市及计划单列市外经贸委（厅、局），各特派员办事处，配额许可证局，各有关总公司，各进出口商会：

为保证重要商品进口工作的顺利开展，维护良好的进口经营秩序，根据外经贸部发布的《进口商品经营管理暂行办法》和有关部委、总公司及地方进口工作的要求，我部对钢材等5种实行核定公司经营的进口商品的经营情况进行了全面的清理和核查。现将钢材等5种商品一般贸易进口核定公司名单和经济特区自行核定公司名单（见附件一、附件二）予以公布，并就有关问题通知如下：

一、外经贸部根据申请企业的经营能力、经营业绩及对国内用户的服务质量，结合不同商品的敏感程度，坚持择优竞选、动态调控的原则核定。对已经具备经营能力和条件的企业，本次赋予其进口经营资格；对已不具备经营能力和条件、服务质量低的企业，相应取消其进口经营资格。

二、取消外经贸部《关于明确进口经营有关问题的通知》（〔1996〕外经贸管发第618号）有关“各部委直属总公司经核定可经营国家实行核定公司经营商品的，其二级公司经总公司授权，可适用总公司的经营范围，海关凭二级公司出具的有关单证验放”的规定。我部将进口经营权直接赋予经营企业，今后各中央管理企业、各部委办总公司不得再将经营权赋予二级公司，海关直接凭经营企业出具的有关单证验放，银行和外汇管理部门据此进行付汇和核销管理。

三、取消钢材进料加工的核定经营管理。有关企业开展钢材加工贸易业务，按照国家关于加工贸易的有关规定办理。

四、各级发证机关要严格按本次核定的企业名单发放进口许可证和进口登记证；各地外经贸主管部门要按照外经贸部的有关规定加强对经营企业的指导和协调管理。对违反国家法律和有关规定的企业，外经贸部将取消其进口经营资格。

五、经济特区自行核定的公司和经我部核定的苏州工业园区进口公司限于代理特区和工业园区自用商品的进口。

六、本通知自7月1日起执行，对在本次核定中被取消经营资格的企业且于7月1日前申领进口许可证或登记证明的，须在8月1日前执行完毕。

我部过去发布的有关规定和公布的企业名单，凡与本通知不一致的，一律以本通知为准。

特此通知。

附件：如文

附件一

钢材等5种商品一般贸易进口核定公司名单

一、钢　　材

中央企业及下属二级公司

中国五金矿产进出口总公司
中国国际信托投资公司
中国华通物产集团公司
中国五矿物资进出口有限公司
中国钢铁工贸集团公司
中国对外贸易开发总公司
中国华润总公司
中国轻工物资供销总公司
中国出口商品基地建设总公司
中国工艺美术总公司
中国包装进出口总公司
中国机械进出口总公司
中国五矿石油器材贸易有限公司
中国技术进出口总公司
中国机械设备进出口总公司
中国工艺品进出口总公司
中国水利电力物资总公司
中国轻工业原材料总公司
中国石油物资装备（集团）总公司
中国仪器进出口总公司
中国石化国际事业公司
华垦物资公司
中国兵工物资总公司
中国金山联合贸易公司
中国远东国际贸易总公司
悦生进出口公司
中国商业对外经济技术合作公司
北京中力国贸进出口有限公司
中粮包装实业贸易公司
欣正实业发展总公司
中国化工供销总公司
华星进出口有限责任公司
高新国际贸易有限公司
中国物资储运总公司
五矿钢铁有限责任公司
中化国际贸易股份有限公司
海南南光进出口公司
中海集团国际贸易有限公司

中基得利进出口有限公司
神华国际贸易有限责任公司
中国海外经济合作总公司
中国冶金进出口河北公司
中艺华甬进出口公司
北京同恒源进出口有限责任公司
中国华源集团有限公司
天平进出口有限责任公司

北京市

北京市五金矿产进出口公司
北京国际贸易公司
北京市富亿通达经贸有限责任公司

天津市

天津外总集团有限公司
天津五金矿产进出口集团有限公司
天津文教体育用品进出口公司

河北省

河北省五金矿产进出口公司
河北省进出口贸易公司
河北省包装进出口公司

山西省

山西太钢进出口公司
山西省机械进出口公司

内蒙古自治区

内蒙古物资集团有限责任公司
内蒙古贸发进出口公司

辽宁省

辽宁省对销贸易公司
辽宁省对外贸易总公司
沈阳机械进出口公司
沈阳五金矿产进出口公司
辽宁成大实业有限公司
辽宁外贸威利公司

大连市

大连五金矿产进出口公司
大连轻工业品进出口公司

吉林省

长春市机械化工五矿进出口公司
吉林省五金矿产进出口公司
吉林吉原钢管有限责任公司
长春市对外经济贸易公司

黑龙江省

黑龙江省进出口公司
黑龙江省五金矿产进出口公司
哈尔滨五金矿产进出口公司
黑龙江省国信贸易公司
哈尔滨铁路局对外经济技术合作公司

上海市

上海市五金矿产进出口公司
上海市对外贸易公司
上海机械进出口（集团）有限公司
上海物资（集团）公司
上海电气（集团）进出口公司

江苏省

江苏省海外企业集团有限公司
江苏省五金矿产进出口（集团）公司
江苏舜天国际集团机械进出口股份有限公司
中设江苏机械设备进出口集团公司
南京市对外经济技术贸易公司

浙江省

浙江物产国贸有限公司
浙江省对外贸易公司
浙江省五金矿产进出口公司
浙江省金属材料公司
温州市国际外贸有限公司

宁波市

宁波市五矿机械进出口公司
宁波市工艺品进出口公司

安徽省

安徽省技术进出口股份有限公司
安徽省五矿进出口公司
安徽省机械进出口公司

福建省

福建省五金矿产进出口公司
福建省机械进出口公司
福建省轻工业品进出口集团公司

厦门市

厦门国贸集团股份有限公司
厦门建发股份有限公司
厦门象屿集团有限公司

江西省

江西省五金矿产进出口公司
江西赣南外经贸集团公司

山东省

山东省华隆进出口公司
山东省对外贸易集团有限公司

山东威海进出口集团公司
烟台银河股份有限公司
青岛市
青岛市五金矿产机械进出口公司
青岛市进出口公司
青岛海尔国际贸易有限公司
河南省
河南省五金矿产进出口公司
河南省机械进出口公司
湖北省
湖北省轻工业品进出口公司
武汉市五金矿产品进出口公司
湖北省机械设备进出口公司
湖北天和国际贸易股份有限公司
湖南省
湖南省金环进出口总公司
湖南省五金矿产进出口公司
湖南华升工贸进出口（集团）公司
广东省
广东省五金矿产进出口公司
广东省外贸开发公司
广州市五金矿产进出口公司
广东省机械设备进出口（集团）公司
广东省机械进出口（集团）公司
广东省物资进出口公司
广东省阳江轻工业品进出口（集团）公司
揭东县外贸总公司
江门外贸集团有限公司
深圳市
深圳市仁生实业有限公司
深圳市广盛达实业有限公司
深圳市恒业丰（集团）有限公司
广西壮族自治区
广西进出口贸易股份有限公司
广西五金矿产进出口集团公司
海南省
海南省机械进出口公司
海南中联有限公司
四川省
四川省外贸进出口公司
四川省五金矿产进出口公司
四川华瑞国际贸易有限公司
四川省火炬进出口公司

重庆市
西南技术进出口公司
重庆市万州进出口公司
贵州省
贵州省五金矿产进出口公司
贵州省外贸进出口公司
云南省
云南冶金集团进出口有限公司
云南省德宏州进出口公司
云南省机械进出口公司
西藏自治区
西藏自治区国际经济技术合作公司
西藏远大工贸有限公司
陕西省
西安市五金矿产进出口公司
陕西省进出口公司
陕西省机械设备进出口公司
陕西五金矿产国际贸易股份有限公司
甘肃省
甘肃省进出口贸易集团公司
甘肃省机械设备进出口公司
青海省
青海省新机五金矿产有限公司
宁夏回族自治区
宁夏机械化工进出口公司
宁夏机械设备进出口公司
新疆维吾尔自治区
新疆对外经济贸易公司
新疆机械化工五矿轻工进出口公司
新疆生产建设兵团
新天国际经济技术合作公司
新疆中基股份有限公司
新疆农垦国际贸易公司

二、天然橡胶

中央企业及下属二级公司
中国化工进出口总公司
中国华润总公司
中国化工建设总公司
中国化工供销总公司
中国新时代公司
中国兵工物资总公司

中国泛华经济发展有限公司
中化国际贸易股份有限公司
中化上海浦东贸易公司
华垦物资公司
中国轻工业原材料总公司
海南南光进出口公司
中联橡胶（集团）总公司
中国正联实业有限公司
中国医药保健品进出口公司
中国包装进出口总公司
天平进出口有限责任公司

北京市

北京化学工业集团进出口公司
北京市物资总公司

天津市

天津外总集团有限公司
天津机械进出口集团有限公司

河北省

河北省纺织进出口公司
河北省食品进出口公司

山西省

山西省化工进出口公司
山西省轻工业品进出口公司

内蒙古自治区

内蒙古国际经济技术合作公司
内蒙古轻工工艺机械进出口公司

辽宁省

辽宁省对外贸易总公司
沈阳化工进出口公司
辽宁恒谊对外贸易有限公司
辽宁省化学工业进出口公司

大连市

中国大连国际合作（集团）公司
大连轻工业品进出口公司

吉林省

中国包装进出口吉林公司

黑龙江省

黑龙江省和昌进出口有限公司
哈尔滨国际石油化工贸易有限公司

上海市

上海市对外贸易公司
上海市兰生股份有限公司

江苏省

江苏国泰国际集团有限公司
无锡橡胶集团有限责任公司
无锡中润（集团）有限公司
南京信业集团股份有限公司

浙江省

浙江物产国贸有限公司
浙江东方集团股份有限公司
温州市国际外贸有限公司

宁波市

宁波市工艺品进出口公司

安徽省

安徽省土产进出口公司
安徽省轻工进出口股份有限公司
安徽省技术进出口有限公司

福建省

福建省化工进出口公司
福建省轻工业品进出口集团公司

厦门市

厦门国贸集团股份有限公司
厦门象屿集团有限公司

江西省

江西省丝绸进出口公司
南昌市对外贸易经济总公司

山东省

山东省对外贸易集团有限公司
威海市化工进出口有限公司
济宁市进出口公司

青岛市

青岛益佳集团有限公司
青岛市土畜产进出口公司

河南省

河南凯达国际经贸发展股份有限公司
河南省南光进出口公司

湖北省

湖北省化工进出口公司
湖北省机械设备进出口公司
中国出口商品基地建设湖北公司

湖南省

湖南省化工进出口公司
湖南省轻工业品进出口公司
湖南省进出口集团有限公司

广东省

广州市橡胶工业进出口公司

广东省外贸开发公司
深圳市
中化深圳实业有限公司
深圳市宝安外贸实业股份有限公司
广西壮族自治区
广西壮族自治区轻工业品进出口公司
广西桂海进出口公司
海南省
海口海越经济开发有限公司
海南神鹰实业公司
四川省
四川华瑞国际贸易有限公司
四川茶叶进出口公司
重庆市
重庆轻工业品进出口公司
贵州省
贵州省对外经济贸易发展公司
云南省
云南省德宏州进出口公司
西藏自治区
西藏自治区外贸进出口公司
西藏山海工贸有限公司
陕西省
陕西省化工进出口公司
陕西五金矿产国际贸易股份有限公司
陕西省对外经济贸易广告公司
甘肃省
甘肃五金矿产进出口公司
青海省
青海省医药保健品进出口公司
宁夏回族自治区
宁夏轻工工艺品进出口公司
宁夏圣雪绒国际企业集团公司
新疆维吾尔自治区
新疆机械化工五金矿产轻工进出口公司
新疆对外经济贸易公司
新疆生产建设兵团
新疆农垦粮油食品土畜医保进出口公司
新疆中基股份有限公司

三、羊　毛

中央企业及下属二级公司
中国纺织品进出口总公司
中国土产畜产进出口总公司
中国南光进出口总公司
中国纺织物资总公司
中国工艺品进出口总公司
中国乡镇企业总公司
中国出口商品基地建设总公司
中国仪器进出口总公司
中国华源集团有限公司
北京华源亚太科技有限公司
中国工艺美术总公司
中国地毯进出口公司
中纺原料进出口公司
北京南光物资进出口公司
中土畜华林贸易公司
中纺辅料进出口公司
悦生进出口公司
中国恒天集团公司
中土畜裘皮革皮进出口公司
海南南光进出口公司
中国丝绸物资进出口公司
高新国际贸易有限公司
中艺华甬进出口公司
上海华利达进出口公司
天平进出口有限责任公司
北京市
北京国际贸易公司
北京百福实业公司
天津市
天津外总集团有限公司
天津东亚毛纺厂集团有限公司
天津市纺织工业供销公司
河北省
河北省圣仑进出口公司
山西省
山西省纺织品进出口公司
山西省土畜产进出口公司
内蒙古自治区
内蒙古土畜产进出口公司
内蒙古国际经济技术合作公司
辽宁省
辽宁省对外贸易总公司
辽宁省纺织品进出口公司

辽宁省服装进出口公司

大连市

中国大连国际合作（集团）股份有限公司

吉林省

吉林省纺织品进出口公司

中国包装进出口吉林公司

黑龙江省

哈尔滨铁路局对外经济技术合作公司

上海市

东方国际（集团）有限公司

上海毛麻纺织有限公司

上海市对外贸易公司

上海市纺织原料公司

江苏省

江苏省海外企业集团有限公司

江苏省纺织品进出口集团股份有限公司

南京土产畜产进出口股份有限公司

江苏舜天国际集团服装进出口公司

江苏阳光集团公司

三毛集团公司

浙江省

浙江东方集团股份有限公司

浙江省纺织品进出口公司

宁波市

宁波市丝绸进出口公司

中国包装进出口宁波公司

安徽省

安徽省进出口（集团）公司

安徽省畜产进出口公司

安徽省丝绸进出口公司

福建省

福建省粮油食品进出口集团公司

福建宏达进出口公司

厦门市

厦门建发股份有限公司

厦门国贸集团股份有限公司

江西省

江西省丝绸进出口公司

江西省九江市进出口公司

山东省

山东省对外贸易集团有限公司

山东省畜产进出口公司

青岛市

青岛市经济技术开发区进出口公司

青岛华青实业有限公司

河南省

河南省工艺品进出口公司

河南省化纤毛麻进出口公司

湖北省

湖北省轻工业品进出口股份有限公司

湖北省化工进出口公司

湖南省

湖南省纺织品进出口公司

湖南省轻工业品进出口公司

广东省

广东省纺织品进出口（集团）公司

广州市纺织工业联合进出口公司

广东省畜产品进出口（集团）公司

广东省东莞纺织品进出口公司

广东省佛山纺织品进出口公司

深圳市

深圳土畜产茶叶进出口公司

广西壮族自治区

广西壮族自治区丝绸进出口公司

海南省

海南嘉兴工贸总公司

海南富艺进出口有限公司

四川省

四川华瑞国际贸易有限公司

重庆市

重庆轻工业品进出口公司

贵州省

贵州省纺织品进出口公司

云南省

云南省纺织品进出口公司

西藏自治区

西藏自治区外贸进出口公司

西藏远大工贸有限公司

陕西省

陕西省纺织品进出口公司

陕西省丝绸进出口公司

甘肃省

甘肃省地毯进出口公司

兰州三毛集团进出口公司

青海省

青海省纺织品进出口公司

宁夏回族自治区
宁夏进出口公司
宁夏圣雪绒国际企业集团公司
新疆维吾尔自治区
新疆维吾尔自治区畜产进出口公司
新疆地毯工艺品进出口公司
新疆生产建设兵团
新疆农垦国际贸易公司
新疆农垦纺织五矿化工机械进出口公司

四、腈　　纶

中央企业及下属二级公司
中国纺织物资总公司
中国纺织品进出口总公司
中国南光进出口总公司
中国丝绸进出口总公司
中国华润总公司
中国工艺品进出口总公司
中国工艺美术总公司
中国（福建）对外贸易中心集团
中国华源集团有限公司
上海华利达进出口公司
中国地毯进出口公司
中化国际贸易股份有限公司
中纺原料进出口公司
中国北方工业公司
中纺辅料进出口公司
中国恒天集团公司
北京南光物资进出口公司
中国丝绸物资进出口公司
高新国际贸易有限公司
中艺华甬进出口公司
北京市
北京针棉织品进出口集团公司
北京市富亿通进出口有限责任公司
天津市
天津亿利达集团有限公司
天津服装进出口公司
河北省
河北省方达进出口公司
山西省
山西省纺织品进出口公司
山西省服装针棉织品进出口公司
内蒙古自治区
内蒙古自治区五矿化工进出口公司
内蒙古物资集团有限责任公司
内蒙古贸发进出口公司
辽宁省
辽宁省成大股份有限公司
辽宁省丝绸进出口公司
辽宁省纺织品进出口公司
辽宁省对外贸易总公司
大连市
中国大连国际合作（集团）股份有限公司
大连化工进出口公司
吉林省
长春市纺织品进出口公司
中国包装进出口吉林公司
吉林省延边对外贸易进出口公司
黑龙江省
黑龙江省远达进出口公司
上海市
东方国际（集团）有限公司
上海市对外贸易公司
上海市纺织原料公司
江苏省
江苏省海外企业集团有限公司
南京纺织品进出口股份有限公司
江苏汇鸿国际集团毛针织品进出口有限公司
常州大华进出口（集团）有限公司
浙江省
浙江东方集团股份有限公司
浙江省丝绸进出口公司
浙江省纺织品进出口公司
浙江省对外贸易公司
宁波市
宁波市工艺品进出口公司
余姚市对外贸易（集团）有限公司
安徽省
安徽省轻工业品进出口股份有限公司
安徽省服装进出口公司
安徽省化工进出口股份有限公司
福建省
福建省轻工进出口集团公司
福建省漳州市轻工业品进出口公司

福建省纺织品进出口公司

厦门市

厦门建发股份有限公司

厦门国贸集团股份有限公司

厦门特贸有限公司

江西省

江西省针棉进出口公司

江西丝绸进出口公司

江西省进出口公司

山东省

山东省对外贸易集团有限公司

山东威海进出口集团公司

山东省畜产进出口公司

青岛市

青岛纺织品联合进出口公司

青岛经济技术开发区进出口公司

河南省

河南省畜产品进出口公司

河南省工艺品进出口公司

湖北省

湖北省轻工业品进出口股份有限公司

湖北省畜产进出口公司

湖北省化工进出口公司

湖南省

湖南省纺织品进出口公司

湖南省化工进出口公司

湖南省进出口集团有限公司

湖南省工业品进出口公司

广东省

广州市纺织工业联合进出口公司

广东省纺织工贸进出口公司

广州市纺织品进出口公司

广东省轻工业品进出口（集团）公司

广东省南海外贸开发公司

深圳市

深圳土畜产茶叶进出口公司

广西壮族自治区

广西壮族自治区纺织品进出口梧州公司

广西桂林市纺织品进出口公司

海南省

海南省纺织工业总公司

海南省纺织品进出口公司

四川省

四川省纺织品进出口公司

四川华瑞国际贸易有限公司

四川茶叶进出口公司

重庆市

重庆轻工业品进出口公司

贵州省

贵州省对外经济贸易发展公司

云南省

云南省进出口公司

云南省纺织品进出口公司

西藏自治区

西藏自治区国际经济技术合作公司

西藏刚坚发展总公司

陕西省

陕西省纺织进出口公司

陕西省化工进出口公司

陕西省畜产进出口公司

甘肃省

甘肃维尼纶进出口公司

甘肃省进出口贸易集团公司

青海省

青海省化工进出口公司

宁夏回族自治区

宁夏圣雪绒国际企业集团公司

新疆维吾尔自治区

新疆机械化工五矿轻工进出口公司

新疆生产建设兵团

新疆农垦粮油食品土畜医保进出口公司

新疆中基股份有限公司

五、胶 合 板

中央企业及下属二级公司

中国土产畜产进出口总公司

中国轻工业品进出口总公司

中国对外贸易开发总公司

中国南光进出口总公司

中国上海对外贸易中心股份有限公司

中国建筑材料及设备进出口公司

中国工艺品进出口总公司

中国（福建）对外贸易中心集团

中国仪器进出口总公司

中国兵工物资总公司

华垦物资公司
中国医药保健品进出口总公司
广州中轻进出口公司
中国木材进出口公司
中土畜华林贸易公司
悦生进出口公司
中国化工供销总公司
海南南光进出口公司
中艺华海进出口有限公司

北京市

北京市土产进出口公司
北京市富亿通进出口有限责任公司

天津市

天津工艺品进出口集团有限公司
天津市物资集团总公司

河北省

河北省方达进出口公司

山西省

山西省土产畜产进出口公司

内蒙古自治区

内蒙古物资集团有限责任公司
内蒙古贸发进出口公司
内蒙古国际经济技术合作公司

辽宁省

辽宁成大股份有限公司
辽宁省轻工业品进出口公司
辽宁恒谊对外贸易有限公司

大连市

大连天巳国际贸易有限公司

吉林省

中国包装进出口吉林公司
吉林省土产畜产进出口集团有限责任公司

黑龙江省

黑龙江省进出口公司
哈尔滨工艺品进出口公司

上海市

上海市土产进出口公司
上海物资（集团）总公司
东方国际（集团）有限公司

江苏省

江苏省海外企业集团有限公司
江苏国泰国际集团有限公司
江苏省工艺品进出口集团股份有限公司
中设江苏机械设备进出口集团公司
南京物资实业集团总公司

浙江省

浙江省对外贸易公司
浙江省土畜产进出口公司
浙江温州市进出口公司

宁波市

宁波市工艺品进出口公司
宁波国际合作（集团）有限公司
宁波海田集团总公司

安徽省

安徽省土产进出口公司
安徽省轻工进出口股份有限公司

福建省

福建省工艺品进出口公司
福建省化工进出口公司
福建省轻工业品进出口（集团）公司

厦门市

厦门特贸有限公司
厦门经济特区对外贸易集团公司
厦门建发股份有限公司
厦门象屿集团有限公司

江西省

江西赣南外经贸集团公司

山东省

山东省对外贸易集团公司

青岛市

青岛市土畜产进出口公司

河南省

中国包装进出口河南公司

湖北省

湖北省技术进出口公司
湖北省粮油食品进出口（集团）公司

湖南省

湖南省轻工业品进出口公司
湖南省国际经济开发（集团）公司
湖南普达实业发展有限公司

广东省

广东省土产进出口（集团）公司
广州轻工业品进出口（集团）公司
广东省轻工业品进出口（集团）公司
广东省外贸开发公司

深圳市

深圳对外贸易（集团）公司
深圳市物资集团公司
深圳土畜产茶叶进出口公司
广西壮族自治区
广西轻工业品进出口公司
广西壮族自治区土产进出口公司
海南省
海南扶轮实业贸易公司
四川省
四川省外贸进出口公司
四川省对外经济贸易总公司
重庆市
西南技术进出口公司
重庆市万州进出口公司
贵州省
贵州省外贸进出口公司
云南省
云南省进出口公司
云南省德宏州进出口公司
西藏自治区
西藏自治区包装进出口公司
西藏自治区外贸进出口公司
西藏自治区国际经济技术合作公司
陕西省
中国包装进出口陕西公司
陕西土产进出口公司
甘肃省
甘肃省进出口贸易集团公司
青海省
青海省轻工业品进出口公司
宁夏回族自治区
宁夏机械设备进出口公司
新疆维吾尔自治区
新疆机械化工五金矿产轻工进出口公司
新疆生产建设兵团
新疆农垦国际贸易公司

附件二

经济特区自行核定公司名单

深　　圳

钢材：深圳市建材保税贸易行、深圳众鹏保税贸易公司、深圳宏兴祥保税贸易公司、深圳物资保税贸易公司、深圳利丰保税贸易公司、深圳市金属保税贸易公司、中国五金矿产进出口深圳公司、深圳市万邦贸易发展公司

天然橡胶：中国深圳对外贸易（集团）公司、深圳奥康德石油贸易集团公司、深圳市物资集团公司、深圳市莱英达（集团）公司、深圳万邦贸易发展公司

胶合板：深圳市木材保税贸易行、深圳市建材保税贸易行、深圳众鹏保税贸易公司、深圳宏兴祥保税贸易公司、深圳物资保税贸易公司、深圳利丰保税贸易公司、深圳市万邦贸易发展公司

羊毛：中国深圳对外贸易（集团）公司、深圳奥康德石油贸易集团公司、深圳市物资集团公司、深圳市莱英达（集团）公司、深圳市纺织（集团）股份有限公司、深圳万邦贸易发展公司

腈纶：中国深圳对外贸易（集团）公司、深圳奥康德石油贸易集团公司、深圳市物资集团公司、深圳市莱英达（集团）公司、深圳市纺织（集团）股份有限公司、深圳万邦贸易发展公司

珠　　海

钢材：珠海金鑫集团公司、珠海市华原发展公司、珠海经济特区珠光公司、珠海经济特区物资总公司、珠海市粤海进出口公司

胶合板：珠海经济特区中兴实业集团有限公司、珠海经济特区物资总公司、珠海市粤海进出口公司

汕　　头

钢材：汕头市大诚有限公司、广东省汕头经济特区物资进出口总公司、广东省汕头五金矿产进出口公司、广东省汕头经济特区发展总公司

天然橡胶：广东省汕头轻工业品进出口公司、广东省汕头经济特区进出口（集团）公司、广东省汕头化工进出口公司

胶合板：广东省汕头经济特区进出口（集团）公司、广东省汕头经济特区发展总公司、广东省汕头经济特区对外商业（集团）公司、中国广澳开发集团公司

羊毛：中国抽纱汕头进出口公司、广东省汕头纺织品进出口公司、广东省汕头经济特区对外商业（集团）公司

厦　　门

钢材：厦门国贸集团股份有限公司、厦门建发股份有限公司、厦门特贸有限公司、厦门象屿集团有限公司、厦门物资进出口总公司

天然橡胶：厦门特贸有限公司、厦门建发股份有限公司、厦门国贸集团股份有限公司、厦门象屿集团有限公司、厦门信达股份有限公司、厦门经济特区对外贸易（集团）公司、厦门物资进出口总公司、厦门橡胶厂

胶合板：厦门特贸有限公司、厦门建发股份有限公司、厦门国贸集团股份有限公司、厦门象屿集团有限公司、厦门经济特区对外贸易（集团）公司、厦门信达股份有限公司、厦门嘉华进出口贸易有限公司

羊毛：厦门建发股份有限公司、厦门特贸有限公司、厦门国贸集团股份有限公司、厦门象屿集团有限公司、厦门信达股份有限公司

腈纶：厦门特贸有限公司、厦门建发股份有限公司、厦门象屿集团有限公司、厦门国贸集团股份有限公司、厦门信达股份有限公司

海　　南

钢材：海南省联合贸易公司、海南省国际经济贸易中心、海南中联有限公司

天然橡胶：海南省对外贸易（集团）公司、海南省国际经济贸易中心、海南企业有限公司

胶合板：海南省土产进出口公司、海南省海信（集团）公司、海南省商贸开发总公司

羊毛：海南省纺织品进出口公司、海南省海信（集团）公司、海南企业有限公司

腈纶：海南省国际经济贸易中心、海南省联合贸易公司、海南企业有限公司

苏州工业园区

钢材：苏州工业园区南光进出口有限公司、苏州工业园区股份有限公司

胶合板：苏州工业园区南光进出口公司、苏州工业园区对外贸易公司、苏州工业园区股份有限公司

注：苏州工业园区核定公司名单由外经贸部核定。

国家经济贸易委员会　对外贸易经济合作部 海关总署关于确定第一批加工贸易禁止类和进口限制类商品目录的通知

国经贸贸易〔1999〕490号

1999年5月26日

各省、自治区、直辖市、计划单列市及新疆生产建设兵团经贸委（经委、计经委）、外经贸委（厅、局），海关总署广东分署、各直属海关、国务院有关部门：

根据《国务院办公厅转发国家经贸委等部门关于进一步完善加工贸易银行保证金台账制度意见的通知》（国办发〔1999〕35号）的有关规定，现将《加工贸易禁止类、进口限制类商品目录》（第一批）下发给你们，自1999年6月1日起执行。6月1日前已经外经贸主管部门批准的合同，仍按原规定执行至合同完毕。

注：1. 根据《国务院办公厅转发国家经贸委等部门关于进一步完善加工贸易银行保证金台账制度意见的通知》（国办发〔1999〕35号），国家对限制类商品的加工贸易实行银行保证金台账"实转"。

2. 根据《关于执行国务院办公厅国办发〔1999〕35号文件有关问题的通知》（国经贸贸易〔1999〕742号），《关于确定第一批加工贸易禁止类和进口限制类商品目录的通知》（国经贸贸易〔1999〕490号）已推迟到1999年10月1日起执行。

附　件

加工贸易禁止类、进口限制类商品目录

（第一批）

一、禁止类商品

1. 进口料件属于我国禁止进口商品（包括旧服装、含淫秽内容的废旧书刊、含有害物、放射性物质的工业垃圾等）；

2. 用于拆解、翻新的废旧汽车、摩托车及其主要部件；

3. 为种植、养殖等出口产品而进口的种子、种苗、化肥、饲料、添加剂、抗生素等。

二、进口限制类商品

商品大类	商品名称	税　号
1. 塑料原料	初级形状的聚乙烯	3901100
		39012000
2. 聚脂切片	聚脂切片	39076010
3. 化纤原料	涤纶长丝	54022000
		54023310
		54023390

		54021200
		54024300
		54025200
		54026200
	化学纤维短纤	55012000－55013000
		55020090
		55032000－55033000
		55041000
		55049000
		55062000－55063000
		5507000
		55092100－55093200
		55095100－55096900
		55101100－55109000
4．棉花		52010000
		52030000
5．棉纱		52051100－52054800
		52061100－52064500
		52071000－52079000
6．棉坯布		52081100－52085900
		52091100－52095900
		52101100－52105900
		52111100－52115900
		52121100－52122500
7．钢材	铁及非合金钢材	72081000－72089000
		72091500－72099000
		72101100－72109000
		72111300－72119000
		72121000－72126000
		72131000－72139900
		72141000－72149900
	不锈钢	72191100－72199000
		72201100－72209000

国家经济贸易委员会　对外贸易经济合作部 海关总署关于调整第一批加工贸易进口 限制类商品目录的补充通知

国经贸贸易〔1999〕930号
1999年9月27日

各省、自治区、直辖市、计划单列市及新疆生产建设兵团经贸委（经委、计经委）、外经贸委（厅、局），海关总署广东分署、各直属海关、国务院有关部门：

为贯彻落实《国务院办公厅转发国家经贸委等部门关于进一步完善加工贸易银行保证金台账制度意见的通知》（国办发〔1999〕35号），国家经贸委、外经贸部、海关总署联合下发了《关于确定第一批加工贸易禁止类和进口限制类商品目录的通知》（国经贸贸易〔1999〕490号，以下简称《目录》）。现对《目录》中“棉坯布”商品税号进行调整，自1999年10月1日起执行。

附件：棉坯布限制类商品税号目录

附　件

棉坯布限制类商品税号目录

商品大类		商品税号				
棉坯布						
	未漂白	52081100	52081200	52081300	52081900	
		52091100	52091200	52091900	52101100	52101200
		52101900	52111100	52111200	52111900	52121100
		52122100				
	漂　白	52082100	52082200	52082300	52082900	
		52092100	52092200	52092900	52102100	52102200
		52102900	52112100	52112200	52112900	52121200
		52122200				

国家经济贸易委员会　对外贸易经济合作部 海关总署关于确定第二批加工贸易进口限制类商品目录的通知

国经贸贸易〔1999〕934号

1999年9月27日

各省、自治区、直辖市、计划单列市及新疆生产建设兵团经贸委（经委、计经委）、外经贸委（厅、局），海关总署广东分署、各直属海关、国务院有关部门：

根据《国务院办公厅转发外经贸部等部门关于进一步采取措施鼓励扩大外贸出口意见的通知》（国办发〔1999〕71号）有关规定，现将《加工贸易进口限制类商品目录》（第二批）下发你们，自1999年10月1日起按有关规定实行银行保证金台账“实转”。10月1日前已经外经贸主管部门批准且在2000年1月1日前在海关备案的加工贸易合同仍按原规定执行至合同完毕，对经批准延期的合同，延长期限不超过半年，申请第二次延期的由海关对尚未加工出口的料件征收应征税款等额的台账保证金。各地海关对10月1日前已批准的加工贸易合同要抓紧办理备案手续。

附　件

加工贸易进口限制类商品目录
（第二批）

商品大类	商品名称	商品税号
1．食糖		
	甘蔗原糖，未加香料或着色剂	17011100
	甜菜原糖，未加香料或着色剂	17011200
	砂　糖	17019910
	绵白糖	17019920
2．植物油（未经化学改性）		
	初榨的豆油	15071000
	其他豆油及其分离品	15079000
	初榨的花生油	15081000
	其他花生油及其分离品	15089000
	初榨的棕榈油	15111000
	其他棕榈油及其分离品	15119000

	初榨的葵花油或红花油	15121100
	初榨的棉子油，不论是否去除棉子酚	15122100
	其他棉子油及其分离品	15122900
	初榨的菜子油	15141010
	初榨的芥子油	15141090
	其他菜子油或芥子油及其分离品	15149000
	初榨的玉米油	15152100
	芝麻油及其分离品	15155000
3. 天然橡胶		
	天然胶乳，不论是否预硫化	40011000
	烟胶片	40012100
	技术分类天然橡胶（TSNR）	40012200
	其他形状的天然橡胶	40012900
4. 羊毛		
	未梳含脂剪羊毛	51011100
	其他未梳含脂羊毛	51011900
	未梳脱脂剪羊毛，未碳化	51012100
	其他未梳脱脂羊毛，未碳化	51012900
	未梳碳化羊毛	51013000
	羊毛落毛	51031010
	粗梳羊毛	51051000
	精梳羊毛片毛	51052100
	羊毛条及其他精梳羊毛	51052900

对外贸易经济合作部关于印发《加工贸易审批管理暂行办法》的通知

〔1999〕外经贸管发第314号

1999年5月27日

各省、自治区、直辖市及计划单列市外经贸厅（委、局），部驻各地特派员办事处，配额许可证事务局：

为贯彻落实《国务院办公厅转发国家经贸委等部门关于进一步完善加工贸易银行保证金台账制度意见的通知》（国办发〔1999〕35号），经商海关总署，我部制定了《加工贸易审批管理暂行办法》，现印发给你们，请遵照执行。

附件：如文

附　件

加工贸易审批管理暂行办法

第一章　总　　则

第一条　为进一步加强加工贸易管理，维护正常的经营秩序，保证加工贸易健康发展，根据《中华人民共和国外贸法》、《中华人民共和国海关法》、《国务院关于对加工贸易进口料件试行银行保证金台账制度的批复》（国函〔1995〕109号）和《国务院办公厅转发国家经贸委等部门关于进一步完善加工贸易银行保证金台账制度意见的通知》（下称国办发〔1999〕35号），特制定本办法。

第二条　本办法所称加工贸易，是指从境外保税进口全部或部分原辅材料、零部件、元器件、包装物料（下称进口料件），经境内企业加工或装配后，将制成品复出口的经营活动，包括来料加工和进料加工。

来料加工是指进口料件由外商提供，即不需付汇进口，也不需用加工费偿还，制成品由外商销售，经营企业收取加工费的加工贸易。

进料加工是指进口料件由经营企业付汇进口，制成品由经营企业外销出口的加工贸易。

第三条　本办法所称经营企业是指负责对外签订加工贸易进出口合同的各类进出口企业和外商投资企业，以及经批准获得来料加工经营许可的对外加工装配服务公司。

本办法所称加工企业是指接受经营企业委托，负责对进口料件进行加工或装配，且具有法人资格的生产企业，以及由经营企业设立的虽不具有法人资格，但实行相对独立核算并已办理工商营业证（执照）的工厂。

第四条　经营企业开展加工贸易，必须事先报外经贸主管部门审批。对外贸易经济合作部（以下简称外经贸部）负责管理全国的加工贸易业务审批工作。

第二章　审批机关及分级审批

第五条　各省级外经贸主管部门负责管理、审批本地区的加工贸易业务，并可根据实际需要，授予部分地（市）和县（市）级外经贸主管部门加工贸易审批权，但需事先报外经贸部备案。

第六条　经授权审批加工贸易业务的各级外经贸主管部门（简称加工贸易审批机关，下同）须按照外经贸部规定的统一规格、样式刻制加工贸易业务审批专用章，并由省级外经贸主管部门统一报外经贸部备案。

第七条　各级加工贸易审批机关名单及其加工贸易业务审批专用章（印模）由外经贸部统一送海关总署备案。

第八条　各级加工贸易审批机关，应具备使用计算机审批管理系统审批加工贸易的条件，须配备相应的计算机管理设备，加入中国国际电子商务网，并与外经贸部联网。

第九条　开展进口原料属于国家对加工贸易进口实行总量平衡管理的棉花、食糖、植物油、羊毛、天然橡胶、原油和成品油等商品的加工贸易业务，由经营企业（包括原部委总公司及其子公司）注册地省级加工贸易审批机关审批，各省级审批机关不得将审批权下放。

其他加工贸易业务由经营企业（包括原部委总公司及其子公司）注册地的加工贸易审批机关审批。

第三章　申报文件和材料

第十条　经营企业申请开展加工贸易业务时，必须提供下列证明文件和材料：

（一）经营企业出具的书面申请报告及加盖经营企业公章的《加工贸易业务申请表》（格式见附1）。

（二）经营企业进出口经营权批准文件（或外商投资企业批准证书）和工商营业执照（复印件）。

（三）加工企业注册地县级以上外经贸主管部门出具的加工企业生产能力证明正本（格式见附3），加工企业的工商营业执照（复印件）。

（四）经营企业对外签定的进出口合同（正本）。

（五）经营企业与加工企业签定的加工协议（合同）正本。

（六）审批机关认为需要出具的其他证明文件和材料。

第十一条 如经营企业或加工企业属于外商投资企业，除出具本办法第十条所规定的证明文件或材料外，须同时提供外经贸主管部门批准的能说明生产经营范围和规模的合同、章程，以及能确认已建成投产，投资方资金已如期到位，联合年检合格的证明文件。

第十二条 开展下列特定商品的加工贸易，除按本办法第十条和第十一条规定出具证明文件和材料外，须同时按下列规定相应提供其他证明文件和材料：

（一）开展进口料件属于废旧金属或物品的加工贸易，须按有关规定提供国家环保局出具的料件进口批准文件。

（二）开展进口料件或出口制成品属于易制毒化学品、军民通用化学品的加工贸易，须按有关规定提供有关部门出具的料件进口或制成品出口的批准文件。

第四章 加工贸易业务（合同）审批

第十三条 各级加工贸易审批机关在审批加工贸易业务时，须严格按照本办法第十条、第十一条和第十二条的规定，审核经营企业提供的有关证明文件和材料，严禁“三无”（无工厂、无加工设备、无工人）企业开展加工贸易，防止企业以加工贸易名义进行走私等违法活动。

第十四条 《加工贸易业务批准证》（格式见附2）是海关等部门据以办理加工贸易银行保证金台账相关手续的有效证明文件。对能够按规定提交各项证明文件和材料，且确有加工复出口能力的经营企业，由加工贸易审批机关审核签发《加工贸易业务批准证》，并加盖加工贸易业务审批专用章。

第十五条 加工贸易审批机关应认真填制《进口料件申请备案清章》和《出口制成品及对应进口料件消耗备案清单》（格式见附2），并加盖加工贸易业务审批专用章。

第十六条 加工贸易审批机关须严格按照海关总署、国家经贸委会同有关国家工业局制订并分批公布的全国统一的单耗标准审批加工贸易。对尚没有全国统一单耗标准的，加工贸易审批机关要严格审核企业所申报的单耗，征求生产行业主管部门和主管海关的意见后予以审批，海关凭加工贸易审批机关签发的《加工贸易业务批准证》予以备案。海关监管中发现单耗不符的，将意见函告原审批机关，由原审批机关予以调整，海关也相应办理有关内容的变更手续。

第十七条 加工贸易审批机关在审批时，必须认真审核《加工贸易加工企业生产能力证明》。《加工贸易加工企业生产能力证明》的有效期为一年。

加工企业注册地县级以上外经贸主管部门，应在严格查验加工企业生产能力和经营状况的基础上签发《加工贸易加工企业生产能力证明》，必要时，可征求生产行业主管部门的意见。

第十八条 国家将加工贸易进口商品分为禁止类、限制类和允许类，将加工贸易企业分为A类、B类、C类、D类（具体分类原则和分类目录按照国办发〔1999〕35号文件的规定另行对外公布并进行动态调整）；国家对开展限制类商品的加工贸易和C类企业开展的加工贸易实行银行保证金台账“实转”管理。

加工贸易审批机关在审批时，应认真审核加工贸易进口商品和企业的类别，如属于限制类商品或C类企业，应在《加工贸易业务批准证》备注栏内加注“实转”字样。

第十九条 各级加工贸易审批机关均不得批准D类加工贸易企业（包括经营企业和加工企业）开展加工贸易业务，不得批准任何经营企业开展进口料件属于禁止类商品的加工贸易业务。

第二十条 A类企业开展加工贸易，不实行银行保证金台账制度，但其加工贸易合同事先仍需报加工贸易审批机关审批。

第五章 批准证变更及延期审批

第二十一条 《加工贸易业务批准证》上规定的出口制成品返销期限原则上按企业出口合同有效期审批，一般不得超过一年，其中，食糖、棉花、植物油、羊毛和天然橡胶加工贸易的制成品返销期限原则上不超过6个月。

第二十二条 经营企业必须按《加工贸易业务批准证》规定的期限加工、返销制成品并办理核销手续。如因客观原因确需延长制成品返销期限，须在规定的制成品返销期限内报原审批机关批准，海关凭批件办理延期手续。

第二十三条 延期一般不得超过两次，每次延长期限一般不超过6个月。

第二十四条 经营企业必须按《加工贸易业务批准证》规定的内容加工出口，如因客观原因确需变更部分项目内容，须在《加工贸易业务批准证》规定的期限内报原审批机关批准，海关凭批件办理变更手续。

第六章 配额许可证管理

第二十五条 加工贸易进口料件原则上不实行配额许可证管理，但另有规定的除外。

第二十六条 国家对食糖、棉花、植物油、羊毛、天然橡胶和原油、成品油等加工贸易进口实行总量平衡和配额许可证管理。配额总量由国务院确定，具体分配管理办法按有关规定执行。

第二十七条 加工贸易进口配额当年有效，不得跨年度使用。外经贸部驻各地特派员办事处和配额许可证事务局负责按照加工贸易进口配额和省级加工贸易审批机关签发的《加工贸易业务批准证》签发加工贸易进口许可证。

加工贸易进口许可证有效期不得超过《加工贸易业务批准证》规定的制成品返销期限，对需跨年度的，不得超过次年2月底。

第二十八条 外经贸部驻各地特派员办事处应通过中国国际电子商务网，逐日向配额许可证事务局上报加工贸易进口发证数据，配额许可证事务局负责向外经贸部提供全国的加工贸易进口发证数据(包括配额许可证事务局的发证数据)。外经贸部将对发证情况进行定期或不定期检查，严禁越权、无配额或超配额等各种违规发证行为。

第二十九条 加工贸易制成品如属出口配额管理的，经营企业应凭出口配额和《加工贸易业务批准证》申领出口许可证，海关凭有效出口许可证验收。

第三十条 加工贸易进口料件或出口制成品如属于易制毒化学品、军民通用化学品，海关凭《加工贸易业务批准证》和有关部门出具的料件进口或制成品出口的批准文件办理备案手续。

第七章 统计监督及跟踪管理

第三十一条 各省级加工贸易审批机关须逐日汇总本地区加工贸易业务的审批情况和到期加工贸易业务的核销情况，并通过中国国际电子商务网，统一上报外经贸部。

第三十二条 各级加工贸易审批机关要加强对本地区加工贸易核销情况的监督检查和跟踪管理，要求经营企业在出口核销后的30天内将海关的核销通知单报原审批机关核销备案。对逾期未能办理核销备案的企业，要查清原因，并暂停批准其开展新的加工贸易业务。

第三十三条 外经贸部对各地的加工贸易审批情况进行定期或不定期检查，严禁越权、无配额和超配额等违规审批行为。

第三十四条 各级加工贸易审批机关要积极与海关、税务、银行和外汇等部门配合，加强部门间的信息交流与协作，加大对加工贸易的综合监管力度。

第八章 附 则

第三十五条 加工贸易保税进口料件应全部加工后复出口。如确有特殊原因，需将保税进口料件(或其制成品)在国内销售或转用于生产内销产品，按《加工贸易保税进口料件内销审批暂行办法》的有关规定办理。

第三十六条 国家允许开展加工贸易结转深加工复出口业务。但经营企业必须事先报经外经贸主管部门批准。具体管理办法另行制定。

第三十七条 保税区内企业开展加工贸易不实行银行保证金台账制度，按《保税区海关监管办法》执行。

第三十八条 加工贸易项下进口，不受一般贸易进口经营分工管理规定的限制，经营企业可自行组织进口。

第三十九条 外经贸部对违反本办法的审批机关，将予以通报批评，暂停或取消其加工贸易审批权；对发证机关，将予以通报批评，暂停或取消其进口发证权。

第四十条 对违反本办法的加工贸易企业，将予以通报批评，并通知海关记录违规一次，对情节严重的，暂停或取消其加工贸易经营权；对触犯刑律的，移交司法机关处理。

第四十一条 本办法自1999年6月1日起执行。

第四十二条 本办法由外经贸部负责解释。此前所发《对外贸易经济合作部关于印发对外加工装配业务有关问题的规定的通知》(〔89〕外经贸进出灵字第212号)等五个文件(清单见附4)同时废止；此前所发其他有关文件规定凡与本办法不一致的，均以本办法为准。

(附1、附2、附3略)

附4

自6月1日起废止文件目录(共5个)

一、《对外贸易经济合作部关于印发对外加工装配业务有关问题的规定的通知》(〔89〕外经贸进出灵字第212号)

二、《关于委托省、自治区、直辖市及计划单列市外经贸主管部门审批管理部委直属公司来料加工业务的通知》(〔1997〕外经贸政发第798号)

三、《关于统一使用加工贸易业务(合同)批准证的通知》(〔1998〕外经贸政发第21号)

四、《来料加工装配项目分类指导目录》(〔1998〕外经贸政发第193号)

五、《关于加工贸易业务审批工作有关事项的通知》(〔1999〕外经贸管发第64号)

海关总署 对外贸易经济合作部 国家经济贸易委员会关于加工贸易企业分类管理评定标准和审定程序问题的通知

署监〔1999〕522号

1999年7月12日

广东分署，各直属海关，各省、自治区、直辖市、计划单列市外经贸委(厅局)，经贸委(经委、计经委)：

为贯彻执行《国务院办公厅转发国家经贸委等部门关于进一步完善加工贸易银行保证金台账制度的意见》(国办发〔1999〕35号)，根据国务院领导指示精神，加工贸易部际联席会第二次会议通过了加工贸易企业分类管理的评定标准和审定程序，现就有关问题通知如下：

一、加工贸易企业不实行银行保证金台账制度的条件

经海关依据海关总署、外经贸部和国家经贸委联合下发的《中华人民共和国海关对企业实施分类管理办法》(署监〔1999〕240号)第六条的规定评定适用A类管理的加工贸易企业，且符合下列条件之一的，海关可不对其实行银行保证金台账制度：

(一)实行海关派员驻厂监管或与主管海关实行计算机联网管理的保税工厂；

(二)从事飞机、船舶等特殊行业加工贸易的；

(三)企业年进出口总额在3000万美元(含

3000万美元）以上，自营生产型企业年出口额在1000万美元（含1000万美元）以上，或年加工贸易出口额在1000万美元（含1000万美元）以上的。

二、加工贸易企业适用C类管理的审定标准

（一）企业有署监240号文件第九条所列情形之一的，海关对该企业实施C类管理；

（二）署监240号文件第九条（一）款所称“违规”，以海关依据《中华人民共和国海关法行政处罚实施细则》第三章的规定对企业违规行为进行的处罚且该处罚决定书已生效为准；但对违规行为处罚金额在人民币1000元（含1000元）以下的不作为企业管理类别评定的记录；

（三）审定适用C类、D类管理企业违规走私行为的时间界限为1998年8月1日。即：以企业在此时间后发生的违规和走私行为作为企业分类管理评定的记录。

三、加工贸易企业管理类别评定程序

（一）各海关成立企业分类管理委员会；

（二）企业主管海关提出不实行银行保证金台账制度的A类管理企业名单，在7个工作日内将企业名单抄送企业所在地（地、市级及以上，下同）外经贸、经贸委、税务、外汇管理、中国银行等有关部门征求意见。上述部门应在7个工作日内反馈意见，对确定的企业管理类别有异议时，应向海关提供详细的说明和有关证明材料，由海关进行复审；上述部门在规定期限内无反馈意见的，视为无不同意见。

（三）海关发现企业有违规或走私行为的，应随时对企业的管理类别按有关规定调整为C类或D类进行管理。对审定适用C类或D类管理的企业，海关于审定之日将企业名单抄送所在地外经贸、经贸委、税务、外汇管理、中国银行等有关部门，并自审定之日起三日后开始对企业实施C类或D类管理。

（四）海关不向社会公告企业所适用的管理类别，但应通知有关企业（适用B类管理的企业除外）。如企业对海关审定的管理类别不服时，可根据《中华人民共和国行政复议法》的有关规定申请复议。

以上请遵照执行。

对外贸易经济合作部关于发布《白银出口管理暂行办法》的通知

〔1999〕外经贸管发第702号

1999年11月26日

各省、自治区、直辖市及计划单列市外经贸委（厅、局），各有关外经贸企业：

现将国务院批准的《白银出口管理暂行办法》印发给你们，请遵照执行。

特此通知。

附件：一、《白银出口管理暂行办法》

二、2000年度白银出口企业名单

附件一

白银出口管理暂行办法

为贯彻落实国务院关于白银管理改革的指示精神，对白银实行出口管理，根据《中华人民共和国对外贸易法》的有关规定，制定本办法。

第一条 本办法所称白银系指银粉、未锻造银及银的半制成品（具体管理名录见附件）。

第二条 人民银行库存白银的出口仍按现行规定办理。

第三条 国家对白银出口实行配额许可证管理，具体按照外经贸部《关于出口商品配额编报、下达和组织实施暂行办法的实施细则》（〔1998〕外经贸管发第980号）执行。

第四条 经外经贸部核定具有白银出口经营资格的企业方可经营白银一般贸易出口。按照优胜劣汰的原则，外经贸部每年对白银一般贸易出口企业核定一次并予以公布。

第五条 外经贸部授权配额许可证事务局核发白银出口许可证。海关凭出口许可证验放。

第六条 外经贸部授权的发证机关，要严格审核企业白银出口经营资格和配额数量，审核企业的出口合同，核发出口许可证。

第七条 加工贸易企业进口本办法第一条所列以外的含白银商品，需要加工复出口白银，由企业提出申请，其加工贸易业务由企业注册地省级外经贸主管部门审批。海关凭《加工贸易业务批准证》办理合同登记备案手续。考虑到白银生产的特殊性，外经贸主管部门在批准证的备注栏内注明“复出口白银以进口料件商检后核定的数量为准”。

加工贸易进口料件进口后180天内，省级外经贸主管部门需将企业加工出口白银的数量、进口料件商检证明、企业加工工艺及单耗情况等报外经贸部，同时抄报国家有色金属工业局。外经贸部征求国家有色局意见后，办理批复手续。如批复的白银进口含量、单耗、应加工出口数量等与原审批、备案情况不一致的，外经贸部将批件抄送备案主管海关，企业需办理相应的合同变更手续，海关按修改后的单耗予以监管核销。企业凭外经贸部批件到配额许可证事务局申领出口许可证。海关凭出口许可证验放。

第八条 对违反本办法及其他有关出口管理规定的出口企业，一经查实，将根据情节轻重，处以扣减出口配额、直至取消其白银出口经营权的处罚。

第九条 凡以前的有关规定与本办法不一致的，以本办法为准。

第十条 本办法自2000年1月1日起执行。在此日期之前已向海关办理了白银加工贸易合同备案手续的仍按原规定执行。

附：《出口白银管理名录》

附

出口白银管理名录

名　　称	协调制度编码
银　粉	71061000
未锻造的银（包括块、锭、粒及铸条等）	71069100
银的半制成品（包括经锻轧的条、棒、丝、板、片、带、管、箔及型材等）	71069200

上述所称“银”是指纯银，不包括镀金、镀铂的银，也不包括银合金及以其他金属或材料为底包银或镀银的制品。

附件二

2000年度白银出口企业名单

中国印钞造币总公司
中国铜铅锌集团公司

国家环境保护总局　对外贸易经济合作部海关总署关于印发《消耗臭氧层物质进出口管理办法》的通知

环发〔1999〕278号
1999年12月3日

各省、自治区、直辖市环境保护局、外经贸委(厅、局)，海关总署广东分署、各直属海关：

为履行《关于消耗臭氧层物质的蒙特利尔议定书》(伦敦修正案)，加强对我国消耗臭氧层物质的进出口管理，根据国务院批准的《中国逐步淘汰消耗臭氧层物质的国家方案(修订稿)》，制定了《消耗臭氧层物质进出口管理办法》。现将该办法印发给你们，请遵照执行。

附：消耗臭氧层物质进出口管理办法

附　件

消耗臭氧层物质进出口管理办法

第一条　为履行《关于消耗臭氧层物质的蒙特利尔议定书》(伦敦修正案)(以下简称《议定书》)，加强对我国消耗臭氧层物质的进出口管理，根据国务院批准的《中国逐步淘汰消耗臭氧层物质国家方案》(修订稿)，制定本办法。

第二条　在中华人民共和国领域内从事《议定书》缔约国之间的受控消耗臭氧层物质进出口的经营活动，适用本办法。

本办法所称消耗臭氧层物质，包括消耗臭氧层物质及生产和消费消耗臭氧层物质的相关设备和产品。

第三条　国家环境保护总局、对外贸易经济合作部和海关总署对受控消耗臭氧层物质的进出口实行统一监督管理。

(一)制定并发布《中国进出口受控消耗臭氧层物质名录》(以下简称《名录》)；对列入《名录》的消耗臭氧层物质，实行进出口配额许可证管理；

(二)制定并发布禁止进出口的消耗臭氧层物质名录。

第四条　申请《名录》中所列消耗臭氧层物质

进出口的企业，必须按照国家有关规定，提前三个月向国家环境保护总局和对外贸易经济合作部提出消耗臭氧层物质进出口配额书面申请，并提供1995—1997年及提出申请时上一年度相应消耗臭氧层物质的进出口、销售和使用情况及其证明。

第五条 对外贸易经济合作部会同国家环境保护总局负责确定《名录》所列消耗臭氧层物质的国家年度进出口配额总量和申请企业的进出口配额量；受理企业对《名录》中所列消耗臭氧层物质的进出口配额申请；签发《受控消耗臭氧层物质进出口审批单》(以下简称《进出口审批单》)。

第六条 持有国家环境保护总局和对外贸易经济合作部签发的《进出口审批单》的企业，应向对外贸易经济合作部授权的发证机构申领《进出口许可证》。

对外贸易经济合作部凭国家环境保护总局和对外贸易经济合作部签发的《进出口审批单》，签发《进出口许可证》。

《进出口许可证》实行一批一证制。进出口许可证的申领和管理按照对外贸易经济合作部有关进出口许可证管理办法执行。

第七条 出口回收的消耗臭氧层物质的企业，须持有国家环境保护总局签发的回收证明，直接向对外贸易经济合作部授权的发证机构申请出口许可证；

出口回收的消耗臭氧层物质的容器上必须贴有由国家环境保护总局统一印制的“回收的消耗臭氧层物质”的标志，并准确标示物质名称和含量。

第八条 海关对《名录》所列的受控消耗臭氧层物质的进出口，凭对外贸易经济合作部签发的《进出口许可证》监管验放。

第九条 经营消耗臭氧层物质进出口的企业，必须按照《议定书》有关规定，进行消耗臭氧层物质的进出口贸易；不得转让或买卖进出口配额和进出口许可证。

第十条 违反本办法规定的，由有关部门按照国家有关法律、法规的规定进行处理。

第十一条 国家环境保护总局、对外贸易经济合作部和海关总署有权对经营企业的进出口经营情况进行监督和检查。

第十二条 国家环境保护总局、对外贸易经济合作部和海关总署根据管理需要联合设立专门办事机构负责本办法的实施，并制定本办法的实施细则。该办事机构设在国家环境保护总局。

第十三条 本办法由国家环境保护总局、对外贸易经济合作部和海关总署根据各自的职责分工进行解释。

第十四条 本办法自发布之日起施行。

对外贸易经济合作部关于印发《蚕丝类出口经营管理暂行办法》及有关事项的通知

〔1999〕外经贸管发第714号

1999年12月9日

各省、自治区、直辖市及计划单列市外经贸委（厅、局）：

为维护蚕丝类出口经营秩序，推动茧丝绸贸工农一体化进程，外经贸部决定调整现行蚕丝类出口经营管理体制，制订了《蚕丝类出口经营管理暂行办法》，现印发给你们。有关事项通知如下：

一、蚕丝类出口，按照《蚕丝类出口经营管理暂行办法》(见附件一）执行。

二、根据各省、自治区、直辖市和计划单列市人民政府的推荐意见，外经贸部核定了2000年蚕丝类出口经营企业名单（见附件二)。

三、2000年1月1日起，蚕丝类出口许可证由配额许可证事务局和外经贸部驻各地特派员办事处负责发放。

特此通知，请遵照执行。

附件：一、蚕丝类出口经营管理暂行办法

二、2000年蚕丝类核定出口经营企业名单（不包括三资企业）

附件一

蚕丝类出口经营管理暂行办法

第一条 为加强蚕丝类出口经营管理，推动茧丝绸行业贸工农一体化进程，根据《中华人民共和国对外贸易法》，特制定本办法。

第二条 本办法所称蚕丝类包括蚕茧和蚕丝，包括海关编码前四位为5001－5005的商品。

第三条 国家对蚕丝类出口实行配额和许可证管理。蚕丝类出口配额的申报和下达，按照外经贸部《关于出口商品配额编报、下达和组织实施暂行办法的实施细则》（〔1998〕外经贸管发第980号）执行。

第四条 为维护我国蚕丝类出口经营秩序，蚕丝类出口由外经贸部核定的具有蚕丝类出口经营资格的企业按照有关规定经营。根据企业出口经营状况，按照优胜劣汰的原则，外经贸部将每年或两年对蚕丝类出口企业经营资格重新核定，实行动态管理。

第五条 中国纺织品进出口商会丝绸分会，全面负责蚕丝类出口协调工作，包括：研究制定蚕丝类出口价格、市场协调办法；根据举报，负责调查低价出口等违规行为，将调查结果和处理建议上报外经贸部（贸管司）；跟踪研究国际、国内市场动态；调查了解蚕丝类出口中的问题，并向外经贸部提出建议；了解、反映出口企业的困难，做好服务工作。

第六条 蚕丝类出口企业须加入中国纺织品进出口商会丝绸分会，自觉遵守丝绸分会的协调管理规定，积极反映出口情况和问题。

第七条 企业出口蚕丝类要按规定进行法定检验。

第八条 出口许可证发证机关要严格审核出口企业的出口合同等有关单据，按有关规定签发出口许可证。

第九条 蚕丝类出口继续实行限定报关口岸。具体按照1997年国家经贸委、对外贸易经济合作部和海关总署联合发布的《关于丝类商品出口报关口岸的通知》（国经贸〔1997〕84号）和《关于丝类商品出口报关口岸的补充通知》（国经贸〔1997〕386号）的有关规定执行。

第十条 企业申领出口许可证和出口报关时，必须详细注明品种、规格。海关严格凭出口许可证、出入境检验检疫部门出具的“出境货物通关单”等验放。

第十一条 企业有如下行为者，视为违反本办法：

（一）违反协调价格，低价出口的；

（二）串证出口的；

（三）伪报货名、逃避出口配额许可证管理的；

（四）无出口经营资格擅自经营蚕丝类出口业务的；

（五）其它违反有关外贸管理规定的行为。

对有上述行为的企业，一经查实，将根据情节轻重，予以通报批评、扣减出口配额、取消其蚕丝类出口经营资格、直至取消对外贸易经营许可等处罚。

第十二条 三资企业和边贸出口蚕丝类，仍按现行有关规定办理。

第十三条 本办法自2000年1月1日起执行，由外经贸部负责解释。

附件二

2000年蚕丝类核定出口经营企业名单（不包括三资企业）

序号	地区	企业名称	进出口企业代码	海关注册代码
1	北京	北京市丝绸进出口公司	1100101120079	1105910024
2	天津	北方国际集团天津丝绸进出口股份有限公司	1200103064808	1201910019
3	河北	河北省纺织品进出口集团公司	1300104324106	1301915003
4	山西	山西省丝绸进出口集团公司	1400110017620	1401910031
5	内蒙古	内蒙古自治区新纺业进出口集团股份有限公司	150011412583X	1501910032
6	辽宁	辽宁省丝绸进出口公司	2100117563579	2102912014
7	吉林	吉林省纺织品进出口公司	2200123918559	2201918009
8		长春市纺织品进出口公司	2201123999571	2201910021
9		东方国际集团上海市丝绸进出口有限公司	3100132212400	3101915037
10	上海	上海国丝国际贸易有限公司	3100630631712	3122210467
11		上海绢纺织厂	3100132917312	3106915006
12	江苏	江苏省丝绸进出口集团股份有限公司	3200134778088	3201919024
13		南京纺织品进出口股份有限公司	3201134967428	3201910012
14	浙江	浙江省丝绸进出口公司	3300142928090	3301910042
15		浙江威莱集团公司	3300146974916	3305950027
16	宁波	宁波市丝绸进出口公司	3302144073938	3302910024
17	安徽	安徽省丝绸进出口公司	3400148940883	3401910009
18	福建	福建省丝绸进出口公司	3500158142201	3501912720
19	江西	江西省丝绸进出口公司	3600158266597	3601910024
20	山东	山东省丝绸进出口公司	3700163049650	3702910026
21	河南	河南省丝绸进出口公司	4100169952955	4101910008
22	湖北	湖北省丝绸进出口集团公司	4200177589199	4201910518
23	湖南	湖南省丝绸进出口公司	4300183764176	4301910096
24	广东	广东省丝绸进出口集团公司	4400190341008	4401913297
25		广州绢麻工贸有限公司	4401190504129	4401913297
26	广西	广西壮族自治区丝绸进出口公司	4500198224009	4501910011
27	海南	海南丝绸进出口公司	4600201285313	4601111008
28	四川	四川省丝绸进出口公司	5100201813657	5101910025
29		成都市丝绸进出口公司	5101201935742	5101910047
30	重庆	重庆茧丝绸集团有限公司	5102202803506	5102910254
31	贵州	贵州省丝绸进出口公司	5200214400077	5201919077
32	云南	云南省纺织品进出口公司	5300216526482	5301910008
33	陕西	陕西省丝绸进出口公司	6100220532033	6101918013

续表

序号	地区	企业名称	进出口企业代码	海关注册代码
34	中国丝绸	中丝生丝进出口公司	1100101126841	1101919053
35	进出口	中国蚕丝绸缎进出口公司	1100101255758	1101919095
36	总公司	中丝深圳进出口公司	440312220680	4403119070

备注：黑龙江、新疆未推荐上报，此次暂不予核定。

海关总署　国家经贸委　外经贸部关于企业分类管理标准若干问题的补充通知

署监〔1999〕817号

1999年12月13日

广东分署、各直属海关，各省、自治区、直辖市、计划单列市经贸委（经委、计经委），外经贸委（厅、局）：

为进一步做好企业分类管理工作，配合完善加工贸易银行保证金台账制度的实施，在具体评定企业管理类别中更好地体现区分企业技术性违规和实质性违规的精神，经请示国务院同意，现就企业管理类别评定标准问题补充通知如下：

一、企业符合《中华人民共和国海关对企业实施分类管理办法实施细则》（署监〔1999〕345号）第二十九条规定条件的，海关不对其实行银行保证金台账制度。

对依据《中华人民共和国海关对企业实施分类管理办法》（署监〔1999〕240号）第六条的规定评定适用A类管理的加工贸易企业，海关仍实行银行保证金台账“空转”制度，其进口限制类商品的，也免缴保证金。

评定适用A类管理企业时，应严格按照有关文件规定的标准执行；同时，对企业实行动态管理。企业发生走私、违规行为的，海关应随即调整其管理类别。

二、企业违规行为处罚金额在人民币10000元（含10000元）以下的，不作为C类管理企业的评定记录。

三、对企业一年内出现两次及以上违规行为，但其违规次数不超过上年报并次数1‰的，可不定为C类管理企业。

四、1999年6月1日后发生的违规行为作为C类管理企业的评定记录。

五、各关应按本通知规定对原评定的企业管理类别进行相应调整。

六、请各海关于1999年12月20日将本通知所附公告稿对外公告。

以上请遵照执行。执行中有何问题，请及时上报。

附件：公告稿

附　件

中华人民共和国海关公告

接中华人民共和国海关总署通知，自2000年1月1日起，海关对企业分类评定标准进行部分调整。现将所调整内容公告如下：

一、企业符合《中华人民共和国海关对企业实施分类管理办法实施细则》第二十九条规定条件的，海关不对其实行银行保证金台账制度。

对依据《中华人民共和国海关对企业实施分类管理办法》第六条的规定评定适用A类管理的加工贸易企业，海关仍实行银行保证金台账“空转”制度，其进口限制类商品的，也免缴保证金。

评定适用A类管理企业时，应严格按照有关文件规定的标准执行；同时，对企业实行动态管理。企业发生走私、违规行为的，海关应随即调整其管理类别。

二、企业违规行为处罚金额在人民币10000元（含10000元）以下的，不作为C类管理企业的记录。

三、对企业一年内出现两次及以上违规行为，但其违规次数不超过上年报关次数1‰的，可不定为C类管理企业。

四、1999年6月1日后发生的违规行为作为C类管理企业的评定记录。

中华人民共和国　海关
1999年12月20日

对外贸易经济合作部关于印发《国际招标机构资格审定办法》的通知

〔1999〕外经贸机电发第599号
1999年10月14日

国务院各有关部委、直属机构，各省、自治区、直辖市及计划单列市外经贸委（厅、局），各部门、各地方机电产品进出口办公室，各招标机构：

为建立良好的招标竞争机制，保障国际招标规范有序进行，现将《国际招标机构资格审定办法》印发给你们，请遵照执行。

特此通知

附件：如文

附　件

国际招标机构资格审定办法

第一章　总　　则

第一条　为了保证招标机构的服务质量，建立良好的招标竞争机制，保障国际招标规范有序进行，维护招标的公开、公平、公正性，依据中华人民共和国《对外贸易法》和对外贸易经济合作部1999年第1号令《机电产品国际招标管理办法》(以下简称1号令)，制定本办法。

第二条　国际招标机构是指从事机电产品国际招标业务和从事其他国际招标采购业务的招标机构。凡从事上述业务的招标机构均实行资格审定制。

第三条　招标机构资格审定是指招标机构资格等级审定和定期复审。招标机构资格等级分为甲、乙两级。

第四条　对外贸易经济合作部（以下简称外经贸部）负责全国国际招标机构的资格审定工作。

第五条　各省、自治区、直辖市、计划单列市外经贸主管部门或机电产品进出口管理机构负责本地区招标机构的初审工作。

第二章　资格条件

第六条　招标机构资格申请需具备以下条件：

（一）招标机构与行政机关和其他国家机关没有行政隶属关系。

（二）必须是独立核算的企业法人。

（三）必须有健全的组织机构和内部管理的规章制度。

（四）必须有固定的营业场所和开展国际招标业务所需的设施、资金以及连通专业信息网络的现代化办公条件。

（五）具备编制中、英文招标文件的专业人员。

第七条　申请甲级招标资格，除具备第六条款外，还需具备以下条件：

（一）具有5年以上机电产品国际招标业绩，或具有5年以上外贸经营权，且进出口商品主要为机电产品、高新技术产品。

（二）注册资本800万元（人民币）以上。

（三）近三年年均外贸进出口总额在8亿美元以上，或近三年机电产品国际招标业绩累计在1.2亿美元以上（以1号令附件二“评标报告”中预计合同价为依据，下同）。

（四）中级职称及以上外贸专业人员、专职招标人员不得少于职工总数的70%。

第八条　甲级招标机构，可从事利用国外贷款和国内资金采购机电产品的国际招标业务和其他国际招标采购业务，具有与国外中标厂商签订招标项下合同的进出口经营权。

第九条　申请乙级招标资格，除具备第六条款外，还需具备以下条件：

（一）具有3年以上机电产品国际招标业绩，或具有3年以上外贸经营权，且进出口商品主要为机电产品、高新技术产品。

（二）注册资本500万元（人民币）以上。

（三）近三年年均外贸进出口总额在5亿美元以上，或近三年机电产品国际招标业绩累计在5000万美元以上。

（四）中级职称及以上外贸专业人员、专职招标人员不得少于职工总数的60%。

第十条　乙级招标机构，可从事利用国内资金采购机电产品的国际招标业务。

第十一条　近三年机电产品国内招标业绩累计在3亿元人民币以上的招标机构可预申请乙级资格。当第一年机电产品国际招标业绩达到2000万美元时，可正式申请乙级资格。

第三章　资格申请及审定

第十二条　招标机构在申请或预申请国际招标资格时需提交以下材料：

（一）省、自治区、直辖市、计划单列市外经贸主管部门或机电产品进出口管理机构的初审函件。

（二）申请书。内容包括：组建时间、人员结构情况，专家支持系统和计算机、信息网络等配置情况，国际、国内招标业绩或机电产品、高新技术产品进出口业绩综述。

（三）招标机构章程。

（四）企业法人营业执照（复印件加盖原注册机关的确认章）。

（五）进出口企业资格证书。

（六）机电产品国际招标业绩一览表（附一）及分项表（附二、三，以统计月报为准）或进出口贸易业绩一览表（附四）。

（七）近三年外贸 500 强排列次序和进出口金额。

（八）机构设置表（附五）。

（九）其他有关招标机构的文件。

第十三条 外经贸部接到招标机构符合要求的资格申请后，在一个月内组织审核。对符合条件者，由外经贸部颁发《国际招标资格甲级证书》或《国际招标资格乙级证书》（以下简称证书）。证书自签发之日起生效，有效期 3 年。

第十四条 对预申请乙级资格的招标机构，经外经贸部审核认为符合条件的，颁发《国际招标资格乙级证书》，证书自签发之日起生效，有效期为一年。

第四章 资格复审、变更和终止

第十五条 外经贸部每 3 年对招标机构的资格进行复审。对符合其资格等级条件的，重新颁发相应的等级证书。

第十六条 招标机构在有效期届满后的第一个月向外经贸部提出复审申请。外经贸部接到招标机构符合要求的资格复审申请后，在一个月内组织审核。

第十七条 资格复审所需申报的材料，除依照本办法第十二条款申报外，还需提交经工商税务部门年审通过的财务报表（即损益表、资产负债表）及报表说明。

第十八条 招标机构在变更机构名称时，应向外经贸部申请更换证书；招标机构在组织机构发生重大变化时，应向外经贸部重新申请证书。

第十九条 招标机构在终止国际招标业务后的一个月内，应将证书交回外经贸部。

第五章 违规处罚

第二十条 下列行为之一者，属违规：

（一）资格申请或资格复审时弄虚作假的；

（二）涂改、转让资格证书的；

（三）在招标业务中有下列违反 1 号令行为的：

1．相互串通虚假招标的；

2．未按《机电产品国际招标管理办法》评标规则评标的；

3．评标报告不如实反映招标文件、投标书实际情况的；

（四）其他违反《对外贸易法》、1 号令和本办法的行为。

第二十一条 处罚

（一）属第十九条（一）款者，取消申请或暂停一年资格，并在一年内不再接受其申请。

（二）属第十九条（二）款者，取消其国际招标资格，并在 3 年内不再接受其申请。

（三）属第十九条（三）、（四）款者，视情节进行通报批评、暂停或取消其国际招标资格。

（四）未按规定时间参加资格复审的，被视为自动放弃其国际招标资格。

（五）一年内累计 3 次不按规定逐月上报统计资料的，暂停其招标资格一年。

第六章 附 则

第二十二条 本办法由外经贸部负责解释。过去有关规定与本办法不符的，均以本办法为准。

第二十三条 本办法自 2000 年 1 月 1 日起施行。

（附一至附五略）

对外贸易经济合作部　国家经济贸易委员会
财政部　公安部　国家工商行政管理局　海关总署
关于印发《关于执行<关于禁止非法拼（组）装汽车、摩托车的通告>的实施细则》的通知

〔1999〕外经贸机电发第628号

1999年10月25日

国务院有关部门机电产品进出口办公室，各省、自治区、直辖市及计划单列市机电产品进出口办公室、经贸委（经委、计经委），财政厅（局），公安厅（局），工商行政管理局，广东海关分署，各直属海关，外经贸部驻各地特派员办事处，配额许可证事务局：

为认真贯彻落实党中央、国务院对打击走私工作的部署，更好地执行《关于禁止非法拼（组）装汽车、摩托车的通告》，打击汽车、摩托车非法拼（组）装与走私行为，经国务院批准，现将《关于执行<关于禁止非法拼（组）装汽车、摩托车的通告>的实施细则》印发给你们，请认真贯彻执行。

特此通知。

附件：如文

附　件

关于执行《关于禁止非法拼（组）装汽车、摩托车的通告》的实施细则

第一条　根据《关于禁止非法拼（组）装汽车、摩托车的通告》，制定本实施细则。

第二条　国家机械工业局负责对现行《全国汽车、民用改装车和摩托车生产企业及产品目录》（以下简称《目录》）进行整顿，并尽快修改制定新的《目录管理办法》。

第三条　申请进口汽车、摩托车关键件的生产企业，根据国家批准项目确定的车型，按照机电产品进口管理渠道和程序，向对外贸易经济合作部（以下简称“外经贸部”）提出进口汽车、摩托车关键件的申请。

外经贸部审批进口汽车、摩托车关键件并签发《进口配额证明》或《机电产品进口登记表》，实行一型一证。

《进口配额证明》和《机电产品进口登记表》不得更改。

第四条　外经贸部及其授权的许可证发证机关凭《进口配额证明》发放《进口许可证》，并在备注栏内注明《进口配额证明》的编号。

不得越权发放《进口许可证》；越权发放的，要追究主管单位和当事者的责任。

第五条　申请进口汽车、摩托车关键件的生产企业，向国家限定的汽车、摩托车零件报关口岸办理进口报关纳税手续。

海关凭《进口配额证明》和《进口许可证》或《机电产品进口登记表》验放汽车、摩托车关键件，并签发《关税缴纳证明书》和《货物进口证明书》，实行一型一证。

第六条　凡未持有效《进口配额证明》和《进口许可证》或《机电产品进口登记表》的，或在非指定港口接卸进口汽车、摩托车关键件的，由海关按海关法等有关规定予以处罚。

第七条 下列情况之一者，属非法拼（组）装汽车、摩托车行为：

一、未列入《目录》的企业利用进口关键件组装生产汽车、摩托车的；

二、列入《目录》的企业利用进口关键件组装生产汽车、摩托车，但未经国家批准立项的；或虽经国家批准列项但不能提供外经贸部签发的《进口配额证明》或《机电产品进口登记表》以及许可证发证机关签发的《进口许可证》和海关签发的《关税缴纳证明书》、《货物进口证明书》的；

三、虽持有上述证明文件，但生产的产品与批准进口的车型、数量、规格或用途不符的，或不按规定使用上述证明文件的；

四、生产企业采用国家批准的进口关键总成生产的汽车、摩托车，其关键总成和非关键进口件的总价值超过原进口车型60%，又无整车进口证明和按整车完税证明的。

第八条 国家禁止进口右置方向盘汽车和二手(旧）汽车、二手（旧）摩托车，执法部门一经发现，应按照走私予以没收，并拆解，不得以整车形式销售；公安交通管理部门对以上车辆不予办理牌证。国家不再批准进口用于维修的汽车车身。

第九条 对以废钢铁名义进口的旧汽车及其部件，必须压扁后才能进口，并实行裸装，否则海关不予接受报关。

第十条 国家工商行政管理局对利用进口汽车车身、发动机和摩托车车架、发动机生产的车辆实行号码备案制。列入《目录》的企业，利用上述进口件生产车辆的，须持《进口配额证明》和《进口许可证》或《机电产品进口登记表》以及《货物进口证明书》和《关税缴纳证明书》，将合法生产的汽车车辆识别号《或底盘号）和发动机号码，摩托车车架号及发动机号码报国家工商行政管理局备案，以备办案查询。

第十一条 走私、无进口证明、非法拼（组）装车辆套用国产车商标、国产车《合格证》的，是套用国产车《目录》行为，按走私、无进口证明、非法（组）装车辆予以没收。

国家机械工业局对易被套用《目录》内的国产车辆的车型，实行车辆识别号码备案制。具体办法由国家机械工业局商公安部另行制定。

第十二条 公安交通管理部门对国家批准利用进口关键件组装的汽车、摩托车和易被套用国产车《目录》的汽车、摩托车，根据国家机械工业局颁发的《目录》及配套光盘数据，办理注册登记。对不符合规定的车辆予以没收。

公安交通管理部门发现有非法拼（组）装或有套用《目录》嫌疑的车型，应及时向国家机械工业局查询取证。

第十三条 公安、海关、工商行政管理等执法部门查获的非法拼（组）装车辆一律没收，由查获的部门处理。各执法部门按照公安部、海关总署、国家工商行政管理局《关于启用新版＜没收走私汽车、摩托车证明书＞的通知》（公通字〔1995〕20号）的规定办理没收手续和申领没收的非法拼（组）装车辆的证明书，为了便于管理非法拼（组）装车辆的证明书，其证明书也使用《没收走私汽车、摩托车证明书》，一车一证。

第十四条 《没收走私汽车、摩托车证明书》由国家工商局、海关总署、公安部按系统审核发放。海关总署、国家工商局每月将发放的《没收走私汽车、摩托车证明书》的数量、编号、车牌型号、车身颜色、发动机号码、底盘（车架）号码、裁定没收证明文书编号、签发日期等情况汇总后送公安部，公安部汇总后通过《全国进口机动车计算机核查系统》通报各地公安交通管理部门。

第十五条 执法部门没收的非法拼（组）装汽车、摩托车，要按照《公安部、海关总署、国家工商行政管理局关于贯彻实施＜国务院办公厅关于加强进口汽车牌证管理的通知＞有关问题的通知》（公发〔1993〕7号）的规定，交由国家指定的销售部门统一销售。禁止销售给从事非法拼（组）装汽车、摩托车的当事人。

第十六条 对没收处理的非法拼（组）装汽车、摩托车，公安交通管理部门凭《没收走私汽车、摩托车证明书》和国家指定销售部门的销售发票，并与公安部的通报核实无误后，办理注册登记。对不具备上述手续的车辆，公安交通管理部门不予办理注册登记，并按规定予以没收。

公安交通管理部门对这些车辆按没收走私汽车、摩托车的有关规定进行统计。

第十七条 对生产和买卖非法拼（组）装汽车、摩托车的，视情节应当给予下列处罚：

一、工商行政管理机关查扣非法拼（组）装汽车、摩托车，没收全部销售货款、未销售的车辆及进口的汽车、摩托车关键件；

二、工商行政管理机关对于从事生产和经销非法拼（组）装汽车、摩托车的单位，给予生产或经销金额一倍以上的罚款。情节严重者，吊销其营业执照。

三、对于构成犯罪的有关人员，移送司法部门依法追究刑事责任；

四、国家机械工业局对《目录》内企业从事非法拼（组）装汽车、摩托车的，或以出卖、提供本企业的产品商标、名称、型号和产品合格证等方式参与非法拼（组）装汽车、摩托车的，分别处以取消该车型产品目录、取消部分车型产品目录、直至取消生产企业及产品目录。

对伪造、变造、买卖《进口配额证明》、《机电产品进口登记表》、《进口许可证》、《关税缴纳证明书》、《货物进口证明书》和《没收走私汽车、摩托车证明书》的，按《刑法》第二百八十条的规定处罚。

对转让、涂改、冒用上述证件的，按其他有关规定处理。

第十八条 非法拼（组）装车辆的没收款和罚款的上缴，应按照财政部《罚没财物和追回脏款脏物管理办法》〔（86）财预字第228号〕、《罚款代收代缴管理办法》（财预字〔1998〕201号）规定执行。

第十九条 工商行政管理、公安和海关等执法部门要相互配合，及时交换情况信息，共同做好打击非法拼（组）装汽车、摩托车的工作。

第二十条 执法部门的工作人员违反本细则，利用职权徇私舞弊、玩忽职守的，根据情节给予行政处分，触犯刑律的，移送司法机关，依法追究刑事责任。

第二十一条 本细则所指汽车、摩托车关键件是指汽车底盘、汽车车身（含驾驶室）及发动机和摩托车车架及发动机。

第二十二条 以前各部门所发文件与本《实施细则》相抵触的，以本《实施细则》规定为准。

第二十三条 本细则由对外贸易经济合作部会同有关部门负责解释。

第二十四条 本细则自2000年1月1日起施行。

科学技术部　对外贸易经济合作部关于印发《国家高新技术产业开发区高新技术产品出口基地认定暂行办法》的通知

国科发火字〔1999〕523号

1999年11月16日

各省、自治区、直辖市、计划单列市人民政府：

科技兴贸行动计划实施方案已经确定，在国家高新技术产业开发区，选择培养一批国家高新技术产品出口基地，给予重点扶持，使之在短期内形成有特色并拥有出口产品的高新技术产品出口基地。为规范高新技术产品出口基地的审批手续，现将《国家高新技术产业开发区高新技术产品出口基地认定暂行办法》印发给你们，请予试行。

附　件

国家高新技术产业开发区高新技术产品出口基地认定暂行办法

第一条　为实施科技兴贸行动计划，促进我国高新技术产品的出口，加快国家高新技术产业开发区的国际化进程，规范国家高新技术产业开发区高新技术产品出口基地的管理，制定本办法。

第二条　本办法适用于国家高新技术产业开发区（以下简称国家高新区）。

第三条　国家高新区高新技术产品出口基地由科学技术部和对外贸易经济合作部批准设立，科学技术部火炬高技术产业开发中心（以下简称火炬中心）负责日常管理及指导工作。

第四条　申报国家高新区高新技术产品出口基地，应当具备下列条件：

（一）国家高新区总体发展迅速，软硬环境建设良好，高新技术产品发展强劲，孵化、创新体系比较健全，能为出口企业提供优良服务。

（二）区内高新技术企业产品出口增长较快，能在短短内形成有较大规模的出口主导产品，30%以上的出口产品拥有自主知识产权。

（三）区内年出口额超过1亿美元；低于1亿美元者，年出口额达到300万美元的骨干出口企业应超过10家。

（四）出口产品以高新技术产品为主，高新技术产品出口创汇额占区内创汇总额的50%以上。

（五）当地政府重视出口基地的建设和发展，制定相应的政策措施并给予必要的资金支持。

（六）具备一支精干高效、有外贸经验的管理人员队伍。

第五条　国家高新区高新技术产品出口基地的申报，由所在省、自治区、直辖市、计划单列市人民政府向科学技术部、对外贸易经济合作部提出申请并抄送火炬中心。受科学技术部、对外贸易经济合作部委托，火炬中心组织审核工作。对符合本办法第四条规定条件者，由科学技术部、对外贸易经济合作部批准设立国家高新区高新技术产品出口基地。

第六条　科学技术部、对外贸易经济合作部对国家高新区高新技术产品出口基地实行动态管理。对发展缓慢的国家高新区高新技术产品出口基地予以警告，直至取消其资格。

第七条　科学技术部、对外贸易经济合作部在认定国家高新区高新技术产品出口基地的过程中，根据产业结构的合理布局，对中西部地区适度放宽认定条件。

第八条　国家对国家高新区高新技术产品出口基地实行的重点扶植政策另行制定。

第九条　本办法自发布之日起施行。

利 用 外 资

国家旅游局 对外贸易经济合作部 关于更正《中外合资旅行社试点暂行办法》的通知

旅办发〔1999〕061号
1999年4月19日

各省、自治区、直辖市旅游局、外经贸委（厅、局）：

经国务院批准，国家旅游局、外经贸部于1998年12月2日联合发布了《中外合资旅行社试点暂行办法》（以下简称《暂行办法》），该《暂行办法》文字有误，现将全文更正，请遵照执行。

特此通知。

附件：如文

附 件

中外合资旅行社试点暂行办法

第一条 为了进一步扩大旅游业的对外开放，促进旅游业的发展，根据《中华人民共和国中外合资经营企业法》和《旅行社管理条例》及有关法律、法规，制定本办法。

第二条 本办法适用于外国公司、企业同中国公司、企业在中国境内设立的中外合资旅行社（以下简称“合资旅行社”）。

第三条 申请设立合资旅行社，中国合营者应当符合下列条件：

（一）为国际旅行社；

（二）申请前3年平均每年外联人数超过3万人/天；

（三）申请前3年平均每年旅游业务销售总额超过5000万元；

（四）为中国旅游行业协会的正式会员。

第四条 申请设立合资旅行社，外国合营者应当符合下列条件：

（一）为经营国际旅游的旅行社或拥有全资的经营国际旅游的旅行社的企业；

（二）旅游业务年销售总额5000万美元以上；

（三）加入国际或本国的电脑预订网络，或者已经形成自己的电脑预订网络；

（四）为其本国旅游行业协会的正式会员。

第五条 设立的合资旅行社应当符合以下条件：

（一）注册资本不少于500万元人民币；

（二）企业形式为有限责任公司；

（三）中方出资占注册资本的比例不低于51%；

（四）法定代表人由中方委派；

（五）有符合要求的营业场所、营业设施、经营人员；

（六）合资期限不超过20年。

第六条 合资旅行社按国际旅行社经营入境旅游的规定，交纳旅行社质量保证金。

第七条 合资旅行社的审批程序为：

（一）中国合营者向所在地的省（自治区、直辖市）或计划单列市旅游行政管理部门呈报设立合资旅行社的项目建议书和可行性研究报告等文件。省级旅游行政管理部门初审后转报国家旅游局。

中国合营者为中央企业的，由其主管部门初审后转报国家旅游局。

国家旅游局依据国家有关旅游管理的法律、法规对上报文件进行审批。

（二）中国合营者在得到国家旅游局的同意批复后，向所在地的省级外经贸主管部门呈报设立合资旅行社的合同、章程等文件。省级外经贸主管部门初审后转报外经贸部。

中国合营者为中央企业的，由其主管部门初审后转报外经贸部。

外经贸部依照国家有关外商投资的法律、法规对上报文件进行审批。

（三）获得批准同意设立的项目，中国合营者凭外经贸部颁发的《外商投资企业批准证书》和国家旅游局颁发的《旅行社业务经营许可证》，按照规定办理注册登记和税务登记手续。

第八条 申请设立合资旅行社应当提交以下文件：

（一）中国合营者资格证明材料，包括：营业执照副本、旅行社业务经营许可证、申请前3年的业务年检报告、有关旅游行业协会的会员证明；

（二）外国合营者的资格证明材料，包括：注册登记副本、银行资信证明、会计师事务所出具的财务状况证明材料、相关电脑公司提供的入网证明、本国旅游行业协会会员证明、申请前1年的年度报告；

（三）合资旅行社项目建议书；

（四）合资旅行社可行性研究报告；

（五）合资旅行社的合同与章程；

（六）法律、法规和审批机构要求提供的其他材料。

第九条 每个外国合营者只能在中国境内投资设立一家合资旅行社。

第十条 试点阶段暂不允许合资旅行社设立分支机构。

第十一条 合资旅行社可以经营入境旅游业务和国内旅游业务。

第十二条 合资旅行社暂不允许经营中国公民赴外国及香港特别行政区、澳门、台湾地区旅游业务。

第十三条 合资旅行社经营特种旅游项目和到特殊地区旅游的项目，须报国家旅游局及有关部门审批。

第十四条 合资旅行社不得组织安排含有淫秽、赌博、吸毒内容及其他有害于社会道德和人民身心健康的项目；不得组织含有损害中华人民共和国的国家利益和民族尊严内容的项目；不得组织含有中国法律、法规禁止内容的项目。

第十五条 合资旅行社在中国境内聘用导游员，按国家有关规定办理。

第十六条 合资旅行社须接受旅游行政管理部门的行业管理。

第十七条 合资旅行社须按规定向旅游行政管理等有关部门上报财务、会计和统计报表，接受业务检查。

第十八条 合资旅行社的外汇收支按照外商投资企业的有关办法办理。

第十九条 合资旅行社须遵守中华人民共和国法律、法规，受中国法律、法规管辖，其正当经营活动和合法权益受中国法律、法规的保护。

合资旅行社如有违反中国法律、法规的行为，按有关法律、法规处理。

第二十条 违反本办法规定的，由旅游行政管理部门根据《旅行社管理条例》和《旅行社管理条例实施细则》予以处罚。

第二十一条 本规定实施期间，《关于在国家旅游度假区内开办中外合资经营的第一类旅行社的审批管理暂行办法》继续有效。

第二十二条 香港特别行政区、澳门、台湾地区的投资者在祖国大陆投资设立合资旅行社，参照本规定执行。

第二十三条 本规定由国家旅游局和对外贸易经济合作部负责解释。

第二十四条 本规定自发布之日起实施。

中华人民共和国国家经济贸易委员会
中华人民共和国对外贸易经济合作部 令

第12号

1999年6月25日

《外商投资商业企业试点办法》已于1999年6月17日经国务院批准，现予发布，自发布之日起施行。

外商投资商业企业试点办法

第一条 为进一步扩大对外开放，促进商业企业的改革和发展，推动国内市场建设，使扩大商业领域利用外商投资试点健康有序地进行，根据《中华人民共和国中外合资经营企业法》和《中华人民共和国中外合作经营企业法》等有关法律、法规，制定本办法。

第二条 本办法适用于外国公司、企业同中国公司、企业在中国境内设立中外合资或合作商业企业（以下简称合营商业企业）。暂不允许外商独资设立商业企业。

第三条 设立的合营商业企业必须符合所在城市的商业发展规划，能够引进国际上先进的营销技术和管理经验，促进国内商业现代化，带动国内产品出口，产生良好的经济效益和社会效益。

第四条 设立合营商业企业的地区由国务院规定，目前暂限于省会城市、自治区首府、直辖市、计划单列市和经济特区（以下简称试点地区）。

第五条 合营商业企业的投资者应具备以下条件：

（一）外国合营者或外国合营者中的主要合营者（以下简称外国合营者）应为具有较强的经济实力、先进的商业经营管理经验和营销技术、广泛的国际销售网络、良好的信誉和经营业绩的企业，且能够通过拟设立的合营商业企业带动中国产品出口。

申请设立从事零售业务的合营商业企业的外国合营者，申请前3年年均商品销售额应在20亿美元以上，申请前一年资产额应在2亿美元以上。

申请设立从事批发业务的合营商业企业的外国合营者，申请前3年年均商品批发额应在25亿美元以上，申请前一年资产额应在3亿美元以上。

（二）中国合营者或中国合营者中的主要合营者（以下简称中国合营者）应为具有较强经济实力和经营能力的流通企业，申请前一年的资产额应在5000万元（中西部地区3000万元）人民币以上。其中，中国合营者为商业企业的，申请前3年年均销售额应在3亿元（中西部地区2亿元）人民币以上；为外贸企业的，申请前3年年均自营进出口额应在5000万美元以上（其中出口额不低于3000万美元）。

第六条 合营商业企业应符合以下条件：

（一）符合中国有关法律、法规及有关规定；

（二）符合所在城市商业发展规划；

（三）从事零售业务的合营商业企业的注册资本不低于5000万元人民币，中西部地区不低于3000万元人民币；从事批发业务的合营商业企业的注册资本不低于8000万元人民币，中西部地区不低于6000万元人民币；

（四）采取3家以上分店连锁方式经营的合营商业企业（便民店、专业店和专卖店除外），中国合营者出资比例应达到51%以上；其中对合营商业企业本身经营情况较好，外国合营者已从国内大量采购产品，并能借助外国合营者的国际营销网络，进一步扩大国内产品出口的合营连锁商业企业，经国务院批准后，可允许外国合营者控股；

开设3家以下分店（包括3家）的合营商业企业和连锁方式经营的便民店、专业店、专卖店，中国合营者出资比例应不低于35%；

从事批发业务（包括零售企业兼营批发业务）

的合营商业企业，中国合营者出资比例应达到51%以上；

（五）合营商业企业的分店只限于中外双方直接投资、直接经营的直营连锁形式，暂不允许发展自由连锁、特许连锁等其它连锁形式；

（六）经营年限不超过30年，中西部地区不超过40年。

第七条 外国合营者与合营商业企业签定商标、商号使用许可合同、技术转让合同的，外国合营者提取的相关费用总计不得超过合营商业企业当年销售额（不包括增值税）的0．3%，提取年限不超过10年。

第八条 设立合营商业企业按照以下程序办理：

中国合营者向所在试点地区经济贸易委员会（经济委员会、计划与经济委员会，下同）报送可行性研究报告（代项目建议书）及有关文件，试点地区经济贸易委员会会同内贸主管部门按规定程序报国家经济贸易委员会。国家经济贸易委员会征求对外贸易经济合作部意见后审批。

可行性研究报告（代项目建议书）经批准后，由试点地区外经贸部门按规定程序向对外贸易经济合作部上报合同、章程，对外贸易经济合作部对合同、章程予以审批。

获得批准设立的合营商业企业，应自收到批准证书之日起1个月之内，凭对外贸易经济合作部颁发的《外商投资企业批准证书》，到国家工商行政管理部门办理注册登记手续。

第九条 申请设立合营商业企业，应报送下列文件：

（一）可行性研究申报文件

1．合营各方共同编制的可行性研究报告（代项目建议书）；

2．合营各方的银行资信证明、登记注册证明（复印件）、法定代表人证明（复印件）；

3．合营各方经会计师事务所审计的最近三年的年度资产负债表和损益表；

4．（如果中国合营者以国有资产投资）国有资产管理部门对中方拟投入国有资产的评估报告确认文件；

5．拟设立合营商业企业经营的商品种类；

6．其他有关文件。

（二）合同、章程申报文件

1．可行性研究申报文件及其批准文件；

2．由合营各方授权代表签署的拟设立合营商业企业的合同、章程；

3．进出口商品目录；

4．拟设立合营商业企业董事会成员名单及合营各方董事委派书；

5．国家工商行政管理局出具的企业名称预先核准通知书；

6．其他有关文件。

上述文件除已注明为复印件的，一律为正式文件。非法定代表人签署文件的，应出具法定代表人委托授权书。

第十条 国有流通企业投资设立合营商业企业的，须按《国有资产评估管理办法》的规定，由国有资产管理部门确认的评估机构，对国有流通企业投入的有形和无形资产进行科学、公正的评估。评估结果经省级以上国有资产管理部门确认后，作为投入国有资产作价的依据。

第十一条 已设立合营商业企业申请兼营批发业务、开设分店、更改合营方，对外贸易经济合作部征得国家经济贸易委员会同意后予以审批；已设立合营商业企业的其他变更，按现行外商投资企业的有关规定，报原审批机关审批。报批时合营商业企业需提交以下文件：

（一）申请报告；

（二）企业经营状况报告；

（三）企业验资报告；

（四）企业出口情况报告及证明文件；

（五）董事会有关决议；

（六）合同、章程修改协议；

（七）其他有关文件。

企业应自修改后的合同、章程批准之日起1个月内向国家工商行政管理部门办理登记变更等手续。

第十二条 合营商业企业的经营范围：

（一）从事零售业务的合营商业企业的经营范围

1．商业零售（包括代销、寄售）经营；

2．组织国内产品出口业务；

3．自营商品的进出口业务；

4．经营相关的配套服务。

（二）经营批发业务的合营商业企业的经营范围

国内商品和自营进口商品的国内批发，组织国内产品出口。

第十三条 从事零售业务的合营商业企业经批准可兼营批发业务。

第十四条 合营商业企业不得从事商品进出口代理业务。

第十五条 合营商业企业经营国家有特殊规定的商品以及涉及配额、许可证管理的进出口商品，应按国家有关规定办理审批手续。

合营商业企业年度商品进口总额不得超过本企业当年商品销售额的30%。

第十六条 合营商业企业应遵守中华人民共和国法律、法规，受中国法律、法规管辖，其正当经营活动及合法权益受中国法律、法规的保护。

合营商业企业如有违反中国法律、法规的行为，按中国有关法律、法规处理。

第十七条 各地要严格按本办法规定设立合营商业企业。违反本办法规定的，由国家经济贸易委员会、对外贸易经济合作部会同国家工商行政管理局进行查处。各地经济贸易委员会、外经贸部门要会同有关部门及时跟踪试点情况，认真总结试点经验，妥善解决试点中出现的问题。

第十八条 国家经济贸易委员会、对外贸易经济合作部、国家工商行政管理局或其授权机构依法对外商投资商业企业进行监督和管理。

第十九条 香港特别行政区、澳门、台湾地区的投资者在祖国大陆投资设立合营商业企业，参照本办法执行。

第二十条 本办法由国家经济贸易委员会、对外贸易经济合作部负责解释。

第二十一条 本办法自发布之日起施行。

中华人民共和国对外贸易经济合作部令

第　3　号

1999年8月24日

现将《对外贸易经济合作部<关于外商投资举办投资性公司的暂行规定>的补充规定》予以公布。本规定自公布之日起施行。

对外贸易经济合作部《关于外商投资举办投资性公司的暂行规定》的补充规定

为促进跨国公司来华投资，引进国外先进技术和管理经验，完善投资性公司的功能，现对对外贸易经济合作部1995年4月4日发布的《关于外商投资举办投资性公司的暂行规定》作如下补充规定：

一、投资性公司的注册资本不低于3000万美元，投资性公司的贷款额不得超过已缴付注册资本额的4倍。投资性公司因经营需要，贷款额拟超过已缴付的注册资本额的4倍，应当报对外贸易经济合作部批准。

二、鼓励投资性公司在中国境内设立科研开发中心或部门，从事新产品及高新技术的研究开发，转让其研究开发成果，并提供相应的技术服务。

三、投资性公司可在国内外市场以代理或经销的方式销售其所投资企业生产的产品。

四、投资性公司可为其所投资企业提供运输、仓储等综合服务。

五、投资性公司可在境内收购不涉及出口配额、出口许可证管理的商品出口。

六、投资性公司从事本规定中第三条、第四条、第五条所列经营活动，应将修改后的投资性公司的合同、章程等有关申请文件按程度报对外贸易经济合作部审查批准，并应当符合以下条件：

投资性公司的注册资本已按照合同、章程的规定按期缴付，并且实际缴付的注册资本额不低于

3000万美元。申请为其所投资企业提供本规定第三条、第四条所列经营活动的投资性公司，其在所投资企业的注册资本中的出资比例不应低于10%，并应有其所投资企业的书面委托（经所投资企业董事会一致通过）。

七、本规定与1996年2月16日对外贸易经济合作部发布的《＜关于外商投资举办投资性公司的暂行规定＞有关问题的解释》规定不一致的，以本规定为准。

八、本规定自公布之日起施行。

对外贸易经济合作部　国家工商行政管理局
关于印发《关于外商投资企业合并与分立的规定》的通知

〔1999〕外经贸法发第395号

1999年9月23日

各省、自治区、直辖市及计划单列市外经贸委（厅、局）、工商行政管理局：

为规范涉及外商投资企业合并与分立的行为，保护企业投资者和债权人的合法权益，现将《关于外商投资企业合并与分立的规定》印发给你们，请遵照执行。

附件：如文

附　件

关于外商投资企业合并与分立的规定

第一条　为了规范涉及外商投资企业合并与分立的行为，保护企业投资者和债权人的合法权益，根据《中华人民共和国公司法》和有关外商投资企业的法律和行政法规，制定本规定。

第二条　本规定适用于依照中国法律在中国境内设立的中外合资经营企业、具有法人资格的中外合作经营企业、外资企业、外商投资股份有限公司（以下统称公司）之间合并或分立。

公司与中国内资企业合并，参照有关法律、法规和本规定办理。

第三条　本规定所称合并，是指两个以上公司依照公司法有关规定，通过订立协议而归并成为一个公司。

公司合并可以采取吸收合并和新设合并两种形式。

吸收合并，是指公司接纳其他公司加入本公司，接纳方继续存在，加入方解散。

新设合并，是指两个以上公司合并设立一个新的公司，合并各方解散。

第四条　本规定所称分立，是指一个公司依照公司法有关规定，通过公司最高权力机构决议分成两个以上的公司。

公司分立可以采取存续分立和解散分立两种形式。

存续分立，是指一个公司分离成两个以上公司，本公司继续存在并设立一个以上新的公司。

解散分立，是指一个公司分解为两个以上公司，本公司解散并设立两个以上新的公司。

第五条　公司合并或分立，应当遵守中国的法律、法规和本规定，遵循自愿、平等和公平竞争的原则，不得损害社会公共利益和债权人的合法权益。

公司合并或分立，应符合《指导外商投资方向暂行规定》和《外商投资产业指导目录》的规定，不得导致外国投资者在不允许外商独资、控股或占主导地位的产业的公司中独资、控股或占主导地位。

公司因合并或分立而导致其所从事的行业或经营范围发生变更的，应符合有关法律、法规及国家产业政策的规定并办理必要的审批手续。

第六条 公司合并或分立，应当符合海关、税务和外汇管理等有关部门颁布的规定。合并或分立后存续或新设的公司，经审批机关、海关和税务等机关核定，继续享受原公司所享受的各项外商投资企业待遇。

第七条 公司合并或分立，须经公司原审批机关批准并到登记机关办理有关公司设立、变更或注销登记。

拟合并公司的原审批机关或登记机关有两个以上的，由合并后公司住所地对外经济贸易主管部门和国家工商行政管理局（以下简称国家工商局）授权的登记机关作为审批和登记机关。

拟合并公司的投资总额之和超过公司原审批机关或合并后公司住所地审批机关审批权限的，由具有相应权限的审批机关审批。

拟合并的公司至少有一家为股份有限公司的，由中华人民共和国对外贸易经济合作部（以下简称外经贸部）审批。

第八条 因公司合并或分立而解散原公司或新设异地公司，须征求拟解散或拟设立公司的所在地审批机关的意见。

第九条 在投资者按照公司合同、章程规定缴清出资、提供合作条件且实际开始生产、经营之前，公司不得合并或分立。

第十条 有限责任公司之间合并后为有限责任公司。股份有限公司之间合并后为股份有限公司。

上市的股份有限公司与有限责任公司合并后为股份有限公司。非上市的股份有限公司与有限责任公司合并后可以是股份有限公司，也可以是有限责任公司。

第十一条 股份有限公司之间合并或者公司合并后为有限责任公司的，合并后公司的注册资本为原公司注册资本额之和。

有限责任公司与股份有限公司合并后为股份有限公司的，合并后公司的注册资本为原有限责任公司净资产额根据拟合并的股份有限公司每股所含净资产额折成的股份额与原股份有限公司股份总额之和。

第十二条 根据本规定第十一条第一款合并的，各方投资者在合并后的公司中的股权比例，根据国家有关规定，由投资者之间协商或根据资产评估机构对其在原公司股份价值的评估结果，在合并后的公司合同、章程中确定，但外国投资者的股权比例不得低于合并后公司注册资本的25%。

第十三条 分立后公司的注册资本额，由分立前公司的最高权力机构，依照有关外商投资企业法律、法规和登记机关的有关规定确定，但分立后各公司的注册资本额之和应为分立前公司的注册资本额。

第十四条 各方投资者在分立后的公司中的股权比例，由投资者在分立后的公司合同章程中确定，但外国投资者的股权比例不得低于分立后公司注册资本的25%。

第十五条 公司合并，采取吸收合并形式的，接纳方公司的成立日期为合并后公司的成立日期；采取新设合并形式的，登记机关核准设立登记并签发营业执照的日期为合并后公司的成立日期。

因公司分立而设立新公司的，登记机关核准设立登记并签发营业执照的日期为分立后公司的成立日期。

第十六条 涉及上市的股份有限公司合并或分立的，应当符合有关法律、法规和国务院证券监督管理部门对上市公司的规定并办理必要的审批手续。

第十七条 公司与中国内资企业合并必须符合我国利用外资的法律、法规规定和产业政策要求并具备以下条件：

（一）拟合并的中国内资企业是依照《中华人民共和国公司法》规范组建的有限责任公司或股份有限公司；

（二）投资者符合法律、法规和部门规章对合并后公司所从事有关产业的投资者资格要求；

（三）外国投资者的股权比例不得低于合并后公司注册资本的25%；

（四）合并协议各方保证拟合并公司的原有职工充分就业或给予合理安置。

第十八条 公司吸收合并，由接纳方公司作为申请人，公司新设合并，由合并各方协商确定一个申请人。

申请人应向审批机关报送下列文件：

（一）各公司法定代表人签署的关于公司合并的申请书和公司合并协议；

（二）各公司最高权力机构关于公司合并的决

议；

（三）各公司合同、章程；

（四）各公司的批准证书和营业执照复印件；

（五）由中国法定验资机构为各公司出具的验资报告；

（六）各公司的资产负债表及财产清单；

（七）各公司上一年度的审计报告；

（八）各公司的债权人名单；

（九）合并后的公司合同、章程；

（十）合并后的公司最高权力机构成员名单；

（十一）审批机关要求报送的其他文件。

第十九条 公司合并协议应包括下列主要内容：

（一）合并协议各方的名称、住所、法定代表人；

（二）合并后公司的名称、住所、法定代表人；

（三）合并后公司的投资总额和注册资本；

（四）合并形式；

（五）合并协议各方债权、债务的承继方案；

（六）职工安置办法；

（七）违约责任；

（八）解决争议的方式；

（九）签约日期、地点；

（十）合并协议各方认为需要规定的其他事项。

第二十条 拟合并的公司有两个以上原审批机关的，拟解散的公司应当在依照本规定第十八条向审批机关报送有关文件之前，向其原审批机关提交因公司合并而解散的申请。

原审批机关应自接到前款有关解散申请之日起15日内做出是否同意解散的批复。超过15日，原审批机关未作批复的，视作原审批机关同意该公司解散。

如果原审批机关在前款规定期限内，作出不同意有关公司解散的批复，拟解散公司可将有关解散申请提交原审批机关与公司合并的审批机关共同的上一级对外经济贸易主管部门，该部门应自接到有关公司解散申请之日起30日内作出裁决。

如果审批机关不同意或不批准公司合并，则有关公司解散的批复自行失效。

第二十一条 拟分立的公司应向审批机关报送下列文件：

（一）公司法定代表人签署的关于公司分立的申请书；

（二）公司最高权力机构关于公司分立的决议；

（三）因公司分立而拟存续、新设的公司（以下统称分立协议各方）签订的公司分立协议；

（四）公司合同、章程；

（五）公司的批准证书和营业执照复印件；

（六）由中国法定验资机构为公司出具的验资报告；

（七）公司的资产负债表及财产清单；

（八）公司的债权人名单；

（九）分立后的各公司合同、章程；

（十）分立后的各公司最高权力机构成员名单；

（十一）审批机关要求报送的其他文件。

因公司分立而在异地新设公司的，公司还必须向审批机关报送拟设立公司的所在地审批机关对因分立而新设公司签署的意见。

第二十二条 公司分立协议应包括下列主要内容：

（一）分立协议各方拟定的名称、住所、法定代表人；

（二）分立后公司的投资总额和注册资本；

（三）分立形式；

（四）分立协议各方对拟分立公司财产的分割方案；

（五）分立协议各方对拟分立公司债权、债务的承继方案；

（六）职工安置办法；

（七）违约责任；

（八）解决争议的方式；

（九）签约的日期、地点；

（十）分立协议各方认为需要规定的其他事项。

第二十三条 合并后存续的公司或者新设的公司全部承继因合并而解散的公司的债权、债务。

分立后的公司按照分立协议承继原公司的债权、债务。

第二十四条 审批机关应自接到本规定第十八条或第二十一条规定报送的有关文件之日起45日内，以书面形式作出是否同意合并或分立的初步批复。

公司合并的审批机关为外经贸部的，如果外经贸部认为公司合并具有行业垄断的趋势或者可能形成就某种特定商品或服务的市场控制地位而妨碍公平竞争，可于接到前款所述有关文件后，召集有关部门和机构，对拟合并的公司进行听证并对该公司及其相关市场进行调查。前款所述审批期限可延长至180天。

第二十五条 拟合并或分立的公司应当自审批机关就同意公司合并或分立作出初步批复之日起10日内，向债权人发出通知书，并于30日内在全国发行的省级以上报纸上至少公告3次。

公司应在上述通知书和公告中说明对现有公司债务的承继方案。

第二十六条 公司债权人自接到本规定第二十五条所述通知书之日起30日内、未接到通知书的债权人自第一次公告之日起90日内，有权要求公司对其债务承继方案进行修改，或者要求公司清偿债务或提供相应的担保。

如果公司债权人未在前款规定期限内行使有关权利，视为债权人同意拟合并或分立公司的债权、债务承继方案，该债权人的主张不得影响公司的合并或分立进程。

第二十七条 拟合并或分立的公司自第一次公告之日起90日后，公司债权人无异议的，拟合并公司的申请人或拟分立的公司应向审批机关提交下列文件：

（一）公司在报纸上3次登载公司合并或分立公告的证明；

（二）公司通知其债权人的证明；

（三）公司就其有关债权、债务处理情况的说明；

（四）审批机关要求提交的其他文件。

第二十八条 审批机关应自接到本规定第二十七条所列文件之日起30日内，决定是否批准公司合并或分立。

第二十九条 公司采取吸收合并形式的，接纳方公司应到原审批机关办理外商投资企业批准证书变更手续并到登记机关办理公司变更登记；加入方公司应到原审批机关缴销外商投资企业批准证书并到登记机关办理公司注销登记。

公司采取新设合并形式的，合并各方公司应到原审批机关缴销外商投资企业批准证书并到登记机关办理公司注销登记；新设立的公司应通过申请人到审批机关领取外商投资企业批准证书并到登记机关办理公司设立登记。

公司采取存续分立形式的，存续的公司应到审批机关办理外商投资企业批准证书变更手续并到登记机关办理公司变更登记；新设立的公司应到审批机关领取外商投资企业批准证书并到登记机关办理公司设立登记。

公司采取解散分立形式的，原公司应到原审批机关缴销外商投资企业批准证书并到登记机关办理公司注销登记；新设立的公司应到审批机关领取外商投资企业批准证书并到登记机关办理公司设立登记。

第三十条 公司合并的申请人或拟分立的公司，应自审批机关批准合并或分立之日起30日内，就因合并或分立而解散、存续或新设公司的事宜，到相应的审批机关办理有关缴销、变更或领取外商投资企业批准证书手续。

第三十一条 公司应自缴销、变更或领取外商投资企业批准证书之日起，依照《中华人民共和国企业法人登记管理条例》和《中华人民共和国公司登记管理条例》等有关规定，到登记机关办理有关注销、变更或设立登记手续。

设立登记应当在有关公司变更、注销登记办理完结后进行。

公司合并或分立协议中载明的有关公司财产处置方案及债权、债务承继方案和审批机关批准公司合并或分立的文件，视为注销登记所需提交的清算报告。

第三十二条 公司为新设合并或分立办理注销、变更登记后，当事人不依法办理有关公司设立登记的，应承担相应的法律责任。

第三十三条 公司投资者因公司合并或分立而签署的修改后的公司合同、章程自审批机关变更或核发外商投资企业批准证书之日起生效。

第三十四条 合并或分立后存续或新设的公司应自变更或领取营业执照之日起30日内，向因合并或分立而解散的公司之债权人和债务人发出变更债务人和债权人的通知并在全国发行的省级以上报纸上公告。

第三十五条 合并或分立后存续或新设的公司应自换发或领取营业执照之日起30日内，到税务、海关、土地管理和外汇管理等有关机关办理相应的登记手续。

第三十六条 在公司合并或分立过程中发生股权转让的，依照有关法律、法规和外商投资企业投资者股权变更的规定办理。

第三十七条 香港、港门、台湾地区的投资者在中国其他地区投资举办的公司合并或分立，参照本规定办理。

第三十八条　本规定由外经贸部和国家工商局负责解释。

第三十九条　本规定自1999年11月1日起执行。

对外贸易经济合作部关于外商投资企业技术引进有关问题的通知

〔1999〕外经贸资发第573号

1999年9月28日

各省、自治区、直辖市及计划单列市外经贸委（厅、局）：

我部就解决目前外商投资企业技术引进购付汇问题与国家外汇管理局进行了协商，该局今日发出《关于简化外商投资企业技术引进售付汇管理手续的通知》，为配合作好此项工作，现将有关问题通知如下：

一、各地外经贸主管部门应认真按照国家有关吸收外资法律法规和国家外汇管理局《关于简化外商投资企业技术引进售付汇管理的通知》的规定，做好外商投资企业技术引进合同审批工作。

二、在新批外商投资企业设立（合营合同、章程）时，凡技术引进合同作为合营合同附件的，必须在批文中明确所批准的合营合同包括技术引进合同附件（写明该技术引进合同的名称）。

三、对过去已批准的作为外商投资企业合营合同附件的技术引进合同，由原审批机关的外资管理部门对该技术引进合同出具确认函，确认函中应注明该技术引进合同的名称。

四、各地外经贸主管部门应加强对技术引进合同真实性的审核。外方以技术出资的，不属于确认范围。

特此通知。

对外贸易经济合作部关于地方自行审批鼓励类外商投资企业报外经贸部备案有关问题的通知

〔1999〕外经贸资发第615号

1999年10月15日

各省、自治区、直辖市及计划单列市外经贸委（厅、局）：

按照《关于当前进一步鼓励外商投资的意见》（国发〔1999〕73号）的规定，各省自行批准鼓励类不需要国家综合平衡的外商投资企业的设立（批准合营合同和章程及其附件）须报外经贸部备案。根据国家吸收外商投资法律、法规和外经贸部1988年下发的关于外商投资企业备案的有关规定，现将有关问题通知如下：

一、鼓励类不需要国家综合平衡的限上外商投资企业的设立应由各省、自治区、直辖市及计划单列市外经贸主管部门（以下简称“地方外经贸主管部门”）审批，审批权不得层层下放。

二、地方外经贸主管部门须在合同、章程批准当日将报外经贸部备案的有关材料寄出。

三、所需上报的备案材料：

（一）可行性研究报告批文；

（二）合同、章程批文（批文内容应写明投资方、投资方式、投资总额、注册资本、各方出资比例、出资方式、贷款筹措、经营范围、生产规模、外销比例、经营期限及其它需特别批复的事项；如技术引进合同作为合同附件一并批准，批文中应说明技术引进合同的名称）；

（三）地方外经贸主管部门出具的不需要国家综合平衡的说明。

四、外经贸部收到备案材料后，将在两个工作日之内通知上报单位确认备案材料已收 到及材料是否齐全；对备案项目如有不同意见，外经贸部自收到完整的备案材料之日起在一个月之内予以书面答复，并抄送国家工商行政管理局、海关总署、外汇管理局和国家税务总局。

五、外经贸部在收到备案材料之日起一个月内对备案企业的设立无异议，地方外经贸主管部门方可颁发外商投资企业批准证书。外经贸部有不同意见的项目，一律不得颁发外商投资企业批准证书。

六、地方外经贸主管部门应在每月 5 号之前将其上月所批鼓励类备案企业清单（格式附后）传真外经贸部外资司（办公室）并同时电话确认已送达。

七、外经贸部外资司将对清单中所列企业进行核对，对未收到备案材料的项目将及时通知上报单位及工商、海关、外汇等有关部门。凡未向外经贸部备案的企业或备案未予通过的企业，工商、海关、外汇等部门不予注册、登记或办理其它事宜。

八、工商、海关、外汇、税务等有关部门凭外商投资企业批准证书及其要求的其它文件受理企业登记注册和备案。

九、地方外经贸主管部门审批的鼓励类且不涉及国家综合平衡的现有外商投资企业合同、章程条款的重大变更及增资，按上述有关规定报外经贸部备案。批准增资的备案材料按有关规定提交。

十、地方外经贸主管部门按上述要求以书面形式报外经贸部备案的同时，须按照《关于地方外经贸部门与外经贸部外资司联网有关事项的通知》（〔1998〕外经贸资综函字第 521 号）的规定，将备案企业的有关信息及数据传送给外资司。待条件成熟后，将在全国实行网络备案。

附件：（略）

对外贸易经济合作部办公厅
关于转发《国家税务总局关于外商投资企业技术开发费抵扣应纳税所得额有关问题的通知》的通知

〔1999〕外经贸资字第 107 号

1999 年 12 月 15 日

各省、自治区、直辖市及计划单列市外经贸委（厅、局），国家级经济技术开发区：

为贯彻《国务院办公厅转发外经贸部等部门关于当前进一步鼓励外商投资意见的通知》（国办发〔1999〕73 号）精神，国家税务总局印发了《关于外商投资企业技术开发费抵扣应纳税所得额有关问题的通知》（国税发〔1999〕173 号），现将该文转发给你们，请遵照执行。执行中有何问题，请及时向我部（外资司）反映。

特此通知。

附件：如文

附　件

国家税务总局关于外商投资企业技术开发费抵扣应纳税所得额有关问题的通知

国税发〔1999〕173号

各省、自治区、直辖市和计划单列市国家税务局、深圳市地方税务局：

最近，国务院决定，外商投资企业技术开发费比上年增长10%以上（含10%）的，经税务机关批准，允许再按技术开发费实际发生额的50%抵扣当年度的应纳税所得额。现就实施这一税收优惠政策的有关问题通知如下：

一、企业进行技术开发当年在中国境内发生的技术开发费比上年实际增长10%（含10%）以上的，经税务机关审核批准，允许再按当年技术开发费实际发生额的50%，抵扣当年度的应纳税所得额。具体申报期限、审核程序及审批权限由省（自治区、直辖市或计划单列市）级主管税务机关依据有关税收法律、法规及本通知规定，结合当地实际情况制定，报国家税务总局备案。

适用上款规定的技术开发费是指：企业在一个纳税年度中研究开发新产品、新技术、新工艺所发生的新产品设计费，工艺规程制定费，设备调试费，原材料和半成品的试制费，技术图书资料费，未纳入国家计划的中间实验费，研究机构人员的工资，研究设备的折旧，与新产品的试制和技术研究有关的其他经费；不含企业从其他单位购进技术或受让技术使用权而支付的购置费或使用费，以及从事技术开发业务的企业发生的属于技术开发服务业务的营业成本、费用。

二、企业技术开发费比上年增长达到10%以上、其实际发生额的50%如大于企业当年应纳税所得额的，可准予抵扣其不超过应纳税所得额的部分；超过部分，当年和以后年度均不再予以抵扣。

对按照《中华人民共和国外商投资企业和外国企业所得税法》第十一条规定弥补以前年度亏损后，当年没有应纳税所得额的企业，其发生的技术开发费不适用本通知第一条第一款的规定。

三、外国企业在中国境内设立机构、场所，从事生产经营活动所发生的技术开发费，比照本通知规定执行。

四、本通知自2000年1月1日起执行。

国家税务总局

1999年9月17日

对外经济合作

对外贸易经济合作部
关于赋予国家确定的1000家重点企业对外
承包劳务经营权有关事项的通知

〔1998〕外经贸政发第984号

1999年1月8日

国务院各部委、各直属机构，各省、自治区、直辖市及计划单列市外经贸委（厅、局）：

为进一步扩大对外开放，使企业更多地参与国际市场竞争，现将赋予国家确定的1000家重点企业对外工程承包、对外劳务合作经营权有关事项通知如下：

一、凡属国家确定的1000家重点企业（以下简称千家企业），经批准，均可赋予其对外工程承包和劳务合作经营权，经营本行业的对外工程承包和劳务合作业务。

二、申报及审批程序

（一）千家企业中的中央直属企业直接向外经贸部申报。

（二）千家企业中的地方企业通过各省、自治区、直辖市及计划单列市外经贸委（厅、局）向外经贸部申报。

（三）申报材料包括：企业申请报告、企业法人营业执照（复印件）、可行性报告、公司章程等。

特此通知。

对外贸易经济合作部　国家经济贸易委员会
关于境外带料加工装配项目申报
程序及有关事项的通知

〔1999〕外经贸政发第263号

1999年5月4日

各省、自治区、直辖市及计划单列市外经贸委（厅、局），经贸委（经委、计经委），中央企业：

根据《国务院办公厅转发外经贸部、国家经贸委、财政部关于鼓励企业开展境外带料加工装配业务意见的通知》（国办发〔1999〕17号）的有关规定，为明确境外带料加工装配项目申报程序及有关事项，现通知如下：

一、申报程序

（一）中央企业，直接向外经贸部、国家经贸委申报。申报材料一式两份，同时报送外经贸部、国家经贸委。

（二）其它企业向企业注册地的省级外经贸主管部门（外经贸委、厅或局，下同）、经贸主管部门（经贸委、经委或计经委，下同）同时申报。

省级外经贸主管部门会同经贸主管部门对项目进行审理，并形成一式两份的正式申报文件，联合上报外经贸部、国家经贸委。

（三）国家经贸委对项目的立项和可行性研究报告进行审查，并将符合条件的项目送外经贸部核准。

（四）外经贸部根据国家经贸委的初审意见，向我驻外使馆经商机构征询意见，并参考其回复意见，对项目进行最终审核，向通过审核的项目颁发《境外带料加工装配企业批准证书》。

各级经贸主管部门侧重对项目投资主体的生产经营、发展潜力和境外项目的投资规模、自有资金来源、产品结构等国内问题进行审核；各级外经贸主管部门侧重对项目的投资国别地区的政局状况、国别政策、当地及周边市场、投资环境、主办单位进出口情况等涉外问题进行审核。

二、申报材料

（一）境外项目有关材料

1．项目建议书、项目可行性研究报告；

中方投资额在300万美元（含300万美元）以上的项目，项目建议书经批准后方可进行可行性研究报告的编制；300万美元以下项目的项目建议书与可行性研究报告原则上可合并编制。

2．境外合资企业中、外方合资合同或协议（草签文本）；

3．境外企业中方企业间协议；

4．境外企业章程（草签文本）；

5．合资伙伴背景及其资信材料；

6．外汇管理部门外汇风险审查意见。

（二）项目国内主办单位有关材料

1．项目主办单位营业执照；

2．项目主办单位近三年进出口情况及拟在境外生产的主要产品的出口情况；

3．股份制企业董事会决议；

4．项目主办单位上一年年度报告及注册会计师事务所出具的审计报告；

5．境外带料加工装配项目主要负责人简历。

（三）审批部门要求的其它材料

三、审批时限

（一）在接到境外带料加工装配项目申报材料后，各地方外经贸主管部门应会同经贸主管部门于15个工作日内形成正式申报文件，联合上报外经贸部（发展司）、国家经贸委（外经司）。

（二）国家经贸委应于10个工作日内提出初审意见，并将符合条件的项目送外经贸部。

（三）外经贸部在接到国家经贸委初审意见后，应在3个工作日内征求有关驻外经商机构意见；驻外经商机构应于10个工作日内向外经贸部（发展司）反馈书面意见。

（四）外经贸部在接到驻外经商机构意见后，应于10个工作日内对项目进行最终审核，并对审核通过的项目颁发《境外带料加工装配企业批准证书》。

国家经济贸易委员会　对外贸易经济合作部
关于印发《国家鼓励开展境外带料加工装配产品目录（第一批）》的通知

国经贸外经〔1999〕379号

1999年5月6日

各省、自治区、直辖市及计划单列市经贸委（经委、计经委）、外经贸委（厅、局），国务院各有关部门，委管国家工业局：

为贯彻落实《国务院办公厅转发外经贸部、国家经贸委、财政部关于鼓励企业开展境外带料加工装配业务意见的通知》（国办发〔1999〕17号）精神，我们在征求有关部门意见的基础上，制订了《国家鼓励开展境外带料加工装配产品目录（第一批)》，现印发给你们，请遵照执行。

国家鼓励开展境外带料加工装配产品目录（第一批）

一、机械类

1．装载机、叉车、挖掘机、拖拉机

2．胶带输送机、破碎机、筛分机、手拉葫芦、电动葫芦、千斤顶、工业泵

3．普通机床、机械压力机、量具、刃具、磨料磨具

4．轴承、紧固件、链条、钢丝及钢丝绳

5．汽车、摩托车

6．电度表、水表、光学仪器、照相机、复印机

7．仓储物流设备和大型超市设备

二、电子类

1．微机、显示器、打印机、软件

2．程控交换机、电话机、图文传真机、卫星电视接收机、广播电视发射机

3．激光影碟机、录像机、收音机、收录机、彩色电视机、黑白电视机

4．扬声器、电阻、电容器、印刷电路版、磁头、荧光灯

5．电子系统工程

三、轻工类

1．电冰箱、空调器、洗衣机、微波炉、电风扇、吸尘器、电熨斗、电饭锅

2．自行车及各类零部件、缝纫机、钟表

3．家用燃气灶具、吸油烟机、打火机

4．普通电池、可充电电池、蓄电池、太阳能电池

5．合成洗衣粉、三聚磷酸钠

6．火柴

7．铅笔、自来水笔

8．塑料编织袋、吹塑薄膜

9．玩具

10．日用玻璃、日用搪瓷

四、纺织类

1．服装

2．印染、针复制

3．纺织机械

4．化学纤维

五、烟草类

1．卷烟

2．烟用丝束

3．烟草机械

中华人民共和国对外贸易经济合作部关于我边境地区与毗邻国家开展经济技术合作有关问题的通知

〔1999〕外经贸合函字第1号

1999年1月11日

内蒙古自治区、辽宁省、吉林省、黑龙江省、广西壮族自治区、云南省、西藏自治区、甘肃省、新疆维吾尔自治区、新疆生产建设兵团外经贸委（厅、局)、机电产品进出口办公室，海南省商业贸易厅、机电产品进出口办公室：

为贯彻落实《关于进一步发展边境贸易的补充规定的通知》(〔1998〕外经贸政发第844号，以下简称《补充通知》中有关与毗邻国家开展经济技术合作的规定，保证我边境省（区）与毗邻国家的经济技术合作业务的顺利开展，现就有关问题作如下通知：

一、关于边境小额贸易企业开展与毗邻国家边境地区的承包工程和劳务合作问题。

（一）边境小额贸易企业签订的承包工程和劳务合作项目合同须报所在省（自治区）的外经贸委(厅、局）审核。

（二）边境小额贸易企业凭各省（自治区）外经贸委（厅、局）的批文、项目合同、《国外承包工程劳务合作经营许可证》申请表（一式两份)、企业营业执照（副本）到外经贸部国外经济合作司（以下简称合作司）办理《国外承包工程劳务合作经营许可证》。

二、关于边境外经企业和边境小额贸易企业(以下简称边境外经贸企业）与毗邻国家边境地区开展承包工程和劳和合作项下换回的物资属进口配额和限量登记管理的商品的审批问题。

（一）边境外经贸企业与毗邻国家边境地区开展承包工程和劳务合作项下换回的物资属进口配额和限量登记管理的商品，须在承包工程和劳务合作项目实施前报部合作司，由合作司研究提出意见后转对外贸易管理司（以下简称贸管司）审批。报批材料包括：

1.所在省（自治区）外经贸委（厅、局）的申请报告；

2.经所在省（自治区）外经贸委（厅、局）批准的项目意向书或合同；

3.进口商品清单和数量。

（二）边境外经贸企业凭贸管司下达的进口配额或限量登记额度的批文向其所在省（区）的外经贸委（厅、局）申领进口许可证或进口商品登记证。

（三）边境外经贸企业与毗邻国家边境地区开展承包工程和劳务合作项下进口属配额管理的机电产品，须按机电产品进口管理有关规定申报，经合作司对其项目进行审核后，由外经贸部机电产品进出口司（以下简称机电司）办理进口审批手续。进口单位凭机电司发放的《配额进口证明》向许可证发证机关申领进口许可证。

三、本通知未涉及的内容，仍按《国务院关于边境贸易有关问题的通知》（国发〔1996〕2号)、《关于印发＜边境小额贸易和边境地区对外经济技术合作管理办法＞的通知》（〔1996〕外经贸政发第222号）及《补充通知》规定执行。

本通知自1999年1月1日起执行。执行中有何问题请及时与我部（合作司、发展司、贸管司、机电司）联系。

财政部　外交部　国家外汇管理局
海关总署关于发布《境外国有资产管理
暂行办法》的通知

财管字〔1999〕311号

1999年9月27日

国务院各部委、各直属机构、各办事机构、各直属事业单位，各省、自治区、直辖市、计划单列市财政厅（局）、国有资产管理局（办公室、处）、外事办公室、外汇管理分局、海关总署广东分署、各直属海关：

为规范境外国有资产管理，切实维护国家境外国有资产的合法权益，保障境外国有资产的安全完整和保值增值，我们制定了《境外国有资产管理暂行办法》，现印发给你们，请遵照执行。执行中有何问题，请及时告知我们。

附件：境外国有资产管理暂行办法

附　件

境外国有资产管理暂行办法

第一章　总　　则

第一条　为了规范境外国有资产管理，维护国家境外国有资产的合法权益，保障境外国有资产的安全完整和保值增值，制定本办法。

第二条　本办法所称境外国有资产，是指我国企业、事业单位和各级人民政府及政府有关部门（以下称境内投资者）以国有资产（含国有法人财产，下同）在境外及港、澳、台地区投资设立的各类企业和非经营性机构（以下称境外机构）中应属国有的下列各项资产：

一、境内投资者向境外投资设立独资、合资、合作企业或购买股票（或股权）以及境外机构在境外再投资形成的资本及其权益；

二、境内投资者及其境外派出单位在境外投资设立非经营性机构（包括使馆、领事馆、记者站、各种办事处、代表处等）所形成的国有资产；

三、在境外以个人名义持有的国有股权及物业产权；

四、境外机构中应属国家所有的无形资产；

五、境外机构依法接受的赠予、赞助和经依法判决、裁决而取得的应属国家所有的资产；

六、境外其他应属国家所有的资产。

第三条　对境外国有资产的管理遵循国家统一所有、政府分级监管的原则。财政部统一制定境外国有资产管理规章制度，各级财政（国有资产管理）部门负责对本级政府管辖的境外国有资产进行监督管理。

第四条　财政（国有资产管理）部门对境外国有资产管理履行下列职责：

一、制定境外国有资产管理规章、制度，并负责组织实施和检查监督；对违法违规行为责任人给予经济、行政的处罚；

二、建立境外国有资产经营责任制，组织实施境外企业国有资本金效绩评价；

三、审核境外企业重大国有资本运营决策事项；

四、组织境外机构开展国有资产产权界定、产权登记、资产统计、资产评估等各项基础管理工作；

五、从总体上掌握境外国有资产的总量、分布和构成；

六、检查监督境外国有资产的运营状况，并向本级政府和上级财政（国有资产管理）部门反映情况和提出建议；

七、办理政府授权管理的其他事项。

第二章　经营与监管

第五条　境外国有资产经营实行政企职责分开、出资者所有权与企业法人财产权分离、政府分级监管、企业自主经营的原则。

第六条　占用国有资产的境外机构，可以注册为独资公司、股份有限公司、有限责任公司或其他形式的经营性和非经营性实体，但不得以“无限责任公司”形式办理注册登记。

第七条　国家建立境外投资资质审查和规模准入制度，保障境外企业达到经济规模。对过小、过散、无发展前途的企业，实行关闭、清算；对业务正常、管理规范的小企业，实行兼并或合并，以达到经济规模。

第八条　境外机构的中方负责人是国有资产经营责任人，对境外机构占用的国有资产负有安全有效使用和保值增值的责任。

第九条　境内投资者对所属境外机构行使出资者职能，必须明确管理的职能部门及其工作职责，严禁法定代表人及其他任何人超过职能部门，对境外机构采用个人单线联系方式进行管理。

第十条　中央管理的规模大、在当地有重要影响的境外企业，可以实行授权经营。授权经营办法另行制定。

第十一条　中央管理的境外企业的重大资本运营决策事项需由财政部或由财政部会同有关部门审核，必要时上报国务院批准。

重大决策事项包括：

一、境外发行公司债券、股票和上市等融资活动；

二、超过企业净资产50%的投资活动；

三、企业增、减资本金；

四、向外方转让国有产权（或股权），导致失去控股地位；

五、企业分立、合并、重组、出售、解散和申请破产；

六、其他重大事项。

以上需审核事项，有关部门在收到企业申报的有效必备文件后，应于10个工作日内予以批复。

第十二条　中央管理境外企业的下列事项须报财政部备案：

一、不超过企业净资产50%的境外投资活动；

二、企业子公司发生第十一条中列举的重大决策事项。

第十三条　地方政府管理的境外企业发生第十一条、第十二条所列事项，参照上述办法进行管理。

第十四条　境内企业以国有资产在境外投资设立企业或在境外发行股票和上市，须按国家有关境外投资管理规定报政府有关部门审核批准。

境内企业投资设立的境外企业，其日常监管和考核由其境内母企业负责，但涉及第十一条中列举的重大决策事项，应由其境内母企业报财政（国有资产管理）部门备案。

第十五条　经政府或政府授权部门批准的境外投资项目，原则上均须以企业、机构名义在当地持有国有股权或物业产权。确需以个人名义持有国有股权或物业产权的，须经境内投资者报省级人民政府或国务院有关主管部门批准后，由境内投资者（委托人）与境个机构产权持有人（受托人）按国家规定在境内办理国有资产产权委托协议法律手续，并经委托人所在地公证机关公证。同时，须按驻在国（地区）法律程序，及时办理有关产权委托代理声明或股权声明等法律手续，取得当地法律对该部分国有资产产权的承认和保护。公证文件（副本）须报财政（国有资产管理）部门备案。

第十六条　境外企业为解决自身资金需求，可自行决定在境外进行借款。但需以其不动产作抵押的，应报境内投资者备案。

境外企业为其全资子公司借款设立抵押或为其非全资子公司借款按出资比例设立抵押，应报境内投资者备案。

第十七条　境外机构为企业的，其在境外以借款、发行公司债券等方式筹集资金的，其所筹集资金不得调入境内使用。境外机构为非经营性机构的，不得以其自身名义直接对外筹集资金。境外企业将其所筹资金调入境内给境内机构使用，或者境外非经营性机构以其境内投资机构的名义对外筹资的，境内机构应当按照《境内机构发行外币债卷管理办法》、《境内机构借用国际商业贷款管理办法》及《境内机构对外担保管理办法》等规定办理外债的筹借、使用和偿还。

第十八条　除国家允许经营担保业务的金融机

构外，境外机构不得擅自对外提供担保，确需对外提供担保时，境内投资者应按照财政部境外投资财务管理的有关规定执行。

第十九条 境外企业发生的涉及减少国有资本金的损失，应及时报告境内投资单位和财政（国有资产管理）部门。

第二十条 境内投资单位应对境外机构中方负责人进行任期审计和离任审计。审计工作应尊重所在国（地区）的法律。

第三章 基础管理

第二十一条 境外国有资产基础管理的主要内容包括产权界定、产权登记、资产统计和资产评估等。

第二十二条 境外国有资产的产权界定遵循“谁投资、谁拥有产权”的原则进行；按照分级监管的原则，由各级财政（国有资产管理）部门负责组织实施。

第二十三条 凡占有、使用国有资产的境外机构，都必须按照《境外国有资产产权登记管理暂行办法》和实施细则的规定由境内投资者及时办理境外国有资产产权登记（以下简称“境外产权登记”）。

境外产权登记表及有关资料是境内投资者向外汇管理部门申办登记和投资外汇资金汇出手续的必备文件。

向境外投资的货物出境时，收发货人或者其代理人应当主动向海关提交境外产权登记表，并接受海关的监管。

第二十四条 境外机构发生分立、合并、整体出售、撤资、解散或申请破产情形时，须报境内投资者审核批准，并及时进行清算，清理财产和各项债权、债务，同时办理境外国有资产产权注销登记。清理后归中方所有的财产、收入，按照国家有关规定，及时由其投资者足额收回，并报国家有关部门备案。

第二十五条 境外机构应执行企业、单位年度会计信息报告制度，境内投资者应如实、及时向财政（国有资产管理）和外汇管理部门报送境外机构年度会计报表。

第二十六条 境内投资者向境外投资，须按《国有资产评估管理办法》要求进行资产评估。资产评估应遵循独立、客观、公正原则，依照国家法律、法规和国家规定的标准、程序和方法进行。驻在国（地区）对资产评估有法律规定的从其规定。

第四章 效绩评价

第二十七条 财政部负责组织实施境外企业国有资产效绩评价，从总体上考核境外国有资产的经营情况。

第二十八条 境内投资者应按《国有资本金效绩评价规则》的要求，做好境外企业国有资产效绩评价工作，并向财政（国有资产管理）部门报告。

对境外非经营性国有资产，境内投资者重点是做好基础管理工作，考核其完好性和使用效率。

第二十九条 财政（国有资产管理）部门既要做好效绩评价办法实施情况的监督检查，又要做好本级政府管理的境外企业国有资产效绩评价工作，并将评价结果报送政府，同时抄送人事、党务管理部门，作为对企业经营者进行任免和奖惩的参考依据。

第三十条 为建立健全激励和约束机制，在财务数据真实可靠的前提下，境内投资者可以选择经营业绩显著的境外企业，对其经营者试行“期权”激励和约束办法，具体实施办法由财政部会同有关部门另行制定。

第五章 法律责任

第三十一条 财政（国有资产管理）部门及政府有关部门的公务人员由于工作失职、滥用职权或违反国家法律，造成严重后果，导致国有资产损失，应追究责任人员行政、经济责任直至刑事责任。

第三十二条 境内投资者违反国有资产管理和境外投资法规、制度，因下列行为导致国有资产流失和造成恶劣影响的，财政（国有资产管理）部门可根据不同情节给予通报批评，建议监察、审计部门立案审查，对责任人员可建议有关部门给予经济和行政的处分，触犯刑律的，移送司法机关依法追究刑事责任。

一、未经政府或政府授权部门批准擅自对外投资；

二、对所属境外机构国有资产总体情况和流失情况不掌握，不报告，不处理；

三、对所属境外机构不明确管理职能机构及其工作职责，造成管理失控；

四、未按规定程序批准和登记，擅自同意将其所属机构国有资产向境外转移；

五、未经可行性论证，盲目决策，致使国有资产遭受损失；

六、向境外投资时，弄虚作假，逃避审批，擅自转移资产或不按规定进行资产评估；

七、对政府规定报告、备案事项不按要求报告或备案；

八、其他。

第三十三条 境外机构中方负责人，因下列行为导致国有资产损失的，财政（国有资产管理）部门会同政府有关部门根据不同情节给予通报批评或经济、行政处罚。重大案件可联合监察、审计部门进行立案审查。触犯刑律的，移送司法机关依法追究刑事责任。

一、不如实填报境外机构会计信息统计报表和对规定报告、备案事项不按要求办理，隐瞒真实情况；

二、不按规定办理境外产权登记手续；

三、未经政府有关部门批准或未办理有关法律手续，将国有资产产权以个人名义注册；

四、未经批准向外方担保，造成国有资产流失；

五、未按规定在境外发行股票上市；

六、未按规定权限处置国有资产；

七、逃避国家监督、检查，私立账户，转移资产；

八、发生境外人员携款潜逃事件，造成资产损失；

九、其他。

第六章 附 则

第三十四条 国务院有关部门、各省、自治区、直辖市、计划单列市财政（国有资产管理）部门，可根据本办法制定补充规定或实施细则，报财政部备案。

第三十五条 本办法发布前关于境外国有资产管理的行政规章与本办法相抵触的，以本办法为准。

第三十六条 本办法自发布之日起施行。

对外贸易经济合作部 中国人民银行 关于下发《对外承包工程项目投标（议标）许可暂行办法》的通知

〔1999〕外经贸合发第699号

1999年12月14日

铁道部、信息产业部、民航总局，各省、自治区、直辖市及计划单列市外经贸委（厅、局），中国人民银行各分行、营业管理部，国有独资商业银行、中国进出口银行、国家开发银行、中国农业发展银行，其他商业银行，各有关外经贸企业：

为加强对对外承包工程业务的管理，规范经营秩序，增强企业的总体对外竞争能力，降低银行风险，外经贸部、中国人民银行共同制定了《对外承包工程项目投标（议标）许可暂行办法》，现印发你们，请遵照执行。

特此通知。

附件：对外承包工程项目投标（议标）许可暂行办法

附　件

对外承包工程项目投标（议标）许可暂行办法

第一条　为维护对外承包工程业务经营秩序，保障业务健康发展，增强企业的对外竞争能力，降低银行风险，特制定本办法。

第二条　本办法所称“对外承包工程项目投标（议标）许可”（以下简称项目许可）是指由对外贸易经济合作部（以下简称外经贸部）根据项目所在国情况及有关业务管理规定，审理企业项目申请后所颁发的许可。企业凭本项目许可，向国内中资银行（以下简称银行）申请开具保函。

第三条　本办法所称企业是指经工商管理部门登记注册，由外经贸部赋予对外承包工程经营权的企业（以下简称企业）。

第四条　本办法所称项目是指企业在国（境）外以投、议标方式参与的、且报价金额在500万美元以上（含500万美元）工程的项目。

第五条　本办法所称保函是指企业为参加项目的投标或实施，向银行申请开具的保函，包括投标项目的投标保函、议标项目的预付款保函或履约保函。

第六条　项目许可申请程序

参加投、议标的企业，在向银行申请开具保函前，须向外经贸部提出项目许可的申请。

一、企业申请所需的材料

（一）项目许可申请报告：

1. 介绍本企业对外承包工程业务方面的业绩、专业实力；

2. 项目的基本情况、组织方式及企业前期接触筹备情况；

3. 实施项目的融资方案。

（二）对外承包工程项目投标（议标）许可申请表（见附表）。

（三）我驻外使、领馆经商参处（室）对我企业参与该项目投标（议标）的书面意见。

（四）有关商会的书面协调意见。

（五）企业上两个会计年度经会计师事务所审计的资产负债表、损益表。

（六）外经贸部要求提供的其他材料。

二、申请程序

（一）中央管理的企业及尚未脱钩的国务院有关部委的企业直接向外经贸部提出申请。

（二）地方企业直接向外经贸部提出申请，同时将项目许可申请报告抄报地方外经贸委。

第七条　外经贸部收到企业报来的齐全材料后，按以下内容进行审理，并在3个工作日内对企业的申请予以答复。

一、企业的专业优势和管理技术水平。

二、企业的财务状况和以往承包工程的业绩。

三、业主的资信与实施项目的资金来源。

四、项目所在国的政治、经济风险。

五、有关单位的书面意见。

第八条　经审理合格，外经贸部将出具《对外承包工程项目投标（议标）许可》（样式及有关规定另行下发）。

企业凭项目许可，向银行申请开具保函。

第九条　银行凭外经贸部出具的项目许可，按照银行业务的有关规定，对获准企业的保函申请予以审理，并根据审理结果决定是否为企业出具有关保函。

银行不得受理未获许可企业的保函申请。

第十条　境内机构的对外承包工程涉及对外担保、筹措外债及对外支付定金等，应按国家外汇管理有关规定办理相应手续。

第十一条　各企业要严格遵守本办法的各项规定。对违反上述规定的企业，外经贸部将按有关规定给予处罚。

第十二条　本办法由对外贸易经济合作部和中国人民银行负责解释。

第十三条　本办法自2000年5月1日起试行。

（附表略）

中华人民共和国主席令

第 21 号

1999 年 8 月 30 日

《中华人民共和国招标投标法》已由中华人民共和国第九届全国人民代表大会常务委员会第十一次会议于 1999 年 8 月 30 日通过，现予公布，自 2000 年 1 月 1 日起施行。

中华人民共和国招标投标法

（1999 年 8 月 30 日第九届全国人民代表大会常务委员会第十一次会议通过）

目　　录

第一章　总　　则

第一条　为了规范招标投标活动，保护国家利益、社会公共利益和招标投标活动当事人的合法权益，提高经济效益，保证项目质量，制定本法。

第二条　在中华人民共和国境内进行招标投标活动，适用本法。

第三条　在中华人民共和国境内进行下列工程建设项目包括项目的勘察、设计、施工、监理以及与工程建设有关的重要设备、材料等的采购，必须进行招标：

（一）大型基础设施、公用事业等关系社会公共利益、公众安全的项目；

（二）全部或者部分使用国有资金投资或者国家融资的项目；

（三）使用国际组织或者外国政府贷款、援助资金的项目。

前款所列项目的具体范围和规模标准，由国务院发展计划部门会同国务院有关部门制订，报国务院批准。

法律或者国务院对必须进行招标的其他项目的范围有规定的，依照其规定。

第四条　任何单位和个人不得将依法必须进行招标的项目化整为零或者以其他任何方式规避招标。

第五条　招标投标活动应当遵循公开、公平、公正和诚实信用的原则。

第六条　依法必须进行招标的项目，其招标投标活动不受地区或者部门限制。任何单位和个人不得违法限制或者排斥本地区、本系统以外的法人或者其他组织参加投标，不得以任何方式非法干涉招标投标活动。

第七条 招标投标活动及其当事人应当接受依法实施的监督。

有关行政监督部门依法对招标投标活动实施监督，依法查处招标投标活动中的违法行为。

对招标投标活动的行政监督及有关部门的具体职权划分，由国务院规定。

第二章 招　　标

第八条 招标人是依照本法规定提出招标项目、进行招标的法人或者其他组织。

第九条 招标项目按照国家有关规定需要履行项目审批手续的，应当先履行审批手续，取得批准。

招标人应当有进行招标项目的相应资金或者资金来源已经落实，并应当在招标文件中如实载明。

第十条 招标分为公开招标和邀请招标。

公开招标，是指招标人以招标公告的方式邀请不特定的法人或者其他组织投标。

邀请招标，是指招标人以投标邀请书的方式邀请特定的法人或者其他组织投标。

第十一条 国务院发展计划部门确定的国家重点项目和省、自治区、直辖市人民政府确定的地方重点项目不适宜公开招标的，经国务院发展计划部门或者省、自治区、直辖市人民政府批准，可以进行邀请招标。

第十二条 招标人有权自行选择招标代理机构，委托其办理招标事宜。任何单位和个人不得以任何方式为招标人指定招标代理机构。

招标人具有编制招标文件和组织评标能力的，可以自行办理招标事宜。任何单位和个人不得强制其委托招标代理机构办理招标事宜。

依法必须进行招标的项目，招标人自行办理招标事宜的，应当向有关行政监督部门备案。

第十三条 招标代理机构是依法设立、从事招标代理业务并提供相关服务的社会中介组织。

招标代理机构应当具备下列条件：

（一）有从事招标代理业务的营业场所和相应资金；

（二）有能够编制招标文件和组织评标的相应专业力量；

（三）有符合本法第三十七条第三款规定条件、可以作为评标委员会成员人选的技术、经济等方面的专家库。

第十四条 从事工程建设项目招标代理业务的招标代理机构，其资格由国务院或者省、自治区、直辖市人民政府的建设行政主管部门认定。具体办法由国务院建设行政主管部门会同国务院有关部门制定。从事其他招标代理业务的招标代理机构，其资格认定的主管部门由国务院规定。

招标代理机构与行政机关和其他国家机关不得存在隶属关系或者其他利益关系。

第十五条 招标代理机构应当在招标人委托的范围内办理招标事宜，并遵守本法关于招标人的规定。

第十六条 招标人采用公开招标方式的，应当发布招标公告。依法必须进行招标的项目的招标公告，应当通过国家指定的报刊、信息网络或者其他媒介发布。

招标公告应当载明招标人的名称和地址、招标项目的性质、数量、实施地点和时间以及获取招标文件的办法等事项。

第十七条 招标人采用邀请招标方式的，应当向3个以上具备承担招标项目的能力、资信良好的特定的法人或者其他组织发出投标邀请书。

投标邀请书应当载明本法第十六条第二款规定的事项。

第十八条 招标人可以根据招标项目本身的要求，在招标公告或者投标邀请书中，要求潜在投标人提供有关资质证明文件和业绩情况，并对潜在投标人进行资格审查；国家对投标人的资格条件有规定的，依照其规定。

招标人不得以不合理的条件限制或者排斥潜在投标人，不得对潜在投标人实行歧视待遇。

第十九条 招标人应当根据招标项目的特点和需要编制招标文件。招标文件应当包括招标项目的技术要求、对投标人资格审查的标准、投标报价要求和评标标准等所有实质性要求和条件以及拟签订合同的主要条款。

国家对招标项目的技术、标准有规定的，招标人应当按照其规定在招标文件中提出相应要求。

招标项目需要划分标段、确定工期的，招标人应当合理划分标段、确定工期，并在招标文件中载明。

第二十条 招标文件不得要求或者标明特定的生产供应者以及含有倾向或者排斥潜在投标人的其他内容。

第二十一条　招标人根据招标项目的具体情况，可以组织潜在投标人踏勘项目现场。

第二十二条　招标人不得向他人透露已获取招标文件的潜在投标人的名称、数量以及可能影响公平竞争的有关招标投标的其他情况。

招标人没有标底的，标底必须保密。

第二十三条　招标人对已发出的招标文件进行必要的澄清或者修改的，应当在招标文件要求提交投标文件截止时间至少15日前，以书面形式通知所有招标文件收受人。该澄清或者修改的内容为招标文件的组成部分。

第二十四条　招标人应当确定投标人编制投标文件所需要的合理时间；但是，依法必须进行招标的项目，自招标文件开始发出之日起至投标人提交投标文件截止之日止，最短不得少于20日。

第三章　投　　标

第二十五条　投标人是响应招标、参加投标竞争的法人或者其他组织。

依法招标的科研项目允许个人参加投标的，投标的个人适用本法有关投标人的规定。

第二十六条　投标人应当具备承担投标项目的能力；国家有关规定对投标人资格条件或者招标文件对投标人资格条件有规定的，投标人应当具备规定的资格条件。

第二十七条　投标人应当按照招标文件的要求编制投标文件。投标文件应当对招标文件提出的实质性要求和条件作出响应。

招标项目属于建设施工的，投标文件的内容应当包括拟派出的项目负责人与主要技术人员的简历、业绩和拟用于完成招标项目的机械设备等。

第二十八条　投标人应当在招标文件要求提交投标文件的截止时间前，将投标文件送达投标地点。招标人收到投标文件后，应当签收保存，不得开启。投标人少于3个的，招标人应当依照本法重新招标。

在招标文件要求提交投标文件的截止时间后送达的投标文件，招标人应当拒收。

第二十九条　投标人在招标文件要求提交投标文件的截止时间前，可以补充、修改或者撤回已提交的投标文件，并书面通知招标人。补充、修改的内容为投标文件的组成部分。

第三十条　投标人根据招标文件载明的项目实际情况，拟在中标后将中标项目的部分非主体、非关键性工作进行分包的，应当在投标文件中载明。

第三十一条　两个以上法人或者其他组织可以组成一个联合体，以一个投标人的身份共同投标。

联合体各方均应当具备承担招标项目的相应能力；国家有关规定或者招标文件对投标人资格条件有规定的，联合体各方均应当具备规定的相应资格条件。由同一专业的单位组成的联合体，按照资质等级较低的单位确定资质等级。

联合体各方应当签订共同投标协议，明确约定各方拟承担的工作和责任，并将共同投标协议连同投标文件一并提交招标人。联合体中标的，联合体各方应当共同与招标人签订合同，就中标项目向招标人承担连带责任。

招标人不得强制投标人组成联合体共同投标，不得限制投标人之间的竞争。

第三十二条　投标人不得相互串通投标报价，不得排挤其他投标人的公平竞争，损害招标人或者其他投标人的合法权益。

投标人不得与招标人串通投标，损害国家利益、社会公共利益或者他人的合法权益。

禁止投标人以向招标人或者评标委员会成员行贿的手段谋取中标。

第三十三条　投标人不得以低于成本的报价竞标，也不得以他人名义投标或者以其他方式弄虚作假，骗取中标。

第四章　开标、评标和中标

第三十四条　开标应当在招标文件确定的提交投标文件截止时间的同一时间公开进行；开标地点应当为招标文件中预先确定的地点。

第三十五条　开标由招标人主持，邀请所有投标人参加。

第三十六条　开标时，由投标人或者其推选的代表检查投标文件的密封情况，也可以由招标人委托的公证机构检查并公证；经确认无误后，由工作人员当众拆封，宣读投标人名称、投标价格和投标文件的其他主要内容。

招标人在招标文件要求提交投标文件的截止时间前收到的所有投标文件，开标时都应当当众予以拆封、宣读。

开标过程应当记录，并存档备查。

第三十七条 评标由招标人依法组建的评标委员会负责。

依法必须进行招标的项目，其评标委员会由招标人的代表和有关技术、经济等方面的专家组成，成员人数为5人以上单数，其中技术、经济等方面的专家不得少于成员总数的2/3。

前款专家应当从事相关领域工作满8年并具有高级职称或者具有同等专业水平，由招标人从国务院有关部门或者省、自治区、直辖市人民政府有关部门提供的专家名册或者招标代理机构的专家库内的相关专业的专家名单中确定；一般招标项目可以采取随机抽取方式，特殊招标项目可以由招标人直接确定。

与投标人有利害关系的人不得进入相关项目的评标委员会；已经进入的应当更换。

评标委员会成员的名单在中标结果确定前应当保密。

第三十八条 招标人应当采取必要的措施，保证评标在严格保密的情况下进行。

任何单位和个人不得非法干预、影响评标的过程和结果。

第三十九条 评标委员会可以要求投标人对投标文件中含义不明确的内容作必要的澄清或者说明，但是澄清或者说明不得超出投标文件的范围或者改变投标文件的实质性内容。

第四十条 评标委员会应当按照招标文件确定的评标标准和方法，对投标文件进行评审和比较；设有标底的，应当参考标底。评标委员会完成评标后，应当向招标人提出书面评标报告，并推荐合格的中标候选人。

招标人根据评标委员会提出的书面评标报告和推荐的中标候选人确定中标人。招标人也可以授权评标委员会直接确定中标人。

国务院对特定招标项目的评标有特别规定的，从其规定。

第四十一条 中标人的投标应当符合下列条件之一：

（一）能够最大限度地满足招标文件中规定的各项综合评价标准；

（二）能够满足招标文件的实质性要求，并且经评审的投标价格最低；但是投标价格低于成本的除外。

第四十二条 评标委员会经评审，认为所有投标都不符合招标文件要求的，可以否决所有投标。

依法必须进行招标的项目的所有投标被否决的，招标人应当依照本法重新招标。

第四十三条 在确定中标人前，招标人不得与投标人就投标价格、投标方案等实质性内容进行谈判。

第四十四条 评标委员会成员应当客观、公正地履行职务，遵守职业道德，对所提出的评审意见承担个人责任。

评标委员会成员不得私下接触投标人，不得收受投标人的财物或者其他好处。

评标委员会成员和参与评标的有关工作人员不得透露对投标文件的评审和比较、中标候选人的推荐情况以及与评价有关的其他情况。

第四十五条 中标人确定后，招标人应当向中标人发出中标通知书，并同时将中标结果通知所有未中标的投标人。

中标通知书对招标人和中标人具有法律效力。中标通知书发出后，招标人改变中标结果的，或者中标人放弃中标项目的，应当依法承担法律责任。

第四十六条 招标人和中标人应当自中标通知书发出之日起30日内，按照招标文件和中标人的投标文件订立书面合同。招标人和中标人不得再行订立背离合同实质性内容的其他协议。

招标文件要求中标人提交履约保证金的，中标人应当提交。

第四十七条 依法必须进行招标的项目，招标人应当自确定中标人之日起15日内，向有关行政监督部门提交招标投标情况的书面报告。

第四十八条 中标人应当按照合同约定履行义务，完成中标项目。中标人不得向他人转让中标项目，也不得将中标项目肢解后分别向他人转让。

中标人按照合同约定或者经招标人同意，可以将中标项目的部分非主体、非关键性工作分包给他人完成。接受分包的人应当具备相应的资格条件，并不得再次分包。

中标人应当就分包项目向招标人负责，接受分包的人就分包项目承担连带责任。

第五章 法律责任

第四十九条 违反本法规定，必须进行招标的项目而不招标的，将必须进行招标的项目化整为零或者以其他任何方式规避招标的，责令限期改正，可以处项目合同金额5‰以上10‰以下的罚款；对全部或者部分使用国有资金的项目，可以暂停项目执行或者暂停资金拨付；对单位直接负责的主管人员和其他直接责任人员依法给予处分。

第五十条 招标代理机构违反本法规定，泄露应当保密的与招标投标活动有关的情况和资料的，或者与招标人、投标人串通损害国家利益、社会公共利益或者他人合法权益的，处5万元以上25万元以下的罚款，对单位直接负责的主管人员和其他直接责任人员处单位罚款数额5%以上10%以下的罚款；有违法所得的，并处没收违法所得；情节严重的，暂停直至取消招标代理资格；构成犯罪的，依法追究刑事责任。给他人造成损失的，依法承担赔偿责任。

前款所列行为影响中标结果的，中标无效。

第五十一条 招标人以不合理的条件限制或者排斥潜在投标人的，对潜在投标人实行歧视待遇的，强制要求投标人组成联合体共同投标的，或者限制投标人之间竞争的，责令改正，可以处1万元以上5万元以下的罚款。

第五十二条 依法必须进行招标的项目的招标人向他人透露已获取招标文件的潜在投标人的名称、数量或者可能影响公平竞争的有关招标投标的其他情况的，或者泄露标底的，给予警告，可以并处1万元以上10万元以下的罚款；对单位直接负责的主管人员和其他直接责任人员依法给予处分；构成犯罪的，依法追究刑事责任。

前款所列行为影响中标结果的，中标无效。

第五十三条 投标人相互串通投标或者与招标人串通投标的，投标人以向招标人或者评标委员会成员行贿的手段谋取中标的，中标无效，处中标项目金额5‰以上10‰以下的罚款，对单位直接负责的主管人员和其他直接责任人员处单位罚款数额5%以上10%以下的罚款；有违法所得的，并处没收违法所得；情节严重的，取消其1年至2年内参加依法必须进行招标的项目的投标资格并予以公告，直至由工商行政管理机关吊销营业执照；构成犯罪的，依法追究刑事责任。给他人造成损失的，依法承担赔偿责任。

第五十四条 投标人以他人名义投标或者以其他方式弄虚作假，骗取中标的，中标无效，给招标人造成损失的，依法承担赔偿责任；构成犯罪的，依法追究刑事责任。

依法必须进行招标的项目的投标人有前款所列行为尚未构成犯罪的，处中标项目金额5‰以上10‰以下的罚款，对单位直接负责的主管人员和其他直接责任人员处单位罚款数额5%以上10%以下的罚款；有违法所得的，并处没收违法所得；情节严重的，取消其1年至3年内参加依法必须进行招标的项目的投标资格并予以公告，直至由工商行政管理机关吊销营业执照。

第五十五条 依法必须进行招标的项目，招标人违反本法规定，与投标人就投标价格、投标方案等实质性内容进行谈判的，给予警告，对单位直接负责的主管人员和其他直接责任人员依法给予处分。

前款所列行为影响中标结果的，中标无效。

第五十六条 评标委员会成员收受投标人的财物或者其他好处的，评标委员会成员或者参加评标的有关工作人员向他人透露对投标文件的评审和比较、中标候选人的推荐以及与评标有关的其他情况的，给予警告，没收收受的财物，可以并处3千元以上5万元以下的罚款，对有所列违法行为的评标委员会成员取消担任评标委员会成员的资格，不得再参加任何依法必须进行招标的项目的评标；构成犯罪的，依法追究刑事责任。

第五十七条 招标人在评标委员会依法推荐的中标候选人以外确定中标人的，依法必须进行招标的项目在所有投标被评标委员会否决后自行确定中标人的，中标无效，责令改正，可以处中标项目金额5‰以上10‰以下的罚款；对单位直接负责的主管人员和其他直接责任人员依法给予处分。

第五十八条 中标人将中标项目转让给他人的，将中标项目肢解后分别转让给他人的，违反本法规定将中标项目的部分主体、关键性工作分包给他人的，或者分包人再次分包的，转让、分包无效，处转让、分包项目金额5‰以上10‰以下的罚款；有违法所得的，并处没收违法所得；可以责令停业整顿；情节严重的，由工商行政管理机关吊销营业执照。

第五十九条 招标人与中标人不按照招标文件和中标人的投标文件订立合同的，或者招标人、中标人订立背离合同实质性内容的协议的，责令改正；可以处中标项目金额5‰以上10‰以下的罚款。

第六十条 中标人不履行与招标人订立的合同的，履约保证金不予退还，给招标人造成的损失超过履约保证金数额的，还应当对超过部分予以赔偿；没有提交履约保证金的，应当对招标人的损失承担赔偿责任。

中标人不按照与招标人订立的合同履行义务，情节严重的，取消其2年至5年内参加依法必须进行招标的项目的投标资格并予以公告，直至由工商行政管理机关吊销营业执照。

因不可抗力不能履行合同的，不适用前两款规定。

第六十一条 本章规定的行政处罚，由国务院规定的有关行政监督部门决定。本法已对实施行政处罚的机关作出规定的除外。

第六十二条 任何单位违反本法规定，限制或者排斥本地区、本系统以外的法人或者其他组织参加投标的，为招标人指定投标代理机构的，强制招标人委托招标代理机构办理招标事宜的，或者以其他方式干涉招标投标活动的，责令改正；对单位直接负责的主管人员和其他直接责任人员依法给予警告、记过、记大过的处分，情节较重的，依法给予降级、撤职、开除的处分。

个人利用职权进行前款违法行为的，依照前款规定追究责任。

第六十三条 对招标投标活动依法负有行政监督职责的国家机关工作人员徇私舞弊、滥用职权或者玩忽职守，构成犯罪的，依法追究刑事责任；不构成犯罪的，依法给予行政处分。

第六十四条 依法必须进行招标的项目违反本法规定，中标无效的，应当依照本法规定的中标条件从其余投标人中重新确定中标人或者依照本法重新进行招标。

第六章　附　　则

第六十五条 投标人和其他利害关系人认为招标投标活动不符合本法有关规定的，有权向招标人提出异议或者依法向有关行政监督部门投诉。

第六十六条 涉及国家安全、国家秘密、抢险救灾或者属于利用扶贫资金实行以工代赈、需要使用农民工等特殊情况，不适宜进行招标的项目，按照国家有关规定可以不进行招标。

第六十七条 使用国际组织或者外国政府贷款、援助资金的项目进行招标，贷款方、资金提供方对招标投标的具体条件和程序有不同规定的，可以适用其规定，但违背中华人民共和国的社会公共利益的除外。

第六十八条 本法自2000年1月1日起施行。

海关、税收

海　关　总　署
公　　告

1999 年 1 月

国务院关税税则委员会决定，自 1999 年 1 月 1 日起，调整《中华人民共和国海关进出口税则》的部分税率税目。（详见 1999 年《中华人民共和国海关进出口税则》）

特此公告。

附件一

1999 年进口关税税率调整表

税　号	货　品　名　称	1998 税则税率	1999 税则税率
42021210	以塑料或纺织材料作面的衣箱	35	30
42021290	塑料或纺织材料作面的其他箱包	35	30
42022200	以塑料片或纺织材料作面的手提包	35	30
42023200	以塑料或纺织品作面的钱包等物品	35	30
42029200	以塑料或纺织材料作面的其他容器	35	30
44011000	薪柴	8	0
44012100	针叶木木片或木粒	1	0
44012200	非针叶木木片或木粒	1	0
44013000	锯末、木废料及碎片	1	0
44031000	用油漆、着色剂等方法处理的原木	2	0
44032000	用其他方法处理的针叶原木	2	0
44034100	深红色红柳桉木等	2	0
44034910	柚木原木	2	0
44034990	其他原木	2	0
44039100	栎木原木	2	0
44039200	山毛榉木原木	2	0

续表

税号	货品名称	1998税则税率	1999税则税率
44039910	楠木原木	2	0
44039920	樟木原木	2	0
44039930	红木原木	2	0
44039940	泡桐木原木	2	0
44039990	其他原木	2	0
44061000	未浸渍的铁道及电车道枕木	3	0
44069000	已浸渍的铁道及电车道枕木	3	0
44071000	针叶木木材	3	0
44072400	美洲桃花心木等木材	3	0
44072500	深红色红柳桉木等木材	3	0
44072600	白柳桉木等木材	3	0
44072910	柚木木材	9	0
44072990	其他热带木木材	3	0
44079100	栎木木材	3	0
44079200	山毛榉木木材	3	0
44079910	樟木、楠木、红木木材	9	0
44079920	泡桐木木材	3	0
44079990	其他木材	3	0
44151000	木箱及类似的包装容器，电缆卷筒	18	10
44152000	托盘	18	10
44184000	水泥构件的木模板	20	10
44190010	木制一次性筷子	21	10
47010000	机械木浆	1	0
47020000	化学木浆，溶解级	1	0
47031100	未漂白针叶木碱木浆或硫酸盐木浆	1	0
47031900	未漂白非针叶木碱木浆等	1	0
47032100	漂白针叶木碱木浆或硫酸盐木浆	1	0
47032900	漂白非针叶木碱木浆或硫酸盐木浆	1	0
47041100	未漂白的针叶木亚硫酸盐木浆	1	0
47041900	未漂白的非针叶木亚硫酸盐木浆	1	0
47042100	漂白的针叶木亚硫酸盐木浆	1	0
47042900	漂白的非针叶木亚硫酸盐木浆	1	0
47050000	半化学木浆	1	0
47061000	棉短绒纸浆	1	0
47062000	从回收纸及纸板提取的纤维浆	1	0
47069100	机械浆	1	0
47069200	化学浆	1	0
47069300	半化学浆	1	0
47071000	未漂白牛皮纸或纸板的废碎品	1	0
47072000	漂白的其他纸和纸板废碎品	1	0

续表

税　号	货　品　名　称	1998税则税率	1999税则税率
47073000	由机械木浆制的纸，纸板的废碎品	1	0
47079000	其他纸及纸板的废碎品	1	0
50040000	非供零售用丝纱线	13	12
50050010	非供零售用䌷丝纱线	13	12
50050090	非供零售用其他绢纺纱线	13	12
50060000	零售用丝纱线，绢纺纱线蚕胶丝	13	12
50071010	未漂白或漂白的䌷丝机织物	27	26
50071090	其他纯chou丝机织物	27	26
50072011	未漂白或漂白桑蚕丝机织物	27	26
50072019	其他纯桑蚕丝机织物	27	26
50072021	未漂白或漂白纯柞蚕丝机织物	27	26
50072029	其他纯柞蚕丝机织物	27	26
50072031	未漂白或漂白纯绢丝机织物	27	26
50072039	其他纯绢丝机织物	27	26
50072090	其他纯丝机织物	27	26
50079010	未列名未漂白或漂白丝机织物	27	26
50079090	其他丝机织物	27	26
51053010	已梳兔毛	13	12
51053021	已梳无毛山羊绒	13	12
51053029	其他已梳山羊绒	13	12
51053090	其他已梳动物细毛	13	12
51054000	已梳动物粗毛	13	12
51111100	重量≤300g/平方米粗梳全毛布	30	28
51111900	重量＞300g/平方米粗梳全毛布	30	28
51112000	与化纤长丝混纺粗梳毛布	30	28
51113000	与化纤短纤混纺粗梳毛布	30	28
51119000	与其他纤维混纺的粗梳毛布	30	28
51121100	重量≤200g/平方米精梳全毛布	30	28
51121900	重量＞200g/平方米精梳全毛布	30	28
51122000	与化纤长丝混纺精梳毛布	30	28
51123000	与化纤短纤混纺精梳羊毛布	30	28
51129000	与其他纤维混纺精梳毛布	30	28
51130000	动物粗毛或马毛机织物	30	28
52041100	非零售棉制缝纫线，含棉≥85％	10	9.8
52041900	其他非零售棉制缝纫线	10	9.8
52042000	零售用绵制缝纫线	10	9.8
52051100	非零售粗梳粗纯棉单纱	10	9.8
52051200	非零售粗梳中支纯棉单纱	10	9.8
52051300	非零售粗梳细支纯棉单纱	10	9.8
52051400	非零售粗梳较细纯棉单纱	10	9.8

续表

税　号	货　品　名　称	1998 税则税率	1999 税则税率
52051500	非零售粗梳特细支纯棉单纱	10	9.8
52052100	非零售精梳粗支纯棉单纱	10	9.8
52052200	非零售精梳中支纯棉单纱	10	9.8
52061100	非零售粗梳粗支混纺棉单纱	13	12
52061200	非零售粗梳中支混纺棉多股纱	13	12
52061300	非零售粗梳细支混纺棉单纱	13	12
52061400	非零售粗梳较细支混纺棉单纱	13	12
52061500	非零售粗梳特细支混纺棉单纱	13	12
52062100	非零售精梳粗支混纺棉单纱	13	12
52062200	非零售精梳中支混纺棉单纱	13	12
52062300	非零售精梳细支混纺棉单纱	13	12
52062400	非零售精梳较细支混纺棉单纱	13	12
52062500	非零售精梳特细支混纺棉单纱	13	12
52063100	非零售粗梳粗支混纺棉多股纱	13	12
52063200	非零售粗梳中支混纺棉多股纱	13	12
52063300	非零售粗梳细支混纺棉多股纱	13	12
52063400	非零售粗梳较细混纺棉多股纱	13	12
52063500	非零售粗梳特细混纺棉多股纱	13	12
52064100	非零售精梳粗支混纺棉多股纱	13	12
52064200	非零售精梳中支混纺棉多股纱	13	12
52064300	非零售精梳细支混纺棉多股纱	13	12
52064400	非零售精梳较细混纺棉多股纱	13	12
52064500	非零售精梳特细混纺棉多股纱	13	12
52079000	供零售用混纺棉纱线	13	12
52081100	未漂白全棉平纹布	19	18
52081200	未漂白全棉平纹布	19	18
52081300	未漂白三四线全棉斜纹布	19	18
52081900	未漂白其他全棉机织物	19	18
52082100	漂白的全棉平纹布	19	18
52082200	漂白的全棉平纹布	19	18
52082300	漂白的全棉三四线斜纹布	19	18
52082900	漂白的其他全棉机织物	19	18
52083100	染色的全棉平纹布	19	18
52083200	染色的全棉平纹布	19	18
52083300	染色的全棉三四线斜纹布	19	18
52083900	染色的其他全棉机织物	19	18
52084100	色织的全棉平纹布	19	18
52084200	色织的全棉平纹布	19	18
52084300	色织的全棉三四线斜纹布	19	18
52084900	色织的其他全棉机织物	19	18

续表

税号	货品名称	1998税则税率	1999税则税率
52085100	印花的全棉平纹布	19	18
52085200	印花的全棉平纹布	19	18
52085300	印花的全棉三四线斜纹布	19	18
52085900	印花的其他全棉机织物	19	18
52091100	未漂白的全棉平纹布	19	18
52091200	未漂白的全棉三四线斜纹布	19	18
52091900	未漂白的其他棉机织物	19	18
52092100	漂白的全棉平纹布	19	18
52092200	漂白的全棉三四线斜纹布	19	18
52092900	漂白的其他棉机织物	19	18
52093100	染色的全棉平纹布	19	18
52093200	染色的全棉三四线斜纹布	19	18
52093900	染色的其他棉机织物	19	18
52094100	色织的全棉平纹布	19	18
52094200	色织的全棉粗斜纹布	18	17
52094300	色织的全棉三四线斜纹布	19	18
52094900	色织的其他棉机织物	19	18
52095100	印花的全棉平纹布	19	18
52095200	印花的全棉三四线斜纹布	19	18
52095900	印花的其他棉机织物	19	18
52101100	与化纤混纺未漂白的棉平纹布	23	22
52101200	化纤混纺未漂白三四线斜纹布	23	22
52101900	与化纤混纺未漂白的其他棉布	23	22
52102100	与化纤混纺漂白的平纹棉布	23	22
52102200	化纤混纺漂白三四线斜纹棉布	23	22
52102900	与化纤混纺漂白的其他棉布	23	22
52103100	与化纤混纺染色的平纹棉布	23	22
52103200	化纤混纺染色三四线斜纹棉布	23	22
52103900	与化纤混纺染色的其他棉布	23	22
52104100	与化纤混纺色织的平纹棉布	23	22
52104200	化纤混纺色织三四线斜纹棉布	23	22
52104900	与化纤混纺色织的其他棉布	23	22
52105100	与化纤混纺印花的平纹纹布	23	22
52105200	化纤混纺印花三四线斜纹棉布	23	22
52105900	与化纤混纺印花的其他棉布	23	22
52111100	与化纤混纺未漂白的棉平纹布	23	22
52111200	化纤混纺未漂白三四线斜纹棉布	23	22
52111900	与化纤混纺未漂白的其他棉布	23	22
52112100	与化纤混纺漂白的棉平纹布	23	22
52112200	化纤混纺漂白三四线斜纹棉布	23	22

续表

税号	货品名称	1998 税则税率	1999 税则税率
52112900	与化纤混纺漂白的其他棉布	23	22
52113100	与化纤混纺染色的棉平纹布	23	22
52113200	化纤混纺染色三四线斜纹棉布	23	22
52113900	与化纤混纺染色的其他棉布	23	22
52114100	与化纤混纺色织的棉平纹布	23	22
52114200	与化纤混纺色织的粗斜纹棉布	23	22
52114300	与化纤混纺色织的斜纹棉布	23	22
52114900	与化纤混纺色织的其他棉布	23	22
52115100	与化纤混纺印花的棉平纹布	23	22
52115200	化纤混纺印花三四线斜纹棉布	23	22
52115900	与化纤混纺印花的其他棉布	23	22
52121100	未漂白的其他混纺棉布	19	18
52121200	漂白的其他混纺棉布	19	18
52121300	染色的其他混纺棉布	19	18
52121400	色织的其他混纺棉布	19	18
52121500	印花的其他混纺棉布	19	18
52122100	未漂白的其他混纺棉布	19	18
52122200	漂白的其他混纺棉布	19	18
52122300	染色的其他混纺棉布	19	18
52122400	色织的其他混纺棉布	18	17
52122500	印花的其他混纺棉布	19	18
53052100	生的蕉麻	5	4．2
53052900	经加工、未纺制的蕉麻、短纤等	5	4．2
53071000	黄麻及其他纺织用韧皮纤维单纱	10	9．8
53072000	黄麻及其他韧皮纤维多股纱或缆线	10	9．8
53081000	椰壳纤维纱线	10	9．8
53082000	大麻纱线	10	9．8
53083000	纸纱线	10	9．8
53089090	其他植物纺织纤维纱线	10	9．8
53091110	未漂白的纯亚麻机织物	22	21
53091120	漂白的纯亚麻机织物	22	218
53091900	其他纯亚麻机织物	22	21
53092110	未漂白的混纺亚麻机织物	22	21
53092120	漂白的混纺亚麻机织物	22	21
53092900	其他混纺亚麻机织物	22	21
53101000	未漂白的黄麻及其他韧皮纤维织物	19	15
53109000	其他黄麻机织物	19	15
53110012	纯苎麻未漂白机织物	22	21
53110013	其他纯苎麻机织物	22	21
53110014	非纯苎麻未漂白机织物	22	21

续表

税　　号	货　　品　　名　　称	1998 税则税率	1999 税则税率
53110015	其他非纯苎麻机织物	22	21
53110020	纸纱线机织物	19	17
53110090	其他纺织用植物纤维机织物	19	17
54011010	非供零售用合纤长丝缝纫线	21	20
54011020	供零售用合纤长丝缝纫线	21	20
54012010	非供零售用人纤长丝缝纫线	14	13
54012020	供零售用人纤长丝缝纫线	14	13
54021010	聚己内酰胺（尼龙－6）纺制的尼龙和高强力纱	19	18
54021020	聚己二酰己二胺（尼龙－66）纺制的尼龙	19	18
54021030	芳香族聚酰胺纺制的尼龙和高强力纱	19	18
54021090	其他非零售用尼龙高强纱	19	18
54022000	非零售聚酯高强力纱	21	20
54023111	聚己内酰胺（尼龙－6）纺制的弹力丝	17	14
54023112	聚己二酰己二胺（尼龙－66）纺制的弹力丝	17	14
54023113	芳香族聚酰胺纺制的弹力丝	17	14
54023119	其他非零售细尼龙弹力丝	17	14
54023190	非零售其他细尼龙变形纱线	17	14
54023211	聚己内酰胺（尼龙－6）纺制的弹力丝	17	15
54023212	聚己二酰己二胺（尼龙－66）纺制的弹力丝	17	15
54023213	芳香族聚酰胺纺制的弹力丝	17	15
54023219	其他非零售粗尼龙弹力丝	17	15
54023290	非零售其他粗尼龙变形纱线	17	15
54023310	非零售聚酯弹力丝	23	22
54023390	非零售其他聚酯变形纱线	21	17
54023910	聚丙烯纱线	21	17
54023920	氨纶纱线	21	17
54023990	其他非零售其他合成纤维长丝变形纱	21	17
54024110	聚己内酰胺（尼龙－6）纺制的单纱	17	16
54024120	聚己二酰己二胺（尼龙－66）纺制的单纱	17	16
54024130	芳香族聚酰胺纺制的单纱	17	16
54024190	其他非零售其他尼龙纱线	17	16
54024200	非零售未捻的部分定向聚酯纱线	21	18
54024300	非零售未捻的其他聚酯纱线	21	20
54024910	聚丙烯纱线	21	20
54024920	氨纶纱线	21	20
54024990	非零售未捻的其他合纤长丝单纱	21	20
54025110	聚己内酰胺（尼龙－6）纺制的单纱	17	16
54025120	聚己二酰己二胺（尼龙－66）纺制的单纱	17	16
54025130	芳香族聚酰胺纺制的单纱	17	16
54025190	其他尼龙或其他聚酰胺纱线单纱	17	16

续表

税　号	货　品　名　称	1998 税则税率	1999 税则税率
54025200	非零售加捻的其他聚酯纱线	21	20
54025910	聚丙烯纱线	21	20
54025920	氨纶纱线	21	20
54025990	非零售加捻的其他合纤长丝单纱	21	20
54026110	聚己内酰胺（尼龙－6）制单纱	19	18
54026120	聚己二酰己二胺（尼龙－66）制单纱	19	18
54026130	芳香族聚酰胺制单纱	19	18
54026190	其他尼龙或其他聚酰胺制单纱	19	18
54026200	非零售聚酯多股纱线	21	20
54026910	聚丙烯纱线	21	20
54026920	氨纶纱线	21	20
54026990	非零售其他合纤长丝多股纱线	21	20
54031000	非零售粘胶纤维高强力纱	15	14
54032000	非零售人造纤维长丝变形纱线	15	14
54033100	非零售未捻的粘胶纤维单纱	15	14
54033200	非零售加捻的粘胶纤维单纱	15	14
54033390	非零售其他醋酸纤维单纱	15	14
54033900	非零售其他人造纤维长丝单纱	15	14
54034100	非零售粘胶长丝多股纱线或缆线	15	14
54034200	非零售醋酸长丝多股纱线或缆线	15	14
54034900	非零售其他人造纤维长丝多股纱或缆线	15	14
54041000	细度≥67 分特的合成纤维单丝	23	22
54049000	合成纺织材料制扁条及类似品	23	22
54061000	供零售用合成纤维长丝纱线	21	20
54074400	印花的纯尼龙布	36	33
54075400	印花的纯涤纶变形丝布	36	33
54077400	印花的其他纯合成纤维长丝布	36	33
54078400	印花的与棉混纺合成纤维布	36	33
54079400	印花的其他混纺合成纤维布	36	33
54081000	粘胶纤维高强力纱的机织物	35	34
54082110	粘胶纤维制未漂白或漂白机织物	35	34
54082120	醋酸纤维制未漂白或漂白机织物	35	34
54082190	其他未漂白或漂白机织物	35	34
54082210	粘胶纤维制染色机织物	35	34
54082220	醋酸纤维制染色机织物	35	34
54082290	其他染色机织物	35	34
54082310	粘胶纤维制色织机织物	35	34
54082320	醋酸纤维制色织机织物	35	34
54082390	其他色织机织物	35	34
54082410	粘胶纤维制印花机织物	35	31

续表

税号	货品名称	1998税则税率	1999税则税率
54082420	醋酸纤维制印花机织物	35	31
54082490	其他印花机织物	35	31
54083100	未漂白或漂白人纤长丝混纺布	35	34
54083200	染色的人纤长丝混纺布	35	34
54083300	色织的人造纤维混纺布	35	34
54083400	印花的人造纤维混纺布	35	31
55012000	聚酯长丝丝束	19	18
55013000	聚丙烯腈长丝丝束	15	13
55019000	其他合成纤维长丝丝束	19	18
55020010	二醋酸纤维丝束	13	12
55032000	未梳的聚酯短纤	19	18
55033000	未梳的聚丙烯腈及其变性短纤	15	13
55039000	未梳的其他合成纤维短纤	19	18
55041000	未梳的粘胶短纤	11	9.6
55051000	合成纤维废料	15	14
55062000	已梳的聚酯短纤	19	18
55063000	已梳的聚丙烯腈及其变性短纤	15	13
55069000	已梳的其他合成纤维短纤	19	18
55070000	已梳的人造纤维短纤	11	10
55081000	合成纤维短纤纺制的缝纫线	23	22
55082000	人造纤维短纤纺制的缝纫线	19	18
55092100	非零售纯聚酯短纤单纱	23	22
55092200	非零售纯聚酯短纤多股纱线	23	22
55093100	非零售纯聚丙烯腈短纤单纱	23	22
55093200	非零售纯聚丙烯腈短纤多股纱线	23	22
55094100	非零售其他纯合成短纤单纱	23	22
55094200	非零售其他纯合成短纤多股纱线	23	22
55095100	非零售与人造纤维短纤混纺聚酯短纤纱	23	22
55095200	非零售与毛混纺聚酯短纤纱线	23	22
55095300	非零售与棉混纺聚酯短纤纱线	23	22
55095900	非零售与其他混纺聚酯短纤纱线	23	22
55096100	非零售与毛混纺腈纶短纤纱线	23	22
55096200	非零售与棉混纺腈纶短纤纱线	23	22
55096900	非零售与其他混纺腈纶短纤纱线	23	22
55099100	非零售与毛混纺合成纤短维纤纱线	23	22
55099200	非零售与棉混纺合成纤维短纤纱线	23	22
55099900	非零售与其他混纺合成纤短纤纱线	23	22
55101100	非零售纯人造纤维短纤单纱	19	18
55101200	非零售纯人造纤维短纤多股纱或缆线	19	18
55102000	非零售与毛混纺人造纤维短纤纱线	19	18

续表

税号	货品名称	1998税则税率	1999税则税率
55103000	非零售与棉混纺人造纤维短纤纱线	19	18
55109000	非零售与其他混纺人造纤维短纤纱线	19	18
55111000	零售用纯合成纤维短纤纱线	23	22
55112000	零售用混纺合成纤维短纤纱线	23	22
55113000	零售用人造纤维短纤纱线	19	18
55121100	未漂或漂白的纯聚酯布	36	34
55121900	其他纯聚酯布	36	34
55122100	未漂或漂白的纯腈纶布	35	34
55122900	其他纯腈纶布	35	34
55129100	未漂或漂白的其他纯合纤布	36	34
55129900	未列名其他纯合纤布	36	34
55131110	与棉混纺未漂白的轻质聚酯平纹布	36	34
55131120	与棉混纺漂白的轻质聚酯平纹布	36	34
55131210	与棉混纺未漂白的轻质聚酯斜纹布	36	34
55131220	与棉混纺漂白的轻质聚酯斜纹布	36	34
55131310	与棉混纺未漂白的其他轻质聚酯布	36	34
55131320	与棉混纺漂白的其他轻质聚酯布	36	34
55131900	棉混纺未漂或漂白轻质其他合纤布	36	34
55132100	与棉混纺染色的轻质聚酯平纹布	36	34
55132200	与棉混纺染色的轻质聚酯斜纹布	36	34
55132300	与棉混纺染色的其他轻质聚酯布	36	34
55132900	与棉混纺染色的轻质其他合纤布	36	34
55133100	与棉混纺色织的轻质聚酯平纹布	36	34
55133200	与棉混纺色织的轻质聚酯斜纹布	36	34
55133300	与棉混纺色织的其他轻质聚酯布	36	34
55133900	与棉混纺色织的轻质其他合纤布	36	34
55134100	与棉混纺印花的轻质聚酯平纹布	34	31
55134200	与棉混纺印花的轻质聚酯斜纹布	34	31
55134300	与棉混纺印花的其他轻质聚酯布	34	31
55134900	与棉混纺印花的轻质其他合纤布	34	31
55141110	与棉混纺未漂白的重质聚酯平纹布	36	34
55141120	与棉混纺漂白的重质聚酯平纹布	36	34
55141210	与棉混纺未漂白的重质聚酯斜纹布	36	34
55141220	与棉混纺漂白的重质聚酯斜纹布	36	34
55141310	与棉混纺未漂白的重质其他聚酯布	36	34
55141320	与棉混纺漂白的重质其他聚酯布	36	34
55141900	与棉混纺未漂或漂重质其他合纤布	36	34
55142100	与棉混纺染色的重质聚酯平纹布	36	34
55142200	与棉混纺染色的重质聚酯斜纹布	36	34
55142300	与棉混纺染色的其他重质聚酯布	36	34

续表

税　号	货　品　名　称	1998税则税率	1999税则税率
55142900	与棉混纺染色的重质其他合纤布	36	34
55143100	与棉混纺色织的重质聚酯平纹布	36	34
55143200	与棉混纺色织的重质聚酯斜纹布	36	34
55143300	与棉混纺色织的其他重质聚酯布	36	34
55143900	与棉混纺色织的重质其他合纤布	36	34
55144100	与棉混纺印花的重质聚酯平纹布	34	31
55144200	与棉混纺印花的重质聚酯斜纹布	34	31
55144300	与棉混纺印花的其他重质聚酯布	34	31
55144900	与棉混纺印花的重质其他合纤布	36	34
55151100	与粘胶短纤混纺的聚酯布	36	34
55151200	与化纤长丝混纺的聚酯布	36	34
55151300	与毛混纺的聚酯布	36	34
55151900	与其他纤维混纺的聚酯布	36	34
55152100	与化纤长丝混纺的腈纶布	35	34
55152200	与毛混纺的腈纶布	35	34
55152900	与其他纤维混纺的腈纶布	35	34
55159100	与化纤长丝混纺的其他合纤短纤布	36	34
55159200	与毛混纺的其他合纤短纤布	36	34
55159900	与其他纤维混纺的其他合纤短纤布	36	34
55161100	未漂或漂白纯人纤短纤布	32	31
55161200	染色的纯人纤短纤布	32	31
55161300	色织的纯人纤短纤布	32	31
55161400	印花的纯人纤短纤布	30	28
55162100	与化纤长丝混纺未漂或漂白人纤布	32	31
55162200	与化纤长丝混纺的染色人纤布	32	31
55162300	与化纤长丝混纺的色织人纤布	32	31
55162400	与化纤长丝混纺的印花人纤布	30	28
55163100	与毛混纺的未漂或漂白人纤布	32	31
55163200	与毛混纺的染色人纤布	32	31
55163300	与毛混纺的色织人纤布	32	31
55163400	与毛混纺的印花人纤布	30	28
55164100	与棉混纺的未漂或漂白人纤布	32	31
55164200	与棉混纺的染色人纤布	32	31
55164300	与棉混纺的色织人纤布	32	31
55164400	与棉混纺的印花人纤布	30	28
55169100	与其他纤维混纺未漂或漂白人纤布	32	31
55169200	与其他纤维混纺的染色人纤布	32	31
55169300	与其他纤维混纺的色织人纤布	32	31
55169400	与其他纤维混纺的印花人纤布	30	28
56011000	絮胎制卫生巾，止血塞等卫生用品	26	24

续表

税　　号	货　品　名　称	1998税则税率	1999税则税率
56012100	棉制的絮胎及其他絮胎制品	22	20
56012210	化学纤维制的卷烟滤嘴	32	31
56012290	化学纤维制的絮胎及其他絮胎制品	32	31
56012900	毛及其他纤维制絮胎及其制品	28	26
56013000	纺织纤维屑，纤维粉末及球结	28	26
56021000	针刺机制毡呢及纤维缝编织物	28	26
56022100	未浸、涂的毛制其他毡呢	28	26
56022900	未浸、涂的其他纺织材料制其他毡呢	30	28
56029000	经浸、涂，包覆或层压的其他毡呢	30	28
56031110	经浸渍等的化纤轻质无纺织物	30	28
56031190	其他化纤轻质无纺织物	30	29
56031210	经浸渍等的化纤较轻质无纺织物	30	28
56031290	其他化纤较轻质无纺织物	30	29
56031310	经浸渍等的化纤较重质无纺织物	30	28
56031390	其他化纤较重质无纺织物	30	29
56031410	经浸渍等的化纤重质无纺织物	30	28
56031490	其他化纤重质无纺织物	30	29
56039110	经浸渍等的其他纤维轻质无纺织物	28	26
56039190	其他纤维轻质无纺织物	22	20
56039210	经浸渍的其他纤维较轻质无纺织物	28	26
56039290	其他纤维较轻质无纺织物	22	20
56039310	经浸渍的其他纤维较重质无纺织物	28	26
56039390	其他纤维较重质无纺织物	22	20
56039410	经浸渍等的其他纤维重质无纺织物	28	26
56039490	其他纤维重质无纺织物	22	20
56041000	用纺织材料包覆的橡胶线及绳	24	22
56042000	用橡、塑浸渍或涂布的高强力纱	24	22
56049000	用橡、塑浸渍涂布的其他纺织纱线	24	22
56050000	含金属纱线	24	22
56060000	绳绒线及粗松螺旋花线	24	22
56071000	黄麻或韧皮纤维纺制线，绳，索，缆	17	16
56072100	剑麻或其他龙舌兰纤维制包扎用绳	17	16
56072900	剑麻或龙舌兰纤维制其他线绳索缆	17	16
56073000	蕉麻或硬质纤维制线，绳，索，缆	17	16
56074100	聚乙烯或聚丙烯制包扎用绳	27	26
56074900	聚乙烯或聚丙烯制线，绳，索，缆	27	26
56075000	其他合纤制线，绳，索，缆	27	26
56079000	其他纺织材料制线，绳，索，缆	27	26
56081100	化纤材料制成的渔网	22	20
56081900	化纤材料制成的其他网	27	26

续表

税　　号	货　　品　　名　　称	1998 税则税率	1999 税则税率
56089000	其他纤维制成的网	27	26
56090000	用纱线，扁条，绳，索，缆制其他物品	27	26
57011000	羊毛结织栽绒地毯及其他铺地制品	32	31
57019010	化纤结织栽绒地毯及其他铺地制品	30	28
57019090	其他材料结织栽绒地毯及铺地制品	32	31
57021000	“开来姆”等手织地毯	32	31
57022000	椰壳纤维制的铺地制品	28	27
57023100	未制成的羊毛起绒地毯及铺地制品	32	31
57023200	未制成的化纤起绒地毯及铺地制品	32	31
57023900	未制成其他纺织材料起绒铺地制品	32	31
57024100	制成的羊毛起绒地毯及铺地制品	32	31
57024200	制成的化纤起绒地毯及铺地制品	32	31
57024900	制成的其他纺织材料起绒铺地制品	32	31
57025100	未制成羊毛非起绒地毯及铺地制品	32	31
57025200	未制成化纤非起绒地毯及铺地制品	32	31
57025900	未制成其他非起绒地毯及铺地制品	32	31
57029100	制成的羊毛非起绒地毯及制地制品	32	31
57029200	制成的化纤非起绒地毯及铺地制品	32	31
57029900	制成的其他非起绒地毯及铺地制品	32	31
57031000	羊毛簇绒地毯及其他簇绒铺地制品	32	31
57032000	尼龙簇绒地毯及其他簇绒铺地制品	30	28
57033000	化纤簇绒地毯及其他簇绒铺地制品	30	28
57039000	其他簇绒地毯及其他簇绒铺地制品	30	25
57041000	小块毡呢地毯及其他毡呢铺地制品	30	28
57049000	大块毡呢地毯及其他毡呢铺地制品	32	31
57050010	羊毛制其他地毯及其他铺地制品	32	31
57050020	化纤制其他地毯及其他铺地制品	32	31
57050090	其他材料制其他地毯及铺地制品	32	31
58011000	毛制起绒机织物及绳绒织物	32	31
58012100	不割绒的纬起绒棉织物	24	22
58012200	割绒的棉灯芯绒	24	22
58012300	未列名纬起绒棉织物	24	22
58012400	不割绒的棉制经起绒织物	24	22
58012500	割绒的棉制经起绒织物	24	22
58012600	棉制绳绒织物	24	22
58013100	不割绒的化纤制纬起绒织物	32	31
58013200	割绒的化纤制灯芯绒	32	31
58013300	其他化纤纬起绒织物	32	31
58013400	不割绒的化纤经起绒织物（棱纹绸）	32	31
58013500	割绒的化纤制经起绒织物	32	31

续表

税　号	货　品　名　称	1998 税则税率	1999 税则税率
58013600	化纤绳绒织物	32	31
58019010	丝（绢丝）起绒机织物及绳绒织物	32	31
58019090	其他材料起绒机织物及绳绒织物	30	28
58021100	未漂棉毛巾织物及类似毛圈机织物	24	22
58021900	其他棉毛巾织物及类似毛圈机织物	24	22
58022010	丝（绢丝）毛巾织物及类似毛圈织物	32	31
58022020	羊毛等毛巾织物及类似毛圈机织物	32	31
58022030	化纤毛巾织物及类似毛圈机织物	32	31
58022090	其他材料毛巾织物及类似毛圈织物	30	28
58023010	丝（绢丝）制簇绒织物	32	31
58023020	羊毛或动物细毛制簇绒织物	32	31
58023030	棉或麻制簇绒织物	24	22
58023040	化学纤维制簇绒织物	32	31
58023090	其他纺织材料制簇绒织物	30	28
58031000	棉制纱罗	24	22
58039010	丝及绢丝制纱罗	32	31
58039020	化学纤维制纱罗	32	31
58039090	其他纺织材料制纱罗	30	28
58041010	丝（绢丝）网眼薄料及其他网眼织物	32	31
58041020	棉制网眼薄纱及其他网眼织物	24	22
58041030	化纤制网眼薄纱及其他网眼织物	32	31
58041090	其他材料网眼薄纱及其他网眼织物	30	28
58042100	化纤机制花边	32	31
58042910	丝及绢丝机制花边	32	31
58042920	棉机制花边	24	22
58042990	其他纺织材料机制花边	30	28
58043000	手工制花边	30	29
58050010	手工针绣嵌花装饰毯	28	26
58050090	“哥白林”等手织装饰毯	30	28
58061010	棉或麻制狭幅起绒机织及绳绒织物	24	22
58061090	其他材料制狭幅起绒及绳绒织物	26	24
58062000	弹性纱线或橡胶线高含量狭幅织物	30	29
58063100	棉制其他机狭幅织物	24	22
58063200	化纤制其他机织狭幅织物	32	31
58063910	丝（绢丝）制其他机织狭幅织物	32	31
58063920	羊毛制其他机织狭幅织物	32	31
58063990	其他材料制其他机织狭幅织物	30	28
58064010	棉或麻粘合有经纱无纬纱狭幅织物	24	22
58064090	其他材料粘合有经无纬狭幅职物	30	28
58071000	机织非绣制纺织材料标签，徽章等	30	29

续表

税　　号	货　　品　　名　　称	1998 税则税率	1999 税则税率
58079000	非机织非绣制纺织材料标签，徽章等	30	29
58081000	成匹的编带	30	29
58089000	非绣制成匹装饰带，流苏，绒球	30	29
58090010	与棉混制金属线布及含金属纱线布	30	28
58090020	与化纤混制金属线布及含金属纱布	30	28
58090090	其他金属线布及含金属纱线布	30	28
58101000	不见底布的刺绣品	32	31
58109100	棉制见底布的刺绣品	28	27
58109200	化学纤维制见底布的刺绣品	32	31
58109900	麻制见底布的刺绣品	28	27
58110010	丝及绢丝制被褥状纺织品	30	28
58110020	羊毛或动物细毛制被褥状纺织品	30	28
58110030	棉制被褥状纺织品	26	24
58110040	化学纤维制被褥状纺织品	30	28
58110090	其他纺织材料制被褥状纺织品	30	28
59011010	用胶或淀粉涂布的棉或麻纺织物	25	21
59011020	用胶或淀粉涂布的化纤纺织物	32	25
59011090	用胶或淀粉涂布的其他纤维纺织物	32	25
59019010	制成的油画布	19	14
59019091	棉或麻制描图布，帽里硬衬布等	23	21
59021000	尼龙等高强力纱制的帘子布	20	19
59022000	聚酯高强力纱制的帘子布	20	19
59029000	粘胶纤维高强力纱制帘子布	20	19
59031010	聚氯乙烯制绝缘布或带	15	10
59031020	聚氯乙烯制人造革	25	21
59031090	用聚氯乙烯浸渍的其他纺织物	26	24
59032010	聚氨基甲酸酯制绝缘布或带	15	10
59032020	聚氨基甲酸酯制人造革	25	21
59032090	用聚氨基甲酸酯浸渍的其他纺织物	26	24
59039010	其他塑料制绝缘布或带	15	10
59039020	其他塑料制人造革	25	21
59039090	用其他塑料浸渍的其他纺织物	26	24
59041000	列诺伦（亚麻油地毡）	26	24
59049100	以毡呢或无纺布为底涂布的铺地品	30	28
59049200	以其他纺织物为底涂布的铺地品	30	28
59050000	糊墙织物	28	26
59061010	用橡胶处理宽≤20cm 纺织绝缘带	15	10
59061090	用橡胶处理宽≤20cm 其他胶粘带	28	26
59069100	用橡胶处理的针织或钩编的纺织物	28	26
59069910	橡胶处理宽＞20cm 绝缘布或带	15	10

续表

税　号	货　品　名　称	1998 税则税率	1999 税则税率
59069990	用橡胶处理的其他纺织物	29	27
59070010	其他材料浸涂的绝缘布或带	15	10
59070020	其他材料浸涂的已绘制画布	17	14
59070090	其他材料浸涂的其他纺织物	30	25
59080000	灯芯，炉芯等和煤气灯纱筒及纱罩	17	16
59090000	纺织材料制水龙软管及类似管子	14	13
59100000	纺织材料制的传动带或输送带	14	13
59111010	浸胶的起绒狭幅织物	23	17
59111090	其他涂布、包覆织物	14	8．4
59112000	筛布	16	8．4
59113100	轻的环状或有联接装置的布或毡呢	16	8．4
59113200	重的环状或有联接装置的布或毡呢	16	8．4
59114000	用于榨油机器或类似机器的滤布	16	8．4
59119000	其他专门技术用途纺织产品及制品	16	8．4
60011000	针织或钩编的长毛绒织物	30	29
60012100	棉制针织或钩编的毛圈绒头织物	24	22
60012200	针织或钩编化纤制毛圈绒头织物	30	29
60012900	针织或钩编其他纺材毛圈绒头织物	32	31
60019100	棉制针织或钩编起绒织物	24	22
60019200	针织或钩编化纤起绒织物	30	29
60019900	针织或钩编其他纺织材料起绒织物	32	31
60021010	宽≤30cm 弹性棉制针织或钩编织物	24	22
60021090	宽≤30cm 弹性其他纺材针织钩编物	30	29
60022010	宽≤30cm 非弹性棉针织、钩编织物	24	22
60022090	宽≤30cm 非弹性其他纺材针织钩编物	30	29
60023010	宽＞30cm 弹性棉针织、钩编织物	24	22
60023090	宽＞30cm 弹性其他纺材针织钩编物	30	29
60024100	毛制经编织物	30	29
60024200	棉制经编织物	24	22
60024300	化纤制经编织物	30	29
60024900	其他材料制经编织物	30	29
60029100	毛制其他针织或钩编织物	30	29
60029200	棉制其他针织或钩编织物	24	22
60029300	化纤制其他针织或钩编织物	30	29
60029900	其他材料制其他针织或钩编织物	32	31
61011000	毛制针织或钩编男式大衣、防风衣	36	33
61012000	棉制针织或钩编男式大衣、防风衣	31	28
61013000	化纤制针织或钩编男式大衣等	36	33
61019000	其他针织或钩编男式大衣、防风衣	36	33
61021000	毛制针织或钩编女式大衣、防风衣	36	33

续表

税　　号	货　品　名　称	1998 税则税率	1999 税则税率
61022000	棉制针织或钩编女式大衣、防风衣	31	28
61023000	化纤制针织或钩编女式大衣等	36	33
61029000	其他针织或钩编女式大衣、防风衣	36	33
61031100	毛制针织或钩编男式西服套装	36	33
61031200	合纤制针织或钩编男西服套装	36	33
61031900	人纤制针织或钩编男西服套装	36	33
61032100	毛制针织或钩编男式便服套装	36	33
61032200	棉制针织或钩编男式便服套装	31	28
61032300	合纤制针织或钩编男便服套装	36	33
61032900	人纤制针织或钩编男便服套装	36	33
61033100	毛制针织或钩编男式上衣	36	33
61033200	棉制针织或钩编男式上衣	31	28
61033300	合纤制针织或钩编男式上衣	36	33
61033900	其他针织或钩编男式上衣	36	33
61034100	毛制针织或钩编男长裤、工装裤等	35	33
61034200	棉制针织或钩编男长裤、工装裤等	31	28
61034300	合纤制针织或钩编男长裤等	35	33
61034900	其他针织或钩编男长裤等	35	33
61041100	毛制针织或钩编女式西服套装	36	33
61041200	棉制针织或钩编女式西服套装	31	28
61041300	其他针织或钩编女西服套装	36	33
61041900	其他针织或钩编女西服套装	36	33
61042100	毛制针织或钩编女式便服套装	36	33
61042200	棉制针织或钩编女式便服套装	31	28
61042300	合纤制针织或钩编女便服套装	36	33
61042900	其他针织或钩编女西服套装	36	33
61043100	毛制针织或钩编女式上衣	36	33
61043200	棉制针织或钩编女式上衣	31	28
61043300	其他合纤制针织或钩编女式上衣	36	33
61043900	其他纺材制针织或钩编女式上衣	36	33
61044100	毛制针织或钩编连衣裙	35	33
61044200	棉制手工钩编连衣裙	31	28
61044300	合纤制手工钩编连衣裙	35	33
61044400	其他人纤制针织或钩编的连衣裙	35	33
61044900	其他纺材制针织或钩编的连衣裙	35	33
61045100	毛制针织或钩编裙子及裙裤	35	33
61045200	棉制针织或钩编的裙子及裙裤	31	28
61045300	合纤制针织或钩编裙子及裙裤	35	33
61045900	人纤制针织钩编裙子及裙裤	35	33
61046100	毛制针织或钩编女长裤、工装裤等	35	33

续表

税号	货品名称	1998 税则税率	1999 税则税率
61046200	棉制针织或钩编女长裤、工装裤等	31	28
61046300	合纤制针织或钩编女长裤等	35	33
61046900	其他纺材制针织或钩编女长裤等	35	33
61051000	棉制针织或钩编男衬衫	30	21
61052000	化纤制针织或钩编男衬衫	35	33
61059000	其他纺材制的针织或钩编男衬衫	35	25
61061000	棉制针织或钩编女衬衫	30	21
61062000	合纤制针织或钩编女衬衫	35	25
61069000	其他针织或钩编女衬衫	35	25
61071100	棉制针织或钩编男内裤及三角裤	28	21
61071200	化纤制针织或钩编男内裤及三角裤	32	25
61071900	其他纺材针织或钩编男内裤及三角裤	33	31
61072100	棉制针织或钩编男长睡衣及睡衣裤	28	21
61072200	化纤制针织或钩编男睡衣裤	32	25
61072900	其他针织或钩编男长睡衣及睡衣裤	33	31
61079100	棉制针织或钩编男浴衣、晨衣	28	21
61079200	化纤制针织或钩编男浴衣、晨衣	32	25
61079900	其他针织或钩编男浴衣、晨衣	32	25
61081100	化纤制针织或钩编长衬裙及衬裙	32	25
61081910	棉制针织或钩编长衬裙及衬裙	28	21
61081990	其他针织或钩编长衬裙及衬裙	32	25
61082100	棉制针织或钩编女三角裤及短衬裤	28	21
61082200	化纤制针织或钩编女三角裤等	32	25
61082900	其他针织或钩编女三角裤及短衬裤	33	31
61083100	棉制针织或钩编女睡衣及睡衣裤	28	21
61083200	化纤制针织或钩编女睡衣及睡衣裤	32	25
61083900	其他针织或钩编女睡衣及睡衣裤	33	31
61089100	棉制针织或钩编女浴衣、晨衣	28	21
61089200	化纤制针织或钩编女浴衣、晨衣	32	25
61089900	其他针织或钩编女浴衣、晨衣	33	31
61091000	棉制针织或钩编 T 恤衫、汗衫等	28	21
61099000	其他针织或钩编 T 恤衫、汗衫等	32	25
61101010	羊绒制针织或钩编套头衫等	33	31
61101020	羊毛制针织或钩编套头衫等	33	31
61101030	兔毛制针织或钩编套头衫等	33	31
61101090	其他毛制针织或钩编套头衫等	33	31
61102000	棉制针织或钩编套头衫等	28	21
61103000	合纤制针织或钩编套头衫等	32	25
61109000	其他针织或钩编套头衫等	32	25
61111000	毛制婴儿手套、袜子和内衣等	33	31

续表

税号	货品名称	1998税则税率	1999税则税率
61112000	棉制婴儿手套、袜子和内衣等	28	26
61113000	合纤制婴儿针织或钩编手套等	33	31
61119000	其他纺材制婴儿针织或钩编手套等	33	31
61121100	棉制针织或钩编运动服	31	28
61121200	合纤制针织或钩编运动服	35	33
61121900	其他纺材制针织或钩编运动服	35	33
61122010	棉制针织或钩编滑雪服	31	28
61122090	合纤制针织或钩编滑雪服	35	33
61123100	合纤制男式针织或钩编游泳服	35	33
61123900	其他纺材制男式针织或钩编游泳服	35	33
61124100	合纤制女式针织或钩编游泳服	35	33
61124900	其他纺材制女式针织或钩编游泳服	35	33
61130000	毛或化纤制经处理针织服装等	35	33
61141000	毛制针织或钩编的其他服装	35	33
61142000	棉制针织或钩编的其他服装	31	28
61143000	合纤制针织或钩编的其他服装	35	33
61149000	其他针织或钩编的其他服装	35	33
61151100	单丝67分特以下合纤制连裤袜等	33	31
61151200	单丝67分特及以上合纤制连裤袜等	33	31
61151910	棉制针织或钩编连裤袜及紧身裤袜	26	24
61151990	毛或化纤制弹性处理连裤袜等	33	31
61152000	其他纺织材料制女针织或钩编统袜	33	31
61159100	毛制针织或钩编短袜及其他袜等	30	29
61159200	棉制针织或钩编短袜及其他袜等	26	24
61159300	化纤制针织或钩编短袜等	33	31
61159900	其他针织或钩编短袜及其他袜等	33	31
61161000	用塑橡浸渍的手套	30	29
61169100	毛制其他针织或钩编手套	30	29
61169200	棉制其他针织或钩编手套	26	24
61169300	合成纤维制其他针织或钩编手套	33	31
61169900	其他纺材制其他针织或钩编手套	33	31
61171000	其他纺织材料针织，钩编披巾，头巾	33	31
61172000	其他纺织材料针织，钩编领带，领结	33	31
61178000	其他纺织材料针织或钩编衣着附件	33	31
61179000	其他纺织材料针织或钩编衣着零件	33	31
62011100	毛制男式大衣，斗篷及类似品等	36	33
62011210	棉制男式羽绒服	31	28
62011290	棉制男式大衣，斗篷及类似品等	31	28
62011310	化纤制男羽绒服	36	33
62011390	化纤制男大衣、斗篷及类似品	36	33

续表

税　号	货　品　名　称	1998税则税率	1999税则税率
62011900	其他材料制男大衣、斗篷及类似品	36	33
62019100	毛制男带风帽防寒短上衣、防风衣	36	33
62019210	棉制男式其他羽绒服	31	28
62019290	棉制男带风帽防寒短上衣、防风衣	31	28
62019310	化纤制男式其他羽绒服	36	33
62019390	化纤制男防寒短上衣、防风衣	36	33
62019900	其他材料制男防寒短上衣、防风衣	36	33
62021100	毛制女式大衣，斗篷及类似品等	36	33
62021210	棉制女式羽绒服	31	28
62021290	棉制女式大衣，斗篷及类似品等	31	28
62021310	化纤制女羽绒服	36	33
62021390	化纤制女大衣，斗篷及类似品	36	33
62021900	其他材料制女大衣，斗篷及类似品	36	33
62029100	毛制女带风帽防寒短上衣，防风衣	36	33
62029210	棉制女式羽绒服	31	28
62029290	棉制女带风帽防寒短上衣，防风衣	31	28
62029310	化纤制女式其他羽绒服	36	33
62029390	化纤制女式带风帽防寒短大衣	36	33
62029900	其他材料制防风衣，防风短上衣等	36	33
62031100	毛制男式西服套装	36	33
62031200	合纤制男式西服套装	36	33
62031900	其他纺织材料制男式西服套装	36	33
62032100	毛制男式便服套装	36	33
62032200	棉制男式便服套装	31	28
62032300	合纤制男式便服套装	36	33
62032910	丝制男式便服套装	36	33
62032990	其他纺织材料制男式便服套装	36	33
62033100	毛制男式上衣	36	33
62033200	棉制男式上衣	31	28
62033300	毛型合纤制男式上衣	36	33
62033910	丝制男式上衣	36	33
62033990	其他纺织材料制男式上衣	36	33
62034100	毛制男式长裤，工装裤等	35	33
62034210	棉制阿拉伯裤	31	28
62034290	棉制男式长裤，工装裤等	31	28
62034310	合纤制阿拉伯裤	35	33
62034390	合纤制男式长裤，工装裤等	35	33
62034910	其他材料制阿拉伯裤	35	33
62034990	其他材料制男式长裤，工装裤等	35	33
62041100	毛制女式西服套装	36	33

续表

税　　号	货　品　名　称	1998 税则税率	1999 税则税率
62041200	棉制女式西服套装	31	28
62041300	合纤女式西服套装	36	33
62041900	其他材料制女式西服套装	36	33
62042100	毛制女式便服套装	36	33
62042200	棉制女式便服套装	31	28
62042300	合纤制女式便服套装	36	33
62042910	丝制女式便服套装	36	33
62042990	其他材料制女式便服套装	36	33
62043100	毛制女式上衣	36	33
62043200	棉制女式上衣	31	28
62043300	合纤制女式上衣	36	33
62043910	丝制女式上衣	36	33
62043990	其他材料制女式上衣	36	33
62044100	毛制连衣裙	35	33
62044200	棉制连衣裙	31	28
62044300	合纤制女式连衣裙	35	33
62044400	人纤制女式连衣裙	35	33
62044910	丝制连衣裙	35	33
62044990	其他材料制连衣裙	35	33
62045100	毛制裙子及裙裤	35	33
62045200	棉制裙子及裙裤	31	28
62045300	合纤制裙子及裙裤	35	33
620045910	丝制裙子及裙裤	35	33
62045990	其他材料制裙子及裙裤	35	33
62046100	毛制女式长裤，工装裤等	35	33
62046200	棉制女式长裤，工装裤等	31	28
62046300	合纤制女式长裤，工装裤等	35	33
62046900	其他材料制女式长裤，工装裤等	35	33
62051000	毛制男衬衫	35	33
62052000	棉制男衬衫	31	28
62053000	人纤制男衬衫	35	33
62059010	丝制男衬衫	35	33
62059090	其他材料制男衬衫	35	33
62061000	丝制女式衬衫	35	33
62062000	毛制女衬衫	35	33
62063000	棉制女衬衫	31	28
62064000	化纤制女衬衫	35	33
62069000	其他材料制女衬衫	35	33
62071100	棉制男式内裤及三角裤	28	26
62071910	丝制男式内裤及三角裤	33	31

续表

税　　号	货　品　名　称	1998 税则税率	1999 税则税率
62071920	化纤制男式内裤及三角裤	33	31
62071990	其他材料制男式内裤及三角裤	33	31
62072100	棉制男式长睡衣及睡衣裤	28	26
62072200	化纤制男式长睡衣及睡衣裤	33	31
62072910	丝制男式长睡衣及睡衣裤	33	31
62072990	其他材料制男式长睡衣及睡衣裤	33	31
62079100	棉制男式浴衣，晨衣及类似品	28	26
62079200	化纤制男浴衣，晨衣及类似品	33	31
62079910	丝制男浴衣，晨衣及类似品	33	31
62079990	其他材料制男浴衣，晨衣及类似品	33	31
62081100	化纤制长衬裙及衬裙	33	31
62081910	丝制长衬裙及衬裙	33	31
62081920	棉制长衬裙及衬裙	28	26
62081990	其他材料制长衬裙及衬裙	33	31
62082100	棉制女式睡衣及睡衣裤	28	26
62082200	化纤制女式睡衣及睡衣裤	33	31
62082910	丝制女式睡衣及睡衣裤	33	31
62082990	其他材料制女式睡衣及睡衣裤	33	31
62089100	棉制女式浴衣，晨衣及类似品	28	26
62089200	化纤制女浴衣，晨衣及类似品	33	31
62089910	丝制女式浴衣，晨衣及类似品	33	31
62089990	其他材料制女式浴衣，晨衣及类似品	33	31
62091000	毛制婴儿服装及衣着附件	30	29
62092010	棉制婴儿尿布	28	26
62092090	棉制其他婴儿服装及衣附件	28	26
62093000	合纤制婴儿服装及衣着附件	33	31
62099000	其他材料制婴儿服装及衣着附件	33	31
62101010	毛制毡呢或无纺织物服装	35	33
62101020	棉或麻制毡呢或无纺织物服装	28	26
62101030	化纤制毡呢或无纺织物服装	35	33
62101090	其他材料制毡呢或无纺织物服装	30	29
62102000	用各种材料处理织物制男外装	35	33
62103000	用各种材料处理织物制女外装	35	33
62104000	各种材料处理织物制男其他服装	35	33
62105000	各种材料处理织物制女其他服装	35	33
62111100	男式游泳服	35	33
62111200	女式游泳服	35	33
62112010	棉制滑雪服	31	28
62112090	其他材料制化纤制滑雪服	35	33
62113100	毛制男式运动服及其他服装	35	33

续表

税　号	货　品　名　称	1998 税则税率	1999 税则税率
62113210	棉制阿拉伯袍	31	28
62113290	棉制其他男式运动服及其他服装	31	28
62113310	化纤制阿拉伯袍	35	33
62113390	化纤制其他男式运动服及其他服装	35	33
62113910	丝制男运动服及其他服装	35	33
62113990	其他材料制男式其他服装	35	33
62114100	毛制女式运动服及其他服装	35	33
62114200	棉制女式运动服及其他服装	31	28
62114300	化纤制女式运动服及其他服装	35	33
62114910	丝制女式运动服及其他服装	35	33
62114990	其他材料制其他女式运动服滑雪服	35	33
62121010	化纤制胸罩	33	31
62121090	其他材料制胸罩	33	31
62122010	化纤制束胸带及腹带	33	31
62122090	其他材料制束胸带及腹带	33	31
62123010	化纤制紧身胸衣	33	31
62123090	其他材料制紧身胸衣	33	31
62129010	化纤制吊裤带，吊袜带等	33	31
62129090	其他材料制吊裤带，吊袜带等	33	31
62131010	丝制刺绣手帕	33	31
62131090	其他丝及绢丝制手帕	33	31
62132010	棉制刺绣手帕	28	26
62132090	其他棉制手帕	28	26
62139010	其他材料制刺绣手帕	33	31
62139090	其他材料制其他手帕	33	31
62141000	丝制披巾，头巾，围巾及类似品	33	31
62142000	毛制披巾，头巾，围巾及类似品	33	31
62143000	合纤制披巾，头巾及类似品	33	31
62144000	人纤制披巾，头巾及类似品	33	31
62149000	其他材料制披巾，头巾及类似品	33	31
62151000	丝制领带及领结	33	31
62152000	化纤制领带及领结	33	31
62159000	其他材料制领带及领结	33	31
62160000	纺织材料制手套	33	31
62171010	其他材料制袜子及袜套	33	31
62171020	其他材料制和服腰带	33	31
62171090	其他材料制服装或衣着附件	33	31
62179000	毛或毛型化纤制服装或衣着零件	33	31
63011000	电暖毯	28	27
63012000	毛制毯子及旅行毯	33	31

续表

税　　号	货　品　名　称	1998 税则税率	1999 税则税率
63013000	棉制毯子及旅行毯	30	29
63014000	合纤制毯子及旅行毯	33	31
63019000	其他材料制毯子及旅行毯	33	31
63021010	棉制针织或钩编的床上用织物制品	26	24
63021090	其他材料制床上用织物制品	33	31
63022110	棉制印花床单	25	21
63022190	棉制印花床上用织物制品	25	21
63022210	化纤制印花床单	32	25
63022290	化纤制印花床上用织物制品	33	31
63022910	丝制印花床上用织物制品	33	31
63022920	麻制印花床上用织物制品	26	24
63022990	其他材料制用织物制品	33	31
63023110	棉制刺绣的其他床上用织物制品	25	21
63023191	棉制其他床单	25	21
63023192	棉制毛巾被	25	21
63023199	棉制其他床上用织物制品	25	21
63023210	化纤制刺绣床上用织物制品	32	25
63023290	化纤制其他床上用织物制品	32	25
63023910	丝制其他床上用织物制品	33	31
63023921	麻制刺绣床上用织物制品	26	24
63023929	麻制其他床上用织物制品	26	24
63023991	其他材料制刺绣床上用织物制品	33	31
63023999	其他材料制床上用织物制品	33	31
63024010	其他材料制手工针织餐桌制品	33	31
63024090	其他材料制其他针织餐桌制品	33	31
63025110	棉制刺绣餐桌用织物制品	26	24
63025190	棉制其他餐桌用织物制品	26	24
63025210	亚麻制刺绣餐桌用织物制品	26	24
63025290	亚麻制其他餐桌用织物制品	26	24
63025310	其他材料制刺绣餐桌用织物制品	33	31
63025390	化纤制其他餐桌用织物制品	33	31
63025900	其他材料制餐桌用织物制品	33	31
63026010	棉制浴巾	25	21
63026090	棉制盥洗及厨房用毛巾织物制品	25	21
63029100	棉制其他盥洗及厨房制品等	25	21
63029200	亚麻制其他盥洗及厨房制品等	26	24
63029300	化纤制其他盥洗及厨房制品等	33	31
63029900	其他材料制盥洗及厨房其他制品等	33	31
63031110	棉制针织的窗帘	25	21
63031120	棉制钩编的窗帘	25	21

续表

税　　号	货　品　名　称	1998 税则税率	1999 税则税率
63031210	合纤制针织的窗帘	32	25
63031220	合纤制钩编的窗帘	32	25
63031910	其他材料制针织窗帘	32	25
63031920	其他材料制钩编窗帘	32	25
63039100	棉制非针织或钩编的窗帘等	25	21
63039200	合纤制非针织或钩编窗帘	32	25
63039900	其他材料制非针织或钩编窗帘	33	31
63041121	其他材料制手工针织的床罩	33	31
63041129	其他材料制其他针织的床罩	33	31
63041131	其他材料制手工钩编的床罩	33	31
63041139	其他材料制其他钩编的床罩	33	31
63041910	丝制非针织或钩编床罩	33	31
63041921	棉制手绣非针织或钩编床罩	26	24
63041929	棉制其他非针织或钩编床罩	26	24
63041931	化纤制刺绣非针织或钩编床罩	33	31
63041939	化纤制其他非针织或钩编床罩	33	31
63041991	其他材料制刺绣非针织或钩编床罩	33	31
63041999	其他材料制其他非针织或钩编床罩	33	31
63049121	手工针织的其他装饰用织物制品	33	31
63049129	非手工针织的其他装饰用织物制品	33	31
63049131	手工钩编的其也装饰用织物制品	33	31
63049139	非手工钩编的其他装饰用织物制品	33	31
63049210	棉制刺绣非针织或钩编装饰制品	26	24
63049290	棉制其他非针织或钩编的装饰制品	26	24
63049310	其他合纤制刺绣装饰制品等	33	31
63049390	合纤制其他非针织装饰制品等	33	31
63049910	丝制非针织或钩编的装饰制品	33	31
63049921	麻制刺绣非针织装饰制品	26	24
63049929	麻制其他非针织或钩编的装饰制品	26	24
63049990	其他材料制非针织或钩编装饰制品	33	31
63051000	黄麻或其也韧皮纤维制货物包装袋	18	16
63052000	棉制货物包装袋	26	24
63053200	化纤制柔性包装袋	30	29
63053300	聚乙烯聚丙烯制包装袋	30	29
63053900	其他包装袋	30	29
63059000	其他材料制货物包装袋	28	26
63061100	棉制油苫布、天篷及遮阳篷	26	24
63061200	合纤制油苫布、天篷及遮阳篷	30	29
63061910	麻制油苫布、天篷及遮阳篷	26	24
63061990	其他材料制油苫布、天篷及遮阳篷	30	29

续表

税　　号	货　　品　　名　　称	1998税则税率	1999税则税率
63062100	棉制帐篷	26	24
63062200	合纤制帐篷	30	29
63062900	其他材料制帐篷	30	29
63063100	合纤制风帆	30	29
63063900	其他材料制风帆	30	29
63064100	棉制充气褥垫	26	24
63064910	化纤制充气褥垫	30	29
63064990	其他材料制充气褥垫	30	29
63069100	棉制其他野营用品	26	24
63069910	麻制其他野营用品	26	24
63069920	化纤制其他野营用品	30	29
63069990	其他材料制其他野营用品	30	29
63071000	其他材料制擦地布，擦碗布等	30	29
63072000	其他材料制救生衣及安全带	25	22
63079000	其他材料制其他制成品	30	29
63080000	其他材料制零售包装成套物品	30	29
63090000	旧衣物	36	33
63101000	纺织材料制经分拣的碎织物等	22	20
63109000	纺织材料制其他碎织物等	22	20
94049010	羽绒或羽毛填充的寝具及类似品	30	28
94049020	兽毛填充的寝具及类似品	30	28
94049030	丝棉填充的寝具及类似品	30	28
94049040	化纤棉填充的寝具及类似品	30	28
94049090	其他材料制的寝具及类似品	30	28
95010000	供儿童乘骑的带轮玩具及玩偶车	21	10
95021000	玩偶	21	10
95029100	玩偶服装及其附件	21	10
95029900	其他玩偶零件、附件	21	10
95031000	玩具电动火车	21	10
95032000	缩小（按比例缩小）的全套模型组件	21	10
95033000	其他建筑套件及建筑玩具	21	10
95034100	填充的玩具动物	21	10
95034900	其他玩具动物	21	10
95035000	玩具乐器	21	10
95036000	智力玩具	21	10
95037000	组装成套的其他玩具	21	10
95038000	其他带动力装置的玩具及模型	21	10
95039000	其他未列名玩具	21	10

附件二

1999年税则暂定税率（原材料、零部件及部分设备）商品一览表

序号	税则号列	货　品　名　称	税则税率（%）	税则暂定税率（%）
1	15131100	椰子油	20	7
2	15131900	椰子油	20	7
3	18040000	可可脂	35	15
4	23099090	已配制的饲料	8	5
5	25281000	天然硼砂及其精矿	6	1
	25289000	天然硼砂及其精矿	6	1
6	26011100	未烧结铁矿砂及其精矿	0	1
	26011200	已烧结铁矿砂及其精矿	0	1
	26012000	焙烧的黄铁矿	0	1
7	27075000	芳烃混合物	8	3
8	27076000	混合甲酚	8	3
9	28251010	水合肼	9	3
10	28332500	硫酸铜	9	3
11	29012910	异戊烯	5	3
12	29025000	苯乙烯	9	6
13	29031500	1，2－二氯乙烷	10	3
14	29033090	二溴甲烷	10	3
15	29036110	邻二氯苯	9	3
16	29036910	对氯甲苯	9	3
17	29036920	3，4－二氯三氟甲苯	9	3
18	29042020	邻、对硝基甲苯	9	3
19	29049010	邻、对硝基氯化苯	9	3
20	29051210	正丙醇	8	3
21	29051400	叔丁醇	8	3
22	29053200	丙二醇	8	3
23	29053990	1－4，丁二醇	8	3
24	29309090	乙硫醇	9	3
25	29071212	邻甲酚	9	3
26	29071310	壬基酚	10	3
27	29094100	二甘醇	10	3
28	29094990	2－正丙氧基乙醇	10	3
29	29121900	乙二醛	10	3
30	29126000	多聚甲醛	9	3

续表

税号	税则号列	货品名称	税则税率（%）	税则暂定税率（%）
31	29141300	甲基异丁基甲酮	9	3
32	29155010	丙酸	6	3
33	29159000	辛酸	9	5
34	29211990	三乙胺、月桂胺、一乙胺、正丁胺	9	3
35	29212110	乙二胺	8	3
36	29212900	二乙烯三胺	9	3
37	29214300	邻甲苯胺	9	3
38	29221100	一乙醇胺	9	3
39	29221200	二乙醇胺	9	3
40	29221310	三乙醇胺	9	3
41	29221320	芳基聚氧乙烯磷酸酯	9	3
42	29241000	二甲基甲酰胺	9	3
43	29269090	己二腈	9	3
44	29333990	氰基吡啶、甲基吡啶、吡啶硫铜锌	9	4
45	32061110	金红石型钛白粉	14	5
46	32089000	光导纤维用涂料（主要成分为聚胺脂丙烯酸酯类化合物）	15	6
47	33013010	鸢尾凝脂（香膏类）	25	10
48	34021100	十二烷基苯磺酸钙	10	7
49	34029000	十二烷基苯磺酸钙甲醇溶液（十二烷基苯磺酸钙含量应高于70%）	30	7
50	35030010	明胶（感光胶片用）	18	5
51	37019920	超微粒干板	18	8
52	37024220	光致抗蚀干膜（印刷线路板制造用）	49元/M²	5元/M²
	37024429	光致抗蚀干膜（印刷线路板制造用）	43元/M²	5元/M²
53	38099300	制革工业用助剂	10	5
54	38180010	直径≥6英寸单晶硅片	6	3
55	38237000	工业用脂肪醇	16	9
56	39021000	电工级初级形状聚丙烯树脂（灰分含量不大于30ppm）	16	9
57	39119000	芳基酸与芳胺预缩聚物	16	6
58	39119000	改性三羟基乙酸类预缩聚物	16	6
59	39119000	聚苯并噻唑	16	10
60	39119000	聚苯硫醚	16	6
61	39119000	偏苯三酸酐和异氰酸预缩聚物	16	6
62	39121100	未塑化二、三醋酸纤维素	14	5
63	39121200	已塑化二、三醋酸纤维素	14	7
64	39206200	涤纶片基、薄膜	16	7
65	39207300	三醋酸纤维片基	16	10
66	39209910	聚四氟乙烯制非泡沫塑料的板、片、膜、箔及扁条	16	10

续表

税号	税则号列	货品名称	税则税率（%）	税则暂定税率（%）
67	40119100	断面宽度24英寸及以上的巨型轮胎	22	6
68	48052900	照相原纸	15	5
69	48113110	彩色相纸用双面涂塑纸	20	7
70	48113911	电解电容器纸	12	8
71	55041000	未梳的粘胶短纤维	9.6	6
	55070000	已梳的粘胶短纤维	10	6
72	70200010	导电玻璃	16	9
73	72091800	冷轧卷板，厚度<0.35mm	8	4
74	72101100	马口铁，厚度=0.5mm	10	7
	72101200	马口铁，厚度<0.5mm	10	7
	72121000	马口铁，厚度≤0.5mm	10	7
75	72269900	铁镍合金带材（生产集成电路框架用）	10	4
76	73043910	锅炉管（包括内螺纹），截面外径≥219mm	10	5
	73044110	锅炉管（包括内螺纹）	12	5
	73044910	锅炉管（包括内螺纹）	10	5
	73045910	锅炉管（包括内螺纹）截面外径≥133mm或截面外径<76mm	10	5
77	74040000	按重量计含铜量大于80%的铜废碎料	2	1
78	81089090	钛管，壁厚≤0.5mm	10	5
79	84079090	转速<3600r/min的发电机用汽油发动机、转速<4650r/min的工程机械用汽油发动机	20	10
80	84089092	转速<4650r/min工程机械用柴油发动机	18	10
81	84122990	载重4万吨及以上船舶用舱口盖液压装置	16	8
82	84143011	冰箱压缩机	22	12
	84143012	冰箱压缩机	25	12
	84143013	空调压缩机	25	12
	84143019	冰箱、空调压缩机	20	12
83	84149010	压缩机零件：集尘圈、排气坐圈、叶片弹簧、精密铸件、涡旋盘、涡旋盘轴芯、卸载衬套、浮动密封、密封接线柱	12	7
84	84248999	高能等离子喷涂设备	12	10
85	84281090	飞机集装箱装卸机	15	10
86	84335100	功率≥160马力的联合收割机	12	5
87	84335910	甘蔗收获机	14	6
	84335990	棉花收获机、自走式青储饲料收获机	14	6
88	84483200	精梳机钳板、顶梳装置、精梳机锡林部件、精梳机车头凸轮传动、行星齿轮部件，清梳联合机梳理装置，清梳联合机给棉装置，清梳联合机盖板清洁装置	6	3
89	84483310	络筒锭	6	3

续表

税号	税则号列	货　品　名　称	税则税率（%）	税则暂定税率（%）
90	84483920	电子清纱器	6	3
91	84483930	空气捻接器	6	3
92	84484910	接、投梭箱	6	3
93	84484920	引纬、送经装置	6	3
94	84484990	自动寻纬、补纬装置、打纬装置	6	3
95	84798990	海水淡化装置、飞机客舱环境控制系统	18	10
96	85023100	风力发电设备	10	6
97	85144000	焊缝中频退火装置	18	5
98	85175090	光通信数字同步设备	15	10
99	85229030	视频信号录制或重放设备的零件	35	10
100	85299099	移动通讯基地站零件	9	7
101	85371010	船用主机控制系统	7	5
102	85371010	纺机数控装置	7	3
103	85401100	监视器用显像管（荧光点间距在0.21mm及以下）	18	12
104	85461000	钢化玻璃绝缘子伞盘	14	6
105	87019000	飞机牵引车	15	10
106	87019000	功率大于150马力的拖拉机	15	5
107	87042240	混凝土泵车、搅拌车用底盘（装有驾驶室）	30	10
	87042300	混凝土泵车、搅拌车用底盘（装有驾驶室）	30	10
	87060090	混凝土泵车、搅拌车用底盘（不装有驾驶室）	60	10
108	87042300	起重25吨及以上汽车起重机用底盘（装有驾驶室）	30	10
109	87059090	跑道除冰车	25	10
110	87084050	扭距≥90kgm的变速箱、分动箱的零件	20	6
	87089950	扭距≥90kgm的变速箱、分动箱的零件	15	6
111	87085020	轴荷≥10t的中后驱动桥	35	8
	87089920	轴荷≥10t的中后驱动桥的零件	35	8
112	87085050	轴荷≥6t的前驱动桥	20	8
	87089950	轴荷≥6t的前驱动桥及零件、轴荷≥10t的中后驱动桥及零件	15	8
113	87086020	30座及以上客车用非驱动桥及零件	35	8
114	87086050	总重≥14t的货车用非驱动桥及零件	20	8
115	87088090	30座及以上的客车用悬挂减震器	40	8
116	87088090	总量≥14t的柴油型货车用减震器	40	8
117	87089320	30座及以上客车用离合器及零件	35	8
118	87089350	总量≥14t的柴油型货车用离合器及零件	20	8
119	87089420	30座及以上客车用转向器	35	8
	87089920	30座及以上客车用转向器的零件	35	8
120	87089450	总量≥14t柴油货车转向器零件	20	8
	87089950	总量≥14t柴油货车转向器的零件	15	8

续表

税号	税则号列	货品名称	税则税率（%）	税则暂定税率（%）
121	87089930	非公路用自卸车未列名零部件	6	3
122	87089950	总量≥14t 柴油型货车用其他零部件	15	8
123	89020010	载重≥2500 吨的拖网加工船	7	5
	89020010	载重≥300 吨的金枪鱼围网船	7	3
	89020010	载重≥300 吨的金枪鱼延绳钓船	7	3
	89020010	载重≥300 吨的鱿鱼钓船	7	3
124	89051000	挖泥船	5	1
125	90011000	光导纤维	15	10
126	90099090	复印机定影、显影组件	12	10
127	90104200	分步重复光刻机	22	1
128	90261000	船舶货油舱液位测量仪器及装置	12	6
129	90308990	电磁兼容测试仪	12	6
130	90318090	跑道摩擦系数测试仪	12	3
		非零售包装农药成药：		
131	38081090	非零售包装的杀虫剂	6	4
132	38082090	非零售包装的杀菌剂	6	4
133	38083019	非零售包装的除草剂	5	4
134	38083099	非零售包装抗萌剂植物生长调节剂	6	4
		零售包装农药成药：		
135	38081019	零售包装的杀虫剂	12	4
136	38082010	零售包装的杀菌剂	12	4
137	38083011	零售包装的除草剂	12	4
138	38083091	零售包装抗萌剂及植物生长调节剂	12	4
		农药原药：		
139	29214300	氟乐灵原药	9	3
140	29242990	叶蝉散原药	9	3
141	29269090	功夫原药	9	3
142	29269090	来福灵原药	9	3
143	29269090	氯氰菊酯、百树菊酯原药	9	3
144	29269090	灭扫利原药	9	3
145	29309090	拿扑净	9	3
146	29309090	杀草丹、巴丹原药	9	3
147	29310000	益收宝原药	9	3
148	29332900	扑海因原药	9	3
149	29333990	精稳杀得、乐思本原药	9	3
	29339000	精禾草克	9	3
150	29341000	尼索朗原药	9	3
151	29349090	农思它、硫丹原药	9	3
		农药中间体：		

续表

税号	税则号列	货 品 名 称	税则税率（%）	税则暂定税率（%）
152	28121010	氯化亚砜	9	2
153	29071910	邻仲丁基酚、邻异丙基酚	4	2
154	29072910	邻苯二酚	4	2
155	29124900	间苯氧基苯甲醛	9	2
156	29141200	甲基乙基酮	6	2
157	29162010	二溴菊酸、DV菊酸甲酯	4	2
158	29162090	二氯菊酰氯（DV菊酰氯）	9	2
159	29172010	四氢苯酐	4	2
160	29211910	二正丙胺	4	2
161	29211920	异丙胺	9	2
162	29214920	2，4、2，6—二甲基苯胺	7	2
163	29214940	2，6－二乙基苯胺	7	2
164	29329910	呋喃酚	4	2
165	29333210	六氢吡啶	4	2
166	29336910	三聚氰氯	9	2
		化肥：		
167	31031000	过磷酸钙	5	3
168	31039000	其他矿物磷肥及化学磷肥	5	3
169	31042000	氯化钾	5	3
170	31043000	硫酸钾	5	3
171	31052000	复合肥	5	3
172	31053000	磷酸氢二铵	5	3
173	31054000	磷酸二氢铵及磷酸二氢铵与磷酸氢二铵的混合物	5	3
174	31055100	含有硝酸盐及磷酸盐的矿物肥料或化学肥料	5	3
175	31055900	其他含氮、磷两种肥效的矿物肥料或化学肥料	5	3
176	31056000	含磷、钾两种肥效的矿物肥料或化学肥料	5	3
		飞机、机载设备、机舱设备及零部件：		
177	40113000	航空用新的充气橡胶轮胎	3	1
178	40129010	航空用实心或半实心橡胶轮胎	6	1
179	40139010	航空用橡胶内胎	3	1
180	84111110	涡轮风扇发动机	3	1
	84111190	涡轮风扇发动机	3	1
	84111210	涡轮风扇发动机	3	1
	84111290	涡轮风扇发动机	3	1
181	84119100	涡轮喷气或涡轮螺桨发动机零件	2	1
182	84119910	涡轮轴发动机用零件	7	1
183	84714140	飞机机载大气数据专用计算机	15	1
184	85252099	飞机机载无线通讯设备	9	1

续表

税号	税则号列	货　品　名　称	税则税率（%）	税则暂定税率（%）
185	85261090	机载雷达（包括气象雷达、地形雷达和空中交通管制应答系统）	9	1
186	85438990	飞行数据记录器、报告器	18	1
187	88024010	空载重量在25吨及以上，但重量不超过45吨的客运飞机	5	1
188	88024020	空载重量超过45吨的飞机	3	1
189	88031000	飞机用推进器、水平旋翼及零件	2	1
190	88032000	飞机用起落架及其零件	2	1
191	88033000	飞机用其他零件	2	1
192	90328900	飞机自动驾驶系统（包括自动驾驶、电子控制飞行、自动故障分析、警告系统、配平系统及推力监控设备及其相关仪表）	12	1
193	90330000	飞机自动驾驶系统（包括自动驾驶、电子控制飞行、自动故障分析、警告系统、配平系统及推力监控设备及其相关仪表）的零件	9	1
194	94011000	飞机用坐具	22	15
195	94032000	飞机机内厨房用家具	22	15
196	94039000	飞机用坐具、机内厨房用家具的零件	22	10

附件三

1999年出口税则暂定税率一览表

序号	税则号列	货　品　名　称	1999年税则税率（%）	1999年暂定税率（%）
1	03019210	鳗鱼苗	20	10
2	26070000	铅矿砂及其精矿	30	5
3	26080000	锌矿砂及其精矿	30	10
4	26090000	锡矿砂及其精矿	50	20
5	29022000	苯	40	0
6	72022000	硅铁	25	10
7	72022000	稀土镁硅铁	25	0
8	74070000	铜条、杆、型材及异型材	30	0
9	74080000	铜丝	30	0

续表

序号	税则号列	货品名称	1999年税则税率（%）	1999年暂定税率（%）
10	74090000	铜板、片及带，厚度超过0.15毫米	30	0
11	75089010	电镀用镍阳极	40	0
12	76010000	未锻轧铝	30	0
13	76020000	铝废碎料	30	0
14	76040000	铝条、杆、型材及异型材	20	0
15	76050000	铝丝	20	0
16	76060000	铝板、片及带，厚度超过0.2毫米	20	0
17	79010000	未锻轧锌	20	0
18	81100020	未锻轧锑	20	5

注：72022000的硅铁和稀土镁硅铁由国家经贸委、外经贸部共同组织出口招标事宜，海关凭中标通知书办理暂定税率手续。

财政部　国家税务总局
关于提高部分货物出口退税率的通知

财税字［1999］17号

1999年1月29日

各省、自治区、直辖市、计划单列市财政厅（局）、国家税务局：

为加大对外贸出口的扶持力度，增强外贸出口对经济增长的拉动作用，缓解国内重点行业和重点企业的生产经营困难，经国务院批准，决定提高部分货物的出口退税率。现将有关问题通知如下：

一、机械及设备、电器及电子产品、运输工具、仪器仪表4大类机电产品的出口退税率提高到17%；

农机的出口退税率提高到13%；

纺织原料及制品、钟表、鞋、陶瓷、钢材及其制品、水泥的出口退税率提高到13%；

有机化工原料、无机化工原料、涂料、染料、颜料、橡胶制品、玩具及运动用品、塑料制品、旅行用品及箱包的出口退税率提高到11%；

目前执行6%出口退税率的货物，包括以农产品为原料加工生产的工业品及其他货物的出口退税率提高到9%。

农产品的出口退税率提高到5%。

二、以上提高出口退税率货物适用的《中华人民共和国海关进出口税则》税号见附件，其执行中有关具体问题的解释及附件中未列举货物适用的税号，由国家税务总局另行下达。

三、本通知自1999年1月1日起执行（具体执行日期按“出口货物报关单（出口退税联）”上注明的海关离境日期为准）。凡与本通知有抵触的，一律按本通知执行。

附件：部分提高出口退税率货物适用的税号

附　件

部分提高出口退税率货物适用的税号

序号	货物名称	税号
1	机械及设备、电器及电子产品、运输工具、仪器仪表4大类机电产品	84章—90章（农机、89019090、89031000、89039100、89039900、89060090、8907、8908、9001、9003、9004、890200901除外）
2	钢材制品	73章
3	无机化工原料	29章
4	无机化工原料	28章（2843—2851、28271010、28342110除外）
5	涂料、染料及颜料	32章（3214、3215、3201、3202除外）
6	橡胶制品	40章（4001除外）
7	玩具及运动用品	95章
8	塑料制品	3918、3922—3925、3926（39262000除外）
9	旅行用品及箱包	4202

中华人民共和国海关总署令

第71号

1999年4月2日

现发布《中华人民共和国海关对企业实施分类管理办法》，自1999年6月1日起实施。海关总署1988年5月1日实施的《中华人民共和国海关对信得过企业管理办法》同时废止。

署长：钱冠林

附　件

海关总署　对外贸易经济合作部
国家经济贸易委员会关于印发
《中华人民共和国海关对企业
实施分类管理办法》的通知

署监〔1999〕240号

广东分署，各直属海关，各省、自治区、直辖市及计划单列市外经贸委（厅局），经贸委（计委、计经委）：

为促进企业守法自律，提高海关监管效率，海关总署和外经贸部、国家经贸委联合制定了《中华人民共和国海关对企业实施分类管理办法》（以下简称“办法”），现印发给你们，请以海关总署第71号令对外发布，并于1999年6月1日起实施。现就有关事项通知如下：

一、本办法所称主管海关为总署管理的直属海关。企业分类管理工作涉及面广，综合性强，各关务必加强组织领导，建立海关内部对企业的共管机制。要求各海关主管关长牵头负责，成立关一级的企业分类管理委员会，负责处理企业分类管理工作中出现的重大问题。日常实施工作由分管企业注册登记管理的部门统一归口负责。其职责范围包括：

（一）受理企业申请，并对企业报送的有关文件和资料进行审核；

（二）提出适用A类、D类管理的企业名单，经本关分类管理委员会审核后报总署；

（三）审定适用B类或C类管理的企业名单，组织本关区的实施工作；

（四）归口协调各职能部门的相关工作，汇总反馈的意见，维护本关区的企业数据库。

（五）与外经贸、经贸委、税务、工商、外汇等有关部门建立联系制度，互通情况，共享信息。

二、对从事加工贸易企业的分类评定工作由企管部门会同加工贸易主管部门共同进行。

三、本办法强调对企业实施动态的分类管理。因此要求各职能部门之间加强协作配合，确保各业务环节所做的有关企业的详细记录，例如，审单记录、查验记录、缴税情况记录、核销记录、稽查记录、调查和侦查记录等能及时反馈归口管理部门，对发现有走私违规行为的企业，随时进行管理类别的调整。

四、在执行本办法第十五条第三、四款关于“暂停企业报关资格”或“取消企业报关资格”时，应根据海关总署《关于对未年审报关单位及报关员实施行政处罚的法律依据问题的通知》（署法〔1996〕1021号文）和《中华人民共和国海关稽查条例》的有关规定办理。

五、为做好企业分类管理工作，总署将成立由各有关业务司参加的企业分类管理委员会。有关适用A类和D类管理的企业名单如何报送总署及如何在全国海关范围执行的问题，总署监管司和通关司将另行制定操作规程并下发。

本办法第六条所述企业年进出口额标准以海关统计为准。

六、《企业状况调查表》（见附件）是由总署原稽查司与社科院共同设计的，并配套开发了“企业分类评定系统”。该系统已在部分海关试用。因此，各关在审定适用A类管理的企业时可参考使用该系统，操作时可采取人机结合的方式。同时，总署将进一步完善该系统。

尚未领取该系统软件的海关请尽快向总署监管司申领。

七、为发挥海关对企业实施分类管理在引导企业守法经营，促进企业自警自律方面的作用，各关在评审工作中务必认真负责，严格执行办法规定的标准，实事求是开展评审工作。

八、自本办法实施之日起，各海关原自行制定的企业分类管理办法一律停止执行。

九、海关对企业的分类管理工作需要依靠有关部门的支持和协助。各关应加强与外经贸部门的联系配合，听取外经贸、经贸委、税务、外汇管理、工商和银行等有关主管部门的意见和建议，协同努力，共同做好有关工作。

以上请遵照执行。执行中如遇有问题，请及时上报。

附件一：中华人民共和国海关对企业实施分类管理办法

附件二：进出口企业状况调查表（略）

附件一

中华人民共和国海关对企业实施分类管理办法

第一条 为了便利企业货物的合法进出口，促进企业自律守法，有效实施海关管理，根据《中华人民共和国海关法》和其他有关法律、法规，制定本办法。

第二条 本办法所称“企业”系指与进出口活动直接有关的企业、单位，包括外商投资企业、外贸公司、有进出口权的商业物资企业、自营进出口生产企业和科研院所、加工贸易经营单位和接受委托加工企业、经营保税仓储业务的企业、使用或者经营减免税进口货物的企业、从事报关业务的企业、承接海关监管货物运输的企业、设有存放海关监管货物仓库的企业、免税外汇商品经营单位及海关总署规定的从事与进出口活动直接有关的其他企业。

第三条 海关根据企业的经营管理状况、报关情况、遵守海关法律法规情况等，设置A、B、C、D四个管理类别，对企业实施动态的分类管理。

第四条 企业适用的管理类别由企业所在地主管海关审定，其中适用A类、D类管理的企业名单报海关总署备案。海关总署将适用A类管理的企业名单抄送外经贸部。

第五条 B类和C类管理由主管海关统一布置在本关区范围内实施。A类和D类管理由海关总署统一布置在全国海关范围内实施。

第六条 符合下列条件的企业经向主管海关申请并经海关审核确定的，海关实施A类管理，其中年进出口总额3000万美元以上或出口总额达到2000万美元以上的外贸公司和自营出口额1000万美元以上（机电产品自营出口额达到500万美元以上）的生产企业可予以优先考虑。

（一）注册登记两年以上，并且(1)连续两年无走私违规行为记录，(2)连续两年无拖欠海关税款情事，(3)连续两年加工贸易合同按期核销，(4)进口海关必检商品签定免验协议后两年内无申报不实记录；

（二）向海关提供的单据、证件真实、齐全、有效；

（三）有正常的进出口业务；

（四）会计制度完善：财务账册健全，科目设置合理，业务记录真实可信；

（五）指定专人负责海关事务；

（六）连续两年报关单差错率在5%以下；

（七）凡设有存放海关监管货物仓库的企业，其仓库管理制度健全，仓库明细账目清楚，入库单、出库单（包括领料单）等实行专门管理，做到账货相符。

第七条 企业向海关申请实施A类管理时应当向主管海关提交书面申请报告。企业申请时有弄虚作假或所呈不实者，海关两年内不受理对其实施A类管理的申请。企业提交申请报告应随附下列文件一式两份：

（一）外经贸主管部门或其他主管部门批准经营的有效文件的副本或复印件；

（二）企业年审合格证明；

（三）企业对照本办法第六条所列条件进行自我评估的报告；

（四）经本企业法定代表人或其授权代表签字并加盖公章的《企业状况调查表》；

（五）企业注册所在地外经贸主管部门出具的书面意见。

第八条 海关应严格审核企业提交的有关文件

和档案资料，根据企业实际通关情况进行审定，符合条件的予以核准，并在30日内通知企业。

第九条 企业有下列情形之一者，海关实施C类管理：

（一）一年内出现两次违规行为，或偷逃应缴税款5万元人民币以上及不满50万元人民币的；

（二）拖欠海关税款100万元人民币以下的；

（三）账册管理混乱，账簿、资料不能真实有效地反映进出口业务情况的；

（四）遗失重要业务单证或拒绝提供有关账簿、资料，致使海关无法监管的；

（五）不按规定办理加工贸易合同核销手续的；

（六）一年内报关单差错率在10%以上的；

（七）出借企业名义，供他人办理进出口货物报关纳税等事宜的；

（八）在进出口经营活动中被外经贸主管部门给予通报批评、或警告等行政处罚的。

第十条 企业有下列情形之一者，海关实施D类管理：

（一）两年内走私偷逃应缴税款50万元人民币以上的（多次走私应累计）；

（二）伪造、涂改进出口许可证或批件的；

（三）走私国家禁止进出口物品的；

（四）拖欠海关税款100万元人民币以上的；

（五）利用假手册、假报关单、假批件骗取加工贸易税收优惠的；

（六）在承运监管货物的运输工具上私设夹层、暗格的；

（七）被外经贸主管部门暂停或撤销对外贸易经营许可的；

（八）已构成走私罪并经司法机关依法追究刑事责任的。

第十一条 凡经审核不符合A类管理条件且未发生本办法第九条和第十条所列情形者，海关实施B类管理。

第十二条 适用A类管理的企业名单由海关总署下发各海关执行，在实行常规管理制度的基础上，提供以下便利：

（一）在海关业务现场设专门窗口，优先办理货物申报、查验和放行手续；并应企业要求，优先实行“门对门”验货。

（二）对从事加工贸易的企业，经海关总署批准，可实行海关派员驻厂监管或计算机联网管理。除国家另有规定者外，不实行银行保证金台账制度。

（三）对按规定允许担保的货物，海关凭企业提交的保函验放，免收保证金。

（四）对企业进口海关必检商品目录中的商品可免予取样化验。

（五）为企业优先提供EDI联网报关的便利。

（六）自营进出口生产企业和科研院所可向外经贸部申报成立进出口公司，海关优先为其办理报关注册登记手续。

第十三条 海关对适用B类管理企业实行常规管理制度。

第十四条 海关对适用C类管理的企业实行包括以下措施在内的重点监管：

（一）对按规定允许担保的货物必须提交保证金；

（二）办理加工贸易合同登记备案必须按规定的比例交纳保证金；

（三）对其经营活动列入稽查重点；

（四）对其进出口货物实行重点查验；

（五）不予办理异地报关备案；

（六）将有关情况通报国家经贸委和外经贸部。

第十五条 海关对适用D类管理的企业采取以下措施：

（一）不予办理新的加工贸易合同备案；

（二）进出口货物逐票开箱查验；

（三）按有关规定暂停企业报关资格，或暂停企业载运海关监管货物业务资格，暂停企业保税存储业务资格；

（四）情节严重的按有关规定取消企业报关资格，或取消企业载运海关监管货物的业务资格，取消企业保税存储的业务资格；

（五）将有关情况通报国家经贸委和外经贸部。由外经贸部或其授权的省级外经贸主管部门根据《对违规、走私企业给予警告、暂停或撤销对外贸易、国际货运代理经营许可行政处罚的暂行规定》对企业进行行政处罚。

第十六条 海关对企业实施动态的分类管理。一经发现企业发生本办法第九条和第十条所列情事的，海关立即对其管理类别进行相应调整，实施C类或D类管理。其中对调整前适用A类管理的企业，主管海关应通知企业不再对其实施A类管理，并将调整结果7日内报海关总署。由海关总署通报全国海关，同时抄送外经贸部。

第十七条 适用D类管理的企业在两年内没有再发生本办法第十条所列情事的，海关对其实施C类管理；适用C类管理的企业在一年内没有发生本办法第九条和第十条所列情事的，海关对其实施B类管理。

第十八条 本办法由海关总署负责解释。

第十九条 本规定自1999年6月1日起实施。1988年5月1日起实施的《中华人民共和国海关对信得过企业管理办法》同时废止。

海关总署关于做好出口退税工作支持扩大外贸出口的通知

署通〔1999〕339号

1999年5月12日

广东分署，各局、处级海关：

出口退税政策是国家为鼓励外贸企业扩大出口而采取的一项重要措施。为做好海关有关工作，加快出口退税，支持企业扩大出口，保证国家出口退税政策的贯彻落实，特通知如下：

一、加快实现出口货物舱单电子数据传输

（一）已实现舱单电子数据传输的口岸，海关要积极、主动加强与港务、航空、铁路、船代、货代等有关部门的联系与协调，建立经常性的、定期的联系和联络制度，共同制定数据传输的具体保障措施，定期检查落实舱单数据传输情况，确保数据传输的及时和准确。

（二）尚未实现舱单电子数据传输的口岸，海关要加快移植使用5.0版H883/EDI系统，以解决舱单报文入库和与报关单核销问题。总署正在加紧开发统一的联网传送软件，并解决利用公网的通信及身份认证问题，以彻底完成舱单电子数据联网传输。目前作为过渡措施，各海关必须采用人工录入舱单数据并由H883/EDI系统进行核销处理。

二、尽快实现实时向国税部门提供报关单电子数据

总署决定，2000年1月1日起在全国海关范围内推广使用出口报关单联网核查系统，以网络方式实现实时向国税部门提供出口报关单证明联电子数据，提高报关单核查的时效性和准确率。各海关通关管理部门要密切配合，提前做好技术和业务各项准备，保证该系统按时在全国海关推广使用。

三、确保企业及时领取出口退税证明联

各海关要严格按照总署要求，在收到清洁舱单后5个工作日内必须完成核销和保证签发出口报关单证明联的工作，确保出口企业及时领取证明联。各关要将此项工作时限要求作为服务承诺对外公布，接受社会监督。

四、提高报关单电子数据质量

要进一步规范企业报关行为，严格按照《报关单填制规范》要求报关企业填报进出口货物报关单。加强审核，明确责任，确保数据准确性，防止因电子数据质量问题延误企业办理出口退税手续。现场海关要保证出口报关单证明联与电子数据的一致性，直属海关职能部门要保证报关单电子数据的完整性，技术部门要保证网络畅通，总署通关管理部门要保证各关上报数据的及时入库上网。

五、加强技术保障

各海关要在网络技术和通关管理部门以及各海关现场，指定专人和专用电话，与总署通关业务查控室对口建立热线电话值班及联系制度，及时解决有问题的电子数据和报关单的核销问题。要通过信息上网等技术和通讯手段，使企业能及时获得出口货物结关信息。

六、做好转关运输货物出口报关单证明联的签发工作

各口岸海关要严格执行转关运输计算机管理系

统的操作规范，及时核销转关货物数据，使启运地海关及时获得货物实际出口信息，为企业及时签发出口报关单证明联。总署将进一步研究完善出口货物转关运输的管理制度，指导各关尽快实现转关运输计算机网络管理系统并与H883/EDI系统的联接，以加快转关货物结关出境回执反馈速度。

七、进一步推进国家口岸专网建设工作

总署信息管理部门要进一步加强与信息产业部的合作，加紧组织实施国家口岸专网工程，力争在今年上半年基本完成全国600多个基层海关的入网工作，从技术上保证海关通关数据的顺利上网交换，为相关部门和进出口企业提供准确、快捷的服务。

国家税务总局关于提高部分出口货物退税率的通知

国税明电〔1999〕11号

1999年7月20日

各省、自治区、直辖市和计划单列市国家税务局：

为增强我国产品在国际市场上的竞争力，促进国民经济发展，经国务院批准，决定提高部分出口货物退税率。现将有关问题通知如下：

一、机械设备、电器及电子产品、运输工具、仪器仪表等四大类机电产品出口退税率维持17%不变，服装的出口退税率提高到17%；

服装以外的纺织原料及制品、四大类机电产品以外的其他机电产品及法定征税率为17%且现行退税率为13%或11%的货物的出口退税率提高到15%；

法定征税率为17%且现行退税率为9%的其他货物和农产品以外的法定征税率为13%且现行退税率未达到13%的货物的出口退税率提高到13%；

农产品的出口退税率维持5%不变。

二、上述调整出口退税率货物所适用的商品代码，我局将放在总局广域网上，请各地税务机关直接在总局广域网上领取。

三、本通知自1999年7月1日起执行。具体执行日期以“出口货物报关单（出口退税联）”上海关注明的出口日期为准。

中华人民共和国海关总署令

第77号

1999年8月5日

现发布《中华人民共和国海关对外国政府、国际组织无偿赠送及我国履行国际条约规定进口物资减免税的审批和管理办法》，自1999年9月15日起实施。

海关总署关于印发《中华人民共和国海关对外国政府、国际组织无偿赠送及我国履行国际条约规定进口物资减免税的审批和管理办法》的通知

署税〔1999〕565号
1999年8月5日

广东分署，各直属海关，院校：

为进一步贯彻《国务院关于改革和调整进口税收政策的通知》（国发〔1995〕34号），严格执行“依法行政、为国把关”的海关工作指导方针，切实做到规范审批，方便通关，我署在征求有关部委和部分海关意见的基础上制定了《中华人民共和国海关关于对外国政府、国际组织无偿赠送及我国履行国际条约规定进口物资减免税的审批和管理办法》，现印发给你们，请以中华人民共和国海关总署令第77号对外公布，自1999年9月15日起实施。现将执行中的有关问题通知如下：

1. 外国政府、国际组织无偿赠送及我国履行国际条约规定进口物资的减免税，包括减免关税、进口环节增值税和消费税。上述免税物资的范围不受国家停止减免税的20种商品和汽车的限制。

2. 各海关在审批和管理工作中要认真执行三级审批制度，不得擅自扩大减免税范围。凡不属于外国政府、国际组织无偿赠送或所签协定、协议中没有减免税条款的均不能按本办法办理；对界限不清的，须报总署审批。所在地直属海关与进口地海关要运用《减免税管理系统》加强联系，密切配合，同时做好有关政策的宣传工作。

3. 我国政府主管部委（包括部委代管局）和国务院直属机构，需指定一个司局级单位具体负责此项工作，并由该单位向有关直属海关出具《外国政府、国际组织无偿赠送及我国履行国际条约进口物资证明》（以下简称《证明》，《证明》由上述主管部委和国务院直属机构按照本文所附的格式自行印制和管理，并将加盖在《证明》上的印章印模样本送海关总署备案，由海关总署发文通知各直属海关。

4. 本办法实施后，此前海关总署下发的有关管理规定（详见附件二）即行废止。各海关要及时反映执行的情况，执行中有何问题，请及时与总署关税征管司联系。

特此通知。

附件：如文

附件一

中华人民共和国海关对外国政府、国际组织无偿赠送及我国履行国际条约规定进口物资减免税的审批和管理办法

第一条 根据《中华人民共和国海关法》和《中华人民共和国进出口关税条例》的有关规定，为

加强海关对外国政府、国际组织无偿赠送及我国履行国际条约规定进口物资减免税的审批和管理工作，特制订本办法。

第二条 本办法下列用语的含义是：

外国政府是指外国国家的中央政府；

国际组织是指联合国各专门机构以及长期与我国有合作关系的其他国际组织（见附件1)；

国际条约是指依据《中华人民共和国缔结条约程序法》(见附件2）以“中华人民共和国”、“中华人民共和国政府”以及“中华人民共和国政府部门”名义同外国缔结协定或协议以及参加的国际条约。

第三条 外国政府、国际组织无偿赠送及我国履行国际条约规定进口物资的减免税范围包括：

(一）根据中国与外国政府、国际组织间的协定或协议，由外国政府、国际组织直接无偿赠送的物资或由其提供无偿赠款，由我国受赠单位按照协定或协议规定用途自行采购进口的物资；

(二）外国地方政府或民间组织受外国政府委托无偿赠送进口的物资；

(三）国际组织成员受国际组织委托无偿赠送进口的物资；

(四）我国履行国际条约规定减免税进口的物资。

第四条 外国政府、国际组织无偿赠送及我国履行国际条约规定进口物资减免税的审批单位：

(一）由受赠单位或项目执行单位向其所在地直属海关申请办理，经所在地直属海关审批。

(二）对于受赠单位或项目执行单位是多个且跨省、市、自治区的，可由我国政府主管部委统一向海关总署申请办理。经海关总署审批后，通知有关直属海关和进口地海关执行。

第五条 外国政府、国际组织无偿赠送及我国履行国际条约规定进口物资减免税的办理程序如下：

(一）受赠单位或项目执行单位应于首批物资进口前向所在地直属海关提交外国政府、国际组织的赠送函或含有减免税条款的协定、协议、国际条约的复印件备案。

(二）外国政府、国际组织临时无偿赠送进口的物资。如不能及时提交外国政府、国际组织的赠送函，也可提交外国驻我国大使馆、国际组织驻中国代表处的证明函。

(三）外国地方政府或民间组织受外国政府委托无偿赠送进口的物资，受赠单位或项目执行单位应向所在地直属海关提交外国政府的委托书，或外国驻我国大使馆的证明函。

(四）国际组织成员受国际组织委托无偿赠送进口的物资，受赠单位或项目执行单位应向所在地直属海关提交国际组织的委托书，或国际组织驻中国代表处的证明函。

(五）受赠单位或项目执行单位应于上述无偿赠送物资进口前，向所在地直属海关提出申请，除提交上述协定、协议和证明函外，应同时提交我国政府主管部委出具的《外国政府、国际组织无偿赠送及我国履行国际条约进口物资证明》(见附件3）和进口物资清单，经所在地直属海关审核无误后出具《进口货物征免税证明》，进口地海关凭以减免税验放。

第六条 海关对上述减名税审批工作，一般应在接到申请单位的申请之日起10个工作日内办结。如申请单位提交的有关材料不完整或不准确的，海关应在接到申请之日起5个工作日内通知申请单位补办。

第七条 上述减免税进口物资属海关监管货物，未经批准不得擅自转让、出售或移作他用。对违反本规定的，海关将依照《中华人民共和国海关法》及国家有关法律、法规的规定予以处罚。

第八条 本办法由海关总署负责解释。

第九条 本办法自1999年9月15日起实施。

附　一

国际组织（部分）

一、联合国有关组织

1. 联合国开发计划署 (United Nations Development Programme-UNDP)

2. 联合国环境规划署

(United Nations Environment Programme - UNEP)

3. 联合国贸易和发展会议

(United Nations Conference on Trade and Development - UNCTAD)

4. 联合国人口基金

(United Nations Population Fund - UNFPA)

5. 联合国儿童基金会

(United Nations Children's Fund - UNICEF)

6. 联合国难民事务高级专员公署

(Office of the United Nations High Commissioner for Refugees - UNHCR)

7. 联合国欧洲经济委员会

(United Nation's Economic Commission for Europe - UN/ECE)

8. 世界粮食计划署

(World Food Programme - WFP)

9. 亚洲及太平洋经济社会委员会

(Economic and Social Commission for Asia and the Pacific - ESCAP)

10. 和平利用外层空间委员会

(The Committee on the Peaceful Uses of Outer Space - COPUOS)

二、同联合国建立关系的政府间机构

1. 国际劳工组织

(International Labour Organization - ILO)

2. 联合国粮食及农业组织

(Food and Agriculture Organization of the United Nations - FAO)

3. 联合国教育、科学及文化组织

(United Nations Educational, Scientific and Cultural Organization - UNESCO)

4. 世界卫生组织

(World Health Organization - WHO)

5. 国际货币基金组织

(International Monetary Fund - IMF)

6. 国际开发协会

(International Development Association - IDA)

7. 国际复兴开发银行（世界银行）

(International Bank for Reconstruction and Development - IBRD) (World Bank)

8. 国际金融公司

(International Finance Corporation - IFC)

9. 国际民用航空组织

(International Civil Aviation Organization - ICAO)

10. 万国邮政联盟

(Universal Postal Union - UPU)

11. 国际电信联盟

(International Telecommunication Union - ITU)

12. 世界气象组织

(World Meteorological Organization - WMO)

13. 国际海事组织

(International Maritime Organisation - IMO)

14. 世界知识产权组织

(World Intellectual Property Organization - WIPO)

15. 国际农业发展基金会

(International Fund for Agricultural Development - IFAD)

16. 联合国工业发展组织

(United Nations Industrial Development Organization - UNIDO)

17. 国际原子能机构

(International Atomic Energy Agency - IAEA)

18. 世界贸易组织

(World Trade Organization - WTO)

三、其他有关国际组织和金融机构

1. 红十字会与红新月会国际联合会（简称国际联合会）

(The International Federation of Red Cross And Red Crescent Societies - IFRCS)

2. 红十字国际委员会

(The International Committee of The Red Cross - ICRC)

3. 欧洲联盟

(European Union - EU)

4. 亚太经济合作组织

(Asia Pacific Economic Cooperation - APEC)

5. 亚洲开发银行

(Asia Development Bank - ADB)

6. 日本协力团

(Japan International Cooperation Agency - JICA)

7. 韩国协力团

(Korea International Cooperation Agency-KOICA)

8. 国际计生联组织

(International Planned Parenthood Federation - IPPF)

9. 国际移动卫星组织

(International Mobile Satelite Organization - INMARSAT)

10. 阿拉伯国家联盟

(League of Arab States - LAS)

附 二

中华人民共和国缔结条约程序法

(1990年12月28日第七届全国人民代表大会
常务委员会第十七次会议通过　1990年12月28日
中华人民共和国主席令第三十七号公布
自公布之日起施行)

第一条　根据中华人民共和国宪法，制定本法。

第二条　本法适用于中华人民共和国同外国缔结的双边和多边条约、协定和其他具有条约、协定性质的文件。

第三条　中华人民共和国国务院，即中央人民政府，同外国缔结条约和协定。

中华人民共和国全国人民代表大会常务委员会决定同外国缔结的条约和重要协定的批准和废除。

中华人民共和国主席根据全国人民代表大会常务委员会的决定，批准和废除同外国缔结的条约和重要协定。

中华人民共和国外交部在国务院领导下管理同外国缔结条约和协定的具体事务。

第四条　中华人民共和国以下列名义同外国缔结条约和协定：

(一) 中华人民共和国；

(二) 中华人民共和国政府；

(三) 中华人民共和国政府部门。

第五条　谈判和签署条约、协定的决定程序如下：

(一) 以中华人民共和国名义谈判和签署条约、协定，由外交部或者国务院有关部门会同外交部提出建议并拟订条约、协定的中方草案，报请国务院审核决定；

(二) 以中华人民共和国政府名义谈判和签署条约、协定，由外交部提出建议并拟订条约、协定的中方草案，或者由国务院有关部门提出建议并拟订条约、协定的中方草案，同外交部会商后，报请国务院审核决定。属于具体业务事项的协定，经国务院同意，协定的中方草案由国务院有关部门审核决定，必要时同外交部会商；

(三) 以中华人民共和国政府部门名义谈判和签署属于本部门职权范围内事项的协定，由本部门决定或者本部门同外交部会商后决定；涉及重大问题或者涉及国务院其他有关部门职权范围的，由本部门或者本部门同国务院其他有关部门会商后，报请国务院决定。协定的中方草案由本部门审核决定，必要时同外交部会商。

经国务院审核决定的条约、协定的中方草案，经谈判需要作重要改动的，重新报请国务院审核决定。

第六条　谈判和签署条约、协定的代表按照下列程序委派：

(一) 以中华人民共和国名义或者中华人民共和国政府名义缔结条约、协定，由外交部或者国务院有关部门报请国务院委派代表。代表的全权证书由国务院总理签署，也可以由外交部长签署；

(二) 以中华人民共和国政府部门名义缔结协定，由部门首长委派代表。代表的授权证书由部门首长签署。部门首长签署以本部门名义缔结的协定，各方约定出具全权证书的，全权证书由国务院总理签署，也可以由外交部长签署。

下列人员谈判、签署条约、协定，无须出具全权证书：

（一）国务院总理、外交部长；

（二）谈判、签署与驻在国缔结条约、协定的中华人民共和国驻该国使馆馆长，但是各方另有约定的除外；

（三）谈判、签署以本部门名义缔结协定的中华人民共和国政府部门首长，但是各方另有约定的除外；

（四）中华人民共和国派往国际会议或者派驻国际组织，并在该会议或者该组织内参加条约、协定谈判的代表，但是该会议另有约定或者该组织章程另有规定的除外。

第七条 条约和重要协定的批准由全国人民代表大会常务委员会决定。

前款规定的条约和重要协定是指：

（一）友好合作条约、和平条约等政治性条约；

（二）有关领土和划定边界的条约、协定；

（三）有关司法协助、引渡的条约、协定；

（四）同中华人民共和国法律有不同规定的条约、协定；

（五）缔约各方议定须经批准的条约、协定；

（六）其他须经批准的条约、协定。

条约和重要协定签署后，由外交部或者国务院有关部门会同外交部，报请国务院审核；由国务院提请全国人民代表大会常务委员会决定批准；中华人民共和国主席根据全国人民代表大会常务委员会的决定予以批准。

双边条约和重要协定经批准后，由外交部办理与缔约另一方互换批准书的手续；多边条约和重要协定经批准后，由外交部办理向条约、协定的保存国或者国际组织交存批准书的手续。批准书由中华人民共和国主席签署，外交部长副署。

第八条 本法第七条第二款所列范围以外的国务院规定须经核准或者缔约各方议定须经核准的协定和其他具有条约性质的文件签署后，由外交部或者国务院有关部门会同外交部，报请国务院核准。

协定和其他具有条约性质的文件经核准后，属于双边的，由外交部办理与缔约另一方互换核准书或者以外交照会方式相互通知业已核准的手续；属于多边的，由外交部办理向有关保存国或者国际组织交存核准书的手续。核准书由国务院总理签署，也可以由外交部长签署。

第九条 无须全国人民代表大会常务委员会决定批准或者国务院核准的协定签署后，除以中华人民共和国政府部门名义缔结的协定由本部门送外交部登记外，其他协定由国务院有关部门报国务院备案。

第十条 缔约双方为使同一条约、协定生效需要履行的国内法律程序不同的，该条约、协定于缔约双方完成各自法律程序并以外交照会方式相互通知后生效。

前款所列条约、协定签署后，应当区别情况依照本法第七条、第八条 第九条的规定办理批准、核准、备案或者登记手续。通知照会的手续由外交部办理。

第十一条 加入多边条约和协定，分别由全国人民代表大会常务委员会或者国务院决定。

加入多边条约和协定的程序如下：

（一）加入属于本法第七条第二款所列范围的多边条约和重要协定，由外交部或者国务院有关部门会同外交部审查后，提出建议，报请国务院审核；由国务院提请全国人民代表大会常务委员会作出加入的决定。加入书由外交部长签署，具体手续由外交部办理；

（二）加入不属于本法第七条第二款所列范围的多边条约、协定，由外交部或者国务院有关部门会同外交部审查后，提出建议，报请国务院作出加入的决定。加入书由外交部长签署，具体手续由外交部办理。

第十二条 接受多边条约和协定，由国务院决定。

经中国代表签署的或者无须签署的载有接受条款的多边条约、协定，由外交部或者国务院有关部门会同外交部审查后，提出建议，报请国务院作出接受的决定。接受书由外交部长签署，具体手续由外交部办理。

第十三条 中华人民共和国同外国缔结的双边条约、协定、以中文和缔约另一方的官方文字写成，两种文本同等作准，必要时，可以附加使用缔约双方同意的一种第三国文字，作为同等作准的第三种正式文本或者作为起参考作用的非正式文本；经缔约双方同意，也可以规定对条约、协定的解释发生分歧时，以该第三种文本为准。

某些属于具体业务事项的协定，以及同国际组织缔结的条约、协定，经缔约双方同意或者依照有关国际组织章程的规定，也可以只使用国际上较通用的一种文字。

第十四条 以中华人民共和国或者中华人民共和国政府名义缔结的双边条约、协定的签字正本，以及经条约、协定的保存国或者国际组织核证无误的多边条约、协定的副本，由外交部保存；以中华人民共和国政府部门名义缔结的双边协定的签字正本，由本部门保存。

第十五条 经全国人民代表大会常务委员会决定批准或者加入的条约和重要协定，由全国人民代表大会常务委员会公报公布。其他条约、协定的公布办法由国务院规定。

第十六条 中华人民共和国缔结的条约和协定由外交部编入《中华人民共和国条约集》。

第十七条 中华人民共和国缔结的条约和协定由外交部按照联合国宪章的有关规定向联合国秘书处登记。

中华人民共和国缔结的条约和协定需要向其他国际组织登记的，由外交部或者国务院有关部门按照各该国际组织章程的规定办理。

第十八条 中华人民共和国同国际组织缔结条约和协定的程序，依照本法及有关国际组织章程的规定办理。

第十九条 中华人民共和国缔结的条约和协定的修改、废除或者退出的程序，比照各该条约、协定的缔结的程序办理。

第二十条 国务院可以根据本法制定实施条例。

第二十一条 本法自公布之日起施行。

附　三

外国政府　国际组织无偿赠送及我国履行国际条约进口物资证明

编号（　　）字　　号

所在地直属海关		到货口岸	
赠送国家或国际组织			
协定或国际条约名称			
受赠或项目执行单位			
进口物资提单号			
进口物资品名			
物资数量		物资金额	

主管单位审批盖章

经办人：　　　　　　　　电话：　　　　　　　　年　　月　　日

备注：

1. 本证明一次性使用，自审批之日起半年内有效，允许跨年度使用。如物资品名栏不能填写详尽的，应附盖有公章的物品清单。
2. 物资进口前，受赠单位或项目执行单位应持《证明》正本向所在地直属海关申请办理免税手续，证明内容不得更改，复印件无效。
3. 证明一式两联，第一联由所在地直属海关留存，第二联由主管单位留存。

附件二

废止文件目录

1.《关于接受援助项目进口设备的征免税规定》(〔80〕署税字第207号)

2.《关于我国与联合国系统多边经济技术合作活动进口的物资设备办理海关手续的通知》(〔81〕署货字第716号)

3.《关于免税放行国际红十字会组织提供援助物资的通知》(〔81〕署税字第32号)

4.《关于接受日本国际协力事业团援助项目进口设备、器材准予免税的暂行办法的通知》(〔82〕署税字第119号)

5.《关于联合国粮农机构向我国援助的粮食、设备等办理进口手续的通知》(〔82〕署货联字第718号)

6.《关于卫生部系统接受国外援助医疗、卫生物资设备等办理进口手续的通知》(〔84〕署货联字第103号)

7.《关于联合国系统多边经济技术援助项目等改由中国国际经济技术交流中心负责管理的通知》(〔85〕署货字第406号)

财政部　国家税务总局关于贯彻落实《中共中央　国务院关于加强技术创新，发展高科技，实现产业化的决定》有关税收问题的通知

财税字〔1999〕273号

1999年11月2日

海关总署，各省、自治区、直辖市、计划单列市财政厅(局)、国家税务局、地方税务局，新疆生产建设兵团：

为了贯彻落实《中共中央国务院关于加强技术创新，发展高科技，实现产业化的决定》(中发〔1999〕14号)的精神，鼓励技术创新和高新技术企业的发展，现对有关税收问题通知如下：

一、关于增值税

(一)一般纳税人销售其自行开发生产的计算机软件产品，可按法定17%的税率征收后，对实际税负超过6%的部分实行即征即退。

(二)属生产企业的小规模纳税人，生产销售计算机软件按6%的征收率计算缴纳增值税；属商业企业的小规模纳税人，销售计算机软件按4%的征收率计算缴纳增值税，并可由税务机关分别按不同的征收率代开增值税发票。

(三)对随同计算机网络、计算机硬件、机器设备等一并销售的软件产品，应当分别核销售额。如果未分别核算或核算不清，按照计算机网络或计算机硬件以及机器设备等的适用税率征收增值税，不予退税。

(四)计算机软件产品是指记载有计算机程序及其有关文档的存储介质(包括软盘、硬盘、光盘等)。对经过国家版权局注册登记，在销售时一并转让著作权、所有权的计算机软件征收营业税，不征收增值税。

二、关于营业税

（一）对单位和个人（包括外商投资企业、外商投资设立的研究开发中心、外国企业和外籍个人）从事技术转让、技术开发业务和与之相关的技术咨询、技术服务业务取得的收入，免征营业税。

技术转让是指转让者将其拥有的专利和非专利技术的所有权或使用权有偿转让他人的行为。

技术开发是指开发者接受他人委托，就新技术、新产品、新工艺或者新材料及其系统进行研究开发的行为。

技术咨询是指就特定技术项目提供可行性论证、技术预测、专题技术调查、分析评价报告等。

与技术转让、技术开发相关的技术咨询、技术服务业务是指转让方（或受托方）根据技术转让或开发合同的规定，为帮助受让方（或委托方）掌握所转让（或委托开发）的技术，而提供的技术咨询、技术服务业务。且这部分技术咨询、服务的价款与技术转让（或开发）的价款是开在同一张发票上的。

（二）免征营业税的技术转让、开发的营业额为：

1. 以图纸、资料等为载体提供已有技术或开发成果的，其免税营业额为向对方收取的全部价款和价外费用。

2. 以样品、样机、设备等货物为载体提供已有技术或开发成果的，其免税营业额不包括货物的价值。对样品、样机、设备等货物，应当按有关规定征收增值税。转让方（或受托方）应分别反映货物的价值与技术转让、开发的价值，如果货物部分价格明显偏低，应按《中华人民共和国增值税暂行条例实施细则》第16条的规定，由主管税务机关核定计税价格。

3. 提供生物技术时附带提供的微生物菌种母本和动、植物新品种，应包括在免征营业税的营业额内。但批量销售的微生物菌种，应当征收增值税。

（三）免税的审批程序

1. 纳税人从事技术转让、开发业务申请免征营业税时，须持技术转让、开发的书面合同，到纳税人所在地省级科技主管部门进行认定，再持有关的书面合同和科技主管部门审核意见证明报当地省级主管税务机关审核。

外国企业和外籍个人从境外向中国境内转让技术需要免征营业税的，需提供技术转让或技术开发书面合同、纳税人或其授权人书面申请以及技术受让方所在地的省级科技主管部门审核意见证明，经省级税务主管机关审核后，层报国家税务总局批准。

2. 在科技和税务部门审核批准以前，纳税人应当先按有关规定缴纳营业税，待科技、税务部门审核后，再从以后应纳的营业税款中抵交，如以后一年内未发生应纳营业税的行为，或其应纳税款不足以抵顶免税额的，纳税人可向负责征收和税务机关申请办理退税。

三、关于所得税

（一）对社会力量，包括企业单位（不含外商投资企业和外国企业）、事业单位、社会团体、个人和个体工商户（下同），资助非关联的科研机构和高等学校研究开发新产品、新技术、新工艺所发生的研究开发经费，经主管税务机关审核确定，其资助支出可以全额在当年度应纳税所得额中扣除。当年度应纳税所得额不足抵扣的，不得结转抵扣。

非关联的科研机构和高等学校是指，不是资助企业所属或投资的，并且其科研成果不是惟一提供给资助企业的科研机构和高等学校。

企业向所属的科研机构和高等学校提供的研究开发经费资助支出，不实行抵扣应纳税所得额办法。

企业等社会力量向科研机构和高等学校资助研究开发经费，申请抵扣应纳税所得额时，须提供科研机构和高等学校开具的研究开发项目计划、资金收款证明及其他税务机关要求提供的相关资料，不能提供相关资料的，税务机关可不予受理。

（二）软件开发企业实际发放的工资总额，在计算应纳税所得额时准予扣除。

四、关于外商投资企业和外国企业所得税

外商投资企业和外国企业资助非关联科研机构和高等学校研究开发经费，参照《中华人民共和国外商投资企业和外国企业所得税法》中有关捐赠的税务处理办法，可以在资助企业计算企业应纳税所得税额时全额扣除。

五、关于进出口税收

（一）对企业（包括外商投资企业、外国企业）为生产《国家高新技术产品目录》的产品而进口所需的自用设备及按照合同随设备进口的技术及配套件、备件，除按照国发〔1997〕37号文件规定《国内投资项目不予免税的进口商品目录》所列商品外，免征关税和进口环节增值税。

（二）对企业（包括外商投资企业、外国企业）引进属于《国家高新技术产品目录》所列的先进技术，按合同规定向境外支付的软件费，免征关税和进口环节增值税。

软件费是指进口货物的纳税义务人为在境内制造、使用、出版、发行或者播映该项货物的技术和内容，向境外卖方支付的专利费、商标费以及专有技术、计算机软件和资料等费用。

（三）对列入科技部、外经贸部《中国高新技术商品出口目录》的产品，凡出口退税率未达到征税率的，经国家税务总局核准，产品出口后，可按征税率及现行出口退税管理规定办理退税。

六、科研机构转制问题

（一）中央直属科研机构以及省、地（市）所属的科研机构转制后，自1999年至2003年5年内，免征企业所得税和科研开发自用土地的城镇土地使用税。

本条所指科研机构不包括：已经转制和已并入企业的科研机构，以及所有从事社会科学研究的科研机构。

（二）享受上述税收优惠政策的科研机构，需持转制变更后的企业工商登记材料报当地主管税务机关，并按规定办理有关减免税手续。

七、本通知自1999年10月1日起开始执行。

中华人民共和国海关总署令

第73号

现发布《中华人民共和国海关审定加工贸易进口货物完税价格办法》，自1999年6月1日起实施。海关总署1997年5月1日起实施的《中华人民共和国海关审定加工贸易进口货物完税价格暂行办法》同时废止。

署长　钱冠林

1999年5月26日

附　件

中华人民共和国海关
审定加工贸易进口货物完税价格办法

第一条　为落实《国务院办公厅转发国家经贸和等部门关于进一步完善加工贸易银行保证金台账制度意见的通知》精神，促进加工贸易的健康发展，便利加工贸易进口货物的通关，打击价格瞒骗，保证国家税收，根据《中华人民共和国海关法》、《中华人民共和国进出口关税条例》和《中华人民共和国海关审定进出口货物完税价格办法》的有关规定，制定本办法。

第二条　海关审定加工贸易进口货物完税价格的范围：

（一）按规定在进口时需按比例征税的加工贸易货物；

（二）因故不能出口，经外经贸主管部门批准内销需予补税的加工贸易进口货物；

（三）海关处理的案件中需予补税的加工贸易进口货物；

（四）其他需由海关审价的加工贸易进口货物。

第三条　加工贸易进口货物以海关审定的成交价格为基础确定完税价格。成交价格经海关审查未能确定的，由海关依次采用同一时期从同一出口国或地区进口的相同货物成交价格方法、类似货物成交价格方法、相同或类似货物在国内市场批发价格倒扣方法及其他合理方法估定。

第四条 海关审定加工贸易进口货物完税价格的具体环节：

（一）按规定在进口时需按比例征税的加工贸易料件，在料件申报进口时由海关按规定审定完税价格。

（二）加工贸易进口货物经批准内销申报进口时，海关按以下原则审定完税价格：

1. 对进料加工进口料件或其制成品，以海关审定的料件申报进境时的成交价格为基础的到岸价格作为完税价格；

2. 对来料加工进口料件或其制成品，以内销申报之日海关按照本办法第三条的规定审定的料件价格作为完税价格；

3. 对加工贸易加工过程中产生的边角废料及副产品，经批准内销需予补税的，经内销申报之日海关按照本办法第三条的规定审定的价格作为完税价格。

（三）海关处理的案件中需予补税的加工贸易进口货物，以案件查获之日海关按照本办法第三条的规定审定的该货物所含进口料件的价格作为完税价格。

第五条 加工贸易进口货物的收货人或其代理人应向海关如实申报成交价格及有关费用，提供有关合同、发票、加工贸易登记手册等。必要时，还应提供购进料件的厂家发票和反映加工贸易双方关系及成交活动的有关情况。

为确定申报价格的真实性，海关有权检查加工贸易的有关合同、发票、账册、单据、业务函电、文件和其他资料。

第六条 加工贸易进口货物的买卖双方如有特殊经济关系，加工贸易进口货物的收货人或其代理人应如实向海关申报。海关经调查认定加工贸易双方的特殊经济关系影响到成交价格时，有权不接受申报价格。

第七条 加工贸易进口货物的收货人或其代理人向海关提供虚假或伪造的合同、发票及其他单证、资料、伪瞒报价格以偷逃税款的，海关按照《中华人民共和国海关法行政处罚实施细则》的有关规定予以处罚，并按《中华人民共和国海关对企业实施分类管理办法》实行分类管理。

第八条 本办法由海关总署负责解释。

第九条 本办法自 1999 年 6 月 1 日起实施，1997 年 5 月 1 日起实施的《中华人民共和国海关审定加工贸易进口货物完税价格暂行办法》同时废止。

海关总署关于印发《中华人民共和国海关对企业实施分类管理办法实施细则》的通知

署监〔1999〕345 号

1999 年 7 月 28 日

广东分署，各直属海关：

为贯彻执行《国务院办公厅转发国家经贸委等部门关于进一步完善加工贸易银行保证金台账制度的意见》(国办发〔1999〕35 号)，实施《中华人民共和国海关对企业实施分类管理办法》（以下简称“办法”)，总署制定了《中华人民共和国海关对企业实施分类管理办法实施细则》（以下简称“细则”，见附件一)，现印发你们，请各关于 1999 年 8 月 10 日前将本《细则》对外公告（公告文稿见附件二)，并做好有关宣传解释工作。现将有关问题通知如下：

一、各海关应根据《细则》的规定和要求，加强领导，落实责任，规范操作，制作规范的联系单证，建立各职能部门间的联系配合制度，共同做好企业分类管理工作。

二、为保障企业分类管理工作在起步阶段能够有序、稳妥地进行，目前先对已办理报关注册登记的企业进行分类管理。对尚待明确海关登记办法的企业，暂不进行管理类别评审工作。有关登记办法，总署将陆续制定下发。企业取得海关登记编码后，海关即可对其进行分类管理。海关对企业分类管理不涉及保税区内加工贸易企业。

经确定的企业管理类别，应录入至企业档案数据库的“企业级别”数据项中。该数据项中原有的记录应在8月10日前清空。

《细则》第三十五条（二）款所指“规定的程序”，总署将另行下发。

三、鉴于目前海关尚未与企业签订进出口海关必检商品免予取样化验的协议，各关在起步阶段执行《办法》第六条第一项第四点时，暂可视同企业无申报不实记录。

四、根据《细则》第十七条规定的程序，海关评定企业适用A类管理时须征求企业所在地外经贸等主管部门意见。鉴于《办法》第七条（五）款内容已包含在该程序中，为避免重复，经商外经贸部，企业申请A类管理时，可不要求其提交“外经贸主管部门出具的书面意见”。

《企业状况调查表》适用范围为申请A类管理的企业。有关该调查表的印制和使用以及填写要求，按《监管司关于印发〈企业状况调查表〉的通知》（监管〔1999〕115）号的规定办理。

海关受理企业申请及实施企业分类管理中应当保守企业的商业秘密。

五、对加工贸易企业申请实行海关派员驻厂监管或与主管海关实行计算机联网管理保税工厂的，按《海关总署关于派驻海关监管人员在保税工厂审批原则的通知》（署监〔1996〕612号）、《海关总署关于海关派员驻厂监管的保税工厂审批原则的补充通知》（署监〔1996〕902号）、《海关总署关于对加工贸易保税工厂试行计算机联网监管有关问题的通知》（署监〔1997〕453号）的规定办理。

六、起步阶段审定适用C类、D类管理企业以1998年8月1日为界，企业在此后发生的违规和走私行为作为企业分类管理评定的记录。

七、海关不向社会公告企业所适用的管理类别，但应通知本企业（适用B类管理的企业除外）。如企业对海关审定的管理类别不服时，可根据《中华人民共和国行政复议法》的有关规定申请复议。

八、为使外经贸等主管部门在其有关工作环节中能及时掌握企业所适用的管理类别，根据加工贸易部际联席会第二次会议决定，海关应于审定企业适用C类或D类管理之日将企业名单抄送所在地外经贸等有关部门，并自审定之日起3日后开始实施，以便有关主管部门在此期间内对本部门记录的企业管理类别进行调整。

九、对已经调查、稽查、侦查等部门立案调查有重大违规、走私嫌疑的企业，在案件未审结前，海关暂不改变企业管理类别，由各关对其进行布控处理。必要时海关对涉嫌重大违规案件的加工贸易企业，要求提交备案进口料件应征税款百分之五十的风险担保全；对涉嫌走私案件的加工贸易企业，要求提交备案进口料件应征税款等值的风险担保金。一旦海关处罚决定生效，即按《办法》规定的标准对其进行管理类别的调整。

以上请遵照执行。执行中有何问题，请及时报总署监管司。

附件：一、中华人民共和国海关对企业实施分类管理办法实施细则

二、中华人民共和国海关公告

附件一

中华人民共和国海关对企业实施分类管理办法实施细则

第一章　总　则

第一条　为了实施《中华人民共和国海关对企业实施分类管理办法》（以下简称《办法》），制定本实施细则。

第二条　海关通过对企业经营管理状况和遵守海关法律法规情况的评估，核定企业的信誉程度，设置A、B、C、D四个管理类别。

第三条　海关对企业实施动态的分类管理制度，

依据企业在从事与海关业务有关的经营活动中的守法和违法记录，及时调整对企业的管理类别。

第四条 海关以公开、公正、公平的原则实施企业分类管理。全国海关实行统一的企业分类管理评定程序、评定标准和管理措施。

第二章 职责分工

第五条 海关总署成立由各有关业务部门参加的企业分类管理委员会，协调各部门做好企业分类管理工作，处理企业分类管理工作中出现的重大问题，监督、检查各关企业分类管理工作。

委员会的日常工作及企业分类管理工作的组织实施统一由企业管理主管部门归口负责。

第六条 直属海关成立由主管关长牵头，各职能部门参加的关一级企业分类管理委员会。其主要职责为：

（一）审定本关企业管理部门提交的企业管理类别的初审名单；

（二）协调有关业务部门做好企业分类管理工作；

（三）处理企业分类管理工作中出现的问题；

（四）监督落实企业的分类管理措施。

委员会下设办公室，负责委员会的日常工作。办公室设在企业管理部门。

第七条 直属海关企业管理部门统一归口负责企业的分类管理工作，其职责范围包括：

（一）受理企业申请，审核企业提交的有关文件和资料；

（二）汇总各职能部门提供的信息和记录，向企业分类管理委员会提交企业适用的管理类别的初审意见；

（三）保存企业评定的原始材料；

（四）及时维护企业档案数据库企业管理类别标志；

（五）通知企业适用的管理类别（B类除外）；

（六）跟踪企业分类管理措施落实情况；

（七）与所在地外经贸、经贸委、税务、工商、外汇管理等有关部门建立联系制度，互通情况，共享信息。

第八条 海关各有关职能部门应指定专人负责企业分类管理的联系工作，及时向企业管理部门提供与企业分类管理有关的记录和信息。

第九条 隶属海关的企业分类管理工作由直属海关依据本细则的规定确定。

第三章 管理类别评定标准

第十条 海关评定适用A类管理的企业时应严格按照《办法》第六条所规定的标准进行。

《办法》第六条所称“连续二年”，系指海关接受企业申请之日前两年。企业在两年前发生违反海关法律法规情事但至提交申请之日仍未结案的，不具备申请适用A类管理的资格。

第三项“有正常的进出口业务”，系指企业年进出口总额在100万美元以上。

进出口总额以海关统计数据为准。

第十一条 凡不符合《办法》第六条规定的各项条件，且未发生《办法》第九条和第十条所列情形之一的企业适用B类管理。

企业第一次办理报关注册登记时可按B类管理。企业注册登记后发生《办法》第九条或第十条所列情形之一的，海关应对其实施C类或D类管理。

第十二条 企业有《办法》第九条所列情形之一的，海关实施C类管理。

《办法》第九条第一项所称“违规”，以海关依据《中华人民共和国海关法行政处罚实施细则》第三章的规定对企业违规行为进行的处罚（处人民币一千元以下罚款的除外）且该处罚决定书已生效为准。

第二项“拖欠海关税款”系指超过三个月仍未缴纳正常进出口应缴税款，包括经海关认定违反海关监管规定，除给予处罚外，尚需补交的税款。

该项同样适用于超过三个月仍未交付海关罚款、没收的违法所得和追缴的私货等值价款。

第三项“账册管理混乱”，以海关根据《中华人民共和国海关稽查条例》对企业所作稽查报告的结论为依据。

第四项“遗失重要业务单证，”所指情形为藏匿、损毁或不能提供有关单证，致使海关无法监管。

第七项“出借企业名义，供他人办理进出口货物报关纳税等事宜”，系指以收取代理费方式，让委托企业（或货主）自带客户、自带货源、自带汇票、自行报关，或以任何形式出让其名义供他人办理进出口业务中付汇、收汇、报关等手续。

第八项“被外经贸主管部门给予通报批评或警告等行政处罚”，系指外经贸部或其授权的省级外经贸主管部门根据《对违规、走私企业给予警告、暂停或撤销对外贸易、国际货运代理经营许可行政处罚的暂行规定》（外经贸政发）（〔1998〕929号）对企业进行的批评或处罚。

第十三条 企业有《办法》第十条所列情形之一的，海关实施D类管理。

《办法》第十条所称“走私”，以海关处罚决定书或法院判决书生效为准。第一项所称“二年内”，系指海关审核企业管理类别之日前两年。

企业以成立新企业或变更企业名称逃避海关分类管理和监督，海关掌握确凿证据的，对其成立的新企业或变更名称后的企业实施D类管理。

第四章　评定程序

第十四条 海关必须实行公开、透明的企业管理类别评定程序。关一级企业分类管理委员会每季度定期召开会议，以多数通过的方式对本关区企业适用管理类别进行审定。

第十五条 海关在开展企业适用管理类别评定工作中，应加强与外经贸、经贸委、税务、外汇管理、中国银行等部门的协作配合；并商上述部门向海关推荐监督员，列席有关企业管理类别评定会议，对评定工作进行监督。

第十六条 主管海关接受企业提出适用A类管理的申请时向企业发放申请表（格式见附件1）。海关受理企业申请后各职能部门应进行下列工作：

（一）企业管理部门负责审核企业提交的文件和资料；

（二）调查、侦查、稽查、监管、关税、保税、审单、统计等各有关职能部门负责提供企业走私违规、拖欠税款、加工贸易合同核销、进口海关必检商品签订免予取样化验协议后二年内的申报记录、企业会计制度和仓库管理、年进出口量、报关单差错率等信息资料及处理意见。

（三）企业管理部门汇总有关职能部门提供的信息资料及意见，结合企业分类管理计算机评定程序进行初审，初审意见提交关一级企业分类管理委员会评定。

第十七条 主管海关应自评定企业适用A类管理之日起7个工作日内将有关企业名单抄送所在地外经贸、经贸委、税务、外汇管理、中国银行等有关部门征求意见；并请上述部门在7个工作日内反馈意见。反馈意见中对评定的企业管理类别出现异议时，海关应要求其说明理由并提供有关证明材料。上述部门在规定期限内无反馈意见的，视为无不同意见。

第十八条 海关汇总反馈意见后，对无异议的企业立即组织实施分类管理；对有异议的企业名单进行复审。

对核准适用A类管理的企业，海关应自核准之日起30日内通知该企业（通知书式样见附件2）。

第十九条 海关各有关职能部门发现企业有《办法》第九条或第十条所列行为，应在制发的处罚决定书生效后7个工作日内将处罚决定书复印件及有关材料提交企业管理部门。企业管理部门据此对有关企业管理类别进行实时调整，实施C类或D类管理。

第二十条 对审定适用C类或D类管理的企业，海关应自审定之日起7个工作日内组织实施，并在7个工作日内通知有关企业（通知书式样见附件3）。

第二十一条 企业管理部门应结合年审工作，根据《办法》规定的标准，对企业适用的管理类别进行年度核定，并根据实际情况对企业的管理类别进行调整。调整意见提交企业分类管理委员会讨论通过。

（一）适用A类管理的企业在年度核定中未发现有《办法》第九条或第十条所列行为、但不符合《办法》第六条第二至七项条件的，调整按B类管理。

对经调整后不再按A类管理的企业，海关应自调整之日起7个工作日内通知有关企业取消对其实施A类管理（通知书式样见附件4）。

（二）适用D类或C类管理的企业在年度核定中符合《办法》第十七条有关条件的，转为按C类或B类管理（通知书式样见附件5）。

《办法》第十七条所称“二年内”和“一年内”，系指自企业被审定适用D类或C类管理之日起二年内或一年内。

第二十二条 企业管理部门应对企业评定的原始材料进行归档并保存，以备必要时进行调阅。原始材料保存期二年。

第五章 管理措施

第二十三条 海关对经评定适用A类管理的企业应认真执行《办法》第十二条所列的各项便利措施。

第二十四条 海关对适用B类管理的企业按《办法》第十三条规定进行监管。

第二十五条 海关对适用C类管理的企业按《办法》第十四条规定实施重点监管。

其中第四项“重点查验”按《海关总署关于试行〈海关监管工作查验、检查、核销量化标准〉(试行)的通知》(署监〔1998〕247号)和《海关总署关于印发〈海关对进出境货物查验规程〉(试行)的通知》(署监〔1999〕270号)规定办理。

第五项“不予办理异地报关备案”,系指经海关审定适用C类管理的企业不得在异地自行开展报关业务,必须在备案地委托专业报关企业或委托承运其货物的代理报关企业报关。

第二十六条 海关对适用D类管理的企业按《办法》第十五条规定采取监控措施。

对《办法》第十五条第三、四项“暂停”或“取消企业报关资格”的,各海关执行时应按规定制发处罚决定书。

第二十七条 凡办理异地报关备案的企业在备案地发生《办法》第九条和第十条所列情形之一的,备案地海关应在制发的处罚决定书生效后7个工作日内将处罚决定书复印件及有关材料寄送企业注册地海关,由注册地海关对企业的管理类别进行调整。

第二十八条 各海关发现异地企业在本地发生《办法》第九条和第十条所列情形之一的,应在制发的处罚决定书生效后7个工作日内将处罚决定书复印件及有关材料寄送企业注册地海关,由注册地海关对企业的管理类别进行调整。

第六章 加工贸易企业管理类别的评定和实施

第二十九条 经海关评定适用A类管理的加工贸易企业,且符合下列条件之一的,海关可不对其实行银行保证金台账制度:

(一)实行海关派员驻厂监管或与主管海关实行计算机联网管理保税工厂的;

(二)从事飞机、船舶等特殊行业加工贸易的;

(三)企业年进出口总额3000万美元(自营生产型企业出口额1000万美元)及以上,或年加工贸易出口额1000万美元及以上的。

第三十条 适用B类管理的加工贸易企业,除开展加工贸易限制类商品外,继续实行现行的银行保证金台账“空转”制度。

第三十一条 适用C类管理的加工贸易企业向海关办理合同登记备案时,海关对其备案进口料件收取应征进口关税和进口环节增值税税款等值的保证金。

《办法》第九条第五项“不按规定办理加工贸易合同核销手续”,系指加工贸易经营单位(广东、福建两省的加工生产企业在“对外加工装配服务公司”名义项下开展对外加工装配业务的,加工生产企业可视同经营单位)超出海关规定的合同核销期限,经海关催核,仍不向海关办理合同核销手续并无正当理由的。

第三十二条 适用D类管理的加工贸易企业,海关不予办理新的加工贸易合同备案。

第三十三条 加工贸易经营单位与承接委托加工的生产企业管理类别不一致时,以A、B、C、D为顺序,海关按较后的管理类别采取相应的监管措施。

经营单位不得委托适用D类管理的生产企业加工。

第七章 企业名单的报送

第三十四条 企业管理部门应自企业管理类别审定或调整之日起7个工作日内将企业管理类别录入企业档案数据库并通知各有关执行部门实施。

第三十五条 各直属海关审定的企业管理类别每日通过企业档案数据库传输至总署。各海关通过“异地备案网上查询系统”查询异地备案企业的管理类别。

总署每日将企业管理类别的增量文件反馈各海关。各海关打印出在本关区备案的异地企业的管理类别调整结果,按规定的程序进行修改并执行。

第三十六条 注册地海关对企业管理类别审定或对原适用的管理类别进行调整后,对其中经本关办理异地备案手续的企业,应在7个工作日内通报备案地海关（通报单式样见附件6）。

第八章　附　　则

第三十七条　经营单位与其委托代理报关企业、运输企业管理类别不一致时，海关按经营单位的管理类别采取相应的监管措施。

第三十八条　本细则由海关总署负责解释。

第三十九条　本细则自1999年8月10日起施行。

附件一：适用A类管理企业申请表

附件二：海关实施A类管理通知书

附件三：海关实施C类/D类管理通知书

附件四：海关取消A类管理通知书

附件五：海关企业管理类别调整通知书

附件六：企业管理类别通报单

（附件略）

中华人民共和国海关总署令

第74号

现发布《中华人民共和国海关关于异地加工贸易的管理办法》，自1999年10月1日起实施。

署长　钱冠林

1999年9月22日

海关总署关于下发《中华人民共和国海关关于异地加工贸易的管理办法》的通知

署税［1999］648号

广东分署，各直属海关：

为贯彻执行《国务院办公厅转发国家经贸委等部门关于进一步完善加工贸易银行保证金台账制度意见的通知》（国办发［1999］35号），海关总署制定了《中华人民共和国海关关于异地加工贸易的管理办法》，并随文下发，请以第74号中华人民共和国海关总署令对外发布，现将有关问题明确如下：

一、海关对开展异地加工贸易的经营单位和加工企业实行分类管理，当两者的管理类别发生调整时，其主管海关应及时按《海关总署关于印发〈中华人民共和国海关对企业实施分类管理办法实施细则〉的通知》（署监［1999］345号）有关规定通知对方海关，以便采取相应的监管措施。

二、加工企业主管海关要加强对备案合同的后续监管，合同核销结案后一个月内，将合同执行情况填写《中华人民共和国海关异地加工贸易回执》（以下简称《回执》），反馈给经营单位主管海关。

三、加工企业主管海关发现合同执行过程中有异常情况的，应于发现之日起7个工作日内填写《回执》反馈给经营单位主管海关。

四、《中华人民共和国海关异地加工贸易申请表》（以下简称《申请表》和《回执》未实行网络异地传输之前，主管海关应将《申请表》或《回执》制作关封，送交给对方海关；实行网络异地传输后，主管海关必须将《申请表》或《回执》的有关内容通过电脑网络传输给对方海关。

五、海关总署于1999年5月25日所发署税（1999）382号文予以作废。

六、《中华人民共和国海关异地加工贸易申请表》、《中华人民共和国海关异地加工贸易回执》由各关自行印制。

以上请遵照执行。

附件：《中华人民共和国海关关于异地加工贸易的管理办法》

海关总署

1999年9月22日

附　件

中华人民共和国海关关于异地加工贸易的管理办法

第一条　为了促进加工贸易健康发展，加强和规范海关对异地加工贸易的管理，根据《中华人民共和国海关法》和国务院批准的国家经贸委等部门《关于进一步完善加工贸易银行保证金台账制度的意见》及其他有关规定，制定本办法。

第二条　本办法中的“异地加工贸易”是指加工贸易经营单位（以下简称经营单位）将进口料件委托另一直属海关关区内加工生产企业（以下简称加工企业）开展的加工业务。不包括加工出口产品过程中某一加工工序以外发加工业务（外发加工业务管理办法另行制定）。

第三条　经营单位与加工企业开展异地加工业务，双方须签定符合《中华人民共和国合同法》规定的“委托加工合同”。

第四条　经营单位与加工企业双方必须遵守国家对加工贸易管理的有关规定，经营单位不得将保税进口料件转卖给加工企业。

第五条　经营单位开展异地加工贸易，须凭其所在地外经贸主管部门核发的《加工贸易业务批准证》和加工企业所在地外经贸主管部门出具的《加工贸易加工企业生产能力证明》，填制《中华人民共和国海关异地加工贸易申请表》（格式见附件1，以下简称《申请表》）向经营单位主管海关提出异地加工申请。

第六条　经营单位主管海关在核准其异地加工申请时，对于办理过异地加工贸易业务的经营单位，须查阅由加工企业主管海关反馈的《中华人民共和国海关异地加工贸易回执》（格式见附件2，以下简称《回执》）。经核实合同执行情况正常的，在《申请表》（一式两联）内批注签章，与《加工贸易业务批准证》、《加工贸易加工企业生产能力证明》一并制作关封，交经营单位凭以向加工企业主管海关办理合同登记备案。

第七条　加工企业主管海关凭经营单位提供的《加工贸易业务批准证》、“委托加工合同”、《加工贸易加工企业生产能力证明》、《申请表》及其他有关单证办理合同登记备案。如由加工企业向海关办理合同备案手续的，必须持有经营单位出具的委托书。

第八条　海关对开展异地加工贸易的经营单位和加工企业实行分类管理，如果两者的管理类别不相同，按其中较低类别采取临管措施。如需实行保证金台账“实转”的，经营单位应按规定交付备案进口料件税款等额的台账保证金。经营单位不得委托按D类管理的加工企业开展异地加工贸易。

第九条　异地加工贸易合同执行过程中，如有走私违规行为或无法正常核销结案的，加工企业主管海关应负责将台账保证金转税和罚款。台账保证金转税数额不足的，由加工企业主管海关负责向经营单位追缴税款，经营单位主管海关应予协助。

第十条　对违反本规定，构成走私、违规的，由海关依照《中华人民共和国海关法》及《中华人民共和国海关法行政处罚实施细则》有关规定处理。经营单位和加工企业在执行本办法和海关各项规定时，负有共同责任。对其违法行为，海关可根据实际情况分别追究法律责任。

第十一条　经营单位与加工企业不在同一直属关区，但属同一法人开展异地加工贸易业务的，可比照上述规定办理。

第十二条　本办法由海关总署负责解释。

第十三条　本办法自1999年10月1日起实施。

附件：1.《中华人民共和国海关异地加工贸易申请表》

2.《中华人民共和国海关异地加工贸易回执》

附件一

海关编号：______

中华人民共和国海关异地加工贸易申请表

__________海关：

我__________（公司、厂）需将加工贸易合同（合同号：______________）委托____________（公司、厂）进行加工、委托合同号：__________。我们保证遵守《海关法》及有关规定，如有违反，我们愿承担相应的法律责任。

主要进口料件名称	数　量	价　值	出口成品名称	数　量	价值

经营单位：

地址：　　　　　　　　　　　　　　　　电话：

企业法定代表人（签名）：

年　　月　　日（盖章）

企业管理类别

经营单位主管海关意见：

年　　月　　日（盖章）

1. 本申请表一式两联：第一联经营单位主管海关留存，第二联加工企业主管海关留存。
2. 企业管理类别由海关填写。

（请各关按此表实样印制）

附件二

海关编号：______

中华人民共和国海关异地加工贸易回执

______海关：

你关区内______公司的异地加工贸易申请表（海关编号：______），我关已同意并办理了合同登记备案（手册号为：______），现将全同履行过程中的情况反馈如下：

合同履行正常情况	正在履约中	〔 〕
	正在核销中	〔 〕
	已核销结案	〔 〕 结案号：
合同履行异常情况	合同逾期未报核	〔 〕
	内销补税欠税	〔 〕
	内销补税待补证	〔 〕
	走私违规（附处罚通知书）	〔 〕
	企业解散、倒闭	〔 〕
	其他情况	〔 〕 说明：

注：1．填制本表时，根据实际情况在相应的栏目〔 〕内打“√”；

2．本回执一式两联，一联加工地海关留存，一联交经营单位所在地海关。

______海关（盖章）

（请各关按此表实样印制）

中华人民共和国海关公告

1999年10月1日

根据《国务院办公厅转发国家经贸委等部门关于进一步完善加工贸易银行保证金台账制度意见的通知》(国办发[1999]35号),从1999年10月1日起,对部分企业、部分商品的加工贸易实行银行保证金台账“实转”,现将有关规定公告如下:

一、加工企业登记

根据保证金台账“实转”规定对企业实行分类管理的要求,从1999年10月1日起,加工贸易经营单位必须委托已在所在地主管海关办理了加工企业登记手续的加工企业加工。没有办理企业登记手续的加工企业,应向主管海关企管部门办理加工企业登记手续,申请加工企业编码。

二、合同备案审批

(一)从1999年10月1日起,没有企业编码的加工企业不予办理合同备案。

适用D类管理的企业和涉及禁止类商品的合同,不再予以办理新合同的备案手续。经营单位不得委托按D类管理的加工企业进行加工。

(二)备案合同预审。企业在申请办理加工贸易合同备案手续时,应先到海关进行备案合同预审,由海关按有关规定审核确定企业填报的贸易方式、征免性质、商品编码、品名规格、计量单位等内容是否符合规范。

(三)1万美元以下(含1万美元,金额以海关核定为准。)合同备案。适用A、B类管理企业,进口料件无论是否涉及限制类商品,均不开设台账,其中对外商提供的价值5000美元以下(含5000美元)辅料品种在规定78种范围内的,仍按原规定办理;适用C类管理企业,一律开设台账,并实行保证金台账“实转”。

(四)进料加工非对口合同的进口料件按比例征税的,征税部分不再收取保证金。

三、备案合同的变更

1. 对因企业管理类别调整,备案合同进口料件从保证金“空转”转为“实转”的,应对原备案合同按规定收取台账保证金。经主管海关关(处)长批准,可只对原合同未履行出口部分按规定收取台账保证金。对管理类别调整为按D类管理的企业,对已备案的合同,经主管海关关(处)长批准,允许收取全额台账保证金后继续执行完毕,但不得变更和延期。

2. 对允许类商品转为限制类商品的,已备案的合同不再征收台账保证金。对原限制类或允许类商品转为禁止类的,已备案的合同按有关部门的规定办理。

3. 对增加进口料件或合同金额涉及保证金台账“实转”的,海关按台账“实转”规定对增加部分征收台账保证金或重新核发《登记手册》。对合同项下其他变更,不再收取台账保证金。

4. 适用B类管理企业,1万美元以下(含1万美元)的合同发生变更后进口料件总值超过1万美元的,需开设台账,如果增加的进口料件涉及限制类商品的,海关按台账“实转”规定对增加部分征收台账保证金或重新核发《登记手册》。

5. 合同延期除另有规定外,仍按现行有关规定办理。

6. 保证金台账合同执行过程中发生变更,如涉及增加台账保证金的,应按规定补交增加部分台账保证金。对因企业类别调整、限制类商品转为允许类商品或变更后台账保证金减少的,备案合同已收取的台账保证金暂不退还,待合同核销结案后方予退还。

四、对1999年10月1日前备案的老合同原则上按原台账制度规定履行完毕

但对10月1日后因增加进口料件引起台账“实转”的要对增加部分收取台账保证金;涉及限制类商品的老合同原则上不允许延期,遇特殊情况经外经贸主管部门批准办理延期的,由主管海关关(处)长同意后予以办理,但延长期限不超过半年,申请第二次延期的,对尚未进口但确需进口的以及进口后未加工复出口的限制类商品，同主管海关征收税款等额的台账保证金后予以办理延期手续；对C类企业经批准办理老合同首次延期的，对尚未进口但确需进口的以及进口后未加工复出口的料件要收取台账保证金；对调整为D类企业的老合同变更或延期按本公告第三条第1款内容办理。

五、内销补税及补缓税利息

计息期限：从加工贸易企业合同手册记录首次进口料件之日起至补征税之日止。1999年10月1日前备案合同涉及内销补税缓税利息的，不征收缓税利息。

利率：以海关总署定期确定的银行活期存款利率计征。

特此公告

国家税务总局关于外商投资企业出口货物若干税收问题的通知

国税发［1999］189号

1999年10月8日

各省、自治区、直辖市和计划单列市国家税务局：

为进一步加强外商投资企业出口货物退（免）税管理，支持外商投资企业扩大出口，根据国务院有关决定精神，现对1993年12月31日前批准成立的外商投资企业（以下简称老外商投资企业）出口货物税收问题通知如下：

一、关于出口货物退（免）税办法问题

自1999年11月1日起，老外商投资企业自营或委托出口货物由原出口免税办法改为出口退税办法。具体退（免）税的计算办法按现行自营生产企业“先征后退”或“免、抵、退”税办法执行。

如老外商投资企业要求对出口货物继续免税，可在1999年11月底前向主管征税机关提出申请，经批准同意后，其出口货物在2000年底前，也可继续按照财政部、外经贸部、国家税务总局《关于1993年12月31日前批准成立的外商投资企业有关税收政策问题的通知》（财税字［1998］184号）的规定执行。从2001年1月1日起，其出口货物改按退税办法。

二、关于出口货物实行退（免）税后几个具体政策问题

（一）来料加工、进料加工退（免）税问题

老外商投资企业直接承接来料加工复出口的，免征本环节增值税和消费税；老外商投资企业承接来料加工后委托其他外商投资企业或国内企业加工再收回复出口的，可持凭主管退税的税务机关出具的“来料加工免税证明”免征消费税和委托加工工缴费的增值税。

老外商投资企业以进料加工进口料件生产出口货物的，可分别按如下公式调整计算应退税款：

1. 执行“先征后退”办法的计算公式为：

当期应纳税额＝当期内销货物的销项税额＋当期出口货物离岸价×外汇人民币牌价×征税税率-（当期全部进项税额＋当期海关核销免税进口料件组成计税价格×征税税率）

当期应退税额－当期出口货物离岸价×外汇人民币牌价×退税税率－当期海关核销免税进口料件组成计税价格×退税税率

2. 执行“免、抵、退”税办法的计算公式为：

当期不予抵扣或退税的税额－当期出口货物离岸价×外汇人民币牌价×（征税税率－退税税率）－当期海关核销免税进口料件组成计税价格×（征税税率－退税税率）

其具体计算步骤及公式仍按《财政部、国家税务总局关于出口货物税收若干问题的补充通知》（财税字［1997］014号）等有关规定执行。

上述征税税率和退税税率是指复出口货物所适用的征税税率和退税税率。

（二）中标机电产品退（免）税问题

对利用外国政府贷款或国际金融组织贷款通过国际招标由老外商投资企业中标的机电产品，实行“先征后退”管理办法。对其申报退税所需凭证及审核、审批程序等具体管理办法，依照《国家税务总局关于印发〈出口货物退（免）税管理办法〉的通知》(国税发［1994］031号)、《国家税务总局关于印发〈出口货物退（免）税若干问题的具体规定〉的通知》（国税发［1999］101号）的有关规定执行。

（三）出口保税区货物退（免）税问题

对老外商投资企业运往保税区的货物不予退（免）税。保税区内企业从区外老外商投资企业购进货物时必须向主管税务机关申报备案增值税专用发票的有关内容，待该批货物出口或加工后再出口，再按规定办理退（免）税。

（四）钢材“以产顶进”退（免）税问题

老外商投资企业利用已免税“以产顶进”钢材加工生产的出口货物，比照现行有关加工贸易税收管理办法进行征、退税管理、具体按照国家税务总局等五部委《关于印发〈钢材“以产顶进”改进办法实施细则〉的通知》（国税发［1999］68号）第十八条第（一）款的有关规定执行。

（五）修理修配业务退税问题

老外商投资企业承接国外修理修配业务，修理修配劳务收入免征增值税，不退税。对其用于修理修配的零部件、原材料等，按照购货增值税专用发票和适用退税税率办理退税。

（六）“免、抵”税款调库问题

老外商投资企业实行“免、抵、退”税办法后，对其“免、抵”的税款，按照财政部、国家税务总局、中国人民银行《关于实行“免、抵、退”税办法有关预算管理问题的通知》（财预字［1998］242号）进行调库处理。

三、关于出口货物退（免）税管理问题

（一）老外商投资企业应按照国家税务总局国税发［1994］031号文件的规定，持工商营业执照等有关资料在1999年底前向主管退税的税务机关办理退税登记手续。未办理退税登记手续的企业一律不予办理出口货物的退（免）税。

老外商投资企业如发生撤并、变更情况，应于批准撤并、变更之日起30日内向主管退税的税务机关办理注销或变更退税登记手续。

（二）老外商投资企业应设专职或兼职办理出口退税人员（以下简称办税员），经主管退税的税务机关培训考试合格后发给《办税员证》。没有《办税员证》的人员不得办理出口退税业务。企业更换办税员，应及时通知主管税务机关注销原《办税员证》。凡未及时通知的，原办税员在被更换后与税务机关发生的一切退税活动和责任仍由企业负责。

（三）老外商投资企业出口退（免）税的日常管理，如办证、检查、清算及资料的审核、保管等工作，由各地国家税务局涉外税收管理机关具体负责。涉外税收管理机关负责按月接收“免、抵、退”企业退（免）税预申报及“先征后退”企业纳税申报和退税申报，并审核办理免、抵、退税及应纳税额或将未抵扣完的进项税额结转下期继续抵扣的手续。进出口税收管理机关负责按季接收“免、抵、退”企业退（免）税汇总申报及按月接收“先征后退”企业退税申报，并审核审批免、抵及退税额，通知征税机关调整免、抵税额，办理退税手续。

（四）老外商投资企业出口退（免）税，实行计算机管理，具体按照《国家税务总局关于印发〈出口退税电子化管理办法〉的通知》（国税发［1996］79号）执行。

四、关于出口货物清理问题

（一）各地要对实行退（免）税办法的老外商投资企业1999年11月1日前出口的货物进行清理。企业1999年11月1日前报关离境，1999年11月1日后在财务上作销售的出口货物，仍按出口免税办法执行。

（二）对1999年11月1日前购进，日前尚未核销的进口料件，老外商投资企业应持海关核发的《进料加工登记手册》等有关凭证，到其主管退税机关补申请开具《进料加工贸易申请表》。

海关总署关于进一步鼓励外商投资有关进口税收政策的通知

署税［1999］791号

1999年11月22日

广东分署，各直属海关、院校：

根据国务院指示精神，为了鼓励外商投资，决定进一步扩大对外商投资企业的进口税收优惠政策，经商外经贸部、国家经贸委、财政部，现就有关问题通知如下：

一、对已设立的鼓励类和限制乙类外商投资企业、外商投资研究开发中心、先进技术型和产品出口型外商投资企业（以下简称五类企业）技术改造、在原批准的生产经营范围内进口国内不能生产或性能不能满足需要的自用设备及其配套的技术、配件、备件，可按《国务院关于调整进口设备税收政策的通知》（国发［1997］37号）的规定免征进口关税和进口环节税。

（一）享受本条免税优惠政策应符合以下条件：

1. 资金来源应是五类企业投资总额以外的自有资金（具体是指企业储备基金、发展基金、折旧和税后利润，下同）；

2. 进口商品用途：在原批准的生产经营范围内，对本企业原有设备更新（不包括成套设备和生产线）或维修；

3. 进口商品范围：国内不能生产或性能不能满足需要的设备（即不属于《国内投资项目不予免税的进口商品目录》的商品），以及与上述设备配套的技术、配件、备件（包括随设备进口或单独进口的）。

（二）征免税手续办理程序：

1. 进口证明的出具：由有关部门根据本条第（一）款第1、2点的规定出具《外商投资企业进口更新设备、技术及配备件证明》（格式见附件一），其中：鼓励类、限制乙类外商投资企业由原出具项目确认书的部门出具（1997年12月31日以前批准设立的上述企业由原审批部门出具）；外商投资研究开发中心由原审批部门（具体部门详见本通知第二条第（一）款第1点）出具；产品出口型企业和先进技术型企业由颁发《外商投资产品出口企业确认书》和《外商投资先进技术企业确认书》的外经贸部或省、自治区、直辖市、计划单列市的外经贸厅局出具。

2. 征免税证明的办理：企业所在地直属海关凭企业提交的上述进口证明、合同和进口许可证明等有关资料，并审核进口商品范围符合本条第（一）款第3点的规定后出具征免税证明。

（三）特殊规定：

1. 凡五类企业超出本条第（一）款第2点界定范围进行技术改造的，其进口证明应由国家或省级经贸委按审批权限出具《技术改造项目确认登记证明》（格式见附件二）。

2. 五类企业利用自有资金进行设备更新维修或技术改造，需进口属于《国内投资项目不予免税的进口商品目录》内的商品，如确属国内同类产品的性能不能满足需要的，由归口管理该类产品的国家行业主管部门审核并出具《外商投资企业设备更新或技术改造进口国内不能生产的同类设备证明》（格式见附件三），直属海关凭上述证明和《外商投资企业进口更新设备、技术及配备件证明》或《技术改造项目确认登记证明》及合同和进口许可证明等有关资料办理设备及配套技术的免税审批手续。

二、外商投资设立的研究开发中心，在投资总额内进口国内不能生产或性能不能满足需要的自用设备及其配套的技术、配件、备件，可按《国务院关于调整进口设备税收政策的通知》（国发［1997］37号）的规定免征进口关税和进口环节税。

（一）享受本条免税优惠政策应符合以下条件：

1. 享受单位应是经国家计委、国家经贸委、外经贸部以及各省、自治区、直辖市、计划单列市计委、经贸委、外经贸厅局批准，设立在外商投资企业内部或单独设立的专门从事产品或技术开发的研究机构；

2. 资金来源限于在投资总额内；

3. 进口商品范围：国内不能生产或性能不能满足需要的自用设备（指不属于《外商投资项目不予免税的进口商品目录》中的商品）及其配套的技术、配件、备件，但仅限于不构成生产规模的实验室或中试范畴，也不包括船舶、飞机、特种车辆和施工机械等。

（二）征免税手续办理程序：

1. 项目确认书的出具：按照上述研究机构的审批权限由国家计委、国家经贸委、对外经贸部以及各省、自治区、直辖市、计划单列市计委、经贸委、外经贸厅局按照本条第（一）款第1、2点的规定出具外商投资研究开发中心项目确认书。项目确认书的格式和内容与署税（1997）1062号文所附《国家鼓励发展的内外资项目确认书》相同。

2. 征免税证明的办理：企业所在地直属海关凭上述项目确认书及有关资料，比照署税［1997］1062号文的规定办理。

三、对符合中西部省、自治区、直辖市利用外资优势产业和优势项目目录（由国务院批准后另行发布，下同）的项目，在投资总额内进口国内不能生产或性能不能满足需要的自用设备及其配套的技术、配件、备件，除国发（1997）37号文规定的《外商投资项目不予免税的进口商品目录》外，免征进口关税和进口环节税。有关手续比照署税［1997］1062号文对外商投资项目的有关规定办理。

四、对符合中西部省、自治区、直辖市利用外资优势产业和优势项目目录的项目，在投资总额外利用自有资金进口享受税收优惠政策商品范围及免税手续比照本通知第一条对五类企业的有关规定办理。

五、符合本通知规定免税进口的货物为海关监管货物，企业不能擅自出售和转让。设备更新或技术改造而被替换的设备，如在本企业内继续使用，海关按监管年限进行管理，在监管年限内出售和转让给其他可享受进口设备税收优惠政策企业的，可免予补税，否则应照章征税。

六、企业所在地直属海关与进口地海关要加强联系配合，提高办理效率，直属海关经审核无误出具《进口货物征免税证明》后，尽快通知进口地海关办理免税验放。如企业所在地系非直属海关所在地，可由所在地处级海关受理初审，报送直属海关核准，出具征免税证明。总署将组织力量，尽快补充和调整《减免税管理系统》，将此项税收优惠政策纳入计算机管理。

七、此项税收优惠政策涉及的部门多、政策性强，各海关要认真学习领会文件精神，严格遵照执行，不得擅自扩大免税范围。要主动与地方政府和有关主管部门联系，做好宣传工作。

八、本通知自1999年9月1日起实施，但已征收的税款不予退还。在此日期以后报关进口、尚未办结征税手续的，按本通知的规定办结免税手续后，予以免税结案，已征收的保证金准予退还。

执行中的问题和情况，请及时报总署关税征管司。

附件一：外商投资企业进口更新设备、技术及配备件证明（略）

附件二：技术改造项目确认登记证明（略）

附件三：外商投资企业设备更新或技术改造进口国内不能生产的同类设备证明（略）

金融、外汇

中国人民银行　对外贸易经济合作部关于下发《关于支持境外加工贸易的信贷指导意见》的通知

银发〔1999〕230号
1999年6月30日

中国人民银行各分行、营业管理部，中国进出口银行、国有独资商业银行、其他商业银行；各省、自治区、直辖市及计划单列市外经贸委（厅、局）：

为支持扩大出口，提高对外开放水平，鼓励我国轻工、纺织、家用电器等机械电子以及服装加工等行业具有比较优势的企业到境外开展加工贸易业务，中国人民银行和对外贸易经济合作部根据《国务院办公厅转发外经贸部、国家经贸委、财政部关于鼓励企业开展境外带料加工装配业务意见的通知》（国办发〔1999〕17号），制定了《关于支持境外加工贸易业务的信贷指导意见》。现印发你们，有关银行和外经贸部门要按照国家产业政策和外贸政策的需要，在切实有效防范风险的前提下，对国家确定的境外加工贸易业务给予积极支持，促进境外加工贸易业务的发展。

特此通知。

附件：关于支持境外加工贸易业务的信贷指导意见

附　件

关于支持境外加工贸易业务的信贷指导意见

随着我国经济水平的提高，经济结构的改善和对外经贸合作关系的扩大，境外加工贸易业务正逐步成为外贸出口的重要形式和扩大出口的新的增长点。根据《国务院办公厅转发外经贸部、国家经贸委、财政部关于鼓励企业开展境外带料加工装配业务意见的通知》（国办发〔1999〕17号）文件精神，现就信贷支持境外加工贸易业务工作提出如下意见：

一、境外加工贸易业务是指我国企业以国内成熟的技术和设备及适用的料件到国外投资办厂，在境外以加工装配的形式，带动和扩大国内设备、技术、零配件、原材料出口的国际经贸合作方式。

各商业银行和中国进出口银行要高度重视境外加工贸易业务在扩大出口、促进国内产业结构调整中的积极作用，按照国家产业政策和外贸政策的需要，在切实有效防范风险的前提下，对国家确定的境外加工贸易业务给予积极支持，促进境外加工贸易业务的发展。

二、对境外加工贸易业务的信贷支持重点是我国在设备、技术上有较强优势的轻工、纺织、家用电器等机械电子及服装加工等行业。

（一）取得外经贸部颁发的《境外带料加工装配企业批准证书》；

（二）企业生产经营状况良好，管理水平较高，能对境外投资贷款提供必要的担保；

（三）境外加工贸易项目具有良好的经济效益和发展前景，稳定的现金流量和符合国家政策要求的收汇水平；

（四）企业有良好的银行信用记录，没有逃废银行债务的行为；

（五）银行要求的其他条件。

四、对符合境外加工贸易业务条件的企业，银行可以发放中长期贷款和短期贷款。中长期贷款主要用于境内采购建厂所需设备、技术以及设备安装等，期限在1年以上；短期贷款主要用于购买境外加工贸易业务所需的原材料、零部件以及支付其生产经营费用等，以支持这些产品的出口和生产，期限在1年以内（含1年）。贷款以人民币为主，对项目确有需要的，银行可发放短期外汇贷款。外汇贷款的发放和使用，以及外汇资金汇出必须符合国家有关外汇管理规定。对贷款金额大的，银行可以积极组织银团贷款。除此之外，银行还可根据实际情况采取多种信贷方式和手段支持境外加工贸易业务的发展。

五、贷款银行要严格按照有关贷款规定对境外加工贸易业务的贷款自主审定、自主发放，严格控制和防范风险，保障信贷资金安全。

银行可在对企业统一授信的基础上，根据企业日常流动资金的需求状况、出口规模以及预计境外加工贸易项目的加工能力等，核定企业境外加工贸易业务的信贷额度。信贷额度每年核定一次，特殊情况可以临时追加。企业使用额度内的信贷资金，银行要逐笔核贷，但可视情况简化核贷程序和手续。

如在境外加工贸易业务所有地有我国内银行的分支业务机构，则应安排由该机构直接承做当地企业的授信业务。需由国内单位对外出具担保的，应按规定到外汇管理部门办理担保的审批、登记等手续。

六、对境外加工贸易业务的贷款利率按照国家规定的同档次利率执行。对资信状况和经营状况良好的企业，其境外带料加工项目效益明显，还本付息有保证的，贷款利率可在国家规定的范围内适当下浮。

七、为了保证贷款安全、防范投资风险，对境外加工贸易业务的贷款，应以国内投资主体的资产作抵押，或由国内第三方企业作担保，或有银行认可的其他担保。银行认为必要时，企业还应投保出口信用险。

八、企业要定期、如实向银行提供信贷资金使用情况，特别要提供境外加工贸易项目的生产情况和与之有关的出口情况，以便银行掌握企业经营活动和资信状况。企业必须及时归还银行贷款，并支付利息。借用外汇贷款的，应以境外加工贸易项目的外汇收益偿还，不得以人民币购汇还贷。

贷款银行要加强和改进服务，积极探索和完善服务方式和手段，加强对贷款的监督和管理。对非法转移资金、拖欠银行本息、逃避银行债务、逃汇和套汇等违反金融法规和政策的行为，贷款银行要及时采取收回贷款、要求担保单位承担担保责任、处置抵押物等保全措施，并向人民银行、外汇管理局和外经贸主管部门通报。

九、外经贸主管部门要及时向银行通报境外加工贸易业务的有关政策、项目以及境外投资国家的经济、政治、法律等有关情况和资料。对违反境外加工贸易有关规定的企业，外经贸主管部门应视情节轻重给予处罚。

人民银行各级分支行要会同当地有关部门，积极支持境外加工贸易业务，对境外加工贸易业务中遇到的困难和问题，应及时向上级报告。

国家经济贸易委员会　对外贸易经济合作部　海关总署　中国人民银行　国家外汇管理局　中国银行　关于印发《关于加工贸易企业以多种形式缴纳税款保证金实施办法》的通知

国经贸贸易〔1999〕1271号

1999年12月29日

各省、自治区、直辖市、计划单列市及新疆生产建设兵团经贸委(经委、计经委)、外经贸委(厅、局)、海关总署广东分署、各直属海关、中国人民银行分行、外汇分局、中国银行分行,国务院有关部门:

为落实《国务院办公厅转发国家经贸委等部门〈关于进一步完善加工贸易银行保证金台账制度〉的通知》(国办发〔1999〕35号)和《国务院办公厅转发外经贸部等部门〈关于进一步采取措施鼓励扩大出口意见〉的通知》(国办发〔1999〕71号)精神,国家经贸委、外经贸部、海关总署、中国人民银行、国家外汇管理局、中国银行根据《中华人民共和国海关法》、《中华人民共和国担保法》等有关法律、法规,制定了《关于加工贸易企业以多种形式缴纳税款保证金实施办法》。本实施办法规定,经海关总署确认的、具有担保资格的金融机构或其他具有代为清偿债务能力的法人(以下简称"担保机构"),均可为加工贸易企业向海关提供担保。目前,海关总署会同中国人民银行已确认中国银行为加工贸易提供担保的金融机构,其他担保机构的担保资格经确认后亦参照本办法执行。

现将《关于加工贸易企业以多种形式缴纳税款保证金实施办法》印发你们,自2000年1月1日起执行。

关于加工贸易企业以多种形式缴纳税款保证金实施办法

第一条　为完善加工贸易银行保证金台账制度,允许开展加工贸易业务的企业(以下简称"企业")以多种形式向海关缴纳关税及其他税费保证金(以下简称"税款保证金"),根据《中华人民共和国海关法》、《中华人民共和国担保法》等有关法律、法规的规定,制定本办法。

第二条　企业开展加工贸易业务因故无法向海关缴纳税款保证金的,可凭中国银行出具的以海关为受益人的税款保付保函办理海关备案手续。税款保付保函及索赔函格式见附件。

第三条　中国银行下列机构可根据企业资信,经自行评估,向海关出具保函:

(1)中国银行总行营业部;

(2)各省、自治区、直辖市分行;

(3)深圳市分行;

(4)珠海、汕头、苏州、无锡、宁波、厦门、沈阳市分行。

第四条　中国银行提供担保的金额包括税款及

利息两部分。其中税款指海关核定的企业应缴关税和其他税费的金额。利息和利率适用按海关有关规定执行。

第五条 担保期限至台账核销期满后60天。

第六条 担保期限内，企业加工合同增额或展期的，应向原出具保函的中国银行申请办理相应的保函增额或展期手续后，方可向海关、中国银行办理台账变更手续。为简化手续，经企业申请，中国银行提供的保函金额可大于保证金金额。

第七条 对符合法律、法规及本办法的，中国银行根据海关开出的《银行保证金台账开设联系单》或《银行保证金台账变更联系单》，对企业资信情况及提供的保证、抵押、质押、留置和定金（包括企业自有外汇资金、其他非金融机构担保人为其出具的担保）等多种形式的担保进行评估，经评估符合风险控制要求的，可为其出具以海关为受益人的税款保付保函，并转往有关台账业务点。对不符合国家法律、法规及本实施办法的，中国银行可以拒绝受理。

第八条 中国银行台账业务点收到本行保函业务授权分行开立的银行台账保证金保付保函后，开具《银行保证金台账登记通知单》或《银行保证金台账变更通知单》。企业凭上述《银行保证金台账登记通知单》或《银行保证金台账变更通知单》和保付保函向海关办理加工贸易合同备案手续。

第九条 在担保期限内，企业出口合同执行完毕或履行缴纳税款义务的，中国银行的担保责任自行解除；在担保期限内，企业未能全部或部分履行出口义务的，海关按应补税额及缓税利息向中国银行开出《索赔书》和《海关专用缴款书》（进口料件未经批准内销的，需加开《税款缴纳扣划通知书》），中国银行凭此履行保函项下的赔付责任。中国银行履行了保函项下的赔付责任后，可以依法向被担保人追索。

第十条 海关与中国银行间建立的现行台账联系制度不变。海关与中国银行按照《关于印发〈加工贸易进口料件保证金台账“实转”联系配合办法实施细则〉的通知》（中银发〔1999〕89号）及有关配套办法的各项规定处理银行保证金台账事宜。

第十一条 未能取得中国银行出具的税款保付保函的加工贸易企业应以现金、转账支票、汇票、汇款等方式缴纳税款保证金。

第十二条 本办法自2000年1月1日起执行。实施细则由海关总署、中国银行制定并颁布。

附件：一、税款保付保函

　　　二、索赔函

附件一

税 款 保 付 保 函

致：________________海关　　　　日期：

　　　　　　　　　　　　　　　　　　编号：

应________________（申请人）的要求，根据________________海关________________号《银行保证金台账开设联系单》，我行兹开立你方为受益人的不可撤销的担保函，担保金额为《银行保证金台账开设联系单》申请人应缴纳的台账保证金________________及利息________________（计息日为自申请人进口报关日至《银行保证金台账开设联系单》上核定的核销日，利率适用海关有关规定）。　　本保函自开立之日起生效，至________________（海关核定的台账核销期满后60天）失效。本保函的担保金额将随申请人在海关核定的核销期内出口或已向海关支付税款金额而自动递减。

我行保证，如果申请人未能在海关核定的有效期内出口或海关支付税款，我行将在收到你方的书面索赔函和《海关专用缴款书》（注有“台账保证金转税专用”字样）或《海关征税缴款书》、《税款缴纳扣划通知书》后，向你方支付上述税款及利息。任何索赔，务必于本保函到期日前送达我行。

　　　　　　　　　　　　　　　　　　担保人：中国银行____________分行

附件二

索赔函

致：中国银行＿＿＿＿＿＿＿＿分行

＿＿＿＿＿＿＿＿公司在你行办理的＿＿＿＿＿＿＿＿号（加工贸易手册号）加工贸易业务没有在规定的期限内复出口，应按规定补缴税款。我关现凭贵行第＿＿＿＿＿＿＿＿号保函，请你行支付税款＿＿＿＿＿＿＿＿元，缓税利息＿＿＿＿＿＿＿＿元，（利息计算方法为：＿＿＿＿＿＿＿＿），金额合计＿＿＿＿＿＿＿＿元。

请贵行将上述金额一次性划转中央金库。

＿＿＿＿＿＿＿＿海关

年　　月　　日

对外贸易经济合作部办公厅　科学技术部办公厅关于转发《关于高新技术产品出口信贷执行利率的通知》的通知

〔1999〕外经贸技字第14号

1999年9月24日

各省、自治区、直辖市及计划单列市、沈阳市、苏州市、武汉市、南京市、广州市、成都市、西安市外经贸委（厅、局）、科委，中央管理的外经贸企业：

为实施“科技兴贸”战略，推动高新技术产品出口，中国进出口银行最近下发《关于高新技术产品出口信贷执行利率的通知》（进出银计发〔1999〕第205号）。现将该通知转发给你们，请加强与中国进出口银行及其各地代表处的沟通与协调。执行中有何情况，请及时向外经贸部（科技司）或科技部（发展计划司）联系。

特此通知。

附　件：如文

附　件

中国进出口银行
关于高新技术产品出口信贷执行利率的通知

进出银计发〔1999〕第205号
1999年9月17日

各部、室，国内各代表处：

根据《国务院办公厅转发外经贸部等部门关于进一步采取措施鼓励扩大外贸出口意见的通知》（国办发〔1999〕71号）文件，高新技术产品出口列入我行出口信贷和优惠贷款业务范围。经请示人民银行同意，我行对科技部等部门联合制定的《中国高新技术产品出口目录》中的产品发放的人民币出口信贷，按人民银行确定的人民币出口卖方信贷第一档利率（大型成套设备和技术含量高的机电产品）执行，现行利率为4.05%。请遵照执行。

检验、检疫

国家药品监督管理局 国家中医药管理局 对外贸易经济合作部 海关总署 关于出口中药实行凭企业证照放行办法的通知

国药管安〔1999〕95号

1999年1月20日

各省、自治区、直辖市药品监督管理局或卫生厅(局)、医药管理部门、外经贸委(厅、局)、广东海关分署、各直属海关:

为规范中药出口程序,促进我国中药出口,根据《中华人民共和国对外贸易法》及国际惯例,现决定,改变我国中药(指以中药为原料生产的中成药产品)的现行出口放行制度,自1999年5月1日起,国家中医药局、外经贸部、原国家进出口商品检验局、海关总署下发的《关于实行出口中药产品质量注册和检验放行制度的通知》(国中医药质〔1996〕4号)予以废止。与此同时,各类经营对外贸易的企业(包括自营出口生产企业)在办理上述通知所附"列入管理的中药产品目录"所列五种中药产品出口手续时,海关不再加验商检证书。改为凭企业合法证照放行。届时,海关自动化报关系统参数库亦做相应调整。

出口中药产品的质量问题,由出口企业自负。对进口国索取我出口药品生产企业资格及产品自由销售证明者,由国家药品监督管理局负责办理。

请各省、自治区、直辖市外经贸委(厅、局)、药品监督管理局或卫生厅(局)、医药管理部门将本通知及时转发有关单位和企业。

特此通知。

中华人民共和国 国家出入境检验检疫局令

第1号

现发布《进口汽车检验管理办法》,自2000年1月1日起施行。

局长 李长江

1999年11月22日

附　件

进口汽车检验管理办法

第一条　为加强进口汽车检验管理工作，根据《中华人民共和国进出口商品检验法》（以下简称《商检法》）及其实施条例，制定本办法。

第二条　国家出入境检验检疫局（以下简称国家检验检疫局）主管全国进口汽车检验监管工作，进口汽车入境口岸检验检疫机构负责进口汽车入境检验工作，用户所在地检验检疫机构负责进口汽车质保期内的检验管理工作。

第三条　对转关到内地的进口汽车，视通关所在地为口岸，由通关所在地检验检疫机构按照本办法负责检验。

第四条　进口汽车的收货人或代理人在货物运抵入境口岸后，应持合同、发票、提（运）单、装箱单等单证及有关技术资料向口岸检验检疫机构报检，口岸检验检疫机构审核后签发《入境货物通关单》。

第五条　进口汽车入境口岸检验检疫机构对进口汽车的检验包括：一般项目检验、安全性能检验和品质检验。

第六条　一般项目检验。在进口汽车入境时逐台核查安全标志，并进行规格、型号、数量、外观质量、随车工具、技术文件和零备件等项目的检验。

第七条　安全性能检验。按国家有关汽车的安全环保等法律法规、强制性标准和《进出口汽车安全检验规程》（SN/T0792－1999）实施检验。

第八条　品质检验。品质检验及其标准、方法等应在合同或合同附件中明确规定，进口合同无规定或规定不明确的，按《进出口汽车品质检验规程》（SN/T0791－1999）检验。

整批第一次进口的新型号汽车总数大于300台（含300台，按同一合同、同一型号、同一生产厂家计算）或总值大于100万美元（含100万美元）的必须实施品质检验。

批量总数小于300台或总值小于100万美元的新型号进口汽车和非首次进口的汽车，检验检疫机构视质量情况，对品质进行抽查检验。

品质检验的情况应抄报国家检验检疫局及有关检验检疫机构。

第九条　检验检疫机构对进口汽车的检验，可采取检验检疫机构自检、与有关单位共同检验和认可检测单位检验等方式，由检验检疫机构签发有关检验单证。

第十条　对大批量进口汽车，外贸经营单位和收用货主管单位应在对外贸易合同中约定在出口国装运前进行预检验、监造或监装，检验检疫机构可根据需要派出检验人员参加或者组织实施在出口国的检验。

第十一条　经检验合格的进口汽车，由口岸检验检疫机构签发《入境货物检验检疫证明》，并一车一单签发《进口机动车辆随车检验单》；对进口汽车实施品质检验的，《入境货物检验检疫证明》须加附《品质检验报告》。

经检验不合格的，检验检疫机构出具检验检疫证书，供有关部门对外索赔。

第十二条　进口汽车的销售单位凭检验检疫机构签发的《进口机动车辆随车检验单》等有关单证到当地工商行政管理部门办理进口汽车国内销售备案手续。

第十三条　用户在国内购买进口汽车时必须取得检验检疫机构签发的《进口机动车辆随车检验单》和购车发票。在办理正式牌证前，到所在地检验检疫机构登检、换发《进口机动车辆检验证明》，作为到车辆管理机关办理正式牌证的依据。

第十四条　经登记的进口汽车，在质量保证期内，发现质量问题，用户应向所在地检验检疫机构申请检验出证。

第十五条　各直属检验检疫局根据工作需要可委托或指定经考核符合条件的汽车检测线承担进口汽车安全性能的检测工作，并报国家检验检疫局备案。国家检验检疫局对实施进口汽车检验的检测线的测试和管理能力进行监督抽查。

第十六条　检验检疫机构对未获得进口安全质量许可证书或者虽然已获得进口安全质量许可证书但未加贴检验检疫安全标志的、未按本办法检验登记的进口汽车，按《商检法》及《商检法实施条例》的有关规定处理。

第十七条 进口摩托车等其他进口机动车辆由收货人所在地检验检疫机构参照本办法负责检验。

第十八条 各直属检验检疫机构每半年将进口汽车质量分析报国家检验检疫局，并于7月15日和次年1月15日以前报出。

第十九条 本办法由国家检验检疫局负责解释。

第二十条 本办法自2000年1月1日起施行。原国家商检局下发的《国家商检局关于贯彻全国进出口汽车检验工作会议精神的通知》（国检检［1990］468号文）和《国家商检局关于启用新的〈进口机动车辆随车检验单〉和统一制作〈进口车辆检验专用章〉的通知》（国检检［1994］30号文）同时废止。

国家出入境检验检疫局
对外贸易经济合作部
海　关　总　署
关于对出口小家电产品实施法定检验的通知

国检检联［1999］383号

1999年12月16日

各直属检验检疫局，各省、自治区、直辖市及计划单列市外经贸委（厅、局），各地机电产品进出口办公室，海关总署广东分署，各直属海关：

随着我国对外贸易的发展，作为重要的机电产品之一的小家电产品，出口量越来越大，并已进入了欧美等世界各地的市场。由于小家电产品直接涉及使用者的人身安全，出口小家电产品出现的安全质量问题，已影响了我国机电产品的出口。

为了促进外贸发展，提高出口小家电产品的质量水平，并进一步扩大出口，充分发挥检验把关职责，根据《中华人民共和国进出口商品检验法》的规定，将出口小家电列入法定检验，现将有关检验事宜通知如下；

一、对出口小家电产品（具体商品HS编码名称见附件），自2000年1月1日起实施出口法定检验。

二、对于出口小家电产品，检验时其安全性能项目不能低于GB4706.1及GB4706的系列产品标准规定。

三、对出口的小家电产品，海关凭国家出入境检验检疫机构出具的《出境货物通关单》验放。有关《出境货物通关单》的样式将另文下达。

四、出口小家电产品的报验、检验、出具证书等按照国家出入境检验检疫局的有关规定执行。

附件：实施出口法定检验的小家电产品目录

附　件

实施出口法定检验的小家电产品目录

编　码	商　品　名　称
84145130	功率≤125W 具有旋转导风轮的风扇（本身装有一个不超过 125 瓦的电动机）
84145199	功率≤125 瓦其他风机、风扇（本身装有一个不超过 125 瓦的电动机）
84221100	家用型洗碟机
84248910	家用型喷射、喷雾机械器具
85091000	真空吸尘器
85092000	地板打蜡机
85093000	厨房废物处理器
85094000	食品研磨机，搅拌器及果、菜榨汁器
85098000	其他家用电动器具
85101000	电动剃须刀
85102000	电动毛发推剪
85103000	电动脱毛器
85161000	电热水器（指电热的快速热水器、储存式热水器、浸入式液体加热器）
85162100	电气储存式空间加热散热器
85162990	其他电气空间加热器
85163100	电吹风机
85163200	其他电热理发器具
85163300	电热干手器
85165000	微波炉
85166010	电磁炉
85166030	电饭锅
85166040	电炒锅
85167100	电咖啡壶或茶壶
85167200	电热烤面包器
85167900	未列名电热器具
90191010	按摩器具
95069110	健身及康复器械

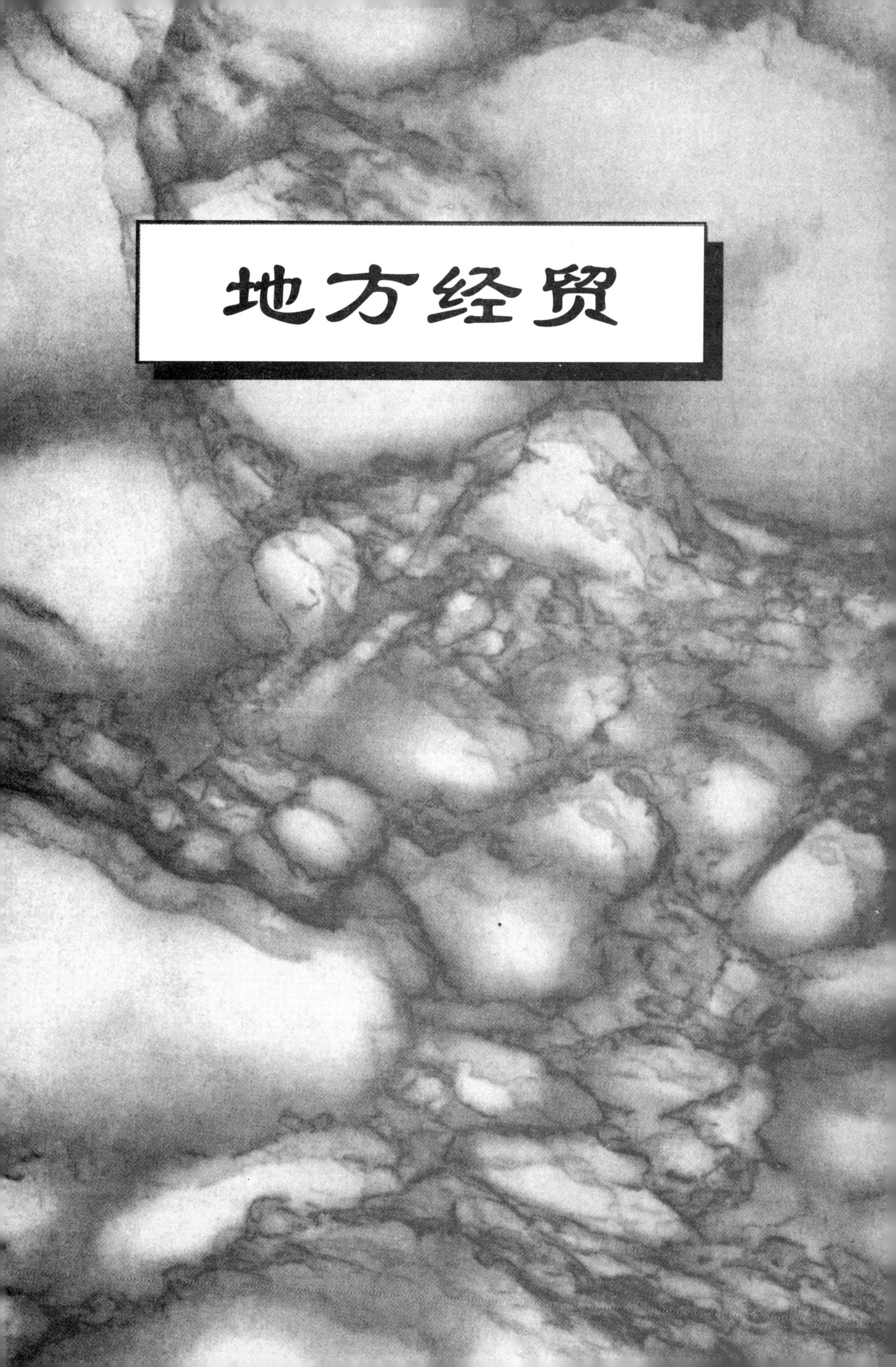
地方经贸

1999年北京市对外经济贸易

北京市对外经济贸易委员会

【对外贸易】

进出口总额 1999年北京市进出口总额84.42亿美元，比1998年的65.05亿美元增长29.8%。

出口总额 出口总额32.61亿美元，比1998年的28.29亿美元增长15.2%，占全市国内生产总值2169.7亿元的12.4%，占全国出口额的1.67%。

出口商品结构 初级产品出口额2.49亿美元，占出口总额的7.6%，工业制成品出口额30.12亿美元，占出口总额的92.4%。

出口额在1000万美元以上主要商品情况表

金额分类	商品名称	出口金额（亿美元）	占出口总额%
1000－3000万美元（34种）	彩色阴极射线电视显像管，扬声器，片式多层瓷介电容器，有液晶装置或发光二极管的显示板，视频信号录制或重放设备零附件，计算机及部件的零附件，移动通讯基地站，断电器，无绳电话机，照相机，多相交流电动机，普通钢铁的半制成品，未锻轧非合金锌，稀土永磁铁，机动散货船，羊毛针织或钩编套头衫、开襟衫及马甲等，羊绒制针织或钩编套头衫、开襟衫及马甲等，棉制男衬衫，棉制男裤，棉制针织或钩编套头衫、开襟衫及马甲等，针织或钩编的运动服，合成纤维制针织或钩编女式便服套装，合成纤维制男裤，化纤制男式服装，合成纤维制针织或钩编男式便服套装，合成纤维制男式上衣，化纤胸罩，未漂平纹布，未漂或漂白的布，短纤混纺布，填充的玩具动物，塑料或纺织面的提箱及小手袋等，鸡肉及食用杂碎，冻鱼片	5.84	17.91
3000万美元以上（14种）	手持及车载无线电话，手机零件，录像机，显示器，半导体集成电路，数字式单片集成电路，机动多用船，黄金首饰及零件，皮革或再生皮革衣服，化纤制针织或钩编套头衫、开襟衫、马甲等，男式毛制西服套装，化纤男衬衫，皮革面鞋靴，冻鸡块及杂碎	8.73	26.77
合　　计	**48种**	**14.57**	**44.68**

出口商品市场 出口商品销往173个国家和地区。

主要出口国别（地区）情况表

单位：万美元

国别（地区）	出口额	占总额（%）
日　本	72643	22.3
美　国	47033	14.4
香　港	41721	12.8
俄罗斯	40837	12.5
德　国	13491	4.1
伊　朗	10750	3.3
韩　国	7235	2.2
英　国	7169	2.2
荷　兰	6676	2.0

主要出口国别（地区）情况表（续）

单位：万美元

国别（地区）	出口额	占总额（%）
意大利	4569	1.4
合　计	**252124**	**77.2**

进口总额　进口总额51.81亿美元，比1998年的36.76亿美元增长40.9%。

进口商品结构　初级产品进口额3.55亿美元，占进口总额的6.8%；工业制成品进口额48.26亿美元，占进口总额的93.2%。

进口额在1000万美元以上主要商品情况表

金额分类	商品名称	进口金额（亿美元）	占进口总额（%）
1000－3000万美元（38种）	印刷电路，视频信号录制或重放设备零附件，半导件集成电路，有液晶装置或发光二极管的显示板，电视显示管零件，无线电通讯专用的仪器及装置，有线载波通信及有线数字通信设备，系统形式的巨型机、大型机及中型机，计算机零件及附件，数控装置，数字式自动数据处理设备，彩色阴极射线电视显像管，稳压电源，电感器，发动机零件，飞机零件，蓄电池，针式打印机，自动柜员机，激光盘，有接头电缆，载客电梯，插头及插座，X射线断层检查仪，X光发生器及检测仪器等，已烧结的铁矿砂及精矿，混合或非混合产品构成的药品，人用疫苗，机织物，染色布，短纤混纺布，未漂或漂白的布，初级形状的聚乙烯，小麦及混合麦，棕榈油及分离品，非零售除草剂，对苯二甲酸，冻鳕鱼	6.65	12.84
3000万美元以上（16种）	数字式单片集成电路，手持及车载无线电话，手机零件，数字式移动通讯交换机，移动通讯基地站，有接收装置的发送设备，数字式程控电话或电报交换机零件，单片集成电路，彩色数据/图形显示管，片式多层瓷介电容器，混合集成电路，未烧结的铁矿砂及精矿，铝合金矩形板，含氮、磷、钾的矿物肥料或化肥，磷酸氢二铵，氯化钾	22.53	43.49
合　计	**54种**	**29.18**	**56.33**

进口商品市场　进口商品来自88个国家和地区。

主要进口国别（地区）情况表

单位：万美元

国别（地区）	进口额	占总额（%）
日　本	99713	19.2
芬　兰	97218	18.8
美　国	56948	11.0
瑞　典	56351	10.9
韩　国	30963	6.0
德　国	29047	5.6
香　港	18161	3.5
台湾省	17127	3.3
马来西亚	14030	2.7
新加坡	11314	2.2
合　计	**430872**	**83.2**

技术进出口　1999年技术进出口总额5.99亿美元，比1998年的4.5亿美元增长33%。其中，签订引进技术和进口设备合同项目365个，比1998年增加170个；合同金额2.25亿美元，比1998年的2.11亿美元增长6.6%。签订技术出口合同项目294个，比1998年减少42个；合同金额3.73亿美元，比1998年的2.39亿美元增长56.1%。

技术进口　引进技术和进口设备来自21个国家和地区。主要国家和地区的项目数和合同金额情况是：美国90项，4630万美元；香港65项，4105万美元；德国55项，1276万美元；日本46项，869万美元；芬兰18项，4698万美元；法国14项，1249万美元；台湾省10项，814万美元；加拿大5项，1089万美元；瑞典32项，1633万美元。技术引进的主要行业有纺织、轻工、机械、仪器仪表、电子、医药、印刷、化工及城市基础设施等。

技术出口　技术出口实际收汇21211万美元，出口主要国家和地区是：美国9973万美元，香港7188万美元，日本2567万美元，新加坡404万美元，比利时401万美元，马来西亚387万美元，德国104万美元。

【利用外资】

1999年利用外资情况表

利用外资方式	批准签订的合同			实际利用外资	
	项目数（个）	外资金额（万美元）	金额比1998年（±%）	金额（万美元）	金额比1998年（±%）
对外借款	2	964.00	+8.3	43945.52	−23.2
外商直接投资	645	181684.57	−14.8	223123.80	+8.1
合资企业	336	54613.13	−11.1	53477.40	−33.8
合作企业	96	63013.33	−72.9	81938.90	+21.4
外资企业	210	57337.33	−45.9	58385.50	+10.7
外资银行	3	3708.00		3723.00	
外商投资股份制		3012.75		25599.00	
外商其他投资				26612.29	+13.9
国际租赁					
补偿贸易					
加工贸易					
对外发行股票				26612.29	+13.9
合　计	**647**	**182648.57**	**−55.5**	**293681.61**	**+2.3**

外商直接投资行业 外商直接投资项目中，生产型项目388个，非生产型项目257个。按行业划分：农林牧渔水利业16个；采掘业3个，制造业363个，建筑业8个，运输邮电业7个，商业饮食业23个，金融、保险业3个，房地产业36个，社会服务业169个，卫生业2个，综合技术服务业2个，其他行业13个。

外商直接投资来源 外商直接投资来自44个国家和地区。主要投资国家和地区的项目及合同外资金额的情况是：香港154项，合同外资额46018万美元；美国130项，合同外资额27955万美元；台湾省58项，合同外资额3587万美元；英属维尔京群岛53项，合同外资额30256万美元；韩国45项，合同外资额3160万美元；日本39项，合同外资额10246万美元；加拿大24项，合同外资额850万美元；澳大利亚20项，合同外资额1990万美元；德国16项，合同外资额12086万美元；新加坡15项，合同外资额2052万美元；法国11项，合同外资额7602万美元；荷兰7项，合同外资额7692万美元；英国6项，合同外资额7283万美元；瑞典2项，合同外资额3220万美元。

外商直接投资企业生产经营情况 截至1999年底，已有5300家外商投资企业开业投产，职工总数为43万人。全年完成工业产值755亿元，比上年增长17%；实现销售收入1170亿元，比上年增长23%；缴纳税金总额78亿元，比上年增长7%。

【对外经济合作】

承包工程和劳务合作 1999年签订对外承包工程和劳务合作项目90个，金额25230万美元，比1998年的25526万美元下降1.2%；完成营业额26165万美元，比1998年的31030万美元下降15.7%；当年派出劳务人员2084人，年末在外3476人，派往的主要国家和地区是新加坡、香港、日本、毛里求斯、津巴布韦、也门等；主要对外承包工程项目有新加坡的住房工程，阿尔及利亚五星级酒店工程，多米尼克的拉由酒店工程等。

对外经济技术援助 承担援外项目14个。受援国有毛里求斯、刚果（金）、加蓬、贝宁、纳米比亚、扎伊尔、孟加拉、佛得角、尼日尔、加纳、安哥拉、莫桑比克和和赤道几内亚，涉及的行业有建筑、公路、住房和设计咨询等，完成项目14个；当年派出援外人员81人，年末在外103人。

对外投资 1999年在海外举办非贸易型企业18个，中方投资305.8万美元。这些企业分布在美国、阿尔及利亚、多米尼克、俄罗斯、新加坡和澳大利亚。

【其他】

经济技术开发区 北京经济技术开发区1999年竣工5条道路的市政工程，建筑工程竣工面积16万平方米；批准入区企业224个（其中外商投资企业49个），增长96.5%；投资额为6.5亿美元，增长64%；实现国内生产总值15亿元，增长72%；完成销售收入56亿元，增长33%；出口创汇7100万美元，增长10.7%。

港口运输 1999年外贸货运总量249.7万吨，比上年增长24.8%。其中出口运量144.8万吨，进口运量104.9万吨。按运输方式，海运量246.1万吨，陆运量2.5万吨，空运量1.1万吨。

涉外旅游 1999年接待海外旅游者及台港澳同胞252万人次，比1998年220万人次增长14.5%；旅游收入25亿美元，比1998年23.8亿美元增长5%。

1999年天津市对外经济贸易

天津市对外经济贸易委员会

【对外贸易】

进出口总额 1998年天津市进出口总额126.01亿美元，比1998年的106.14亿美元增长18.72%。

出口总额63.31亿美元，比1998年的54.99亿美元增长9.56%，占全市国内生产总值1450.1亿元（相当于173.04亿美元）的36.14%。

出口商品结构 初级产品出口额5.87亿美元，占出口总额的9.3%，工业制成品的出口额57.45亿美元，占出口总额的90.7%。

出口额在1000万美元～2000万美元的商品共77种，出口金额10.7亿美元，占出口总额的15.8%；出口额在2000万美元～5000万美元的商品共35种，出口金额10.46亿美元，占出口总额的16.52%；出口额在5000万美元以上的商品共17种，出口金额20.44亿美元，占出口总额的32.28%。

出口商品市场 出口商品到174个国家和地区。

主要出口市场情况表

国别（地区）	金额（亿美元）	占出口总额（%）
美　国	15.88	25.1
日　本	11.21	17.7
香　港	6.89	10.9
韩　国	5.76	9.1
德　国	3.56	5.6
新加坡	1.97	3.1
英　国	1.84	2.9
荷　兰	1.37	2.2
法　国	1.05	1.7
合　计	**49.52**	**78.2**

进口总额 进口总额62.7亿美元，比1998年的51.15亿美元增长22.6%。

进口商品结构 初级产品进口额20.57亿美元，占进口总额32.8%；工业制成品的进口额42.16亿美元，占进口总额的67.2%。

进口额在5000万美元以上的商品共17种，进口金额18.63亿美元，占进口总额的14.18%。

进口商品市场 进口商品来自108个国家和地区。

主要进口市场情况表

国别（地区）	金额（亿美元）	占总进口值的（%）
日　本	15.84	25.26
韩　国	13.17	21.93
美　国	9.55	15.23
台湾省	6.03	9.62
香　港	3.45	5.59
新加坡	2.5	3.99
英　国	2.43	3.88
德　国	1.67	2.66
马来西亚	1.42	2.26
菲律宾	1.08	1.72
合　计	**57.72**	**92.6**

技术进出口 1999年天津市技术进出口总额14.23亿美元，比1998年的11.78亿美元增长20.8%；签订引进技术和设备合同项目217个，合同金额11.86亿美元，比1998年的9.73亿美元增长21.9%；签订技术出口合同项目55个，合同金额2.37亿美元，比1998年的2.05亿美元增长15.6%。

【利用外资】

1999年利用外资情况表

利用外资方式	项目数（个）	外资金额（亿美元）	金额比1998年（±%）	实际利用外资	
				金　额（亿美元）	金额比1998年（±%）
对外借款	272	10.25	-22.9	2.13	-60.6
外商直接投资	575	36.20	-0.5	25.32	0.5
合资企业	159	8.70	-41.7		
合作企业	26	16.01	87.4		
外资企业	390	11.45	-11.2		
合　计	**847**	**46.45**	**-6.5**	**27.45**	**-10.2**

外商直接投资行业　农业项目10个，外商投资0.15亿美元；工业及建筑业项目300个，外商投资13.72亿美元；国际贸易及服务项目237个，外商投资1.95亿美元；房地产项目14个，外商投资15.26亿美元；交通运输业项目10个，外商投资4.45亿美元；其他行业4个，外商投资0.31亿美元。

外商直接投资来源

外商直接投资的主要国家和地区情况表

国别（地区）	项目数（个）	总投资金额（亿美元）	外商投资金额（亿美元）
香　港	95	2.88	2.35
美　国	143	2.40	2.12
荷　兰	4	0.69	0.69
韩　国	91	0.64	0.62
法　国	8	0.57	0.55
维尔京岛	9	0.46	0.39
加拿大	24	0.42	0.38
新加坡	24	0.40	0.37
日　本	48	0.44	0.36

外商直接投资企业生产情况　1999年天津市已开业的三资企业完成生产总值968.95亿元，比1998年增长17.5%，其中工业生产总值954.33亿元，占天津市工业总产值的42.66%；销售收入1070.87亿元，比1998年增长18.5%；利税总额118.67亿元；外商投资企业出口44.91亿美元，比1998年增长17.5%；占全市出口总值的70.93%。

截至1999年底，天津市共计批准外商投资企业12989家，协议投资总额343.99亿美元，其中协议外资额267.46亿美元，全市累计外资实际到位132.73亿美元。

【对外经济合作】

承包工程和劳务合作　1999年签订对外承包工程和劳务合作项目386个，金额2.11亿美元，比1998年的1.93亿美元增长10%；营业额1.98亿美元，比1998年的1.77亿美元增长12%；当年外派劳务4602人次，年末在外人数11282人。派往的主要国家和地区：韩国、新加坡、香港、日本、塞班。承包工程主要项目及国别：天津国际经济技术合作公司老挝公路项目，1698万美元；水泥设计院埃及2000吨水泥厂项目，12730万美元；尼日利亚日产2000吨水泥项目，4521.8万美元；铁道部第18局巴基斯坦上斯瓦特饮水隧洞工程，270万美元；尼日利亚铁路修复改造工程261万美元；大港油田伊朗综合技术服务项目，201万美元。

对外经济援助　1999年天津完成国家下达的对外经济援助项目5个，合同金额6517.37万元，受援国家有：几内亚、加蓬、西撒摩亚、圣卢西亚、喀麦隆，涉及的行业：建筑业、制药业、仓储等。

境外投资 1999年在海外举办生产性企业16家，总投资1152.84万美元，其中中方投资682.91万美元。这些企业遍布亚洲、欧洲、美洲、非洲的11个国家和地区。

【其他】

经济技术开发区 新批外商投资企业104家，合同外资额7.27亿美元；工业生产总值608.55亿元，比1998年增长17%；销售收入580.21亿元，比1998年增长幅度1.9%；出口25.54亿美元，比1998年增长22.7%；固定资产投入50.28亿元，比1998年减少33.3%。

天津港保税区 新批外商投资企业207个，合同外资额8.35亿美元，固定资产投资3.84亿元，进出口货物总值完成1.88亿美元，销售收入77.73亿元。

对外经贸洽谈会 1999年3月8日至3月15日，在天津举办"'99中国天津进出口商品交易会"，该会由华北、西北地区各省市和中国纺织品、食品土畜、轻工工艺三个进出口商会共同主办。交易会共有342家海内外企业参展，设置475个摊位，来自世界五大洲20多个国家和地区的1000多名客商到会。各参展企业共签订进出口合同2.5亿美元，其中出口成交2.2亿美元，进口成交3000万美元，本届交易会还邀请到俄罗斯、荷兰以及香港、台湾地区的16家海外客商在会上设立22个摊位，为国内企业进行进出口业务洽谈提供了条件。

港口运输 1999年天津港共有各类泊位140个，其中万吨级以上的深水泊位50个，年吞吐能力6000万吨，1999年实际完成货物吞吐总量7297.7万吨，其中完成外贸进出口货物吞吐总量3859.4万吨，出口量2549.5万吨，进口量1309.9万吨。

涉外旅游 1999年入境的国际旅游人数为32.08万人；旅游收入2.09亿美元，比1998年的2.02亿美元增长3.5%。

1999年河北省对外经济贸易

河北省对外贸易经济合作厅

【对外贸易】

进出口总额 1999年河北省进出口总额为45.80亿美元，比1998年的42.27亿美元增长8.3%。

出口总额 出口总额31.19亿美元，比1998年的31.16亿美元增长0.1%，占全省国内生产总值4556.62亿元（相当于551.26亿美元）的5.66%；占全国出口额的1.6%，居全国第10位。

出口商品结构 初级产品出口额8.20亿美元，占出口总额的26.3%，工业制成品出口额22.99亿美元，占出口总额的73.7%。

出口额在1000万美元以上的商品情况表

金额分类	商　品　名　称	出口金额（万美元）	占出口总额（%）
10000万美元以上的4种	服装及衣着附件、纺织纱线织物及制品、煤、医药品	140954	45.19

出口额在1000万美元以上的商品情况表（续）

金额分类	商品名称	出口金额（万美元）	占出口总额（%）
5000－10000万美元的4种	钢材、家用陶瓷器、肠衣、贵金属首饰	27908	8.95
1000万－5000万美元的23种	鲜干水果及坚果、山羊绒、铝、原油、钢坯及精锻件、干豆、水海产品、手用或机用工具、冻鸡、食用油籽、塑料制品、玻璃制品、家具、焦炭半焦炭、蔬菜、电动机及发电机、合成有机染料、鞋、工业用缝纫机、半导体器件、金属加工机床、汽车零件、药材	53828	17.26
合　计	**31种**	**222690**	**71.40**

出口商品市场　出口商品销往181个国家和地区。

主要出口市场情况表

国别（地区）	金额（万美元）	占出口总额（%）
日　本	53616	17.19
美　国	40067	12.85
香　港	39236	12.58
韩　国	32306	10.36
东　盟	18147	5.82
台湾省	13729	4.40

主要出口市场情况表（续）

国别（地区）	金额（万美元）	占出口总额（%）
德　国	13015	4.17
意大利	10422	3.34
合　计	**220538**	**70.71**

进口总额　进口总额14.61亿美元，比1998年的11.11亿美元增加31.5%。

进口商品结构　初级产品进口额3.65亿美元，占进口总额的25%；工业制成品进口额10.96亿美元，占进口总额的75%。

进口额在1000万美元以上的商品情况表

金额分类	商品名称	进口金额（万美元）	占进口总额（%）
3000万美元以上的6种	金属轧机及零件、香蕉、铁矿砂、钢材、初级形状的塑料、纸及纸板	37480	25.66
1000万－3000万美元的17种	纺织用合成纤维、铝、金属加工机床、谷物及谷物粉、灯泡及类似品玻璃外壳、成品油、有线电话或电极交换机、旋转式电力设备零件、肥料、橡胶或塑料加工机械、其他植物油、计量检测分析自控仪器、玻璃热加工机械、通断及电路保护装置、纺织机械、蒸汽及过热水锅炉设备、牛皮革及马皮革	29240	20.02
合　计	**23种**	**66720**	**45.68**

进口商品市场 进口商品来自78个国家和地区。

主要进口市场情况表

国别（地区）	金　额（万美元）	占进口总额（%）
欧　盟	51400	35.19
日　本	20912	14.32
美　国	15068	10.31
韩　国	13483	9.23
东　盟	7969	5.46
澳大利亚	6448	4.41
加拿大	5690	3.89
台湾省	3866	2.65
合　计	**124836**	**85.46**

技术进出口 1999年河北省技术进出口总额34589万美元，比1998年的28306万美元增长22.2%。其中，签订引进技术和进口设备合同项目113个，比1998年增加21个；合同金额23116万美元，比1998年的20139万美元增长14.78%。签订技术出口合同项目83个，比1998年增加38个；合同金额11473万美元，比1998年的8167万美元增长40.47%。

【利用外资】

1999年利用外资情况表

利用外资方式	批准签订的合同			实际利用外资	
	项目数（个）	外资金额（万美元）	金额比1998年（±%）	金　额（万美元）	金额比1998年（±%）
对外借款		49400	18.8	49400	18.8
外商直接投资	520	88946	-29.84	104202	-29.58
合资企业	370	41735	-35.74	75775	-26.90
合作企业	46	18301	-32.90	13460	-54.26
外资企业	104	28910	-16.32	14967	52.93
合　计		**138346**	**-17.83**	**153602**	**-16.73**

外商直接投资行业 外商直接投资项目中，生产型项目457个，非生产型项目63个。按行业分，农林牧渔业19个，采掘业7个，制造业427个，电力、煤气及水的生产和供应业4个，建筑业7个，交通运输、仓储及邮电通信业4个，批发和零售贸易、餐饮业7个，房地产业13个，社会服务业26个，卫生、体育和社会福利业1个，教育、文化艺术及广播电影电视业1个，科学研究和综合技术服务业3个，其他行业1个。

外商直接投资来源 外商直接投资来自44个国家和地区。投资额居前十位的是：香港25869万美元；美国11594万美元；台湾省9599万美元；韩国6345万美元；英国5880万美元；日本5272万美元；加拿大5215万美元；澳大利亚2678万美元；澳门2345万美元；新加坡2027万美元。

外商直接投资企业生产经营情况 截至1999年底，全省已开业投产的外商投资企业共2579家，职工总数28.65万人。1999年销售（营业）收入428.76亿元，比1998年的337.66亿元增长27%；出口8.00亿美元，比1998年的7.20亿美元增长11.1%，占全省出口总额的25.65%。

【对外经济合作】

承包工程和劳务合作 1999年签订对外承包工程和劳务合作合同项目280个，金额11643万美元，比1998年的10048万美元增长15.9%；营业额7136万美元，比1998年的5198万美元增长39.4%；当年派出劳务人员4263人次，比1998年的3912人次增长8.97%；年末在外人数6613人，比上年末的6412人增加3.1%。劳务人员分布在日本、新加坡、阿联酋、毛里求斯、越南等30个国家和地区。承包工程的主要项目及国家是：马里的打井与农田整治、马来西亚的普通厂房建设、蒙古的石油油井修理等。

接受经济援助 1999年接受国际经济援助项目共11项，总金额5200万元人民币。主要项目是：澳大利亚援助张家口水利发展项目，日本援助职业教育项目。

对外投资 1999年在海外兴办非贸易企业5家，中方投资310万美元，分布在蒙古、南非、越南等3个国家，涉及医药、化工、建材等行业。

【其他】

对外经贸洽谈会 1999年5月在石家庄举办了河北省对外经贸洽谈会，到会外商达806人，分别来自日本、香港、韩国、马来西亚等42个国家和地区，出口成交额达2.01亿美元。

涉外旅游 1999年全省共接待境外旅游者35万人次，比1998年的32.1万人次增长9.03%；旅游外汇收人1.1亿美元，比1998年的0.95亿美元增长15.8%。

1999年秦皇岛市对外经济贸易

秦皇岛市对外贸易经济合作局

【对外贸易】

进出口总额 1999年河北省秦皇岛市进出口总额48377万美元，比1998年的43858万美元增长10.30%

出口总额 出口总额为19201万美元，比1998年的18368万美元增长4.54%，占全市国内生产总值2620730万元（相当于216542万美元）的6.07%，占全省出口额的6.19%。

出口商品结构 出口商品达110种，初级产品出口额11630万美元，占出口总额的60.57%；工业制成品的出口额15759万美元，占出口总额的82.07%。出口额在100万美元以上的商品有23种，金额15739万美元，占出口总额的81.97%，比上年下降30.63%；出口额在500万美元以上的商品有9个，出口金额12062万美元，占出口总额的62.82%，比上年下降27.05%；出口额在1000万美元以上的商品有3种，出口金额8179万美元，占出口总额的42.60%，比上年下降25.47%。其中，铝箔出口金额3941万美元，冻鸡出口金额2741万美元，占出口总额的14.28%；革皮服装出口金额1497万美元，占出口总值的7.80%。

出口商品市场 出口商品销往78个国家和地区。出口前10名的国家有：日本6775万美元，占出口总额35.28%；韩国2630万美元，占出口总额的13.75%；美国2601万美元，占出口总额的13.65%；德国1963万美元，占出口总额的13.55%；香港1681万美元，占出口总额的8.75%；比利时719万美元，占出口总额的3.74%；希腊444万美元，占出口总额的2.31%；沙特399万美元，占出口总额的2.08%；法国366万美元，占出口总额的1.91%；俄罗斯312万美元，占出口总额的1.60%。

进口总额 进口总额 29176 万美元，比 1998 年的 25490 万美元增长 14.46%。

进口商品结构 进口商品有 21 个品种，初级产品进口金额 17895 万美元，占进口总额的 61.33%，工业制成品进口金额 14901 万美元，占进口总额的 51.07%。其中，香蕉进口额 6998 万美元，占进口总额 24.00%；化工原料进口金额 4131 万美元，占进口金额的 14.16%；铝锭进口金额 2872 万美元占进口金额的 9.84%；豆粕 1802 万美元占进口总额的 6.18%；木板及制品 1453 万美元，占进口总额的 4.98%。

进口商品市场 进口商品来自 23 个国家和地区，主要来自亚洲、欧美国家和地区。其中，新加坡进口金额 3520 万美元，占进口金额的 12.06%；菲律宾进口金额 3437 万美元，占进口总额的 11.78%；香港进口金额 2699 万美元，占进口总额的 9.25%；厄瓜多尔进口金额 2408 万美元，占进口总额的 8.25%；日本进口金额 1592 万美元，占进口金额的 5.46%；美国进口金额 1385 万美元，占进口金额的 4.75%；哥伦比亚进口金额 1154 万美元，占进口金额的 3.96%。

技术进出口 技术进出口总额 2451 万美元，比上年的 3804 万美元下降 25.51%。签订引进技术和进口设备项目 12 个，与 1998 年相同，合同金额 555.50 万美元，比 1998 年的 523.73 万美元增长 5.11%。签订技术出口合同项目 4 个，合同金额 8.03 万美元，比 1998 年的 0.76 万美元增长 956.58%。

【利用外资】

利用外资方式 批准外资项目 76 个，投资总额 43124 万美元，比 1998 年的 57836 万美元下降 0.25%，合同利用外资金额 42478 万美元，比 1998 年的 45745 万美元下降 0.07%，外商直接投资 13224 万美元，比 1998 年 19608 万美元下降 0.32%。合资企业 40 个，外资金额 14517.63 万美元，合作企业 4 个，外资金额 2964.36 万美元，外资企业 32 个，外资金额 18942.8 万美元。

外商投资的行业 属于生产型项目 54 个，非生产型项目 22 个。轻工 20 项，建材 3 项，机械 12 项，食品 6 项，房地产 2 项，化工 3 项，服务、电子各 3 项；娱乐 3 项，服装 2 项，能源 4 项，医药 2 项，餐饮 4 项，其他 9 项。

外商直接投资来源 外商投资来自 18 个国家和地区。其中，香港 14 项，合同外资金额 8141.01 万美元；韩国 15 项，合同外资金额 5670.91 万美元；美国 16 项，合同外资金额 8203.36 万美元；日本 6 项，合同外资金额 3738.00 万美元；台湾省 5 项，合同外资金额 1218.86 万美元；英国 3 项，合同外资金额 4952.20 万美元；泰国 3 项，合同外资金额 469.00 万美元；新加坡 2 项，合同外资金额 1195.00 万美元；维尔京 2 项，合同外资金额 247.00 万美元；加拿大 2 项，合同外资金额 59.27 万美元；奥地利、澳门、德国、阿根廷、俄罗斯、马来西亚、新西兰、伊朗各 1 项，合同外资金额 2529.68 万美元。

外商直接投资企业生产经营情况 企业已投产的 243 家外商投资企业，1999 年实现产值 58899.90 万元，销售收入 554623.00 万元，上缴税金 18225.74 万元，创汇 16224 万美元，比 1998 年的 14259 万美元增长 13.87%，占全市出口总额的 84.50%。

【对外经济合作】

承包工程和劳务合作 签订对外承包工程和劳务合作合同额 4641.68 万美元，比 1998 年的 2314.64 万美元增长 100.50%；营业额 557.68 万美元，比 1998 年的 537.24 万美元增长 2.60%；当年派出劳务人员 534 人次，年末在外人数 560 人；主要派往蒙古、日本、俄罗斯、柬埔寨、印度、保加利亚、南非、科威特等 18 个国家和地区。承包工程的主要项目是，市安装公司在科威特承包的市政工程项目，合同额 4000 万美元。

对外投资 1999 年在海外举办非贸易性企业项目 3 个，其中投资 50 万美元的“中南塑钢门窗有限公司”已在南非加工出第一批产品。

【其他】

经济技术开发区 1999 年秦皇岛经济技术开发区投资 11549 万元，用于开发区的基础设施建设，改善投资环境。

1999年，批准利用外资合同35项，合同外资金额16646万美元，实际投入外资10285万美元。其中，食品1项、娱乐服务2项、黑色金属冶炼1项、船舶2项、房地产2项，化工3项，其他社会服务6项，其他制造业20项。

批准内联企业165家，总投资2.4亿元。1999年全年实现工业产值4.6亿元，利税0.67亿元，创汇13144万美元。

对外经贸洽谈会 1999年秦皇岛举办的第十一届“北戴河之夏”对外经济技术合作洽谈会暨商品交易会，出口成交额2578.63万美元，签订利用外资合同57项，总投资32527.50万美元，合同外资26998.00万美元，接待了美国、日本、韩国、香港、台湾、新加坡、意大利、澳门等33个国家和地区的客商290人，接待国内客户465人。签订对外承包工程和劳务合作项目2个，合同额44万美元，可外派劳务100人，签订境外办企业项目2个，总投资78万美元，其中，中方投资42.8万美元。

港口运输 1999年秦皇岛市港口有生产泊位29个，港口吞吐能力12445万吨。全年实际完成货运吞吐总量8261.40万吨，比1998年的7792.2万吨增长0.60%，其中，完成外贸进出口吞吐量2483.9万吨，比1998年的2241.8万吨增长0.11%，出口量完成2085.5万吨，比1998年的1814.3万吨增长0.15%，进口量完成398.3万吨，比1998年的427.5万吨下降0.07%。

旅游 全年接待国内外游客662.17万人次，其中，接待日本、韩国、美国、英国、俄罗斯、新加坡、台湾省、香港、澳门等30个国家和地区的国际游客11.60万人次，比1998年的10.70万人次增长8.44%。其中，港、澳、台同胞和华侨5993人次，比1998年的4001人次增长49.78%，全年旅游收入33.62亿美元，比1998年31.10万美元，增长8.1%。

1999年山西省对外经济贸易

山西省对外贸易经济合作厅

【对外贸易】

进出口总额 1999年山西省进出口总额128739万美元，比1998年增长15.86%。

出口总额 出口总额为83940万美元，比1998年下降6%，占全省国内生产总值1641.4亿元人民币（相当于196.79亿美元）的4.27%，占全国出口总额的0.43%。在全省出口总额中，外商投资企业出口完成8088万美元，占出口总额的9.64%，比上年10617万美元减少23.82%。

出口商品结构 初级产品出口额41764万美元，占出口总额的49.75%；工业制成品出口额42175万美元，占出口总额的50.25%。

出口额在500万美元以上的商品情况表

金额分类	商品名称	出口额（万美元）	占出口总额（%）
1亿美元以上商品2种	焦炭、煤	36557	43.55

出口额在500万美元以上的商品情况表（续）

金额分类	商品名称	出口额（万美元）	占出口总额（%）
1000万美元至1亿美元商品6种	粘土及其他耐火矿物、轮胎、纺织及制品、生铁、钢材、服装	13515	16.10
500万美元至1000万美元商品4种	烟花爆竹、玻璃制品、核桃仁、干豆	3370	4.01
合计	**12种**	**53442**	**63.66**

出口机电产品133种，出口金额10124万美元，占出口总额的12.06%，比1998年8339万美元增长21.41%。

出口商品市场 出口商品销往124个国家和地区。出口额在1000万美元以上的国家和地区20个，出口额70200万美元，占83.63%。

主要出口市场情况表

国别（地区）	出口金额（万美元）	占出口总额（%）
韩国	14488	17.26%
美国	11252	13.40
日本	9798	11.67
荷兰	5723	6.82
印度	3175	3.78
英国	2801	3.34
德国	2775	3.31
比利时	2281	2.72
台湾省	2098	2.50
香港	1997	2.38

主要出口市场情况表（续）

国别（地区）	出口金额（万美元）	占出口总额（%）
意大利	1821	2.17
土耳其	1452	1.73
马来西亚	1438	1.71
菲律宾	1432	1.71
法国	1389	1.65
印度尼西亚	1382	1.65
巴西	1362	1.62
巴基斯坦	1308	1.56
俄罗斯	1209	1.44
澳大利亚	1019	1.21
合计(20个)	**70200**	**83.63**

进口总额 进口总额44799万美元，比上年增长110.31%。

进口商品结构 初级产品进口额6629万美元，占进口总额的14.80%；工业制成品38170万美元，占进口总额的85.20%。

进口额在500万美元以上的商品表

金额分类	商品名称	进口额（万美元）	占进口总额（%）
1000万美元以上商品5种	汽轮机零件、蒸汽及过热水锅炉辅助设备、铁矿砂、氧化铝、医疗器械	24053	53.69

进口额在500万美元以上的商品表（续）

金额分类	商 品 名 称	进口额（万美元）	占进口总额（%）
500－1000万美元商品2种	钢材、变压、整流器及零件	1273	2.84
合 计	**7种**	**25326**	**56.53**

进口商品市场 进口商品来自47个国家和地区。进口额在1000万美元以上的市场7个。

主要进口商品市场情况表

国别（地区）	进口额（万美元）	占进口总额（%）
美 国	16826	37.56
德 国	15812	35.30
澳大利亚	2462	5.50
印 度	1830	4.08
日 本	1339	2.99
意大利	1119	2.49
韩 国	1052	2.35
合计(7个)	**40440**	**90.27**

【技术进出口】

技术进口 技术进口总额为1669.15万美元。签订引进技术和进口设备合同29项，比1998年增加11项；合同金额为1669.15万美元，比上年2333.46万美元减少28.47%。

技术进口国别（地区）及行业 引进技术和设备来自7个国家和地区。主要有：美国13项，合同金额756.82万美元；德国6项，合同金额339.68万美元；意大利3项，合同金额245.48万美元；加拿大2项，合同金额181.98万美元；日本3项，合同金额127.38万美元；澳大利亚1项，合同金额12.10万美元；英国1项，合同金额5.71万美元。

引进技术和设备的主要行业分布为：邮电行业9项，合同金额628.68万美元；煤炭工业7项，合同金额235.55万美元；机械工业5项，合同金额为380.08万美元；水利工程1项，合同金额160万美元；建材工业2项，合同金额153.1万美元；医药行业1项，合同金额15.6万美元；化工行业1项，合同金额47.54万美元；有色工业1项，合同金额28万美元；电子工业1项，合同金额12.1万美元；轻工行业1项，合同金额8.5万美元。引进技术和设备的主要项目有：山西省万家寨引黄工程联接段施工监理咨询服务合同；长治市邮电局引进SDH传输设备；大同矿务局引进水泥混凝土摊铺机、搅拌台；山西省邮电局引进山西280M高速寻呼网；大同市三星力源炭素厂引进粉末成型压力机；晋城矿务局五台辅总公司引进自动压砖机；山西省广灵化工总公司引进镁合金熔化炉；山西临汾地区宏远混凝土制造厂引进海斯RH500VA混凝土砌块生产线；大同市电信局引进2.5Gb/sSDH传输设备；太原市天龙油墨有限公司引进分散机RM266合同；太原理工大学引进HORIZON图书馆自动化系统；大同齿轮集团有限责任公司引进剃刀磨床；山西潞安矿务局引进瓦斯安全监测系统；太原重型机械（集团）有限公司引进TR2000CWC2H－E.S.V型立式数控磨床；太原矿山机器厂引进美国吉丁斯·路易斯公司G60－RT卧式加工生产线；太原市电信局接入163.169服务器及163、169扩容工程配套系统等。

【利用外资】

1999年利用外资情况表

利用外资方式	批准签订的合同			实际利用外资	
	项目数（个）	外资金额（万美元）	金额比1998年（±%）	金额（万美元）	金额比1998年（±%）
对外借款					
外商直接投资	79	23444	-43.15	39129	60.03
合资企业	54	6093		3154	
合作企业	12	9396		25306	
外资企业	13	7955		10669	
外商投资股份制					
外商其他投资	41	4171.32		4171.32	
国际租赁					
补偿贸易					
加工贸易	41	4171.32		4171.32	
对外发行股票					
合　计	**120**	**27615.32**	**-43.26**	**43300.32**	**66.60**

外商直接投资　批准签订利用外资合同120项，比上年增加8项；批准签订合同外资金额27615万美元，比上年减少43.26%；实际利用外资43300万美元，比上年增长66.60%。

外商直接投资来源　外商直接投资来自19个国家和地区。其中美国15项，合同外资金额3476万美元；加拿大4项，金额3773万美元；香港20项，金额3468万美元；台湾省10项，金额3965万美元；日本7项，金额299万美元；维尔京群岛4项，金额2860万美元；澳大利亚1项，金额462万美元；英国2项，金额115万美元等。

外商直接投资的规模和行业　外商直接投资的79个项目中，外商投资额在100万美元以上的项目28项。生产型项目67项，非生产型项目12项。按行业分：农林牧渔业5项，金额2342万美元；工业62项，金额11854万美元；交通运输邮电通信业2项，金额1615万美元；建筑业2项，金额391万美元；商业饮食服务业2项，金额238万美元；房地产开发与经营业1项，金额3244万美元；公用社会服务业2项，金额241万美元；科技研究和综合技术服务业2项，金额463万美元。1999年“三资”企业出口创汇8088万美元，比1998年的10617万美元减少23.82%，占全省出口总额的9.64%。

截至1999年底，山西省已累计审批“三资”企业项目2026个，项目总投资额为65.18亿美元，合同外资额为33.94亿美元，外商投资实际到位额为14.66亿美元。

【对外经济合作】

承包工程和劳务合作　全年签订对外承包工程和劳务合作合同51项，合同金额4678万美元，比上年4063万美元增长15.14%；完成营业额2420万美元，比上年2128万美元增长13.72%；当年派出劳务人员687人次，年末在外人数1353人。劳务人员主要分布在以色列、日本、新加坡、韩国、阿联酋等13个国家和地区。

接受经济援助　澳大利亚援助大同煤气化环保项目500万澳元；加拿大援助左权县、和顺县扶贫项目第一期200万元人民币；联合国人口基金援助沁县妇女参与项目30万美元；日本援助和顺县人民医院项目1000万日元；澳大利亚援助方山县开府乡兽医站5.4万元人民币；德国援助山区林业土地综合开发项目1000万马克等。正在申请中的项目即：日本政府援助山西粮食增产项目3亿日元；德国政府援助山西省垃圾发电清洁示范项目500万马克；日本政府援助山西林业示范苗圃，优化生态环境项目1000万日元。

【其他】

内陆开放地区 山西省太原市1999年进出口总额为103138万美元，比1998年81725.8万美元增长26.2%。

出口商品94种，比1998年增加16种。出口额在100万美元以上的商品10种，金额7054.8万美元，占出口总额的11.29%。

出口商品销往74个国家和地区。出口额在100万美元以上的市场15个，金额16172万美元，占出口总额的25.88%。

外商投资企业进出口总额完成34887.3万美元，比上年增长293.7%，占全市进出口总额的33.8%。1999年新批准成立外商投资企业27家，项目投资总额21313万美元，合同外资金额10150万美元。当年实际利用外资15500万美元；外派劳务305人，同太原市直接进行劳务合作的国家和地区主要有喀麦隆、日本、俄罗斯等。外派劳务人员涉及的行业主要有计算机、机械加工、建筑和医疗卫生等。

港口运输 全省进出口货运量为1805.18万吨，比上年1493.97万吨增长20.8%。其中，出口货运量为1614.38万吨，进口货运量为190.8万吨。按运输方式分：当年出口海运量1610.75万吨、陆运量4.2万吨、空运量0.11万吨。

旅游 全年接待港澳台同胞和国外旅游者13.7785万人次，比上年增长10.4%。其中外国人101081人次，比上年增长16.48%；华侨1942人次，比上年下降11.74%；港澳同胞14639人次，比上年下降2%；台湾同胞19923人次，比上年下降5%。1999年旅游外汇收入4256.83万美元，比上年增长11.25%。

1999年内蒙古自治区对外经济贸易

内蒙古自治区对外贸易经济合作厅

【对外贸易】

进出口总额 1999年内蒙古自治区进出口总额12.94亿美元，比1998年的9.63亿美元增长34.37%。

出口总额 出口总额5.35亿美元，比1998年的5.26亿美元增长1.67%，占全区国内生产总值1271亿元（相当于153.54亿美元）的3.48%；占全国出口额的0.34%。

出口商品结构 初级产品出口额1.78亿美元，占出口总额的33.27%，工业制成品出口额3.57亿美元，占出口总额的66.73%。

出口额在500万美元以上的商品情况表

金额分类	商品名称	出口金额（亿美元）	占出口总额（%）
1000万美元以上	玉米、无毛绒、羊绒毛纱线、羊绒围巾、羊绒衫、金首饰、铝、动力煤、无烟煤	3.27	61.21

出口额在500万美元以上的商品情况表（续）

金额分类	商品名称	出口金额（亿美元）	占出口总额（%）
500－1000万美元	荞麦、蕃茄酱罐头、甜菜粕、涤粘混纺布、钢坯、混合稀土金属、饲料金霉素	0.49	9.14
合　计		**3.76**	**70.35**

出口商品市场　出口商品主要销往俄罗斯、日本、蒙古、香港、韩国、美国、意大利、英国，金额7.71亿美元，占出口总额的85.03%。

进口总额　进口总额7.59亿美元，比1998年的4.37亿美元增长73.68%。

进口商品结构　初级产品进口额3.79亿美元，占进口总额的50%，工业制成品进口额3.79亿美元，占进口总额的50%。

进口额在500万美元以上的商品情况表

金额分类	商品名称	进口金额（亿美元）	占进口总额（%）
1000万美元以上	原木、铝、铜精矿砂、氧化铝、环氧氯丙烷、高压聚乙烯、聚氯乙烯、冶金设备	2.58	33.98
500－1000万美元	未漂白长纤维牛皮浆、丁醇、己内酰胺、低压聚乙烯、复合肥、毛纺织设备、奶制品设备	0.45	5.87
合　计		**3.03**	**39.85**

进口商品市场　进口商品主要来自俄罗斯、蒙古、德国、美国、香港、澳大利亚、日本、英国，金额6.86亿美元，占进口总额的90.36%。

边境贸易　1999年内蒙古自治区边境贸易进出口额6.64亿美元，比1998年的3.91亿美元增长69.82%。其中，出口额3.33亿美元，比1998年的2.62亿美元增长27.05%；进口额3.31亿美元，比1998年的1.29亿美元增长156.36%。主要出口商品有苹果、面粉、冻猪肉、涤棉针织外衣；主要进口商品有绵羊皮、原木、羊绒、铜合金、铝、环氧氯丙烷、高压聚乙烯、聚氯乙烯。

技术进出口　技术进出口总额6468万美元，比1998年的8168万美元下降20.81%。签订引进技术和进口设备合同项目52个，比1998年增加10个，合同金额4945万美元，比1998年的6613万美元下降25.22%；签订技术出口项目22个，比1998年增加7个，合同金额1524万美元，比1998年的1555万美元下降1.99%。

技术进口　技术进口涉及15个国家（地区），其中，德国12项，合同金额1959万美元，电信、印刷、食品和玻璃加工设备；美国6项，合同金额989万美元，通讯、毛纺设备；日本11项，合同金额512万美元，医疗、电子、毛纺、食品加工设备；瑞典3项，合同金额301万美元，食品加工设备；意大利3项，合同金额260万美元，电子、电信、陶瓷生产设备；香港5项，合同金额232万美元，毛纺设备；丹麦1项，合同金额230万美元，食品加工设备；加拿大3项，合同金额215万美元，草场、石油生产设备；澳大利亚2项，合同金额45万美元，草场设备；韩国1项，合同金额22万美元，电子设备；比利时1项，合同金额10万美元，玻璃加工设备；法国1项，合同金额8万美元；西班牙1项，合同金额6万美元，食品加工设备；以色列1项，合同金额2万美元，通讯设备；瑞士1项，合同金额6000美元，食品加工设备。

【利用外资】

1999 年 利 用 外 资 情 况 表

利用外资方式	批准签订的合同			实际利用外资	
	项目数（个）	外资金额（万美元）	金额比 1998 年（%）	金　额（万美元）	金额比 1998 年（%）
外商直接投资	68	19344	3	9450	4
合资企业	28	6735	-36	5334	
合作企业	18	7058	7	2628	
外资企业	22	5551	227	1488	
合　计	**68**	**19344**	**3**	**9540**	**4**

外商直接投资行业　外商直接投资的 68 个项目中，生产型项目 52 个，非生产型项目 16 个。按行业分，主要是制造业、社会服务业、农林牧渔业等 9 个行业。

1999 年利用外商直接投资分行业情况表

行　　业	项目数（个）	合同外资额（万美元）	实际利用外资额（万美元）
农林牧渔业	8	865	99
采掘业	2	164	30
制造业	41	8806	4974
电力煤气水生产	1	3083	3194
交通运输、仓储及邮电通讯业	1	885	
批发零售餐饮业	1	25	
房地产业	1	18	439
社会服务业	12	5442	630
卫生体育社会福利业	1	56	

外商直接投资来源　外商直接投资来自 17 个国家和地区。

1999 年利用外商直接投资分国别和地区情况表

国别（地区）	项目数（个）	合同外资额（万美元）	实际利用外资额（万美元）
香港	18	9343	4737
澳门	2	115	16
台湾省	11	2228	822
泰国	1	821	70

1999年利用外商直接投资分国别和地区情况表（续）

国别（地区）	项目数（个）	合同外资额（万美元）	实际利用外资额（万美元）
马来西亚	1	2416	
新加坡	3	181	203
日本	5	80	404
沙特	1	22	22
韩国	6	70	154
以色列	1	5	
英国	2	68	361
意大利	1	9	
俄罗斯	4	223	
维尔京群岛	1	12	181
美国	7	2370	1823
加拿大	2	847	238
澳大利亚	2	532	126

【对外经济合作】

承包工程和劳务合作　签订对外承包工程和劳务合作合同项目102个，金额5298万美元，比1998年的4540万美元增长16.69%；营业额3173万美元，比1998年的2393万美元增长32.59%；当年派出劳务人数3207人次，年末在外1971人，主要派往俄罗斯、蒙古国和日本；承包工程的主要项目是建筑、电力安装；主要分布在俄罗斯、蒙古国。

对外经济技术援助　承担我国援助蒙古国建筑材料项目，合同额5000万元人民币，1998年5月实施，1999年12月2日完成。

接受经济援助　接受国际经济组织及双边援助项目11个，金额1701万美元。其中当年完成项目5个，金额为1171万美元，为接受援助的地区改善文化教育和医疗条件，改变贫困落后状况，恢复灾后重建等发挥了重要作用。

对外投资　在海外举办企业7家，中方投资金额230万美元，投资国别是蒙古国、俄罗斯、马达加斯加，均取得较好的经济效益。

【其他】

对外经贸洽谈会　1999年5月在大连举办内蒙古自治区招商引资洽谈会，签订外商投资项目11项，协议利用外资金额9277万美元。9月在香港举办了内蒙古招商引资洽谈会，签订外商投资项目36个，协议利用外资金额3.34亿美元。

口岸运输　1999年口岸过货量644万吨，其中，进口货物543万吨，出口货物101万吨。全区外贸运输货运总量252万吨，比上年增长10%，其中，出口量122万吨，进口量130万吨。

涉外旅游　1999年入境的外国以及台港澳同胞37.15万人次，国际旅游外汇收入1.20亿美元，比1998年的1.26亿美元下降4.76%。

1999 年辽宁省对外经济贸易

辽宁省对外贸易经济合作厅

【对外贸易】

进出口总额 1999 年辽宁省进出口总额 137.31 亿美元，比 1998 年的 127.41 亿美元增长 7.77%。

出口总额 出口总额 82.00 亿美元，比 1998 年的 80.52 亿美元增长 1.84%，占全省国内生产总值 4135.5 亿元（相当于 499.56 亿美元）的 16.4%，居全国第七位。

出口商品结构 初级产品出口额 21.45 亿美元，占出口总额的 26.16%，工业制成品的出口额 60.55 亿美元，占出口总额的 73.84%。

出口额在 5000 万美元以上的商品情况表

金额分类	商品名称	出口金额（万美元）	占出口总额（%）
1 亿美元以上 16 种	鱼类、服装、鞋类、钢材、锌、重烧镁、原油、石蜡、船舶、成品油、集装箱、微电机、复印机、零件、电子原器件、家用电器、电视机及音响设备	409678	49.96
5000 万美元－1 亿美元 14 种	粮谷类、豆类、贝类、木材、棉布、化纤布、小五金、金属制品、铸铁制品、电熔镁、塑料、医药原料、医疗器械、计算机	79347	9.68
合　计	**30 种**	**489025**	**59.64**

出口商品市场 出口商品销往 163 个国家和地区。

主要出口市场情况表

国别（地区）	出口金额（万美元）	占出口总额（%）
日　本	338846	41.32
美　国	103365	12.61
韩　国	73508	8.96
新加坡	39702	4.84
香　港	32637	3.98
荷　兰	31949	3.90
德　国	23032	2.81
台湾省	17304	2.11

主要出口市场情况表（续）

国别（地区）	出口金额（万美元）	占出口总额（%）
马来西亚	14377	1.75
朝　鲜	13825	1.69
合　计	**688545**	**83.97**

进口总额 进口总额 55.31 亿美元，比 1998 年的 46.89 亿美元增长 17.96%。

进口商品结构 初级产品进口额 10.05 亿美元，占进口总额的 18.17%；工业制成品进口额 45.26 亿美元，占进口额的 81.83%。

进口额在3000万美元以上的商品情况表

金额分类	商品名称	进口金额（万美元）	占进口总额（%）
1亿美元以上13种	水产品、纺织品、钢材、有色金属、原油、塑料、船舶、各类机械、成套设备、矿砂、电子管、微电子组件、家用电器	329278	59.53
3000万－1亿美元10种	纺织原料、黑色金属、化工原料、航空设备、汽车零件、大豆、饲料、畜产品、纸张、医药原料	58367	10.55
合　计	**23种**	**387645**	**70.08**

进口商品市场　进口商品来自99个国家和地区。

主要进口市场情况表

国别（地区）	进口金额（万美元）	占进口总额（%）
日　本	213306	38.57
韩　国	102297	18.50
美　国	43255	7.82
香　港	31542	5.70
德　国	20604	3.73
沙特阿拉伯	13368	2.42
台湾省	12397	2.24
澳大利亚	10138	1.83
伊拉克	9324	1.69
俄罗斯	7742	1.40
合　计	**464043**	**83.90**

边境贸易　1999年我省与朝鲜的边境小额贸易额为5802万美元，其中出口4343万美元，进口1459万美元，分别比1998年下降32%、34%、22%。出口的主要商品有：大米、玉米、焦炭、服装、成品油、煤炭、面粉等。进口的主要商品有：废钢铁、水海产品、中药材、蚕茧、木材等。

港口运输　1999年我省口岸货物吞吐量累计11662.1万吨，比上年增长14.4%。外贸进出口货运量3716.6万吨，比上年减少2.7%，其中外贸进口1325万吨，比上年增长0.6%，出口2391.6万吨，比上年减少4.5%。外贸进出口按货物运输方式完成情况：海运口岸完成3606.7万吨，陆运口岸完成105.9万吨，空运口岸完成4万吨。

【利用外资】

1999年利用外资情况表

利用外资方式	批准签订的合同			实际利用外资	
	项目（个）	外资金额（亿美元）	金额比1998年（±%）	金额（亿美元）	金额比1998年（±%）
对外借款	44	5.12	－37.3	6.28	
外商直接投资	1738	44.4	1.2	23.1	－3.8
合资企业	1000	23.0	14.4		
合作企业	146	6.4	－33.6		
外资企业	590	14.3	15.6		
外商投资股份制	2	0.7	－59.7		
外商其他投资		1.0	－50.3	1.0	

1999年利用外资情况表（续）

利用外资方式	批准签订的合同			实际利用外资	
	项目（个）	外资金额（亿美元）	金额比1998年（±%）	金额（亿美元）	金额比1998年（±%）
国际租赁		0.8	-44.5	0.8	
补偿贸易		0		0	
加工贸易		0.2		0.2	
对外发行股票		0		0	
合　计	**1782**	**50.52**	**-6.5**	**30.38**	**-3.2**

外商直接投资行业　1999年在外商直接投资的项目中，投资于第一产业的项目合同金额为2.22亿美元，占当年外资总投资额的5%；投资于第二产业的项目合同金额为25.34亿美元，占当年外资总投资额的57%；投资于第三产业的项目合同金额为16.89亿美元，占当年外资总投资额的38%。具体的投资行业主要有：农林牧渔业项目76个，合同额2.24亿美元，实际利用外资额5071万美元；制造业项目1141个，合同额21.72亿美元，实际利用外资额11.66亿美元；建筑业项目65个，合同额1.95亿美元，实际利用外资额3105万美元；交通运输、仓储、邮电通讯业项目10个，合同额7165万美元，实际利用外资额1129万美元；商业及餐饮业项目189个，合同额3.60亿美元，实际利用外资额2.19亿美元；房地产业项目75个，合同额6.12亿美元，实际利用外资额2.85亿美元；社会服务业项目134个，合同额5.33亿美元，实际利用外资额1.39亿美元；科学研究和综合技术服务业项目6个，合同额3245万美元，实际利用外资额500万美元；其他行业项目40个，合同额2.46亿美元，实际利用外资额1.56亿美元。

外商直接投资来源　来自亚洲的投资1999年为21.68亿美元，累计项目达到15025项，累计合同额246.1亿美元。主要国家和地区有，港澳投资额为9.36亿美元，累计项目6132项，累计合同额110.9亿美元；日本投资额为3.63亿美元，累计项目3031项，累计合同额55.5亿美元；韩国投资额为4.92亿美元，累计项目3441项，累计合同额31.4亿美元；台湾省投资额为2.59亿美元，累计项目1800项，累计合同额16.4亿美元；新加坡投资额为0.47亿美元，累计项目数409项，累计合同额8.7亿美元。来自大洋洲的投资2.45亿美元，累计项目310项，累计合同额6.6亿美元。主要国家有，澳大利亚投资2.35亿美元，累计项目275项，累计合同额6.0亿美元，来自欧洲的投资额为5.53亿美元，累计项目870项，累计合同额24.6亿美元。主要国家有，法国投资0.35亿美元，累计项目78项，累计合同额6.7亿美元；英国投资0.48亿美元，累计项目118项，累计合同额4.2亿美元；德国投资0.63亿美元，累计项目122项，累计合同额3.7亿美元；荷兰投资0.69亿美元，累计项目40项，累计合同额2.4亿美元；意大利投资0.88亿美元，累计项目94项，累计合同额2.4亿美元。来自北美洲的投资，美国投资11.32亿美元，累计项目2622项，累计合同额53.1亿美元；加拿大投资1.96亿美元，累计项目352项，累计合同额7.8亿美元。

外商直接投资企业生产经营情况　到1999年底，辽宁省外商投资企业开业投产8037家，产值达925亿元，占全省国内生产总值GDP的22.4%，比上年增长21.2%；完成出口创汇43.61亿美元，占全省地方产品出口的57.8%，比上年增长22.8%；实现税收57.7亿元，占全省各项税收总额的11.4%，比上年增长24.8%。

【对外经济合作】

承包工程和劳务合作　1999年全省签订对外工程与劳务合作合同项目1362项，签订工程承包与劳务合作合同额4.47亿美元，比1998年的5.67亿美元下降21.2%；完成营业额3.56亿美元，比

1998年的4.44亿美元下降19.9%；派出劳务人员3.11万人，增长19%；年末在外3.7万人，增长15.8%。外派劳务的主要国家和地区有日本、韩国、新加坡、香港、俄罗斯。对外工程承包的主要国家和地区有日本、韩国、巴基斯坦、塞舌尔、新加坡、香港、加蓬、俄罗斯、泰国。

对外经济技术援助 承担援外项目19项，援外贷款合同额3.35亿元人民币。这些项目主要分布在非洲的科特迪瓦、南非、尼日尔、塞舌尔、赞比亚、纳米比亚、喀麦隆、莫桑比克、博茨瓦那、多哥，亚洲的越南、老挝、蒙古、哈萨克斯坦，拉美的秘鲁、特立尼达和多巴哥。主要行业是农田水利项目、建筑材料项目、服装项目、冶金项目、食品项目等。

接受经济援助 接受国际无偿援助7项，新增援款1222.4万美元。接受援助的主要捐赠国和国际组织有联合国开发署、世界银行、欧洲委员会、英国和德国政府。援款主要用于基础设施建设、环境保护、国企改造及职业培训。

对外投资 1999年全省在海外举办的非贸易性企业有6家，总投资额为525.91万美元，其中中方投资352.58万美元。主要的投资国家有俄罗斯、泰国、老挝、南非、吉尔吉斯和柬埔寨。

【其他】

经济技术开发区 1999年辽宁省国家级经济技术开发区（大连、沈阳、营口、丹东）新批利用外资项目238项，新批合同外资额12.4亿美元，外商实际投资5.23亿美元，实现工业总产值（现价）467.1亿元，实现税收28.46亿元，财政收入27.85亿元，出口创汇19.44亿美元。

保税区 1999年经国务院批准成立的大连保税区在基础设施建设和业务方面取得了显著进步。当年新批利用外资项目100项，合同外资额2.56亿美元，外商实际投资0.8亿美元，实现工业总产值10.1亿元，税收总额达2.1亿元，财政收入1.15亿元，出口创汇3亿美元。

1999年沈阳市对外经济贸易

沈阳市对外经济贸易委员会

【对外贸易】

进出口总额 1999年辽宁省沈阳市进出口总额为17.90亿美元，比1998年15.87亿美元增长12.8%。

出口总额 出口总额7.73亿美元，比1998年的7.75亿美元下降0.3%，占全市国内生产总值1013.1亿元（相当于122.20亿美元）的6.33%；占全省出口额的5.64%。

出口商品结构 初级产品出口额0.69亿美元，占出口总额的9%；工业制成品的出口额7.04亿美元，占出口总额的91%。

出口额在100万美元以上的商品情况表

金额分类	商品名称	出口金额（万美元）	占出口总额（%）
100－500万美元（16种）	水海产品、煤、家用木制品、地毯、塑料纺织袋、玻璃制品、铝材、金属加工机床、干豆、药材	4608	5.9

出口额在100万美元以上的商品情况表（续）

金额分类	商品名称	出口金额（万美元）	占出口总额（%）
500-1000万美元（1种）	蔬菜	546	0.7
1000万美元以上（9种）	服装、医药品、纺织纱线、蓄电池、鞋类、汽车零件、冻鸡、钢材、塑料制品	31072	40.2
合计	**26种**	**36226**	**46.8**

出口商品市场

主要出口市场情况表

国别（地区）	出口金额（万美元）	占出口总额（%）
韩国	13696	17.7
美国	13135	17.0
日本	12712	16.4
德国	4848	6.3
香港	2515	3.3
朝鲜	2345	3.0
俄罗斯	1717	2.2
台湾省	1564	2.0

主要出口市场情况表（续）

国别（地区）	出口金额（万美元）	占出口总额（%）
加拿大	1181	1.5
意大利	1087	1.4
合计	**54782**	**70.8**

进口总额　进口总额10.17亿美元，比1998年的8.12亿美元增长25.3%。

进口商品结构　初级产品进口额1.29亿美元，占进口总额的12.7%；工业制成品的进口额8.88亿美元，占进口总额的87.3%。

进口额在100万美元以上的商品情况表

金额分类	商品名称	进口金额（万美元）	占进口总额（%）
100-500万美元（19种）	鱼粉、锯材、纸浆、铁矿砂、废铜、成品油、氧化铝、汽车及汽车底盘	4722	4.6
500-1000万美元（10种）	皮革、纺织用合成纤维、纸类、内燃机零件、印刷机械、搬运机零件、橡胶加工机械、电线、电缆、合成纤维长丝织物	7882	7.8
1000万美元以上（14种）	医药品、初级形状塑料、自动数据设备、电子元件、汽车零件、铜矿砂及矿用机械	26388	25.9
合计	**43种**	**38992**	**38.3**

进口商品市场

主要进口市场情况表

国别（地区）	进口金额（万美元）	占进口总额（%）
日　本	26968	26.5
韩　国	18368	18.1
美　国	15553	15.3
德　国	10469	10.3
台湾省	4393	4.3
澳大利亚	2188	2.2
新加坡	1997	1.9
俄罗斯	1706	1.7
英　国	1563	1.5
法　国	1547	1.5
合　计	**84752**	**83.3**

技术进出口　1999年沈阳市技术进出口总额18157万美元，比1998年的16730万美元增长10.9%，其中，进口4219万美元，比1998年5664万美元减少25.5%；出口13938万美元，比1998年的11066万美元增长25.9%。

技术进口　引进技术和设备来自13个国家和地区。其中，从日本引进4G6发动机缸体生产线一条，金额1998万美元，从德国、日本引进的数控铣床，金额300万美元。从德国引进五面体加工中心，金额250万美元。

技术出口　技术出口项目主要有：向香港出口蓄电池，共2676万美元；向韩国出口的电子元器件，共3066万美元；向香港出口的电感元件，共617万美元，向日本出口计算机软件，共300万美元。

【利用外资】

1999年利用外资情况表

利用外资方式	批准签订的合同			实际利用外资	
	项目（个）	外资金额（亿美元）	金额比1998年（±%）	金额（亿美元）	金额比1998年（±%）
对外借款	10	2.56	201	4.54	434
外商直接投资	586	7.69	73	4.98	-26
合资企业	278	3.32	71	3.23	-23
合作企业	27	1.03	43	0.67	-58
外资企业	281	3.34	384	1.08	14
外商其他投资	2	0.38	-44	0.83	-44
国际租赁	2	0.38	-44	0.83	-44
合　计	**598**	**11.08**	**63**	**10.35**	**14**

外商直接投资行业　外商直接投资项目中，生产型项目478个，非生产型项目108个。按行业分：农业17个，制造业407个，商业及餐饮业43个，建筑业32个，房地产业18个，社会服务业61个，其他行业8个。

外商直接投资来源　外商直接投资来源于39个国家和地区。投资额居前10位的是：香港87个，17746万美元；韩国208个，14304万美元；美国90个，10751万美元；澳大利亚19个，8496万美元；意大利5个，7610万美元；台湾省57个，4121万美元；日本36个，3037万美元；英属维尔京群岛9个，2236万美元；加拿大21个，2208万美元；新加坡11个，1933万美元。

外商直接投资企业生产经营情况　截至1999年底，已开业投产的外商企业1796家，全年总产值208亿美元，比1998年的176.8亿美元增长17.6%，出口销售收入40854万美元，比1998年的33013万美元，增长23.8%。

【对外经济合作】

1999年沈阳累计签订对外工程承包和劳务合作合同6671万美元，比1998年的7475万美元下降10.75%；实现营业额6462万美元，比1998年的6249万美元增长3.41%；派出劳务人员6287人次，比1998年的5831人次增长7.87%；年末在外人数为5932人。劳务人员分布在韩国、日本、新加坡、塞舌尔、柬埔寨、俄罗斯、美国等65个国家和地区。主要对外工程承包项目有：塞舌尔的莱蒙斯住宅项目，塞舌尔环岛供水工程项目，喀麦隆市政广场的改造工程项目，布基纳法索多里医院项目，南非饼干厂项目等。

【其他】

经济开发区　1999年沈阳经济技术开发区实现社会总产值150亿元，比1998年的100亿元增长50%。实现利润总额16.15亿元，比1998年的10.77亿美元增长50%。实际利用外资：2.60亿美元，比1998年的2.26亿美元增长15%，占全市利用外资的25%。实现出口创汇：1.91亿美元，比1998年的1.55亿美元增长23.2%，占全市出口的24.7%。

1999年高新技术产业开发区实现社会总产值157亿元，比1998年的121亿元增长30%，实现利税总额15.7亿元，比1998年的7.20亿元增长118%。实际利用外资1.90亿美元，比1998年的1.60亿美元增长18.7%，占全市实际利用外资总额的10.3%。

涉外旅游　1999年沈阳市接待境外旅游者13.8万人次，比1998年增长14%。旅游外汇收入6862万美元，比1998年增长14.2%。

1999年大连市对外经济贸易

大连市对外经济贸易委员会

【对外贸易】

进出口总额　1999年大连市进出口总额69.7亿美元，比1998年的56.7亿美元增长22.94%。

出口总额　出口总额40.6亿美元，比1998年的34.5亿美元增长17.65%，占全市国内生产总值1000亿元（相当于120.9亿美元）的33.6%；占全国出口额的2.08%。

出口商品结构　初级产品出口额8.06亿美元，占出口总额的19.85%；工业制成品的出口额32.54亿美元，占出口总额的80.15%。

出口额在1000万美元以上的商品情况表

商品名称	出口金额（万美元）	占出口总额（%）
服装	47147	11.7
船舶	30872	7.6
电动机及发电机	28353	6.9

出口额在1000万美元以上的商品情况表（续）

商品名称	出口金额（万美元）	占出口总额（%）
自动数据处理设备的零件	20991	5.2
成品油	17752	4.4
录放音、像机及唱机的零附件	16434	4.1
蔬菜	10427	2.6
彩色电视机	9003	2.3
冻鱼、冻鱼片	7797	1.9
集装箱	7616	1.8
运动鞋	7159	1.7
医疗器械	5787	1.4
皮鞋	5421	1.3
合计	**214774**	**52.9**

出口商品市场 出口商品销往148个国家（地区）。

出口市场情况表

国别（地区）	出口金额（万美元）	占出口总额（%）
日本	201067	49.5
美国	44534	10.9
香港	23870	5.8
新加坡	29751	7.3
韩国	30683	7.5
德国	13755	3.3
荷兰	13966	3.4

出口市场情况表（续）

国别（地区）	出口金额（万美元）	占出口总额（%）
马来西亚	9391	2.3
英国	5147	1.2
丹麦	4663	1.1
合计	**376827**	**93**

进口总额 进口总额29.1亿美元，比1998年的22.2亿美元增长31.16%。

进口商品结构 初级产品进口额6.6亿美元，占进口总额的22.68%；工业制成品的进口额22.5亿美元，占进口总额的77.32%。

进口商品情况表

商品名称	进口金额（万美元）	占进口总额（%）
原油	32187	11
钢材	15979	5.4
录放音、像机及唱机的零附件	13771	4.7
自动数据处理设备的零件	8340	2.8
集成电路及微电子组件	7607	2.6
旋转式电力设备的零件	6164	2.1
冻鱼	5811	1.9
合成纤维长丝机织物	5703	1.9
大豆	5582	1.9

进口商品情况表（续）

商品名称	进口金额（万美元）	占进口总额（%）
针织或钩编织物	4725	1.6
合　计	**105869**	**35.9**

进口商品市场　进口商品来自87个国家（地区）。

进口市场情况表

国别（地区）	进口金额（万美元）	占进口总额（%）
日　本	154509	53
韩　国	54007	18.5
美　国	21578	7.4
台湾省	9604	3.3
伊拉克	9324	3.2
德　国	7795	2.6
印尼	4866	1.6
俄罗斯	4737	1.6
澳大利亚	4515	1.5

进口市场情况表（续）

国别（地区）	进口金额（万美元）	占进口总额（%）
新加坡	4005	1.3
合　计	**274940**	**94**

技术进出口　1999年大连市技术进出口总额12.1亿美元，比1998年的7.83亿美元，增长36%（包括高新技术产品出口6.6亿美元，比1998年的3.48亿美元增长48%）。签订的技术引进和设备进口合同项目121个，比1998年减少106项，合同金额1.7亿美元，比1998年的2.04亿美元下降17%。签订技术进出口合同项目163个，比1998年减少110项，合同金额5.5亿美元，比1998年的4.51亿美元增长18%。

【利用外资】

1999年利用外资情况表

利用外资方式	批准签订的合同			实际利用外资	
	项目（个）	外资金额（万美元）	金额比1998年（±%）	金额（万美元）	金额比1998年（±%）
对外借款				10537	-13.8
外商直接投资	621	245761	-2.3	117415	-5.1
合资企业	316	131077	+7.5	74632	+21.3
合作企业	66	22272	-17.1	9439	-47.5
外资企业	239	92412	-10.1	33344	-23.4
外商投资股份制					
外商其他投资	918	1995		3709	-22.3
加工贸易	918	1995		3709	-22.3
合　计	**1539**	**247756**	**-1.5**	**131661**	**-6.5**

外商直接投资行业 外商直接投资项目中生产型项目426项，非生产型项目195个，其中，第一产业26项，第二产业378项，第三产业217项。

外商直接投资来源 1999年共有38个国家或地区投资。

外商直接投资主要来源情况表

国别（地区）	投资项目数（个）	投资金额（亿美元）
美 国	123	8.03
港 澳	103	5.27
日 本	134	2.86
台湾省	48	1.88
韩 国	121	1.76
加拿大	23	1.01
澳大利亚	10	0.84
英 国	8	0.46
荷 兰	5	0.33
俄罗斯	8	0.11
新加坡	7	0.11
意大利	4	0.11

外商直接投资企业生产经营情况 新开业外商投资企业250家，累计开业3850家，产值454亿元，增长24.2%；销售收入464亿元，增长21.1%，利润2.5亿元，增长5.5倍，出口30.2亿美元，增长19.4%。

【对外经济合作】

承包工程和劳务合作 1999年签订对外承包工程和劳务合作合同项目838个，金额21917万美元，比1998年的16472万美元增长33%；营业额15680万美元，比1998年12677万美元增长23.7%；当年派出劳务人员数15100人次，年末在外人数13295人，劳务主要派往日本、新加坡、韩国、台湾省、港澳、以色列等国家和地区；承包工程主要是苏里南、巴勒斯坦等国家和地区。

对外投资 1999年在海外举办企业（系指非贸易性企业）的项目7个，中方投资金额4192万美元。

【其他】

经济技术开发区 新批外商投资企业113家，协议外资金额7.8亿美元。累计批准外商投资企业1310家，其中528家开业投产。当年实现总产值256亿元，出口创汇额15.8亿美元。全区全年国内生产总值140.2亿元，工业总产值285亿元。

保税区 大连保税区全年完成基础设施投资11874万元，实现国内生产总值15.54亿元，税收1.53亿元，进出口总额7.18亿美元。

对外经贸洽谈会 '99中国大连进出口商品交易会于1999年5月23日至28日在大连星海会展中心举行。共设标准摊位500个，来自54个国家和地区的1488名客商到会。国内有24个省市自治区400余家企业参展。交易会共签订进出口贸易合同5.1亿美元，签订利用外资项目30项，合同外资7426万美元。

港口运输 港口泊位72个，港口吞吐能力8505.2万吨、当年实际完成的货物吞吐总量8505.2万吨，其中完成外贸进出口货物吞吐量2411.5万吨，其中出口量1509.3万吨、进口量901.9万吨。1999年本地区外贸运输货运总量比上年增长13.2%。

涉外旅游 共接待海外旅游者26万人次，旅游收入1.8亿美元，比1998年的1.53亿美元增长17.6%。

1999 年吉林省对外经济贸易

吉林省对外贸易经济合作厅

【对外贸易】

进出口总额　1999 年吉林省进出口总额为 221698 万美元，比 1998 年的 165229 万美元增长 34.1%。

出口总额　出口总额为 101956 万美元，比 1998 年的 74847 万美元增长 36.1%。

出口商品结构　工业制成品出口 57704 万美元，占总额的 57%。初级产品出口 44252 万美元，占总额的 43%。

出口贸易结构　一般贸易 69670 万美元，占出口总额的 68%；加工贸易 27303 万美元，占总额的 27%；其他贸易 4983 万美元，占出口总额的 5%。

出口市场结构　亚洲市场占 72%；欧洲市场占 15%；北美洲市场占 9%；非洲市场占 2%；拉丁美洲市场占 0.7%；大洋洲及太平洋岛屿占 0.6%。

出口商品市场　出口商品销往 122 个国家和地区。

主要出口市场情况表

国别（地区）	出口金额（万美元）	占出口总额（%）
日　本	22844	22.40
韩　国	19542	19.16
美　国	8091	7.93
马来西亚	6039	5.92
朝　鲜	5779	5.66
德　国	5756	5.65
印　尼	4964	4.87
香　港	3499	3.43
荷　兰	1810	1.78
台湾省	1526	1.50
泰　国	1433	1.41
俄罗斯	883	0.82
合　计	**82166**	**80.59**

出口额在 500 万美元以上的商品情况表

金额分类	商　品　名　称	出口金额（万美元）	占出口总额（%）
500－1000 万美元（9 种）	水果、食用油籽、药材、锯材、山羊绒、成品油、钢材、铝、电线电缆	6317	6.20
1000 万美元以上（11 种）	冻鸡、大米、玉米、杂豆、家用装饰用木制品、纺织纱线、汽车、家具、服装、塑料制品	55413	54.35
合　计	**20 种**	**61730**	**66.55**

进口总额　进口总额 119742 万美元，比 1998 年的 90382 万美元增长 32.5%。

进口商品结构　工业制成品进口 100574 万美元，占总额的 84%；初级产品 19085 万美元，占总额的 16%。

进口贸易结构　一般贸易 76752 万美元，占总额的64%；加工贸易16309万美元，占总额的13.6%；其他贸易26659万美元，占总额的22.26%。

进口市场结构 亚洲市场占36%；欧洲市场占50%；北美洲市场占8%；非洲市场占1%；拉丁美洲市场占2%；大洋洲及太平洋岛屿占3%。

主要进口市场情况表

国别（地区）	进口金额（万美元）	占进口总额（%）
德　国	46714	39
日　本	21016	17.55
美　国	8435	7.04
韩　国	6995	5.84
俄罗斯	5644	4.71
澳大利亚	3063	2.58
台湾省	2499	2.09
朝　鲜	2062	1.72
墨西哥	1874	1.57
意大利	1251	1.04
合　计	**99553**	**83.14**

进口额在500万美元以上的商品情况表

金额分类	商　品　名　称	进口金额（万美元）	占进口总额（%）
500－1000万美元（9种）	纺织用合成纤维、铝矿砂、肥料、初级形状塑料、废铝、食品加工机械、集成电路、汽车	6498	5.42
1000万美元以上（16种）	原木、纸浆、铬矿砂、氧化铝、钢材、活塞内件、建筑机械、金属加工机床、橡胶或塑料加工机械、焊接机器、电线电缆、汽车零件、医疗仪器、印刷设备、氧化铝、型模	61865	51.67
合　计	**25种**	**68363**	**57.09**

边境贸易 1999年吉林省边境小额贸易进出口总额为16234万美元，比1998年的14106万美元上升31%，其中出口为8095万美元，比1998年增长8%，进口8138万美元，比1998年的5398万美元增长65%。

技术进出口 1999年吉林省共签订技术进出口项目57项，进出口总额13210.3万美元。其中签订引进技术和进口设备合同项目24项，合同金额8095.3万美元；签订技术出口项目23项，合同金额5115万美元。

【利用外资】

1999年利用外资情况表

利用外资方式	批准签订的合同			实际利用外资	
	项目数（个）	外资金额（万美元）	比上年增长（±%）	金　额（万美元）	比上年增长（±%）
合资	142	25397	－6.6	20216	－1.3
合作	26	5709	－17.2	1495	－87.7

1999年利用外资情况表（续）

利用外资方式	批准签订的合同			实际利用外资	
	项目数（个）	外资金额（万美元）	比上年增长（±%）	金额（万美元）	比上年增长（±%）
独资	187	13943	-9.2	8409	1.4
合计	**355**	**45049**	**-9.1**	**30120**	**-26.4**

外商直接投资行业 在1999年的355个外商直接投资项目中，生产型项目323个，非生产型项目32个。主要分布在：农林牧渔水利业20个，工业293个，建筑业10个，商业、饮食、供销仓储业10个，房地产公用服务业5个，其他行业17个。

外商直接投资来源 外商直接投资来自23个国家和地区，主要有韩国195项，香港53项、美国32项、日本18项、台湾省16项，上述项目外资金额38209万美元，占总额的84.8%。

【对外经济合作】

1999年吉林省共签订对外工程承包和劳务合作项目306个，合同金额39283万美元，完成营业额17978万美元。当年外派劳务人员16518人，年末在外劳务人员27340人次。外派劳务人员主要派往朝鲜、俄罗斯、美国塞班、新加坡、日本等。

1999年长春市对外经济贸易

长春市对外贸易经济合作局

【对外贸易】

进出口总额 1999年吉林省长春市进出口总额为123732万美元，比1998年的80966万美元增长52.82%。

出口总额 出口总额41146万美元，比1998年的20973万美元增长96.19%，占全市国内生产总值707亿元人民币（相当于85亿美元）的4.84%，占吉林省出口总额的40.3%。

出口商品结构 初级产品出口额23849万美元，占出口总额的57.96%；工业制成品出口额17297万美元，占出口总额的42.04%。

出口额在1000万美元以上的商品有玉米、鸡块、汽车发动机及零件，出口额24986万美元，占出口总额的60.73%；出口额在500万—1000万美元的商品有保藏鸡肉、接头电缆，出口额为1425万美元，占出口总额的3.46%；出口额在300万—500万美元的商品有冷冻设备及零件、柴油货车、柴油客车、汽车货车、其他硅、家具零件、女式便服装、塑料小雕制品、筷子、套头衫、木制拼花地块，出口额为4197万美元，占出口总额的10.2%。

出口商品市场 出口商品销往世界93个国家和地区。

进口总额 进口总额82586万美元，比1998年59993万美元增长37.66%。

进口商品结构 初级产品进口额4437万美元，占进口总额的5.37%；工业制成品进口额78149万美元，占进口总额的94.63%。

主要出口市场情况表

国别（地区）	出口金额（万美元）	占出口总额（%）
日　本	7435	18.07
韩　国	6716	16.32
马来西亚	4271	10.38
德　国	4250	10.33
印度尼西亚	4109	9.99
美　国	1835	4.46
香　港	1288	3.13
泰　国	1059	2.57
伊　朗	1000	2.43
南　非	980	2.38
合　计	**32943**	**80.06**

进口额在5000万美元以上的商品为其他车辆用零件、金属用注模、独立功能的机器及机械，进口额35901万美元，占进口总额的43.47%；进口额在1000—5000万美元的商品有大豆、手绘设计用纸、车用往复式活塞、点燃式发动机零件、工件夹具、半自动电阻焊接机，进口额为19909万美元，占进口总额的24.11%。

进口商品市场　进口商品来自48个国家（地区）。

技术进出口　1999年吉林省长春市技术进出口总额2835万美元，比1998年1076万美元增长163.48%。其中，签订引进技术和进口设备合同项目3个，比1998年的2个增加1项；合同金额315万美元，比1998年的222万美元增长41.89%。签订技术出口合同项目19个，比1998年的16项增加3项；合同金额2520万美元，比1998年的854万美元增长195.08%。

主要进口市场情况表

国别（地区）	进口金额（万美元）	占进口总额（%）
德　国	43742	52.96
日　本	16218	19.64
美　国	5929	7.18
香　港	2209	2.68
台湾省	1968	2.38
合　计	**70066**	**84.84**

技术进口　技术引进项目包括：澳大利亚1项，食品加工业，金额172万美元；德国1项，汽车制造业，金额128万美元；日本1项，汽车制造业，金额15万美元。

技术出口　技术出口主要项目包括：对香港、韩国、印度出口基因干扰素、乙肝疫苗、水痘疫苗等生物制药产品，金额1779万美元；对香港、韩国出口LCD汽车用显示器，金额527万美元；对韩国、香港、美国、日本出口液晶显示器、光电编码器，金额87万美元；对美国、日本出口观察仪器，金额60万美元。

【利用外资】

1999年利用外资情况表

利用外资方式	批准签订的合同			实际利用外资	
	项目（个）	外资金额（万美元）	金额比1998年（±%）	金额（万美元）	金额比1998年（±%）
外商直接投资	119	16366	－7.64	12627	－4.61
合资企业	66	13084	＋44.38	10575	＋4.9
合作企业	9	1262	－61.33	116	－93.87
外资企业	44	2020	－62.56	1936	＋53.28

外商直接投资行业　在外商直接投资项目中，生产型项目95个，非生产型项目24个。按行业分：工业95个，农林牧渔水利业5个，建筑、工程、房地产业10个，商业服务业9个。

外商直接投资来源　外商直接投资来自10个国家和地区。投资额居前4位的是：香港29项，金额6796万美元；美国15项，金额3527万美元；英属维尔京群岛4项，金额3519万美元；韩国46项，金额1673万美元。

外商投资企业生产经营情况　截至1999年底，已开业投产的外商投资企业共416家，职工总数30167人，全年销售（营业）收入43.7亿元，比1998年的42.3亿元增长3.31%；利税总额2.29亿元，比1998年的2.89亿元减少20.77%。

【对外经济合作】

承包工程和劳务合作　1999年签订对外承包工程和劳务合作项目合同29个，金额3146万美元，比1998年的3767万美元减少16.49%；营业额2714万美元，比1998年的1785万美元增长52.05%；当年派出劳务人员3419人次，年末在外5303人，分别比1998年的1815人次和3111人增长88.38%和70.46%。劳务人员分布在新加坡、韩国、以色列、日本、坦桑尼亚、古巴、尼日利亚、柬埔寨、俄罗斯、罗马尼亚、阿联酋、萨尔瓦多、洪都拉斯等14个国家。

对外投资　1999年在俄罗斯兴办豆制品加工厂1项，中方投资1.6万美元。

【其他】

经济技术开发区　长春经济技术开发区1999年完成固定资产投资24.6亿元，为1998年29.9亿元的82.2%。新批入区企业270户。其中外商投资企业46个，合同外资金额16558万美元，实际利用外资8200万美元。截至1999年底，累计兴办外商投资企业313家，其中106家已投产开业。全区全年实现社会总产值205.26亿元，比1998年的147.37亿元增长39.28%；出口创汇7000万美元；利税30.8亿元，比1998年的23.65亿元增长30.23%。

长春高新技术产业开发区　长春高新技术产业开发区1999年完成固定资产投资总额11.8亿元，比1998年的6.9亿元增长71.02%。新批入区企业334个，其中外商投资企业26个，合同外资金额15426万美元，实际利用外资7370万美元。截至1999年底，累计兴办外商投资企业263家，其中84家已投产开业。全区全年实现科工贸总收入161.6亿元，比1998年的130亿元增长24.31%；出口创汇3251万美元；利税28.8亿元，比1998年的21.8亿元增长32.11%。

涉外旅游　1999年长春市接待海外旅游者44887人次，比1998年的34323人次增长30.78%；旅游外汇收入1992万美元，比1998年的1527万美元增长30.45%。

1999年黑龙江省对外经济贸易

黑龙江省对外贸易经济合作厅

【对外贸易】

进出口总额　1999年黑龙江省进出口总额21.9亿美元，比1998年的20.1亿美元增长8.9%。

出口总额　出口总额9.5亿美元，比1998年的9.1亿美元增长4.8%，占全省（市）国内生产总值2897.4亿元（相当于349.51亿美元）的2.72%；占全国出口额的0.49%。

出口商品结构 初级产品出口额2.88亿美元，占出口总额的30.35%；工业制成品的出口额6.62亿美元，占出口总额的69.65%。

出口额在1000万美元以上的商品情况表

金额分类	商品名称	出口金额（万美元）	占出口总额（%）
1000－5000万美元（9种）	大豆、计算机零件、装饰用木制品、玉米、铝材、鲜蔬菜、石蜡、烤烟、锯材	19351	20.36
5000万美元以上（5种）	鞋、大米、服装、录放映（像）机零件、亚麻织物	32430	34.13
合　计	**14种**	**51781**	**54.49**

出口商品市场 出口商品销往136个国家和地区。

主要出口市场情况表

国别（地区）	出口金额（万美元）	占出口总额（%）
俄罗斯	23197	24.41
日　本	17148	18.05
韩　国	10991	11.57
香　港	6830	7.18
美　国	6399	6.73
菲律宾	3061	3.22
德　国	2577	2.71
泰　国	2165	2.28

主要出口市场情况表（续）

国别（地区）	出口金额（万美元）	占出口总额（%）
荷　兰	1514	1.59
印度尼西亚	1475	1.55
合　计	**75357**	**79.29**

进口总额 进口总额12.4亿美元，比1998年的11.06亿美元增长12.2%。

进口商品结构 初级产品进口额4.53亿美元，占进口总额的36.55%；工业制成品的进口额7.87亿美元，占进口总额的63.45%。

进口额在1000万美元以上的商品情况表

金额分类	商品名称	进口金额（万美元）	占进口总额（%）
1000－5000万美元（16种）	计算机设备、废钢、牛皮纸、成品油、钢材、对苯二甲酸、计量检测分析仪器、废铝、化肥、模型金属铸造箱、抗菌素、纺织机械、合成橡胶、大豆、建筑采矿设备、原油	38996	31.42
5000万美元以上（5种）	纸浆、原木、塑料、计算机零件、己内酰胺	45952	37.03
合　计	**21种**	**84948**	**68.45**

进口商品市场

主要进口市场情况表

国别（地区）	进口金额（万美元）	占进口总额（%）
俄罗斯	68472	55.17
韩　国	13231	10.66
日　本	9359	7.54
美　国	8238	6.64
香　港	4810	3.88
德　国	4387	3.53
意大利	3524	2.84
法　国	2377	1.92
泰　国	1213	0.98
台湾省	1138	0.92
合　计	**116749**	**94.08**

边境贸易　1999年边境贸易进出口总额7.71亿美元，比1998年的6.07亿美元增长27.15%。其中出口1.2亿美元，比1998年的1.25亿美元下降3.6%。主要出口商品有大米、鲜蔬菜、冻猪肉、鲜苹果等。进口6.51亿美元，比1998年4.82亿美元增长35.1%。进口的主要商品有纸浆、原木、己内酰胺、废钢等。

技术进出口　1999年黑龙江省技术进出口总额27384万美元，比1998年的23657万美元增长15.75%。其中，签订引进技术和进口设备合同项目30个，比1998年减少23个，合同金额1818万美元，比1998年的1469美元增长23.82%。

技术进口　引进项目和设备来自14个国家和地区。主要有：意大利3项，合同金额946万美元，涉及汽车制造行业；韩国2项，合同金额333万美元，涉及造纸、汽车制造行业；德国3项，合同金额244万美元，涉及电站设备、汽车行业等。

【利用外资】

1999年利用外资情况表

利用外资方式	批准签订的合同			实际利用外资	
	项目（个）	外资金额（万美元）	金额比1998年（±%）	金额（万美元）	金额比1998年（±%）
对外借款	18	29414	-13.5	29414	86.4
外商直接投资	313	93237	16.4	81895	5.0
合资企业	167	39492	-30.4	36231	-37.7
合作企业	17	9432	20.70	2922	-41.3
外资企业	129	12713	15.0	11142	7.7
外商投资股份制					
其他		31600		31600	
合　计	**331**	**122651**	**3.31**	**111309**	**13.43**

外商直接投资行业　外商直接投资的313个项目中，生产型项目247项，非生产型项目66项。按行业分，农林牧渔业12项，合同外资额1068万美元；制造业227项，合同外资额78456万美元；建筑业8项，8133万美元；地质水利1项，合同外资额100万美元；交通邮电2项，合同外资额191万美元；零售餐饮23项，合同外资额771万美元；房地产5项，合同外资额1158万美元；社会服务25项，合同外资额2463万美元；科研技术6项，合同外资额737万美元；其他4项，合同外资额165万美元。

外商直接投资来源　外商直接投资来自27

个国家和地区。主要国家和地区是：香港75项，合同外资额75787万美元；日本37项，合同外资额3448万美元；韩国72项，合同外资额3120万美元；美国31项，合同外资额3025万美元；维尔京群岛2项，合同外资额2245万美元；台湾省26项，合同外资额1527万美元；荷兰1项，合同外资额1175万美元。

外商直接投资企业生产经营情况 外商直接投资企业1999年实现产值295亿元，占全省GDP的10.1%。涉外企业税收10.6亿元，占全省地方财政收入的6.6%。

【对外经济合作】

承包工程和劳务合作 1999年签订对外承包工程和劳务合作合同项目206个，合同金额33566万美元，比1998年的15464万美元增长117.1%。营业额20099万美元，比1998年的14468万美元增长38.7%；当年派出劳务人员9892人次；年末在外8678人。派往的主要国家和地区是：俄罗斯、韩国、蒙古、新加坡、老挝、孟加拉、日本、菲律宾等。主要承包工程项目有：承建蒙古公路维修项目、巴基斯坦540MW燃气联合循环电厂工程、伊朗水电站工程15台设备供货项目、越南协福燃煤电厂工程、菲律宾87号变电站工程等。

对外经济技术援助 承担援外项目1项，在建项目是：承担我国援建孟加拉国第五座桥梁工程。

接受经济援助 接受国际经济组织及双边援助项目10项，合同外资金额737万美元。

对外投资 1999年新批境外投资项目（非贸易性企业）10项，总投资额4670万美元，其中，中方投资金额3344万美元。主要投资国别和地区是：蒙古、俄罗斯、博茨瓦纳、坦桑尼亚、菲律宾、加拿大、德国等。

【其他】

对外经贸洽谈会 1999年6月15日至21日，第10届中国哈尔滨经济贸易洽谈会在哈尔滨召开。设有1000个展位，其中境外展位100个。有51个国家和地区的6200多名客商与会，共展出20大类2万个品种，成交额30.70亿美元。

口岸运输 1999年全省口岸货运量328.5万吨，比1998年增长37.6%。其中，铁路运输209万吨，比1998年增长30.2%；船舶运输42.2万吨，比1998增长31.9%；汽车运输77.2万吨，比1998年增长67.5%；航空运输711吨，比1998年增长38.5%。

涉外旅游 1999年入境外国人36.1万人次，台港澳同胞46353人次，旅游收入1.5亿美元，比1998年的1.23亿美元增长22.3%。

1999年哈尔滨市对外经济贸易

哈尔滨市对外贸易经济合作局

【对外贸易】

进出口总额 1999年黑龙江省哈尔滨市进出口总额为89394万美元，比1999年的87500万美元增长2.16%。

出口总额 出口总额42022万美元，比1998年的41605万美元增长1%，占全市国内生产总值883.3亿元（相当于106.7亿美元）的3.94%。

出口商品结构 初级产品出口额2951万美元，占出口总额的7.02%；工业制成品出口额39071万美元，占出口总额的92.98%。

出口额在1000万美元以上商品情况表

金额分类	商品名称	出口金额（万美元）	占出口总额（%）
1亿美元以上（1种）	计算机附属设备	17203	40.94
1000万至1亿美元（6种）	亚麻细布、棉麻混纺布、棉服装、铝材、电力成套设备、日用杂品	10239	24.37
合　计	**7种**	**27442**	**65.31**

出口商品市场　出口商品销往91个国家和地区。

主要出口市场情况表

国别（地区）	出口金额（万美元）	占出口总额（%）
韩　国	11409	27.15
日　本	5372	12.78
香　港	5094	12.12
美　国	3369	8.02
德　国	1836	4.37

主要出口市场情况表（续）

国别（地区）	出口金额（万美元）	占出口总额（%）
巴基斯坦	1644	3.91
越　南	361	0.86
南　非	293	0.7
合　计	**29378**	**69.91**

进口总额　进口总额47372万美元，比1998年的45941万美元增长3.11%。

进口额在1000万美元以上商品情况表

金额分类	商品名称	进口金额（万美元）	占进口总额（%）
5000万美元以上（3种）	电讯设备及器材、化工原料、成套设备	26323	55.57
1000万－5000万美元（8种）	钢材，其它油品，塑料原料，化肥农药，橡胶及制品，医药原料，汽车、电车、摩托车零件，各类机械	13848	29.23
合　计	**11种**	**40171**	**84.8**

进口商品市场　进口商品市场主要来自29个国家和地区。

主要进口市场情况表

国别（地区）	进口金额（万美元）	占进口总额（%）
俄罗斯联邦	19444	41.05

主要进口市场情况表（续）

国别（地区）	进口金额（万美元）	占进口总额（%）
韩　国	13589	28.69
德　国	2962	6.25
美　国	2942	6.21
香　港	2201	4.65

主要进口市场情况表（续）

国别（地区）	进口金额（万美元）	占进口总额（%）
意大利	2080	4.39

主要进口市场情况表（续）

国别（地区）	进口金额（万美元）	占进口总额（%）
日　本	2003	4.23
合　计	**43141**	**95.47**

【利用外资】

1999年利用外资情况表

利用外资方式	批准签订的合同			实际利用外资	
	项目数（个）	外资金额（万美元）	金额比1998年（±%）	金　额（万美元）	金额比1998年（±%）
对外借款					
外商直接投资	144	18548	+103.69	15095	+0.63
合资企业	65	5026	+37.89	8212	-20.7
合作企业	10	8349	+183.11	795	+35.4
外资企业	69	5173	+105.93	6088	+78
合　计	**144**	**18548**	**103.69**	**15095**	**0.63**

外商直接投资行业　外商直接投资项目中生产型项目109个，其中各类加工制造工业104个，农业5个；非生产型项目35个，其中餐饮业14个、社会服务业10个、科学研究和技术服务5个、建筑业4个、房地产业2个。

外商直接投资主要来源　韩国37家，金额3552万美元；香港35家，金额3333万美元；美国13家，金额2264万美元；台湾省9家，金额1767万美元；日本16家，金额1699万美元；加拿大5家，金额1107万美元；澳大利亚5家，金额412万美元；澳门1家，金额401万美元；俄罗斯4家，金额384万美元。

外商直接投资企业生产经营情况　外商投资开业34户，出口创汇19010万美元。

【对外经济合作】

承包工程和劳务合作　签订对外承包工程和劳务合作合同项目4个，金额13200万美元，比1998年的14300万美元减少7.69%；营业额11400万美元，比1998年的8864万美元增长28.61%；当年派出劳务人员1832人，主要派往俄罗斯、韩国、日本、美国等国家；主要对外承包工程项目有孟加拉3000MW燃油发电机组交钥匙工程、巴基斯坦古杜电厂大修技术指导合同、巴基斯坦贾姆肖罗电站大修工程。

对外投资　在海外举办非贸易性企业6个，中方投资金额275万美元，投资国别为俄罗斯。

【其他】

经济技术开发区　经济技术开发区继续保持稳定增长的态势，各项主要经济指标持续增长。全年实现工业总产值58亿元，比上年增长20.83%；税收4.8亿元，比上年增长23%，财政收入5.2亿元，比上年增长23%，约占全市10.4%；全年筹措建设资金2.4亿元，比上年增长92%；新开工面积56.2万平方米，竣工面积26万平方米。出口创汇 842 万美元，比上年增长 24%，新增劳动就业人数 1800 人。

招商引资取得重大进展。1999 年开发区新批三资企业 24 家，协议外资额 7473 万美元，比上年增长 15.5%；外资实际到位金额 5200 万美元，比上年增长 15.6%；新批内联企业 159 家，总注册资本 6.2 亿元。

对俄出口加工园区稳步发展。进一步发挥对俄经贸合作的区位优势，不断加强对俄出口加工园区的宣传招商力度，努力完善金融、会计、审计等服务保障体系，基本形成从哈尔滨内陆港（验关）及绥纷河公路到海参崴（保税库）至海参崴中国城的对俄出口大通道。目前，在对俄出口加工园区内，初步形成了以伊达药业、华泰药业、大洋药业、红太阳药业为代表的制药产业。

对外经贸洽谈会 1999 年 6 月 15 日至 21 日，第十届中国哈尔滨经济贸易洽谈会在哈尔滨举行。我市交易团为大会邀请到会经贸和政府团组外宾 1525 人，签定对外经济技术合作合同 11.63 亿美元，比上届增长 18.67%，其中：进出口贸易合同金额 4.01 亿美元，比上届增长 6.93%，出口成交 2.14 亿美元，进口成交 1.87 亿美元；签订利用外资项目 64 项，利用外资合同总额 3.57 亿美元，比上届增长 0.56%，引进外资额 2.7 亿美元，比上届增长 39.9%；签订对外工程承包和劳务输出项目 7 项，合同金额 3.25 亿美元，比上届增长 79.56%，合同外派劳务人数 4200 人。是上届哈洽会的 15.7 倍。签订国内横向经济联合项目 203 项，合同金额为 6.54 亿元人民币，折合 7876 万美元。引进资金 4.21 亿元人民币，折合 5076 万美元，分别比上年增长 18.5% 和 87.9%。

港口运输 水、陆、空口岸外贸货运量完成 31074 吨（其中水运完成 89 吨，空运完成 711 吨，铁路货运完成 30274 吨、2485 标箱），同比增加 112.2%。其中出口 16385 吨（空运完成 229.3 吨，铁路货运完成 16067.6 吨、1296 标箱，水运完成 89 吨），进口 14688.1 吨（空运完成 481.7 吨，铁路货运完成 14206.4 吨、1189 标箱）

涉外旅游 1999 年人境人数为 14.46 万人，比上年增长 9%。其中，外国人 10.03 万人次，增长 9%；华侨、港澳台同胞 4.43 万人次，增长 9%。旅游外汇收入 4442 万美元，比上年增长 10%。

1999 年上海市对外经济贸易

上海市对外经济贸易委员会

【对外贸易】

进出口总额 1999 年上海市进出口总额为 386.04 亿美元，比 1998 年的 313.44 亿美元增长 23.16%。

出口总额 出口总额 187.85 亿美元，比 1998 年的 159.56 亿美元增长 17.7%，占全市国内生产总值 4034.96 亿元（相当于 488.14 亿美元）的 38.48%，占全国出口总额的 9.64%，居全国第二位。

出口商品结构 初级产品出口额 7.63 亿美元，占出口总额的 4.06%；工业制成品的出口额 180.22 亿美元，占出口总额的 95.93%。

出口额在5000万美元以上商品情况表

金额分类	商品名称	出口金额（亿美元）	占出口总额（%）
5000万－10000万美元47种	电池、家具及零件、石油制品、滚动轴承、紧固件、纺织面料鞋、皮鞋、羊毛衫、复印机、显示器、激光唱机、扫描仪等	34.38	18.51
10000万美元以上33种	集成电路及微电子组件、集装箱、空调、船舶、半导体器件、打印机、长西裤、汽车零部件、照相机、小家电等	65.90	35.08
合计	**80种**	**100.68**	**53.60**

出口商品市场 出口商品销往206个国家和地区。

主要出口市场情况表

国别（地区）	出口金额（亿美元）	占出口总额（%）
日本	45.86	24.41
美国	43.48	23.15
香港	16.08	8.56
德国	7.54	4.01
韩国	6.35	3.38
新加坡	4.91	2.61
英国	4.33	2.31
菲律宾	4.31	2.29

主要出口市场情况表（续）

国别（地区）	出口金额（亿美元）	占出口总额（%）
荷兰	4.15	2.21
台湾省	3.75	1.20
合计	**140.76**	**74.93**

进口总额 进口总额198.19亿美元，比1998年的153.88亿美元增长28.8%。

进口商品结构 初级产品进口额24.89亿美元，占进口总额的12.56%；工业制成品进口额173.3亿美元，占进口总额的87.44%。

进口额在5000万美元以上的商品情况表

金额分类	商品名称	进口金额（亿美元）	占进口总额（%）
5000万－10000万美元20种	生橡胶、原油、天然气、皮革制品、橡胶制品、压缩机、制冷机、载客电梯、激光打印机、硬盘驱动器等	13.48	6.8
10000万美元以上21种	软木及木材、纸浆及废纸、纺织纤维、金属矿砂、燃料油、对苯二甲酸、医药品、钢铁、电解铜、电力机械等	86.72	43.76
合计	**41种**	**100.2**	**50.56**

进口商品市场 进口商品来自197个国家和地区。

主要进口市场情况表

国别（地区）	进口金额（亿美元）	占进口总额（%）
日　本	47.09	23.76
美　国	31.21	15.75
德　国	20.45	10.32
韩　国	14.16	7.14
台湾省	10.91	6.51
香　港	9.73	4.81
法　国	8.19	4.13
新加坡	5.97	3.01
澳大利亚	5.55	2.80
巴　西	2.74	1.38
合　计	**158.0**	**79.72**

技术进出口 1999年上海市技术进出口总额28.86亿美元，比1998年的18.36亿美元增长57.19%。签订引进技术和进口设备合同项目1634个，比1998年的940个增长74%；合同金额17.99亿美元，比1998年的10.03亿美元增长79%。签订技术出口合同项目443个，比1998年的316个增长40.19%；合同金额10.87亿美元，比1998年的8.33亿美元增长30.5%。

技术进口 引进技术和设备来自29个国家和地区。主要有：美国468项，56550万美元；日本293项，36181万美元；德国195项，32001万美元；法国58项，25073万美元；香港250项，6866万美元；荷兰27项，5403万美元；英国41项，3240万美元；新加坡51项，2501万美元；瑞士23项，2133万美元；意大利25项，2052万美元；西班牙17项，958万美元；奥地利21项，686万美元。

引进技术和设备的主要行业分布是：机电工业199项，30575万美元；仪表电子工业146项，21450万美元；轻工业109项，12308万美元；冶金工业30项，9115万美元；建筑业83项，5925万美元；医药工业50项，3437万美元；石化工业8项，679万美元。

技术出口 签订技术出口主要有美国、日本、德国、香港、新加坡、法国、荷兰、泰国、澳大利亚、瑞士、朝鲜、伊拉克、台湾省、马来西亚、奥地利等35个国家和地区。签订技术出口的主要项目有：向美国等出口计算机硬件和软件，金额3500多万美元；向美国出口集装箱门吊，金额3160万美元；向美国、巴西出口港机设备；向泰国出口污水处理系统、向非洲地区出口运输设备、电站设备等。

【利用外资】

1999年利用外资情况表

利用外资方式	批准签订的合同			实际利用外资	
	项目数（个）	外资金额（万美元）	金额比1998年（±%）	金　额（万美元）	金额比1998年（±%）
对外借款	556	352400	37.23	295000	150.42
外商直接投资	1472	410375	-29.82	304772	-16.2
合资企业	399	151056	-40.27	151747	2.1
合作企业	255	48397	-33.81	34852	-27.5
外资企业	817	192888	29.01	113205	-11.1
股份制企业	1	18034	-83.49	4968	-87.5
合　计	**2028**	**762775**	**-9.36**	**334272**	**-30.59**

外商直接投资行业 在外商直接投资的项目中，生产型项目913个，非生产型项目559个。按行业分，农林牧渔水利业15个，工业834个，建筑业7个，交通运输邮电通讯72个，商业饮食物资供销54个，房地产、公用事业254个，卫生体育社会福利3个，教育文艺广播电视4个，科学研究技术服务5个，其他行业224个。

外商直接投资来源 外商直接投资来自85个国家和地区。投资额居前10位的是：香港347个，10.72亿美元；美国228个，8.78亿美元；英属维尔京86个，3.26亿美元；德国37个，2.88亿美元；新加坡78个，2.44亿美元；荷兰10个，2.44亿美元；日本144个，2.35亿美元；台湾省220个，1.92亿美元；澳大利亚78个，1.11亿美元；法国14个，0.79亿美元。

外商直接投资企业生产经营情况 截止1999年底，已开业投产的外商投资企业共15000多家，1999年上海外商投资企业销售收入2991.02亿元，同比增长7.3%；同期实现利润103.03亿元，同比增加45.4%；缴纳税金136.6亿元，同比增加13%；外贸出口103.47亿美元，同比增长26.73%。

【对外经济合作】

承包工程和劳务合作 1999年上海签订对外承包工程和劳务合作合同项目1068个，合同金额94908万美元，比1998年的71062万美元增长33.5%；完成营业额60362万美元，比1998年的55728万美元增长8.3%；当年派出劳务人员8528人次，比1998年的8132人增长4.8%，年末在外人数27458人，比1998年增长13.8%。劳务人员主要分布在日本、塞班岛、新加坡、港澳地区和毛里求斯等国家和地区。主要对外承包工程项目有孟加拉国国际会议中心、孟加拉国程控交换电话线及泰国污水处理工程等项目。

对外经济技术援助 承担援外项目10个，主要是援助项目及无偿援助物资，总金额2.63亿人民币，受援国是孟加拉国、也门、苏丹、摩洛哥、马里等国。

对外投资 1999年上海共举办海外非贸易型项目12个，总投资5280万美元，其中中方投资3490万美元。这些企业主要分布在南非、纳米比亚、洪都拉斯、斯里兰卡、柬埔寨、摩洛哥、美国等国家和地区。

【其他】

经济技术开发区 1999年浦东新区经济持续健康发展，国内生产总值达800亿元，比上年增长16.1%；全年完成工业总产值1451亿元，比上年增长17.3%；其中工业高新技术产值增长29%，占工业总产值的25%；外贸出口总值66.67亿美元，增长26.4%；签订外商直接投资项目470项，吸引外资合同金额10.73亿美元，其中引进1000万美元以上的大项目29个；社会消费品零售总额198.38亿元，比上年增长10.9%。

浦东新区功能开发取得新进展，张江高科技园区1平方公里技术创新区建设已全面展开，同步光源等重大项目基本选定，累计已引进15家研发机构及包括国际著名跨国集团、大公司、国内大企业的50多个项目；金桥加工贸易区高新技术企业产值比重达68.3%。同时，浦东新区的重点工程进展顺利，浦东国际机场一期、外高桥港区二期、地铁二号线、合流污水二期、国际会议中心、世纪大道、中央公园等一大批重大项目已顺利竣工或基本完成。

漕河泾新兴技术开发区 经过12年的开发建设，累计有各类企业700多家，其中科技开发型企业300多家，高科技生产项目和研究开发机构达254家，投资来自20多个国家和地区，项目总投资14亿美元，外商投资额为9.3亿美元。世界排名前500位的国际跨国公司已有28家在区内设立了35个项目，投资额达5亿美元。1999年，新批准外商投资企业20家，外商投资金额2073万美元；实现销售收入150亿元，比上年增长19%；利税16亿元，比上年增长14%；出口总值6.9亿美元，比上年增长11%。该开发区在土地利用率、通用厂房租售率、单位面积土地产出率和人均经济效益等均居全国开发区前茅。

闵行经济技术开发区 总面积为3.5平方公里，创建15年已建成一个外向型、集约化、综合性的现代化工业园区。到1999年底，累计引进外资项目145个，吸收外资19.62亿美元，其中，1000万美元以上项目有20个，全球500强企业有28家在区内落户，有60%以上的企业增资100多次，金额达11.5亿美元，美国强生从初创时的700万美元增加到2.3亿美元。1999年，完成销售收入160.5亿元，利润15.89亿元，实缴税收14.5亿元，外汇收入5.9亿美元，劳动生产率达55万元。据1999年底统计，该区每平方公里工业用地投资额7.85亿美元，销售额超过64亿元。按单位面积计，各项经济指标在全国开发区名列前茅。

虹桥经济技术开发区 是以外贸中心为主要特征，集展览展示、办公、居住、购物、餐饮娱乐为一体的多功能外向型商贸区。开发15年来已累计引进投资项目102个，建造了世界贸易商城、国际贸易中心、国际展览中心和7幢办公楼、7幢商住楼、4幢宾馆等20多幢高层建筑。有1000多家中外商社和贸易机构进驻区内。1999年，举办了50多个大型国际国内商品展览。实现销售收入42.38亿元，其中，外商投资企业40.42亿元。

保税区 上海外高桥保税区进一步扩大开放，规范管理和优化投资环境，积极推动开发建设的进程，1999年保税区各项综合经济指标持续稳定增长，全年完成国内生产总值63.2亿元，比1998年增长24.2%；实现销售（经营）收入468.3亿元，增长29.9%；完成工业总产值96.8亿元，增长41.8%；全区完成进出口总额29.61亿美元，增长7%，其中出口10.46亿美元，增长45.3%。外高桥保税区日益受到国内外众多船公司的关注，1999年港口吞吐量579.9万吨，增长21.8%；集装箱装卸量67.5万标准箱，增长37.5%；外贸吞吐量451.4万吨，年增长34.2%。保税仓储企业货物存储充沛，月均储存量达30万吨，同比增长43.7%；年货运量98.4万吨，增长16.7%。全年批准项目461个，吸引合同外资4.53亿美元，其中外商当年增资1.5亿美元。累计到1999年底，已有109家企业投入生产，比1998年增长22.5%；有11家企业年产值超亿元，12家高科技企业全年完成工业产值73.1亿元，比上年增长33.9%，占工业总产值的76.1%。

对外经贸洽谈会 1999年3月5日～3月11日由上海、江苏、浙江、安徽、福建、江西、山东、南京、宁波9省市共同主办，在上海举办了第九届中国华东进出口商品交易会，外商来自130多个国家和地区6108人，成交金额12.06亿美元。本届华交会更名为“中国华东进出口商品交易会”，增加了进口功能，首次设立了境外馆，来自13个国家和地区的61个参展企业共租用78个摊位。

1999年12月13日～17日在上海举办了第一届国际工业博览会，参展企业400多家，参观人次达22.5万。本届工博会设立了产权交易馆和技术交易馆，突破单一的产品交易模式，通过“因特网”工博会开设“在线工博会”，接受3.6万人次的访问。在工博会上，产品、技术和产权三大类总成交25亿人民币，达成成交意向超20亿人民币。第一届上海国际工业博览会被评为1999年度上海市十大新闻之一。

分别在日本、泰国、土耳其和科特迪瓦举办对外经贸洽谈会，共有73家外贸企业参展，累计成交金额4500万美元。

港口运输 1999年，上海港口泊位数317个，港口吞吐能力1.64亿吨。当年实际完成货物吞吐总量1.86亿吨，比1998年的1.64亿吨增长11.8%。其中，完成外贸进出口货物吞吐量6285万吨（出口量2386万吨，进口量3899万吨）。全年本地区外贸运输货运总量为4738.9万吨，比1998年的3756.9万吨增长20.7%。其中，出口货运量2089万吨，进口货运量2649.9万吨；按运输方式分：当年海运量4696.4万吨，空运量34.5万吨，陆运量8万吨。全年国际集装箱吞吐量为421.6万个国际标准箱，比1998年的306.6万个增长27.27%。

涉外旅游 全年共接待世界各地旅游者165.68万人次，比1998年的152.7万人次增长8.5%，其中，外国人128.73万人次，港澳台同胞32.31万人次。国际旅游外汇收入13.64亿美元，比1998年的12.18增长12%。

1999年江苏省对外经济贸易

江苏省对外经济贸易委员会

【对外贸易】

进出口总额 1999年江苏省进出口总额为3126400万美元，比1998年的2642600万美元增长18.30%。

出口总额 出口总额为1831000万美元，比上年的1565100万美元增长16.90%，占全省国内生产总值77006000万元的33.7%，占全国出口总额的9.4%，居全国第三位。

出口商品结构 高技术含量、高附加值产品出口33.66亿美元，比上年增长20.2%；机电产品出口76.9亿美元，占全省出口总值的42%，同比增长24%；有9种机电产品出口超亿美元。

主要出口商品是梭织服装、计算机、电子元器件、针织服装、化纤布、棉布、玩具、鞋类、家用小电器、棉制品、电视机及音响设备、集装箱及零备件、塑料制品、各类船、手工具、小五金、电动工具、毛纱线、有线通讯设备、化纤制品、金属制品、化纤纱线、电工设备、蔬菜、汽车零件、绸缎、染料中间体、动力机械等。

出口商品市场 出口商品销往的主要国家和地区依次为日本、美国、香港、荷兰、韩国、德国、新加坡、英国、台湾省、法国、意大利、澳大利亚、加拿大、比利时、印度、泰国、西班牙、孟加拉国、印度尼西亚、阿联酋、马来西亚、墨西哥等，出口额161.49亿美元，占全省出口总额的88.20%。

进口总额 进口总额1295000万美元，比1998年的1077499万美元增长20.2%。

进口商品结构 主要进口商品是自动数据处理设备的零件、制造纸及纸制品用机械、钢材、原油、合成纤维长丝机织物、初级形状塑料、飞机、纺织机械、通断及保护电路装置、集成电路及微电子组件、纸浆、成品油、棉机织物、计量检测分析自控仪器及器具、羊毛、纺织用合成纤维、针织或钩编织物、原木、纸及纸板、金属加工机床等。

进口商品市场 进口商品主要来自日本、台湾省、韩国、美国、新加坡、瑞典、香港、德国、印度尼西亚、泰国、意大利、马来西亚、澳大利亚、加拿大、俄罗斯、英国、芬兰、巴西、法国、荷兰等国家和地区，进口额120.37万美元，占全省进口总额的92.95%。

技术进出口 技术出口总额336600万美元，同比增长20.24%，占全省出口总额的18.4%；签订引进技术和进口设备合同项目数306个，合同金额356075万美元，分别比上年增长215.46%和288.25%。

【利用外资】

1999年利用外资情况表

利用外资方式	批准签订的合同			实际利用外资	
	项目数（个）	外资金额（万美元）	金额比1998年（±%）	金额（万美元）	金额比1998年（±%）
外商直接投资	1926	697000	-8.0	640500	-3.69
合资企业	912	238876		284047	
合作企业	112	52574		55826	

1999年利用外资情况表（续）

利用外资方式	批准签订的合同			实际利用外资	
	项目数（个）	外资金额（万美元）	金额比1998年（±%）	金额（万美元）	金额比1998年（±%）
外资企业	901	405460		297667	
外商投资股份制	1	162		2916	
合计	**1926**	**697000**	**-8.0**	**640500**	**-3.69**

外商直接投资的行业和规模 外商在江苏的投资实现了从第二产业向第一、第二、第三产业全方位投资的转变，从劳动密集型向技术密集型的转变以及下游工业（制造加工业）向上游工业（原材料、基础设施）的转变，投资领域进一步优化。外商直接投资仍以第二产业为主，新批协议外资59.34亿美元，占全年新批协议外资总额的85%；实际利用外资额48.33亿美元，占全年实际利用外资的75%。第三产业吸引外资保持适度规模，全年新批协议外资额9.3亿美元，比上年增长17.0%，实际利用外资额6.5亿美元。

外商直接投资来源 外商直接投资来自61个国家和地区。其中，新批协议外资有香港地区16.27亿美元，美国8.2亿美元，台湾省8.1亿美元，英属维尔京群岛7.1亿美元，新加坡6.1亿美元，日本6.0亿美元。

三资企业生产经营和出口 新投产开业的三资企业406家，全省三资企业自营出口总值达98.6亿美元，比上年增长22.3%，三资企业自营出口已占全省外贸出口总额的54%。出口超过1000万美元的三资企业达173家，出口超1亿美元的有11家。1999年全省三资企业主营业务收入2498.61亿元。比上年同期上升23.15%。涉外税收112亿元，同比增长39.11%，占全省财政收入的16.48%。

【对外经济技术合作】

对外承包工程和劳务合作 签订对外承包工程、劳务合作、设计咨询合同额81500万美元，同比增长30.5%；营业额61300美元，同比增长17.44%；年末在外人数32435人，同比增长39.6%。劳务人员主要派往新加坡、科威特、日本、阿联酋、以色列、毛里求斯、乌干达、津巴布韦、肯尼亚等国家。

对外经济技术援助 承担了对外经援项目5个，完成投资额4800万元人民币。

接受国际援助 加拿大援助江苏省的“中加江苏中小企业应用管理与环保项目”已有3个项目开始启动，共使用环保周转金900万元人民币。

对外投资 1999年经批准的江苏海外非贸易企业为13家，总投资1281.49万美元，其中中方投资947.8万美元，经营情况良好。

1999年全省经外经贸部确认的境外加工贸易项目24家，总投资3304.42万美元，其中中方投资1607.1万美元。境外加工贸易企业已有21家投产开业，带动3500多万美元国内产品出口。

【其他】

经济技术开发区 江苏省已有经国务院批准的11个经济技术开发区和江苏省政府批准的69个经济技术开发区。1999年，新批进区企业5695家，比上年增加1982家；进区企业总投资545.8亿元。其中新批外商投资项目726个，合同外资42.98亿美元，占全省新批合同外资总额的61.6%；外商实际出资34.58亿美元，同比下降23.4%，占全省实际利用外资总额的54%。开发区企业实现的自营进出口额（按业务统计口径）144.29亿美元，比上年增长41%；其中出口73.07亿美元，比上年增长36.7%，占全省出口比重达39.9%。全省大多数开发区进入产出期，1999年全省开发区实现业务总收入3052.09亿元，比上年增长41.4%；其中工业产品销售收入2150亿元，同比增长41.2%。开发区已经成为江苏省与国际接轨的新兴工业区，也是全省经济发展的重要增长点。此外，开发区还提供了大量的就业岗位，截至1999年底，全省开发区进区企业从业人数已达96.82万人，比上年增加17万人。

对外经贸洽谈会 1999年江苏省分别在6个国家举办和参加展览（博览）会，展团人数452人，成交金额达1585.9万美元，意向成交3580万美元。各展览（博览）会主要参展的商品有机械设备、五金矿产、机电、工具、医药保健、轻工、服装、家纺以及畜产品等。

涉外旅游 1999年，江苏省接待海外游客134.4万人次，创汇6.2亿美元，分别比上年增长16.4%和17.2%，均居全国第五位。

1999年南京市对外经济贸易

南京市对外经济贸易委员会

【对外贸易】

进出口总额 1999年江苏省南京市进出口总额269486万美元，比1998年的190569万美元增长41.41%。

出口总额 出口总额115338万美元，比1998年的100154万美元增长15.16%；占全市国内生产总值的10.70%；占江苏省出口额的6.30%。

出口商品结构 初级产品出口额1442万美元，占出口总额的1.25%；工业制成品出口额113896万美元，占出口总额的98.75%。

出口额在1000万美元以上的商品情况表

金额分类	商品名称	出口金额（万美元）	占出口总额%
2000万美元以上8种	移动通讯基地站、玩具、收录（放）机、水泥、彩色电视机、程控电话及零件、玩偶、彩色显像管	23766	20.61
1000万美元－2000万美元10种	显示器、棉坯布、化纤针织品、陶餐具、镁、肝素纳、彩色数据图形显示管、女式服装、充气橡胶轮胎、手提砂磨工具	14433	12.51
合计	**18种**	**38199**	**33.12**

出口商品市场 出口商品销往132个国家和地区。

主要出口市场情况表

国别（地区）	出口额（万美元）	占出口总额（%）
美 国	22574	19.57
香 港	18083	15.68
日 本	17230	14.94
德 国	6370	5.52
韩 国	4812	4.17
法 国	3719	3.22
英 国	2928	2.54
意大利	2775	2.41
台湾省	2581	2.24

主要出口市场情况表（续）

国别（地区）	出口额（万美元）	占出口总额（%）
加拿大	2005	1.74
合 计	**83077**	**72.03**

进口总额 进口总额154148万美元，比1998年的90415万美元增长70.49%。

进口商品结构 初级产品进口额3391万美元，占进口总额的2.20%；工业制成品进口额150757万美元，占进口总额的97.80%。

进口额在1000万美元以上的商品情况表

金额分类	商 品 名 称	进口金额（万美元）	占进口总额%
3000万美元以上7种	程控电话及零件、显像管零件、阴极射线管玻璃外壳、移动通讯基地站、手持无线电话、彩色电视机显像管、未列名装置备用零件	58082	37.68
1000万美元－3000万美元8种	正构烷烃、彩色数据显示管、射线管零件、苯乙烯、手持无线电话零件、防眩玻壳、精炼铜阴极、机械器具	13702	8.89
合 计	**15种**	**71784**	**46.57**

进口商品市场 进口商品来自59个国家和地区。其中瑞典45027万美元，占进口总额的29.21%；日本19147万美元，占12.42%，台湾省11603万美元，占7.53%；韩国9758万美元，占6.33%；香港7598万美元，占4.93%；荷兰7488万美元，占4.86%；美国5053万美元，占3.28%；德国4240万美元，占2.75%；英国2697万美元，占1.75%；意大利2547万美元，占1.65%。合计115158万美元，占74.70%。

【利用外资】

1999年利用外资情况表

利用外资方式	批准签订的合同			实际利用外资	
	项目（个）	外资金额（万美元）	金额比1998年（±%）	金 额（万美元）	金额比1998年（±%）
外商直接投资	335	75374	38.95	77088	3.00
合资企业	157	36036	55.63	41076	－18.30

1999 年利用外资情况表（续）

利用外资方式	批准签订的合同			实际利用外资	
	项目（个）	外资金额（万美元）	金额比1998年（±%）	金额（万美元）	金额比1998年（±%）
合作企业	26	6420	-43.33	4610	1.50
外资企业	152	32919	77.37	31382	56.70
合计	**335**	**75374**	**38.95**	**77088**	**3.00**

外商直接投资行业 在外商直接投资的 335 个项目中，生产型项目 286 个，非生产型项目 49 个。按行业分，化工医药业 33 个，机械制造业 28 个，电子通信业 38 个，其他制造业 137 个，房地产业 11 个，社会服务业 17 个，农林牧渔业 26 个，其他 45 个。

外商直接投资来源 外商直接投资来自 26 个国家和地区。主要有：香港 98 个，外资金额 23648 万美元；美国 56 个，11413 万美元；台湾省 78 个，11067 万美元；英属维尔京群岛 12 个，3829 万美元；英国 3 个，2841 万美元；菲律宾 1 个，2404 万美元；新加坡 7 个，2324 万美元；日本 17 个，2323 万美元；澳大利亚 11 个，1991 万美元；德国 9 个，1072 万美元；法国 4 个，1045 万美元。

外商直接投资企业生产经营情况 截止 1999 年底，已开业投产的外商投资企业共 2891 家，其中 1999 年开业的有 146 家。全年销售（营业）收入 431 亿元，比 1998 年的 351 亿元增长 22.79%；纳税总额 27.60 亿元，比 1998 年的 18.30 亿元增长 50.82%；出口创汇 5.64 亿美元，比 1998 年的 4.33 亿美元增长 30.25%，占全市出口总额的 48.92%。

【对外经济合作】

承包工程和劳务合作 1999 年签订对外承包工程和劳务合作合同 119 个，合同金额 15009 万美元，比 1998 年的 9682 万美元增长 55.02%；完成营业额 11003 万美元，比 1998 年的 9029 万美元增长 21.86%；当年派出劳务人员 2449 人，年末在外 6016 人。劳务人员分布在黎巴嫩、科威特、莫桑比克、毛里求斯、苏里南、乌干达等 52 个国家和地区。承包工程的主要项目有：新加坡政府组屋工程项目、莫桑比克 45 幢住宅工程项目、苏里南政府住宅工程项目、伊拉克 36KW 燃气轮发电机组工程项目、乌干达 MBALE 卫生学校工程项目。

对外投资 批准在美国、阿根廷举办非贸易企业 2 家，中方总投资 119 万美元。

【其他】

经济技术开发区 南京高新技术开发区全年投入基础设施建设资金 6.77 亿元，技工贸销售总额 221 亿元，比上年增长 33.94%；实现利税 21 亿元，增长 23.53%。1999 年批准进区外商投资企业 10 家，实际利用外资金额 2288 万美元，出口创汇 11157 万美元。

对外经贸洽谈会 1999 年 9 月在南京举办“南京金秋经贸洽谈会”，接待了来自 64 个国家和地区的客商 2433 人，批准利用外资立项以上项目 302 个，合同外资金额 5.38 亿美元。

港口运输 南京港拥有生产泊位 66 个，其中万吨级以上泊位 16 个，集装箱泊位 4 个，港口年吞吐能力 6700 万吨，集装箱吞吐能力 30 万个标准箱。全年实际完成货物吞吐总量 5922 万吨，其中外贸货物进出口吞吐量 716 万吨（出口量 290 万吨，进口量 426 万吨）。

涉外旅游 1999 年南京市共接待海外旅游者 37.89 万人次，比 1998 年的 30.52 万人次增长 24.15%。其中外国人 20.91 万人次，华侨和港澳台同胞 16.98 万人次。旅游收入 2.01 亿美元，比 1998 年的 1.47 亿美元增长 36.73%。

1999年连云港市对外经济贸易

连云港市对外经济贸易委员会

【对外贸易】

进出口总额 1999年江苏省连云港市进出口总额41872万美元，比1998年32813万美元增长27.61%。

出口总额 出口总额32052万美元，比1998年的26523万美元增长20.85%，占全市国内生产总值的285亿元（合美元34.76亿元）的10.84%；

出口商品结构 初级产品出口额6410万美元，占出口总额的20%，工业制成品的出口额25642万美元，占出口总额的80%。出口额在8000万美元以上的有煤炭，金额为8316万美元，占出口总额的25.95%；1000万美元以上的有柠檬酸，金额为1754万美元，占5.47%；500万美元以上的有碳化硅、机动车及零部件、冻龙虾、其他食品、动物内脏、鲜紫菜、淀粉、玻璃，金额为5210万美元，占16.25%；

出口商品市场 出口商品销往日本、美国、韩国、德国、泰国、荷兰、马来西亚、比利时、台湾省、印度等100多个国家和地区。主要出口市场为：日本11197万美元，占出口总额的34.93%；美国4539万美元，占13.73%；韩国4374万美元，占13.65%；德国1633万美元，占5.09%；泰国1276万美元，占3.98%；荷兰498万美元，占1.55%；马来西亚490万美元，占1.53%；比利时479万美元，占1.49%，台湾省460.8万美元，占1.44%；印度460万美元，占1.44%。

进口总额 进口总额9820万美元，比1998年6291万美元，增长56.10%。

进口商品结构 初级产品进口额2998万美元，占进口总额的30.53%；工业制成品进口额6822万美元，占进口总额的69.47%。

主要进口商品中，1000万美元以上的有机器设备、燃料、塑料及制品、光学医疗仪器，金额为5609万美元，占进口总额的57.12%；500万美元以上的有电气电讯设备、硫磺，金额为1355万美元，占13.80%；200万美元以上的有无机化学制品，有机化学制品、纸浆、短化纤、制鞋原料和配件、钢材，金额为1552万美元，占15.80%；100万美元以上的有金属工具、皮革、钢铁制品、活性剂，金额为547万美元，占5.57%。

进口商品市场 进口商品来自日本、韩国、加拿大、美国、俄罗斯、新加坡、法国、香港、荷闫等20个国家和地区。主要是日本4785万美元，占进口总额48.73%；韩国1838万美元，占18.72%；加拿大594万美元，占6.05%；美国531万美元，占5.41%；台湾省513万美元，占5.22%；俄罗斯209万美元，占2.13%；新加坡208万美元，占2.12%；法国147万美元，占1.50%；香港130万美元，占1.32%；荷兰105万美元，占1.07%。

【利用外资】

1999年利用外资情况表

利用外资方式	批准签订的合同			实际利用外资	
	项目（个）	外资金额（万美元）	金额比1998年（±%）	金额（万美元）	金额比1998年（±%）
对外借款	3	11512	444.56	11512	307.94

1999年利用外资情况表（续）

利用外资方式	批准签订的合同			实际利用外资	
	项目（个）	外资金额（万美元）	金额比1998年（±%）	金额（万美元）	金额比1998年（±%）
外商直接投资	118	11020	18.99	4668	-54.7
合资企业	64	2330		3160	
合作企业	2	60		54	
外资企业	52	8630		1454	
合　计	**121**	**22532**	**97.82**	**16180**	**23.09**

外商直接投资行业　在外商直接投资的项目中，生产型项目104个，非生产型项目14个。按行业分，工业制造业97个；农林业7个；房地产业8个；其他6个。

外商直接投资来源　外商直接投资来自17个国家和地区。主要是香港33个，实际利用外资1422万美元；日本17个，944万美元；台湾省17个，567万美元；韩国16个，513万美元；美国11个，367万美元；加拿大7个，104万美元；澳大利亚3个，150万美元。

外商直接投资企业生产经营情况　1999年全市有50家外商投资企业投产，出口创汇9190万美元，比1998年8067万美元，增长13.92%，占全市出口总额28.67%；进口5433万美元，占进口总额55.33%。涉外税收1.86亿元人民币，有12家外资企业增资扩股，增资额486万美元。到1999年底，连云港市累计批准外商直接投资项目1833个，合同外资11.53亿美元。实际利用外资5.87亿美元。

【对外经济合作】

承包工程和劳务合作　1999年签订对外承包工程和劳务合作项目104个，合同金额7176万美元，比1998年的6395万美元增长12.21%；完成营业额6831万美元，比1998年6179万美元增长10.55%；当年派出劳务人员2817人，年末在外5661人，派往的主要国家和地区是新加坡、日本、科威特、韩国等。

【其他】

经济技术开发区　全年完成固定资产投资4.06亿元人民币，比1998年5.08亿人民币下降20.08%；全区新批利用外资企业40个，实际利用外资7012万美元，比1998年的6006万美元增长16.75%；全区共完成工业总产值60.5亿人民币，比1998年50.38亿人民币增长20.09%。实际财政收入1.81亿元人民币，比1998年1.74亿人民币增长4.02%。全区出口总额5775万美元，外商投资企业出口5245万美元。

港口运输　到1999年底，连云港港口共有35个泊位，其中生产泊位30个，非生产泊位5个。在生产泊位中，万吨级以上有25个，万吨级以下5个。港口吞吐能力2265万吨，当年实际完成货物吞吐总量2016.7万吨，比1998年1775.8万吨增长13.57%。其中完成外贸进出口货物总量997.4万吨（出口552.4万吨，进口445万吨）比1998年1006.8万吨下降0.94%，标准集装箱11.05万个，比1998年91616个增长20.61%。

涉外旅游　1999年入境的外国人数以及台港澳同胞1.4万人次，旅游收入506万美元，比1998年的480万美元增长5.42%。

1999年南通市对外经济贸易

南通市对外经济贸易委员会

【对外贸易】

进出口总额 1999年江苏省南通市进出口总额24.11亿美元，比1998年的21.84亿美元增长10.4%。

出口总额 出口总额为15.96亿美元，比1998年13.31亿美元增长19.8%，占全市国内生产总值666.8亿元（相当于80.43亿美元）的19.84%，占江苏省出口总额的8.72%，出口总额在江苏省各市中居第3位。

出口商品结构 初级产品出口额0.71亿美元，占出口总额的4.46%。工业制成品的出口额15.25亿美元，占出口总额的95.54%。

出口额在1000万美元以上商品情况表

商品名称	出口金额（万美元）	占出口总额（%）
纺织原料服装及纺织制品	81780	51.26
机器电器及零件	15484	9.7
车辆航空器船舶及运输设备	15469	9.7
贱金属及制品	9367	5.87
杂项制品	8893	5.57
化学工业及相关工业产品	5274	3.31
塑料、橡胶及其制品	5103	3.2
鞋帽伞等制品	5015	3.14
生皮皮革、毛皮及制品	3439	2.16
活动物、动物产品	3082	1.93
食品饮料酒、烟草及制品	2832	1.78
植物产品	1194	0.75
精密仪器设备及零件	1053	0.66
合　计	**157985**	**99.02**

出口商品市场 出口商品销往117个国家和地区，比上年的119个减少2个。

出口主要市场表

国别（地区）	出口额（万美元）	占出口总额（%）
日本	71319	44.7

出口主要市场表（续）

国别（地区）	出口额（万美元）	占出口总额（%）
美国	17396	10.9
香港	10469	6.56
韩国	6115	3.83
英国	4908	3.08

出口主要市场表（续）

国　别（地区）	出口额（万美元）	占出口总额（%）
新加坡	4006	2.51
德　国	3779	2.37
台湾省	1876	1.18
泰　国	1793	1.12
法　国	1692	1.06
荷　兰	1602	1.0
印度尼西亚	1566	0.98
澳大利亚	1436	0.9
意大利	1423	0.89
马来西亚	1194	0.75
合计	**130574**	**81.84**

进口总额　进口总额8.16亿美元，比1998年的8.53亿美元下降4.4%。

进口商品结构　初级产品为0.38亿美元，占进口总额的4.72%；工业制成品为7.77亿美元，占进口总额的95.28%。

主要进口商品表

商　品　名　称	进口金额（万美元）	占进口总额（%）
纺织原料服装及纺织制品	26335	32.29
化学工业及相关工业产品	16022	19.65
机器电器及零件	13264	16.27
贱金属及制品	6543	8.02
木及木制品编结材料制品	5292	6.49
塑料、橡胶及制品	3769	4.62
木浆纸及制品	3053	3.74
矿产品	1987	2.44
生皮皮革、毛皮及制品	1736	2.13
合　计	**78001**	**95.65**

进口商品市场　进口商品来自40个国家和地区，与上年持平。

主要进口市场情况表

国　别（地区）	进口金额（万美元）	占进口总额（%）
日　本	36722	45.02
韩　国	11484	14.08
台湾省	7975	9.78
美　国	7306	8.96
印度尼西亚	1917	2.35
香　港	1738	2.13
德　国	1667	2.04
俄罗斯	1156	1.42
合计	**69965**	**85.78**

技术进口　1999年南通签订技术引进项目11个，分别为从瑞士引进的高浓度钾生产技术、从英国引进的百草枯生产技术、从美国引进的代森锰锌生产技术、吡啶生产技术、从加拿大引进的吡虫琳生产技术、从日本引进的高压型铝解电容器生产技术、从泰国引进的饲料生产技术等。

【利用外资】

1999年全市协议利用外资金额3.49亿美元，其中1999年以前批准的项目增资金额为4818万美元。

1999年利用外资情况表

利用外资方式	批准签订的合同			实际利用外资	
	项目数（个）	外资金额（万美元）	金额比1998年（±%）	金额（万美元）	金额比1998年（±%）
对外借款	16	867	-55.77	2373	374.6
外商直接投资	120	34016	-33.59	28322	-53.23
合资企业	70	21770	-45.42	23752	17.7
合作企业	6	1318	217.59	586	-81.21
外资企业	44	10928	0.06	3983	-72.52
合计	**136**	**34882**	**-34.41**	**30694**	**-49.75**

外商直接投资行业 外商直接投资120个项目中，生产型项目113个，占94.2%，非生产型项目7个，占5.8%。按行业分：服装及其他纤维制造业24个，纺织业和普通机械制造业各12个，化学原料及化学制品制造业、专业设备制造业、电器及机械制造业各6个，塑料制品业5个，渔业、食品加工业和金属制造业各4个，非金属矿物制造业、房地产开发与经营业、土木工程业、农业、餐饮业、电子及通信设备制造业、娱乐服务业等其他行业39个。

外商直接投资来源 外商直接投资来自21个国家和地区。主要有日本26项，协议外资金额16651万美元；香港23项，金额6485万美元；美国22项，金额2544万美元；台湾省13项，金额1983万美元；韩国9项，金额485万美元；德国5项，金额1026万美元；英国2项，金额592万美元；开曼群岛1项，金额2803万美元；新加坡1项，金额579万美元；西班牙1项，金额464万美元等。

外商直接投资企业生产经营情况 1999年全市外商投资企业实现主营业务收入245.36亿元，增长48.7%；出口创汇10.06亿美元，比上年增长20.98%；实现利税26.25亿元，增长96.5%，其中净利润6.33亿元，利税超千万元的企业有19家，其中净利润超千万元的有11家。

【对外经济合作】

承包工程和劳务合作 签订对外承包工程和劳务合作项目391个，合同金额1.85亿美元，比上年增长22.44%；完成营业额1.71亿美元，比上年增长29.22%；当年派出劳务5477人，主要派往新加坡、日本、俄罗斯、以色列、毛里求斯、阿联酋等49个国家和地区。主要行业涉及建筑业、纺织服装业、远洋捕捞业、农业种植、商业服务等。全年签订200万美元以上大中型项目8个，合同额5216万美元，占全市总数的28.12%。全市有对外承包劳务签约权的公司已发展到13家，居全省各市首位，新签合同额、实现营业额分别占全市总数的55.3%和56.2%。

对外投资 举办海外非贸易性企业2家，中方总投资76万美元，主要涉及服装、轻工行业。

【其他】

经济技术开发区 南通经济技术开发区完成基础设施投资2880万元。区内新批三资企业16家，协议外资金额1219万美元，实际利用外资3005万美元。1999年全区实现工业总产值41.07亿元，比上年增长38.2%，其中外商投资企业完成工业产值29.97亿元，比上年增长57.6%。全区进出口总额 5.35 亿美元，其中出口 2.85 亿美元，比上年增长 36.63%。全区共完成财政收入 2.46 亿元，比上年增长 27.9%。

港口运输 南通港完成旅客吞吐量 126.5 万人次，比上年下降 24.6%。货物吞吐量 2277 万吨，比上年增长 12.9%，其中外贸吞吐量 371 万吨，增长 5.9%，占全港吞吐量的 16.29%；集装箱吞吐量 15.8 万标准箱，比上年增长 21.3%，其中国际航线集装箱吞吐量为 3.7 万标准箱，下降 4.9%，占 17.37%。集装箱吞吐量在全国内河港口中继续名列第一。

涉外旅游 共接待海外旅游者 4.8 万人次，比上年的 7.23 万人次下降 33.6%。

1999 年浙江省对外经济贸易

浙江省对外贸易经济合作厅

【对外贸易】

进出口总额 1999 年浙江省进出口总额 183.05 亿美元，比 1998 年的 148.53 亿美元增长 23.24%。

出口总额 出口总额 128.71 亿美元，比 1998 年的 108.61 亿美元增长 18.50%，占全省国内生产总值 5310 亿元的 19.8%；占全国出口额的 6.60%，居全国外贸出口第四位。

出口商品结构 初级产品出口额 14.67 亿美元，占出口总额的 11.39%；工业制成品的出口额 114.03 亿美元，占出口总额的 88.61%。

主要出口商品情况表

商品名称	出口金额（亿美元）	占出口总额（%）
机电产品	36.10	28.05
服装及衣着附件	34.67	26.94
纺织针线、织物及制品	13.38	10.40
水海产品	3.35	2.76
鞋类	3.31	2.57
旅行用品及箱包	2.42	1.88
塑料制品	2.24	1.74
灯具、照明装置及类似品	2.23	1.73
医药品	1.92	1.49
家具	1.73	1.34
合计	**101.58**	**78.93**

出口商品市场 出口商品销往 180 多个国家和地区。

主要出口商品市场情况表

国 别 (地区)	出口金额 (万美元)	占出口总额 (%)
美 国	24.16	18.77
日 本	22.76	17.69
香 港	9.17	7.13
德 国	6.06	4.71
韩 国	4.26	3.31
意大利	4.01	3.12
荷 兰	3.73	2.89
英 国	3.57	2.78
法 国	3.10	2.42
澳大利亚	2.83	2.20

主要出口商品市场情况表（续）

国 别 (地区)	出口金额 (万美元)	占出口总额 (%)
东 盟	5.80	4.51
欧 盟	27.88	21.67
合计	**83.68**	**65.02**

进口总额 进口总额54.34亿美元，比1998年的39.87亿美元增长36.28%。

进口商品结构 初级产品进口14.04亿美元，占进口总额的25.83%；工业制成品的进口额40.30亿美元，占进口总额的74.17%。

主要进口商品情况表

商 品 名 称	进口金额 (亿美元)	占进口总额(%)
机电产品	17.59	32.37
初级形状的塑料	4.09	7.52
钢材	2.55	4.69
纺织机械	2.00	3.68
纸浆	1.90	3.49
原油	1.79	3.29
电视及无线通讯设备	1.74	3.20
纸及纸板	1.45	2.66
原木	1.25	2.30
棉机织物	1.03	1.89

进口商品市场

主要进口商品市场情况表

国 别 (地区)	进口金额 (万美元)	占进口总额 (%)
日 本	11.49	21.15
韩 国	6.54	12.03
美 国	5.79	10.65
台湾省	4.27	7.86
英 国	3.30	6.08
德 国	2.79	5.13

主要进口商品市场情况表（续）

国 别 (地区)	进口金额 (万美元)	占进口总额 (%)
印度尼西亚	1.87	3.44
意大利	1.79	3.29
加拿大	1.43	2.63
马来西亚	1.24	2.28

技术进出口 签订引进技术和进口设备合同项目50个，比1998年的18个增加了32个，合同

金额3.01亿美元，比1998年4573万美元增长558%。引进项目的国别地区为：日本、韩国、美国、法国、新加坡、英国、瑞典、德国、挪威、瑞士、意大利、香港、台湾省、马来西亚、俄罗斯。

技术引进情况表

国别（地区）	项目数	金额（亿美元）	行　业
日本	11	1.24	邮电、机械、化工
韩国	1	1.2	轮胎
美国	8	0.80	医药、计算机软件、通信
法国	7	0.22	机械电子、医药、化工
新加坡	6	0.029	通信、食品
英国	2	0.024	机械、轻工业
瑞典	1	0.02	电力

【利用外资】

1999年利用外资情况表

利用外资方式	实　际　外　资				
	项目数（个）	合同外资（万美元）	金额比1998年（±%）	实际外资（万美元）	金额比1998年（±%）
对外借款	41	85528	103.6	97036	-11.3
外商直接投资	1113	214793	17.1	153262	16.3
合资企业	687	96414	33.3	85510	42.2
合作企业	51	21029	-56.9	16281	-35.4
外资企业	375	97350	56.3	51471	10.8
外商其他投资		2518	520.2	2201	442.1
补偿贸易			-100		-100
加工装配		490	30.3	173	-54
对外发行股票		2028		2028	
合　计	**1154**	**302839**	**34.1**	**252499**	**4.5**

外商直接投资来源表

国家和地区	合同外资金额(万美元)
香港	78590
美国	26799
台湾省	21630
英属维尔京群岛	12167
日本	11263
韩国	8839
新加坡	7182
荷兰	5264

外商直接投资来源表（续）

国家和地区	合同外资金额(万美元)
凯曼群岛	3853
法国	3509
其他	35697

1999年浙江省外商企业自营出口33.27亿美元，销售收入1380.16亿元，盈利868140万元，上缴税金719720万元。

1999年外商投资企业生产经营情况表

指标名称	计算单位	本年实际
销售收入	万元	13801564
其中：出口产品收入	万美元	414227
销售（营业）成本	万元	11185752
税金总额	万元	719720
利润总额	万元	868140
资产总额	万元	22969091
负债余额	万元	11807915
从业人员人数	人	770850

投产企业6960家，盈利企业3068家，盈利1075222万元，亏损企业2175家，亏损207082万元。

【对外经济技术合作】

承包工程和劳务合作 1999年全省共签订对外承包工程和劳务合作项目809个，合同额28132万美元，比1998年的25205万美元增长12%，完成营业额33824万美元，比1998年的30027万美元增长12.6%，居全国第六位；当年派出劳务人员为11532人次，年末在外人数达21904人，首次突破2万人，居全国第七位。1999年我省对外劳务合作的主要海外市场为新加坡、美国塞班、日本、柬埔寨、保加利亚、毛里求斯及我国的台湾省。对外工程承包1999年完成营业额达到14800万美元，主要项目有科威特住宅项目，柬埔寨石矿开采项目，香港赤柱监仓工程、青山道玻璃幕墙项目，新加坡Bakit Panj ahg组屋项目、houg ang Ave7公寓项目、裕廊西二期组屋项目、Ju Yong West二期组屋项目、裕廊东组屋项目、巴西立车库组屋项目、女皇镇组屋项目、亚太变电所项目、亚太公司重建局大厦工程、亚太住宅小区项目，老挝小水电项目，也门立交桥工程，关岛别墅区项目，沙特商场利亚得商业楼项目，新加坡汽车库等项目。

对外经济技术援助 1999年1月我国援尼泊尔中华寺项目竣工验收，当年完成营业额为15万美元，派出援外人员6人；援非洲贝宁马维尔农垦项目开始执行，当年派出援外人员11人；援密克罗尼西亚体育场设计项目当年派出援外人员3人。

对外投资 1999年在经批准的境外非贸易性项目为23个，中方投入878万美元，行业主要涉及服装、食品、家电、建筑、化工等，分布在柬埔寨、香港、新加坡、越南、约旦、埃及、尼日利亚、博茨瓦纳等18个国家和地区。1999年全省经批准的境外加工贸易项目为9个，中方投入697万美元，带动国内出口2500万美元。

【其他】

1999年浙江省国家级经济技术开发区、保税区业务进展情况表

	已开发区面积	基础设施投入	批准进区项目	其中：外资项目	合同外资	实际外资	出口总值	工业总产值
单位	平方公里	亿元	个	个	万美元	万美元	万美元	亿元
杭州开发区	2.97	1.84	201	22	25157	12007	15126	140
宁波开发区	2.77	23.9	297	23	15579	15287	48200	175

1999 年浙江省国家级经济技术开发区、保税区业务进展情况表（续）

	已开发区面积	基础设施投入	批准进区项目	其中：外资项目	合同外资	实际外资	出口总值	工业总产值
单位	平方公里	亿元	个	个	万美元	万美元	万美元	亿元
温州开发区		0.4	93	11	734	258	11303	39
萧山开发区	1	0.55	42	13	10114	5020	23000	41
大榭开发区	7.44	10406	196	1	1420	822	12085	14
宁波保税区		0.059	383	47	10267	5509	24638	8

对外经贸洽谈会　1999 年 10 月 19 日－23 日，浙江省外经贸厅组团参加了在南非约翰内斯堡举办的 SAITEX99 博览会。这次参展共实现出口成交 1175.95 万美元，其中实际签约出口成交 503.2 万美元，意向出口成交 672.75 万美元。浙江的棉纺织品、丝绸产品、小五金、土畜产等出口商品受到客户的好评。

港口运输　1999 年浙江省外贸运输出口量为 490 万吨，比上年增长 18%；其中海运出口 479.7 万吨，空运出口 1.3 万吨，陆运出口 9.2 万吨。

涉外旅游　1999 年到浙江旅游的外国人数 94.8 万人，台港澳同胞人数 40.8 万人，旅游收入 4.1 亿美元，比 1998 年的 3.6 亿美元增长 13.5%。

1999 年宁波市对外经济贸易

宁波市对外贸易经济合作委员会

【对外贸易】

进出口总额　1999 年浙江省宁波市进出口总额 500421 万美元，比 1998 年 421237 万美元增长 18.80%。

出口总额　出口总额 347721 万美元，比上年的 296386 万美元增长 17.3%，占全市国内生产总值 1070 亿元（相当于 1292560 万美元）的 26.90%；占全省出口额的 27.02%。

出口商品结构　初级产品出口额 34110 万美元，占出口总额的 9.81%；工业制成品的出口额 313611 万美元，占出口总额的 90.19%。

出口额在500万美元以上的商品情况表

金额分类	商品名称	出口金额（万美元）	占出口总额（%）
出口额在1000万美元以上的商品（37种）	服装及衣着附件、塑料制品、轴承、鞋类、成品油、水海产品、灯具、照明装置及类似品、通断及保护电路装置、旅行用品及箱包、棉机织物、蔬菜、手用或机用工具、合成有机染料、玩具、圣诞用品、汽车零件、棉纱线、钢铁或铜制标准紧固件、床垫、寝具及类似品、医药品、家具、手电筒、原电池、录放音、像机及唱机的零附件、家用或装饰用木制品、扬声器、电线和电缆、丝绸、制作或保藏的河鳗、锁、伞、铜材、茶叶、静止式变流器	198303	57.03
出口额在500－1000万美元的商品（10种）	地毯、钢材、医疗仪器及器械、金属加工机床、不锈钢厨具、餐具等家用器具、摩托车、摩托车及自行车的零件、电动机及发电机、玻璃制品	6745	1.94
合计	**47种**	**205048**	**58.97**

出口商品市场 出口商品销往167个国家和地区，其中出口额在1000万美元以上的国家和地区有48个，金额328380万美元，占出口总额的94.44%。

主要出口市场情况表

国别（地区）	出口金额（万美元）	占出口总额（%）
日本	64047	18.42
美国	53953	15.52
香港	23999	6.90
德国	16234	4.67
韩国	13104	3.77
荷兰	11750	3.38
意大利	10428	3.00

主要出口市场情况表（续）

国别（地区）	出口金额（万美元）	占出口总额（%）
英国	10067	2.90
澳大利亚	9512	2.74
西班牙	9330	2.68
合计	**222424**	**63.97**

进口总额 进口总额152700万美元，比上年的124851万美元增长22.3%。

进口商品结构 初级产品进口额55019万美元，占进口总额的36.03%，工业制成品的进口额为97681万美元，占进口总额的63.97%。

进口额在500万美元以上的商品情况表

金额分类	商品名称	进口金额（万美元）	占进口总额（%）
进口额在1000万美元以上的商品(24种)	初级形状的塑料、原油、纸浆、羊毛（包括羊毛条）、钢材、纸及纸板（未切成形的）、苯乙烯、钢坯及粗锻件、废铜、纺织机械、己内酰胺、大豆、纺织用合成纤维、食用植物油、大麦、金属加工机床、录放音、像机及唱机的零附件、集成电路及微电子组件、成品油、计量检测分析自控仪器及器具、橡胶或塑料加工机械、通断及保护电路装置及零件、自动数据处理设备及其部件	97126	63.61
进口额在500－1000万美元的商品(15种)	液化石油气及其他烃类气、合成纤维纱线、医疗仪器及器械、制冷设备用压缩机、合成橡胶（包括胶乳）、合成纤维长丝机织物、制造纸及纸制品用机械、印刷、装订机械、针织或钩编织物、铜材、异氰酸酯、未锻造的铝（包括铝合金）、型模及金属铸造用型箱、机械提升搬运装卸设备及零件	10644	6.97
合　计	**39种**	**107770**	**70.58**

进口商品市场　进口商品来自80个国家和地区，其中进口额在1000万美元以上的国家和地区有27个，合计金额145440万美元，占进口总额的95.25%。

主要进口市场情况表

国　别（地区）	进口金额（万美元）	占进口总额（%）
日　本	29103	19.06
韩　国	18152	11.89
台湾省	17897	11.72
美　国	14308	9.37
印度尼西亚	9719	6.36
澳大利亚	6939	4.54
英　国	6853	4.49
加拿大	6670	4.37
德　国	5006	3.28
香　港	3137	2.05
合　计	**117784**	**77.13**

技术进口　1999年签订引进技术和进口设备合同项目数173个，比1998年多107个，合同金额6024万美元，比上年增长86.1%。引进项目的国家和地区有19个，其中从美国引进项目44个，金额993万美元；德国引进项目36个，金额1694万美元；日本引进项目30个，金额594万美元；意大利引进项目13个，金额181万美元；奥地利引进项目2个，金额479万美元；加拿大引进项目8个，金额312万美元；澳大利亚引进项目2个，金额21万美元；法国引进项目6个，金额554万美元；丹麦引进项目4个，金额21万美元；荷兰引进项目1个，金额29万美元；瑞士引进项目5个，金额139万美元；英国引进项目7个，金额338万美元；马来西亚引进项目1个，金额7万美元；西班牙引进项目1个，金额60万美元；瑞典引进项目1个，金额19万美元；芬兰引进项目3个，金额4万美元；台湾省引进项目26个，金额413万美元；香港引进项目8个，金额169万美元；韩国引进项目1个，金额0.1万美元。涉及的行业分别为电子及通信设备制造业、邮电通信设备制造业、交通运输设备制造业、电器机械及器材制造业、造纸及纸制品业、纺织业、化学工业、机械工业、金属制品业、塑料制品业、食品制品业、橡胶制品业、烟草加工业、交通运输业等。

【利用外资】

1999年利用外资情况表

利用外资方式	批准签订的合同			实际利用外资	
	项目数（个）	外资金额（万美元）	金额比1998年（±%）	金额（万美元）	金额比1998年（±%）
外商直接投资	364	65660	28.25	52035	3.39
合资企业	194	22044	10.23	26760	15.68
合作企业	20	5795	-59.63	6860	-33.69
外资企业	150	37821	124.51	18415	9.27
合　计	**364**	**65660**	**28.25**	**52035**	**3.39**

外商直接投资行业　在外商直接投资项目中，生产型项目288个，非生产型项目76个，按行业分，主要有电子及通信设备制造业、化学原料及化学制品制造业、普通机械制造业、纺织及服装制造业、塑料制品业、交通运输业、食品制造业、建筑业等，外商直接投资来自44个国家和地区，投资居前5位的是：香港109项，合同外资14700万美元；台湾省76项，合同外资为10671万美元；美国53项，合同外资6867万美元；维尔京群岛5项，合同外资4792万美元；荷兰4项，合同外资4757万美元。

截止1999年底，已开业投产的外商投资企业共1788家，职工总数为19.58万人，全年销售营业收入为39.4亿元，其中自营出口为86525万美元，利润总额为20.3亿美元。

【对外经济合作】

承包工程和劳务合作　1999年签订对外承包工程和劳务合作项目335份，金额9662万美元，比上年的10946万美元下降11%；营业额17200万美元，比上年的16000万美元增长7.5%；当年派出劳务人员5164人次，年末在外劳务人数12100万人，比上年增长10%，劳务人民分布在52个国家和地区，主要有新加坡、日本、柬埔寨、毛里求斯、马达加斯加、阿联酋、塞班等。

对外经济技术援助　承担援外项目2个，受援国是贝宁马维尔农垦和密克罗尼西亚体育馆设计，项目都已完成，金额111万美元，当年派出援外人员14名，年末在外人员3名。

对外投资　1999年在海外设立贸易型企业7家，非贸易型生产企业5家，境外经贸办事处8家，项目总投资616万美元。其中中方投资488万美元，这些企业分布在新加坡、美国、香港、罗马尼亚、荷兰、土库曼斯坦、法国、德国、俄罗斯、日本、柬埔寨、波兰、马来西亚、南非等14个国家和地区。

【其他】

经济技术开发区　1999年宁波经济技术开发区新投入基础设施资金1亿元，建设了一批道路和市政设施。全区新批外商投资企业23家，同比增长35.2%，协议利用外资1.56亿美元，同比增长10.7%，实际利用外资1.53亿美元。全年实现国内生产总值58.1亿元，同比增长13.8%；工业总产值175亿元，同比增长16.7%；财政收入6.58亿元，同比增长10.3%。

保税区　基础设施建设力度加大，投资软硬环境进一步改善，1999年完成固定资产投资总额3.2亿元，比上年增长27.4%。全年引进各类企业383家，其中外商投资企业总投资2.03亿美元，协议利用外资1.03亿美元，实际利用外资0.55万美元，分别比上年增长116.4%、40.8%、32.8%。全年完成进仓货物总值为9.5亿元，出仓货物总值9.3亿元。全年实现工业总产值8.02亿无，比上年同期增长 27.9%。

对外经贸洽谈会 1999 年 6 月 8 日至 6 月 10 日'99 浙江投资贸易洽谈会在宁波市举行，到会的外宾和外商有 3861 人，签订合资项目 457 个，总投资 44.39 亿美元，协议外资 23.87 亿美元，贸易成交额 5380 万美元。

10 月 18 日至 22 日我市举行第三届宁波国际服装节，有 28 个国家和地区 1200 余名海外人士参加，其中展示了国外 13 个国家、地区（64 家企业 51 个品牌）和国内 15 个省、市共 117 个服饰及面辅料品牌。本届博览会签订外资项目 17 个，总投资 17190 万美元，协议外资 12614 万美元。实现成交额 40.2 亿元。

港口运输 1999 年港口从 3000 吨到 25 万吨的泊位共有 39 个，港口吞吐能力 8608 万吨。当年实际完成货物吞吐量 9660 万吨，列全国第三位，比上年增长 11%，其中完成外贸进出口货物吞吐量 3852 万吨（其中进口 3460 万吨，出口 392 万吨），占宁波港吞吐量的 39.87%。全年集装箱吞吐量达 60 万标箱，比上年增长 70%，列全国第八位。当年空运量 1.78 万吨。为了增加运输能力，新开通国际集装箱干线 6 条，其中欧洲 3 条，美洲 2 条，东南亚和中东 1 条。现每月国际集装箱班轮已达 100 班。

涉外旅游 全年接待入境的外国人以及港澳台胞 11.2 万人次，比上年增长 12%，旅游收入 4810 万美元，比上年增长 9.32%。

1999 年温州市对外经济贸易

温州市对外贸易经济合作局

【对外贸易】

进出口总额 1999 年浙江省温州市进出口总额 122653 万美元，比 1998 年的 85688 万美元增长 43.1%。

出口总额 出口总额 82338 万美元，比上年的 68270 万美元增长 20.6%，占全市国内生产总值 732.4 亿元（相当于 88.6 亿美元）的 9.3%，占全省出口额的 6.4%。

出口商品结构 初级产品出口额 7564 万美元，占出口总额的 9.2%；工业制成品的出口额 74774 万美元，占出口总额的 90.8%。

出口额在 1000 万美元以上商品情况表

金额分类	商　品　名　称	出口金额（万美元）	占出口总额（%）
2000 万美元以上	生牛皮、布胶鞋、皮鞋、打火机、眼镜、电工用具、针织服装、梭织服装、水产品、小五金	37137	45.1
1000－2000 万美元	合成革鞋、运动鞋、公文包、家用小电器、日用皮制品、塑料制品、汽摩配件、文教用品	11340	13.8
合　计	**18 种**	**48477**	**58.9**

出口商品市场 出口商品销往156个国家(地区)。主要出口市场的出口金额60041万美元，占出口总额的72.9%。

主要出口市场情况表

国别（地区）	出口金额（万美元）	占出口总额（%）
美国	9261	11.2
香港	6071	7.4
匈牙利	5234	6.4
日本	4239	5.1
荷兰	3134	3.8
意大利	3090	3.8
捷克	2989	3.6
韩国	2927	3.6
法国	2757	3.3
西班牙	2692	3.3
德国	2556	3.1
俄罗斯	2366	2.9

主要出口市场情况表（续）

国别（地区）	出口金额（万美元）	占出口总额（%）
波兰	2364	2.9
阿联酋	2015	2.4
克罗地亚	1656	2.0
巴西	1534	1.9
英国	1448	1.8
土耳其	1319	1.6
比利时	1262	1.5
台湾省	1128	1.4
合计	**60041**	**72.9**

进口总额 进口总额40315万美元，比上年的17419万美元增长131.5%。

进口商品结构 初级产品进口额26429万美元，占进口总额的66%；工业制成品的进口额13886万美元，占进口总额的34%。

进口额在500万美元以上商品情况表

金额分类	商品名称	进口金额（万美元）	占进口总额（%）
500万美元以上	液化气、化工原料、塑料原料、牛革皮、钢材、化学设备、革制品设备、纸张	31451	78

进口商品市场 进口商品来自39个国家(地区)。

主要进口市场情况表

国别（地区）	进口金额（万美元）	占进口总额（%）
韩国	8652	21.5
日本	4187	10.4
香港	2743	6.8
台湾省	2305	5.7

主要进口市场情况表（续）

国别（地区）	进口金额（万美元）	占进口总额（%）
美国	2219	5.5
阿联酋	1864	4.6
德国	1236	3.1
加拿大	1081	2.7
合计	**24287**	**60.2**

【利用外资】

1999年利用外资情况表

利用外资方式	批准签订的合同			实际利用外资	
	项目数（个）	外资金额（万美元）	金额比1998年（±%）	金 额（万美元）	金额比1998年（±%）
外商直接投资	70	4644	−81	5615	+51.7
合资企业	53	2871	−48.36	2309	−15.98
合作企业		70	−99.56	2292	+18.59
外资企业	17	1703	−39.91	1014	+21.15

外商直接投资行业　在外商直接投资的70个项目中，生产型项目63个，占90%；非生产型项目7个，占10%，按行业分，农业1个，制造业63个，建筑业1个，房地产业4个，社会服务业1个。

外商直接投资来源　外商直接投资来自24个国家和地区。投资额居前6位的是：台湾省13个，合同外资765万美元；香港8个，1422万美元；法国8个，985万美元；西班牙5个，125万美元；美国4个，185万美元；意大利4个，53万美元。

外商投资企业生产经营情况　截止1999年底，累计批准外商投资企业1391家，项目总投资28.78亿美元，合同外资金额14.19亿美元，实际利用外资4.64亿美元。其中已开业投资的外商投资企业共638家，销售收入62.66亿元，比上年64.1亿元下降2.3%。盈利企业340家，盈利额3.45亿元，亏损企业181家，亏损额1亿元，盈亏相抵利润总额2.45亿元，同比下降24.7%。全年上缴税金4.5亿元，比上年的3.5亿元增长12%；直接出口企业278家，自营出口17583万美元，比上年下降11.6%。

【对外经济合作】

承包工程和劳务合作　1999年签订对外承包工程和劳务合作项目132个，金额338.5万美元，比上年的303.7万美元增长11.46%；营业额316.7万美元，比上年的257.6万美元增长22.9%；当年派出劳务人员1404人次，年末在外651人。劳务人员主要分布在老挝、保加利亚、台湾省（渔轮）等国家和地区；承包工程项目主要有老挝小水电工程。

对外投资　1999年温州市在海外举办企业（机构）8家，中方投资额84万美元，分别设在美国、德国、波兰、柬埔寨、尼日利亚、蒙古、埃及等国家。

【其他】

温州经济技术开发区　1999年共引进项目93个，总投资15.6亿元，比上年增长27.7%。其中外资项目11个，投资额1628万美元。到1999年底，开发区累计引进项目658个，总投资74.6亿元。其中外资项目141个，总投资2.88亿美元，合同外资1.5亿美元。内资项目517个，投资49.67亿元。

全年实现国内生产总值16.8亿元，比上年增长34%。工业总产值39.2亿元，同比增长35%。三产销售额32.3亿元，同比增长25%。出口创汇1.13亿美元，同比增长11%。财政收入2.27亿元，同比增长40%。

全年新开工基础设施项目30个，续建项目25个，年内竣工29个，共完成投资额1.4亿元。

港口运输　温州港口泊位114个，其中5万吨级1个，万吨级4个，5000～10000吨级4个，5000吨级以上105个。浮筒泊位2个，为万吨级。全年实际完成货物吞吐量711万吨，其中外贸进出口货物吞吐量104万吨，进口78万吨，出口26万吨。国际集装箱吞吐量36828标准箱，其中进口18969标准箱，出口17859标准箱。

涉外旅游 1999年接待外国旅游者、华侨、港澳台同胞5.44万人次，比上年的4.8万人次增长13.33%；旅游外汇收入2800万美元，比上年2700万美元增长3.7%。

1999年安徽省对外经济贸易

安徽省对外经济贸易委员会

【对外贸易】

进出口总额 1999年安徽省进出口总额26.49亿美元，比上年的22.57亿美元增长17.4%

出口总额 出口总额16.77亿美元，比上年的14.86亿美元增长13.1%，占全省国内生产总值2910亿元（相当于351.52亿美元）的4.77%；占全国出口额1949亿美元的0.86%。

出口商品结构 初级产品出口额2.59亿美元，占出口总额的15.5%；工业制成品出口额14.17亿美元，占出口总额的84.5%。

出口商品品种共1750种，其中出口额在1000万美元以上的商品25种，这25种商品出口额13.03亿美元，占全省出口总额的77.7%。

出口额在1000万美元以上商品情况表

金额分类	商品名称	出口金额（亿美元）	占出口总额（%）
1000万－5000万美元（17）种	柠檬酸、运输工具、芝麻、箱包、蔬菜、钢材、玩具、羽绒制品、塑料及制品、生铁、地毯、电冰箱、茶叶、自行车、纸及纸浆、花生仁、空调器	3.91	23.31
5000万－1亿美元（5种）	机械设备、大米、鞋类、电器及电子产品、轮胎	3.54	21.11
1亿美元以上3种	服装、金属制品、铜及铜材	5.58	33.23
合计	**25种**	**13.03**	**77.65**

出口商品市场 出口商品销往179个国家（地区）。主要出口市场是欧盟30728万美元，占18.3%；北美28169万美元，占16.8%；日本21426万美元，占12.8%；韩国11849万美元，占7.1%；东盟10191万美元，占6.1%；香港9548万美元，占5.7%。

进口总额 进口总额9.7亿美元，比上年的7.7亿美元增长25.5%。

进口商品结构 初级产品进口额3.03亿美元，占进口总额的31.2%；工业制成品进口额6.69亿美元，占进口总额的68.8%。

主要进口商品

进口额在1000万美元以上的商品情况表

金额分类	商品名称	进口金额（亿美元）	占进口总额（%）
1000万－5000万美元14种	天然橡胶、纸浆、塑料、纸及纸板、合成纤维长丝机织物、钢材、未锻造的铜及铜材、压缩机、金属加工机床、橡胶或塑料加工机械、型模、阀门、汽车零件、计量检测分析自控仪器	2.56	26.34
5000万－1亿美元3种	气轮机零件、铁矿砂、建筑及采矿用机械	1.93	19.89
1亿美元以上1种	铜矿砂	1.72	17.72
合　计	**18种**	**6.21**	**63.95**

进口商品市场　主要进口市场是日本16253万美元，占16.7%；欧盟25169万美元，占25.9%；韩国8279万美元，占8.5%；拉美13561万美元，占13.9%；北美7848万美元，占8.1%；东盟6736万美元，占6.9%。

技术进出口　技术进出口总额4.46亿美元，比上年的4.22亿美元增长5.7%。签订引进技术和进口设备合同190项，比上年减少4项；合同金额3.64亿美元，比上年的363亿美元增长0.3%。签订技术出口合同393项，比上年增加335项；合同金额0.82亿美元，比上年的0.59亿美元增长39.5%。主要技术出口项目有船舶、钢化玻璃生产线、计算机整机和软件、生化制品等。

【利用外资】

1999年利用外资情况表

利用外资方式	实际利用外资额（万美元）	比1998年（+%）
外商直接投资		
合资企业	30326	222.86
合作企业	11949	352.79
外资企业	13593	10.80
外商其他投资		
对外发行股票	11249	
合　计	**67117**	**108.24**

当年新批外商投资企业199家，利用外资合同金额5.59亿美元，比上年的2.69亿美元增长129.9%。其中，新批合资企业93家、3.09亿美元，合作企业25家、1.19亿美元，外资企业81家、1.36亿美元，对外发行股票企业1家、1.12亿美元。

外商直接投资行业　1999年新批外商直接投资协议项目中，第一、二产业的协议项目133项、协议外商直接投资额40790万美元，第三产业的协议项目66项、协议外商直接投资额15070万美元。

外商直接投资主要行业投向表

国制（地区）	协议项目数（个）	协议外商投资额（万美元）
电力煤气热水生产供应	3	15606
房地产	19	6396
食品加工	33	5988
社会服务业	32	5410
机械设备	28	4495
有色冶炼及延压	老项目增资	3648
化学原料及制品	8	2922
塑料制品	14	2560

外商直接投资来源

外商直接投资主要来源国别（地区）表

国别（地区）	协议项目数（个）	协议外商投资额（万美元）
香港	71	25439
美国	33	9302
日本	13	5287
台湾省	33	4498
维尔京群岛	4	3176
英国	2	2867
荷兰	1	1300
新加坡	7	1118

外商投资企业出口 1999年安徽外商投资企业完成出口额2.91亿美元，比上年的2.6亿美元增长10.7%；在全省出口总额中的比重由上年的19.7%下降到17.4%。

【对外经济合作】

承包工程和劳务合作 1999年签订对外承包工程和劳务合作合同额8550万美元，比上年的6864万美元增长24.6%；完成营业额9920万美元，比1996年的4926万美元增长101.4%；当年派出劳务人员2168人次，年末在外4276人。承包工程和劳务合作的主要市场是新加坡、马达加斯加、以色列、莫桑比克、津巴布韦和台湾省。

【其他】

经济技术开发区 合肥高新技术产业开发区 到1999年底，进区企业累计570家，协议投资额74.85亿元人民币。其中外商投资企业累计143家，协议利用外资额2.78亿美元。

1998、1999年国家和安徽省有关部门先后批准在区内建设高新技术农业园、留学生园、软件园、大学园区、国家级民营科技园，高新区正逐步建设“一区多园”的格局。其中软件园已吸引30多家软件企业入驻，还有10余家在外排队等候入驻。区内软件大厦一期工程8000平方米和二期工程2500平方米的装修即将竣工，将为软件企业提供良好的工作场所。

1999年区内新开工道路建设20万平方米，新开工房屋建设9万平方米，新增绿化面积1.8万平方米。区内空调、电冰箱、洗衣机、叉车等产业持续发展。同时，安科生物、凯立电子、显臣制药等一批科技型中小企业在产品开发、管理体制、企业融资等方面不断创新，顺利跨越初创阶段，进入了规模发展的良性循环。以中圜永信、硅谷天音、汇隆药业、医工所为代表的一批信息产业、生物工程及新医药企业纷纷入区发展，为高新区产业发展注入新的活力。

1999年全区技工贸总收入80亿元，出口4489万美元。

芜湖经济技术开发区 1999年开发区新增开发面积3平方公里，协议引进工业项目46个，协议引进资金19.1亿元，比上年协议引进资金增长67.8%。进区项目规模质量进一步提高。在协议引进项目中，1亿元以上的工业项目6个。广东科龙集团电机项目、美的集团工业园项目、铜陵铜业集团铜精加工项目等一批投资规模大、科技含量高的项目进区落户。形成了汽车及零部件、新型建材、电子电气等三个支柱产业。一批区内企业由租赁厂户发展到购地建厂，使优势产品加快发展，产业链在区内扩大延伸。1999年区内共出让土地21宗，计1470亩，是建区以来土地出让最多的一年。以“产业链”招商成为开发区引资工作的一大特色。

对外经贸洽谈会 1999年安徽举办的对外经贸洽谈活动主要有两次：10月26日至28日，安徽经贸代表团参加在日本神户举办的“中国商务良机交易会”，与参展的安徽企业开展经贸洽谈的日本客商201人次，意向成交220万美元。11月23～26日，安徽经贸代表团参加德国纽伦堡国际玩具博览会，与参展的安徽企业开展经贸洽谈的各国客商100多人次，成交25万美元。

港口运输 全省港口1999年共完成外贸货运量（包括直接外运和转关运输）124.5万吨，比上年的125万吨基本持平。合肥、黄山两空港运送出入境旅客2.99万人次，比上年的2.15万人次增长38%。芜湖港新增三个专用码头对外开放，并顺利接纳外国籍船舶靠泊作业。

涉外旅游 接待来省的外国人及港澳台同胞

25.12 万人次，旅游收入 9015.8 万美元，比上年的 7036.1 万美元增长 28.1%。

1999 年福建省对外经济贸易

福建省对外经济贸易委员会

【对外贸易】

进出口总额 1999 年福建省进出口总额 176.45 亿美元，比 1998 年的 171.60 亿美元增长 2.82%。

出口总额 出口总额 103.76 亿美元，比上年的 99.59 亿美元增长 4.19%，占全省国内生产总值 3628.04 亿元（相当于 437.64 亿美元）的 23.71%，占全国出口总额的 5.32%，居全国第 6 位。

出口商品结构 初级产品出口额 12.60 亿美元，占出口总额的 12.14%；工业制成品的出口额 91.16 亿美元，占出口总额的 87.86%。

出口额在 1000 万美元以上的大宗商品 80 种，合计金额 90.69 亿美元，占全省出口总额的 87.40%。其中出口额在 1 亿美元以上的商品有河鳗（烤鳗）、花岗岩石材及制品、装饰用陶瓷制品、显示器、电热烤面包器、飞机及直升机的装配零件、船舶、家具、旅行用品及箱包、非针织或钩编织物制服装、针织或钩编的服装、鞋、塑料制品、贵金属或包贵金属的首饰、伞等 15 种，合计出口金额 68.87 亿美元，占出口总额的 66.37%；出口额在 5000 万－1 亿美元的商品有食用菌农产品、茶叶、蘑菇罐头、家用或装饰用木制品、数字或自动数据处理设备、电动机及发电机、静止式变流器、推进器扬声器、录音机及收录（放）音机、太阳镜、玩具等 11 种，合计金额 6.85 亿美元，占出口总额的 6.60%；出口额在 1000 万－5000 万美元的有芦笋罐头、食用植物油、地毯、显微镜、电熨斗、测量器、望远镜、电子计算器、变压器、有线电话机、圣诞用品、人造花、竹编结品等 54 种，合计金额 15.24 亿美元，占出口总额的 14.69%。

出口商品市场 出口商品销往 180 个国家和地区。主要出口市场：美国 25.54 亿美元、日本 20.56 亿美元、香港 14.64 亿美元、德国 5.22 亿美元、台湾省 3.03 亿美元、新加坡 2.48 亿美元、荷兰 2.27 亿美元、英国 2.15 亿美元、意大利 1.72 亿美元、加拿大 1.68 亿美元、西班牙 1.53 亿美元、澳大利亚 1.28 亿美元、韩国 1.21 亿美元、比利时 1.17 亿美元、马来西亚 1.08 亿美元、菲律宾 1.01 亿美元，合计 86.57 亿美元，占出口总额的 83.43%。

进口总额 进口总额 72.69 亿美元，比上年的 72.01 亿美元增长 0.94%。

进口商品结构 初级产品进口 9.78 亿美元，占进口总额的 13.45%；工业制成品进口 62.91 亿美元，占进口总额的 86.55%。

进口额在 1 亿美元以上的大宗商品有饲料，生橡胶，石油、石油产品及有关原料，天然气及人造气，有机化学品，初级形状的塑料，皮革、皮革制品及已鞣毛皮，纸浆、纸及纸制板，纺纱、织物及有关产品，非金属矿物制品，钢铁，有色金属，金属制品，动力机械及设备，特种工业专用机械，通用工业机械设备及零件，办公用机械及自动数据处理设备，电信及声音的录制和重放装置设备，电力机械、器具及其电气零件等 19 类，合计金额 56.01 亿美元，占进口总额的 77.05%。

进口额在 5000 万美元的商品有鱼及其制品，纺织纤维，天然肥料及矿物，染料、鞣料及着色料，非初级形态的塑料，橡胶制品，金工机械，鞋靴，专业、科学及控制用仪器和装置，摄影器材及光学制品等 10 类，合计进口额 7.09 亿美元，占进口总额的 9.75%。

进口额在1000万－5000万美元的商品有乳品及蛋品，谷物及制品，软木及木材，纸浆及废纸，金属矿砂及金属废料，植物油、脂，无机化学品，精油、香料等光洁制品，软木及木制品，陆路车辆，服装及衣着附件等11类，合计金额3.23亿美元，占进口总额的4.44%。

进口商品市场 进口商品来自93个国家和地区。主要进口市场：台湾省20.22亿美元、日本11.72亿美元、韩国8.25亿美元、美国7.13亿美元、香港3.10亿美元、马来西亚2.03亿美元、德国1.80亿美元、英国1.67亿美元、新加坡1.67亿美元、泰国1.33亿美元、俄罗斯1.27亿美元、法国1.21亿美元、印度尼西亚1.10亿美元。合计金额62.5亿美元，占进口总额的85.98%。

技术进出口 1999年技术进出口总额2.53亿美元，比上年的1.68亿美元增长50.59%。其中，签订引进技术进口设备合同60项，合同金额5453.23万美元，比上年的5545万美元下降1.66%；签订技术出口合同17项，金额1.98亿美元，比1998年的1.13亿美元增长75.22%。

技术进口 引进技术进口设备来自美国、德国、英国、澳大利亚、日本、泰国、新加坡、香港、台湾省等国家和地区。其中主要的有：美国11项、合同金额2280.65万美元，德国7项、611.32万美元，香港3项、54.65万美元，英国2项、71.4万美元，台湾省2项、50.48万美元等。主要涉及化工、邮电、船舶、金融、冶金、印刷、医疗、农业、陶瓷、建筑等行业的生产技术与设备。

技术出口 主要出口法国、加拿大、德国和孟加拉等国家，涉及船舶、电站、软件、激光器等技术、成套设备。

【利用外资】

1999年利用外资情况表

利用外资方式	批准签订的合同			实际利用外资	
	项目（个）	外资金额（万美元）	金额比1998年（±%）	金额（万美元）	金额比1998年（±%）
对外借款		1100	－88.56	1100	－88.56
外商直接投资	1439	489996	－2.03	402403	＋0.03
合资企业	250	103378	－1.7	99542	＋12.56
合作企业	37	37356	＋0.96	42121	－1.67
外资企业	997	379262	－2.44	260180	－0.08
外商投资股份制				560	
合计	**1439**	**491096**	**－3.66**	**403503**	**0.06**

外商直接投资行业 在外商直接投资项目中，生产型项目1175个，非生产型264个。按行业分，农林牧渔业132项，采掘业22项，制造业1021项，电力、煤气及水的生产11项，建筑业11项，地质勘查业、水利1项，交通、运输、仓储9项，批发和零售贸易40项，房地产业97项，社会服务业85项，卫生、体育和社会福利业2项，教育、文化、艺术2项，科学研究和综合技术服务业1项，其他行业5项。

外商直接投资来源 投资者来自49个国家和地区。其中香港647项、合同外资金额23.99亿美元，台湾省378项、7.14亿美元，美国56项、5.59亿美元，维尔京群岛24项、2.74亿美元，英国12项、2.52亿美元，新加坡49项、1.69亿美元，菲律宾53项、9376万美元，日本65项、6908万美元，澳门29项、5931万美元，马来西亚16项、5921万美元，澳大利亚30项、3045万美元，加拿大12项、2672万美元等。

外商直接投资企业生产经营情况 1999年新开业投产的外商投资企业765家。到1999年底止，全省累计已开业投产的外商投资企业15159家。1999年外商投资企业实现工业产值1382.28亿元，比1998年的1220.20亿元增长13.28%，占全省乡及乡以上工业产值的62.2%；出口58.87亿美元，比上年的54.49亿美元增长8.04%，占全省出口总额的56.74%。

【对外经济合作】

承包工程和劳务合作 1999年签订对外承包工程和劳务合作合同2249项，合同金额3.61亿美元，比上年的4.39亿美元下降17.74%。完成营业额4.47亿美元，比上年的5.19亿美元下降13.89%。当年派出劳务人数3.12万人次，年末在外劳务人数5.67万人。劳务人员分布在新加坡、澳门、香港、以色列、柬埔寨、博茨瓦纳、毛里求斯、格鲁吉亚等80个国家和地区。主要对外承包工程项目有马来西亚岭顶地产、菲律宾6PY1－2道路工程、澳大利亚圣嘉利湖地产开发、香港渣甸街46－52工程等。

对外投资 1999年新批准在澳门、柬埔寨、马达加斯加等地举办海外企业3家，中方投资160万美元。其中生产加工型企业1家，进出口贸易企业1家，建筑设计咨询1家。

【其他】

经济技术开发区 福建省经国务院批准的经济技术开发区有福州经济技术开发区、福清融侨经济技术开发区和福建东山经济技术开发区等。其中东山经济技术开发区继续加强基础设施建设，新投资2000多万元用于区内水、电、路、环境保护设施等项目建设，目前区内水、电、路、通讯等设施基本配套。开发区重点开发食品、通用器材、水产品和工业城等项目。1999年新批外商投资项目11项，合同外资金额8178万美元，外商实际到资6020.8万美元。外贸出口2500万美元。

对外经贸洽谈会 由“福建投资贸易洽谈会”更名的“中国投资贸易洽谈会”，于1999年9月8日在厦门市举行。本届洽谈会由国家对外经贸部主办、福建省人民政府和厦门市人民政府共同承办、福建及各省市等44个成员单位组成。洽谈会共接待来自港澳台、东南亚、欧美、日本、韩国、澳大利亚、新西兰等80多个国家和地区的境外客商6410多人。会上共签订外商投资合同项目1228项，利用外资51.83亿美元；外贸进出口成交8.13亿美元，其中出口成交7.09亿美元，进口成交1.04亿美元。福建省在会上共签订外商投资合同项目704项，利用外资26.12亿美元；进出口成交5.02亿美元，其中出口成交4.01亿美元，进口成交1.01亿美元。

港口运输 沿海主要港口货物吞吐量5253万吨，比上年的4517.69万吨增长16.27%。

全年进出口货运总量2014万吨，比1998年的1743.4万吨增长15.52%。其中出口货运量998万吨，进口货运量1016万吨。主要运输方式为海运。

涉外旅游 全年接待观光、探亲访友以及洽谈投资贸易的各类海外人士135.60万人次，比上年的121.78万人次增长11.34%。其中外国人35.30万人次，比上年的32.68万人次增长8.02%；港澳同胞53.24万人次，比上年的48.83万人次增长9.03%；台湾同胞41.46万人次，比上年的35.36万人次增长17.25%。

1999年厦门市对外经济贸易

厦门市贸易发展委员会

【对外贸易】

进出口总额 1999年厦门市进出口总额79.63亿美元，比1998年76.14亿美元增长4.8%

出口总额 出口总额44.36亿美元。比上年的42.96亿美元增长3.4%。

出口商品结构 初级产品出口额42415万美元，占出口总额的9.6%；工业制成品的出口额401172万美元，占出口总额的90.4%。

出口额在3000万美元以上商品情况表

金额分类	商品名称	出口金额（亿美元）	占出口总额（%）
1亿美元以上（3种）	飞机及直升机的其他零件、花岗岩碑石或建筑用石及其制品、电热烤面包器	5.350	12.06
5000万－1亿美元（9种）	塑料制小雕塑品及其他装饰品、制作或保藏的（河）鳗鱼整条或切块的、其他微型数字式自动数据处理机、合成纤维制帐篷、橡胶或塑料制外底及鞋面的其他运动鞋靴、未列名橡胶或塑料制外底及鞋面的鞋靴、其他橡、塑或再生皮革外底，皮革鞋面的鞋靴、未列名塑料制品、太阳镜	6.084	13.72
3000万－5000万美元（13种）	塑料或纺织材料作面的提箱、小手袋等、其他运动或户外游戏用设备；游泳池或戏水池、未列名静止式变流器、小白蘑菇（洋蘑菇）罐头、电熨斗、其他硅、其他收录（放）音组合机、龙头、旋塞及类似装置、其他电感器、草地网球拍、其他扬声器、人造纤维短纤≥85%未漂白或漂白布、瓷制塑像及其他装饰品	4.905	11.06
合　计	**25种**	**16.339**	**36.82**

主要出口市场情况表

国别（地区）	出口金额（美元）	占出口总额（%）
美国	1073062448	24.19
日本	848048869	19.12
香港	691202779	15.58
德国	170616741	3.85
台湾省	139908084	3.15
新加坡	111777431	2.52

主要出口市场情况表（续）

国别（地区）	出口金额（美元）	占出口总额（%）
英国	99540531	2.24
荷兰	98697366	2.22
韩国	75486004	1.70
意大利	68198736	1.54
合　计	**3376538989**	**76.11**

进口总额 进口总额35.27亿美元，比上年的33.18亿美元增长6.5%。

进口商品结构 初级产品出口额27263万美元，占出口总额的7.7%；工业制成品的出口额325403万美元，占出口总额的92.3%。

进口额在3000万美元以上商品情况表

金额分类	商品名称	进口金额（亿美元）	占进口总额（%）
1亿美元以上（1种）	飞机及直升机的其他零件	2.333	6.61
5000万～1亿美元（6种）	对苯二甲酸、彩色阴极射线电视显像管、混合集成电路、其他单片集成电路、8471所列其他机器的零件及附件、其他燃料油	3.959	11.22
3000万～5000万美元（9种）	未列名塑料制品、原状或粗加修整的花岗岩、1，2－乙二醇、整张牛皮革，表面积≤28sq ft（2.6平方米）、硬盘驱动器、未锻轧的精炼铜阴极及阴极型材、初级形状的聚氯乙烯，未掺其他物质、8535、8536或8537所列装置的其他零件、未锻轧的铝合金	3.212	9.11
合　计	**16种**	**9.504**	**26.94**

主要进口市场情况表

国别（地区）	进口金额（美元）	占进口总额（%）
台湾省	853339377	24.20
日　本	522823934	14.82
韩　国	414601060	11.76
美　国	363071421	10.30
香　港	218563848	6.20
英　国	118646344	3.36

主要进口市场情况表（续）

国别（地区）	进口金额（美元）	占进口总额（%）
新加坡	116342396	3.30
德　国	110014530	3.12
马来西亚	103032165	2.92
泰　国	90810988	2.57
合　计	**2911246063**	**82.55**

【利用外资】

1999年利用外资情况表

利用外资方式	批准签订的合同			实际利用外资	
	项目数（个）	外资金额（万美元）	金额比1998年（±%）	金额（万美元）	金额比1998年（±%）
外商直接投资	209	128655	－23.19	134196	－2.84

1999 年利用外资情况表

利用外资方式	批准签订的合同			实际利用外资	
	项目数（个）	外资金额（万美元）	金额比 1998 年（±%）	金额（万美元）	金额比 1998 年（±%）
合资企业	54	47916		41381	
合作企业	12	10852		30930	
外资企业	143	69887		61885	

1999 年利用外资分国别/情况表

单位：万美元

国别地区	项目数	总投资	协议外资
总计	**209**	**148081**	**128655**
香　港	57	45518	33367
台湾省	75	20675	20275
新加坡	12	8297	8116
美　国	14	44797	37869
菲律宾	3	1012	1004
日　本	9	1403	1238
英　国	14	16334	16265
马来西亚	8	887	538
澳　门	1	1700	1671
澳大利亚	2	110	110

1999 年利用外资分行业情况表

单位：万美元

	项目数	总投资	协议外资
总计	**209**	**148081**	**128655**
农业	6	1135	833
工业	161	124541	108165
建筑业	0	0	0
交通运输	1	51	51
饮食服务	28	8981	7474
房地产	13	133395	12131
其他	0	0	0

【对外经济合作】

承包工程和劳务合作　签订对外承包工程和劳务合作项目 136 个，金额 4658 万美元，比上年的 2673 万美元增长 74%；营业额 7069 万美元，比 1998 年 8026 万美元下降 12%；当年派出劳务人员 2974 人次，年末在外人数 8547 人，派往的主要国家和地区：香港、澳门、以色列、毛里求斯、越南、柬埔寨等。

【其他】

港口运输　1999 年厦门海港完成外贸进出口货物吞吐量 1773.38 万吨，比上年增长 8.2%。其中出口 662.08 万吨，增长 22.9%，进口 1111.30 万吨，增长 1.0%。集装箱吞吐量 84.85 万标箱，增长 29.8%。

1999年福州市对外经济贸易

福州市对外经济贸易委员会

【对外贸易】

进出口总额 1999年福州市进出口总额343160万美元，比1998年361484万美元，下降5.1%。

出口总额 出口总额208856万美元，比上年194800万美元增长7.2%，占福州市国内生产总值的18.27%，占全省出口总值的20.13%。其中外贸专业公司和工贸公司出口24496万美元，比上年同期增长0.7%；外商投资企业出口184360万美元，比1998年增长8.1%。

出口商品结构 初级产品出口额10000万美元，占出口总额的4.79%；工业制成品的出口额198856万美元，占出口总额的95.21%。

出口商品有60多类，1000多种。其中主要出口商品有光电产品52779万美元，箱包鞋帽40302万美元，粮油水产22585万美元，家用电器20325万美元，工艺陶瓷17385万美元，文化用品13946万美元，五金矿产7833万美元，纺织服装5764万美元，钟表4214万美元。共计185133万美元，占出口总额88.64%。

出口商品市场 出口商品销往102个国家和地区。

主要出口商品市场情况表

国别（地区）	出口金额（万美元）	占出口总额（%）
香港	79288	37.96
美　国	55252	26.45
日　本	38099	18.24
德　国	15122	7.25
台湾省	8112	3.88
合　计	**195873**	**93.78**

进口总额 进口总额134304万美元，比上年167377万美元下降19.76%。其中国有外贸企业进口7091万美元，外商投资企业进口127213万美元，分别占进口总额的5.3%和94.7%。

主要进口商品有光电设备产品44450万美元、化工产品16180万美元、家用电器15944万美元、土畜产品5852万美元、粮油食品1986万美元。共计84412万美元，占进口总额62.85%。

进口商品市场 进口商品主要来自香港、日本、台湾省、美国、韩国、德国、法国、马来西亚等国家（地区）。

技术进口 1999年签订引进设备及配品备件合同610项，合同金额8046万美元。引进技术设备主要来自台湾省、香港、日本、美国、澳大利亚、新加坡、马来西亚、德国、奥地利、意大利等国家和地区；引进项目主要分布在机械设备、电机、电讯、电子等设备及其他配品备件。

【利用外资】

1999年批准签订外商投资企业合同338项，比上年的481项减少29.73%。合同外资93426万美元，比上年111031万美元减少15.86%。其中，合资企业80项，合同外资金额13434万美元；合作经营企业8项，合同外资金额5030万美元；独资企业250项，合同外资金额74962万美元。外商投资企业全年实际利用外资90036万美元，比上年90384万美元减少0.35%。

外商直接投资行业 外商直接投资的338项中，制造业219项，金额49682万美元；农牧业26项，金额8560万美元；建筑业6项，金额3970万美元；采掘业4项，金额330万美元；地质勘探1项，金额687万美元；科学研究2项，金额86万美元；房地产业39项，金额22465万美元；批发零售17项，金额4178万美元；社会服务23项，金额3348万美元；卫生体育1项，金额120万美元。其中生产型、出口创汇型项目占76.62%。

外商直接投资来源 投资者主要来自香港、澳门、台湾省、老挝、日本、菲律宾、泰国、马来西亚、新加坡、印度尼西亚、韩国、马达加斯加、德国、法国、意大利、荷兰、英国、多米尼加、巴西、阿根廷、巴拿马、维尔京岛、加拿大、美国、澳大利亚、新西兰、西萨摩亚等27个国家和地区。其中香港144项,金额56983万美元;台湾省81项,金额8701万美元;美国22项,金额7672万美元;新加坡8项,金额5142万美元;日本27项,金额2033万美元;加拿大3项,金额2006万美元;马来西亚5项,金额1896万美元。

外商直接投资企业生产经营情况 全年有243家外商投资企业投产。至1999年底已开业投产的外商投资企业2962家,工业产值460亿元人民币,占福州市同期乡以上工业总产值的70%;出口创汇184360万美元,比上年170549万美元增长8.1%,占全市出口总额的88.27%。

【对外经济技术合作】

承包工程和劳务合作 1999年签订对外承包合同和劳务合作合同735个,金额5142万美元,比上年5644万美元减少5.6%;营业额6509万美元,比上年6284万美元增长3.6%;全年派出劳务人员6011人次,年末在外8986人。主要派往台湾省、澳门、新加坡、香港、也门、日本、孟加拉、印尼、马来西亚、越南、马尔代夫、柬埔寨、菲律宾、以色列、泰国、毛里求斯、南非、塞浦路斯、莱索托、喀麦隆、毛里塔尼亚、赤道几内亚、加纳、贝宁、多哥、几内亚、乌干达、利比利亚、塞舌尔、摩尔多瓦、匈牙利、保加利亚、英国、土耳其、俄罗斯、阿塞拜疆、丹麦、圣巴丁、捷克、苏里南、希腊、罗马尼亚、美国、加拿大、牙买加、墨西哥、阿根廷、玻利维亚、马达加斯加、澳大利亚、斐济、巴布亚新几内亚等国家和地区。主要从事渔工、海员、建筑、制衣、机械、针织、电子、餐饮等业务。

【其他】

经济技术开发区 福州经济技术开发区是目前全国惟一集国家级经济技术开发区、保税区、台商投资区、高科技园区和地方行政区于一体的特殊开放区域。十五年来,福州经济技术开发区在抓基础设施和公用设施的硬环境建设同时,大力加强软环境建设。实行了“项目登记制”、“一个窗口收费制”、“外商投资接待日”等项制度,加大了改善外商投资环境力度。在项目建设方面,坚持了“以工业项目为主,以吸引外资为主和出口创汇为主”的方针,广泛吸引外商前来投资。十五年来,福州开发区(含台商投资区、保税区、高科技园区)先后有香港、台湾省、美、日、德、英、法等国家和地区的跨国公司和知名企业前来开发区投资。截止1999年底,累计审批内外资项目1108项,总投资37.8亿美元。其中外商投资项目762项,总投资34.4亿美元,合同外资16.5亿美元,实际利用外资近10亿美元。全区实现国内生产总值71.2亿元人民币,工业总产值153.7亿元,出口总值5.19亿美元。其中已投产的台资企业中,产值超亿元的6家,超千万元以上的21家。

福州融侨开发区 坚持“以侨引台”、“以台促侨”、“侨台外”共同发展的开放开发的路子,使开发区外向型经济迅速发展。全年新批外商投资项目8项,合同外资2939万美元,历年累计批准外商投资项目206项,合同外资11.19亿美元,实际利用外资9.4亿美元。区内涌现出了冠捷电子、福耀玻璃、太平洋塑胶、明达塑胶等一批大型骨干企业。1999年外商投资企业出口82691万美元,工业产值124亿元,占福州市工业产值38.7%。

地处闽江经济圈的元洪投资区,已累计审批外商投资项目26项,合同外资47357万美元,实际利用外资21470万美元,出口4973万美元,外商投资企业工业产值8.23亿元人民币。

福州海峡两岸农业合作试验区自批准成立以来,发展势头良好。实验区成立后,首期推出福清、闽侯、马尾琅岐作为三地示范重点培植地,建成一批具有较高科技含量和示范辐射功能的项目。如福清洪宽海峡两岸农业合作试验农场、闽侯雪峰农场、琅岐华琅农业综合开发项目等,这些项目均取得了较好的效益。截止1999年底,全市共引进农业合资项目324项,合同台资4.4亿美元,实际利用台资2.9亿美元。

对外经贸洽谈会 1999年5月,在福州举办的中国福州国际招商月、9月福州代表团参加外经贸部在厦门举办的第三届中国投资贸易洽谈会,福州市接待了来自香港、澳门和台湾省以及美国、加拿大、英国、法国、西班牙、阿根廷、德国、澳大利亚、泰国、日本、韩国等47个国家和地区5000多名境外来宾。签订外商投资企业合同200项,总投资9.26亿美元,协议外资8.22亿美元。

港口运输 1999年大小生产性泊位103个,其中万吨级以上深水泊位16个。港口吞吐量1480万吨,实际进出口货物总运量1480万吨,其中外贸进出口吞吐量510万吨,出口340万吨,进口170万吨。

涉外旅游 在办好原有福州国家森林公园、鳄鱼公园、左海水族娱乐城、琅岐龙鼓渡假村重点景点基础上,同时推出一批"海乐梦"大型豪华游轮闽江一日游、大穆溪漂流、屏山公园猕猴世界、新东阳卡丁赛车等旅游项目。

1999年全市接待国内游客536万人次,营业额收入12.2亿元;接待国际游客24.8万人次,旅游创汇1.17亿美元。

1999年江西省对外经济贸易

江西省对外贸易经济合作厅

【对外贸易】

进出口总额 1999年江西省进出口总额131382万美元,比1998年的124718万美元增长5.34%。

出口总额 出口总额90606万美元,比上年的101822万美元下降11.02%,占全省国内生产总值1967.7亿元(相当于237.66亿美元)的3.81%,占全国出口额的0.46%。

出口商品结构 初级产品的出口额16306万美元,占出口总额的18.0%;工业制成品的出口额74300万美元,占出口总额的82.0%。出口175种主要商品,金额在100万美元以上的出口商品有66种,计65171万美元,占出口商品总额的71.93%。

出口额在500万美元以上的商品情况表

金额分类	商品名称	出口金额(万美元)	占出口总额(%)
5000万美元以上(3种)	服装、棉织品、鞋	28559	31.52
1000万美元至5000万美元(11种)	大米、烟花爆竹、铜材、活大猪、抗菌素、河鳗、苎麻织品、陶瓷、茶叶、床垫寝具、手工具	19892	21.85
500万美元至1000万美元(10种)	碲石、仲钨酸铵、合成织物、装饰木制品、纸及纸板、灯具、棉坯布、食用油籽、塑料制品、人造花	6180	6.82
合 计	**24种**	**54631**	**60.29**

出口商品市场 出口商品销往153个国家和地区,。出口金额在100万美元以上的65个国家和地区,计78496万美元,占出口总额的86.63%。

主要出口市场情况表

国别(地区)	出口金额(万美元)	金额比1998年(±%)	占出口总额(%)
香　港	15649	-43.40	17.27
日　本	10749	7.38	11.86
美　国	9347	2.90	10.32
韩　国	4346	8.57	4.80
德　国	4253	-7.50	4.69
印度尼西亚	3040	-25.03	3.36
巴拿马	2594	-13.07	2.86
菲律宾	2118	-45.44	2.34
阿联酋	2019	14.07	2.23
荷　兰	1969	-24.70	2.17
新加坡	1881	87.35	2.08
英　国	1771	16.51	1.95
孟加拉国	1658	72.89	1.83
合　计	**61394**	**-17.19**	**67.76**

进口总额 进口总额40776万美元,比上年的22896万美元增长78.09%。占全国进口额的0.25%。

进口商品结构 初级产品的进口额8015万美元,占进口总额的19.66%;工业制成品的进口额32761万美元,占进口总额的80.34%。进口129种主要商品,金额在100万美元以上的进口商品有44种,计26960万美元,占进口商品总额的66.18%。

进口额在500万美元以上的商品情况表

金额分类	商品名称	进口金额(万美元)	占进口总额(%)
1000万美元以上(6种)	汽车零件、金属铸造用型箱、铜矿砂、液泵及液体提升机、纸浆、汽车	10888	26.70
500万美元至1000万美元(13种)	集成电路、铁矿砂、成品油、钢材、自动数据处理设备、塑料、合成纤维、内燃机零件、纸及纸板、钢板、机械设备、建设机械、锰矿砂	9054	22.20
合　计	**19种**	**19942**	**48.90**

进口商品市场 进口商品来自51个国家和地区,进口额在100万美元以上的32个国家和地区,

计 40004 万美元，占进口总额的 98.4%。

主要进口市场情况表

国别(地区)	进口金额(万美元)	金额比 1998 年(±%)	占进口总额(%)%
日　本	9945	101.97	24.39
美　国	4729	52.30	11.60
德　国	4489	421.98	11.01
台湾省	2872	48.73	7.04
英　国	2639	-3.69	6.47
香　港	2505	72.64	6.14
韩　国	2435	91.28	5.97
加拿大	1624	53.64	3.98
南　非	1137	96.71	2.79
秘　鲁	834	100.00	2.05
巴　西	759	860.76	1.86
法　国	616	3.88	1.51
澳大利亚	533	-41.43	1.31
合　计	**35117**	**80.08**	**86.12**

技术进出口　技术进出口总额 12171 万美元，比上年的 13966 万美元下降 12.85%。其中签订引进技术和进口设备合同项目 16 个，比上年减少 17 个；合同金额 1132 万美元，比上年的 3223 万美元下降 64.88%。签订技术出口合同项目 913 个，比上年增加 278 个，合同金额 11039 万美元，比上年的 10743 万美元增长 2.76%。

技术进口　技术引进和设备进口来自 7 个国家和地区，涉及 9 个行业。

技术引进和设备进口分行业汇总表

行　业	项目数(个)	合同金额(万美元)
广　播	2	329
汽　车	1	245

技术引进和设备进口分行业汇总表(续)

行　业	项目数(个)	合同金额(万美元)
航　空	1	123
印　刷	1	111
冶　金	5	110
有　色	2	85
仪　器	1	55
轻　工	2	36
邮　电	1	27
合　计	**16**	**1132**

技术出口 技术出口对外签订项目全部履约。技术出口主要项目有:金属制品2876万美元、电子机械及器材2036万美元、仪器仪表1607万美元、电子及通讯设备1260万美元、普通机械999万美元、专用设备515万美元。技术出口到69个国家和地区,主要出口国别地区是:美国1561万美元;德国785万美元、英国522万美元、津巴布韦451万美元、荷兰344万美元、法国273万美元、意大利214万美元。

【利用外资】

签订利用外资合同项目 250 个,合同外资额 38147 万美元,比上年的 65244 万美元下降 38.91%;实际利用外资 56829 万美元,比上年的 70865 万美元下降 19.81%。

1999 年利用外资情况表

利用外资方式	批准签订的合同			实际利用外资	
	项目(个)	外资金额(万美元)	金额比1998年(±%)	金额(万美元)	金额比1998年(±%)
对外借款	2	2890	-85.76	12610	-4.05
外商直接投资	245	35136	-16.18	32080	-31.00
合资企业	88	11679	-24.06	11452	-47.45
合作企业	21	3554	-28.48	6344	11.71
外资企业	136	17855	-17.22	14284	-24.91
外商投资股份制		2048			
外商其他投资	3	121	-47.39	12139	8.09
国际租赁					
补偿贸易					
加工贸易	2	121	14.15	113	6.60
对外发行股票	1			12026	9.33
合计	**250**	**38147**	**-38.91**	**56829**	**-19.81**

外商直接投资行业 在外商直接投资项目中,生产型 166 项占 67.76%、非生产型 79 项占 32.24%。

外商直接投资分行业情况表

行业	项目数(个)	合同外资(万美元)	占合同外资总额(%)
农、林、牧、渔业	13	1585	4.51
制造业	135	19325	54.93
其中:饮料	7	971	2.76
纺织	8	883	2.51
服装	11	985	2.80
竹木加工	8	1014	2.88
化学原料及制品	12	556	1.58

外商直接投资分行业情况表(续)

行业	项目数(个)	合同外资(万美元)	占合同外资总额(%)
非金属矿物制品	10	3547	10.08
交通运输设备	2	1262	3.59
电气机械及器材	6	821	2.33
电子及通讯设备	8	3299	9.38
电力煤气业	7	1064	3.02
建筑业	9	904	2.57
房地产业	29	7340	20.86
社会服务业	43	4112	11.69
其他行业	9	852	2.42
合　计	**245**	**35182**	**100.00**

外商直接投资来源　外商签约直接投资来自25个国家和地区,投资额居前五位是:香港21033万美元,占59.78%;美国4121万美元,占11.71%;台湾省3453万美元,占9.81%;新加坡2316万美元,占6.58%;英属维尔京群岛1045万美元,占2.97%。

外商直接投资企业生产经营情况　1999年全省有75家外商投资企业投资开业。截至1999年底,全省累计批准外商投资企业4945家,其中投产开业的1456家。外商投资企业1999年出口创汇9989万美元。比上年的8659万美元增长15.36%,占全省出口总额的比重由1998年的8.50%上升到11.02%,提高2.52个百分点。据487家外商投资企业统计,1999年实现销售(营业)收入76.46亿元,缴纳税金3.49亿元,利润1.93亿元,从业人员68195人,其中外籍员工369人。

【对外经济合作】

承包工程和劳务合作　签订对外承包工程和劳务合作合同项目117个,比上年增加14项,合同金额11665万美元,比上年的7725万美元增长50.98%;完成营业额8537万美元,比上年的7615万美元增长12.03%;当年派出劳务人员2712人,年末在外人数5419人,比上年增加1322人。劳务人员派往45个国家和地区,主要国家和地区是:日本、台湾省、新加坡、美国塞班和马来西亚;承包工程主要项目有:尼泊尔的印德拉瓦迪水利、马里的体育场、沙特阿拉伯的利雅得宾馆和马来西亚的2872住宅楼项目。

对外经济技术援助　承担对外援助项目2个,受援国家及其项目是:斐济农村供电项目,已建成移交斐方使用;赞比亚经商处综合楼项目,已竣工验收合格。当年派出援外人员18人,年末在外人数14人。

接受经济援助　接受国际经济组织及双边援助项目9个,金额555万美元,比上年的679万美元下降18.26%。接受援助已经执行完毕的4个项目是:联合国开发计划署援助8万美元的灾区学校恢复项目、日本政府援助69万元人民币的修水县上杭乡乡村公路建设项目、澳大利亚政府援助84万元人民币的黎川县洵口镇电站恢复项目和余干县蛇塘小学重建项目;正在执行的5个项目是:日本政府援助2亿日元的粮食增产项目、德国政府援助600万马克的江西山区可持续发展项目、澳大利亚政府援助44万元人民币的弋阳县湖山乡饮用水建设项目和援助50万澳元的都昌县可持续生态改善项目以及血吸虫感染区治理项目。

对外投资　1999年批准中国江西国际经济技术合作公司在埃塞俄比亚设立中埃阳光制药私人有限公司,从事境外带料加工装配业务,中方投资135万美元。

【其他】

高新技术产业开发区　南昌国家级高新技

术产业开发区,1999年继续加大固定资产投资,广泛开展招商引资活动,促进了经济快速发展。1999年技工贸总收入完成52万元,比1998年增长36.84%;工业总产值完成42亿元,增长34.2%;实现利税4.1亿元,增长28.13%;财政收入9527万元,增长10%;签订利用外资合同10项,金额4319万美元,增长93.16%,实际利用外资1540万美元,下降39.08%;签订利用内资合同19项,金额7.35亿元,增长48.48%,实际利用内资6.99亿元,增长82.51%;出口创汇1312万美元,增长21.71%。

全社会固定资产投资1.13亿元,确保了高新区内基础设施、工业建设和企业技改项目的顺利实施。完成道路5000米,铺设面积22万平方米,各类管线2.7万米,构建了辐射全区的道路网络总体框架;新开工业建设项目7项,建筑面积4.9万平方米,竣工建设项目8项,竣工建筑面积22.74万平方米;完成企业技改项目5项,投资4300万元。截至1999年底,南昌高新技术产业开发区建有396家企业,其中外资企业72家,属省级高新技术企业173家,占43.69%。年技工贸总收入超千万元的有34家企业,逾亿元的企业12家,最高一家企业达16亿元。

对外经贸洽谈会 1999年5月11日至12日,在深圳举办'99江西(深圳)招商引资新闻发布会,五百余位客商到会,签订利用外资合同140项,合同外资额2.26亿美元。此外,分别参加华东交易会、广州交易会、厦门投资贸易洽谈会、'99中国昆明世博会江西活动周、深圳首届中国国际高新技术成果交易会和意大利米兰马契夫秋季国际博览会、日本神户中国商务良机洽谈会、迪拜秋季国际博览会以及出国推销,共签订利用外资合同89项,合同外资额1.88亿美元;成交出口商品4.52亿美元,占1999年出口成交总额12.36亿美元的36.57%。

港口运输 1999年长江九江港有12个泊位,港口年吞吐能力1250万吨,实际完成货物吞吐总量611.6万吨,比1998年增长75.75%,其中完成外贸进出口货物吞吐量为7.01万吨,比上年增长29.81%,其中出口量4.03万吨下降1.49%,进口量2.98万吨,增长127.21%。1999年江西省外贸运输货运总量96.55万吨,比上年增长16.33%,其中出口量59.05万吨,增长4.88%、进口量37.5万吨,增长40.45%;按运输方式分:海运量79.59万吨,增长15.68%、空运量68吨,下降77.78%、陆运量16.96万吨,增长19.44%。

涉外旅游 1999年江西省接待旅游、参观、访问及从事各项交流活动的外国人、海外侨胞和台港澳同胞13.86万人次,比1998年的11.4923万人次增长20.6%;旅游外汇收入5037.76万美元,比1998年的4284万美元,增长17.59%。

1999年山东省对外经济贸易

山东省对外贸易经济委员会

【对外贸易】

进出口总额 1999年山东省进出口总额为182.71亿美元,比1998年的166.29亿美元增长9.9%。

出口总额 出口总额115.79亿美元,比上年的103.59亿美元增长11.8%,占全省国内生产总值7662.3亿元人民币(相当于924亿美元)的12.5%,占全国出口总额的5.9%,居全国第五位。

出口商品结构 初级产品出口额26.4亿美元,占出口总额的22.8%;工业制成品出口额89.4亿美元,占出口总额的77.2%。出口额在5000万美元以上的商品有:水海产品、冻鱼、蔬菜、冻鸡、鲜干水果及坚果、花生及花生仁、食用油籽、煤、轮胎、棉纱线、棉机织物、地毯、水泥、玻璃制品、家用陶瓷器皿、生铁、钢材、锁、电视及无线电讯零附件、集装箱、汽车零件、家具、旅行用品及箱包、服装、鞋类、塑料制品、玩具、棉坯布等。出口额在3000～5000万美元的商品有:合成短纤85%及以上的纱线、人造短纤机织物、棉浴巾、钢坯及粗锻件、钢铁管配件等。出口额在1000～3000万美元的商品有:原油、鲜冻兔肉、冻虾仁、辣椒、啤酒、肠衣、药材、烤烟、生丝、天然石墨、焦炭、合成有机染料、抗菌素、医用敷料、家用及装饰用木制品、丝绸、塑料编织带、珍珠及宝石、半宝石、铜材、钢铁及铜制标准紧固件、纺织机械、金属加工机床、轴承、电动机及发电机、原电池、静止式变流器、扬声器、收录机、电容器、电线和电缆、船舶、手表、医疗器械、带编织品、人造花、锯材、坯绸等。

出口商品市场 1999年出口商品销往187个国家和地区。

主要出口市场情况表

国别(地区)	出口金额(万美元)	占出口总额(%)
日　本	341801	29.5
美　国	224243	19.4
韩　国	157869	13.6
欧　盟	154962	13.4
香　港	57559	5.0
东南亚	57529	5.0
非洲	21298	1.8
南美洲	20174	1.7
独联体及东欧	15519	1.3
澳大利亚	14920	1.3
合　计	**1065874**	**92.1**

进口总额 进口总额66.9亿美元,比上年的62.7亿美元增长6.7%。

进口商品结构 进口额在5000万美元以上的商品有:机械、成套设备、电器及电子产品、塑料、牛皮革、纺织用合成纤维、钢材、针织或钩编织物、铁矿砂、计量监测分析仪器、合成纤维、长丝机织物、合成纤维纱线、纸及纸板、原棉、纸浆、天然橡胶、塑料制品、谷物及谷粉、棉机织物、食用植物油。进口额在3000～5000万美元的商品有:肥料、农药、纺织用人造纤维、医疗器械、钻石等。进口额在1000～3000万美元的商品有:裘皮及制品、腈纶长丝、棉纱布、服装、文体用品、电工设备、箱包鞋帽等。

进口商品市场 进口商品来自75个国家和地区。

主要进口市场情况表

国别(地区)	进口金额(万美元)	占进口总额(%)
韩国	267134	39.9
日本	109127	16.3
美国	63452	9.5
台湾省	25946	3.9
德国	20670	3.1
俄罗斯	20390	3.0
澳大利亚	15191	2.3
意大利	15129	2.3
香港	14918	2.2
加拿大	12769	1.9
合计	**564726**	**84.4**

技术进出口 1999年山东省签订技术出口合同102项,合同金额15031万美元,技术出口项目主要分布在机械、电子、化工、运输、能源、轻工、纺织等行业。出口过1000万美元的商品有:发电设备、工程机械、船舶、挖掘机。出口主要国家有:新加坡、伊拉克、印尼、孟加拉国、缅甸、美国、印度、巴基斯坦。1999年签订技术引进合同11项,合同金额9530万美元,项目主要分布在电子、化工、水泥设备等行业,进口国家主要有:日本、韩国、以色列、德国、西班牙。

【利用外资】

1999年利用外资情况表

利用外资方式	批准签订的合同			实际利用外资	
	项目数(个)	外资金额(万美元)	金额比1998年(±%)	金额(万美元)	金额比1998年(±%)
外商直接投资	1717	311087	+40	246878	+11
合资企业	733	124225	+59	92752	-20
合作企业	120	43750	+6	66168	+118
独资企业	863	142529	+40	86365	+16
合作开发	0	0	-66	1000	-49
股份制企业	1	583		593	
外商其他投资	0		-38	50793	-12
补偿贸易			-36	1368	-69
加工贸易			-36	1025	+114
对外发行股票			-5	29900	-2
国际租赁			-69	18500	-17
合　计	**1717**	**357398**	**+20**	**297671**	**+6**

外商直接投资行业　在外商直接投资项目中,第一产业项目89个,第二产业项目1430个,第三产业项目198个。按行业划分:农林牧渔水利业89个;采掘业8个;制造业1396个;建筑业26个;交通运输邮电业7个;商业餐饮业86个;房地产业31个;社会服务业43个;其他行业8个。

外商直接投资来源　主要有来自香港298个,合同金额8.9亿美元;美国194个,合同金额5.7亿美元;韩国593个,合同金额4.6亿美元;台湾省182个,合同金额2.2亿美元;德国26个,合同金额1.6亿美元,日本156个,合同金额1.5亿美元。

【对外经济合作】

承包工程和劳务合作　签订对外承包工程和劳务合作项目合同额9.3亿美元,比上年的7.4亿美元增长39.4%,完成营业额6.4亿美元,比上年的4.7亿美元增长91.6%。当年外派劳务人员19699人次,比上年增长30.1%。项目主要分布在韩国、日本、新加坡、香港、以色列等国家和地区,涉及建筑、水产、电子、渔业、服装、宾馆服务、石油工程等行业。

全年全省新获国家正式批准境外企业(机构)62家,比上年增加21家,占当年全国新批准310家的20%,在各省市中位居第一;投资总额8367万美元,占改革开放以来全省境外投资总额的43%。截至年底,全省共有各类境外企业(机构)497家,总投资2.88亿美元,注册资本2.02亿美元,中方投资2.17亿美元,占总投资的75.3%。

【其他】

经济技术开发区　1999年,全省各类经济开发区新批外商投资项目384个,合同外资额11.4亿美元,实际利用外资8.6亿美元,合同外资额和实际利用外资分别占全省的36.7%和34.8%,比上年提高了3.4个和1.8个百分点。在新批准外商投资项目中,1000万美元以上的大项目39个,合同外资额7.4亿美元,占开发区全部合同外资额的64.8%。项目平均规模由上年的228万美元提高到296万美元,比全省平均水平高出115万美元。全省经济开发区实现工业总产值692.7亿美元,比上年增长23.4%;销售收入645.9亿元,增长153.4%;利税

64.5亿元,增长31.6%;财政收入13.4亿元,增长17.5%。

港口运输 山东省对外开放口岸29个,港口年吞吐能力1.5亿吨,当年完成货物吞吐量1.25亿吨,其中完成外贸货物运输5828.2万吨,进口货物运量3145.7万吨,出口货物货运量2682.5万吨。

涉外旅游 全年共接待海外过夜旅游者56.2万人次,比上年增长25.2%。接待海外一日游旅客6万人次。旅游外汇收入2.65亿美元,比上年增长20.8%。

1999年青岛市对外经济贸易

青岛市对外经济贸易委员会

【对外贸易】

进出口总额 1999年山东省青岛市进出口总额77.56亿美元,比1998年的68.17亿美元增长13.77%。

出口总额 出口总额44.63亿美元,比1998年的40.97亿美元增长8.93%,占全市国内生产总值990亿元(相当于119.58亿美元)的37.32%;占全省出口额的38.54%

出口商品结构 初级产品出口额5.87亿美元,占出口总额的13.15%;工业制成品的出口额38.75亿美元,占出口总额的86.85%。

出口额在1000万美元以上商品情况表

金额分类	商品名称	出口金额(万美元)	占出口总额(%)
5000万美元以上(11种)	冻鱼片、箱包、皮革服装、涤纶布、汗衫背心、鞋靴、假发制品、集装箱、填充玩具动物、健身器械、塑料制品	172316	38.61
2000~5000万美元(26种)	干蔬菜、鱼、花生、调味品、橡胶轮胎、牛皮革、缆绳、棉混平纹布、套头衫、运动服、棉制男衬衫、帐篷、仿首饰、空调器、家用冷藏箱、软盘驱动器、变压器、耳机耳塞、音像设备零附件、铝电解电容器、电路开关、非机械驱动车辆及零件、医疗器械、家具、电子游戏机、钓鱼狩猎用品	74366	16.66
1000-2000万美元(38种)	冻鸡块、冻对虾仁、冷冻蔬菜、辣椒干辣椒粉、花生仁、鸡肉、啤酒、鳞片石墨、焦炭、二氧化硅、碳酸钠、碳酸钡、藻酸类产品、木制画框、植物编结品、纸袋、棉纱线、棉布、地毯、化纤花边、女式上衣、男内裤、袜子、男式防寒衣、毛制男式西服套装、胸罩、毯子、钻石、钢铁、洗衣机、计算机及部件、电热设备、电力控制盘、娱乐用品、床上用品、台布、毛巾、不锈钢厨房用具	53854	12.07
合计	**75种**	**300536**	**67.34**

出口商品市场 出口商品销往178个国家和地区。出口额居前10名的国家和地区依次是：日本123616万美元，占出口总额（下同）27.70%；美国122582万美元，占27.47%；韩国56523万美元，占12.66%；德国19024万美元，占4.26%；香港17202万美元，占3.85%；比利时10424万美元，占2.34%；荷兰9078万美元，占2.03%；英国8495万美元，占1.90%；加拿大7007万美元，占1.57%；法国6079万美元，占1.36%。

进口总额 进口总额32.93亿美元，比上年的27.20亿美元增长21.07%。

进口商品结构

进口额在2000万美元以上商品情况表

金额分类	商品名称	进口金额（万美元）	占进口总额比重（%）
3000万美元以上（11种）	生皮及皮革、冻鱼、压缩机、程控电话交换机零件、铁矿砂、鞋靴零件、制冷设备、对苯二甲酸、尼龙染色布、塑料制品、计算机及零附件	97787	29.70
2000－3000万美元（7种）	纸袋、聚丙烯腈、人造革、化纤织品、普通钢铁卷材、电视显像管、电子游戏机	16298	4.95
合　计	**18种**	**114085**	**34.65**

进口商品市场 进口商品的国家和地区共89个，主要进口商品的国家和地区依次是：韩国156856万美元，占进口总额（下同）的47.63%；日本55740万美元，占16.93%；美国31374万美元，占9.53%；台湾省12844万美元，占3.90%；俄罗斯10952万美元，占3.33%；香港6909万美元，占2.10%；意大利6872万美元，占2.09%；泰国4523万美元，占1.37%；新加坡4196万美元，占1.27%；德国3919万美元，占1.19%。

【利用外资】

1999年利用外资情况表

利用外资方式	批准签订的合同			实际利用外资	
	项目数（个）	外资金额（万美元）	金额比1998年（±%）	金额（万美元）	金额比1998年（±%）
对外借款	1	2398	－43.15	2069	－77.72
外商直接投资	714	172734	75.46	91742	25.97
合资企业	206	55284	128.16	27390	7.53
合作企业	45	19363	27.81	5810	87.78
外资企业	463	98087	66.06	58542	32.26
外商投资股份制					
外商其他投资	4	116		224	
国际租赁					
补偿贸易				129	

1999年利用外资情况表(续)

利用外资方式	批准签订的合同			实际利用外资	
	项目数(个)	外资金额(万美元)	金额比1998年(±%)	金额(万美元)	金额比1998年(±%)
加工贸易	4	116		95	
对外发行股票					
合计	**719**	**175248**	**70.70**	**94035**	**14.51**

外商直接投资分行业情况表

行业	项目数(个)	合同外资(万美元)
农、林、牧、渔业	41	9021
农业	27	7168
采掘业	3	278
制造业	548	116269
纺织业	20	3728
化学原料及化学制品制造业	20	7816
医药制造业	2	543
普通机械制造业	21	4938
专用设备制造业	13	2400
电子及通信设备制造业	29	10697
电力、煤气及水的生产和供应业	2	366
建筑业	11	5772
交通运输、仓储及邮电通信业	4	2656
批发和零售贸易、餐饮业	65	13871
房地产业	9	4296
房地产开发与经营业	7	4238
社会服务业	20	13645
卫生、体育和社会福利业	2	2964
科学研究和综合技术服务业	1	1000
其他行业	8	2596

1999年,全市共批准利用外资项目719个,增长27.71%;合同外资17.52亿美元,增长70.70%;实际利用外资9.40亿美元,增长14.51%。

外商直接投资来源 1999年在青岛直接投资的国家和地区有50个。按合同外资额排列,前5位依次是:香港,101个项目,4.78亿美元;美国,72个项目,3.37亿美元;韩国,328个项目,2.53亿美元;台湾省,52个项目,1.32亿美元;加拿大,18个项目,6911万美元。

外商直接投资企业生产经营情况 全市累计投产经营外商投资企业3143家。全年实际出口32.99亿美元,增长9.09%;缴纳税金13.3亿元,比上年的11亿元增长20.91%;销售收入464亿元,比上年的414亿元增长12.08%。

【对外经济合作】

承包工程和劳务合作 1999年签订对外承包工程和劳务合作项目482个,金额9036万美元,比上年的5921万美元增长52.61%;营业额6851万美元,比上年的5404万美元增长26.78%;当年派出5149人次,年末在外人数7874人,派往的主要国家是:韩国、巴拿马、新加坡、日本、利比里亚、以色列、俄罗斯;承包工程的主要项目是:塞舌尔的虾池工程;以色列的阿什道德海滨住宅;以色列的ORT10栋公寓楼;以色列的特拉维夫综合楼;博茨瓦纳的BHC88套住宅。

对外投资 1999年在海外举办企业项目9项,中方投资金额3695万美元,投资的国家有:美国、埃及、摩洛哥、伊朗、保加利亚、越南、突尼斯、俄罗斯。

【其他】

经济技术开发区 青岛经济技术开发区自1984年建区以来已累计投入130多亿元人民币,建成了一批大型能源、交通等配套设施。其中,前湾港为国家一类开放口岸,拥有煤炭、矿石专用码头、杂货码头、集装箱码头和原油、成品油码头,年吞吐量达到7310万吨。重点扶持的石油、化工、化纤、机械、电子、建材六大主导产业已初具规模,形成了产业群体优势。截至1999年12月末,全区合同外资累计22.41亿美元,实际利用外资累计12.07亿美元,世界500强公司中已有12家前来投资。包括1999年建成的海尔工业园在内,已 有澳柯玛、颐中、双星、轻骑等知名国内大企业纷纷在开发区建立了工业园。1999年全区完成工业总产值166亿元,同比增长64%,完成国内生产总值65亿元,同比增长29.2%。全年出口创汇5.54亿美元,同比增长2.3%。

保税区 全年共批准项目110个,项目总投资1.56亿美元,其中,三资项目42个,合同外资1.01亿美元,实际利用外资4576万美元。区内大部分工业企业运行良好,松下电子、茂治电子、黄海铅塑等企业相继投产,区内完成工业产值7.7亿元,实现销售收入7.39亿元。区内贸易企业业务稳中有升,贸易额5.5亿元,出口货物总值8000万美元,完成市场交易额1.8亿元。区内仓储功能发挥顺畅,11家仓储企业,室内面积10万平方米。全年共完成基础设施投资1000万元,前一路、保四路及三水工程已完成,完成了保税区主大门施工图设计,并已开工建设,区内的绿化、美化、亮化工程初步实施。

港口运输 1999年青岛港拥有营运泊位46个,其中万吨级以上泊位30个。港口吞吐能力超过亿吨。当年实际完成货物吞吐总量7257万吨,其中完成外资吞吐量为3716万吨,出口量为1272万吨、进口量为2444万吨。1999年青岛进出口空运货邮总量为1.77万吨。

涉外旅游 接待海外游客22.8万人次,比上年增长14.1%。其中,外国人16.5万人次,同比增长14.5%;华侨和港澳台胞6.3万人次,比上年增长13.2%。国际旅游收入11448万美元,比上年的10231万美元增长12.0%。

1999年烟台市对外经济贸易

烟台市对外经济贸易委员会

【对外贸易】

进出口总额 山东省烟台市1999年进出口总额为22.88亿美元,比上年的22.28亿美元增长2.7%。

出口总额 出口总额为14.66亿美元,比上年的12.84亿美元增长14.2%,占全市国内生产总值的15.2%,占全省出口总额的12.6%。

出口商品结构 出口商品有17大类600多个品种,其中初级产品出口额5.17亿美元,占出口总额的35.3%;工业制成品出口额9.49亿美元,占出口总额的64.7%。

出口额在1000万美元以上的出口商品情况表

金额分类	商品分类	出口金额(万美元)	占出口总额(%)
2亿美元以上(1种)	服装	28341	19.3
1亿美元以上(1种)	水海产品	14453	9.9
5000-1亿美元(3种)	纺织品、蔬菜、汽车配件	17637	12
1000-5000万美元(17种)	水泥、锁头、玩具、家具、粉丝、鞋类、电子元器件、塑料制品等	36043	24.6
合计	**22种**	**96465**	**65.8**

出口商品市场 出口商品销往128个国家和地区,比1998年增长10个。

主要出口市场情况表

国别(地区)	出口金额(万美元)	占出口总额(%)
日本	53992	36.8
美国	25849	17.6
韩国	22254	15.2
香港	4468	3
德国	3690	2.5
荷兰	3225	2.2
加拿大	2560	1.7

主要出口市场情况表(续)

国别(地区)	出口金额(万美元)	占出口总额(%)
新加坡	2409	1.6
阿联酋	2360	1.6
澳大利亚	2220	1.5
合计	**123027**	**83.7**

进口总额 全年进口总额为8.2亿美元,比上年的9.4亿美元下降12.8%。

进口商品结构 初级产品进口额为1.95亿美元,工业制成品进口额为6.28亿美元,分别占进口总额的23.7%和76.3%。

进口商品市场 进口商品来自56个国家和地区。

主要进口市场情况表

国别(地区)	进口金额(万美元)	占进口总额(%)
韩　国	37776	45.9
日　本	12604	15.3
美　国	4629	5.6
澳大利亚	3449	4.2
台湾省	3103	3.8
意大利	2692	3.3
俄罗斯	2654	3.2
德　国	2133	2.6
加拿大	1193	1.4
香　港	1065	1.3
合　计	**71298**	**86.6**

技术进出口 1999年山东省烟台市实现成套设备技术出口3088万美元,比上年增长2倍,主要出口美国、香港、新加坡、泰国、南非、马来西亚等国家和地区。

【利用外资】

1999年利用外资情况表

利用外资方式	批准签订的合同			实际利用外资	
	项目数(个)	外资金额(万美元)	金额比1998年(±%)	金额(万美元)	金额比1998年(±%)
对外借款	3	3168	22.1	802	-72.5
外商直接投资	230	32509	5.9	31439	-31.4
合资企业	124	19455	8.8	25868	-29.8
合作企业	19	2880	-10.4	1631	15
外资企业	87	10174	6	3940	-47.7
外商其他投资	-	-	-	-	-
国际租赁	-	-	-	-	-
补偿贸易	-	3023	+67.6	1149	-21
加工装配	-	-	-	-	-
对外发行股票	-	-	-	-	-
合　计	**233**	**38700**	**+10.3**	**33390**	**-33.4**

外商直接投资行业 在外商直接投资的230个项目中,生产型项目221项,非生产型项目9项。按行业划分,农业18项,工业202项,第三产业10项。

外商直接投资来源 外商投资来自23个国家和地区。主要有:香港38项,合同外资9478万美元;美国20项,6434万美元;韩国64项,4653万美元;日本34项,4215万美元,台湾省32项,4534万美元。

外商直接投资企业生产经营情况 全年共有30家外商投资企业投产,全市累计投产的外商投资企业达到1890家,1999年完成销售收入200.66

亿元,实现利润8.45亿元,税收7.89亿元,分别增长3.1%、82%和5.5%,出口13459万美元。

【对外经济合作】

承包工程与劳务合作 1999年共签订对外承包工程与劳务合作项目137个,合同额9693万美元,比上年的7327万美元增长32.3%;营业额6227万美元,比上年的4919万美元增长26.7%;共派出各类劳务人员3208人次,比上年的2700人次增长18.7%;年末在外人数达到3571人,比上年的2734人增长30.6%。对外经济合作涉及的国家和地区主要有日本、韩国、香港、新加坡、美国、台湾省、玻利维亚、巴巴多斯、以色列、厄立特里亚、尼泊尔、也门等。

【其他】

经济技术开发区 烟台经济技术开发区1999年实现国内生产总值37亿元,其中工业增加值28.5亿元,引进外商投资项目总投资1.38亿美元,合同外资额6631万美元,增长11%和9.8%。其中500万美元以上项目4个,1000万美元以上项目2个。完成进出口贸易额6.4亿美元,其中出口2.3亿美元,增长15.6%。全区完成固定资产投资25亿元。实际利用外资1.43亿美元,实现了3~5个大中项目开工建设、3~5个大中项目建成投产的目标。

港口运输 1999年烟台各港口吞吐量完成2504.5万吨,比上年增长17.2%,外贸货物运量完成702万吨。国际集装箱运输完成12.3万标准箱,比上年增长16.5%。海空港出入境旅客13.8万人次,比上年增长102%,其中外籍旅客97302人次。龙口港是全国最大的地方港口,1999年完成吞吐量488.3万吨,外贸货运量53.1万吨,增长10.4%。

对外经贸洽谈会 1999年10月12日至16日,在烟台市举办了果蔬加工与产业化国际研讨会暨展览会。本次果蔬研展会由联合国亚太经社会、联合国亚太技术转让中心、中国工程院和山东省人民政府共同主办,烟台市人民政府具体承办。共成交利用外资项目112个,总投资6.5亿美元,外资额4.66亿美元。进出口贸易成交额5.69亿美元,其中出口成交5.07亿美元。签订对外承包工程与劳务合作合同(协议)额1615万美元。国内贸易成交7.07亿元人民币。

涉外旅游 1999年共接待观光旅游的外国人和港澳同胞14万人次,比上年增长17.7%;旅游外汇收入5723万美元,比上年增长21.35%。

1999年河南省对外经济贸易

河南省对外贸易经济合作厅

【对外贸易】

进出口总额 1999年河南省进出口总额为175194万美元,比1998年的173436万美元增长1.01%。

出口总额 出口总额113040万美元,比上年118669万美元下降4.74%。占全省国内生产总值4580亿元的2.14%,占全国出口总额的1949.30亿美元的0.58%。

出口商品结构 初级产品出口额19784万美元,占出口总额的17.50%;工业制成品的出口额93257万美元,占出口总额的82.50%。

出口额在500万美元以上的商品情况表

金额分类	商品名称	出口金额(万美元)	占出口总额(%)
5000万美元以上(3种)	人发制品,核反应堆,锅炉机械器具及零件,非针织或钩编织物制服装	21348	18.89
1000－5000万美元(28种)	针织或钩编服装,鞋,电机,电气,音响设备及其零附件,家用器皿,人造刚玉,棉坯布,未锻造的铜及铜材,未锻造的铝及铝材,地毯,活大猪,食用油籽,滚动轴承,碳化物,玻璃及其制品,棉机织物,棉纱线,医药品,毛皮制品,锯材,味精,烤烟,肠衣,金属陶瓷及其制品,未锻轧铅,镁及其制品,钢材,干豆,用于8425至8430所列机械的零件	56708	50.17
500万－1000万美元(20种)	摩托车及脚踏车,合成短纤与棉混纺机织物,未锻轧镁,家具,蔬菜,蓄电池,钢铁铸造制品,灯具及照明装置,无可锻性铸铁制品,聚脂短棉纤坯布,光学、照相医疗设备及零附件,固体矿物分选处理器,铸造砂模成型机,钻探及凿井机械零件,氨基酸,原电池,鲜、冻猪肉,玩具,芦笋罐头,棉浴巾	14902	13.18
合　计	**51种**	**92958**	**82.24**

出口商品市场　出口商品销往158个国家和地区。

主要出口商品市场情况表

国别(地区)	出口金额(万美元)	占出口总额(%)
美　国	23623	20.90
欧　盟	17886	15.82
香　港	16717	14.79
日　本	12732	11.26
东　盟	9013	7.97
韩　国	7214	6.38
台湾省	2182	1.93
澳大利亚	1839	1.63
俄罗斯	1495	1.32

主要出口商品市场情况表(续)

国别(地区)	出口金额(万美元)	占出口总额(%)
加拿大	1377	1.22
合　计	**94078**	**83.23**

进口总额　进口总额62155万美元,比上年的54469万美元增长14.11%,占全国进口总额的0.37%。

进口商品结构　初级产品进口额13987万美元,占进口总额的22.50%;工业制成品的进口额48168万美元,占进口总额的77.50%。

进口额在500万美元以上的商品情况表

金额分类	商品名称	进口额（万美元）	占进口总额（%）
1000万美元以上（31种）	谷物及谷物粉，二醋酸纤维丝束，铁矿砂，氧化铝，异氧酸酯，其他腈基化合物，感光材料，初级形状的塑料，绵羊生皮，未锻造的钢及钢材，未锻造的铝及铝材，印刷装订机械，纺织机械，金属冶炼铸造设备及零件，玻璃热加工机械，自动数据处理设备及其部件，汽车零件，计量检测分析自控仪器及器具，空气泵，气体压缩机、风机、洗碟机、包装机，印刷机，化学纺织纤维挤压、拉伸变形或切割机器，金属冶炼及铸造用转炉、锭 模及铸造机，自动数据处理设备及其部件，灯泡封装机，玻璃及制品制造或热加工机，有线电话、电报设备，有线载波通信或有线数字通信设备，车辆及其零附件，光学照相，医疗设备及零附件	48016	77.25
500－1000万美元（18种）	大豆，纸浆、石油沥青，生牛、羊皮，活塞式内燃机的零件，制冷设备用压缩机，建筑及采矿用机械，金属加工机床，烟草加工机械，模型及金属铸造用型箱，钢材，电动机 P≤0.4KW，包装或打包机，用于8425至8430所列机械的零件，人造纤维纺丝机，钢坯连铸机用零件，金属、硬质合金用注模或压模，用于8407或8408发动机的零件	13297	21.39
合　计	**49种**	**61313**	**98.64**

进口商品市场　进口商品来自61个国家和地区。

主要进口市场情况表

国别（地区）	进口金额（万美元）	占进口总额（%）
欧　盟	17405	28.00
美国	11304	18.18
日　本	10989	17.67
东南亚联盟	5120	8.24
澳大利亚	4169	6.70
韩　国	2900	4.67
加拿大	2284	3.67
台湾省	1588	2.55
香　港	1158	1.86
合　计	**56917**	**91.54**

技术进出口　1999年全省技术进出口总额为8633万美元。比上年的6011万美元，增长43.62%。签订引进技术合同项目19个，比上年增加8个，合同金额4486万美元，比上年的1042万美元增长330.52%。

技术进口　引进项目主要来自日本、美国、英国、韩国、荷兰等5个国家，合同金额4486万美元，涉及石油、电力、机械制造、家电、信息、农业种值与加工等7个行业。1999年所签订项目19个，当年全部投产并产生较好的经济效益。

技术出口　1999年全省完成高新技术产品出口1599万美元，为企业带来较好的经济效益。

地方经贸

【利用外资】

1999 年利用外资情况表

利用外资方式	批准签订的合同			实际利用外资	
	项目(个)	外资金额(万美元)	金额比1998年(±%)	金额(万美元)	金额比1998年(±%)
对外借款	11	10880	55.12	5752	
外商直接投资	261	64664	22.00	53100	-14.60
合资企业	160	37261	26	24573	-24.40
合作企业	33	16927	51	14310	-13.90
外资企业	68	10476	-15	13252	
外商投资股份制				965	
外商其他投资	2	524	-91.30	8000	-39
国际租赁					
补偿服务	1	168	-81.30		
加工贸易	1	356	-33.60		
对外发行股票				8000	-30.30
合　计	**272**	**76068**		**66852**	

外商直接投资行业　1999 年河南省外商直接投资项目涉及 40 多个行业。生产型项目 224 个，合同外资金额 57190 万美元，占总合同外资金额的 88.44%，其中，制造业 192 个，合同外资金额 30662 万美元；农、林、牧、渔业项目 14 个，合同外资金额 3552 万美元；采掘业 3 个，合同外资金额 404 万美元；电力、煤气及水的生产和供应业项目 10 个，合同外资金额 20662 万美元；建筑业项目 5 个，合同外资金额 1910 万美元。非生产型项目 37 个，合同外资金额 7474 万美元，占 11.56%。其中，交通运输、仓储及邮电通信业 2 个，合同外资金额 694 万美元，批发和零售贸易、餐饮业 9 个，合同外资金额 537 万美元；房地产业 10 个，合同外资金额 2381 万美元；社会服务业 12 个，合同外资金额 3305 万美元；科学研究和综合技术服务业 1 个，合同外资金额 5 万美元；其他行业 3 个，合同外资金额 552 万美元。

外商直接投资来源　外商直接投资来源于 41 个国家和地区。主要国家和地区是：美国 41 个，实际利用外资金额 3786 万美元；香港 81 个，实际利用外资金额 34788 万美元；新加坡 10 个，实际利用外资金额 2944 万美元；台湾省 41 个，实际利用外资金额 1872 万美元；日本 8 个，实际利用外资金额 901 万美元；泰国 4 个，实际利用外资金额 891 万美元；加拿大 10 个，实际利用外资金额 670 万美元；英国 4 个，实际利用外资金额 588 万美元。

外商投资企业生产经营情况　截止 1999 年底，全省建成投产的外商投资企业 6413 家，其中已投产开业的外商投资企业 2000 余家，从业职工 30 多万人；外商投资企业出口创汇 23700 万美元，比上年出口 24684 万美元下降 3.99%；占全省出口总值的比重为 20.97%。以外商投资企业为主体的涉外税收 20.90 亿元人民币，比上年的 16.41 亿元增加 27.36 个百分点。

【对外经济合作】

承包工程和劳务合作　1999 年签订对外承包工程和劳务合作项目 154 个，金额 11451 万美元，比上年的 11148 万美元增长 2.72%;营业额 8607 万美元,比上年的 6994 万美元增长 23.06%;当年派出劳务人数 6052 人次,年末在外人数 12683 人,分布在 15 个国家和地区,主要集中在马里、苏丹、卡塔尔、印度尼西亚、菲律宾、哥伦比亚、阿尔及利亚、老挝和台湾省等国家和地区。承包工程主要有:柬埔寨水利工程、苏丹石油勘探工程、阿尔及利亚及马里建筑工程、尼泊尔公路整修工程等。

接受经济援助 接受日本政府对华粮食增产项目、联合国儿童基金会 SPPA 项目、澳大利亚政府 SAS 扶贫项目、德国 EZE 民间组织培训等 6 个援助项目,授援资金 327 万美元,项目受益区覆盖了全省 13 个国家级和省级贫困县,受益人达到 60 多万。

对外投资 在阿尔及利亚、匈牙利、吉尔吉斯斯坦、韩国、日本和澳门等 7 个国家和地区投资兴办企业 7 个,中方投资金额 38 万美元,有些企业投资当年已初见效益。

【其他】

经济技术开发区 郑州高新技术产业开发区完成基础设施等固定资产投资 22200 万元,累计协议投资额 913600 万元。新批准成立企业 135 家,建成投产企业 18 家。实现技工贸总收入 923500 万元,较上年同期 820103 万元增长 12.61%;实现财税收入 18691 万元,较上年同期 15183 万元增长 23.10%。全年批准外商投资企业 8 家,实际利用外资 1968 万美元,比上年同期 2200 万美元下降 10.55%。出口创汇 1866 万美元,比上年同期 3286 万美元下降 43.21%。

洛阳高新技术产业开发区 完成基础设施等固定资产投资 2250 万元,累计投资额 3425 万元。新批准成立企业 88 家,建成投产企业 41 家。实现技工贸总收入 502295 万元,比上年同期 451014 万元增长 11.37%;实现财税收入 3350 万元,较上年同期 3136 万元增长 6.82%。新批准外商投资企业 3 家,合同外资金额 780 万美元,比上年同期 859 万美元下降 9.20%;实际利用外资 564 万美元,比上年同期 706 万美元下降 20.11%。出口创汇 5042 万美元,比上年同期 5098 万美元下降 1.10%。进口到货 609 万美元,比上年同期 1096 万美元下降 44.43%。

对外经贸洽谈会 1999 年 6 月 29 日至 7 月 1 日,在北京举办了'99 北京河南省情说明会暨投资项目洽谈会。130 多家国有生产企业带去 122 个项目参加了本次洽谈活动,并进行与会洽谈。120 家跨国公司、外国公司驻京办事处以及外国驻京银行、商社、商会、驻华使馆等派出 180 多人参加了洽谈会。此次活动共签订项目 25 个,合同外资金额 12760 万美元,协议项目 14 个,协议金额 5309 万美元。在签订的合同和协议中,1000 万美元以上的项目 7 个。

1999年3月30日至31日,在美国纽约市举办'99 河南省(纽约)经济贸易洽谈会。全省 37 家有进出口经营权的企业参加了本次洽谈会。到会客商达 370 多人,其中有一半以上为新客户。本次洽谈会共签订出口合同 211 份,出口成交总额 1854 万美元。

涉外旅游 1999 年共接待境外旅游者 30 多万人次,比上年同期 27 万人次增长 11.11%,其中来自港澳台地区同胞 14 万人次。比上年同期的 13 万人次增长 7.69%。旅游外汇收入 11350 万美元,比上年同期的 10001 万美元增长 13.49%。

1999年湖北省对外经济贸易

湖北省对外贸易经济合作厅

【对外贸易】

进出口总额 1999年湖北省进出口总额268107万美元,比1998年的281329万美元下降4.7%。

出口总额 出口总额151378万美元,比上年的170663万美元下降11.3%,占全省国内生产总值3857.99亿元(相当于466.5亿美元)的3.24%。

出口商品结构 初级产品出口16349万美元,占出口总额的10.8%;工业制成品出口135029万美元,占出口总额的89.2%。

主要出口商品情况表

金额分类	商品名称	出口金额(万美元)	占出口总额(%)
1000至2000万美元(19种)	白肋烟、磷灰石、三磷酸钠、充气橡胶轮胎、猪皮革、棉坯布、铅酸蓄电池、药棉、棉色织布、化纤针织品、合成纤维针织品、粘胶纤维纱、防寒短上衣、维生素、女式裙裤、女裤、鞋靴、硅铁、黄金首饰	26140	17.27
2000至3000万美元(6种)	活大猪、提箱、男式西服套装、女式便服套装、光纤光缆、大米	14932	9.86
3000万美元以上(6种)	棉针织品、男式上装、男裤、女式上装、机动集装箱船、初级形状普通钢铁	28327	18.71
合计	**31种**	**69399**	**45.84**

出口商品市场 出口商品销往160个国家和地区。

主要出口市场情况表

国别(地区)	出口金额(万美元)	占出口总额(%)
日本	25878	17.09
香港	24290	16.05
美国	15378	10.16
德国	9070	5.99
韩国	7361	4.86
荷兰	3226	2.13
意大利	2743	1.81

主要出口市场情况表(续)

国别(地区)	出口金额(万美元)	占出口总额(%)
澳大利亚	2068	1.37
英国	2065	1.36
马来西亚	2064	1.36
合计	**94143**	**62.19**

进口总额 进口总额116729万美元,比上年的110749万美元增长5.4%。

进口商品结构 初级产品进口23836万美元,占进口总额的20.42%;工业制成品进口92893万美元,占进口总额的79.58%。

主要进口商品情况表

金额分类	商品名称	进口金额（万美元）	占进口总额（%）
1000万至2000万美元（14种）	油菜籽、热带木原木、二醋酸长丝丝束、服装、涂无机物书写印刷纸、粗梳毛的机织物、铝合金矩形板片、软木处理机、机械器具、机器零件、数字式移动通讯交换机，装有接收装置的发送设备、机动车辆用变速箱、光纤光缆	23993	20.55
2000万美元以上（6种）	含聚酯非变形长丝的机织物、光端机及脉冲编码调制设备、手持无线电话机、车辆用零附件、铁矿砂、铜矿砂	24207	20.74
合　计	**20种**	**48200**	**41.29**

进口商品市场　进口商品来自66个国家和地区。

主要进口市场情况表

国别（地区）	进口金额（万美元）	占进口总额（%）
日本	21389	18.32
法国	15037	12.88
德国	13718	11.75
美国	11703	10.03
英国	6363	5.45
韩国	5865	5.02
台湾省	4777	4.09
意大利	4318	3.70
瑞典	2983	2.56
香港	2396	2.05
合　计	**88549**	**75.85**

技术进出口　技术进出口总额28936万美元，比上年的52071.7万美元下降44.43%。其中，签订引进技术和进口设备合同205个，比上年增加192个；合同金额24659.7万美元，比上年的6445万美元增长282.62%。

技术进口　引进的项目来自美国、俄罗斯、日本、德国、法国和英国，合同金额分别为12001万美元、5562万美元、3652万美元、1500万美元、1000万美元和945万美元。涉及的行业有电讯，通讯导航、汽车零部件、饮料、农业和化工。

【利用外资】

1999年利用外资情况表

利用外资方式	批准签订的合同			实际利用外资	
	项目数（个）	外资金额（万美元）	金额比1998年（±%）	金　额（万美元）	金额比1998年（±%）
外商直接投资	260	82178	59	91488	－0.5
中外合资企业	133	24316	70	59153	－6
中外合作企业	18	4546	－78	6892	－35
外资企业	109	53316	218	25443	2

1999 年利用外资情况表(续)

利用外资方式	批准签订的合同			实际利用外资	
	项目数(个)	外资金额(万美元)	金额比1998年(±%)	金额(万美元)	金额比1998年(±%)
外商其他投资		10926	-43	11426	22
补偿贸易		11			
加工装配		10915	-21	7426	88
对外发行股票				4000	-26
合　计	260	93104	31	102914	1.5

外商直接投资行业　在外商直接投资中，生产型项目 193 个，非生产型项目 67 个。按行业分：农林牧渔业 7 个，采掘出 5 个，制造业 166 个，电力煤气及水供应业 6 个，建筑业 9 个，交通运输仓储业 4 个，批发零售贸易餐饮业 7 个，房地产业 18 个，社会服务业 34 个，卫生体育福利业 2 个，科技服务业 1 个，其他行业 1 个。

外商直接投资　外商投资来源于 36 个国家和地区。主要有美国 27 项 24328 万美元，日本 9 项 23115 万美元，香港 126 项 18189 万美元，新加坡 15 项 4855 万美元，英国 7 项 3042 万美元，台湾省 39 项 1481 万美元，英属维尔京群岛 3 项 1450 万美元，马来西亚 3 项 1319 万美元。

外商直接投资企业生产经营情况　截至 1999 年底，外商投资企业已开业投产的有 3144 个，销售额 30997 万美元。

【对外经济合作】

承包工程和劳务合作　1999 年签订对外承包和劳务合作合同项目 227 个，金额 18099 万美元，比上年的 17403 万美元增长 4%；营业额 12173 万美元，比上年的 9510 万美元增长 28%；当年派出劳务人员 2908 人次，年末在外人数 5718 人，派往的主要国家和地区有新加坡、毛里求斯、尼泊尔，孟加拉、美国、保加利亚、乌克兰、香港、澳门等。承包工程的主要项目有瑞典的船舶制造工程、斯里兰卡电力机厂、广州内环公路建设、宁夏古王一级公路建设。

对外经济技术援助　承担援外项目有 5 个，受援的国家有几内亚比绍、缅甸、佛德角、喀麦隆和刚果。涉及的行业有建筑业、医疗卫生和农业等。全年外派援外人数 50 人，年末在外人数 30 人。

接受经济援助　接受联合国人口基金和和童基金、日本、欧盟的多边及双边援助项目 4 个，即联合国的妇女参与发展项目 1 个，贫困地区社会发展项目 1 个，日本粮食增产项目 1 个，欧盟援助技术项目 1 个，共有金额 347 万元。

对外投资　1999 年在海外举办的企业有 1 个，即尼日利亚纺织厂。中方用 15000 纱锭及配套纺织设备作价 145 万美元作投资，现正在筹建中。

【其他】

对外经贸洽谈　1999 年，湖北在德国汉堡慕尼黑举办“99 湖北对外经贸洽谈会”；参加美国俄亥俄州博览会；在毛里求斯、也门、吉布提兴办“湖北商品展销会”；接待法国巴黎工商会、英中贸易协会、韩国大韩商工会议所赴内陆考察团的来访；开展了对外组团出访及考察和对外经贸洽谈等活动。不仅增进了双方相互了解，扩大了交流与合作，而且为湖北扩大了招商引资。1999 年共签利用外资项目 15 个，总投资额 20300 万美元，其中协议利用外资金额 10600 万美元。进出口贸易成交总额 4700 万美元，其中出口成交 3600 万美元。

港口运输　1999 年湖北完成外贸进出口货物吞吐量 133.78 万吨，其中，出口 123 万吨，比上年的 125.2 万吨下降 1.76%；进口 10.78 万吨，比上年的 9.25 万吨增长 16.54%。

涉外旅游　1999 年共接待外国及台港澳同胞 30 万人次，旅游外汇收入 10400 万美元，比 1998 年的 8800 万美元增长 18.18%。

1999年武汉市对外经济贸易

武汉市对外经济贸易委员会

【对外贸易】

进出口总额 1999年武汉市进出口总额110661万美元。

出口总额 出口总额50065万美元，比1998年的48227万美元增长3.8%，占全市国内生产总值1086亿元（相当于131.19亿美元）的3.8%，占全省出口额的33%。

出口商品结构 初级产品出口额2287万美元，占出口总额的4.57%；工业制成品的出口额47778万美元，占出口总额的95.43%。

出口额在1000万美元以上商品情况表

金额分类	商品名称	出口金额（万美元）	占出口总额（%）
8000万美元以上的商品1个	钢锭	8480	16.94
2000－5000万美元的商品2个	船舶	4024	8.04
	光纤	2968	5.93
1000－2000万美元的商品3个	黄金首饰	1361	2.72
	塑料及纺织面料	1074	2.15
	蓄电池	1043	2.08
合　计	**6种**	**18950**	**37.85**

出口商品市场 出口商品销往120个国家和地区。

主要出口商品市场情况表

国别（地区）	出口金额（万美元）	占出口总额（%）
香港	8759	17.50
台湾省	6918	13.82
德国	5573	11.13
美国	5135	10.26
韩国	2767	5.53
日本	2647	5.29

主要出口商品市场情况表（续）

国别（地区）	出口金额（万美元）	占出口总额（%）
印尼	1063	2.12
新加坡	976	1.95
合　计	**33838**	**67.59**

进口总额 进口总额60596万美元，比1998年增长0.3%。

进口商品结构 初级产品进口额10567万美元，占进口总额的16.7%；工业制成品的进口额50029万美元，占进口总额的83.3%。

进口商品市场

主要进口商品情况表

商品名称	进口金额（万美元）	占进口总额（%）
铁矿砂	7387	14.6
船舶	2243	4.43
成材	1528	3.02
各类机械	1441	2.85
纸浆纸张	849	1.68
塑料	255	0.5
板石	235	0.5
合　计	**13938**	**23.21**

主要进口市场情况表

国别（地区）	进口金额（万美元）	占进口总额（%）
香港	42617	70.33
澳大利亚	3316	5.47
南非	2572	4.24
德国	2194	3.62
印尼	1160	1.91
意大利	823	1.36
美国	746	1.23
合　计	**53428**	**88.17**

技术进出口　1999 年武汉市技术进出口总额 14735 万美元，比 1998 年的 13012 万美元增长 13.2%。

【利用外资】

1999 年利用外资情况表

利用外资方式	批准签订的合同			实际利用外资	
	项目（个）	外资金额（万美元）	金额比 1998 年（±%）	金额（万美元）	金额比 1998 年（±%）
对外借款	14	70555	180.1	56654	22.9
外商直接投资	125	36880	6.0	47550	4.7
合资企业	59	20268		28151	
合作企业	3	945		4718	
外资企业	63	15667		14681	
外商其他投资	61	12478	2.3	12381	1.4
国际租赁	2	11997		11997	
加工贸易	59	481		384	
合　计	**200**	**119913**	**49.6**	**116585**	**10.4**

外商直接投资行业　外商直接投资中生产型项目数为 95 个、非生产型项目数为 30 个，其中按行业分：农业 1 个；工业 87 个；建筑业 7 个；交通邮电业 1 个；商业饮食供销仓储业 2 个；房地产公用服务业 20 个；卫生体育福利事业 1 个；科研技术服务事业 5 个；其他行业 1 个。

外商直接投资来源　外商直接投资来自世界 18 个国家和地区，主要外资分布的国别或地区为：香港，58 个项目，合同外资 6298 万美元；台湾省，19 个项目，合同外资 414 万美元；美国，13 个项目，合同外资 8588 万美元；新加坡，7 个项目，合同外资 1576 万美元；英国，4 个项目，合同外资 3934 万美元。

外商直接投资企业生产经营情况 1999 年外商直接投资企业上缴各类工商税收 15.28 亿元人民币。

【对外经济技术合作】

承包工程和劳务合作 1999 年武汉市共签订对外承包工程和劳务合作项目 85 个，合同额 7030 万美元，比 1998 年的 14832 万美元下降 52.6%；完成营业额 6377 万美元，比 1998 年的 5206 万美元增长 22.5%；当年新派出劳务人员 1644 人，年末在外 3237 人，承包工程和劳务业务涉及东南亚、非洲、南美、中东等 27 个国家和地区；主要承包工程项目 2 个，分别是：武汉国际公司承包的瑞典船舶制造项目，合同额 2436 万美元；武汉建工集团承包的新加坡南洋理工大学宿舍楼项目，合同额 1223 万美元。

对外经济技术援助 1999 年武汉市共承担援外项目 3 个，分别是：1. 佛得角图书馆建设项目，合同额为 155 万美元，当年派出援外人员 28 人，该项目已于 1999 年 5 月竣工，目前，其二期工程即佛得角图书馆国父纪念碑项目正在执行中。2. 塞拉利昂农机站项目，1999 年完成营业额 36 万美元，当年派出援外人员 4 人，期末在外 4 人。3. 莫桑比克外交大楼设计项目，合同额 34 万美元，派出 8 人，该项目现已完成。

对外投资 1999 年武汉市在海外举办非贸易企业 3 个，中方投资金额 137 万美元，投资国别（地区）为津巴布韦和新加坡。

【其他】

经济技术开发区 1999 年武汉经济技术开发区工业总产值（现行价）1055288 万元人民币，工业增加值 370406 万元，工业产品销售率比上年增长 11%，工业投产企业 10 个，其中外商投资企业有 2 个，与上年持平，固定资产投资完成额 95075 万元人民币，其中基础设施项目完成额 27363 万元人民币，比上年增长 68.55%。1999 年武汉经济开发区共批准外商投资企业 12 个，比 1998 年下降 29.41%；实际使用外资金额 8905 万美元，比上年下降 32.11%，其中外商直接投资 1952 万美元，比 1998 年下降 39.99%；境外借资 6953 万美元，比上年下降 28.18%。1999 年武汉经济开发区工业企业实现税收 55934 万元，比上年增长 38.24%；外商投资企业实现税收 48561 万美元，比上年增长 30.99%。

对外经贸洽谈会 1999 年 10 月 10 日至 12 日，'99 武汉金秋经贸洽谈会在武汉市华中国际博览中心举行，这是武汉市首次举办的大规模、高层次、宽领域的对外经贸洽谈会，它的成功举办标志着走向新世纪的武汉对外开放又翻开了新的一页。本届交易会共设 374 个摊位，来自武汉经济协作区的 26 个城市以及全国其他省市的有关企业 1200 多名客商参加了洽谈会。来自世界五大洲 30 个国家和地区的 800 多名客商到会。各参展企业共签订进出口合同 9600 万美元，其中出口成交 8850 万美元，进口成交 750 万美元。共签订利用外资项目 39 个，合同外资额 8.16 亿美元，协议外资 4.6 亿美元。利用内资有 73 个项目签约，协议总金额达 37.9 亿元人民币，内资合同中武汉市占协议总金额的 90%；房地产销售共签订合同 2.1 亿元人民币，其中现房销售 2000 万元，期房销售 1.3 亿元，意向合同 6000 万元。

港口运输 1999 年武汉港口泊位 374 个，港口吞吐能力平均每年 5000 万吨（最大为 7000 万吨），当年实际完成的货物吞吐总量 1820 万吨。1999 年武汉地区外贸货物运输总量 68.7 万吨，比 1998 年下降 18.7%，其中按运输方式分：海运量 66.8 万吨、空运量 58 吨、陆运量 1.67 万吨。

涉外旅游 1999 年入境的外国人数为 16.08 万人次，台港澳同胞人数为 43264 人次；旅游出口创汇 7336 万美元，比上年的 6413 万美元增长 14.39%。

1999年湖南省对外经济贸易

湖南省对外经济贸易委员会

【对外贸易】

进出口总额 1999年，湖南省进出口总额195584万美元，比1998年的17897万美元增长9.8%。

出口总额 出口总额128190万美元，与上年的128280万美元基本持平；出口总额占全省国内生产总值3422亿元人民币（相当于413.32亿美元）的3.10%；占全国出口总额的0.66%。

出口商品结构 初级产品出口额18211万美元，占出口总额的14.21%，比上年比重下降0.87个百分点；工业制成品出口额109979万美元，占出口总额的85.79%，比上年比重上升0.87个百分点。其中：机电产品出口21417万美元，占出口总额的16.71%，比上年比重上升1.43个百分点。

出口额500万美元以上的大宗骨干商品共34种，出口金额109369万美元，占全省出口总额的85.32%。

出口额500万美元以上商品情况表

金额分类	商品名称	出口金额（万美元）	占出口总额（%）
1000万美元以上商品22种	活猪、水海产品、大米、茶叶、鞭炮烟花、亚麻及苎麻纱线、亚麻及苎麻机织物、棉机织物、陶瓷、钢材、未锻造的锌及锌合金、未锻造的锰、手用或机用工具、旅行用品及箱包、服装及衣着附件、鞋类、金属制品、机械及设备、电器及电子电讯设备、运输工具、化工原料、蔬菜及水果	101122	78.89
500万～1000万美元商品12种	鲜冻猪肉、天然石墨、仲钨酸铵、氧化锌及过氧化锌、轴承、汽车零件、塑料制品、仪器仪表、烟草及其制品、纺织纤维及废料、橡胶制品、软极木制品	8247	6.43
合计	**34种**	**109369**	**85.32**

出口商品市场 出口商品销往158个国家（地区），比上年增加14个。主要市场有：港澳地区19939万美元，占出口总额15.55%；美国19124万美元，占出口总额14.92%；欧共体24598万美元，占出口总额19.19%；东盟13335万美元，占出口总额10.40%；日本12663万美元，占出口总额9.88%；独联体及东欧2693万美元，占出口总额2.10%，对以上六大市场共出口92352万美元，占全省出口总额72.04%，出口比重比上年下降8.85个百分点。

出口主要国别（地区）表

单位：万美元

国别（地区）	出口额	比重（%）
香港	19139	14.93
美国	19124	14.92
日本	12663	9.88
韩国	8722	6.80
德国	7262	5.67

出口主要国别（地区）表（续）

单位：万美元

国别（地区）	出口额	比重（%）
荷兰	6824	5.32
新加坡	5933	4.63
台湾省	4307	3.36
印度尼西亚	3271	2.55
意大利	2809	2.19

进口总额 进口到货总额67394万美元，比上年的49917万美元增长35.01%。

进口商品结构 初级产品进口额9852万美元，占进口总额的14.62%；工业制成品进口额57542万美元，占进口总额的85.38%。

进口额300万美元以上商品情况表

金额分类	商品名称	进口金额（万美元）	占进口总额（%）
1000万美元以上商品9种	自动数据处理设备及其部件、铁矿砂、扬声器、未铸造的铜及铜材、钢铁棒材、干豆、电视收音机及无线电讯设备、黑白电视机、纺织机械	16955	25.16
300万～1000万美元商品14种	鲜冻猪肉、活鱼、大米、蔬菜、松子仁、天然蜂蜜、茶叶、纸烟、天然碳酸镁、焦炭、仲钨酸铵、装饰用陶瓷制品、珠宝、工具	7441	11.04
合　计	**23种**	**24396**	**36.20**

进口商品市场 进口商品来自49个国家和地区，进口到货500万美元以上的主要市场有17个国家（地区），进口金额共61754万美元，占全省进口总额的91.63%。

进口主要国别(地区)表

单位：万美元

国别（地区）	进口额	比重（%）
日本	16495	24.48
美国	8257	12.25
韩国	7668	11.38
英国	5232	7.76
德国	4272	6.34
台湾省	4140	6.14
意大利	2996	4.45
法国	2297	3.41

进口主要国别(地区)表(续)

单位：万美元

国别（地区）	进口额	比重（%）
澳大利亚	2157	3.20
香港	1828	2.71

技术进出口 对外签订技术进出口合同项目共117个，合同金额34001.67万美元，比上年的31676.84万美元增长7.34%。其中：签订技术引进和进口设备合同项目78个，比上年增加16个；合同金额26379.37万美元，比上年的24904.03万美元增长5.92%；实际用汇26379万美元，比上年的24904万美元增长5.92%。签订技术出口合同项目39个，比上年减少17个；合同金额7622.3万美元，比上年的6772.81万美元增长12.54%；年内收汇6772.81万美元，比上年的6005万美元增长12.79%。

技术进口 技术设备引进的主要国别（地区）有美国、德国、瑞士、日本、香港等发达国家和地区。技术引进项目分布在邮电、轻工、机械、电子、冶金、化工等10多个行业。其中，引进项目金额最多的前五位是：邮电行业27个项目，21897.14万美元，占引进总金额的80.01%；机械行业26个项目，1837.15万美元，占6.96%；化工行业4个项目，953万美元，占2.61%；电子行业11个项目，545.18万美元，占2.01%；冶金行业6个项目，876.7万美元，占3.32%。这些重点技术项目的引进，对湖南科学技术进步和产业结构调整发挥了重要作用，特别是邮电行业多年来引进项目金额居于首位，加速了全省邮电业的现代化进程。

技术出口 技术出口主要方式为大型设备、机电产品、成套设备、国际招标、国内中标等；分布行业为机械、轻工、电子等；主要出口孟加拉国、伊拉克、越南等发展中国家，并逐步向美国、日本、加拿大等发达国家转移。1999年出口高新技术产品2300万美元，比上年增长27.8%。

【利用外资】

全年批准利用外资项目共364个，比上年421个减少57个；合同利用外资金额171298万美元，比上年的143026万美元增长19.77%；实际利用外资金额163974万美元，比上年的100918万美元增长62.48%。其中，外国政府贷款项目43个，合同贷款金额121100万美元，比上年的20877万美元增长480.06%，实际贷款98600万美元，比上年的3005万美元增长3181.20%；直接利用外资项目321个，比上年减少95个，合同利用外资金额56949万美元，比上年的122149万美元下降53.38%；实际利用外资金额71945万美元，比上年的97913万美元下降26.52%。

1999年利用外资情况表

利用外资方式	批准签订的合同			实际利用外资	
	项　目（个）	外资金额（万美元）	金额比1998年（±%）	金　额（万美元）	金额比1998年（±%）
对外借款	43	121100	480.06	98600	3181.20
其中：					
外国政府贷款	43	121100	480.06	98600	3181.20
外商直接投资	321	50198	-54.15	65374	-20.18
合资企业	123	13269	-53.11	30534	-17.09
合作企业	33	11504	-66.39	8227	-52.81
外资企业	165	25425	-45.87	26613	-3.42
外商其他投资 其中补偿贸易		6751	-46.66	6571	-59.18
加工装配		6751	-46.66	6571	-59.10
合　计	**364**	**171298**	**19.77**	**163974**	**62.48**

外商直接投资行业 外商直接投资项目中，属于生产型的235个，合同外资金额37667万美元，实际利用外资金额46783万美元；属于非生产型的86个，合同外资金额12531万美元，实际利用外资金额18591万美元。这些项目分布在10大行业：农林牧渔业28个项目，合同外资金额6973万美元，实际利用外资金额5211万美元；制造业182个项目，合同外资金额24164万美元，实际利用外资金额29545万美元；采掘业9个项目，合同外资金额1337万美元，实际利用外资金额1180万美元；建筑业8个项目，合同外资金额1673万美元，实际利用外资金额4172万美元；电力、煤气及水的生产和

供应业4个项目，合同外资金额1521万美元，实际利用外资金额1630万美元；交通运输、仓储及邮电通讯业3个项目，合同外资金额1914万美元，实际利用外资金额5045万美元；房地产业15个项目，合同外资金额1837万美元，实际利用外资金额9189万美元；社会服务业61个项目，合同外资金额9456万美元，实际利用外资金额8707万美元；批发和零售贸易、餐饮业6个项目，合同外资金额188万美元，实际利用外资金额341万美元；教育、文化、艺术及广播影视业3个项目，合同外资金额327万美元，实际利用外资金额354万美元；科学研究及综合技术服务业1个项目，合同外资金额65万美元；其他1个项目，合同外资金额723万美元。

外商直接投资来源 外商直接投资来源于六大洲27个国家和地区。合同外资金额在500万美元以上的有11个国家和地区，依金额大小排序为：香港171个项目，合同外资金额31419万美元，实际投资金额31039万美元；台湾省61个项目，合同外资金额6978万美元，实际投资7600万美元；加拿大11个项目，合同外资金额2785万美元，实际投资金额2276万美元；美国28个项目，合同外资金额1982万美元，实际投资金额3822万美元；澳门14个项目，合同外资金额1950万美元，实际投资金额906万美元；维尔京群岛3个项目，合同外资金额1592万美元，实际投资金额2491万美元；韩国合同外资金额1015万美元，实际投资3764万美元；澳大利亚7个项目，合同外资金额656万美元，实际投资922万美元；泰国3个项目，合同外资金额599万美元，实际投资695万美元；毛里求斯1个项目，合同外资金额600万美元，实际投资金额150万美元；意大利1个项目，合同外资金额573万美元，实际投资270万美元。

外商直接投资企业生产经营状况 全省累计投产开业的“三资”企业共2000多家，其中有进出口实绩的199家，全年共完成进出口总额29860万美元，比上年增长1.71%，其中出口12900万美元，比上年增长12.13%；年销售收入214亿元，比上年的194亿元增长10.31%；实现税收9.8亿元，比上年的8.94亿元增长9.62%。

【对外经济合作】

承包工程与劳务合作 对外承包工程与劳务合作业务继续保持了持续发展的良好势头，全省22家外经企业对外签订承包劳务合同项目共653个，比上年增长68.30%；合同金额12571万美元，比上年的12743万美元下降1.35%；完成营业额12220万美元，比上年的10563万美元增长15.69%；当年外派承包劳务人员2062人（次），比上年的1868人（次）增长10.39%；年末在外人数3912人，比上年的3265人增长19.82%。对外承包劳务项目分布在越南、柬埔寨、阿联酋、马尔代夫、新加坡、巴基斯坦、泰国、印度尼西亚、孟加拉国、日本、香港、澳门、毛里求斯、埃及、马里、喀麦隆、坦桑尼亚、尼日利亚、塞拉利昂、阿尔及利亚、德国、法国、意大利、荷兰、美国、加拿大、澳大利亚、墨西哥、秘鲁、牙买加、尼加拉瓜、巴巴多斯、巴布亚新几内亚、斐济、密克罗西尼亚等74个国家和地区。

对外经济技术援助 执行中的援外项目4个，其中新增项目2个，援外金额604万元。援外项目主要分布在阿尔及利亚、喀麦隆、加纳等10多个国家（地区），项目进展顺利，得到受援国的好评，援助加纳农田水利项目被评为国家优秀项目。

接受国外经济援助 正在执行的国际双边和多边的无偿援助项目31个，受援金额6195.21万美元，其中当年新增受援项目13个，受援金额732.16万美元。配合灾后重建工作，先后争取了联合国儿童基金会给益阳、郴州各两个区的灾后防病、供水改水项目2个；澳大利亚援助南县明山头中心卫生院灾后重建项目、平江县伍市镇中心卫生院灾后重建项目、汝城县三星镇梓槽小学灾后重建项目3个；日本援助的粮食增产项目覆盖沅陵、安化、新化、桃源、攸县五个县；此外，还有到德国进行中型企业经理培训项目、中荷人才开发项目、武陵大学器材装备续援项目和农村金融体系建设项目等。

对外投资 新批海外企业3家：香港长丰实业发展有限公司，中方投资50万美元；香港勤隆发展有限公司；湘潭神州龙服装有限公司在阿尔及利亚开办1家境外加工贸易企业，中方投资75万美元，派出人员3人。

【其他】

经济技术开发区 截止1999年底，长沙高新技术产业开发区累计完成技工贸总收入434.4亿元，实现利税67.1亿元，上缴国家税金22.5亿元，出口创汇2.5亿美元。全区拥有493家高新技术企业，在研项目280个，其中处于国际国内领先和先进水平的有231个，累计开发高新技术项目933个，列入国家、省（部）重点计划的200个，主要产品处于国际领先和先进水平的116个，处于国内领先和先进水平的334个。全区累计创办“三资”企业158家，总投资7.13亿美元，其中外商投资3.3亿美元，实际到位2.6亿美元，开发高新技术项目182个。全年完成工贸总收入152.1亿元，实现利润15.6亿元，上缴税金7.2亿元，分别比上年增长27.8%、34.5%、31%。有30多种高新技术产品出口美国、日本、欧洲、东南亚、港澳台等国家和地区，全年出口额达6700万美元，上缴涉外税收3.29亿元。

涉外旅游 旅游业紧扣“生态环境旅游年”主题，全年旅游业的各项指标较上年全面增长。共接待国（境）外旅游者38万人（次），比上年的34.86万人（次）增长9.01%；涉外旅游创汇1.8亿美元，比上年的1.56亿美元增长15.38%。接待国内旅游者4300万人（次），国内旅游收入95亿元，分别比上年增长2.38%和9.20%。

1999年广东省对外经济贸易

广东省对外贸易经济合作厅

【对外贸易】

进出口总额 1999年广东省进出口总额1403.40亿美元，比1998年的1298.27亿美元增长8.1%。

出口总额 出口总额776.75亿美元，比上年的756.4亿美元增长2.69%，占全国出口总额的39.85%，居全国首位。

出口商品结构 初级产品出口额30.54亿美元，占出口总额的3.93%；工业制成品的出口额746.21亿美元，占出口总额的96.07%。

出口额在500万美元以上的商品情况表

金额分类	商品名称	出口金额（万美元）	占出口总额（%）
1亿美元以上（160）种	8471所列其他机器的零件、附件，其他玩具，未列名橡胶或塑料制外底及鞋面的鞋靴，显示器，塑料或纺织材料作面的提箱、小手袋等，无绳电话机，大、中、小型计算机及其部件的零件、附件等	5006157	64.45
5000万美元～1亿美元（136种）	放电灯或放电管用镇流器，其他钢铁丝制品，氯化钾，16、18、20英寸越野自行车，合成纤维制针织或钩编的女式便服套装，其他微型数字式自动数据处理机，按摩器具等	961671	12.38
1000万美元～5000万美元（548种）	未列名电动的钟，木制的画框、相框及类似品，不间断供电电源，太阳镜，化学纤维制其他男式服装，瓦楞纸或纸板制的箱、盒、匣等	1234397	15.89

出口额在500万美元以上的商品情况表(续)

金额分类	商品名称	出口金额（万美元）	占出口总额（%）
500万美元～1000万美元（356种）	其他装有计算装置的现金出纳机，螺母，初级形状的聚甲醛，棉制其他袜等	254847	3.28
合　计	**1200种**	**7457072**	**96.00**

出口商品市场　出口商品销往214个国家（地区）。

主要出口市场情况表

国别（地区）	出口金额（万美元）	占出口总额（%）
香港	2636524	33.94
美国	2022262	26.04
欧盟	1090968	14.05
日本	678363	8.73
新加坡	168746	2.17
台湾省	163355	2.10
澳大利亚	99959	1.29

主要出口市场情况表(续)

国别（地区）	出口金额（万美元）	占出口总额（%）
加拿大	95666	1.23
合　计	**6955843**	**89.55**

进口总额　进口总额626.65亿美元，比上年的541.87亿美元增长15.65%。

进口商品结构　初级产品进口额64.35亿美元，占进口总额的10.27%；工业制成品的进口额562.3亿美元，占进口总额的89.73%。

进口额在500万美元以上的商品情况表

金额分类	商品名称	进口金额（万美元）	占进口总额（%）
1亿美元以上（115种）	其他单片集成电路，8471所列其他机器的零件、附件，石油原油及从沥青矿物提取的原油，其他初级形状的聚苯乙烯，其他燃料油，初级形状的聚丙烯，未列名具有独立功能的机器及机械器具，混合集成电路等	3279683	52.34
5000万美元～1亿美元（87种）	光盘驱动器，其他镀或涂锌普通钢铁板材，铝电解电容器，其他未列名测量或检验仪器、器具及机器，未列名浸涂、染、饰面或印花纸、纸板、纤维纸，其他非工业用钻石等	681955	10.88

进口额在500万美元以上的商品情况表（续）

金额分类	商品名称	进口金额（万美元）	占进口总额（%）
1000万美元～5000万美元（657种）	人造纤维短纤≥85%的多股纱线或缆线，棉制女裤，涂漆或涂塑普通钢铁板材，成卷或成张的新闻纸，已组装电动的光电显示器表的完整表芯等	1590645	25.38
500万美元～1000万美元（434种）	其他未锻轧的精炼铜，玻璃纤维粗纱，小麦及混合麦的细粉，其他灌装机、包装机，使用液体燃料的炉用燃烧器等	307669	4.91
合计	**1293种**	**5859951**	**93.51**

进口商品市场 进口商品来自151个国家（地区）。

主要进口市场情况表

国别（地区）	进口金额（万美元）	占进口总额（%）
日本	1337621	21.35
台湾省	1231577	19.65
韩国	554635	8.85
欧盟	544249	8.69
美国	541402	8.64
香港	405579	6.47
新加坡	169285	2.70
泰国	164816	2.63
合计	**4949164**	**78.98**

技术进出口 1999年广东省技术进出口总额138.03亿美元，比上年的35.45亿美元增长2.89倍。

技术进口 签订技术引进合同222项，比上年的115项增长93.04%；合同金额14.32亿美元，比上年的11.78亿美元增长21.56%。引进的技术来自24个国家（地区），其中美国47项、日本75项，香港29项，台湾省20项，法国10项，从上述5个国家和地区引进合同金额共9.96亿美元，占技术引进合同总金额的69.55%。技术引进涉及电子、轻工、邮电、化工等28个行业，其中电子行业引进金额8.14亿美元、轻工行业3.29亿美元，共占引进合同总金额的79.82%。在技术引进合同总金额中，技术费为12.68亿美元，占88.55%。

技术出口 技术出口合同总金额123.71亿美元，比上年的23.67亿美元增长4.23倍。其中高技术产品出口额120.3亿美元，占全省技术出口合同总金额的97.24%。

【利用外资】

1999年利用外资情况表

利用外资方式	批准签订的合同			实际利用外资	
	项目（个）	外资金额（万美元）	金额比1998年（±%）	金额（万美元）	金额比1998年（±%）
对外借款	68	100117	－45.95	103595	－49.34

1999 年利用外资情况表(续)

利用外资方式	批准签订的合同			实际利用外资	
	项目（个）	外资金额（万美元）	金额比 1998 年（±%）	金 额（万美元）	金额比 1998 年（±%）
外商直接投资	3013	617451	-32.61	1220300	+1.52
合资企业	824	108507	-51.65	408392	+17.84
合作企业	423	132919	-47.85	387885	-14.71
外资企业	1766	374756	-12.98	417725	+6.45
外商投资股份制		1269	-79.48	6298	-23.35
外商其他投资	11743	154024	+12.92	123488	+19.35
国际租赁					
补偿贸易				23	-98.90
加工装配	11743	154024	+17.99	123465	+24.84
对外发行股票					
合　计	**14824**	**871592**	**-29.59**	**1447383**	**-4.14**

外商直接投资行业　在批准的 3013 个外商直接投资项目中，生产性项目占 80%以上，按行业分，农林牧渔业 104 个，采掘业 13 个，制造业 2335 个，电力、煤气及水的生产和供应业 16 个，建筑业 19 个，交通运输、仓储及邮电通讯业 30 个，批发和零售贸易、餐饮业 65 个，房地产业 103 个，社会服务业 254 个，卫生、体育和社会福利业 2 个，科学研究和综合技术服务业 15 个，其他行业 57 个。

外商直接投资来源　外商直接投资来自 45 个国家（地区）。其中香港 1922 个，合同外资金额 314660 万美元；维尔京群岛 170 个，125140 万美元；台湾省 388 个，39563 万美元；美国 152 个，35678 万美元；西萨摩亚 32 个，12664 万美元；日本 37 个，11683 万美元；澳门 119 个，11056 万美元；加拿大 34 个，6725 万美元。

外商直接投资企业生产经营情况　截至 1999 年底，全省登记注册的外商投资企业 5.36 万家，大批技术和管理先进的外商投资企业取得较好的经济效益。当年全省外商投资企业出口总额 393.98 亿美元，占全省出口总额的 50.72%

【对外经济合作】

承包工程和劳务合作　1999 年签订对外承包工程、劳务合作和设计咨询合同 5714 个，金额 62696 万美元，比上年的 26658 万美元增长 135.19%；营业额 35305 万美元，比上年的 32329 万美元增长 9.21%。当年派出劳务人员 5961 人次，年末在外 19731 人。

对外经济技术援助　承担援助柬埔寨体育项目，密克罗尼西亚体育馆施工项目和圣卢西亚农业技术合作项目。柬埔寨体育项目，合同金额 35 万元人民币，已派出 3 名体育教练；密克罗尼西亚多功能体育馆施工项目合同额 2779 万元人民币，已派出 101 人；圣卢西亚农业技术合作项目，已派出农业专家 6 名。

接受经济援助　1999 年获德国提供的援助项目 2 项，金额折合 13 万元人民币，分别用于和平县公白镇饮水工程和龙门县地派中学校舍建设；获澳大利亚提供的援助项目 2 项，金额折合 53 万元人民币，分别用于东源县蓝口良田小学和乳源县侯公渡卫生院的大楼建设。

对外投资　1999 年经批准在柬埔寨、巴基斯坦、印度、巴西共举办境外加工贸易企业 6 家，总投资额 4541 万美元，内含中方投资总额 3793 万美元。其中，佛山纺织工业发展公司在柬埔寨金边举办的金禅制衣有限公司，总投资额 105 万美元，其中中方投资 53 万美元。

【其他】

经济技术开发区 广州、湛江、大亚湾、南沙经济技术开发区在加快建设。其中惠州市大亚湾经济技术开发区1999年保持良好的发展势头，南海石化项目、天然气发电项目、东风汽车城建设等在稳步推进，惠州港的整体形象大为改观；当年该开发区批准合同外资额15049万美元，实际利用外资10090万美元，出口总额5415万美元。

保税区、高新技术产业开发区 深圳沙头角、深圳福田、深圳盐田港、广州、汕头、珠海保税区和深圳科技工业园、广州天河、中山“火炬”、惠州仲恺、佛山、珠海高新技术产业开发区的各项优势和功能作用得到了进一步的发挥。其中中山“火炬”高新技术产业开发区，1999年设立了“科技创新基金”，已初步建立有利于科技进步的管理体制和运行机制，全区已有高新技术企业44家；年内批准利用外资合同21个，合同外资额8507万美元，实际利用外资1.26亿美元，出口总额2.91亿美元；当年全区实现国内生产总值38亿元，科技进步对经济增长的贡献率达50%。佛山高新技术产业开发区至1999年末，入区企业已有53家，其中技工贸总收入超亿元的有12家，经认定的高新技术企业有15家，已初步形成电子信息、光机电一体化、新材料、生物医药技术等主导产业和一批在国内外市场有较强竞争力的高新技术产品；全年利用外资合同金额5.28亿美元，实际利用外资额5.06亿美元，产品出口额1.2亿美元。

对外经贸洽谈会 1999年5月18～21日在香港举办广东经济技术贸易洽谈会，共接待来自20多个国家（地区）的公司3177家、客商8000多人次，签订外商直接投资合同770个，外资金额37亿美元；协议186个，外资金额15.4亿美元；意向书159个，外资金额11.4亿美元。此外，还签订“三来一补”协议224个，外资金额2.5亿美元；贸易成交14.8亿美元。10月17～31日，广东经贸考察团赴巴西、智利、秘鲁考察，先后召开了广东—圣保罗、广东—圣地亚哥、广东—利马经贸合作洽谈会，到会客商共300多家，签订了美的牌空调、拉舍尔毛毯、DVD、功放器、麦克风、服装、轻工产品等出口合同及意向书4300万美元。12月7日和12月14日，广东经贸代表团分别在英国伦敦和法国巴黎举办广东投资推介会和投资项目、贸易洽谈会，共签订各种利用外资项目47个，投资总额5.45亿美元，外资金额4.45亿美元；贸易成交1.88亿美元。

港口运输 1999年全省沿海主要港口货物吞吐量16258万吨，比1998年增长26.36%。

涉外旅游 1999年入境旅客5923万人次，其中外国人242万人次，华侨4万人次，港澳台胞5677万人次。旅游外汇收入32.73亿美元，比上年的29.42亿美元增长11.25%。

1999年广州市对外经济贸易

广州市对外经济贸易委员会

【对外贸易】

进出口总额 1999年广东省广州市进出口总额为144.07亿美元，比1998年129.43亿美元增长11.3%。

出口总额 出口总额78.22亿美元，比上年75.2亿美元增长4.47%。出口占全市国内生产总值2063.37亿元的32.38%，占全省出口总额的10.07%。

出口商品结构 初级产品出口额2.67亿美元，占出口总额的3.41%；工业制成品的出口总额75.55亿美元，占出口总额的96.59%。

出口额在1000万美元以上的商品情况表

金额分类	商品名称	出口金额（万美元）	占出口总额（%）
1亿美元以上（16种）	鞋类、服装、玩具、电子电器、电子元器件等	447800.39	57.25
5千万～1亿美元（17种）	电视机及音响设备、各类船、化工原料，有线通讯设备、自行车，办公用品及设备等	116795.29	14.93
1千万美元～5千万美元（57种）	化纤布、小五金、轮胎，棉制品、食用植物油，金属制品等	137026.54	17.52
合　计	**90种**	**701622.22**	**89.70**

出口商品市场　出口商品销往196个国家和地区。

主要出口市场情况表

国别（地区）	出口金额（万美元）	占出口总额（%）
香港	277776.30	35.5
美国	219118.66	28.01
日本	68530.31	8.76
德国	23397.94	2.99
比利时	16912.62	2.16
英国	14216.00	1.82
加拿大	13914.56	1.78
澳大利亚	12865.85	1.64
荷兰	11833.30	1.51
新加坡	6932.19	1.23
合　计	**665497.73**	**85.4**

进口总额　进口总额为65.85亿美元，比上年的54.23亿美元增长21.43%。

进口商品结构　初级产品进口额4.77亿美元，占进口总额的7.25%；工业制成品的进口总额61.08亿美元，占进口总额的92.75%。

主要进口商品情况表

商品名称	进口金额（万美元）	占进口总额（%）
纺织品	64429.3	9.78

主要进口商品情况表（续）

商品名称	进口金额（万美元）	占进口总额（%）
塑料	60404.4	9.17
有色金属	31007.4	4.71
黑色金属	28854.8	4.38
各类机械	23953.2	3.64
畜产品	34664.6	5.26
工艺品类	34874.8	5.30
电信设备及器材	57251.8	8.69
纺织原料	5593.2	0.85
纸浆纸张及制品	19706.9	3.0
汽车、电车、摩托车及零件	12705.4	1.93
船舶	12094.5	1.84

进口商品市场　进口商品来自120个国家和地区。

主要进口市场情况表

国别（地区）	进口金额（万美元）	占进口总额（%）
香港	412377.5	62.62
日本	37290.1	5.66
台湾省	19964.3	3.03
美国	15086.6	2.29
韩国	9962.3	1.51
德国	4561.5	0.69
比利时	11840.1	1.80

主要进口市场情况表(续)

国别（地区）	进口金额（万美元）	占进口总额（%）
澳大利亚	4025.14	0.61
法国	4187.5	0.64
合　计	**519295.04**	**78.86**

技术进出口 1999年广东省广州市技术进出口总额为9.76亿美元。签订引进技术和设备合同项目158个，比上年的80个增加78个；合同金额2.67亿美元，比上年的6.95亿元下降61.58%。签订技术出口合同项目（不包括高技术产品）136个，合同金额3.11亿美元。

技术进口 引进项目的国家（地区）15个。其中日本63个，金额10775万美元；美国26个，金额8019万美元；台湾省22个，金额1036万美元；香港21个，金额2675万美元；瑞士3个，金额824万美元；德国8个，金额1407万美元；新加坡3个，金额887万美元；澳大利亚3个，金额65万美元；法国3个，金额43万美元；其他6个国家金额共993万美元。引进的行业有：轻纺15个，金额5704万美元；原材料16个，金额3141万美元；交通运输4个，金额3432万美元；机械电子114个，金额13859万美元；其他9个，金额587万美元。

【利用外资】

1999年利用外资情况表

利用外资方式	批准签订的合同			实际利用外资	
	项目数（个）	外资金额（万美元）	金额比1998年（±%）	金额（万美元）	金额比1998年（±%）
对外借款	1	26507	-15.6	18118	-42.3
外商直接投资	537	141377	-26.8	298687	10
合资企业	119	27119	-44.7	121412	104.7
合作企业	122	54189	-35.6	120096	-20.7
外资企业	296	60096	0.1	57179	-6.1
外商其他投资	515	4924	-76	795	-45.7
加工贸易	343	4924	-76	795	-38.2
合　计	**1053**	**172808**	**-29.5**	**317600**	**4.3**

外商直接投资行业 在新批准的537个外商投资项目中，生产型项目394个，占总数的73.37%。

广州市1999年外商直接投资行业分析表

单位：万美元

行　业	项目		合同外资金额		实际使用外资金额	
	个数	比重（%）	金额	比重（%）	金额	比重（%）
农业	13	2.4	989	0.7	1010	0.3

广州市1999年外商直接投资行业分析表(续)

单位：万美元

行业	项目		合同外资金额		实际使用外资金额	
	个数	比重（%）	金额	比重（%）	金额	比重（%）
制造业	377	70.2	92984	65.8	135093	45.2
其中：纺织	15	2.8	3338	2.4	6067	2.0
化工	40	7.4	12028	8.5	9889	3.3
机械	14	2.6	2324	1.6	6629	2.2
电子	49	9.1	17999	12.7	15225	5.1
房地产开发	28	5.2	23140	16.4	71678	24
社会服务业	49	9.1	8754	6.2	7276	2.4
建筑业	4	0.7	4603	3.3	10399	3.5
交通邮电业	4	0.7	2001	1.4	3580	1.2
其他	52	11.5	2899	6.3	26379	23.4
合　计	**537**	**100**	**141377**	**100**	**298687**	**100**

外商直接投资来源　外商直接投资的国家和地区有43个。其中主要以港澳台和新加坡为主的境外华人投资，以日本、美国和西欧发达国家为代表的国际资本，以及维尔京群岛、凯曼群岛为代表的国际游资分居外商直接投资来源的前三位。

外商直接投资企业生产经营情况　截至1999年底，广州市登记注册的外商投资企业累计11163家，其中投产开业的5326家，累计实际利用外资176.8亿美元。1999年广州市外商投资企业出口总额51.82亿美元，占全市出口总额的66.24%。

外商直接投资来源情况表

单位：万美元

国别（地区）	项目数		合同利用外资		实际利用外资	
	个数	比重（%）	金额	比重（%）	金额	比重（%）
香港	537	59.2	66959	47.4	135976	45.5
维尔京群岛	32	6.0	16176	11.4	43184	14.5
美国	35	6.5	13941	9.9	10782	3.6
台湾省	77	14.3	7817	5.5	6322	2.1
澳门	5	0.9	5943	4.2	2295	0.8
日本	9	1.7	4456	3.2	8399	2.8
新加坡	14	1.6	4367	3.1	8215	2.8
开曼群岛	4	0.7	3398	2.4	6470	2.2
瑞士	2	0.4	3224	2.3	4062	1.4
马来西亚	5	0.9	3101	2.2	1268	0.4
荷兰	2	0.4	2233	1.6	2188	0.7
毛里求斯	2	0.4	1945	1.4	1175	0.4
英国	8	1.5	1707	1.2	2359	0.8

外商直接投资来源情况表(续)

单位：万美元

国别(地区)	项目数		合同利用外资		实际利用外资	
	个数	比重（%）	金额	比重（%）	金额	比重（%）
芬兰	1	0.2	1200	0.8		0
其他	14	4.3	4910	3.5	65992	22.1
合　计	**537**	**100.0**	**141377**	**100.0**	**298687**	**100.0**

【对外经济合作】

承包工程和劳务合作　1999年签定对外承包工程和劳务合作合同项目5051个，金额3338万美元，是上年918万美元的3.636倍；对外劳务营业额1515万美元，下降30.66%；对外承包工程营业额2078万美元，上升7.8%。当年派出劳务人员566人次，比上年的1309人次下降56.76%。年末在外人数2106人。派往的国家和地区为：香港、澳门、越南、柬埔寨、菲律宾、泰国等近30个国家(地区)。

对外投资　1999年在海外开办企业数为3家，投资金额271万美元，投资的国别（地区）有香港、美国。

【其他】

广州经济技术开发区　1999年是广州经济技术开发区、广州高新技术产业开发区“合署办公”后的第一年，开发区全年实现国内生产总值105.5亿元，比上年增长15.42%；高新技术产业开发区完成工业总产值53.1亿元，比上年增长19.59%。两区出口5.96亿美元，比上年5.57亿美元增长7%；进口8.93亿美元，比上年6.50亿美元增长37.38%；实际利用外资4.35亿美元，比上年4.18亿美元增长4.1%。1999年底，全区累计批准外商投资企业1154个，实际利用外资28亿美元。

广州保税区　1999年是广州保税区历年来经济发展最好的一年，由于国家出台了打击走私、以产顶进及保税汽车等一系列政策，使保税区的投资环境更具吸引力，保税区建设趋于完善。1999年广州保税区引进外资项目43个，比上年59个下降27.12%，投资总额8087万美元，比上年5696万美元上升42%；实际利用外资11284万美元，比上年2169万美元上升420.24%；出口货值10686万美元，比上年11341万美元下降5.78%；进口货值20986万美元，比上年15610万美元上升34.44%。

广州南沙经济技术开发区　1999年广州南沙经济技术开发区各项主要经济指标完成较好。国内生产总值和工业生产总值分别是13.64亿元和23.82亿元，比上年增长13.1%和16.1%；全年实现了进口总值1.42亿美元，比上年增长11.6%，出口总值1.71亿美元，比上年增长4.7%。引进外资项目31个，合同利用外资1.3亿美元，实际利用外资3000万美元，比上年增长30.83%。

对外经济洽谈会　1999年初，广州市在美国、香港设立两个招商办事处，年末在法国巴黎的招商办事处开始启动。上半年，广州市市长带队赴美国拜会跨国大公司、大财团，在硅谷举办留学人员座谈会和广州经济发展介绍会。年中，在香港举行招商洽谈会、来料加工专题招商会和加工贸易政策介绍会。11月，在南沙开发区举办广州南沙科技投资洽谈会，签定利用外资合同8个，合同利用外资金额4亿美元。

港口运输　1999年广州港口货物吞吐量11324万吨，比上年增长29.9%；其中进口7368万吨，比上年增长33.2%，出口3955万吨，比上年增长24.2%。

涉外旅游　1999年入境的外国人数以及港澳台同胞人数为313万人次，比上年增长3.09%。旅游外汇收入11.67亿美元，比上年增长9.8%。

1999年深圳市对外经济贸易

深圳市贸易发展局

【对外贸易】

进出口总额 1999年深圳市进出口总额504.28亿美元，比1998年452.74亿美元增长11.38%。

出口总额 出口总额282.08亿美元，比1998年的263.96亿美元增长6.86%，占全市国内生产总值1436.51（相当于173.70亿美元）的162.39%。占全省出口额776.80亿美元的36.32%；占全国出口总额1949亿美元的14.47%。

出口商品结构 初级产品出口额12.14亿美元，占出口总额282.08亿美元的4.30%；工业制成品的出口额269.95亿美元，占出口总额282.08亿美元的95.69%。

出口额在1亿美元以上的商品情况表

金额分类	商品名称	出口金额（万美元）	占出口总额（%）
出口10亿美元以上的商品	电讯设备及器材	851777	30.20
	文体用品	251287	8.91
	家用电器	172409	6.11
	箱包及鞋帽	161885	5.73
	各类机械	143479	5.09
	服装	135086	4.79
	塑料	110108	3.90
	钟表	102426	3.63
出口1～10亿美元的商品	成套设备	83963	2.98

出口额在 1 亿美元以上的商品情况表(续)

金额分类	商品名称	出口金额（万美元）	占出口总额（%）
出口 1～10 亿美元的商品	工艺品类	81591	2.89
	日用杂品	72822	2.58
	家具类	66618	2.36
	纺织品	63436	2.25
	未分类商品	54353	1.93
	黑色金属	46205	1.63
	自行车类	45834	1.63
	照相制版及电影器材	31489	1.12
	日用五金器皿	22181	0.79
	纸浆、纸张及制品	21998	0.78
	出版物	18928	0.67
	船舶	18415	0.65
	食品制成品	17659	0.63
	陶瓷类	17006	0.60
	光学仪器	15846	0.56
	非金属矿产品及制品	15610	0.55
	电子设备及仪器	15564	0.55
	工农具	14577	0.52
	有色金属	13556	0.48
	化工原料	13112	0.46
	化肥、农药	12022	0.43
	食用动物及其产品	10523	0.37
	医疗器械	10262	0.36

出口商品市场

主要出口市场情况表

国别（地区）	出口金额（万美元）	占出口总额（%）
香港	840049	29.78
美国	818616	29.02
日本	270033	9.57
德国	122264	4.33
新加坡	103022	3.65
英国	102024	3.62

主要出口市场情况表(续)

国别（地区）	出口金额（万美元）	占出口总额（%）
荷兰	80320	3.20
台湾省	70645	2.50
法国	43935	1.56
加拿大	36364	1.29

进口总额　进口总额 222.19 亿美元，比 1998 年的 188.78 亿美元增长 17.70%。

进口商品结构

进口额在1亿美元以上的商品情况表

商品名称	进口金额（万美元）	占进口总额（%）
电讯设备及器材	690727	31.09
塑料	245820	11.06
各类机械	147475	6.64
有色金属	145796	6.56
黑色金属	131965	5.94
纸浆、纸张及制品	99348	4.50
未分类商品	84968	3.82
纺织品	68668	3.09
成套设备	66608	3.00
化工原料	56941	2.56
钟表	45242	2.03
石油及制品	43190	1.94
丝织品	38276	1.72
木材	32747	1.47
畜产品	25508	1.15
非金属矿产品及制品	25012	1.13
电子设备及仪器	22353	1.00
照相制版及电影器材	19245	0.87
化肥、农药	19055	0.86
油漆、油墨及染料	15978	0.72
航空设备	15394	0.69
光学仪器	14456	0.65
食用动物及其产品	14241	0.64
家用电器	12928	0.58
服装	11680	0.53
物理化工仪器	11284	0.51
汽车、电车、摩托车及零件	10612	0.48
粮油	10181	0.46

进口商品市场

主要进口市场情况表

国别（地区）	进口金额（万美元）	占进口总额（%）
日本	529340	23.82
台湾省	401176	18.06
美国	208300	9.37
韩国	157775	7.10
香港	122077	5.49
新加坡	91658	4.13
澳大利亚	68571	3.09
泰国	67094	3.02
马来西亚	57744	2.60
法国	49369	2.22

高新技术产品出口 1999年高新技术产品出口总额60.18亿美元，比1998年的55.59亿美元增长8.26%。

【利用外资】

1999年利用外资情况表

利用外资方式	批准签订的合同			实际利用外资	
	项目（个）	外资金额（万美元）	金额比1998年（±%）	金额（万美元）	金额比1998年（±%）
外商直接投资	797	121017	-40.52	177839	6.9
合资企业	321	16345	-79.05	74848	1.47
合作企业	15	7242	-14.64	18954	-15.21
外资企业	461	96585	-16.23	82556	22.19
外商投资股份制		845	-49.76	1481	-44.74

【对外经济合作】

承包工程和劳务合作 1999年签订对外承包工程和劳务合作项目91个，金额20508万美元，比1998年的2619万美元增长683%；营业额6055万美元，比1998年的1115万美元增长443%；当年派出劳务人员496人，年末在外人数721人，派往的主要国家和地区是：香港、澳门、泰国、马来西亚、巴基斯坦、孟加拉、俄罗斯、肯尼亚、南斯拉夫、美国、约旦、沙特阿拉伯、柬埔寨。承包工程的主要国别和地区是：香港，深圳河治理工程，金额为5866万美元，牛潭尾渠务工程，金额为3861万美元；南斯拉夫，90万线GSM项目，金额为7500万美元。

对外投资 1999年在海外举办企业的项目9个，中方投资金额3754万美元，投资国别（地区）为：香港、印度、巴基斯坦、美国、南非、刚果。

1999年珠海市对外经济贸易

珠海市对外经济贸易委员会

【对外贸易】

进出口总额 1999年珠海市进出口总额为62.86亿美元，比1998年的59.17亿美元增长6.24%

出口总额 出口总额26.99亿美元，比上年的29.95亿美元下降9.86%。占全市国内生产总值34.62亿美元的77.96%；占全省出口额776.75亿美元的3.47%。

出口商品结构 初级产品出口额20985万美元，占出口总额的7.78%；工业制成品的出口额209450万美元，占出口总额的77.62%。

出口额在1000万美元以上的商品情况表

金额分类	商品名称	出口金额（万美元）	占出口总额（%）
1亿美元以上（4种）	服装、机械、电讯设备、家用电器	134424	49.8
5000万～1亿美元（6种）	纺织品、箱包及鞋帽、钟表、照相电影器材、电讯设备、各类机械	46949	17.38
1000万～5000万美元（19种）	食用动物及产品、纺织品、陶瓷、工艺品、箱包及鞋帽、文体用品、日用五金器皿、家具、日用杂品、黑色金属、有色金属、非金属矿产品、化工原料、塑料、工农具、家用电器、食品及制成品、成套设备、电子设备及仪器	56610	20.97
合　计	**29种**	**237983**	**88.15**

出口商品市场 出口商品销往133个国家和地区。

主要出口市场情况表

国别（地区）	出口金额（万美元）	占出口总额（%）
香港	199664	73.99
澳门	22410	8.30
荷兰	10760	3.99
美国	6961	2.58
日本	6356	2.35
瑞士	3737	1.38
德国	1502	0.56

主要出口市场情况表(续)

国别（地区）	出口金额（万美元）	占出口总额（%）
台湾省	1473	0.55
总　计	**252863**	**93.7**

进口总额 进口总额35.87亿美元，比上年的29.22亿美元增长22.74%。

进口商品结构 初级产品进口额58499万美元，占进口总额的16%；工业制成品的进口额185948万美元，占进口总额的52%。

进口额达1000万美元以上的商品情况表

金额分类	商　品　名　称	进口金额（万美元）	占进口总额（%）
1亿美元以上（7种）	纺织品、有色金属、石油及制品、化工原料、塑料、各类机械、电讯设备及器材	70394	19.63
5000万～1亿美元(3种)	纸浆、纸张及制品、黑色金属、成套设备	25516	7.11
1000万～5000万美元（24种）	粮油、食品制成品、饲料、畜产品、木材、纺织原料、丝织品、服装、钟表、日用杂品、非金属矿产品及制品、物理化工仪器、油漆油墨及染料、橡胶及制品、中成药、药酒、医药原料、西成药、医疗器械、船舶、航空设备、汽车、电车、摩托车等、照相制版及电影器材、家用电器。	58090	16.19
合　计	**34种**	**154000**	**42.93**

进口商品市场 进口商品来自34个国家和地区。

主要进口市场情况表

国别（地区）	进口金额（万美元）	占进口总额（%）
香港	232329	64.76
伊朗	51756	14.41
澳门	19857	5.51
日本	9986	2.76
美国	6333	1.76
沙特阿拉伯	5677	1.56

主要进口市场情况表(续)

国别（地区）	进口金额（万美元）	占进口总额（%）
马来西亚	3828	1.07
瑞士	3808	1.06
韩国	3527	0.98
印度尼西亚	3402	0.95
合　计	**340503**	**94.82**

【利用外资】

1999 年利用外资情况表

利用外资方式	批准签订的合同			实际利用外资	
	项目（个）	外资金额（万美元）	金额比1998年（±%）	金额（万美元）	金额比1998年（±%）
对外借款	57	9012	-77.49	17666	-55.87
外商直接投资	240	31101	-17.92	75157	8.03
合资企业	58	8215	18.54	11212	-36.99
合作企业	19	2510	-79.07	35825	55.29
外资企业	163	19952	5.18	25440	-11.38
外商投资股份制		424		2680	
外商其他投资	44				
补偿贸易					
加工贸易	44	2501	136.84	2616	147.96
合　计	**341**	**42614**	**-46.04**	**95439**	**-13.75**

外商直接投资行业　1999 年外商直接投资的 240 个项目中，属生产型项目 160 个，非生产项目 80 个。按行业分，农林牧渔业 7 项，制造业 153 项，建筑业 4 项，交通运输、仓储及邮电通信业 6 项，批发和零售贸易、餐饮业 10 项，房地产业 22 项，社会服务业 36 项，卫生体育和社会福利业 1 项。

外商直接投资来源　外商直接投资来自 15 个国家和地区，项目主要有来自香港 91 个，合同利用外资 16720 万美元；澳门 78 个，合同利用外资 626 万美元；台湾省 29 个，合同利用外资 712 万美元；美国 19 个，合同利用外资 1318 万美元；日本 7 个，合同利用外资 868 万美元；英属维尔京群岛 5 个，合同利用外资 2660 万美元；加拿大 4 个，合同利用外资 946 万美元；新加坡 3 个，合同利用外资 5495 万美元；马来西亚 2 个，合同利用外资 26 万美元；韩国 2 个，合同利用外资 19 万美元；澳大利亚 2 个，合同利用外资 2749 万美元；开曼群岛 1 个，合同利用外资 178 万美元；意大利 1 个，合同利用外资 140 万美元；柬埔寨 1 个，合同利用外资 15 万美元，洪都拉斯 1 个，合同利用外资 13 万美元。

【对外经济合作】

承包工程和劳务合作　1999 年签订对外承包工程和劳务合作合同 167 份，与上年增加 20 份，合同金额 2063 万美元，比上年的 5086 万美元减少 59.44%，营业额 4291 万美元，比上年的 4205 万美元增长 2.05%；年末在外劳务人数 2861 人，比上年的 2839 人增加了 22 人。对外劳务合作由去年的 8 个国家和地区增加至 11 个国家和地区。对外承包工程主要在缅甸和港澳地区。

【其他】

高新技术开发区　珠海高新技术产业开发区占地 9.8 平方公里。1999 年经过区位调整后，高新区下设南屏科技工业园、三灶科技工业园、新青科技工业园、白蕉科技工业园和广东珠海高科技成果产业化示范基地。各科技工业园自 1999 年 3 月 5 日、6 日挂牌，截至 1999 年 12 月 31 日，已有 51 个项目正式落户园区及基地，新增投资 19.7 亿元，总产值达 38.3 亿元；新增产值 26 亿元，出口创汇 2.5 亿美元。

保税区 截至 1999 年 12 月底，珠海保税区直接投入建设资金 3300 多万元，完成区内吹填工程的 70%，完成 15 万平方米土地平整，按海关总署对保税区监管条件验收标准，完成隔离设施、巡逻通道、出入卡口、办公设施、海关员工 10 套住房等建设配套任务，并于 1999 年 5 月 8 日通过了海关总署的验收，正式开始开关运作。全区动工项目占地面积 31 万平方米，在建厂房及仓库面积 12218 平方米，其中跨国企业西门子松下电子一期 1 万平方米厂房已于 1999 年 10 月完工并投入使用。区内注册企业 20 家，合同投资总额 12449 万美元，其中国内企业投资 5621 万美元，外商投资 6828 万美元，实际利用外资 1400 万美元。在边建设边营运的情况下，1999 年完成工业产品销售总额 1.8 亿元，仓储加工及进出口货物总值 5000 万美元，财政税收 60 万元。

对外经贸洽谈会 1999 年珠海市举办和参加对外经贸洽谈会 12 个。其中在 1999 年 5 月 18 日在香港展览中心举办的“'99 广东经济技术洽谈会”上，珠海代表团签订利用外资合同 25 个，投资总额 2.58 亿美元，合同外资金额 2.25 亿美元。在 1999 年 8 月 3 日至 5 日在澳门举办的“'99 珠海（澳门）投资贸易洽谈会”上签订利用外资合同 32 项，投资总额 3.37 亿美元，合同外资金额 1.67 亿美元。

涉外旅游 1999 年共接待过夜国际游客 79.41 万人次，比上年增长 13.9%。在国际游客中，外国人 8.2 万人次，比上年增长 17.9%；港澳同胞 48.84 万人次，比 1998 年减少 3.34%；台湾同胞 22 万人次，比上年增长 8.09%；华侨 3168 人次，比上年增长 515.15%。国际旅游外汇收入 7.56 亿美元，比上年的 3.32 亿美元增长 127.71%。

1999 年汕头市对外经济贸易

汕头市对外经济贸易委员会

【对外贸易】

进出口总额 1999 年，广东省汕头市进出口总值 43.91 亿美元，比 1998 年 66.10 亿美元下降 33.6%。

出口总额 出口总值 26.94 亿美元，比上年的 34.49 亿美元下降 21.9%。按贸易方式分，一般贸易出口 18.93 亿美元，增长 41.7%；加工贸易出口 7.97 亿美元，下降 59.3%。出口总值占全市国内生产总值 454 亿元（相当于 54.76 亿美元）的 49.2%，占全省出口总额的 3.5%。

出口额在 500 万美元以上的商品情况表

金额分类	商品名称	出口金额（万美元）	占出口总额（%）
500 万美元～1000 万美元 8 种	家具，收音机、录、放像机，二极管、晶体管及类半导体器件，贵金属或包贵金属的首饰，电子计算器，游戏机，电视机（包括整套散件）	5932	2.2

出口额在500万美元以上的商品情况表(续)

金额分类	商品名称	出口金额(万美元)	占出口总额(%)
1000万美元～5000万美元7种	电视、收音机及无线电讯设备零附件，印刷电路，扬声器，自动数据处理设备及其部件，电话机，人造花，灯具、照明装置及类似品	16681	6.2
5000万美元～1亿美元6种	塑料制品，陶瓷，汽车零件，鞋类，旅行用品及箱包，圣诞用品	42589	15.8
1亿美元以上5种	服装及衣着附件、机电产品、纺织纱线、织物及制品、玩具，渔农产品	173922	64.6
合　计	**26种**	**239124**	**88.8**

出口商品市场　出口商品销往153个国家和地区。

主要出口市场情况表

国别(地区)	出口金额(万美元)	占出口总额(%)
港澳地区	171099	63.5
美　国	18619	6.9
日　本	15070	5.6
巴拿马	6674	2.5
新加坡	5290	2.0
沙特阿拉伯	4725	1.8
英　国	4623	1.7
澳大利亚	3595	1.3

主要出口市场情况表(续)

国别(地区)	出口金额(万美元)	占出口总额(%)
德　国	2846	1.1
阿拉伯酋长国	2730	1.0
合　计	**235271**	**87.3**

进口总额　进口总额16.97亿美元，比上年下降46.3%。进口额在1000万美元以上的商品有24种，金额15.79亿美元，占进口总额93%。

进口1000万美元以上的商品表

金额分类	商品名称	进口金额(万美元)	占进口总额(%)
1000～5000万美元16种	成品油，合成纤维纱线，胶合板，自动数据处理设备及其部件，石油气，塑料制品，医药品，电线和电缆，棉机织物，电视、收音机及无线电讯设备，铜，发电机组及旋转式变流机，通断及保护电路装置，铝，未录的磁带及类似品，橡胶或塑料加工机械	36504	21.5

进口1000万美元以上的商品表(续)

金额分类	商品名称	进口金额（万美元）	占进口总额（%）
5000万～1亿美元3种	农渔产品，合成纤维长丝机织物，塑料板、片、薄膜	19480	11.5
1亿美元以上5种	机电产品、初级形态的塑料，化工产品，钢材，纸及纸板（未切成形的）	101957	60
合计	**24种**	**157941**	**93**

进口商品市场 进口商品来自69个国家和地区。

主要进口市场情况表

国别（地区）	进口金额（万美元）	占进口总额（%）
泰国	3864	2.3
俄罗斯	4091	2.4
德国	4341	2.6
马来西亚	4850	2.9
印度尼西亚	8660	5.1
美国	14234	8.4
香港	15046	8.9
台湾省	16638	9.8

主要进口市场情况表(续)

国别（地区）	进口金额（万美元）	占进口总额（%）
日本	23882	14.1
韩国	46686	27.5
合计	**142292**	**83.8**

【利用外资】

全市签订利用外资项目111项，合同外资金额2.86亿美元，实际利用外资6.69亿美元。

1999年利用外资情况表

利用外资方式	批准签订的合同			实际利用外资	
	项目数（个）	外资金额（万美元）	金额比上年（±%）	金额（万美元）	金额比上年（±%）
对外借款	0	0		230	-97
外商直接投资	85	28428	-60.5	66393	-29.4
合资企业	31	4102	-26.2	37995	109.5
合作企业	12	11646	-70.7	15843	-60.6
外资企业	42	12680	-68.2	12555	-64.9
外商其他投资	26	138	-68.3	248	-88
国际租赁					

1999 年利用外资情况表(续)

利用外资方式	批准签订的合同			实际利用外资	
	项目数（个）	外资金额（万美元）	金额比上年（±%）	金　额（万美元）	金额比上年（±%）
补偿贸易				23	-98.4
加工装配	26	138	-53.6	225	-66.2
合　计	**111**	**28566**	**-42.3**	**66871**	**-35.6**

外商直接投资行业　在外商直接投资的85个项目中，按产业分，第一产业3项，第二产业68项，第三产业14项。属生产型项目71项，非生产型项目14项。按行业分，农林牧渔业3项，制造业66项，电力、煤气及水的生产和供应业2项，批发和零售贸易、餐饮业2项，房地产2项，社会服务业7项，其他行业3项。

外商直接投资来源　外商直接投资来自14个国家和地区。分别是：香港59项，合同外资14723万美元；美国7个，6055万美元；台湾省6个，466万美元；加拿大2个，532万美元；日本2个，28万美元；泰国2个，23万美元；新加坡1个，3351万美元；印度尼西亚1个，27万美元；韩国1个，20万美元；波兰1个，15万美元；德国1个，1185万美元；巴拿马2个，401万美元；澳大利亚1个，45万美元；西萨摩亚1个，100万美元。

外商直接投资企业生产经营情况　截至1999年底，已批准的外商投资企业共5174家，1999年总产值为119.99亿元，比上年150.91亿元下降20.5%；销售（营业）收入101.73亿元，比1998年141.67下降20.5%，其中出口销售收入7.90亿美元，下降37.2%。

【对外经济合作】

承包工程和劳务合作　对外签订劳务合作合同15个，合同金额394万美元，营业额254万美元，当年派出劳务人员116人，年末在外人数479人。

劳务人员主要派往澳门、越南、毛里求斯、泰国、新加坡、马来西亚、牙买加、柬埔寨、圣卢西亚、厄瓜多尔等国家和地区，主要从事制衣、毛织、建筑、饮食、捕捞、维修等工作。

【其他】

对外经贸洽谈　5月18日至21日，广东省政府在香港举办’99广东经济贸易技术洽谈会。洽谈会期间全市共签订外商投资项目24项，投资总额11382万美元，利用外资6206万美元，其中，有8个属于卫星定位监测器、笔记式电脑、互联网、新型弹性水泥防水材料、光缆监控设备等生产性项目，技术档次、产品档次较高。此外，还签订出口贸易合同5个，合同总金额3395万美元，取得较好成效。

此外，两届广交会汕头市企业共成交3.52亿美元，比上年增加70%，达到历史最高水平。其中，远洋市场成交额3.17亿美元，约占90%。秋交会期间汕头陶瓷（集团）公司、汕头土产进出口公司、中国抽纱汕头进出口公司、汕头经济特区陶瓷公司、汕头轻工业品进出口公司等5家企业成交金额超过1000万美元。

港口运输　全市港口1999年实际完成货物吞吐量1191万吨，比上年1290万吨下降7.7%，其中，完成外贸进出口货物吞吐量276.7万吨（进口230.1万吨，出口46.6万吨）。

1999年湛江市对外经济贸易

湛江市对外经济贸易委员会

【对外贸易】

进出口总额 1999年广东省湛江市进出口总额74725万美元，比1998年90082万美元下降17.05%。

出口总额 出口总额25492万美元，比上年的33581万美元下降24.09%，占全市国内生产总值384.03亿元（相当于46.38亿美元）的5.50%，占全省出口额的0.33%。

出口商品结构 初级产品出口额5196万美元，占出口总额的20.38%；工业制成品的出口额20296万美元，占出口总额的79.62%。

出口额在500万美元以上商品情况表

金额分类	商品名称	出口金额（万美元）	占出口总额（%）
500～1000万美元 3种	氯化钾、羽绒、木家具	2172.71	8.52
1000万美元以上 5种	精梳棉纱、冻鱼、造纸木片、灯用镇流器、螺栓	8774.34	34.42
合　计	**8种**	**10947.05**	**42.94**

出口商品市场 出口商品销往107个国家和地区。

主要出口市场情况表

国别（地区）	出口金额（万美元）	占出口总额（%）
香港	7468	29.30
美国	4773	18.72
日本	3211	12.60
台湾省	1466	5.75
韩国	765	3.00
英国	625	2.45
德国	507	1.99
奥地利	506	1.9
新加坡	480	1.88
越南	427	1.68
合　计	**20228**	**79.35**

进口总额 进口总额49238万美元，比上年的56500万美元下降12.86%

进口商品结构 初级产品进口额3260万美元，占进口总额的6.62%；工业制成品进口额45973万美元，占进口总额的93.38%。

进口额在500万美元以上商品情况表

金额分类	商品名称	进口金额（万美元）	占进口总额（%）
500～1000万美元（5种）	石油采掘零件、聚丙烯、铜碎料、小麦、氨纶长丝	3113	6.32
1000～3000万美元（6种）	氯化钾、棉花、甘蔗糖蜜、苯乙烯、摩托车发动机零件、纸张	8177	16.61
3000万美元以上（2种）	液化石油气、原油	24580	49.92
合　计	**13种**	**35870**	**72.92**

进口商品市场　进口商品来自56个国家和地区。

主要进口市场情况表

国别（地区）	进口金额（万美元）	占进口总额（%）
澳大利亚	11220	22.79
也　门	8123	16.49
美　国	4227	8.58
日　本	3978	8.08
马来西亚	3090	6.27
泰　国	2954	5.99
加拿大	2160	4.39
韩　国	1921	3.90
新加坡	1421	2.89
德　国	800	1.62
合　计	**29894**	**81.02**

技术进出口　1999年湛江市技术进出口总额306.75万美元，比上年的1213.7万美元下降74.73%。

技术进口　签订引进技术和进口设备合同1个，比上年减少2个，合同金额66.7万美元，比上年的869.56万美元下降92.33%。引进技术来自日本汽车部件生产，该项引进技术已投产。

技术出口　签订技术和成套设备出口合同8个，比上年增加1个，合同金额240万美元，比上年的344.14万美元下降30.26%。出口技术和成套设备主要有方便面生产线、港口散货灌装设备、高速离心机、摩托车装配线、高压电器、橡胶加工设备等。分别出口到俄罗斯、印度尼西亚、马来西亚、泰国、越南、菲律宾等国家。

【利用外资】

1999年利用外资情况表

利用外资方式	批准签订的合同			实际利用外资	
	项目（个）	外资金额（万美元）	金额比1998年（±%）	金额（万美元）	金额比1998年（±%）
外商直接投资	28	7029	27.64	7510	－28.44
合资企业	10	1883	－24.38	3427	－42.99
合作企业	7	2612	596.53	1331	－54.20
外资企业	11	2534	－4.09	2752	74.51
外商其他投资					
加工贸易	6	312		527	25.35
合　计	**34**	**7341**	**33.3**	**8037**	**－23.41**

外商直接投资行业　在外商直接投资项目中，生产型项目24个，非生产型项目4个。按行业分，农林牧渔业1个，采掘业2个，制造业18个，建筑业1个，仓储业2个，餐饮业2个，社会服务业1个，其他行业1个。

外商直接投资来源　外商直接投资来自15个国家和地区。合同外资额居前5位的是：香港18个，1716万美元；英属维尔京群岛2个，1430万美元；巴哈马1个，1295万美元；马来西亚1个，1200万美元；美国1个，1000万美元。

外商投资企业生产经营情况　截至1999年底，已开业投产的外商投资企业共576家，1999年销售（营业）收入62.27亿元，比1998年的55.54亿元下降12.12%。其中，出口销售收入7845万美元。外商投资企业盈利总额31033万元，比上年的11417万元增长171.81%，亏损总额18436万元，比上年的27800万元下降33.68%。全市外商投资企业盈亏相抵利润总额12597万元。

【其他】

经济技术开发区　湛江经济技术开发区1999年工业总产值34.53亿元，比上年的43.06亿元下降19.8%。外贸出口4947万美元，比1998年40.82下降29.55%。固定资产投资完成10.25亿元，比上年的9.47亿元增长8%。新批准外商直接投资项目8个，合同外资金额1548万美元，比上年下降52.54%，实际利用外资4375万美元，比上年下降37.25%。

对外经贸洽谈会　1999年4月16～17日，湛江市组团参加省政府在深圳市举行的粤台经济技术贸易交流会，签订利用外资项目合同（协议）12个，合同（协议）总投资金额2784万美元，其中外资2554万美元；签订来料加工合同8个，合同工缴费576万美元。1999年5月18日～21日组团参加广东省政府在香港展览中心举办的广东经济技术贸易洽谈会。共接待香港、澳门、台湾省以及美国、日本、加拿大、马来西亚、以色列等数十个国家和地区的客商300多人次，洽谈公司112家。共签订利用外资合同28个，合同外资金额1.58亿美元。出口成交3110万美元。1999年6月8日～10日参加在香港举行的中国投资贸易洽谈会暨政策研讨会，签订利用外资协议4个，合同外资金额767万美元，出口成交850万美元。

港口运输　湛江市共有海运港口泊位128个，港口吞吐能力2874万吨，其中万吨级港口泊位24个，最大靠泊能力7万吨。1999年全市港口实际完成货物吞吐总量1917.8万吨，比上年的2256万吨下降15%，其中完成外贸进出口货物吞吐量996.2万吨（出口325.2万吨，进口671万吨），占全年货物吞吐量51.94%。比上年提高9.54%。港口集装箱运输量49344标准箱，比上年的33460箱增长47.47%。

涉外旅游 1999年湛江市接待来自24个国家和香港、澳门、台湾省地区的境外旅游者16.5万人次，比上年的5.32万人次增长2.1倍。其中过夜的入境游客3.95万人次。1999年旅游收入25.4亿元，比上年的24.4亿元增长4.1%。旅游外汇收入986.35万美元，比上年940万美元增长5%。

1999年广西壮族自治区对外经济贸易

广西壮族自治区对外贸易经济合作厅

【对外贸易】

进出口总额 1999年广西壮族自治区进出口总额17.53亿美元，比1998年的24.09亿美元下降27.2%。

出口总额 出口总额12.47亿美元，比上年的18.04亿美元下降30.9%。出口占全自治区国内生产总值2001.68亿元的5.2%。按贸易性质分，一般贸易出口9.11亿美元，占出口总额的73%；加工贸易出口2.14亿美元，占出口总额的17.2%；边境贸易出口1.2亿美元，占出口总额的9.6%。按企业性质分，国有企业出口9.77亿美元，占出口总额的78.3%；外商投资企业出口2.2亿美元，占出口总额的17.7%；其他企业出口0.5亿美元，占出口总额的4%。

出口商品结构 初级产品出口2.19亿美元，占出口总额的17.6%；工业制成品出口10.28亿美元；占出口总额的82.4%；其中机电产品出口1.67亿美元，占出口总额的13.4%，比1998年上升了5.1个百分点。

出口额在500万美元以上的商品有24种，出口金额5.92亿美元，占出口总额的47.5%。

出口额在500万美元以上的商品情况表

金额分类	商品名称	出口金额（万美元）	占出口总额（%）
500万～1000万美元（7种）	珍珠宝石及制品、钢材、电线及电缆、皮手套、锑、竹编织品、藤编织品	4903	3.93
1000万～2000万美元（10种）	活猪、蔬菜、苹果、水泥、重晶石、滑石、塑料制品、锌及锌合金、原电池、合成短纤维与棉混纺	15654	12.55
2000万美元以上（7种）	氧化锌及过氧化锌、松香及树脂酸、鞋、烟花爆竹、家用陶瓷、锡及锡合金、织物服装	38623	30.97
合　计	**24种**	**59180**	**47.45**

出口商品市场 出口商品销往120个国家和地区。其中十大主要出口市场出口额9.76亿美元，占出口总额的78.3%。

主要出口市场情况表

国别（地区）	出口金额（万美元）	占出口总额（%）
香　港	23888	
越　南	21810	
美　国	14817	
荷　兰	10743	
日　本	9122	
德　国	4993	
台湾省	4327	
英　国	2970	
韩　国	2534	
法　国	2393	
合　计	**97597**	**78.26**

进口总额 进口总额5.06亿美元，比1998年的6.05亿美元下降16.3%。

进口商品结构 初级产品进口额1.27亿美元，占进口总额的25.1%；工业制成品进口额3.79亿美元，占进口总额的74.9%。

进口额在500万美元以上的商品有10种，进口金额12250万美元，占进口总额的24.2%。

进口额在500万美元以上商品情况表

金额分类	商　品　名　称	进口金额（万美元）	占进口总额（%）
500万～1000万美元（5种）	天然橡胶、铁矿砂、成品油、初级形状塑料、通断及保护电路装置	3265	6.45
1000万美元以上（5种）	食用植物油、钻石、锰矿砂、钢材、牛皮革及马皮革	8985	17.75
合　计	**10种**	**12250**	**24.2**

进口商品市场 进口商品来自40个国家和地区。其中十大主要进口市场进口额36158万美元，占进口总额的71.43%。

主要进口市场情况表

国别（地区）	进口金额（万美元）	占进口总额（百分比）
法　国	5175	10.22
台湾省	5001	9.88
美　国	4635	9.16
越　南	4621	9.13
日　本	4085	8.07
芬　兰	2781	5.49
英　国	2629	5.19
南　非	2500	4.94
韩　国	2480	4.9
德　国	2251	4.43
合　计	**36158**	**71.43**

边境贸易 1999年广西对越南边境贸易进出口总额16076万美元，比上年的13767万美元增长16.8%。其中出口额11992万美元，比上年的10018万美元增长19.7%，占全自治区出口总额的9.6%；进口额4084万美元，比上年的3749万美元

增长8.9%，占全自治区进口总额的8.1%。

【利用外资】

批准签订外商直接投资项目223个，比上年减少43个。其中合资项目106个，合作项目42个，独资项目75个。合同外资额6.74亿美元，比上年的6.42亿美元增长5%；实际直接利用外资6.35亿美元，比上年的8.86亿美元下降28.3%。

1999年利用外资情况表

利用外资方式	批准签订的合同			实际利用外资	
	项目数（个）	外资金额（万美元）	金额比1998年（±%）	金额（万美元）	金额比1998年（±%）
外商直接投资	223	67363	5	63512	-28.3
合资企业	106	15702		23460	
合作企业	42	33674		9272	
外资企业	75	17987		30780	
合　计	**223**	**67363**		**63512**	

外商直接投资行业　在新批准的223个外商直接投资项目中，生产型项目占76%，合同外资额51282万美元，非生产型项目占24%，合同外资额16081万美元。按行业分，农林牧副渔业占9%，合同外资额6301万美元；制造业占18%，合同外资额11816万美元；电力、水的生产和供应占8%，合同外资额5077万美元；建筑业占28%，合同外资额19082万美元；交通运输、仓储业占2%，合同外资额1483万美元；房地产业占11%，合同外资额7523万美元；社会服务业占14%，合同外资额9423万美元；其他类占10%，合同外资额6658万美元。与1998年相比，建筑业、农业项目有较大增长，能源项目下降，基础设施建设和工业制造业仍是外资主要投向。

外商直接投资来源　外商直接投资来自28个国家和地区。其中实际投入外资较大的国家和地区有：香港119项，实际投入资金24560万美元；法国2项，实际投入资金15862万美元；美国14项，实际投入资金4464万美元；英国2项，实际投入资金4541万美元；台湾省43项，实际投入资金4026万美元；维尔京群岛5项，实际投入资金2281万美元；毛里求斯3项，实际投入资金1562万美元；西萨摩亚4项，实际投入资金1211万美元；德国1项，实际投入资金999万美元。

【对外经济合作】

承包工程和劳务合作　签订对外承包工程和劳务合作项目98个，合同总金额2292万美元，比上年的1413万美元增长62.2%；完成营业额4570万美元，比上年的2949万美元增长55%；派出劳务人员639人次，比上年增加120人次；年末在国（境）外劳务人员1006人，比上年末增加166人；承包工程带动进口405万美元，比上年稍有下降；带动出口229万美元，比上年增长56.8%。对外承包工程和劳务合作业务主要分布在越南、柬埔寨、孟加拉、波利尼西亚、澳门、香港等国家和地区。

接受经济援助　1999年，广西新获批准的接受国际无偿援助项目6个，援助金额76万美元和56万人民币。其中包括联合国人口基金援助“妇女参与发展项目”、联合国儿童基金援助“综合发展项目”、澳大利亚政府无偿援助桂林市社会福利院“儿童住宅扩建及培训项目”和无偿援助南丹县“少数民族妇女识字及卫生教育”项目等等。同时，日本政府无偿援助广西5.8亿日元粮食增产项目，于

1997年底获得批准后，1999年顺利完成了项目管理办法的制订、项目管理机构的成立以及日援物资的接受和配发等工作。另外，联合国开发署无偿援助广西扶贫项目和一批接受国际无偿援助项目继续顺利实施。

对外投资 1999年广西在境外举办企业5家，合同总额595万美元；其中中方协议投资560万美元，占合同总额的94%。这几家企业分布在越南、澳大利亚、东非等国家。主要生产销售药品、纸制品、服装、电线电缆等。

对外经贸洽谈会 1999年广西组织了6次重大的招商洽谈活动。分别是：3月在越南举办的“经贸洽谈会”、8月在北京、上海举办的“投资项目招商会”、9月上旬组团参加外经贸部在厦门举办的“第三届中国投资贸易洽谈会”、9月中下旬在美国夏威夷州、休斯敦市举办的“投资项目洽谈会”、10月在香港展览中心举办的'99香港投资项目洽谈会、11月在南宁举办的'99南宁国际民歌艺术节经贸洽谈商品展销会。这6次招商洽谈活动共有来自美国、加拿大、英国、法国、德国、意大利、西班牙、澳大利亚、日本、韩国、泰国、新加坡、马来西亚、印度尼西亚、越南、阿联酋、台湾省、香港、澳门等几十个国家和地区的近2000名外商参加，与外商签订合作项目共248项。其中签合同项目124项，投资总额10亿美元，合同外资额8亿美元；协议项目124项，投资总额32亿美元，协议外资额8亿美元。

港口运输 外贸运输总量398.85万吨，比上年下降38%。其中出口量247.89万吨，进口量150.96万吨。按运输方式分，海运量384.94万吨，陆运量13.92万吨，空运量199吨。

涉外旅游 共接待国（境）外旅游游客人数77.68万人次，比上年增长48.2%。其中接待国外游客37.17万人次，比上年增长33%；接待港澳同胞16.71万人次，比上年增长42.1%；接待台湾同胞23.52万人次，比上年增长94.6%。国际旅游收入15.15亿元，比上年增长26.7%。

1999年北海市对外经济贸易

北海市对外贸易经济合作局

【对外贸易】

进出口总额 1999年广西壮族自治区北海市进出口总额为11926.2万美元，比1998年的11685.4万美元增长2.06%。

出口总额 出口总额8566.9万美元，比上年的7575.2万美元增长13.09%，占全市国内生产总值110.45亿元（相当于133605万美元）的6.41%，占全自治区出口总额12.47亿美元的6.87%。

出口商品结构 初级产品出口额436万美元，占全市出口总额的5.09%；工业制成品的出口额8130.9万美元，占出口总额的94.91%。

出口额在100万美元以上的商品情况表

金额分类	商品名称	出口金额（万美元）	占出口总额（%）
1000万美元以上（2种）	鞭炮烟花、除草剂	6019.6	70.26
100万～1000万美元（12种）	杀虫剂、棉布、藤制品、化肥、塑料制品、革皮及制品、针织服装、汽车零件、家具、水产品、梭织服装、非金属矿及其产品	1921.8	22.43
合计	**14种**	**7941.4**	**92.69**

出口商品市场

主要出口商品市场情况表

国别（地区）	出口金额（万美元）	占出口总额（%）
美国	4494	52.46
香港	2630.5	30.71
德国	452	5.27
日本	332	3.87
越南	166	1.94
阿根廷	137	1.60

主要出口商品市场情况表(续)

国别（地区）	出口金额（万美元）	占出口总额（%）
孟加拉国	129	1.51
合计	**8340.5**	**97.36**

进口总额　进口总额3359.3万美元，比上年的4110.2万美元下降18.27%。

进口商品结构　初级产品进口额1129.3万美元，占进口总额的33.62%；工业制成品进口总额2230万美元，占进口总额的66.38%。

进口额在50万美元以上的商品情况表

金额分类	商品名称	进口金额（万美元）	占进口总额（%）
1000万美元以上（2种）	化肥农药、畜产品	2317	70.21
100万～1000万美元（3种）	化工原料、农业机械零配件、棉花	606	18.36
50万～100万美元（2种）	医疗器械、液化石油气	162	4.91
合计	**7种**	**3085**	**93.48**

进口商品市场

主要进口商品市场情况表

国别（地区）	进口金额（万美元）	占进口总额（%）
香　港	3017	91.42
美　国	255	7.73
合　计	**3272**	**99.15**

【利用外资】

1999年全市共批准签订利用外资合同项目16个，比上年的24个下降33.33%，新批项目合同外资金额6084万美元，比上年的6078万美元增长0.10%，实际利用外资4340万美元，比上年的2768万美元增长56.79%。其中：合资经营项目12个，比上年的13个下降6.69%，合同外资金额1150万美元，比上年的807万美元增长42.50%，实际利用外资2314万美元；外资项目4个，比上年的9个下降55.56%，合同外资金额5134万美元，比上年的3846万美元增长33.49%，实际利用外资1863万美元。

外商直接投资行业　外商直接投资项目中生产型项目14个，非生产型项目2个；按行业划分：种植业2项，畜牧业1项，加工业2项，工业制造业8项、汽车修理业1项，旅游业1项，娱乐服务业1项。

外商直接投资来源　外商直接投资主要来自于亚洲、拉丁美洲、北美洲等五大洲10个国家和地区。具体为：香港8项，合同外资金额3390万美元，实际利用外资金额1451万美元；台湾省4项，合同外资金额7万美元，实际利用外资金额22万美元；维尔京群岛2项，合同外资金额2120万美元，实际利用外资1294万美元；美国3项，合同外资金额416万美元，实际利用外资金额172万美元；秘鲁1项，合同外资金额118万美元，加拿大1项，合同外资金额6万美元。此外，新加坡、日本、意大利、大洋洲等国家和地区分别在上年原有项目上增加合同外资金额及外资到位率，实际利用外资金额共计1401万美元。

外商投资企业生产经营情况　截止1999年底，全市累计批准的外商投资企业1296家，目前实有513家，合同投资总额490872万美元，已建成并开业投产经营的外商投资企业255家，比上年的260家减少1.92%，1999年实现工业产值70850万元，亏损12506万元，全年出口总额5010万美元，比1998年的5001万美元增长0.18%，现外商投资企业从业人员11215人。

【对外经济合作】

承包工程和劳务合作　签订对外承包工程和劳务合同项目3个，合同金额28万美元，比上年的97万美元减少71.13%，营业额8万美元，比上年的21万美元下降61.9%；当年共派出各类劳务人员20人，年末在境外各类劳务人员达17人，主要派驻国别为柬埔寨、越南。

【其他】

对外商贸洽谈会　1999年，北海市组队参加了昆明世界园艺博览会、深圳高新技术交易会、香港商贸洽谈会等招商会，共签订利用外资项目14项，其中合同13项，合同投资总额5302万美元，合同外资金额3903万美元，协议类项目1个，合同投资总额365万美元，外资金额300万美元。

港口运输　1999年北海港港口吞吐总量405万吨，比上年的301万吨增长34.55%，其中完成外贸进出口货物吞吐总量121万吨，比上年的106万吨增长14.15%，货物总值达2.56亿美元，比上年增长2500万美元，同比增长11%（出口量66万吨，比上年的54.09万吨增长22%；进口量为55万吨，比上年的53.92万吨增长2%），按运输方式分全部是海运量。

涉外旅游　1999年接待境外旅游人数2.1万人次，比上年的1万人次增长110%，国际旅游外汇收入435.2万美元，比上年的270.98万美元增长60.6%。

1999年海南省对外经济贸易

海南省对外贸易经济合作厅

【对外贸易】

进出口总额 1999年海南省进出口总额为121867万美元，比1998年的173859万美元下降29.91%。

出口总额 出口总额74860万美元，比上年75777万美元下降1.21%，占全省国内生产总值471.69亿元（相当于56.98亿美元）的13%。

出口商品结构 初级产品出口额20047万美元，占出口总额的26.78%；工业制成品出口额54813万美元，占出口总额的73.22%。

出口商品涉及54个大类765种。

出口额在1000万美元以上商品情况表

金额分类	商品名称	出口金额（万美元）	占出口总额（%）
5000万美元以上（1种）	天然气	21113	28.20
1000～5000万美元（4种）	木材、锡锭、木家具、锌锭	7365	9.84
合　计	**5种**	**28478**	**38.04**

出口商品市场 出口商品销往149个国家（地区）。

主要出口市场情况表

国别（地区）	出口金额（万美元）	占出口总额（%）
香　港	30955	41.35
日　本	8239	11.01
美　国	8096	10.81
韩　国	2216	2.96
台湾省	2165	2.89
新加坡	1448	1.94
德　国	1421	1.90
印　尼	1179	1.57
荷　兰	1050	1.40

主要出口市场情况表（续）

国别（地区）	出口金额（万美元）	占出口总额（%）
英　国	884	1.18
合　计	**57653**	**77.01**

进口总额 1999年海南进口总额47007万美元，比上年的98032万美元下降52.08%。

进口商品结构 进口商品涉及1793种商品。其中，初级产品进口额9790万美元，占进口总额的20.82%；工业制成品进口额37217万美元，占进口总额的79.18%。

主要进口商品情况表

金额分类	商品名称	进口金额（万美元）	占进口总额（%）
1000～10000万美元的8种	钢铁板材；钢铁棒材；棕榈油；液化石油气；点燃式活塞；内燃发动机的零件；对苯二甲酸；原木；其他药品	15575	33.13
合　计	**15种**	**92389**	**33.13**

进口商品市场　进口商品来自54个国家（地区）。

主要进口市场情况表

国别（地区）	进口金额（万美元）	占进口总额（%）
日　本	8249	17.55
美　国	6843	14.56
韩　国	5091	10.83
台湾省	4530	9.64
马来西亚	2567	5.46
俄罗斯	2213	4.70
德　国	2107	4.48
英　国	2048	4.36

主要进口市场情况表(续)

国别（地区）	进口金额（万美元）	占进口总额（%）
泰　国	1806	3.84
香　港	1688	3.59
越　南	1617	3.44
意大利	1264	2.69
荷　兰	1250	2.66
合　计	**41273**	**87.80**

技术进出口　1999年海南省技术引进合同13项，合同总额为978.33万美元，其中引进计算机软件合同8项。

【利用外资】

1999年利用外资情况表

利用外资方式	批准签订的合同			实际利用外资	
	项目数（个）	外资金额（万美元）	金额比1998年（±%）	金额（万美元）	金额比1998年（±%）
对外借款		–	–	35700	－6.10
外商直接投资	158	79176	453.00	48449	－32.4
合资企业	52	6697	－12.20	15753	－41.90
合作企业	5	5397	553.00	411	－72.10
外资企业	101	66708	1037.00	29848	－22.20
外商投资股份制企业		374		2437	－48.50
合　计	**158**	**79176**	**–**	**84149**	**－23.30**

1999年外商直接投资主要行业情况表

投资产业	项目数	外资实际投资金额	占外商实际投资总额（%）
第一产业	57	4623	9.54
其中：农业	42	4137	8.5
第二产业	49	16875	34.83
其中：（一）工业	42	16512	34.1
采掘业	2	135	0.3
制造业	40	16377	33.8
（二）建筑业	6	363	0.7
第三产业	52	26951	55.63
其中：交通运输仓储业	6	2253	4.7
批零贸易餐饮业	7	265	0.5
房地产业	7	4826	9.9
其他服务行业	32	19607	40.4
合　计	**158**	**48449**	**100**

外商直接投资分国别（地区）主要情况表

国别（地区）	项目数	外资实际投资金额（万美元）	占外商直接投资总额（%）
香　港	80	14299	29.5
新加坡	9	12088	24.9
美　国	8	8276	17.1
台湾省	35	4930	10.2
英　国	6	3302	6.8
泰　国	3	2116	4.4
加拿大	1	1197	2.5
日　本	2	716	1.5
印度尼西亚	-	431	0.8
马来西亚	1	314	0.6
韩　国	3	184	0.38
荷　兰	-	100	0.2

【对外经济合作】

承包工程和劳务合作　1999年签订对外承包工程和劳务合作合同14个，合同金额2751.71万美元，完成营业额114641万美元，上年共派出劳务127人（次），年末在外人数114人。

对外经济援助　利用国家援外合资合作基金项目一个，金额为130万美元。

对外投资　1999年共在海外举办企业2个，投资金额140万美元，投资国别为美国和南非。

1999年重庆市对外经济贸易

重庆市对外贸易经济委员会

【对外贸易】

进出口总额 1999年重庆市进出口总额为121023万美元，比1998年的103370万美元增长17.08%。

出口总额 出口总额49028万美元，比上年的51395万美元下降4.61%，占全市国内生产总值1488亿（相当于179.9亿美元）的2.72%；占全国出口额的0.25%。

出口商品结构 初级产品出口额为4952万美元，占出口总额的10.10%；工业制成品出口额44076万美元，占出口总额的89.90%。

出口额在500万美元以上的商品情况表

金额分类	商品名称	出口金额（万美元）	占出口总额（%）
5000万美元以上2种	摩托车、合成药及中间体	12778	26.06
1000万～5000万美元9种	汽柴油机及其零件、肝素及其盐、染料和颜料、聚乙烯醇、桑蚕丝及机织物、苎麻及其机织物、钢材、铝材、锌材	12782	26.07
500万～1000万美元7种	电池、耐火粘土、人造刚玉、胱氨酸、锰材、猪鬃、肠衣	4658	9.50
合　计	**18种**	**30218**	**61.63**

出口商品市场 出口商品销往132个国家和地区。

主要出口市场情况表

国别（地区）	出口金额（万美元）	占出口总额（%）
美　国	6156	12.56
香　港	5303	10.82
日　本	4893	9.98
韩　国	4012	8.18
德　国	3202	6.53
越　南	2338	4.77
意大利	2039	4.16

主要出口市场情况表（续）

国别（地区）	出口金额（万美元）	占出口总额（%）
荷　兰	1968	4.01
印度尼西亚	1622	3.31
泰　国	1550	3.16
合　计	**33083**	**67.48**

进口总额 进口总额为72005万美元，比上年的51975万美元增长38.54%。

进口商品结构 初级产品进口额为5065万美元，占进口总额的7.03%，工业制成品进口额66940万美元，占进口总额的92.97%。

进口额在500万美元以上的商品情况表

金额分类	商品名称	进口金额(万美元)	占进口总额(%)
1亿美元以上2种	汽车零件、汽柴油发动机零件	23005	31.95
1000万~1亿美元8种	密封垫、车用视觉信号装置、铁矿砂、往复式活塞引擎、海水淡化装置、重油及其制品、滑轮、车用刮水器	18411	26.57
500万~1000万美元10种	数据处理设备、螺钉及螺栓、金属加工中心、医疗设备、丙烯腈、对苯二甲酸、载客电梯、摩托车车架、冷轧非卷材、轴承	7397	10.27
合计	**20种**	**48813**	**67.79**

进口商品市场 进口商品来自48个国家和地区。

主要进口市场情况表

国别(地区)	进口金额(万美元)	占进口总额(%)
日本	46218	64.19
香港	5152	7.16
美国	4051	5.63
韩国	2785	3.87
德国	2777	3.86

主要进口市场情况表(续)

国别(地区)	进口金额(万美元)	占进口总额(%)
台湾省	2021	2.81
澳大利亚	1495	2.08
印度	810	1.13
英国	809	1.12
新加坡	566	0.79
合计	**66684**	**92.61**

【利用外资】

1999年利用外资情况表

利用外资方式	批准签订的合同			实际利用外资	
	项目(个)	外资金额(万美元)	金额比1998年(±%)	金额(万美元)	金额比1998年(±%)
对外借款	2	19100	-26.14	8564	-5.12
外商直接投资	169	50688	6.54	23893	-44.57
合资企业	96	27895	6.04	16505	-42.26
合作企业	12	12757	177.39	1201	-73.27
外资企业	61	10036	-39.81	6187	-38.30
外商投资股份制					

1999 年利用外资情况表(续)

利用外资方式	批准签订的合同			实际利用外资	
	项目（个）	外资金额（万美元）	金额比 1998 年（±%）	金　额（万美元）	金额比 1998 年（±%）
外商其他投资	28	327	-80.31	242	-84.61
国际租赁					
补偿贸易					
加工贸易	28	327	-80.31	242	-84.61
对外发行股票					
合　计	**199**	**70115**	**-6.64**	**32699**	**-39.11**

外商直接投资行业　在外商投资项目中，生产型项目 114 个，非生产型项目 55 个。合同外资金额在 1000 万美元以上的行业分布为：制造业 104 个，合同外资金额 25811 万美元；建筑业 5 个，合同外资金额 3681 万美元；交通运输、仓储及邮电通信业 3 个，合同外资金额 2233 万美元；批发和零售贸易、餐饮业 10 个，合同外资金额 4246 万美元；房地产业 15 个，合同外资金额 9665 万美元；社会服务业 22 个，合同外资金额 3970 万美元。

外商直接投资来源　外商直接投资来自 34 个国家和地区。投资额居前 5 位的国家和地区是：香港 59 项，24967 万美元；美国 21 项，6338 万美元；英国 6 项，5040 万美元；日本 8 项，3643 万美元；台湾省 32 项，2867 万美元。

外商直接投资企业生产经营情况　1999 年外商直接投资企业出口创汇 6326 万美元，比上年下降 7.10%，涉外税收 26.45 亿元，比上年增长 19.60%。

【对外经济合作】

承包工程与劳务合作　签订对外承包工程、劳务合作合同项目 224 个，金额 4591 万美元，比上年的 1969 万美元增长 133.16%；营业额 3842 万美元，比上年的 3203 万美元增长 19.95%；当年派出劳务人员 1509 人，年末在外人数 3006 人。对外承包工程、劳务合作分布在 38 个国家和地区，营业额在 100 万美元以上的有韩国、马来西亚、新加坡、印度尼西亚、苏丹、坦桑尼亚、美国和阿根廷，营业额最高的为美国，达 1028 万美元；主要承包工程项目有：马来西亚排屋、巴库住宅、苏丹道路和坦桑尼亚道路等工程，其中马来西亚排屋工程合同金额达 600 万美元。

对外经济援助　1999 年重庆承担的对外经济援助项目有 1 个，受援国为纳米比亚农业项目。由重庆建工集团承担、合同金额 200 万美元，当年派出 2 人，年末在外人数 2 人。

接受经济援助　接受国外经济援助项目有 2 个，分别是日本政府无偿援助石柱民族中学教育器材设备项目和澳大利亚政府援助石柱县沿溪乡沿江村人畜饮水项目，共计 106 万美元。

对外投资　批准在海外举办非贸易性企业 1 家。由重庆涪陵三峡物资协作有限公司与缅甸钻龙陶瓷合作有限公司合资兴办仰光 MBC 实业发展有限公司，中方投资金额 15.53 万美元，占总投资比重 53%，目前运作正常。

【其他】

经济技术开发区　1999 年重庆经济技术开发区兴办外商投资企业 11 家，合同外资金额 7197 万美元，实际利用外资 4880 万美元。开发区实施项目招商、网上招商、代理招商等有效办法，引进了庆德实业、新华多媒体、航伟科技等投资额超过 1000 万美元的外商投资企业和中药研究所、中正物业、力思特制药、江南汽车、长江紧固件等注册资本超过1000万元的内资企业。开发区在培育高新技术企业和开发高新技术产品方面取得较大进展，1999年新增高新技术企业6户，高新技术企业产值占工业总产值比重提高到24%，10项产品纳入市重点企业新产品和改造产品计划，3项产品评为国家级新产品。

高新技术产业开发区 1999年重庆高新技术产业开发区兴办外商投资企业12家，合同外资金额6078万美元，实际利用外资4604万美元，出口创汇4000万美元。诺基亚、野村证券、深圳华侨城、三爱海陵等一批中外知名企业来区投资、法国圣丹尼市代表团、美国华尔街金融代表团、英国BTR集团、欧洲经济研究所等客商前来考察。有4个项目被列入2000年国家高新技术产业发展计划，分别是嘉顿公司的洋茉莉醛项目被列为“产业化专项”，信威公司的SCDMA无线用户环路系统项目和海扶公司的聚焦超声肿瘤治疗系统项目被列为“产业化示范工程”，杜克公司的杜氏高压油封项目被列为“产业化推进项目”。目前，开发区形成了以电子信息、生物生化制药及医疗器械、新材料及节能与环保、汽车摩托车配套高新技术产品为主的四大产业群，成为重庆市重要的高新技术产业化基地。

对外经贸洽谈会 1999年4月28日～5月2日举行了重庆市对外经济贸易洽谈会。来自美国、日本、德国等38个国家和地区的2000多名客商到会，洽谈会实现出口成交6318万美元，协议引进外资金额11.8亿美元。

农业投资洽谈会 11月19日～21日举行重庆农业投资洽谈暨优质农产品展示会。来自日本、意大利、匈牙利等10多个国家和地区208名客商到会，匈牙利驻华大使及其夫人参加了开幕式。洽谈会签订投资项目52个，引进国内资金10.8亿元，外资1376万美元。

港口运输 进出口货物运输总量为899389吨，比上年下降22.50%。进口运量682433吨，比上年下降33.14%，陆运量、水运量和空运量分别为4962吨、680771吨和185吨。出口运量216950吨，比上年增长55%。陆运量、水运量和空运量分别为8542吨、198340吨和706吨。

涉外旅游 接待旅游、参观访问及从事各项活动的海外游客18.49万人，旅游外汇收入9726万美元，分别比上年增长12.95%和10.06%。

1999年四川省对外经济贸易

四川省对外贸易经济合作委员会

【对外贸易】

进出口总额 1999年四川省进出口总额314080万美元，比1998年的285888万美元增长9.86%。

出口总额 出口总额173126万美元，比上年的167464万美元增长3.38%，占全省国内生产总值3711.6亿元（相当于447.72亿美元）的3.87%，占全国出口总额的0.89%。

出口商品结构 初级产品出口额32083万美元，占出口总额的18.5%；工业制成品出口141043万美元，占出口总额的81.5%。

出口商品市场 出口商品销往世界136个国家和地区。主要出口商品市场是：香港、美国、日本、尼泊尔、韩国、德国、印度、荷兰、台湾省、伊朗。四川省对上述10个国家和地区出口总额合计为131093万美元，占出口总额的75.72%。

出口额在1000万美元以上商品情况表

金额分类	商品名称	出口金额（万美元）	占出口总额（%）
1亿美元以上4种	纺织品、服装、钢材、化工原料	56754	32.78
5000万美元～1亿美元7种	电讯设备及器材、医药原料、航空设备、各类机械、纺织原料、成套设备、铁合金	56137	32.43
1000万美元～5000万美元17种	丝织品、工农具、有色金属矿产品、干菜及制品、木材、家用电器、中药材、电视机及散件、猪肠衣、白酒、有色金属材及制品、蔬菜、塑料制品、高纯金属、汽车零件、工艺品类、生化药物	37668	21.75
合　计	**28种**	**150559**	**86.96**

主要出口商品市场情况表

国别（地区）	出口金额（万美元）	占出口总额（%）
香　港	32278	18.64
美　国	23843	13.77
日　本	22052	12.74
尼泊尔	10061	5.81
韩　国	9648	5.57
德　国	7484	4.32
印　度	7397	4.27
荷　兰	6689	3.86
台湾省	6461	3.73

主要出口商品市场情况表(续)

国别（地区）	出口金额（万美元）	占出口总额（%）
伊　朗	5180	2.99
合　计	**131093**	**75.72**

进口总额　进口总额140954万美元，比上年的118423万美元增长19.03%。

进口商品结构　初级产品进口额4434万美元，占进口总额的3.1%；工业制成品进口额136520万美元，占进口总额的96.9%。

进口额在1000万美元以上的商品情况表

金额分类	商品名称	进口金额（万美元）	占进口总额（%）
1亿美元以上3种	航空设备、电子元器件、钢材	81532	57.84
5000万美元～1亿美元2种	成套设备、塑料	15573	11.05

进口额在1000万美元以上的商品情况表(续)

金额分类	商品名称	进口金额（万美元）	占进口总额（%）
1000万美元～5000万美元11种	化工原料、电工设备、矿山机械、电子仪器、钒铁、纸浆、通用机械、物理化工仪器、核子仪器、医药原料、有色金属及制品	20801	14.76
合　计	**16种**	**117906**	**83.65**

进口商品市场　1999年，四川省进口商品来自世界39个国家和地区。

主要进口商品市场情况表

国别（地区）	进口金额（万美元）	占进口总额（%）
法　国	35892	25.46
香　港	24292	17.23
美　国	21691	15.39
日　本	19293	13.69
德　国	8525	6.05
台湾省	5228	3.71
新加坡	3609	2.56

主要进口商品市场情况表(续)

国别（地区）	进口金额（万美元）	占进口总额（%）
韩　国	3284	2.33
西班牙	2580	1.83
意大利	2472	1.75
合　计	**126866**	**90.01**

技术进口　1999年，四川省签订引进技术和进口设备合同项目98个，比上年增加41个，合同金额6347.96万美元，比上年的6673.15万美元下降4.87%。

【利用外资】

1999年利用外资情况表

利用外资方式	批准签订的合同			实际利用外资	
	项目数（个）	外资金额（万美元）	金额比1998年（±%）	金额（万美元）	金额比1998年（±%）
对外借款		87042	9.66	51374	3.79
外商直接投资	195	59288	－16.75	45378	－9.96
合资企业	113	27247	－45.31	24730	－18.40
合作企业	10	8545	－20.78	6552	－41.12
外资企业	72	23496	121.58	14096	57.25
外商其他投资		10407	46.41	10197	55.04
合　计		**156737**	**－0.61**	**106949**	**0.44**

外商直接投资行业　批准外商直接投资项目195项。其中，生产型项目155个，非生产型项目40个。外商投资主要分布在：工业（占74.55%）、城市建设（占16.17%）、能源交通通讯（占10.90%）、社会服务（占6.41%）、农林牧渔（占0.61%）。

外商直接投资分行业情况表

行　　业	项目数量（家）	合同利用外资额（万美元）	实际到位外资额（万美元）
农林牧渔业	6	861	278
采掘业	3	856	1510
制造业	129	34478	21042
电力、煤气及水生产和供应业	3	12874	3923
建筑业	4	1471	1187
交通运输仓储及邮电通信业	1	1209	1025
批发零售贸易、餐饮业	5	500	1177
房地产业	10	1358	2228
社会服务业	33	5168	1716
科学研究和综合技术服务业	1	513	15
其他行业			11277
总　计	**195**	**59288**	**45378**

外商直接投资来源　外商直接投资来自51个国家和地区。前10位的国家和地区是：香港62项，投资金额8236万美元，占18.15%；维尔京群岛6701万美元，占14.77%；美国6254万美元，占13.78%；日本3405万美元，占7.50%；台湾省2743万美元，占6.04%；新加坡1543万美元，占3.40%；法国1535万美元，占3.38%；澳大利亚501万美元，占1.10%；英国326万美元，占0.72%；德国322万美元，占0.71%。

1999年四川省外商投资企业完成进出口总额为53380万美元，同比增长17%。其中出口30682万美元，比上年出口25069万美元，增长22.39%。

【对外经济合作】

承包工程和劳务合作　1999年新签对外承包工程和劳务合作合同项目161个，比上年增加44个。其中，承包工程合同83个，劳务合作合同77个。新签对外承包劳务合作合同总金额38237万美元，比上年增加7489万美元。其中，承包工程合同额为33693万美元，劳务合作合同额为4544万美元。1999年完成营业额21688万美元，比上年减少772万美元。其中，承包工程完成16883万美元，劳务合作完成4843万美元。当年四川省共派出劳务10074人次，比上年增加991人次，同比增长10.9%。

对外经济技术援助　1999年获得了援肯尼亚基恩公路项目、援尼泊尔国际会议中心维修项目的授标，填补了四川省自国家实行援外方式改革以来尚无经援项目的空白。上述项目的合同金额分别为371万美元和100万美元。此外，中川国际公司通过积极争取和不懈努力，获准实施援肯尼亚莫伊国际体育中心体育馆维修和更换体育场计时记分牌项目的施工任务。

接受国际无偿援助情况　争取国际无偿援助项目7个，受援金额共计约1640万美元，是四川省争取国际无偿援助总金额最多的一年。主要项目有：英国政府援助四川国企改革项目（约950万英镑）、新西兰援助甘孜县包虫病控制示范项目（150万新元）、联合国人口基金援助仪陇广安妇女发展项目（60万美元）、日本援助内江红十字医院和宜宾市聋哑学校建设项目（共16万美元）等。

对外投资 1999年在海外举办非贸易性企业项目1个，注册资本375万美元。其中中方投资300万美元，外方投资75万美元。

【其他】

1999年，四川省人境的外国及台港澳同胞37万人次，涉外旅游收入9700万美元。

1999年成都市对外经济贸易

成都市对外贸易经济合作委员会

【对外贸易】

进出口总额 1999年四川省成都市进出口总额为16.13亿美元，比1998年的14.89亿美元增长8.33%。

出口总额 出口总额7.42亿美元，比上年的7.72亿美元下降3.89%，占全市国内生产总值1090亿元人民币（相当于131.8亿美元）的5.63%，占全省出口额的65.03%

出口商品结构 初级产品出口额3.55亿美元，占出口总额的47.94%；工业制成品出口额3.86亿美元，占出口总额的52.02%。

出口额在1000万美元以上的商品情况表

金额分类	商品名称	出口金额（万美元）	占出口总额（%）
1000万至3000万美元	肠衣、锯材、钢材、手用或机用工具、电视机	6555	8.84
3000万至4000万美元	蔬菜、生丝、医药品	9845	13.28
4000万美元以上	纺织纱线、织物及制品、服装及衣着附件、机电产品	44115	59.49
合计		**60515**	**81.61**

出口商品市场

主要出口商品市场情况表

国别（地区）	出口金额（万美元）	占出口总额（%）
美国	10805	14.57
日本	9671	13.04

主要出口商品市场情况表(续)

国别（地区）	出口金额（万美元）	占出口总额（%）
香港	7815	10.54
尼泊尔	7362	9.93
伊朗	4788	6.46
韩国	4258	5.74

主要出口商品市场情况表(续)

国别（地区）	出口金额（万美元）	占出口总额（%）
印　度	4088	5.51
德　国	3184	4.29

进口总额　进口总额8.71亿美元，比上年的7.16亿美元增长21.65%。

进口商品结构　初级产品进口额0.39亿美元，占进口总额的4.52%；工业制成品的进口额8.32亿美元，占进口总额的95.48%。

进口额在500万美元以上的商品情况表

金额分类	商　品　名　称	进口金额（万美元）	占进口总额（%）
500万至1000万美元	豆饼、豆粕、初级形状的塑料、钢材	2928	3.36
1000万至2000万美元	对苯二甲酸、纸及纸板	2385	2.74
2000万美元以上	机电产品	69885	80.19
合　计		**75198**	**86.29**

进口商品市场

主要进口商品市场情况表

国别（地区）	进口金额（万美元）	占进口总额（%）
法　国	32710	37.53
美　国	14433	16.56
德　国	9024	10.36
日　本	8401	9.64

主要进口商品市场情况表(续)

国别（地区）	进口金额（万美元）	占进口总额（%）
台湾省	2938	3.37
西班牙	2765	3.17
意大利	2427	2.78
韩　国	2244	2.58

【利用外资】

1999年利用外资情况表

利用外资方式	批准签订的合同			实际利用外资	
	项目（个）	外资金额（亿美元）	金额比1998年（±%）	金　额（亿美元）	金额比1998年（±%）
外商直接投资	107	3.87	+45	1.92	+29
合资企业	57	1.73	+22	0.91	+21
合作企业	6	0.45	−30	0.36	−9.7

1999 年利用外资情况表(续)

利用外资方式	批准签订的合同			实际利用外资	
	项目(个)	外资金额(亿美元)	金额比 1998 年(±%)	金额(亿美元)	金额比 1998 年(±%)
外资企业	44	1.70	+175	0.65	+89
合计	**107**	**3.87**	**+45**	**1.92**	**+29**

外商直接投资行业情况表

行业类别	项目数		合同外资		实到外资	
	数量	占比重%	金额(万美元)	占比重%	金额(万美元)	占比重%
农业	4	3.7	672	1.7	240	1.2
制造业	71	66.3	22029	56.9	9678	50.4
房地产业	8	7.5	542	1.4	1798	9.4
城市基础设施	2	1.9	10758	27.8	3474	18.1
交通运输业	1	0.9	1209	3.1	1025	5.3
贸易、餐饮业	5	4.7	500	1.3	1147	6
社会服务业	14	13.1	2014	5.2	906	4.7
其他	2	1.9	944	2.4	930	4.8

外商直接投资来源情况表

国别(地区)	项目数		合同外资		实到外资	
	数量	占比重%	金额(万美元)	占比重%	金额(万美元)	占比重%
亚洲	67	62.6	18355	47.5	10629	55.4
香港	33	30.8	5179	13.4	4563	23.8
台湾省	14	13	1917	5	1842	9.6
菲律宾	1	0.9	5	0.01	—	—
泰国	1	0.9	6	0.01	—	—
马来西亚	—	—	—	—	8	0.04
新加坡	5	4.7	944	2.4	884	4.6
日本	10	9.3	10179	26.3	3323	17.3
韩国	3	2.8	125	0.3	9	0.05
欧洲	9	8.4	2924	7.6	1920	10
德国	3	2.8	171	0.4	235	1.2
法国	2	1.9	1934	5	1316	6.8
意大利	1	0.9	38	0.1	—	—
荷兰	—	—	—	—	25	0.1
比利时	1	0.9	3	—	3	0.01
英国	2	1.9	764	2	326	1.7

外商直接投资来源情况表(续)

国别（地区）	项目数		合同外资		实到外资	
	数量	占比重%	金额（万美元）	占比重%	金额（万美元）	占比重%
瑞士	—	—	12	0.03	15	0.09
哈萨克	—	—	2	—	—	—
拉丁美洲	8	7.5	14527	37.6	4517	23.5
维京群岛	6	5.6	13812	35.7	4217	22
凯曼群岛	2	1.9	715	1.8	300	1.6
北美洲	19	17.8	2336	6	2036	10.6
加拿大	3	2.8	11	0.03	—	—
美国	16	14.9	2325	6	1986	10.3
百慕大	—	—	—	—	50	0.3
大洋洲	5	4.7	526	1.4	96	0.5
澳大利亚	3	2.8	154	0.4	21	0.1
新西兰	2	1.9	372	1	75	0.4

【对外经济合作】

承包工程和劳务合作 1999年签定对外承包工程和劳务合作合同项目11个，合同金额363万美元，比上年的1670万美元下降78.26%；营业额479万美元，比上年的614万美元下降21.99%；当年派出劳务人数868人，年末在外人数1098人，派往的主要国家和地区为日本、以色列、柬埔寨、新加坡、越南、缅甸等。

【其他】

经济技术开发区 成都高新技术开发区是经国务院批准的经济技术开发区。1999年成都高新区完成了人民南路南沿线高新段6.7公里管道敷设，完成投资11714万元。1999年共新认定高新技术企业69家，比上年增长92%；申报各级科技计划项目81项，落实、安排区本级科技三项费399万元，比上年增长20%，资助了雌三醇栓产业化工程等14个高新技术项目。为区内高新技术企业落实无偿项目资金879万元，协助成都国腾通信有限公司等10家企业落实科技开发贷款和流动资金7000余万元。

高新区1999年实现工业增加值22.6亿元，比上年增长29.8%；利税11.3亿元，增长23.5%；引进外资总额10429.3万美元，合同外资5561.2万美元，到位外资3438.68万美元，比上年分别增长26%、72%、25%；引进外资项目30个，其中增资项目6个。

建成了留学人员创业园，首批入住项目初见成效。1999年共接纳23家留学人员创办的企业入园发展。项目主要涉及电子信息、生物制药和新材料三大领域。据初步统计，留学人员创业园首批入住企业总产值已达3000万元。

高新区西部软件园已经成功挂牌运作，情况良好，成为高新区“一区多园”模式的重要组成部分。目前，西部软件园已全面承担国家863计划、“九五”重要攻关计划、火炬计划和技术改造、技术创新等多项计划项目。

实现乡镇企业总产值17.56亿元，比上年同期增长32.1%，其中，工业总产值为13.17亿元，比上年同期增长30.6%，利税总额13851.6万元，比上年同期增长38.1%。

涉外旅游 1999年成都市共接待国际游客22.19万人次（包括港、澳、台），旅游收入6919.83万美元，比1998年增长1.28%。

1999年贵州省对外经济贸易

贵州省对外贸易经济合作厅

【对外贸易】

进出口总额 1999年贵州省进出口总额54758万美元，比1998年62248万美元下降12.03%。

出口总额 出口总额35775万美元，比上年的38796万美元下降7.79%，占全省国内生产总值907亿元（相当于109.55亿美元）的3.27%；占全国出口额的0.18%。

出口商品结构 初级产品出口额11534.88万美元，占出口总额的32.24%；工业制成品的出口额24239.86万美元，占出口总额的67.76%。

出口额在1000万美元以上的商品情况表

金额分类	商品名称	出口金额（万美元）	占出口总额（%）
1000～2000万美元4种	烤烟、黄磷、棕刚玉、硅锰铁	6691	18.70
2000～3000万美元2种	硅铁、汽车轮胎	4970	13.99
3000万美元以上1种	磷灰石	6115	17.09
合　计	**7种**	**17776**	**49.68**

出口商品市场 出口商品销往114个国家和地区。

主要出口商品市场情况表

国别（地区）	出口金额（万美元）	占出口总额（%）
日　本	5409	15.12
韩　国	4427	12.38
香　港	3641	10.18
美　国	3293	9.20
印度尼西亚	2114	5.91
台湾省	1827	5.11
印　度	1553	4.34

主要出口商品市场情况表(续)

国别（地区）	出口金额（万美元）	占出口总额（%）
荷　兰	1450	4.05
沙特阿拉伯	1087	3.04
波　兰	763	2.13
合　计	**25564**	**71.46**

进口总额 进口总额18983万美元，比上年的23452万美元下降19.06%。

进口商品结构 初级产品进口额9884.99万美元，占进口总额的52.07%；工业制成品的进口额9098.26万美元，占进口总额的47.93%。

进口额在1000万美元以上商品情况表

金额分类	商品名称	进口金额（万美元）	占进口总额（%）
1000～2000万美元3种	塑料、橡胶及其制品、纺织品	2447	12.89
2000万美元以上2种	矿产品、贱金属及其制品	9374	49.38
合　计	**5种**	**11821**	**62.27**

进口商品市场　进口商品来自34个国家和地区。

主要进口商品市场情况表

国别（地区）	进口金额（万美元）	占进口总额（%）
香　港	6728	35.44
阿富汗	2119	11.16
印　度	1548	8.16
日　本	1209	6.37
澳大利亚	933	4.91
美　国	922	4.86
英　国	795	4.19
阿根廷	743	3.91

主要进口商品市场情况表(续)

国别（地区）	进口金额（万美元）	占进口总额（%）
加拿大	738	3.89
德　国	597	3.15
合　计	**16332**	**86.04**

技术进口　技术引进项目有：从台湾省引进新型CNC自动绕线机电控制系统及生产技术，合同金额为12万美元；从美国引进片式钽电容器制造技术，合同金额3.6万美元；从美国引进PCS2000技术，合同金额为5.2万美元；从澳大利亚引进波尔山羊胚胎移植技术，金额为9.9万澳元（折合6.07万美元），以上四项引进的技术均已投产使用。

【利用外资】

1999年利用外资情况表

利用外资方式	批准签订的合同			实际利用外资	
	项目（个）	外资金额（万美元）	金额比1998年（±%）	金额（万美元）	金额比1998年（±%）
对外借款	5	16125	303.12	2486	100
外商直接投资	43	6685	-56.34	4090	-9.81
合资企业	23	1691	-41.12	3184	4.67
合作企业	5	4475	-37.45	709	60.05
外资企业	15	519	-90.18	197	-81.24
外商投资股份制					
外商其它投资					
国际租赁					
补偿贸易					

1999 年利用外资情况表(续)

利用外资方式	批准签订的合同			实际利用外资	
	项目（个）	外资金额（万美元）	金额比 1998 年（±%）	金额（万美元）	金额比 1998 年（±%）
加工贸易					
对外发行股票					
合计	48	12810	78.03	6576	73.67

外商直接投资行业 外商直接投资的 43 个项目中，生产型项目 34 个，非生产型项目 9 个。按行业分：农、林、牧、渔业 5 个；采掘业 1 个；制造业 26 个；电业、煤气及水生产和供应业 1 个；建筑业 1 个；批发零售贸易、餐饮业 1 个；房地产业 3 个；社会服务业 5 个。

外商直接投资来源 外商直接投资来自17个国家和地区。主要投资的国家和地区及金额有：日本1722万美元、新加坡813万美元、澳门386万美元、香港364万美元、美国287万美元、台湾省226万美元、维尔京群岛(英属)137万美元、马来西亚86万美元、法国31万美元、加拿大28万美元。

外商直接投资企业生产经营情况 外商直接投资企业出口额 3456 万美元，进口额 1118 万美元。

【对外经济合作】

承包工程和劳务合作 签订对外承包工程和劳务合作合同项目22个，金额1742万美元，比上年的8769万美元下降80.14%；完成营业额2789万美元，比上年的956万美元增长191.74%；当年派出劳务人员277人次，年末在外人数110人，派往的主要国家和地区有：澳门、越南、柬埔寨、菲律宾、斯里兰卡、香港、新加坡。涉及的行业、项目有老挝的巴色机场和1999年开发启动的香港地铁等。

接受经济援助 接受日本政府提供 1442 万元人民币援助的粮食增长项目。

对外投资 对尼日利亚投资5万美元，用于技术售后服务；对美国投资6.67万美元，用于机电售后服务及技术咨询服务；对澳大利亚投资140万澳元(折合85.85万美元)，用于学生公寓餐饮业服务。

【其他】

经济技术开发区 贵州省经国务院批准的国家级开发区有二个：一是贵阳国家高新技术产业开发区（位于贵阳市新天寨）；二是贵阳国家经济技术开发区（位于贵阳市小河区）。1999 年，两个开发区完成投资额分别为：6160 万元、8300 万元人民币，比 1998 年分别增长 9.8%、120%；招商引资的到位资金总额分别为 16500 万元、11600 万元；比 1998 年分别增长 9.8%、43.2%；完成国内生产总值分别为 301483 万元、110200 万元，比 1998 年分别增长 1.4%、8.25%；完成工业总产值分别为 300000 万元、181000 万元，比 1998 年分别增长 1.25%、9.7%；完成利税总额分别为：31000 万元、10400 万元，比 1998 年分别增长 2.8%、16.85%；创汇分别为 93 万美元、144.94 万美元，比 1998 年分别增长 10%、6%。

对外经贸洽谈会 1999 年 6 月由贵州省贸促会组织 9 家企业组成贵州分团前往美国参加由中国贸促会在纽约举办的‘99 中国贸易展览会，会上成交 67.9 万美元，达成意向协议 33.5 万美元，共接待新老客户 250 人，其中 80%是新客户。

港口运输 外贸货物运输总量为 257 万吨，其中，出口 102 万吨，进口 155 万吨，按运输方式：海运量 256.5 万吨，陆运量 0.49 万吨，空运量 0.01 万吨。

涉外旅游 接待海外旅游者16.73万人次，比上年15.14万人次增长10.50%。其中外国人6.61万人次，港澳同胞4.76万人次，台胞5.29万人次，华侨0.07万人次，比 1998 年分别增长 －2.79%、24.61%、17.04%、357.52%，旅游外汇收入5500万美元，比上年的4831万美元增长13.85%。

1999年云南省对外经济贸易

云南省对外贸易经济合作厅

【对外贸易】

进出口总额 1999年云南省进出口总额165969万美元，比1998年165227万美元增长0.45%。

出口总额 出口总额103444万美元，比上年的113066万美元下降8.5%，占全省国内生产总值的4.6%，占全国出口总额的0.53%。

出口商品结构 初级产品出口额28000万美元，占出口总额的27.1%；工业制成品的出口额75444万美元，占出口总额的72.9%。

出口100万美元以上的商品有94种，金额85521万美元，占出口总额的82.7%。其中出口1000万美元以上的商品有：锡、烤烟、黄磷、铅、松茸、棉绦纶布、铝、焊锡、锌、三磷酸钠、卷烟、茶叶、过磷酸钙、磷酸、磷矿石、望远镜、棉纱、石蜡、电池、服装、磷酸氢二铵、钢材、内燃机及配件等23种，金额63465万美元，占出口总额的61.4%；出口500万美元～1000万美元的商品12种，金额7848万美元，占出口总额的7.6%；出口100万美元～500万美元的商品59种，金额14208万美元，占出口总额的13.7%。

出口商品市场 出口商品销往111个国家和地区。

主要出口商品市场情况表

国别（地区）	出口额（万美元）	占出口总额（%）
缅甸	24599	23.8
香港	17351	16.8
日本	11154	10.8
印度尼西亚	6424	6.3
越南	6252	6.1
美国	4858	4.7
韩国	3173	3.1
荷兰	2950	2.9
台湾省	2423	2.4
新加坡	2084	2.1
合计	**81268**	**79**

进口总额 进口总额62525万美元，比1998年的52161万美元增长19.9%。

进口商品结构 初级产品进口额12693万美元，占进口总额的20.3%；工业制成品进口额49832万美元，占进口总额的79.7%。

进口100万美元以上的商品53种，金额48957万美元，占进口总额的78.3%。进口1000万美元以上的商品有：烟用丝束、铜矿砂、氧化铝、未锻轧铝、打印机零附件、醋酸纤维素、铁矿砂、烟草加工机、通讯设备、石油沥青、非针叶木原木等11种，金额32910万美元，占进口总额的52.6%；进口500万美元～1000万美元的商品12种，金额8876万美元，占进口总额的14.2%；进口100万美元～500万美元的商品30种，金额7171万美元，占进口总额的11.5%。

进口商品市场 进口商品来自40个国家和地区。

主要进口商品市场情况表

国别（地区）	进口额（万美元）	占进口总额（%）
香　港	11895	19.1
美　国	7978	12.8
澳大利亚	5365	8.58
缅　甸	5353	8.57
德　国	4097	6.56
俄罗斯	3138	5.02
意大利	3114	4.98
加拿大	3002	4.81
日　本	2313	3.7
智　利	2069	3.31
合　计	**48324**	**77.43**

边境贸易　1999年全省边境小额贸易进出口总额28777万美元，比上年的13089万美元增长119.8%。其中，出口23183万美元，比上年的8896万美元增长160.6%；进口5594万美元，比上年的4193万美元增长33.4%。主要出口商品有：化纤布、棉纱、石蜡、各类机械、家用电器、干电池、水果、水稻种籽、化纤纱、烤烟等；主要进口商品有：原木、铬矿砂、锯材、铁矿砂、锰矿砂、银粉、藤条、豆类等。

技术进出口　1999年共签订技术引进和进口设备合同47项，合同总额2467万美元，比上年同期减少60.3%。主要是烟草、电力、轻工、冶金、有色、化工、机械等方面的技术和设备，引进项目主要来自德国、美国、意大利、瑞士、英国等。其中包括16份项目咨询或技术转让合同，金额459万美元。

【利用外资】

1999年利用外资情况表

利用外资方式	批准签订的合同			实际利用外资	
	项目数（个）	外资金额（万美元）	金额比1998年（±%）	金　额（万美元）	金额比1998年（±%）
对外借款					
外商直接投资	138	33219	0.5	15385	5.6
合资企业	67				
合作企业	16				
外资企业	55				

外商直接投资行业　外商直接投资项目中生产型项目95项，非生产型项目43项。按行业分，农林牧渔业13项，采掘业2项，制造业68项，电力、煤气及水的生产和供应2项，建筑业3项，地质勘查业、水利管理业1项，批发和零售贸易、餐饮业9项，房地产业6项，社会服务业25项，科学研究和综合技术服务业3项，其他行业6项。

外商直接投资来源　外商直接投资来自香港、美国、台湾省、新加坡、泰国、日本、维尔京群岛、德国、缅甸、加拿大、澳门、毛里求斯、意大利、英国、澳大利亚、菲律宾、开曼群岛、以色列、法国、荷兰、俄罗斯、丹麦等22个国家和地区。合同外资额居前十位的国家及地区依次为：香港48项，10877万美元；维尔京群岛4项，4217万美元；美国11项，3641万美元；日本7项，3009万美元；毛里求斯2项，1803万美元；台湾省20项，1745万美元，缅甸6项，1709万美元；德国2项，1632万美元；新加坡8项，1086万美元；澳门2项，657万美元。

【对外经济合作】

承包工程和劳务合作　1999年对外签订合

同207项，总金额33915万美元，比上年的31000万美元增长9.4%。营业额16688万美元，比上年的10000万美元增长66.8%。当年派出劳务人员1450人，年末在外人数1442人。派往主要国家和地区为毛里求斯、老挝、缅甸、泰国、巴基斯坦、阿尔巴尼亚等；承包工程的主要项目为老挝文化中心、老挝ADB五号公路、缅甸邦郎水电站、阿尔巴尼亚布显特水电站勘查设计、毛里求斯纺织项目等。

对外经济技术援助 1999年承担援外项目1个，总金额964万美元，项目为老挝万荣水泥厂二期工程。

接受经济援助 1999年接受国际组织及双边援助项目4个，金额420万美元，主要来自日本、新西兰、联合国国际贸易中心等组织。

【其他】

对外经贸洽谈会 1999年6月6日～10日，在昆明举办了'99中国昆明出口商品交易会，到会境外客商、来宾达9500余人。其中缅甸、老挝、越南、马来西亚、美国、巴基斯坦、法国、日本、澳大利亚等16个国家和香港特别行政区、澳门特别行政区和台湾省的参展展位156个。交易会各项业务成交总额18.28亿美元，其中：出口4.08亿美元；进口1.19亿美元；利用外资12.02亿美元；对外承包工程和劳务合作28项，金额0.94亿美元。

海外旅游 1999年入境的外国人及台港澳同胞104万人次，旅游外汇收入33800万美元，比上年的26100万美元增长29.5%。

1999年西藏自治区对外经济贸易

西藏自治区对外贸易经济合作厅

【对外贸易】

进出口总额 1999年西藏自治区进出口总额为16622万美元，比1998年的10963万美元增长51.62%。

出口总额 出口总额8605万美元，比上年的4587万美元增长87.59%；占全区国内生产总值103亿元人民币的6.90%

出口商品结构 初级产品出口额为1105万美元，占出口总额的12.84%；工业制成品出口额为7500万美元，占出口总额的87.16%。

出口商品市场 出口商品主要销往：尼泊尔，7143万美元，占出口总额的83.01%；香港，1040万美元，占出口总额的12.09%；韩国，420万美元，占出口总额的4.88%。

进口总额 进口总额8017万美元，比上年的6376万美元增长25.74%。

进口商品结构 初级产品进口额1200万美元，占进口总额的14.96%；工业制成品进口额6817万美元，占进口总额的85.03%。

进口商品市场 进口商品主要来自：日本，1810万美元，占进口总额的22.58%；韩国，1690万美元，占进口总额的21.08%；澳大利亚，920万美元，占进口总额的11.48%；尼泊尔，901万美元，占进口总额的11.24%；香港900万美元，占进口总额的11.23%；台湾省，840万美元，占进口总额的10.48%；俄罗斯，760万美元，占进口总额的9.48%。

边境贸易 1999年全区边境贸易进出口额为8044万美元，比上年的2349万美元增长242.44%，主要进出口商品有农产品、畜产品、纺织品、轻工业品、机电产品、建材、医药等。

【利用外资】

外商投资概况 1999年外商在西藏自治区的投资项目8个，协议利用外资684万美元，比上年的2463万美元下降72.23%。其中中外合资项目7个，外商投资614万美元；外商独资企业1个，外商投资70万美元。

外商直接投资行业 外商投资项目中生产型企业2个，非生产型企业6个；其中服务业项目6个，运输行业项目1个，食品加工项目1个。

外商直接投资来源 外资分别来自5个国家和地区。其中香港投资项目1个，投资额325万美元；日本投资项目1个，投资额180万美元；荷兰投资项目1个，投资额80万美元；尼泊尔投资项目4个，投资额74万美元；美国投资项目1个，投资额25万美元。

【对外经济合作】

接受经济援助 1999年西藏自治区共接受国际援助项目10个，援助金额1007.32万美元。援助国别来自联合国儿童基金会和新西兰、德国、加拿大、日本、澳大利亚、荷兰等国政府。援助项目涉及农牧林业综合开发、妇幼保健、教师培训等行业。

【其他】

涉外旅游 1999年西藏自治区共接待境外游客及台港澳同胞10.8万多人次，旅游收入3600万美元，比上年的3302万美元增长9.02%。

1999年陕西省对外经济贸易

陕西省对外贸易经济合作厅

【对外贸易】

进出口总额 1999年陕西省进出口总额20.33亿美元，比1998年的20.51亿美元下降0.90%。

出口总额 出口总额11.77亿美元，比上年的11.76亿美元略有增加，占全省国内生产总值1487.6亿元（相当于179.88亿美元）的6.54%；占全国出口总额的0.60%。

出口商品结构 初级产品出口额1.40亿美元，占出口总额的11.93%；工业制成品出口额10.37亿美元，占出口总额的88.17%。

出口额在1千万美元以上的商品情况表

金额分类	商品名称	出口金额（万美元）	占出口总额（%）
（1）出口额在5千万美元以上的商品（3种）	电子管、棉机织物、棉混纺织物	19610	16.66

出口额在1千万美元以上的商品情况表（续）

金额分类	商品名称	出口金额（万美元）	占出口总额（%）
(2) 出口额在1千万至5千万美元的商品（25种）	果汁、玻璃器皿、未锻轧锌、钼矿砂、滚动轴承、缝纫机、钛及其制品、钢铁铸造制品、铁合金、服装、手工工具、干豆、已梳的羊毛及动物毛、电力控制器、未锻轧铅、鞋靴、钢铁管子附件、传声器	41292	35.08

出口商品市场　出口商品销往155个国家（地区）。

主要出口市场情况表

出口国别（地区）	出口金额（万美元）	占出口总额（%）
香　港	20785	17.66
美　国	13873	11.79
日　本	9413	7.99
韩　国	8587	7.29
荷　兰	5997	5.09
德　国	4803	4.08
土耳其	3995	3.39

主要出口市场情况表（续）

出口国别（地区）	出口金额（万美元）	占出口总额（%）
意大利	3186	2.71
英　国	3050	2.59
新加坡	2672	2.27

进口总额　进口总额8.56亿美元，比上年的8.75亿美元下降2.10%。

进口商品结构　初级产品进口额0.23亿美元，占进口总额的2.65%；工业制成品的进口额8.33亿美元，占进口总额的97.31%。

进口额在1千万美元以上的商品情况表

金额分类	商品名称	进口金额（万美元）	占进口总额（%）
(1) 进口额在5千万美元以上的商品（2种）	航空器、杂环化合物	27623	32.27
(2) 进口额在1千万至5千万美元的商品（13种）	电子管、机器及机械器具、数据处理设备、精炼铜及铝合金、未锻轧铝、纤维素、航空器零部件、铝板、机动车辆零附件、内燃发动机、集成电路及微电子组件、合成纤维短纤、氧化铝	22431	26.20

进口商品市场　进口商品来自40个国家（地区）。

主要进口市场情况表

国家（地区）	进口金额（万美元）	占进口总额（%）
法国	22504	26.28
日本	13789	16.11
美国	10853	12.68
德国	5856	6.84
比利时	5059	5.91
韩国	3971	4.64
瑞典	3965	4.63
澳大利亚	2678	3.13
俄罗斯	2238	2.61
爱尔兰	2009	2.35

技术进出口　1999年陕西省签订引进技术和进口设备合同项目数32个，比上年增加18个；合同金额3388万美元，比上年的627万美元增长440.35%。签订技术出口合同金额12118万美元，比上年的6093万美元增长98.9%。

技术进口　引进项目的国别包括美国、日本、德国、澳大利亚、法国、比利时等6个国家。其中美国11个项目，合同金额共计160万美元，涉及电子、飞机制造、制药、航空、电器、机械等行业；德国4个项目，合同金额共计44.64万美元，涉及有色金属机械、电子等行业；日本13个项目，合同金额共计2843.64万美元，涉及电子、有色金属、制冷、电器等行业；澳大利亚2个项目，合同金额共计99.25万美元，涉及电信、机械等行业；比利时1个项目，合同金额7.7万美元，属医药行业；法国1个项目，合同金额232.63万美元，属印刷行业。

技术出口　1999年技术出口合同金额12118万美元，比上年增长98.9%；收汇金额5878万美元，比上年增长167.8%。其中高新技术产品出口3500万美元。

【利用外资】

1999年利用外资情况表

利用外资方式	批准签订的合同			实际利用外资	
	项目（个）	外资金额（万美元）	金额比1998年（±%）	金额（万美元）	金额比1998年（±%）
外商直接投资	157	42693	13.87	24197	-11.66
合资企业	84	9033	-16.5	10598	-29.6
合作企业	39	28742	44.3	9016	24.9
外资企业	34	4918	-29.5	4583	-15.9
合　计	**157**	**42693**	**13.87**	**24197**	**-11.66**

外商直接投资行业　外商直接投资项目中农、林、牧、渔业项目8个；采掘业项目3个；制造业项目95个；建筑业项目1个；交通运输、仓储及邮电通信业项目1个；批发和零售贸易、餐饮业项目3个；房地产业项目22个，社会服务业项目21个；卫生、体育和社会福利业项目1个；科学研究和综合技术服务业项目1个；其他行业1个。

外商直接投资来源　外商直接投资来自21个国家（地区），主要国别（地区）有：香港，51项，合同外资5550万美元；台湾省，16项，合同外资3847万美元；欧盟，15项，合同外资3296万美元；加拿大，9项，合同外资6212万美元；美国，21项，合同外资7721万美元；澳大利亚，9项，合同外资912万美元。

外商直接投资企业生产经营情况　1999年外商直接投资企业进出口总额32942万美元，其中进口23929万美元，出口9014万美元。

【对外经济合作】

承包工程和劳务合作 1999年签订对外承包工程和劳务合作合同项目101个，金额8011万美元，比上年的6348万美元增长26.20%；营业额8607万美元，比上年的8684万美元下降0.89%；当年派出劳务人员1390人次，年末在外1777人，派往的主要国家和地区有日本、新加坡、塞班、沙特阿拉伯、苏丹、巴布亚新几内亚等；承包工程的主要项目有巴布亚新几内亚的亚柏马公路项目、博茨瓦纳的图图梅中学项目、突尼斯的经援坝项目。

对外经济技术援助 承担援外项目4个，其中援外合资合作项目1个，即柬埔寨砖瓦厂项目，已完成考察、立项、资金落实等工作。

接受经济援助 接受国际经济组织及双边援助的项目数7个，计划援助金额1091万美元。正在执行项目1个，援助金额28万美元，项目进展顺利。

对外投资 1999年在海外举办企业（系指非贸易性企业）11个，投资国别（地区）为罗马尼亚、津巴布韦、吉尔吉斯、法国、加纳、柬埔寨等，经济效益均为良好。

【其他】

经济技术开发区 西安经济技术开发区2000年被晋升为国家级经济技术开发区。

对外经贸洽谈会 1999年4月6日至10日，在西安举行'99中国东西部合作与投资贸易洽谈会。共签订利用外资项目合同131个，总投资额10.75亿美元，其中外资额6.91亿美元；外贸进出口成交总额4.85亿美元，其中出口4.40亿美元，进口0.45亿美元。

涉外旅游 1999年接待境外游客63万人次，旅游收入2.7亿美元，比上年的2.5亿美元增长10%。

1999年西安市对外经济贸易

西安市对外贸易经济合作局

【对外贸易】

进出口总额 西安市1999年进出口总额37283万美元，比1998年的34269万美元增长8.8%。

出口总额 出口总额22934万美元，比上年的22414万美元增长2.3%，占全市国内生产总值617亿元（相当于74.58亿美元）的3.08%；占全省出口总额115083万美元的19.93%。

出口商品结构 初级产品出口1906万美元，占出口总额的8.31%；工业制成品出口21028万美元，占出口总额的91.69%。

出口额200万美元以上的商品情况表

金额分类	商品名称	出口金额（万美元）	占出口总额（%）
200万美元～500万美元（12种）	果汁、胶合板、棉涤坯布、搪瓷器皿、铸铁制品、建筑小五金、铝材、精萘、磷酸二铵、飞机零备件、变压器、工业缝纫机	3656	15.94

出口额 200 万美元以上的商品情况表（续）

金额分类	商品名称	出口金额（万美元）	占出口总额（%）
500 万美元～1000 万美元（3 种）	合纤绸女内衣、铁制玩具、扬声器	1672	7.09
1000 万美元以上（3 种）	缝纫机头、玻璃器皿、滚动轴承	3895	16.98
合计	**18 种**	**9178**	**40.01**

出口商品市场 出口商品销往 100 个国家（地区）。

主要出口国家（地区）情况表

国家（地区）	出口金额（万美元）	占出口总额（%）
香港	4698	20.48
美国	4079	17.79
日本	2970	12.95
德国	1187	5.18
英国	1034	4.51
新加坡	913	3.98
意大利	860	3.75
马来西亚	745	3.25
荷兰	671	2.93

主要出口国家（地区）情况表（续）

国家（地区）	出口金额（万美元）	占出口总额（%）
印度	513	2.24
合计	**17670**	**77.05**

进口总额 进口总额 14349 万美元，比上年的 7759 万美元增长 84．93%。

进口商品结构 初级产品进口额 282 万美元，占进口总额的 1．97%；工业制成品进口额 14067 万美元，占进口总额的 98．03%。

进口额 200 万美元以上的商品情况表

金额分类	商品名称	进口金额（万美元）	占进口总额（%）
200 万美元～500 万美元 4 种	氧化铝、无线电通讯设备、缝纫机零件、铝	1487	10.36
500 万美元以上 4 种	铜 电子成套设备、航空设备及零件、通用机械零配件	4695	32．72
合计	**8 种**	**6182**	**43.08**

进口商品市场 进口商品来自 30 个国家（地区）。

主要进口国家（地区）情况表

国家（地区）	进口金额（万美元）	占进口总额（%）
日本	3416	23.81
美国	2439	16.99
德国	1835	12.79
英国	931	6.49
俄罗斯	893	6.22
韩国	811	5.65

主要进口国家（地区）情况表（续）

国家（地区）	进口金额（万美元）	占进口总额（%）
台湾省	463	3.23
瑞典	461	3.21
澳大利亚	382	2.66
意大利	358	2.49
合　计	**11989**	**83. 55**

【利用外资】

1999年利用外资情况表

利用外资方式	批准签订的合同			实际利用外资	
	项目（个）	外资金额（万美元）	金额比1998年（±%）	金　额（万美元）	金额比1998年（±%）
对外借款	5	1080	-46.61	800	-52.91
外商直接投资	98	28269	-3.14	13751	-37.91
合资企业	56	5881	0.02	6000	-44.98
合作企业	22	20487	22.45	4793	7.49
外资企业	20	1901	-71. 08	2958	-31. 95
合　计	**103**	**29349**	**-6.48**	**14551**	**-38.98**

外商直接投资行业　在外商直接投资项目中，生产型项目64个，非生产型项目34个。按行业分，农林牧渔水利业3个，工业64个，房地产管理业13个，服务业9个，咨询服务业5个，其他行业4个。

外商直接投资来源　外商直接投资来自20个国家和地区。投资额前10位的是：香港32个，9094万美元；英国6个，6429万美元；加拿大6个，6162万美元；美国12个，5908万美元；澳门3个，3225万美元；新加坡5个，3157万美元；台湾省10个，2217万美元；印度尼西亚1个，1500万美元；维尔京群岛1个，881万美元；澳大利亚6个，626万美元。

外商直接投资企业生产经营情况　截止1999年底，已开业投产的外商投资企业共695家，全年完成销售收入42亿元，其中出口销售收入5660万美元，完成税收5.8亿元。

【对外经济合作】

承包工程和劳务合作　1999年签订对外承包工程和劳务合作合同项目60个，金额5670万美元，比上年的2034万美元增长178.76%；营业额2264万美元，比上年的3618万美元下降37.42%；当年派出劳务人员600人，年末在外人数为1030人，主要分布在印度尼西亚、泰国、马来西亚、菲律宾、新加坡、毛里求斯、日本、阿联酋、沙特阿拉伯、莫桑比克、吉尔吉斯斯坦、孟加拉、塞班等国家和地区。

对外投资　1999年在海外举办企业1个，中方投资金额98.6万美元，投资国为南非。

【其他】

经济技术开发区 1999年15项重点科技转化工程计划项目完成总投资2.29亿元，高新技术产业开发区全年技工贸总收入完成201亿元，工业增加值达41亿元，分别比上年增长41.13%和37.56%。新批外商投资项目30个，合同外资额9741万美元，实际进资3539万美元，截至1999年，外商投资企业累计达到371家。

对外经贸洽谈会 '99中国西安投资与贸易洽谈会于1999年9月12日至17日在西安举行。来自香港、日本、美国、英国、法国、德国、韩国、加拿大、澳大利亚、新西兰、马来西亚、泰国、瑞典、俄罗斯、乌克兰、比利时、丹麦等23个国家和地区的商社、协会共1500余人参加了本届洽谈会。本届洽谈会西安市共签订外商直接投资合同项目87个，合同总额5.59亿美元，其中外资额4.68亿美元；签订出口合同总额1716万美元。

涉外旅游 1999年接待海外旅游者55万人次，比上年增长14.58%。旅游外汇收入2.25亿美元，比1998年的1.94亿美元增长15.98%。

1999年甘肃省对外经济贸易

甘肃省对外贸易经济合作厅

【对外贸易】

进出口总额 1999年甘肃省进出口总额40623万美元，比1998年的45573万美元下降11%。

出口总额 出口总额31699万美元，比上年的35261万美元下降10%，占全省国内生产总值931亿元的2.79%，占全国出口额的0.16%。

出口商品结构 初级产品出口额5695万美元，占出口总额的18%；工业制成品出口额26007万美元，占出口总额的82%。

出口额在500万美元以上的商品情况表

金额分类	商品名称	出口金额（万美元）	占出口总额（%）
1000万美元以上	硅铁	5947	19
	镍	4420	14
	锌	3213	10
500万美元至1000万美元	合成纤维	794	3
	铝	784	2
	石墨电极	756	2
合计		**15914**	**50**

出口商品市场 出口商品销往107个国家(地区)。

主要出口商品市场情况表

主要出口市场	出口金额(万美元)	占出口总额(%)
日　本	9583	30
美　国	4165	13
韩　国	3341	11
台湾省	2074	7
香　港	1809	6
意大利	1237	4
新加坡	1155	4

主要出口商品市场情况表(续)

主要出口市场	出口金额(万美元)	占出口总额(%)
荷　兰	629	2
伊　朗	598	2
德　国	579	2
合　计	**25170**	**81**

进口总额 进口总额8924万美元，比上年的10084万美元下降13%。

进口商品结构 初级产品进口额2941万美元，占进口总额的33%；工业制成品的进口额5983万美元，占进口总额的67%。

主要进口商品情况表

金额分类	商品名称	进口金额(万美元)	占进口总额(%)
1000万美元以上	机　电	5131	57
	氧化铝	1017	11
500万美元以下	钢材	440	4.9
	大麦	442	4.9
	羊毛	275	3
合　计		**7308**	**80.8**

主要进口市场情况表

主要进口市场	进口金额(万美元)	占进口总额(%)
澳大利亚	1755	19.6
美　国	1640	18.3
德　国	1544	17.3
日　本	909	10.2
芬　兰	381	4.2
法　国	361	4
俄罗斯	274	3
英　国	249	2.7
台湾省	198	2.2
韩　国	178	1.9

技术进出口 1999年甘肃省技术进出口总额5711.25万美元，比1998年的7822.31万美元下降26.9%。

技术进口 1999年引进项目15个，主要是美国5项，合同金额625.38万美元；西班牙1项，合同金额850万美元；意大利1项，合同金额40万美元；韩国1项，合同金额400万美元；捷克2项，合同金额106.5万美元；香港5项，合同金额34.84万美元。

技术出口 1999年对外签约项目22个，合同总金额4340.26万美元。

【利用外资】

1999 年利用外资情况表

利用外资方式	批准签订的合同			实际利用外资	
	项目（个）	外资金额（万美元）	金额比 1998 年（±%）	金 额（万美元）	金额比 1998 年（±%）
对外借款					
外商直接投资	68	9442	13	4104	6.2
合资企业	36	1192	-44	854	-45
合作企业	14	4829	+82.6	2764	+102
外资企业	18	2215	-42.9	486	-60.7
合 计	**68**	**9442**	**+13**	**4104**	**+6.2**

外商直接投资行业 外商直接投资项目中生产型项目 47 项，非生产型项目 21 项。农、林、牧、渔 1 项；制造业 37 项；电力、煤气及水的生产和供应业 2 项；采掘业 3 项；建筑业 3 项；餐饮业 3 项；房地产 5 项；社会服务 12 项；教育、文化、科研服务业 2 项。

外商直接投资来源情况表

国 别（地区）	项目数（个）	金 额（万美元）
美 国	20	3885
香 港	21	2259
英 国	3	1272
菲律宾	1	301
台湾省	8	226
韩 国	3	124
日 本	3	67
澳 门	1	30
德 国	1	15
加拿大	1	14
澳大利亚	2	14
阿根廷	1	13
新加坡	2	10
泰 国	1	6

【对外经济合作】

承包工程和劳务合作 1999 年签订的对外承包工程和劳务合作合同项目 53 个，执行合同金额 6030 万美元，比上年增长 20.6%，实现营业额 5685 万美元，比上年增长 47%；当年派出各类劳务人员 1000 人，派往的国家和地区主要是津巴布韦、科特迪瓦、加纳、几内亚和新加坡。

对外经济技术援助 承担援外项目 4 项，受援国家和地区是几内亚、科特迪瓦、多哥。涉及的主要行业是建筑、打井及设计。当年派出援外人员 120 人。

接受经济援助 1999 年接受国际经济组织及多、双边援助的项目 54 个，完成执行额 860 万美元，项目执行情况良好。

对外投资 1999 年在海外投资项目达到 34 项，合同额 2645 万美元，比上年增长 9%，其中中方投资额 1869 万美元，比上年增长 11%。主要投资在吉尔吉斯、科特迪瓦、厄里特里亚、津巴布韦等国家。

【其他】

对外经贸洽谈会 中国兰州投资贸易洽谈

会于1999年8月26日至30日在兰州举办。到会中外宾客8000多人，其中来自美国、日本、法国、匈牙利、澳大利亚、韩国、马来西亚及香港、澳门、台湾省等近40个国家和地区的外商510多人。共签约引进国外资金项目32项，总投资12.09亿元，其中引进外资8991万美元。商品成交总额达17.97亿元。

涉外旅游 1999年入境的外国人以及台港澳同胞14.5万人，比上年增长11.66%，旅游收入3735万美元，比上年增长12.45%。

1999年青海省对外经济贸易

青海省对外贸易经济合作厅

【对外贸易】

进出口总额 1999年青海省进出口总额为10785万美元，比1998年的11800万美元下降了8.6%。

出口总额 出口总额8686万美元，比上年的10400万美元下降16.48%，占全省国内生产总值238亿元（相当于28.79亿美元）的3.02%，占全国出口总额的0.04%。

出口商品结构 初级产品出口额1763万美元，占出口总额的20.3%；工业制成品的出口额为6923万美元，占出口总额的79.7%。

出口额在100万美元以上的商品情况表

金额分类	商品名称	出口金额（万美元）	占出口总额（%）
1000万美元以上（1种）	铅锭	1955	22.51
500万美元～1000万美元（5种）	硅铁	976	11.24
	服装	807	9.29
	金属硅	789	9.08
	锌	747	8.64
	氯化镁	583	6.71
100万美元～500万美元（6种）	蚕豆、碳化硅、镁锭、虫草、铸铁件、羊绒	1575	17.65
合计	**12种**	**7432**	**85.56**

出口商品市场 出口商品销往60个国家和地区。

主要出口市场情况表

国别（地区）	出口金额（万美元）	占出口总额（%）
日　本	2402	27.65
韩　国	1661	19.12
美　国	948	10.91
新加坡	632	7.28
哈萨克斯坦	513	5.91
埃　及	367	4.32
香　港	347	3.99
巴　西	196	2.26
德　国	174	2.00
英　国	169	1.95
合　计	**7409**	**85.30**

进口总额　进口总额2099万美元，比上年的1400万美元增长49.93%。

进口商品结构　工业制成品的进口额为2099万美元，占进口总额的100%。

进口额在100万美元以上的商品情况表

金额分类	商　品　名　称	进口金额（万美元）	占进口总额（%）
200万美元～500万美元（3种）	食品加工设备	360	17.51
	其他土建机械	324	15.44
	起重机	214	10.20
100万美元～200万美元（5种）	其他电讯设备及器材	169	8.05
	压缩机	130	6.19
	医疗器械	113	5.38
	氧化铝	56	2.67
	钢铁	51	2.43
合　计	**8种**	**1417**	**67.51**

进口商品市场　进口商品国别和地区18个。

主要进口市场情况表

国别（地区）	进口金额（万美元）	占进口总额（%）
日　本	552	26.30
德　国	522	24.87
香　港	347	16.53
美　国	297	13.29
新加坡	119	5.67
澳大利亚	81	3.86
合　计	**1900**	**90.52**

【利用外资】

1999年利用外资情况表

利用外资方式	批准签订的合同		
	项目数（个）	外资金额（万美元）	金额比1998年（±%）
外商直接投资	15	1421	-81
合资企业	10	570	-50
外资企业	4	609	-89
合作企业	1	242	-79
合计	**15**	**1421**	**-86**

外商直接投资行业 生产型项目5个，非生产型项目10个；能源1个，；农业1个，纺织1个，房地产开发3个，服务性行业6个，其他3个。

外商直接投资来源 香港地区5个项目，协议外资751.48万美元；葡萄牙1项，72万美元；台湾省2项，62.77万美元；日本1项，15万美元；德国1项，24.1万美元；美国3项，275.49万美元；加拿大1项，3.25万美元；泰国1项，16.78万美元。

【对外经济合作】

接受经济援助 新接受国际双边援助项目6个，合计受援金额720万美元。主要项目有：省文化厅争取的日本友人小岛镣次郎先生赠款7亿日元修建省博物馆馆舍，建筑面积约2万平方米；省卫生厅实施的卫VIII项目（英国援助）62.7万美元；青海师大争取的英语教师培训项目8.3万美元（美国利众）和日本利民项目（理化实验设备援助）7.5万美元，以及大通计生委争取的联合国人口基金援助30万美元的生殖健康——计划生育项目。

1999年宁夏回族自治区对外经济贸易

宁夏回族自治区对外贸易经济合作厅

【对外贸易】

进出口总额 1999年宁夏回族自治区进出口总额为37710万美元，比1998年的31728万美元增长18.9%。

出口总额 出口总额为31919万美元，比上年的28650万美元增长11.4%，占全区国内生产总值的10.9%，占全国出口总额的0.16%。

出口商品结构 初级产品出口额为6990万美元，占出口总额的21.9%；工业制成品出口额为24929万美元，占出口总额的78.1%。

出口额在500万美元以上的商品情况表

金额分类	商品名称	出口金额（万美元）	占出口总额（%）
1000万美元以上（9种）	无烟煤、钽粉、钽材、镁、无毛绒、硅铁、羊绒衫、铸铁件、轮胎	19330	60.6
500万美元～1000万美元（6种）	双氰胺、电石、碳化硅及磨料、四环素、活性炭、柠檬酸	4918	15.4
合　计	**15种**	**24248**	**76**

出口商品市场　出口商品主要销往76个国家和地区。

主要出口市场情况表

国别（地区）	出口金额（万美元）	占出口总额（%）
美　国	7348	23.3
日　本	5672	17.9
英　国	2480	7.8
德　国	2449	7.8
韩　国	1808	5.7
以色列	1616	5.1
香　港	1272	4

主要出口市场情况表（续）

国别（地区）	出口金额（万美元）	占出口总额（%）
法　国	1120	3.5
加拿大	1097	3.5
意大利	1087	3.4
合　计	**25949**	**82**

进口总额　进口总额为5792万美元，比上年的3074万美元上升88.4%。

进口商品结构　初级产品的进口额为1478万美元，占进口总额的25.5%；工业制成品的进口额为4314万美元，占进口总额的74.5%。

主要进口商品情况表

金额分类	商品名称	进口金额（万美元）	占进口总额（%）
500万美元～1000万美元（3种）	钽铌矿砂、氧化铝、成套设备	4135	71.4
100万美元～500万美元（6种）	铝粉、医疗器械、纸浆及纸制品、天然橡胶、农药、羊绒	943	16.3
合　计	**9种**	**5078**	**87.7**

进口商品市场 进口商品来自20个国家和地区。

主要进口市场情况表

国别（地区）	进口金额（万美元）	占进口总额%
香　港	1175	20.3
美　国	805	13.9
比利时	700	12.1
英　国	597	10.3

主要进口市场情况表（续）

国别（地区）	进口金额（万美元）	占进口总额%
日　本	437	7.5
奥地利	306	5.3
荷　兰	190	3.3
加拿大	189	3.3
澳大利亚	188	3.3
合　计	**4587**	**79.3**

【利用外资】

1999年利用外资情况表

利用外资方式	批准签订的合同			实际利用外资	
	项目数（个）	外资金额（万美元）	金额比1998年（±%）	金　额（万美元）	金额比1998年（±%）
对外借款	9	4318	-59.3	3097	-40
外商直接投资	28	6185	18.9	1031	-44.5
合资企业	14	729	-66.8	618	66.6
合作企业	11	5424	102.6	304	-74.6
外资企业	3	32	-90.2	109	-62.2
外商其他投资	13	60	-77.5	24	-7
加工装配	13	60	-77.5	24	-7
合　计	**50**	**10563**	**-34.3**	**4152**	**-41**

【对外经济合作】

承包工程和劳务合作 1999年签订对外承包工程和劳务合同项目8个，金额3395万美元。当年派出劳务人员149个，派往的主要国家是沙特、卢旺达、乌干达等。

接受经济援助 接受国外援助项目1个，总金额780万美元。

对外投资 1999年批准在境外投资项目2个。

【其他】

运输 1999年全区完成进出口货运量118.2万吨，比上年增长18.2%，其中出口量为92.4万吨，进口量为25.8万吨。按运输方式分：海运114.2万吨，陆运2万吨。

涉外旅游 1999年入境的外国人及港澳同胞6027人次，增长18.9%。旅游收入1442万美元，比上年的1175万美元增长22.7%。

1999年新疆维吾尔自治区对外经济贸易

新疆维吾尔自治区对外经济贸易合作厅

【对外贸易】

进出口总额 1999年新疆维吾尔自治区进出口总额17.65亿美元，比1998年的15.25亿美元增长15.76%。

出口总额 出口总额102743万美元，比上年的74771万美元增长37.41%，占全区国内生产总值的7.28%，占全国出口总额的0.53%。

出口商品结构 初级产品出口额23042万美元，占出口总额的22.43%；工业制成品的出口额79701万美元，占出口总额的77.57%。

出口额在2000万美元以上的商品情况表

金额分类	商品名称	出口金额（万美元）	占出口总额（%）
1亿美元以上（4种）	棉花、服装、箱包及鞋帽、日用杂品	64186	62.47
3000万美元—5000万美元（4种）	蕃茄酱罐头、化纤布、棉纱线、漆木家俱	16487	16.05
2000万美元—3000万美元（2种）	棉布、化工原料	4790	4.66
合　计	**10种**	**85463**	**83.18**

出口商品市场 出口商品销往98个国家和地区。

主要出口市场情况表

国别（地区）	出口金额（万美元）	占出口总额（%）
哈萨克斯坦	46359	45.12
香　港	10155	9.88
吉尔吉斯斯坦	9989	9.72
韩　国	6634	6.46
美　国	4841	4.71
印度尼西亚	3730	3.63
日　本	3424	3.33

主要出口市场情况表（续）

国别（地区）	出口金额（万美元）	占出口总额（%）
俄罗斯	2910	2.83
合　计	**88042**	**85.69**

进口总额 进口总额73791万美元，比上年的77732万美元下降5.07%。

进口商品结构 初级产品进口额28633万美元，占进口总额的38.80%；工业制成品的进口额45158万美元，占进口总额的61.20%。

进口额在 1000 万美元以上的商品情况表

金额分类	商品名称	进口金额（万美元）	占进口总额（%）
5000 万美元以上（3 种）	薄钢板、化肥、铜材	22225	30.12
2000 万美元～5000 万美元（4 种）	铜、废钢、铝、铝材	17562	23.80
1000 万美元～2000 万美元（11 种）	生牛皮、绒毛、球团矿、有色金属、化工原料、塑料原料、电工设备、拖拉机、石油机械、粮油食品、成套设备、电讯设备及器材	16174	21.92
合　计	**18 种**	**55961**	**75.84**

进口商品市场　进口商品来自 47 个国家和地区。

主要进口市场情况表

国别（地区）	进口金额（万美元）	占进口总额%
哈萨克斯坦	46274	62.71
俄罗斯	6028	8.17
美　国	4970	6.74
德　国	3783	5.13
吉尔吉斯斯坦	3197	4.33
意大利	2884	3.91
澳大利亚	880	1.19
法　国	687	0.93
合　计	**68703**	**93.11**

【边境贸易】

全区边境贸易进出口额 102305 万美元，占全区进出口贸易总额的 57.95%，比上年的 62091 万美元增长 64.77%。其中出口额 57329 万美元，比上年的 32917 万美元增长 74.16%。出口的主要商品有：服装、鞋帽箱包、日用杂品、棉纱线、化工原料、各类机械、家用电器、粮油、食品制成品等。进口额 44976 万美元，比上年的 29174 万美元增长 54.16%。进口的主要商品有：薄钢板、化肥、铜材、铜、铝、铝材、生牛皮、绒毛、球团矿、有色金属等。

技术进出口　签订引进技术和进口设备合同项目 7 个，比上年增加 1 个；合同金额 110 万美元，比上年的 3252 万美元下降 96.62%。引进技术和设备来自 2 个国家，加拿大 1 项 10 万美元；美国 6 项 100 万美元。引进技术和设备的行业是计算机软件 12 项 10 万美元；石油化工 6 项 100 万美元。

【利用外资】

外商直接投资行业　外商直接投资的 52 个项目中，生产型项目 40 个，占 76.92%；非生产型项目 12 个，占 23.08%。按行业划分为农业 7 项、制造业 33 项、社会服务业 10 项、其他行业 2 项。

1999 年利用外资情况表

利用外资方式	批准签订的合同			实际利用外资	
	项目数（个）	外资金额（万美元）	金额比 1998 年（±%）	金　额（万美元）	金额比 1998 年（±%）
外商直接投资	52	6151	-55.51	2404	10.94
合资企业	33	3304		1289	
合作企业	7	1195		90	
外资企业	12	1652		532	
外商投资股份制				493	
合　计	**52**	**6151**	**-55.51**	**2404**	**10.94**

外商直接投资来源　外商直接投资分别来自19个国家和地区。主要有香港特别行政区 13 项，金额 1621 万美元；美国 9 项，金额 1171 万美元；英国 2 项，646 万美元；维尔京群岛 2 项，598 万美元；澳门特别行政区 2 项，388 万美元；台湾省 3 项，545 万美元；新加坡 2 项，30 万美元；日本 1 项，216 万美元；韩国 1 项，10 万美元；以色列 1 项，4 万美元；德国 1 项，127 万美元；意大利 1 项，20 万美元；瑞典 1 项，95 万美元；哈萨克斯坦 4 项，117 万美元；库拉索 1 项，7 万美元；加拿大 3 项，233 万美元；澳大利亚 4 项，305 万美元；新西兰 1 项，4 万美元；新西兰增资 6 万美元；泰国增资 8 万美元。

外商直接投资企业生产经营情况　外商投资企业出口收汇 11777 万美元，比上年增长 7.83%，占全区出口收汇总额的 29.05%。

【对外经济合作】

承包工程和劳务合作　签订对外承包工程和劳务合同 10 个，金额 672 万美元，比上年的 92 万美元增长 630.43%，营业额 801 万美元，比上年的 276 万美元增长 190.22%；当年派出劳务人员 389 人，派往的主要国家是：塔吉克斯坦、哈萨克斯坦、沙特阿拉伯王国。承包的主要项目是：塔吉克烟厂技改工程、哈萨克油井测试工程。

对外经济技术援助　承担援外项目 7 个，总金额 4000 万元人民币。受援国家和地区是：哈萨克斯坦、阿富汗。涉及的行业有：加油站、对难民援助。目前这些项目正在执行。

接受经济援助　接受外国政府援助项目 5 个，总金额 589 万美元。其中：澳大利亚政府无偿援助福海县阿尔达乡改水项目 50 万元人民币、新西兰政府无偿援助福海县阿尔达乡卫生院建设项目 15 万元人民币、日本政府无偿援助乌鲁木齐市中学器材装备项目 800 万元人民币、澳大利亚政府无偿援助新疆爱滋病防治项目 4000 万元人民币、新西兰政府无偿援助巴里坤县妇女创收项目 14 万元人民币。

对外投资　1999 年全区批准在境外兴办企业 7 家，总投资额 1010 万美元，其中中方投资 839 万美元，比上年的 182 万美元增长 360.99%。这些企业主要分布在哈萨克斯坦、吉尔吉斯斯坦、澳大利亚。

【其他】

经济技术开发区　高新技术产业开发区完成基础设施投资额 2600 万元。新批生产型项目 20 个，总投资额 2.62 亿元，注册资本 1.64 亿元，其中：三资企业 8 个，投资额 1.44 亿元，注册资本 8018 万元。项目涉及化工、有色金属加工、黑色金属加工、锅炉制造等行业。整个开发区内企业 1999 年共实现工业总产值 7.48 亿元，实现税收 1.26 亿元；财政收入 7337 万元。外贸完成进出口总额 7184 万美元，其中进口 4588 万美元；出口 2596 万美元。内贸销售额 7.34 亿元。

乌鲁木齐经济技术开发区完成基础设施投资额6769万元。新批生产型项目17个，总投资额7.77亿元，注册资本2.23亿元，其中：三资企业7个，投资额3.65亿元，注册资本1.67亿元。项目涉及风力发电、风力发电机制造、亚麻深加工、金属制品等行业。整个开发区内企业1999年共实现工业总产值6.13亿元；实现税收1.21亿元；财政收入7200万元。外贸完成进出口额4223万美元，其中进口664万美元；出口3559万美元。内贸销售额3.97亿元。

伊宁市边境经济合作区完成基础设施投资额200万元。新批生产型项目7个，总投资额1690万元，注册资本576万元。项目涉及供热、食品加工、毛皮加工等行业。整个开发区企业1999年共实现工业总产值3008万元；实现税收466万元；财政收入312万元。外贸完成出口额312万美元。内贸销售额376万元。

塔城市边境经济合作区完成基础设施投资额180万元。整个开发区企业1999年共实现工业总产值6423万元；实现税收627万元；财政收入298万元。外贸完成进口额3088万美元。内贸完成销售额3.79亿元。

博乐市经济合作区完成基础设施投资额51万元。新批建设项目3个，总投资额2846万元。注册资本1500万元。项目涉及蕃茄酱生产、汽车维修、客运站建设等行业。整个开发区内企业1999年共实现工业总产值2.45亿元；实现税收3048万元；财政收入3048万元。

对外经贸洽谈会　1999年9月1日至9月8日在乌鲁木齐举办的'99乌鲁木齐对外经济贸易洽谈会，有40个国家和地区以及国内28个省、区、市13000多名中外客商和政府官员到会。共签订对外经济贸易合同总额12.12亿美元，其中：对外贸易出口成交4.68亿美元；进口订货4.28亿美元；对外经济技术合作项目成交3.16亿美元。国内贸易和经济技术合作项目成交135.02亿元人民币，其中：国内贸易成交95.02亿元人民币；国内经济技术合作项目成交40亿元人民币。

港口运输　全区已经国家批准开放的一类口岸16个，其中：航空港2个；陆路口岸14个；现已建成开通的有13个。到2005年16个一类口岸的货物吞吐能力为1052万吨。1999年13个口岸完成外贸进出口货物运输总量为392万吨，比上年的306万吨增长12.81%，其中：出口48万吨；进口344万吨。按运输方式分：陆运387万吨；空运2万吨；海运3万吨。

涉外旅游　接待入境旅游和旅游购物者22万人次，旅游外汇收入8500万美元，比上年的8046万美元增长5.64%。

1999年香港对外经济贸易

国务院港澳事务办公室港澳研究所

1999年香港经济在经历了半个世纪以来最严峻的困境后走出衰退，本地生产总值从第三季起结束了持续长达六个季度的负增长，开始步入良性增长的轨道。1999年经济实质增长率达2.9%。

【对外贸易】

1999年香港出口总值13490亿元（港元，下同），扣除出口货物价格下跌因素后，比上年实质增长4%。在出口总值中，转口货值11784亿元，上升1.7%，扣除价格因素实质上升5%；港产品出口货值1706亿元，下跌9.5%，扣除价格因素实质下跌7%。进口总值13930亿元，下跌2.5%，扣除价格因素为微增0.2%。有形贸易赤字437亿元，相当于进口货值的3.1%，比上年的814亿元下降了46.3%。香港对外贸易明显好转，主要得益于亚洲各国经济复苏、祖国大陆、美国和欧盟等传统市场进口需求殷切，以及香港本地经济调整后成本下降导致的出口竞争力加强等因素。

港产品出口 港产品出口总值1706亿元，在上年下跌10.9%的基础上再跌9.5%，这也是自1996年以来连续第四年下跌。主要出口市场中，美国和祖国大陆仍占较大比重，其中对美国出口513.58亿元（占30.1%），比上年下降6.4%；对祖国大陆出口504.15亿元（占29.6%），比上年下降10.1%。

1999年港产品五大出口市场

国家或地区	金 额（亿港元）	比上年（%）	占总值（%）	
			1999年	1998年
美 国	513.58	-6.4	30.1	29.1
中 国	504.15	-10.1	29.6	29.8
英 国	103.92	3.3	6.1	5.3
德 国	85.43	-12.9	5.0	5.2
日 本	54.59	-15.2	3.2	3.4
总 计	**1706.00**	**-9.5**	**100.0**	**100.0**

转口贸易 1999年香港转口贸易持续好转，转口额11784.0亿元，在上年下降6.9%的基础上转为增长1.7%，扣除价格因素后实质增长为5%。在各主要转口市场中，祖国大陆由于下半年起出口明显好转，使得香港对祖国大陆供加工用的物料及资本设备的转口货值大幅增加，1999年转口货物实质增长3%；输往美国的转口货物由于美国内部需求殷切而大幅增长，1999年实质增长6%，大大超过1998年2%的增幅；对日本转口由于日元大幅升值而显著好转，1999年实质增长11%，与1998年12%的跌幅呈鲜明对比；此外，对亚洲、欧洲其他国家的转口因这些地区经济情况改善也有不同程度的升幅。

按转口货物的用途类别分析，转口总值中消费品所占比例最大，达46%，其次是原料及半成品、资本货物，分别占29%和23%。输往祖国大陆和台湾省的转口货物主要是工业加工用原料及半成品，其他市场主要为消费品。

祖国大陆仍是香港转口货物的最大来源地，占经港转口货物总值的61%。其他主要来源地包括日本（10%）、台湾省（6%）、美国（5%）及韩国（3%）。

1999年香港五大转口市场

国家或地区	金 额（亿港元）	比1998年（%）	占总值（%）	
			1999年	1998年
中 国	3991.88	-2.0	33.9	35.1
美 国	2694.44	3.7	22.9	22.4
日 本	675.06	5.2	5.7	5.5
英 国	455.41	7.8	3.9	3.6
德 国	441.22	4.7	3.7	3.6
总 计	**11784.00**	**1.7**	**100.0**	**100.0**

1999 年香港五大转口来源地

国家或地区	金　额（亿港元）	比上年（%）	占总值（%）	
			1999 年	1998 年
中　国	7201.26	4.2	61.1	59.6
日　本	1212.65	-2.1	10.3	10.7
台湾省	719.57	0.2	6.1	6.2
美　国	563.37	4.0	4.8	4.7
韩　国	388.22	-2.1	3.3	3.4
总　计	**11784.00**	**1.7**	**100.0**	**100.0**

进口　1999 年香港进口总值为 13927.18 亿元，同比下跌 2.5%。在主要进口国家和地区中，祖国大陆仍然是香港进口货物的最大来源地，占进口总值的 41.6%，比上年增长 4.6%，扣除价格因素则实质增长超过 8%。

在全部本地留用的进口货品中，按用途类别分析，食品下跌 4%、消费品下跌 16%、建筑机器下跌 14%、工业机器下跌 30%，只有办公室设备和燃料的货值分别增长 7% 和 26%。

1999 年香港五大进口国家或地区

国家或地区	金　额（亿港元）	比上年（%）	占总值（%）	
			1999 年	1998 年
中　国	5791.40	4.6	41.6	38.8
日　本	1699.05	-9.0	12.2	13.1
美　国	1013.26	-8.8	7.3	7.8
台湾省	995.07	-4.1	7.1	7.3
韩　国	686.22	-3.8	4.9	5.0
合　计	**13927.18**	**-2.5**	**100.0**	**100.0**

【旅游】

香港旅游业 1999 年持续复苏，访港旅客总人数 1068 万人次，比上年上升 12%；酒店房间平均入住率达 79%，较 1998 年的 76% 也有提高。按访港旅客来源地分析，祖国大陆和台湾省人数最多，分别占总数的 29% 和 19%，其余依次是南亚及东南亚、日本、美国及英国，分别占 13%、10%、8% 及 3%。按访港旅客人数升幅计，依次为南亚及东南亚（19%）、祖国大陆（19%）、台湾省（10%）、日本（8%）、美国（4%），来自英国的人数继续下降，跌幅为 5%。

1999 年香港居民外出旅游人数继 1998 年上升 14% 后，再增 12%，达 5314 万人次。其中，到祖国大陆旅游的人数增幅最大，达 15%，其余依次为台湾省（10%）及南亚和东南亚（5%）；前往澳门和北亚的人数分别减少了 12% 和 11%，前往美洲、欧洲以及大洋洲等长途目的地的人数分别下降了 8%、4% 及 3% 不等。赴祖国大陆的香港居民占香港居民离境总人数的 85%。

1999 年台湾省对外经济贸易

外经贸部国际贸易经济合作研究院

【对外贸易】

1999 年台湾省对外贸易已恢复到金融危机前稳步增长的态势。1999 年对外贸易总额为 2323.4 亿美元，比 1998 年的 2153.8 亿美元增长 7.9%。其中出口 1216.4 亿美元，较 1998 年的 1106.4 亿美元增长 10%；进口 1107 亿美元，比 1998 年的 1047.4 亿美元增长 5.8%，贸易顺差 109.4 亿美元，增长 84.9%，创近三年新高。截至 1999 年底台湾省外汇储备达 1062 亿美元。

出口商品结构 1999 年台湾省除农产加工品出口有所下降外，其他商品出口均有一定幅度增长。农产品出口 3.7 亿美元，占出口总额的 0.3%，比上年的 3.2 亿美元增长 15.2%；农产加工品出口 15.8 亿美元，占出口总值的 1.3%，比上年的 16.3 亿美元下降 3.0%；重化工业品出口 819.4 亿美元，占出口总值的 67.4%，比上年的 711 亿美元增长 15.3%；非重化工产品出口 377.4 亿美元，占出口总值的 31.0%，比上年的 375.8 亿美元增长了 0.5%。

1999 年台湾省出口商品结构

单位：亿美元

	1999 年		1998 年		增减比较	
	金额	%	金额	%	金额	%
出口金额	1216.4	100	1106.4	100	110	10.0
农产品	3.7	0.3	3.2	0.3	0.5	15.2
农产加工品	15.8	1.3	16.3	1.5	-0.5	-3.0
重化工业产品	819.4	67.4	711.0	64.3	108.4	15.3
非重化工业产品	377.4	31.0	375.8	34.0	1.6	0.5

1999 年台湾省主要出口商品

单位：亿美元

	1999 年		1998 年		增减比较	
	金额	%	金额	%	金额	%
出口总额	1216.4	100.0	1106.4	100.0	110.0	10.0
机械及电机设备	641.8	52.8	552.7	50.0	89.1	16.1
纺织品	141.8	11.7	145.5	13.2	-3.6	-2.5
基本金属及其制品	116.1	9.5	108.7	9.8	7.4	6.8
塑胶橡胶及其制品	75.3	6.2	68.7	6.2	6.6	9.6
车辆及运输设备	51.6	4.2	52.2	4.7	-0.6	-1.1
化学品	32.7	2.7	28.6	2.6	4.1	14.4

1999年台湾省主要出口商品（续）

单位：亿美元

	1999年		1998年		增减比较	
	金额	%	金额	%	金额	%
精密仪器、钟表	29.7	2.4	24.6	2.2	5.1	20.5
玩具、运动用品	17.8	1.5	19.0	1.7	-1.2	-6.3
皮革、毛皮制品	12.0	1.0	12.9	1.2	-0.9	-7.0
家具	17.2	1.4	15.8	1.4	1.4	9.1

进口商品结构 1999年台湾省除消费品进口有大幅度下降外，其他商品进口均有一定幅度增长。资本设备进口292.4亿美元，占进口总值的26.4%，比上年的234.1亿美元增长20.3%；农工原料进口710.4亿美元，占进口总值的64.2%，比上年的668.3亿美元增长6.4%，消费品进口104.2亿美元，占进口总值的9.4%，比上年的135.9亿美元下降23.4%。

1999年台湾省进口商品结构

单位：亿美元

	1999年		1998年		增减比较	
	金　额	%	金　额	%	金　额	%
进口总额	1107	100	1047.4	100.0	59.6	5.8
资本设备	292.4	26.4	243.1	23.2	49.3	20.3
农工原料	710.4	64.2	668.3	63.8	42.1	6.4
消费品	104.2	9.4	135.9	13.0	-31.7	-23.4

1999年台湾省主要进口商品

单位：亿美元

	1999年		1998年		增减比较	
	金　额	%	金　额	%	金　额	%
进口总额	1107	100.0	1047.4	100.0	59.6	5.8
机械及电机设备	506.0	45.7	429.3	41.0	76.7	17.9
化学品	106.0	9.6	99.5	9.5	6.5	6.5
基本金属及其制品	95.1	8.6	95.0	9.1	0.09	0.1
矿产品	91.5	8.3	78.1	7.5	13.4	17.1
精密仪器及钟表	61.9	5.6	51.8	4.9	10.1	19.4
车辆及运输设备	40.2	3.6	55.9	5.3	15.7	-28.1
纸浆、纸及印刷品	19.0	1.7	18.1	1.7	0.9	4.9
塑胶及其制品	30.1	2.7	27.2	2.6	2.8	10.4
珍珠、首饰、黄金	11.7	1.1	9.7	0.9	1.9	20.0
木材及其制品	11.7	1.1	12.2	1.2	-0.5	-4.1

进出口贸易市场 1999年台湾省的主要出口市场是美国、香港（含祖国大陆，下同）、欧洲、东盟五国及日本。其中对美国、香港、欧洲出口金额分别占台湾省出口总额的25.4%、21.4%、16.7%。1999年台湾省对外出口增长最快的国家是韩国、日本及东盟五国，分别较1998年增长75%、27.8%和21.4%。对美国、香港、欧洲出口也分别增长了5.2%、4.9%及3.5%。主要进口国家和地区为日本、美国、欧洲和东南亚地区。日本和美国是台湾省最大的进口市场，台湾省1999年自日本和美国进口金额分别为306亿美元及197亿美元，分别占台进口总额的27.6%及17.8%。

1999年台湾省的贸易顺差主要来自香港和美国，分别达到239亿美元和109亿美元。日本仍是台湾省最大的贸易逆差来源地，1999年逆差总额达186.9亿美元，创历年新高。

台湾省与祖国大陆的贸易情况 1999年台湾省与祖国大陆贸易总额为234.8亿美元，比上年增长14.5%，其中，大陆对台湾省出口39.5亿美元，较1998年增长2.1%，自台湾省进口195.3亿美元，较1998年增长17.4%，台湾省对大陆贸易顺差为15.8亿美元。

1999年台湾省输出到大陆的商品主要包括电机设备及其零部件、机械设备及其零件、塑料、橡胶及其制品、纺织原料及纺织制品、化工产品及相关工业产品、钢铁等，合计177.7亿美元，占台湾省输出到大陆商品金额的89.5%；台湾省自大陆输入的商品主要为电机设备及其零件、钢铁、机械设备及其零件、矿物燃料与矿油及其蒸馏产品、石灰及水泥等，合计29.15亿美元，占台湾省自大陆输入商品金额的74.7%。

【利用外资】

海外华侨和外国人在台湾省直接投资

1999年海外华侨和外国人在台湾投资总额为41.8亿美元，较上年增长26%，创近年来较高增幅，仅次于1997年的42.6亿美元。

台湾省对外投资 1999年经台湾省“经济部”核准的对外投资金额（不含祖国大陆）达到30.68亿美元，较上年同期增长0.88%。其中对美国投资4.08亿美元，下降25.73%，对欧洲5793万美元，增长89.6%；对大洋洲投资4060万美元，增长379.3%。在亚洲地区，对日本投资1.22亿美元，增长367%；新加坡3.2亿美元，增长161.5%；香港地区8544万美元，增长32%；马来西亚1324万美元，下降28.3%；泰国1.97亿美元下降0.7%；越南3427万美元，下降68.8%；菲律宾2920万美元，下降80.6%，台湾省对东南亚地区投资总体呈衰退趋势。

从行业上看，运输仓储业、营造业和商业是台商投资增长较快的三个行业。金融保险业和制造业对外投资则分别下降15.5%及37.1%。

台商在祖国大陆的投资 1999年经台湾省“经济部”核准的台商到大陆投资488件，投资金额为12.5亿美元，与上年相比，投资件数及投资金额分别下降了23.8%及17.5%。台商投资的减少主要与亚洲金融危机，台湾当局岛内爆发的财务危机，以及台湾当局继续实施“戒急用忍”政策等因素相关。台商到大陆投资主要集中在电子业、金属工业、塑胶制品业、精密器械等行业。台商投资金额最多的省份为福建、广东、江苏。

1999年澳门对外经济贸易

国务院港澳事务办公室港澳研究所

【对外贸易】

据澳门特区政府统计，1999年澳门对外贸易总值为338.80亿元（澳门元，下同，约合43.44亿美元），比上年的326.8亿元增长3.54%。其中进口总值为163亿元，同比增长4.5%；出口总值175.80亿元，同比增长2.9%。在总出口中，澳门本地产品出口货值150.44亿元，同比增长0.9%；转口货值23.36亿元，同比大增16.3%。贸易逆差12.80亿元，比上年减少了13.9%。

1999年澳门对外贸易主要指标

单位：亿澳门元

	1999年	1998年	变动率（%）
总出口	175.80	170.84	2.9
本地产品出口	150.44	149.04	0.9
转口	25.36	21.80	16.3
进口	163.00	155.97	4.5
贸易差额	12.80	14.87	-13.9

出口 年内澳门对外贸易增长主要得益于周边地区经济回升，以及主要贸易伙伴进口需求强劲。根据出口货物类别分析，占总出口货值比重83.8%的“纺织品及成衣”类别出口比上年上升2.0%；“非纺织品”类别的出口货值虽占总出口比重不大，但升幅为7.9%，其中“水泥”、“鞋类”出口货值大幅增加。

按主要商品类别统计的出口货值

单位：亿澳门元

	1999年	比重%	1998年	比重%	变动率（%）
纺织品及成衣	147.28	83.8	144.42	84.5	2.0
成衣：					
针织	75.78	43.1	76.17	44.6	-0.5
梭织	53.47	30.4	54.29	31.8	-1.5
纺织布料	11.23	6.4	7.63	4.5	47.2
纺织纱及线	5.68	3.2	5.36	3.1	6.0
其他	1.13	0.6	0.97	0.6	17.0
非纺织品	28.51	16.2	26.42	15.5	7.9
机器及设备	6.59	3.7	6.01	3.5	9.6

按主要商品类别统计的出口货值（续）

单位：亿澳门元

	1999年	比重%	1998年	比重%	变动率（%）
鞋类	5.03	2.9	3.83	2.2	31.2
水泥	1.40	0.8	0.99	0.6	41.5
其他	15.50	8.8	15.58	9.1	-0.6
总　计	**175.80**	**100.0**	**170.84**	**100.0**	**2.9**

按出口目的地统计，澳门出口货值的77.1%集中在美国和欧盟两大市场，其中美国占46.9%，欧盟占30.2%。对这两个市场的出口分别比上年增长了1.3%和1.8%。祖国大陆和香港共占澳门总出口货值的16.0%，其中祖国大陆占9.2%，香港占6.8%。1999年对祖国大陆出口大增39.7%，而对香港却减少了8.1%。

按主要市场统计的出口货值

单位：亿澳门元

	1999年	比重%	1998年	比重%	变动率（%）
美　国	82.49	46.9	81.41	47.7	1.3
欧　盟	53.04	30.2	52.10	30.5	1.8
中　国	16.17	9.2	11.57	6.8	39.7
日　本	1.12	0.6	1.40	0.7	-2.1
台湾省	2.13	1.2	2.51	1.5	-14.7
香　港	11.95	6.8	13.01	7.6	-8.1
澳大利亚	0.40	0.2	0.40	0.2	0.2
其　他	8.50	4.8	8.71	5.1	-2.4
总　计	**175.80**	**100.0**	**170.84**	**100.0**	**2.9**

进口　1999年澳门总进口货值上升了4.5%。上升的原因主要是在进口货值中占较大比重的“资本货物”、“消费品”及“燃料及润滑油”分别增加了43.0%、7.9%和2.3%。但由于受经济衰退影响，内部需求持续疲软，用于加工出口的“原料及半成品”进口则下跌32%。

按主要商品类别统计的进口货值

单位：亿澳门元

	1999年	比重%	1998年	比重%	变动率（%）
消费品	40.40	26.6	40.24	25.8	7.9
原料及半成品	87.81	53.9	90.68	58.1	-3.2
燃料及润滑油	10.12	6.2	9.89	6.3	2.3
资本货物	21.66	13.3	15.15	9.7	43.0
总　计	**163.00**	**100.0**	**155.97**	**100.0**	**4.5**

澳门进口主要来自邻近的亚洲国家与地区，其中祖国大陆与香港占澳门进口总值的比重为53.7%。1999年，澳门从大陆进口与1998年相比增长了14.1%，而从香港进口却下跌了20.3%。其他增长比较多的国家和地区有欧盟、美国、韩国等。

按主要来源地统计的进口货值

单位：亿澳门元

	1999年	比重%	1998年	比重%	变动率（%）
中　国	58.09	35.6	50.92	32.6	14.1
香　港	29.45	18.1	36.96	23.7	-20.3
欧　盟	21.03	12.9	16.41	10.5	28.1
台湾省	15.50	9.5	15.37	9.9	0.8
日　本	10.84	6.7	12.08	7.7	-10.3
美　国	8.31	5.1	7.33	4.7	13.3
韩　国	5.02	3.1	4.08	2.6	22.9
澳大利亚	1.79	1.1	1.17	0.8	52.5
其　他	12.98	8.0	11.63	7.5	11.6
总　计	**163.00**	**100.0**	**155.97**	**100.0**	**4.5**

【旅游】

据澳门旅游局统计，1999年入境旅客总人数为744.39万人次，比上年的695万人次增加7.13%，其中第四季度与1998年同期相比上升12.86%，呈加速上升趋势。1999年平均酒店房间入住率为58.52%，略高于上年，但旅客平均留宿时间则只有1.43晚，比上年的0.24晚略有下降。

祖国大陆到澳旅客人数刷新历史纪录，达164万人次，比上年增加100%，成为澳门第二大客源市场。1999年是澳门的“回归年”，治安状况的好转是澳门旅游市场在沉寂了两年后开始回升的主要因素。

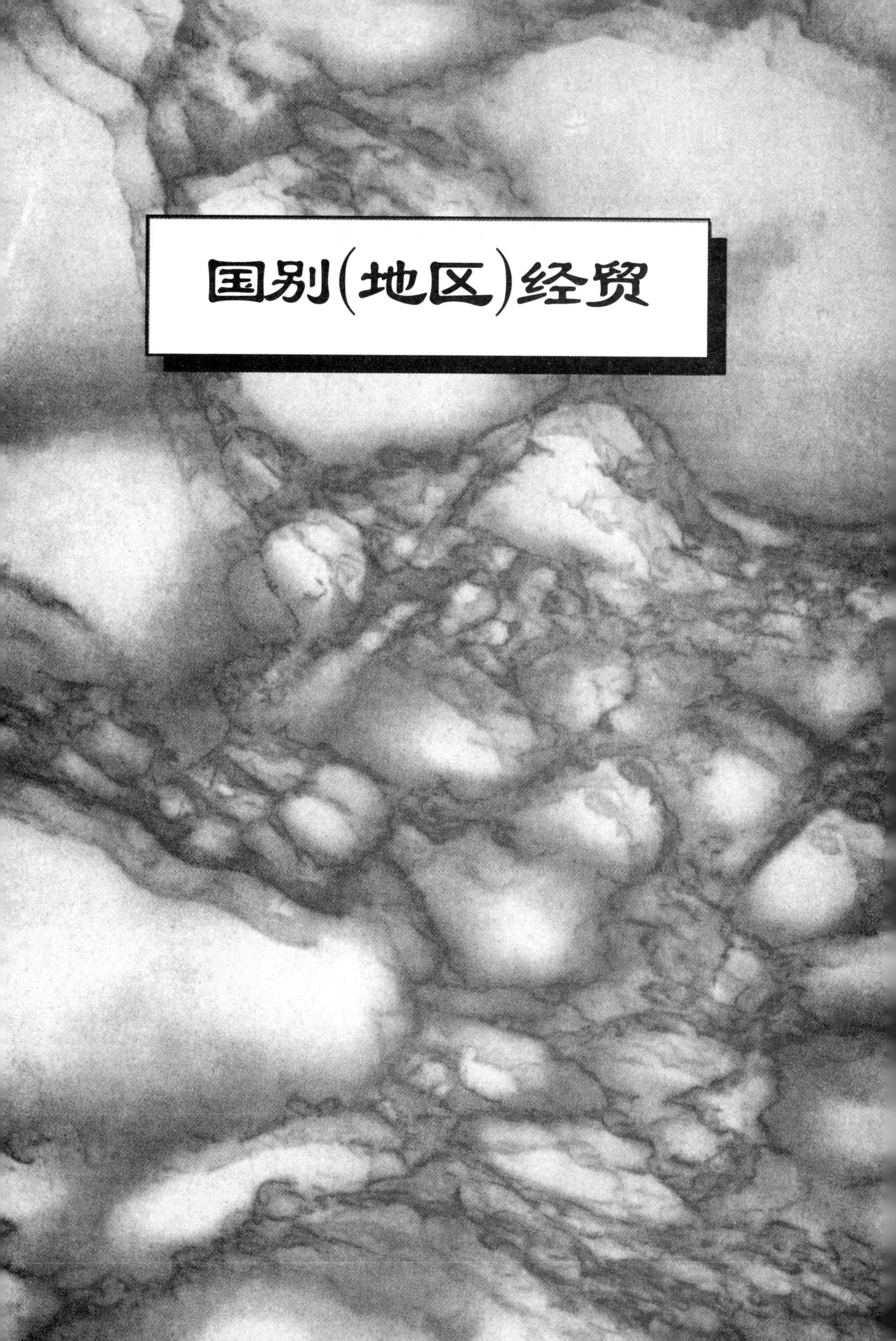

国别(地区)经贸

1999 年中国内地与港、澳地区的经济贸易关系

国务院港澳事务办公室港澳研究所

1999 年，尽管面对复杂多变的内外经济环境，祖国内地与香港地区的经贸合作仍取得了长足发展；这一年，澳门顺利回归祖国，使祖国内地与澳门的经贸关系进入了一个新的历史阶段。祖国内地与港澳地区在贸易、投资、金融、旅游等领域合作关系的不断增强及合作层次的提高，也促进了内地及港澳地区经济、贸易的稳定增长。

一、贸易往来

据我海关统计，1999 年内地与香港进出口贸易额为 437.83 亿美元，比上年下降 3.6%，占当年我进出口总额的 12.1%；其中内地对香港出口 368.91 亿美元，比上年下降 4.8%，占当年我出口总额的 18.9%；内地从香港进口 68.92 亿美元，比上年增加 3.5%，占我当年进口总额的 4.2%，香港仍是内地第三大贸易伙伴及第二大出口市场。内地对香港出口的回升及进口额的增加，显示了两地贸易开始摆脱上年的颓势，逐步恢复增长。

另据香港特区政府统计，内地仍为香港最大的转口来源地和转口市场。1999 年香港转口内地商品 7201.26 亿港元，较上年增加 4.2%；海外经港转口运往内地商品 3991.88 亿港元，较上年下降 2.0%。内地产品经港转口市场主要集中在欧美地区，其中美国占 1/3 以上，其余依次为日本、德国、英国等国家。香港对内地转口产品则来自日本、台湾、韩国等亚洲国家和地区。加工贸易是两地贸易的一项重要内容。据香港特区政府统计 1999 年 1—9 月两地加工贸易值达 10547 亿港元，其中运往内地加工的港产原料及半成品总值为 277 亿港元，经港转口内地的外地原材料及半制成品总值为 1700 亿美元，内地加工后返销香港的制成品总值为 3496 亿港元，加上转口毛利再转销海外的产品总值达 4123 亿港元。从近年内地与香港贸易的发展看，有形商品贸易的增长有逐渐放缓的趋势。其原因在于：一是随着内地对外贸易条件的改善，经港转口比重下降；二是离岸贸易和转运贸易增多，部分取代了转口贸易；三是香港产业升级缓慢，加工贸易的互补优势减弱；四是香港本地贸易商经营成本商，利润回报低；五是两地口岸、交通、海关等基础设施和管理服务亟待改善。

1999 年祖国内地与澳门进出口总额为 7.34 亿美元，比上年下降 15.7%；其中内地对澳门出口 6.37 亿美元，较上年下降 14.7%；内地自澳门进口 0.97 亿美元，较上年下降 21.2%。据海关统计，1999 年内地对香港出口的前 15 种主要商品为：纺织原料及纺织制品 112.18 亿美元；机电产品 99.51 亿美元；家具、玩具及杂项制品 18.75 亿美元；贱金属及其产品 17.97 亿美元；珠宝、贵金属及其制品 16.99 亿美元；光学、医疗仪器、钟表等 14.25 亿美元；塑料及其制品、橡胶及其制品 11.31 亿美元；化学工业及其相关工业产品 10.02 亿美元；车辆、航空器、船舶及运输设备等 9.39 亿美元；矿物燃料、矿物油及其产品 9.39 亿美元，上述商品的出口额总计为 319.76 亿美元，占当年内地对香港出口额的 86.7%。

1999 年内地从香港进口的前 10 种主要商品为：机电产品 26.75 亿美元；纺织原料及纺织制品 17.93 亿美元；塑料及其制品、橡胶及其制品 4.68 亿美元；光学、医疗等仪器、钟表及乐器等 4.62 亿美元；化学工业及相关工业的产品 3.68 亿美元；贱金属及其制品 3.08 亿美元；纤维素浆、纸等产品 2.90 亿美元；珠宝贵金属及制品 1.43 亿美元；家具、玩具及杂项制品 0.99 亿美元；生皮、皮革及其制品、旅行箱包等 0.65 亿美元。上述商品进口额合计 66.75 亿美元。占当年内地从香港进口的 96.8%。

1999 年内地对澳门出口的主要商品为：纺织原料及纺织制品、活动物及动物产品、机电产品、食品及饮料等。

1999 年内地自澳门进口的主要商品为：纺织原料及纺织制品、玻璃及其制品、纤维素浆、纸产品等。

二、相互投资

香港是内地吸引境外投资的首要来源地。据外经贸部统计，从 1979 年到 1999 年底，香港在内地累计投资项目数为 184823 个，占同期全国引进外资总数的 54%；协议港资金额 3096 亿美元，占同期全国协议外资总额的 50%；实际利用港资金额为 1545.58 亿美元占同期全国实际利用外资总额的 50%。其中，1999 年内地吸收香港地区直接投资的项目数为 5876 个，较上年下降 24.9%，占全国同期引进外资项目数的 34.3%；协议港资金额为 130.48 亿美元，较上年下降 21.0%，占全国同期协议外资金额的 31.6%；实际利用港资金额 158.43 亿美元，较上年下降 15.7%，占同期全国实际利用外资总额的 39.2%。

另据香港政府统计，截至 1998 年底按市值计算的香港对外直接投资总额为 17344 亿港元，其中对中国内地的投资占香港对外直接投资总额的 32%，是香港除英属维尔京群岛外第二大对外投资地；同期香港外来投资总额为 17440 亿港元，其中来自中国内地的投资占 12%，是香港除英属维尔京群岛和百慕大群岛外第三大投资来源地。

1999 年，内地引进澳门直接投资项目 255 个，较上年下降 3.4%；协议金额 4.35 亿美元，较上年下降 0.6%；实际利用澳门资金 3.3 亿美元，与上年持平。从 1979 年到 1999 年底，澳门对内地累计直接投资项目 6419 个，协议澳门投资金额 93.41 亿美元，实际利用澳门投资金额 36.74 亿美元。

另一方面，内地也是港澳地区外来投资的主要来源地之一。目前经内地有关部门正式批准的驻港澳中资企业分别为 1800 多家和 200 多家。据香港中资企业协会调查显示，1997 年中资企业的贸易额占香港贸易总额的 5.2%；中资银行的资产、存款和贷款分别占 10%、23% 和 8%；中资控股的上市公司约 80 家；中资旅游业收入约占香港旅游业收入的 25%；中资建筑企业承建的工程约占香港建筑工程总值量的 12%。

在澳门，中资是第一大外来资金，在工业、贸易、金融、旅游、建筑、交通运输、保险等领域都占有相当的比重。其中在金融保险业占 50%、贸易占 45%、旅游酒店业占 50%、房地产建筑业占 50%。长期以来，中资企业在沟通港澳与中国内地的经济联系、保持港澳地区繁荣稳定等方面起着积极的不可低估的作用。

三、金融合作

香港一直是中国内地在境外筹集资金的主要地点，除通过发行债券、筹组银团贷款等传统融资形式外，国企在香港证券市场挂牌上市成为 90 年代以来内地利用香港资本市场融资的一种重要方式。截至 1999 年底，已有 44 家内地国有企业在港发行 H 股，还有 50 多家香港中资企业通过不同形式实现上市，H 股和红筹股总市值达 12000 多亿港元，占港股总市值 48000 亿港元的 25%左右。

内地对香港金融业的参与程度也在不断提高。现在与内地有关的银团贷款、项目融资、贸易融资等已成为许多香港银行的主要业务。截至 1998 年底，香港认可机构对内地机构的对外负债约 2910 亿港元，对外债权达 3240 亿港元；中资企业在香港已拥有 90 多家金融机构，其中持牌银行 19 家；中资保险公司的保费收入占香港保费总额的 21%。

另一方面，据中国人民银行业务统计，截至 1999 年底，有 13 家香港银行在中国内地开设分支机构 36 家，占 182 家外资银行在华开设营业性金融机构家数总和的 20%。

四、旅游及其他

旅游 据香港旅游协会统计，1999 年内地因公及旅游探亲访港人数为 308.39 万人次，占全部访港旅客人数的 28.9%，较上年增长 18.7%，内地仍为香港第一大旅客来源地；同年香港居民到内地进行商务活动、旅游和探亲者为 4517.52 万人次，占香港居民离港外出 5314.37 万总人次的 85%。

据澳门方面统计，1999 年内地居民访澳为 164.52 万人次，占访澳旅客总人次 744.39 万的 22.1%，比上年增长 101.4%；内地旅客在澳人均消费为 2395 澳门元，比全部访澳旅客人均消费额 1327 澳门元多 1068 元。内地客源已成为振兴澳门旅游市场的一个重要因素。

承包工程与劳务合作 据外经贸部业务统计，1999 年内地新签对港承包工程、劳务合作和设计咨询合同 1012 份，合同金额 29.27 亿美元，完成营业额 21.92 亿美元，分别占全国同期对外承包工程和劳务合作总数的 4.8%、15.9% 和 19.5%；同年内地对澳门新签承包工程、劳务合作、设计咨询合同 670 份，合同金额 1.27 亿美元，完成营业额 2.49

亿美元，分别占全国总数的3.2%、0.98%和2.22%。

航运　香港是著名的国际航运中心，1999年在激烈的角逐中超过新加坡，再次成为全球最大的货柜港。香港港口及航运局统计表明，1999年香港集装箱吞吐总量为1621.1万个标准集装箱，比上年增长10.4%，而内河航运的集装箱运量却大增25%。因此香港集装箱运输量的增长主要得益于中国内地外贸活动的出色表现。

五、前景展望

从今后内地与香港经贸合作的发展前景看，仍有较大的增长潜力。双方经济具有很强的互补性，互为对方最重要的贸易、投资和经济合作伙伴的格局在相当长的时间内不会改变，也很难有第三者能取代两地目前的这种关系。随着内地加入世贸组织，及香港产业升级和结构调整，两地合作将由现在的与贸易有关的领域向更高层次发展，内地对香港国际金融中心、航运中心和信息中心的需求进一步加强。内地中心城市和中西部地区有望成为港商投资的新热点。两地进出口贸易，转口贸易及转运贸易仍将继续增长，同时无形贸易所占比重将增长。这些经贸合作无疑将促进两地经济更加繁荣发展。

2000年是澳门回归祖国的第一年，特区政府提出致力于建立一个自由开放、公平竞争的市场环境，以此来推动和引导经济复苏和发展。可以预期澳门将有望摆脱经济持续低迷不景的困境，实现社会经济的和谐、稳定增长。在此基础上，澳门与内地的经贸合作将开创出层次提高、领域广泛、规模扩大的新局面。

1999年中国与日本的经济贸易关系

对外贸易经济合作部亚洲司一处

一、双边贸易情况

（一）中日贸易统计

1999年中日贸易实现全面增长，扭转了1998年大幅下滑的局面并创历史新高。据中国海关统计，双边进出口贸易总额达661.67亿美元，同比增长14.2%；其中中方出口323.99亿美元，增长9.2%；进口337.68亿美元，增长19.4%。中方逆差13.69亿美元，是自1995年以来中国首次对日入超。1999年中日贸易额占中国对外贸易总额的18.4%，日本连续七年保持中国第一大贸易伙伴地位。

（二）主要进出口商品情况

1999年中国对日主要出口商品为：机电产品（94.4亿美元）、服装及衣着附件（88.1亿美元）、鞋类（16.1亿美元）、纺织品纱线、织物及制品（14.8亿美元）、蔬菜（9.3亿美元）、水海产品（8.4亿美元）、原油（5.6亿美元）、旅行用品及箱包（5.4亿美元）、电动机及发电机（4.7亿美元）、煤炭（3.9亿美元）等。服装、纺织品、鞋类等生活消费品出口由衰转盛，成为出口增长的首要拉动力；机电产品增势强劲，粮油食品类增长放缓；能源产品不景气状况依然持续，原材料产品出口出现改善迹象。1999年8月，日本政府宣布终止针对进口中国棉府绸的设限调查，这对于保持中日纺织品贸易的稳定发展具有积极意义。

1999年中国自日主要进口商品为：机电产品（203.2亿美元）、集成电路及微电子组件（24.7亿美元）、钢材（23.3亿美元）、初级形状的塑料（17.7亿美元）、自动数据处理设备零件（8.5亿美元）、通断及保护电路装置及零件（7.3亿美元）、二极管晶体管及类似半导体器件（6.9亿美元）、电视收音机无线电讯设备零附件（5.9亿美元）、合成纤维长丝机织物（5.9亿美元）、未锻造的铜及铜材（5.4亿美元）等。机电设备及零件进口全面增长，其中运输工具相关零配件进口增长最为迅猛；原材料进口保持增势，而纺织用合成纤维、聚丙烯腈纤维等纺织用化纤原料进口大幅减少，金属加工机床、金属轧机及零件以及汽车和汽车底盘减幅较大。

（三）中日技术贸易

据外经贸部业务统计，1999年中国从日本引进技术设备共994项，较上年下降28.3%，合同金额19.4亿美元，较上年下降7%。自日引进的主要项目有秦山三期项目（气体绝缘开关）、北京燕山乙烯装置回收系统改造项目、安徽氯碱化工集团日产150吨烧碱项目、北京地铁项目（车辆电气设备）、广州本田汽车技术转让项目、华东电力集团公司500千伏变压器项目等。

二、中日资金合作情况

（一）日本对华直接投资

受亚洲金融动荡和国内经济结构调整等因素的影响，日本企业对华投资开始进入调整期。1999年日本企业对华投资继续下降，全年投资项目数1136个，较上年下降4.4%；合同外资金额24.89亿美元，下降7.8%；实际使用外资金额30.03亿美元，下降4.9%。对华投资合同金额在中国吸引外资国（地区）别中居第五位，实际使用金额居第三位。截至1999年底，中国累计批准日本企业对华投资项目18738个，合同金额350.32亿美元，实际使用249.15亿美元。经历一个时期的调整后，中日两国在技术资金密集型领域以及中西部地区的资金合作可望有更大发展。

（二）中日政府资金合作

日元贷款是中日经济合作的重要内容。从1979年至2000年，中国已利用四批日元贷款。累计协议金额达22609亿日元，项目109个，用于中国五年计划中的重点和骨干项目的建设，分布在交通、能源等制约国民经济发展的领域。日本政府贷款约占外国政府向中国承诺贷款额的50%，居首位。第四批日元贷款于1996至2000年的五年间分前三年和后两年即“3+2”方式两次承诺实施。

从1981年至今，中国共接受日本无偿援助约1120.63亿日元，用于98个项目的建设，涉及教育、医疗、农业、环保等领域。其中，1999年度日本对华无偿援助金额为43.5亿日元，项目为6个。

三、重要经贸往来

3月，外经贸部首席谈判代表龙永图与日本驻华大使谷野作太郎就中日无偿资金合作“中国长江大堤加固计划”和“粮食增产援助”项目签字换文，4月双方就“卫生部预防接种扩大计划”项目换文确认。

4月，外经贸部陈新华副部长主持外经贸部与日本国际贸易促进协会访华团的座谈会，双方就如何扩大中日贸易和对华投资等问题交换了意见。

7月，外经贸部石广生部长会见随同小渊首相来访的日本外相高村正彦和邮政相野田圣子，就结束关于中国加入世界贸易组织的中日双边谈判交换意见。7月9日，朱镕基总理与小渊首相举行会谈，会后双方发表联合新闻公报，宣布两国就中国加入世界贸易组织的双边谈判达成协议。

10月，外经贸部马秀红部长助理率团访日参加大阪商务大会和东京中国投资洽谈会、演讲会。

10月，外经贸部孙振宇副部长会见日中经济协会访华团，介绍了中国外经贸形势和中日双边经贸发展趋势以及中国入世谈判进展、吸引外资新措施、规范加工贸易管理的新办法等。

11月，外经贸部石广生部长出席在北京举行的中日投资促进机构第九次联席会议。

1999年中国与东盟国家的经济贸易关系

对外贸易经济合作部亚洲司二处

1999年4月30日，柬埔寨正式加入东盟，10国（文莱、柬埔寨、印尼、老挝、马来西亚、缅甸、菲律宾、新加坡、泰国和越南）大东盟最终形成。随着东盟各国经济的复苏，1999年我与东盟各国的经贸往来也出现了回升的势头。

一、双边贸易

1999年，我与东盟国家的双边贸易大幅回升，全年贸易总额达272亿美元，比上年增长15%，创历史最高水平。其中我出口123亿美元，进口149亿美元，分别比上年增长11%和18%。我对东盟出口的主要商品有机电产品、纺织品和服装、成品油和粮食等，其中机电产品的出口比上年增长20%，达60亿美元，占总出口的49%。我从东盟进口的主要商品为电子产品、原油、液化石油气和成品油、植物油、木材及其制品和化工原料等。

二、经济技术合作

1999年，东盟来华投资继续下降。东盟国家共新签来华投资项目931项，比上年下降6%；协议投资金额31.3亿美元，下降21%；实际投入金额32.9亿美元，下降20%。

1999年我与东盟国家承包工程和劳务合作出现恢复性增长，全年我与东盟国家共签订承包劳务、设计咨询合同2817份，比上年增长21%，合同金额25亿美元，完成营业额18亿美元，分别比上年增长10%和5%。

三、重要经贸往来

1999年，中国与东盟各国政府经贸主管部门继续保持着频繁密切的高层经贸往来。

1月，外经贸部副部长张祥与陪同老挝总理西沙瓦来访的贸易旅游部长富米·提帕汶举行了对口会谈。中国－东盟经贸研讨会在北京举行，外经贸部首席谈判代表龙永图出席开幕式并致词。

2月，外经贸部副部长孙广相会见了随越共中央总书记黎可漂访华的越贸易部长张庭选。

4月，外经贸部副部长刘向东率中国经贸代表团访泰并出席在曼谷召开的“中国与东盟国家经贸合作研讨会暨项目洽谈会”。孙广相副部长率中国政府经贸代表团赴新加坡、柬埔寨访问。泰国商业部副部长巴威集访华。

6月，外经贸部副部长陈新华与随同缅甸国家和平与发展委员会第一秘书长钦纽访华的缅“和发会”主席府部长埃博尔及缅商务部部长觉丹举行了会谈。马来西亚初级产品工业部部长林敬益率团访华。

8月，应外经贸部石广生部长邀请，新加坡贸工部长杨荣文准将率政府及企业家代表团访华。陈新华副部长会见了陪同马哈蒂尔总理来访的马来西亚贸工部副部长郭洙镇。孙广相副部长会见并宴请了来访的柬埔寨农村发展部国务秘书李图一行。

9月，陈新华副部长会见了来访的越南农业与农村发展部副部长阮善伦。

12月，陈新华副部长与到访的缅甸外长吴温昂就双边经贸合作举行了会谈。

1999年中国与南亚及部分西亚国家的经济贸易关系

对外贸易经济合作部亚洲司三处

一、双边贸易

1999年，中国与南亚8国（印度、巴基斯坦、孟加拉国、尼泊尔、斯里兰卡、马尔代夫、阿富汗和不丹）的贸易总额为41.78亿美元，较上年增长6.64%，其中我出口29.28亿美元，进口12.50亿美元，分别较上年增长13.23%和下降6.16%。1999年中国与南亚国家贸易主要呈现如下几个特点：一是由于国内经济形势稳定，我对南亚国家的出口呈现旺盛增长势头；二是国际社会因核试验对印、巴的制裁趋于松动，其外汇短缺状况有所缓和，对中国商品需求上升较快，1999年我对印、巴出口增长均超过10%；三是中尼（泊尔）贸易额达创纪录水平，成为我与南亚国家贸易的一个亮点，其中我对尼出口增长209.6%，达2.07亿美元。

中国对南亚国家出口的主要商品有机电产品、化工及医药原料、生丝、焦炭、钢材、水泥、纺织品等。中国从南亚国家进口的主要商品有铁矿砂、铬矿石、皮革和纺织原料等。

1999年我同西亚国家三国（土耳其、伊朗、塞浦路斯）的贸易额为21.34亿美元，其中我出口14.01亿美元，进口7.33亿美元，较上年分别增长了6.81%、0.4%和21.76%。其中我对伊朗贸易再创历史新高，达到13.47亿美元，较上年增长10.9%；中国对土贸易有所下降，但我自土进口增长了10.6%，贸易不平衡状况有所改善。

我对上述三国主要的出口商品有纺织品、机电产品及成套设备、五矿及化工产品、仪器仪表、工农具等；主要进口商品有原油、钢材、铬矿石等。

二、经济技术合作

1999年我同南亚国家新签承包劳务合同297项，合同金额4.82亿美元，营业额6.17亿美元，派出劳务人员5635人次；我同西亚三国新签承包劳务合同57项，合同金额1.16亿美元，营业额2.18亿美元，派出劳务人员1156人次。该地区继续保持我承包工程重要市场的地位。1999年，中国政府继续向南亚部分国家提供力所能及的援助，同巴基斯坦、尼泊尔、孟加拉等国政府签订了新的援助协议，新提供无偿援助1.38亿元人民币，优惠贷款1亿元人民币。

三、重要经贸往来

1999年1月，孙广相副部长会见了应外交部邀请来访的土耳其外交部次长哈吉·塔内尔一行；3月，陈新华副部长率政府经贸代表团访问伊朗和土耳其；6月，石广生部长会见了随同塞浦路斯总统访华的塞工商旅游部长尼科斯·罗兰迪斯；11月，中、印度经贸研讨会在京举行，周可仁副部长出席并致辞；11月29日，中国和伊朗经贸科技合作联委会第十次会议在京举行，吴仪国务委员和来访的伊朗副总统哈什米共同主持了会议，期间，江泽民主席、胡锦涛副主席、钱其琛副总理分别会见了哈什米。

1999年中国与西亚国家的经济贸易关系

对外贸易经济合作部西亚非洲司一处

西亚国家包括海湾合作委员会六国（沙特、阿联酋、科威特、巴林、卡塔尔、阿曼）、约旦、叙利亚、黎巴嫩、伊拉克、也门、巴勒斯坦、以色列等13个国家。1999年中国与上述国家的经贸合作取得可喜的进展。

一、双边贸易

据中国海关统计，1999年中国与西亚13国的进出口贸易额为67.8亿美元，比上年增长11.9%。其中，中国出口38.9亿美元，比上年增长14%；中国进口28.9亿美元，比上年增长9.3%。

1999年中国对这一地区出口额最大的国家是阿联酋，达14.4亿美元，其次是沙特和以色列，分别为9.5亿美元和4.9亿美元。

中国从这一地区进口额最大的国家是沙特，达9.1亿美元，其次是阿曼和也门，进口额分别为6.4亿美元和5.6亿美元。

中国对西亚13国出口的主要产品是机电产品，约占中国对这一地区出口总额的37.5%；其次是服装和纺织品，约占中国对这一地区出口总额的28.4%，其中服装6.78亿美元，纺织品4.28亿美元。除此之外，中国向西亚13国鞋类出口达3.57亿美元，轮胎出口超过1亿美元。

中国从西亚13国进口的主要产品是原油和成品油，金额达17.3亿美元，占中国从其进口总额的59.9%；其次是液化石油气，金额为4.9亿美元；其他还有聚乙烯、聚丙烯、铝锭等。

中国与西亚13国双边贸易有较大的互补性，西亚地区的原油、成品油、化肥及各种石化产品是中国需求较多的商品，同时上述西亚国家（特别是海湾六国）具有较强的购买力，是中国开展市场多元化战略的重点市场。此外，海湾六国拥有庞大的海外资本，是我开展外资引进的重要地区；而西亚13

国的加工工业水平都较低，我应重视在这些国家开展境外加工贸易。

二、经济技术合作

（一）承包劳务

截止1999年底，中国公司在西亚13国共签订承包工程、劳务合作及设计咨询合同4877项，合同额累计67.97亿美元，完成营业额累计48.57亿美元。其中，1999年签订合同540项，合同金额5.8亿美元。完成营业额5.5亿美元，比上年增长41%。1999年在西亚13国执行合同的中国承包劳务人员有29000多人。

（二）对外援助

1999年，中国向西亚地区的约旦、叙利亚、伊拉克、也门提供了经济援助。当年竣工的项目有叙利亚哈马毛纺厂更新梳棉设备项目，目前正在援建的项目有也门萨那立交桥项目。

三、重要经贸往来

1999年，中国与西亚国家的重要经贸往来包括：

10月，江泽民主席出访沙特，随访的外经贸部石广生部长与沙特财经大臣共同主持召开中沙第二届经贸混委会，并签署会议纪要，石部长还与沙油矿大臣签署了《中沙混委会四个工作组工作文件》和《中沙两国政府石油合作备忘录》。3月和11月，李鹏委员长先后出访叙利亚、以色列、巴勒斯坦和阿曼。6月，外经贸部孙广相副部长率技术贸易代表团出访以色列。8月，外经贸部龙永图副部长率团赴黎巴嫩出席77国集团会议，并与黎方就发展双边经贸合作进行了探讨。10月，外经贸部周可仁副部长率政府经贸代表团出访伊拉克，主持召开中伊第十届经贸混委会。

3月，也门副总统访华，外经贸部孙广相副部长与随访的也门工业部长举行了两次对口会谈。4月，卡塔尔埃米尔访华，双方签署两国政府《鼓励和相互保护投资协定》。3月，以色列总统魏茨曼访华，石广生部长出席中以企业家经贸研讨会并致辞。6月，巴林财经大臣访华，双方签署两国政府《鼓励和相互保护投资协定》。9月，沙特商业大臣访华并参加99投资洽谈会。12月，约旦计划部秘书长访华，与外经贸部何晓卫部长助理共同主持召开中约第四届经贸混委会。此外，4月巴勒斯坦总统访华，12月约旦国王访华，外经贸部孙振宇副部长和周可仁副部长分别参加了有关活动。

1999年中国与非洲国家的经贸关系

对外贸易经济合作部西亚非洲司协调处

中国和非洲国家互补性强，合作潜力很大。非洲大陆自然资源丰富，中国的成套设备和技术已具有较高的质量和水平，机电、轻工产品及服装、纺织品也十分适合非洲的需要。随着经济“全球化”趋势的不断加强和各自经济和社会的发展，双方合作的领域会越来越宽。

一、双边贸易

据中国海关统计，1999年中国与非洲国家的进出口贸易总额为64.84亿美元，比上年增长17.2%，其中向非洲出口41.09亿美元，同比增长1.3%；自非洲进口23.75亿美元，同比增长60.9%。1999年，中国同非洲地区进出口额超过1亿美元的国家有14个，居前四位的分别为南非、埃及、尼日利亚和安哥拉，其中以南非为最大贸易伙伴，双边贸易额为17.22亿美元。中国向非洲出口较多的国家有南非（8.61亿美元）、埃及（7.16亿美元）、尼日利亚（3.96亿美元）、摩洛哥（2.54亿美元）、苏丹（2.29亿美元）、科特迪瓦（1.98亿美元）、阿尔及利亚（1.60亿美元）、贝宁（1.59亿美元）、加纳（1.10亿美元）和肯尼亚（1.01亿美元）等国家；中国自该地区进口较多的国家有南非（8.61亿美元）、安哥拉（3.56亿美元）、加蓬

(2.27 亿美元)、尼日利亚（1.82 亿美元）、赤道几内亚（1.67 亿美元）等。

1999 年中国对非洲贸易的一大特点是，我从非洲进口有较大幅度的增长，比上年增长 60.9%，非洲与中国的贸易逆差进一步缩小。据中国海关统计，1999 年，中国从该地区进口原油 725 万吨，金额 8.76 亿美元，占中国从非洲进口总额的 36.9%，比上年增长 205.2%。其他大宗进口商品有：原木(3.11 亿美元)、矿产品（2.11 亿美元)、钻石(0.87 亿美元)、液化石油气（0.72 亿美元)、肥料(0.51 亿美元）等。中非双边贸易的另一个显著特征是中国出口商品结构逐步优化。近年来中国对非洲地区的出口已由过去的以纺织品、轻工业品等劳动密集型产品为主转到以技术含量和附加值较高的机电产品为首位。据中国海关统计，1999 年中国向该地区出口机电产品 14.84 亿美元，约占对该地区出口总额的 36.1%，位于出口榜首。其次是纺织品和服装，出口额为 10.28 亿美元，占出口总额的 25%，其他还有轻工业产品（出口额 5.52 亿美元，占 13.4%)、鞋类（出口额 4.32 亿美元，占 10.5%)、粮油食品（出口额 2.26 亿美元，占 5.5%)、茶叶（出口额 1.26 亿美元，占 3%）和药品（出口额 0.64 亿美元，占 1.6%）等。

在中非双方政府和经贸界的共同努力下，中国与非洲地区的贸易有了长足的发展。但中国对非贸易规模仍很小，双边贸易整体水平还很低，在各自对外贸易中所占份额较小。中国政府有关部门十分重视并将继续采取措施，改善双边经贸关系的环境，促进双边贸易的进一步发展。

二、经济技术合作

(一) 对外援助

截至 1999 年底，中国共向 24 个非洲国家提供优惠贷款援助，已拨款的优惠贷款项目有 33 个，部分项目取得了较好的社会和经济效益。1999 年，中国对非援助项目 27 个，建成项目 22 个。

(二) 承包劳务

非洲是中国对外承包工程和劳务合作具有巨大潜力的市场。据不完全统计，1999 年，中国同非洲国家的承包劳务合同 1206 份，合同金额 18.64 亿美元，营业额为 20.36 亿美元。全年共向非洲派出各类劳务 22994 人。

三、贸易中心

1995 年以来，中国相继在非洲成立了 11 个“中国投资开发贸易促进中心”，目前，这 11 个“中心”已经或即将开业。“中心”是在国家资金支持下建立的服务经营实体，主要职责是为国内各类企业贯彻市场多元化战略、开拓非洲市场提供各类服务。其服务范围包括：提供保税存仓设施、经贸洽谈、商品展示；提供办公、住宿条件、提供安全保障；提供报关、保险、运输、旅游服务；提供结汇、结算服务；提供法律、会计、经贸咨询服务。现在正根据“中心”运行的实际情况，在明确承建单位责、权、利的前提下，探索“中心”发展的新模式，为促进中非双边经贸合作的良性发展做出努力。

四、对非投资

截至 1999 年底，中国对非洲投资累积达 4.4 亿美元，设立企业 351 家。1999 年，中国对非洲投资 0.95 亿美元，设立企业 54 家。中国企业在非洲 16 个国家建立了 47 个境外加工贸易项目，双方投资总额 7414 万美元，其中中方投资 4314 万美元，占中国对外投资总额的 16.89%。境外加工贸易项目不仅为有关国家增加了税收，而且还为它们创造了就业机会，取得了较好的经济效益和社会效益，同时还带动了我相关技术、设备和原材料的出口。

五、重要经贸往来

1999 年，党和国家领导人多次访问非洲，为我开展对非经贸合作创造了良好的大环境。1 月，胡锦涛副主席访问加纳、科特迪瓦、马达加斯加和南非，与南非政府签署了《贸易、经济和技术合作协定》和《关于成立经贸联委会协定》；11 月，李鹏委员长访问肯尼亚、毛里求斯和南非；5 月，全国政协主席李瑞环出访埃及；10 月，人大常委会副委员长田纪云出访埃及。在党中央的高度重视和中国政府的正确领导下，中国与非洲的经贸关系不断巩固和加强，非洲已经成为中国市场多元化和开拓“两种资源，两个市场”的重要地区。

2 月，何晓卫部长助理出访苏丹、博茨瓦纳和赞比亚，主持召开中苏第五届经贸混委会。5 月，徐秉金部长助理出访佛得角、布隆迪、肯尼亚和南非，主持召开中布第八届经贸混委会。8 月，国家经贸委副主任陈邦柱出访利比亚，主持召开中利第六届经贸混委会。10 月，周可仁副部长出访突尼斯；孙广相副部长出访几内亚、加蓬、刚果（金)、毛里求斯四国，主持召开中几第二届、中毛第五届、中刚第六届经贸混委会，与刚果（金）签署了《中刚贸易、经济与技术合作协定》。12 月，徐秉金部长助理出访埃塞俄比亚、肯尼亚和马达加斯加，主持召开中埃第四届经贸混委会。

1999年，毛里求斯副总理兼外交与国际贸易部长、科特迪瓦工业发展和中小企业部长、几内亚比绍财经部长、尼日尔工商部长、坦桑尼亚工商部长、莱索托贸工大臣、塞舌尔工商部长、津巴布韦工商部长、桑几巴尔财政部长、中非经济计划和国际合作部部长级代表、刚果（布）外交合作部长率经贸代表团访华。

1999年中国与欧洲联盟国家的经贸关系

对外贸易经济合作部欧洲司四处

欧盟一直是中国经济建设所需资金和技术的主要提供者之一，经济技术合作发展总体呈持续快速增长态势，双边贸易额逐年增长。目前，欧盟是中国的第三大贸易伙伴和最重要的经济技术合作伙伴之一。

一、双边贸易

据中国海关统计，1999年，中欧双边贸易额达556.8亿美元，比上年增长13.9%，其中我出口302.1亿美元，增长7.3%，进口254.7亿美元，增长22.7%。欧盟是我国第三大贸易伙伴，居日本、美国之后，香港之前。

二、对华投资

1999年，欧盟来华直接投资项目数为877个，协议外资金额42.33亿美元，下降28.4%，实际投入44.7亿美元，增长4.03%。截止1999年底，欧盟成员国来华投资项目数达10207项，协议外资金额405.8亿美元，实际投入218.8亿美元。欧盟对华投资继续保持项目平均规模大，技术含量高，经济和社会效益好的特点。

三、双边经济技术合作

（一）引进技术

欧盟国家是中国引进先进技术、设备的最大供应者。截止1999年底，中国从欧盟成员国引进技术共10128项，合同总金额约542.8亿美元。其中1999年，我从欧盟成员国引进技术1564项，合同总金额为87.64亿美元，占我国同期引进技术总额的51.1%，高于1998年的46%。

（二）贷款合作

欧盟是中国利用外国政府贷款较集中的地区。截至1999年年底，欧盟成员国及官方金融组织累计向中国提供政府贷款协议金额161.58亿美元，占外国政府和官方金融组织向中国提供贷款总额的44%。其中1999年，欧方提供贷款协议金额11.7亿美元，占全国同期的41%。

（三）其他合作

自1985年中国与欧盟签署《贸易与经济合作协定》以来，中欧双方已举行了16次经贸混委会。目前，双方在混委会下成立了经贸、科技、环保、能源和信息通讯技术5个工作组，在培训、科技、发展援助等领域也开展了广泛的合作。1999年10月，中国成功举行了首届亚欧科技部长会议。自1993年以来，我共接受欧委会及其成员国对华无偿援助约计4亿美元。

四、重要经贸往来

1999年，江泽民主席两度出访西欧，先后对意、瑞（士）、奥、英、法、葡等六国进行了国事访问，李鹏委员长访问希腊。德国总理施罗德年内两次访华，荷兰女王自两国建交以来首次访华均表明西欧国家政府对发展对华关系的高度重视。5月，欧盟委员会副主席布里坦访华。10月，石广生部长出席了在柏林举行的亚欧经济部长会议。12月21日，朱镕基总理与来访的欧盟轮值主席国芬兰总理利波宁及欧委会新任主席普罗迪举行了第二次中欧领导人会晤，双方就进一步发展中欧关系和其他共同关心的问题深入交换了意见。双方高层互访对增进了解，促进双方在多个领域的合作与交流具有重要意义，也为中欧经贸合作创造了良好的氛围。

五、中欧经贸关系中的主要问题

（一）反倾销调查

欧盟是最早也是对中国出口产品实行反倾销调查最多的地区，1999 年有愈演愈烈之势，分别对我输欧黄磷、塑料 CD 盒、非合金钢板、马钢管件、部分彩电显像管、发刷、甘氨酸、电子秤、焦炭、自行车车架、前叉和车轮、铝箔等十二个商品进行反倾销立案调查，对我电脑磁盘零部件和钢铁管接头两种商品进行反规避调查，矛头直指我大宗出口产品，使中国成为欧盟反倾销措施的主要打击对象。

1999 年 4 月，欧盟决定给予我生产黄磷的云南马龙化建公司市场经济地位。此案不仅是非市场经济问题上的一个重大突破，更重要的是获得市场经济待遇的是一家国有企业。这是改革开放以来我国企业首次在欧美对华反倾销案中获得市场经济地位，标志着我国长期的对外反倾销交涉取得重大进展。但同时，欧盟的对华反倾销政策仍具有较强的歧视性，中国企业仍不能自动享有市场经济待遇，中国企业在反倾销应诉中仍需为获得公正待遇而付出艰苦的努力。

（二）农产品

欧盟自 1996 年 8 月起相继停止从我进口禽肉和部分水产品。我有关部门和企业按欧盟法规进行了全面整改，并多次接受了欧盟兽医代表团的考察，但欧盟只做出了恢复从我三家工厂进口兔肉的决定。1999 年 6 月和 10 月，欧盟兽医代表团两度来华考察，但欧方无视中方在加强监管、提高产品质量和制订实施卫生检疫检测标准方面所做努力，至今尚未解除我禽肉、兔肉对欧出口禁令。

（三）数量限制

欧盟目前仍对我部分鞋类、陶餐具、瓷餐具、蘑菇罐头、大蒜实行配额或单边数量限制。

1999 年中国与独联体国家的经济贸易关系

对外贸易经济合作部欧洲司二处

一、中国和独联体国家的经贸关系

据中国海关统计，1999 年中国与独联体国家（见注释）的贸易总额为 75.16 亿美元，比 1998 年增加 11.6%。其中，中国出口 22.33 亿美元，比 1998 年下降 6.9%；进口 52.82 亿美元，比 1998 年增加 21.8%，中方逆差 30.49 亿美元。

中国向独联体国家主要出口服装、鞋类等轻纺产品、食品和机电产品等；自这些国家主要进口化肥、钢材、棉花、有色金属、木材等原材料性商品。

目前中国在这些国家注册的合（独）资企业约 2300 家，主要从事进出口贸易、服务性行业，生产型企业数量不多，涉及石油开采、家电组装、服装生产、食品加工、通讯等领域。

1999 年中国与独联体国家新签劳务、工程承包合同 78 项，合同金额 13992 万美元，完成营业额 5114 万美元。至 1999 年底，在外工程、劳务人数 1904 人。

1999 年，中国国家主席江泽民和国务院总理朱镕基分别对吉尔吉斯斯坦和俄罗斯进行了友好访问，吴仪国务委员对俄罗斯、乌克兰、白俄罗斯和波罗的海三国进行了访问。哈萨克斯坦总统纳扎尔巴耶夫、乌兹别克斯坦总统卡里莫夫、塔吉克斯坦总统拉赫莫诺夫、哈萨克斯坦副总理兼外长托卡耶夫、白俄罗斯经济部长希莫夫、吉尔吉斯斯坦外长伊马纳利耶夫等分别访问了中国。上述高层互访对加深相互间了解，增进友谊，进一步扩大中国与上述国家间的经济贸易合作起到了积极的推动作用。

现将中国与独联体重点国家和地区的经贸关系分述如下：

俄罗斯是中国在独联体国家中的第一大贸易伙伴。中俄贸易在我国对外贸易发展中起着比较重要作用。双边经贸合作基础良好，发展相对平稳。1999 年中俄贸易额为 57.2 亿美元，比上年增长 4.4%，其中中国向俄罗斯出口 14.97 亿美元，比上年下降18.6%，进口42.22亿美元，比上年增长16%。中方逆差达27亿美元。中国对俄罗斯出口以轻纺产品和食品为主，自俄罗斯进口的主要商品有钢材、化肥、成品油、木材等。两国进出口商品结构仍以传统商品为主。

目前中俄相互投资规模不大，在俄中资企业约1300家，总投资超过1亿美元，主要从事进出口贸易、微电子、通讯、服装加工、家用电器组装、餐饮业、木材加工、农业等。俄罗斯在中国投资项目约1108个，实际投入近2.2亿美元。主要涉及核电、汽车、农机组装、维修、化工、建材、食品加工和餐饮服务等。

1999年中国与俄罗斯劳务、工程承包合作比上年有所下降，全年新签合同339份，合同金额3.6亿美元，完成营业额9095万美元，在外劳务人员13108人。

1999年，中国与俄罗斯签订自俄罗斯技术引进112项，合同总额7835.7万美元，中国自俄罗斯进口的技术产品主要涉及军工、核电、航空、电子等领域。

1999年中俄贸易自1997年来首次实现恢复性增长，特别自下半年开始增势明显，随着俄罗斯经济进一步好转，预计双边贸易增长势头将在2000年得以继续保持。

1999年中国与中亚地区的经贸合作进一步发展，尤其是中国出口大幅增长，使往年中国巨额逆差局面得以改善。1999年中国与中亚地区贸易额达13.3亿美元，比上年增长39.2%，其中出口6.34亿美元，比上年增长39%，进口6.97亿美元，比上年增长39.4%。中国自中亚进口商品主要有棉花、短绒、羊毛、牛羊皮、钢材、化肥、石油、有色金属和黑色金属等，出口商品主要有食品、轻纺产品、机械产品、日用消费品等。

哈萨克斯坦、吉尔吉斯斯坦和乌兹别克斯坦分别为中国在独联体国家中第二、第四和第五大贸易伙伴，贸易额分别为6.36亿美元、1.98亿美元和0.9亿美元。

中国在中亚各国已注册了850余家中资企业，总投资额达4亿美元以上，但是实际运营的不到200家。投资领域主要涉及石油开采、汽车组装、机场改造、轻工业品生产、国际贸易等领域。

1999年中国与中亚地区劳务、工程承包合作方面新签合同39项，合同金额13152万美元，完成营业额4259万美元，在外劳务人员806人。

截至目前，中国向中亚地区共提供15笔政府商品和援外优惠贷款，总金额达9亿元人民币。

乌克兰是中国在独联体国家中的第三大贸易伙伴。1999年中乌贸易额4.21亿美元，比上年增长53.2%，其中中国出口0.81亿美元，比上年下降10.1%，进口3.4亿美元，比上年增长84%。中国主要出口鞋、机电产品、服装和纺织品、耐火材料等，主要进口钢材、钢坯、变压器等。中国在乌注册的企业60多家。

二、中国与独联体国家经贸合作中存在的问题

1. 商品结构单一

中国出口以传统的轻纺产品和食品为主，而进口以原材料性商品为主。单一的商品结构易受市场需求变化及两国相关产业政策调整的影响，这已成为双边贸易发展的制约因素。

2. 贸易方式不正规

中国与独联体银行间无直接帐户往来，信用证等符合国际贸易规范的支付方式很少采用，现钞贸易、易货贸易仍占很大比重，中国与独联体国家的贸易方式有待进一步规范。

3. 双方对各自优势和互补性了解不够

目前双方企业对对方国家的优势行业和优势产品还很不了解，各自优势未充分反映在双边经贸合作中，这也是双边贸易规模不大、进出口商品结构单一、双边经贸合作没有大的突破的重要原因之一。

4. 独联体国家企业支付能力下降

受俄罗斯金融危机的影响，独联体国家企业进口支付能力进一步下降，双边贸易中往往要求中方货到付款甚至售后付款，给中方向这些国家出口带来极大困难。

5. 中国商品形象问题

各国独立之初，市场处于饥饿状态，双方倒爷将许多中国假冒伪劣商品贩运到独联体国家，严重损害了中国商品形象，加之中国企业缺乏品牌意识，不愿为商品做广告。因此，重塑中国商品在上述国家消费者中的形象的任务还很重。

6. 双边经贸合作服务体系不完善

目前中国与独联体国家在银行、信贷、保险、贸易结算等方面的服务机制尚不尽完善，双方企业难以利用各种融资手段开展经贸业务和合作，在一定程度上制约了一些项目的实施，不利于经贸合作

的健康稳定发展。

（注释：独联体国家包括俄罗斯、乌克兰、白俄罗斯、哈萨克斯坦、乌兹别克斯坦、吉尔吉斯斯坦、土库曼斯坦、塔吉克斯坦、格鲁吉亚、阿塞拜疆、亚美尼亚、摩尔多瓦12国，文中统计数字均为与12国的情况；波罗的海三国：爱沙尼亚、拉脱维亚、立陶宛三国亦为原苏联国家，1999年，我国与波海三国的贸易额为5862万美元，比1998年下降3.2%，其中我国向其出口4812万美元，进口1050万美元，分别比1998年下降1.5%和35.8%。）

1999年中国与欧洲其他国家的经济贸易关系

对外贸易经济合作部欧洲司办公室

一、中国和瑞士的经贸关系

瑞士是最早承认中国的西方国家之一。1950年9月14日，中瑞两国建交。1974年12月，两国签订贸易协定并成立了中瑞贸易混合委员会，至今双方已先后在北京和伯尔尼召开过14次会议。1999年3月，江泽民主席成功地对瑞士进行了国事访问；11月，瑞士联邦委员兼经济部长库什潘应外经贸部石广生部长邀请访华。这些重要互访有力地推动了中瑞双边经贸关系的顺利发展。

瑞士是我国在西欧除欧盟外最大的贸易伙伴。在双边贸易中，转口贸易占有一定比重。根据我国海关统计，1999年中瑞双边贸易额达16.9亿美元，较上年增长17.9%，创历史最高纪录。其中，我国出口6.8亿美元，增长6.4%；进口10.1亿美元，增长27.1%。我国主要出口商品包括纺织品、机电产品、化工原料、玩具、体育器材和皮革制品等，我国主要进口商品包括机电产品、化工医药产品、光学和医疗设备及钟表等。

随着双边贸易的发展，瑞士企业在华投资的步伐也不断加快。ABB、雀巢等一批瑞士大公司相继在我国机电、食品等工业领域成立了多家合资企业。同时，瑞士中小企业的对华投资也日渐活跃。1999年，我国共批准瑞士在华投资项目35个，较上年下降18.6%；协议瑞资金额1.2亿美元，下降55.3%；实际投入2.5亿美元，增长7.9%。截至1999年底，我国累计批准瑞士在华投资项目405个，协议瑞资金额17.6亿美元，实际投入11.2亿美元。瑞士在华投资项目主要集中在医药、化工、机械、电子、食品和服务业等领域，投资区域主要在沿海省市。

为促进中瑞企业，尤其是中小企业之间建立合资企业及其他形式的合作，1997年12月，中瑞双方签署了成立中瑞合作基金（SSPE）的有关文件。基金的投资总额为9375万瑞士法郎，其中首期规模3125万瑞士法郎，中瑞双方分别持股20%和80%。基金由中瑞双方专家组成的投资委员会委托国家开发银行国际基金管理部进行管理。

两国财政合作稳步发展。自1984年8月至1999年底，瑞士政府已向我国提供了四笔政府贷款，协议金额共计2.16亿美元，已建成和在建的项目有56个，主要为纺织、通讯、医疗、机械、电力、环保和市政等类型的项目。

瑞士还一直是我国技术引进的主要来源国之一。1999年我国共批准从瑞技术引进合同83个，合同总金额2.3亿美元。从1979年至1999年底，我国累计批准从瑞技术引进合同723个，金额约16.4亿美元。

二、中国与挪威的经济贸易关系

中挪贸易始于19世纪初。自两国于1954年10月5日建立外交关系以来，双方签订了一系列贸易协议和协定。目前，中挪经贸关系良好，贸易额逐年增加，挪威商界对华投资兴趣不断增强，挪威政府向中国提供的优惠贷款保持在稳定的水平，金融、技术和海运等方面的合作也在发展。

据中国海关统计，1999年中挪双边贸易总额为8.27亿美元，增长30.4%。其中中国对挪威出口

3.43亿美元，增长3.9%；进口4.84亿美元，增长59.1%。

中国对挪威出口主要商品有船舶、纺织服装、机电产品、鞋类、箱包、焦炭和蘑菇罐头；中国从挪威进口主要商品有原油、机电产品、肥料、建筑及采矿用机械、装卸设备及零件、铁矿砂。

1986至1999年底，中国与挪威共签订技术设备引进合同81个，合同金额为1.6亿美元。其中1999年引进技术设备项目29个，合同金额3242万美元。引进的技术和设备主要用于邮电、电子、机械、交通、轻工、农业和环保等领域。

中国自1986年开始使用挪威政府混合贷款。到目前为止，中挪双方共签订贷款项目50个，协议金额2.53亿美元，生效额2.03亿美元。中国使用挪威混合贷款的主要领域是能源、通讯、轻工、农业、城市建设、运输等。

挪威对华投资起步晚、规模小、金额少。截至1999年底，中国累计批准挪威在华投资项目88个，协议挪资金额2.25亿美元，挪方实际投资1.48亿美元。1999年，中国共批准挪企业对华投资项目9个；协议挪资金额3400万美元，下降5.6%；实际利用挪资金额1859万美元，下降28.3%。挪威在华投资的主要领域有航运、电子、机械、通讯及化工等。

1974年,中挪就每年轮流在各自首都举行政府间司局级贸易混合委员会达成了协议。1975年在奥斯陆召开了第一次中挪贸易混委会。1980年9月，双方签订协议成立中挪经济、工业和技术合作混委会,代替1975年建立的中挪贸易混委会,并于1981年9月在北京举行了第一次混委会会议,至今共召开了十三次会议。第十三次混委会会议于1998年6月18日在北京召开,双方就共同关心的双边贸易、经济技术及财政金融合作等问题广泛地交换了意见。

三、中国与中东欧国家经贸关系

中东欧国家历史上与中国关系良好，是与中国最早相互建立外交关系的地区。至80年代末，该地区大部分国家与中国的贸易为政府记账贸易，当时，中国与该地区的贸易额曾达到较高的水平，如与罗马尼亚、波兰、捷克等国的年贸易额曾达10亿美元以上，中国从该地区进口了大量的机械设备、钢材、化肥、运输工具以及许多生产技术。自80年代末，中国和该地区国家的经济、外贸体制等均发生了巨大变化，双边贸易形式也由政府记账贸易转为为现汇贸易。

90年代初期，除波黑外，中国与该地区所有国家均签订了双边政府间经贸合作协定、投资保护协定、避免双重征税协定等经济领域里的基础文件，并成立了双边政府间经济贸易合作委员会，混委会定期举行会议，讨论双边经贸合作中的问题，提出相应的建议。

中国与中东欧国家贸易形式改为现汇贸易后，双边贸易曾一度下滑。经过双方的努力，贸易额开始回升。据我国海关统计，1998年双边贸易额19.6亿美元，1999年双边贸易额为22.8亿美元，较上年增长16.7%，其中中国出口19.0亿美元，较上年增长3.9%，中国进口3.81亿美元，较上年增长200.5%。

中国在该地区最大的贸易伙伴是波兰，1999年两国贸易额为8.6亿美元，其次为匈牙利、捷克、罗马尼亚。1999年中国与上述四国的贸易额为20.2亿美元，占中国与该地区贸易额的88.6%，与中国贸易额最少的国家是波黑，仅88万美元。

随着中国和该地区国家经济、市场的变化，中国与该地区的进出口商品结构发生了较大的变化。1999年中国向该地区主要出口商品为：纺织品、服装、鞋、食品、医药、玩具、陶瓷、家用电器、通讯设备、电站及化工设备等；中国从该地区主要进口商品为：有色金属、小轿车、机械设备、化工产品、鱼粉、医药品等。

中国与中东欧国家贸易方式转变后，双方企业开展了多种形式的合作，并开始相互投资。据中国统计，截至1999年底，中东欧国家在华投资799个项目，协议额为4.86亿美元，实际投资额为1.91亿美元，涉及机械、食品、医药、化工等领域，据不完全统计，中国各类企业在该地区投资2.6亿美元，多为餐饮业和贸易公司，另外也有少量机械、纺织领域的生产企业。但总的来讲，双方相互投资的规模均不大，只有个别投资效益较好。中国大型机电设备以出口信贷方式开始进入该地区，如我国在马其顿承建的2X40MW的水电站（总金额8100万美元）和在南斯拉夫承建的氮肥厂（金额1900万美元）。

双边经贸关系中存在的主要问题：贸易额小，合作形式单一，缺乏大型的生产性的合作项目，进出口商品结构不够优化，我对该地区的贸易有较大顺差等。

1999年中国与美国的经济贸易关系

对外贸易经济合作部美洲大洋洲司三处

一、双边贸易

1999年中美双边经贸关系继续呈快速稳定的发展态势。根据中国海关统计，1999年，中美双边贸易总额为614.3亿美元，比上年增长12%。其中中国对美国出口419.5亿美元，比上年增长10.5%；中国自美国进口195亿美元，比上年增长15.4%。对美国贸易顺差224.5亿美元，比上年增长6.8%。

1999年中国对美国出口的商品主要是：机电产品（194亿美元）、鞋类（87亿美元）、服装（39亿美元）、玩具（28亿美元）、塑料制品（15亿美元）、家具（14亿美元）、纺织纱线织物及制品（11亿美元）、灯具照明装置及类似品（9亿美元）、旅行用品及箱包（6亿美元），其他出口额超过亿美元的商品还有医药品、水海产品、轮胎、家用或装饰用木制品、未切成形的纸及纸板、水泥、玻璃制品、家用陶瓷器皿、装饰用陶瓷制品、钢材、床垫寝具及类似品、手表等。

1999年中国自美国进口的商品主要是：机电产品（112亿美元）、肥料（11亿美元）、初级形状的塑料（6亿美元）、未切成形的纸及纸板（6亿美元）、大豆（5亿美元），其他进口额超过亿美元的商品有：食用植物油、纸浆、成品油、牛皮革及马皮革、废铜、未锻造的铝及铝材等。

二、双边投资

1999年，美国在华投资项目数2047个，比上年下降7.58%，协议美资61亿美元，同比下降1.55%，实际投入美资44亿美元，比上年增长12.14%。截止到1999年底，美国在华投资项目累计达28628个，协议美资金额524亿美元，美方实际投入资金258亿美元。近年来，美国在华投资领域广阔，涉及机械、冶金、石油、电子、通讯、化工、纺织、轻工、食品、农业、医药、房地产以及金融、保险、外贸、会计、货运代理等试点开放的行业。在华美国企业多以美方控股为主，多数企业经营状况良好，并不断追加投资。

近年来，中国在美国开设的贸易型和非贸易型公司也呈不断增长趋势。截止1999年底，经批准的我国在美国投资举办的海外企业共计590家。协议投资总额7.91亿美元，其中中方投入资金总额达5.65亿美元，涉及的行业有工业、科技、承包工程、服装、农业、餐饮业、食品、旅游、金融、保险和运输等等。

三、双边经贸合作及重要经贸往来

1999年4月6日至14日，中国国务院总理朱镕基对美国进行了正式访问。访问期间，中美双方就双边经贸关系中的一系列问题进行了广泛而深入的讨论，双方愿意在平等互惠的基础上进一步加强交流与合作，共同推动中美经贸关系的不断向前发展。两国政府签署了《中美农业合作协议》，朱总理还与克林顿总统发表了联合声明，美方表示将坚定地支持中国加入世界贸易组织。访问期间，朱总理还与美国副总统戈尔共同主持了中美环境和发展讨论会第二次会议，两国领导人表示要进一步加强双方在环保方面的合作，为两国的发展创造更为良好的条件。朱总理的成功访问对中美关系的发展产生了积极的推动作用，同时为中美经贸关系的发展注入了新的活力，也大大加快了中美两国关于中国加入世界贸易组织双边谈判的进程。

受两国关系总体气氛的影响，1999年中美经贸交往经历了波折。5月8日以美国为首的北约悍然用导弹袭击了中国驻南联盟大使馆，造成中国人员和财产的严重损失，两国关系进入最低点，双边经贸关系也受到了严重影响，各种形式的合作与交流都因此而中止。7月美国商务部阿伦副部长访问中国，双边经贸交流合作才开始逐步恢复。11月15日，在两国最高领导人从世纪的高度亲自领导下，双方代表经过几天几夜的艰苦谈判，历时十三年之久的中美关于中国加入世界贸易组织的双边谈判终于有了结果，双方代表在北京签署了双边协议。这个协议不仅符合中美两国的根本利益，有利于世界的和平与发展，也有利于世界贸易组织本身的发展，对中美经贸关系的发展具有历史性的意义。

四、中美经贸关系中存在的主要问题

（一）关于对华永久正常贸易关系

相互给予无条件最惠国待遇是世界贸易组织的基本原则之一，也是《中美贸易关系协定》的核心条款和发展中美经贸关系的基本保证。但美国1974年贸易法中的杰克逊－瓦尼克修正案规定，每年由总统视中国是否违反该修正案中关于自由移民的规定来决定是否给予最惠国待遇。1998年，美国国会通过方案，将中国最惠国待遇更名为“正常贸易关系”（NTR），但仍未改变年度审议的法律程序。美方一年一度的审议是中美经贸关系的一个主要的不稳定因素，严重影响了工商企业界人士发展中美经贸关系的信心和热情。近几年来，美国国内包括美国政界和工商界都为永久解决对华正常贸易关系作出了努力。

1999年11月15日，中美两国达成了关于中国加入世界贸易组织的双边协议，协议执行的基础和前提是美国必须无条件解决对华永久正常贸易关系（PNTR）问题，美国政府对此也做出了明确的承诺。中国政府希望美国政府能切实履行承诺，推动国会尽早无条件解决对华永久正常贸易关系问题，促进中美双边经贸关系健康稳定地向前发展。

（二）对华反倾销及“非市场经济”问题

自1980年以来，中国产品已在美国遭受反倾销、保障措施调查74起，美国是仅次于欧盟的对华反倾销最为严重的国家之一。1999年美国对来自中国的8项产品正式立案进行反倾销调查，其中包括一起对蟹肉进行的201条款（即保障措施）调查。这些反倾销调查严重影响了中美双边的经贸往来，影响了中国产品对美国的正常出口，损害了中国有关企业的合法权益。

中国20年的改革开放和多年市场经济建设已取得巨大成就。但美国一直将中国视为非市场经济国家，采用替代国的方法确定正常价值，这是许多案件被征税的最重要原因。

中国政府希望美国政府在今后的对华反倾销调查中正视中国市场经济建设的成就，不再使用替代国方法确定正常价值，给予中国企业公正合理的待遇，为中美两国正常双边经贸关系的健康发展创造良好的环境。

（三）美国对华出口管制和最终用户访问

美国对华仍执行不合理的出口管制政策，并且有日趋严厉之势，使两国正常的技术贸易受到了严重干扰。1999年5月25日美方部分公布了美国会众院特委会的考克斯报告，报告诬蔑中国非法窃取军事技术、核技术、卫星及导弹技术以及高性能计算机。考克斯报告对中美科技交流与合作产生了严重影响，极大地破坏了中美科技合作的气氛。

1998年6月，中美两国就最终用户访问事达成谅解，中国政府有条件地安排美方对最终用户进行许可前访问和对计算机用户进行到货后核实。1999年5月8日，以美为首的北约悍然用导弹袭击中国驻南联盟使馆，中国政府推迟了安排最终用户访问项目。8月美国商务部副部长阿伦访华后，中国政府重新启动了最终用户访问。1999年共安排了29项访问，共查看了46台高性能计算机。

1998年以来，美国加严了对华出口管制。1999年3月，美国政府将卫星出口许可审批权由美国商务部转至美国国务院。其结果直接影响了中国商业卫星发射服务的市场开发服务业务。

1999年美国政府在放宽对华出口管制方面做出了一些积极的举动，但中美两国之间业已存在的问题仍未获得实质性的突破。中美在商业卫星发射的合作至今仍未恢复，美方对中国的出口审批时间过长，拒批项目过多等问题依然存在。

1999年11月，在中美关于中国加入世贸组织的双边谈判期间，美方曾允诺以信函方式表示将放宽对华出口管制。

中国政府希望美国政府从中美经贸关系乃至中美关系的大局出发，摒弃冷战思维，采取切实有效的措施，真正从根本上改变针对中国的歧视性的出口管制政策，放宽直至彻底取消对华高技术出口限制。

在相互尊重、平等协商、互谅互让的基础上处理双边经贸关系中存在的问题是促进和发展国与国之间经贸关系的基本原则。尽管目前中美双边经贸关系中还存在这样或那样的问题和矛盾，但中美经贸合作不仅符合中美两国的根本利益，也有利于世界的和平与发展。中美两国的经济互补性很强，双边经贸合作的潜力巨大。经验告诉我们，只要双方能排除非经济贸易因素的影响，以平等协商、积极务实的态度解决所遇到的问题，中美经贸关系就能得到健康稳定的发展，中美双边经贸合作就有光明的前景。

1999年中国与加拿大的经济贸易关系

对外贸易经济合作部美洲大洋洲司二处

1999年中加双边经贸合作发展顺利。1999年11月26日中加双方达成并签署了中加两国就中国加入世贸组织的双边市场准入协议。

一、双边贸易

据中国海关统计，1999年中加双边贸易额为47.67亿美元，比上年增长9.2%，创历史最高纪录；其中中国对加拿大出口24.33亿美元，比上年增长14.4%；从加拿大进口23.34亿美元，比上年增长4.3%。目前加拿大为中国第十大贸易伙伴。

从进出口商品结构来看，从加拿大进口的主要商品为机电产品、粮食、化肥、纸浆、纸张等。1999年从加拿大进口机电产品达7.25亿美元，比上年同期增长了12.7%。1999年从加拿大进口了12万吨小麦，价值2093万美元，较往年有较大幅度下降；但谷物贸易中，从加拿大进口大麦数量上升，1999年进口达38万吨，金额5435万美元。1999年我国进口加拿大钾肥156万吨，价值1.94亿美元，比上年下降了22%。1999年我国进口加拿大纸浆87万吨，4亿多美元，比上年增长了近60%。

中国对加拿大出口的主要商品是：机电产品、服装、纺织品、鞋类、塑料制品、玩具、箱包等。机电产品已占我国对加拿大出口的第一位，1999年共向加拿大出口机电产品9.62亿美元，较上年增长39%，占对加拿大出口总额的39.6%；纺织服装仍是我国对加拿大出口的重要商品，1999年，纺织服装出口共计5.4亿多美元，比上年同期增长11%，占对加拿大出口总额的22.3%。其它轻工类产品也表现出一定的增长潜力。

二、经济技术合作

（1）双向投资：

加拿大对华直接投资始于1980年。截至1999年底，共批准加拿大在中国直接投资项目4328项，协议加资金额70.41亿美元，加方实际投入20.57亿美元。1999年，加拿大在华新设投资项目346个，比1998年下降16.43%，合同金额6.69亿美元，实际投入2.90亿美元，分别比1998年下降29.80%和17.03%。加拿大投资企业分布在广东、上海、江苏、福建、山东、河北、北京、陕西、安徽、新疆、海南等20多个省市自治区。覆盖的行业有石油开发、机械、电子、通讯、化工、轻工、食品、纺织、农业、水产养殖、房地产、金融保险业、服务业等。生产性项目约占总数的80%。

1999年我国外经贸部新批3家在加拿大投资企业，均在服务贸易领域，双方协议投资总额为92.19万美元，中方协议投资总额约51.97万美元。自1983年至1999年底，经我国外经贸部批准或在我国外经贸部备案的我国在加拿大投资兴办的贸易和非贸易性企业共120多家，中方协议投资总额为3350多万美元。我国在加拿大投资涉及的行业有：资源开发、工业生产、建筑承包、农牧渔业、餐饮业、科技文化交流、交通运输、咨询服务等。

（2）贷款合作

1997年4月，双方签署了第五批中加政府贷款协议。根据协议，加方承诺向中国提供一笔与7500万加元等值的美元的优惠贷款，有效期两年。目前已有30个项目向EDC提出申请并签商务合同，涉及金额1.65亿美元；其中12个项目已经生效，金额为5960万美元。自1986年至1999年，加拿大政府通过其出口发展公司（EDC）共对华提供五批优惠混合贷款，总计承诺金额22.6亿美元。第一至四批贷款共安排项目145个，使用贷款约12.83亿美元，项目主要集中在邮电通讯、水电、能源、石化、纸浆造纸、轻工建材、城市建设等领域。

（3）加对华援助

中加两国从1982年起开始进行发展合作，1983年中加两国政府签署《中国和加拿大政府关于发展合作总协定》。十多年来，双方已进行了两个周期的合作，1995年开始了第三周期（1995～1999年）的项目安排。双方合作涉及到农业、林业、能源、交通、通讯、环保、人才开发、扶贫等多个领域，项目总数已达84个。其中已完成合作项目54个，正在执行的项目30个。另外还有8个项目正在规划中。据统计，加方对已签署备忘录的84个项目拟投入资金5.6亿加元（约合4.1亿美元）。

三、高层经贸互访

1999年11月，石广生部长应加拿大国贸部长佩蒂格鲁的邀请访问了加拿大，双方签署了中加两国关于中国加入世贸组织的双边市场准入协议，并参加了加中贸易理事会年会。同年5月，孙广相副部长率中国工业技术代表团访问了加拿大。

1999年中国与拉美国家的经济贸易关系

对外贸易经济合作部美洲大洋洲司一处

一、中拉贸易略有下降，但双边贸易额仍保持一定水平

1999年，受部分拉美国家经济增长停滞，甚至出现经济衰退等因素影响，中拉贸易与上年相比略有下降。根据中国海关统计，去年中拉贸易总额为82.6亿美元，同比下降0.6%。其中我国对拉美出口52.69亿美元，同比下降1%，我国从拉美进口29.91亿美元，同比增长0.1%。

在拉美主要贸易伙伴中，中国与巴西、智利、阿根廷和巴拿马的双边贸易额均超过10亿美元，分别为18.45亿美元、12.69亿美元、10.68亿美元和10.38亿美元。与墨西哥的双边贸易额也达到9.51亿美元，与秘鲁、古巴、乌拉圭、委内瑞拉、哥伦比亚、厄瓜多尔和危地马拉的双边贸易额均超过1亿美元。在上述国家中，巴拿马是我国在拉美地区最大的出口市场，中方出口为10.37亿美元。我国对巴西、墨西哥、智利和阿根廷的出口额分别为8.76亿美元、7.92亿美元、6.05亿美元和4.96亿美元。此外，我国对古巴、秘鲁、乌拉圭、哥斯达黎加、伯利兹、圭亚那和海地等国的出口有了较大幅度的增长。我国对拉美出口的大宗商品有机电产品（20亿美元）、服装和纺织品（15亿美元）、医药和化工品（2.5亿美元）、轻工产品（1.1亿美元）、谷物和蔬菜（0.9亿美元）以及焦炭（0.5亿美元）等。

1999年我国从拉美进口与上年相比略有增加。其中从巴西进口9.69亿美元，从智利、阿根廷、秘鲁和墨西哥进口也分别为6.64亿美元、5.90亿美元、3.10亿美元和1.59亿美元。我国从上述五国的进口约占我国从拉美地区进口总额的90%。中国从拉美进口的主要商品有矿产品（5.33亿美元）、大豆（3.59亿美元）、铜材（2.79亿美元）、纸浆（2.48亿美元）、植物油（2.44亿美元）、鱼粉（2.15亿美元）、机电产品（1.52亿美元）、皮革（0.98亿美元）、钢材（0.77亿美元）、香蕉（0.77亿美元）、羊毛（0.72亿美元）、食糖（0.55亿美元）和化肥（0.16亿美元）等。

二、双边经济技术合作取得积极进展

1999年，中拉经济技术合作在上年基础上继续取得进展。中国与巴西联合研制的地球资源勘探卫星成功发射，既是发展中国家高科技领域合作的典范，又是两国航天技术合作的新飞跃；深圳华为技术有限公司和巨龙公司积极参加巴西和哥伦比亚电信项目投标，带动我国高技术机电产品出口；南京金城集团在哥伦比亚项目获得成功的基础上又在阿根廷兴办了第二家摩托车组装厂；石油天然气集团公司在委内瑞拉和秘鲁等国的石油开采项目展现出良好的开发前景；中国成套设备进出口公司在委内瑞拉的经济住房建设项目进展顺利。此外，中国纺织机械（集团）总公司在秘鲁的棉纺厂项目、小天鹅集团在阿根廷的洗衣机组装项目以及格力集团在巴西的空调机组装项目等也正在顺利实施中。

1999年，我国在拉美国家建立了30个投资项目，双方投资额为2.5亿美元，其中中方投资2.25亿美元。同期，拉美国家在华投资项目642个，合同外资金额42亿美元，实际投资金额32亿美元。拉美地区外资主要来自维尔京群岛、凯曼群岛、巴哈马和巴拿马，上述国家和地区的直接投资协议金额达40.55

亿美元,实际投资金额31.70亿美元,此外,来自哥斯达黎加、巴西、玻利维亚、多米尼加共和国的直接投资协议金额也均超过1000万美元。

1999年，中国企业在拉美地区共新签承包工程和劳务合作合同278份，合同总金额2.98亿美元。其中承包工程合同57份，合同总金额2.40亿美元，完成营业额7184万美元；劳务合作合同207份，合同总金额5636万美元，完成营业额6969万美元。

1999年，中国在力所能及范围内向部分拉美国家提供了经济援助。其中与古巴签订了优惠贷款框架协议，向古巴、玻利维亚、苏里南、秘鲁、特里尼达和多巴哥、圣卢西亚、巴哈马、哥伦比亚、厄瓜多尔、乌拉圭提供了无息贷款援助或无偿援助。此外，中国还向古巴、圭亚那、墨西哥、哥伦比亚和厄瓜多尔提供了多边技术援助，共有14名学员参加了各类技术培训。

三、双方继续保持经贸领域高层频繁互访，政治关系进一步加强

1999年，国家主席江泽民在亚太经合组织第七次领导人非正式会议期间，分别会见了秘鲁总统藤森、墨西哥总统塞迪略和智利总统弗雷。中共中央政治局常委、书记处书记尉健行对古巴、乌拉圭和阿根廷进行了正式友好访问。此外，我国外经贸部刘山在副部长和陈新华副部长先后率团访问了巴西、阿根廷、乌拉圭、厄瓜多尔、秘鲁、圭亚那、巴哈马和安提瓜和巴布达。中国与哥伦比亚、玻利维亚、厄瓜多尔、智利和古巴召开了双边经贸混合委员会。此外，哥伦比亚总统帕斯特拉纳、牙买加总督库克、厄瓜多尔总统马瓦德、安提瓜和巴布达总督莱尔、委内瑞拉总统查韦斯、巴哈马总督腾奎斯特、巴拿马当选第一副总统巴利亚里诺、乌拉圭副总统法因戈德、哥伦比亚副总统莱穆斯、巴西副总统马西埃尔、圣卢西亚总理安东尼、古巴国务委员会副主席兼部长会议执委会秘书拉赫、智利外长因苏尔萨、乌拉圭外长奥佩蒂、特多工贸部长阿萨姆、古巴外贸部长卡布里萨斯等相继访华，就发展双边经贸关系与中方交换了意见，这些高层交往起到了增进了解、加深友谊和推动合作的作用。

1999年中国与澳大利亚、新西兰的经济贸易关系

对外贸易经济合作部美洲大洋洲司二处

一、中国与澳大利亚经济贸易关系

1999年，两国经贸关系继续顺利发展。1999年9月，国家主席江泽民对澳大利亚进行了国事访问，双方一致同意建立面向21世纪的长期稳定、健康发展的全面合作关系。7月，澳大利亚外长唐纳在访华期间与我国就中国加入WTO达成双边协议。这些为双边经贸合作的进一步发展奠定了坚实的基础。

（一）双边贸易

在经历了1998年亚洲金融危机影响之后，1999年中澳双边贸易强劲回升。据中国海关统计，全年双边贸易总额达到63.11亿美元，比1998年增长25.5%，再创历史新高。其中中国对澳大利亚出口27.04亿美元，增长14.3%；从澳大利亚进口36.07亿美元，增长34.5%。澳大利亚升为我国第八大贸易伙伴。

从进出口贸易的构成来看，机电产品已超过服装而成为中国对澳大利亚出口的第一大类商品，其他主要商品依然是纺织品和轻工产品。据中国海关统计，1999年中国向澳大利亚出口机电产品8.3亿美元、服装7.6亿美元、纺织品2.2亿美元、鞋类2.2亿美元。1999年中国从澳大利亚进口的主要商品为：铁矿砂5.9亿美元（2434万吨）、羊毛4.2亿美元（11.8万吨）、氧化铝2.99亿美元（146万吨）、大麦1.89亿美元（141万吨）、铝及铝材1.7亿美元（10.6万吨）等，另进口了价值为2.2亿美元的机电产品。

（二）经济技术合作

1. 双向投资

1999年澳大利亚在华新设直接投资项目405个，澳方协议投资额6.35亿美元，实际投入2.6亿美元。截至1999年底，中国累计批准澳商在华直接投资项目3873个，澳方协议投资额58.4亿美元，实际投入超过18亿美元。投资行业分布在农业、建材、纺织、电子、服务业等领域。澳大利亚是中国吸收外资的主要来源地之一。

同时，澳大利亚也是中国在海外投资最多的国家之一。截至1999年底，经外经贸部批准的中国在澳大利亚设立的各种贸易性和非贸易性机构共177家，中方协议投资金额为3.6亿美元。中国在澳大利亚投资以资源开发为主，波特兰炼铝厂和恰那铁矿是中国在澳大利亚投资的两个最大的资源开发项目；在工业生产、交通运输、餐馆旅馆服务业及建筑承包等方面也有所投资。

2. 技术合作

自1981年10月中澳两国政府正式签署《中澳技术合作促进发展计划协定》以来，由于两国政府的重视及双方的共同努力，中澳技术合作进展顺利，成果显著。十几年来，合作领域不断扩大，已涉及农业、林业、牧业、能源、矿产、交通、纺织、建材、教育、卫生、审计、城市改造等方面。澳大利亚1999/2000年度预算中对华援款额度比上年度又略有增加。截至1999年底，中国利用澳大利亚援助已完成合作项目71个，澳方投入资金1.9亿澳元；正在执行项目37个，澳大利亚投入1.3亿澳元；待执行项目22个，澳方拟投入1.5亿澳元。

（三）重要经贸访问

1999年9月，国家主席江泽民在对澳大利亚进行国事访问期间出席了在墨尔本举行的中澳贸易投资研讨会。

1999年5月，澳大利亚副总理兼贸易部长费希尔访华并与外经贸部石广生部长共同主持了中澳部长级经济联委会第9次会议。

1999年7月，澳大利亚外长唐纳访华，并在访华期间与我国就中国加入WTO达成双边协议。

二、中国与新西兰经济贸易关系

（一）双边贸易

1999年，中国和新西兰的经贸关系继续发展。据中国海关统计，1999年两国双边贸易额为8.24亿美元，创历史最高纪录，同比增长20.3%；其中中国对新西兰出口3.43亿美元，从新西兰进口4.81亿美元，同比分别增长24.7%和17.4%。

从商品结构看，1999年中国对新西兰的出口商品仍以轻纺产品为主，主要包括：服装及衣着附件（10696万美元）、纺织品（3115万美元）、鞋类（2601万美元）、塑料制品（5475吨，737万美元）、玩具（466万美元）等，占对新西兰出口的一半左右。近几年来，中国对新西兰的机电产品出口增长较快，1999年出口金额为9316万美元，同比增长49.1%。中国对新西兰出口商品结构得到进一步改善。

中国从新西兰进口的主要商品多是原料性产品，包括：羊毛（27842吨，6929万美元）、纸浆（8万吨，3122万美元）、纸及纸板（7万吨，2909万美元）、锯材（133470立方米，2791万美元）、饲料用鱼粉（20341吨，1808万美元）、原木（23万立方米，1694万美元）、煤（13万吨，661万美元）、铁矿砂（36万吨，659万美元）等。羊毛一直是我国从新西兰进口的最大宗商品。但近几年占我国从新西兰进口总额的比例有所下降。同时，新西兰机电产品等制成品在不断扩大其在中国市场的份额。

（二）经济技术合作

1. 相互投资

1999年，我国新批新西兰来华投资项目49个，协议金额3668万美元，实际投入1839万美元；截至1999年12月底，我国批准新西兰在华投资项目总数为471个，协议金额3.38亿美元，实际投入1.79亿美元。在华投资主要分布在农林、轻工、纺织、冶金、食品加工、医药、计算机等领域。截至1999年12月，中国在新西兰设立的各种贸易性机构和生产性企业19家，中方投资额约10.3亿美元。其中最大的项目包括中信公司与新西兰雄狮公司和新西兰BRIERLEY投资公司组成的财团买下的新西兰森林公司（BRIERLEY投资公司已将其股份卖给中信公司与新西兰雄狮公司，目前两公司各占50%）和中国对外贸易运输总公司经营的威尼达林业公司。目前新西兰已成为中国在海外最大的投资目的地之一。

2. 技术合作

截至新西兰98/99财政年度，新西兰共向中国提供了近1200万新元的无偿援助，用于对中国经济不发达地区的扶贫，并将其先进的农牧业技术和设备介绍到中国，收到了很好的经济和社会效益。1998/1999年度，新西兰援华资金额度为137万新元，援助项目主要分为综合扶贫、体制改革研讨和促进双边投资合作等三大类。

（三）高层互访

1999年9月，国家主席江泽民对新西兰进行了国事访问，双方一致同意建立面向21世纪的长期稳定、健康发展的全面合作关系。同年7月，应朱镕基总理的邀请，新西兰总理希普利访华。这些都为双边经贸合作的进一步发展奠定了坚实的基础。

其他主要经贸互访还有：

1999年3月，新西兰国贸部长史密斯访华；4月，新西兰外交贸易部秘书长诺塔奇访华；9月，我国外交部长唐家璇，外经贸部部长石广生出席了在新西兰举行的APEC外长和贸易部长会议；11月，新西兰贸发局首席执行官范·威尔德女士访华，并与外经贸部孙振宇副部长举行了会谈。

中国船舶工业贸易公司

China Shipbuilding Trading Co., Ltd. (CSTC)

中国船舶工业贸易公司（CSTC）是中国船舶工业系统从事进出口业务的专业工贸公司。经营业务包括：出口各种民用和军用船舶、船用和非船用设备及其它机电产品，进口船用材料和设备，技术转让，合作生产，合资经营，“三来一补”，劳务出口，转口贸易、对销贸易、物业管理、售后技术服务，承包各类船厂、船用设备厂、大型钢结构、桥梁，工业成套设备、高层建筑物等建筑工程。中国船舶工业贸易公司在国内设有九个子公司或分公司，在境外设有九个代表处或公司。公司自1982年成立以来，已向40多个国家和地区出口了各类船舶300多艘，共800多万载重吨，近年在缅甸建桥6座，质量优良，获缅方高度评价。累计出口创汇约93亿美元。1999年完成进出口总额13.5亿美元。其中出口总额10.7亿美元，进口总额2.8亿美元。

China Shipbuilding Trading Co., Ltd. (CSTC) is an industry specialized trading company dedicated to import and export of items relating to ship for China Shipbuilding industry. The scope of business includes: export of civil and military ships/marine and non-marine equipment/other mechanical and electrical equipment and electronics; import of shipbuilding materials and equipment; transfer of technology; compensatory trade; co-production; joint venture; processing of foreign materials; labor service export; entrepot trade, counter trade, estate management, after-sales service; contracting for construction projects of various shipyards/ marine equipment works/large steel structures/bridge structures/industrial package/multi-storied building. CSTS has all of nine branch companies home, and nine representative offices or companies abroad. Since founding in 1982, CSTC has exported more than 300 varies types of ships, 8 million and more dwt to more than 40 countries and regions. In recent years, it also won the high reputation from Myanmar government in construction of high quality of 6 bridges. It has received the aggressive amount of all about 9.3 billin USD export over the past years. The total import-export value in 1999 equaled to 1.35 billion US dollars. The total export value covered 1.07 billion US dollars, import value is 0.28 billion US dollars. CSTC was awarded the honorary Title "Flower of China National Economy" by China Ministry of Foreign Trade and Economy.

董事长： 陈小津　Chairman of the Board : Chen Xiaojin

总经理： 李柱石　President : Li Zhushi

地址： 北京海淀区白石桥路甲54号方圆大厦22-27层

Add : 22nd-27th Floor, Fangyuan Mansion No.54 (jia) , Baishiqiao Lu, Haidian District, Beijing, P.R. of China

邮编 (Postcode) : 100044

电话 (Tel) : (010) 88026088, 88026688

传真 (Fax) : (010) 88026000, 88026001

网址 (Web Site) : www.chinaships.com

电子信箱 (E-mail) : webmaster@cstc.com.cn

中国南方航空进出口贸易公司

China Southern Airlines (Group) Import & Export Trading Corp.

中国南方航空进出口贸易公司是南方航空集团公司经营进出口贸易的全资性子公司。自1993年成立以来，公司坚持“顾客权益至上”的经营宗旨，积极开展以航空业务为主的国内贸易和进出口业务。为国内各航空公司、空管局、机场提供各类进出口（商品的订货、送修、仓储）服务；并为国内外企业、公司提供产品代理、运输、报关服务。1995年荣获海关“A级企业”称号，1999年被评为出口收汇核销“A级企业”。

公司下设有广州南方航空报关有限公司、深圳南方航空器材有限公司、海南南方航空器材有限公司、珠海南方航空器材有限公司及深圳飞机轮胎服务中心。我们热诚欢迎与国内外客户携手合作，共创世界航空市场的辉煌。

公司总理：周明亮
公司总部地址：中国广州白云国际机场
邮政编码：510405
电话：广州 (020) 86124769 86124755
报关 (020) 86128186
深圳 (0755) 6640988
海南 (0898) 8520251
珠海 (0756) 8110193
传真：020-86633587
E-mail：maoyico@cs-air.com

As one of the subsidiaries of China Southern Airlines (Group), China Southern Airlines (Group) Import & Export Trading Corporation Specializes in import and export business. Since our foundation in 1993, we adhere to the principle of "For the rights of customer", and take an active part in developing civil trade as well as import and export business with an emphasis in aviation field. We render import and export service for all domestic airlines, air traffic control administration, and airport (purchasing, repair, storage). We also provide service of product agency, transportation and customs declaration for enterprises at home and abroad. Having setting up good business relationship with lots of domestic and overseas customers, we were granted the title of: "Grade A Enterprise" by the Customs.

We now have several subsidiaries as such: Guangzhou Southern Airlines Customs Declaration Company, Southern Airlines (Group) Aviation Supplies Corp. Shenzhen, China Southern Airlines (Group) Hainan Aviation Supplies Co. Ltd, China Southern Airlines (Group) Aviation Supplies Corp-ZH, and Shenzhen Aircraft Tyre Service Center.

We warmly and sincerely invite all the civil and foreign client to work with us for a brilliant world aviation market.

General Manager: Mr. Zhou Mingliang
Add: Guangzhou Baiyun International Airport, China
Postcode: 510405
Tel: Guangzhou(8620)86124769 86124755
Customs Declaration(8620)86128186
Shenzhen(86755)6640988
Hainan(86898)8520251
Zhuhai(86756)8110193
Fax: (8620)86633587
E-mail: maoyico@cs-air.com

YUNNAN HONGTA IMPORT & EXPORT CO., LTD.

云南红塔进出口有限公司是云南红塔集团的全资子公司，于1996年2月成立，经营集团成员企业自产产品及相关技术的进出口业务。代理进口纸张等原辅材料，机械设备，仪器仪表，零配件。

在经贸部发表的中国进出口总额最大的500家企业中，98年名列第148位；出口额最大的200家企业中，98年名列第119位。

Yunnan Hongta Import & Export Co., Ltd. that founded in Feb. 1996, mainly manages the import and export business for Hongta Group's member enterprises as the Group's full-capitalized subsidiary corporation. Specifically, the corporation imports the following commodities as the agent: the raw and auxiliary materials such as the acetate tow and plug wrap; machinery, instruments, export the high quality tobacco and cigarette of Yunnan etc.

The corporation was ranked the 148th among the 500 largest import and export enterprises and listed the 119th among the largest export enterprises in 1998 in China.

法人代表：陈效贤
Corporate Representative : Chen Xiaoxian
地址：云南省玉溪市玉江东路
邮编 (Post Code)：653100
Add : Yujing East Rd., Yuxi City, Yunnan, China
电话 (Tel)：86-877-2050726, 2051480
传真 (Fax)：86-877-2050296
E-mail : wjiang@hongta.com、zhmin@hongta.com

青岛纺联集团有限公司

青岛纺联集团有限公司（原青岛纺织品联合进出口公司）是国家批准、具有法人地位的工贸结合、进出结合，拥有对外贸易权的大型企业。经营各类纺织品进出口贸易，并承办来料、进料、来样加工、合资经营、补偿贸易、合作生产、技术和设备引进等业务。

本公司拥有历史悠久，设备先进，技术力量雄厚的纺织、印染、色织、针织、绒布、巾被、床单、台布、毛纺织、服装等生产企业。花色品种齐全，品质优良，款式新颖，信守合同，服务周到，在国际市场上久负盛誉。

本公司热诚欢迎世界各地贸易金融界友好人士与本公司发展贸易往来，以及进行技术交流合作。

Approved by the State Council, Qingdao Associated Textiles Import and Export Group Co., Ltd. is a large-scal enterprise combining industry and trading, and an independent economic entity with legal status, engages in various textiles imports & export business, QATEX deals mainly in importing material exporting textiles, transacting business of pressing with customer's materials, joint venture, compensation trade, cooperation in production and importing technology and equipments as well.

QATEX now possesses hundreds of manufacturers mills and factories with advanced equipments, a large number of technical personnel and a long history in porduction raning from spinning weaving to dyeing, printing, knitting and yar-dyedweaving, as well as fowelling bed sheeting, table cover, corduroy and raised fabrics, wollen fabrics, synthetic fabrics and garments. With various designs, fine quality elegant styles, well-timed delivery, the products have already enjoyed a high prestige on the domestic and world market.

We are sincerely looking forward to establishing and developing trade relationship, technique exchange and cooperation in production with trade and financial circles all over the world.

董事长：王磊　Chairman of the borad：Wanglei

总经理：林得知　General manager：Lin de zhi

地址：青岛市馆陶路3号　邮编（Post Code）：266011

Add：No.3 GuanTao Road Qingdao China

电话（Tel）：0532-2800412　传真（Fax）：0532-2802141

电子邮件（E-mail）：qatex@ns.qd.sd.cn

联系人：付斌　Fu Bin

中国石油技术开发公司

China Petroleum Technology and Development Corporation

中国石油技术开发公司（简称CPTDC）是中国石油开然气集团公司（简称CNPC）全资子公司，是从事国际贸易的专业化公司，在世界各地拥有21个海外机构。公司成立以来，作为CNPC的对外贸易的窗口，为CNPC引进先进技术和设备及出口中国的石油设备和技术。自1992年来共为CNPC进口了20亿美元的石油设备和技术，向世界各地累计出口额接近10亿美元。在经贸部发表的中国进出口总额最大的500家企业中，98年名列第28位。

CPTDC建立了以国内150多家石油设备和材料的生产厂家为基础的出口产品网络系统。八十年代以来，CPTDC为CNPC所属机械制造厂先后从国外引进了60余项先进的生产线、制造技术及设备。CPTDC对国外提供成套石油装备和单机设备、石油管材、油田化学品和炼油化工设备以及石油工程技术服务。目前，CPTDC已经将中国生产的石油装备出口到了美国、加拿大、委内瑞拉、俄罗斯、哈萨克斯坦、伊朗、苏丹和印度尼西亚等国家和地区，这些产品及工程技术服务受到各地用户的好评，目前已与世界48个国家和地区建立了贸易关系。

China Petroleum Technology and Development Corporation (CPTDC), a 100% owned subsidiary company of China National Petroleum Corporation (CNPC), is a professional company engaged in international trade with 21 overseas offices and branches all over the world. As the foreign trade "window" of CNPC, CPTDC has been responsible of exporting China's petroleum equipment and technology to the outside world as well as introducing advanced technologies and equipment to China. Since 1992, its total import of petroleum equipment and technologies has amounted to US$2,000,000,000 and the export about US$ 1,000,000,000. In 1998, CPTDC was ranked the 28th of the nation's top 500 foreign trade companies by the total imports and exports. At the same time, it was also the 6th largest exporter of electromechanical products in all the foreign trade companies directly under the administration of the central government of China.

CPTDC has established a national export network system consisting of over 150 member manufacturers of petroleum equipment and materials all over China. Since the 1980's, CPTDC has imported more than 60 items of advanced production lines, manufacturing technologies and equipment. Its exports range from complete sets of petroleum equipment, machinery products, tubular goods, oilfield chemicals and refining and chemical equipment to technical engineering services. Till now, CPTDC has exported China's petroleum equipment to various countries and regions including the United States, Canada, Venezuela, Russia, Kazakhsta, Iran, Sudan, and Indonesia. CPTDC has now established trade relations with 48 countries and regions around the world.

地址：北京市西城区鼓楼外大街5号
邮编：100029
电话：010-62096922, 62096878
传真：010-62096922, 62096784
网址：http ://www.cptdc.cnpc.com.cn

Add：5, Culouwai Dajie, Beijing
Post Code：100029
Tel：010-62096922, 62096878
Fax：010-62096922, 62096784
Web Site：http ://www.cptdc.cnpc.com.cn

仪征化纤股份有限公司

Yizheng Chemical Fibre Company Limited

仪征化纤股份有限公司（本公司）及其附属公司（本集团）是中华人民共和国（中国）大型的现代化化纤和化纤原料生产基地，以一九九九年聚酯聚合装置产能计，本集团是世界第七大聚酯生产商，本公司一地聚酯聚合产能居世界前茅。

本公司位于江苏省仪征市，是原仪征化纤工业联合公司（仪化）改组后，以其全部聚酯生产单位和辅助生产单位注入，于一九九三年十二月十一日注册登记成立的。本公司于一九九四年三月、一九九五年一月和一九九五年四月分别发行10亿H股、2亿A股和4亿新H股，并于一九九四年三月二十九日、一九九五年四月十一日和一九九五年四月二十六日分别在香港联合交易所有限公司（联交所）和上海证券交易所（上交所）挂牌上市。

本公司主要从事生产及销售聚酯切片和涤纶纤维业务，经营范围包括化纤及化工产品的生产及销售，原辅材料与纺织机械的生产，纺织技术开发，自产产品运输及技术服务。

本公司是国家六五、七五、八五及九五计划期间重点建设项目，生产装置分别从德国、日本、意大利和法国等国家引进，工艺技术达到国际先进水平。主产品质量体系顺利通过了ISO9002国际认证，产品质量在业内处于领先地位。截至一九九九年底，本集团具备了93.8万吨／年聚酯聚合能力、5.8万吨／年瓶级切片固相缩聚能力、54.2万吨／年涤纶纤维抽丝能力、4万吨／年加弹能力和32.5万吨／年精对苯二甲酸（PTA）氧化精制能力，规模效益显著。

Yizheng Chemical Fibre Company Limited (the "Company") and its subsidiaries ("the Group") is the largest modernized manufacturer of chemical fibre and its raw materials in the People's Republic of China (the "PRC"). In terms of polyester capacity in 1999, the Group ranks as the seventh largest polyester manufacturer in the world, and the Company is the largest polyester manufacturer in one site all of the world. (Source: PCI 1999)

Located in Yizheng City, Jiangsu Province, the Company was established on 31 December 1993 following a reorganization of Yizheng Joint Corporation of Chemical Fibre Industry (currently Yihua Group Corporation ("Yihua")) and an injection of the entire polyester production units and ancillary production lines by Yihua. The Company issued 1 billion "H" shares in March 1994, 200 million "A" shares in January 1995 and a further 400 million new "H" shares in April 1995. The Company's "H" shares, "A" shares, and new "H" shares were listed and commenced trading on the Stock Exchange of Hong Kong Limited (the "HKSE") and the Shanghai Stock Exchange (the "SSE") on 29 March 1994, 11 April 1995 and 26 April 1995 respectively.

The Company is principally engaged in the production and sales of polyester chips and polyester fibre. The business includes production and distribution of chemical fibre and petrochemical products, production of raw materials, ancillary raw materials and textile machinery, research and development ("R&D") in textile technology, transportation and technological support for products manufactured by the Company.

The Company was constructed and developed as a major project under the PRC's Sixth, Seventh, Eighth and Ninth Five-Year Plans. Its production facilities were mostly imported from Germany, Japan, Italy and France, and its technology has reached advanced international levels. The Company obtained ISO9002 certification for the quality of its principal products, and its product quality commands a leading position in the market. At the end of 1999, the Group owned polymerization facilities with annual capacity of 938,000 tonnes, solid-state-polymerization facilities with annual capacity of 58,000 tonnes, spinning and drawing facilities with annual capacity of 542,000 tonnes, texturing facilities with annual capacity of 40,000 tonnes and oxidation and purification facilities with annual capacity of 325,000 tonnes. As a result the Group further strengthened its leading market position, improved its market share and benefited from the economies of scale.

法人代表：傅兴堂先生

地址：中国江苏省仪征市　　邮编：211900

电话：86-514-3232235　　传真：86-514-3233880

网址：http ://www.ycfc.com

Legal representative: Mr. Fu Xing-tang

Address: YIzheng City, Jiangsu Province, PRC, 211900

Tel: 86-514-3232235　　Fax: 86-514-3233880

Website: http://www.ycfc.com

涤纶长丝生产线

中央控制室

仪化产品

辽宁成大集团有限公司
辽宁成大股份有限公司

Liaoning Chengda Group co., Ltd
Liaoning Chengda co., Ltd

辽宁成大集团有限公司（以下简称集团公司）是1995年9月经批准设立的。1996年11月，辽宁省政府以辽政[1996]198号文批准授予集团公司为国有资产投资主体，集团公司系国有独资公司，注册资本为16800万元人民币。主要经营管理集团公司和所属全资、控股子公司的国有资产，依法行使法人财产的占有、使用、收益和处置权。集团公司内部实行母子公司管理体制。

辽宁成大股份有限公司（以下简称股份公司）为集团公司的控股子公司和骨干企业。股份公司是1993年6月，在改组具有40多年经营历史的辽宁省针棉毛织品进出口公司的基础上以定向募集方式创立的。经中国证监会批准，公司于1996年8月6日成功地向社会公开发行了1200万股A股股票，并于8月19日在上交所挂牌上市，成为辽宁外经贸行业第一家上市公司。现注册资本为24757万元人民币。

董事长、党委书记：尚书志

股份公司主要从事针棉毛织品和服装进出口业务，同时从事外经业务。在经贸部发表的中国进出口总额最大的500家企业中，99年名列第163位；出口额最大200家企业中，99年名列第108位；99年为辽宁外贸出口额领先的企业。辽宁成大是国家外经贸部和辽宁外经贸系统先进企业。公司股票价格逐年攀升，已由上市时每股13.16元上升到106.70元；99年每股收益达到1.06元，居中国逾千家上市公司前列。公司一贯恪守"平等互利"的原则，在与各方交往中素负盛名。同世界五大洲上百家客商有着良好的合作关系，在国内与10几个省市的400多家厂商有着密切的业务往来。

股份公司具有很强的融资能力，每年证券市场直接融资可达3-5亿元，同时还具有较强的信贷实力。良好的经济实力，使公司不仅具备高成长性，同时更具有较强的国际竞争实力。

辽宁成大总部——成大大厦，高30层，座落在素有中国"北方香港"之称的大连市金融、商贸、旅游业集中的黄金地段。

辽宁成大将在市场经济条件下，按照公司发展战略实业商业资本与金融资本、产业资本的结合，可持续发展，把辽宁成大建成一个对国家有突出贡献，对社会有较大影响，对股东和职工有丰厚回报的大型企业集团。

地址： 中国·大连人民路71号
邮编： 116001
电话（Tel）： 0411-2641609, 2647441
传真（Fax）： 0411-2656116, 2641533
Add：No. 71 Renmin Road, Dialian China
Post Code：116001
Tel：0411-2641609, 2647441
Fax：0411-2656116, 264153311

Liaoning Chengda Group Co., Ltd (hereafter referred as the Group) was founded in 1995. In November of 1996 the Group was authorized to become a state-wholly-invested and state-wholly-owned company by the approval of Liaoning government with the registered capital of RMB168 million. Its activity covers managing the state asset of the group, its wholly-owned subsidiary and holding company; It is offered the right to maintain, to utilize, to grow and to manage the asset legally with following the managing model as company/sub-company.

Liaoning Chengda Co., Ltd (hereafter referred as the holding company) is the holding subsidiary and backbone of the Group. The holding company was set up in June of 1993 on the basis of reconstructing the former 40-year-history Liaoning Knitwear and Home-Textile Imp./Exp. Company by raising funds directionally. On Aug 12, 1996 the holding company successfully issued 12 million shares to the society and was listed on Shanghai Exchange on Aug 19 so that becomes the first listed company in Liaoning foreign-trade territory with the present registered asset RMB247.57 million.

The holding company is mainly concentrating on the knitwear and garments Imp./Exp. business and engaged in foreign business as well. The holding company is appointed as one of the top 500 companies with greatest Imp./Exp. amount and the top 200 companies with greatest exporting amount in China and the No.1 company with greatest exporting amount of its field in Liaoning province. It is also appointed to be the pioneer enterprise by Liaoning foreign trade commission and the national foreign trade bureau. The company's stock is keeping hot and the stock price being up year by year with the initial 13.16/share up to 106.70/share until today. In 1999 the stock profit is 1.06/share which is No.3 best-profit stock among thousands of listed companies in China. The company achieved steady and friendly business relationship with over 400 customers in more than 10 provinces in China and 100 customers all over the world by adopting "Equality and Mutual Benefit" policy.

The holding company is enjoying strong substantial capability of raising funds. Every year it benefits 300-500 million direct funds from the security market meanwhile has good integrity and credit. The strong economic advantage bring the company with great potential of growth and strong competence in international market as well.

Liaoning Chengda's headquarter-Chengda Mansion is a 30-storey building which is located in the center of finance, business and tourist in Dalian, Northern H.K. in China.

Under the condition of market economy and the devepment strategy of the company Liaoning Chengda will dedicate to achieve the combination and continuable growth of the commercial financial and industrial assets of the company Liaoning Chengda will develop itself into a large-diversified business group by contributing to the country and benefiting the soceity and bringing the Share-holder and the employel with greatest profit.

新疆对外经济贸易（集团）有限责任公司

新疆对外经济贸易（集团）有限责任公司是由国家外经贸部和新疆维吾尔自治区人民政府批准经营进出口贸易的综合性企业，具有法人资格和对外贸易经营权，公司注册资本11905万元人民币。公司位于乌鲁木齐繁华地段，交通便利，拥有一座现代化的办公大楼，管理机构和设施齐全。职工总人数791人，平均年龄32岁，是一个由10个民族组成的大家庭。公司拥有一批精通外语和外贸、国际商务和经济管理的专业人才队伍。

在经贸部发表的中国进出口总额最大的500家企业中，公司连续10年榜上有名，99年名列第90位；出口额最大的200家企业中，99年名列第48位。公司曾多次被授予中华人民共和国海关信得过企业的光荣称号，并荣获自治区双文明单位、国家外经贸系统优秀企业等几十项荣誉称号。

公司近年来不断加大改革力度，积极探索"大经贸战略"格局，逐步向国际化、集团化、实业化方向发展，由商品经营向资产经营转变，对外贸易主要经营自治区工农业大宗生产资料、物资及高科技产品，如：钢材、棉花、化肥、建材、塑料、纺织、粮油、畜产、机械、计算机等并加大了对农业和工业出口基地建设的投入。公司还开展：生产合作、新建项目、技术转让、合资经营、加工贸易、国外工程承包等业务，贸易形式灵活多样，易货、现汇、对销、转口、代理等均可受理。

一九九七年以来，集团公司加快了推进改制上市的进程并开拓探索投资实业，以低成本扩张、高效率发展为目标，以投资、控股等不同方式进行资产重组，组建了集团公司最大的控股子公司－新疆国际实业股份有限公司。先后向新疆和硕麻黄素制品有限公司，新疆凯泽番茄酱制品有限公司投资近亿元，用于技术改造和引进生产设备，使麻黄素与番茄酱成为股份公司的支柱产业和集团公司新的利润增长点。新疆国际实业股份有限公司已经自治区人民政府和国家证监会批准将于2000年上市。

集团公司有八个全资子公司和两个控股公司。在北京、广州、上海、天津、阿拉木图、塔什巴、巴库、莫斯科、汉城、香港、洛杉矶等地设立了办事机构和代表处。并在自治区主要口岸：霍尔果断、阿拉山口、奎顿、巴克图、吐尔尕特等地建立了分公司、仓库及中转站。与国内数百家进出口企业和供货部门建立了紧密的贸易关系。同几十个国家和地区的外贸公司及大中型企业建立了稳定的经济贸易和经济技术合作关系，公司贸易伙伴遍及欧亚大陆，赢得了国内外贸易界人士的信赖。

公司愿在"平等互利，互通有无"的基础上，继续发展同世界各国经济界人士的友好交流与合作。

Approved by Ministry of Foreign Trade and Economic Co-operation and the people's Government of Xinjiang Uygur Autonomous Region, Xinjiang Foreign Economic & Trade (Group) Co. Ltd is a complex enterprise with legal personality to enjoy the right of egaging in import and export trade and it has RMB one hundred and nineteen million and fifty thousand yuan of its registered capital. Located in downtowm of Urumqi, the office building of the corporation is equipped with modern facilities. Composed of 10 different nationalities, the corporation staff amount to 791 with an average age of 32 years and they are expert in foreign languages, foreign trade and economic administration.

In the past 10 years the corporation has been listed among the top 500 foreign trade enterprises with the largest import and export value by Ministry of Foreign Trade and Economic Co-operation and in these recent 3 years it has been consistently among the top 100 largest ones and in 1999 it was ranked No. 90 concerning import and export volume and ranked No 48 with regard to export. For many times the corporation was awarded by General Administration of Customs of China as "Trustworthy Enterprise" and has won dozens of titles including "Double-Civilization Unit and Outstanding Enterprise" in MOFTEC Circel.

The Group has been continuously laying a stress on economic reform, actively searching for a "Grand Economic & Trade Strategy", gradually moving toward international, industrial and grouped direction and transforming from commodity management to capital operation. It mainly engages in agricultural and industrial means of production and high-tech products, such as: steel products, cotton, chemical, fertilizer, building material, plastic products, textile, oil and cereal, animal by products, machinery and computers. The corporation has increased the investment in developing agricultural and industrial export base. The Group also deals in co-operation, new construction project, technology transfer, joint venture and processing with materials, samples and assembling parts conducting supplied by investors or clients and compensation trade. Business form is flexibly practiced as barter, spot, counter, transit and agent etc.

Since 1997, The Group has sped up the process of reforming and going public, expanding with low cost, aiming at high efficiency development, reorgnizing the assets in terms of investment & stock holding and having established the Group's biggest subsidary-Xinjiang International Industry Co. Ltd. The Group has invested nearly 100 million RMB to Xinjiang Heshuo Ephedrine Products Co. Ltd and Xinjiang Kaize Tomato Procuts Co. Ltd respectively for purpose of technical reform and advanced equipment import so that the epedrine products and tomato paste have become the pillar industry and the new profit-growing points of the Group. Having been approved by the provincial government and the State Securities Supervision Committee, Xinjiang International Industry Co. Ltd will go public in the year 2000.

There are eight full-capital subsidiaries and two stock-holding companies. Offices and agencies have been distributed in Beijing, Guangzhou, Shanghai, Tianjing, Alma-ata, Tashgan, Baku, Moscow, Seoul, Hongkong and Los Angeles. The Group also has sub-compaines, warehouses and transfer stations respectively in the passes including Horgos, Alashankou, Baketu, Turgat and the city of Kuitun. It has established close Trade relations with hundreds of import-export enterprises and trade partners all over Europe and Asia. Besides it has been keeping stable economic and trade relations with dozens of foreign trade companies and medium-sized and large-sized enterprises and has won the trust of people from the trade circles both home and abroad.

On the basis of equality and mutual benefits and mutually supplying each other's needs, the Group will sincerely continue to develop the friendly exchange and cooperation with the friends of economic and trade circles from all over the world.

地址：乌鲁木齐市团结路45号
电话 (Tel)：0991-2860039
传真 (Fax)：0991-2863669

金城集团有限公司

THE FOREIGN CURRENCY EARNING AND EXPORT VOLUME RANKS FIRST IN CHINA'S MOTORCYCLE MANUFACTURING SECTOR

金城集团有限公司，是中国500家大型工业企业之一，国家重点扶持的300家国有企业之一。公司主要从事航空机载设备、摩托车及发动机、工程液压产品的研制、生产于销售，以及进出口贸易、国内外投资和第三产业。拥有8家中外合资企业和19家参控股企业，总资产36亿元，净资产17亿元，是中国摩托车行业的重点骨干企业。“金城”牌摩托车拥有从36CC-250CC排量近80个品种，畅销40多个国家和地区，年出口创汇3000万美元，在海外设有多个合资公司和摩托车组装厂。出口创汇和出口量位居中国摩托车行业前列，并受到国家外经贸部的通报表彰。“金城”牌摩托车被认定为国家重点支持的出口名牌产品。一九九九年底，“金城”牌摩托车荣获“中国驰名商标”。“建世界级企业，创世界级名牌”——金城人的目标!

中国驰名商标

Jincheng Corporation is among top 500 large scale enterprise in China.It is also one of 300 key state-owned enterprise that enjoy our govemment's aid. It primarily involves in production and sales of air -borne equipment, motorcycles and engines, hydraulic products for construction machines. It is also engaged in import and export owns 8 sino-foreign joint ventures and 19 share holding companies. The total fixed assets in Jincheng reaches 3.6 billion yuan and its net assets total 1.7 billion yuan.

Jincheng Corporation is the key motorcycle enterprise in China. Jincheng brand motorcycles have 80 models in the displacements from 36cc-25cc, and they are being well exported to nearly 40 countries and regions. Annual foreign exchange earned of Jincheng reaches 30 million US dollars. Jincheng Corporation has established several joint ventures and motorcycle assembly plants in overseas. In terms of its foreign exchange earned and export volume, Jincheng ranks in the forefront in Chinese motorcycle manufacturing sector and has been highly praised by Ministry of Foreign Trade and Economic Co-operation of China, Jincheng brand motorcycles are certified as the Government-promoted Export Commodity. In 1999, JINCHENG brand was assessed as the CHINA WELL-KNOWN TRADEMARK.

"To be a world class enterprise and produce a world class branded product"is our Jincheng object.

地址：中国南京市中山东路518号
邮编：210002
电话：86-25-4594165 4593388
传真：86-25-4591758

Add: 518 East Zhongshan RD,Nanjing, China PC: 210002
Tel: 86-25-4594165 4593388 Fax: 86-25-4591758
Email: jieco@publicl.ptt.js.cn
Http: //w w w. jincheng.com

安徽省外经建设（集团）公司

Anhui Foreign Economic Construction (Group) Corporation

安徽省外经建设（集团）公司是具有国家建筑施工壹级资质，并拥有承包境外工程、开展国际劳务合作和进出口贸易经营权的国有企业，已通过ISO9002质量体系认证。公司具有丰富的工程建设施工管理经验，先后成功实施了马达加斯加体育馆、多哥体育场、莫桑比克议会办公楼、毛里塔尼亚总统府办公楼、圣卢西亚仓库和办公用房等我国的大中型援外项目，得到各受援国政府和人民的高度赞扬。现在马达加斯加、莫桑比克、多哥、新加坡等地都建立了海外发展基地，卓有成效地开展了房地产开发、承包工程、劳务合作、进出口贸易等业务，并于1997年联合18家大中型企业组建了安徽外经建设集团，以强大的整体优势和竞争实力全面开拓海内外市场。

安徽外经建设集团总裁兼（集团）公司总经理蒋庆德

President of AFECG and General Manager of the Corporation：Mr. Jiang Qingde

Anhui Foreign Economic Construction (Group) Corporation (AFECG) is a state-owned enterprise with National 1st Class Construction Qualification and has the right to undertake overseas construction project, develope international labour cooperation and carry out import and export business. It has gained ISO9002 Quality Authentication Certificate. With ample construction management experience, AFEGC has successfully undertaken many large and middle scale foreign-aid project of our country, such as Madagasgar Gymnasium, Togo Stadium, Mozambique Parliament Office Building, Warehouse and Office Building in Saint Lucia and has been highly appraised by the governments and people of the aided country. AFEGC has established voerseas development bases in Madagasgar, Mozambique, Togo and Hongkong, making great achievements in real estate development, project contract, labour cooperation and import and export business. In 1997, consisting of eighteen large and middle scale enterprises, Anhui Foreign Economic Construction Group was established to fully exploit both domestic and voerseas markets with its great group advantage and competitive strength.

公司承建的马达加斯加体育馆

Madagasgar Gymnasium constructed by AFECG

公司承建的总建筑面积36104m²，可容纳三万观众的多可体育场

Togo Stadium constructed by AFECG with a construction area of 36104m² and an audience capacity of thirty thousand

地址：安徽省合肥市东流路28号外经大厦
Add : 28 Dongliu Road, Hefei City, China
邮编 (Post Code)：230022
电话 (Tel)：0551-3492558
传真 (Fax)：0551-3492537
电子信箱 (E-mail)：afecc@mail.hf.ah.cn

中国有色金属工业贸易集团公司

中国有色金属工业贸易集团公司是由中国有色金属进出口总公司等国内有色金属贸易公司和生产企业组成的大型工贸集团公司，在国内外设有几十个下属企业或分支机构。中色贸易集团公司以经营有色金属商品的进出口贸易为主，出口商品有：铜、铝、铅、锌、钨、锡、锑、镁、铜材、铝材、铁合金、机电产品等；进口商品有：氧化铝、铜精矿、锌矿砂、铅矿砂、锰矿、成套设备和机电产品等，同时兼营有色冶金原辅材料的国内贸易。一九九九年度，中色贸易集团的进出口总额为19.07亿美元，在经贸部发表的中国进出口总额最大的500家企业中，99年名列前10名。另外，中色贸易集团的实业开发涉及矿山、冶炼、加工等行业，以及高新技术产业、仓储运输、房地产、广告展览、期货经纪和信息产业等多种领域。中色贸易集团将进一步深化改革，为中国有色金属行业的发展作出新的贡献。

董事长、总经理：陈胜年
Managing Director : Chen Shengnian
公司注册资本：1亿元人民币
Registered Capital : 100 million RMB yuan
公司地址：北京复兴路乙12号
Address : 12B, Fuxing Rd., Beijing, China
邮编 (Post Code) : 100814
电话 (Tel) : (010) 63963835
传真 (Fax) : (010) 63965363
网址 (Web Site) : www.cnitc.com
E-mail : office@cnitc.com

China National Nonferrous Metals Industry Trading Group Corporation (CNITC) is a large-scale industrial trading enterprise composed of leading China National Nonferrous Metals Import and Export Corporation (CNIEC) and other major nonferrous metals dealers and producers in China. The Group is engaging in import and export of nonferrous metals and related products as its mainstay business. The Main articles for export are copper, aluminum, lead, zinc, tungsten, tin, antimony, magnesium, copper products, aluminum products, ferroalloys, electrical and mechanical products, etc.; the main import commodities are alumina, copper concentrate, zinc concentrate, lead concentrate, manganese concentrate, complete sets of equipment, electrical and mechanical products, etc.; the goods on the domestic market are raw and auxiliary materials supported for the industry. In 1999, the total I/E value chalked up 1.907 billion US dollars, listing itself high in the top ten among China's 500 largest state-owned foreign trade enterprises. In addition, CNITC has promoted efforts in mining, melting, deep-processing, new-high technology, storage & transportation, real estate, advertisement & exhibition, future brokerage, information industry, etc. CNITC and its subsidiaries will do every endeavors to forward in-depth reform to make its contributions to the further development of the nonferrous metals industry in China.

发展中的天津水泥工业设计研究院

该院设计的大宇（山东）7200t/d新型干法水泥生产线为目前国内最大规模

The largest cement plant of China-Daewoo (Shandong) 7200t/d new dry cement production line designed by TCDRI

天津水泥工业设计研究院具有工程设计、技术咨询、工程总承包、环境评价、建筑智能化、施工监理等多种甲级资质。承担了国内外各种规模水泥厂工程设计、技术服务、装备配套等综合性项目。1992年以来一直跻身于我国“勘察设计综合实力百强”之列。

联合国工发组织援建的“中国水泥发展中心”建在该院。天津院已与许多国家和地区建立了技术合作与业务往来。承建的汶莱国40万吨/年水泥粉磨站，马来西亚、巴基斯坦2000t/d新型干法水泥生产线等建设工程，获得了业主的赞誉。成功地设计了国内规模最大的7200t/d新型干法水泥生产线。为中国水泥行业占领国际市场奠定了基础。

该院设计的马来西亚2000t/d新型干法水泥生产线

Malaysia 2000t/d new dry cement production line designed by TCDRI

天津水泥工业设计研究院
院长：刘志江
电话：022-26391311
传真：022-26390071
邮编：300400
电挂：天津8940
电子邮箱：TCDRI@public. tpt.tj.cn
网址：WWW.TCDRI.com.cn

Tianjin Cement Industry Design and Research Institute (TCDRI) is a first grade institute on the qualification of engineering design, technical consultation, turnkey project contracting, environmental assessment, construct intellectualization and construction supervision. TCDRI has made many comprehensive projects on engineering design, technical serivce and installation completion for each scaled cement plants both in China and abroad. Since 1992 TCDRI is in the ranks of "One Hundred Powerful Units on Overall Strength of Prospecting and Design" in China.

China Cement Development Center was established in TCDRI which is assisted by UNDP. TCDRI has made many technical cooperations and business with the countries and regions in the world. These projects obtained great reputation from the owner, such as Brunei 400,000t/y cement grinding plant, 2000t/d new dry cement production lines in Malaysia and Pakistan. The Institute has designed a largest 7200t/d new dry cement production line in China by success. This laid a foundation on occupying international market for China cement industry.

Tianjin Cement Industry Design & Research Institute
President: Liu Zhijiang
Telephone: 022-26391311
Telefax: 022-26390071
Post code: 300400
Cable address: Tianjing 8940
E-mail: TCDRI@public.tpt.tj.cn
http://www.TCDRI.com.cn

天津水泥工业设计研究院办公楼 Office building of TCDRI

浙江中大集团股份有限公司

Zhejiang Zhongda Group Co., Ltd.

中大股份董事长：陈继达
Chairman of Zhejiang Zhongda Group Co. Ltd.

浙江中大集团股份有限公司于1992年由国有企业改制为股份制企业，并于1996年6月成为国家外经贸部推荐的上市公司。

公司拥有“人地”和“汉能”两大品牌，主要经营领域为国际化经营、房地产业、高科技产业及金融等方面投资。

中大股份始终坚持“**诚信互利，知识为本**”的经营理念，发扬“和谐、创新、高效、立誉”的企业精神，开拓创新，努力奋斗，立志把中大股份建成新世纪有一定知名度的跨国公司。

国际化经营：公司领导正在与外商洽谈合作事宜
Transnational Transaction: The Group Leaders Hold a Business Talk with a Foreign Customer

Zhejiang Zhongda Group Co., Ltd. was reformed from a state-owned company to a stock-share enterprise in 1992, and was authorized to be a the first public listed share enterprise of foreign trade industry upon the approval of China Securities Requlatory Commission, recommended by the Ministry of Foreign Trade and Economic Cooperation of PRC. in June, 1996.

The main scope of business inculdes: transnational transaction such as export & import trade, labor service exports; real estate; high & new technology development; financial and other investment etc.

Series of products such as garments, foodstuffs, beverages branded by “SENDI” and battery branded by “HANNENG” etc. have been promulgated as “the double-nice brands in quality and service in Zhejiang market” and “the most deeply-influenced brands to Zhejiang citizens” in 1999 by government and other authorities.

It was evaluated as one of the best 50 enterprises in China (Shanghai Stocks Market) and one of the best 50 enterprises with development potentiality in “China Stock” and other authorities in 1999.

Facing with the challenge of economic globalization and knowledge economy, Zhejiang Zhongda Group Co., Ltd. will stick to the management belief as “Benefiting each other through honesty and trust, Taking knowledge as the base”, carry forward the enterprise spirits of “Harmony, Innovation, Efficiency, Reputation”, and resolve to become a famous transnational corporation at home and abroad on the basis of Zhongda Staff's pioneering, innovating and striving.

房地产业：开发项目之一——气势恢宏的中大广场
One Project of Zhongda Real Estate: An Imposing Zhongda Plaza

高科技产业：国家科技部镍氢电池三大产业化示范基地之一——中大电源公司
Hi-tech Industry: One of the three National Exemplary Ni-MH Battery Base Evaluated by National Science and Technology Department – Zhongda Power Sources Co., Ltd.

董事长：陈继达　　总裁：马金龙
公司地址：中国·杭州·中大广场A座
邮编：310003
电话：0571-5155000（总机）5777018，5777029
传真：0571-5777050
公司网站：http://zhongda.com
公司电子信箱：zdinc@mail.hz.zj.cn

Chairman of the Board: Mr. Chen Jida
Chief Executive Officer: Mr. Ma Jinlong
Add: Tower A, Zhongda Plaza, Hangzhou, China
P.code: 310003
Tel: 0571-5155000(tel. exchange), 5777018, 5777029
Fax: 0571-5777050
Web site: http://www.zhongda.com
E-mail box: zdinc@mail.hz.zj.cn

CEIEC

中国电子进出口总公司

CHINA NATIONAL ELECTRONICS IMP. & EXP. CORP.

公司总裁：钱本源

中国电子进出口总公司——中国电子行业大型的进出口企业，是以电子技术及产品进出口为主，兼营其它的综合型外贸公司。

公司成立以来，坚持为我国电子工业和国民经济发展服务；坚持改革，坚持贸工结合、贸技结合、进出结合；坚持以进出口业务为主，开展多种经营，全面发展；坚持两个文明一起抓，加强经营管理。公司业务不断发展，规模不断扩大，从1980年至1999年，公司进出口总额达 221.62 亿美元，其中进口105.04 亿美元，出口 116.61 亿美元，为我国电子工业的技术改造和生产能力、产品质量、经济效益的提高，为我国电子产品走向世界做出了重要贡献。一九九二年以来，公司进出口总额在全国500家最大进出口企业中名列前茅，出口连年过 10 亿美元。同世界上 140 多个国家和地区建立了贸易关系。出口商品 600 多种。一九八七年以来，公司多次被评为经贸行业的先进单位，机电产品出口先进企业，首都文明单位，中央国家机关文明单位标兵，中国对外经贸行业先进单位，中国对外经贸行业质量效益型企业。

经过多年的发展，公司已发展成为一个具有 49 个子公司、4000 多名职工，200 多个独资、合资、控股、参股企业，20 多个驻外点的综合型大型外贸企业。

公司的精神是：团结、开拓、求实、奉献；服务、信誉、效益、效率。

公司的发展目标是：以国际贸易为龙头，以实业为基础，以科技为先导，以金融为依托，以国际、国内两个市场为目标，实行流通、生产、科研、金融、服务相结合。把公司发展成为综合化、实业化、国际化、国内一流、国际一流的集团公司。

公司法人代表、总裁：钱本源

副总裁：冯学昌、张志杰、陈旭、兰树立

地址:北京市复兴路甲 23 号电子大楼

邮编:100036

电话:(010)68219550，68219532

传真:(010)68212352 68223907

电子信箱：ceiec@ceiec.com.cn

网址：//www.ceiec.com.cn

中国长江三峡工程开发总公司

China Yangtze Three Gorges Project Development Corporation

中国长江三峡工程开发总公司是经国务院批准，负责三峡工程建设的业主单位。公司内部设有国际合作部，又于 1996 年成立了三峡国际招标有限公司，专门从事三峡工程所需的设备、物资国际招标采购。截止到2000年，三峡工程国际招标采购合同额累计逾9亿美元。2000年上半年又完成三峡工程左岸水轮发电机组辅助设备、高强度钢板等国际招标采购，签约金额达 2500 万美元，下半年将进行电站自动控制系统国际招标。同时中国长江三峡工程开发总公司也积极在工程建设中，就一些重大技术课题、施工方案等与国际著名科研机构、咨询公司合作，2000 年上半年签订国际咨询合同共 17 项，合同额近 400 万美元，有效地促进了工程建设技术攻关和质量控制。

China Yangtze Three Gorges Project Development Corporation (CTGPC) approved by State Council, is the owner in charge of the construction of Three Gorges Project. CTGPC set up International Cooperation Department, and Three Gorges International Tendering Limited Company (TGT) in 1996 as well, which specifically undertake procurement of equipment and materials needed by Three Gorges Project by way of international bidding. By the year of 2000, The sum of Three Gorges international bidding contracts amounts to 0.9 billion USD. In the first half year of 2000, CTGPC finished the procurement by way of international bidding for subsidiary equipment to turbine units and generator units of Three Gorges Project Left Bank Power Station and high intensity steel plates etc., with the contractual sum of 25 million USD. The international bidding of auto control system on power station will be carried on in the second part of this year. At the same time, during the construction, CTGPC cooperates with world famous science and technology research institutions and consulting company in respect of major technological subjects and working plans. In the first half year of 2000, seventeen international consulting contracts were concluded with the sum of 4million USD, which effectively enhanced the development of technology and quality control on project constructions.

地址：北京市崇文区广渠门内大街 25 号
电话：67153569
传真：67124392

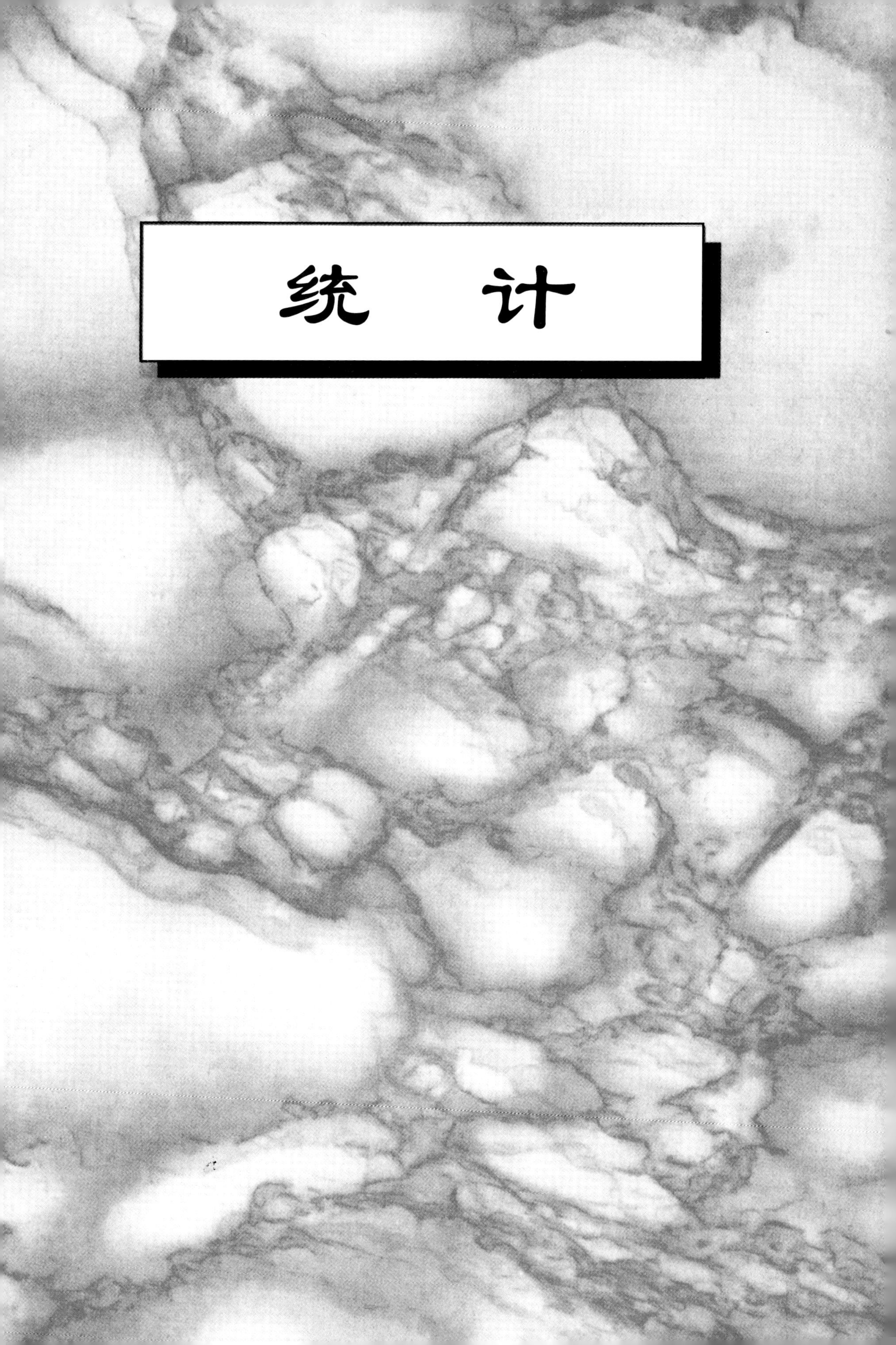

统　　计

1994－1999中国对外贸易进出口情况

进出口总额（金额单位：亿美元）

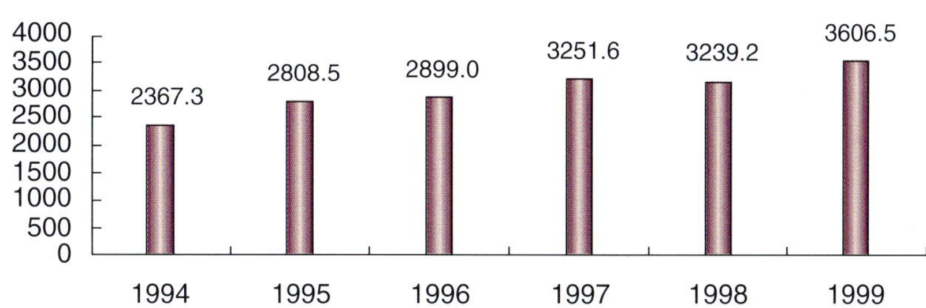

出口总额（金额单位：亿美元）

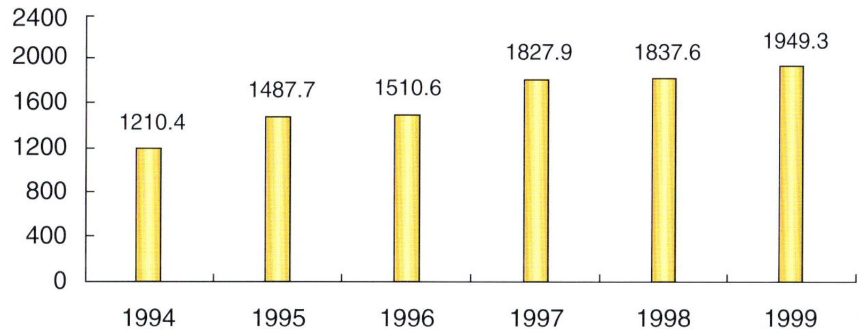

进口总额（金额单位：亿美元）

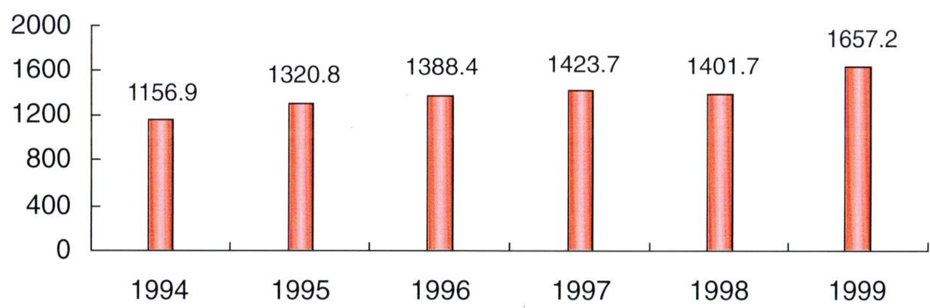

1999年中国对外贸易构成情况（一）

按国际贸易标准分类划分

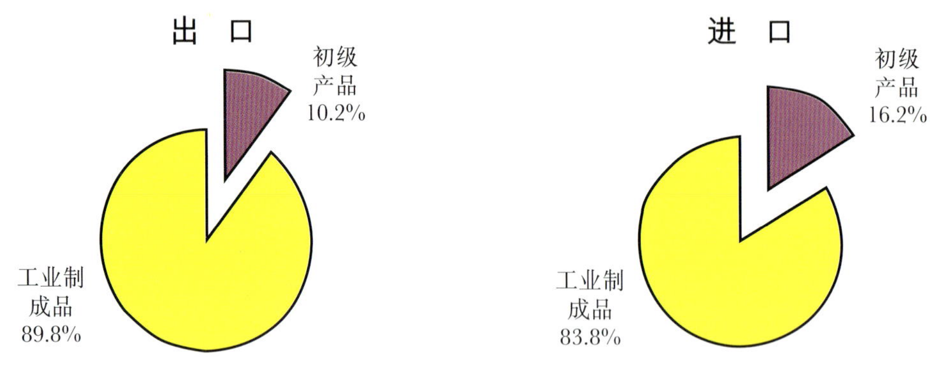

按贸易方式划分

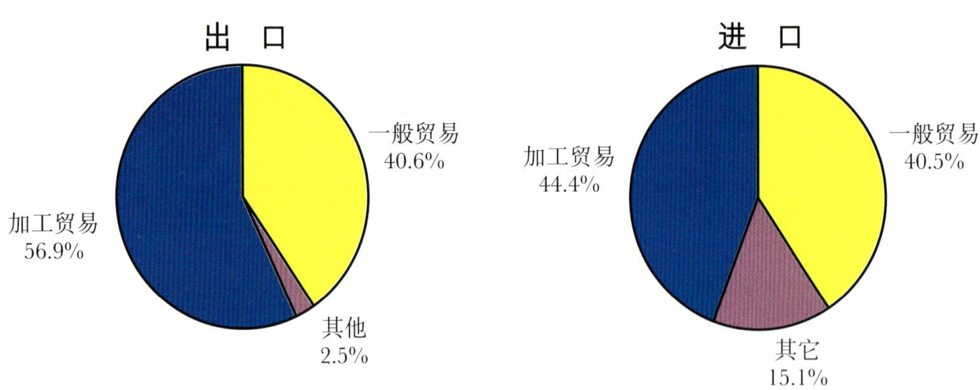

按企业性质划分

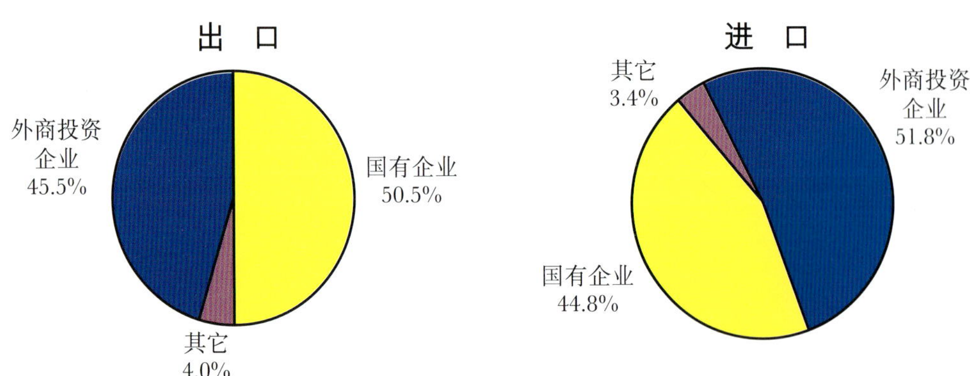

1999年中国对外贸易构成情况（二）

按主要贸易伙伴划分

出 口

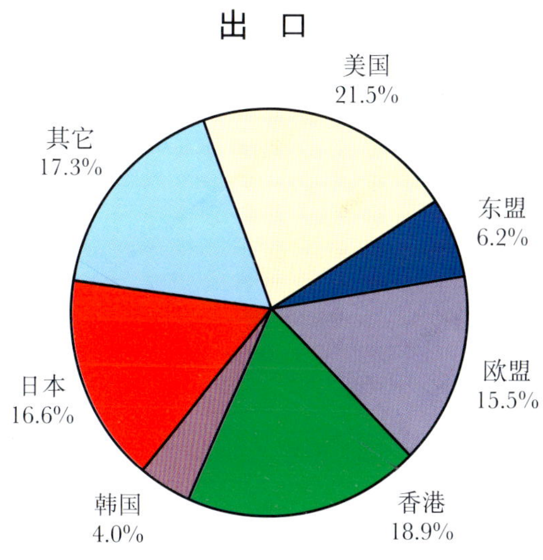

进 口

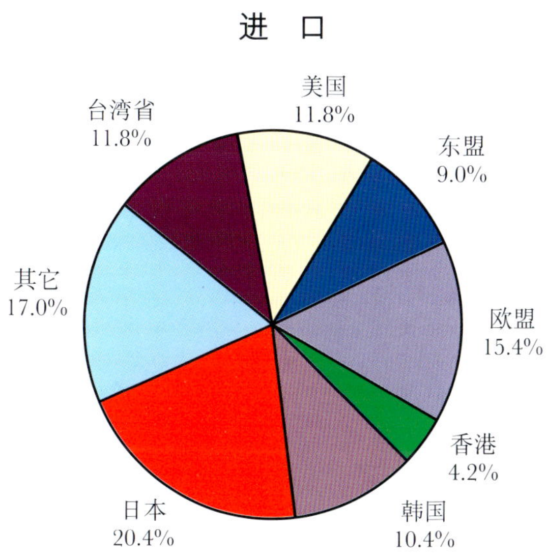

1999年中国对外贸易构成情况（三）

按主要省市划分

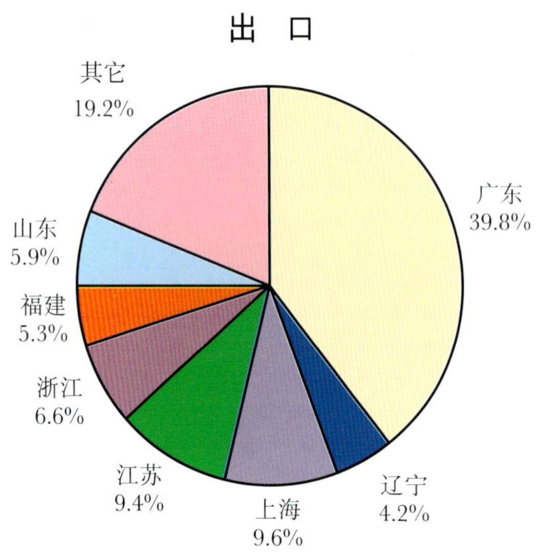

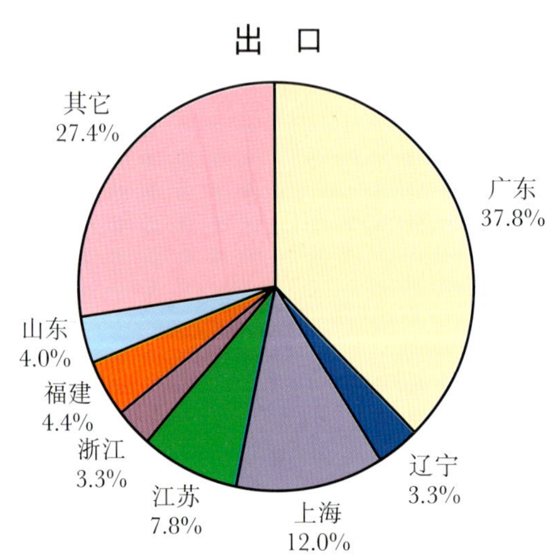

1994—1999年中国实际利用外资情况

利用外资总额（金额单位：亿美元）

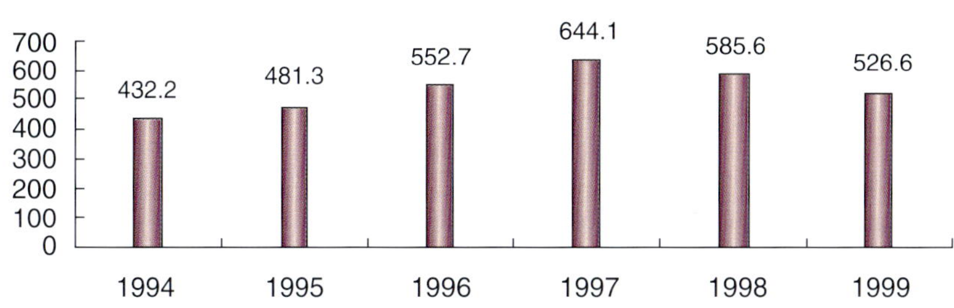

对外借款（金额单位：亿美元）

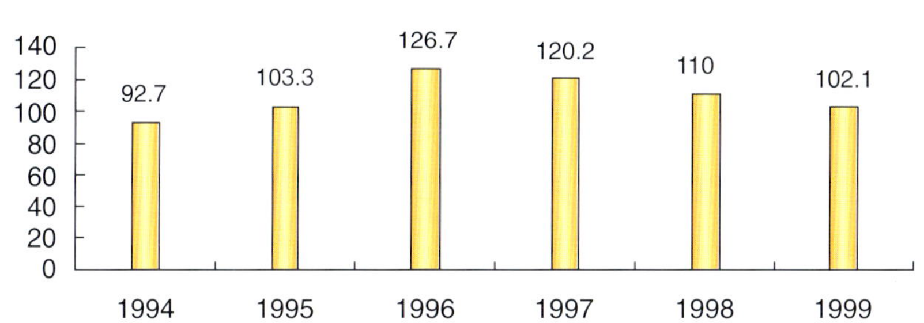

外商直接投资（金额单位：亿美元）

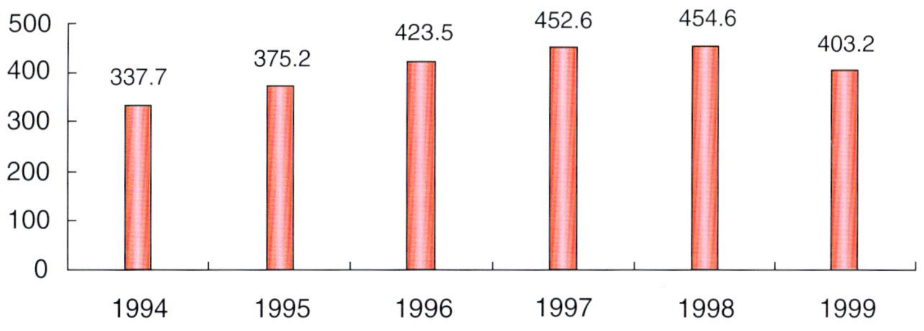

1999年实际利用外资构成

按利用外资方式划分

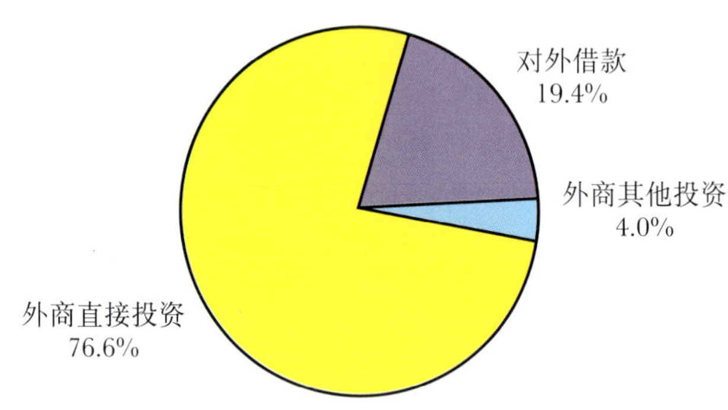

按主要投资方划分（外商直接投资）

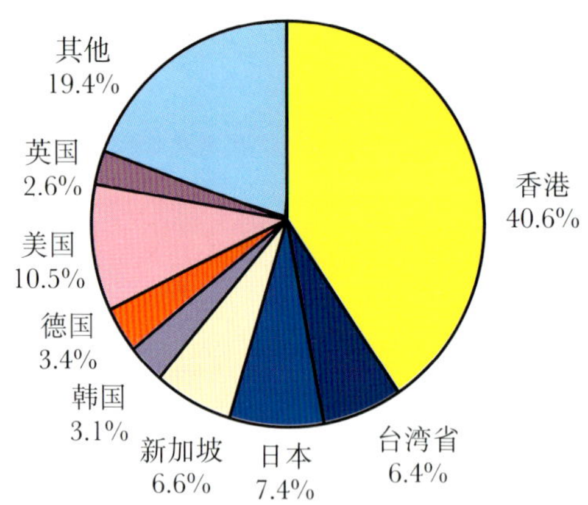

按主要利用外资省市划分（外商直接投资）

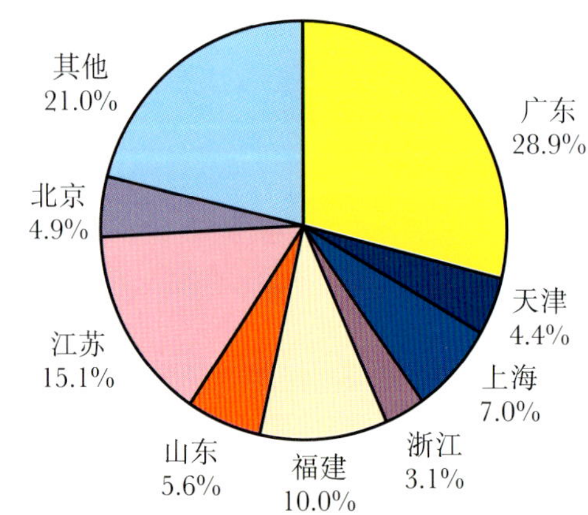

1994—1999年中国批准签订利用外资协议（合同）情况

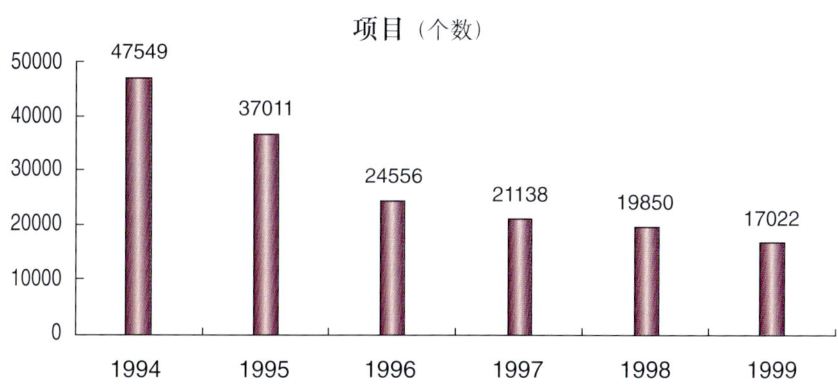

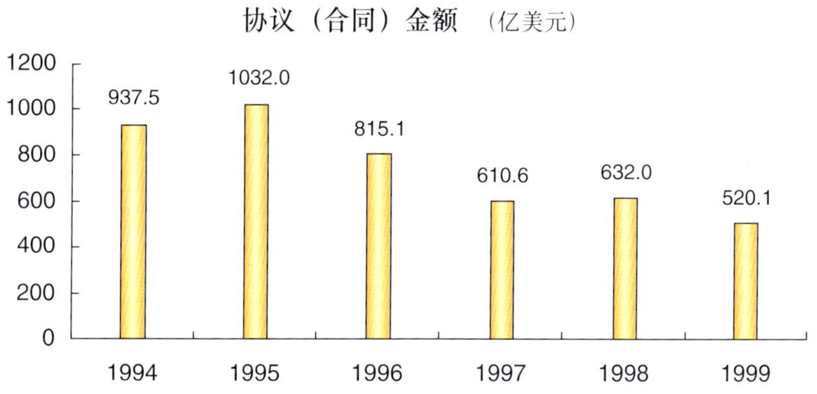

1994 —1999年中国签订对外经济合作合同情况

承包工程合同额（金额单位：亿美元）

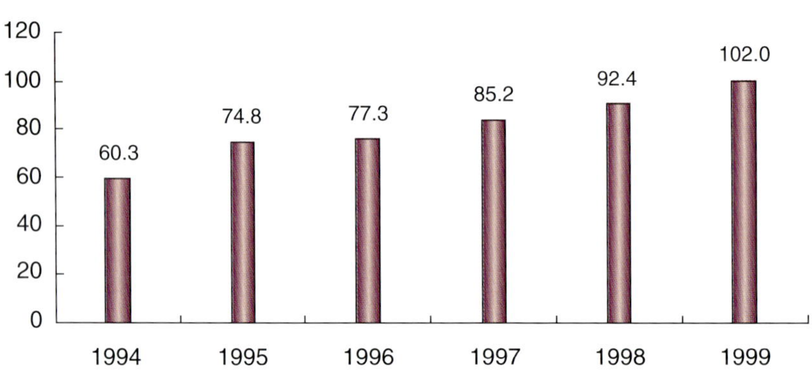

劳务合作合同额（金额单位：亿美元）

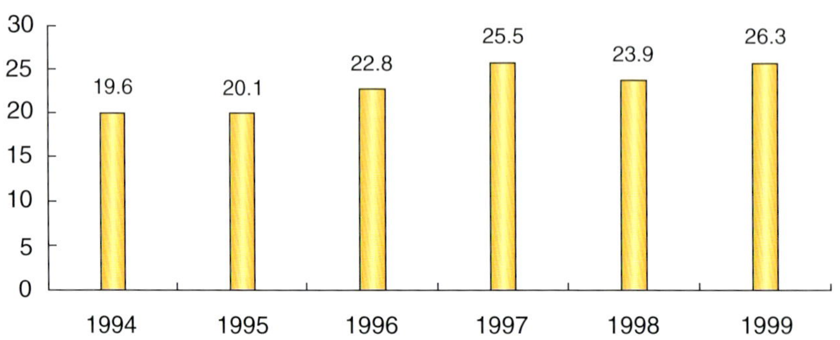

1994—1999 年中国对外经济合作实际完成情况

承包工程营业额（金额单位：亿美元）

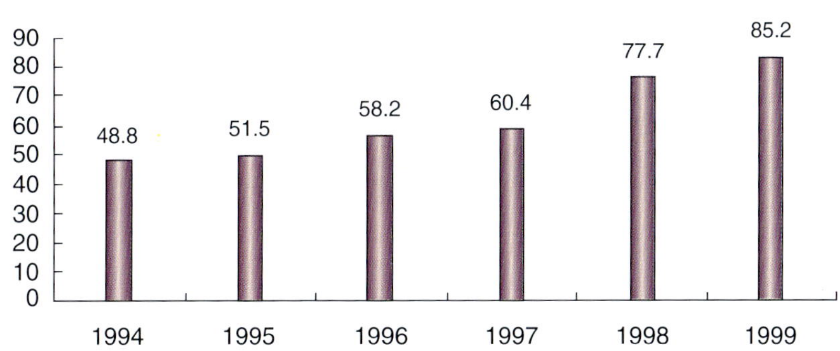

劳务合作营业额（金额单位：亿美元）

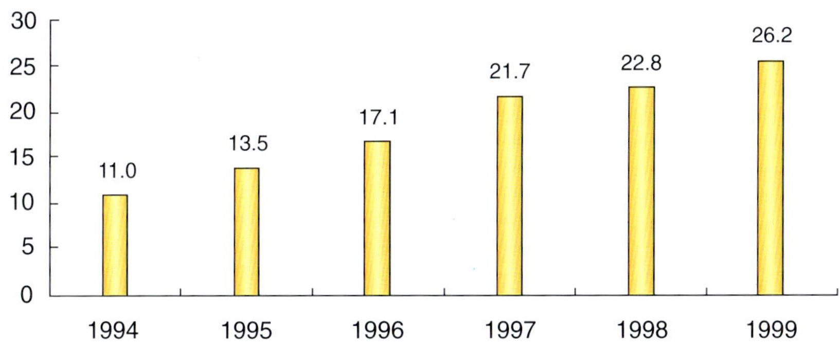

1999年中国签订对外经济合作合同构成情况

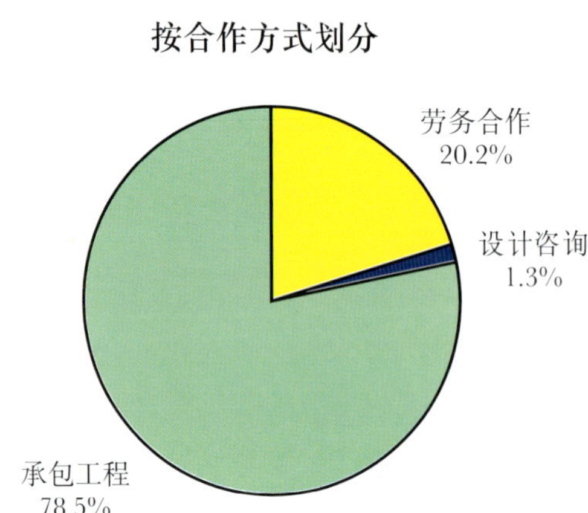

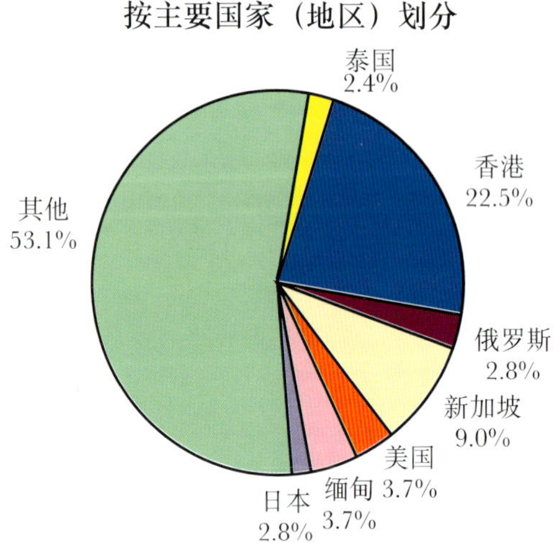

1999年中国实际完成对外经济合作构成情况

按合作方式划分

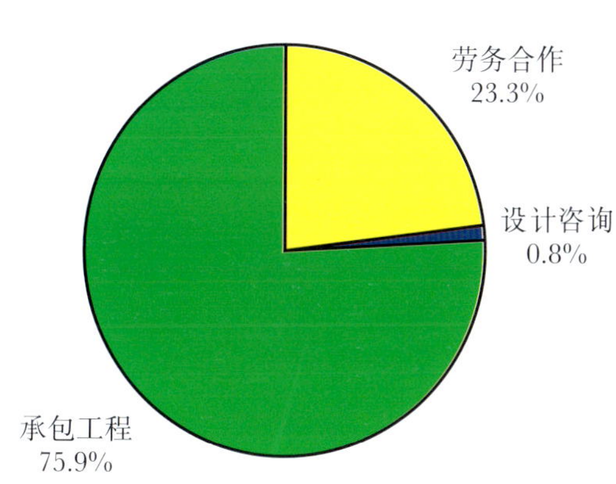

按主要国家（地区）划分

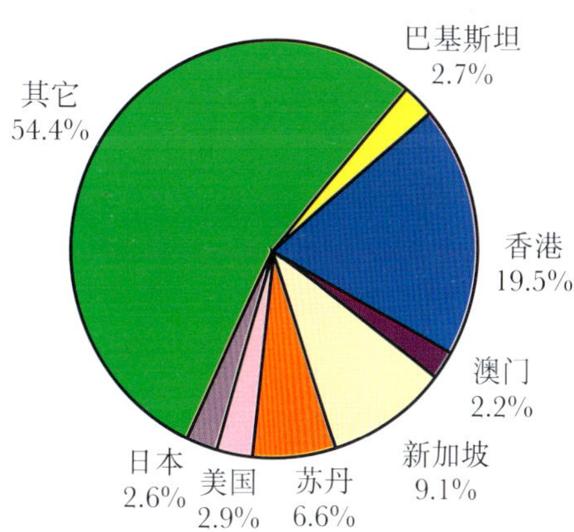

1980年—1999年中国进出口总额

金额单位:亿美元

年份	进出口额	出口额	进口额
1980	381.4	181.2	200.2
1981	440.2	220.1	220.1
1982	416.2	223.2	192.8
1983	436.1	222.2	213.9
1984	535.5	261.4	274.1
1985	696.0	273.5	422.5
1986	738.4	309.4	429.0
1987	826.5	394.4	432.1
1988	1028.0	475.2	552.8
1989	1116.8	525.4	591.4
1990	1154.4	620.9	533.5
1991	1356.3	718.4	637.9
1992	1655.3	849.4	805.9
1993	1957.1	917.6	1039.5
1994	2367.3	1210.4	1156.9
1995	2808.5	1487.7	1320.8
1996	2899.0	1510.7	1388.3
1997	3251.6	1827.9	1423.7
1998	3239.3	1837.6	1401.7
1999	3606.5	1949.3	1657.2

1980年—1999年中国进出口总额指数
(1980=100)

年份	进出口额	出口额	进口额
1980	100.0	100.0	100.0
1981	115.4	121.5	109.9
1982	109.1	123.2	96.3
1983	114.3	122.6	106.8
1984	140.4	144.3	136.9
1985	182.5	150.9	211.0
1986	193.6	170.8	214.3
1987	216.7	217.7	215.8
1988	269.5	262.2	276.1
1989	292.8	289.9	295.4
1990	302.7	342.7	266.5

1980 年—1999 年中国进出口总额指数
(1980 = 100)

年　份	进出口额	出口额	进口额
1991	355.6	396.5	318.6
1992	434.0	468.8	402.5
1993	513.1	506.4	519.2
1994	620.7	668.0	577.9
1995	736.4	821.0	659.7
1996	760.1	833.7	693.5
1997	852.3	1008.3	711.1
1998	856.5	1005.8	717.0
1999	945.6	1075.8	827.9

1981 年—1999 年中国进出口总额增长速度
(比上年增长%)

年　份	进出口额	出口额	进口额
1981	15.4	21.5	9.9
1982	-5.4	1.4	-12.4
1983	4.8	-0.4	10.9
1984	22.8	17.6	28.1
1985	30.0	4.6	54.2
1986	6.1	13.1	1.5
1987	11.9	27.5	0.7
1988	24.4	20.5	27.9
1989	8.7	10.6	7.0
1990	3.4	18.2	-9.8
1991	17.5	15.7	19.6
1992	22.0	18.2	26.3
1993	18.2	8.0	28.9
1994	21.0	31.9	11.3
1995	18.6	22.9	14.2
1996	3.2	1.5	5.1
1997	12.1	20.9	2.5
1998	-0.4	0.5	-1.5
1999	11.3	6.1	18.2

1980年—1999年中国出口总额占世界出口总额的比重和位次

金额单位:亿美元

年　份	世界出口总额	中国出口总额	中国出口总额占世界出口总额比重%	位　次
1980	19906	181.2	0.9	26
1981	19724	220.1	1.1	19
1982	18308	223.2	1.2	17
1983	18078	222.2	1.2	17
1984	19019	261.4	1.4	18
1985	19277	273.5	1.4	17
1986	21157	309.4	1.5	16
1987	24969	394.4	1.6	16
1988	28382	475.2	1.7	16
1989	30361	525.4	1.7	14
1990	34700	620.9	1.8	15
1991	35300	718.4	2.0	13
1992	37000	849.4	2.3	11
1993	36870	917.6	2.5	11
1994	41683	1210.4	2.9	11
1995	50200	1487.7	3.0	11
1996	52540	1510.7	2.9	11
1997	54550	1827.9	3.3	10
1998	54050	1837.6	3.4	9
1999	54600	1949.3	3.6	9

1990 年—1999 年中国出口商品构成
（按国际贸易标准分类）

金额单位：亿美元

年份	出口总额	初级产品		1. 食品及活动物		2. 饮料及烟草		3. 非食用原料（燃料除外）		4. 矿物燃料、润滑油及有关原料		5. 动植物油、脂及蜡	
		金额	比重%	金额	比重%	金额	比重%	金额	比重%	金额	比重%	金额	比重%
1990	620.9	158.9	25.6	66.1	10.6	3.4	0.5	35.4	5.7	52.4	8.4	1.6	0.4
1991	718.4	161.5	22.5	72.3	10.1	5.3	0.7	34.9	4.9	47.5	6.6	1.5	0.2
1992	849.4	170.0	20.0	83.1	9.8	7.2	0.8	31.4	3.7	46.9	5.5	1.4	0.2
1993	917.6	166.7	18.2	84.1	9.2	9.0	1.0	30.5	3.3	41.1	4.5	2.0	0.2
1994	1210.4	197.1	16.3	100.2	8.3	10.0	0.8	41.3	3.4	40.6	3.4	5.0	0.4
1995	1487.7	214.9	14.4	99.5	6.7	13.7	0.9	43.8	2.9	53.4	3.6	4.5	0.3
1996	1510.7	219.3	14.5	102.3	6.8	13.4	0.9	40.5	2.7	59.3	3.9	3.8	0.3
1997	1827.9	239.3	13.1	110.5	6.0	10.5	0.6	41.9	2.3	69.9	3.8	6.5	0.4
1998	1837.6	206.0	11.2	106.2	6.0	9.8	0.5	35.2	1.9	51.8	3.0	3.1	0.2
1999	1949.3	199.3	10.2	104.6	5.4	7.7	0.4	39.2	2.0	46.5	2.4	1.3	0.1

1990年—1999年中国出口商品构成
（按国际贸易标准分类）

金额单位：亿美元

年份	工业制成品		1．化学成品及有关产品		2．按原料分类的制成品		3．机械及运输设备		4．杂项制品		5．未分类的商品	
	金额	比重%	金额	比重%	金额	比重%	金额	比重%	金额	比重%	金额	比重%
1990	461.8	74.4	37.3	6.0	125.8	20.3	55.9	9.0	126.9	20.4	116.3	18.7
1991	556.9	77.0	38.2	5.3	144.6	20.1	71.5	10.0	166.2	23.1	136.5	19.0
1992	679.4	80.0	43.5	5.1	161.4	19.0	132.2	15.6	342.3	40.3	—	—
1993	750.9	81.8	46.2	5.0	164.0	17.8	152.9	16.7	387.8	42.3	—	—
1994	1013.3	83.7	62.3	5.1	232.2	19.2	219.3	18.1	499.4	41.3	0.1	0.0
1995	1272.8	85.6	90.9	6.1	322.4	21.7	313.9	21.1	545.5	36.7	0.1	0.0
1996	1291.4	85.5	88.8	5.9	285.1	18.9	353.1	23.4	564.3	37.3	0.1	0.0
1997	1587.7	86.9	102.3	5.6	344.1	18.9	437.0	23.9	704.3	38.5	0.1	0.0
1998	1631.6	88.8	103.2	5.6	323.8	17.6	502.3	27.3	702.2	38.2	0.1	0.0
1999	1750.0	89.8	103.7	5.3	332.6	17.1	588.3	30.2	725.3	37.2	0.1	0.0

1990年—1999年中国进口商品构成
（按国际贸易标准分类）

金额单位：亿美元

年份	工业制成品		1．化学成品及有关产品		2．按原料分类的制成品		3．机械及运输设备		4．杂项制品		5．未分类的商品	
	金额	比重%	金额	比重%	金额	比重%	金额	比重%	金额	比重%	金额	比重%
1990	434.9	81.6	66.5	12.5	89.1	16.7	168.4	31.6	21.0	3.9	89.9	6.9
1991	529.6	83.0	92.8	14.5	104.9	16.4	196.0	30.7	24.4	3.8	111.5	21.1
1992	673.3	83.6	111.6	13.8	192.7	23.9	313.1	38.8	55.9	6.9	—	—
1993	897.3	86.3	97.1	9.3	285.4	27.5	449.9	43.3	64.9	6.2	—	—
1994	992.2	85.8	121.3	10.5	280.8	24.3	515.6	44.6	67.7	5.9	6.8	0.6
1995	1076.7	81.5	173.0	13.1	287.7	21.8	526.4	39.8	82.7	6.3	6.9	0.5
1996	1134.0	81.7	181.1	13.0	313.9	22.6	547.7	39.5	84.8	6.1	6.5	0.5
1997	1137.4	79.9	193.0	13.6	322.2	22.6	527.6	37.1	85.5	6.0	9.1	0.6
1998	1172.1	83.6	201.7	19.4	310.7	22.2	567.7	40.5	84.6	6.0	7.5	0.5
1999	1388.7	83.8	240.3	14.5	343.2	20.7	694.7	41.9	97.0	5.9	13.5	0.8

1990 年—1999 年中国进口商品构成
（按国际贸易标准分类）

金额单位：亿美元

年份	进口总额	初级产品		1. 食品及活动物		2. 饮料及烟草		3. 非食用原料（燃料除外）		4. 矿物燃料、润滑油及有关原料		5. 动植物油、脂及蜡	
		金额	比重%	金额	比重%	金额	比重%	金额	比重%	金额	比重%	金额	比重%
1990	533.5	98.6	18.3	33.4	6.2	1.6	0.3	41.1	7.7	12.7	2.3	9.8	1.8
1991	637.9	108.3	17.0	28.0	4.4	2.0	0.3	50.0	7.8	21.1	3.3	7.2	1.1
1992	805.9	132.6	16.4	31.5	3.9	2.4	0.3	57.7	7.2	35.7	4.4	5.3	0.6
1993	1039.5	142.2	13.7	22.1	2.1	2.5	0.3	54.4	5.2	58.2	5.6	5	0.5
1994	1156.9	164.7	14.2	31.2	2.7	0.7	0.1	74.4	6.4	40.3	3.5	18.1	1.6
1995	1320.8	244.1	18.5	61.3	4.6	3.9	0.3	101.6	7.7	51.3	3.9	26	2.0
1996	1388.4	254.4	18.3	56.7	4.1	5.0	0.4	107.0	7.7	68.8	4.9	17	1.2
1997	1423.7	286.2	20.1	43.0	3.0	3.2	0.2	120.1	8.4	103.1	7.2	16.8	1.2
1998	1401.7	229.5	16.4	37.9	2.7	1.8	0.0	107.2	7.7	67.7	4.8	14.9	1.1
1999	1657.2	268.4	16.2	36.2	2.2	2.1	0.1	127.4	7.7	89.1	5.4	13.7	0.8

1999年中国进出口分国家(地区)总值表

金额单位:万美元

国家(地区)	1999			1998		
	进出口	出口	进口	进出口	出口	进口
总值	**36064944**	**19493143**	**16571801**	**32392342**	**18375711**	**14016630**
亚洲	**20426881**	**10257861**	**10169020**	**18523504**	**9818040**	**8705464**
阿富汗	1958	1668	290	2455	2434	21
巴林	7068	3177	3891	5704	2971	2733
孟加拉国	71513	70087	1425	68715	66068	2647
不丹	74	72	2	28	28	
东南亚国家联盟	2704167	1217046	1487121	2348213	1092110	1256103
文莱	810	810		915	914	1
缅甸	50803	40655	10148	58090	51886	6204
印度尼西亚	482983	177893	305090	362792	117122	245670
老挝	3172	2216	956	2573	1783	790
马来西亚	527940	167362	360578	426432	159635	266798
菲律宾	228692	137938	90754	201311	150116	51195
新加坡	856334	450216	406118	815433	393004	422429
泰国	421618	143570	278048	356087	114807	241280
越南	131815	96385	35429	124579	102844	21736
柬埔寨	16012	10433	5579	16188	11369	4818
塞浦路斯	10253	10201	52	8122	8059	62
朝鲜	37037	32866	4171	41302	35571	5731
香港	4378301	3689063	689238	4541163	3875321	665842
印度	198768	116189	82579	192230	101660	90570
伊朗	134746	66274	68472	121502	65669	55832
伊拉克	26408	14795	11612	16453	10467	5986
以色列	68187	49062	19125	52382	35279	17103
日本	6616726	3239901	3376825	5789918	2969199	2820720
约旦	18026	14931	3095	15981	13568	2413
科威特	28857	13744	15113	23015	11030	11985
黎巴嫩	15740	15732	8	14853	14828	25
澳门	73422	63727	9695	87044	74748	12296
马尔代夫	86	86	1	59	54	5
蒙古	26310	6883	19427	24329	6254	18075
尼泊尔	21536	20702	834	7210	6688	522
阿曼	66245	2708	63537	74589	3942	70646
巴基斯坦	97081	58061	39020	91276	52376	38900
巴勒斯坦	614	614	1	866	865	1
卡塔尔	9112	2786	6326	6134	1621	4513

1999年中国进出口分国家(地区)总值表

金额单位:万美元

国家(地区)	1999			1998		
	进出口	出口	进口	进出口	出口	进口
沙特阿拉伯	185533	94373	91160	169973	89614	80358
韩国	2503560	780800	1722761	2126433	626898	1499536
斯里兰卡	26807	25889	918	29858	29279	579
叙利亚	20833	20334	499	17588	17441	148
土耳其	68381	63649	4732	70190	65911	4278
阿拉伯联合酋长国	163307	144361	18946	145244	129080	16164
也门共和国	68322	12635	55687	63036	10671	52366
中华人民共和国	414033		414033	301526		301526
台湾省	2347855	395008	1952848	2049917	386956	1662961
亚洲其他国家(地区)	5	5		12	12	
非洲	**648362**	**410849**	**237513**	**553587**	**405933**	**147654**
阿尔及利亚	22217	15998	6219	11680	11668	12
安哥拉	37203	1638	35565	19036	3666	15370
贝宁	16167	15925	242	15713	15364	349
博茨瓦那	817	816		1124	1124	
布隆迪	146	146		209	209	
喀麦隆	9647	2015	7631	6757	1892	4865
加那利群岛	2118	2112	6	1762	1762	
佛得角	315	315		197	197	
中非共和国	101	101		107	106	1
塞卜泰(休达)	196	196		134	134	
乍得	24	24		15	15	
科摩罗	64	64		12	12	
刚果	7072	1079	5993	8807	4674	4133
吉布提	3835	3834		3092	3092	1
埃及	75022	71586	3436	60653	57484	3169
赤道几内亚	16960	250	16710	7185	294	6891
埃塞俄比亚	5422	5345	77	6875	6827	48
加蓬	28564	653	27912	15733	1016	14717
冈比亚	5719	5719		5064	5064	
加纳	11433	10952	482	12007	11155	852
几内亚	5422	4631	791	3813	3718	95
几内亚(比绍)	338	318	20	145	145	
科特迪瓦共和国	20564	19772	793	17613	15207	2406
肯尼亚	10553	10061	492	11971	11821	149
利比里亚	1237	1237		2778	2778	

1999年中国进出口分国家(地区)总值表

金额单位:万美元

国家(地区)	1999			1998		
	进出口	出口	进口	进出口	出口	进口
利比亚	8162	6475	1687	9314	7160	2154
马达加斯加	4551	4060	491	3447	3273	175
马拉维	500	500		251	251	
马里	1986	1850	136	2925	2439	486
毛里塔尼亚	2264	1779	485	1076	955	121
毛里求斯	9348	7109	2239	6651	6588	63
摩洛哥	30930	25381	5549	25160	16554	8606
莫桑比克	2224	1894	330	1377	1334	43
纳米比亚	1056	736	320	1699	923	777
尼日尔	1476	1476		741	741	
尼日利亚	57843	39594	18249	38468	35726	2742
留尼汪	553	553		448	448	
卢旺达	349	175	174	402	212	191
圣多美和普林西比	6	6		6	6	
塞内加尔	3985	3932	54	4376	4336	40
塞舌尔	202	201		132	132	
塞拉利昂	435	435		441	441	
索马里	55	49	6	22	18	5
南非	172178	86059	86118	155827	86722	69106
西撒哈拉	6	6		4	4	
苏丹	28262	22933	5330	35105	34958	147
坦桑尼亚	6940	6365	574	7967	6998	969
多哥	7032	7026	6	6223	5909	314
突尼斯	12576	9737	2839	12972	393	4579
乌干达	1085	1065	20	1092	1078	13
布基纳法索	337	138	200	939	514	426
民主刚果	2006	1875	132	6325	6100	224
赞比亚	2602	840	1762	2835	2213	622
津巴布韦	7160	2726	4434	13273	10487	2787
莱索托	377	375	2	902	899	3
梅利利亚	219	219		172	172	
斯威士兰	244	244		234	234	
厄立特里亚	76	74	2	264	260	4
非洲其他国家(地区)	182	176	6	39	37	2
欧洲	**6812874**	**3547498**	**3265376**	**5973512**	**3342877**	**2630634**
欧洲联盟	5567601	3021549	2546546	4886322	2814790	2071532

1999年中国进出口分国家(地区)总值表

金额单位:万美元

国家(地区)	1999			1998		
	进出口	出口	进口	进出口	出口	进口
比利时	279286	182240	97045	251951	164110	87841
丹麦	101527	61504	40023	77629	45744	31885
英国	787406	487915	299491	658407	463219	195187
德国	1611422	777809	833613	1434755	735392	699363
法国	670549	292017	378532	602749	282276	320473
爱尔兰	41966	21248	20718	30201	19627	10573
意大利	561609	292912	268697	485437	257734	227703
卢森堡	8655	3814	4841	8222	3671	4551
荷兰	642289	541194	101096	599522	516151	83370
希腊	39102	36780	2322	40642	38594	2048
葡萄牙	25828	21996	3832	22756	20061	2696
西班牙	233614	179474	54140	200410	152388	48022
奥地利	68541	24719	43821	48340	21141	27198
芬兰	219635	36441	183194	157847	31855	125992
瑞典	276175	60993	215182	267455	62826	204629
阿尔巴尼亚	1040	1040		884	883	
安道尔	58	58		157	157	
保加利亚	6266	5344	922	4799	4518	280
直布罗陀	49	49		376	376	
匈牙利	62207	55060	7146	40986	39705	1281
冰岛	1459	669	790	1266	536	730
列支敦士登	54	39	16	41	41	
马耳他	6067	5072	995	2703	2529	175
摩纳哥	243	186	57	202	172	30
挪威	82701	34277	48424	63450	32996	30454
波兰	86023	70244	15779	81453	75867	5586
罗马尼亚	19127	14564	4563	25966	23975	1992
圣马力诺	34	33	1	11	10	
瑞士	168568	67440	101128	142955	63399	79556
爱沙尼亚	1039	723	316	1468	692	776
拉脱维亚	2111	1436	675	2178	1359	820
立陶宛	2713	2653	60	2408	2369	39
格鲁吉亚	373	223	150	773	613	161
亚美尼亚	1159	1158	1	84	78	6
阿塞拜疆	113	99	15	131	115	16
白俄罗斯	2602	533	2069	1734	646	1088

1999年中国进出口分国家(地区)总值表

金额单位:万美元

国家(地区)	1999			1998		
	进出口	出口	进口	进出口	出口	进口
哈萨克斯坦	113878	49438	64440	63554	20468	43086
吉尔吉斯斯坦	13487	10290	3197	19810	17241	2569
摩尔多瓦	38	38		70	19	51
俄罗斯	572006	149749	422257	548123	184037	364086
塔吉克斯坦	804	230	574	1923	1104	819
土库曼斯坦	949	747	202	1252	1029	222
乌克兰	42133	8100	34033	27505	9011	18494
乌兹别克斯坦	4034	2739	1295	9025	5788	3236
南斯拉夫	3733	3055	678	3333	2882	451
斯洛文尼亚	5805	4791	1014	3608	3412	196
克罗地亚	5282	4752	530	2027	1987	40
捷克	35683	28455	7228	29196	26590	2605
斯洛伐克	2907	2710	197	3457	3224	233
马其顿共和国	441	394	46	251	238	12
波斯尼亚—黑塞哥维那	88	57	31	33	21	13
拉丁美洲	**826022**	**526894**	**299127**	**831215**	**532299**	**298916**
安提瓜和巴布达	94	86	8	224	216	9
阿根廷	108562	49594	58969	127450	55004	72446
阿鲁巴岛	333	333		258	258	
巴哈马	540	540		2786	2786	
巴巴多斯	204	202	1	205	205	
伯利兹	288	288		210	184	26
玻利维亚	751	504	248	754	746	8
博内尔	2	2				
巴西	184471	87614	96857	221867	108556	113310
开曼群岛	3	3		20	20	
智利	126863	60506	66358	104135	61990	42145
哥伦比亚	12501	10433	2068	10097	9275	822
多米尼克国	4077	3937	140	4657	4634	23
哥斯达黎加	7043	6327	715	6329	4646	1684
古巴	28874	23209	5665	22128	12736	9392
库腊索岛	1480	1480		1227	1227	
多米尼加共和国	5746	5694	52	6191	6159	33
厄瓜多尔	11852	3989	7862	14704	7393	7311
法属圭亚那	25	24		85	85	
格林纳达	14	14		24	23	1

1999年中国进出口分国家(地区)总值表

金额单位:万美元

国家(地区)	1999			1998		
	进出口	出口	进口	进出口	出口	进口
瓜德罗普	76	76		57	57	
危地马拉	10363	10333	30	9534	9497	38
圭亚那	1125	815	310	597	552	45
海地	1168	1168		944	944	
洪都拉斯	6115	6115		5958	5861	97
牙买加	5837	5000	837	6425	4632	1793
马提尼克	54	54		35	35	
墨西哥	95088	79161	15927	83681	68935	14747
蒙特塞拉特	1	1		2	2	
尼加拉瓜	1659	1659		1834	1834	
巴拿马	103838	103731	107	104876	104756	119
巴拉圭	5881	5698	183	8026	7841	186
秘鲁	44075	13079	30996	39540	10726	28814
波多黎各	6602	5733	870	3629	3595	34
萨巴	7	7				
圣卢西亚	121	121		57	57	
圣马丁岛	124	124		55	55	
圣文森特和格林纳丁斯	1121	1108	13	562	536	26
萨尔瓦多	5169	5168	1	4432	4424	8
苏里南	692	690	2	949	850	99
特立尼达和多巴哥	2842	1747	1095	1671	1671	
特克斯和凯科斯群岛	11	11		12	10	2
乌拉圭	21277	14231	7046	16500	12047	4453
委内瑞拉	18836	16070	2766	18290	17043	1247
英属维尔京群岛	174	173	1	107	107	
圣其茨—尼维斯	9	9		1	1	
拉丁美洲其他国家(地区)	36	36		92	91	1
北美洲	**6620407**	**4438768**	**2181639**	**5930284**	**4010439**	**1919845**
加拿大	476677	243273	233404	436486	212766	223720
美国	6142573	4194576	1947997	5493699	3797587	1696112
格陵兰	256	18	238	26	13	13
百慕大	897	897		72	72	
北美洲其他国家(地区)	4	4		2	2	
大洋洲	**730361**	**311274**	**419087**	**580150**	**266124**	**314027**
澳大利亚	631137	270416	360721	502976	234167	268809
库克群岛	22	22		27	27	

1999年中国进出口分国家(地区)总值表

金额单位:万美元

国家(地区)	1999			1998		
	进出口	出口	进口	进出口	出口	进口
斐济	2099	2009	90	1785	1385	400
盖比群岛	21	21		13	13	
马克萨斯群岛	1	1		2	2	
瑙鲁	6	6		2	2	
新喀里多尼亚	309	308	1	252	251	1
瓦努阿图	125	122	3	130	110	19
新西兰	82417	34285	48133	68493	27502	40992
诺福克岛	5	5		17	15	2
巴布亚新几内亚	11474	2923	8551	5244	1904	3340
社会群岛	133	133		101	101	
所罗门群岛	1709	120	1589	564	110	454
汤加	61	60		51	51	
土阿莫土群岛	2	2				
土布艾群岛						
萨摩亚	231	231		124	115	10
基里巴斯	143	143		131	131	
图瓦卢				8	8	
密克罗尼西亚联邦	16	16		17	17	
马绍尔群岛共和国	33	33		29	29	
贝劳共和国	102	102		48	48	
大洋洲其他国家(地区)	317	317		137	137	

1999年中国出口主要商品数量金额

金额单位:万美元

品名	单位	1999		1998	
		数量	金额	数量	金额
粮谷	公吨	7376298	118663	8886399	157618
大米	公吨	2703202	64564	3745387	92506
玉米	公吨	4304987	44997	4686261	53164
高粱	公吨	16888	239	18607	246
荞麦	公吨	105751	2081	106337	2474
谷子	公吨	20845	457	18597	446

1999年中国出口主要商品数量金额

金额单位:万美元

品　　名	单位	1999		1998	
		数量	金额	数量	金额
面粉	公吨	163534	4555	268967	7389
豆类	公吨	1015249	33994	642205	28042
黄大豆	公吨	204366	6189	169874	6339
蚕豆	公吨	164636	3833	17574	580
绿豆	公吨	289038	10897	114279	6598
红小豆	公吨	61593	2902	53438	2428
芸豆	公吨	214859	8073	222850	9851
扁豆	公吨	21888	496	26310	722
食用植物油	公吨	96615	7577	309314	22545
花生油	公吨	12978	1517	10165	1199
豆油	公吨	53394	3433	185891	13475
芝麻油	公吨	3962	764	4171	767
食用植物油籽	公吨	674368	35469	439694	26982
花生仁	公吨	285933	16564	148573	11273
花生果	公吨	54624	2835	66296	4278
芝麻	公吨	96795	8484	44471	4424
葵花籽	公吨	22957	1241	8550	612
工业用油	公吨	33190	4352	35903	5839
桐油	公吨	24176	2184	21176	2963
工业用油籽	公吨	31260	1341	24797	1020
活畜禽	金额		38515		44101
活大猪	头	1627030	21540	1748965	25880
活中猪	头	327130	2052	433502	2967
活牛	头	65581	3878	74491	4107
活鸡	万只	4312	9305	4114	9154
活鸭	万只	87	242	89	255
活鸽	万只	231	249	211	272
肉食	金额		105266		113953
冻猪肉	公吨	53743	6744	104975	18082
冻牛肉	公吨	19161	2572	43041	7266
冻山羊肉	公吨	3392	429	2756	396
冻兔肉	公吨	16583	3271	15029	2660
冻鸡	公吨	301928	47379	274443	46017
冻鸭	公吨	4011	620	4499	701
灌腊肠	公吨	9660	2003	9742	2146
鲜蛋	万个	46577	1228	57755	1875

1999年中国出口主要商品数量金额

金额单位:万美元

品名	单位	1999		1998	
		数量	金额	数量	金额
鸡蛋	万个	44078	1193	54899	1803
皮蛋	万个	9434	544	9643	592
咸蛋	万个	15951	552	17510	758
苹果	公吨	219196	7593	170329	6456
桔柑橙	公吨	166448	3957	161159	4612
梨	公吨	121435	3020	112675	3503
香蕉	公吨	12360	438	16660	559
荔枝	公吨	12763	672	2990	290
荸荠	公吨	11407	551	11125	586
西瓜	公吨	33854	437	47001	693
栗子	公吨	33729	6426	38581	6903
葡萄干	公吨	1300	205	1345	182
柿饼	公吨	9886	1110	6561	731
蜜饯	公吨	42031	4512	41229	4886
蜜枣	公吨	5114	438	5933	598
核桃	公吨	2399	281	1359	178
核桃仁	公吨	8282	2087	9969	2851
苦杏仁	公吨	5273	829	5797	1092
松子仁	公吨	4877	3142	4897	4909
白果	公吨	3327	1042	2586	923
红枣	公吨	23400	2177	19943	2268
山核桃	公吨	2399	281	1359	178
山核桃仁	公吨	8282	2087	9969	2851
蔬菜	公吨	2269978	149330	2034171	148779
土豆	公吨	63630	899	37134	515
洋葱	公吨	190647	4304	128860	2890
萝卜	公吨	48200	1050	41350	1117
鲜姜	公吨	82310	4334	53059	3681
蕃茄	公吨	14285	239	28025	634
大蒜	公吨	290847	10681	157627	8450
咸蕨菜	公吨	6947	828	6285	622
榨菜	公吨	16402	782	17755	829
速冻蔬菜	公吨	301603	29373	262746	27462
黑木耳	公吨	5576	2027	4781	1920
蘑菇	公吨	45229	11086	45149	10866
蘑菇干片	公吨	10343	5012	14981	5853

1999年中国出口主要商品数量金额

金额单位:万美元

品名	单位	1999		1998	
		数量	金额	数量	金额
辣椒干	公吨	43447	3482	52983	4810
辣椒粉	公吨	7545	1255	6340	953
笋干丝	公吨	2650	899	2467	1113
水产品	金额		194702		173668
大闸蟹	公吨	145	280	207	437
活鳗鱼	公吨	8184	5292	5929	4859
冰鲜鱼	公吨	69855	11918	62150	13672
冻鱼	公吨	366846	36973	120404	20977
冻鱼片	公吨	240091	47659	226253	46321
冻对虾	公吨	4818	4553	5160	4838
冰鲜虾	公吨	10285	1355	19212	2506
冻小虾	公吨	44741	16475	33567	14072
冻虾仁球	公吨	3618	3345	3659	3390
冻小虾仁	公吨	33465	13118	25298	11245
鱼翅	公吨	2014	3345	2005	3174
海蛰皮	公吨	3867	1513	3842	1570
猪肉罐头	公吨	38338	6238	33394	5914
牛肉罐头	公吨	5487	807	7489	1196
菠萝罐头	公吨	34189	1826	52730	3210
桔子罐头	公吨	119540	9840	112234	7954
桃子罐头	公吨	35296	3146	31543	2676
荔枝罐头	公吨	14995	1255	4787	652
蘑菇罐头	公吨	142981	13278	137745	13038
蕃茄酱罐头	公吨	106764	7241	92345	6628
芦笋罐头	公吨	77632	8881	78813	9300
核桃仁罐头	公吨	603	238	967	397
花生米罐头	公吨	1746	218	2192	314
糖	金额		7819		12321
砂糖	公吨	338246	6687	409428	11220
原糖	公吨	9777	390	13509	521
啤酒	公吨	61083	3030	56412	2629
米酒及黄酒	公吨	18920	2403	16352	2266
葡萄酒	公吨	5722	697	4385	767
果汁	公吨	139993	11451	116197	8836
食盐	公吨	392355	1484	332649	1266
味素	公吨	13432	1739	10735	1520

1999年中国出口主要商品数量金额

金额单位:万美元

品名	单位	1999		1998	
		数量	金额	数量	金额
酱油	公吨	51199	2749	47705	2522
醋	公吨	9110	548	7989	470
鲜奶	公吨	25195	1816	24495	1820
奶粉	公吨	10008	1950	8408	1366
炼乳	公吨	2561	310	2412	345
花生制品	公吨	138245	12980	105972	11873
蜂蜜	公吨	87188	7476	78678	8307
淀粉	公吨	42358	1793	32131	1624
麦麸	公吨	20952	232	14554	213
豆粕	公吨	13490	219	18493	462
甜菜粕	公吨	517828	5215	592514	4539
棉子仁饼粕	公吨	91367	785	52508	679
菜籽饼粕	公吨	339034	2590	6881	118
玉米蛋白粉	公吨	49406	292	29048	297
混合饲料	金额		7510		9730
骨粉	公吨	9276	202	13946	312
茶叶	公吨	199608	33834	217437	37028
红茶	公吨	33594	4658	69591	10263
绿茶	公吨	121632	18943	111685	18065
花茶	公吨	18665	4098	15645	3712
乌龙茶	公吨	20130	4744	17134	4277
咖啡	公吨	4437	822	2685	739
可可	公吨	14548	3976	18966	4380
胡椒	公吨	2402	696	645	234
薄荷脑	公吨	2771	3842	1804	2612
香茅油	公吨	949	344	1071	390
桂油	公吨	549	1132	627	1304
山苍子油	公吨	817	498	606	467
桉叶油	公吨	3784	1147	2811	992
松油	公吨	10633	502	24650	1256
香叶油	公吨	144	450	73	229
天然樟脑(粉、块)	公吨	7404	992	7524	1297
柠檬酸	公吨	182826	15904	130008	11707
松香	公吨	261060	14168	254145	13568
明胶	公吨	2406	305	3056	503
蜂蜡	公吨	2508	706	2591	808

1999 年中国出口主要商品数量金额

金额单位:万美元

品名	单位	1999		1998	
		数量	金额	数量	金额
鞭炮烟花	公吨	210908	31272	137432	22131
蚊香	公吨	8540	874	10008	1001
神纸(土纸)	公吨	90079	6182	79780	7676
观赏鱼	金额		232		304
猪鬃	公吨	10103	6771	12293	8383
马鬃尾	公吨	1410	705	1532	735
鬃刷	万把	33905	4899	33120	4824
肠衣	公吨	52333	33422	45502	34278
猪肠衣	公吨	39071	19887	32647	20670
绵羊肠衣	公吨	7463	10042	6469	10160
山羊肠衣	公吨	1242	1953	1045	1647
鹅鸭绒毛	公吨	32066	17538	30232	17074
羽绒睡袋	个	449965	1064	402351	1047
骨粒粉	公吨	65625	1288	70025	1671
猪革皮	公吨	7072	4745	5504	5513
羊革皮	公吨	1209	1331	1635	2839
牛革皮	公吨	63512	28485	47609	25556
生牛皮	公吨	27208	753	33938	1285
原木	立方米	23016	801	31926	1246
桐原木	立方米	8407	253	9395	303
锯材	立方米	310146	13749	254545	11439
胶合板	立方米	423658	12365	176857	6496
梧桐木拼板	公吨	58229	8781	50654	9051
箱板	金额		2310		1573
木板门	公吨	84013	9714	70548	7196
烟类	金额		33632		57836
烟草	公吨	131634	20834	106289	18202
烤烟	公吨	109585	19135	85969	16355
烟草制品	金额		11202		37392
卷烟	万支	743719	11197	2286031	37392
烟草辅料	金额		1596		2242
棉花	公吨	237762	28387	45115	5631
苎麻	公吨	1493	580	1650	679
茧类	金额		372		570
桑蚕茧	公吨	448	360	591	559
丝类	金额		39193		35195

1999年中国出口主要商品数量金额

金额单位:万美元

品名	单位	1999		1998	
		数量	金额	数量	金额
桑蚕丝	公吨	7991	16242	8481	19909
柞蚕丝	公吨	513	701	534	1007
羊毛	公吨	12259	3506	15659	5867
羊绒	公吨	5074	23996	2003	10005
兔毛	公吨	5185	5489	2808	4044
纺织品	金额		1231688		1200729
棉纱线	件	958924	52802	735159	42086
麻纱线	件	134461	8820	142635	9896
亚麻纱线	件	29810	3000	31100	3121
棉麻混纺纱线	件	14555	291	14181	361
苎麻纱线	件	81944	5008	88569	5904
毛纱线	件	261617	47044	258162	40149
棉涤纶纱线	件	30353	1216	19612	946
棉布	万米	256462	229255	221206	213225
坯布	万米	103635	59898	82122	51281
漂布	万米	18991	13428	11386	9227
色布	万米	72018	79768	63801	69943
花布	万米	16683	12287	17796	13068
色织布	万米	43155	61658	43966	67029
其他棉布	万米	1980	2217	2134	2677
麻布	万米	19770	28360	16968	28977
浴巾	打	11593318	18799	9776852	17632
毛巾被	条	9244495	3788	6768643	3324
床单	条	30641131	8277	28025219	7983
床罩	条	22365472	6403	21243057	6527
棉毯	条	14547195	6542	12278684	6533
毛毯	条	15041244	13362	10369187	12300
纤维毯	条	1287189	1070	887138	487
绸缎	万米	11442	31561	12110	38268
服装	金额		3005785		3005720
日用瓷	金额		74509		66550
日用陶	金额		7057		5656
美术陶瓷	金额		57855		60856
建筑陶瓷	金额		10547		10200
陶瓷砖	金额		6812		7572
卫生洁具	金额		3594		2417

1999年中国出口主要商品数量金额

金额单位:万美元

品名	单位	1999		1998	
		数量	金额	数量	金额
地毯及装饰毯	金额		42129		44165
宝石	金额		42046		32091
钻石	金额		37193		26529
养殖珍珠	公斤	250026	2761	368151	5517
天然植物编织品	金额		46466		46339
稻草制品	金额		3758		4175
藤制品	金额		5268		5241
柳制品	金额		8526		9152
竹编制品	金额		8843		8709
鞋类	金额		867270		839179
帽类	金额		47554		45466
圆珠笔	打	172518529	8052	97220425	5893
铅笔	公斤	28858080	7205	20271284	5547
电子计算器	台	441918082	49090	385107371	45709
乒乓球	万个	14467	542	14769	570
玩具	金额		511214		514246
电动玩具	金额		3321		3213
机械玩具	金额		39361		46984
智力玩具	金额		10660		5402
布绒玩具	金额		147601		140659
童车	金额		2105		2345
乐器	金额		35150		30715
钢琴	台	48702	4473	36170	3849
口琴	打	653932	615	642852	653
手风琴	架	110150	334	74055	320
提琴	套	751903	1722	435748	1121
管乐器	个	118398	448	85975	470
铜响乐器	金额		1175		669
电子乐器	金额		12315		10673
帐篷	顶	14438556	23523	13711624	24669
太阳伞	个	19333573	8743	17136477	9628
纸浆类	公吨	5692	303	19786	935
纸张	公吨	202511	16166	240857	19893
纸制品	公吨	762162	85158	762878	87581
玻璃器皿	金额		16096		12565
保温瓶类	金额		15915		14676

1999年中国出口主要商品数量金额

金额单位:万美元

品名	单位	1999		1998	
		数量	金额	数量	金额
钟类	金额		49634		50037
闹钟	个	237104719	16373	186031586	15759
表类	金额		90813		98167
机械手表	个	23376474	3479	26638790	5423
电子手表	个	806663069	87335	830479361	92744
家具类	金额		270781		219026
清洁用品	金额		3872		3517
香皂	公吨	9226	1142	10927	1736
肥皂	公吨	6678	469	6689	460
牙膏	公吨	21553	3786	18286	3468
化妆品	金额		10845		10871
美容用品	金额		8218		7988
护发美发用品	金额		1656		2369
香水	金额		240		235
锁类	公吨	153501	37233	138161	36401
灯具	金额		193222		148798
衡器类	金额		10121		8539
皮手套	打付	49444543	36356	46468053	37210
钢材	公吨	3684396	141320	3565997	168698
钢坯	公吨	1725992	31721	1644296	35143
钢锭	公吨	602272	11136	528586	10994
废钢	公吨	62873	886	24922	651
铁丝	公吨	182446	8615	124955	6544
铅矿砂	公吨	22906	286	34371	465
锌矿砂	公吨	233150	3349	201325	2714
钼矿砂	公吨	9300	2982	4567	2080
生铁	公吨	1638470	19468	2444244	33642
铁合金	公吨	963945	61402	959958	69931
钨铁	公吨	4111	1746	3617	1571
钼铁	公吨	38586	16157	31739	17204
锰铁	公吨	122257	5056	130658	5634
铬铁	公吨	73813	4597	102083	7248
硅铁	公吨	349231	17189	265981	14536
钒铁	公吨	2125	1586	2308	3780
锡	公吨	64584	31448	53573	26695
锑	公吨	45339	4810	22365	3060

1999年中国出口主要商品数量金额

金额单位：万美元

品　　名	单位	1999		1998	
		数量	金额	数量	金额
氧化锑	公吨	36704	4312	28062	3871
铜	公吨	115189	18148	131903	21834
铜合金	公吨	4957	1010	2336	486
铝	公吨	99540	13721	237756	33696
铅	公吨	468368	24274	250941	14152
锌	公吨	507501	51901	370612	38816
镍	公吨	14455	6910	15051	7762
镁	公吨	109013	19117	85036	18407
钼	公吨	637	714	546	458
铋	公吨	2694	1585	1344	911
铬	公吨	5240	2319	3418	2044
锰	公吨	80626	7706	73214	8072
铝合金	公吨	107062	13599	89142	11073
锌合金	公吨	19641	2004	12282	1415
氧化铝	公吨	14406	524	32613	936
氧化钼	公吨	7976	2538	17147	7448
三氧化钨	公吨	3648	1750	3668	1985
仲钨酸铵	公吨	10507	4418	12675	5918
铜材	公吨	101974	34362	93143	30393
铜管	公吨	9474	2382	8825	2982
铜棒	公吨	6092	1169	10177	1742
铜丝	公吨	12261	2586	21336	4451
铝材	公吨	94796	21785	109354	24272
铝板	公吨	21392	5069	22688	5768
铝管	公吨	2375	802	1047	435
铝丝	公吨	1827	296	2078	379
铝箔	公吨	22954	6216	20841	5468
锌材	公吨	10216	777	9952	979
镍材	公吨	3329	1258	1127	643
镁材	公吨	3556	625	3673	725
锡材	公吨	9237	4322	7028	3492
银	公斤	308335	4879	88574	1402
钯	公斤	2345	2517	2515	2088
钯合金	公斤	2345	2517	2515	2088
水泥	公吨	6356530	20092	8199725	29046
平板玻璃	平方米	44175749	10969	36450929	9738

1999年中国出口主要商品数量金额

金额单位:万美元

品名	单位	1999		1998	
		数量	金额	数量	金额
重烧镁	公吨	1187845	12143	1198985	12446
白云石	公吨	495921	529	357394	567
鳞片石墨	公吨	100043	2840	123298	3848
无定形石墨	公吨	105847	836	57455	439
滑石块	公吨	418698	2763	385273	2482
滑石粉	公吨	294383	3085	311210	3109
长石块	公吨	539041	684	608501	1091
轻烧镁	公吨	281541	2888	310606	3270
砩石块	公吨	1221491	11541	1315972	12947
重晶石	公吨	1286782	4707	1774289	6868
煤	公吨	37407072	108375	27995790	106779
焦炭	公吨	9974197	55122	11463981	79839
电力	万度	485105	55088	717364	44630
石油及制品	金额		207636		246880
原油	公吨	7166181	75240	15600712	152745
成品油	公吨	6451581	109541	4360976	73891
汽油	公吨	4138310	64575	1819730	28081
煤油	公吨	1249695	26934	921877	20243
轻柴油	公吨	604541	9097	984769	16325
重柴油	公吨	7581	861	12286	1809
润滑油脂	公吨	74543	2805	22190	1603
石脑油	公吨	98385	1898		
液化石油气	公吨	75930	1441	502177	8261
磷酸	公吨	114504	4242	94287	3970
氢氟酸	公吨	15231	740	9808	512
金属钠	公吨	3074	418	1551	247
烧碱	公吨	222129	3682	262142	4465
纯碱	公吨	1044002	10281	705537	8069
硫化碱	公吨	69835	1330	60651	1224
硅酸钠	公吨	17922	242	9133	144
次亚磷酸钠	公吨	8150	1150	6924	1185
氯化钠	公吨	392355	1484	332649	1266
氰化钠	公吨	3231	480	504	72
氯化钾	公吨	860051	9510	452094	4881
氯酸钾	公吨	11633	620	7975	491
硝酸钾	公吨	10518	375	5515	209

1999年中国出口主要商品数量金额

金额单位:万美元

品名	单位	1999		1998	
		数量	金额	数量	金额
高锰酸钾	公吨	9454	855	10396	1040
电石(碳化钙)	公吨	97879	2821	62937	2030
氯化钙	公吨	55178	694	55681	717
硫酸钡	公吨	14890	327	17253	401
碳酸钡	公吨	200582	4309	174499	3808
电解二氧化锰	公吨	18015	1714	17149	1488
氯化镍	公吨	6433	309	1676	383
碳酸镁	公吨	20558	1519	19045	1116
氯化镁	公吨	94767	1170	57621	812
硫酸铝	公吨	22663	207	26071	277
工业氢氧化铝	公吨	35225	724	40552	823
氟化铝	公吨	4287	301	817	66
钼酸铵	公吨	1367	648	795	466
硝酸钴	公吨	30092	1009	29159	1038
氧化钴	公吨	238	519	287	739
钨酸钠	公吨	1367	380	1508	459
氢氧化锂	公吨	2195	619	1913	606
五氧化二钒	公吨	6167	2796	7586	8213
碳酸锶	公吨	48872	2133	43207	2046
工业硝酸铵	公吨	31150	533	47997	874
氯化铵	公吨	143984	1176	171202	1405
磷酸二氢铵	公吨	39097	884	3280	148
磷酸氢二铵	公吨	105850	2303	68007	1553
活性碳	公吨	100358	6043	104745	5626
石蜡	公吨	587961	23843	593032	24678
石油焦	公吨	887910	4544	984355	5786
锻烧焦	公吨	239619	3188	180042	2774
沥青焦	公吨	31342	496	18063	322
石油沥青	公吨	260288	1277	166318	985
煤焦沥青	公吨	120005	1930	85835	1371
乙醇(酒精)	升	40334089	1669	105652309	4342
环乙醇	公吨	40409	1703	105685	4398
糠醇	公吨	35816	3124	33792	3648
糠醛	公吨	35569	2119	56389	4203
甲酸(蚁酸)	公吨	7489	338	5632	303

1999 年中国出口主要商品数量金额

金额单位：万美元

品名	单位	1999		1998	
		数量	金额	数量	金额
苯甲酸	公吨	14140	1584	12034	1568
水杨酸	公吨	2765	594	2959	741
草酸(乙二酸)	公吨	26710	1133	23885	1209
酒石酸	公吨	2350	342	1707	283
癸二酸	公吨	19254	5032	14555	3195
丙烯酸酯	公吨	15977	1051	9670	735
对苯二酚	公吨	1479	420	785	234
丁二烯	公吨	6344	379	11488	452
双氰胺	公吨	15370	1875	12843	1837
三聚氰胺	公吨	16669	1405	23348	3956
己内酰胺	公吨	14359	1508	24304	3351
硫脲	公吨	941	359	531	137
纯苯	公吨	95066	1968	26956	563
粗苯	公吨	22771	332	35192	514
二甲苯(含邻间对)	公吨	57169	1979	69463	2048
防老剂	公吨	4643	779	5212	1172
催化剂	公吨	3607	1363	3897	1359
虫胶	公吨	500	204	228	60
塑料	金额		517488		521611
低压聚乙烯	公吨	9164	718	20779	1540
聚丙烯	公吨	8712	699	28302	1881
ABS 树脂	公吨	21283	2271	28933	3636
电木粉(酚醛树脂)	公吨	13737	1011	11056	978
电玉粉	公吨	8677	595	7155	576
聚氯乙烯(树脂)	公吨	32150	3066	42796	3888
聚苯乙烯	公吨	54898	4648	127843	10650
聚四氟乙烯	公吨	1088	609	911	650
环氧树脂	公吨	10436	2143	3831	812
聚碳酸脂	公吨	33544	7214	23096	5630
塑料雨衣	公吨	179387	36148	161068	37908
塑料雨帽	打	17293776	1203	20597495	1898
尼龙牙刷	罗	5232465	3934	4140737	3457
各种染料	公吨	155715	46682	131690	49727
硫化染料	公吨	24714	2512	21724	2602
还原染料	公吨	10726	6290	11387	7717

1999 年中国出口主要商品数量金额

金额单位:万美元

品　　名	单位	1999		1998	
		数量	金额	数量	金额
直接染料	公吨	6065	2119	6236	2539
酸性染料	公吨	18392	6633	16071	6795
盐基染料	公吨	9750	4326	7228	3862
活性染料	公吨	5291	2891	4316	2862
分散染料	公吨	75319	19752	58853	20539
增白粉	公吨	2666	1211	1516	560
二萘酚(B 萘酚)	公吨	17760	1692	12458	1331
苯胺	公吨	991	320	1395	607
二苯胺	公吨	2187	628	951	558
甲萘胺(1－萘胺)	公吨	9964	2085	7308	1716
三聚氯氰	公吨	22675	3912	11759	2472
立德粉	公吨	78840	2604	70186	2370
钛白粉	公吨	42087	4348	31967	3251
氧化锌	公吨	68499	5110	57445	4800
群青	公吨	3939	225	4059	239
油漆	公吨	62899	9982	74210	11820
油墨	公吨	8647	2827	9178	2999
化肥	公吨	1834102	23648	1342851	16811
尿素	公吨	53772	705	125051	1861
氯化钾	公吨	860051	9510	452094	4881
硝铵(硝酸铵)	公吨	31150	533	47997	874
过磷酸钙	公吨	325824	4621	238818	2437
农药	公吨	146948	43960	107479	32530
除草剂	公吨	54614	17727	34418	13318
杀虫剂	公吨	54616	13688	43890	10170
天然橡胶	公吨	3879	221	19043	1383
合成橡胶	公吨	45550	3326	29486	2609
轮胎	金额		78824		64210
整套轮胎	万套	8634	72183	7397	57516
轮胎内胎	万条	9109	5456	7963	5191
胶管	公吨	9316	1806	8419	1680
运输带	公吨	4705	1157	2927	882
传动带	公吨	6281	1760	4012	1289
乳胶手套	万付	83952	5443	86397	6227
甘草	公吨	5692	682	3917	496

1999年中国出口主要商品数量金额

金额单位:万美元

品名	单位	1999		1998	
		数量	金额	数量	金额
半夏	公吨	647	280	636	570
虫草	公吨	9	620	7	414
菊花	公吨	2812	357	2444	412
黄芪	公吨	3207	480	3291	458
枸杞	公吨	3382	578	3936	837
党参	公吨	1330	277	1001	296
茯苓	公吨	2724	327	3245	519
白术	公吨	2590	298	1904	270
姜黄	公吨	2100	220	1909	271
啤酒花颗粒	公吨	492	232	339	151
动物药材	金额		1886		1702
鲜王浆	公斤	1884237	1794	2163323	1546
槟榔	公吨	10734	4461	9868	6111
片仔癀	公斤	2106	783	1595	610
清凉油	公斤	2657339	1098	3110292	1472
药酒	金额		496		395
抗菌素药	公吨	60129	53287	30381	52931
磺胺药	公吨	10367	8119	9574	7804
磺胺嘧啶	公斤	1199875	923	1221495	1000
磺胺二甲基嘧啶	公斤	1818657	1143	2182572	1422
维生素	金额		33318		29785
医疗器械	金额		35845		32382
体温表	万支	4356	1913	3550	2123
血压表	万支	973	7921	952	7542
听诊器	万个	209	202	229	241
心电瞬时记录仪	台	8887	2179	9574	1547
注射器	万支	31909	1128	18647	882
注射针头	金额		610		425
畜牧专用器械	金额		227		340
医用敷料	金额		24001		25545
各类船	艘	34968	160620	30158	173160
客船	艘	66	825	35	2008
客货船	艘	382	85678	403	120279
冷藏船	艘	2	2568	1	1540
挖泥船	艘	187	578	135	1129

1999年中国出口主要商品数量金额

金额单位:万美元

品名	单位	1999		1998	
		数量	金额	数量	金额
拖轮	艘	86	5065	70	4466
渔船	艘	69	1868	115	3239
海洋平台	金额		365		12421
集装箱	只	639617	147783	569706	158689
飞机	架	72	24393	31	10610
汽车	辆	6239	10016	9833	15470
载重汽车	辆	4165	3230	6951	6417
小轿车	辆	1352	1450	1592	1916
客车	辆	415	2536	743	2694
汽车底盘	金额		252		267
摩托车	辆	258218	12734	110143	6460
摩托车零件	金额		9155		8822
汽车零件	金额		78020		53049
显像管	万只	623	21597	615	25619
集成电路	金额		205807		115004
电线电缆	公吨	438151	125846	363381	97983
蓄电池	金额		65168		47346
铅酸蓄电池	万个	2292	12171	1454	7267
起重机械	台	13896126	35212	10965597	39129
金属切削机床	台	3392962	22735	2255084	23507
车床	台	38957	5513	38123	6615
钻床	台	951382	5032	566261	3629
镗床	台	889	231	979	262
磨床	台	2123622	4209	1519752	4091
铣床	台	3640	861	3243	1058
铸造机械	台	4665954	2288	8831114	4896
木工机械	台	1205409	6617	451745	3371
各种泵	金额		102371		105866
滚动轴承	套	1108140918	49863	850993241	44542
印刷机械	金额		3193		2849
制革制鞋机械	金额		243		205
金属轧机	金额		2804		3667
玻璃加工机械	金额		1442		931
橡胶或塑料加工机械	金额		10830		9072
电动机及发电机	万台	219045	149186	200488	129022

1999年中国出口主要商品数量金额

金额单位:万美元

品名	单位	1999		1998	
		数量	金额	数量	金额
发电机组	台	62166	2693	12826	6176
电动机和发电机零件	金额		15165		17061
有线电话电报交换机	台	147702736	190127	110175329	155565
有线电话电报交换机零件	金额		41023		32757
计算机	金额		792203		706797
微型电子计算机	台	345202	16669	248111	20397
显示器	台	27386831	256461	17381051	173777
打印机	台	15257026	108982	11050770	97839
键盘	个	235582808	64859	177220758	52726
磁盘	万片	67308	7385	62915	8263
文字处理机	金额		4343		4055
有线通讯设备	金额		231150		188322
电话机	台	134219041	152202	106861882	130412
各种电子交换机	金额		4719		1551
载波机	台	11653828	11629	1196803	5451
传真机	台	1495622	20889	1291746	17725
复印机	台	1296689	58902	1508751	62009
调制解调器	台	19402	5562	11168	2575
雷达	金额		2483		1045
电台对讲机	金额		9392		8311
电池	金额		50371		42711
测绘仪器	金额		16824		13731
望远镜	金额		17491		17689
放大镜	只	17539831	710	12060241	433
照相机	架	59511512	99031	67465551	99400
照相机零件	金额		10503		7763
彩色冲洗扩印系统	金额		445		639
自行车类	金额		125622		109917
自行车	辆	22902345	77799	17825640	61507
自行车外胎	条	44564919	5094	40432021	5193
自行车内胎	条	73390588	3292	61632928	2936
自行车零配件	金额		42705		43295
缝纫机类	金额		28500		27669
缝纫机	金额		23706		23590
家用缝纫机	台	3390763	10487	3157512	10187

1999年中国出口主要商品数量金额

金额单位:万美元

品名	单位	1999		1998	
		数量	金额	数量	金额
工业缝纫机	台	1032050	13218	895070	13403
缝纫机零件	金额		4794		4078
缝纫机针	金额		722		516
电风扇	台	140075173	65082	151846680	72974
吊扇	台	25536195	29190	24145831	32836
台扇	台	14048727	7929	11781226	8401
落地电扇	台	13459366	11718	9510221	10786
排风扇	台	1584274	1474	1023597	1391
电冰箱	台	1243394	10382	881914	7179
洗衣机	台	640474	5934	525320	5050
空调器	台	1063845	21378	683317	16419
吸尘器	台	21425869	25435	18095204	23614
空气加湿器	台	2480574	2505	2719854	2316
空气干燥器	台	18774	284	5003	557
电水壶	个	39785069	19625	32954444	15673
电炉	个	20461636	13772	18099616	10571
电热水器	个	7290780	1977	4465976	1792
煤气热水器	台	73271	483	13705	68
电面包烤炉	台	48593605	39655	38727881	31211
洗碗机	台	20302	266	1612	75
电吹风	个	55743875	14142	50041175	11449
电动剃须刀	个	16335127	8307	13999652	7167
电熨斗	个	32807023	15571	28256221	13293
电筒	个	482180106	17054	374403485	12707
台灯	金额		38901		29783
吊灯	金额		34406		25398
节日灯	金额		57749		40629
卤钨灯	万只	38378	11621	26477	9000
收音机	台	127780074	29919	121452947	28202
录音机	金额		205329		221097
收录两用机	台	20946989	6526	24206528	8387
电视机及散件	金额		80312		68665
彩色电视机	台	5689236	63784	4388198	52590
黑白电视机	台	7287748	16528	5815482	16075
投影电视机	台	4504	326	6464	161

1999 年中国出口主要商品数量金额

金额单位:万美元

品名	单位	1999		1998	
		数量	金额	数量	金额
录像机	台	10585176	45838	7934754	42005
摄像机	台	1157931	14305	355432	9586
音箱	万台	121590	90140	91533	66874
组合音响	万套	14	664	15	558
录像带	万盒	31589	12418	28849	16212
耳塞机	万个	46715	24685	31360	10657
麦克风	个	220887831	6623	145135383	3935
量具	金额		13819		10097
刃具	金额		4390		3734
磨具	金额		4899		4550
砂布	公吨	3929	583	3662	560
电动工具	金额		78481		59451
电钻	个	22717775	32928	14779517	26059
各种锤	金额		5067		5169
各种钳	金额		10487		9105
各种扳手	金额		5683		5235
各种螺丝批	金额		5212		5213
各种钻	金额		1879		4094
各种锉和刀	金额		17319		21113
各种锯和锯条	金额		8563		8629
农具	金额		9031		8910
出版物	金额		26270		22604

1999 年中国进口主要商品数量金额

金额单位:万美元

品名	单位	1999		1998	
		数量	金额	数量	金额
粮谷	公吨	3394613	52414	3883057	71602
大米	公吨	168031	7810	243815	11996
小麦	公吨	448121	8565	1489403	27857
玉米	公吨	70183	807	250613	3174
大麦	公吨	2268776	29364	1519141	24097
面粉	公吨	57121	1707	58903	1549
豆类	公吨	4375407	90603	3294343	82713
黄大豆	公吨	4318634	89030	3192594	80481
豌豆	公吨	47896	1095	78417	1742
食用植物油	公吨	2080813	107434	2055237	129877
花生油	公吨	9616	1306	8723	847
豆油	公吨	803691	42104	829189	52124
菜油	公吨	49912	2662	246291	15292
芝麻油	公吨	522	118	348	62
玉米油	公吨	2762	219	1536	113
食用植物油籽	公吨	6928163	152715	4604676	122124
葵花籽	公吨	12234	760	10768	597
油菜籽	公吨	2595305	62836	1386413	40246
工业用油	公吨	194869	13443	298051	19309
蓖麻油	公吨	33803	3028	41417	3085
亚麻油	公吨	52479	3009	11876	526
椰子油	公吨	25097	1808	48763	3131
棕榈油	公吨	41392	2374	166718	10571
工业用油籽	公吨	11566	374	1209	261
亚麻籽	公吨	10580	273	32	2
活畜禽	金额		6560		5447
活羊	头	2317	318	1868	341
肉食	金额		50310		14467
冻猪肉	公吨	58421	2435	15789	682
冻牛肉	公吨	4554	631	3548	506
冻绵羊肉	公吨	9972	774	9192	490
冻鸡	公吨	788495	40465	193621	10741
苹果	公吨	27433	1027	8587	281
桔柑橙	公吨	25630	1029	3989	137
香蕉	公吨	431737	14051	539093	16312
荔枝	公吨	6752	244	598	26

1999年中国进口主要商品数量金额

金额单位:万美元

品名	单位	1999		1998	
		数量	金额	数量	金额
葡萄	公吨	44156	2358	7023	330
李子	公吨	7060	291	1210	47
西瓜	公吨	7220	120	13879	276
栗子	公吨	1157	136	745	78
松子仁	公吨	2138	230	59	11
红枣	公吨	9900	800	4016	328
蔬菜	公吨	111821	5933	80486	3527
速冻蔬菜	公吨	27356	1430	20983	794
水产品	金额		88156		66635
活鳗鱼苗、种	公斤	154275	18487	88934	3407
冰鲜鱼	公吨	5107	713	8699	700
冻鱼	公吨	454798	40838	572344	42910
冻鱼片	公吨	2900	399	2711	249
冻对虾	公吨	4579	1658	4439	1832
冰鲜虾	公吨	692	170	59	21
冻小虾	公吨	12200	4213	10704	2549
冻小虾仁	公吨	2317	688	1281	417
鱼翅	公吨	4063	2182	4236	2475
糖	金额		8518		14516
砂糖	公吨	52967	1523	59618	2033
原糖	公吨	360725	6901	445291	12367
啤酒	公吨	58917	6305	33143	2150
葡萄酒	公吨	46237	3462	51563	3831
果汁	公吨	15896	1339	11973	913
味素	公吨	1029	119	6313	616
酱油	公吨	14924	2839	16165	2878
醋	公吨	858	118	541	56
鲜奶	公吨	14942	853	8884	326
奶粉	公吨	56616	8010	31053	3901
奶油	公吨	1504	208	92	7
蜂蜜	公吨	850	102	494	74
淀粉	公吨	147089	4215	83365	2851
麦麸	公吨	76668	756	36359	386
豆粕	公吨	571821	10031	3733302	86374
花生饼粕	公吨	6110	107	9403	100
菜籽饼粕	公吨	29498	354	107246	1274

1999年中国进口主要商品数量金额

金额单位:万美元

品名	单位	1999		1998	
		数量	金额	数量	金额
木薯干片	公吨	372699	3787	300501	3172
混合饲料	金额		9196		6099
鱼粉	公吨	631271	36077	416188	31168
骨粉	公吨	129566	3808	154003	5841
茶叶	公吨	1872	349	1185	246
红茶	公吨	1003	248	345	161
咖啡	公吨	4816	815	4973	1122
可可	公吨	39235	5349	37645	6419
胡椒	公吨	815	136	239	26
薄荷脑	公吨	1116	1173	790	857
柠檬桉油	公吨	122	196	143	58
松香	公吨	1365	264	1400	250
明胶	公吨	1510	742	1469	810
肠衣	公吨	90695	7183	65319	4835
猪肠衣	公吨	17449	2120	14836	1899
绵羊肠衣	公吨	10182	1563	10989	1425
鹅鸭绒毛	公吨	2883	1880	1366	1256
猪革皮	公吨	6779	6731	9605	9720
羊革皮	公吨	12367	27690	8840	22482
牛革皮	公吨	524375	156409	445231	152832
生猪皮	公吨	8718	619	15632	1889
生牛皮	公吨	250354	26675	204355	23938
绵羊皮	公吨	97101	6078	62759	6309
水貂皮	公吨	1505	3110	987	2846
原木	立方米	10135683	124863	4823042	59909
锯材	立方米	2720149	65864	1678992	34692
胶合板	立方米	1042463	41586	1691113	54363
梧桐木拼板	公吨	34289	2630	53817	3733
箱板	金额		338		150
木板门	公吨	1430	213	1748	242
烟类	金额		8769		10571
烟草	公吨	10480	5176	6708	3510
烤烟	公吨	9565	4783	6004	3236
烟草制品	金额		3305		6954
卷烟	万支	180544	3282	343980	6933
烟草辅料	金额		288		107

1999年中国进口主要商品数量金额

金额单位:万美元

品名	单位	1999		1998	
		数量	金额	数量	金额
棉花	公吨	52206	7958	209418	35697
茧类	金额		167		204
桑蚕茧	公吨	519	152	744	183
丝类	金额		965		1331
桑蚕丝	公吨	97	162	31	32
羊毛	公吨	198624	63772	168606	60300
羊绒	公吨	1597	1555	775	893
兔毛	公吨	149	131	50	44
纺织品	金额		1095885		1094971
棉纱线	件	2054090	71157	2092500	74142
麻纱线	件	94481	3666	91537	3343
亚麻纱线	件	14821	547	22038	922
苎麻纱线	件	67171	2794	62263	2209
毛纱线	件	198635	17643	282557	20994
棉涤纶纱线	件	125632	3500	119613	3279
棉布	万米	140457	137380	138395	133841
坯布	万米	41163	26198	33997	24106
漂布	万米	8249	6483	8978	6754
色布	万米	48405	57344	53328	55385
花布	万米	5529	9430	5635	8646
色织布	万米	35537	35810	35052	37028
其他棉布	万米	1574	2116	1404	1922
麻布	万米	7831	9186	8449	15741
绸缎	万米	3538	10420	3951	11428
服装	金额		109455		106592
日用瓷	金额		212		199
美术陶瓷	金额		173		48
建筑陶瓷	金额		3200		4291
陶瓷砖	金额		2066		2965
陶瓷管	金额		188		94
卫生洁具	金额		892		1223
地毯及装饰毯	金额		2262		2191
宝石	金额		51828		35579
钻石	金额		44995		30115
养殖珍珠	公斤	96267	696	68532	565
天然植物编织品	金额		507		447

1999 年中国进口主要商品数量金额

金额单位:万美元

品名	单位	1999		1998	
		数量	金额	数量	金额
鞋类	金额		30601		29043
帽类	金额		184		114
圆珠笔	打	5905376	435	4216486	315
铅笔	公斤	1253520	216	1232784	245
电子计算器	台	6829740	629	4175799	392
玩具	金额		5172		6947
电动玩具	金额		239		324
机械玩具	金额		181		125
智力玩具	金额		204		180
布绒玩具	金额		119		36
乐器	金额		8604		7007
钢琴	台	5028	431	3027	272
电子乐器	金额		218		82
纸浆类	公吨	3097908	141460	2199310	92368
纸张	公吨	6489151	335020	5754765	300781
纸制品	公吨	480929	70563	558688	65483
玻璃器皿	金额		10609		7871
保温瓶类	金额		334		244
钟类	金额		12824		16324
闹钟	个	705968	151	273808	83
表类	金额		3912		4504
机械手表	个	564023	1092	968492	1882
电子手表	个	14126544	2820	11667454	2623
家具类	金额		10285		9274
清洁用品	金额		648		335
香皂	公吨	5746	508	5659	425
牙膏	公吨	1529	315	761	133
剃须膏	公斤	270642	135	91076	30
去污粉	公斤	1065302	149	1050524	139
化妆品	金额		3818		3246
美容用品	金额		2491		2264
护发美发用品	金额		890		705
香水	金额		178		141
锁类	公吨	11915	4311	8347	3488
灯具	金额		5936		5452
衡器类	金额		2554		1931

1999年中国进口主要商品数量金额

金额单位：万美元

品名	单位	1999		1998	
		数量	金额	数量	金额
钢材	公吨	14862716	700775	12415481	628677
钢坯	公吨	2048016	39923	661657	14896
钢锭	公吨	86939	2493	29171	1753
废钢	公吨	3339113	31666	2018655	21378
铁丝	公吨	193046	12306	167505	10542
铁矿砂	公吨	55274004	137899	51770715	146776
铬矿砂	公吨	816230	7431	711544	8089
锰矿砂	公吨	1056873	8776	1179051	9033
铜矿砂	公吨	1250148	47436	1182867	45831
钴矿砂	公吨	7573	983	2787	781
铝矿砂	公吨	243489	641	148533	539
铅矿砂	公吨	169669	2991	236034	4226
锌矿砂	公吨	44003	835	52508	1274
铬矿砂	公吨	816230	7431	711544	8089
钼矿砂	公吨	15680	3131	10843	2807
生铁	公吨	85198	4135	43052	2138
铁合金	公吨	9003	1974	6974	1356
硅铁	公吨	3256	172	2749	149
镍铁	公吨	354	301	635	143
钒铁	公吨	274	198	10	4
锡	公吨	3788	1489	2988	1121
水银	公吨	883	330	524	212
锑	公吨	1246	191	2782	356
氧化锑	公吨	1312	356	1038	224
铜	公吨	2251077	136835	1226635	73751
铜合金	公吨	13011	2205	9892	1964
铝	公吨	380626	48950	203208	27647
铅	公吨	15774	660	15414	772
锌	公吨	16091	1592	12091	1157
镍	公吨	4498	2098	4983	2341
铬	公吨	969	159	598	125
铝合金	公吨	153378	18625	103780	12070
锌合金	公吨	91347	9171	75385	7515
锡矿砂	公吨	871	205	692	41
氧化铝	公吨	1623186	33791	1574909	35422
铜材	公吨	631944	159471	546625	137470

1999年中国进口主要商品数量金额

金额单位:万美元

品名	单位	1999		1998	
		数量	金额	数量	金额
铜管	公吨	43870	16315	30705	11343
铜棒	公吨	120708	21515	122884	22873
铜丝	公吨	223319	44323	207875	44088
铝材	公吨	426952	106193	341294	84492
铝板	公吨	274643	62183	216860	47923
铝管	公吨	12818	4677	12224	4130
铝丝	公吨	2660	1130	1956	752
铝箔	公吨	55546	23970	35592	16394
铅材	公吨	5754	383	4734	484
锌材	公吨	77894	5060	63475	4567
镍材	公吨	6327	4942	8175	4693
镁材	公吨	233	173	145	113
锡材	公吨	14568	4800	13463	4280
金	公斤	1387	525	43	2
银	公斤	299879	5627	156546	3035
钯	公斤	1687	1694	537	167
钯合金	公斤	1687	1694	537	167
水泥	公吨	499665	1477	179775	1143
平板玻璃	平方米	22891104	10300	17361645	8977
鳞片石墨	公吨	1018	212	1482	177
滑石粉	公吨	10100	497	8797	363
长石块	公吨	11253	728	20256	744
煤	公吨	1671046	6086	1582133	6845
电力	万度	36615	2119	1713	40
石油及制品	金额		853733		650369
原油	公吨	36613688	464124	27322632	327454
成品油	公吨	20815201	269768	21739869	240518
煤油	公吨	2111910	37685	1290823	19774
轻柴油	公吨	308352	4914	3104241	44777
重柴油	公吨	40794	8549	40058	8353
润滑油脂	公吨	181981	20556	175961	20465
石脑油	公吨	372306	5424	779492	12379
液化天然气	公吨	9700	190	41442	787
液化石油气	公吨	5542594	119649	4781684	81542
硫酸	公吨	262536	835	297227	909
硝酸	公吨	1447	153	1577	133

1999年中国进口主要商品数量金额

金额单位:万美元

品名	单位	1999		1998	
		数量	金额	数量	金额
磷酸	公吨	74017	1808	152321	3915
硼酸	公吨	47071	2377	47631	2510
烧碱	公吨	24123	707	26403	814
纯碱	公吨	35705	490	84238	1293
硝酸钠	公吨	24147	404	10297	180
次亚磷酸钠	公吨	648	105	502	92
氰化钠	公吨	20684	2068	14213	1656
氯化钾	公吨	5195481	60841	5120377	60627
硫酸钾	公吨	197238	4035	534354	11459
氢氧化钾	公吨	12250	883	10528	767
碳酸钙	公吨	89588	2437	69313	2083
硫酸钡	公吨	1370	110	902	74
电解二氧化锰	公吨	8952	1034	5585	796
氯化镍	公吨	1804	250	1667	222
氧化镍	公吨	2154	1175	1642	857
碳酸镁	公吨	1244	178	1532	158
工业氢氧化铝	公吨	9605	421	2351	166
氧化钴	公吨	98	279	52	137
五氧化二钒	公吨	143	103	35	25
氯化铵	公吨	3143	223	7130	229
磷酸二氢铵	公吨	50471	856	84858	1790
磷酸氢二铵	公吨	5282200	112876	5440556	125472
活性碳	公吨	1904	558	1692	328
硫磺	公吨	154811	818	241132	1205
溴素	公吨	2538	219	1920	171
石蜡	公吨	17389	1411	13046	1032
锻烧焦	公吨	7801	425	6808	377
沥青焦	公吨	19879	932	18850	928
石油沥青	公吨	1470078	19919	871601	11126
煤焦沥青	公吨	33733	527	109660	1578
甲醇(木精)	公吨	1373932	14898	704531	8403
乙醇(酒精)	升	5079735	166	1746500	126
乙二醇	公吨	566887	24047	308172	13447
丁醇(正丁醇)	公吨	660497	6442	104892	4224
季戊四醇	公吨	10097	855	1246	148
环乙醇	公吨	5136	189	1794	139

1999年中国进口主要商品数量金额

金额单位:万美元

品名	单位	1999		1998	
		数量	金额	数量	金额
甲醛	公吨	1253	120	2521	142
甲酸(蚁酸)	公吨	6375	268	3339	164
甲酸钠	公吨	13463	246	21554	408
苯甲酸	公吨	1159	307	694	173
水杨酸	公吨	332	106	1025	54
冰醋酸(乙酸)	公吨	105861	3328	135396	4869
草酸(乙二酸)	公吨	653	104	274	18
己二酸	公吨	17968	1902	22080	2313
对苯二甲酸	公吨	1542362	62585	728742	26861
丙烯酸酯	公吨	124841	9771	80372	6654
丙酮	公吨	73745	2535	67149	2595
环己酮	公吨	34723	2011	21203	1176
苯酚(石碳酸)	公吨	73825	3385	37197	2400
间苯二酚(雷锁辛)	公吨	1628	657	2335	473
二氯甲烷	公吨	97266	4115	35524	1794
二氯乙烷	公吨	193681	4453	133793	2300
三氯甲烷(氯仿)	公吨	95192	4658	43687	2541
三氯乙烷	公吨	6234	397	5211	310
环乙烷	公吨	7220	352	1389	110
乙烯	公吨	37156	1603	32848	1269
丙烯	公吨	96295	3353	67469	2063
丁二烯	公吨	87695	2575	41141	1039
苯乙烯	公吨	1026947	50615	583395	23812
三氯乙烯	公吨	15037	874	12250	709
丙烯腈	公吨	158211	6922	99031	4891
乙二胺	公吨	11519	1593	5737	840
双氰胺	公吨	574	150	448	113
三聚氰胺	公吨	3986	354	3763	420
己内酰胺	公吨	220817	22713	175850	22118
纯苯	公吨	51704	1414	74414	1593
甲苯	公吨	495354	11746	369380	8357
二甲苯(含邻间对)	公吨	278739	8837	204741	5609
粗萘(工业萘)	公吨	26958	613	21831	563
四氢呋喃	公吨	4737	680	2974	856
羧甲基纤维素	公吨	1548	567	884	330
防老剂	公吨	95489	16861	77261	13174

1999 年中国进口主要商品数量金额

金额单位:万美元

品名	单位	1999		1998	
		数量	金额	数量	金额
催化剂	公吨	30170	16417	26444	9847
塑料	金额		1161178		1045876
高压聚乙烯	公吨	962403	58754	650436	42080
低压聚乙烯	公吨	1636572	104409	1810737	120744
聚丙烯	公吨	1472438	92918	1544122	99147
ABS 树脂	公吨	1333856	125437	1069033	108356
电木粉(酚醛树脂)	公吨	63526	7300	51406	6344
电玉粉	公吨	10171	956	6756	660
聚氯乙烯(树脂)	公吨	1841506	115309	1605107	106648
聚苯乙烯	公吨	3068876	254387	2603173	230133
聚四氟乙烯	公吨	12145	2957	8534	2160
环氧树脂	公吨	98318	21994	72510	16964
聚碳酸脂	公吨	160558	28735	108507	19580
醇酸树脂	公吨	34892	3834	31406	3236
塑料雨衣	公吨	3387	1675	42192	1472
尼龙牙刷	罗	107179	124	105030	86
各种染料	公吨	37659	16451	36832	15410
硫化染料	公吨	806	127	717	110
还原染料	公吨	756	521	952	453
直接染料	公吨	7251	2353	6498	1900
酸性染料	公吨	4487	2857	4357	2373
盐基染料	公吨	1181	457	2058	737
活性染料	公吨	12347	5834	10167	4983
分散染料	公吨	5750	2768	7452	3285
增白粉	公吨	4642	1845	2345	962
二甲基苯胺	公吨	555	283	293	139
苯胺	公吨	6521	309	4819	406
三聚氯氰	公吨	15879	847	11580	748
钛白粉	公吨	109517	18516	79766	12283
氧化锌	公吨	10752	1134	9875	1019
油漆	公吨	181372	38236	156969	33327
油墨	公吨	22842	11315	18790	7983
化肥	公吨	13352093	224823	13871429	250567
尿素	公吨	68100	936	119104	1722
氯化钾	公吨	5195481	60841	5120377	60627
硝酸钠	公吨	24147	404	10297	180

1999 年中国进口主要商品数量金额

金额单位:万美元

品　　名	单位	1999		1998	
		数量	金额	数量	金额
硫酸钾	公吨	197238	4035	534354	11459
农药	公吨	47714	24258	44173	18614
除草剂	公吨	27514	12884	24995	11528
杀虫剂	公吨	11188	6411	10679	3387
天然橡胶	公吨	429068	28189	430079	31928
合成橡胶	公吨	652104	60201	513622	46552
再生胶	公吨	16157	851	2898	285
轮胎	金额		4726		3546
整套轮胎	万套	639	4138	321	2050
轮胎内胎	万条	486	337	128	105
胶管	公吨	2891	2202	2355	1611
运输带	公吨	3100	2245	3125	1763
传动带	公吨	1661	2415	1352	1208
乳胶手套	万付	9261	299	3095	240
槐米	公吨	569	120	578	168
动物药材	金额		350		296
鲜王浆	公斤	97633	308	42386	255
血竭	公吨	1723	166	938	109
槟榔	公吨	8616	674	9894	883
清凉油	公斤	37864	108	29934	42
抗菌素药	公吨	1971	22621	2325	20249
磺胺药	公吨	527	885	3706	428
维生素	金额		5519		3900
医疗器械	金额		66642		39567
血压表	万支	169	1539	66	3075
心电瞬时记录仪	台	1159	610	2169	750
体外反搏装置	万个	1	584		205
注射器	万支	2023	304	2414	153
注射针头	金额		592		467
畜牧专用器械	金额		1167		880
医用敷料	金额		895		626
各类船	艘	1409	12809	968	12163
客船	艘	5	102	38	931
客货船	艘	299	6851	252	5730
挖泥船	艘	14	3058	17	1493
拖轮	艘	45	616	30	1133

1999 年中国进口主要商品数量金额

金额单位:万美元

品　　名	单位	1999		1998	
		数量	金额	数量	金额
渔船	艘	7	709	20	634
集装箱	只	752	545	1203	633
飞机	架	74	231683	81	260279
汽车	辆	34375	79051	39375	81512
载重汽车	辆	2752	8691	4634	10090
小轿车	辆	27194	45710	27498	42489
客车	辆	2749	6151	4608	9558
汽车底盘	金额		2043		1224
摩托车	辆	1756	232	308	32
摩托车零件	金额		6474		3956
汽车零件	金额		125250		93499
显像管	万只	949	89183	596	46527
集成电路	金额		792412		477824
电线电缆	公吨	281504	110039	246721	92484
蓄电池	金额		58763		37971
铅酸蓄电池	万个	285	1098	174	605
起重机械	台	33625	28285	38125	23179
金属切削机床	台	89411	150644	79112	139077
车床	台	8264	12804	7320	12527
钻床	台	6146	6682	6026	4879
镗床	台	484	4113	605	6012
磨床	台	14472	19929	13875	20080
齿轮加工机床	台	343	1905	301	2823
螺纹加工机床	台	2761	1072	2595	1424
铣床	台	5664	9544	4622	7579
刨床	台	247	220	317	168
插床	台	114	105	46	107
拉床	台	99	365	231	764
铸造机械	台	1635734	12850	2800022	11504
木工机械	台	25686	15719	26782	13689
各种泵	金额		134174		104991
滚动轴承	套	645418618	34083	376280681	23192
纺织机械	台	1276	19158	4871	12643
印刷机械	金额		71986		42533
制革制鞋机械	金额		8698		8142
金属轧机	金额		44464		34283
玻璃加工机械	金额		11949		12516

1999年中国进口主要商品数量金额

金额单位:万美元

品　名	单位	1999		1998	
		数量	金额	数量	金额
橡胶或塑料加工机械	金额		104310		92601
烟草加工机械	金额		8530		20890
电动机及发电机	万台	97806	74175	73904	58044
发电机组	台	22546	27952	12502	31893
电动机和发电机零件	金额		59818		61438
有线电话电报交换机	台	2971436	162246	1113176	136582
有线电话电报交换机零件	金额		115633		91176
计算机	金额		325308		181010
大、中型电子计算机	台	88	4609	54	3600
小型电子计算机	台	2567	11869	780	4609
微型电子计算机	台	54194	6315	49513	7584
显示器	台	467773	9077	1544810	8182
打印机	台	1883975	43023	934736	23262
键盘	个	8016154	3774	3185662	1958
磁盘	万片	34414	9909	21481	7968
文字处理机	金额		668		376
有线通讯设备	金额		277879		227758
电话机	台	1685344	4168	871837	16595
各种电子交换机	金额		53526		47028
载波机	台	859905	87183	115298	66280
传真机	台	282353	4835	82747	1215
复印机	台	72837	6678	20859	2379
调制解调器	台	196950	8489	27833	8371
雷达	金额		3283		3068
导航设备	金额		1871		2314
电台对讲机	金额		955		213
电池	金额		25332		25122
测绘仪器	金额		14289		12241
望远镜	金额		721		1214
放大镜	只	320210	102	921250	127
照相机	架	1703207	1270	92672	688
照相机零件	金额		50859		47073
彩色冲洗扩印系统	金额		200		185
自行车类	金额		16102		13595
自行车外胎	条	5849188	773	2865455	442
自行车内胎	条	4731937	293	1176094	70
自行车零配件	金额		14989		12970
缝纫机类	金额		20600		15969

1999年中国进口主要商品数量金额

金额单位:万美元

品名	单位	1999		1998	
		数量	金额	数量	金额
缝纫机	金额		14830		10333
家用缝纫机	台	344771	1515	211915	1139
工业缝纫机	台	182774	13315	134888	9194
缝纫机零件	金额		5771		5635
电风扇	台	25556407	7373	20768682	8462
排风扇	台	97827	490	207345	585
电冰箱	台	13340	366	16398	435
洗衣机	台	24211	619	40710	866
空调器	台	37573	1254	5954	235
吸尘器	台	56067	260	69584	376
空气加湿器	台	42679	715	10572	720
空气干燥器	台	27840	8004	12453	5267
电炉	个	83892	325	80426	309
电热水器	个	216785	1435	257114	1637
煤气热水器	台	66088	490	29208	234
洗碗机	台	3730	265	3704	215
消毒柜	台	2470	1039	1844	712
电吹风	个	347652	122	65137	50
电动剃须刀	个	131917	342	37007	85
电熨斗	个	83021	169	116092	188
电筒	个	1579792	101	1334283	44
台灯	金额		121		167
吊灯	金额		496		490
节日灯	金额		146		43
卤钨灯	万只	889	817	1091	721
录音机	金额		4216		3025
电视机及散件	金额		14378		13175
彩色电视机	台	256746	14266	303434	13041
黑白电视机	台	4099	111	10842	134
投影电视机	台	5082	922	1250	356
录像机	台	3706	1547	8880	683
摄像机	台	79850	4854	26216	1626
音箱	万台	55699	14012	42384	8561
组合音响	万套	4	637	4	280
录像带	万盒	18195	5828	17361	8905
耳塞机	万个	7749	2691	5410	2181
麦克风	个	231948276	4504	156523478	2736
量具	金额		2023		1657

1999 年中国进口主要商品数量金额

金额单位:万美元

品名	单位	1999		1998	
		数量	金额	数量	金额
刃具	金额		6150		5381
磨具	金额		7381		5485
砂布	公吨	3409	1130	2267	823
电动工具	金额		6006		6688
电钻	个	140864	449	45024	150
各种锤	金额		111		104
各种钳	金额		562		351
各种扳手	金额		1625		1118
各种螺丝批	金额		231		175
各种钻	金额		100		167
各种锉和刀	金额		1230		940
各种锯和锯条	金额		1233		904
出版物	金额		10322		11130

1999 年中国主要出口商品输往地

粮谷

输往地	1999		1998	
	数量(公吨)	金额(美元)	数量(公吨)	金额(美元)
总值	**7376298**	**1186630224**	**8886399**	**1576182797**
孟加拉国	123180	13259284	120	306450
缅甸	2122	537468	7703	1729237
朝鲜	305411	53552642	404304	75975715
香港	125067	38117972	114939	43020795
印度	147232	14829202	11996	2762493
印度尼西亚	1314445	200632356	1405384	318030312
伊朗	103175	10000000	268745	28213982
伊拉克	102880	30367500	98690	29123695
以色列	125	44360	100	37659
日本	285966	69458149	400353	90532814
科威特	13732	3185375	20	4305
老挝	320	75602	524	127230
澳门	2222	602181	1844	655231
马来西亚	1570677	179761146	1253653	145888848

1999年中国主要出口商品输往地

粮谷

输往地	1999		1998	
	数量(公吨)	金额(美元)	数量(公吨)	金额(美元)
蒙古	14057	3346525	36255	9400701
巴基斯坦	0	40	500	241610
菲律宾	249412	48457390	1453734	325110066
新加坡	20874	3090935	1411	379932
韩国	1385496	174146703	2640937	324966870
斯里兰卡	64550	6632643	83527	9495807
泰国	134002	13795906	1106	412686
土耳其	21071	4955946	41	9532
阿拉伯联合酋长国	885	272564	536	162687
越南	126215	19562912	72691	11869221
台湾省	15120	1867581	17410	2279709
吉布提	0	59	4	1080
赤道几内亚	24	4116	3150	709065
几内亚	99513	17729968	23625	5315625
科特迪瓦	421054	85394288	179941	41706564
利比亚	84000	24584060	73164	25682380
毛里求斯	35723	8490785	11420	2948600
南非	417	140992	334	106875
苏丹	8	1928	1	720
坦桑尼亚	14668	3449373	35824	9253919
比利时	5257	1227562	2412	603680
丹麦	114	37164	83	32721
英国	1619	527724	2215	813759
德国	1461	589775	1101	543404
法国	454	225988	31	17348
意大利	1372	318914	1372	307133
荷兰	7519	1528889	13808	3079466
西班牙	18	11665	9	3040
波兰	24398	6082818	19999	5283200
罗马尼亚	46005	9814459	3	2775
哈萨克斯坦	2972	966335	1052	372299
吉尔吉斯斯坦	2408	906950	891	348970
俄罗斯	164493	56726209	25806	8038117
塔吉克斯坦	60	5963	8	1975
乌兹别克斯坦	200	32942	120	40823
斯洛文尼亚共和国	2550	563347	17843	4602276

1999年中国主要出口商品输往地

粮谷

输往地	1999		1998	
	数量(公吨)	金额(美元)	数量(公吨)	金额(美元)
安提瓜和巴布达	13	5167	5	1510
巴西	3	1833	10	7626
智利	6	2470	26	6530
哥斯达黎加	1	702	0	293
古巴	226933	51742970	145375	33573108
加拿大	274	120379	339	154798
美国	667	336970	815	393437
澳大利亚	346	136528	206	98745
新西兰	73	52841	61	46947
其他	103443	24315709	48827	11346402

豆类

输往地	1999		1998	
	数量(公吨)	金额(美元)	数量(公吨)	金额(美元)
总值	**1015249**	**339939865**	**642205**	**280422194**
孟加拉国	1227	389934	59	12142
缅甸	510	101205	279	38238
朝鲜	49482	10241847	41253	11089935
香港	9614	2995393	12199	4475892
印度	160595	50317358	37868	12589213
印度尼西亚	24529	7096003	5222	1424259
伊拉克	3000	1200000	28806	17632199
以色列	548	244937	379	147336
日本	239251	104815949	217208	113280047
约旦	613	176656	726	265071
科威特	179	69450	426	173836
黎巴嫩	1136	619674	1221	671631
澳门	159	34427	102	38887
马来西亚	11696	4148229	8012	2773431
尼泊尔	50	21508	28	8856
巴基斯坦	41302	12488124	23131	8367334
菲律宾	22147	7231182	9053	3277899
沙特阿拉伯	2997	893423	327	91188
新加坡	4552	1306812	2811	1094541

1999 年中国主要出口商品输往地

豆类

输往地	1999		1998	
	数量(公吨)	金额(美元)	数量(公吨)	金额(美元)
韩国	74354	19471359	36905	10393562
斯里兰卡	168	52602	765	245025
泰国	1562	609354	1342	492122
土耳其	5349	2124981	6292	3069069
阿拉伯联合酋长国	7011	2462971	848	345017
也门共和国	11520	3955473	9273	3318438
越南	12916	4564892	4076	1849052
台湾省	20962	6960197	17728	6873256
阿尔及利亚	1564	541688	200	105500
安哥拉	3413	996326	1852	796231
博茨瓦那	0	120	0	68
刚果	319	103220	145	81550
埃及	138702	33268940	4963	1902573
毛里求斯	441	191056	424	194485
摩洛哥	511	122185	298	71489
南非	30831	10349535	43366	16641410
苏丹	2	748	61	17622
扎伊尔	57	14600	223	90141
比利时	18555	5939485	18620	7115019
丹麦	104	33724	40	22980
英国	7403	3383362	4599	2675324
德国	1659	713665	2132	1064782
法国	7105	2360450	5827	2238957
爱尔兰	60	39123	20	15539
意大利	28206	10694618	19375	9269806
荷兰	7674	3313971	7926	4324375
希腊	934	439175	514	319493
葡萄牙	7437	3354506	5923	2541324
西班牙	5658	2367159	3323	1508079
奥地利	40	27440	60	47899
波兰	24	3242	120	72000
罗马尼亚	1	760	2	1400
瑞典	10	4750	5	2250
瑞士	60	27600	60	29314
俄罗斯	1272	201728	30	15062
斯洛文尼亚共和国	8	2760	21	11361

1999年中国主要出口商品输往地

豆类

输往地	1999		1998	
	数量(公吨)	金额(美元)	数量(公吨)	金额(美元)
阿根廷	499	221255	327	188341
巴西	12247	2974192	17819	4820072
智利	252	115319	119	69988
哥伦比亚	5525	2477042	5370	2629633
多米尼加共和国	448	98604	420	130200
墨西哥	1770	606665	203	107222
乌拉圭	238	156460	260	171364
委内瑞拉	2310	873798	11373	4600907
加拿大	7737	2426559	3459	2136371
美国	12360	6127470	12116	8250560
澳大利亚	12	10006	82	61341
新西兰	150	67753	90	50720
其他	2223	694866	4103	1991966

蔬菜

输往地	1999		1998	
	数量(公吨)	金额(美元)	数量(公吨)	金额(美元)
总值	**2269978**	**1493300858**	**2034171**	**1487788793**
巴林	450	212978	112	76280
孟加拉国	4595	1192957	78	20659
文莱	345	118495	265	147182
缅甸	11764	3741376	2654	1060644
柬埔寨	24	16339	47	28189
塞浦路斯	12	9608	15	13760
朝鲜	5323	1681179	340	369429
香港	400978	67305271	456706	107094111
印度	10914	3978875	1	16211
印度尼西亚	40052	12046284	21894	8881821
以色列	1706	1318440	1550	1340164
日本	929909	931501010	850164	918198624
约旦	109	66947	176	110277
科威特	872	517151	552	406763
老挝	1042	253558	2684	641887
黎巴嫩	95	92820	167	112241
澳门	30279	6147345	27469	7240261

1999年中国主要出口商品输往地

蔬菜

输往地	1999		1998	
	数量(公吨)	金额(美元)	数量(公吨)	金额(美元)
马来西亚	57242	16036050	35185	14061359
蒙古	4798	579117	11138	1447617
尼泊尔	4854	1846655	2710	747183
阿曼	1420	876469	578	413699
巴基斯坦	4704	1535268	1219	624910
菲律宾	15583	4089166	10960	2939764
沙特阿拉伯	6983	3116309	3652	2163394
新加坡	109321	29819812	83550	27241226
韩国	115418	70105495	61179	48703636
斯里兰卡	2813	719609	945	318159
叙利亚	128	133498	104	133831
泰国	4385	5373252	3576	4728497
土耳其	540	485336	499	652504
阿拉伯联合酋长国	35384	14023373	13497	7877589
也门共和国	830	365608	191	108687
越南	29122	5108929	24070	4996480
台湾省	20358	20053232	23375	23396619
阿尔及利亚	27	21518	64	114628
博茨瓦那	0	1032	1	783
埃及	408	274800	138	146675
加纳	72	23602	3	1088
几内亚	50	19500	170	199360
肯尼亚	269	93370	89	47039
毛里求斯	62	131103	59	69076
摩洛哥	392	330572	80	42500
纳米比亚	11	3780	12	5736
南非	1723	1313717	1498	1325292
苏丹	496	372678	57	17728
突尼斯	187	78515	14	13630
比利时	5410	5630792	6000	7424541
丹麦	780	778224	546	619489
英国	12368	8411934	9698	8640813
德国	32193	40336554	36257	45084151
法国	16112	21440852	17547	24848715

1999年中国主要出口商品输往地

蔬菜

输往地	1999		1998	
	数量(公吨)	金额(美元)	数量(公吨)	金额(美元)
爱尔兰	15	7398	64	66824
意大利	23755	35754258	21018	34441537
荷兰	56583	34830690	45429	33024290
希腊	260	223307	246	233315
葡萄牙	1241	729745	770	590935
西班牙	6506	5857176	4982	4649356
奥地利	47	83604	16	48469
保加利亚	2	7688	188	138812
芬兰	211	176135	263	207843
匈牙利	96	136049	61	50505
马耳他	1	886	16	21440
挪威	195	427005	513	737723
波兰	842	603269	818	789270
罗马尼亚	728	369277	629	425585
瑞典	1352	1253813	1130	1239805
瑞士	740	2024717	782	2244236
拉脱维亚	13	14074	20	29120
立陶宛	0	360	109	74581
白俄罗斯	26	20200	92	94656
哈萨克斯坦	89	34517	437	213014
吉尔吉斯斯坦	6	3356	23	12500
俄罗斯	121050	20165676	116834	19729903
乌克兰	37	48663	141	82241
南斯拉夫	10	6600	27	23191
斯洛文尼亚共和国	163	77019	40	29083
克罗地亚共和国	0	48	10	7883
捷克共和国	4	24958	14	20680
斯洛伐克共和国	1	2736	2	1069
阿根廷	972	915072	2755	1710961
阿鲁巴岛	73	28565	40	20200
伯利兹	0	140	1	844
巴西	22643	9250578	23074	13643254
智利	763	344245	333	245799
哥伦比亚	11735	4403546	6645	3553935

1999年中国主要出口商品输往地

蔬菜

输往地	1999		1998	
	数量(公吨)	金额(美元)	数量(公吨)	金额(美元)
多米尼克	1283	815639	508	208280
哥斯达黎加	1968	733811	284	168184
古巴	109	76727	64	45380
多米尼加共和国	252	90720	2237	2893383
厄瓜多尔	2208	722023	329	180435
危地马拉	585	255140	123	71250
圭亚那	73	27669	0	2247
洪都拉斯	254	114783	92	47513
墨西哥	577	287858	163	147437
巴拿马	1001	474051	178	141210
秘鲁	1386	586637	399	244711
波多黎各	120	74692	112	102135
苏里南	26	17001	18	19844
特立尼达和多巴哥	57	26783	193	117750
乌拉圭	192	201439	169	155664
委内瑞拉	528	498647	249	271148
加拿大	16441	11574651	12894	10073877
美国	59739	66262717	68121	71753526
澳大利亚	8064	7387927	6212	7015108
新西兰	945	848437	672	762911
其他	1102	667782	101	49040

水产品

输往地	1999		1998	
	数量	金额(美元)	数量	金额(美元)
总值		**1947020614**		**1736683979**
柬埔寨		721		161
朝鲜		87600		15291
香港		159604925		215154130
印度		56850		152107
印度尼西亚		993389		205601
以色列		432199		615948
日本		839243635		737104505
约旦		3569		2180

1999年中国主要出口商品输往地

水产品

输往地	1999		1998	
	数量	金额(美元)	数量	金额(美元)
澳门		5066319		6504649
马来西亚		5982448		2809643
菲律宾		2422448		320803
沙特阿拉伯		1591		186659
新加坡		7149726		6717506
韩国		362708971		170754977
斯里兰卡		43697		33770
泰国		5146602		7068924
阿拉伯联合酋长国		153923		29179
越南		81945		142414
台湾省		31529686		38342973
留尼汪		324596		128071
南非		631805		298388
比利时		11290514		11246904
丹麦		5413719		5687912
英国		17201791		10626577
德国		63833050		113381863
法国		20372541		20158201
意大利		8052747		2128419
卢森堡		119200		24
荷兰		13953782		22383758
希腊		1769641		2514196
葡萄牙		4354134		4316648
西班牙		61724059		64475647
芬兰		23401		4944440
匈牙利		220124		1801
马耳他		82306		27219
挪威		1356968		736299
波兰		3984248		2129089
罗马尼亚		55915		29552
瑞典		6607364		4619950
瑞士		6909		176471
立陶宛		3360		205511
俄罗斯		778963		23578834
乌克兰		56421		72
捷克共和国		2248329		543382

1999年中国主要出口商品输往地

水产品

输往地	1999		1998	
	数量	金额(美元)	数量	金额(美元)
墨西哥		413633		350683
巴拿马		133550		2928
波多黎各		1405542		392034
乌拉圭		3		320084
委内瑞拉		7643		2566
加拿大		20253255		20744539
美国		273298274		230189188
澳大利亚		3860793		2129836
斐济		95362		59952
新西兰		1261673		691050
巴布亚新几内亚		559439		889708
其他		555316		410763

茶叶

输往地	1999		1998	
	数量(公吨)	金额(美元)	数量(公吨)	金额(美元)
总值	**199608**	**338338001**	**217437**	**370275800**
阿富汗	2600	2606617	4414	4964917
缅甸	227	103708	44	37634
柬埔寨	4	39194	4	30994
香港	9665	20649588	11700	22849082
印度	269	213281	542	855630
印度尼西亚	60	98302	857	908679
伊朗	416	335955	124	128603
伊拉克	1999	3528140	9816	18671139
以色列	90	154874	30	56915
日本	28498	63327723	20833	48168992
澳门	318	609105	265	473658
马来西亚	1915	4234704	1203	2610047
蒙古	206	116620	643	536887
尼泊尔	22	45638	17	55002
巴基斯坦	5863	4744331	5369	5813661
菲律宾	29	97289	44	129438
沙特阿拉伯	594	1738854	967	2342755

1999年中国主要出口商品输往地

茶叶

输往地	1999		1998	
	数量(公吨)	金额(美元)	数量(公吨)	金额(美元)
新加坡	752	1876630	2017	4654683
韩国	427	561930	213	262754
斯里兰卡	828	1032000	534	608030
叙利亚	161	250546	59	65867
泰国	225	455636	257	529785
土耳其	40	39251	1	8452
阿拉伯联合酋长国	2896	2499785	5021	7099820
也门共和国	256	253382	1164	1411923
越南	141	171140	71	68270
阿尔及利亚	2235	4251222	6308	12861040
贝宁	274	470271	9	19780
喀麦隆	336	185913	0	240
吉布提	150	92963	13	10128
埃及	75	72375	714	1037498
加蓬	12	27000	35	75241
冈比亚	3763	7216534	4177	8490154
加纳	246	438564	126	291788
几内亚	193	391274	1850	3178939
科特迪瓦	2307	6004424	2622	5538456
肯尼亚	24	13322	550	609447
利比里亚	35	73884	138	238602
利比亚	735	1507730	551	913848
马里	5928	9852791	7069	13466275
毛里塔尼亚	3293	5869824	998	1802586
摩洛哥	31709	59629910	15447	24077692
尼日尔	417	664447	130	244080
尼日利亚	6454	2983417	4990	2926944
留尼汪	1	4500	1	4500
塞内加尔	7429	14527267	12632	24176108
南非	8	18383	3	6882
多哥	4082	7276298	4369	7904087
突尼斯	3334	4567306	4297	6484140
比利时	1740	3994040	3728	8277727
丹麦	242	441269	329	590415
英国	5826	8745292	7590	11932964
德国	7721	18581872	6526	13217501

1999年中国主要出口商品输往地

茶叶

输往地	1999		1998	
	数量(公吨)	金额(美元)	数量(公吨)	金额(美元)
法国	8037	15963501	15179	29531051
爱尔兰	0	1702	547	1016640
意大利	131	305445	325	644676
荷兰	2860	6280813	3564	7689521
希腊	13	27723	17	24354
西班牙	620	1369445	1190	2721694
奥地利	10	104067	0	1099
芬兰	154	290729	41	104807
直布罗陀	17	36647	9	27541
匈牙利	7	25721	2	8677
挪威	5	27791	3	9733
波兰	3221	5695047	3286	5881679
瑞典	7	23087	10	32518
瑞士	3	25839	3	28277
立陶宛	57	58887	118	102713
白俄罗斯	152	193886	134	189388
哈萨克斯坦	1016	1179712	1154	1687165
吉尔吉斯斯坦	177	208015	103	160650
俄罗斯	6008	7810651	6780	9994485
塔吉克斯坦	136	115050	59	52180
土库曼斯坦	4081	3440295	2244	2224459
乌克兰	567	938261	1927	2379743
乌兹别克斯坦	10928	9532408	9872	12052690
捷克共和国	11	26596	4	14297
巴西	2	52087	1	6045
智利	1	4149	2	12410
巴拿马	24	45175	26	47428
秘鲁	6	39220	6	39567
加拿大	369	1048458	468	1148119
美国	13455	14748621	17888	18429646
澳大利亚	307	691455	535	1536421
新西兰	59	92351	425	559151
其他	96	248852	105	196297

1999年中国主要出口商品输往地

纺织品

输往地	1999		1998	
	数量(公吨)	金额(美元)	数量(公吨)	金额(美元)
总值		**12316878821**		**12007289886**
阿富汗		395746		1150843
巴林		8135057		9156695
孟加拉国		361349275		353296844
文莱		265796		261282
缅甸		93002981		67888240
柬埔寨		44911392		28417808
塞浦路斯		12343166		16033930
朝鲜		17045025		21767511
香港		4096678446		4465875908
印度		61556691		42712350
印度尼西亚		122745362		72447046
伊朗		12399099		10394777
伊拉克		287862		1219155
以色列		40794668		33297025
日本		1385504077		1284641157
约旦		13012313		14024295
科威特		13836280		12708247
老挝		3374125		2174780
黎巴嫩		13779348		14291712
澳门		130971949		118982665
马来西亚		102247637		81172812
马尔代夫		98917		278693
蒙古		21269291		7595443
尼泊尔		54898175		19537308
阿曼		8318457		7001390
巴基斯坦		21521539		8476433
巴勒斯坦		229565		259480
菲律宾		118900348		121227092
卡塔尔		5060968		5078932
沙特阿拉伯		63807970		72261140
新加坡		188731513		203583103
韩国		922898990		740399525
斯里兰卡		125604979		115787288
叙利亚		13485042		15787193
泰国		151478979		124198527

1999年中国主要出口商品输往地

纺织品

输往地	1999		1998	
	数量(公吨)	金额(美元)	数量(公吨)	金额(美元)
土耳其		89312991		107419423
阿拉伯联合酋长国		212200276		173040593
也门共和国		13631467		6109276
越南		100436293		122497242
台湾省		82598753		72807130
阿尔及利亚		18653427		16244500
安哥拉		1127620		4176968
贝宁		90473433		89017635
博茨瓦那		597699		52897
布隆迪		36		143230
喀麦隆		2409036		2014475
加那利群岛		10778725		8853672
佛得角		75343		73844
塞卜泰(休达)		1003109		453785
乍得		198267		4834
刚果		1406833		3353887
吉布提		6135136		3081007
埃及		42990846		40880190
赤道几内亚		71477		28675
埃塞俄比亚		4280287		4846978
加蓬		492220		383776
冈比亚		35780130		30796923
加纳		18962659		19537217
几内亚		5472010		1975458
几内亚(比绍)		236197		170552
科特迪瓦		31283046		35174032
肯尼亚		25706264		21944390
利比里亚		556334		413497
利比亚		13986553		12919954
马达加斯加		21582138		12398951
马拉维		1592840		453402
马里		395573		3101640
毛里塔尼亚		5255517		2423065
毛里求斯		36764597		36426714
摩洛哥		30277926		17435110
莫桑比克		2041463		1766530

1999年中国主要出口商品输往地

纺织品

输往地	1999		1998	
	数量(公吨)	金额(美元)	数量(公吨)	金额(美元)
纳米比亚		1022766		467568
尼日尔		3445745		3849509
尼日利亚		26999578		13325471
留尼汪		125382		126748
卢旺达		48953		112122
塞内加尔		9891729		5848643
塞舌尔		41978		43368
塞拉利昂		498036		609303
南非		76288871		78728926
苏丹		4297597		4988662
坦桑尼亚		10885564		10874890
多哥		29486806		19565853
突尼斯		7790572		7618174
乌干达		1107875		281478
扎伊尔		2521512		6412007
赞比亚		992619		1315445
津巴布韦		4941804		5081902
莱索托		2660169		1792127
梅利利亚		225571		190479
斯威士兰		2275049		1468421
比利时		97179353		98553883
丹麦		14426169		12369849
英国		137073403		127111922
德国		237054750		256617190
法国		103624731		108771835
爱尔兰		2118389		1238651
意大利		179882418		174366932
卢森堡		233889		128310
荷兰		54492012		58581692
希腊		28734729		24656685
葡萄牙		14973632		15177390
西班牙		59583854		50454765
阿尔巴尼亚		2508040		2896887
安道尔		164998		55812
奥地利		6436686		6455117
保加利亚		1414288		779237

1999年中国主要出口商品输往地

纺织品

输往地	1999		1998	
	数量(公吨)	金额(美元)	数量(公吨)	金额(美元)
芬兰		4140027		3698028
直布罗陀		208346		1005333
匈牙利		35942106		28705259
冰岛		3151418		1331068
马耳他		11089506		2937020
摩纳哥		373276		64608
挪威		13865003		12424921
波兰		33608090		34582973
罗马尼亚		12921631		28750084
瑞典		11750029		11420030
瑞士		9147678		9890945
爱沙尼亚		80973		229980
拉脱维亚		1069373		3390284
立陶宛		1350328		1786378
格鲁吉亚		108022		29302
亚美尼亚		560247		200690
阿塞拜疆		760		204165
哈萨克斯坦		29027268		21384240
吉尔吉斯斯坦		31940825		47625058
俄罗斯		37186042		83825507
塔吉克斯坦		1764568		2729870
土库曼斯坦		299382		106519
乌克兰		12765930		12163424
乌兹别克斯坦		2000596		2294880
南斯拉夫		677195		2318070
斯洛文尼亚共和国		2484060		1958652
克罗地亚共和国		856864		951722
捷克共和国		13243292		7445852
斯洛伐克共和国		435008		1007882
马其顿共和国		1534617		878492
安提瓜和巴布达		164179		168267
阿根廷		26606504		35957510
阿鲁巴岛		5774		50240
巴哈马		131187		37620
巴巴多斯		336028		527081
伯利兹		94924		25666

1999年中国主要出口商品输往地

纺织品

输往地	1999		1998	
	数量(公吨)	金额(美元)	数量(公吨)	金额(美元)
玻利维亚		353093		585001
巴西		37614071		46997789
智利		52656822		60801393
哥伦比亚		4619776		2979271
多米尼克		12828434		20434872
哥斯达黎加		12075174		10170035
古巴		13839639		7782093
库腊索岛		873308		1281592
多米尼加共和国		33978705		35519222
厄瓜多尔		2834055		3734363
危地马拉		46082761		40838355
圭亚那		906464		941295
海地		3497739		4184906
洪都拉斯		40625389		40970359
牙买加		19739098		20378296
墨西哥		43578346		29091675
尼加拉瓜		11804930		13674683
巴拿马		99263189		102979377
巴拉圭		2092686		4421663
秘鲁		8615059		7332553
波多黎各		266740		491993
圣卢西亚		230557		3928
圣马丁岛		273958		154402
圣文森特和格林纳丁斯		38201		44311
萨尔瓦多		30254504		25514830
苏里南		771528		1238469
特立尼达和多巴哥		4970783		3734254
乌拉圭		6872630		5165898
委内瑞拉		10672010		9830162
加拿大		122357646		117987285
美国		861744916		751354774
澳大利亚		218172613		188938270
斐济		7787366		5677474
瑙鲁		3018		2055
新喀里多尼亚		307645		278419
瓦努阿图		49995		55414

1999年中国主要出口商品输往地

纺织品

输往地	1999		1998	
	数量(公吨)	金额(美元)	数量(公吨)	金额(美元)
新西兰		30243144		28729318
巴布亚新几内亚		2803051		2320773
社会群岛		267062		620593
所罗门群岛		58945		77629
汤加		17153		2708
萨摩亚		729275		32855
密克罗尼西亚联邦		27846		33393
马绍尔群岛共和国		9147		7666
贝劳共和国		357827		278
其他		3634401		1060988

棉纱线

输往地	1999		1998	
	数量(件)	金额(美元)	数量(件)	金额(美元)
总值	**958924**	**528016949**	**735159**	**420864608**
孟加拉国	3280	1713939	370	219732
缅甸	41009	14326734	26750	14090875
柬埔寨	142	73143	77	23615
朝鲜	1090	382379	613	263157
香港	700803	397084322	588526	336554956
印度	134	59456	918	408553
印度尼西亚	3094	1582601	49	41325
伊朗	67	59307	201	171035
以色列	82	98586	39	34257
日本	83583	44696850	56576	32971682
科威特	24	30348	15	20802
黎巴嫩	57	39830	91	40588
澳门	2947	1454508	4496	1668645
马来西亚	12694	7420953	3422	2212653
蒙古	905	643780	590	346660
尼泊尔	8	9764	33	14460
阿曼	11	14958	12	17300
巴基斯坦	75	49591	14	21173
菲律宾	2139	961127	2190	1137477
卡塔尔	8	13481	2	2799

1999年中国主要出口商品输往地

棉纱线

输往地	1999		1998	
	数量(件)	金额(美元)	数量(件)	金额(美元)
沙特阿拉伯	42	31954	9	3730
新加坡	2977	1331576	1049	594034
韩国	64088	32784962	28129	16838672
斯里兰卡	313	193011	396	358207
叙利亚	651	592611	151	178169
泰国	2681	2321712	3375	1701093
土耳其	124	91827	110	44000
阿拉伯联合酋长国	1265	953858	281	274452
也门共和国	70	81343	80	92127
越南	166	144512	11	16532
台湾省	702	636497	54	34475
贝宁	18	21660	302	181361
喀麦隆	574	314683	111	46200
加蓬	56	29820	1	288
加纳	49	30340	225	116476
几内亚	172	64294	63	33978
科特迪瓦	715	434623	694	415609
肯尼亚	53	29576	4	7648
利比亚	438	326196	2931	2078290
马达加斯加	691	333321	43	29707
毛里求斯	1438	855908	73	102051
尼日利亚	2788	1563773	1272	820114
留尼汪	6	7558	2	2756
南非	14	16290	61	44040
苏丹	107	90487	72	65550
坦桑尼亚	39	30240	111	46549
突尼斯	1132	525132	1836	979855
英国	44	46197	33	48252
德国	322	257723	244	237195
法国	11	17197	8	12483
意大利	57	25066	65	68355
荷兰	20	25227	14	17017
西班牙	2128	741927	2620	1020311
芬兰	10	9987	2	3378

1999年中国主要出口商品输往地

棉纱线

输往地	1999		1998	
	数量(件)	金额(美元)	数量(件)	金额(美元)
匈牙利	483	103004	2	1296
冰岛	80	51680	122	75019
马耳他	8	6414	0	75
哈萨克斯坦	355	159742	4	3925
捷克共和国	17	6300	18	3564
智利	93	119519	132	171591
古巴	3	3545	193	121890
厄瓜多尔	114	121795	86	100644
危地马拉	80	129397	75	127269
海地	6	6840	10	13594
洪都拉斯	27	45013	22	37051
牙买加	183	73060	19	13846
巴拿马	7	10038	11	14327
特立尼达和多巴哥	6	9784	12	20347
加拿大	225	259636	201	236273
美国	9917	5522686	2150	1623201
澳大利亚	10212	4980950	1667	767808
斐济	74	41840	423	327636
新西兰	6	8983	7	10678
其他	919	679978	591	419876

棉布

输往地	1999		1998	
	数量(万米)	金额(美元)	数量(万米)	金额(美元)
总值	**256462**	**2292553434**	**221206**	**2132250017**
阿富汗	9	68343	10	126569
巴林	388	4756802	428	6191061
孟加拉国	13629	146826005	10533	123715516
缅甸	1358	8182832	751	5859123
柬埔寨	1512	18502600	591	8112124
塞浦路斯	40	337603	232	2319264
朝鲜	233	1767998	102	569886
香港	98055	1017070563	99619	1073469129
印度	1087	14501573	661	9618296
印度尼西亚	3337	30188419	1650	20247182

1999年中国主要出口商品输往地

棉布

输往地	1999		1998	
	数量(件)	金额(美元)	数量(件)	金额(美元)
伊朗	3	9900	9	180904
以色列	396	5672325	205	2933136
日本	17087	100410534	17172	102835584
约旦	70	606358	168	2030807
科威特	528	5354901	356	3120433
老挝	369	1149326	29	353713
黎巴嫩	57	805281	80	1246100
澳门	1514	20741798	1638	26270536
马来西亚	1628	14772484	1848	19597587
蒙古	455	6621541	192	2425765
尼泊尔	145	1709583	143	1336895
阿曼	279	3817538	198	2472978
巴基斯坦	80	1196499	68	768511
菲律宾	2258	26684042	2387	26059377
卡塔尔	127	1422773	271	3272382
沙特阿拉伯	280	1828959	190	1431411
新加坡	3342	22378314	6332	40557860
韩国	35614	187021326	14954	84235999
斯里兰卡	2894	32925031	2252	24254846
叙利亚	10	170374	3	66751
泰国	3071	22021414	1516	13421848
土耳其	1286	10951498	1041	9607063
阿拉伯联合酋长国	1375	16532803	1121	12669520
越南	986	11543998	1287	13405829
台湾省	311	2672232	221	2340775
阿尔及利亚	34	297679	13	147538
安哥拉	29	166797	392	2460037
贝宁	4383	45131368	3618	39865598
喀麦隆	6	69665	68	356779
加那利群岛	49	347323	26	225942
刚果	113	616863	152	875537
埃及	1653	19593982	1290	15598156
埃塞俄比亚	2	48110	1	34266
冈比亚	2151	19125665	1962	15055497
加纳	1778	11251294	1321	8372633
几内亚	345	3424198	62	447070

1999年中国主要出口商品输往地

棉布

输往地	1999		1998	
	数量(件)	金额(美元)	数量(件)	金额(美元)
科特迪瓦	1962	14383822	1970	15485838
肯尼亚	1984	12111371	1244	8509640
利比里亚	57	365816	11	58200
利比亚	42	422174	50	348024
马达加斯加	64	864892	70	1167719
马里	11	47512	362	2079223
毛里塔尼亚	1208	3941965	103	402782
毛里求斯	921	20743079	977	24523171
摩洛哥	253	3085980	111	1785114
莫桑比克	11	54423	18	186233
纳米比亚	3	33600	18	103581
尼日尔	411	2356302	557	3440065
尼日利亚	521	3678524	156	1577951
塞内加尔	791	5567454	241	1650153
塞拉利昂	60	325678	68	461776
南非	932	11273019	639	6677629
坦桑尼亚	546	2890370	608	3759700
多哥	888	6156466	626	5050695
突尼斯	24	324301	78	601024
扎伊尔	17	72153	88	586813
赞比亚	34	156613	67	370721
津巴布韦	80	780123	193	1866623
莱索托	75	1287503	26	466163
比利时	2362	19784512	2511	24436049
丹麦	103	1025308	80	846405
英国	1594	12809527	1549	13705329
德国	1219	9280449	883	7551457
法国	744	7547833	895	9014193
爱尔兰	4	72918	1	11272
意大利	985	8215539	1018	10684949
荷兰	434	2472317	493	4313026
希腊	56	501552	54	520156
葡萄牙	11	168291	51	792048
西班牙	380	3011330	336	2959754
阿尔巴尼亚	62	434971	31	277683
奥地利	53	289603	80	581782

1999年中国主要出口商品输往地

棉布

输往地	1999		1998	
	数量(件)	金额(美元)	数量(件)	金额(美元)
芬兰	14	65335	3	30683
匈牙利	69	818093	23	434831
冰岛	37	618918	0	2431
马耳他	365	2997193	80	701509
挪威	474	3040174	586	3765371
波兰	102	946544	29	316947
罗马尼亚	24	206945	10	66732
瑞典	79	538942	36	283376
瑞士	70	661411	64	588430
爱沙尼亚	0	15	3	22704
立陶宛	6	120121	10	241317
俄罗斯	45	420370	51	660577
乌克兰	174	1896800	425	4535141
南斯拉夫	11	64575	25	349669
斯洛文尼亚共和国	22	172348	39	433089
克罗地亚共和国	24	244808	10	78108
捷克共和国	25	280377	2	48598
马其顿共和国	73	1250932	42	536395
阿根廷	50	486367	79	691056
巴西	1358	8265689	1652	10485726
智利	464	6245427	254	3167009
哥伦比亚	27	462567	21	309744
多米尼克	500	5278054	307	3621008
哥斯达黎加	93	820653	106	936926
古巴	273	1820680	235	1680754
多米尼加共和国	1096	12508747	852	9602730
厄瓜多尔	10	160391	10	143547
危地马拉	1691	22862414	1408	16741299
圭亚那	19	174888	15	52592
海地	118	1238847	71	717074
洪都拉斯	1938	23615560	1585	17575602
牙买加	190	3428056	351	8056037
墨西哥	624	7529553	294	3177765
尼加拉瓜	594	6682386	837	10641153
巴拿马	206	3217371	243	2925351
巴拉圭	3	32918	27	291232

1999年中国主要出口商品输往地

棉布

输往地	1999		1998	
	数量(件)	金额(美元)	数量(件)	金额(美元)
秘鲁	9	121452	12	193115
萨尔瓦多	1206	14115053	689	8506065
苏里南	66	350379	73	492491
特立尼达和多巴哥	11	98874	33	339972
乌拉圭	176	1110308	12	98260
委内瑞拉	115	1434673	97	1569295
加拿大	1427	14345155	1224	12504775
美国	14565	93701292	11908	77158344
澳大利亚	4137	44883194	3394	35616393
斐济	154	871327	180	1075048
新喀里多尼亚	27	96916	1	4290
瓦努阿图	1	3035	2	10243
新西兰	159	1987371	160	2022717
巴布亚新几内亚	77	371888	118	528865
社会群岛	3	13662	1	7816
其他	207	2040582	85	793061

绸缎

输往地	1999		1998	
	数量(万米)	金额(美元)	数量(万米)	金额(美元)
总值	**11442**	**315608239**	**12110**	**382676024**
阿富汗	4	83487	0	13134
文莱	1	35390	0	8207
塞浦路斯	0	2897	2	132041
香港	3580	114996367	4784	163828301
印度	271	6081749	314	7345776
印度尼西亚	4	110321	2	98738
以色列	12	307675	9	285946
日本	1454	32498882	1142	26482756
约旦	13	89697	1	5006
科威特	12	300009	2	51217
黎巴嫩	0	3767	1	24350
澳门	2	84839	3	98488
马来西亚	106	2042295	62	1535555
尼泊尔	896	17617819	306	6594356

1999年中国主要出口商品输往地

绸缎

输往地	1999		1998	
	数量(万米)	金额(美元)	数量(万米)	金额(美元)
菲律宾	4	65405	20	353637
沙特阿拉伯	137	2657421	225	4172322
新加坡	333	7010929	108	2806371
韩国	2322	67750213	2473	79293135
斯里兰卡	1	49521	0	3600
泰国	4	147390	2	67547
土耳其	15	419956	28	784249
阿拉伯联合酋长国	158	3685703	119	3178927
越南	5	296774	2	70859
台湾省	9	199565	8	325493
埃及	27	782333	1	36903
摩洛哥	89	2305098	143	2813263
南非	6	72166	1	22665
突尼斯	9	149914	9	128351
丹麦	5	209438	8	324929
英国	44	1720377	75	2739488
德国	227	6409770	265	7958085
法国	114	2736688	168	4467528
爱尔兰	2	26904	1	21173
意大利	758	20890391	772	25428123
荷兰	1	24712	12	301794
希腊	3	82219	7	217946
西班牙	14	336138	13	281562
奥地利	1	48031	4	100389
芬兰	2	35668	2	64382
波兰	22	488428	35	771354
罗马尼亚	0	3640	4	32515
瑞典	2	105624	2	83544
瑞士	61	1509180	69	1825186
吉尔吉斯斯坦	108	4215809	476	20895013
俄罗斯	8	208423	1	58441
斯洛文尼亚共和国	2	75405	2	74733
克罗地亚共和国	2	30487	0	6061
巴西	3	100170	1	44638
巴拿马	0	2993	1	18590
加拿大	12	354986	6	235032
美国	378	13764973	370	14529697
澳大利亚	30	870576	21	691310
新西兰	7	144501	6	143345
其他	163	1365126	23	799973

1999 年中国主要出口商品输往地

服装

输往地	1999 金额(美元)	1998 金额(美元)	输往地	1999 金额(美元)	1998 金额(美元)
总值	**30057854590**	**30057203416**	阿拉伯联合酋长国	201602318	176057250
阿富汗	120694	90113	也门共和国	12915651	8511093
巴林	3096756	2867265	越南	86210449	157509822
孟加拉国	7827054	9322266	台湾省	186866561	192316632
文莱	228928	101811	阿尔及利亚	24123974	12672509
缅甸	4182637	1408726	安哥拉	2087757	9096754
柬埔寨	4407493	13930484	贝宁	1586554	2304051
塞浦路斯	7691317	3873746	博茨瓦那	3201507	1260394
朝鲜	2750533	1841249	布隆迪	222	24665
香港	7151546753	9302036225	喀麦隆	917507	1055646
印度	1659827	36286317	加那利群岛	7216190	5897561
印度尼西亚	12438174	4371386	佛得角	2088161	85920
伊朗	337808	1796868	中非共和国	2278	386014
以色列	49359477	22659757	塞卜泰(休达)	671847	453349
日本	8811769024	7447414477	乍得	40972	39790
约旦	22522653	14824084	刚果	1343983	27680530
科威特	41219821	35808283	吉布提	6343495	4142066
老挝	800910	21588	埃及	147647357	110806901
黎巴嫩	18561207	18092846	赤道几内亚	20631	7049
澳门	252261552	237902164	埃塞俄比亚	5288311	3402440
马来西亚	67499126	36342783	加蓬	81811	122892
马尔代夫	52750	46899	冈比亚	696480	207622
蒙古	7877728	1134079	加纳	2641725	1678618
尼泊尔	15350266	2951420	几内亚	2904252	5246427
阿曼	882200	955591	几内亚(比绍)	16647	28909
巴基斯坦	3137704	1621664	科特迪瓦	1480340	1096535
巴勒斯坦	425837	83368	肯尼亚	3578144	13896814
菲律宾	27299694	13726531	利比里亚	83558	254856
卡塔尔	565768	815733	利比亚	4711079	13154868
沙特阿拉伯	327554454	292319448	马达加斯加	4138513	1150475
新加坡	335706632	243826729	马拉维	255971	11100
韩国	665713927	516616682	马里	133367	385865
斯里兰卡	6627132	6219515	毛里塔尼亚	457341	405553
叙利亚	755120	660400	毛里求斯	749800	575696
泰国	22738616	16408676	摩洛哥	33904020	16902959
土耳其	12838334	9286789	莫桑比克	3213804	795649

1999年中国主要出口商品输往地

服装

输往地	1999	1998
	金额(美元)	金额(美元)
纳米比亚	718768	484009
尼日尔	60015	55209
尼日利亚	15272999	5475206
留尼汪	20684	79058
卢旺达	574	432733
塞内加尔	387634	118648
塞舌尔	95708	48391
南非	114044393	108330814
西撒哈拉	36992	3175
苏丹	4368820	1520525
坦桑尼亚	945177	360301
多哥	8494867	6238368
突尼斯	11988454	5547248
乌干达	850996	263207
扎伊尔	471761	8610999
赞比亚	2684797	14974094
津巴布韦	315805	223286
莱索托	267359	123302
梅利利亚	751539	563700
斯威士兰	107294	30206
比利时	115075600	102357076
丹麦	123154141	109720765
英国	409017196	399684412
德国	883505324	908867889
法国	396705966	334115011
爱尔兰	17356975	14597446
意大利	375780861	375649828
卢森堡	9359542	10132628
荷兰	272686773	271773452
希腊	23647679	22715158
葡萄牙	11094873	11798966
西班牙	195009929	159631025
阿尔巴尼亚	2742108	2860932
安道尔	137893	761644
奥地利	38626851	42209949
保加利亚	14684657	11705222

输往地	1999	1998
	金额(美元)	金额(美元)
芬兰	61608654	72659623
直布罗陀	140868	18988
匈牙利	194299118	164910739
冰岛	1360239	1305392
马耳他	14679486	8897898
摩纳哥	344435	271491
挪威	112264509	104203970
波兰	265259924	313440423
罗马尼亚	28626857	61344793
瑞典	137658803	152372567
瑞士	261909491	218195933
爱沙尼亚	2389536	2849937
拉脱维亚	1903627	1928695
立陶宛	8966018	10009037
格鲁吉亚	217335	147491
亚美尼亚	267686	435915
阿塞拜疆	10960	76318
白俄罗斯	29465	169623
哈萨克斯坦	149987582	44797545
吉尔吉斯斯坦	20502747	30839539
摩尔多瓦	28460	57397
俄罗斯	735169128	888539868
土库曼斯坦	62388	621966
乌克兰	8806320	16849562
乌兹别克斯坦	1089468	3230783
南斯拉夫	6003574	7850448
斯洛文尼亚共和国	22173217	10658791
克罗地亚共和国	31202805	9218182
捷克共和国	153473196	132970658
斯洛伐克共和国	13591811	14395206
马其顿共和国	897548	662129
波斯尼亚—黑塞哥维那	137185	39318
阿根廷	50500553	54161309
阿鲁巴岛	536705	770739
巴哈马	963264	1678350

1999年中国主要出口商品输往地

服装

输往地	1999 金额(美元)	1998 金额(美元)
伯利兹	18008	9253
玻利维亚	882856	151079
巴西	83076273	153459393
智利	172687841	175957396
哥伦比亚	1887231	2644024
多米尼克	1525525	1431725
哥斯达黎加	1209359	692211
古巴	9470791	8710761
库腊索岛	10194624	6395713
多米尼加共和国	1277200	4832792
厄瓜多尔	2671590	7882001
危地马拉	11442189	13109947
圭亚那	88501	267629
海地	220043	46790
洪都拉斯	3243736	963754
牙买加	16701974	11117904
墨西哥	91407976	43457695
尼加拉瓜	581320	2195473
巴拿马	441661974	417125700
巴拉圭	3106790	4622981
秘鲁	4118225	7030771
波多黎各	326177	363653
圣卢西亚	197	29100
圣马丁岛	592221	173130
萨尔瓦多	2472012	1526741
苏里南	290886	290846
特立尼达和多巴哥	1105378	709066
特克斯和凯科斯群岛	86719	3944
乌拉圭	30167982	15431360
委内瑞拉	32104663	21950715
加拿大	414384937	365760385
美国	3872142357	3747916055
格陵兰	60833	50097
百慕大	248392	552299
澳大利亚	760686820	611986685
库克群岛	13320	77518
斐济	592035	2096738
盖比群岛	68555	2326
新喀里多尼亚	447717	290085
瓦努阿图	26124	37711
新西兰	106963827	92982444
巴布亚新几内亚	2404818	1973224
社会群岛	2520	27259
所罗门群岛	33832	53263
汤加	8138	11316
萨摩亚	155374	45020
马绍尔群岛共和国	9132	4436
贝劳共和国	4374	10080
其他	416775	807187

日用瓷

输往地	1999 金额(美元)	1998 金额(美元)
总值	**745090188**	**665500783**
阿富汗	249870	72675
巴林	268020	454341
孟加拉国	2677523	644217
文莱	26575	7122
缅甸	3671372	832902
柬埔寨	1273443	1314649
塞浦路斯	1431323	1773817
朝鲜	12123	4138
香港	22767802	25541369
印度	409223	199202
印度尼西亚	11807906	1447003
伊朗	1611635	581071
以色列	12372234	14112125
日本	15906406	9141753
约旦	6686141	6432068

1999年中国主要出口商品输往地

日用瓷

输往地	1999 金额(美元)	1998 金额(美元)	输往地	1999 金额(美元)	1998 金额(美元)
科威特	1906348	2374631	肯尼亚	2310375	4381145
老挝	73132	37490	利比亚	320388	368826
黎巴嫩	20117007	14542817	马达加斯加	178169	74177
澳门	151450	109520	马拉维	21748	22598
马来西亚	6129755	3184995	毛里求斯	745218	710555
蒙古	747	2626	摩洛哥	15928075	13206866
尼泊尔	353869	69840	莫桑比克	60983	51967
阿曼	375448	92355	尼日尔	253000	989
巴基斯坦	5686267	3142803	尼日利亚	3934523	2471666
巴勒斯坦	68260	25754	留尼汪	66141	44238
菲律宾	11015064	6606156	卢旺达	14618	10064
卡塔尔	213098	90729	南非	35561897	22985967
沙特阿拉伯	12768711	11307148	苏丹	3402326	1053079
新加坡	7124603	4589386	坦桑尼亚	1489436	1468606
韩国	1839363	1216242	突尼斯	5350433	4258349
斯里兰卡	3884966	2928579	乌干达	438674	370691
叙利亚	44903	60958	扎伊尔	44839	114141
泰国	3013644	497706	赞比亚	75867	167928
土耳其	5163878	11165902	津巴布韦	68848	210810
阿拉伯联合酋长国	25843134	27768498	比利时	6016449	4713177
也门共和国	616880	511114	丹麦	1015581	1374776
越南	1721873	1736575	英国	19343619	13108436
台湾省	1811733	1358234	德国	29698135	27384439
阿尔及利亚	12992835	7727959	法国	10401118	11744261
安哥拉	158947	238908	爱尔兰	628143	510283
贝宁	1810	75	意大利	26920568	20985526
喀麦隆	832898	902806	荷兰	18029442	17943479
佛得角	12026	26591	希腊	7043795	3610987
刚果	82336	39581	葡萄牙	3890067	4634042
吉布提	368477	237641	西班牙	16364420	9220660
埃及	21458592	18597592	阿尔巴尼亚	20906	52964
埃塞俄比亚	207847	770107	安道尔	10656	13745
加蓬	139854	129785	奥地利	2072274	1702443
加纳	462634	225783	保加利亚	1473412	809925
几内亚	94282	119784	芬兰	642002	464332
科特迪瓦	172247	267211	匈牙利	445160	330795

1999年中国主要出口商品输往地

日用瓷

输往地	1999	1998
	金额(美元)	金额(美元)
冰岛	11193	12799
马耳他	438054	69296
摩纳哥	43702	8124
挪威	2363432	2806753
波兰	3996800	1118850
罗马尼亚	662052	1022393
瑞典	2292069	2154147
瑞士	826486	667133
爱沙尼亚	13755	53099
拉脱维亚	153070	257104
立陶宛	235091	300407
哈萨克斯坦	4245148	1173759
吉尔吉斯斯坦	2971	159594
俄罗斯	2197651	2078271
土库曼斯坦	9413	1275
乌克兰	112325	236669
乌兹别克斯坦	4470	30480
南斯拉夫	483292	141634
斯洛文尼亚共和国	612690	322421
克罗地亚共和国	520035	203417
捷克共和国	1229862	542989
斯洛伐克共和国	115386	42124
安提瓜和巴布达	14656	11250
阿根廷	9019090	10955319
巴哈马	16643	5262
巴巴多斯	13152	36680
玻利维亚	20680	64357
巴西	2053663	4590185
智利	13564735	12759120
哥伦比亚	639351	1427276
多米尼克	3726955	4349929
哥斯达黎加	560807	1132715
古巴	67240	119819
库腊索岛	13722	16609
多米尼加共和国	648517	749553
厄瓜多尔	1318920	3190645
瓜德罗普	19820	11017
危地马拉	4081253	4851787
圭亚那	99671	38697
海地	257552	165989
洪都拉斯	953315	550106
牙买加	519675	790720
墨西哥	3651074	3983130
尼加拉瓜	1138	150
巴拿马	12107825	17632828
巴拉圭	177184	99840
秘鲁	7314230	6378158
波多黎各	1047650	2153892
萨尔瓦多	328125	291646
苏里南	40720	3298
特立尼达和多巴哥	120894	192574
乌拉圭	2066531	1904002
委内瑞拉	3695933	5482137
加拿大	28663646	24648144
美国	158586642	169615464
澳大利亚	23399981	15483996
斐济	338608	354071
新喀里多尼亚	8668	5311
新西兰	2499386	1945144
巴布亚新几内亚	248670	128532
所罗门群岛	5080	12747
其他	248020	126681

地毯及装饰毯

输往地	1999	1998
	金额(美元)	金额(美元)
总值	**421293826**	**441650842**
巴林	72680	12617
文莱	121654	51370
缅甸	106198	5330
柬埔寨	2322	80

1999年中国主要出口商品输往地

地毯及装饰毯

输往地	1999 金额(美元)	1998 金额(美元)
塞浦路斯	193662	288529
朝鲜	22035	62043
香港	13471441	14423802
印度尼西亚	1086976	117760
以色列	587276	459220
日本	62628315	60351093
约旦	449531	253429
科威特	513867	843009
黎巴嫩	678853	1181984
澳门	82815	60487
马来西亚	1818445	439982
蒙古	379150	498413
尼泊尔	27796	7930
阿曼	41664	194226
巴基斯坦	64988	19235
菲律宾	71807	71515
卡塔尔	169697	247908
沙特阿拉伯	6487791	7800177
新加坡	703849	623931
韩国	1560479	653157
斯里兰卡	31454	1208
泰国	295918	360406
土耳其	2802095	5580804
阿拉伯联合酋长国	3551545	9458505
也门共和国	252593	58439
越南	23635	17186
台湾省	2869321	1836088
阿尔及利亚	691	19065
埃及	2441859	2862291
加纳	27572	5861
肯尼亚	48485	3470
利比亚	141411	150
马达加斯加	7382	3720
毛里求斯	382097	796987
留尼汪	42797	7990
南非	351307	354948
突尼斯	16190	3379
比利时	3743656	4483218
丹麦	230088	281756
英国	26175499	28589806
德国	41415222	49708692
法国	4702772	3698580
爱尔兰	73612	14110
意大利	13273197	15093369
卢森堡	23203	18390
荷兰	4339277	7866092
希腊	990366	1045678
葡萄牙	5898953	4304809
西班牙	3597368	4246839
阿尔巴尼亚	9830	32400
奥地利	601754	1134938
保加利亚	84036	284847
芬兰	100289	79671
匈牙利	162058	162557
马耳他	234529	52626
挪威	337318	151707
波兰	126332	314495
罗马尼亚	50124	161547
瑞典	1809730	1164621
瑞士	3545663	3634609
拉脱维亚	4400	5339
立陶宛	3940	29171
哈萨克斯坦	46620	14371
吉尔吉斯斯坦	8368	49181
俄罗斯	319707	1306125
乌克兰	52969	46940
乌兹别克斯坦	65269	64700
南斯拉夫	301849	128349
斯洛文尼亚共和国	108635	58898
克罗地亚共和国	147798	35042
捷克共和国	42440	27331
马其顿共和国	90091	28844

1999年中国主要出口商品输往地

地毯及装饰毯

输往地	1999	1998
	金额(美元)	金额(美元)
阿根廷	396790	630972
玻利维亚	437	4856
巴西	1020918	2166181
智利	159312	184299
圭亚那	36518	21327
墨西哥	462691	561587
巴拿马	226316	21251
乌拉圭	114512	65565
委内瑞拉	69346	58907
加拿大	5713058	6483192
美国	189998850	189907131
澳大利亚	4341285	2388273
斐济	837	790
新西兰	761854	516180
巴布亚新几内亚	4909	13097
其他	639588	269862

鞋类

输往地	1999	1998
	金额(美元)	金额(美元)
总值	**8672699694**	**8391789934**
巴林	588086	716552
孟加拉国	521930	319248
文莱	182395	137823
缅甸	4120487	1165083
柬埔寨	7021512	1579380
塞浦路斯	1698146	1148284
朝鲜	1726536	921681
香港	594419964	663822819
印度	2653276	4064485
印度尼西亚	12628395	6068200
伊朗	607795	1587404
伊拉克	32544	84678
以色列	25850534	21866062
日本	842222390	727828074

输往地	1999	1998
	金额(美元)	金额(美元)
约旦	14611234	14300487
科威特	4816626	4869964
老挝	165570	80249
黎巴嫩	9010270	10529548
澳门	27919020	23705989
马来西亚	21883543	9820480
马尔代夫	15956	16347
蒙古	83928	155457
尼泊尔	8412873	3603055
阿曼	318694	102937
巴基斯坦	3076765	1661107
巴勒斯坦	225240	52463
菲律宾	24845007	19529456
卡塔尔	83484	70388
沙特阿拉伯	61715327	62193529
新加坡	27889272	15265851
韩国	118595291	91493414
斯里兰卡	913930	457989
叙利亚	158672	214900
泰国	7219101	9063202
土耳其	8745427	10817289
阿拉伯联合酋长国	54855973	56143974
也门共和国	7852420	6232440
越南	12765619	11521180
台湾省	46537928	65508246
阿尔及利亚	9573789	9922709
安哥拉	3222481	6056845
贝宁	3275597	1896232
博茨瓦那	1582577	1150245
喀麦隆	1677339	1413751
加那利群岛	51522	141027
佛得角	404164	232227
中非共和国	7500	6813
塞卜泰(休达)	174805	214548
刚果	1090474	2742715
吉布提	3842720	4125465

1999 年中国主要出口商品输往地

鞋类

输往地	1999	1998
	金额(美元)	金额(美元)
埃及	33615674	27000105
赤道几内亚	15521	40627
埃塞俄比亚	1721205	1684534
加蓬	528214	723938
冈比亚	4204170	4452705
加纳	9744236	6363416
几内亚	5156169	3809706
几内亚(比绍)	82149	27146
科特迪瓦	11480125	11071681
肯尼亚	1782703	2638529
利比里亚	661320	404126
利比亚	3122431	7563174
马达加斯加	1039602	2033071
马拉维	932942	130170
马里	718892	682715
毛里塔尼亚	1473196	1309085
毛里求斯	1234728	1228771
摩洛哥	2545153	924449
莫桑比克	3337831	3587540
纳米比亚	1198551	1817034
尼日尔	49765	185789
尼日利亚	17432535	9519922
留尼汪	299472	234563
卢旺达	79212	167874
塞内加尔	3335803	2830195
塞舌尔	29373	74284
塞拉利昂	354260	339902
索马里	129942	103609
南非	64792232	46193506
苏丹	1445833	642683
坦桑尼亚	2037866	2237902
多哥	10687732	11206134
突尼斯	6943784	10901254
乌干达	216132	118243
布基纳法索	295718	202108
扎伊尔	662227	1435068
赞比亚	1205107	789798
津巴布韦	987794	291336

输往地	1999	1998
	金额(美元)	金额(美元)
莱索托	778322	5765328
梅利利亚	80169	91980
比利时	140718003	114832736
丹麦	10245225	8780138
英国	127379389	117429900
德国	171539553	183095466
法国	114087278	108025017
爱尔兰	6262264	4429440
意大利	104084432	87720888
荷兰	114788897	92896556
希腊	22872405	16376028
葡萄牙	10935116	11909387
西班牙	78036741	68662682
阿尔巴尼亚	1644706	1007104
奥地利	9440371	8899710
保加利亚	6250460	5987242
芬兰	11814346	19573379
匈牙利	44447629	64576180
冰岛	119338	116931
马耳他	722217	734918
摩纳哥	91637	221516
挪威	9230368	8518276
波兰	88417158	132715017
罗马尼亚	22638005	76112590
瑞典	22373879	15670039
瑞士	15877492	6914647
爱沙尼亚	529167	710626
拉脱维亚	956795	679825
立陶宛	2002371	1182745
格鲁吉亚	15296	68048
亚美尼亚	269887	1080
阿塞拜疆	760	73542
白俄罗斯	4813	29665
哈萨克斯坦	195419400	37078394
吉尔吉斯斯坦	26625584	42896055
俄罗斯	178781378	164174460
土库曼斯坦	48492	80012
乌克兰	10037161	7895145

1999 年中国主要出口商品输往地

鞋类

输往地	1999	1998
	金额(美元)	金额(美元)
乌兹别克斯坦	292496	1274651
南斯拉夫	2719501	3382121
斯洛文尼亚共和国	2522696	2587382
克罗地亚共和国	1963756	2114219
捷克共和国	31270611	34736490
斯洛伐克共和国	7580244	8714807
马其顿共和国	86036	113059
波斯尼亚—黑塞哥维那	69867	14369
安提瓜和巴布达	74470	1759
阿根廷	15798028	22055156
阿鲁巴岛	104267	260360
巴哈马	67678	39535
巴巴多斯	92188	19794
伯利兹	50357	129966
玻利维亚	852518	1078708
巴西	13076655	30560583
智利	68444405	76003956
哥伦比亚	4104552	3652440
多米尼克	743133	1038802
哥斯达黎加	3694874	3513074
古巴	3095207	5614412
库腊索岛	1199447	1581338
多米尼加共和国	336869	653304
厄瓜多尔	1286143	4283116
瓜德罗普	43067	34864
危地马拉	5248332	4179844
圭亚那	1593912	374350
海地	397710	51058
洪都拉斯	1189952	1037695
牙买加	1106805	1277223
马提尼克	20807	17280
墨西哥	3395055	780331
尼加拉瓜	288994	82018
巴拿马	128936397	138229471
巴拉圭	2800139	5852129
秘鲁	751970	1488822
波多黎各	2517358	2197648
萨尔瓦多	2509925	3415565
苏里南	408389	358582
特立尼达和多巴哥	817040	855562
乌拉圭	8830345	12740302
委内瑞拉	5555397	10989329
加拿大	134696481	127166978
美国	4356633846	4317317806
澳大利亚	111428248	91926200
斐济	1390246	1017021
瑙鲁	852	2610
新喀里多尼亚	239533	225275
瓦努阿图	41677	29611
新西兰	13023226	7966699
巴布亚新几内亚	1606907	768744
社会群岛	11575	22613
所罗门群岛	153917	87374
汤加	9240	1918
萨摩亚	131666	93954
马绍尔群岛共和国	3030	3996
贝劳共和国	1073	1250
其他	350354	250736

玩具

输往地	1999	1998
	金额(美元)	金额(美元)
总值	**5112142419**	**5142463692**
阿富汗	27503	10063
巴林	450026	596527
孟加拉国	129273	217594
文莱	19407	35260
缅甸	3298879	580669
柬埔寨	33780	51402
塞浦路斯	1468923	1512229
朝鲜	8735	29956
香港	732210968	829599424

1999 年中国主要出口商品输往地

玩具

输往地	1999 金额(美元)	1998 金额(美元)
印度	2938403	1302446
印度尼西亚	4844020	1479107
伊朗	147153	90088
以色列	8548892	7670735
日本	252422222	251942010
约旦	1020586	939711
科威特	1688691	2226397
老挝	85118	36168
黎巴嫩	2403958	2202887
澳门	748617	26083016
马来西亚	13747297	6565926
马尔代夫	8211	1440
蒙古	1600	78567
尼泊尔	517190	41371
阿曼	72544	14508
巴基斯坦	1780389	750506
巴勒斯坦	80768	14456
菲律宾	10969140	4271654
卡塔尔	40493	59636
沙特阿拉伯	14379630	14308290
新加坡	7362193	18451219
韩国	34484925	37771269
斯里兰卡	155029	347153
叙利亚	92346	115942
泰国	3557292	4741913
土耳其	14745375	9012880
阿拉伯联合酋长国	18123272	24649775
也门共和国	235189	148120
越南	1296533	3098897
台湾省	28516244	24372509
阿尔及利亚	286859	271363
安哥拉	20259	87702
博茨瓦那	19051	1100
喀麦隆	52049	19377
加那利群岛	144363	69378
佛得角	6280	3346
中非共和国	76124	16129
刚果	9335	13506
埃及	8540693	7565669
埃塞俄比亚	1170	13548
加蓬	24692	3693
加纳	261867	95419
几内亚	18986	14740
科特迪瓦	134173	102581
肯尼亚	138357	53866
利比里亚	12146	821
马达加斯加	83314	137731
毛里求斯	358759	165907
摩洛哥	2029887	2018057
莫桑比克	13174	51511
纳米比亚	3696	7148
尼日尔	14025	14096
尼日利亚	270632	162010
留尼汪	8890	14333
塞内加尔	18512	71140
塞舌尔	1680	6342
南非	11294754	7559621
苏丹	3323	5542
坦桑尼亚	2829	1822
突尼斯	944824	639652
赞比亚	8234	898
津巴布韦	97537	12261
比利时	28920450	27381849
丹麦	11774811	8309978
英国	240888037	216443324
德国	202195825	187695728
法国	98040504	94027370
爱尔兰	2047482	2721659
意大利	98011568	81224205
卢森堡	30637	144913
荷兰	62468809	54974417
希腊	11988380	10730571
葡萄牙	7493583	7487166
西班牙	64970168	53442636
阿尔巴尼亚	84388	314063
奥地利	4540070	3085054
保加利亚	1273408	1369682
芬兰	3720400	3902676

1999年中国主要出口商品输往地

玩具

输往地	1999 金额(美元)	1998 金额(美元)
直布罗陀	40343	28550
匈牙利	2720975	1964498
冰岛	34234	75150
马耳他	201738	146031
摩纳哥	62252	45687
挪威	4489073	3655059
波兰	13178686	14179258
罗马尼亚	2627131	3055855
瑞典	9864104	7939355
瑞士	4634634	4346985
爱沙尼亚	66412	60874
拉脱维亚	69418	36508
立陶宛	194117	279755
格鲁吉亚	3075	13804
阿塞拜疆	101719	22912
白俄罗斯	35253	35346
哈萨克斯坦	9279390	5491275
吉尔吉斯斯坦	326106	1153272
摩尔多瓦	7319	9141
俄罗斯	8311498	18262359
乌克兰	773238	1798481
乌兹别克斯坦	2420	99352
南斯拉夫	460423	603122
斯洛文尼亚共和国	936887	733385
克罗地亚共和国	613737	499881
捷克共和国	2526249	2467452
斯洛伐克共和国	521589	896749
马其顿共和国	34717	26632
波斯尼亚—黑塞哥维那	21118	55542
阿根廷	19102335	26624469
阿鲁巴岛	2937	11640
玻利维亚	76696	89701
巴西	15862478	35387210
智利	19048740	22054541
哥伦比亚	1629717	2377961
多米尼克	274291	425701
哥斯达黎加	783497	870971

输往地	1999 金额(美元)	1998 金额(美元)
古巴	219234	251644
多米尼加共和国	386080	536350
厄瓜多尔	1131581	1950296
法属圭亚那	2685	16930
危地马拉	657038	514543
圭亚那	33043	16782
海地	22727	38448
洪都拉斯	73067	274364
牙买加	315904	87778
墨西哥	19110582	11566814
尼加拉瓜	27774	5147
巴拿马	6556416	7888890
巴拉圭	5281542	10659179
秘鲁	1223645	1634569
波多黎各	2005837	2238804
萨尔瓦多	500529	119295
苏里南	49192	54825
特立尼达和多巴哥	97591	259768
乌拉圭	3977847	5205313
委内瑞拉	5550366	4410857
加拿大	76142796	65048615
美国	2797497872	2783991980
格陵兰	33713	7834
百慕大	77	20160
澳大利亚	41143759	36650330
库克群岛	1059	22078
斐济	141640	23887
瑙鲁	731	6234
新喀里多尼亚	21079	30008
瓦努阿图	1858	1567
新西兰	4663361	4999698
巴布亚新几内亚	58504	100787
所罗门群岛	15993	1082
贝劳共和国	139	332
其他	268804	126720

1999 年中国主要出口商品输往地

纸制品

输往地	1999		1998	
	数量(公吨)	金额(美元)	数量(公吨)	金额(美元)
总值	**762162**	**851580718**	**762878**	**875813271**
阿富汗	0	23	12	19626
巴林	171	183420	63	68499
孟加拉国	2347	2052624	3207	4063038
文莱	35	29779	86	101593
缅甸	1382	1232518	564	514320
柬埔寨	790	1102627	347	783304
塞浦路斯	71	183295	24	41459
朝鲜	1528	1395955	1065	1255306
香港	321157	317175365	357876	355263318
印度	546	615031	1149	1855672
印度尼西亚	5069	4430037	2396	2421876
伊朗	102	123925	6	18583
伊拉克	3	1208	2	16297
以色列	660	879977	639	1009268
日本	39208	84263600	45514	86646254
约旦	161	240106	140	248611
科威特	497	556337	577	664059
老挝	52	132837	321	697013
黎巴嫩	106	190320	54	173141
澳门	18265	10561458	28355	21963598
马来西亚	10134	11290871	8213	10151148
蒙古	262	239834	348	270583
尼泊尔	97	122112	51	47737
阿曼	219	232930	36	29401
巴基斯坦	365	368979	262	331577
菲律宾	4809	5007321	2966	3183116
卡塔尔	100	76234	79	110730
沙特阿拉伯	4425	4299834	2268	2789651
新加坡	21893	25395022	24546	34652699
韩国	3063	5711069	3086	4703395
斯里兰卡	318	367789	244	236814
叙利亚	17	38834	16	40084
泰国	3820	4621522	6950	9814624
土耳其	222	389775	153	343326
阿拉伯联合酋长国	1191	1633256	933	1307205

1999年中国主要出口商品输往地

纸制品

输往地	1999		1998	
	数量(公吨)	金额(美元)	数量(公吨)	金额(美元)
也门共和国	29	26945	61	64059
越南	2562	2362912	2747	3167473
台湾省	55329	27828487	48261	31165453
阿尔及利亚	122	151260	133	237848
安哥拉	12	19377	7	64481
贝宁	197	173710	158	163351
布隆迪	21	21524	0	977
喀麦隆	37	70456	6	14599
加那利群岛	11	33606	0	2022
佛得角	11	4665	1	750
刚果	36	61297	402	533108
吉布提	37	56532	178	225683
埃及	704	1072009	378	634771
赤道几内亚	12	21792	0	121
埃塞俄比亚	48	57239	223	260966
加蓬	1	1732	3	826
冈比亚	13	22619	2	3156
加纳	63	75349	84	122681
几内亚	4	7021	43	108980
科特迪瓦	17	36600	31	61902
肯尼亚	92	131589	60	92660
利比里亚	119	137183	7	4671
利比亚	10	16238	166	214309
马达加斯加	62	101619	47	65866
马里	4	35171	0	4807
毛里求斯	56	91870	84	111485
摩洛哥	218	338872	50	155518
莫桑比克	3	16760	18	24591
尼日尔	1	1009	1	22500
尼日利亚	440	769262	370	612976
留尼汪	64	62494	91	85373
塞内加尔	7	5998	1	1349
塞舌尔	16	13705	0	400
塞拉利昂	90	109539	45	62015
南非	872	1098552	1559	2370510
苏丹	16	48031	63	82755

1999 年中国主要出口商品输往地

纸制品

输往地	1999		1998	
	数量(公吨)	金额(美元)	数量(公吨)	金额(美元)
坦桑尼亚	54	69330	283	412879
突尼斯	36	54323	36	62528
乌干达	111	139858	18	19804
扎伊尔	62	105579	323	369987
赞比亚	3	1495	0	417
津巴布韦	15	17757	14	8785
比利时	1712	4809399	1463	4137163
丹麦	1101	1630255	644	932065
英国	29986	36076905	26252	32137982
德国	14803	20198601	11286	19129865
法国	8546	12662091	5617	9175940
爱尔兰	54	58354	34	42909
意大利	3252	6959028	5003	7089392
卢森堡	1	720	30	46773
荷兰	15616	14283483	11658	10700880
希腊	720	1256177	426	939663
葡萄牙	431	685561	248	366342
西班牙	4891	6344563	4771	6290919
阿尔巴尼亚	4	11620	10	38430
奥地利	431	919000	387	893406
保加利亚	45	84052	31	71361
芬兰	478	667909	570	781820
匈牙利	177	161559	152	210622
马耳他	31	38462	15	17233
挪威	492	644347	328	513414
波兰	987	1306059	683	972882
罗马尼亚	128	194363	150	293861
瑞典	897	1978235	772	1693744
瑞士	414	649370	330	721105
爱沙尼亚	1	971	15	23776
拉脱维亚	32	32327	76	74919
立陶宛	7	7950	101	76584
哈萨克斯坦	1993	3763417	554	801737
吉尔吉斯斯坦	59	149405	415	891294
俄罗斯	1205	2099294	4157	4582424
塔吉克斯坦	5	24200	52	138320

1999 年 中 国 主 要 出 口 商 品 输 往 地

纸制品

输 往 地	1999		1998	
	数量(公吨)	金额(美元)	数量(公吨)	金额(美元)
土库曼斯坦	3	14107	5	25894
乌克兰	109	111400	132	174480
乌兹别克斯坦	3	1176	37	19753
南斯拉夫	26	25256	50	43828
斯洛文尼亚共和国	16	32329	28	59506
克罗地亚共和国	46	95354	13	8829
捷克共和国	63	79732	25	41610
斯洛伐克共和国	18	12268	155	122959
马其顿共和国	0	145	0	2020
阿根廷	1357	1568270	1088	1532587
阿鲁巴岛	1	2363	0	419
巴巴多斯	1	2681	2	2548
伯利兹	7	11454	20	30875
巴西	659	865052	2157	1965029
智利	454	692541	367	689223
哥伦比亚	58	64841	82	119538
多米尼克	3	3805	5	50224
哥斯达黎加	32	36212	35	34857
古巴	494	934991	245	614237
多米尼加共和国	15	24957	33	83896
厄瓜多尔	46	54520	27	64471
危地马拉	18	24788	43	59870
圭亚那	19	13720	0	331
海地	4	10350	4	8775
洪都拉斯	12	19666	35	26271
牙买加	81	124063	7	8530
墨西哥	713	1191624	235	474219
巴拿马	380	623962	334	459224
巴拉圭	47	66960	272	393616
秘鲁	50	48767	3	12127
波多黎各	35	29903	21	26901
萨尔瓦多	2	1067	3	5800
苏里南	29	27264	9	20436
特立尼达和多巴哥	28	22306	2	1939
乌拉圭	235	254860	282	309223
委内瑞拉	167	183522	64	110311

1999年中国主要出口商品输往地

纸制品

输往地	1999		1998	
	数量(公吨)	金额(美元)	数量(公吨)	金额(美元)
加拿大	7615	8544265	7688	9465072
美国	140036	182056584	112607	154457261
澳大利亚	15179	14398791	11237	11811788
斐济	15	23590	54	67997
瑙鲁	0	180	0	6
瓦努阿图	23	16546	2	2174
新西兰	661	671542	624	967201
巴布亚新几内亚	44	37034	80	121570
所罗门群岛	9	10020	8	9654
汤加	30	47378	2	3495
萨摩亚	0	2741	2	1310
马绍尔群岛共和国	5	10785	0	693
其他	115	170119	22	57552

家具类

输往地	1999	1998
	金额(美元)	金额(美元)
总值	**2707811998**	**2190259333**
巴林	197471	199963
孟加拉国	30949	21303
文莱	945370	224289
缅甸	78390	21394
柬埔寨	10368	12124
塞浦路斯	412780	338766
朝鲜	336257	327417
香港	399129386	392732684
印度	499205	49590
印度尼西亚	2013622	1464962
以色列	2943471	1772207
日本	272605454	225386347
约旦	666391	198137
科威特	1695862	890432
黎巴嫩	2212499	605392
澳门	4720344	6420388
马来西亚	4544904	1993125
蒙古	257640	625086
尼泊尔	31472	3149
阿曼	834032	1268412
巴基斯坦	70970	68433
巴勒斯坦	52173	19546
菲律宾	2131278	1234068
卡塔尔	511163	141961
沙特阿拉伯	5410659	4987136
新加坡	28431542	37390758
韩国	13000545	9839342
斯里兰卡	281900	304529
叙利亚	28884	29007
泰国	854739	3200762
土耳其	422220	386652
阿拉伯联合酋长国	6130367	8183182
也门共和国	55140	65279
越南	639355	337392
台湾省	75525464	70938727

1999年中国主要出口商品输往地

家具类

输往地	1999 金额(美元)	1998 金额(美元)
阿尔及利亚	826164	416380
安哥拉	233933	45884
贝宁	1730	16146
博茨瓦那	21980	276
喀麦隆	50176	33735
加那利群岛	136400	70047
佛得角	65120	464
吉布提	26903	63511
埃及	391692	289215
埃塞俄比亚	160290	1089
加蓬	82789	133303
加纳	95465	151997
几内亚	347393	2926
科特迪瓦	81291	14401
肯尼亚	30979	258244
利比里亚	420	479
利比亚	1925528	11019
马达加斯加	47181	53470
毛里塔尼亚	28364	12875
毛里求斯	196876	142000
摩洛哥	514827	396714
莫桑比克	22637	5712
纳米比亚	89332	56635
尼日利亚	188969	113908
留尼汪	444572	199369
卢旺达	357	14901
塞内加尔	17320	4568
塞舌尔	12111	142345
南非	3000412	3316582
苏丹	687513	1418030
坦桑尼亚	29791	22343
多哥	32915	3314
突尼斯	85403	42889
扎伊尔	21788	75255
赞比亚	23630	36807
津巴布韦	11401	35102

输往地	1999 金额(美元)	1998 金额(美元)
比利时	22196952	18324679
丹麦	5124531	4664176
英国	85416394	72340204
德国	49729288	38918928
法国	45807227	45209659
爱尔兰	1557006	1292777
意大利	24337203	21042705
卢森堡	860462	615848
荷兰	45155263	41363979
希腊	2728430	2503014
葡萄牙	1673213	2019992
西班牙	15688355	13852209
阿尔巴尼亚	20277	6270
奥地利	585895	455586
保加利亚	32261	27858
芬兰	1545562	1250288
匈牙利	202346	304897
冰岛	59204	43642
马耳他	235470	121690
挪威	1533215	1715188
波兰	682140	448619
罗马尼亚	252453	102051
瑞典	9644818	8247674
瑞士	894965	850771
爱沙尼亚	17493	38482
拉脱维亚	16700	463
立陶宛	5258	13212
哈萨克斯坦	300675	532206
吉尔吉斯斯坦	104049	49058
俄罗斯	857479	4408948
乌克兰	32161	20567
乌兹别克斯坦	3392	55406
南斯拉夫	50869	25482
斯洛文尼亚共和国	79392	33971
克罗地亚共和国	7777	13491
捷克共和国	357984	43867

1999年中国主要出口商品输往地

家具类

输往地	1999	1998
	金额(美元)	金额(美元)
安提瓜和巴布达	27328	446
阿根廷	2639976	3136935
阿鲁巴岛	21689	13328
巴巴多斯	5794	7386
伯利兹	434	6412
巴西	1355223	2905605
智利	2813898	3779915
哥伦比亚	403788	490413
多米尼克	417221	958818
哥斯达黎加	336444	160169
古巴	108462	61652
库腊索岛	58676	159040
多米尼加共和国	283490	670593
厄瓜多尔	118398	337345
瓜德罗普	85712	53190
危地马拉	11974	50682
圭亚那	131570	9867
海地	17689	35417
牙买加	227811	67503
墨西哥	1108213	1320552
巴拿马	2175074	2902381
巴拉圭	83485	50310
秘鲁	195817	319476
波多黎各	1592468	1452373
萨尔瓦多	25785	34225
苏里南	28599	46952
特立尼达和多巴哥	49996	31441
乌拉圭	722490	975175
委内瑞拉	1429196	1464217
加拿大	43232367	30294569
美国	1443514950	1040431826
格陵兰	1288	3665
百慕大	22122	14454
澳大利亚	42503541	34274665
斐济	34477	6458
瑙鲁	1488	295
新喀里多尼亚	53526	58167
瓦努阿图	18404	8892
新西兰	4113143	3078504
诺福克岛	21560	34477
巴布亚新几内亚	44270	30733
社会群岛	9048	37838
所罗门群岛	2410	1822
汤加	420	12620
萨摩亚	87193	6087
马绍尔群岛共和国	11413	27727
贝劳共和国	10476	16661
其他	2211125	176322

钢材

输往地	1999		1998	
	数量(公吨)	金额(美元)	数量(公吨)	金额(美元)
总值	**3684396**	**1413199662**	**3565997**	**1686980064**
巴林	947	455492	618	385552
孟加拉国	12651	7622440	21539	12399928
文莱	3177	630036	1329	351202
缅甸	35432	12284658	55645	29426538
柬埔寨	49643	10391520	65053	16782949
塞浦路斯	1471	1014207	1065	598322

1999年中国主要出口商品输往地

钢材

输往地	1999		1998	
	数量(公吨)	金额(美元)	数量(公吨)	金额(美元)
朝鲜	32993	12260852	34077	12769861
香港	570905	202021570	621160	244512559
印度	49230	21094696	31438	22096744
印度尼西亚	71617	32310939	46809	23287004
伊朗	23886	20053913	14801	14233540
伊拉克	3210	2635170	525	435235
以色列	11142	5869661	14449	6324309
日本	389551	130765132	397261	154152076
约旦	2233	1134790	6192	3885618
科威特	13073	7758175	4341	2634109
老挝	578	233779	689	225301
黎巴嫩	4787	2269529	5793	2782418
澳门	23106	5932965	10595	4579464
马来西亚	85897	28643847	55524	21762483
蒙古	2246	1926701	8351	3808706
尼泊尔	328	210996	1449	567688
阿曼	175	84435	87	41419
巴基斯坦	18484	10745768	24615	14132394
巴勒斯坦	34	43293	73	103502
菲律宾	36862	14245799	31946	14014452
卡塔尔	743	363418	686	446200
沙特阿拉伯	22383	10268399	23843	8906648
新加坡	83953	35684109	68840	38526482
韩国	743368	177694796	145122	54679097
斯里兰卡	4889	2174731	5353	3206109
叙利亚	30075	18411803	27392	16710823
泰国	31587	14184472	30164	12472923
土耳其	60623	16198776	64154	21570317
阿拉伯联合酋长国	24730	15529431	23709	16089567
也门共和国	3078	1397605	2545	1533737
越南	23667	10779545	43780	15427000
台湾省	74781	44960640	100782	63539890
阿尔及利亚	771	508202	852	774363
安哥拉	300	103030	100	98880
贝宁	221	86293	127	49770
布隆迪	39	20414	1238	872730

1999年中国主要出口商品输往地

钢材

输往地	1999		1998	
	数量(公吨)	金额(美元)	数量(公吨)	金额(美元)
喀麦隆	135	106474	244	193725
刚果	110	63173	338	141905
吉布提	1714	727198	2689	788896
埃及	13281	8804782	27695	17059907
埃塞俄比亚	1816	831103	2806	1019846
加蓬	214	96371	49	78722
冈比亚	42	24066	41	26240
加纳	2041	1630497	912	519584
几内亚	1	183	30	8625
科特迪瓦	824	366753	746	529543
肯尼亚	952	653848	1135	753590
利比亚	975	2595181	387	744950
马达加斯加	1279	542188	439	234371
马里	197	152023	6	12604
毛里塔尼亚	89	136121	77	31856
毛里求斯	540	257763	447	282398
摩洛哥	1492	916926	1270	784157
莫桑比克	100	65938	393	165431
尼日利亚	5490	2869601	2538	2368192
塞内加尔	728	396347	535	333827
塞舌尔	186	108125	1	718
南非	5617	5675739	12611	20101959
苏丹	27615	21541878	237828	185054788
坦桑尼亚	4160	2131959	649	317339
多哥	145	79585	120	59376
突尼斯	1338	832122	794	556843
乌干达	45	32824	20	11660
扎伊尔	101	56899	101	79309
赞比亚	104	120737	6	5968
津巴布韦	321	264137	1084	534049
比利时	17595	10728156	139426	51512681
丹麦	1088	1226963	1066	4635600
英国	15962	11708312	65925	29114434
德国	8565	11603348	11238	15374428
法国	3831	4875077	11189	6380161
爱尔兰	512	697330	346	584995

1999年中国主要出口商品输往地

钢材

输往地	1999		1998	
	数量(公吨)	金额(美元)	数量(公吨)	金额(美元)
意大利	89348	33703591	69895	33082748
荷兰	5256	4540460	34917	12646207
希腊	3195	2180178	2187	2269562
葡萄牙	1606	1014407	5034	1987078
西班牙	62961	24732480	58145	20624871
奥地利	108	57293	16	67833
芬兰	160	184082	227	288549
匈牙利	749	897383	450	607872
冰岛	10	3000	0	43
马耳他	300	183160	180	170168
挪威	22	33852	105	134146
波兰	6618	2455149	816	1335766
罗马尼亚	756	1595523	136	136941
瑞典	281	181245	5353	1653769
瑞士	17	11454	51	54193
哈萨克斯坦	374	510663	41	9853
吉尔吉斯斯坦	2	1714	318	109908
俄罗斯	2326	1710064	826	1054606
土库曼斯坦	7	35991	141	272668
乌克兰	20	45096	0	5381
南斯拉夫	467	761942	245	856611
斯洛文尼亚共和国	167	153287	60	33880
克罗地亚共和国	36	45977	15	21071
捷克共和国	48	71920	21	35758
阿根廷	1909	2747063	3013	4842115
巴哈马	20	6800	8	10770
巴巴多斯	42	21651	28	15549
伯利兹	12	9450	21	18535
玻利维亚	238	588728	33	22831
巴西	1272	1361607	4803	3069047
智利	1862	1594618	1980	1651942
哥伦比亚	947	1573138	3357	3779475
多米尼克	351	192808	82	121615
哥斯达黎加	95	75143	115	111917
古巴	53861	33682658	2758	2021525
库腊索岛	40	23982	95	68345

1999年中国主要出口商品输往地

钢材

输往地	1999		1998	
	数量(公吨)	金额(美元)	数量(公吨)	金额(美元)
多米尼加共和国	408	278676	399	482540
厄瓜多尔	380	320449	1262	1256564
危地马拉	291	235148	180	138644
圭亚那	55	42296	60	41831
海地	484	190511	176	105685
洪都拉斯	460	272437	96	99807
牙买加	81	44091	3459	4054040
墨西哥	3908	1676128	9382	3871408
尼加拉瓜	62	53241	126	85221
巴拿马	466	260734	286	167510
巴拉圭	28	28002	54	61862
秘鲁	1990	1217293	836	873964
波多黎各	2101	1196476	124	127916
圣卢西亚	279	230267	270	137133
萨尔瓦多	349	184199	189	102366
苏里南	104	45320	42	26151
特立尼达和多巴哥	257	172626	8466	2656743
乌拉圭	224	166421	174	169863
委内瑞拉	2917	3594809	4217	3899494
加拿大	39999	18240757	39101	20343951
美国	693879	279754588	726441	328659116
澳大利亚	29422	12573983	41411	16111510
斐济	131	58739	143	64826
瓦努阿图	11	9338	131	36957
新西兰	2030	1017542	1544	704264
巴布亚新几内亚	12	9386	0	153
所罗门群岛	4	1826	1	1045
其他	513	411068	12659	7905766

水泥

输往地	1999		1998	
	数量(公吨)	金额(美元)	数量(公吨)	金额(美元)
总值	**6356530**	**200916828**	**8199725**	**290457117**
孟加拉国	1510	139634	365451	9122766
文莱	11999	366974	44421	1569431

1999 年中国主要出口商品输往地

水泥

输往地	1999		1998	
	数量(公吨)	金额(美元)	数量(公吨)	金额(美元)
缅甸	88154	3836725	140586	5126467
朝鲜	8380	355776	5411	232778
香港	1356341	51126006	1406349	59024428
印度尼西亚	546	79983	141	13338
伊朗	401	45000	80	11048
日本	139061	3727311	142343	4567084
老挝	680	32749	1498	81245
澳门	77746	3042705	151195	5770957
马来西亚	1104	171656	8389	374912
蒙古	1478	60313	6966	320357
巴基斯坦	440	56910	579	75822
菲律宾	508	46212	55773	2075997
新加坡	23	3343	425413	12849551
韩国	319955	8372260	195735	6225323
也门共和国	800	61600	132179	3733114
越南	6144	315583	3961	173330
台湾省	120377	2447145	1115672	32138853
喀麦隆	15000	390000	13000	377000
刚果	20200	484900	20000	609985
冈比亚	7700	180950	9500	275090
尼日利亚	108698	2893294	63020	1798688
南非	3021	313605	200	18000
苏丹	39675	978622	14	959
比利时	45	6680	38	780
英国	0	94	0	30
德国	3	800	2	53
法国	1	69	0	80
意大利	100	19924	160	28000
荷兰	6091	646592	1646	161242
希腊	50	6000	250	30000
葡萄牙	220	27500	60	7370
西班牙	76321	1666097	50	12250
俄罗斯	225	12049	8347	434839
美国	3819669	114923989	3682699	136034868
澳大利亚	35411	1477935	57399	2493449
新西兰	100	11500	8148	398918
马绍尔群岛共和国	11	396	30	1052
其他	88343	2587947	133020	4287663

1999 年中国主要出口商品输往地

焦炭

输往地	1999		1998	
	数量(公吨)	金额(美元)	数量(公吨)	金额(美元)
总值	**9974197**	**551217298**	**11463981**	**798389639**
孟加拉国	10930	939938	11951	1246997
不丹	12738	716000	4479	259760
缅甸	1740	55611	2060	137322
朝鲜	72970	4050231	84127	5860330
香港	40438	1430521	42444	2170533
印度	1240863	65529440	1373827	95349803
印度尼西亚	46748	3569498	20651	2318503
伊朗	170836	9034446	190095	13330762
以色列	147	14638	32	4022
日本	1053524	64646869	1053715	79449794
约旦	195	14400	114	7676
黎巴嫩	7	786	35	3724
马来西亚	76287	4715050	37707	2261639
蒙古	155	12673	500	56503
巴基斯坦	46155	3047769	20414	2027175
菲律宾	22446	1694790	16736	1484283
新加坡	1878	49017	2400	229360
韩国	166435	11911095	120067	9912543
斯里兰卡	254	19027	100	10320
泰国	70000	4610462	52650	4136515
土耳其	356211	19449296	312525	21696630
越南	12269	925366	4588	301856
台湾省	221313	13377881	95469	7568921
埃及	71918	3292562	57018	3961611
南非	524086	27798891	485292	34128618
坦桑尼亚	25	1850	184	16275
比利时	657872	34927252	582995	37578397
英国	375810	18893089	510705	34596073
德国	310099	16537844	369780	25351935
法国	725661	39464467	789310	53868795
意大利	232316	12952688	525588	38305495
荷兰	581872	30412016	368681	22712314
保加利亚	96244	4864996	105868	7027599
挪威	116037	6945823	112750	7134631
瑞典	80806	4437329	268279	18715670

1999 年中国主要出口商品输往地

焦炭

输往地	1999		1998	
	数量(公吨)	金额(美元)	数量(公吨)	金额(美元)
瑞士	293757	16446156	719120	51618078
俄罗斯	15	750	162	13932
巴西	543498	24804160	1250046	82201380
墨西哥	76414	4713097	332805	23087192
秘鲁	186970	10832630	225578	15770496
加拿大	69099	3248479	29498	1913300
美国	1122020	65748150	1232794	87317232
澳大利亚	99990	5157004	42017	2621345
其他	185148	9923261	8826	624300

成品油

输往地	1999		1998	
	数量(公吨)	金额(美元)	数量(公吨)	金额(美元)
总值	**6451581**	**1095410632**	**4360976**	**738906453**
巴林	40	22734	79	45540
孟加拉国	437	321240	28	14820
缅甸	23934	5478004	23112	5383621
柬埔寨	2537	462485	2081	357225
塞浦路斯	30505	3791069	27628	3738539
朝鲜	122950	24865005	149757	25723252
香港	776243	139516720	829953	127282031
印度	44178	4337593	4319	582828
印度尼西亚	28604	7448480	1876	814857
伊朗	280053	43328293	4976	1664382
以色列	2327	847212	2547	969403
日本	331384	55679953	250298	35265282
约旦	26	13979	26	15340
科威特	1149	126806	32	7025
黎巴嫩	21	12842	13	7313
澳门	50314	7002656	46114	7183796
马来西亚	7937	2670886	7990	2689330
蒙古	13002	3196349	7231	1938365
尼泊尔	1477	538960	1963	766345
巴基斯坦	3987	1287163	3790	1282278
菲律宾	8107	1042088	70718	11190095

1999 年中国主要出口商品输往地

成品油

输往地	1999		1998	
	数量(公吨)	金额(美元)	数量(公吨)	金额(美元)
新加坡	2303595	362491392	909648	138231755
韩国	896079	145802456	586766	95879389
泰国	66278	13892295	42973	9980423
土耳其	5276	1455335	2669	328791
也门共和国	158	96175	1083	217090
越南	715513	104661124	522752	73843049
台湾省	74185	11416704	184096	32059401
埃及	136	279518	587	100991
埃塞俄比亚	211	93060	823	334963
利比里亚	15627	2459318	24483	3668830
马里	4	7029	5	11682
毛里求斯	17	12649	4	2880
苏丹	148	72617	2	1799
丹麦	1153	247849	1651	318927
英国	14076	5057706	11491	4515300
德国	48458	17237546	39189	14655126
法国	29982	10860723	26741	9908668
意大利	11063	3974911	12916	5025007
荷兰	16861	5758376	12928	4236864
希腊	5126	822204	14353	1954137
奥地利	9268	3317865	11190	4194364
芬兰	6052	2169199	5641	2162439
匈牙利	2732	969895	608	221027
马耳他	33851	4705562	11073	1860950
挪威	2356	398288	2178	395673
波兰	559	106181	2992	995048
罗马尼亚	3548	1238247	1679	601660
瑞典	11231	4009653	10559	3948866
瑞士	21987	7795586	25188	9551262
格鲁吉亚	389	138095	688	258340
白俄罗斯	261	95696	474	185082
哈萨克斯坦	9349	1883162	1772	681511
吉尔吉斯斯坦	1013	367549	591	226632
俄罗斯	20546	4770639	78167	13585762
土库曼斯坦	128	49281	44	17355
乌克兰	2064	713324	3920	1329739

1999 年中国主要出口商品输往地

成品油

输往地	1999		1998	
	数量(公吨)	金额(美元)	数量(公吨)	金额(美元)
乌兹别克斯坦	1327	471204	1085	415013
南斯拉夫	3726	1345034	2413	919161
安提瓜和巴布达	639	105079	696	68931
巴哈马	5727	816241	9059	1141786
伯利兹	11049	1676991	7268	1005988
洪都拉斯	3576	537564	2642	413180
巴拿马	119264	17535261	167218	28411444
圣文森特和格林纳丁斯	21179	3018750	35676	5091491
加拿大	19147	6618566	17073	6445270
美国	160634	34108871	99109	22775677
澳大利亚	36800	5599786	18792	7336260
瓦努阿图	1007	104218	579	102969
马绍尔群岛共和国	239	60180	969	116541
其他	8774	1995161	11939	2250293

塑料

输往地	1999	1998	输往地	1999	1998
	金额(美元)	金额(美元)		金额(美元)	金额(美元)
总值	**5174882902**	**5216105056**	科威特	3419479	2801173
阿富汗	122821	508502	老挝	154068	22342
巴林	472413	739942	黎巴嫩	6244334	5084285
孟加拉国	5052519	3633366	澳门	10146571	32422883
文莱	231031	261445	马来西亚	22020093	21009471
缅甸	3243749	1844583	马尔代夫	4007	12231
柬埔寨	1037861	561693	蒙古	998330	1586118
塞浦路斯	1378028	1100128	尼泊尔	604642	245694
朝鲜	13940211	15427527	阿曼	244508	157448
香港	1023905527	1312668043	巴基斯坦	10802671	8628033
印度	5960782	17052280	巴勒斯坦	133610	160256
印度尼西亚	18970878	13382605	菲律宾	27472532	24473328
伊朗	4757999	3091789	卡塔尔	333661	93525
伊拉克	1035298	1511774	沙特阿拉伯	20136482	17432286
以色列	12276161	10307155	新加坡	53106067	55453197
日本	475383827	448355358	韩国	49911200	58457621
约旦	4020460	3151610	斯里兰卡	2556403	2373635

1999年中国主要出口商品输往地

塑料

输往地	1999 金额(美元)	1998 金额(美元)	输往地	1999 金额(美元)	1998 金额(美元)
叙利亚	4057145	2723048	尼日利亚	6996885	4542758
泰国	20490454	33435247	留尼汪	267574	136019
土耳其	14010587	10333367	卢旺达	188403	80930
阿拉伯联合酋长国	27887181	24415184	塞内加尔	186491	184867
也门共和国	1225707	1043150	塞舌尔	73836	76776
越南	15099918	24704649	塞拉利昂	17031	40153
台湾省	70852202	74381812	南非	15232078	23783410
阿尔及利亚	3749022	2213864	苏丹	6073677	5499727
安哥拉	471221	759578	坦桑尼亚	843455	871651
贝宁	451370	333456	多哥	118167	107117
博茨瓦那	45211	48022	突尼斯	4416421	2414501
喀麦隆	562362	335670	乌干达	117482	40194
加那利群岛	436076	175213	扎伊尔	454276	668722
佛得角	92444	59885	赞比亚	89274	111131
中非共和国	22266	60182	津巴布韦	796441	527736
刚果	62920	701813	梅利利亚	15527	6450
吉布提	385970	276397	比利时	54428231	48511277
埃及	13963367	15976155	丹麦	20468137	14982289
赤道几内亚	35864	9989	英国	234402980	265604809
埃塞俄比亚	129103	488483	德国	204249828	201698318
加蓬	257812	145156	法国	116144089	109584043
冈比亚	89178	116653	爱尔兰	9602527	5801522
加纳	1621597	874269	意大利	82522538	87032251
几内亚	354484	188093	卢森堡	10832704	11647885
几内亚(比绍)	16647	4888	荷兰	197441770	140832364
科特迪瓦	1269953	1348205	希腊	12232270	10507749
肯尼亚	1279750	1119552	葡萄牙	8423149	7251431
利比里亚	5790	52018	西班牙	65541523	57723005
利比亚	369506	460804	阿尔巴尼亚	177510	159418
马达加斯加	692036	585050	安道尔	12238	10186
马拉维	73785	4510	奥地利	5221942	3850445
马里	49347	9535	保加利亚	1177759	899351
毛里塔尼亚	132471	40634	芬兰	12088754	11044163
毛里求斯	974200	669728	匈牙利	1917592	1707190
摩洛哥	5037062	4197663	冰岛	112704	175009
莫桑比克	310516	81104	马耳他	535980	355889
纳米比亚	234252	444390	摩纳哥	28049	266927
尼日尔	173769	17385	挪威	8651807	11262217

1999年中国主要出口商品输往地

塑料

输往地	1999 金额(美元)	1998 金额(美元)
波兰	8902654	12011500
罗马尼亚	3740408	7364943
瑞典	19581169	29085757
瑞士	5951022	6672738
爱沙尼亚	90611	111068
拉脱维亚	733018	545663
立陶宛	195217	480323
格鲁吉亚	23707	7053
亚美尼亚	2619	280
阿塞拜疆	4432	333
白俄罗斯	525715	6288
哈萨克斯坦	12683884	6046352
吉尔吉斯斯坦	733623	3045574
俄罗斯	21633145	24068864
土库曼斯坦	34675	64629
乌克兰	3103365	2023226
乌兹别克斯坦	755388	21058035
南斯拉夫	572604	403576
斯洛文尼亚共和国	426123	386263
克罗地亚共和国	594869	138087
捷克共和国	3034157	3419333
斯洛伐克共和国	225613	357963
马其顿共和国	104745	191498
波斯尼亚—黑塞哥维那	454	11712
安提瓜和巴布达	13072	12302
阿根廷	17181374	17489252
阿鲁巴岛	44218	5405
巴哈马	36407	53833
巴巴多斯	157107	185146
伯利兹	19138	23765
玻利维亚	41402	27077
巴西	16124644	25207928
智利	15583448	17253259
哥伦比亚	2490227	1716502
多米尼克	664469	342203
哥斯达黎加	919523	607316
古巴	1547463	2049199
库腊索岛	301905	134356
多米尼加共和国	608200	575572
厄瓜多尔	1653931	2714848
法属圭亚那	10538	28000
瓜德罗普	10240	6467
危地马拉	1583968	775084
圭亚那	377504	301036
海地	303172	112988
洪都拉斯	386695	123647
牙买加	642383	630817
墨西哥	14501846	9665499
尼加拉瓜	114047	127846
巴拿马	22759459	15901836
巴拉圭	1978833	3019907
秘鲁	1581691	1886383
波多黎各	4597041	2891740
圣卢西亚	81872	13253
圣马丁岛	5674	17915
萨尔瓦多	627089	281156
苏里南	149542	181795
特立尼达和多巴哥	870619	394969
乌拉圭	4497599	4064479
委内瑞拉	4600428	3774558
加拿大	114932805	175044683
美国	1713100896	1418742890
澳大利亚	85496103	83444607
斐济	553685	573850
瑙鲁	2539	3049
新喀里多尼亚	93520	137983
瓦努阿图	19220	22290
新西兰	9215256	9569690
巴布亚新几内亚	520668	299966
社会群岛	412364	30225
所罗门群岛	43243	32939
汤加	19112	11886
萨摩亚	61671	72645
密克罗尼西亚联邦	6510	12103
马绍尔群岛共和国	78741	52299
贝劳共和国	26161	43882
其他	428556	1065666

1999年中国主要出口商品输往地

各种染料

输往地	1999		1998	
	数量(公吨)	金额(美元)	数量(公吨)	金额(美元)
总值	**155715**	**466821158**	**131690**	**497269310**
孟加拉国	2785	4121278	2440	4231730
缅甸	1081	1582888	555	1100568
朝鲜	100	743293	97	382023
香港	9398	30576506	12222	48624864
印度	4160	15128038	3061	13228630
印度尼西亚	11163	27624895	7634	20317997
伊朗	2664	6826899	2230	7171263
以色列	10	56452	32	240908
日本	7212	28932674	8619	33275763
约旦	109	379664	116	642206
澳门	10	23905	11	52207
马来西亚	515	1790635	349	1474515
尼泊尔	22	66073	21	138160
巴基斯坦	6639	13011870	5296	12928416
菲律宾	478	1587685	227	940277
沙特阿拉伯	18	17435	4	8149
新加坡	1045	4231479	840	4352552
韩国	30171	76908081	20141	65222570
斯里兰卡	145	419776	68	298128
叙利亚	548	1425381	664	2177364
泰国	5119	14387616	3424	9813257
土耳其	2098	6407202	1407	7100471
阿拉伯联合酋长国	74	167823	318	1041760
也门共和国	2	10864	14	65235
越南	1927	4583552	1835	5416654
台湾省	19667	50466718	13907	50779047
阿尔及利亚	1	9300	9	45859
贝宁	8	34910	9	45574
吉布提	2	10345	1	10932
埃及	1957	4232530	1698	4965780
埃塞俄比亚	5	31680	12	76487
加纳	16	98019	4	44992
几内亚	18	107712	25	90814

1999 年中国主要出口商品输往地

各种染料

输往地	1999		1998	
	数量(公吨)	金额(美元)	数量(公吨)	金额(美元)
科特迪瓦	76	543822	197	857343
肯尼亚	41	119692	55	195841
马里	44	193175	8	19480
毛里求斯	160	790950	162	404551
摩洛哥	424	765978	310	1055048
尼日利亚	588	2219064	312	1367163
南非	497	1765096	301	1528354
苏丹	105	274265	29	89142
坦桑尼亚	16	73640	23	47340
突尼斯	83	56499	29	45477
津巴布韦	32	169450	12	85319
比利时	1080	5281191	885	4419812
英国	4289	15089107	4437	19022056
德国	2923	16749784	3831	21704231
法国	118	302293	206	1118963
爱尔兰	13	60331	20	92844
意大利	3553	10565693	3372	11989334
荷兰	4179	19960419	5204	30915138
希腊	204	949073	267	1176718
葡萄牙	528	475061	448	527257
西班牙	2248	5719790	1843	5680394
奥地利	7	35122	1	11787
芬兰	0	1272	10	58318
匈牙利	1	2440	10	19136
波兰	185	446333	128	422122
瑞典	83	588741	37	89832
瑞士	1973	8706821	2442	14199773
哈萨克斯坦	4	19000	3	25088
吉尔吉斯斯坦	1	2269	0	402
俄罗斯	37	133353	83	190746
捷克共和国	28	77030	0	762
阿根廷	1121	2406959	964	2656073
巴西	3420	9711491	2520	7883325
智利	174	539830	111	476363

1999年中国主要出口商品输往地

各种染料

输往地	1999		1998	
	数量(公吨)	金额(美元)	数量(公吨)	金额(美元)
哥伦比亚	458	1492093	285	856780
厄瓜多尔	147	365365	156	449557
危地马拉	391	575021	187	268531
海地	13	25208	0	1615
墨西哥	2653	6512601	1550	4850627
巴拿马	163	638502	101	343596
秘鲁	262	1005339	96	406873
乌拉圭	32	110587	45	126758
委内瑞拉	89	445603	103	443240
加拿大	540	1465446	339	1263021
美国	12879	51069832	12654	61061017
澳大利亚	589	1917143	523	2162302
新西兰	8	57115	7	48210
巴布亚新几内亚	0	2727	1	4741
其他	92	340364	93	301758

各类船

输往地	1999		1998	
	数量(艘)	金额(美元)	数量(艘)	金额(美元)
总值	**34968**	**1606204647**	**30158**	**1731599433**
孟加拉国	1	83870	1	436050
缅甸	211	26306293	128	25238347
塞浦路斯	3	43340000	3	29701075
朝鲜	4	400720	12	23034
香港	742	107022860	404	154461626
印度	3	394690	10	108777
印度尼西亚	54	45536396	79	54391190
以色列	9	1172	4	1040
日本	14128	27391438	12923	22979347
黎巴嫩	2	9521	16	23750
澳门	51	1694561	76	2097700
马来西亚	56	39728178	16	152197900
蒙古	17	18966	2	4824

1999年中国主要出口商品输往地

各类船

输往地	1999		1998	
	数量(艘)	金额(美元)	数量(艘)	金额(美元)
菲律宾	3	21544647	4	38667198
新加坡	263	285334187	181	226307475
韩国	913	9654636	378	3719332
斯里兰卡	25	155041	5	6506300
泰国	22	21234243	28	8521667
阿拉伯联合酋长国	154	337061	78	156146
越南	67	56967	13	40752
台湾省	102	2961141	829	3514291
比利时	205	78957	111	79771
丹麦	704	171581391	374	78683460
英国	2226	1216366	1636	89616863
德国	1492	312193971	1211	374959294
法国	3720	1005072	3754	66323306
爱尔兰	75	16425	3	23119488
意大利	653	833011	1070	531535
荷兰	2353	38668236	2314	763990
希腊	386	182467	567	89900571
葡萄牙	200	63380	100	21613
西班牙	1538	439515	544	3113464
奥地利	259	84696	40	7800
马耳他	25	10150	21	2450
挪威	523	85818259	1436	81400258
瑞典	208	17156747	165	105395
俄罗斯	34	34076	9	293000
斯洛文尼亚共和国	100	21900	1	258400
捷克共和国	100	21900	1	20737700
哥伦比亚	1	1250000	2	2630946
墨西哥	724	89791	115	15050
巴拿马	78	56852626	41	69327893
加拿大	339	25920819	63	5414749
美国	1472	7365402	998	44670811
澳大利亚	206	14712935	235	3371649
新西兰	1	5035	46	136111
其他	516	237374932	111	47016045

1999年中国主要出口商品输往地

集装箱

输往地	1999		1998	
	数量(只)	金额(美元)	数量(只)	金额(美元)
总值	**639617**	**1477831624**	**569706**	**1586890412**
香港	202722	491295839	182458	557380470
印度	502	1479510	6174	14668962
印度尼西亚	40	56400	1251	3461230
以色列	1410	3995800	990	2154400
日本	45585	70093356	10346	33304319
科威特	2580	4403456	385	850775
马来西亚	119	463415	216	812260
巴基斯坦	1	1085	14	27500
菲律宾	80	716710	583	2693695
新加坡	5723	15607971	1575	9561126
韩国	115045	259610702	108626	301630813
泰国	7624	15055774	1347	4166890
台湾省	54644	130520827	47191	131990793
喀麦隆	25	275000	40	362325
埃及	48	71982	88	245520
南非	279	2139281	1	19000
比利时	2270	7149270	3452	11307494
丹麦	6113	12554770	3704	7748804
英国	20586	43003060	25837	52558201
德国	29517	65835917	51837	123517460
法国	11274	21021847	7948	18552195
意大利	1814	5751550	512	3587417
荷兰	1739	5912302	577	5927888
西班牙	36	178163	232	2199693
瑞典	587	5905050	36	211200
瑞士	2569	4565976	5535	12504364
古巴	8	8000	8	8000
巴拿马	12512	29771466	9506	20534201
加拿大	279	1083900	68	421400
美国	108540	259689851	96897	250343674
澳大利亚	1153	6514407	1610	9038460
新西兰	382	1343370	327	1375560
其他	3811	11755617	335	3724323

1999年中国主要出口商品输往地

汽车

输往地	1999		1998	
	数量(辆)	金额(美元)	数量(辆)	金额(美元)
总值	**6239**	**100157509**	**9833**	**154700682**
孟加拉国	116	556111	86	1573072
缅甸	101	1220541	286	5762402
柬埔寨	19	166753	53	347640
塞浦路斯	9	113856	16	115416
朝鲜	509	3368792	993	7155613
香港	838	29079893	949	34616416
印度尼西亚	10	1566074	3	679000
伊朗	8	1376657	17	13270719
日本	53	684218	48	741344
约旦	13	81813	1	9225
科威特	11	89605	17	236573
老挝	249	2220785	145	1351750
黎巴嫩	5	160000	95	639600
蒙古	66	654305	79	1621971
尼泊尔	38	383115	75	811304
阿曼	6	43475	24	201519
巴基斯坦	61	8632821	2	56109
菲律宾	45	1006308	58	781016
沙特阿拉伯	118	1340324	475	4075672
韩国	56	1013295	82	3454544
斯里兰卡	82	118831	3	21308
叙利亚	6	378933	64	259790
泰国	3	27908	1	23976
土耳其	11	62590	19	4501040
阿拉伯联合酋长国	8	61815	40	1083586
也门共和国	16	1033121	12	116749
越南	58	654263	255	4195963
台湾省	3	35074	8	134000
安哥拉	24	178971	7	233550
博茨瓦那	11	266000	4	37067
喀麦隆	54	1007729	16	234230
刚果	134	1396812	4	146736
埃及	456	1845627	1313	5506862
赤道几内亚	5	76997	15	386002
埃塞俄比亚	122	4038189	211	2983105

1999年中国主要出口商品输往地

汽车

输往地	1999		1998	
	数量(辆)	金额(美元)	数量(辆)	金额(美元)
加纳	27	231885	64	1421403
几内亚	4	38673	33	517794
科特迪瓦	24	255951	96	1003717
肯尼亚	9	78450	31	1081309
马达加斯加	25	254965	39	610863
马里	21	410533	17	559264
毛里塔尼亚	1	10630	4	81320
摩洛哥	2	57984	18	247864
莫桑比克	18	276282	6	52307
塞内加尔	2	51395	8	51375
塞舌尔	7	440459	1	7463
塞拉利昂	1	25835	15	92900
南非	138	1508599	772	8470155
苏丹	413	4585591	240	7896140
坦桑尼亚	42	305771	153	2291268
乌干达	1	8937	52	1266760
扎伊尔	12	272827	100	1863846
赞比亚	1	18072	10	31562
津巴布韦	176	2279663	90	1193703
比利时	18	55500	1	10800
英国	71	120520	17	218166
德国	20	1200982	7	1024602
法国	5	13580	17	165914
意大利	13	34822	7	54300
荷兰	5	75162	1	125540
马耳他	32	504196	8	42344
瑞典	7	148500	6	99500
哈萨克斯坦	13	123104	20	242113
吉尔吉斯斯坦	5	81000	4	35600
俄罗斯	19	156900	62	1000030
南斯拉夫	15	14197	5	18340
阿根廷	499	3177012	1583	10025062
巴西	1	29000	11	43019
哥伦比亚	1	217000	11	30515
古巴	36	1566637	6	50316
危地马拉	3	20751	11	59298

1999年中国主要出口商品输往地

汽车

输往地	1999		1998	
	数量(辆)	金额(美元)	数量(辆)	金额(美元)
巴拉圭	30	180664	57	346980
秘鲁	2	68180	22	56098
苏里南	14	132661	5	137605
乌拉圭	41	354075	68	536394
委内瑞拉	16	240020	27	352273
美国	117	784678	70	1942697
澳大利亚	95	65188	1	5315
其他	913	14739077	581	11971979

汽车零件

输往地	1999	1998
	金额(美元)	金额(美元)
总值	**780201628**	**530486376**
阿富汗	1219273	453827
巴林	19291	22869
孟加拉国	1132398	479801
缅甸	4954704	1574623
柬埔寨	42942	22063
塞浦路斯	12624	689
朝鲜	52541	159622
香港	17307779	11608453
印度	510938	233425
印度尼西亚	8222513	2306651
伊朗	1261749	111248
伊拉克	183492	125000
以色列	780559	1691163
日本	140652598	105847905
约旦	651625	437690
科威特	235899	115509
老挝	127517	115573
黎巴嫩	735827	199621
澳门	168092	1876
马来西亚	5851173	2549895
蒙古	567992	106866
尼泊尔	61465	152966
阿曼	878	27196
巴基斯坦	2388214	1456076
菲律宾	5189528	3614823
卡塔尔	35659	20573
沙特阿拉伯	3633201	1786419
新加坡	8011108	4678387
韩国	3381340	1886422
斯里兰卡	660222	874732
叙利亚	579795	271821
泰国	4384668	3993083
土耳其	1397722	1155214
阿拉伯联合酋长国	5951321	3996993
也门共和国	375997	180069
越南	1345519	4618448
台湾省	10654956	8728842
阿尔及利亚	929272	783121
安哥拉	22386	4575
贝宁	30000	3176
博茨瓦那	4284	69278
喀麦隆	152185	117238
吉布提	49075	14081
埃及	1395612	2503967
埃塞俄比亚	401756	149141

1999年中国主要出口商品输往地

汽车零件

输往地	1999	1998	输往地	1999	1998
	金额(美元)	金额(美元)		金额(美元)	金额(美元)
冈比亚	1202	7380	阿尔巴尼亚	57244	39609
加纳	114221	516071	奥地利	686823	166040
几内亚	13070	131223	保加利亚	266496	128536
科特迪瓦	113280	329767	芬兰	706666	319193
肯尼亚	412340	371893	匈牙利	999952	563024
利比里亚	266	22070	冰岛	28364	29469
马达加斯加	128584	31012	马耳他	42002	6282
马里	180713	77353	挪威	116716	202664
毛里塔尼亚	14799	30999	波兰	1101529	308938
毛里求斯	3597	39707	罗马尼亚	102489	18263
摩洛哥	334241	140001	瑞典	1166736	636319
莫桑比克	54678	6700	瑞士	71566	81744
纳米比亚	4905	15405	拉脱维亚	93452	40692
尼日利亚	2800183	2574650	立陶宛	127445	1742
卢旺达	13000	3398	哈萨克斯坦	12044	96261
南非	5858693	4830741	俄罗斯	82146	113220
苏丹	267368	348477	土库曼斯坦	78890	226969
坦桑尼亚	218866	791026	乌兹别克斯坦	46108	80
多哥	10599	4815	南斯拉夫	23400	400
突尼斯	139605	73900	斯洛文尼亚共和国	107468	78083
乌干达	76068	35210	捷克共和国	560082	102393
扎伊尔	26733	3586	阿根廷	1686311	1418086
赞比亚	52011	22056	巴巴多斯	855	7552
津巴布韦	294606	164856	巴西	634302	734490
厄立特里亚	1696	42138	智利	811499	961910
比利时	2363559	1046812	哥伦比亚	164172	635424
丹麦	1673136	725720	多米尼克	88602	41273
英国	13157630	8310267	哥斯达黎加	231337	70312
德国	36514741	19711067	古巴	3097503	1659024
法国	10346307	6472445	多米尼加共和国	190653	35475
爱尔兰	457984	287559	厄瓜多尔	426623	558989
意大利	15500080	9144057	危地马拉	58001	80689
荷兰	7193471	4258276	洪都拉斯	110609	84569
希腊	1631991	552218	牙买加	132754	5661
葡萄牙	522079	157205	墨西哥	1900849	536318
西班牙	28936289	18252979	巴拿马	1431528	706554

1999年中国主要出口商品输往地

汽车零件

输往地	1999	1998
	金额(美元)	金额(美元)
巴拉圭	53498	122566
秘鲁	418781	464981
波多黎各	181470	35608
乌拉圭	401789	155488
委内瑞拉	1515970	997507
加拿大	25271901	25164975
美国	352727202	237236542
澳大利亚	15883918	6169803
新喀里多尼亚	1911	2193
新西兰	485761	389413
巴布亚新几内亚	79456	21485
其他	576475	245519

电线电缆

输往地	1999		1998	
	数量(公吨)	金额(美元)	数量(公吨)	金额(美元)
总值	**438151**	**1258463013**	**363381**	**979828560**
巴林	77	115841	5	9243
孟加拉国	2369	5376529	1137	2898673
文莱	1	2189	16	18108
缅甸	968	3850378	879	2968143
柬埔寨	1	8694	307	669387
塞浦路斯	145	264506	58	189166
朝鲜	849	1824357	239	708417
香港	92593	195246081	80074	174282331
印度	1596	2817541	446	993926
印度尼西亚	3450	6265749	894	1925555
伊朗	2957	8585445	2296	11276952
伊拉克	779	2176566	4	17243
以色列	1090	1552909	443	740602
日本	55423	332662292	45625	266367260
约旦	155	228285	203	284857
科威特	279	425437	206	350207
老挝	529	964030	17	50192
黎巴嫩	192	323873	304	535960
澳门	1291	4328780	445	999394
马来西亚	3253	11285853	2530	7439227
蒙古	122	262882	110	325931
尼泊尔	46	49898	48	189933
阿曼	46	76581	28	60031
巴基斯坦	3064	6468088	4875	10371626

1999年中国主要出口商品输往地

电线电缆

输往地	1999		1998	
	数量(公吨)	金额(美元)	数量(公吨)	金额(美元)
菲律宾	1948	4584557	1552	2996416
卡塔尔	1	2533	39	83599
沙特阿拉伯	1274	1875034	896	1415812
新加坡	13580	39679617	16080	38428660
韩国	14682	36946231	15601	45378743
斯里兰卡	304	642856	259	603328
叙利亚	279	703186	818	4098229
泰国	4829	9289203	2621	6835405
土耳其	277	594734	116	195540
阿拉伯联合酋长国	3319	4716059	2969	4961708
也门共和国	409	582371	407	649135
越南	410	1109290	549	1806383
台湾省	31665	73525419	30707	72656148
阿尔及利亚	262	337362	276	456307
安哥拉	18	40728	2	3430
贝宁	60	77676	61	75978
喀麦隆	10	31637	11	28786
刚果	19	38851	38	80540
吉布提	64	101916	0	2095
埃及	1777	7297229	354	683714
赤道几内亚	5	14368	10	22967
埃塞俄比亚	10	18716	30	63175
加蓬	1	6843	33	94597
加纳	92	233520	52	104555
几内亚	2	18987	2	4978
科特迪瓦	42	68548	64	172323
肯尼亚	32	46388	46	108556
马达加斯加	150	204090	83	88037
马里	1	2100	3	41978
毛里塔尼亚	10	34460	1	5634
毛里求斯	30	56005	51	91765
摩洛哥	710	895060	454	739135
莫桑比克	13	39572	0	200
尼日利亚	986	1591824	532	891435
塞舌尔	2	2567	7	18221

1999 年中国主要出口商品输往地

电线电缆

输往地	1999		1998	
	数量(公吨)	金额(美元)	数量(公吨)	金额(美元)
南非	651	827769	493	776746
苏丹	1397	6385753	13	71093
坦桑尼亚	26	50875	1	3171
多哥	32	92847	11	27727
突尼斯	18	33093	22	27669
赞比亚	2	6880	7	33344
津巴布韦	90	327136	2	15651
比利时	1349	2315455	1069	2111469
丹麦	338	591762	232	556564
英国	16321	26744313	11440	17650263
德国	22759	58939549	17518	39650541
法国	4938	9918625	3844	8422688
爱尔兰	428	3043099	375	1544464
意大利	2760	4655848	2085	3874951
卢森堡	2	22770	4	6346
荷兰	3950	6621592	2663	4912440
希腊	442	623478	372	609017
葡萄牙	233	328149	152	251801
西班牙	1819	6342323	1212	3828006
阿尔巴尼亚	9	22785	7	12439
奥地利	247	478664	116	274290
保加利亚	320	747719	229	532783
芬兰	236	357798	185	362283
匈牙利	659	2745109	596	1467687
马耳他	19	40848	41	121766
挪威	310	524000	242	464076
波兰	374	482379	412	630207
罗马尼亚	52	80025	9	15755
瑞典	1746	14580424	1317	8650768
瑞士	345	617368	242	477237
拉脱维亚	81	118606	30	62989
立陶宛	84	143321	57	106084
哈萨克斯坦	5	14196	10	45172
俄罗斯	179	1884643	247	767582
乌克兰	126	285129	66	126516

1999年中国主要出口商品输往地

电线电缆

输往地	1999		1998	
	数量(公吨)	金额(美元)	数量(公吨)	金额(美元)
斯洛文尼亚共和国	97	171739	28	68545
克罗地亚共和国	42	58349	4	9396
捷克共和国	536	696416	562	672137
斯洛伐克共和国	15	22276	14	19970
安提瓜和巴布达	0	740	3	17000
阿根廷	184	387253	185	249905
玻利维亚	0	593	2	2895
巴西	975	1767124	844	1436191
智利	896	1426660	655	1109891
哥伦比亚	77	159782	146	291174
多米尼克	36	77929	140	370868
哥斯达黎加	13	23700	29	55391
古巴	329	1101054	47	241365
多米尼加共和国	68	140196	47	104763
厄瓜多尔	34	56486	58	142972
危地马拉	301	503254	10	11921
圭亚那	0	1140	45	135694
牙买加	9	20464	1	6827
墨西哥	1714	6987580	906	2506231
巴拿马	128	255407	204	407798
巴拉圭	28	32234	8	7884
秘鲁	148	300234	65	113932
波多黎各	26	43823	35	105133
苏里南	24	112642	126	528482
乌拉圭	9	18820	18	33455
委内瑞拉	105	203990	109	238941
加拿大	2274	4679888	2089	4065064
美国	111769	299468012	91090	189028101
澳大利亚	7089	17156822	4012	10254240
斐济	59	175420	0	56
新西兰	208	634960	473	755245
巴布亚新几内亚	0	39	27	447189
密克罗尼西亚联邦	2	8649	0	152
其他	57	202687	165	338291

1999年中国主要出口商品输往地

金属切削机床

输往地	1999		1998	
	数量(台)	金额(美元)	数量(台)	金额(美元)
总值	**3392962**	**227353705**	**2255084**	**235073457**
巴林	1	168	1	9291
孟加拉国	7599	816105	2543	1073418
缅甸	877	2928492	280	4067651
柬埔寨	34	27737	94	166229
塞浦路斯	68	46580	143	58018
朝鲜	27	491229	19	190350
香港	8105	9569940	63890	18161660
印度	1467	1423558	767	2280499
印度尼西亚	13592	3692673	446	1364141
伊朗	4282	8112517	5923	6996500
以色列	4436	289774	301	348458
日本	42558	11723288	33684	8201906
约旦	978	298383	676	160967
科威特	621	35808	63	47038
老挝	24	68801	20	18362
黎巴嫩	795	146103	690	127458
澳门	57	162336	67	149417
马来西亚	19628	4607388	5060	3018918
蒙古	8	90807	18	7282
尼泊尔	588	90345	9	27277
巴基斯坦	292	1223502	241	2204532
菲律宾	17403	1332787	4084	786884
沙特阿拉伯	8860	982574	7621	1028801
新加坡	5099	5546140	1244	5020394
韩国	6489	2816975	70	526421
斯里兰卡	6535	451022	2447	400771
叙利亚	1978	1700074	582	815528
泰国	11187	2857464	2245	12751974
土耳其	7820	274014	17172	733690
阿拉伯联合酋长国	7169	1098161	6422	1058602
也门共和国	107	300432	115	300023
越南	14296	1616181	7699	3503586
台湾省	4045	1383192	3836	2180607
阿尔及利亚	2245	87422	16	55733
博茨瓦那	2	414	13	24231

1999年中国主要出口商品输往地

金属切削机床

输往地	1999		1998	
	数量(台)	金额(美元)	数量(台)	金额(美元)
喀麦隆	1	4843	14	278756
吉布提	218	152963	10	20164
埃及	4171	3677543	3261	2452988
埃塞俄比亚	180	179830	251	259342
加蓬	5	3010	18	31677
加纳	63	159349	175	244204
几内亚	5	7466	4	17579
科特迪瓦	47	145874	459	393904
肯尼亚	106	274968	374	56336
马达加斯加	101	7985	22	30070
马里	1	268	7	15563
毛里塔尼亚	3	246	3	36520
毛里求斯	118	26918	103	35233
摩洛哥	1767	230149	1539	72396
纳米比亚	43	98581	6	2237
尼日利亚	548	399026	113	774645
塞舌尔	19	15361	3	1435
南非	26575	2413398	18727	3585664
苏丹	441	3735553	87	5379082
坦桑尼亚	31	2819	14	12206
突尼斯	3095	248209	1291	137614
津巴布韦	210	32023	31	27761
比利时	23276	2085074	33856	2550758
丹麦	15927	745576	5207	667521
英国	247121	9272275	127124	14287930
德国	415891	18727529	360618	18094379
法国	221494	6504125	116926	3464268
爱尔兰	201	44130	314	119055
意大利	90616	5409713	63434	5036456
荷兰	154712	4400449	94935	4019931
希腊	5512	856745	1950	425101
葡萄牙	19010	1023918	8019	801513
西班牙	52025	2523726	41738	2019417
阿尔巴尼亚	2	1995	3	4600
奥地利	20929	1255653	15651	1207191
芬兰	9681	513324	9157	530157

1999年中国主要出口商品输往地

金属切削机床

输往地	1999		1998	
	数量(台)	金额(美元)	数量(台)	金额(美元)
匈牙利	26	17053	3810	104422
冰岛	8	39990	9	870
马耳他	482	15948	105	9447
挪威	15057	592658	10031	461348
波兰	22494	699398	7467	671752
瑞典	24671	979116	21066	961153
瑞士	6130	194657	5483	799484
哈萨克斯坦	1	500	12	22199
吉尔吉斯斯坦	10	10693	1	1084
俄罗斯	185	258519	2373	118916
克罗地亚共和国	1	3000	1	5000
捷克共和国	1934	116806	352	38594
阿根廷	31633	2682357	29953	5396336
巴西	38538	938259	76299	2840472
智利	22502	1372588	13135	1671488
哥伦比亚	1194	193366	1992	737695
多米尼克	217	11608	2	474
哥斯达黎加	871	50511	176	5412
厄瓜多尔	127	185165	2725	329502
危地马拉	373	86925	627	232637
洪都拉斯	227	58385	15	51651
墨西哥	11248	5305572	10114	3007433
巴拿马	559	51856	36	123919
巴拉圭	1245	17841	585	41539
秘鲁	2746	229948	8807	767537
乌拉圭	6835	576304	7072	806783
委内瑞拉	8025	303583	10653	689585
加拿大	178366	8728630	126680	8813350
美国	1373461	62811523	774910	53189587
澳大利亚	119689	8024762	57338	6940883
斐济	40	2685	1	120
新西兰	10082	695045	8121	768062
巴布亚新几内亚	8	3160	31	21746
其他	560	622294	1157	482707

1999 年中国主要出口商品输往地

照相机

输往地	1999		1998	
	数量(架)	金额(美元)	数量(架)	金额(美元)
总值	**59511512**	**990307194**	**67465551**	**994004682**
巴林	42108	352809	615069	3082321
孟加拉国	1400	62758	851	36355
香港	8645939	121782653	10227066	177571206
印度	74493	838503	70592	1369284
印度尼西亚	30	960	5000	29500
以色列	23004	88119	26182	216756
日本	6528949	198627800	10816554	204979994
约旦	11	156	19580	297062
科威特	28846	299483	19935	193562
黎巴嫩	24359	544805	4770	59650
澳门	6438	194216	131373	677545
马来西亚	508175	16883218	1072756	9285185
尼泊尔	34848	477712	320	11365
阿曼	76863	1550240	50500	492340
巴基斯坦	22823	258501	13070	43842
巴勒斯坦	2200	12541	2500	18300
菲律宾	5490	31035	5632	34666
沙特阿拉伯	243154	3548410	15320	121730
新加坡	1073721	26497822	1309086	30030512
韩国	468942	11848690	164570	5143602
斯里兰卡	99	13973	17	4960
叙利亚	15778	159254	5640	94004
泰国	8954	297758	999	44252
土耳其	53716	219432	77303	746633
阿拉伯联合酋长国	1477501	11849745	2688162	22049645
越南	1028	3491	16546	267290
台湾省	1113828	10355133	1356001	10929945
加那利群岛	150	8156	1220	43894
埃及	13698	72382	1350	30748
摩洛哥	4114	15223	1	62
南非	5394	58147	10843	98578
比利时	1487946	29841386	1666128	39873937
丹麦	31746	906908	29328	735307

1999 年中国主要出口商品输往地

照相机

输往地	1999		1998	
	数量(架)	金额(美元)	数量(架)	金额(美元)
英国	1466222	28484045	1036706	21664901
德国	11924011	161279230	12413555	124827188
法国	702993	16180359	829496	17281137
意大利	196529	6435146	241077	3694846
荷兰	1576447	35325435	1742325	39845703
希腊	62750	450087	38867	643589
葡萄牙	14580	352067	7364	214616
西班牙	257910	6997603	308821	6680930
奥地利	14703	593340	6920	311214
芬兰	21656	739066	285639	3877600
匈牙利	17630	76755	20791	469190
冰岛	1060	23016	160	7208
挪威	25855	955783	7005	175739
波兰	148680	1922224	230102	2396510
罗马尼亚	9176	43117	100	350
瑞典	53633	1122799	56242	1435145
瑞士	66446	1546763	20205	776688
立陶宛	34151	561923	23092	477597
俄罗斯	20	1000	77939	522001
南斯拉夫	457	10137	135	2136
捷克共和国	7838	61992	7183	32432
阿根廷	81188	831576	205201	3004596
巴西	143837	1580696	148374	1439282
智利	179423	881313	311684	1729558
墨西哥	1099447	9399800	620947	5320389
巴拉圭	110672	736124	22000	196086
秘鲁	3100	21074	2000	1404
委内瑞拉	4142	15427	34855	278706
加拿大	349975	8340659	224572	6527176
美国	18765209	265243048	17946257	238270224
澳大利亚	70604	1535395	109936	2108107
新西兰	2240	49370	13121	79646
其他	73183	809406	48616	1098756

1999年中国主要出口商品输往地

自行车

输往地	1999		1998	
	数量(辆)	金额(美元)	数量(辆)	金额(美元)
总值	**22902345**	**777988333**	**17825640**	**615069023**
阿富汗	90240	3480682	96683	3921146
巴林	3120	82337	6124	179343
孟加拉国	113016	3724494	117747	4317641
缅甸	7769	215255	37425	1068437
柬埔寨	9305	265822	1803	48455
塞浦路斯	10334	373544	1651	37425
朝鲜	41659	1302435	13260	470290
香港	1947554	55688603	939700	25619298
印度尼西亚	116926	3064997	335	11428
伊朗	43760	641485	143791	4568588
以色列	40268	1153764	54810	1477292
日本	2202420	112158545	1298872	77700594
约旦	41596	726339	33787	640345
科威特	71227	1281082	61343	1436891
老挝	50	1208	2724	112745
黎巴嫩	67652	1289554	65223	1358272
澳门	170	4410	325	8722
马来西亚	160229	2055745	16339	269824
马尔代夫	2175	40632	690	10230
蒙古	800	22590	57	1152
尼泊尔	5543	197810	7095	257402
巴基斯坦	40083	1244753	25161	892972
菲律宾	23543	397119	17470	352206
卡塔尔	475	18035	780	31347
沙特阿拉伯	460207	8817202	378700	7301162
新加坡	44118	1096396	34637	1083081
韩国	418760	16202922	292828	7006918
斯里兰卡	59226	1164815	42550	952514
泰国	633	37245	610	14452
土耳其	10098	189112	5000	91000
阿拉伯联合酋长国	885526	16561049	991728	18439342
也门共和国	23205	385707	10850	221817
越南	16408	429060	15557	934880
台湾省	187253	6214894	25546	558423

1999年中国主要出口商品输往地

自行车

输往地	1999		1998	
	数量(辆)	金额(美元)	数量(辆)	金额(美元)
阿尔及利亚	52742	1062248	18008	413320
安哥拉	12414	260393	14862	374745
贝宁	9084	371657	12924	589632
博茨瓦那	8588	128737	4788	93868
喀麦隆	7141	141320	3205	73910
中非共和国	372	14592	3523	308596
刚果	2880	95378	1612	69197
埃及	168580	4652644	124299	4242630
埃塞俄比亚	9677	392338	17457	726536
加蓬	2955	48583	1156	29447
冈比亚	2786	102436	2876	109457
加纳	94500	3010046	153652	5738139
几内亚	9672	302541	11724	370752
科特迪瓦	21480	444274	18643	352243
肯尼亚	31882	884183	40057	1203245
利比亚	1785	27452	1032	15652
马达加斯加	20216	525143	10131	367704
毛里求斯	35207	974554	13355	290192
摩洛哥	145383	2979234	61766	1678356
莫桑比克	2923	69574	700	24337
纳米比亚	1312	21823	2140	42268
尼日利亚	100040	2879559	87702	2926066
塞内加尔	2730	39810	1109	30755
塞拉利昂	2487	99924	3226	101914
南非	263210	5634558	311107	7276951
苏丹	56440	1898571	31107	1128570
坦桑尼亚	72021	2644951	53052	2054232
多哥	26	857	7226	308327
突尼斯	13462	191489	10374	173667
乌干达	2188	79979	5144	204234
津巴布韦	5479	163358	8231	269113
比利时	2205	69962	2601	103709
丹麦	2129	118468	191	11482
英国	12175	234749	10047	255342
德国	78111	2076805	62289	1527886

1999 年中国主要出口商品输往地

自行车

输往地	1999		1998	
	数量(辆)	金额(美元)	数量(辆)	金额(美元)
法国	2242	99701	1907	53598
意大利	11551	392800	323	33981
荷兰	35327	918194	54499	866984
希腊	77075	1290586	88454	1757987
葡萄牙	1652	35606	2080	22630
西班牙	6635	187304	6109	127606
阿尔巴尼亚	1850	45700	3423	95206
奥地利	3660	56817	3508	137545
保加利亚	26558	561512	11807	191480
芬兰	8843	180517	12582	208320
匈牙利	90629	1717985	88255	1553093
冰岛	1810	155695	211	25950
马耳他	1575	36729	600	10939
挪威	47352	2251335	95298	1610143
波兰	34502	1489030	70995	2352826
罗马尼亚	62810	1647757	80394	1851443
瑞典	1119	58578	342	7420
瑞士	5253	292030	9057	509848
爱沙尼亚	7151	162434	3086	57487
拉脱维亚	4680	86880	8899	180607
立陶宛	14349	307847	25508	484727
哈萨克斯坦	431	13212	12205	393197
吉尔吉斯斯坦	1547	24890	2282	45654
俄罗斯	19555	1091224	31408	973426
乌克兰	8800	161613	47134	1859107
南斯拉夫	4460	142023	1212	18777
斯洛文尼亚共和国	8555	183947	4600	83400
克罗地亚共和国	30348	645300	14870	365666
捷克共和国	62362	3345710	18780	707058
阿根廷	24384	359763	28110	463976
巴哈马	1349	49472	1150	23500
伯利兹	8135	210613	2735	77280
玻利维亚	3423	122887	17106	708555
巴西	173144	2551061	95643	1449505
智利	333858	6202974	445047	8308875

1999 年中国主要出口商品输往地

自行车

输往地	1999		1998	
	数量(辆)	金额(美元)	数量(辆)	金额(美元)
哥伦比亚	20081	295188	8250	120853
多米尼克	125765	1714966	70843	1151576
哥斯达黎加	51673	913685	49552	1044673
古巴	6710	286210	17372	626602
库腊索岛	610	20478	2626	103726
多米尼加共和国	109800	1553199	101615	1662700
厄瓜多尔	71429	1402099	101079	1932141
危地马拉	30375	412000	34527	652918
圭亚那	14202	401673	13772	396695
洪都拉斯	29189	455915	25565	595854
牙买加	24569	698327	12657	347705
墨西哥	346676	6465905	53939	790980
巴拿马	748137	17034223	1002100	22171353
巴拉圭	46702	946157	52573	1012686
秘鲁	29986	561248	40270	860296
波多黎各	33541	774425	17920	362953
萨尔瓦多	26319	277191	15358	283757
苏里南	1090	30292	4722	149203
特立尼达和多巴哥	12640	223778	13901	237311
乌拉圭	43384	617214	56049	897965
委内瑞拉	352913	7180736	182538	3888896
英属维尔京群岛	24267	1465114	15967	948746
加拿大	370382	11960326	335358	12415389
美国	9914805	388538272	7645682	307947754
澳大利亚	809757	29031699	704122	27951497
斐济	5625	204274	2025	43117
新喀里多尼亚	1976	53522	210	6787
瓦努阿图	564	14710	1382	60703
新西兰	59517	2852617	71902	3087360
巴布亚新几内亚	19771	436556	10960	222945
基里巴斯	789	25553	50	4100
马绍尔群岛共和国	200	4315	3	109
其他	42297	884908	18615	589769

1999 年中国主要出口商品输往地

电风扇

输往地	1999		1998	
	数量(台)	金额(美元)	数量(台)	金额(美元)
总值	**140075173**	**650821698**	**151846680**	**729742354**
巴林	17595	149733	4427	64646
孟加拉国	36648	290186	25694	154350
缅甸	54910	535210	21713	418253
柬埔寨	7578	51573	7846	178403
塞浦路斯	15759	118105	6261	30934
朝鲜	66723	701810	42383	442355
香港	46521026	246024845	46154317	240409891
印度	22362	107995	10722	25631
印度尼西亚	771858	1914071	230258	489698
伊朗	1147	212898	266	2827438
以色列	272841	1397147	310858	1252512
日本	8294927	35043808	17261783	44402895
约旦	106533	774554	94155	886731
科威特	9669	50789	13310	202027
老挝	18	1087	10	32282
黎巴嫩	236599	1603910	162383	1576336
澳门	55590	557233	48718	628311
马来西亚	146626	1946718	439831	2173310
马尔代夫	400	2950	2306	21212
蒙古	90	2675	5	5091
尼泊尔	44874	449221	19548	288368
阿曼	14953	95654	11017	106221
巴基斯坦	48642	149096	28984	292141
菲律宾	149314	1634791	350049	1851185
卡塔尔	600	5940	6474	49207
沙特阿拉伯	833789	5994624	592556	5982560
新加坡	1174411	2889310	2260874	6455731
韩国	3044012	2342796	1600280	1309550
斯里兰卡	47682	471401	26771	307838
叙利亚	179498	2106886	49757	431531
泰国	4834169	1114894	7175899	3428385
土耳其	276869	1172398	109679	652908
阿拉伯联合酋长国	1401184	11405950	1504836	15072351
也门共和国	16148	132359	8228	73069
越南	2168	78616	218217	2361756

1999年中国主要出口商品输往地

电风扇

输往地	1999		1998	
	数量(台)	金额(美元)	数量(台)	金额(美元)
台湾省	12572032	3772061	10914445	6437672
阿尔及利亚	47764	421865	53222	437553
安哥拉	7358	55043	9938	49843
喀麦隆	10324	76419	26971	103406
刚果	690	7935	85998	261899
埃及	677691	4033398	342830	3763785
埃塞俄比亚	4999	41898	1808	14610
加蓬	4538	28359	3723	140968
冈比亚	7514	22740	4	144
加纳	162722	1053054	90947	680806
几内亚	250	2800	300	3328
科特迪瓦	26982	193402	12717	107310
肯尼亚	13247	97940	4196	46968
马达加斯加	970	7465	969	8129
毛里求斯	5071	62356	10165	125218
摩洛哥	18303	142476	10191	94858
莫桑比克	23	380	680	7020
尼日利亚	278703	1854323	721124	7968457
留尼汪	8490	82201	8208	74001
塞舌尔	2160	22193	738	10605
南非	372483	2431747	319855	2377600
苏丹	70007	1440106	13315	139595
坦桑尼亚	1708	15667	6	14738
突尼斯	123935	989059	96490	875383
扎伊尔	2598	17710	1408	5632
赞比亚	2	34	2	34
津巴布韦	42	166082	7014	169162
比利时	194597	1271307	155587	1328979
丹麦	171784	255674	279501	474983
英国	1513478	4011852	4759592	14526761
德国	808398	3971661	1043128	4614137
法国	1141757	6271712	2472177	9662132
意大利	1634417	6163560	612719	1354404
荷兰	517706	1757182	957518	2696500
希腊	447903	3056270	128174	1070622
葡萄牙	21212	111406	43206	228464

1999年中国主要出口商品输往地

电风扇

输往地	1999		1998	
	数量(台)	金额(美元)	数量(台)	金额(美元)
西班牙	347518	1915174	584054	2680757
奥地利	12240	34705	132112	346558
保加利亚	7611	3069	1950	24454
芬兰	50381	259807	108125	458026
匈牙利	17350	106155	1	102
马耳他	14782	82832	6252	76798
挪威	8206	32727	50706	251882
波兰	73648	161021	19057	48178
罗马尼亚	20212	303933	950	6508
瑞典	68929	462632	108731	654978
瑞士	8010	29120	6416	74826
俄罗斯	234712	179086	25275	93012
南斯拉夫	2500	483	202	57
克罗地亚共和国	10191	18787	4000	4000
捷克共和国	12150	2057	5500	1043
阿根廷	590361	4307235	770834	6938303
巴巴多斯	1270	7515	1200	11430
伯利兹	775	13560	550	7298
玻利维亚	2000	392	4335	56132
巴西	906845	7695345	394842	1984187
智利	41664	219942	139010	677552
哥伦比亚	4700	5582	22458	111610
多米尼克	5946	71036	34795	391945
哥斯达黎加	4960	21292	20587	42663
古巴	511880	4584324	318757	3608917
多米尼加共和国	6800	62538	16244	151760
厄瓜多尔	2688	15705	7810	50861
瓜德罗普	1500	7965	1810	18516
危地马拉	5100	39570	5892	49998
洪都拉斯	9463	70105	15955	122637
牙买加	31481	197600	28399	196939
墨西哥	885257	8131084	686278	6422128
巴拿马	170546	1205351	479826	4032884
巴拉圭	80396	1367124	225601	3207809
秘鲁	25486	193204	37960	393704
波多黎各	224877	1204855	198087	1173677

1999年中国主要出口商品输往地

电风扇

输往地	1999		1998	
	数量(台)	金额(美元)	数量(台)	金额(美元)
特立尼达和多巴哥	640	3588	6168	79199
乌拉圭	86131	239204	25448	243406
委内瑞拉	11636	59114	19413	189758
加拿大	686587	4361565	318135	1339669
美国	43540670	233760440	43039347	277490384
澳大利亚	1663331	13161011	1888436	20205605
新喀里多尼亚	5962	53759	8603	97245
新西兰	62874	480304	33998	367532
巴布亚新几内亚	2350	20009	1630	17007
所罗门群岛	402	3530	10	118
贝劳共和国	1090	7426	680	6242
其他	31995	218266	50970	573247

1999年中国主要进口商品来源地

小麦

来源地	1999		1998	
	数量(公吨)	金额(美元)	数量(公吨)	金额(美元)
总值	**448121**	**85654164**	**1489403**	**278570132**
墨西哥	0	2	0	22
加拿大	124301	20934840	961661	179826254
美国	180577	29502372	319002	57876513
澳大利亚	110808	20603675	203115	39836065
其他	32436	14613275	5625	1031278

黄大豆

来源地	1999		1998	
	数量(公吨)	金额(美元)	数量(公吨)	金额(美元)
总值	**4318634**	**890303816**	**3192594**	**804805878**
韩国	1	205	0	55
俄罗斯	8209	1497770	64961	11396735
阿根廷	964043	187542456	391111	95490250
巴西	860105	171931145	941207	238791758
加拿大	41174	11369410	17355	6442493
美国	2444717	517878271	1750012	446167602
澳大利亚	20	12231	0	215
新西兰	362	69925	86	16568
其他	3	2403	27863	6500202

食用植物油

来源地	1999		1998	
	数量(公吨)	金额(美元)	数量(公吨)	金额(美元)
总值	**2080813**	**1074341947**	**2055237**	**1298769892**
香港	6530	3910480	32489	16465876
印度	50	57734	1737	1196885
印度尼西亚	355172	164779781	188466	111177376
日本	312	405512	704	880372
马来西亚	794083	408601950	741217	476635889

1999年中国主要进口商品来源地

食用植物油

来源地	1999		1998	
	数量(公吨)	金额(美元)	数量(公吨)	金额(美元)
新加坡	29308	14841232	10088	6714341
韩国	310	386765	4080	2782057
泰国	7	9517	1974	985778
越南	34710	20713689	31465	21280775
台湾省	62	76866	165	190419
南非	82	106871	424	334532
比利时	0	501	5007	3665845
英国	0	12320	0	155
德国	14275	9022063	86849	54525982
法国	16	29240	16	17840
意大利	68	110306	34	68662
荷兰	25793	16021842	111003	72064662
西班牙	18	64693	8975	5507067
瑞典	158	1049301	212	1692600
阿根廷	362524	184054793	202813	128919997
巴西	133999	60041890	161962	101571304
加拿大	13696	7286683	44597	28404805
美国	309393	182376749	412937	257837287
澳大利亚	134	214541	122	125236
新西兰	20	29948	40	50142
其他	92	136680	7861	5674008

食用植物油籽

来源地	1999		1998	
	数量(公吨)	金额(美元)	数量(公吨)	金额(美元)
总值	**6928163**	**1527151424**	**4604676**	**1221237766**
缅甸	231	90252	2660	1180499
香港	69	33098	22	14789
印度	787	403183	8182	4661589
印度尼西亚	511	151800	540	242120
日本	129	27442	133	96560
马来西亚	19	7333	186	82392
蒙古	89	19278	76	18720

1999年中国主要进口商品来源地

食用植物油籽

来源地	1999		1998	
	数量(公吨)	金额(美元)	数量(公吨)	金额(美元)
菲律宾	0	129	58	39672
新加坡	3	6270	13	24865
韩国	1	205	1074	596329
泰国	139	59846	164	72995
越南	277	121132	943	383691
台湾省	25	9992	409	74484
德国	324141	72161002	133141	39373958
法国	395630	90133457	232775	69447748
俄罗斯	8308	1515242	65901	11520075
阿根廷	964263	187701853	391111	95490250
巴西	860105	171931145	941207	238791758
加拿大	957884	244239303	946387	274612639
美国	2456191	524122818	1760057	451912482
澳大利亚	502523	129519285	90523	25393430
新西兰	362	69925	86	16568
其他	456478	104827434	29028	7190153

糖

来源地	1999	1998
	金额(美元)	金额(美元)
总值	**85175036**	**145160106**
香港	295627	361464
日本	1689636	2427434
马来西亚	14674	231824
尼泊尔	23622	87933
新加坡	86350	1091616
韩国	11231736	13870334
泰国	7952882	12532324
台湾省	10007	138998
南非	60033	385303
比利时	758142	624166
英国	1012618	1310370
德国	71793	301567
法国	154368	267381
瑞士	871	2002
巴西	570	5933277
古巴	55527188	88852904
美国	21839	136775
澳大利亚	5726449	16029137
其他	536631	575297

1999年中国主要进口商品来源地

胶合板

来源地	1999		1998	
	数量(立方米)	金额(美元)	数量(立方米)	金额(美元)
总值	**1042463**	**415859409**	**1691113**	**543632030**
柬埔寨	10691	7000536	957	210583
香港	3028	1639049	1684	672506
印度	440	144470	2044	508906
印度尼西亚	588432	246077333	920345	309113657
日本	1419	679430	2903	1174314
马来西亚	331316	101663570	669189	187637375
菲律宾	49	2034	11	10403
新加坡	1136	411489	2969	1281422
韩国	72259	43440351	54292	30018527
泰国	2101	645648	3338	1179676
越南	1588	457078	665	211341
台湾省	14316	5467246	17991	5923387
南非	258	147171	33	12592
比利时	38	34898	481	111490
英国	1031	452997	1064	394537
德国	1381	920990	1101	693854
法国	15	28359	191	55277
意大利	557	191143	97	75118
荷兰	282	194634	102	76175
奥地利	120	23280	285	70925
芬兰	1449	1033702	954	721627
瑞典	382	194080	327	258347
瑞士	55	22968	39	13725
俄罗斯	888	879744	306	335309
巴西	184	115673	21	19114
智利	62	18652	85	30688
加拿大	1263	270567	1263	277026
美国	2972	1497151	3683	1079571
澳大利亚	1033	320024	2274	544368
新西兰	781	275689	675	189843
其他	2937	1588453	1744	730347

1999年中国主要进口商品来源地

棉花

来源地	1999		1998	
	数量(公吨)	金额(美元)	数量(公吨)	金额(美元)
总值	**52206**	**79584496**	**209418**	**356972376**
香港	0	40	66	130053
印度	340	387417	5520	8769674
日本	0	112	552	984664
韩国	917	4596455	597	302587
叙利亚	48	62672	1049	1369356
土耳其	99	133271	340	569254
台湾省	8	6314	389	367730
贝宁	1674	2422371	1962	3489858
喀麦隆	2264	3010135	1449	2556550
埃及	363	1091095	199	612380
科特迪瓦	1887	2596430	4491	8021375
马里	800	1352396	2899	4769757
多哥	40	62658	1840	3122366
布基纳法索	1288	1997249	2532	4258756
意大利	1	4605	0	17
俄罗斯	427	686371	1638	2435774
土库曼斯坦	101	207175	1029	1803475
乌兹别克斯坦	4771	6982458	16047	25998525
阿根廷	1740	2072812	2035	2732986
墨西哥	3426	4488588	6195	10451577
美国	13668	20490434	107161	186120346
澳大利亚	17525	25688450	30444	50896227
其他	820	1244988	20984	34488089

羊毛

来源地	1999		1998	
	数量(公吨)	金额(美元)	数量(公吨)	金额(美元)
总值	**198624**	**637723681**	**168606**	**602996523**
香港	1	2087	77	332074
日本	533	3797910	834	6312410
马来西亚	67	355381	536	3340324

1999年中国主要进口商品来源地

羊毛

来源地	1999		1998	
	数量(公吨)	金额(美元)	数量(公吨)	金额(美元)
蒙古	4845	2177735	4661	2316795
韩国	1094	6147989	677	2947857
泰国	751	4039699	1016	6629456
台湾省	5559	22987059	3690	16817126
南非	1935	7103619	1215	5625409
英国	2608	5575301	3764	9874603
德国	167	926880	372	2962426
法国	316	2510662	200	1586382
爱尔兰	3487	6755391	1703	4461656
意大利	663	7030108	180	2214271
荷兰	50	124708	54	109102
西班牙	12	26436	63	139408
哈萨克斯坦	4248	2520702	4374	2751091
吉尔吉斯斯坦	81	56614	1374	1106279
俄罗斯	230	169861	1672	1508096
阿根廷	6310	18433889	2874	10951890
智利	651	1823250	123	480790
秘鲁	37	406702	305	2485496
乌拉圭	17227	51722280	5416	22230360
美国	455	1508426	891	4716626
澳大利亚	118398	419010075	89916	371413404
新西兰	27842	69294409	41854	116960764
其他	1057	3216508	767	2722428

纺织品

来源地	1999	1998
	金额(美元)	金额(美元)
总值	**10958848915**	**10949707019**
孟加拉国	983458	2181861
缅甸	9930	310
柬埔寨	11144	228516
塞浦路斯	8565	32759
朝鲜	105109	136631
香港	1230035290	1335150722
印度	145766267	147577645
印度尼西亚	140033133	142703328
伊朗	49674	79320

1999年中国主要进口商品来源地

纺织品

来源地	1999 金额(美元)	1998 金额(美元)
以色列	567874	161860
日本	2346283770	2102600054
科威特	4998	104
黎巴嫩	482	242
澳门	55549800	70104489
马来西亚	83344384	81945684
蒙古	3465221	25503
尼泊尔	346034	216299
阿曼	283300	197908
巴基斯坦	340094113	350570905
菲律宾	3593645	3588138
沙特阿拉伯	795808	158975
新加坡	19896151	19474986
韩国	2182919954	2141340546
斯里兰卡	486470	469444
泰国	80022656	89728310
土耳其	2349732	1120040
阿拉伯联合酋长国	1902650	1876630
越南	7309687	5947191
台湾省	2938924139	3032847342
埃及	27381	30842
加纳	9629	7904
马达加斯加	4	24989
毛里求斯	17862	3032
莫桑比克	443	14000
南非	810620	2633997
苏丹	435154	426509
比利时	6831199	3167482
丹麦	1901295	754589
英国	30720762	28824519
德国	36594321	32858977
法国	15228571	16899856
爱尔兰	690202	506847
意大利	129882758	133415021
卢森堡	5683018	5744934
荷兰	9075154	6641354
希腊	64037	29799
葡萄牙	851507	785793
西班牙	4993035	4178776
奥地利	3069862	2415633
保加利亚	223404	86718
芬兰	2543186	1608219
匈牙利	90712	66578
冰岛	143	929
马耳他	4859	1034
挪威	1029539	453811
波兰	128665	121522
罗马尼亚	194935	493721
瑞典	5045709	1793957
瑞士	4876951	4148142
爱沙尼亚	70036	118029
立陶宛	9257	1074
白俄罗斯	1286673	299502
哈萨克斯坦	67088	43333
吉尔吉斯斯坦	101186	269686
俄罗斯	3903370	1755679
塔吉克斯坦	1858937	118
乌兹别克斯坦	1360055	2542258
南斯拉夫	89445	103964
斯洛文尼亚共和国	255312	92778
捷克共和国	973092	323221
阿根廷	493306	31750
巴西	1096229	413322
智利	595539	724781
哥伦比亚	14897	33756
古巴	209	10365
厄瓜多尔	2710	4496
危地马拉	35306	188098
牙买加	83136	21945
墨西哥	1158730	4371792
巴拿马	43932	5461
巴拉圭	3444	18506

1999年中国主要进口商品来源地

纺织品

来源地	1999 金额(美元)	1998 金额(美元)
秘鲁	660830	379231
乌拉圭	100534	237903
委内瑞拉	129	410195
加拿大	3745364	18613140
美国	118406913	123749412
澳大利亚	13052208	24550515
新西兰	1233215	2738199
巴布亚新几内亚	3239	54935
其他	961976239	988994349

棉纱线

来源地	1999		1998	
	数量(件)	金额(美元)	数量(件)	金额(美元)
总值	**2054090**	**711569277**	**2092500**	**741421862**
香港	192147	67528156	226953	82132997
印度	365048	120970079	379817	125416223
印度尼西亚	127273	40953299	119229	39806369
日本	17916	15872530	13325	13434735
澳门	8972	3358457	13679	5152257
马来西亚	22376	9155852	17469	6026639
巴基斯坦	634739	180171791	689931	215575073
菲律宾	283	138289	1013	411910
新加坡	1110	340912	573	196797
韩国	72224	33899007	68424	33530169
斯里兰卡	110	39366	182	41644
泰国	44994	21544585	47660	23278858
土耳其	258	60818	304	120785
阿拉伯联合酋长国	1	2162	100	47213
越南	693	166308	232	52349
台湾省	80275	32884279	82135	30281414
南非	83	28340	146	31946
苏丹	2264	435154	1186	426509
比利时	67	27830	7	2448
丹麦	1	2411	1	1650
英国	474	393886	335	331424
德国	146	427007	144	249497
法国	135	181701	1403	478332

1999年中国主要进口商品来源地

棉纱线

来源地	1999		1998	
	数量(件)	金额(美元)	数量(件)	金额(美元)
爱尔兰	9	15897	4	10541
意大利	1329	1754811	1385	1475247
荷兰	12	1795	13	1807
葡萄牙	1	393	1	12893
西班牙	99	27643	5	2386
奥地利	235	47946	34	11963
芬兰	35	49907	70	84262
瑞典	3	1312	41	37739
瑞士	570	184465	277	103344
吉尔吉斯斯坦	49	7488	359	110664
乌兹别克斯坦	2161	858404	6119	2542258
巴西	298	201769	189	90654
墨西哥	0	125	18	3962
秘鲁	306	164556	20	33678
加拿大	34	13218	403	104148
美国	1233	530062	4715	1825544
澳大利亚	5224	2161850	6705	2869531
新西兰	1	397	6	2595
其他	470899	176965020	407887	155071408

棉布

来源地	1999		1998	
	数量(万米)	金额(美元)	数量(万米)	金额(美元)
总值	**140457**	**1373801016**	**138395**	**1338408587**
孟加拉国	54	350864	0	752
香港	38129	321863742	40885	345245041
印度	3766	19675065	2555	15345400
印度尼西亚	1414	13820680	1199	12406297
伊朗	1	29898	0	1160
日本	16022	370298720	15433	315481589
澳门	1859	10476819	2840	15670874
马来西亚	103	1160463	96	1212294

1999年中国主要进口商品来源地

棉布

来源地	1999		1998	
	数量(万米)	金额(美元)	数量(万米)	金额(美元)
巴基斯坦	22984	150630496	16089	126580055
菲律宾	0	3318	0	6029
沙特阿拉伯	23	354942	3	38497
新加坡	160	1128268	93	1549906
韩国	4717	70957622	5137	56452558
斯里兰卡	35	315051	30	183347
泰国	519	7210510	542	8210985
土耳其	3	213128	1	12246
阿拉伯联合酋长国	167	1897849	140	1798036
越南	26	356356	13	265718
台湾省	15184	123895537	15524	136373225
毛里求斯	3	17570	0	3032
南非	5	67238	193	1758220
比利时	10	428853	10	294150
丹麦	3	112904	1	12742
英国	18	222521	28	354192
德国	50	872966	68	1439759
法国	25	609424	37	837827
意大利	265	6394509	242	8433155
荷兰	5	72502	6	161836
葡萄牙	1	45480	4	222648
西班牙	25	432885	8	280956
奥地利	4	187699	3	77551
保加利亚	0	762	0	1985
芬兰	1	20557	2	55303
挪威	0	29136	2	20343
波兰	0	9324	1	15160
罗马尼亚	0	9057	0	7623
瑞典	13	225545	4	57959
瑞士	3	143901	11	251264
爱沙尼亚	1	10515	0	1216
吉尔吉斯	33	93698	49	159022
俄罗斯	10	56390	0	1843
捷克共和国	5	231669	2	99188
巴西	0	507	12	199132

1999年中国主要进口商品来源地

棉布

来源地	1999		1998	
	数量(万米)	金额(美元)	数量(万米)	金额(美元)
智利	4	137178	1	64246
厄瓜多尔	0	2710	0	4179
牙买加	2	49454	1	20574
墨西哥	0	851	1	42995
加拿大	8	125080	54	1243688
美国	251	3231532	452	5716986
澳大利亚	89	1509313	48	1048482
新西兰	0	22942	0	24
其他	34456	263787016	36574	278687298

服装

来源地	1999	1998
	金额(美元)	金额(美元)
总值	**1094548926**	**1065922727**
孟加拉国	1590154	2259204
柬埔寨	2033038	2141917
香港	549288909	495488991
印度	4422558	7298786
印度尼西亚	2015064	526317
以色列	3507501	54927
日本	309676952	327885908
科威特	18	277
黎巴嫩	2586	3008
澳门	25716473	17075005
马来西亚	2339308	1789443
蒙古	2089282	2504620
尼泊尔	74398	2043
巴基斯坦	152318	7097
菲律宾	3106581	2336836
沙特阿拉伯	888	243
新加坡	536819	1202337
韩国	72971467	76224729
斯里兰卡	46828	37170
泰国	1180206	1178778
土耳其	149335	9044
阿拉伯联合酋长国	1341	9896
越南	2656020	2160183
台湾省	45302314	58586604
埃及	6629	5896
埃塞俄比亚	50	47
摩洛哥	7	146
南非	4698	13190
津巴布韦	89	35
比利时	86559	101714
丹麦	174979	340680
英国	5105832	2632248
德国	2507121	2983168
法国	2774189	2083812
爱尔兰	12374	3615
意大利	11699233	12452255
卢森堡	132	523
荷兰	216253	210894
希腊	34687	25052

1999年中国主要进口商品来源地

服装

来源地	1999 金额(美元)	1998 金额(美元)
葡萄牙	239863	36514
西班牙	714599	969387
奥地利	310337	69407
芬兰	64956	86510
匈牙利	714	970
冰岛	59	5
挪威	19793	61820
波兰	180421	63846
罗马尼亚	36654	12836
瑞典	117907	197510
瑞士	1157959	379147
俄罗斯	133176	109065
斯洛文尼亚共和国	5660	77
捷克共和国	5534	80
阿根廷	1287	5933
巴西	2482	10361
智利	911	218
哥伦比亚	12279	13245
哥斯达黎加	6802	187
牙买加	337	921
墨西哥	15019	17656
巴拿马	19851	480
秘鲁	8441	22832
乌拉圭	48454	226
加拿大	344236	658529
美国	6472993	7736044
澳大利亚	12089334	6366185
新西兰	44166	79126
其他	21011512	29386972

鞋类

来源地	1999 金额(美元)	1998 金额(美元)
总值	**306011368**	**290429462**
缅甸	172446	100283
塞浦路斯	2432	984
香港	12979352	8419826
印度	17062	43606
印度尼西亚	3145626	2973975
以色列	43	115
日本	8485424	10468471
澳门	64632	35001
马来西亚	80359	137861
巴基斯坦	21670	3959
菲律宾	20592	123389
新加坡	140562	310723
韩国	113197077	115763947
斯里兰卡	214	101275
泰国	1929721	891451
阿拉伯联合酋长国	21441	31735
越南	1084176	862226
台湾省	71015184	81056600
南非	1	904
比利时	33162	21308
丹麦	252053	40794
英国	895710	980105
德国	1111997	911579
法国	792486	559127
意大利	10394946	9019658
荷兰	254012	122282
希腊	1270	285
葡萄牙	218387	29789
西班牙	773982	638781
奥地利	54600	28256
芬兰	691361	259084
匈牙利	1283	4305
挪威	400	224
罗马尼亚	23779	23183
瑞典	42172	14223
瑞士	53517	63705
捷克共和国	210441	88338
阿根廷	494	245448

1999年中国主要进口商品来源地

鞋类

来源地	1999	1998
	金额(美元)	金额(美元)
巴西	757952	702267
智利	21594	4345
加拿大	717438	249566
美国	71638005	52611253
澳大利亚	87579	138235
其他	4604734	2346991

纸张

来源地	1999		1998	
	数量(公吨)	金额(美元)	数量(公吨)	金额(美元)
总值	**6489151**	**3350200921**	**5754765**	**3007806346**
朝鲜	98	54574	44	24600
香港	191597	81899447	320954	142399107
印度	7775	5243587	2365	1148461
印度尼西亚	985628	455660376	751491	350615571
伊朗	1	650	1	361
以色列	11	10659	3	5422
日本	633271	432396634	494910	343654522
黎巴嫩	0	191	0	164
澳门	100	83040	233	140527
马来西亚	34247	24504302	18356	10657227
菲律宾	32162	16933587	13233	7675026
沙特阿拉伯	893	232399	43	14452
新加坡	22723	10538229	23748	11681775
韩国	1162265	665002094	1137336	661941081
泰国	337566	124842256	279862	98639562
土耳其	137	128781	420	434286
越南	1168	787770	2951	1382437
台湾省	633626	305314004	609285	293737688
南非	32691	11399331	25569	11388633
比利时	14606	12005337	4931	3765851
丹麦	4120	1659571	310	663718
英国	20698	21858596	27827	43198633
德国	11894	57961171	78127	54222439
法国	69034	31571220	27425	22380874
爱尔兰	40	103133	0	3223
意大利	29126	16063181	7224	7424489

1999年中国主要进口商品来源地

纸张

来源地	1999		1998	
	数量(公吨)	金额(美元)	数量(公吨)	金额(美元)
卢森堡	19	92020	3	10938
荷兰	125582	49545823	59468	24721088
葡萄牙	1153	830621	559	327434
西班牙	9058	3729661	5177	13673306
奥地利	48759	27132236	9478	5685494
芬兰	127336	99618778	89236	73517833
匈牙利	5	3644	5	3534
挪威	13917	7665077	16593	10462341
波兰	4393	1703882	539	229631
罗马尼亚	494	274750	91	64369
瑞典	147587	82839886	88664	48951772
瑞士	6632	4316033	3182	1922461
白俄罗斯	25	9534	37	35040
哈萨克斯坦	46	25929	270	159429
俄罗斯	187914	77503218	141763	61695330
捷克共和国	36	86633	68	103108
阿根廷	1467	591035	46	18102
巴西	28458	11744552	11819	5215267
智利	2000	1042788	4	2756
墨西哥	110	170225	51	104831
加拿大	133979	62358328	113314	58328624
美国	1094939	552729715	1138897	544980106
澳大利亚	114974	40324551	154460	47281995
新西兰	71314	29071069	70186	30380724
其他	43479	20536813	24209	12730704

纸制品

来源地	1999		1998	
	数量(公吨)	金额(美元)	数量(公吨)	金额(美元)
总值	**480929**	**705628747**	**558688**	**654829112**
塞浦路斯	0	215	0	34
香港	126598	126966932	138652	125809308

1999年中国主要进口商品来源地

纸制品

来源地	1999		1998	
	数量(公吨)	金额(美元)	数量(公吨)	金额(美元)
印度	8	19472	90	103443
印度尼西亚	13616	6975930	21190	12349047
伊朗	0	158	14	9101
以色列	32	152824	35	75602
日本	47639	131296984	70006	137218869
黎巴嫩	0	662	0	362
澳门	1120	1423087	1097	1137475
马来西亚	1897	2790664	2709	3037574
蒙古	0	14	0	140
尼泊尔	0	168	0	107
巴基斯坦	1	3063	1	2655
菲律宾	596	1607915	211	344265
沙特阿拉伯	8	13620	4	3727
新加坡	4023	13800256	4043	8964200
韩国	66470	103667362	92512	97585459
斯里兰卡	14	49747	1	2043
泰国	5553	6419998	3866	3181822
土耳其	27	107044	14	5021
阿拉伯联合酋长国	204	53555	114	51238
越南	4	12688	6	3913
台湾省	94225	112484205	111068	114299480
毛里求斯	0	76	0	416
南非	8	16176	2193	1027657
突尼斯	34	16126	34	15004
比利时	908	2726162	833	2099545
丹麦	1620	2380651	2247	3450087
英国	4722	14105944	3068	6820688
德国	6760	12909608	4133	8882742
法国	11780	19851521	5164	7792038
爱尔兰	154	612403	44	339623
意大利	1814	3133672	1322	3494868
卢森堡	105	429924	38	63692
荷兰	2112	2859500	1512	3045213
希腊	0	993	0	1192
葡萄牙	313	194310	80	57546

1999年中国主要进口商品来源地

纸制品

来源地	1999		1998	
	数量(公吨)	金额(美元)	数量(公吨)	金额(美元)
西班牙	535	956676	363	663766
奥地利	4979	10189639	967	1875933
芬兰	1819	1935864	3183	2138293
匈牙利	6	19431	2	13209
挪威	192	415658	138	207640
波兰	6	7994	0	10619
瑞典	1458	2719639	1301	2002034
瑞士	1105	1158225	198	881790
白俄罗斯	7	4118	0	5506
俄罗斯	45	11332	175	354369
乌克兰	0	86	0	40833
南斯拉夫	0	861	0	749
斯洛文尼亚共和国	7	19811	7	20432
克罗地亚共和国	0	464	0	12
捷克共和国	18	72823	1	6807
阿根廷	3	24373	8	21126
巴西	171	177619	146	112724
智利	0	2290	1	1766
墨西哥	288	390232	37	94482
秘鲁	0	378	0	650
加拿大	2402	2779016	4058	3338915
美国	49177	84041389	50149	68736696
澳大利亚	974	3526407	1492	2970701
新西兰	327	251918	748	545111
其他	25043	29838875	29412	29509753

钢材

来源地	1999		1998	
	数量(公吨)	金额(美元)	数量(公吨)	金额(美元)
总值	**14862716**	**7007752547**	**12415481**	**6286773774**
缅甸	2	1861	35	14301
朝鲜	20	40961	2037	881993

1999年中国主要进口商品来源地

钢材

来源地	1999		1998	
	数量(公吨)	金额(美元)	数量(公吨)	金额(美元)
香港	31958	29406601	34566	28289216
印度	9943	8013186	12421	8891179
印度尼西亚	73163	24903517	108388	34700118
伊朗	215	104885	150	171213
以色列	144	204082	20	99205
日本	3807544	2328196110	3606412	2311577201
澳门	37	35409	7	9668
马来西亚	31629	14073196	56940	33012031
菲律宾	3175	1155057	3345	1639522
卡塔尔	2	687	90	19164
沙特阿拉伯	5313	1645776	703	231086
新加坡	9448	12229747	8716	11137442
韩国	2732543	1455128751	2531033	1276290273
叙利亚	0	230	0	11
泰国	119340	59657153	58239	33345111
土耳其	12404	3496324	11623	3504646
阿拉伯联合酋长国	81	32640	3	7492
越南	8	18323	1191	572316
台湾省	2784226	1424277954	1826698	1034872636
埃及	8	4128	10	15144
南非	40130	15510566	24445	11136660
苏丹	0	258	0	181
比利时	19321	20221233	28350	26261567
丹麦	447	974487	543	1281206
英国	67639	37961807	66300	43238080
德国	135196	167825410	156118	165443574
法国	40015	49211029	39812	53571702
爱尔兰	6	17759	62	84617
意大利	11482	22345192	15292	19126303
卢森堡	17225	8577222	2441	1426535
荷兰	14598	8719875	11751	7536500
希腊	205	136943	51	43533
葡萄牙	207	324694	2	7234
西班牙	15277	18513054	22684	26036615
奥地利	11116	10161539	14932	12530155

1999年中国主要进口商品来源地

钢材

来源地	1999		1998	
	数量(公吨)	金额(美元)	数量(公吨)	金额(美元)
芬兰	3632	4765550	3012	2764317
挪威	3743	2392036	15620	11003129
波兰	17087	4231154	4191	824702
罗马尼亚	568	267909	16996	5508456
瑞典	17726	27999369	11833	18014421
瑞士	1211	2220677	251	1179502
立陶宛	3	1632	16	4506
白俄罗斯	4801	1988056	5428	1625497
哈萨克斯坦	1208744	260236679	854473	185702221
俄罗斯	1907845	440316654	2038248	500966838
乌克兰	1259873	260800451	361760	92398553
捷克共和国	493	142442	408	125413
阿根廷	65369	42967048	70602	52576653
巴西	41307	20412221	37483	15266016
墨西哥	18789	13373251	8355	7331191
秘鲁	3	1137	11	5256
加拿大	10502	6073906	7508	4259363
美国	60165	93737271	60887	119060086
澳大利亚	118339	49759170	132944	59562416
新西兰	4970	1856451	162	98225
其他	123481	51081837	139882	61491583

铁矿砂

来源地	1999		1998	
	数量(公吨)	金额(美元)	数量(公吨)	金额(美元)
总值	**55274004**	**1378986196**	**51770715**	**1467762617**
朝鲜	26253	443379	82770	1363841
香港	1	933	12066	407956
印度	8888821	222491292	6940559	187164606
日本	53713	860656	2	1310
马来西亚	66691	1686970	53346	1400925
韩国	10	34199	2	2829

1999年中国主要进口商品来源地

铁矿砂

来源地	1999		1998	
	数量(公吨)	金额(美元)	数量(公吨)	金额(美元)
越南	285720	4558877	155253	2033659
台湾省	25	31520	3	1744
南非	7037058	162130268	5657525	151411810
德国	0	162	20981	699187
法国	402	118080	66	10956
哈萨克斯坦	389807	16859497	356266	16231379
巴西	11518840	310110249	8958232	281597950
秘鲁	1948527	55980856	2744986	96506770
委内瑞拉	136990	2948214	139852	3917609
加拿大	143393	3016951	622170	23798793
美国	1	1946	1	962
澳大利亚	24340890	588805611	25567496	686901601
新西兰	355497	6593523	259101	5171205
其他	81364	2313013	200040	9137525

铜矿砂

来源地	1999		1998	
	数量(公吨)	金额(美元)	数量(公吨)	金额(美元)
总值	**1250148**	**474364260**	**1182867**	**458312575**
朝鲜	2685	264754	5884	584510
印度尼西亚	9837	4914806	23220	12361968
伊朗	28472	7358987	14996	5755538
马来西亚	355	189798	325	119852
蒙古	425479	143846064	318055	113462441
菲律宾	45680	15694435	22065	7591313
土耳其	25263	7080581	30289	8602814
越南	2696	389011	4810	1057090
南非	52	9314	897	135409
意大利	4214	1369978	2909	954090
俄罗斯	8156	2556600	7431	1753604
智利	275060	125571218	314615	145848654
秘鲁	91824	36570087	49151	17168602

1999年中国主要进口商品来源地

铜矿砂

来源地	1999		1998	
	数量(公吨)	金额(美元)	数量(公吨)	金额(美元)
加拿大	38670	16597218	63677	25537364
美国	1	197	554	170968
澳大利亚	258062	96723737	267596	98637513
其他	33641	15227475	56395	18570845

铜

来源地	1999		1998	
	数量(公吨)	金额(美元)	数量(公吨)	金额(美元)
总值	**2251077**	**1368345684**	**1226635**	**737513936**
缅甸	53	33418	10	5304
朝鲜	3	3300	474	906350
香港	71428	27137934	55583	25370433
印度	21	38365	42	7122
印度尼西亚	158	199899	1078	1249729
日本	644914	242911050	381051	123822128
马来西亚	3630	3824445	2111	1616161
蒙古	26	30565	849	1267593
阿曼	200	341900	680	1204400
菲律宾	71993	116916693	35308	64036592
沙特阿拉伯	41	47351	293	487406
新加坡	8620	12707704	13927	23311909
韩国	109662	174732010	64348	103121052
泰国	1687	3107632	1879	3493524
阿拉伯联合酋长国	145	86363	23	42375
台湾省	19847	16487456	12969	16974577
南非	3836	6079498	2574	4551716
赞比亚	2853	4234268	2248	4103022
比利时	20156	5989279	3629	828538
英国	6578	2783745	4681	7787713
德国	16181	14492860	13931	8287512
法国	4077	1180045	375	616516
意大利	6500	4050579	368	155628

1999年中国主要进口商品来源地

铜

来源地	1999		1998	
	数量(公吨)	金额(美元)	数量(公吨)	金额(美元)
荷兰	75124	18089304	21912	6231125
希腊	2731	406217	43	6510
西班牙	103	86983	483	290783
奥地利	0	263	508	927731
芬兰	78	168533	98	166807
挪威	1	576	145	28743
波兰	40028	66577402	13000	23207983
罗马尼亚	590	329925	96	34466
瑞典	2417	398640	967	193062
瑞士	154	240256	536	805963
哈萨克斯坦	79631	105643952	39605	56924376
吉尔吉斯斯坦	3845	4069896	1877	2304282
俄罗斯	12505	15364614	14793	19497409
阿根廷	253	164175	339	194347
智利	175345	278011083	52241	90990035
墨西哥	797	947412	386	568809
秘鲁	847	1142532	2641	3333816
委内瑞拉	501	561195	384	391093
加拿大	8818	2661053	5282	1297798
美国	835430	219279664	458087	122150262
澳大利亚	13734	8996949	11247	8610060
新西兰	338	110612	407	255592
其他	5196	7678089	3128	5855584

铝

来源地	1999		1998	
	数量(公吨)	金额(美元)	数量(公吨)	金额(美元)
总值	**380626**	**489501091**	**203208**	**276467498**
巴林	1298	1697775	100	111321
朝鲜	491	540116	1335	1468131
香港	2454	2784100	3213	4112673
印度	880	1167792	47	36403

1999年中国主要进口商品来源地

铝

来源地	1999		1998	
	数量(公吨)	金额(美元)	数量(公吨)	金额(美元)
印度尼西亚	1343	1737698	2426	3430833
日本	565	1221226	1310	2168972
马来西亚	21	53785	521	723534
蒙古	272	217544	113	93392
新加坡	2093	2477490	10	14000
韩国	2684	4027336	1566	1890326
阿拉伯联合酋长国	29	47915	1417	2369014
台湾省	3949	5793173	4179	6682998
南非	5296	7550949	994	1361584
比利时	301	315761	22	23876
德国	44	57880	494	533568
荷兰	202	256235	178	256427
瑞典	60	89634	131	206446
白俄罗斯	399	531024	20	39427
俄罗斯	275095	344554598	127719	168969736
巴西	718	873665	649	878543
加拿大	381	534727	619	850883
美国	551	796848	1576	1800103
澳大利亚	64056	87408175	45324	65975617
新西兰	913	1272724	18	31921
其他	16530	23492921	9227	12437770

铜材

来源地	1999		1998	
	数量(公吨)	金额(美元)	数量(公吨)	金额(美元)
总值	**631944**	**1594712627**	**546625**	**1374704204**
缅甸	0	56	1	713
朝鲜	10	32503	4	8959
香港	18531	57152425	22020	64507399
印度	190	1104083	26	49446
印度尼西亚	4330	8419662	3475	7238698
伊朗	247	423310	51	97665

1999年中国主要进口商品来源地

铜材

来源地	1999		1998	
	数量(公吨)	金额(美元)	数量(公吨)	金额(美元)
以色列	1	10392	4	20583
日本	124416	391514767	116400	349553829
澳门	27	26849	8	19718
马来西亚	14650	49616451	8690	29399100
菲律宾	1014	7545378	142	607336
新加坡	1901	7343621	2162	8185526
韩国	135498	274122866	111507	242386167
泰国	2289	9524543	1636	6845521
土耳其	485	1020255	3278	7324519
阿拉伯联合酋长国	19	27182	0	4466
越南	21	39794	44	111531
台湾省	236403	518713229	198543	447119673
南非	1846	2890483	1334	2453122
比利时	358	945771	624	2114956
丹麦	21	285155	12	169612
英国	1240	5570527	1189	5055746
德国	15984	50659810	9092	26361537
法国	4444	12589580	3706	11329383
爱尔兰	10	133175	102	1339965
意大利	1363	2914730	1320	2558443
卢森堡	85	739429	85	824830
荷兰	1965	6665298	1834	6432714
葡萄牙	41	111812	1	1714
西班牙	109	328137	79	345983
奥地利	273	1011288	38	605674
芬兰	346	1427323	227	668103
挪威	25	66093	41	78311
波兰	2670	3238835	906	1469958
瑞典	1177	3475561	898	3287234
瑞士	99	836321	97	681078
哈萨克斯坦	34	65986	5	6175
俄罗斯	284	487041	406	656406
捷克共和国	1	2541	1	17573
巴西	225	327675	37	171690
智利	163	296888	655	1220867

1999 年 中 国 主 要 进 口 商 品 来 源 地

铜材

来源地	1999		1998	
	数量(公吨)	金额(美元)	数量(公吨)	金额(美元)
墨西哥	16	109295	17	102098
加拿大	291	786334	542	1879058
美国	5028	29760741	7057	29842336
澳大利亚	15601	28907631	16826	34741859
新西兰	69	302966	30	127963
其他	38140	113138835	31476	76678967

铝材

来源地	1999		1998	
	数量(公吨)	金额(美元)	数量(公吨)	金额(美元)
总值	**426952**	**1061925980**	**341294**	**844917833**
巴林	3721	6540205	5299	10318786
香港	9142	20584247	9226	24190192
印度	276	907363	32	85274
印度尼西亚	1980	3407037	1674	4418487
以色列	8	17874	13	125224
日本	122236	342596976	101996	258461707
澳门	21	87947	52	97334
马来西亚	9643	25425724	5236	9582753
菲律宾	8	27778	42	81840
沙特阿拉伯	20	15678	11	25052
新加坡	1392	3934341	2676	8906142
韩国	64494	162076529	45165	111885863
泰国	444	783945	311	393732
土耳其	27	62026	186	345510
阿拉伯联合酋长国	67	51531	157	258985
台湾省	85068	170442382	62618	143205553
南非	989	1194567	843	1020108
比利时	1803	5214602	1343	4233891
丹麦	86	465545	74	310363
英国	4026	12661074	3007	10142762
德国	10543	35722792	10575	29455383

1999年中国主要进口商品来源地

铝材

来源地	1999		1998	
	数量(公吨)	金额(美元)	数量(公吨)	金额(美元)
法国	11875	35627138	10366	28065158
意大利	811	4708865	573	3169069
荷兰	2476	8792621	2594	9071199
希腊	1116	2393118	1429	2094841
西班牙	89	293980	6	36445
奥地利	14	76024	3	15999
芬兰	24	87601	1	7510
挪威	64	296407	1	387
波兰	0	114	19	73097
瑞典	6902	16071019	8180	18473572
瑞士	80	359695	112	328896
俄罗斯	2437	3531119	1052	1512410
巴西	51	177123	29	110288
巴拉圭	0	850	49	54764
加拿大	645	987799	1270	2106864
美国	41804	107594574	33361	92954120
澳大利亚	36827	77342852	27346	60822205
新西兰	247	1197115	145	817368
其他	5495	10167803	4225	7658700

原油

来源地	1999		1998	
	数量(公吨)	金额(美元)	数量(公吨)	金额(美元)
总值	**36613688**	**4641235916**	**27322632**	**3274537489**
印度尼西亚	3952948	487615161	3387144	386614968
伊朗	3949291	519837563	3619989	415914820
伊拉克	974155	115845796	607352	59835233
日本	1	4444	55336	5251052
科威特	330443	37731050	282285	36813361
马来西亚	247425	32656428	451096	55667060
蒙古	10531	1273844	5615	561490
阿曼	5020825	633400607	5793430	704309160

1999年中国主要进口商品来源地

原油

来源地	1999		1998	
	数量(公吨)	金额(美元)	数量(公吨)	金额(美元)
巴基斯坦	53874	5867162	26096	3032131
沙特阿拉伯	2496968	332714398	1807618	193861505
新加坡	4767	381360	0	5
也门共和国	4132183	552438029	4043151	520806221
越南	1511950	218890259	865899	109806765
安哥拉	2876005	355615887	1104985	153453062
刚果	384708	50833510	382400	40074642
埃及	112589	10961732	198714	21292684
赤道几内亚	812657	96836573	243204	33339986
利比亚	132592	16441449	138383	21371086
尼日利亚	1369168	155541698	123238	17633820
挪威	2009860	254302495	489779	55900761
哈萨克斯坦	490807	40919125	409153	39280484
俄罗斯	572276	81659552	144578	15845529
美国	360351	39400355	853713	96072344
澳大利亚	901045	131462635	353856	42203060
巴布亚新几内亚	149205	22127276	68792	8234965
其他	3757063	446477528	1866823	237361295

成品油

来源地	1999		1998	
	数量(公吨)	金额(美元)	数量(公吨)	金额(美元)
总值	**20815201**	**2697684894**	**21739869**	**2405175867**
巴林	177012	18646129	88156	12306243
朝鲜	19180	1563043	51226	6889282
香港	43756	39187872	107362	51042247
印度	1	538	36522	2358921
印度尼西亚	205679	26112312	426777	46919429
伊朗	93090	8871399	1	92
以色列	5	38826	5	5365
日本	1200998	182036332	1921988	201050020
科威特	1200	136800	43372	9335362

1999年中国主要进口商品来源地

成品油

来源地	1999		1998	
	数量(公吨)	金额(美元)	数量(公吨)	金额(美元)
马来西亚	430723	59051229	553714	53681807
菲律宾	226966	25769571	93745	9237587
沙特阿拉伯	199847	31205557	40447	4513414
新加坡	4934163	659813657	7515761	850682328
韩国	9480148	1116537379	9139357	900247597
斯里兰卡	0	379	13458	1991740
泰国	40259	10448385	21541	3412943
阿拉伯联合酋长国	57824	5711044	43708	4441537
越南	243	225944	71113	5431427
台湾省	196395	42471097	152663	32428369
南非	506	316287	170	88365
比利时	83877	9338905	2190	2631297
丹麦	67	99443	60	76228
英国	103118	18191272	3170	4438519
德国	7002	10127496	3632	7963394
法国	17633	8663942	6637	8171000
意大利	392	889244	120	303183
荷兰	43977	11919344	4067	7460437
西班牙	586	1031927	908	1301907
奥地利	3	7456	0	1516
挪威	0	1590	0	1171
瑞典	1902	564089	1176	339999
瑞士	3	17924	996	348984
俄罗斯	2068987	239592047	904719	87606237
巴西	19	37335	28	51884
墨西哥	1	3379	0	401
加拿大	344	464623	148	323544
美国	978440	140464852	416519	70931573
澳大利亚	11849	4397474	35221	7100064
新西兰	0	447	24153	4046710
其他	189003	23728325	15035	6013744

1999年中国主要进口商品来源地

塑料

来源地	1999	1998
	金额(美元)	金额(美元)
总值	**11611777379**	**10458763363**
柬埔寨	5100	492
朝鲜	476318	126711
香港	409094090	301955265
印度	7860915	3196829
印度尼西亚	137686862	152305856
伊朗	19287049	10284378
以色列	5371001	2949948
日本	2361609932	2078113021
科威特	97992180	49650277
老挝	26770	32963
黎巴嫩	2091	213
澳门	1279327	1000144
马来西亚	172537589	179916279
尼泊尔	28535	46232
阿曼	17259	68388
巴基斯坦	238943	41226
菲律宾	10595016	9190764
卡塔尔	37265804	39813138
沙特阿拉伯	173941745	180394471
新加坡	356161880	359941706
韩国	2240919924	2535936356
斯里兰卡	168676	140502
泰国	493272769	419307252
土耳其	1687697	789238
阿拉伯联合酋长国	1816285	4247361
也门共和国	11547	3415
越南	1142464	1389949
台湾省	2885380017	2487194786
埃及	12078	833
尼日利亚	435	145175
南非	20521701	9189315
乌干达	193	108250
比利时	110868724	74876090
丹麦	1328831	1664092
英国	44867715	40195859
德国	212392122	156351960
法国	82946852	59808663
爱尔兰	2290356	1004457
意大利	55141345	36724779
卢森堡	20514877	12705040
荷兰	85729696	58341003
希腊	536149	115731
葡萄牙	3161208	4004623
西班牙	12286514	11822302
奥地利	2832346	2147138
保加利亚	31018	18971
芬兰	20510018	11488678
匈牙利	2679426	2017191
冰岛	19946	3424
列支敦士登	204	93
挪威	4309347	2972309
波兰	1970345	367601
罗马尼亚	1957209	26019
瑞典	24706724	21125791
瑞士	11940802	9186792
立陶宛	273	41059
俄罗斯	159748248	87658446
乌克兰	47609	19846
斯洛文尼亚共和国	218256	5572
克罗地亚共和国	1836	4378
捷克共和国	1369623	290975
斯洛伐克共和国	85929	408
阿根廷	2470554	2760342
巴西	18389253	18048048
智利	194488	402942
哥伦比亚	2385861	180640
危地马拉	8976	208
墨西哥	7671838	7780317
巴拉圭	14444	66081
乌拉圭	36895	17981
委内瑞拉	606442	770

1999年中国主要进口商品来源地

塑料

来源地	1999	1998
	金额(美元)	金额(美元)
加拿大	86229157	58996554
美国	964232380	784743627
澳大利亚	37324871	39507532
新西兰	1388980	2078122
其他	189917500	121710176

化肥

来源地	1999		1998	
	数量(公吨)	金额(美元)	数量(公吨)	金额(美元)
总值	**13352093**	**2248225664**	**13871429**	**2505671727**
香港	50781	5340799	81	54012
印度尼西亚	24590	2587978	16197	2084731
以色列	152983	20681164	218814	27312206
日本	283	1412302	259	221047
约旦	260451	30781725	203907	24071600
马来西亚	48	60819	1	968
新加坡	62	87875	26	22525
韩国	28827	5699315	42269	9098264
台湾省	21131	4473428	45753	9805652
摩洛哥	143415	29866854	319567	71918611
突尼斯	100040	21340403	54629	12385063
比利时	244788	49651058	123380	26687152
丹麦	96025	15563191	129979	28292502
英国	10	5411	9	3103
德国	32144	6655519	288456	58516923
法国	115	51684	18579	3474573
意大利	0	75	3	4054
荷兰	28145	7547257	389	413337
希腊	30007	5608807	52411	10709169
芬兰	191317	42186076	38795	8450451
挪威	254720	40153887	333110	65663570
瑞士	9	28973	4	14320
拉脱维亚	63431	6695283	49336	5734403
哈萨克斯坦	59669	9877596	30536	4863277
俄罗斯	4828175	642351197	4485269	637861997
乌克兰	10000	1690000	26999	3077938

1999 年中国主要进口商品来源地

化肥

来源地	1999		1998	
	数量(公吨)	金额(美元)	数量(公吨)	金额(美元)
智利	79739	15753802	83692	22888152
加拿大	1563878	193703906	1992155	249394878
美国	5067152	1084238904	5267986	1214993533
澳大利亚	40	8529	32	18104
新西兰	4	1996	2	784
其他	20113	4119851	48801	7634828

天然橡胶

来源地	1999		1998	
	数量(公吨)	金额(美元)	数量(公吨)	金额(美元)
总值	**429068**	**281890801**	**430079**	**319281527**
缅甸	31	21511	580	429793
柬埔寨	9586	6558781	7296	5734593
香港	28	21291	21	11364
印度尼西亚	46683	29682840	34988	26812450
日本	35	43567	460	350597
马来西亚	84201	55911462	62567	49776603
菲律宾	7750	5165408	4947	3601523
新加坡	2656	1626064	2177	1601551
韩国	445	344094	2325	2013908
斯里兰卡	599	694113	304	233680
泰国	243705	159303387	281903	203685576
越南	24430	16077096	25491	19174321
台湾省	2662	2160888	6336	5239189
尼日利亚	5564	3914421	181	128326
德国	1	2416	16	23549
美国	85	45632	111	92196
其他	608	317830	376	372308

1999年中国主要进口商品来源地

合成橡胶

来源地	1999		1998	
	数量(公吨)	金额(美元)	数量(公吨)	金额(美元)
总值	**652104**	**602009943**	**513622**	**465517420**
香港	3336	3095592	5702	5834665
印度尼西亚	10724	6437202	3686	2313404
伊朗	15438	8600624	5804	3704036
日本	130414	163658846	107800	132619019
澳门	0	1921	2	11337
马来西亚	5183	3366769	2822	1992583
菲律宾	69	66935	4	2961
沙特阿拉伯	0	19	20	12914
新加坡	1748	4658596	1618	3052812
韩国	112955	88252933	78644	68150655
斯里兰卡	131	243867	165	380399
泰国	22346	15170227	9330	6411478
越南	23	30377	35	18552
台湾省	195894	148089561	184156	146608509
南非	253	182005	349	344962
比利时	4620	6689426	2777	5115490
丹麦	0	789	0	1497
英国	9268	20078374	44904	10060533
德国	6364	10172276	3899	7153339
法国	10215	11600677	6424	7390212
意大利	1667	2417437	848	1581765
卢森堡	52	198091	13	44204
荷兰	246	290312	558	730911
西班牙	950	1119025	401	413139
奥地利	0	18485	0	982
波兰	13	23400	13	37050
瑞典	48	122844	69	187559
瑞士	518	1308972	0	856
白俄罗斯	409	428052	79	94480
俄罗斯	70484	46512891	18461	16285509
巴西	1464	1093777	134	144500
墨西哥	3221	2295413	2590	2080911
加拿大	6553	11646207	6263	10414861
美国	28344	37364122	19704	26299878

1999年中国主要进口商品来源地

合成橡胶

来源地	1999		1998	
	数量(公吨)	金额(美元)	数量(公吨)	金额(美元)
澳大利亚	15	54132	133	93708
新西兰	0	1000	24	32890
其他	9138	6718767	6189	5894860

医疗器械

来源地	1999	1998
	金额(美元)	金额(美元)
总值	**666424297**	**395673251**
香港	10301864	8395795
印度	2819140	524997
印度尼西亚	114958	12192
以色列	3274765	18421768
日本	185762208	103551600
马来西亚	4884180	1881664
菲律宾	198	93649
新加坡	5832607	4734415
韩国	3671070	3768993
泰国	1231750	870877
台湾省	3034692	1733192
比利时	1110642	1470762
丹麦	4163766	1888038
英国	6533977	4572647
德国	93567183	51529131
法国	14065988	7657866
爱尔兰	420405	206537
意大利	13647497	3169576
荷兰	24276700	15629478
西班牙	522615	134253
奥地利	3308105	2810933
芬兰	4843563	3072853
匈牙利	97500	14084
挪威	1328868	635213
波兰	1240	15112
瑞典	11986482	5602322
瑞士	3517762	1582864
俄罗斯	118999	30278
南斯拉夫	28340	150537
巴西	173118	64366
古巴	1250	289
多米尼加共和国	432648	112898
墨西哥	6867	18942
加拿大	2722333	344252
美国	251439570	143437483
澳大利亚	1406504	400420
新西兰	15185	11016
其他	5759758	7121959

1999年中国主要进口商品来源地

各类船

来源地	1999		1998	
	数量(艘)	金额(美元)	数量(艘)	金额(美元)
总值	**1409**	**128088806**	**968**	**121631206**
香港	179	6501654	207	9034193
日本	176	43776553	171	23324291
澳门	3	70900	12	258170
新加坡	1	24500	3	803698
韩国	208	452803	80	9099778
台湾省	301	233488	7	561192
丹麦	10	221196	15	470099
德国	50	32529434	68	34948419
法国	2	68278	3	4088
荷兰	14	28456320	11	9957940
西班牙	2	14972	4	326862
挪威	6	266675	25	8654477
波兰	7	11511	4	11350
俄罗斯	38	1173000	31	557650
巴拿马	1	257963	2	515878
圣文森特和格林纳丁斯	1	128982	1	258261
加拿大	47	206109	20	9091697
美国	107	548629	180	3587160
新西兰	3	36958	4	436778

飞机

来源地	1999		1998	
	数量(架)	金额(美元)	数量(架)	金额(美元)
总值	**74**	**2316830053**	**81**	**2602789125**
德国	2	43134004	1	42864528
法国	24	1040891031	25	959942171
俄罗斯	16	151768888	12	317678409
美国	27	1080654740	36	1194720916
其他	5	381390	7	87583101

1999年中国主要进口商品来源地

汽车

来源地	1999		1998	
	数量(辆)	金额(美元)	数量(辆)	金额(美元)
总值	**34375**	**790510462**	**39375**	**815116351**
日本	24080	434710351	31177	533980346
新加坡	5	233200	3	729336
韩国	2112	47229307	2155	34159225
泰国	3	5968380	2	42770
台湾省	134	3823891	99	1817177
比利时	5	904847	6	752795
英国	42	3598113	146	5686649
德国	1671	92213218	1329	89544531
法国	666	18803249	1029	11673979
意大利	85	4489267	48	2777531
荷兰	12	1104000	4	407940
奥地利	20	5680838	8	1320991
芬兰	7	4642042	5	1816926
匈牙利	2808	42428500	2	21053
罗马尼亚	106	367000	100	340000
瑞典	415	11543603	664	18603578
瑞士	1	221265	19	2529532
白俄罗斯	28	13344000	11	1151291
俄罗斯	52	941800	35	9968834
乌克兰	3	5020662	15	6640000
捷克共和国	1032	13582041	120	3706767
巴西	9	151042	4	65000
加拿大	49	5105374	26	566812
美国	1001	69782193	2303	82627359
澳大利亚	4	1676417	31	2048932
其他	25	2945862	34	2136997

1999年中国主要进口商品来源地

汽车零件

来源地	1999 金额(美元)	1998 金额(美元)
总值	**1252501879**	**934985338**
香港	437100	2056995
印度	162203	51882
印度尼西亚	544182	20988
以色列	99	3
日本	326352295	114036253
马来西亚	648573	140327
菲律宾	27400	43880
沙特阿拉伯	276	245
新加坡	1075694	773953
韩国	25981342	7489976
斯里兰卡	5769	106691
泰国	4117127	1634327
土耳其	34903	32220
阿拉伯联合酋长国	598	23
台湾省	11925989	5029602
南非	1448706	125757
比利时	1449132	640882
丹麦	4786	7215
英国	37373923	39080020
德国	503016662	533761897
法国	67202231	143272590
意大利	15435446	18472747
荷兰	3532009	3392518
葡萄牙	213335	508910
西班牙	8572929	5289808
奥地利	2026248	469836
芬兰	73065	209826
匈牙利	45912	319689
波兰	1322	14737
罗马尼亚	15451	26922
瑞典	14686427	13023493
瑞士	15038	84687
白俄罗斯	3347	1890973
俄罗斯	431332	371206
乌克兰	60742	733818
捷克共和国	1754751	1021941
斯洛伐克共和国	1075	54170
巴西	2405935	2523011
墨西哥	741479	33298
加拿大	75268289	1195281
美国	141877310	35975257
澳大利亚	3479145	1010863
新西兰	402	554
其他	51900	56067

集成电路

来源地	1999 金额(美元)	1998 金额(美元)
总值	**7924117601**	**4778243261**
朝鲜	47890	446154
香港	529745888	455745844
印度	210898	69361
印度尼西亚	16569814	2239866
以色列	690587	181798
日本	2583098288	1617506457
澳门	128450	5653625
马来西亚	500029505	241785200
阿曼	893	5704
菲律宾	332351274	71226080
新加坡	360218105	261101202
韩国	587965445	356197186
泰国	81887623	36985729
土耳其	3186032	1164576
阿拉伯联合酋长国	640	10899
越南	39398	37500
台湾省	1132603753	791070473
摩洛哥	6443605	1106854
南非	83367	56545
比利时	7090123	32577773

1999年中国主要进口商品来源地

集成电路

来源地	1999 金额(美元)	1998 金额(美元)
丹麦	490208	90132
英国	54217623	14761083
德国	147108364	73550835
法国	77165077	28392687
爱尔兰	32538754	9244370
意大利	7165864	5166887
荷兰	14866246	5852836
希腊	183710	18943
葡萄牙	682097	1331160
西班牙	724738	237484
奥地利	5519822	1247701
芬兰	315643247	68296058
匈牙利	127640	1377
马耳他	9831897	1050366
摩纳哥	38967	1173
挪威	399020	448968
波兰	13362	2386
瑞典	12672762	4940076
瑞士	1174301	913372
白俄罗斯	88565	522123
俄罗斯	5862135	11380931
乌克兰	3867195	15977
捷克共和国	1849481	10982
巴西	3325	14639
哥斯达黎加	4208887	1248006
墨西哥	17874602	3304299
加拿大	12225582	13924312
美国	979927634	621421114
澳大利亚	4292867	105417
新西兰	18748	74388
其他	70943303	35504353

金属切削机床

来源地	1999		1998	
	数量(台)	金额(美元)	数量(台)	金额(美元)
总值	**89411**	**1506437542**	**79112**	**1390772572**
朝鲜	9	161300	4	2799570
香港	4116	15555964	6183	22859936
印度尼西亚	50	713575	8	128501
以色列	12	267029	22	211963
日本	13585	410679526	12882	480252545
马来西亚	153	2291343	571	3667762
菲律宾	28	114847	49	932150
新加坡	554	8931125	481	10546536
韩国	3871	36591125	4356	99570367
泰国	150	2688011	276	2289128
土耳其	27	140069	1	18796
越南	1	120	5	2017
台湾省	55601	410639277	45604	279385911

1999年中国主要进口商品来源地

金属切削机床

来源地	1999		1998	
	数量(台)	金额(美元)	数量(台)	金额(美元)
比利时	203	6784258	156	11338365
丹麦	45	880107	20	105296
英国	492	27701290	448	17703870
德国	1836	249437174	1553	195524372
法国	242	18580850	135	5673988
爱尔兰	24	313747	1	337368
意大利	970	80598397	545	71960650
卢森堡	1	9607	1	1268
荷兰	65	2968376	74	6055998
葡萄牙	20	127443	3	20300
西班牙	279	6852323	330	18493257
奥地利	22	733327	14	1557951
芬兰	22	2392410	23	1831058
波兰	2	133341	2	5000
瑞典	155	4982383	122	2514229
瑞士	2025	58026133	491	24867201
俄罗斯	100	8439126	174	13222187
捷克共和国	8	7782406	11	1688480
斯洛伐克共和国	1	14749	1	1828
巴西	5	144242	9	214702
墨西哥	183	73117	8	27328
加拿大	70	5880730	81	4423087
美国	2671	125755761	2102	101614102
澳大利亚	64	2949792	113	3344193
其他	1749	6103142	22	5581312

铸造机械

来源地	1999		1998	
	数量(台)	金额(美元)	数量(台)	金额(美元)
总值	**1635734**	**128503115**	**2800022**	**115043468**
香港	2665	3539402	8430	1351381
以色列	714	294232	113	198115

1999年中国主要进口商品来源地

铸造机械

来源地	1999		1998	
	数量(台)	金额(美元)	数量(台)	金额(美元)
日本	379108	35846787	605502	34743619
菲律宾	1	855	2	58
新加坡	20	34307	915	54975
韩国	7414	756408	130320	4609950
泰国	3999	4139	6153	9689
台湾省	269270	11052629	209415	8888244
比利时	38245	1949136	25189	1409861
丹麦	3171	254167	11130	448956
英国	17648	383350	44022	6554486
德国	302395	20575884	1153741	25429854
法国	27752	1794725	6892	754673
意大利	51087	20502130	22652	11135593
卢森堡	301	15837	81468	3158966
荷兰	550	49842	25916	213390
西班牙	7238	782527	4546	55225
奥地利	198456	11475956	16329	1262012
芬兰	9103	459118	6298	490322
瑞典	4584	656836	15	248770
瑞士	228610	7019303	23032	4019682
白俄罗斯	1	518000	1	43000
捷克共和国	1	36163	1540	19808
加拿大	355	191187	196477	272221
美国	82013	7864219	209422	8673827
澳大利亚	1022	1909487	2927	114123
其他	11	536489	7575	882668

橡胶或塑料加工机械

来源地	1999	1998
	金额(美元)	金额(美元)
总值	**1043104251**	**926007754**
香港	72825702	70014110
印度	134693	284215
印度尼西亚	140905	653989
以色列	18073	241829
日本	230781022	208080728
马来西亚	1395803	2636095
菲律宾	31137	167022

1999年中国主要进口商品来源地

橡胶或塑料加工机械

来源地	1999	1998
	金额(美元)	金额(美元)
新加坡	7248629	10945645
韩国	39933949	48045866
泰国	1632029	1858628
台湾省	302672947	226042252
比利时	1057392	2562588
丹麦	462639	252367
英国	9548914	9486333
德国	151104206	117540781
法国	27981525	18790093
爱尔兰	222294	25224
意大利	71050700	128308529
卢森堡	41778	30175
荷兰	9680379	4505395
西班牙	35171	285978
奥地利	49528899	959710
芬兰	1097206	875683
匈牙利	15210	700
挪威	13976	10450
瑞典	3437990	1166448
瑞士	3597236	11907820
俄罗斯	1686052	302314
巴西	24762	107910
加拿大	10755980	11097338
美国	36752593	34103518
澳大利亚	1371124	2458931
新西兰	173467	41603
其他	6649869	3580091

烟草加工机械

来源地	1999	1998
	金额(美元)	金额(美元)
总值	**85304450**	**208903959**
香港	14099	8570
日本	1385	1260055
新加坡	135544	4222
丹麦	3780	33241
英国	9825768	25034986
德国	14615263	56333046
法国	1063258	5299
意大利	57010990	115645256
巴西	2618864	117554
美国	11950	10274977
其他	3549	186753

电动机及发电机

来源地	1999		1998	
	数量(万台)	金额(美元)	数量(万台)	金额(美元)
总值	**97806**	**741754467**	**73904**	**580438698**
香港	18491	100341884	16076	80601845
印度	16	260877	30	108756
印度尼西亚	672	8386395	428	5674926

1999年中国主要进口商品来源地

电动机及发电机

来源地	1999		1998	
	数量(万台)	金额(美元)	数量(万台)	金额(美元)
以色列	0	92304	2	18023
日本	13497	143726686	13909	144376618
澳门	0	11940	4	9975
马来西亚	6387	53275013	2781	32569498
菲律宾	414	16402602	72	3374947
新加坡	2108	11891128	1232	10011416
韩国	1382	35444331	642	14962238
泰国	2121	24941954	1295	20165279
土耳其	0	584	0	60
越南	6	167692	8	37861
台湾省	7069	58441953	6869	49250201
南非	0	45716	0	4653
比利时	0	103664	1	2848803
丹麦	0	1432651	0	1120737
英国	35	5043818	14	8793059
德国	282	33942342	340	28117042
法国	7	5761579	8	5634749
爱尔兰	0	30396	0	1857
意大利	68	7272145	69	8510736
荷兰	214	3258974	135	3042103
西班牙	19	2988865	5	1278707
奥地利	0	2659620	0	5699641
芬兰	51	4288122	11	5925801
匈牙利	0	29285	0	24112
挪威	0	99717	0	344382
波兰	0	451909	0	20404
瑞典	93	8810902	73	5348177
瑞士	33	2192390	25	1848238
俄罗斯	0	83940	0	68924
捷克共和国	0	6137	0	11953
巴西	2	741087	6	983214
加拿大	12	9346461	20	3367049
美国	228	35280153	146	30311782
澳大利亚	0	493044	0	787982
新西兰	0	41526	2	146893
其他	44600	163964681	29703	105036057

1999 年中国主要进口商品来源地

发电机组

来源地	1999		1998	
	数量(台)	金额(美元)	数量(台)	金额(美元)
总值	**22546**	**279521537**	**12502**	**318927169**
香港	92	2387823	192	3078332
日本	15922	26614836	5961	34759717
马来西亚	2	3101	6	41948
新加坡	364	16173688	213	8489120
韩国	33	6133803	1672	11136677
台湾省	131	4101506	270	5823484
比利时	3	7020250	4	3904596
丹麦	49	2766565	56	7572683
英国	2475	42062271	1106	57920510
德国	140	26225945	120	13926343
法国	909	14023739	80	2072139
意大利	189	1706119	242	1676961
荷兰	219	13231490	21	3959000
奥地利	0	2410950	5	6485226
芬兰	13	4236338	51	21032943
挪威	19	963040	4	1265744
波兰	2	475000	3	34239
瑞典	15	1973292	33	1332461
加拿大	59	2115691	81	1871450
美国	1498	71197694	1700	115485748
澳大利亚	349	22945789	213	12592368
其他	63	10752607	469	4465480

有线电话、电报交换机零件

来源地	1999	1998
	金额(美元)	金额(美元)
总值	**1156332959**	**911755040**
香港	44837513	91129344
印度	112437	28788
印度尼西亚	12836	1057029
以色列	4316920	10870637
日本	189508669	156945245

来源地	1999	1998
	金额(美元)	金额(美元)
马来西亚	3486315	2182818
菲律宾	682643	580034
新加坡	4267257	3629059
韩国	26084553	23942992
泰国	1726657	1437806
土耳其	108168	34705

1999年中国主要进口商品来源地

有线电话、电报交换机零件

来源地	1999	1998
	金额(美元)	金额(美元)
越南	85379	451
台湾省	63835957	53416093
比利时	4346021	11690022
丹麦	111535	20649
英国	14015246	8045202
德国	79695124	102797503
法国	57251869	54917523
爱尔兰	1232416	166041
意大利	8400072	5350465
荷兰	2870803	20107332
葡萄牙	3752	13678
西班牙	4158471	6270340
奥地利	548658	3035272
芬兰	76984895	44755260
挪威	1404954	1054956
波兰	649749	765019
瑞典	251852926	87606711
瑞士	2727027	3029885
捷克共和国	528	454
巴西	1534611	13246
墨西哥	522481	57993
加拿大	32101746	60694189
美国	254064056	149832721
澳大利亚	14789406	2654329
新西兰	2962	1200977
其他	7998347	2420272

计算机

来源地	1999	1998
	金额(美元)	金额(美元)
总值	**3253077941**	**1810096712**
朝鲜	18900	95195
香港	97941826	116958162
印度	229919	17300
印度尼西亚	40775400	8185574
以色列	13005677	2545314
日本	415799993	324214376
马来西亚	89290529	49234969
菲律宾	78883753	35473709
新加坡	376784621	209499320
韩国	113962678	46675864
泰国	68449777	62919706
阿拉伯联合酋长国	53572	2300
台湾省	252637483	139455727
比利时	4016221	2952198
丹麦	1935467	1044405
英国	41703027	16127411
德国	61237643	43741558
法国	19114459	15965871
爱尔兰	26597532	4225606
意大利	21511701	9840348
荷兰	4186038	607415
西班牙	1421461	15979647
奥地利	1763792	79155
芬兰	42140203	7475093
匈牙利	6553624	1410812
挪威	6576375	2876763
瑞典	6958496	8654896
瑞士	3183266	1118446
俄罗斯	1568035	280782
巴西	322165	1259
哥斯达黎加	1916543	68550
墨西哥	917826	1094971
波多黎各	26907	904
加拿大	30960801	24847817
美国	1227937095	598285564
澳大利亚	8580481	5659541
新西兰	31489	33051
其他	184083166	52447133

1999年中国主要进口商品来源地

有线通讯设备

来源地	1999 金额(美元)	1998 金额(美元)
总值	**2778789961**	**2277576710**
香港	55860941	98545496
印度	116147	28788
印度尼西亚	54306	1057029
以色列	57960656	56591016
日本	339272856	333677194
澳门	645	5610
马来西亚	10592074	2588828
菲律宾	698825	589194
新加坡	9119378	4158772
韩国	37903333	25651964
泰国	5692030	4677811
土耳其	108168	121321
越南	85379	451
台湾省	88123332	57959366
比利时	11883793	14604378
丹麦	6210136	37377
英国	67242941	58376862
德国	260466497	260905671
法国	77879059	75230668
爱尔兰	12606247	4165787
意大利	45379637	51602730
荷兰	4011577	26906690
葡萄牙	3752	13678
西班牙	4302616	12716990
奥地利	1924878	3816400
芬兰	312893362	132408211
挪威	2551618	1465138
波兰	649749	765019
瑞典	379325113	334209168
瑞士	12142112	6551642
捷克共和国	528	454
巴西	1553684	35270
墨西哥	549303	57993
巴拿马	233	775
加拿大	172170634	147501576
美国	754847611	544649258
澳大利亚	18534585	7133037
新西兰	72302	1200977
其他	25999924	7568121

1999年中国利用外资统计表

金额单位:万美元

方　　式	批准利用外资协议(合同)		实际使用外资金额
	项目个数	外资金额	
总计	**17022**	**5200874**	**5265896**
一、对外借款	104	836000	1021200
外国政府贷款	104	148800	331600
国际金融组织贷款		360400	260600
出口信贷		20000	102500
外国银行商业贷款		226800	246500
对外发行债券		80000	80000
二、外商直接投资	16918	4122302	4031871
合资经营企业	7050	1351520	1582729
合作经营企业	1656	680302	823367
外资企业	8201	2070637	1554475
外商投资股份制企业	3	10285	29233
合作开发	5	5850	38389
其他	3	3708	3678
三、外商其他投资	0	242572	212825
国外发行股票		61000	61000
国际租赁		10697	18500
补偿贸易		4146	1262
加工装配		166729	132063

1999年中国实际利用外资分国别和地区统计表

金额单位:万美元

国家和地区	合　计	对外借款	外商直接投资	外商其他投资
总值	**5265896**	**1021200**	**4031871**	**212825**
香港	1740233		1636305	103928
澳门	33778		30864	2914
台湾省	275857		259870	15987
越南	13		13	
菲律宾	11728		11728	
泰国	14832		14832	
马来西亚	23773		23771	2
新加坡	264252		264249	3
文莱	18		18	
印尼	12917		12917	
朝鲜	368		368	

1999年中国实际利用外资分国别和地区统计表

金额单位:万美元

国家和地区	合　计	对外借款	外商直接投资	外商其他投资
老挝				
柬埔寨	248		248	
蒙古	6		6	
日本	306358		297308	9050
缅甸	1101		1101	
巴基斯坦	189		189	
孟加拉	43		43	
印度	49		49	
尼泊尔				
伊朗				
土耳其	385		385	
塞浦路斯	189		189	
叙利亚	11		11	
黎巴嫩	20		20	
巴勒斯坦				
也门	20		20	
伊拉克	202		202	
沙特	256		256	
科威特	248		248	
阿联酋	221		221	
韩国	128025		127473	552
以色列	327		327	
埃及	16		16	
利比亚	7		7	
阿尔及利亚	35		35	
摩洛哥	5		5	
毛里塔尼亚	156		156	
几内亚(比绍)	176		176	
加纳				
科特迪瓦				
贝宁	7		7	
利比里亚	429		429	
塞拉利昂	105		105	
多哥	10		10	
尼日利亚	200		200	
喀麦隆	6		6	
扎伊尔				
布隆迪				

1999年中国实际利用外资分国别和地区统计表

金额单位:万美元

国家和地区	合　计	对外借款	外商直接投资	外商其他投资
肯尼亚	40		40	
乌干达	26		26	
坦桑尼亚	10		10	
塞舌尔	29		29	
毛里求斯	17025		17025	
马达加斯加	54		54	
津巴布韦	15		15	
博茨瓦纳				
莱索托				
南非	590		590	
纳米比亚	635		635	
非洲其他国家	30		30	
德国	137363		137326	37
法国	88429		88429	
意大利	18744		18744	
荷兰	54168		54168	
比利时	8322		8322	
卢森堡	422		422	
英国	104494		104449	45
爱尔兰	305		305	
丹麦	8491		8491	
芬兰	6765		6765	
瑞典	32478		15580	16898
奥地利	2317		2317	
希腊	3		3	
西班牙	1754		1754	
葡萄牙	831		831	
波兰	354		354	
匈牙利	1204		1204	
捷克	147		147	
保加利亚	10		10	
罗马尼亚	642		642	
南斯拉夫	112		112	
挪威	1859		1859	
冰岛	1		1	
瑞士	24709		24709	
马耳他	279		279	
摩纳哥	10		10	

1999年中国实际利用外资分国别和地区统计表

金额单位:万美元

国家和地区	合　计	对外借款	外商直接投资	外商其他投资
列支敦士登	416		416	
直布罗陀	39		39	
斯洛伐克	10		10	
俄罗斯	1954		1954	
乌克兰	24		24	
白俄罗斯	7		7	
哈萨克斯坦				
吉尔吉斯斯坦				
爱沙尼亚	30		30	
欧洲其他国家				
墨西哥	33		33	
洪都拉斯	90		90	
尼加拉瓜				
哥斯达黎加	250		250	
巴拿马	8951		8951	
古巴				
多米尼加共和国	2		2	
牙买加	300		300	
巴巴多斯	392		392	
委内瑞拉	565		565	
哥伦比亚	228		228	
巴西	338		338	
厄瓜多尔	29		29	
秘鲁	272		272	
玻利维亚	38		38	
智利	208		208	
巴拉圭	502		500	2
阿根廷	177		177	
乌拉圭				
巴哈马	4301		4301	
特克斯和凯科斯岛				
维尔京群岛	267282		265896	1386
安提瓜	7		7	
圣其茨—尼维斯	10		10	
多米尼加联邦	10		10	
伯利兹				
凯曼群岛	37795		37795	
苏里南	45		45	

1999年中国实际利用外资分国别和地区统计表

金额单位:万美元

国家和地区	合　计	对外借款	外商直接投资	外商其他投资
库拉索				
拉丁美洲其他国家	10		10	
加拿大	31449		31442	7
美国	422255		421586	669
格陵兰				
百慕大	8580		8580	
澳大利亚	26676		26331	345
新西兰	1839		1839	
西萨摩亚	20129		20129	
汤加	130		130	
斐济	85		85	
库克群岛	84		84	
巴布亚新几内亚	52		52	
马绍尔群岛	159		159	
东萨摩亚	7		7	
其他太平洋岛屿	1380		1380	
大洋洲其他国家	724		724	
其他	77346		16346	61000

1999年中国实际利用外资分省市统计表

金额单位:万美元

省、市	合　计	对外借款	外商直接投资	外商其他投资
总计	**5265896**	**1021200**	**4031871**	**212825**
北京市	197525		197525	
天津市	176399		176399	
河北省	104202		104202	
山西省	39129		39129	
内蒙古自治区	6456		6456	
辽宁省	106173		106173	
吉林省	30120		30120	
黑龙江省	31828		31828	
上海市	283665		283665	
江苏省	607756		607756	
浙江省	123262		123262	
安徽省	26131		26131	
福建省	402403		402403	

1999 年中国实际利用外资分省市统计表

金额单位:万美元

省、市	合计	对外借款	外商直接投资	外商其他投资
江西省	32080		32080	
山东省	246547		225878	20669
河南省	52135		52135	
湖北省	98914		91488	7426
湖南省	65374		65374	
广东省	1289238		1165750	123488
广西自治区	63512		63512	
海南省	48449		48449	
四川省	34101		34101	
重庆市	24135		23893	242
贵州省	4090		4090	
云南省	15385		15385	
陕西省	24197		24197	
甘肃省	4104		4104	
青海省	459		459	
宁夏自治区	5134		5134	
新疆自治区	2404		2404	

1999 年中国实际利用外资分行业统计表

金额单位:万美元

行业	合计	对外借款	外商直接投资	外商其他投资
总计	**5265896**	**1021200**	**4031871**	**212825**
农林牧渔业	71075		71015	60
采掘业	55714		55714	
制造业	2394515		2260334	134181
电力煤气及水的生产和供应业	370274		370274	
建筑业	91658		91658	
地质勘查业、水利管理业	452		452	
交通运输仓储及邮电通信业	172012		155114	16898
批发和零售贸易餐饮业	96513		96513	
金融保险业	9767		9767	
房地产业	558831		558831	
社会服务业	255066		255066	
卫生体育和社会福利业	14769		14769	
教育文化艺术及广播电影电视业	6072		6072	
科学研究和综合技术服务业	11013		11013	
其他行业	136954		75268	61686

1999年中国批准签订外商投资协议(合同)分国家和地区统计表

金额单位:万美元

国家和地区	合计		对外借款		外商直接投资		外商其他投资	
	项目个数	合同外资金额	项目个数	合同外资金额	项目个数	合同外资金额	项目个数	合同外资金额
总值	**17022**	**5200874**	**104**	**836000**	**16918**	**4122302**		**242572**
香港	5902	1457119			5902	1332892		124227
澳门	254	45974			254	42656		3318
台湾省	2499	361672			2499	337444		24228
越南	1	1688			1	1688		
菲律宾	99	18445			99	18408		37
泰国	119	24781			119	24754		27
马来西亚	133	26679			133	26573		106
新加坡	503	226136			503	225824		312
文莱								
印度尼西亚	54	9621			54	9620		1
朝鲜	12	209			12	209		
老挝	4	975			4	975		
柬埔寨	7	110			7	110		
蒙古	3	35			3	35		
日本	1167	272864			1167	259128		13736
缅甸	11	5146			11	5146		
巴基斯坦	9	291			9	246		45
孟加拉	2	32			2	32		
印度	2	40			2	40		
尼泊尔	1	20			1	20		
伊朗	1	21			1	1		
土耳其	2	23			2	23		
塞浦路斯	5	149			5	149		
叙利亚	1	3			1	3		
黎巴嫩	3	50			3	50		
巴勒斯坦	1	10			1	10		
也门								
伊拉克								
沙特	1	22			1	22		
科威特	1	28			1	10		18
阿联酋	13	1303			13	1303		
韩国	1547	149332			1547	148385		947
以色列	16	1890			16	1890		
埃及	6	637			6	637		

1999年中国批准签订外商投资协议(合同)分国家和地区统计表

金额单位:万美元

国家和地区	合 计		对外借款		外商直接投资		外商其他投资	
	项目个数	合同外资金额	项目个数	合同外资金额	项目个数	合同外资金额	项目个数	合同外资金额
利比亚	1	7			1	7		
阿尔及利亚	1	68			1	68		
摩洛哥								
毛里塔尼亚								
几内亚(比绍)	1	720			1	720		
加纳	1	5			1	5		
科特迪瓦	1	39			1	39		
贝宁	2	27			2	27		
利比里亚	1	126			1	126		
塞拉利昂		95				95		
多哥	1	90			1	90		
尼日利亚	3	88			3	88		
喀麦隆								
扎伊尔	1	723			1	723		
布隆迪	1	6			1	6		
肯尼亚	2	258			2	258		
乌干达	1	6			1	6		
坦桑尼亚	3	135			3	135		
塞舌尔	2	29			2	29		
毛里求斯	27	39798			27	39798		
马达加斯加	1	120			1	120		
津巴布韦	2	102			2	102		
博茨瓦纳	1	87			1	87		
莱索托	1	23			1	23		
南非	20	1031			20	1031		
纳米比亚	1	100			1	100		
非洲其他国家								
德国	196	95229			196	93872		1357
法国	110	47068			110	47031		37
意大利	108	18746			108	18739		7
荷兰	76	67581			76	67581		
比利时	26	22157			26	22157		
卢森堡	9	6029			9	6029		
英国	230	108727			230	108540		187
爱尔兰	1	155			1	155		

1999年中国批准签订外商投资协议(合同)分国家和地区统计表

金额单位:万美元

国家和地区	合计		对外借款		外商直接投资		外商其他投资	
	项目个数	合同外资金额	项目个数	合同外资金额	项目个数	合同外资金额	项目个数	合同外资金额
丹麦	13	8114			13	8114		
芬兰	18	3521			18	3521		
瑞典	30	17158			30	17158		
奥地利	26	3526			26	3526		
希腊	6	3304			6	3304		
西班牙	40	6514			40	6514		
葡萄牙	5	3325			5	3325		
波兰	9	642			9	642		
匈牙利	22	1213			22	1213		
捷克	14	365			14	365		
保加利亚	1	20			1	20		
罗马尼亚	24	1823			24	1823		
南斯拉夫	2	136			2	136		
挪威	9	3409			9	3409		
冰岛								
瑞士	35	11740			35	11740		
马耳他	3	209			3	209		
摩纳哥		10				10		
列支敦士登	1	565			1	565		
直布罗陀								
斯洛伐克	1	7			1	7		
俄罗斯	67	2805			67	2805		
乌克兰	5	116			5	116		
白俄罗斯	1	17			1	17		
哈萨克斯坦	4	119			4	119		
吉尔吉斯斯坦	1	10			1	10		
爱沙尼亚								
欧洲其他国家		608				608		
墨西哥	1	33			1	33		
洪都拉斯	1	13			1	13		
尼加拉瓜	1	19			1	19		
哥斯达黎加	3	2490			3	2490		
巴拿马	15	5193			15	5193		
古巴	1	54			1	54		
多米尼加共和国	2	1268			2	1268		

1999 年中国批准签订外商投资协议(合同)分国家和地区统计表

金额单位:万美元

国家和地区	合计		对外借款		外商直接投资		外商其他投资	
	项目个数	合同外资金额	项目个数	合同外资金额	项目个数	合同外资金额	项目个数	合同外资金额
牙买加	1	100			1	100		
巴巴多斯								
委内瑞拉	3	479			3	479		
哥伦比亚	3	726			3	726		
巴西	17	1807			17	1807		
厄瓜多尔	2	186			2	186		
秘鲁	5	473			5	473		
玻利维亚	7	1510			7	1510		
智利	5	231			5	231		
巴拉圭	3	122			3	120		2
阿根廷	14	688			14	688		
乌拉圭	1	3			1	3		
巴哈马	16	12197			16	12197		
特克斯和凯科斯岛	1	322			1	322		
维尔京群岛	495	351811			495	348749		3062
安提瓜								
圣其茨—尼维斯								
多米尼加联邦	1	14			1	14		
伯利兹	4	143			4	143		
凯曼群岛	38	39418			38	39418		
苏里南	1	36			1	36		
库拉索	1	7			1	7		
拉丁美洲其他国家								
加拿大	367	78551			367	69915		8636
美国	2028	602598			2028	601611		987
格陵兰	1	859			1	859		
百慕大	8	7124			8	7124		
澳大利亚	396	59001			396	58838		163
新西兰	49	3668			49	3668		
西萨摩亚	68	35418			68	35286		132
汤加								
斐济	1	18			1	18		
库克群岛								
巴布亚新几内亚	3	122			3	122		
马绍尔群岛	6	287			6	287		

1999 年中国批准签订外商投资协议(合同)分国家和地区统计表

金额单位:万美元

国家和地区	合计		对外借款		外商直接投资		外商其他投资	
	项目个数	合同外资金额	项目个数	合同外资金额	项目个数	合同外资金额	项目个数	合同外资金额
东萨摩亚	1	544			1	544		
其他太平洋岛屿	4	1052			4	1052		
大洋洲其他国家	1	70			1	70		
其他	11	72263			11	11263		61000

1999 年中国批准签订利用外资协议(合同)分省市统计表

金额单位:万美元

省、市	合计		对外借款		外商直接投资		外商其他投资	
	项目个数	合同外资金额	项目个数	合同外资金额	项目个数	合同外资金额	项目个数	合同外资金额
总计	**17022**	**5200874**	**104**	**836000**	**16918**	**4122302**		**242572**
北京市	645	178672			645	178672		
天津市	575	159054			575	159054		
河北省	520	88946			520	88946		
山西省	79	23444			79	23444		
内蒙古自治区	68	17740			68	17740		
辽宁省	1147	329687			1147	329687		
吉林省	355	45049			355	45049		
黑龙江省	313	39524			313	39524		
上海市	1472	410370			1472	410370		
江苏省	1926	647072			1926	647072		
浙江省	1113	194793			1113	194793		
安徽省	199	55868			199	55868		
福建省	1439	486996			1439	486996		
江西省	245	33136			245	33136		
山东省	1717	327382			1717	311087		16295
河南省	261	64664			261	64664		
湖北省	260	93104			260	82178		10926
湖南省	320	50198			320	50198		
广东省	3013	701475			3013	547451		154024
广西自治区	223	67363			223	67363		
海南省	158	79176			158	79176		

1999 年中国批准签订利用外资协议(合同)分省市统计表

金额单位:万美元

省、市	合计		对外借款		外商直接投资		外商其他投资	
	项目个数	合同外资金额	项目个数	合同外资金额	项目个数	合同外资金额	项目个数	合同外资金额
四川省	195	49288			195	49288		
重庆市	169	51015			169	50688		327
贵州省	43	6685			43	6685		
云南省	138	32594			138	32594		
陕西省	157	42693			157	42693		
甘肃省	67	8236			67	8236		
青海省	15	1421			15	1421		
宁夏自治区	29	6228			29	6228		
新疆自治区	52	6151			52	6151		

1999 年中国批准签订外商投资协议(合同)分行业统计表

金额单位:万美元

行业	合计		对外借款		外商直接投资		外商其他投资
	项目个数	外资金额	项目个数	外资金额	项目个数	外资金额	
总计	**17022**	**5200874**	**104**	**836000**	**16918**	**4122302**	**242572**
农林牧渔业	762	147770			762	147170	600
采掘业	130	32221			130	32221	
制造业	12042	2704745			12042	2533180	171565
电力煤气及水的生产和供应业	116	163519			116	163519	
建筑业	247	109619			247	109619	
地质勘查业、水利管理业	10	5397			10	5397	
交通运输、仓储及邮电通信业	205	120021			205	111401	8620
批发零售贸易餐饮业	825	120413			825	120413	
金融保险业	3	3708			3	3708	
房地产业	669	417785			669	417785	
社会服务业	1474	301680			1474	301680	
卫生体育和社会福利业	28	6727			28	6727	
教育文化艺术及广播电影电视业	29	7258			29	7258	
科学研究和综合技术服务业	62	13372			62	13372	
其他行业	316	210639			316	148852	61787

1999年中国最大500家外商投资企业名录

金额单位:万元人民币

位次	企业名称	销售额
1	上海大众汽车有限公司	2520388
2	摩托罗拉(天津)电子有限公司	1804583
3	广东移动通信有限责任公司	1727183
4	松下电器机电(深圳)有限公司	1219577
5	康佳集团股份有限公司	857389
6	华能国际电力股份有限公司	811146
7	联想(北京)有限公司	770214
8	一汽大众汽车有限公司	768511
9	希捷国际科技(无锡)有限公司	762334
10	深圳希捷科技有限公司	661455
11	北京诺基亚移动通信有限公司	638428
12	上海贝尔有限公司	605889
13	广东核电合营有限公司	603255
14	上海现代集装箱制造有限公司	524371
15	广州宝洁有限公司	524210
16	北京大唐发电股份有限公司	506734
17	中国国际海运集装箱(集团)股份有限公司	491350
18	大连西太平洋石油化工有限公司	487650
19	上海轮胎橡胶(集团)股份有限公司	399759
20	上海阿霍德-中汇超市有限公司	397510
21	韶关钢铁有限公司	396001
22	广东广合电力有限公司	376153
23	华能国际电力开发公司	372164
24	广东科龙电器股份有限公司	366095
25	南京依维柯汽车有限公司	354481
26	苏州飞利浦消费电子有限公司	353758
27	庆铃汽车股份有限公司	353586
28	北京爱立信移动通信有限公司	348617
29	上海真空电子器件股份有限公司	335911
30	沈阳金杯客车制造有限公司	334803
31	上海跃龙有色金属有限公司	332813
32	上海海中海发展股份有限公司	327945
33	冠捷电子(福建)有限公司	320637
34	上海三菱电梯有限公司	315794
35	上海贝尔阿尔卡特移动通讯系统有限公司	308919
36	深圳创维-RGB电子有限公司	294984
37	深圳开发科技股份有限公司	282163
38	重庆钢铁股份有限公司	281166

1999年中国最大500家外商投资企业名录

金额单位:万元人民币

位次	企业名称	销售额
39	上海永新彩色显象管有限公司	280615
40	佳能珠海公司	280069
41	上海汇众汽车制造有限公司	277717
42	深圳三洋华强激光电子有限公司	275868
43	杭州娃哈哈保健食品有限公司	270393
44	华飞彩色显示系统有限公司	266757
45	南海油脂工业(赤湾)有限公司	262956
46	长城国际信息产品(深圳)有限公司	258343
47	爱普生技术(深圳)有限公司	256878
48	阿科中国有限公司	250933
49	福建大丰投资集团有限公司	248236
50	理光(深圳)工业发展有限公司	247786
51	上海申美饮料食品有限公司	244136
52	江西铜业股份有限公司	242781
53	广州钢铁股份有限公司	236560
54	南昌正大畜禽有限公司	235579
55	广东福地彩色显像管股份有限公司	230867
56	吉林德大有限公司	227608
57	上海大江(集团)股份有限公司	227483
58	松下电器(中国)有限公司	216928
59	上海索广电子有限公司	209159
60	江西昌河铃木汽车有限责任公司	208971
61	神龙汽车有限公司	206683
62	北京北大方正电子有限公司	205090
63	上海西门子移动通信有限公司	204072
64	东莞福安纺织印染有限公司	203162
65	上海福华玻璃有限公司	202907
66	上海锦江麦德龙购物中心有限公司	202806
67	上海夏普电器有限公司	202530
68	上海氯碱化工股份有限公司	202107
69	宁波中华纸业有限公司	201829
70	江铃汽车股份有限公司	200603
71	广东高路华电视机有限公司	199566
72	张家港保税区东海粮油工业有限公司	197876
73	福建南靖万利达视听有限公司	196571
74	华懋双汇实业(集团)有限公司	191391
75	中国惠普有限公司	188093
76	河南新飞电器有限公司	187272

1999年中国最大500家外商投资企业名录

金额单位:万元人民币

位次	企业名称	销售额
77	西安杨森制药有限公司	186692
78	翔鹭涤纶纺纤(厦门)有限公司	185998
79	厦门华侨电子股份有限公司	184338
80	上海蜂星国际贸易有限公司	184298
81	湛江东兴石油企业有限公司	183937
82	哈尔滨哈飞汽车制造有限公司	182913
83	宝洁(中国)有限公司	181236
84	山东华能发电股份有限公司	178063
85	飞利浦桑达消费通信(深圳)有限公司	176591
86	重庆长安铃木汽车有限公司	176431
87	友利电子(深圳)有限公司	176149
88	深圳国际商业机器技术产品有限公司	174990
89	青岛啤酒股份有限公司	172271
90	上海联华超市有限公司	170530
91	中国天津奥的斯电梯有限公司	170359
92	联合利华服务(上海)有限公司	168807
93	国际商业机器中国有限公司	168780
94	深圳三星电管有限公司	168301
95	乐金曙光电子有限公司	168075
96	南京熊猫电子股份有限公司	166892
97	三洋电机(蛇口)有限公司	166600
98	深圳长科国际电子有限公司	165971
99	唯冠科技(深圳)有限公司	165047
100	夏普办公设备(常熟)有限公司	164587
101	天津三美电机有限公司	163633
102	顺德格兰仕电器厂有限公司	162364
103	陕西渭河发电有限公司	161276
104	东莞诺基亚移动电话有限公司	157110
105	惠普计算机产品(上海)有限公司	155442
106	南京金城机械有限公司	154649
107	东莞三星电机有限公司	154080
108	丰田通商(上海)有限公司	153942
109	江苏利港电力有限公司	153576
110	和德(集团)有限公司	153201
111	TCL 王牌电器(惠州)有限公司	152870
112	厦新电子有限公司	152820
113	苏州罗技电子有限公司	152120
114	深圳海量存储设备有限公司	151243

1999年中国最大500家外商投资企业名录

金额单位:万元人民币

位次	企业名称	销售额
115	华源凯马机械股份有限公司	151193
116	上海朗讯科技通信设备有限公司	151037
117	金隆铜业有限公司	150605
118	番禺市祈福新村房地产有限公司	150357
119	徐州维维食品饮料有限公司	148557
120	上海美建钢结构有限公司	148501
121	广东健力宝集团有限公司	147836
122	乐金电子(天津)电器有限公司	146716
123	苏州明基电脑有限公司	145951
124	河南安阳彩色显像管玻壳有限公司	141652
125	上海国嘉实业股份有限公司	140940
126	深圳妈湾电力有限公司	139631
127	天津三星电机有限公司	137787
128	福建永恩投资(集团)有限公司	137298
129	上海索广映像有限公司	136942
130	合肥美菱股份有限公司	136883
131	北京万通广场房地产有限公司	136311
132	海南航空股份有限公司	136088
133	佳能大连办公设备有限公司	136006
134	青岛朗讯科技通讯设备服务有限公司	135809
135	深圳赛格日立彩电显示器件有限公司	134339
136	山东中华发电有限公司	133508
137	厦门灿坤实业股份有限公司	133165
138	锦州东港电力有限公司	132167
139	本溪北龙炼铁有限公司	131845
140	伟创力实业(深圳)有限公司	130164
141	杭州中策橡胶有限公司	130138
142	深圳南方中集集装箱制造有限公司	129807
143	富金精密工业(深圳)有限公司	129684
144	上海嘉士德－华海金属制品有限公司	127893
145	广深珠高速公路有限公司	126609
146	江苏富士通通信技术有限公司	125082
147	大连东芝电视有限公司	124386
148	南京爱立信通信有限公司	124214
149	中美天津史克制药有限公司	123764
150	中国－阿拉伯化肥有限公司	123569
151	万宝至马达大连有限公司	123149
152	开平中晖复合纤维母粒有限公司	121635

1999年中国最大500家外商投资企业名录

金额单位:万元人民币

位次	企业名称	销售额
153	雅达电子有限公司	120777
154	上海太平洋百货有限公司	120017
155	青岛三美电机有限公司	119090
156	惠阳联想电脑有限公司	119000
157	厦门华夏国际电力发展有限公司	118183
158	正大集团(天津)实业有限公司	118176
159	上海延锋汽车饰件有限公司	118150
160	本溪北龙钢铁集团有限公司	117163
161	才众电脑(深圳)有限公司	116999
162	广州日立电梯有限公司	116751
163	浙江美可达摩托车有限公司	116102
164	内蒙古鄂尔多斯羊绒制品股份有限公司	115238
165	上海美蓓亚精密机电有限公司	115232
166	奥林巴斯(深圳)工业有限公司	114194
167	广东电力发展股份有限公司	113760
168	日本电产(大连)有限公司	113327
169	天津顶益国际食品有限公司	112646
170	高明高丰纺织染联合企业有限公司	112640
171	宁波森邦国际经贸有限公司	111206
172	厦门正新橡胶工业有限公司	110678
173	仁宝电脑工业(中国)有限公司	109884
174	上海光明乳业有限公司	109287
175	上海伊藤忠商事有限公司	108613
176	上海振华港口机械股份有限公司	108268
177	广州东方电力有限公司	108128
178	江阴兴澄钢铁有限公司	107880
179	山东晨鸣纸业集团股份有限公司	107023
180	张家港润忠钢铁有限公司	106856
181	嘉吉贸易(上海)有限公司	106382
182	凤凰股份有限公司	106198
183	江门市大长江摩托车有限公司	106151
184	上海阿法泰克电子有限公司	105937
185	顺德惠而浦蚬华微波制品有限公司	105877
186	广州珠江电力有限公司	105632
187	石家庄宝石电气硝子玻璃有限公司	103789
188	北海粮油工业(天津)有限公司	103142
189	北京飞机维修工程有限公司	102809
190	湖南湘钢华光线材有限公司	101657

1999年中国最大500家外商投资企业名录

金额单位:万元人民币

位次	企业名称	销售额
191	东芝复印机(深圳)有限公司	101044
192	南通中集顺达集装箱有限公司	100572
193	合肥荣事达洗衣机有限公司	100551
194	洛阳北方易初摩托车有限公司	99642
195	武汉金鹤药业有限公司	99156
196	东风金狮轮胎有限公司	98880
197	上海汽轮机有限公司	97788
198	嘉国实业(深圳)有限公司	97562
199	山东新华制药股份有限公司	97388
200	广州京安豹汽车有限公司	97114
201	上海柴油机股份有限公司	96928
202	包头天诚线材有限公司	96815
203	上海日立家用电器有限公司	96675
204	高标准实业(深圳)有限公司	96194
205	箭牌口香糖有限公司	95612
206	银川中策(长城)橡胶有限公司	95374
207	江阴振华港口机械有限公司	94699
208	卡西欧电子(深圳)有限公司	93171
209	上海第一八佰伴有限公司	93124
210	黑龙江正大实业有限公司	93103
211	杭州松下家用电器有限公司	92026
212	乐金电子沈阳有限公司	92008
213	广西玉柴机器股份有限公司	91975
214	广州造纸有限公司	91835
215	株洲南方雅马哈摩托车有限公司	91592
216	北京燕莎友谊商城有限公司	89819
217	舟山兴业有限公司	89787
218	西门子(中国)有限公司	89770
219	陆氏实业(武汉)有限公司	89544
220	秦皇岛首钢板材有限公司	88833
221	杭州顶益国际食品有限公司	88071
222	上海花王有限公司	88022
223	上海集装箱码头有限公司	87635
224	南通天生港发电有限公司	87635
225	天津电装汽车电机有限公司	87541
226	长飞光纤光缆有限公司	87128
227	赛特集团有限公司	86847
228	上海百事可乐饮料有限公司	86483

1999年中国最大500家外商投资企业名录

金额单位:万元人民币

位次	企业名称	销售额
229	张家港沙太钢铁有限公司	86209
230	上海丽兴房地产有限公司	86018
231	上海屈臣氏日用品有限公司	85999
232	上海易初通用机器有限公司	85330
233	上海易初配销有限公司	84859
234	上海东方商厦有限公司	84834
235	上海自动化仪表股份有限公司	84442
236	上海新建设发展有限公司	84402
237	上海闸电燃气轮机发电有限公司	84127
238	上海利华有限公司	84108
239	上海益昌薄板有限公司	83893
240	黑龙江华润金玉实业有限公司	83628
241	圣韵电子有限公司	83625
242	上海联家超市有限公司	83622
243	诺基亚(中国)投资有限公司	83606
244	珠海华丰食品工业(集团)有限公司	83538
245	广州进道集装箱有限公司	83364
246	番禺潭洲裕纺织印有限公司	83347
247	江苏南钢宝兴钢铁有限公司	83040
248	上海恒立房地产有限公司	82969
249	美国通用电器塑料中国有限公司	82839
250	正大康地(蛇口)有限公司	82557
251	佛山市沙口发电厂有限公司	82389
252	徐州华润电力有限公司	82376
253	中美上海施贵宝制药有限公司	81873
254	百威(武汉)国际啤酒有限公司	81842
255	诸城兴贸玉米开发有限公司	81826
256	青岛海尔电冰箱公司	81532
257	天津雅马哈电子乐器有限公司	81466
258	爱立信(中国)有限公司	81456
259	南通醋酸纤维有限公司	81449
260	靖远第二发电有限公司	80888
261	深圳南天油粕工业有限公司	80389
262	营口渤海油脂工业有限公司	80060
263	杭州娃哈哈饮料有限公司	79924
264	金利来(中国)服饰皮具有限公司	79203
265	宁波雅戈尔服饰有限公司	78587
266	双城雀巢有限公司	78468

1999年中国最大500家外商投资企业名录

金额单位:万元人民币

位次	企业名称	销售额
267	上海派克电气有限公司	78420
268	上海锦海捷业国际货运有限公司	77692
269	上海商城	77618
270	新利实业(深圳)有限公司	77600
271	上海远东集装箱有限公司	77485
272	辽阳忠旺铝型材有限公司	77434
273	源兴电脑科技(东莞)有限公司	77355
274	南太电子(深圳)有限公司	77196
275	上海JVC电器有限公司	76644
276	内蒙古伊泰煤炭股份有限公司	76628
277	中国迅达电梯有限公司	76393
278	中华映管(福州)有限公司	76302
279	天津华利汽车有限公司	76052
280	上海德加拉电器有限公司	75550
281	深圳施乐高科技有限公司	75430
282	中国南玻集团股份有限公司	75411
283	海尔梅洛尼(青岛)洗衣机有限公司	75175
284	北京裕京花园别墅有限公司	75093
285	明达塑胶(福建)有限公司	74921
286	维德木业(苏州)有限公司	73669
287	华南蓝天航空油料有限公司	73350
288	安徽佳通轮胎有限公司	72776
289	合肥日立挖掘机有限公司	72374
290	宁波和邦国际贸易有限公司	72253
291	牧田(中国)有限公司	72155
292	南京华新电线电缆有限公司	72077
293	光大木材工业(深圳)有限公司	71825
294	番禺创倍鞋业有限公司	71727
295	松下.万宝(广州)压缩机有限公司	71582
296	广州华凌空调设备有限公司	71576
297	广州宝洁纸品有限公司	71302
298	天津三星电子有限公司	71032
299	上海新格有色金属有限公司	70932
300	北京JVC电子产业有限公司	70040
301	厦门进雄企业有限公司	70027
302	淮阴利淮钢铁有限公司	69644
303	金桐石油化工有限公司	69528
304	开平亚联复合纤维有限公司	69204

1999年中国最大500家外商投资企业名录

金额单位:万元人民币

位次	企业名称	销售额
305	康惠(惠州)电子实业有限公司	69139
306	嘉陵－本田发动机有限公司	68937
307	无锡夏普电子元器件有限公司	68901
308	黑龙江电力股份有限公司	68897
309	西门子光缆有限公司.成都	68538
310	哈尔滨龙兴化纤有限公司	68470
311	广州正大万客隆(佳景)有限公司	68221
312	昆山统一企业食品有限公司	68098
313	深圳金威啤酒有限公司	67818
314	北京轻型汽车有限公司	67706
315	上海招商局大厦有限公司	67680
316	中讯电子(昆山)有限公司	67293
317	UT斯达康(中国)有限公司	67219
318	天津卡丁车竞技娱乐有限公司	67004
319	杭州中萃食品有限公司	66998
320	北京首钢宝生带钢有限公司	66814
321	鹤山美雅纺织有限公司	66710
322	上海嘉里粮油工业有限公司	66534
323	青岛正大有限公司	66317
324	上海金兴房地产发展有限公司	66182
325	强生(中国)有限公司	65637
326	福建恒安集团有限公司	65539
327	珠海松下马达有限公司	65522
328	上海施乐复印机有限公司	65496
329	福建日立电视机有限公司	65424
330	南京金鹰国际实业有限公司	65396
331	中国南山开发(集团)股份有限公司	65378
332	桂林大宇客车有限公司	65055
333	中乔智威汤逊广告有限公司	64646
334	东芝大连有限公司	64349
335	深圳百仕达实业有限公司	64173
336	渤海铝业有限公司	63733
337	首钢日电电子有限公司	63339
338	深圳易初配销有限公司	63253
339	上海耀华皮尔金顿玻璃股份有限公司	63125
340	至卓飞高线路板(深圳)有限公司	62941
341	深圳东海爱地房地产发展有限公司	62939
342	南京金腾钢铁有限公司	62904

1999年中国最大500家外商投资企业名录

金额单位:万元人民币

位次	企业名称	销售额
343	广东天贸(集团)股份有限公司	62861
344	西安大唐电信有限公司	62672
345	张家港永新钢铁有限公司	62469
346	厦门厦杏摩托有限公司	62429
347	沈阳沈海热电有限公司	62365
348	肇庆蓝带啤酒卢堡有限公司	62170
349	大连华录.松下录像机有限公司	62104
350	济南轻骑铃木摩托车有限公司	62056
351	苏州信越聚合有限公司	61781
352	西安西沃客车有限公司	61511
353	上海兰生大宇有限公司	61470
354	上海陆家嘴金融贸易区开发股份有限公司	61398
355	深圳创华合作有限公司	61199
356	陕西康佳电子有限公司	61182
357	广东正大康地有限公司	61083
358	福建龙马农用车制造有限公司	61052
359	天津天美汽车配件有限公司	61015
360	常熟通润机电有限公司	60975
361	欧姆龙(大连)有限公司	60971
362	广夏(银川)实业股份有限公司	60938
363	日商岩井(上海)有限公司	60662
364	深圳彩虹皇旗电子资讯有限公司	60656
365	重庆建设-雅马哈摩托车有限公司	60617
366	葫芦岛锌厂东方铜业有限公司	60573
367	上海奥美广告有限公司	60460
368	上海三荣电器有限公司	60390
369	信华精机有限公司	60246
370	湖北汉新发电有限公司	59962
371	丹东阿尔派电有限公司	59947
372	青岛海信空调公司	59911
373	福建实达电脑科技有限公司	59905
374	蛇口招商港务股份有限公司	59857
375	台达电子(东莞)有限公司	59822
376	丽都饭店有限公司	59688
377	沈阳顶益国际食品有限公司	59637
378	东莞歌乐东方电子有限公司	59538
379	太平洋塑胶(福建)有限公司	59441
380	武汉广场管理有限公司	59380

1999年中国最大500家外商投资企业名录

金额单位:万元人民币

位次	企业名称	销售额
381	张家港合丰钢铁有限公司	59337
382	青岛海尔电冰箱(国际)有限公司	59275
383	上海纳铁福传动轴有限公司	59258
384	广州珠江轮胎有限公司	59200
385	天津北洋集装箱有限公司	59199
386	广东北电交换系统设备有限公司	59070
387	珠海经济特区红塔仁恒纸业有限公司	59013
388	盐田国际集装箱码头有限公司	58897
389	上海进道集装箱有限公司	58894
390	深圳华安液化石油气有限公司	58864
391	南通正大有限公司	58807
392	天津日电电子通信工业有限公司	58760
393	天津太平(集团)有限公司	58756
394	上海庄臣有限公司	58706
395	上海中集冷藏箱有限公司	58687
396	杭州大厦有限公司	58671
397	中贸联万客隆商业有限公司	58362
398	四川嘉里粮油工业有限公司	58347
399	富士通将军(上海)有限公司	58306
400	吉联(吉林)石油化学有限公司	58123
401	柯达电子(上海)有限公司	58063
402	天津可口可乐饮料有限公司	57994
403	茉织华实业(集团)有限公司	57848
404	顺德市德胜电厂有限公司	57824
405	上海肯德基有限公司	57714
406	秦皇岛正大有限公司	57687
407	辽宁大成农牧实业有限公司	57649
408	洛阳春都实业有限公司	57571
409	索尼精密部件(惠州)有限公司	57434
410	北京可口可乐饮料有限公司	56950
411	天津宝洁有限公司	56916
412	上海动力设备有限公司	56825
413	好孩子儿童用品有限公司	56730
414	天津通广三星电子有限公司	56576
415	上海裕安智盈显示设备有限公司	56519
416	东莞德永佳纺织制衣有限公司	56471
417	北京百盛轻工发展有限公司	56465
418	建泰橡胶(深圳)有限公司	56457

1999年中国最大500家外商投资企业名录

金额单位:万元人民币

位次	企业名称	销售额
419	武汉可口可乐饮料有限公司	56443
420	上海百霖木业有限公司	56438
421	长春长铃摩托车有限公司	56279
422	天津正大饲料科技有限公司	56273
423	广东恒福置业有限公司	56269
424	韶关发电D厂有限公司	56210
425	上海惠普有限公司	56134
426	侨鑫集团有限公司	55938
427	上海－易初摩托车有限公司	55596
428	山东凤祥－爱迪西有限公司	55463
429	上海邮电通信设备股份有限公司	55423
430	三水健力宝富特容器有限公司	55403
431	中山嘉华电子(集团)有限公司	55201
432	亚星－奔驰有限公司	55069
433	开封正大有限公司	54946
434	广州羊城汽车有限公司	54809
435	正大岳阳有限公司	54713
436	华新利乐(佛山)包装有限公司	54684
437	东莞华强三洋马达有限公司	54657
438	苏州爱普生显示元器件有限公司	54559
439	苏州工业园区华能阿莫科清洁能源有限公司	54418
440	上海嘉汇达房地产开发经营有限公司	54212
441	深圳南顺油脂有限公司	53667
442	东莞市石龙京瓷光学有限公司	53666
443	扬子巴斯夫苯乙烯系列有限公司	53503
444	汕头海洋第一聚苯树脂有限公司	53441
445	上海太平国际货柜有限公司	53095
446	武进大众钢铁有限公司	52999
447	广东东芝万家乐制冷设备有限公司	52976
448	常熟松下阪神电器有限公司	52797
449	江苏双良特灵溴化锂制冷机有限公司	52700
450	东洲油脂工业(广州)有限公司	52619
451	飞利浦亚明照明有限公司	52454
452	江阴博丰钢铁有限公司	52357
453	大连中集集装箱制造有限公司	52300
454	厦门建松电器有限公司	52289
455	上海轻骑国际贸易有限公司	52210
456	惠州三星电子有限公司	52004

1999年中国最大500家外商投资企业名录

金额单位:万元人民币

位 次	企 业 名 称	销 售 额
457	上海英雄股份有限公司	51986
458	临沂新程肉制品有限公司	51672
459	深圳南油(集团)有限公司	51643
460	上海奇华顿罗亚有限公司	51563
461	深圳王利电机有限公司	51476
462	上海联吉合纤有限公司	51397
463	广东清连公路发展有限公司	51264
464	唐山国丰钢铁有限公司	51254
465	高明市高丰针织企业有限公司	51204
466	北京松下.电子部品有限公司	51067
467	蛇口南顺面粉有限公司	51038
468	河南新中益电力有限公司	51023
469	丸红(上海)有限公司	51010
470	北京恩德斯豪斯电子有限公司	50959
471	洛阳玻璃股份有限公司	50903
472	本溪北龙烧结有限公司	50889
473	上海福海木业企业有限公司	50695
474	北京麦当劳食品有限公司	50690
475	上海德尔福汽车空调系统有限公司	50656
476	佛山电器照明股份有限公司	50484
477	仪化佛山聚酯有限公司	50476
478	重庆奥妮化妆品有限公司	50332
479	深圳南海粮食工业有限公司	50208
480	北京冠海房地产有限公司	50176
481	广东健力宝饮料有限公司	50136
482	东莞普思电子有限公司	50119
483	深圳方大实业股份有限公司	50076
484	上海瑞侃电缆附件有限公司	50068
485	东南(福建)汽车工业有限公司	50065
486	中法合营王朝葡萄酿酒有限公司	49943
487	广州市东迅房地产发展有限公司	49703
488	南京中萃食品有限公司	49570
489	上海永久自行车股份有限公司	49493
490	台山市金桥铝型材厂有限公司	49467
491	捷安特(中国)有限公司	49322
492	爱芬食品(北京)有限公司	49156
493	苏州迅达电梯有限公司	49108
494	朗讯科技(中国)有限公司	49008

1999年中国最大500家外商投资企业名录

金额单位:万元人民币

位次	企业名称	销售额
495	大连浦金钢板有限公司	48859
496	长营电器(深圳)有限公司	48821
497	杭州旺旺食品有限公司	48814
498	依利安达(广州)电子有限公司	48681
499	长沙旺旺食品有限公司	48554
500	潍坊光澳纸业有限公司	48552

1999年中国对外承包工程和劳务合作合同额分国家(地区)总值

金额单位:万美元

国家和地区	合计	承包工程	劳务合作	设计咨询
合计	**1300198**	**1019897**	**263244**	**17057**
亚洲小计:	**753601**	**579693**	**167832**	**6076**
香港	292683	276704	15792	187
澳门	12746	5471	7260	15
台湾省	14488	0	14481	7
朝鲜	817	600	127	90
越南	11788	9203	2033	552
老挝	9774	9356	205	213
柬埔寨	8428	3974	4427	27
蒙古	7293	3958	3332	3
日本	36115	149	35875	91
菲律宾	5444	5269	175	0
缅甸	48224	45891	835	1498
泰国	30680	29984	640	56
马来西亚	14685	13014	1050	621
新加坡	117560	77197	40245	118
文莱	20	0	20	0
印度尼西亚	7194	3947	3168	79
巴基斯坦	18301	17697	132	472
孟加拉国	13841	12555	798	488
印度	2502	2243	151	108
尼泊尔	6546	6469	67	10
斯里兰卡	6054	5875	128	51
马尔代夫	949	0	947	2
伊朗	11408	10163	37	1208

1999年中国对外承包工程和劳务合作合同额分国家(地区)总值

金额单位:万美元

国家和地区	合　计	承包工程	劳务合作	设计咨询
土耳其	120	0	120	0
塞浦路斯	103	0	103	0
叙利亚	843	821	22	0
黎巴嫩	3144	3130	14	0
约旦	879	532	347	0
巴勒斯坦	12	0	0	12
也门共和国	12286	12169	103	14
伊拉克	11488	11345	0	143
沙特阿拉伯	2930	1291	1639	0
科威特	1981	1012	969	0
卡塔尔	4134	3773	361	0
阿拉伯联合酋长国	7790	4114	3676	0
阿曼	37	0	36	1
韩国	17758	150	17598	10
以色列	12556	1637	10919	0
非洲小计:	**186432**	**166483**	**18306**	**1643**
埃及	3375	3061	87	227
苏丹	15396	14725	77	594
利比亚	981	378	599	4
突尼斯	548	511	37	0
阿尔及利亚	13521	12365	1156	0
摩洛哥	1988	522	1466	0
毛里塔尼亚	1791	921	868	2
塞内加尔	5104	5100	4	0
冈比亚	14	0	14	0
几内亚比绍	5220	5172	35	13
马里	7461	7308	147	6
几内亚	2497	1899	577	21
加纳	6218	5756	439	23
科特迪瓦	6669	6503	159	7
贝宁	484	411	72	1
尼日尔	652	575	76	1
利比里亚	3554	0	3554	0
塞拉利昂	415	415	0	0
多哥	132	104	22	6
尼日利亚	20670	19875	795	0
喀麦隆	1191	229	601	361

1999年中国对外承包工程和劳务合作合同额分国家(地区)总值

金额单位:万美元

国家和地区	合 计	承包工程	劳务合作	设计咨询
赤道几内亚	6213	6200	0	13
中非	293	291	2	0
加蓬	2462	2063	399	0
刚果	53	43	6	4
扎伊尔	78	47	24	7
佛得角	22	4	1	17
圣多美和普林西比	1	1	0	0
布隆迪	1014	1004	10	0
卢旺达	2173	2169	0	4
埃塞俄比亚	16763	15998	750	15
吉布提	742	710	32	0
肯尼亚	5337	4602	735	0
乌干达	2171	2124	45	2
坦桑尼亚	5804	5504	30	270
塞舌尔	4309	4254	55	0
毛里求斯	5267	1228	4038	1
科摩罗	447	443	4	0
马达加斯加	2873	2803	70	0
安哥拉	1385	1381	0	4
莫桑比克	1689	1650	2	37
赞比亚	4823	4820	3	0
马拉维	764	764	0	0
津巴布韦	4109	4071	38	0
斯威士兰	39	0	39	0
博次瓦纳	7529	7399	130	0
莱索托	2123	1502	618	3
南非	7692	7250	442	0
纳米比亚	2031	1983	48	0
厄立特里亚	345	345	0	0
欧洲小计:	**82451**	**56636**	**24236**	**1579**
波兰	540	486	54	0
匈牙利	56	0	56	0
捷克共和国	46	0	46	0
保加利亚	737	3	734	0
阿尔巴尼亚	144	0	8	136
罗马尼亚	832	145	687	0
德国	6396	1073	5298	25

1999年中国对外承包工程和劳务合作合同额分国家(地区)总值

金额单位:万美元

国家和地区	合　计	承包工程	劳务合作	设计咨询
南斯拉夫	9179	8934	185	60
法国	917	2	898	17
意大利	427	79	338	10
荷兰	456	227	187	42
比利时	2243	2100	143	0
卢森堡	20	0	20	0
英国	5098	3843	1255	0
爱尔兰	20	0	20	0
丹麦	36	0	36	0
芬兰	537	513	24	0
瑞典	2630	2502	128	0
挪威	1068	657	411	0
冰岛	2	0	2	0
瑞士	196	58	138	0
奥地利	452	372	80	0
希腊	84	5	79	0
马耳他	5	0	5	0
西班牙	243	0	243	0
葡萄牙	45	0	43	2
俄罗斯联邦	36002	23665	12225	112
乌克兰	358	0	358	0
乌兹别克斯坦	1000	1000	0	0
哈萨克斯坦	8970	7677	118	1175
摩尔多瓦	53	0	53	0
吉尔吉斯斯坦	943	801	142	0
塔吉克斯坦	508	448	60	0
亚美尼亚	31	31	0	0
土库曼斯坦	1731	1710	21	0
爱沙尼亚	10	10	0	0
拉脱维亚共和国	38	0	38	0
阿塞拜疆共和国	315	295	20	0
格鲁吉亚共和国	83	0	83	0
拉丁美洲小计:	**29758**	**23947**	**5636**	**175**
墨西哥	9020	8211	809	0
危地马拉	75	0	75	0
洪都拉斯	172	0	172	0
萨尔瓦多	42	0	42	0

1999年中国对外承包工程和劳务合作合同额分国家(地区)总值

金额单位:万美元

国家和地区	合　计	承包工程	劳务合作	设计咨询
尼加拉瓜	375	0	375	0
巴拿马	1240	0	1240	0
古巴	256	144	112	0
多米尼加共和国	7	0	7	0
牙买加	120	0	120	0
特立尼达和多巴哥	493	492	1	0
巴巴多斯	518	518	0	0
委内瑞拉	5811	5066	678	67
哥伦比亚	64	60	4	0
圭亚那	526	486	34	6
巴西	500	500	0	0
厄瓜多尔	135	11	116	8
秘鲁	3387	3355	32	0
玻利维亚	154	113	39	2
阿根廷	2027	711	1316	0
乌拉圭	27	0	27	0
巴哈马	47	0	47	0
英属维尔京	40	0	40	0
安提瓜	1610	1527	0	83
多米尼加	636	636	0	0
圣卢西亚	322	240	78	4
圣文森特格	59	0	59	0
苏里南	2095	1877	213	5
北美洲小计:	**50074**	**25628**	**24080**	**366**
加拿大	1221	163	1044	14
美国	48533	25465	22716	352
美国塞班	320	0	320	0
大洋洲及太平洋岛屿小计:	**12357**	**6184**	**6127**	**46**
澳大利亚	1581	1100	475	6
新西兰	468	0	468	0
西萨摩亚	330	186	142	2
汤加	1	0	1	0
斐济	1628	1258	364	6
巴布亚新几内亚	1746	1440	304	2
基里巴斯	42	12	0	30
瓦努阿图	24	22	2	0
法属波利尼西亚	47	0	47	0

1999 年中国对外承包工程和劳务合作合同额分国家(地区)总值

金额单位:万美元

国家和地区	合　计	承包工程	劳务合作	设计咨询
马绍尔群岛	29	29	0	0
密克罗尼西亚	2948	1215	1733	0
其他太平洋岛屿	2657	222	2435	0
贝劳	856	700	156	0
其他小计:	**185525**	**161326**	**17027**	**7172**
其他	**6425**	**5135**	**1283**	**7**
国境内	**179100**	**156191**	**15744**	**7165**

1999 年中国对外承包工程和劳务合作营业额分国家(地区)总值

金额单位:万美元

国家和地区	合　计	承包工程	劳务合作	设计咨询
合　　计	**1123458**	**852232**	**262268**	**8958**
亚洲小计:	**624719**	**450209**	**171100**	**3410**
香港	219212	196653	22468	91
澳门	24932	11824	13084	24
台湾省	14112	2	13978	132
朝鲜	1349	1209	140	0
越南	8317	6534	1343	440
老挝	8510	8321	169	20
柬埔寨	4107	1501	2592	14
蒙古	2582	1139	1440	3
日本	28768	316	28330	122
菲律宾	5876	5558	318	0
缅甸	19783	19269	429	85
泰国	12520	10865	1182	473
马来西亚	10760	8793	1450	517
新加坡	101864	53085	48732	47
文莱	1720	1673	47	0
印度尼西亚	5490	2240	3207	43
巴基斯坦	30798	30577	86	135
孟加拉国	15535	14491	649	395
印度	3351	2642	592	117
尼泊尔	6425	6360	41	24
斯里兰卡	5079	4645	419	15
马尔代夫	494	0	492	2
伊朗	20582	20012	25	545

1999年中国对外承包工程和劳务合作营业额分国家(地区)总值

金额单位:万美元

国家和地区	合 计	承包工程	劳务合作	设计咨询
土耳其	363	66	274	23
塞浦路斯	856	669	187	0
叙利亚	806	786	20	0
黎巴嫩	16	0	16	0
约旦	1253	1140	107	6
巴勒斯坦	11	0	5	6
也门共和国	9668	9467	189	12
伊拉克	4391	4316	0	75
沙特阿拉伯	4540	3390	1149	1
科威特	21580	18750	2798	32
巴林	3	0	3	0
卡塔尔	252	203	49	0
阿拉伯联合酋长国	4487	2517	1970	0
阿曼	47	0	46	1
韩国	16740	148	16582	10
以色列	7540	1048	6492	0
非洲小计:	**203629**	**182770**	**20312**	**547**
埃及	1600	1508	61	31
苏丹	74337	72893	1231	213
利比亚	1171	289	878	4
突尼斯	1027	998	29	0
阿尔及利亚	10667	8962	1705	0
摩洛哥	1546	123	1420	3
毛里塔尼亚	2973	1718	1252	3
塞内加尔	5426	5399	27	0
冈比亚	66	49	17	0
几内亚比绍	5016	5000	16	0
马里	9989	9884	95	10
几内亚	1633	1085	527	21
加纳	1473	978	474	21
科特迪瓦	4961	4877	77	7
布基纳法索	250	248	2	0
贝宁	294	220	71	3
尼日尔	935	905	29	1
利比里亚	2055	0	2055	0
塞拉利昂	571	466	105	0
多哥	576	552	18	6
尼日利亚	10881	10372	508	1

1999年中国对外承包工程和劳务合作营业额分国家(地区)总值

金额单位:万美元

国家和地区	合　计	承包工程	劳务合作	设计咨询
喀麦隆	1809	1648	159	2
赤道几内亚	5189	5084	89	16
中非	261	259	2	0
加蓬	3278	2928	350	0
刚果	47	43	4	0
扎伊尔	650	648	2	0
佛得角	101	89	0	12
圣多美和普林西比	50	50	0	0
布隆迪	43	25	18	0
卢旺达	1634	1523	108	3
埃塞俄比亚	3811	3668	127	16
吉布提	676	660	15	1
肯尼亚	5537	5345	192	0
乌干达	1512	1485	25	2
坦桑尼亚	3681	3569	80	32
塞舌尔	3118	2923	195	0
毛里求斯	8193	902	7222	69
科摩罗	66	62	4	0
马达加斯加	1996	1907	84	5
安哥拉	830	827	0	3
莫桑比克	1070	1019	11	40
赞比亚	2048	2027	21	0
马拉维	220	220	0	0
津巴布韦	8490	8449	41	0
斯威士兰	18	0	18	0
博次瓦纳	5740	5525	214	1
莱索托	1013	798	215	0
南非	2157	1746	409	2
纳米比亚	2597	2481	110	6
厄立特里亚	347	334	0	13
欧洲小计:	**30616**	**12593**	**17102**	**921**
波兰	476	434	42	0
匈牙利	213	0	213	0
捷克共和国	62	0	62	0
保加利亚	352	3	349	0
阿尔巴尼亚	226	208	2	16
罗马尼亚	802	125	677	0
德国	3238	392	2801	45

1999年中国对外承包工程和劳务合作营业额分国家(地区)总值

金额单位:万美元

国家和地区	合 计	承包工程	劳务合作	设计咨询
南斯拉夫	1978	1416	112	450
法国	1120	2	1087	31
意大利	682	399	253	30
荷兰	449	218	193	38
比利时	342	210	132	0
卢森堡	19	0	19	0
英国	3324	668	2379	277
爱尔兰	8	0	8	0
丹麦	43	0	43	0
芬兰	367	305	62	0
瑞典	115	10	105	0
挪威	901	388	513	0
冰岛	1	0	1	0
瑞士	172	15	157	0
奥地利	393	300	93	0
希腊	539	5	534	0
马耳他	77	8	69	0
西班牙	453	0	453	0
葡萄牙	10	0	10	0
圣马力诺	24	0	24	0
俄罗斯联邦	9095	3322	5751	22
乌克兰	504	62	442	0
白俄罗斯	19	0	19	0
乌兹别克斯坦	496	495	1	0
哈萨克斯坦	933	871	55	7
摩尔多瓦	99	0	99	0
吉尔吉斯斯坦	50	0	50	0
塔吉克斯坦	583	495	88	0
亚美尼亚	36	36	0	0
土库曼斯坦	2197	2191	1	5
立陶宛	1	0	1	0
拉脱维亚共和国	3	0	3	0
阿塞拜疆共和国	194	15	179	0
格鲁吉亚共和国	3	0	3	0
斯洛文尼亚共和国	17	0	17	0
拉丁美洲小计:	**14366**	**7184**	**6969**	**213**
墨西哥	187	10	177	0
危地马拉	36	0	36	0

1999年中国对外承包工程和劳务合作营业额分国家(地区)总值

金额单位:万美元

国家和地区	合　计	承包工程	劳务合作	设计咨询
洪都拉斯	59	0	59	0
萨尔瓦多	55	0	55	0
尼加拉瓜	105	0	105	0
巴拿马	3407	0	3407	0
古巴	139	90	49	0
多米尼加共和国	2	0	2	0
牙买加	618	9	609	0
特立尼达和多巴哥	415	415	0	0
巴巴多斯	311	286	18	7
委内瑞拉	963	47	826	90
哥伦比亚	2	0	2	0
圭亚那	183	111	66	6
巴西	319	238	81	0
厄瓜多尔	834	713	109	12
秘鲁	873	756	111	6
玻利维亚	23	0	23	0
智利	189	150	39	0
巴拉圭	25	0	25	0
阿根廷	1331	711	620	0
乌拉圭	72	0	72	0
巴哈马	29	0	29	0
英属维尔京	51	0	51	0
安提瓜	970	887	0	83
多米尼加	645	636	9	0
圣卢西亚	1122	993	125	4
圣文森特格	46	0	46	0
伯利兹英属	23	1	22	0
苏里南	1331	1131	195	5
圣马丁	1	0	1	0
北美洲小计:	**33088**	**10367**	**22534**	**187**
加拿大	571	248	323	0
美国	32316	10119	22010	187
美国塞班	201	0	201	0
大洋洲及太平洋岛屿小计:	**18221**	**11950**	**6250**	**21**
澳大利亚	1657	1345	312	0
新西兰	479	0	479	0
西萨摩亚	331	140	189	2
汤加	4	0	4	0

1999年中国对外承包工程和劳务合作营业额分国家(地区)总值

金额单位:万美元

国家和地区	合计	承包工程	劳务合作	设计咨询
斐济	1152	561	585	6
巴布亚新几内亚	8568	8115	451	2
基里巴斯	19	7	1	11
所罗门群岛	1	0	1	0
瓦努阿图	105	99	6	0
法属波利尼西亚	62	0	62	0
马绍尔群岛	19	2	17	0
密克罗尼西亚	2784	779	2005	0
东萨摩亚	239	0	239	0
其他太平洋岛屿	2009	158	1851	0
厄里特立亚	1	0	1	0
贝劳	791	744	47	0
其他小计:	**198819**	**177159**	**18001**	**3659**
其他	5851	4414	1429	8
国境内	192968	172745	16572	3651

1999年中国对外承包工程和劳务合作合同分公司总值

名称	合同数(份)	合同额(万美元)			
		合计	承包工程	劳务合作	设计咨询
合计	**21126**	**1300198**	**1019897**	**263244**	**17057**
中央合计	**4779**	**598973**	**559309**	**36619**	**3045**
中国建筑工程总公司	180	192295	191727	375	193
中国广播电视国际经济技术合作公司	3	273	273	0	0
中国冶金建设集团总公司	5	24947	24926	0	21
中国水产(集团)总公司	11	3990	3900	90	0
中国国际技术智力合作公司	2191	17176	0	17176	0
中国路桥(集团)总公司	54	22496	22496	0	0
中国土木工程集团公司	109	22612	20907	1705	0
中国港湾建设(集团)总公司	43	37429	36426	868	135
中国海外工程总公司	88	10670	10226	444	0
中国水利电力对外公司	16	8711	8711	0	0
中国石化工程建设公司	2	330	300	30	0
中国化学工程(集团)公司	10	7470	7288	182	0
中国轻工业对外经济技术合作公司	104	1644	696	948	0

1999年中国对外承包工程和劳务合作合同分公司总值

名称	合同数(份)	合同额(万美元)			
		合计	承包工程	劳务合作	设计咨询
中国电子国际经济技术合作公司	22	1296	1106	190	0
中国地质工程集团公司	38	9316	9316	0	0
中国国际展览公司	13	77	77	0	0
中国农牧渔业国际合作公司	16	596	566	3	27
中国航空技术国际工程公司	12	1281	1159	122	0
中国国际计算机软件工程公司	20	423	0	423	0
中国林业国际合作公司	3	116	0	116	0
中国建材工业对外经济技术合作公司	17	1244	407	833	4
中国万宝工程公司	21	14167	13759	408	0
中国交远国际经济技术合作公司	20	679	227	452	0
中国海员对外经济技术合作公司	2	168	0	168	0
中国石油工程建设(集团)公司	1	430	400	30	0
科智国际技术合作公司	20	170	0	170	0
中国四达国际经济技术合作公司	139	529	0	529	0
中海国际石油工程有限责任公司	7	253	253	0	0
中国国际工程咨询公司	6	60	0	60	0
中国体育国际经济技术合作公司	7	210	95	115	0
中国海外贸易总公司	11	447	0	447	0
中国电子系统工程总公司	1	296	296	0	0
中国铁道建筑总公司	25	17302	15851	1451	0
中国建筑材料工业建设总公司	3	87	0	87	0
中国化工建设总公司	12	1702	1592	0	110
中国出国人员服务总公司	6	80	0	80	0
中国海外经济合作总公司	8	1512	1447	65	0
中国机械设备进出口总公司	16	4564	4559	5	0
中国寰球化学工程公司	25	3403	3025	33	345
中国机械对外经济技术合作公司	9	2299	2222	77	0
远大国际经济合作有限责任公司	10	156	148	8	0
中国有色金属建设股份有限公司	5	3167	3117	50	0
中国医疗卫生对外经济合作公司	23	157	154	3	0
中国纺织工业对外经济技术合作公司	26	119	109	10	0
长城国际经济技术合作有限公司	0	1	0	1	0
中国化工进出口总公司	46	310	0	310	0
中国航空工业规划设计院	10	112	0	0	112
中国通信建设总公司	2	221	221	0	0
中远对外劳务合作公司	79	3590	0	3590	0
中国成套设备进出口集团总公司	42	8416	8131	280	5

1999 年中国对外承包工程和劳务合作合同分公司总值

名　　称	合同数（份）	合同额(万美元)			
		合计	承包工程	劳务合作	设计咨询
中国对外建设总公司	5	174	174	0	0
轻工业部规划设计院	6	42	0	0	42
北京有色冶金设计研究总院	4	143	136	7	0
燕兴国际经济技术合作公司	1	80	0	80	0
中国铁路工程总公司	81	37405	36692	392	321
北京中民国际经济合作公司	2	460	0	460	0
北京煤炭设计研究院(集团)	5	1048	0	0	1048
中国技术进出口总公司	1	4	0	4	0
北京钢铁设计研究院	6	255	231	0	24
中国电力技术进出口公司	16	6527	6317	210	0
华北电力设计院	4	7694	7680	0	14
中国安能建设总公司	4	3224	3224	0	0
华鑫国际经济贸易公司	3	9	0	9	0
中翰科技经济发展总公司	2	11	0	11	0
中国京冶建设工程承包公司	2	368	368	0	0
中外园林建设总公司	2	331	331	0	0
广播电影电视部设计院	6	5	0	0	5
核工业第二研究设计院	1	2	0	0	2
中交公路规划设计院	4	0	0	0	0
国内贸易部设计院	2	12	0	5	7
建设部综合勘察研究院	1	10	10	0	0
林业部林产工业规划设计院	3	49	0	0	49
中国友发国际工程设计咨询公司	22	54	0	23	31
中国石化北京设计院	1	519	0	0	519
中土畜劳务合作有限公司	102	810	0	810	0
中远工业公司	1	149	149	0	0
中国国际人才开发中心	668	209	0	209	0
中水远洋渔业有限责任公司	18	16948	15390	1558	0
北京市地质矿产勘查开发总公司	1	13	0	0	13
中国机械工业安装总公司	4	69	69	0	0
华北电力国际经贸公司	1	54	0	54	0
中设国际工程有限公司	17	9120	9120	0	0
中国工程与农业机械进出口总公司	14	16066	16066	0	0
北京中水远洋渔业发展公司	1	0	0	0	0
中国新星石油公司	6	5230	5210	20	0
中国燕兴总公司	2	25	0	25	0
中海石油工程设计公司	6	168	168	0	0

1999 年中国对外承包工程和劳务合作合同分公司总值

名　　称	合同数（份）	合同额（万美元）			
		合计	承包工程	劳务合作	设计咨询
中国电力建设工程咨询公司	5	383	374	0	9
中国水利水电工程总公司	10	26014	26014	0	0
中京邮电通信设计院	3	41	0	32	9
中汽对外经济技术合作公司	143	2247	2247	0	0
中国华联国际贸易公司	11	540	0	540	0
中国华阳技术贸易(集团)公司	13	236	0	236	0
中油技术服务有限责任公司	21	9162	9162	0	0
中国石油技术开发公司	5	9354	9354	0	0
中国华润有限公司	2	13855	13855	0	0
中地石油工程公司	2	855	855	0	0
地方合计	**16347**	**701225**	**460588**	**226625**	**14012**
北京市	**90**	**25232**	**18405**	**6517**	**310**
中国北京国际经济合作公司	32	349	0	349	0
北京市建筑工程总公司	25	2089	2022	67	0
北京市政工程设计研究院	5	225	0	6	219
北京市建筑设计院	7	91	0	0	91
北京住宅开发建设集团总公司	7	7464	7464	0	0
北京城建集团总公司	1	8900	8900	0	0
首钢总公司国际经贸部	1	139	0	139	0
四通国际经济技术合作公司	6	90	0	90	0
北京市外国企业服务总公司	5	5866	0	5866	0
北京市第二房修工程公司	1	19	19	0	0
天津市	**385**	**21172**	**10282**	**10429**	**461**
中国天津国际经济技术合作公司	205	10271	1155	9116	0
天津立达国际劳务工程公司	2	258	0	258	0
天津建工集团总公司	20	2999	2234	765	0
天津市建筑设计院	5	10	0	2	8
天津水泥工业设计研究院	8	4876	4754	0	122
铁道部第三勘测设计院	2	9	0	9	0
中国天辰化学工程公司	2	1500	1440	0	60
机械部第五设计研究院	9	93	13	0	80
天津市政设计研究院	4	129	0	0	129
天津市亿利达集团有限公司	20	29	0	29	0
天津市化工设计院	19	76	37	0	39
中国成套天津公司	7	152	0	152	0
天津机械进出口集团有限公司	19	29	0	27	2
天津纺织进出口集团有限公司	1	17	0	17	0

1999年中国对外承包工程和劳务合作合同分公司总值

名　　称	合同数(份)	合同额(万美元)			
		合计	承包工程	劳务合作	设计咨询
天津机械设备进出口公司	1	0	0	0	0
水利部天津水利水电勘测设计研究院	6	15	0	7	8
天津五矿进出口集团有限公司	1	12	0	12	0
大港油田集团有限责任公司	36	433	433	0	0
天海集团股份有限公司	4	35	0	35	0
天津开发区苏伊士国合有限公司	1	54	54	0	0
天津市海岸带公司	1	13	0	0	13
铁道部第十八局	1	148	148	0	0
天津市地质工程勘察院	11	14	14	0	0
河北省	**280**	**11639**	**5769**	**5660**	**210**
中国河北国际经济技术合作公司	47	948	101	847	0
石家庄国际经济技术合作公司	117	1237	192	1045	0
河北公路工程建设集团有限公司	2	60	60	0	0
河北建工集团有限责任公司	34	1692	0	1692	0
核工部第四设计研究院	2	55	55	0	0
唐山国际工程总公司	5	1754	721	1033	0
中国耀华玻璃(集团)公司	1	45	0	45	0
张家口对外劳务工程公司	8	124	0	124	0
秦皇岛国际经济技术合作公司	2	960	750	0	210
地矿河北工程勘测公司	1	77	77	0	0
保定国际经济技术合作公司	21	187	0	187	0
承德对外经济合作公司	3	31	0	31	0
唐山对外合作公司	6	203	0	203	0
铁道部建场工程局	2	421	421	0	0
河北省水利工程局	4	645	615	30	0
河北国际供销合作总公司	4	158	0	158	0
华北石油管理局	1	500	500	0	0
河北省进出口贸易公司	1	2	0	2	0
河北省纺织品进出口公司	1	12	0	12	0
廊坊对外经济技术合作有限公司	2	18	0	18	0
邢台路桥公司	3	1260	1260	0	0
辰光集团公司	5	333	300	33	0
沧州对外经济技术合作公司	6	200	0	200	0
唐山安装工程公司	2	717	717	0	0
山西省	**117**	**4611**	**3681**	**881**	**49**
中国山西国际经济技术合作公司	22	227	186	41	0
山西省建筑工程总公司	2	632	0	632	0

1999年中国对外承包工程和劳务合作合同分公司总值

名称	合同数(份)	合同额(万美元)			
		合计	承包工程	劳务合作	设计咨询
太原市国际经济技术合作公司	15	137	0	137	0
太原钢铁(集团)公司	1	4	0	4	0
山西省电力公司	23	820	820	0	0
山西省送变电工程公司	2	185	185	0	0
山西省公路桥梁工程总公司	4	588	588	0	0
化工部第二设计院	4	347	300	1	46
山西四建集团有限公司	17	16	1	15	0
煤炭部太原设计研究院	12	21	0	18	3
太原重型机器进出口公司	11	1439	1432	7	0
中国第十三冶金建设公司	4	195	169	26	0
内蒙古自治区	**102**	**5298**	**698**	**4576**	**24**
中国内蒙古国际经济技术合作公司	7	148	0	148	0
冶金部包头钢铁设计研究院	3	24	0	0	24
呼伦贝尔盟国际经济技术合作公司	14	821	0	821	0
满洲里国际经济技术合作有限公司	22	325	0	325	0
二连浩特国际经济技术合作公司	12	1121	97	1024	0
锡林郭勒国际经济技术合作公司	5	213	0	213	0
额尔古纳国际经济技术合作公司	3	90	0	90	0
内蒙古高等院校科技开发集团	5	95	0	95	0
二连浩特市华天对外贸易有限责任公司	3	184	60	124	0
满洲里东方国际贸易股份有限公司	2	103	0	103	0
满洲里华运公司	3	500	0	500	0
内蒙古北疆进出口贸易(集团)公司满洲里	1	96	0	96	0
中国内蒙古森林工业集团有限责任公司	5	493	0	493	0
新三维国际经济技术合作股份有限公司	6	245	141	104	0
呼和浩特铁路对外经济技术合作公司	6	438	224	214	0
包头兴业集团股份有限公司	1	85	85	0	0
满洲里远大经贸有限责任公司	1	33	0	33	0
满洲里济合经贸公司	1	91	91	0	0
二连浩特天域贸易有限公司	1	97	0	97	0
巴盟亚欧贸易有限责任公司	1	96	0	96	0
辽宁省	**1288**	**42902**	**20989**	**21869**	**44**
中国辽宁国际合作(集团)股份有限公司	135	6814	4718	2096	0
辽宁省建设集团公司	0	37	0	37	0
辽宁国际建设工程集团公司	2	1600	1600	0	0
鞍山国际经济技术合作公司	6	1084	860	224	0
抚顺对外建设经济合作(集团)股份公司	20	395	38	357	0

1999年中国对外承包工程和劳务合作合同分公司总值

名称	合同数(份)	合同额(万美元)			
		合计	承包工程	劳务合作	设计咨询
本溪对外经济技术合作总公司	5	781	0	781	0
丹东国际经济技术合作公司	36	137	0	137	0
营口国际经济技术合作公司	5	5	0	5	0
鞍山焦化耐火材料设计院	3	19	0	0	19
东北电力集团进出口公司	1	101	101	0	0
锦州华锦国际经贸股份有限公司	21	205	0	203	2
铁岭国际经济技术合作公司	17	72	0	72	0
辽宁华曦集团	6	124	0	124	0
辽阳国际经济技术合作公司	14	1630	200	1430	0
鞍钢集团国际经济贸易公司	2	0	0	0	0
中国第三冶金建设公司	1	92	92	0	0
朝阳建设集团有限公司	5	313	313	0	0
辽宁食品进出口公司	10	114	0	114	0
辽宁粮油进出口公司	13	16	0	16	0
辽宁省国际劳务交流有限公司	4	60	0	60	0
本钢集团国际经济贸易有限公司	5	249	23	226	0
鞍山市对外建设工程承包集团公司	1	350	350	0	0
阜新国际经济技术合作公司	6	45	0	45	0
沈阳市	**132**	**6740**	**2975**	**3743**	**22**
中国沈阳国际经济技术合作公司	122	6231	2975	3256	0
沈阳对外经济建设总公司	2	423	0	423	0
沈阳海外建筑工程承包公司	2	32	0	32	0
煤炭工业部沈阳设计研究院	2	32	0	32	0
沈阳铝镁设计研究院	4	22	0	0	22
大连市	**838**	**21919**	**9719**	**12199**	**1**
中国大连合作(集团)股份有限公司	420	13629	7076	6553	0
瓦房店市国际工程公司	4	15	15	0	0
辽宁省大连海洋渔业集团公司	36	618	0	618	0
大连经济技术开发区劳务公司	104	287	0	287	0
大连工程总承包公司	4	2500	2500	0	0
大化国际经济贸易公司	3	108	0	108	0
大连华南国际经济技术合作公司	8	612	56	556	0
大连港国际经济技术合作公司	10	1377	0	1377	0
大连渤海建筑集团有限公司	3	207	72	135	0
大连远洋船员管理公司	33	110	0	110	0
中国外运大连公司	104	347	0	347	0
中国成套设备进出口大连公司	13	120	0	120	0

1999年中国对外承包工程和劳务合作合同分公司总值

名称	合同数(份)	合同额(万美元)			
		合计	承包工程	劳务合作	设计咨询
大连水产远洋渔业公司	15	909	0	909	0
大连亿达国际合作公司	2	104	0	104	0
辽宁成大股份公司	1	244	0	244	0
中国辽宁国际合作大连开发总公司	33	396	0	396	0
辽宁机械进出口公司	37	107	0	106	1
大连航运集团有限公司	8	99	0	99	0
大连对外服务贸易有限公司	0	130	0	130	0
吉林省	**306**	**39283**	**18029**	**21151**	**103**
中国吉林国际经济技术合作公司	18	1587	16	1571	0
吉林市对外经济技术合作公司	22	7271	0	7271	0
延边对外经济技术合作公司	19	1200	728	472	0
珲春国际经济技术合作公司	7	394	0	394	0
吉林化学工业进出口公司	6	63	0	63	0
吉林冶金建设公司	5	100	0	100	0
吉林省对外招商建设总公司	11	2317	1645	672	0
吉林省建筑总公司	2	70	50	20	0
延边海外经济技术合作公司	3	949	0	949	0
吉林建设开发集团公司	1	14	14	0	0
吉林省对外经济技术合作公司	9	154	26	128	0
吉林国际人才交流公司	5	101	0	101	0
吉林森林工业集团公司	3	7700	7700	0	0
吉林省对外经济发展公司	48	1660	0	1660	0
辽源对外经济技术合作公司	21	1734	500	1234	0
延边国际经济技术合作公司	5	613	0	613	0
吉林省纺织品进出口公司	3	47	30	17	0
四平远东外建合作公司	11	497	0	497	0
吉林化工工程公司	1	265	265	0	0
吉林省农业对外合作公司	16	537	0	537	0
通化金宝国际经济技术合作有限公司	3	599	582	17	0
吉林省新创对外工程公司	2	77	72	5	0
吉林省工程建设有限公司	4	2572	2550	22	0
吉林化工(集团)建设公司	29	3796	3593	100	103
吉林轻工集团股份公司	9	687	0	687	0
珲春对外经贸公司	1	89	0	89	0
吉林省海外工程有限公司	13	1044	258	786	0
长春国际经济技术合作公司	16	2244	0	2244	0
长春建工集团总公司	3	242	0	242	0

1999年中国对外承包工程和劳务合作合同分公司总值

名　　称	合同数(份)	合同额(万美元)			
		合计	承包工程	劳务合作	设计咨询
长春对外劳务合作公司	4	57	0	57	0
长春对外经济技术合作公司	5	426	0	426	0
长春星宇集团股份有限公司	1	177	0	177	0
黑龙江省	**206**	**33567**	**23916**	**9507**	**144**
中国黑龙江国际经济技术合作公司	10	1691	1062	599	30
黑龙江国际工程技术合作公司	9	917	497	420	0
黑龙江东方集团国际经济技术合作公司	3	4827	4640	187	0
黑龙江省森林工对外经济贸易公司	1	201	0	201	0
中国煤炭国际经济技术合作黑龙江公司	7	1841	1512	329	0
哈尔滨铁路局对外经济技术合作公司	6	494	420	74	0
黑龙江省瑞驰建设公司	5	132	132	0	0
齐齐哈尔国际经济技术合作公司	14	95	21	74	0
牡丹江国际经济技术合作公司	16	187	0	187	0
东宁宏达经济贸易公司	2	103	0	103	0
东宁国际经济技术合作公司	26	1080	18	1062	0
密山市经济技术合作公司	3	49	0	49	0
绥芬河国际经济技术合作公司	3	54	0	54	0
黑龙江其他企业	3	41	0	41	0
同江国际经济技术合作公司	9	237	0	237	0
大庆石油技术进出口公司	1	57	0	0	57
大庆油田研究设计院	1	57	0	0	57
黑河国际经济技术合作公司	14	474	219	255	0
伊春市边境贸易公司	11	213	80	133	0
萝北边境贸易公司	1	7	0	7	0
饶河县边境贸易公司	2	34	0	34	0
东宁欣荣经济贸易公司	5	183	0	183	0
同江市北江有限公司	4	155	0	155	0
绥芬河华城国际经济公司	3	1107	10	1097	0
绥芬河兴建经济贸易公司	4	190	55	135	0
绥芬河京鹏经济贸易公司	1	1	0	1	0
绥芬河英泰经贸公司	2	702	0	702	0
同江市农业综合公司	2	164	0	164	0
同江龙华经贸公司	1	41	0	41	0
绥芬河进出口公司	2	33	0	33	0
同江三友物资公司	1	1	0	1	0
绥芬河金地经贸公司	1	24	0	24	0
绥芬河兴远经贸公司	2	50	0	50	0

1999年中国对外承包工程和劳务合作合同分公司总值

名称	合同数（份）	合同额(万美元)			
		合计	承包工程	劳务合作	设计咨询
黑河龙亚经贸公司	1	20	0	20	0
中技贸易股份公司	2	2360	0	2360	0
绥芬河国际工程公司	2	78	0	78	0
黑龙江对外经贸公司	1	49	49	0	0
同江城龙经贸公司	1	10	0	10	0
黑河蓝天公司	2	136	0	136	0
抚远边贸公司	1	45	0	45	0
同江六和实业公司	1	2000	2000	0	0
哈尔滨市	**20**	**13427**	**13201**	**226**	**0**
哈尔滨国际经济技术合作公司	3	37	0	37	0
哈尔滨对外经济技术合作公司	10	73	0	73	0
哈尔滨中建工程公司	1	8	0	8	0
哈尔滨第二建设公司	2	108	0	108	0
哈尔滨电站工程责任有限公司	4	13201	13201	0	0
上海市	**1069**	**95729**	**75175**	**19515**	**1039**
中国上海外经(集团)有限公司	349	34268	23532	10736	0
上海对外劳务合作公司	90	1541	0	1541	0
上海对外建设公司	1	2	0	2	0
上海机械进出口(集团)有限公司	7	723	524	199	0
上海机械设备进出口公司	2	712	700	12	0
上海建筑设计研究院	7	227	0	0	227
上海轻工业设计研究院	17	53	0	0	53
上海电气(集团)总公司	2	2281	2281	0	0
上海市对外服务公司	78	5060	0	5060	0
上海轻纺工业对外经济技术合作公司	18	526	0	526	0
上海核工程研究设计院	5	74	0	0	74
上海医药设计院	4	103	0	0	103
中船第九设计研究院	9	106	0	0	106
华东建筑设计研究院	8	24	0	5	19
上海机电设计研究院	7	367	0	0	367
上海成套设备进出口公司	334	657	199	458	0
上海建工(集团)总公司	42	27486	27486	0	0
上海市政工程设计研究院	1	90	0	0	90
上海航空工业(集团)公司	3	62	0	62	0
上海水产(集团)公司	5	13	0	13	0
上海东方国际(集团)有限公司	34	549	0	549	0
上海浦东国际经济技术合作公司	10	1158	1004	154	0

1999年中国对外承包工程和劳务合作合同分公司总值

名称	合同数(份)	合同额(万美元)			
		合计	承包工程	劳务合作	设计咨询
中国华源集团有限公司	11	8782	8691	91	0
上海隧道工程股份有限公司	3	5209	5209	0	0
上海建筑装饰(集团)总公司	0	80	80	0	0
上海住总(集团)总公司	3	3175	3142	33	0
上海港口机械进出口有限公司	4	2254	2254	0	0
上海黄埔对外经济技术合作公司	11	74	0	74	0
上海园林(集团)公司	4	73	73	0	0
江苏省	**809**	**81592**	**52166**	**29290**	**136**
中国江苏国际经济技术合作公司	132	18351	14827	3524	0
江苏省建筑工程总公司	9	527	105	422	0
南通国际经济技术合作公司	38	2142	660	1482	0
连云港国际经济技术合作公司	13	2361	0	2361	0
镇江国际经济技术合作公司	47	1358	411	947	0
扬州国际经济技术合作公司	36	752	0	752	0
苏州国际经济技术合作公司	29	400	88	312	0
无锡国际经济技术合作公司	3	79	0	79	0
常州国际经济技术合作(集团)有限公司	20	1105	80	1025	0
盐城国际经济技术合作公司	17	1717	0	1717	0
徐州国际经济技术合作公司	4	313	300	13	0
淮阴国际经济技术合作公司	17	772	0	772	0
江苏省建筑材料工业总公司	1	35	0	35	0
南化集团永利进出口公司	2	84	84	0	0
南京水泥工业设计院	5	423	418	0	5
张家港国际经济技术合作公司	4	1017	0	1017	0
江苏公路桥梁工程公司	31	614	611	3	0
江苏水利外经公司	1	131	131	0	0
南京化学工业集团公司设计院	3	63	63	0	0
启东市对外经济技术合作公司	18	1734	0	1734	0
南通第四建筑安装工程公司	5	3707	3607	100	0
南通市第三建筑安装工程公司	24	2851	0	2851	0
武进市建设工程公司	9	1317	1316	1	0
江苏地质工程有限公司	50	187	187	0	0
江苏农业对外经济技术合作公司	8	300	0	300	0
煤炭部南京设计研究院	1	368	368	0	0
常熟国际经济技术合作公司	13	416	0	416	0
江苏省建筑安装工程股份有限公司	2	326	326	0	0
无锡建筑工程公司	3	197	197	0	0

1999年中国对外承包工程和劳务合作合同分公司总值

名称	合同数（份）	合同额（万美元）			
		合计	承包工程	劳务合作	设计咨询
吴县国际经济技术合作公司	7	306	179	127	0
苏州建筑控股集团	11	657	657	0	0
南通建筑工程总承包公司	21	1005	0	1005	0
徐州矿务集团有限公司	2	238	0	238	0
徐州建筑安装工程公司	1	4	0	4	0
徐州工程机械集团公司	10	303	190	113	0
江都市建设工程总公司(集团)	18	1344	1244	100	0
江苏省泰兴市第一建筑安装工程公司	1	1300	0	1300	0
江苏省对外交流公司	51	1189	0	1189	0
中设江苏公司	5	516	477	39	0
江苏第一建筑安装有限公司	2	1949	1719	230	0
化工部连云港设计研究院	6	114	0	0	114
常州市对外经济技术贸易集团公司	12	1238	400	838	0
江苏天目安装集团公司	10	1027	875	152	0
盐城市天虹建筑工程总公司	4	437	250	187	0
江苏邗建集团有限公司	4	84	0	84	0
南通市第六建筑安装工程公司	6	631	200	431	0
苏州进出口(集团)有限公司	9	123	0	106	17
江苏正太股份有限公司	2	423	423	0	0
镇江建筑工程公司	4	510	329	181	0
苏州建设集团有限公司	1	190	190	0	0
江苏舜天机械进出口公司	1	8778	8778	0	0
金坛国际经济技术合作公司	7	1077	61	1016	0
南通市经济技术开发区总公司	4	752	0	752	0
金坛市建筑安装工程公司	3	1136	916	220	0
江苏省工业设备安装公司	2	69	69	0	0
南京市	**60**	**12545**	**11430**	**1115**	**0**
南京国际经济技术合作公司	32	1726	738	988	0
南京海外建筑工程公司	9	7616	7556	60	0
南京市住宅建设总公司	5	802	802	0	0
熊猫电子进出口公司	1	50	50	0	0
南京大地建设(集团)股份有限公司	6	1515	1465	50	0
金城集团进出口有限公司	6	36	19	17	0
南京纺织品进出口股份有限公司	1	800	800	0	0
浙江省	**709**	**22437**	**13825**	**8489**	**123**
中国浙江国际经济技术合作公司	204	3458	1709	1749	0
浙江省建工集团有限责任公司	39	6068	5490	578	0

1999年中国对外承包工程和劳务合作合同分公司总值

名 称	合同数（份）	合同额（万美元）			
		合计	承包工程	劳务合作	设计咨询
浙江省机械设备进出口总公司	3	46	0	46	0
杭州国际经济技术合作公司	19	250	0	250	0
温州国际经济技术合作公司	18	185	0	185	0
绍兴国际经济技术合作公司	7	1269	700	569	0
舟山国际经济技术合作公司	47	181	0	181	0
丽水国际经济技术合作公司	41	514	0	514	0
湖州对外经济技术合作有限公司	2	82	0	82	0
金华对外经济技术合作有限公司	0	70	0	70	0
台州国际经济技术合作公司	33	16	0	16	0
嘉兴市对外经济技术合作有限公司	3	33	0	33	0
浙江省粮油食品进出口股份有限公司	10	197	0	197	0
机械工业部第二设计研究院	3	28	25	0	3
电力工业部华东勘测设计研究院	2	120	0	0	120
浙江中大对外经济技术合作有限公司	9	281	0	281	0
浙江省轻工业品进出口公司	3	33	0	33	0
浙江东方集团股份有限公司	6	98	0	98	0
浙江舜杰建筑集团股份有限公司	6	258	178	80	0
诸暨市建筑安装工程公司	5	654	518	136	0
浙江中雷建筑集团股份有限公司	8	1211	1075	136	0
浙江省对外服务公司	9	142	0	142	0
绍兴市第一建筑安装工程公司	3	493	493	0	0
杭州市对外经济贸易服务公司	5	59	0	59	0
浙江宝业建工集团有限公司	0	557	557	0	0
浙江省其他企业	0	2169	2169	0	0
宁波市	**224**	**3965**	**911**	**3054**	**0**
中国宁波国际合作(集团)有限公司	188	1232	131	1101	0
宁波天地集团股份有限公司	6	168	0	168	0
宁波市建筑安装集团总公司	7	1360	780	580	0
鄞县进出口公司	15	90	0	90	0
宁波市工艺品进出口公司	8	1115	0	1115	0
安徽省	**73**	**8551**	**6309**	**2115**	**127**
安徽国际经济技术合作公司	8	533	62	467	4
化工部第三设计院	3	2131	2131	0	0
安徽省外经建设(集团)公司	15	3149	2277	872	0
合肥对外经济技术合作公司	12	129	0	129	0
冶金部马鞍山钢铁设计研究院	3	98	0	0	98
蚌埠国际经济技术合作公司	1	1020	1020	0	0

1999年中国对外承包工程和劳务合作合同分公司总值

名称	合同数（份）	合同额（万美元）			
		合计	承包工程	劳务合作	设计咨询
安徽省水利水电勘察设计院	1	4	0	0	4
芜湖国际经济技术合作公司	8	201	0	201	0
冶金部第十七冶金建设公司	1	244	244	0	0
安徽建筑设计研究院	2	23	0	15	8
合肥建筑集团公司	1	246	246	0	0
安徽省电力建设二公司	4	141	140	1	0
宿县地区国际经济技术合作公司	2	222	0	222	0
安庆国际经济技术合作公司	6	153	0	153	0
机械部第一设计研究院	1	30	30	0	0
煤炭部合肥设计研究院	0	8	1	0	7
铁道部第四工程局	1	158	158	0	0
安徽省古建园林市政建设总公司	1	6	0	0	6
淮南市国际经济技术合作公司	1	7	0	7	0
安徽华光玻璃集团有限公司	2	48	0	48	0
福建省	**2251**	**36134**	**6227**	**29814**	**93**
中国福建国际经济技术合作公司	378	3235	0	3235	0
福州国际经济技术合作公司	669	3346	0	3346	0
福建省对外劳务合作公司	139	3031	0	3031	0
福建福通对外经济技术合作公司	7	1817	0	1817	0
福建省水利水电勘测设计院	1	22	0	0	22
福建省建筑设计院	3	222	180	0	42
福建华源国际贸易经济合作公司	30	563	0	563	0
中国武夷实业总公司	13	2521	2412	109	0
莆田国际经济技术合作公司	73	1242	0	1242	0
中国泉州国际经济技术合作集团有限公司	478	1209	0	1209	0
中国漳州国际经济技术合作公司	86	1475	0	1475	0
福建厦门轮船总公司	3	3776	0	3776	0
三明国际经济技术合作公司	5	79	0	79	0
南平国际经济技术合作公司	10	54	0	54	0
福建省华洋水产集团公司	4	931	0	931	0
福建省轮船总公司	3	56	0	56	0
福州市劳务技术合作公司	33	668	0	668	0
福州壮安发展有限公司	8	603	0	603	0
福建省投资企业公司	5	52	0	52	0
福建省金福集团公司	16	881	0	881	0
福建省对外劳务咨询服务中心	2	3	0	3	0
福建中旅对外劳务合作公司	9	60	0	60	0

1999年中国对外承包工程和劳务合作合同分公司总值

名称	合同数(份)	合同额(万美元)			
		合计	承包工程	劳务合作	设计咨询
福建省外国机构服务中心	21	84	0	84	0
漳浦国际经济技术合作公司	6	443	0	443	0
福建华旅对外劳务合作公司	2	16	0	16	0
福建三木集团股份有限公司	23	505	0	505	0
莆田对外经济技术合作公司	31	215	0	215	0
福州市建筑设计院	8	29	0	0	29
福建省人才开发中心	4	30	0	30	0
福建轻纺工业经济技术公司	9	96	0	96	0
福建省对外经贸服务公司	8	100	0	100	0
泉州市对外经济技术服务公司	14	443	0	443	0
福建省工业设备安装有限公司	9	1805	1805	0	0
福州市进出口公司	2	21	0	21	0
福州建工集团公司	1	1830	1830	0	0
厦门市	**138**	**4671**	**0**	**4671**	**0**
中国厦门国际经济技术合作公司	120	4096	0	4096	0
厦门建隆发集团公司	11	342	0	342	0
厦门经济特区船务有限公司	3	172	0	172	0
厦门经济特区对外贸易集团公司	2	11	0	11	0
厦门诚毅船务公司	2	50	0	50	0
江西省	**117**	**11665**	**7739**	**3896**	**30**
中国江西国际经济技术合作公司	48	4009	1839	2170	0
南昌对外工程总公司	7	933	900	33	0
江西省建筑工程总公司	6	119	119	0	0
南昌国际经济技术合作公司	14	3111	2800	311	0
南昌有色冶金设计研究院	3	30	0	0	30
江西省轻工业对外经济技术合作公司	6	162	0	162	0
赣州国际经济技术合作公司	16	810	215	595	0
萍乡矿务局建筑安装总公司	3	2177	1727	450	0
宜春海程经贸发展有限公司	1	118	118	0	0
吉安对外经济技术合作公司	6	60	0	60	0
抚州国际经济技术合作公司	0	63	0	63	0
九江市对外经济合作公司	5	44	0	44	0
江西省地质工程(集团)公司	1	8	0	8	0
江西省火电建设公司	1	21	21	0	0
山东省	**1116**	**67727**	**39343**	**28362**	**22**
中国山东国际经济技术合作公司	73	5858	3694	2164	0
齐鲁建设集团公司	12	1445	1411	34	0

1999年中国对外承包工程和劳务合作合同分公司总值

名称	合同数(份)	合同额(万美元)			
		合计	承包工程	劳务合作	设计咨询
山东省建筑工程总公司	12	5500	5500	0	0
山东省外商投资服务公司	16	335	0	335	0
山东省劳务合作公司	57	741	0	741	0
山东省水产企业集团公司	9	2331	0	2331	0
山东省物产进出口公司	9	145	4	141	0
莱芜钢铁总厂	2	633	633	0	0
山东对外贸易集团有限公司	7	136	0	136	0
山东省机械进出口公司	2	7	0	7	0
黄河工程局	1	1300	1300	0	0
山东省纺织品进出口公司	2	4	0	4	0
威海国际经济技术合作公司	68	4294	0	4294	0
烟台国际经济技术合作公司	97	4157	1254	2903	0
烟台市建筑工程公司	8	3057	3057	0	0
潍坊国际经济技术合作公司	31	477	108	369	0
淄博国际经济技术合作公司	36	527	163	364	0
济南国际经济技术合作公司	5	240	0	240	0
日照国际经济 技术合作公司	25	2283	480	1803	0
临沂国际经济技术合作公司	4	304	0	304	0
泰安国际经济技术合作公司	18	1084	0	1084	0
东营国际经济技术合作公司	12	556	0	556	0
潍坊建筑安装工程公司	11	2295	2000	295	0
济南四建集团责任有限公司	4	2500	2500	0	0
荣成市对外经济技术合作公司	13	478	0	478	0
威海火炬高技术开发区进出口公司	22	106	0	106	0
烟台二建实业股份有限公司	4	657	120	537	0
淄博建筑工程公司	4	500	350	150	0
潍坊柴油机厂进出口公司	12	1074	1014	60	0
济南轻骑集团进出口公司	1	60	0	60	0
枣庄国际经济技术合作公司	3	77	0	77	0
诸城市建筑工程公司	12	2028	1905	123	0
菏泽地区对外经济技术合作公司	44	240	0	240	0
威海市进出口集团公司	19	85	0	85	0
泰安建筑工程公司	31	2905	896	2009	0
中国水产烟台海洋渔业公司	27	1802	608	1194	0
胜利油田管理局	2	3050	3050	0	0
日照新亚欧大陆桥有限公司	1	173	0	173	0
烟台环太国际经贸有限公司	1	20	20	0	0

1999年中国对外承包工程和劳务合作合同分公司总值

名称	合同数(份)	合同额(万美元)			
		合计	承包工程	劳务合作	设计咨询
德州市国际经济技术合作公司	5	118	0	118	0
山东省工业设备安装公司	5	800	800	0	0
山东航运集团	1	100	100	0	0
山东电力核电建设集团公司	10	1466	1460	6	0
山东省公路工程总公司	1	1200	1200	0	0
山东省农业实业集团	1	2545	2545	0	0
青岛市	**376**	**8034**	**3171**	**4841**	**22**
中国青岛国际经济技术合作公司	159	2952	637	2315	0
青岛建设集团公司	18	2513	2502	11	0
青岛市五金矿产机械进出口公司	60	1002	32	970	0
青岛国际人才技术合作公司	80	373	0	373	0
青岛海洋渔业公司	10	275	0	275	0
青岛海尔国际贸易有限公司	7	33	0	28	5
青岛市建筑设计研究院	5	17	0	0	17
青岛国际交流中心	15	329	0	329	0
青岛远达对外经济合作公司	22	540	0	540	0
河南省	**98**	**7145**	**5056**	**1989**	**100**
中国河南国际经济技术合作公司	31	2098	879	1219	0
河南省水利电力对外公司	2	1158	1158	0	0
河南省对外劳务合作公司	6	376	0	376	0
河南省建设工程公司	5	647	647	0	0
洛阳国际经济技术合作公司	4	46	0	46	0
商丘国际经济技术合作公司	7	60	15	45	0
机械部第四设计研究院	3	108	108	0	0
洛阳有色金属加工设计院	2	92	62	0	30
中原石油勘探局外经外贸总公司	8	2187	2187	0	0
河南濮阳国际经济技术合作公司	6	138	0	138	0
河南交通规划勘察设计院	18	70	0	0	70
洛阳浮法玻璃公司	5	15	0	15	0
金城国际经济技术合作公司(河南)	1	150	0	150	0
湖北省	**227**	**18099**	**14282**	**2946**	**871**
中国湖北国际经济技术合作公司	4	0	0	0	0
湖北大地国际经济技术合作有限公司	3	237	47	190	0
黄石国际经济技术合作公司	2	10	0	10	0
宜昌国际经济技术合作公司	5	34	22	12	0
葛洲坝水利水电工程集团公司	1	42	42	0	0
中国有色第十五冶金建设公司	3	4680	4680	0	0

1999年中国对外承包工程和劳务合作合同分公司总值

名　　称	合同数(份)	合同额(万美元)			
		合计	承包工程	劳务合作	设计咨询
湖北晴川国际海员劳务开发公司	7	77	0	77	0
孝感国际经济技术合作建筑有限公司	4	15	0	15	0
荆州国际经济技术合作公司	4	47	0	47	0
黄冈国际经济技术合作公司	2	21	0	21	0
十堰国际经济技术合作公司	7	28	0	28	0
湖北省建筑工程集团有限公司	22	789	789	0	0
湖北省国际劳务合作有限公司	15	461	32	429	0
电力工业部中南电力设计院	3	686	0	0	686
武汉地质勘察基础工程(集团)总公司	2	42	42	0	0
湖北国际企业合作公司	55	200	0	200	0
湖北省机械设备进出口公司	3	3699	3600	99	0
武汉市	**85**	**7031**	**5028**	**1818**	**185**
中国武汉国际经济技术合作公司	38	4082	2436	1646	0
中国五环化学工程公司	7	241	240	0	1
武汉建工集团有限公司	3	1223	1223	0	0
武汉钢铁设计研究院	3	67	45	0	22
武汉钢铁(集团)国际经济贸易公司	2	9	0	0	9
铁道部第四勘测设计院	2	7	0	0	7
华中电力国际经贸公司	1	150	150	0	0
煤炭部武汉设计院	1	10	0	0	10
武汉船用机械厂	1	246	246	0	0
长江航运集团对外经济技术合作总公司	21	271	99	172	0
武汉市建筑设计院	3	56	0	0	56
武汉市市政工程总公司	2	589	589	0	0
冶金部武汉勘察研究院	1	80	0	0	80
湖南省	**543**	**5946**	**3277**	**1877**	**792**
中国湖南国际经济技术合作公司	77	491	72	395	24
湖南省公路桥梁建设公司	1	184	184	0	0
湖南建筑工程集团总公司	1	22	22	0	0
第二十三冶金建设公司	2	468	468	0	0
湖南省进出口公司	15	152	0	152	0
湖南环球(集团)公司	370	1177	0	1177	0
长沙冶金设计院	3	20	0	0	20
长沙轻工设计院	5	347	0	0	347
湖南建筑设计院	1	361	0	0	361
湖南机械集团进出口公司	32	104	0	104	0
电力中南设计院	3	69	69	0	0

1999年中国对外承包工程和劳务合作合同分公司总值

名　　称	合同数(份)	合同额(万美元)			
		合计	承包工程	劳务合作	设计咨询
机械工业部第八设计院	3	23	0	0	23
长沙有色冶金设计研究院	4	14	0	0	14
湖南株洲海外国际合作有限公司	12	13	0	13	0
华隆进出口公司	2	36	0	36	0
湖南省机械设备进出口公司	1	600	600	0	0
湖南化学工业设计院	8	88	85	0	3
湖南环达公路桥梁建设公司	3	1777	1777	0	0
广东省	**5714**	**62701**	**52962**	**9329**	**410**
中国广东国际合作(集团)公司	157	8265	7013	1252	0
广东对外劳务经济合作公司	147	4054	0	4054	0
广东海外建设总公司	4	5380	5380	0	0
广东省源大水利水电集团有限公司	6	16845	16845	0	0
广东省岭南综合勘测设计院	7	31	0	0	31
广东省建筑设计研究院	5	376	331	0	45
珠海国际经济技术合作公司	73	639	0	639	0
汕头国际经济技术合作公司	5	194	0	194	0
汕尾市对外劳动服务公司	6	59	0	59	0
江门市对外劳动服务公司	39	429	0	429	0
广东省南粤进出口公司	16	376	0	376	0
中山国际经济技术合作公司	4	171	119	52	0
珠海劳动服务公司	94	646	0	646	0
广东省水利电力勘测设计研究院	4	65	0	0	65
江门甘蔗化工厂(集团)股份有限公司	1	240	240	0	0
广东省第七建筑集团有限公司	4	1083	1083	0	0
广州市	**5051**	**3338**	**2129**	**1051**	**158**
中国广州国际经济技术合作公司	5028	991	53	938	0
广州对外经济发展总公司	21	2189	2076	113	0
广州市设计院	2	158	0	0	158
深圳市	**91**	**20510**	**19822**	**577**	**111**
中国深圳国际合作(集团)股份有限公司	17	6056	5866	190	0
深圳市对外劳动服务公司	6	87	0	87	0
深圳市国际人才劳务经济发展有限公司	43	300	0	300	0
深圳市建设投资控股公司	2	3871	3871	0	0
深圳市建筑设计总院	3	111	0	0	111
深圳市中兴通讯股份有限公司	12	8708	8708	0	0
深圳市华为技术有限公司	8	1377	1377	0	0
广西自治区	**98**	**2451**	**2137**	**310**	**4**

1999 年中国对外承包工程和劳务合作合同分公司总值

名　　称	合同数(份)	合同额(万美元)			
		合计	承包工程	劳务合作	设计咨询
中国广西国际经济技术合作公司	48	449	358	91	0
南宁国际经济技术合作公司	3	38	0	38	0
广西对外建筑工程总公司	5	620	577	43	0
北海海外经济技术合作公司	4	28	0	28	0
防城港国际经济技术合作有限责任公司	6	247	230	17	0
广西建筑综合设计院	1	4	0	0	4
广西水利水电对外有限责任公司	3	314	314	0	0
梧州国际经济技术合作公司	3	83	77	6	0
凭祥市对外经济技术合作公司	3	190	190	0	0
广西玉林国际经济技术合作公司	3	62	0	62	0
桂林国际经济技术合作公司	15	25	0	25	0
广西工艺品进出口防城公司	1	97	97	0	0
广西畜产进出口防城公司	1	99	99	0	0
防城港市京文服务公司	1	98	98	0	0
广西土产防城港仓储供销公司	1	97	97	0	0
海南省	**14**	**2752**	**2731**	**21**	**0**
中国海南国际经济技术合作公司	13	1652	1631	21	0
海南省建筑工程总公司	1	1100	1100	0	0
重庆市	**212**	**8448**	**1848**	**2544**	**4056**
中国重庆国际经济技术合作公司	18	1252	895	357	0
重庆对外建设总公司	10	30	0	30	0
宝钢集团重庆钢铁设计研究院	5	69	0	0	69
万县市国际经济技术合作公司	0	10	0	10	0
涪陵国际经济技术合作公司	4	67	0	67	0
重庆钢铁(集团)有限责任公司	1	77	0	77	0
重庆海外建筑工程承包有限公司	3	953	953	0	0
嘉陵集团公司	159	2003	0	2003	0
中煤设计咨询集团重庆院	6	43	0	0	43
机械部第三设计院	6	3944	0	0	3944
四川省	**144**	**38109**	**31934**	**4057**	**2118**
中国四川国际合作股份有限公司	5	1364	1100	264	0
中国华西企业公司	20	2926	2917	9	0
四川东方电力设备联合公司	7	6351	6351	0	0
中国华西工程设计建设总公司	11	10403	8300	0	2103
中国成达化学工程公司	4	341	326	0	15
四川公路桥梁工程总公司	5	8004	8004	0	0
四川省外经实业股份公司	36	1236	0	1236	0

1999年中国对外承包工程和劳务合作合同分公司总值

名称	合同数(份)	合同额(万美元)			
		合计	承包工程	劳务合作	设计咨询
中国化学工程第七建设公司	4	101	101	0	0
川铁国际经济技术合作公司	12	4080	4080	0	0
攀枝花建设总公司	1	500	0	500	0
成都市建筑工程总公司	2	42		42	0
绵阳国际经济技术合作有限公司	3	109	0	109	0
四川省劳务开发公司	22	1566	0	1566	0
川北电信工程有限公司	1	360	360	0	0
四川德阳国际公司	2	405	395	10	0
成都市	**9**	**321**	**0**	**321**	**0**
中国成都国际经济技术合作公司	9	321	0	321	0
贵州省	**22**	**1741**	**1610**	**131**	**0**
中国贵州国际经济技术合作公司	12	0	0	0	0
铁道部第五工程局	2	1610	1610	0	0
中国贵航集团西秀进出口公司	1	96	0	96	0
贵州省桥梁工程公司	7	35	0	35	0
云南省	**207**	**33914**	**31067**	**247**	**2600**
中国云南国际经济技术合作公司	13	3721	3690	31	0
昆明国际经济技术合作公司	2	423	423	0	0
云南建工集团总公司	2	1490	1490	0	0
云南公路桥梁工程总公司	1	500	500	0	0
中国云南水利水电昆明国际公司	1	225	0	0	225
云南地矿勘查工程总公司(集团)	6	183	0	0	183
云南德宏国际经济技术合作有限责任公司	14	3309	3213	96	0
云南省机械进出口公司	1	120	120	0	0
云南省公路规划勘察设计院	2	224	213	0	11
电力部昆明勘测设计研究院	6	1196	0	120	1076
昆明冶金设计研究院	3	53	0	0	53
林业部昆明勘察设计院	3	1052	0	0	1052
文山州国际股份有限公司	12	3469	3469	0	0
德宏州进出口公司	16	3401	3401	0	0
云南省土产进出口公司	1	159	159	0	0
瑞丽勐卯商号	3	282	282	0	0
裕丰商号	8	1000	1000	0	0
瑞丽市永盛有限责任公司	1	96	96	0	0
陇川县越兴商号	1	85	85	0	0
畹町一德公司	1	45	45	0	0
云南省机床电工设备总公司	1	320	320	0	0

1999 年中国对外承包工程和劳务合作合同分公司总值

名　　称	合同数（份）	合同额（万美元）			
		合计	承包工程	劳务合作	设计咨询
梁河县九保商号	1	100	100	0	0
畹町华昌公司	1	98	98	0	0
潞西市富源商号	1	95	95	0	0
德宏州香料公司	2	196	196	0	0
潞西市贸宏商号	6	588	588	0	0
瑞丽市侨光商号	1	98	98	0	0
河口陆化云星公司	1	91	91	0	0
德宏州龙跃公司	1	99	99	0	0
龙陵县龙山商号	1	97	97	0	0
文山州永瑞边贸有限公司	1	94	94	0	0
临沧地区耿马边贸公司	1	100	100	0	0
保山地区腾冲大同商号	1	98	98	0	0
临沧地区沧源贸源商号	1	98	98	0	0
瑞丽市金星公司	1	86	86	0	0
思茅景谷外贸公司	1	102	102	0	0
紫金商号	1	90	90	0	0
云南省进出口公司德宏公司	2	193	193	0	0
澜沧友联公司	2	100	100	0	0
瑞丽金得利公司	1	96	96	0	0
楚雄外贸河口公司	1	95	95	0	0
河口东亚公司	1	18	18	0	0
思茅澜沧天仁公司	3	120	120	0	0
瑞丽市联发公司	1	97	97	0	0
瑞丽市玉溪商号	1	91	91	0	0
昆明市力车胎厂	1	98	98	0	0
云南粮油食品进出口瑞丽分公司	1	97	97	0	0
瑞丽太阳神边贸公司	1	71	71	0	0
瑞丽利宾公司	1	98	98	0	0
畹町财贸发展有限公司	1	200	200	0	0
畹町盛誉商号	1	98	98	0	0
瑞丽市达兴商号	1	97	97	0	0
版纳州南腊商行	1	99	99	0	0
版纳州勐海报关行	1	91	91	0	0
梁河县顺通商号	3	296	296	0	0
保山地区外经贸公司	1	96	96	0	0
瑞丽市蛉达边贸公司	1	59	59	0	0
瑞丽市振华商号	2	194	194	0	0

1999年中国对外承包工程和劳务合作合同分公司总值

名　　称	合同数（份）	合同额（万美元）			
		合计	承包工程	劳务合作	设计咨询
瑞丽市海利达公司	1	65	65	0	0
芒市边贸商号	1	93	93	0	0
瑞丽市润友公司	1	80	80	0	0
盈江县进出口公司	1	82	82	0	0
云南机设瑞丽进出口公司	1	98	98	0	0
德丽总公司	2	197	197	0	0
梁河昆达商号	2	236	236	0	0
潞西市进出口公司	14	1527	1527	0	0
梁河县进出口公司	3	168	168	0	0
昆明电化厂	1	120	120	0	0
德宏州顺德公司	4	384	384	0	0
瑞丽市联益商号	1	99	99	0	0
德宏州工艺品公司	2	192	192	0	0
畹町富兴工贸有限公司	1	96	96	0	0
畹町利群商号	1	96	96	0	0
思茅孟连建华贸易有限公司	2	68	68	0	0
德宏州德安总公司	1	96	96	0	0
梁河县光大公司	7	837	837	0	0
潞西市德源边贸公司	1	98	98	0	0
瑞丽市洪顺公司	3	283	283	0	0
盈江县永福公司	3	276	276	0	0
畹町市进出口公司	3	2568	2568	0	0
姐告远大科贸公司	1	100	100	0	0
梁河县桂梁商号	1	70	70	0	0
瑞丽市利民商号	1	98	98	0	0
陕西省	**99**	**5387**	**4461**	**803**	**123**
中国陕西国际经济技术合作公司	17	136	40	23	73
秦海国际工程公司	2	279	279	0	0
机械部第七设计院	1	1	0	0	1
中国华陆工程公司	2	58	0	45	13
交通部第一公路设计院	2	31	0	0	31
陕西省机械设备进出口公司	2	323	323	0	0
华山国际工程公司	3	1357	1357	0	0
西飞集团公司	1	5	0	5	0
煤炭工业部西安设计研究院	2	12	0	7	5
中国计算机软件工程公司西安分公司	5	86	0	86	0
中国机械工业第三安装工程公司	4	54	54	0	0

1999年中国对外承包工程和劳务合作合同分公司总值

名　　称	合同数（份）	合同额（万美元）			
		合计	承包工程	劳务合作	设计咨询
西安市	**58**	**3045**	**2408**	**637**	**0**
西安国际技术贸易公司	49	1395	758	637	0
西安电力机械进出口公司	6	1646	1646	0	0
西安天宝国际工程公司	3	4	4	0	0
甘肃省	**34**	**6229**	**6066**	**142**	**21**
中国甘肃国际经济技术合作公司	5	150	100	50	0
甘肃建筑工程总公司	11	2744	2744	0	0
兰州石油化工机械总厂	2	1275	1275	0	0
甘肃省建筑设计研究院	1	21	0	0	21
甘肃金川国际经济技术合作有限公司	1	1561	1561	0	0
甘肃对外经济发展公司	7	171	79	92	0
甘肃地质工程总公司	7	307	307	0	0
宁夏自治区	**1**	**27**	**0**	**27**	**0**
中国宁夏伊斯兰国际经济技术合作公司	1	27	0	27	0
新疆自治区	**16**	**737**	**604**	**131**	**2**
中国新疆国际经济技术合作公司	1	360	360	0	0
新疆机械化工五金矿产轻工进出口公司	9	71	0	71	0
新疆石油管理局	1	244	244	0	0
新疆生产建设兵团	5	62	0	60	2
新天国际经济技术合作公司	3	60	0	60	0
新疆兵团勘测设计院	1	2	0	0	2
阿拉山口中基有限责任公司	1	0	0	0	0

1999年中国对外承包工程和劳务合作营业额分公司总值

金额单位:万美元

名　　称	合　计	承包工程	劳务合作	设计咨询
合　　计	**1123458**	**852232**	**262268**	**8958**
中央合计	**581759**	**529512**	**49997**	**2250**
中国建筑工程总公司	193650	192933	447	270
中国广播电视国际经济技术合作公司	290	290	0	0
中国冶金建设集团总公司	5254	5233	0	21
中国商业对外经济技术合作公司	31	0	31	0
中国水产(集团)总公司	2740	2649	91	0
中国国际技术智力合作公司	20630	6	20621	3

1999年中国对外承包工程和劳务合作营业额分公司总值

金额单位:万美元

名　称	合　计	承包工程	劳务合作	设计咨询
中国路桥(集团)总公司	24771	24600	171	0
中国土木工程集团公司	28928	27039	1889	0
中国港湾建设(集团)总公司	34473	33513	870	90
中国海外工程总公司	15983	15403	580	0
中国水利电力对外公司	15661	15661	0	0
中国石化工程建设公司	82	80	2	0
中国化学工程(集团)公司	1554	1372	182	0
中国轻工业对外经济技术合作公司	1905	583	1322	0
中国电子国际经济技术合作公司	651	530	121	0
中国地质工程集团公司	7641	7641	0	0
中国国际展览公司	77	77	0	0
中国光大国际经济技术合作公司	210	210	0	0
中国农牧渔业国际合作公司	328	305	1	22
中国航空技术国际工程公司	983	840	143	0
中国国际计算机软件工程公司	72	0	72	0
中国林业国际合作公司	29	0	29	0
中国建材工业对外经济技术合作公司	3410	2479	929	2
中国万宝工程公司	11408	10397	1011	0
中国交远国际经济技术合作公司	431	19	412	0
中国海员对外经济技术合作公司	2688	0	2688	0
中国石油工程建设(集团)公司	79951	79916	35	0
科智国际技术合作公司	28	0	28	0
中国四达国际经济技术合作公司	88	0	88	0
中国中原对外工程公司	4268	4268	0	0
中海国际石油工程有限责任公司	1467	1467	0	0
中国国际工程咨询公司	73	1	52	20
中国体育国际经济技术合作公司	86	31	55	0
中国海外贸易总公司	307	0	307	0
中国电子系统工程总公司	2705	2705	0	0
中国铁道建筑总公司	4713	4121	592	0
中国建筑材料工业建设总公司	87	0	87	0
中国化工建设总公司	1567	1567	0	0
中国出国人员服务总公司	12	0	12	0
中国海外经济合作总公司	483	467	16	0
中国机械设备进出口总公司	2462	2457	5	0
中国寰球化学工程公司	3891	3193	24	674
中国机械对外经济技术合作公司	1097	868	229	0
远大国际经济合作有限责任公司	52	51	1	0

1999年中国对外承包工程和劳务合作营业额分公司总值

金额单位：万美元

名　　称	合　计	承包工程	劳务合作	设计咨询
中国有色金属建设股份有限公司	1582	1530	52	0
中国医疗卫生对外经济合作公司	157	154	3	0
中国纺织工业对外经济技术合作公司	94	73	21	0
中国北方工业公司	730	730	0	0
长城国际经济技术合作有限公司	4	1	3	0
中国化工进出口总公司	129	0	129	0
中国航空工业规划设计院	122	0	0	122
中国通信建设总公司	231	217	14	0
中远对外劳务合作公司	12358	0	12358	0
中国成套设备进出口集团总公司	4323	3298	1004	21
中国对外建设总公司	86	86	0	0
轻工业部规划设计院	23	0	0	23
北京有色冶金设计研究总院	9	0	9	0
燕兴国际经济技术合作公司	340	0	340	0
中国铁路工程总公司	21717	21295	174	248
中国机械进出口(集团)有限公司	845	845	0	0
北京中民国际经济合作公司	3	0	3	0
北京煤炭设计研究院(集团)	426	0	0	426
北京钢铁设计研究院	91	53	0	38
中国电力技术进出口公司	2171	1911	260	0
华北电力设计院	20	0	0	20
中国安能建设总公司	491	491	0	0
华鑫国际经济贸易公司	9	0	9	0
中翰科技经济发展总公司	10	0	10	0
中国京冶建设工程承包公司	240	240	0	0
中外园林建设总公司	231	231	0	0
广播电影电视部设计院	5	0	0	5
核工业第二研究设计院	12	0	0	12
中交公路规划设计院	4	0	0	4
国内贸易部设计院	12	0	5	7
建设部综合勘察研究院	10	10	0	0
中国友发国际工程设计咨询公司	54	0	23	31
中国石化北京设计院	180	0	0	180
中土畜劳务合作有限公司	79	0	79	0
中国国际人才开发中心	159	0	159	0
中水远洋渔业有限责任公司	16508	15042	1466	0
北京市地质矿产勘查开发总公司	117	117	0	0
中国机械工业安装总公司	793	793	0	0

1999年中国对外承包工程和劳务合作营业额分公司总值

金额单位:万美元

名　称	合　计	承包工程	劳务合作	设计咨询
华北电力国际经贸公司	72	22	50	0
中设国际工程有限公司	11276	11258	18	0
中国工程与农业机械进出口总公司	6902	6902	0	0
中国新星石油公司	754	752	2	0
中国燕兴总公司	12	0	12	0
中海石油工程设计公司	129	129	0	0
中国电力建设工程咨询公司	39	37	0	2
中国水利水电工程总公司	6404	6404	0	0
中京邮电通信设计院	41	0	32	9
中汽对外经济技术合作公司	2247	2247	0	0
中国华联国际贸易公司	430	0	430	0
中国华阳技术贸易(集团)公司	189	0	189	0
中油技术服务有限责任公司	3063	3063	0	0
中国石油技术开发公司	2554	2554	0	0
中国华润有限公司	5795	5795	0	0
中地石油工程公司	260	260	0	0
地方合计	**541699**	**322720**	**212271**	**6708**
北京市	**26167**	**19344**	**6477**	**346**
中国北京国际经济合作公司	2572	2363	209	0
北京市建筑工程总公司	3071	2708	363	0
北京市政工程总公司	1556	1554	2	0
北京市政工程设计研究院	225	0	6	219
北京市建筑设计院	127	0	0	127
北京住宅开发建设集团总公司	7532	7532	0	0
北京城建集团总公司	3304	3304	0	0
首钢总公司国际经贸部	1136	1074	62	0
北京市外国企业服务总公司	5835	0	5835	0
北京市第二房修工程公司	49	49	0	0
中国燕山联合对外贸易有限公司	600	600	0	0
北京八仙房地产开发公司	160	160	0	0
天津市	**19800**	**10153**	**9274**	**373**
中国天津国际经济技术合作公司	9237	2827	6410	0
天津立达国际劳务工程公司	875	0	875	0
天津建工集团总公司	3017	1390	1627	0
天津市建筑设计院	24	0	2	22
天津水泥工业设计研究院	39	14	0	25
铁道部第三勘测设计院	39	0	26	13
中国天辰化学工程公司	2603	2546	0	57

1999年中国对外承包工程和劳务合作营业额分公司总值

金额单位：万美元

名　　称	合　计	承包工程	劳务合作	设计咨询
机械部第五设计研究院	80	7	0	73
天津港海员对外服务公司	12	0	12	0
天津市政设计研究院	129	0	0	129
天津市亿利达集团有限公司	14	0	14	0
天津市化工设计院	56	32	0	24
天津天航海员技术服务公司	87	0	87	0
中国成套天津公司	152	0	152	0
天津机械进出口集团有限公司	18	0	16	2
天津纺织进出口集团有限公司	19	0	19	0
天津机械设备进出口公司	17	17	0	0
水利部天津水利水电勘测设计研究院	15	0	0	15
大港油田集团有限责任公司	384	384	0	0
天海集团股份有限公司	34	0	34	0
天津开发区苏伊士国合有限公司	44	44	0	0
天津市海岸带公司	13	0	0	13
铁道部第十八局	2830	2830	0	0
天津市地质工程勘察院	14	14	0	0
天津市和平建筑工程有限公司	48	48	0	0
河北省	**7133**	**4001**	**2982**	**150**
中国河北国际经济技术合作公司	948	253	695	0
石家庄国际经济技术合作公司	1010	0	1010	0
河北公路工程建设集团有限公司	40	40	0	0
河北建工集团有限责任公司	404	0	404	0
核工业部第四设计研究院	38	38	0	0
唐山国际工程总公司	485	0	485	0
中国耀华玻璃(集团)公司	30	0	30	0
中国第二十二冶金建设公司	53	53	0	0
张家口对外劳务工程公司	12	0	12	0
秦皇岛国际经济技术合作公司	400	250	0	150
地矿河北工程勘测公司	80	80	0	0
保定国际经济技术合作公司	39	0	39	0
承德对外经济合作公司	7	0	7	0
唐山对外合作公司	70	0	70	0
铁道部建场工程局	1067	1067	0	0
河北省水利工程局	220	200	20	0
中油管道建设有限责任公司	1000	1000	0	0
河北国际供销合作总公司	53	0	53	0
华北石油管理局	50	50	0	0

1999年中国对外承包工程和劳务合作营业额分公司总值

金额单位:万美元

名　　称	合　计	承包工程	劳务合作	设计咨询
河北省进出口贸易公司	1	0	1	0
河北省纺织品进出口公司	2	0	2	0
廊坊对外经济技术合作有限公司	24	0	24	0
邢台路桥公司	551	551	0	0
辰光集团公司	130	127	3	0
沧州对外经济技术合作公司	127	0	127	0
唐山安装工程公司	292	292	0	0
山西省	**2473**	**1398**	**778**	**297**
中国山西国际经济技术合作公司	642	272	106	264
山西省建筑工程总公司	512	0	512	0
太原市国际经济技术合作公司	112	0	112	0
太原钢铁(集团)公司	31	31	0	0
山西省电力公司	443	443	0	0
山西省送变电工程公司	185	185	0	0
山西省公路桥梁工程总公司	124	124	0	0
化工部第二设计院	49	15	1	33
山西四建集团有限公司	15	0	15	0
煤炭部太原设计研究院	18	0	18	0
太原重型机器进出口公司	284	282	2	0
中国第十三冶金建设公司	58	46	12	0
内蒙古自治区	**3174**	**979**	**2138**	**57**
中国内蒙古国际经济技术合作公司	441	341	100	0
冶金部包头钢铁设计研究院	57	0	0	57
呼伦贝尔盟国际经济技术合作公司	362	0	362	0
满洲里国际经济技术合作有限公司	512	150	362	0
内蒙古电力(集团)有限责任公司	181	181	0	0
二连浩特国际经济技术合作公司	140	0	140	0
锡林郭勒国际经济技术合作公司	106	0	106	0
额尔古纳国际经济技术合作公司	63	0	63	0
内蒙古高等院校科技开发集团	54	0	54	0
二连浩特市华天对外贸易有限责任公司	110	0	110	0
额尔古纳市边境贸易公司	23	0	23	0
新巴尔虎右旗边境贸易公司	23	0	23	0
满洲里东方国际贸易股份有限公司	83	0	83	0
满洲里华运公司	314	0	314	0
中国内蒙古森林工业集团有限责任公司	210	0	210	0
新三维国际经济技术合作股份有限公司	228	156	72	0
呼和浩特铁路对外经济技术合作公司	239	151	88	0

1999年中国对外承包工程和劳务合作营业额分公司总值

金额单位:万美元

名　称	合　计	承包工程	劳务合作	设计咨询
内蒙古农牧业科技开发公司	28	0	28	0
辽宁省	**32696**	**15762**	**16871**	**63**
中国辽宁国际合作(集团)股份有限公司	5501	3299	2202	0
辽宁省建设集团公司	404	400	4	0
辽宁国际建设工程集团公司	80	80	0	0
鞍山国际经济技术合作公司	716	135	580	1
抚顺对外建设经济合作(集团)股份公司	821	117	704	0
本溪对外经济技术合作总公司	230	0	230	0
丹东国际经济技术合作公司	114	0	114	0
营口国际经济技术合作公司	12	0	12	0
鞍山焦化耐火材料设计院	8	0	0	8
东北电力集团进出口公司	1330	1330	0	0
锦州华锦国际经贸股份有限公司	19	0	19	0
铁岭国际经济技术合作公司	65	0	65	0
辽宁华曦集团	84	0	84	0
辽阳国际经济技术合作公司	1055	110	945	0
鞍钢集团国际经济贸易公司	425	425	0	0
中国第三冶金建设公司	271	67	204	0
辽河石油勘探局	33	11	22	0
朝阳建设集团有限公司	298	250	48	0
辽宁食品进出口公司	67	0	67	0
辽宁粮油进出口公司	16	0	16	0
抚顺市第二建筑工程公司	20	0	20	0
辽宁省国际劳务交流有限公司	7	0	7	0
本钢集团国际经济贸易有限公司	227	22	205	0
阜新国际经济合作技术公司	22	0	22	0
沈阳市	**5190**	**2444**	**2714**	**32**
中国沈阳国际经济技术合作公司	5051	2444	2607	0
沈阳对外经济建设总公司	76	0	76	0
沈阳海外建筑工程承包公司	6	0	6	0
煤炭工业部沈阳设计研究院	22	0	22	0
沈阳铝镁设计研究院	32	0	0	32
中国建筑东北设计研究院	3	0	3	0
大连市	**15681**	**7072**	**8587**	**22**
中国大连合作(集团)股份有限公司	11994	6433	5561	0
瓦房店市国际工程公司	13	13	0	0
辽宁省大连海洋渔业集团公司	512	0	512	0
大连经济技术开发区劳务公司	22	0	22	0

1999年中国对外承包工程和劳务合作营业额分公司总值

金额单位:万美元

名 称	合 计	承包工程	劳务合作	设计咨询
大连工程总承包公司	560	560	0	0
大化国际经济贸易公司	11	0	11	0
大连华南国际经济技术合作公司	553	46	507	0
大连港国际经济技术合作公司	340	0	340	0
大连渤海建筑集团有限公司	111	0	89	22
大连远洋船员管理公司	20	0	20	0
中国外运大连公司	15	0	15	0
中国成套设备进出口大连公司	145	0	145	0
大连水产远洋渔业公司	711	0	711	0
大连亿达国际合作公司	20	20	0	0
辽宁成大股份公司	88	0	88	0
中国辽宁国际合作大连开发总公司	395	0	395	0
辽宁机械进出口公司	63	0	63	0
大连航运集团有限公司	1	0	1	0
大连对外服务贸易有限公司	107	0	107	0
吉林省	**17978**	**7606**	**10337**	**35**
中国吉林国际经济技术合作公司	3398	873	2525	0
吉林市对外经济技术合作公司	600	0	600	0
延边对外经济技术合作公司	657	113	544	0
珲春国际经济技术合作公司	282	70	212	0
吉林化学工业进出口公司	130	0	130	0
吉林冶金建设公司	112	0	112	0
吉林省对外招商建设总公司	554	126	428	0
吉林省建筑总公司	55	40	15	0
延边海外经济技术合作公司	1318	0	1318	0
吉林省对外经济技术合作公司	42	15	27	0
吉林国际人才交流公司	248	0	248	0
吉林森林工业集团公司	4500	4500	0	0
吉林省对外经济发展公司	723	0	723	0
辽源对外经济技术合作公司	206	50	156	0
延边国际经济技术合作公司	151	0	151	0
吉林省纺织品进出口公司	27	24	3	0
四平远东外建合作公司	52	0	52	0
吉林化工工程公司	120	120	0	0
吉林省农业对外合作公司	157	0	157	0
通化金宝国际经济技术合作有限公司	30	27	3	0
吉林省新创对外工程公司	28	28	0	0
吉林省工程建设有限公司	244	227	17	0

1999年中国对外承包工程和劳务合作营业额分公司总值

金额单位:万美元

名　　称	合　计	承包工程	劳务合作	设计咨询
吉林化工(集团)建设公司	1545	1393	117	35
吉林轻工集团股份公司	107	0	107	0
珲春对外经贸公司	20	0	20	0
吉林省海外工程有限公司	58	0	58	0
长春国际经济技术合作公司	885	0	885	0
长春建工集团总公司	167	0	167	0
长春对外劳务合作公司	140	0	140	0
长春对外经济技术合作公司	1357	0	1357	0
长春星宇集团股份有限公司	65	0	65	0
黑龙江省	**20101**	**15225**	**4762**	**114**
中国黑龙江国际经济技术合作公司	1302	400	902	0
黑龙江国际工程技术合作公司	218	7	211	0
黑龙江东方集团国际经济技术合作公司	1490	1340	150	0
黑龙江省森林工业对外经济贸易公司	201	0	201	0
中国煤炭国际经济技术合作黑龙江公司	1477	1260	217	0
哈尔滨铁路局对外经济技术合作公司	447	420	27	0
黑龙江省瑞驰建设公司	108	2	106	0
齐齐哈尔国际经济技术合作公司	95	21	74	0
牡丹江国际经济技术合作公司	79	0	79	0
东宁宏达经济贸易公司	148	148	0	0
东宁国际经济技术合作公司	496	0	496	0
密山市经济技术合作公司	40	0	40	0
绥芬河国际经济技术合作公司	6	0	6	0
同江国际经济技术合作公司	208	0	208	0
大庆石油技术进出口公司	57	0	0	57
大庆油田研究设计院	57	0	0	57
黑河国际经济技术合作公司	306	167	139	0
伊春市边境贸易公司	113	60	53	0
萝北边境贸易公司	7	0	7	0
饶河县边境贸易公司	22	0	22	0
绥芬河东成经济贸易有限公司	600	0	600	0
东宁欣荣经济贸易公司	80	0	80	0
同江市北江有限公司	78	0	78	0
绥芬河华城国际经贸公司	60	0	60	0
绥芬河兴建经济贸易公司	48	0	48	0
绥芬河英泰经贸公司	40	0	40	0
同江市农业综合公司	82	0	82	0
同江龙华经贸公司	20	0	20	0

1999年中国对外承包工程和劳务合作营业额分公司总值

金额单位：万美元

名　　称	合　计	承包工程	劳务合作	设计咨询
同江三友物资公司	200	0	200	0
绥芬河金地经贸公司	24	0	24	0
绥芬河国际工程公司	51	0	51	0
抚远边贸公司	40	0	40	0
哈尔滨市	**11901**	**11400**	**501**	**0**
哈尔滨国际经济技术合作公司	373	0	373	0
哈尔滨对外经济技术合作公司	37	0	37	0
哈尔滨中建工程公司	8	0	8	0
哈尔滨第二建设公司	83	0	83	0
哈尔滨电站工程责任有限公司	11400	11400	0	0
上海市	**60362**	**38397**	**20444**	**1521**
中国上海外经(集团)有限公司	17468	7961	9051	456
上海对外劳务合作公司	1608	0	1608	0
上海对外建设公司	327	324	3	0
上海机械进出口(集团)有限公司	436	324	112	0
上海机械设备进出口公司	162	150	12	0
上海建筑设计研究院	167	0	0	167
上海轻工业设计研究院	70	0	0	70
上海电气(集团)总公司	2860	2860	0	0
上海市对外服务公司	5667	0	5667	0
上海轻纺工业对外经济技术合作公司	2033	0	2033	0
上海金山石油化工工程公司	1134	1134	0	0
上海核工程研究设计院	100	0	0	100
上海医药设计院	120	0	0	120
中船第九设计研究院	84	0	0	84
华东建筑设计研究院	83	0	0	83
上海机电设计研究院	351	0	0	351
华东电力对外经济贸易公司	8	0	8	0
上海成套设备进出口公司	832	60	772	0
上海建工(集团)总公司	17736	17736	0	0
上海市政工程设计研究院	90	0	0	90
上海航空工业(集团)公司	13	0	13	0
上海水产(集团)公司	401	0	401	0
上海东方国际(集团)有限公司	549	0	549	0
上海浦东国际经济技术合作公司	99	0	99	0
中国华源集团有限公司	626	575	51	0
上海隧道工程股份有限公司	882	882	0	0
上海建筑装饰(集团)总公司	127	127	0	0

1999年中国对外承包工程和劳务合作营业额分公司总值

金额单位:万美元

名　　称	合　计	承包工程	劳务合作	设计咨询
上海住总(集团)总公司	4390	4386	4	0
上海港口机械进出口有限公司	1460	1460	0	0
上海黄埔对外经济技术合作公司	61	0	61	0
上海园林(集团)公司	36	36	0	0
上海城建(集团)公司	382	382	0	0
江苏省	**61291**	**34665**	**26537**	**89**
中国江苏国际经济技术合作公司	16217	13204	3013	0
江苏省建筑工程总公司	787	149	638	0
南通国际经济技术合作公司	1420	520	900	0
连云港国际经济技术合作公司	1647	0	1647	0
镇江国际经济技术合作公司	235	19	216	0
扬州国际经济技术合作公司	1281	231	1050	0
苏州国际经济技术合作公司	730	88	642	0
无锡国际经济技术合作公司	1370	1061	309	0
常州国际经济技术合作(集团)有限公司	601	117	484	0
盐城国际经济技术合作公司	1592	0	1592	0
徐州国际经济技术合作公司	171	85	86	0
淮阴国际经济技术合作公司	1494	0	1494	0
江苏建达建设股份有限公司	1972	1966	6	0
江苏省建筑材料工业总公司	23	0	23	0
南化集团永利进出口公司	113	113	0	0
南京水泥工业设计院	13	5	0	8
张家港国际经济技术合作公司	747	0	747	0
江苏公路桥梁工程公司	495	495	0	0
江苏水利外经公司	5	5	0	0
南京化学工业集团公司设计院	51	51	0	0
启东市对外经济技术合作公司	765	2	763	0
南通第四建筑安装工程公司	2750	2593	157	0
南通市第三建筑安装工程公司	2997	0	2997	0
武进市建设工程公司	455	445	10	0
江苏地质工程有限公司	232	232	0	0
江苏农业对外经济技术合作公司	67	0	67	0
煤炭部南京设计研究院	258	258	0	0
常熟国际经济技术合作公司	156	0	156	0
江苏省建筑安装工程股份有限公司	562	382	180	0
无锡建筑工程公司	226	226	0	0
江苏省矿业总承包公司	130	130	0	0
吴县国际经济技术合作公司	553	519	34	0

1999年中国对外承包工程和劳务合作营业额分公司总值

金额单位:万美元

名　　称	合　计	承包工程	劳务合作	设计咨询
苏州建筑控股集团	714	714	0	0
南通建筑工程总承包公司	818	33	785	0
徐州矿务集团有限公司	180	50	130	0
徐州建筑安装工程公司	57	1	56	0
南通苏中建筑安装工程公司	1722	10	1712	0
徐州工程机械集团公司	129	92	36	1
江都市建设工程总公司(集团)	988	826	162	0
江苏省泰兴市第一建筑安装工程公司	430	0	430	0
江苏省对外交流公司	269	0	269	0
中设江苏公司	34	0	34	0
江苏第一建筑安装有限公司	529	276	253	0
化工部连云港设计研究院	63	0	0	63
常州市对外经济技术贸易集团公司	805	69	736	0
江苏天目安装集团公司	975	950	25	0
盐城市天虹建筑工程总公司	750	219	531	0
江苏邗建集团有限公司	84	0	84	0
南通市第六建筑安装工程公司	573	58	515	0
苏州进出口(集团)有限公司	17	0	0	17
江苏正太股份有限公司	491	82	409	0
镇江建筑工程公司	463	250	213	0
江苏三兴建工集团有限公司	224	0	240	0
苏州建设集团有限公司	205	205	0	0
江苏舜天机械进出口公司	1000	1000	0	0
金坛国际经济技术合作公司	1213	271	942	0
南通市经济技术开发区总公司	12	0	12	0
金坛市建筑安装工程公司	568	374	194	0
江苏省工业设备安装公司	69	30	39	0
南京市	**7794**	**6259**	**1535**	**0**
南京国际经济技术合作公司	2216	1271	945	0
南京海外建筑工程公司	3076	2903	173	0
南京市住宅建设总公司	778	712	66	0
熊猫电子进出口公司	50	50	0	0
南京大地建设(集团)股份有限公司	1155	814	341	0
金城集团进出口有限公司	29	19	10	0
南京纺织品进出口股份有限公司	490	490	0	0
浙江省	**34371**	**14826**	**19274**	**271**
中国浙江国际经济技术合作公司	2769	573	2196	0
浙江省建工集团有限责任公司	5883	4886	997	0

1999 年中国对外承包工程和劳务合作营业额分公司总值

金额单位:万美元

名　　称	合　计	承包工程	劳务合作	设计咨询
浙江省机械设备进出口总公司	9	0	9	0
浙江省建筑设计研究院	20	0	0	20
杭州国际经济技术合作公司	300	0	300	0
温州国际经济技术合作公司	131	63	68	0
绍兴国际经济技术合作公司	933	29	904	0
舟山国际经济技术合作公司	209	0	209	0
丽水国际经济技术合作公司	289	0	289	0
湖州对外经济技术合作有限公司	85	0	85	0
金华对外经济技术合作有限公司	325	0	325	0
台州国际经济技术合作公司	235	114	121	0
嘉兴市对外经济技术合作有限公司	12	0	12	0
浙江省粮油食品进出口股份有限公司	151	0	151	0
机械工业部第二设计研究院	62	61	0	1
电力工业部华东勘测设计研究院	183	0	0	183
浙江中大对外经济技术合作有限公司	259	0	259	0
浙江省轻工业品进出口公司	12	0	12	0
浙江东方集团股份有限公司	98	0	98	0
浙江舜杰建筑集团股份有限公司	332	178	154	0
诸暨市建筑安装工程公司	398	345	53	0
浙江中雷建筑集团股份有限公司	689	489	200	0
浙江省对外服务公司	142	0	142	0
绍兴市第一建筑安装工程公司	397	397	0	0
上虞市第五建筑工程公司	15	0	15	0
杭州市对外经济贸易服务公司	109	0	109	0
浙江环宇建设集团有限公司	91	91	0	0
浙江省其他企业	2484	2193	291	0
宁波市	**17749**	**5407**	**12275**	**67**
中国宁波国际合作(集团)有限公司	3128	115	2946	67
宁波天地集团股份有限公司	2750	9	2741	0
宁波市宁兴集团公司(进出口)	2221	0	2221	0
宁波国际建设经贸公司	3299	0	3299	0
宁波市建筑安装集团总公司	1746	1283	463	0
鄞县进出口公司	359	0	359	0
龙元建设集团股份有限公司	1984	1984	0	0
宏润建设集团股份有限公司	2016	2016	0	0
宁波市工艺品进出口公司	246	0	246	0
安徽省	**9924**	**7114**	**2657**	**153**
安徽国际经济技术合作公司	768	18	743	7

1999年中国对外承包工程和劳务合作营业额分公司总值

金额单位:万美元

名　称	合　计	承包工程	劳务合作	设计咨询
蚌埠玻璃工业设计研究院	46	46	0	0
安徽省外经建设(集团)公司	2593	2142	451	0
合肥对外经济技术合作公司	283	0	283	0
冶金部马鞍山钢铁设计研究院	130	0	0	130
蚌埠国际经济技术合作公司	110	102	8	0
安徽建工集团有限公司	405	12	393	0
安徽省水利水电勘察设计院	7	0	0	7
芜湖国际经济技术合作公司	204	0	204	0
冶金部第十七冶金建设公司	910	910	0	0
安徽建筑设计研究院	25	0	18	7
合肥建筑集团公司	140	140	0	0
中国化学工程第三建筑公司	1402	1402	0	0
安徽省电力建设二公司	129	127	2	0
宿县地区国际经济技术合作公司	401	0	401	0
安庆国际经济技术合作公司	145	0	145	0
机械部第一设计研究院	18	18	0	0
安徽省对外劳务开发中心	3	0	3	0
煤炭部合肥设计研究院	2	0	0	2
铁道部第四工程局	300	300	0	0
安徽省电力建设第一工程公司	1897	1897	0	0
安徽华光玻璃集团有限公司	6	0	6	0
福建省	**44692**	**8570**	**36007**	**115**
中国福建国际经济技术合作公司	7597	0	7597	0
福州国际经济技术合作公司	4949	0	4949	0
福建省对外劳务合作公司	3761	175	3586	0
福建福通对外经济技术合作公司	1246	0	1246	0
福建省水利水电勘测设计院	20	0	0	20
福建省建筑设计院	269	198	0	71
福建华源国际贸易经济合作公司	430	0	430	0
中国武夷实业总公司	6090	6075	15	0
莆田国际经济技术合作公司	1213	0	1213	0
中国泉州国际经济技术合作集团有限公司	1587	0	1587	0
中国漳州国际经济技术合作公司	1880	0	1880	0
福建厦门轮船总公司	529	0	529	0
宁德国际经济技术合作公司	241	0	241	0
三明国际经济技术合作公司	72	0	72	0
南平国际经济技术合作公司	95	0	95	0
福建省华洋水产集团公司	319	0	319	0

1999年中国对外承包工程和劳务合作营业额分公司总值

金额单位:万美元

名　　称	合　计	承包工程	劳务合作	设计咨询
龙岩国际经济技术合作公司	37	0	37	0
福建省轮船总公司	164	0	164	0
福州市劳务技术合作公司	496	0	496	0
福州壮安发展有限公司	529	0	529	0
福建省投资企业公司	75	0	75	0
福建省金福集团公司	392	0	392	0
福建省对外劳务咨询服务中心	476	0	476	0
福建中旅对外劳务合作公司	186	0	186	0
福建省外国机构服务中心	275	0	275	0
漳浦国际经济技术合作公司	259	0	259	0
福建华旅对外劳务合作公司	244	0	244	0
福建三木集团股份有限公司	534	0	534	0
莆田对外经济技术合作公司	570	0	570	0
福州市建筑设计院	22	0	0	22
福建省人才开发中心	29	0	29	0
福建轻纺工业经济技术公司	154	1	153	0
福建省对外经贸服务公司	360	0	360	0
泉州市对外经济技术服务公司	371	0	371	0
福建省工业设备安装有限公司	1984	1984	0	0
福州市进出口公司	2	0	2	0
福州建工集团公司	134	134	0	0
厦门市	**7101**	**3**	**7096**	**2**
中国厦门国际经济技术合作公司	4599	3	4594	2
厦门建隆发集团公司	939	0	939	0
厦门经济特区船务有限公司	87	0	87	0
厦门国贸集团有限公司	672	0	672	0
厦门经济特区对外贸易集团公司	29	0	29	0
厦门特贸有限公司	653	0	653	0
厦门经贸船务公司	36	0	36	0
厦门诚毅船务公司	86	0	86	0
江西省	**8537**	**5250**	**3178**	**109**
中国江西国际经济技术合作公司	3217	1305	1908	4
南昌对外工程总公司	1559	1550	9	0
江西省建筑工程总公司	370	199	171	0
南昌国际经济技术合作公司	1652	1238	414	0
南昌有色冶金设计研究院	105	0	0	105
江西省轻工业对外经济技术合作公司	420	0	420	0
赣州国际经济技术合作公司	559	425	134	0

1999年中国对外承包工程和劳务合作营业额分公司总值

金额单位:万美元

名 称	合 计	承包工程	劳务合作	设计咨询
萍乡矿务局建筑安装总公司	280	252	28	0
宜春海程经贸发展有限公司	268	268	0	0
吉安对外经济技术合作公司	16	0	16	0
抚州国际经济技术合作公司	63	0	63	0
九江市对外经济合作公司	7	0	7	0
江西省地质工程(集团)公司	8	0	8	0
江西省火电建设公司	13	13	0	0
山东省	**63687**	**40694**	**22973**	**20**
中国山东国际经济技术合作公司	3932	2576	1356	0
齐鲁建设集团公司	1343	1323	20	0
山东省国泰集团公司	87	87	0	0
山东省建筑工程总公司	2920	2920	0	0
山东省外商投资服务公司	320	0	320	0
山东省劳务合作公司	1061	0	1061	0
山东省水产企业集团公司	2064	0	2064	0
济南钢铁集团总公司	27	7	20	0
黄河经济协作区联合发展集团公司	12	0	12	0
山东省物产进出口公司	43	4	39	0
莱芜钢铁总厂	392	392	0	0
山东对外贸易集团有限公司	4	0	4	0
山东省机械进出口公司	7	0	7	0
黄河工程局	1268	1268	0	0
山东省纺织品进出口公司	2	0	2	0
兖州矿业集团公司	10800	10800	0	0
威海国际经济技术合作公司	3179	0	3177	2
烟台国际经济技术合作公司	2720	215	2505	0
烟台市建筑工程公司	2051	1891	160	0
潍坊国际经济技术合作公司	610	5	605	0
淄博国际经济技术合作公司	346	32	312	2
济南国际经济技术合作公司	294	83	211	0
日照国际经济 技术合作公司	1552	187	1365	0
临沂国际经济技术合作公司	253	65	188	0
济宁国际经济技术合作公司	13	0	13	0
泰安国际经济技术合作公司	1886	1158	728	0
东营国际经济技术合作公司	294	0	294	0
潍坊建筑安装工程公司	434	13	421	0
济南四建集团责任有限公司	916	916	0	0
荣成市对外经济技术合作公司	474	0	474	0

1999年中国对外承包工程和劳务合作营业额分公司总值

金额单位：万美元

名　　称	合　计	承包工程	劳务合作	设计咨询
威海火炬高技术开发区进出口公司	138	0	138	0
烟台二建实业股份有限公司	425	65	360	0
淄博建筑工程公司	413	240	173	0
潍坊柴油机厂进出口公司	1247	1192	55	0
济南轻骑集团进出口公司	79	0	79	0
枣庄国际经济技术合作公司	118	0	118	0
诸城市建筑工程公司	2506	2214	292	0
菏泽地区对外经济技术合作公司	113	0	113	0
威海市进出口集团公司	33	0	33	0
泰安建筑工程公司	1197	292	905	0
中国水产烟台海洋渔业公司	1011	463	548	0
胜利油田管理局	3889	3873	11	5
烟台环太国际经贸有限公司	20	20	0	0
德州市国际经济技术合作公司	40	0	40	0
山东省工业设备安装公司	413	413	0	0
山东航运集团	3438	3300	138	0
山东电力核电建设集团公司	1972	1966	6	0
山东省公路工程总公司	1000	1000	0	0
莱芜国际经济技术合作公司	50	0	50	0
青岛市	**6281**	**1714**	**4556**	**11**
中国青岛国际经济技术合作公司	2613	10	2603	0
青岛建设集团公司	1718	1704	14	0
青岛市五金矿产机械进出口公司	262	0	262	0
青岛国际人才技术合作公司	318	0	318	0
青岛海洋渔业公司	323	0	323	0
青岛海尔国际贸易有限公司	15	0	12	3
青岛市建筑设计研究院	8	0	0	8
青岛国际交流中心	47	0	47	0
青岛远达对外经济合作公司	977	0	977	0
河南省	**6237**	**3652**	**2455**	**130**
中国河南国际经济技术合作公司	2737	1695	1042	0
河南省水利电力对外公司	1000	470	530	0
河南省对外劳务合作公司	851	0	851	0
河南省建设工程公司	277	277	0	0
洛阳国际经济技术合作公司	16	0	16	0
商丘国际经济技术合作公司	16	16	0	0
洛阳石油化工工程公司	23	0	0	23
机械部第四设计研究院	96	96	0	0

1999年中国对外承包工程和劳务合作营业额分公司总值

金额单位:万美元

名　　称	合　计	承包工程	劳务合作	设计咨询
洛阳有色金属加工设计院	52	15	0	37
中原石油勘探局外经外贸总公司	1083	1083	0	0
河南濮阳国际经济技术合作公司	5	0	5	0
河南交通规划勘察设计院	70	0	0	70
洛阳浮法玻璃公司	3	0	3	0
金城国际经济技术合作公司(河南)	8	0	8	0
湖北省	**12164**	**8422**	**3474**	**268**
中国湖北国际经济技术合作公司	619	536	83	0
湖北建材工贸(集团)公司	23	0	23	0
湖北大地国际经济技术合作有限公司	108	77	31	0
黄石国际经济技术合作公司	51	0	51	0
宜昌国际经济技术合作公司	12	10	2	0
葛洲坝水利水电工程集团公司	833	833	0	0
中国有色第十五冶金建设公司	2536	2536	0	0
湖北晴川国际海员劳务开发公司	76	0	76	0
孝感国际经济技术合作建筑有限公司	26	0	26	0
荆州国际经济技术合作公司	15	0	15	0
黄冈国际经济技术合作公司	10	0	10	0
十堰国际经济技术合作公司	4	0	4	0
湖北省建筑工程集团有限公司	631	631	0	0
湖北省国际劳务合作有限公司	181	4	177	0
电力工业部中南电力设计院	156	0	0	156
铁道部大桥工程局	297	285	0	12
武汉地质勘察基础工程(集团)总公司	51	51	0	0
湖北国际企业合作公司	67	0	67	0
湖北省机械设备进出口公司	99	0	99	0
武汉市	**6369**	**3459**	**2810**	**100**
中国武汉国际经济技术合作公司	2627	123	2504	0
中国五环化学工程公司	506	506	0	0
武汉建工集团有限公司	505	505	0	0
武汉钢铁设计研究院	67	45	0	22
武汉钢铁(集团)国际经济贸易公司	9	0	0	9
中国第一冶金建设公司	480	480	0	0
铁道部第四勘测设计院	17	1	0	16
华中电力国际经贸公司	145	145	0	0
煤炭部武汉设计院	10	0	0	10
武汉凌云集团有限责任公司	1009	980	29	0
长江航运集团对外经济技术合作总公司	357	85	272	0

1999年中国对外承包工程和劳务合作营业额分公司总值

金额单位：万美元

名　　称	合　计	承包工程	劳务合作	设计咨询
武汉市建筑设计院	43	0	0	43
中国出口商品基地武汉公司	5	0	5	0
武汉市市政工程总公司	589	589	0	0
湖南省	**10077**	**8580**	**1246**	**251**
中国湖南国际经济技术合作公司	1044	642	387	15
湖南省公路桥梁建设公司	1379	1379	0	0
湖南建筑工程集团总公司	257	257	0	0
第二十三冶金建设公司	312	312	0	0
湖南省进出口公司	90	0	90	0
湖南环球(集团)公司	708	0	708	0
长沙冶金设计院	45	0	0	45
长沙轻工设计院	87	0	0	87
湖南建筑设计院	15	0	0	15
湖南机械集团进出口公司	30	0	30	0
电力中南设计院	55	35	0	20
中国水利水电第八工程局	2747	2747	0	0
机械工业部第八设计院	18	0	0	18
长沙有色冶金设计研究院	14	0	0	14
湖南交通国际工程合作公司	1907	1907	0	0
湖南株洲海外国际合作有限公司	28	0	28	0
华隆进出口公司	53	50	3	0
湖南省机械设备进出口公司	400	400	0	0
湖南化学工业设计院	111	85	0	26
湖南省农林工业勘察设计研究总院	11	0	0	11
湖南环达公路桥梁建设公司	636	636	0	0
湖南益阳工程公司	130	130	0	0
广东省	**36270**	**22765**	**13285**	**220**
中国广东国际合作(集团)公司	4946	2640	2306	0
广东对外劳务经济合作公司	6116	0	116	0
广东海外建设总公司	2739	2739	0	0
广东省建筑工程总公司	2048	2048	0	0
广东省源大水利水电集团有限公司	3422	3422	0	0
广东省岭南综合勘测设计院	24	0	0	24
广东省建筑设计研究院	120	75	0	45
珠海国际经济技术合作公司	2395	2200	195	0
汕头国际经济技术合作公司	145	0	145	0
汕尾市对外劳动服务公司	82	0	82	0
江门市对外劳动服务公司	1257	0	1257	0

1999年中国对外承包工程和劳务合作营业额分公司总值

金额单位:万美元

名　　称	合　计	承包工程	劳务合作	设计咨询
广东省南粤进出口公司	293	0	293	0
广东省石油化工建设集团公司	37	37	0	0
中山国际经济技术合作公司	116	109	7	0
珠海劳动服务公司	952	0	952	0
广东省水利电力勘测设计研究院	17	1	0	16
江门甘蔗化工厂(集团)股份有限公司	240	240	0	0
广东省第七建筑集团有限公司	671	671	0	0
广州市	**4595**	**2987**	**1570**	**38**
中国广州国际经济技术合作公司	3198	2006	1192	0
广州对外经济发展总公司	381	3	378	0
广州珠江实业集团有限公司	851	851	0	0
广州建筑总公司	96	96	0	0
广州工程总承包集团有限公司	31	31	0	0
广州市设计院	38	0	0	38
深圳市	**6055**	**5596**	**362**	**97**
中国深圳国际合作(集团)股份有限公司	3163	2971	192	0
深圳市对外劳动服务公司	49	0	49	0
深圳市国际人才劳务经济发展有限公司	112	0	112	0
深圳市建设投资控股公司	131	122	9	0
深圳市建筑设计总院	97	0	0	97
深圳市中兴通讯股份有限公司	2503	2503	0	0
广西自治区	**4508**	**4235**	**269**	**4**
中国广西国际经济技术合作公司	313	195	118	0
南宁国际经济技术合作公司	1298	1229	69	0
广西对外建筑工程总公司	478	424	54	0
北海海外经济技术合作公司	7	0	7	0
防城港国际经济技术合作有限责任公司	476	473	3	0
广西建筑综合设计院	4	0	0	4
广西公路桥梁工程总公司	1512	1512	0	0
广西水利水电对外有限责任公司	228	228	0	0
梧州国际经济技术合作公司	11	10	1	0
广西地矿建设工程发展中心	16	16	0	0
凭祥市对外经济技术合作公司	112	112	0	0
广西玉林国际经济技术合作公司	7	1	6	0
桂林国际经济技术合作公司	11	0	11	0
广西工艺品进出口防城公司	15	15	0	0
广西畜产进出口防城公司	8	8	0	0
广西土产防城港仓储供销公司	12	12	0	0

1999年中国对外承包工程和劳务合作营业额分公司总值

金额单位:万美元

名称	合计	承包工程	劳务合作	设计咨询
海南省	**1146**	**1145**	**1**	**0**
中国海南国际经济技术合作公司	1146	1145	1	0
重庆市	**4510**	**1683**	**2757**	**70**
中国重庆国际经济技术合作公司	921	300	621	0
重庆对外建设总公司	684	630	54	0
宝钢集团重庆钢铁设计研究院	14	0	0	14
万县市国际经济技术合作公司	37	0	37	0
涪陵国际经济技术合作公司	13	0	13	0
重庆钢铁(集团)有限责任公司	29	0	29	0
重庆海外建筑工程承包有限公司	753	753	0	0
嘉陵集团公司	2003	0	2003	0
中煤设计咨询集团重庆院	23	0	0	23
机械部第三设计院	33	0	0	33
四川省	**19679**	**16297**	**2715**	**667**
中国四川国际合作股份有限公司	844	85	759	0
中国华西企业公司	547	524	23	0
四川东方电力设备联合公司	12340	12340	0	0
中国华西工程设计建设总公司	651	0	0	651
中国成达化学工程公司	41	25	0	16
四川公路桥梁工程总公司	527	484	43	0
四川省外经实业股份公司	42	0	42	0
四川省电力进出口公司	63	62	1	0
中国化学工程第七建设公司	442	442	0	0
川铁国际经济技术合作公司	2286	2184	102	0
攀枝花建设总公司	476	0	476	0
成都市建筑工程总公司	94	0	94	0
绵阳国际经济技术合作有限公司	3	0	3	0
四川省劳务开发公司	773	0	773	0
川北电信工程有限公司	151	151	0	0
成都市	**399**	**0**	**399**	**0**
中国成都国际经济技术合作公司	399	0	399	0
贵州省	**2788**	**2775**	**13**	**0**
铁道部第五工程局	875	875	0	0
中国贵航集团西秀进出口公司	8	0	8	0
贵州省桥梁工程公司	1905	1900	5	0
云南省	**16687**	**15271**	**331**	**1085**
中国云南国际经济技术合作公司	1115	1079	36	0
昆明国际经济技术合作公司	241	241	0	0

1999年中国对外承包工程和劳务合作营业额分公司总值

金额单位:万美元

名　　称	合　计	承包工程	劳务合作	设计咨询
云南建工集团总公司	66	66	0	0
云南公路桥梁工程总公司	57	57	0	0
中国有色金属工业第十四冶金建设公司	164	164	0	0
中国云南水利水电昆明国际公司	348	191	157	0
云南地矿勘查工程总公司(集团)	103	0	37	66
云南省铁路总公司	152	152	0	0
云南德宏国际经济技术合作有限责任公司	2051	1977	74	0
云南省机械进出口公司	39	39	0	0
云南省机械设备进出口公司	803	803	0	0
云南省公路规划勘察设计院	84	73	0	11
电力部昆明勘测设计研究院	152	0	27	125
昆明冶金设计研究院	25	0	0	25
林业部昆明勘察设计院	858	0	0	858
文山州国际股份有限公司	2041	2041	0	0
德宏州进出口公司	2075	2075	0	0
瑞丽勐卯商号	119	119	0	0
裕丰商号	714	714	0	0
德宏州香料公司	67	67	0	0
潞西市贸宏商号	56	56	0	0
龙陵县龙山商号	20	20	0	0
文山州永瑞边贸有限公司	47	47	0	0
临沧地区耿马边贸公司	59	59	0	0
保山地区腾冲大同商号	72	72	0	0
临沧地区沧源贸源商号	71	71	0	0
瑞丽市金星公司	45	45	0	0
思茅景谷外贸公司	33	33	0	0
紫金商号	20	20	0	0
云南省进出口公司德宏公司	134	134	0	0
澜沧友联公司	23	23	0	0
瑞丽金得利公司	34	34	0	0
楚雄外贸河口公司	46	46	0	0
河口东亚公司	10	10	0	0
思茅澜沧天仁公司	59	59	0	0
瑞丽市联发公司	59	59	0	0
瑞丽市玉溪商号	60	60	0	0
昆明市力车胎厂	63	63	0	0
云南粮油食品进出口瑞丽分公司	79	79	0	0
梁河县顺通商号	229	229	0	0

1999 年中国对外承包工程和劳务合作营业额分公司总值

金额单位:万美元

名　　称	合　计	承包工程	劳务合作	设计咨询
保山地区外经贸公司	39	39	0	0
瑞丽市蛉达边贸公司	29	29	0	0
瑞丽市振华商号	90	90	0	0
瑞丽市海利达公司	30	30	0	0
芒市边贸商号	23	23	0	0
瑞丽市润友公司	30	30	0	0
盈江县进出口公司	41	41	0	0
云南机设瑞丽进出口公司	67	67	0	0
德丽总公司	157	157	0	0
梁河昆达商号	214	214	0	0
潞西市进出口公司	623	623	0	0
梁河县进出口公司	130	130	0	0
昆明电化厂	56	56	0	0
德宏州顺德公司	230	230	0	0
瑞丽市联益商号	12	12	0	0
德宏州工艺品公司	148	148	0	0
畹町富兴工贸有限公司	96	96	0	0
畹町利群商号	21	21	0	0
思茅孟连建华贸易有限公司	35	35	0	0
德宏州德安总公司	96	96	0	0
梁河县光大公司	140	140	0	0
潞西市德源边贸公司	23	23	0	0
瑞丽市洪顺公司	150	150	0	0
盈江县永福公司	210	210	0	0
畹町市进出口公司	1314	1314	0	0
姐告远大科贸公司	100	100	0	0
梁河县桂梁商号	34	34	0	0
瑞丽市利民商号	56	56	0	0
陕西省	**8381**	**7195**	**907**	**279**
中国陕西国际经济技术合作公司	295	53	191	51
秦海国际工程公司	222	213	9	0
机械部第七设计院	115	100	0	15
中国华陆工程公司	207	160	0	47
西北勘测设计院	10	10	0	0
交通部第一公路设计院	36	0	0	36
陕西省机械设备进出口公司	272	263	9	0
华山国际工程公司	2800	2789	11	0
西飞集团公司	9	0	9	0

1999年中国对外承包工程和劳务合作营业额分公司总值

金额单位:万美元

名　　称	合　计	承包工程	劳务合作	设计咨询
煤炭工业部西安设计研究院	10	0	3	7
中国计算机软件工程公司西安分公司	88	0	88	0
陕西省路桥工程总公司	1926	1926	0	0
中国机械工业第三安装工程公司	125	125	0	0
西北电力设计院(陕西)	127	0	4	123
煤航(集团)实业发展有限公司	100	100	0	0
西安市	**2039**	**1456**	**583**	**0**
西安国际技术贸易公司	857	281	576	0
西安电力机械进出口公司	1171	1171	0	0
西安市机械进出口公司	7	0	7	0
西安天宝国际工程公司	4	4	0	0
甘肃省	**5686**	**5616**	**49**	**21**
中国甘肃国际经济技术合作公司	330	305	25	0
甘肃建筑工程总公司	2950	2950	0	0
兰州石油化工机械总厂	880	880	0	0
甘肃省建筑设计研究院	21	0	0	21
甘肃金川国际经济技术合作有限公司	1170	1170	0	0
甘肃对外经济发展公司	67	43	24	0
甘肃地质工程总公司	268	268	0	0
宁夏自治区	**305**	**300**	**5**	**0**
中国宁夏伊斯兰国际经济技术合作公司	305	300	5	0
新疆自治区	**875**	**800**	**75**	**0**
中国新疆国际经济技术合作公司	360	360	0	0
新疆建筑工程总公司	378	378	0	0
新疆机械化工五金矿产轻工进出口公司	15	0	15	0
新疆石油管理局	62	62	0	0
新疆生产建设兵团	60	0	60	0
新天国际经济技术合作公司	60	0	60	0

1999年末中国在外从事对外承包工程和劳务合作的人数

单位:人

名　　称	合　计	承包工程	劳务合作	设计咨询
合　　计	**382275**	**55330**	**326494**	**451**
中央合计	**63730**	**24823**	**38810**	**97**
中国建筑工程总公司	6077	5051	1018	8
中国广播电视国际经济技术合作公司	4	4	0	0

1999年末中国在外从事对外承包工程和劳务合作的人数

单位:人

名　　称	合　计	承包工程	劳务合作	设计咨询
中国冶金建设集团总公司	154	110	15	29
中国商业对外经济技术合作公司	56	0	56	0
中国水产(集团)总公司	489	319	170	0
中国国际技术智力合作公司	4937	0	4937	0
中国路桥(集团)总公司	1550	958	592	0
中国土木工程集团公司	3691	804	2887	0
中国港湾建设(集团)总公司	1827	1722	105	0
中国海外工程总公司	2290	875	1415	0
中国水利电力对外公司	1024	1020	4	0
中国石化工程建设公司	86	84	2	0
中国化学工程(集团)公司	214	214	0	0
中国轻工业对外经济技术合作公司	1632	21	1611	0
中国电子国际经济技术合作公司	216	0	216	0
中国地质工程集团公司	314	314	0	0
中国光大国际经济技术合作公司	23	23	0	0
中国农牧渔业国际合作公司	44	31	11	2
中国航空技术国际工程公司	830	466	364	0
中国国际计算机软件工程公司	588	0	588	0
中国林业国际合作公司	52	0	52	0
中国建材工业对外经济技术合作公司	633	61	572	0
中国万宝工程公司	483	403	80	0
中国交远国际经济技术合作公司	843	104	739	0
中国海员对外经济技术合作公司	2840	0	2840	0
中国石油工程建设(集团)公司	3200	3181	19	0
科智国际技术合作公司	103	0	103	0
中国四达国际经济技术合作公司	1219	0	1219	0
中国中原对外工程公司	349	349	0	0
中海国际石油工程有限责任公司	75	75	0	0
中国国际工程咨询公司	16	5	1	10
中国体育国际经济技术合作公司	39	9	30	0
中国海外贸易总公司	408	0	408	0
中国电子系统工程总公司	1230	1230	0	0
中国铁道建筑总公司	1063	80	983	0
中国建筑材料工业建设总公司	55	0	55	0
中国化工建设总公司	10	10	0	0
中国出国人员服务总公司	70	0	70	0
中国海外经济合作总公司	76	24	52	0
中国机械设备进出口总公司	82	80	2	0

1999年末中国在外从事对外承包工程和劳务合作的人数

单位：人

名　称	合　计	承包工程	劳务合作	设计咨询
中国寰球化学工程公司	380	350	10	20
中国机械对外经济技术合作公司	202	0	202	0
远大国际经济合作有限责任公司	159	6	153	0
中国有色金属建设股份有限公司	1042	582	460	0
中国医疗卫生对外经济合作公司	190	6	184	0
中国纺织工业对外经济技术合作公司	191	170	21	0
中国化工进出口总公司	150	0	150	0
中国航空工业规划设计院	14	0	0	14
中国通信建设总公司	21	21	0	0
中远对外劳务合作公司	11181	0	11181	0
中国成套设备进出口(集团)总公司	3206	975	2231	0
中国对外建设总公司	31	31	0	0
北京有色冶金设计研究总院	4	0	4	0
燕兴国际经济技术合作公司	279	0	279	0
中国铁路工程总公司	1225	846	379	0
中国机械进出口(集团)有限公司	340	340	0	0
北京中民国际经济合作公司	22	0	22	0
北京钢铁设计研究院	3	0	0	3
中国电力技术进出口公司	844	338	506	0
华北电力设计院	7	5	0	2
中国安能建设总公司	14	14	0	0
华鑫国际经济贸易公司	7	0	7	0
中翰科技经济发展总公司	21	0	21	0
中国京冶建设工程承包公司	104	104	0	0
中外园林建设总公司	40	40	0	0
广播电影电视部设计院	1	0	0	1
国内贸易部设计院	4	0	4	0
建设部综合勘察研究院	5	5	0	0
中国友发国际工程设计咨询公司	12	0	12	0
中国石化北京设计院	8	0	0	8
中土畜劳务合作有限公司	442	0	442	0
中国国际人才开发中心	102	0	102	0
中水远洋渔业有限责任公司	3156	2168	988	0
北京市地质矿产勘查开发总公司	11	11	0	0
中国机械工业安装总公司	132	132	0	0
华北电力国际经贸公司	87	8	79	0
中设国际工程有限公司	188	188	0	0
中国工程与农业机械进出口总公司	188	188	0	0

1999年末中国在外从事对外承包工程和劳务合作的人数

单位:人

名　　称	合　计	承包工程	劳务合作	设计咨询
北京中水远洋渔业发展公司	192	167	25	0
中国新星石油公司	37	27	10	0
中国燕兴总公司	85	0	85	0
中国电力建设工程咨询公司	15	15	0	0
中国水利水电工程总公司	252	252	0	0
中国华联国际贸易公司	24	0	24	0
中国华阳技术贸易(集团)公司	13	0	13	0
中油技术服务有限责任公司	119	119	0	0
中国石油技术开发公司	88	88	0	0
地方合计	**318545**	**30507**	**287684**	**354**
北京市	**3476**	**2194**	**1277**	**5**
中国北京国际经济合作公司	722	113	609	0
北京市建筑工程总公司	294	0	294	0
北京市政工程总公司	91	90	1	0
北京市政工程设计研究院	3	1	2	0
北京市建筑设计院	5	0	0	5
北京住宅开发建设集团总公司	1604	1604	0	0
北京城建集团总公司	176	176	0	0
首钢总公司国际经贸部	145	14	131	0
四通国际经济技术合作公司	204	0	204	0
北京市外国企业服务总公司	36	0	36	0
北京城乡建设集团总公司	13	13	0	0
北京市第二房修工程公司	24	24	0	0
中国燕山联合对外贸易有限公司	87	87	0	0
北京八仙房地产开发公司	72	72	0	0
天津市	**11282**	**544**	**10736**	**2**
中国天津国际经济技术合作公司	8354	385	7969	0
天津立达国际劳务工程公司	2198	0	2198	0
天津建工集团总公司	162	106	56	0
天津市建筑设计院	6	0	6	0
铁道部第三勘测设计院	5	0	5	0
机械部第五设计研究院	37	0	37	0
天津港海员对外服务公司	170	0	170	0
天津市亿利达集团有限公司	21	0	21	0
天津天航海员技术服务公司	130	0	130	0
中国成套天津公司	72	0	72	0
天津机械进出口集团有限公司	25	0	25	0
天津纺织进出口集团有限公司	3	0	3	0

1999年末中国在外从事对外承包工程和劳务合作的人数

单位:人

名称	合计	承包工程	劳务合作	设计咨询
水利部天津水利水电勘测设计研究院	6	0	4	2
天津五矿进出口集团有限公司	4	0	4	0
大港油田集团有限责任公司	39	39	0	0
天海集团股份有限公司	36	0	36	0
天津开发区苏伊士国合有限公司	2	2	0	0
铁道部第十八局	12	12	0	0
河北省	**6613**	**837**	**5764**	**12**
中国河北国际经济技术合作公司	1156	15	1141	0
石家庄国际经济技术合作公司	1674	0	1674	0
河北公路工程建设集团有限公司	20	20	0	0
河北建工集团有限责任公司	714	0	714	0
核工业部第四设计研究院	6	6	0	0
唐山国际工程总公司	1191	0	1191	0
中国耀华玻璃(集团)公司	170	0	170	0
中国第二十二冶金建设公司	4	4	0	0
张家口对外劳务工程公司	246	0	246	0
秦皇岛国际经济技术合作公司	12	0	0	12
地矿河北工程勘测公司	5	5	0	0
保定国际经济技术合作公司	180	0	180	0
承德对外经济合作公司	39	0	39	0
唐山对外合作公司	50	0	50	0
铁道部建场工程局	22	22	0	0
河北省水利工程局	60	0	60	0
中油管道建设有限责任公司	630	630	0	0
河北国际供销合作总公司	107	0	107	0
华北石油管理局	35	35	0	0
河北省进出口贸易公司	4	0	4	0
河北省纺织品进出口公司	12	0	12	0
廊坊对外经济技术合作有限公司	36	0	36	0
邢台路桥公司	100	100	0	0
辰光集团公司	27	0	27	0
沧州对外经济技术合作公司	113	0	113	0
山西省	**1340**	**85**	**1253**	**2**
中国山西国际经济技术合作公司	662	48	612	2
山西省建筑工程总公司	456	0	456	0
太原市国际经济技术合作公司	100	0	100	0
山西省公路桥梁工程总公司	16	16	0	0
山西四建集团有限公司	39	1	38	0

1999年末中国在外从事对外承包工程和劳务合作的人数

单位:人

名　　称	合　计	承包工程	劳务合作	设计咨询
太原重型机器进出口公司	39	11	28	0
中国第十三冶金建设公司	28	9	19	0
内蒙古自治区	**1971**	**251**	**1684**	**36**
中国内蒙古国际经济技术合作公司	108	0	108	0
冶金部包头钢铁设计研究院	36	0	0	36
呼伦贝尔盟国际经济技术合作公司	327	0	327	0
满洲里国际经济技术合作有限公司	338	0	338	0
内蒙古电力(集团)有限责任公司	5	5	0	0
二连浩特国际经济技术合作公司	257	36	221	0
锡林郭勒国际经济技术合作公司	136	0	136	0
额尔古纳国际经济技术合作公司	80	0	80	0
内蒙古高等院校科技开发集团	5	0	5	0
二连浩特市华天对外贸易有限责任公司	53	15	38	0
额尔古纳市边境贸易公司	25	0	25	0
新巴尔虎右旗边境贸易公司	50	0	50	0
满洲里华运公司	30	0	30	0
中国内蒙古森林工业集团有限责任公司	328	0	328	0
新三维国际经济技术合作股份有限公司	42	30	12	0
呼和浩特铁路对外经济技术合作公司	142	165	－23	0
内蒙古农牧业科技开发公司	9	0	9	0
辽宁省	**29246**	**1767**	**27466**	**13**
中国辽宁国际合作(集团)股份有限公司	5176	125	5051	0
辽宁省建设集团公司	292	235	57	0
辽宁国际建设工程集团公司	92	2	90	0
鞍山国际经济技术合作公司	863	198	661	4
抚顺对外建设经济合作(集团)股份公司	1352	41	1311	0
本溪对外经济技术合作总公司	1401	0	1401	0
丹东国际经济技术合作公司	530	0	530	0
营口国际经济技术合作公司	459	0	459	0
鞍山焦化耐火材料设计院	1	0	0	1
东北电力集团进出口公司	136	113	23	0
锦州华锦国际经贸股份有限公司	328	0	326	2
铁岭国际经济技术合作公司	70	0	70	0
辽宁华曦集团	921	18	903	0
辽阳国际经济技术合作公司	400	0	400	0
中国第三冶金建设公司	313	0	310	3
辽河石油勘探局	43	43	0	0
朝阳建设集团有限公司	111	90	21	0

1999年末中国在外从事对外承包工程和劳务合作的人数

单位：人

名　　称	合　计	承包工程	劳务合作	设计咨询
辽宁食品进出口公司	168	0	168	0
辽宁粮油进出口公司	13	0	13	0
抚顺市第二建筑工程公司	21	0	21	0
辽宁省国际劳务交流有限公司	86	0	86	0
本钢集团国际经济贸易有限公司	84	18	66	0
阜新国际经济合作技术公司	41	0	41	0
沈阳市	**3050**	**500**	**2550**	**0**
中国沈阳国际经济技术合作公司	2803	500	2303	0
沈阳对外经济建设总公司	91	0	91	0
沈阳海外建筑工程承包公司	67	0	67	0
煤炭工业部沈阳设计研究院	67	0	67	0
中国建筑东北设计研究院	22	0	22	0
大连市	**13295**	**384**	**12908**	**3**
中国大连合作(集团)股份有限公司	6998	295	6703	0
瓦房店市国际工程公司	6	6	0	0
辽宁省大连海洋渔业集团公司	858	0	858	0
大连经济技术开发区劳务公司	829	0	829	0
大化国际经济贸易公司	40	0	40	0
大连华南国际经济技术合作公司	503	78	425	0
大连港国际经济技术合作公司	270	0	270	0
大连渤海建筑集团有限公司	119	0	119	0
大连远洋船员管理公司	635	0	635	0
中国外运大连公司	681	0	681	0
中国成套设备进出口大连公司	108	0	108	0
大连水产远洋渔业公司	780	0	780	0
大连亿达国际合作公司	105	5	100	0
辽宁成大股份公司	203	0	203	0
中国辽宁国际合作大连开发总公司	915	0	915	0
辽宁机械进出口公司	54	0	51	3
大连航运集团有限公司	191	0	191	0
吉林省	**27340**	**2566**	**24755**	**19**
中国吉林国际经济技术合作公司	5161	56	5105	0
吉林市对外经济技术合作公司	886	0	886	0
延边对外经济技术合作公司	1707	299	1408	0
珲春国际经济技术合作公司	328	14	314	0
吉林化学工业进出口公司	229	0	229	0
吉林冶金建设公司	56	0	56	0
吉林省对外招商建设总公司	2220	588	1632	0

1999年末中国在外从事对外承包工程和劳务合作的人数

单位:人

名　　称	合　计	承包工程	劳务合作	设计咨询
吉林省建筑总公司	155	108	47	0
延边海外经济技术合作公司	2011	0	2011	0
吉林建设开发集团公司	71	71	0	0
吉林省对外经济技术合作公司	511	42	469	0
吉林国际人才交流公司	1315	0	1315	0
吉林森林工业集团公司	67	67	0	0
吉林省对外经济发展公司	3702	0	3702	0
辽源对外经济技术合作公司	114	40	74	0
延边国际经济技术合作公司	542	0	542	0
吉林省纺织品进出口公司	15	6	9	0
四平远东外建合作公司	128	0	128	0
吉林化工工程公司	53	53	0	0
吉林省农业对外合作公司	566	0	566	0
通化金宝国际经济技术合作有限公司	61	41	20	0
吉林省新创对外工程公司	75	66	9	0
吉林省工程建设有限公司	516	500	16	0
吉林化工(集团)建设公司	855	615	221	19
吉林轻工集团股份公司	221	0	221	0
珲春对外经贸公司	98	0	98	0
吉林省海外工程有限公司	374	0	374	0
长春国际经济技术合作公司	1377	0	1377	0
长春建工集团总公司	310	0	310	0
长春对外劳务合作公司	138	0	138	0
长春对外经济技术合作公司	3373	0	3373	0
长春星宇集团股份有限公司	105	0	105	0
黑龙江省	**8678**	**726**	**7952**	**0**
中国黑龙江国际经济技术合作公司	571	-85	656	0
黑龙江国际工程技术合作公司	772	150	622	0
黑龙江东方集团国际经济技术合作公司	72	32	40	0
黑龙江省森林工业对外经济贸易公司	280	0	280	0
中国煤炭国际经济技术合作黑龙江公司	43	0	43	0
哈尔滨铁路局对外经济技术合作公司	306	119	187	0
黑龙江省瑞驰建设公司	117	4	113	0
齐齐哈尔国际经济技术合作公司	132	39	93	0
牡丹江国际经济技术合作公司	47	0	47	0
东宁宏达经济贸易公司	34	0	34	0
东宁国际经济技术合作公司	1003	40	963	0
密山市经济技术合作公司	70	0	70	0

1999年末中国在外从事对外承包工程和劳务合作的人数

单位:人

名　　称	合　计	承包工程	劳务合作	设计咨询
绥芬河国际经济技术合作公司	50	0	50	0
黑龙江其他企业	**226**	**0**	**226**	**0**
同江国际经济技术合作公司	317	0	317	0
黑河国际经济技术合作公司	159	0	159	0
伊春市边境贸易公司	286	10	276	0
萝北边境贸易公司	12	0	12	0
饶河县边境贸易公司	70	0	70	0
东宁欣荣经济贸易公司	165	0	165	0
同江市北江有限公司	175	0	175	0
绥芬河华城国际经济公司	495	10	485	0
绥芬河兴建经济贸易公司	108	40	68	0
绥芬河京鹏经济贸易公司	3	0	3	0
绥芬河英泰经贸公司	204	0	204	0
同江市农业综合公司	140	0	140	0
同江龙华经贸公司	40	0	40	0
绥芬河进出口公司	58	0	58	0
同江三友物资公司	75	0	75	0
绥芬河金地经贸公司	18	0	18	0
绥芬河兴远经贸公司	45	0	45	0
黑河龙亚经贸公司	35	0	35	0
中技贸易股份公司	1500	0	1500	0
绥芬河国际工程公司	153	0	153	0
黑龙江对外经贸公司	25	25	0	0
同江城龙经贸公司	12	0	12	0
黑河蓝天公司	140	0	140	0
抚远边贸公司	50	0	50	0
同江六和实业公司	198	198	0	0
哈尔滨市	**472**	**144**	**328**	**0**
哈尔滨国际经济技术合作公司	109	0	109	0
哈尔滨对外经济技术合作公司	192	0	192	0
哈尔滨中建工程公司	18	0	18	0
哈尔滨第二建设公司	9	0	9	0
哈尔滨电站工程责任有限公司	144	144	0	0
上海市	**27458**	**1951**	**25497**	**10**
中国上海外经(集团)有限公司	12556	315	12241	0
上海对外劳务合作公司	5115	0	5115	0
上海对外建设公司	14	12	2	0
上海机械进出口(集团)有限公司	108	0	108	0

1999年末中国在外从事对外承包工程和劳务合作的人数

单位:人

名　　称	合　计	承包工程	劳务合作	设计咨询
上海机械设备进出口公司	60	60	0	0
上海电气(集团)总公司	24	24	0	0
上海市对外服务公司	1793	0	1793	0
上海轻纺工业对外经济技术合作公司	2626	0	2626	0
上海核工程研究设计院	10	0	0	10
华东建筑设计研究院	4	0	4	0
上海成套设备进出口公司	1370	14	1356	0
上海建工(集团)总公司	645	643	2	0
上海航空工业(集团)公司	210	0	210	0
上海水产(集团)公司	683	0	683	0
上海东方国际(集团)有限公司	933	0	933	0
上海浦东国际经济技术合作公司	180	0	180	0
中国华源集团有限公司	125	0	125	0
上海隧道工程股份有限公司	193	193	0	0
上海建筑装饰(集团)总公司	39	39	0	0
上海住总(集团)总公司	667	618	49	0
上海港口机械进出口有限公司	15	15	0	0
上海黄埔对外经济技术合作公司	70	0	70	0
上海园林(集团)公司	18	18	0	0
江苏省	**32424**	**7402**	**25012**	**10**
中国江苏国际经济技术合作公司	6121	1176	4945	0
江苏省建筑工程总公司	711	79	632	0
南通国际经济技术合作公司	1826	445	1381	0
连云港国际经济技术合作公司	1673	0	1673	0
镇江国际经济技术合作公司	387	0	387	0
扬州国际经济技术合作公司	1076	130	946	0
苏州国际经济技术合作公司	1285	0	1285	0
无锡国际经济技术合作公司	208	55	153	0
常州国际经济技术合作(集团)有限公司	428	14	414	0
盐城国际经济技术合作公司	600	0	600	0
徐州国际经济技术合作公司	159	19	140	0
淮阴国际经济技术合作公司	695	0	695	0
江苏建达建设股份有限公司	5	5	0	0
江苏省建筑材料工业总公司	61	0	61	0
南京水泥工业设计院	2	2	0	0
张家港国际经济技术合作公司	536	0	536	0
江苏公路桥梁工程公司	124	77	47	0
启东市对外经济技术合作公司	825	0	825	0

1999年末中国在外从事对外承包工程和劳务合作的人数

单位:人

名　　称	合　计	承包工程	劳务合作	设计咨询
南通第四建筑安装工程公司	149	26	123	0
南通市第三建筑安装工程公司	1384	0	1384	0
武进市建设工程公司	82	69	13	0
江苏地质工程有限公司	49	49	0	0
江苏农业对外经济技术合作公司	67	0	67	0
常熟国际经济技术合作公司	358	0	358	0
江苏省建筑安装工程股份有限公司	232	119	113	0
江苏省矿业总承包公司	74	74	0	0
吴县国际经济技术合作公司	168	126	42	0
苏州建筑控股集团	35	35	0	0
南通建筑工程总承包公司	492	11	481	0
徐州矿务集团有限公司	73	0	73	0
徐州建筑安装工程公司	76	0	76	0
南通苏中建筑安装工程公司	500	44	456	0
徐州工程机械集团公司	80	0	80	0
江都市建设工程总公司(集团)	913	855	58	0
江苏省泰兴市第一建筑安装工程公司	106	0	106	0
江苏省对外交流公司	951	0	951	0
中设江苏公司	13	0	13	0
江苏第一建筑安装有限公司	381	42	339	0
化工部连云港设计研究院	3	0	0	3
常州市对外经济技术贸易集团公司	730	0	730	0
江苏天目安装集团公司	91	-19	110	0
盐城市天虹建筑工程总公司	1055	0	1055	0
江苏邗建集团有限公司	202	0	202	0
南通市第六建筑安装工程公司	431	0	431	0
苏州进出口(集团)有限公司	7	0	0	7
江苏正太股份有限公司	387	64	323	0
镇江建筑工程公司	235	140	95	0
江苏三兴建工集团有限公司	158	0	158	0
江苏舜天机械进出口公司	300	300	0	0
金坛国际经济技术合作公司	1040	3	1037	0
南通市经济技术开发区总公司	16	0	16	0
金坛市建筑安装工程公司	144	52	92	0
南京市	**4720**	**3410**	**1310**	**0**
南京国际经济技术合作公司	3469	2349	1120	0
南京海外建筑工程公司	826	689	137	0
南京市住宅建设总公司	327	317	10	0

1999年末中国在外从事对外承包工程和劳务合作的人数

单位:人

名　　称	合　计	承包工程	劳务合作	设计咨询
熊猫电子进出口公司	2	2	0	0
南京大地建设(集团)股份有限公司	42	0	42	0
金城集团进出口有限公司	1	0	1	0
南京纺织品进出口股份有限公司	53	53	0	0
浙江省	**22406**	**1524**	**20847**	**35**
中国浙江国际经济技术合作公司	2832	230	2602	0
浙江省建工集团有限责任公司	798	458	340	0
浙江省机械设备进出口总公司	33	0	33	0
杭州国际经济技术合作公司	448	0	448	0
温州国际经济技术合作公司	251	17	234	0
绍兴国际经济技术合作公司	1335	0	1335	0
舟山国际经济技术合作公司	344	0	344	0
丽水国际经济技术合作公司	592	2	590	0
湖州对外经济技术合作有限公司	114	0	114	0
金华对外经济技术合作有限公司	816	0	816	0
台州国际经济技术合作公司	207	38	169	0
嘉兴市对外经济技术合作有限公司	37	0	37	0
浙江省粮油食品进出口股份有限公司	293	0	293	0
电力工业部华东勘测设计研究院	－1	0	1	－2
浙江中大对外经济技术合作有限公司	200	0	200	0
浙江省轻工业品进出口公司	37	0	37	0
浙江东方集团股份有限公司	80	0	80	0
浙江舜杰建筑集团股份有限公司	278	0	278	0
诸暨市建筑安装工程公司	67	2	65	0
浙江中雷建筑集团股份有限公司	224	181	43	0
浙江省对外服务公司	57	0	57	0
绍兴市第一建筑安装工程公司	129	129	0	0
上虞市第五建筑工程公司	138	0	138	0
杭州市对外经济贸易服务公司	27	0	27	0
浙江省其他企业	**468**	**190**	**278**	**0**
宁波市	**12602**	**277**	**12288**	**37**
中国宁波国际合作(集团)有限公司	3064	9	3018	37
宁波天地集团股份有限公司	2744	148	2596	0
宁波市宁兴集团公司(进出口)	3152	0	3152	0
宁波国际建设经贸公司	2707	31	2676	0
宁波市建筑安装集团总公司	185	70	115	0
鄞县进出口公司	502	0	502	0
宏润建设集团股份有限公司	19	19	0	0

1999年末中国在外从事对外承包工程和劳务合作的人数

单位：人

名称	合计	承包工程	劳务合作	设计咨询
宁波市工艺品进出口公司	229	0	229	0
安徽省	**4276**	**630**	**3636**	**10**
安徽国际经济技术合作公司	806	4	796	6
安徽省外经建设(集团)公司	1110	172	938	0
合肥对外经济技术合作公司	385	0	385	0
蚌埠国际经济技术合作公司	66	62	4	0
安徽建工集团有限公司	461	7	454	0
安徽省水利水电勘察设计院	2	0	0	2
芜湖国际经济技术合作公司	183	0	183	0
冶金部第十七冶金建设公司	116	116	0	0
安徽建筑设计研究院	33	0	31	2
中国化学工程第三建筑公司	245	245	0	0
安徽省电力建设二公司	1	0	1	0
宿县地区国际经济技术合作公司	579	0	579	0
安庆国际经济技术合作公司	193	0	193	0
机械部第一设计研究院	4	4	0	0
安徽省对外劳务开发中心	41	0	41	0
铁道部第四工程局	20	20	0	0
淮南市国际经济技术合作公司	11	0	11	0
安徽华光玻璃集团有限公司	20	0	20	0
福建省	**56916**	**117**	**56797**	**2**
中国福建国际经济技术合作公司	10484	0	10484	0
福州国际经济技术合作公司	6348	95	6253	0
福建省对外劳务合作公司	7266	0	7266	0
福建福通对外经济技术合作公司	2883	0	2883	0
福建省建筑设计院	4	2	0	2
福建华源国际贸易经济合作公司	1100	0	1100	0
中国武夷实业总公司	34	20	14	0
莆田国际经济技术合作公司	2161	0	2161	0
中国泉州国际经济技术合作集团有限公司	2619	0	2619	0
中国漳州国际经济技术合作公司	3571	0	3571	0
福建厦门轮船总公司	754	0	754	0
宁德国际经济技术合作公司	178	0	178	0
三明国际经济技术合作公司	181	0	181	0
南平国际经济技术合作公司	359	0	359	0
福建省华洋水产集团公司	802	0	802	0
龙岩国际经济技术合作公司	47	0	47	0
福建省轮船总公司	228	0	228	0

1999年末中国在外从事对外承包工程和劳务合作的人数

单位:人

名　　称	合　计	承包工程	劳务合作	设计咨询
福州市劳务技术合作公司	773	0	773	0
福州壮安发展有限公司	1015	0	1015	0
福建省投资企业公司	95	0	95	0
福建省金福集团公司	680	0	680	0
福建省对外劳务咨询服务中心	751	0	751	0
福建中旅对外劳务合作公司	441	0	441	0
福建省外国机构服务中心	705	0	705	0
漳浦国际经济技术合作公司	672	0	672	0
福建华旅对外劳务合作公司	497	0	497	0
福建三木集团股份有限公司	826	0	826	0
莆田对外经济技术合作公司	1182	0	1182	0
福建省人才开发中心	13	0	13	0
福建轻纺工业经济技术公司	250	0	250	0
福建省对外经贸服务公司	647	0	647	0
泉州市对外经济技术服务公司	621	0	621	0
福州市进出口公司	24	0	24	0
厦门市	**8705**	**0**	**8705**	**0**
中国厦门国际经济技术合作公司	5324	0	5324	0
厦门建隆发集团公司	1171	0	1171	0
厦门经济特区船务有限公司	125	0	125	0
厦门国贸集团有限公司	923	0	923	0
厦门经济特区对外贸易集团公司	159	0	159	0
厦门特贸有限公司	760	0	760	0
厦门经贸船务公司	149	0	149	0
厦门诚毅船务公司	94	0	94	0
江西省	**5419**	**609**	**4803**	**7**
中国江西国际经济技术合作公司	2862	106	2750	6
南昌对外工程总公司	133	114	19	0
江西省建筑工程总公司	139	30	109	0
南昌国际经济技术合作公司	1036	281	755	0
南昌有色冶金设计研究院	2	0	1	1
江西省轻工业对外经济技术合作公司	707	0	707	0
赣州国际经济技术合作公司	270	27	243	0
萍乡矿务局建筑安装总公司	42	19	23	0
宜春海程经贸发展有限公司	43	32	11	0
吉安对外经济技术合作公司	31	0	31	0
抚州国际经济技术合作公司	94	0	94	0
九江市对外经济合作公司	52	0	52	0

1999年末中国在外从事对外承包工程和劳务合作的人数

单位:人

名　　称	合　计	承包工程	劳务合作	设计咨询
江西省地质工程(集团)公司	8	0	8	0
山东省	**31127**	**3392**	**27734**	**1**
中国山东国际经济技术合作公司	2449	96	2353	0
齐鲁建设集团公司	365	337	28	0
山东省国泰集团公司	37	36	0	1
山东省建筑工程总公司	578	578	0	0
山东省外商投资服务公司	407	0	407	0
山东省劳务合作公司	1787	0	1787	0
山东省水产企业集团公司	909	0	909	0
济南钢铁集团总公司	60	36	24	0
黄河经济协作区联合发展集团公司	35	0	35	0
山东省物产进出口公司	68	0	68	0
山东对外贸易集团有限公司	34	0	34	0
山东省机械进出口公司	15	0	15	0
山东省纺织品进出口公司	3	0	3	0
威海国际经济技术合作公司	2923	0	2923	0
烟台国际经济技术合作公司	2250	84	2166	0
烟台市建筑工程公司	269	255	14	0
潍坊国际经济技术合作公司	1145	80	1065	0
淄博国际经济技术合作公司	306	39	267	0
济南国际经济技术合作公司	563	23	540	0
日照国际经济技术合作公司	1507	23	1484	0
临沂国际经济技术合作公司	466	0	466	0
济宁国际经济技术合作公司	42	0	42	0
泰安国际经济技术合作公司	1760	87	1673	0
东营国际经济技术合作公司	363	0	363	0
潍坊建筑安装工程公司	931	19	912	0
济南四建集团责任有限公司	151	151	0	0
荣成市对外经济技术合作公司	537	0	537	0
威海火炬高技术开发区进出口公司	213	0	213	0
烟台二建实业股份有限公司	35	0	35	0
淄博建筑工程公司	43	13	30	0
潍坊柴油机厂进出口公司	107	55	52	0
济南轻骑集团进出口公司	322	0	322	0
枣庄国际经济技术合作公司	191	0	191	0
诸城市建筑工程公司	477	316	161	0
菏泽地区对外经济技术合作公司	131	0	131	0
威海市进出口集团公司	78	0	78	0

1999年末中国在外从事对外承包工程和劳务合作的人数

单位：人

名　　称	合　计	承包工程	劳务合作	设计咨询
泰安建筑工程公司	924	231	693	0
中国水产烟台海洋渔业公司	1017	32	985	0
胜利油田管理局	113	109	4	0
德州市国际经济技术合作公司	109	0	109	0
山东航运集团	228	0	228	0
山东省公路工程总公司	10	10	0	0
莱芜国际经济技术合作公司	71	0	71	0
青岛市	**7098**	**782**	**6316**	**0**
中国青岛国际经济技术合作公司	3156	20	3136	0
青岛建设集团公司	805	762	43	0
青岛市五金矿产机械进出口公司	764	0	764	0
青岛国际人才技术合作公司	810	0	810	0
青岛海洋渔业公司	552	0	552	0
青岛海尔国际贸易有限公司	10	0	10	0
青岛国际交流中心	75	0	75	0
青岛远达对外经济合作公司	926	0	926	0
河南省	**7480**	**327**	**7120**	**33**
中国河南国际经济技术合作公司	2688	90	2598	0
河南省水利电力对外公司	530	0	530	0
河南省对外劳务合作公司	3382	0	3382	0
河南省建设工程公司	37	37	0	0
洛阳国际经济技术合作公司	44	0	44	0
商丘国际经济技术合作公司	18	0	18	0
洛阳石油化工工程公司	5	0	0	5
机械部第四设计研究院	10	10	0	0
洛阳有色金属加工设计院	11	0	0	11
中原石油勘探局外经外贸总公司	190	190	0	0
河南濮阳国际经济技术合作公司	162	0	162	0
河南交通规划勘察设计院	17	0	0	17
洛阳浮法玻璃公司	12	0	12	0
金城国际经济技术合作公司(河南)	374	0	374	0
湖北省	**5679**	**556**	**5090**	**33**
中国湖北国际经济技术合作公司	1216	84	1132	0
湖北建材工贸(集团)公司	17	0	17	0
湖北大地国际经济技术合作有限公司	32	9	23	0
黄石国际经济技术合作公司	40	0	40	0
宜昌国际经济技术合作公司	10	6	4	0
葛洲坝水利水电工程集团公司	167	167	0	0

1999年末中国在外从事对外承包工程和劳务合作的人数

单位:人

名称	合计	承包工程	劳务合作	设计咨询
中国有色第十五冶金建设公司	6	6	0	0
湖北晴川国际海员劳务开发公司	103	0	103	0
孝感国际经济技术合作建筑有限公司	37	0	37	0
荆州国际经济技术合作公司	41	0	41	0
黄冈国际经济技术合作公司	35	0	35	0
十堰国际经济技术合作公司	19	0	19	0
湖北省建筑工程集团有限公司	83	83	0	0
湖北省国际劳务合作有限公司	462	2	460	0
电力工业部中南电力设计院	4	0	0	4
铁道部大桥工程局	34	34	0	0
武汉地质勘察基础工程(集团)总公司	11	11	0	0
湖北国际企业合作公司	164	0	164	0
武汉市	**3198**	**154**	**3015**	**29**
中国武汉国际经济技术合作公司	2545	8	2537	0
中国五环化学工程公司	4	0	0	4
武汉建工集团有限公司	71	71	0	0
武汉钢铁(集团)国际经济贸易公司	2	0	0	2
中国第一冶金建设公司	36	36	0	0
铁道部第四勘测设计院	7	0	1	6
华中电力国际经贸公司	13	13	0	0
煤炭部武汉设计院	3	0	0	3
武汉凌云集团有限责任公司	33	0	33	0
武汉船用机械厂	4	0	4	0
长江航运集团对外经济技术合作总公司	412	-6	418	0
武汉市建筑设计院	4	0	-8	12
中国出口商品基地武汉公司	18	0	18	0
武汉市市政工程总公司	44	32	12	0
冶金部武汉勘察研究院	2	0	0	2
湖南省	**2632**	**355**	**2268**	**9**
中国湖南国际经济技术合作公司	854	115	739	0
湖南省公路桥梁建设公司	34	26	8	0
湖南建筑工程集团总公司	48	38	10	0
湖南省进出口公司	235	0	235	0
湖南环球(集团)公司	941	0	941	0
湖南建筑设计院	1	0	0	1
湖南机械集团进出口公司	130	0	130	0
电力中南设计院	8	0	0	8
中国水利水电第八工程局	103	103	0	0

1999年末中国在外从事对外承包工程和劳务合作的人数

单位:人

名　　称	合　计	承包工程	劳务合作	设计咨询
湖南交通国际工程合作公司	64	64	0	0
湖南株洲海外国际合作有限公司	163	0	163	0
华隆进出口公司	42	0	42	0
湖南省机械设备进出口公司	7	7	0	0
湖南环达公路桥梁建设公司	2	2	0	0
广东省	**19765**	**604**	**19161**	**0**
中国广东国际合作(集团)公司	3504	86	3418	0
广东对外劳务经济合作公司	6586	0	6586	0
广东海外建设总公司	44	17	27	0
广东省建筑工程总公司	46	46	0	0
广东省源大水利水电集团有限公司	133	133	0	0
广东省建筑设计研究院	5	5	0	0
珠海国际经济技术合作公司	1005	123	882	0
汕头国际经济技术合作公司	179	0	179	0
汕尾市对外劳动服务公司	76	0	76	0
江门市对外劳动服务公司	2892	0	2892	0
广东省南粤进出口公司	535	0	535	0
广东省石油化工建设集团公司	23	23	0	0
中山国际经济技术合作公司	32	19	13	0
珠海劳动服务公司	1844	0	1844	0
广州市	**2140**	**54**	**2086**	**0**
中国广州国际经济技术合作公司	1811	7	1804	0
广州对外经济发展总公司	296	14	282	0
广州珠江实业集团有限公司	15	15	0	0
广州建筑总公司	14	14	0	0
广州工程总承包集团有限公司	4	4	0	0
深圳市	**721**	**98**	**623**	**0**
中国深圳国际合作(集团)股份有限公司	267	0	267	0
深圳市对外劳动服务公司	20	0	20	0
深圳市国际人才劳务经济发展有限公司	326	0	326	0
深圳市建设投资控股公司	19	9	10	0
深圳市中兴通讯股份有限公司	78	78	0	0
深圳市华为技术有限公司	11	11	0	0
广西自治区	**1006**	**443**	**563**	**0**
中国广西国际经济技术合作公司	414	54	360	0
南宁国际经济技术合作公司	98	61	37	0
广西对外建筑工程总公司	221	163	58	0
北海海外经济技术合作公司	17	0	17	0

1999年末中国在外从事对外承包工程和劳务合作的人数

单位:人

名　称	合　计	承包工程	劳务合作	设计咨询
防城港国际经济技术合作有限责任公司	71	64	7	0
广西公路桥梁工程总公司	22	22	0	0
广西水利水电对外有限责任公司	10	10	0	0
梧州国际经济技术合作公司	5	0	5	0
凭祥市对外经济技术合作公司	9	9	0	0
广西玉林国际经济技术合作公司	62	0	62	0
桂林国际经济技术合作公司	17	0	17	0
广西工艺品进出口防城公司	7	7	0	0
广西畜产进出口防城公司	20	20	0	0
防城港市京文服务公司	6	6	0	0
广西土产防城港仓储供销公司	27	27	0	0
海南省	**114**	**96**	**18**	**0**
中国海南国际经济技术合作公司	114	96	18	0
重庆市	**1535**	**142**	**1393**	**0**
中国重庆国际经济技术合作公司	765	76	689	0
重庆对外建设总公司	224	59	165	0
万县市国际经济技术合作公司	376	0	376	0
涪陵国际经济技术合作公司	141	0	141	0
重庆钢铁(集团)有限责任公司	15	0	15	0
重庆海外建筑工程承包有限公司	7	7	0	0
嘉陵集团公司	7	0	7	0
四川省	**6154**	**1160**	**4994**	**0**
中国四川国际合作股份有限公司	1198	193	1005	0
中国华西企业公司	118	37	81	0
四川东方电力设备联合公司	46	46	0	0
中国成达化学工程公司	11	11	0	0
四川公路桥梁工程总公司	93	85	8	0
四川省外经实业股份公司	1460	0	1460	0
四川省电力进出口公司	10	10	0	0
中国化学工程第七建设公司	24	24	0	0
川铁国际经济技术合作公司	438	362	76	0
攀枝花建设总公司	51	0	51	0
成都市建筑工程总公司	59	0	59	0
绵阳国际经济技术合作有限公司	43	0	43	0
四川省劳务开发公司	1183	0	1183	0
川北电信工程有限公司	376	376	0	0
四川德阳国际公司	15	3	12	0
成都市	**1029**	**13**	**1016**	**0**

1999年末中国在外从事对外承包工程和劳务合作的人数

单位:人

名　　称	合　计	承包工程	劳务合作	设计咨询
中国成都国际经济技术合作公司	1029	13	1016	0
贵州省	**110**	**15**	**95**	**0**
中国贵州国际经济技术合作公司	20	0	20	0
铁道部第五工程局	15	15	0	0
中国贵航集团西秀进出口公司	36	0	36	0
贵州省桥梁工程公司	39	0	39	0
云南省	**1442**	**1145**	**201**	**96**
中国云南国际经济技术合作公司	212	72	138	2
昆明国际经济技术合作公司	40	40	0	0
云南建工集团总公司	25	25	0	0
云南公路桥梁工程总公司	10	10	0	0
中国有色金属工业第十四冶金建设公司	140	140	0	0
中国云南水利水电昆明国际公司	6	0	0	6
云南地矿勘查工程总公司(集团)	53	0	40	13
云南省铁路总公司	468	468	0	0
云南德宏国际经济技术合作有限责任公司	13	2	11	0
云南省机械进出口公司	10	10	0	0
电力部昆明勘测设计研究院	68	0	12	56
昆明冶金设计研究院	4	0	0	4
林业部昆明勘察设计院	15	0	0	15
文山州国际股份有限公司	49	49	0	0
德宏州进出口公司	39	39	0	0
裕丰商号	26	26	0	0
云南省进出口公司德宏公司	8	8	0	0
瑞丽金得利公司	8	8	0	0
楚雄外贸河口公司	7	7	0	0
河口东亚公司	2	2	0	0
思茅澜沧天仁公司	1	1	0	0
瑞丽市联发公司	1	1	0	0
梁河县顺通商号	53	53	0	0
保山地区外经贸公司	12	12	0	0
瑞丽市蛉达边贸公司	12	12	0	0
云南机设瑞丽进出口公司	12	12	0	0
梁河昆达商号	34	34	0	0
潞西市进出口公司	45	45	0	0
梁河县进出口公司	7	7	0	0
德宏州顺德公司	43	43	0	0
德宏州工艺品公司	3	3	0	0

1999年末中国在外从事对外承包工程和劳务合作的人数

单位:人

名 称	合 计	承包工程	劳务合作	设计咨询
德宏州德安总公司	3	3	0	0
盈江县永福公司	4	4	0	0
畹町市进出口公司	5	5	0	0
姐告远大科贸公司	4	4	0	0
陕西省	**1777**	**400**	**1359**	**18**
中国陕西国际经济技术合作公司	256	59	182	15
秦海国际工程公司	35	24	11	0
西北勘测设计院	9	5	1	3
陕西省机械设备进出口公司	11	5	6	0
华山国际工程公司	224	210	14	0
西飞集团公司	5	0	5	0
煤炭工业部西安设计研究院	5	0	5	0
中国计算机软件工程公司西安分公司	146	0	146	0
中国机械工业第三安装工程公司	36	36	0	0
煤航(集团)实业发展有限公司	4	4	0	0
西安市	**1046**	**57**	**989**	**0**
西安国际技术贸易公司	1008	30	978	0
西安电力机械进出口公司	9	9	0	0
西安市机械进出口公司	11	0	11	0
西安天宝国际工程公司	18	18	0	0
甘肃省	**483**	**384**	**98**	**1**
中国甘肃国际经济技术合作公司	187	126	61	0
甘肃建筑工程总公司	186	186	0	0
兰州石油化工机械总厂	6	1	5	0
甘肃省建筑设计研究院	1	0	0	1
甘肃金川国际经济技术合作有限公司	9	9	0	0
甘肃对外经济发展公司	61	29	32	0
甘肃地质工程总公司	33	33	0	0
宁夏自治区	**69**	**39**	**30**	**0**
中国宁夏伊斯兰国际经济技术合作公司	69	39	30	0
新疆自治区	**327**	**246**	**81**	**0**
新疆建筑工程总公司	220	220	0	0
新疆机械化工五金矿产轻工进出口公司	78	0	78	0
新疆石油管理局	4	4	0	0
新疆生产建设兵团	25	22	3	0
新天国际经济技术合作公司	20	17	3	0
阿拉山口中基有限责任公司	5	5	0	0

1999 年中国批准海外投资企业统计表

国别(地区)	截至 1999 年批准		1999 年批准	
	企业数量（个）	中方投资总额（万美元）	企业数量（个）	中方投资总额（万美元）
合计	**2616**	**317446**	**220**	**59064**
香港	221	25497	24	2448
澳门	52	5760	3	19
朝鲜	6	188	1	61
韩国	19	996	1	10
日本	87	1658	1	54
蒙古	43	4329	15	4026
越南	12	1166	2	662
老挝	8	447	1	200
柬埔寨	40	6750	13	3277
缅甸	13	1261	1	663
泰国	139	6927	3	204
马来西亚	78	3160		
新加坡	85	3168	6	294
印度尼西亚	42	4928	0	1895
菲律宾	29	1083		
尼泊尔	3	61		
巴基斯坦	15	888	3	366
印度	7	1248	3	1050
孟加拉	29	1042		
斯里兰卡	14	1022	3	639
伊朗	4	362	2	356
土耳其	7	851		
塞浦路斯	3	32		
也门	8	418		
沙特阿拉伯	2	81		
卡塔尔	2	67	1	46
阿联酋	22	1436	2	619
阿曼	1	5		
叙利亚	2	63		
约旦	6	364	1	250
科威特	3	81		
以色列	1	6		
俄罗斯	271	10338	12	380
白俄罗斯	2	223		

1999年中国批准海外投资企业统计表

国别(地区)	截至1999年批准		1999年批准	
	企业数量(个)	中方投资总额(万美元)	企业数量(个)	中方投资总额(万美元)
乌克兰	16	219		
拉脱维亚	2	564		
爱沙尼亚	1	2		
立陶宛	1	91		
格鲁吉亚	2	95		
乌兹别克斯坦	12	535		
哈萨克斯坦	32	2504	7	1721
吉尔吉斯斯坦	16	996	4	179
塔吉克斯坦	3	248		
土库曼斯坦	2	30		
阿尔巴尼亚	1	250		
英国	12	731	1	6
法国	16	1001	1	3
德国	33	1138	1	27
瑞士	4	300		
荷兰	16	640	1	12
比利时	7	165	1	3
卢森堡	1	20		
奥地利	7	204		
葡萄牙	3	230		
西班牙	12	412		
意大利	7	300	1	1
马耳他	6	181		
丹麦	2	35		
瑞典	6	186		
芬兰	1	24		
挪威	2	65		
波兰	4	64		
捷克	3	56		
保加利亚	2	175	1	150
匈牙利	14	643		
罗马尼亚	8	1127	4	866
南斯拉夫	1	5		
埃及	12	1957	5	380
利比亚	1	10		

1999年中国批准海外投资企业统计表

国别(地区)	截至1999年批准		1999年批准	
	企业数量（个）	中方投资总额（万美元）	企业数量（个）	中方投资总额（万美元）
阿尔及利亚	1	35		
突尼斯	2	30	1	9
摩洛哥	14	258	3	154
毛塔	2	178		
马里	4	2945	1	120
苏丹	7	1082		
埃塞俄比亚	3	224	1	50
肯尼亚	15	1239	1	380
厄立特里亚	2	97		
坦桑尼亚	12	3708	3	1626
乌干达	9	528	1	185
赞比亚	14	4988	4	665
莫桑比克	3	301	1	193
布隆迪	2	72		
卢旺达	4	285		
马达加斯加	15	718	2	495
毛里求斯	19	723		
刚果(民)	7	2424	1	1600
刚果	1	2		
中非	5	179		
乍得	1	17		
塞内加尔	3	24		
冈比亚	5	175		
几内亚比绍	1	420		
几内亚	3	578		
塞拉利昂	2	115		
利比里亚	7	737		
科特迪瓦	12	1409	2	191
布基纳法索	1	3		
加纳	10	1525	4	1246
多哥	3	111		
贝宁	1	99		
尼日尔	2	102		
尼日利亚	24	2211	2	163
喀麦隆	13	1356	2	462

1999年中国批准海外投资企业统计表

国别(地区)	截至1999年批准		1999年批准	
	企业数量(个)	中方投资总额(万美元)	企业数量(个)	中方投资总额(万美元)
赤道几内亚	4	897	1	98
加蓬	10	1160	1	122
佛得角	3	60		
南非	64	6698	14	1277
纳米比亚	7	803	1	70
津巴布韦	7	3025	1	34
安哥拉	1	198		
博茨瓦纳	6	213	2	4
莱索托	6	62		
塞舌尔	1	15		
巴西	24	4250	1	45
阿根廷	16	613	1	99
乌拉圭	2	28		
智利	6	2087		
秘鲁	10	19646	1	7574
哥伦比亚	5	907	1	777
委内瑞拉	4	182		
厄瓜多尔	14	390		
圭亚那	5	1726	2	1215
法属圭亚那	1	388		
玻利维亚	14	558		
墨西哥	34	12292	2	9700
古巴	1	1200	1	1200
牙买加	2	130		
安提瓜和巴布达	3	130		
巴巴多斯	1	20		
百慕大	8	1360	4	9
开曼群岛	6	210	2	110
洪都拉斯	2	198		
巴拿马	7	96	1	1
伯利兹	2	142		
哥斯达黎加	1	30		
维尔京群岛	14	56	4	20
多米尼加共和国	3	91		
密克罗尼西亚	1	10		

1999 年中国批准海外投资企业统计表

国别(地区)	截至 1999 年批准		1999 年批准	
	企业数量(个)	中方投资总额(万美元)	企业数量(个)	中方投资总额(万美元)
巴哈马	3	106		
玻利尼西亚	2	38		
多米尼克	1	10	1	10
美国	295	48214	21	8110
加拿大	83	35658	1	13
澳大利亚	99	33091	3	170
新西兰	15	4588		
巴布亚新几内亚	16	4327		
斐济	13	713		
瓦努阿图	9	497		
西萨摩亚	5	171		
所罗门群岛	3	54		
贝劳	4	107		

1999 年中国对外援助成套项目建成及提供单项设备情况

行　业	建成项目数	规　　模	受援国别
合　计	**32**		
公用民用建筑	12	(1)牌楼高 13 米、跨度 18.8 米	古巴
		(2)改造参议院会议厅	柬埔寨
		(3)政府办公楼泵房 146 平方米,提供并安装所需设备	贝宁
		(4)建筑面积 5650 平方米总统府	几内亚
		(5)老年人活动中心,建筑面积 3015 平方米	毛里求斯
		(6)人民宫维修、更换电声排水设备	吉布提
		(7)残疾妇女宿舍,建筑面积 300 平方米	喀麦隆
		(8)剧场,建筑面积 12500 平方米	科特迪瓦

1999年中国对外援助成套项目建成及提供单项设备情况

行 业	建成项目数	规 模	受援国别
		(9)贸易中心、建筑面积3400平方米	刚果(金)
		(10)议会大厦、建筑面积15475平方米	加蓬
		(11)低造价住房102套,建筑面积6800平方米	纳米比亚
		(12)外交部大楼改造	马里
文教体育卫生	8	(1)中学增建工程	塞舌尔
		(2)包括游泳场、射击场、田径场、灯光、计分牌和扩声系统等的体育设施	尼泊尔
		(3)牙科诊所、建筑面积968平方米	瓦努阿图
		(4)图书馆,建筑面积2300平方米	佛得角
		(5)教室和诊所。教室建筑面积90平方米、诊所建筑面积285平方米	喀麦隆
		(6)中国医生住房,建筑面积638平方米	贝宁
		(7)3万人座体育场	多哥
		(8)师范学校,10间教室、办公室、图书馆、试验室和围墙	马里
水利电力	5	(1)300口民用饮水井	柬埔寨
		(2)高压输变电线路18.81公里、配电线路90公里、升压变电站1座、降压变电站8座	苏里南
		(3)煤矿1-1采区开发和电站锅炉改造、建筑面积3138平方米	坦桑尼亚
		(4)农村供电11千伏电网、延长线9.9公里和8个杆上变电站	斐济
		(5)装机容量500千伏、23公里输	圭亚那

1999 年中国对外援助成套项目建成及提供单项设备情况

行业	建成项目数	规模	受援国别
		电线路	
农牧渔业	3	(1)442 公顷农田、2 个水闸及渠道、仓库、晒场工程等	科特迪瓦
		(2)打井 10 眼	喀麦隆
		(3)恢复 150 公顷农田	贝宁
纺织工业	2	(1)更新梳棉设备	叙利亚
		(2)向坦桑尼亚友谊纺织厂提供设备	坦桑尼亚
交通运输	2	(1)对内罗比三条主要道路进行整修	肯尼亚
		(2)63 公里公路	赤道几内亚

1999 年中国对外承担援外成套项目和单项设备情况

行业	项目数(个)	国别
合计	**45**	
公用民用建筑	19	马里、柬埔寨(2)、佛得角、刚果(金)、萨摩亚(2)、老挝、肯尼亚、南非、蒙古、尼泊尔、科特迪瓦、秘鲁、几内亚比绍、斐济、马尔代夫
文教卫生	6	加蓬、埃塞俄比亚、汤加、埃及、巴勒斯坦、喀麦隆
水利电力	10	老挝、坦桑尼亚(2)、玻利维亚、肯尼亚、喀麦隆、桑给巴尔、布隆迪、突尼斯、科特迪瓦
邮电通讯	3	尼泊尔、赞比亚、巴勒斯坦
交通运输	5	孟加拉国、赤道几内亚、马达加斯加、肯尼亚、坦桑尼亚、赞比亚
工业项目	2	叙利亚、老挝

1999 年中国对外承担援外技术合作项目情况

行业	项目数(个)	国别
合计	**30**	
农牧渔业	7	中非(2)、佛得角、刚果(金)、塞拉利昂、厄立特里亚、贝宁
公用民用建筑	4	喀麦隆、科特迪瓦、几内亚、莱索托
文教体育卫生	11	柬埔寨、乌干达、尼泊尔、肯尼亚、吉布提、塞拉利昂、博茨瓦纳、马达加斯加、尼日尔、蒙古、毛里塔尼亚

1999年中国对外承担援外技术合作项目情况

行　业	项目数(个)	国　　　别
邮电通讯	2	几内亚、赤道几内亚
水利电力	2	安提瓜和巴布达、圭亚那
工业项目	3	几内亚、黎巴嫩、科特迪瓦
交通运输	1	坦桑尼亚、赞比亚

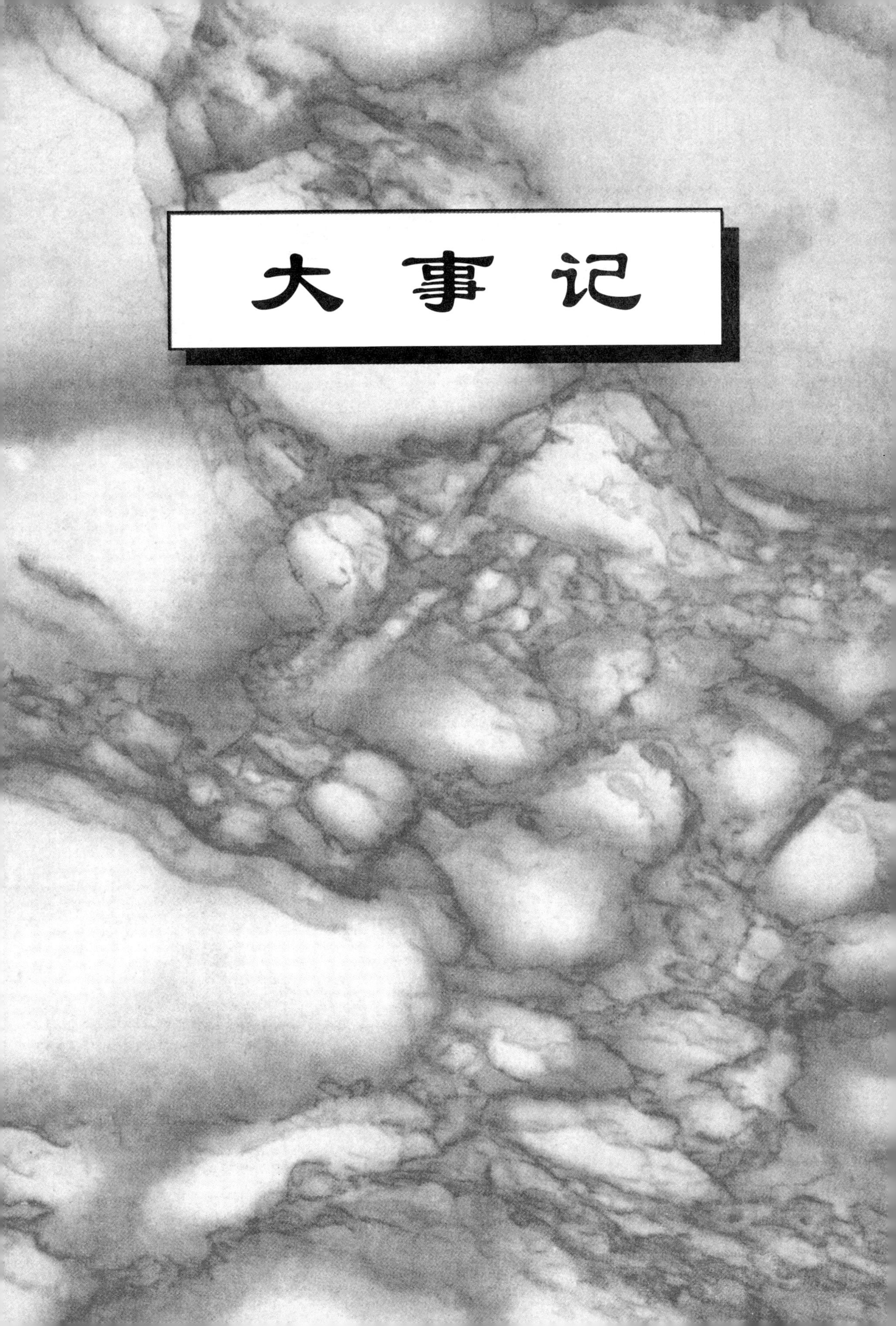

大事记

1999年中国对外经济贸易活动大事记

1 月

11 日 张祥副部长会见荷兰副议长威斯赫拉斯（WEISGLAS）及荷兰企业家代表团一行。张祥副部长向客人介绍当前中国经济形势并回答企业家提出的问题。

13 日 石广生部长与葡萄牙经济部长皮纳·莫拉在北京共同主持中葡第四届经贸混委会。双方就进一步发展双边经贸关系全面交换意见。

14 日 石广生部长参加吴仪国务委员与莫拉部长的会见。

18 日 龙永图首席谈判代表应中国日本人商工会议所邀请，在北京就中国加入 WTO 问题发表演讲。

张祥副部长应约会见土耳其驻华大使达尔亚尔·巴特巴伊（DARYAL BATTBAY）。土大使提出希望1999年我扩大自土的进口，并希望外交部和外经贸部关注土商办理来华签证较困难问题。

19 日 孙广相副部长会见即将离任的毛里塔尼亚驻华大使谢赫·巴巴米内先生。毛大使表示，目前毛中双边经贸合作情况良好，希望双方在文化、卫生领域之外的其他方面开展多样化的合作。

孙广相副部长应约会见尼泊尔新任驻华大使拉杰什瓦尔·阿查里雅（RAJESHWAR ACHARYA）。尼大使提出希望中方企业赴尼开展合资合作，并希望中方银行在尼设立机构。

孙广相副部长应约会见伊朗驻华大使穆罕默德·侯赛因·马拉埃克（MOHAMMAD HOSSEIN）。伊大使提出，伊拟向中方预售5亿美元的原油，中方可在一年内分期提供现汇支付。孙副部长允商有关部门后答复伊方。

何晓卫部长助理在北京会见瓦努阿图外长助理克莱门特·利奥（CLEMENT LEO）。双方就两国经贸合作问题交换意见，并分别代表各自政府就我向瓦政府提供10万美元现汇事换文确认。

20 日 张祥副部长会见英国贸工部副次官兼贸易政策司总司长托尼·哈顿。双方就双边和多边的贸易政策问题交换意见。

张祥副部长会见来访的智利伊基克市市长豪尔赫尔·索里亚·基里奥加（JORGE SORIA QUIRIOGA），为我参加伊基克港口扩建招标项目做推动工作。

21 日 石广生部长会见率荷兰中小企业代表团访华的荷兰外贸大臣易伯玛。双方就两国中小企业合作及其他双边经贸问题交换意见。此后，石部长还会见荷中小企业代表团成员。

22 日 石广生部长会见新日本制铁株式会社社长千速晃。双方就中日经贸合作等问题交换意见。

25 日 张祥副部长与陪同老挝总理西沙瓦来访的贸易旅游部部长富米·提帕汶举行对口会谈。双方就进一步加强双边经贸合作问题交换意见。

张祥副部长和老挝老中合作委员会主席麦燕·因祥分别代表各自政府在北京签署关于我向老挝提供2000万元人民币无偿援助的经济技术合作协定。

张祥副部长和老挝财政部副部长瑶·喷万塔分别代表各自政府在北京签署关于我向老挝提供1亿元人民币优惠贷款的框架协议。

25 日～28 日 龙永图首席谈判代表在北京出席“中国—东盟经贸研讨会”开幕式并致词 。

26 日～29 日 我部在北京召开1999年度全国外经贸工作会议。会议主要任务是：以邓小平理论和党的十五大精神为指导，贯彻落实中央经济工作会议精神，总结1998年全国外经贸工作，分析当前形势，部署1999年全国外经贸工作，进一步动员全国一切从事外经贸工作的干部职工，千方百计扩大出口，更多更好地利用外资，全面完成各项外经贸任务。吴仪国务委员出席会议并做重要指示；石广生部长作题为《坚定信心，全力以赴，全面完成1999年各项外经贸任务》的工作报告；刘山在副部长作会议总结；龙永图首席谈判代表、高虎城部长助理、马秀红部长助理、徐秉金部长助理分别就经济全球化与对外开放、进出口商品管理体制改革、利用外资和机电产品进出口等问题作专题报告；孙振宇副部长、陈新华副部长、刘向东纪检组长、张祥副部长、安民部长助理、何晓卫部长助理出席会议。

27日 石广生部长应邀赴朝鲜使馆参加朱昌骏大使为感谢中国政府无偿援朝的8万吨原油顺利交付完毕举办的宴会。

徐秉金部长助理会见美国西屋公司政府关系总监卡伦（CARON）。双方就加强中美能源合作问题交换意见。

安民部长助理接受台湾《工商时报》记者的采访。安助理就金融危机对祖国大陆的影响、大陆吸收利用外资、台资情况、加入WTO问题、两岸经贸交流前景以及我部对欧元启动的态度等问题回答记者的提问，呼吁台湾当局取消限制台商到大陆投资的“戒急用忍”政策，彻底开放大陆产品进口，全面开放两岸直接“三通”。

28日 龙永图首席谈判代表与来访的美国贸易谈判副代表费希尔（FISCHER）一行举行会谈。双方就我加入WTO及有关双边经贸问题交换意见。

29日 石广生部长会见美国贸易谈判副代表费希尔。费希尔表示美国正加紧按照中方要求，准备“没有水分”的“最后要价单”，预计3月初巴舍夫斯基将到北京向中方提交这份清单。

张祥副部长与俄罗斯贸易部第一副部长米特罗法诺夫会谈。双方就中俄总理定期会晤委员会经贸合作分委会第二次会议有关问题交换意见。

2　月

1月24日～2月4日 孙广相副部长随国家副主席胡锦涛出访马达加斯加、加纳、科特迪瓦、南非四国。1月25日，孙副部长和马达加斯加外长拉齐凡德里亚马纳分别代表各自政府在塔那那利佛签署关于我向马提供2000万元人民币无偿援助的经济技术合作协定和我向马提供5000万元人民币优惠贷款的框架协议；1月27日，孙副部长和加纳贸工部副部长阿布达皮分别代表各自政府在阿克拉签署我向加提供5000万元人民币优惠贷款的框架协议，并就我向加赠送价值200万元人民币一般物资事换文确认。1月29日，孙副部长和科特迪瓦国务部长、外交部长阿马拉·埃西分别代表各自政府在阿比让签署关于我向科提供1亿元人民币优惠贷款的框架协议，并就我向科提供250万元人民币无偿援助、同意帮助科政府在科罗戈镇建一座妇幼中心事分别换文确认。2月2日，孙副部长和南非外交部副部长阿齐兹·帕哈德分别代表各自政府就帮助南非政府在姆普马拉加省格拉斯考普市建设400套低造价社会住宅事在开普敦换文确认。

1日 石广生部长参加朱镕基总理与来访的圣卢西亚总理肯尼·安东尼（KENNY ANTHONY）在人民大会堂举行的工作会谈。石部长与随同圣卢西亚总理来访的圣外交和国际贸易部长乔治·奥德伦（GEORGE ODLUM）分别代表各自政府在北京签署关于我向圣提供3000万元人民币无偿援助的经济技术合作协定，并就我向圣提供200万元人民币无偿援助事换文确认。

龙永图首席谈判代表出席北京德意志工商中心开业典礼并讲话。龙首席谈判代表在讲话中简要介绍我国1998年经济形势以及我国保持人民币汇率稳定的政策，并高度评价中德双边经贸关系。

张祥副部长会见来访的德国巴符州州长托伊费尔。张副部长简要介绍1998年我国经济、外贸形势及我国为促进经济发展所采取的政策措施。

2日 石广生部长与圣卢西亚外交和国际贸易部长乔治·奥德伦举行会谈。双方就发展双边经贸关系特别是我援建圣项目及推动我企业到圣投资等问题交换意见。

2日～7日 高虎城部长助理率由外经贸部、国家经贸委和国家出入境检验检疫局组成的木质包装磋商代表团赴英国，与英贸工部次官哈顿，农渔食品部次官蒂姆斯以及英外交部、林业委员会就英对我输英货物木质包装实施新检疫措施进行磋商。高助理向英方进一步阐述中国政府的立场，希望通过双方共同努力寻求妥善解决办法。并希望英国在讨论整体措施时发挥积极作用。

2日～7日 徐秉金部长助理应邀访问韩国大宇公司举办的机电产品贸易研讨会并实地考察大宇公司等韩国著名大企业下属工厂。徐助理向大宇公司等企业的社长（或总裁）介绍中国经济形势、中国吸引外资的鼓励政策、中国的投资环境及中国增加先进设备的进口与鼓励机电产品出口的政策并高度评价韩国大企业对两国经贸关系发展所做的努力；韩方介绍在中国投资的情况及扩大投资的规划。双方探讨扩大中韩机电产品进出口的潜力、途径。

3 日 石广生部长参加吴仪国务委员会见来华参加中俄经贸合作分委会会议的俄罗斯贸易部长加布尼亚的活动。

3 日～6 日 石广生部长与俄罗斯贸易部长加布尼亚在北京共同主持召开中俄总理定期会晤委员会经贸合作分委会第二次会议。分委会对中俄承包劳务领域合作顺利发展表示满意，强调双方在林业领域合作具有很大潜力，认为两国应积极开展建设、交通、农业等领域的经济技术合作，建议两国主管机构加紧短期劳务协定的商签工作。石部长还向客人介绍 1998 年中国经济和外贸形势，并签署分委会会议纪要。

3 日～12 日 何晓卫部长助理率中国政府经贸代表团访问非洲两国和出席南部非洲发展组织（SADC）协商会议。3 日～6 日访问苏丹。何助理代表中方主持第五届中苏经贸混委会；5 日，何助理和苏丹国际合作和投资部国务部长阿卜杜·贾比尔分别代表各自政府在喀土穆签署关于我向苏丹提供 1 亿元人民币优惠贷款的框架协议和关于我向苏丹提供 1000 万元人民币无偿援助的两国政府经济技术合作协定。7 日～9 日访问博茨瓦纳。9 日，何助理与博财政和发展计划部长凯迪基尔维就我向博提供 200 万元人民币无偿援助事换文确认。11 日～12 日何助理代表唐家璇外长以观察员身份出席在赞比亚召开的南部非洲发展组织（SADC）协商会议。

8 日 孙振宇副部长应约会见加拿大驻华大使贝祥。双方就朱镕基总理访加时将涉及到的双边经贸关系中的重大问题交换意见。

8 日～10 日 龙永图首席谈判代表率中国代表团与以美国助理贸易代表卡希迪为首的美国代表团在华盛顿就中国“入世”问题进行磋商。双方就美方准备提交的“最后要价单”进行讨论，这是中美间第 19 轮中国“入世”问题双边磋商。

9 日 孙广相副部长和柬埔寨王国政府国务秘书兼财政大臣吉春分别代表各自政府在北京签署关于我向柬提供 1.5 亿元人民币优惠贷款的框架协议和我向柬提供 4000 万元人民币无偿援助的经济技术合作协定。

11 日 安民部长助理会见台湾“立法委员”、国民党“中央政策会”副执行长、“公营事业预算委员会”召集人廖福本先生。安助理回顾两岸贸易从对台出口煤炭开始做起的艰难历程，希望廖早日促成台电采用长约方式采购大陆煤，同时希望廖促成两岸直航或变通直航，进而为扩大两岸贸易作出贡献。

马秀红部长助理与部分美国在华企业代表座谈，双方就双边经贸关系中有关问题及如何改善我投资环境交换意见。

12 日 孙振宇副部长会见美国 AT&T 公司高级副总裁克劳西（BILL CLOSSEY）先生，孙副部长向对方介绍 1998 年我国的经贸发展情况，并听取 AT&T 公司在中国的经营活动及存在问题。

22 日 以龙永图首席谈判代表为首的中国代表团与美国助理贸易代表卡希迪为首的美国代表团在北京就中国“入世”问题进行磋商。双方就美方 2 月 12 日提交的“最后要价单”草案进行讨论，这是中美间第 20 轮中国“入世”问题双边磋商。

22 日～27 日 石广生部长出访俄罗斯。23 日，石部长出席在莫斯科举行的中俄总理第四次定期会晤及总理定期会晤委员会第三次会议；25 日，石部长代表中国政府与俄罗斯贸易部长加布尼亚在莫斯科签署中俄政府 1999 年经济贸易合作议定书。

24 日 刘山在副部长出席安提瓜和巴布达驻华大使修维（DAVID K.HSIU）为刘副部长访问拉美送行的宴会。双方就刘副部长访问安巴、如何推动中国和安巴及中国与加勒比的经贸关系交换意见。

26 日 徐秉金部长助理会见德国宝马公司董事特尔切克。双方就宝马在华汽车合作项目以及汽车进口配额问题交换意见。

3 月

1 日 石广生部长在北京会见科特迪瓦工业发展和中小企业部长阿瓦·恩多里·泰奥菲一行。同日孙广相副部长与阿瓦部长就中科合资巧克力项目继续合作事举行会谈。

龙永图首席谈判代表与日本大使就中日无偿资金合作“中国长江大堤加固计划”和“粮食增产援助”项目签字换文。

1 日～12 日 张祥副部长陪同吴仪国务委员

访问爱沙尼亚、拉脱维亚、立陶宛、白俄罗斯、乌克兰五国。4日，张祥副部长与拉外交部国务秘书马利斯·耶克斯京什在里加签署《中华人民共和国政府和拉托维亚共和国政府关于中国向拉托维亚提供300万元人民币无偿援助的换文》；5日，张祥副部长与立经济部副部长盖·米什基尼斯在维尔纽斯签署《中华人民共和国政府和立陶宛共和国政府关于中国向立陶宛提供300万元人民币无偿援助的换文》；7日，张祥副部长与白总统助理兼总统办公厅人道主义合作局局长库钦斯基在明斯克签署《中华人民共和国政府和白俄罗斯共和国政府关于中国向白俄罗斯提供500万元人民币无偿援助的换文》；9日，张祥副部长与乌对外经济联络和贸易部副部长瓦·伊·奥列伊尼克在基辅签署《中华人民共和国政府和乌克兰政府关于中国向乌克兰提供500万元人民币无偿援助的换文》；11日，张祥副部长与乌对外经济联络和贸易部副部长瓦·伊·奥列伊尼克在基辅签署《中华人民共和国政府和乌克兰政府关于中国向乌克兰提供5000万元人民币优惠贷款的协定》。

2日 龙永图首席谈判代表会见美中贸委会会长罗伯特·柯白（Robert Kapp）。双方就中美经贸关系的发展状况及有关问题交换意见。

3日 石广生部长会见美国贸易代表巴舍夫斯基（Barshelfsky）。双方就中国“入世”问题举行会谈。

孙振宇副部长会见参加中国与澳大利亚两国政治磋商的澳外交贸易部秘书长艾斯顿·卡尔弗特（Ashton Calvert），双方就加强两国经贸合作有关议题以及1999年经济联委会的安排问题交换意见。

龙永图首席谈判代表会见澳大利亚外交贸易部秘书长卡尔弗特，双方就中国“入世”的中澳双边磋商事项交换意见。

孙广相副部长会见韩国产业资源部金龙甲审议官。双方就中韩经贸合作有关问题交换意见。

4日 石广生部长与来访的意大利外贸部长皮耶罗·法西诺（Piero Fassino）在北京共同主持中意经济合作混委会第五次会议开幕式。会议期间，双方就两国经贸关系、中欧经贸关系和中国“入世”等问题交换了意见。

5日 石广生部长主持由国家计委、国家经贸委、国防科工委、人民银行、林业局、内贸局、保监委、中国银行、进出口银行等部门负责人以及上海市、山西省、黑龙江省、吉林省、辽宁省、内蒙古自治区、新疆维吾尔族自治区外经贸厅（委）领导和我部有关司、局、公司代表参加的对俄经贸工作会议，布置落实朱镕基总理访俄期间双方达成的经贸合作协议。

石广生部长会见新西兰国际贸易部部长洛克伍德·史密斯（Lockwood Smith），双方就1999年的APEC会议有关事项以及中新经贸合作有关议题交换意见。

龙永图首席谈判代表会见美国前助理贸易代表李森治（Lee Sands），双方就我国“入世”前景及双边经贸关系有关问题交换意见。

安民部长助理会见香港总商会中国委员会北京访问团。双方就内地吸引外资、中国申请“入世”、两地加强科技合作等方面问题交换意见。

安民部长助理会见台资企业宏仁企业集团董事长王文洋（王永庆之子）一行。安助理听取宏仁企业集团投资经营情况介绍，希望王扩大在大陆投资。

5日～14日 陈新华副部长率中国政府经贸代表团访问伊朗和土耳其。5日—8日，访问伊朗。7日，陈副部长参加由我北方公司承建的德黑兰地铁开通仪式；9日—14日，访问土耳其。12日，陈副部长与土外贸署长雅乌兹（A·Yavuz Ege）签署外经贸部与土外贸署建立贸易磋商机制谅解备忘录并参加中方以BOT方式承建的土耳其桑达勒杰克水电站合作意向书签字仪式。

9日 孙振宇副部长会见美国福特汽车公司中国公司总裁程美玮（Cheng Meiwei）。程介绍公司在中国业务发展的情况及向中国出口替代燃料汽车的设想。

孙振宇副部长会见美国波音公司中国公司总裁博睿（Ray Bracy）。博介绍包括波音公司在内的美国大公司为支持我“入世”所做的工作。

孙广相副部长与刚果（布）共和国外交、合作和法语国家事务部长鲁道夫·阿达达在北京举行经贸对口会谈。之后，双方签署中国政府向刚果（布）政府无偿提供200万元人民币物资援助的换文及延长3笔贷款使用期和推迟10笔贷款偿还期的换文。

10日 石广生部长会见德国勃兰登堡州州长施托尔佩，双方就勃兰登堡州与中国经贸关系问题交换了意见。

10日～25日 刘山在副部长率中国政府经

贸代表团访问巴哈马、安提瓜和巴布达、圭亚那、秘鲁和巴西。访问期间，刘副部长主要就双边贸易、经济技术合作，特别是组装加工业务和对外工程承包业务以及经援项目的开展与对方交换意见。

15 日 石广生部长与欧盟委员会主席布里坦(Brittan) 在北京签署："中国与欧盟甘肃基础教育项目"。欧盟向该项目提供 1500 万欧币的无偿援助，支持甘肃的基础教育发展。

17 日 孙振宇副部长会见西班牙亚古利民集团主席贾乐华（Luis Caiulla）一行，双方就该集团在华生产大大泡泡糖的合资企业转股等问题交换了意见。

18 日 孙广相副部长约见巴基斯坦驻华大使伊那姆·哈克（Inanul Haque)。双方就巴基斯坦水电发展署（WAPDA）500KV 输变电线工程买方信贷项目交换意见。

19 日 石广生部长会见德国新任驻华大使于倍寿（Ueberschaer)，双方就中德双边经贸关系和中国加入世贸组织等问题交换意见。

石广生部长会见奥地利新任驻华大使博天豪(Erich Buttenhauser)，双方就江主席即将对奥地利进行的国事访问和中奥双边经贸关系等问题交换了意见。

石广生部长代表中国政府在北京正式签署中华人民共和国政府和法兰西共和国政府关于资助上海地铁三线车辆的财政议定书和两国政府关于资助上海陇西水厂饮水项目的财政议定书。

龙永图首席谈判代表在日内瓦出席由世贸组织中国工作组主席吉拉德（Girard）主持的代表团团长非正式会议。此次会议的主要目的是评估目前中国"入世"谈判的形势，并对今后的谈判做出安排。美国、欧盟、日本、加拿大、澳大利亚、新西兰、阿根廷、智利、马来西亚等代表团的团长出席会议，与会代表一致认为中国入世谈判已出现新的势头，希望中国在新一轮谈判前"入世"。

22 日 孙广相副部长会见莫桑比克副外长帕特里西奥，双方就发展两国经贸关系交换意见。

22 日～28 日 孙振宇副部长与访华的特立尼达和多巴哥贸易和工业部长梅尔文·阿萨姆(Meryn Assam) 举行工作会谈。双方就中特贸易不平衡、中国企业到特多投资及经援问题交换意见。孙副部长还阐述我在台湾问题上的立场。

23 日 孙振宇副部长会见空中客车集团执行副总裁达尔马（Delmas)，达尔马向孙副部长介绍了空客集团的经营情况和业务发展情况。

刘向东纪检组长在上海主持召开全国外经贸系统纪检监察工作会议并作重要讲话。

24 日 孙振宇副部长应约紧急会见美国驻华使馆临时代办麦克海（Mc Cahill)，双方就美国商务部长即将访华的有关问题交换意见。

24 日～31 日 龙永图首席谈判代表为首的中国代表团与美国助理贸易代表卡希迪（Cassidy）为首的美国代表团在北京就中国"入世"问题进行磋商。双方继续就有关中国"入世"的中美一揽子协议中的议定书、市场准入、农业合作协议等问题举行磋商，这是中美间第 21 轮中国"入世"双边磋商。

26 日 孙广相副部长会见喀麦隆对外关系部秘书长约恩·多米尼克一行。孙副部长向客人介绍中非经贸合作情况和中—非经济管理官员研修班的情况。中方原则同意于 1999 年召开中喀经贸混委会。

29 日 何晓卫部长助理会见古巴外国投资和经济合作部副部长诺埃米·贝尼特斯·门多萨一行，双方就加强双边经贸合作交换意见。

30 日 马秀红部长助理会见了来访的瑞士人寿保险公司董事长卢恩斯（Ernst Rueesch）一行。卢向马助理介绍刚刚成立的瑞士人寿中国投资基金的有关情况，并表达了在华从事保险业务的愿望。马助理介绍我吸引外资的现状、政策及厦门投资贸易洽谈会，对瑞士人寿在华开业的意愿表示了理解和支持。

31 日 孙振宇副部长会见来访的英荷壳牌公司总裁布宏达（M.A. Van den Bergh）一行。布向孙副部长汇报了南海石化项目的进展情况。孙副部长希望双方共同努力，通过全面的谈判达成详尽的合同，早日签约。

孙广相副部长与随同也门共和国副总统哈迪访华的也门工业部长奥斯曼举行对口会谈。双方就加强双边经贸合作交换意见。会谈结束后，双方签署《中国政府向也门政府提供 500 万元人民币无偿援助的换文》，也门建设、计划、教育部副部长参加会谈及签字仪式。

4 月

3 月 31 日～4 月 5 日 刘向东纪检组长率中国政府经贸代表团访问泰国。4 月 1 日，刘纪检组长出席在曼谷召开的“中国与东盟国家经贸合作研讨会暨项目洽谈会”，与泰方就如何进一步推动中泰经贸合作问题交换意见。

1 日 张祥副部长出席中国俄罗斯森林资源开发和利用常设工作小组中方小组成立暨第一次会议并作重要讲话，张副部长任中方小组组长。会议讨论通过《中俄森林资源开发和利用常设工作小组条例（草案）》，讨论修改《关于加强中俄森林资源开发和利用合作业务管理的通知》。

2 日 龙永图首席谈判代表与日本驻华大使古野作太郎在北京分别代表双方政府就日无偿援助我卫生部预防接种扩大计划项目换文确认。

孙广相副部长与也门副总统哈迪举行对口会谈，双方就中国参与也门萨那、亚丁两个纺织厂改造、经营事项进行商谈。

5 日 石广生部长与埃及计划、国际合作部国务部长卡扎菲·贝希里分别代表各自政府在北京签署关于我向埃提供 3000 万元人民币无偿援助的经济技术合作协定。

6 日 徐秉金部长助理会见美国波士顿银行常务董事加里·马特森（GARY·MATSON）先生，双方就中美经贸关系、银行与企业合作特别是波士顿银行帮助中国企业融资等方面交换意见。

7 日 张祥副部长会见美国维蒙特工业公司董事长兼首席执行官摩根·贝（MOGENS C·BAY）先生，双方就中美双边经贸关系发展状况及维蒙特工业公司在上海的投资情况交换意见。

8 日 何晓卫部长助理出席开拓欧美发达国家承包工程市场座谈会并作重要讲话。二十余家在欧美发达国家开展承包工程的公司、企业、设计院代表与会。会上总结交流此项业务中的经验和教训，分析进入这一市场的障碍和壁垒并探讨我公司进入该市场的可能性、可行性及今后的发展思路。

9 日 孙广相副部长参加江泽民主席与卡塔尔埃米尔哈马德举行的大组会谈，并与卡能源大臣分别代表本国政府签署中、卡两国政府鼓励和相互保护投资协定。

何晓卫部长助理会见来访的尼日利亚当选总统秘书欧拉佩德，双方就中尼经贸合作问题交换意见。

马秀红部长助理会见德国赫斯特（中国）投资有限公司董事长巴特，巴特向马助理介绍了赫斯特公司与法国罗纳—普朗克公司合并计划，并就两公司在华投资公司的重组设想征求马助理意见。

11 日 张祥副部长会见荷兰副首相兼经济大臣尤里兹玛。张副部长介绍我国外经贸发展形势和中荷双边经贸关系现状，双方就进一步加强经贸合作和欧盟对华贸易限制问题进行积极磋商。

12 日 孙振宇副部长出席并主持尼日利亚当选总统奥巴桑乔与中国工商界人士座谈会。

陈新华副部长会见日本国际贸易促进协会访华团，双方就如何扩大中日贸易和对华投资等问题交换意见。

孙广相副部长会见桑给巴尔财政部长阿里一行，双方就中桑两国经贸合作事宜交换意见，并分别代表各自政府就我向桑政府提供 500 万元人民币事换文确认。

13 日 张祥副部长会见应我农业部之邀来访的匈牙利农业部国务秘书托马斯·卡洛伊（TOMAS KAROJ），双方就中匈农业合作交换意见。

安民部长助理会见即将离任的香港太古集团主席萨秉达。萨介绍太古集团在香港和内地的投资及业务发展情况。安助理感谢萨秉达先生多年来为促进内地和香港的经贸交流所作的努力，并希望其继任者继续拓展两地的经贸合作。

何晓卫部长助理会见苏丹能源和矿产部长贾兹，双方就中苏在能源领域合作，特别是苏丹喀土穆州 200 千瓦联合循环电站项目事交换意见。

13 日～15 日 何晓卫部长助理出席在上海召开的中国对外承包工程商会三届四次理事会并作重要讲话。

13 日～25 日 孙广相副部长率中国政府经贸代表团访问新加坡、柬埔寨。13 日～17 日访问新加坡，代表团与新加坡有关部门就中新在承包工程和劳务合作方面的有关问题进行磋商；18 日～24 日访问柬埔寨；20 日，孙副部长与柬埔寨王国政府国务大臣兼外交国际合作部大臣贺南洪分别代表各自政府就我同意援柬 500 口民用水井事在金边换文确认。22 日，孙副部长与柬埔寨王国政府国务秘书李图分别代表各自政府在金边签署我援柬 300 口民用水井的交接证书。23日，孙副部长与柬埔寨王国政府参议院主席西索瓦·基旺莫尼拉分别代表各自政府在金边签署我援柬参议院会议厅改造项目的交接证书。

14日 张祥副部长会见英外交部主管贸易和出口促进事务的外交国务大臣德利克·法切特(DEREK FACHEH)，就双边、多边经贸问题进行了友好的交谈。

安民部长助理应邀在钓鱼台国宾馆会见台湾宏仁集团董事长王文洋博士（台塑关系企业董事长王永庆先生之子）一行。安助理向台湾客人介绍祖国大陆改革开放的经济形势并回答客人感兴趣的问题。

16日 高虎城部长助理会见巴黎工商会法中交流委员会主任达珂娜（DAGNET），双方就1999年5月高助理赴法举办’99中法投资洽谈会有关筹备工作等问题交换了意见。

19日 周可仁副部长与来访的泰国商业部副部长巴威集（PRAVICH RATTANAPIAN）举行会谈，双方就双边经贸合作等有关问题交换意见。

20日 何晓卫部长助理与来访的刚果（金）石油国务部长皮埃尔—维克多·姆波约举行经贸会谈，双方就中刚双边经贸合作事宜交换意见，并分别代表各自政府就我向刚政府提供300万元人民币无偿援助事在北京换文确认。

22日 石广生部长会见来华访问的联合国儿童基金执行主任贝拉米（BELLARMY）女士，双方就该基金未来向中国提供援助问题交换意见。

张祥副部长前往越南驻华大使馆看望来京治病的越南副总理阮功丹，并同阮就两国经贸合作问题交换意见。

26日 石广生部长参加江泽民主席与来访的以色列总统魏茨曼举行的大组会谈后，出席中以企业家经贸研讨会及午餐会并发表讲话。

孙广相副部长与来华访问的萨摩亚工程部长卡穆进进工作会谈，双方就加强中萨经贸合作及友好关系交换意见。

马秀红部长助理会见纽约金融届妇女协会会长、大通证券公司副总裁雷诺丽·阿尔波姆（LENORE ALBOM）女士一行，马助理简要介绍中国实行改革开放政策以来所取得的成就及在金融、保险业方面开放的情况。

27日 德国驻华大使于倍寿（UEBERSCHAER）紧急约见张祥副部长，双方就我部接待随德国总理施罗德（SCHROEDER）来访的德国联邦经济部长米勒（MUELLER）及经济分团等有关事宜进行磋商。

28日 孙广相副部长会见来访的肯尼亚外长伯纳亚·戈达纳一行，双方就共同关心的经贸合作事宜交换意见，并分别代表各自政府就我向肯政府提供500万元人民币无偿援助事在北京换文确认。

张祥副部长会见来华出席昆明世博会的智利农业部部长卡洛斯·姆拉迪尼克（CARLOS MLADRNIC），张副部长介绍我“入世”进程等情况。

28日～29日 何晓卫部长助理出席在厦门召开的中国外派海员协调机构四届三次理事会并作重要讲话。会议分析当前外派海员工作面临的形势，并对下一步工作做了部署。

29日 刘向东纪检组长会见泰国顺和成集团总裁张锦程，就顺和成集团与中国开展经贸合作问题交换意见。

30日 孙振宇副部长会见美国福特汽车公司副总裁亨利·华莱士（HENRY WALLACE）一行，双方就中国“入世”和福特公司在华投资有关问题交换意见。

孙振宇副部长会见来访的基里巴斯交通部长威廉·托卡塔阿克（WILLIE TOKATAAKE），双方就两国船舶、飞机贸易等事宜交换意见。

5 月

3日 何晓卫部长助理与津巴布韦外交部常务副秘书曼格瓦纳在北京共同主持中津混委会第五次工作会议。

4日 石广生部长和古外贸部部长里卡多·卡布里萨斯（RICARDO CABRISAS）在北京共同主持中古第十一届经贸混委会。双方签署新的贸易协定、会谈纪要和我向古提供1亿元人民币优惠贷款、5000万元人民币无息贷款及1000万元人民币无偿援助等协议，并就进一步促进双边经贸往来和扩大相互投资等问题交换意见。

石广生部长会见美国联合包裹运送服务公司（UPS）总裁兼首席执行官吉姆·凯利（JIM KELLY），双方就中美经贸关系有关问题及UPS在华合作情况交换意见。

孙振宇副部长应约会见澳大利亚驻华大使石励(RICSMITH)，双方就即将举行的中澳部长级经济联委会有关事宜交换意见。

5日 何晓卫部长助理会见突尼斯外交部长赛义德·本·穆斯塔法，双方就进一步加强双边经贸合作交换意见。

6日 石广生部长和津巴布韦外长斯坦·穆登盖（SITAN. MUDENGE）分别代表各自政府在北京签署关于我向津提供1000万元人民币无偿援助的两国政府经济技术合作协定，并就我向津赠送一批价值200万元人民币的农业机械事换文确认。石部长和津外长还共同主持中津混委会第5次工作会议开幕式和闭幕式并签署中津混委会第5次会议纪要。

孙振宇副部长会见美国联合技术公司总裁(GEOGE DAVID）乔治·大卫及中国美国商会主席赖雷明一行，双方就中美经贸关系有关问题交换意见。

陈新华副部长会见来访的日本京都国际贸易促进协会副会长石田明，双方就中日经贸合作交换意见。

何晓卫部长助理和马达加斯加外长莉拉·拉齐方德里亚马纳纳（LILA RATSIFANGRIHAMANANA）分别代表各自政府在北京签署关于我向马提供1000万元人民币无偿援助的两国政府经济技术合作协定，并就我承担援马昂—瓦公路项目事换文确认。

何晓卫部长助理会见玻利维亚副外长索拉雷斯(ANA. M. SOLARES)，双方就发展双边贸易及加强经援项下的合作交换意见。

11日 孙广相副部长会见来华参加中韩第七次贸易实务会谈的韩国代表团团长、韩国外交通商部地域通商局局长崔中华，双方就中韩经贸关系问题交换意见。

何晓卫部长助理与全国总工会书记处书记董力同志就外派劳务人员合法权益保障问题进行会谈。

11日～12日 陈新华副部长在满洲里参加铁道部主持召开的满洲里铁路口岸现场办公会议并签署会议纪要。会议专题研究加大铁路口岸运输工作力度，扩大口岸运输能力，提高进出口运量等问题。

12日 周可仁副部长会见法国埃尔夫阿托化工公司总裁雅克·布沙尔，布向周副部长介绍公司在华开展业务情况。

13日 孙振宇副部长会见来访的南太平洋论坛秘书长莱维（NOEL LEVI），双方就加强中国与南太地区经贸合作以及论坛拟在北京设立代表处等有关议题交换意见。

14日 石广生部长参加了江泽民主席与哥伦比亚总统帕斯特拉纳（ANDRES PASTRANA）的正式会谈。会谈后，石部长和哥外长吉列尔莫·费尔南德斯·德索托（Guillermo Fernandez de Soto）分别代表各自政府就我向哥提供1000万元人民币无偿援助事和我向哥地震灾区提供活动用房和计算机事在北京换文确认。

石广生部长与哥伦比亚外贸部长拉米雷斯(MARTHA RAMIREZ）共同主持了中哥第六届经贸混委会。双方回顾自上届混委会以来的双边经贸关系的发展情况，并就双边贸易、哥对我产品反倾销、经济合作、经援等有关问题具体、深入地交换意见。

张祥副部长会见乌兹别克斯坦新任驻华大使埃尔加舍夫·伊·拉，双方就进一步密切中乌经贸合作广泛交换意见。

张祥副部长会见摩尔多瓦驻华大使绍瓦，双方探讨进一步加强中摩经贸合作等问题。

马秀红助理会见美国安利公司亚太副总裁郑李锦芬，就安利公司在华经营有关问题交换意见。

14日～24日 高虎城部长助理率中国企业家代表团赴法国巴黎和南特举办’99中国投资贸易洽谈会。17日和19日，高助理两次向到会的300多位法国企业家介绍中国的投资环境及吸引外资的有关政策，并回答法国企业家的提问。18日，高助理拜会法国参议院副主席瓦拉德和法国国土整治局局长基古。20日，高助理拜会法国外贸国务秘书董杜。

17日 石广生部长与来访的澳大利亚副总理兼贸易部长费希尔（TIM FISCHER）共同主持两国部长级经济联委会第九次会议，双方就双边经贸合作广泛议题进行商讨。龙永图首席谈判代表参加会议，并与澳方就中国“入世”事进行建设性磋商。

龙永图首席谈判代表会见美国摩托罗拉公司负责政府关系事务副总裁布莱纳（A.R.NORD BRENNER），双方就我驻南联盟使馆被炸事件及中美双方关于WTO谈判情况交换意见。

18日 外经贸部与澳大利亚贸易委员会共同

在北京主办了中澳羊毛研讨会，推广使用中国、澳大利亚、新西兰三方最新制订的羊毛贸易示范合同。首席谈判代表龙永图与澳大利亚副总理兼贸易部长费希尔出席研讨会并发表讲话。

18日～19日 何晓卫部长助理出席对台湾省远洋渔工劳务工作紧急会议并讲话。12个省市外经贸委（厅、局）和有对台湾省远洋渔工劳务经营权的公司参加会议，同时国务院台湾事务办公室、外交部、公安部、交通部、农业部、中华全国总工会的代表应邀出席会议。此次会议的中心议题是贯彻落实中央领导同志有关批示精神，整顿经营秩序，加强管理，保护渔工劳务人员合法权益。

19日 安民部长助理会见台湾顶新国际集团魏应行先生。安助理详细了解顶新国际集团经营中出现的一些情况并回答客人提出的问题。

20日 龙永图首席谈判代表会见美国中部委员会主席托马斯·麦纳（THOMAS MINER），麦纳简要介绍该委员会近来为促进双边经贸关系发展所做的工作。

孙广相副部长、何晓卫部长助理共同主持召开对外经济合作、对外援助领导小组第三次会议。各成员单位代表参加会议，EDI中心代表列席会议。会议原则讨论通过《对外承包工程和劳务合作管理工作改革方案》（征求意见稿）。

21日 石广生部长会见德国驻华大使于倍寿和法国驻华大使毛磊，两位大使代表各自政府向石部长通报德国总理施罗德与法国总统希拉克的会晤情况，并递交18日两位首脑发表的关于中国“入世”问题的联合声明。石部长向两位大使阐述中国在上述问题上的原则立场和态度。

周可仁副部长会见国际金融公司常务副总裁沃奇先生，双方就共同举办投资促进研讨会等具体项目及进一步合作等问题交换意见。

张祥副部长会见捷克外长杨·卡万一行，双方就双边经贸关系的发展交换意见。

何晓卫部长助理会见来访的阿拉伯联合酋长国沙迦自由区管理局局长塔里格·卡西米，双方就继续发展经贸合作问题交换意见。

24日 安民部长助理会见以澳门政府政务司办公室顾问何永安为团长的澳门高级公务员访京团。安助理向客人介绍我部职能、境外脱钩企业情况、两地经贸交流现状等，双方还就如何进一步加强经贸合作交换意见。

25日 张祥副部长会见来访的吉尔吉斯斯坦外长伊马纳利耶夫，双方就双边经贸项目及召开混委会等问题重点交换意见。

26日 张祥副部长会见德国萨尔州内政部长莱普勒，双方就科索沃危机及中德双边经贸关系等问题交换意见。

27日 何晓卫部长助理会见孟加拉化学工业公司主席霍克一行，双方就两国企业合作在孟设化肥厂项目进行商谈。

28日 张祥副部长就中国俄罗斯经贸合作有关问题接受国务院新闻办五洲传播中心采访。

6 月

5月20日～6月10日 徐秉金部长助理率中国政府经贸代表团访问佛得角、布隆迪、肯尼亚和南非四国。5月21日，徐助理与佛贸易、工业与能源部长亚历山大·蒙泰罗举行工作会谈，双方签署《中佛贸易和经济合作协定》和《中佛经济和技术合作协》，中国政府向佛提供1300万元人民币的无偿援助。同日，徐助理与佛总理等政府高级官员出席由中国援建的佛得角国家图书馆揭幕和移交仪式；5月28日，徐助理与布隆迪对外关系和合作部部长塞佛兰·恩塔翁维基耶共同主持中布经贸合作混委会第八次会议，5月30日，双方签署经济技术合作协定和第八次混委会纪要，中国政府向布提供2000万元人民币无偿援助并商定具体项目；6月2日，徐助理分别与肯尼亚农业部长穆萨利·穆达维迪、贸易部长约瑟夫·卡姆索及工业发展部长安德鲁·吉卜图就进一步发展双边经贸合作交换意见；6月7日，徐助理应邀与南非贸工部总司长拉斯托吉博士就双边经贸合作中的有关问题交换意见。

1日 石广生部长会见以西山德光为团长的日本滑石协议会访华团，双方就中日滑石贸易的现状与问题交换意见。

石广生部长会见阿拉伯国家驻华使节，何晓卫部长助理参加会见。石部长向各国使节介绍我国经济发展现状和我“入世”的有关情况。双方还就中阿双边经贸合作进行广泛深入的探讨。

周可仁副部长与到访的塞拉利昂农业、林业和环境部长哈里·威尔（HARRY WILL）举行经贸对口会谈。双方就两国经贸合作与交流广泛地交换意见，还就援塞农技站技术合作项目在北京换文确认。同日，周副部长和塞拉利昂外交与国际合作部长萨马·班亚（SAMA BANYA）分别代表各自政府在北京签署关于我向塞提供2500万元人民币无偿援助的两国政府经济技术合作协定，并就我向塞无偿提供物资援助和援塞体育场技术合作项目换文确认。

3日～15日 何晓卫部长助理陪同钱其琛副总理访问土库曼斯坦、塔吉克斯坦、吉尔吉斯斯坦和乌兹别克斯坦四国。4月，何助理与土库曼斯坦副总理奥拉佐夫分别代表各自政府就我向土提供500万元人民币无偿援助事在阿什哈巴德换文确认；7月，何助理和塔吉克斯坦经济外经部第一副部长马赫穆托夫分别代表各自政府在杜尚别签署关于我向塔提供1000万元人民币无偿援助的两国政府经济技术合作协定；8日，何助理和吉尔吉斯斯坦对外贸易工业部第一副部长苏莱曼库洛夫分别代表各自政府就我向吉提供1000万元人民币无偿援助事在比什凯克换文确认；10日，何助理和乌兹别克斯坦外交部副部长别克穆拉多夫分别代表各自政府就我向乌提供500万元人民币无偿援助事在塔什干换文确认。

4日 陈新华副部长会见以中田庆雄为团长的日本国际贸易促进协会中国花卉产业流通考察暨参加昆明世博会访华团，双方就发展中日花卉方面的合作问题交换意见。

龙永图首席谈判代表会见香港特别行政区财政司司长曾荫权一行，双方就中国“入世”等问题交换意见。

7日 陈新华副部长和缅甸和平与发展委员会主席府部长埃博尔（EBOR）分别代表各自政府在北京签署关于我向缅甸提供5000万元人民币无息贷款的两国政府经济技术合作协定。

8日 石广生部长会见随同塞浦路斯总统访华的塞工商旅游部长尼克斯·罗兰迪斯（NICOS ROLANDIS），双方就中塞经贸合作的有关问题交换意见。

陈新华副部长与缅甸国家和平与发展委员会主席府部长埃博尔和缅商业部长觉丹（JVDAN）举行会谈，双方就发展中缅经济合作有关问题交换意见。

9日 孙振宇部长应约会见加拿大永明保险公司（SUNASSURANCE）董事长兼首席执行官斯图特（DONALAD A.STEWART），双方就该公司在华业务有关事项交换意见。孙副部长还向客人介绍我保险业开放有关情况。

10日 周可仁副部长会见匈牙利总理府部长什敦普夫（LSTVAN STUMPF）一行，双方就进一步加强中匈两国经贸合作关系问题交换意见。

11日 孙广相副部长和朝鲜驻华大使朱昌骏分别代表各自政府就我向朝鲜无偿提供15万吨粮食和40万吨炼焦煤事在北京换文确认。

孙广相副部长和尼日尔外交与合作部长艾沙图·明达乌杜·苏莱曼（AICHATOU MINDAOUDOU SOULEYMANE）分别代表各自政府在北京签署关于我向尼提供1000万元人民币无偿援助的两国政府经济技术合作协定。

高虎城部长助理紧急约见欧盟驻华大使魏根深（WILKINSON），就欧盟委员会6月1日作出决定对中国货物木质包装实行紧急措施一事进行严正交涉，对欧盟未经协商单方面采取不利于双边正常贸易发展的行为和措施表示强烈不满。

14日 孙广相副部长和中非经济、计划与国际合作部部长级代表雅各布·姆巴依塔杰姆（JACOB MBAITADJIM）分别代表各自政府在北京签署了关于我向中非提供1000万元人民币无偿援助的两国政府经济技术合作协定和我向中非提供300万美元现汇援助的换文。

15日 石广生部长会见由香港总商会主席董建成率领的香港总商会访京团，安民部长助理参加会见。石部长向客人介绍我出口形势、内地促进进出口所采取的措施及近期我对加工贸易政策调整的基本情况、中国“入世”问题和内地服务贸易的开放情况及发展趋势，双方还就如何进一步加强两地经贸合作交换意见。

孙广相副部长会见委内瑞拉基础设施部副部长卡洛斯·赫纳蒂奥斯（CARLOS GENADIOS）率领的访华代表团，双方就中成公司承建委住房项目进行友好会谈。

孙广相副部长与来访的中非经济、计划和国际合作部部长级代表雅各布·姆巴伊塔杰姆举行会谈。双方就双边贸易、经援合作和承包劳务等问题广泛深入地交换意见。

张祥副部长在哈尔滨出席第十届哈洽会开幕式并于14日和15日分别会见俄罗斯阿穆尔州州长别

拉洛戈夫和赤塔州州长戈里亚图林。

15日～18日 陈新华副部长率中国政府经贸代表团访问蒙古国。16日～17日，陈副部长与蒙基础设施发展部部长嘎·巴特呼（GA BATHO）共同主持召开中蒙第六届经贸技术联委会。

16日～24日 张祥副部长率中国政府经贸代表团访问俄罗斯赤塔州、阿穆尔州和哈巴罗夫斯克边区，为落实1999年2月朱镕基总理访问俄罗斯期间双方领导人就共同开发和利用俄森林资源达成的协议。17日与18日，张副部长分别和赤塔州第一副州长奥古涅夫和副州长别图霍夫举行会谈；21日，张祥副部长与阿穆尔州州长拉洛戈夫在布拉戈维申斯克举行会谈；22日，张祥副部长与哈巴罗夫斯克边区行政长官伊沙耶夫举行会谈。访问期间，张副部长实地考察俄远东地区林业资源及生产情况，同俄方就合作的原则、方式和渠道等达成共识，同时提出发展中俄森林资源开发和利用合作的下步设想，为此项合作进一步发展奠定基础。

17日 石广生部长与来访的英国贸工大臣斯蒂芬·拜尔斯（STEPHEN BYERS）举行会谈，双方就科索沃问题、中国“入世”问题和中英、中欧间的经贸关系交换意见。

石广生部长会见来访的巴林财经大臣塞义夫一行。双方就如何进一步发展两国经贸关系，尤其是在金融、石油化工、航空运输等领域的合作广泛交换意见。会见结束后，双方签署《中巴两国政府鼓励和相互保护投资协定》。

18日 石广生部长会见日本朝阳贸易株式会社社长华井满，双方就日中投资促进机构会长斋藤裕因健康原因卸任后，日方拟由丰田章一郎接任会长事交换意见。

21日 马秀红部长助理会见瑞士诺华公司董事叶策（JETZER）先生，双方就诺华公司在华业务发展问题交换意见。

22日 孙振宇副部长会见率团参加“中俄面向21世纪地区间合作研讨会”的俄联邦委员会第一副主席科罗廖夫先生及其一行，双方就中俄地方间经贸合作问题交换意见。

23日 何晓卫部长助理会见孟加拉住房和公共工程部总工程师拉赫曼先生一行，双方就我援建孟国际会议中心项目进行商谈。

25日 石广生部长会见前来辞行的美国驻华大使尚慕杰先生（JAMES SESSER），双方就发展中美经贸关系问题交换意见。

周可仁副部长会见率团来华参加中斯混委会第四次会议的斯洛伐克经济部国务秘书（副部级）彼得·布尔诺（PETER BRNO），双方就促进双边经贸关系等问题交换意见。

孙广相副部长和几内亚比绍财政国务秘书鲁伊·杜阿尔特·巴罗斯（RUI DUARTE BARROS）分别代表各自政府就我向几比提供200万元人民币物资援助事在北京换文确认。

28日 孙振宇副部长会见美国布鲁金斯学会学长阿马科斯特（ARMACOST）大使一行，双方就目前中美经贸关系和中国“入世”问题交换意见。

30日 张祥副部长会见德国曼内斯曼公司董事韦金石亲王（PETER PRINZ WITTGENSTEIN），双方就曼内斯曼公司进一步拓展在华业务的有关问题交换意见。

张祥副部长会见阿根廷驻华大使费得里科·卡络斯·巴特费尔德（FEDERICO CARLOS BARTTFELD），双方就阿向中国出口牛肉检疫问题交换意见。

安民部长助理会见台湾中华航空公司董事长蒋洪彝一行。安助理向客人介绍我开放服务业领域的政策并回答客人关心的问题。

7 月

1日 全国人大财经委员会和外经贸部在人民大会堂召开座谈会，纪念中外合资经营企业法颁布实施20周年。外经贸部部长石广生在会上发言说，改革开放以来，我国吸收外资成就瞩目，世界知名跨国公司500家中已有近400家来华投资。

1日 外经贸部新闻发言人胡楚生就欧盟推迟对我国货物木质包装实施新检疫标准一事回答记者问时说，欧盟对中国木质包装实施检疫新标准宽限期延长一个月的决定，将有利于减少中国已候港待运货物所受的损失。欧方在制定双边经贸政策时应避免单方面采取限制措施，影响双边关系的正常发展。

2日 外经贸部部长助理马秀红与英国驻华大使高德年爵士在京签署《大不列颠及北爱尔兰联合王国政府与中华人民共和国政府关于联合王国英联

邦开发公司（CDC）在中华人民共和国开展经营的谅解备忘录）。

6 日 外经贸部副部长孙振宇在京会见第 53 届联合国大会主席、乌拉圭外长迪迪埃·奥佩蒂·巴丹，就进一步发展中国与乌拉圭双边经贸关系交换意见。

8 日 外经贸部部长石广生在京与随同小渊惠三首相来访的日本外务大臣高村正彦、邮政大臣野田圣子举行会谈，就中日双边经贸关系、中国加入世贸组织等问题交换意见。9 日 中国和日本两国政府代表团在京发表《关于中国加入世界贸易组织双边谈判的联合新闻公报》。

9 日 石广生部长与哈萨克斯坦共和国副总理兼外长托卡耶夫在京签署关于中国向哈萨克斯坦共和国提供优惠贷款的框架协定。

12 日 石广生部长在京会见澳大利亚外长亚历山大·唐纳，双方就进一步发展两国经贸关系和中国加入世界贸易组织等问题交换意见。13 日，石广生部长和唐纳外长在京发表《关于中国加入世界贸易组织双边谈判的联合新闻公报》。

15 日 外经贸部日前向海尔集团、金城集团等 50 家海外投资企业颁发批准证书，确认其境外加工贸易企业资格。

15 日 外经贸部和国家外汇管理局在京首次联合召开共同促进进出口和利用外资协作会，外经贸部副部长孙振宇在会上指出，要拓宽汇贸协作形式和内涵，确保外贸出口有新增长和吸收外资保持相当规模。

19 日 外经贸部首席谈判代表龙永图在北京举办的世界贸易组织第二期培训班开学仪式上指出，中国加入世贸组织从根本上说对中国是有利的，当前不少人对加入世贸组织问题存在的一些错误认识，应该得到纠正。

27 日 孙振宇副部长在京与美国商务部副部长戴维·阿龙举行会谈，双方就中美经贸关系等问题交换意见。石广生部长在会谈现场会见阿龙一行时说，中方非常重视发展中美经贸关系，希望中美双方在平等协商、共同发展原则基础上开展建设性对话，推动两国经贸关系发展。

27 日～28 日 全国外经贸年中工作会议在京召开，国务委员吴仪在会上要求确保实现外经贸既定目标。石广生部长在会上部署当前外经贸工作，重点是进一步扩大对外开放，实施科技兴贸战略，调整出口商品结构，并大力推动境外加工贸易。

28 日 外交部发言人朱邦造就美国众议院 27 日以多数票否决关于“取消对华正常贸易关系”议案一事在京表示，美国应顺应时代潮流，早日解决永久对华正常贸易关系问题，为中美经贸关系的持续发展创造有利条件。

29 日 石广生部长在京会见荷兰飞利浦公司总裁布绍昌时说，中国很欢迎外国公司选择目前有一定困难的中国企业进行合作，帮助中国企业发展。

29 日 中国驻美国使馆临时代办刘晓明和世界银行副行长塞维里诺在世行总部分别代表中国政府和世行签署第 9 个卫生项目、高等教育改革项目和第 2 个福建公路项目等 3 个贷款协定。

8 月

3 日～5 日 由珠海市人民政府及珠海经济特区管理委员会主办，由澳门贸易投资促进局协办的’99 珠海（澳门）投资贸易洽谈会在澳门举行。这是正值澳门回归祖国前夕密切珠澳两地经贸合作的一个实质性盛举。

3 日 中国人民银行和对外贸易经济合作部联合发布《关于支持境外带料加工装配业务的信贷指导意见》，以支持扩大出口，鼓励我国轻工、纺织、家电等机械电子以及服装加工等行业具有比较优势的企业到境外开展带料加工装配业务。

5 日 外经贸部举行座谈会批判和声讨李登辉妄图分裂祖国的“两国论”。外经贸部部长石广生指出，一个中国原则是两岸关系发展基础和前提，也是两岸经贸关系发展基石，“两国论”极大地破坏了两岸关系的健康发展。

8 日 由天津市经贸委主办、中国出口国际网承办的“中国天津网上出口商品交易会”正式开幕，此次“网交会”历时一年，是我国出口产品在互联网上面向世界的一次集中展示，它充分体现中国出口企业的行业特点。

8 日 石广生部长在京会见联合国开发署新任署长马克·布朗时谈到，希望开发署继续坚持其技术援助普遍、中立、无偿等原则和宗旨，为发展中国家在发展经济、消除贫困、保护环境、支持妇女参与发展方面作出积极贡献。

9 日 中国人民银行决定，进一步扩大上海、深圳外资银行经营人民币业务的范围，增加外资银行人民币资金来源，以促进外资银行人民币业务健康发展。

9日～12日 77国集团亚洲组第九届部长级会议在黎巴嫩首都贝鲁特举行，来自亚洲成员国300多名代表就债务、私有资本市场、国际贸易规则和高科技发展等问题进行广泛讨论。中国外经贸部首席谈判代表龙永图率团以特别客人身份出席会议并指出，经济全球化所带来的弊端使得建立新的国际经济新秩序比过去任何时候都显得更加重要和迫切。

12日 钓鱼台国宾馆俱乐部联谊活动在京举行，近50位驻华使馆代表、30多位跨国公司总裁和首席代表出席联谊会。石广生部长讲话指出，进一步扩大对外开放，大力发展多双边经贸关系，创造良好的国际环境是当前中国对外经济贸易发展的重要内容。

12日 国务院总理朱镕基在昆明世博园会见塔吉克斯坦总统莫马利·拉赫莫诺夫时说，目前两国的经贸关系发展潜力很大，希望进一步扩大塔中两国经济贸易往来。

17日 中国建设银行与日本输出入银行签定一项22亿美元的担保协议。这是中国建设银行首次为中外合资企业向国外银行借款出具担保，也是目前国内最大的一项境外担保业务。

23日 中国机械进出口（集团）有限公司子公司——中机海川国际船舶公司利用中国政府优惠贷款向孟加拉出口船舶合同在京正式签约。该项目的实施将对改善孟加拉内河航运状况及促进我国船舶出口起到积极作用。

24日 朱镕基总理在京会见文莱达鲁萨兰国苏丹哈桑纳尔·博尔基亚陛下时谈到，中文两国经贸合作很有潜力，中方愿与文莱进一步加强在各个领域的互利合作。

26日 中国、吉尔吉斯斯坦、俄罗斯、哈萨克斯坦和塔吉克斯坦五国元首在吉尔吉斯斯坦首都比什凯克举行第四次会晤。五国元首高度评价五国为巩固地区安全与合作所做的努力，一致认为建立相互协作机制有利于充分发挥多边合作潜力，促进地区稳定和发展。

26日 外经贸部首席谈判代表龙永图在京会见德国经济合作与发展部代表团时谈到，中德在技术合作方面具有非常广泛的前景，今后双方可进一步加强合作，尤其在环保方面应取得进展。

26日 中国—马来西亚经贸会议在大连举行。马来西亚贸工部副部长郭洙镇率领政府代表团和经贸考察团一行出席会议，探讨双方在商品贸易和投资领域合作前景。

30日 石广生部长与马耳他经济部长约瑟夫·邦尼奇在京召开的第一届中马经贸混委会上，一致同意进一步拓展双边经贸关系。

9　月

1日～3日 由上海市人民政府、大阪市政府和大阪商务伙伴城市协议会联合主办的“99商务伙伴城市圆桌会议（BPC）”在上海举行。与会BPC成员代表就加强商务伙伴城市直接交往展开深入讨论，并对亚洲金融危机后的经济恢复状况及经济重建等问题进行广泛商讨。

2日～16日 应泰国国王普密蓬、澳大利亚总督威廉·迪恩和新西兰总督博伊斯的邀请，中国国家主席江泽民对三国进行国事访问。访问期间，江主席同三国国家元首和政府领导人就双边关系和重大国际及地区问题深入交换意见。

6日～11日 江主席在澳大利亚访问期间出席澳中贸易投资研讨会并会见澳中工商委员会成员和公司代表。

3日 由外经贸部和联合国开发计划署共同召开，旨在交流合作经验并探讨未来新的合作模式、方向和潜力的“纪念中国－联合国开发计划署合作20周年研讨会”在京举行。外经贸部部长石广生、联合国开发计划署助理署长兼亚太局局长内通以及来自国内外的有关专家、学者和政府官员等出席研讨会。

6日～7日 由外经贸部和信息产业部共同主办、中国国际电子商务中心承办的首届中国国际电子商务应用博览会在京举行。

8日～12日 第三届中国投资贸易洽谈会在厦门市举行。国务院和有关部门、省市领导以及有关国家政府、国际组织、跨国公司的代表出席开幕式。8日　国务委员吴仪在“迈向21世纪的国际投资合作研讨会”上发表演讲，建议海外投资者在国企技改、中西部开发、高新技术、基础设施、服务贸易方面寻找商机。同日　外经贸部部长助理马秀红发布鼓励外商投资政策出台的消息。9日　外经贸部副部长孙广相在京会见出席第三届投资贸易洽谈会的沙特商业大臣法基一行，双方就劳务合作、双边贸易、科技合作、双向投资等问题交换意见。

12日　’99中国西安投资贸易洽谈会隆重开幕。全国人大、全国政协、国家计委、国务院有关部委、省市领导以及德国、法国、比利时、美国等有关国家政府、商会、金融机构的代表出席开幕式。

13日　亚太经合组织第七次领导人非正式会议在新西兰奥克兰举行。中国国家主席江泽民和亚太经合组织其他成员领导人出席会议，就进一步推进亚太地区经济合作、亚太经合组织如何为新一轮全球贸易谈判作贡献以及亚太经合组织的未来走向等问题展开讨论。会后通过题为《奥克兰挑战》的宣言。

13日　全国人大常委会委员长李鹏在京会见日中经贸中心代表团，希望中日今后能在经贸投资、科技交流、基础设施建设、环保和人才培训等方面加强合作。

14日　在太平洋经济合作理事会的倡导下，由对外贸易经济合作部和天津市人民政府联合主办的“第一届PECC国际贸易投资博览会”在天津开幕。28个国家和地区经贸组织和商会代表出席开幕式。

16日～20日　由山西省政府主办的’99山西国际经济贸易洽谈会在太原举行。美国、英国、德国、荷兰、法国、日本等28个国家和地区共300多位客商代表参加洽谈会，共签订投资合作项目90项、协议及意向71项。

20日　中法经贸混委会第13次会议在京举行，外经贸部副部长周可仁与法国外贸国务秘书于伟特共同主持会议。周可仁积极评价中法两国的经贸关系，并指出中法经济互补性很强，双方在航空、金融、运输、农业等领域有巨大合作潜力。

23日　国务院总理朱镕基在京会见新加坡内阁资政李光耀时指出，中新关系发展势头良好，两国经贸合作取得长足进展。

28日　外经贸部部长石广生同美国贸易谈判代表巴尔舍夫斯基在华盛顿就中国加入世贸组织问题举行会谈，进一步贯彻执行两国元首就恢复双边磋商和加快谈判进程所达成的谅解。

27日～29日　’99《财富》全球论坛在上海举行，来自全球的商界精英、政要、学者荟萃浦东，以“中国：未来50年”为题，探讨中国发展前景、纵论世界经济走势。中国国家主席江泽民参加开幕活动并会见来自美洲、欧洲和亚洲的跨国企业代表50多人。800位世界商界精英与中国企业家、经济学家及政府官员，就上百项议题进行广泛交流。

10　月

5日～10日　由国家对外贸易经济合作部、科学技术部、信息产业部、中国科学院和深圳市政府共同主办的首届中国国际高新技术成果交易会在深圳举行。国务院总理朱镕基出席会议并致辞。本届高交会成交总额64.94亿美元，其中成交高新技术项目1030项，成交金额42.78亿美元，占总成交额的65.9%，其他项目成交429项，成交金额22.16亿美元。10日　外经贸部和科技部联合在深圳召开全国促进高新技术产品出口工作会议。外经贸部部长石广生和科技部部长朱丽兰分别在会议上作报告。

8日　石广生部长与德国经济部长米勒在京共同主持中德经贸混委会第10次会议。双方就进一步推动两国贸易、投资等各种形式经济技术合作进行磋商与交流。

9日　第二届亚欧经济部长会议在德国首都柏林开幕。外经贸部部长石广生率中国代表团与会，并通过《主席声明》。

11日　外经贸部副部长孙振宇与匈牙利国务秘书古拉奇在京共同主持召开中匈经贸混委会第10次会议，双方代表签署《中国和匈牙利政府经济贸易和科技合作委员会第十次会议纪要》。

12日　第五届亚太地区政府合作社部长会议在京开幕。这是亚太地区政府合作会议和中国合作社历史上规模最大、规格最高的一次国际性会议。

13日　由世界知识产权组织和中国国家知识产权局共同举办的知识产权与知识经济国际研讨会在京举行。国务院总理朱镕基在京会见世界知识产权组织总干事加米勒·伊德里斯一行。

14日　首届亚欧科技部长会议在京举行。来自亚欧会议25个成员国科技主管部门的部长及欧盟委员会的官员出席会议，共同就未来合作进行探讨。

15日～30日 第86届中国出口商品交易会在广州举行。到会客商累计91213人，比去年秋交会增长30.3%，出口成交额达127亿美元。

18日～11月3日 应英国女王伊丽莎白二世、法国总统希拉克、葡萄牙总统桑帕约、摩洛哥国王穆罕默德六世、阿尔及利亚总统布特弗利卡和沙特阿拉伯国王法赫德邀请，国家主席江泽民前往上述六国进行国事访问。20日 国家主席江泽民在英中贸易协会举行的欢迎午宴上发表讲话。中英两国在伦敦签署3项经济贸易合作协议。23日 中法两国元首一致同意建立两国元首间的热线电话，以及加强两国常驻联合国代表之间的磋商机制。25日 江泽民主席与法国总统希拉克举行会谈。江泽民强调当前世界应是一个多极世界，希望欧盟就中国加入世贸组织采取积极务实灵活态度，并希望中法加强高新技术合作。26日 江泽民主席与葡萄牙总统在葡举行会谈。双方就澳门问题、双边关系和共同关心的国际问题交换意见。28日 江泽民主席与穆罕默德六世举行会谈。两国首脑签署《中华人民共和国政府与摩洛哥王国政府关于中国向摩洛哥提供优惠贷款的框架协议》、《中华人民共和国政府与摩洛哥王国政府经济技术合作协定》。30日 国家主席江泽民与阿尔及利亚总统布特弗利卡举行会谈。中阿双方签署《中阿经济技术协定》、《中阿贸易协定》。11月2日 国家主席江泽民与阿卜杜拉王储举行会谈。双方签署《中华人民共和国政府与沙特阿拉伯王国政府石油领域合作谅解备忘录》。

20日 国际标准化组织（ISO）第22届大会在京举行。国务院副总理吴邦国出席会议并指出，研究对国际贸易和国际社会发展有重要影响的标准化工作，协调全球标准活动，消除贸易壁垒，促进国际合作，这对全世界都有重要现实意义。

21日 国务院总理朱镕基会见来华参加中美第12次联合经济委员会会议的美国财政部部长劳伦斯·萨默斯一行。

25日 外经贸部副部长周可仁与瑞典大臣雷夫·帕格罗斯在京共同主持召开中瑞第14次经贸混委会，双方就共同关心的问题交换意见。

11　月

2日 外经贸部副部长孙振宇与智利外交部副部长费尔南德斯在京签署两国关于中国加入世贸组织双边市场准入协议。智利是世贸组织成员中第一个与中国结束双边谈判的拉丁美洲国家。

4日 在外经贸部支持下，“中国机电产品展览中心”在阿联酋沙迦酋长国正式成立。

5日 外经贸部部长石广生在京会见匈牙利外长毛尔托尼·亚诺什时指出，中匈两国经贸发展具有广阔发展前景。

5日 中德商会成立典礼在京举行。外经贸部部长石广生、中国贸促会会长俞晓松、德国经济技术部部长米勒等出席成立典礼。商会宗旨是促进中德双边贸易及中德公司间的商务联系。

5日 国务院总理朱镕基在京会见德国总理格哈德·施罗德时表示，中方愿同德方加强中小企业合作，并逐步开展金融、保险等服务领域的合作。

8日 外经贸部部长石广生在京会见克罗地亚经济部部长奈纳德·波尔盖斯时说，中克双方应致力于拓展经贸合作新途径，开展更深入的合作。双方共同主持中克第六届混委会开幕式。

8日 祖国内地与香港特别行政区商贸联委会第一次会议在京召开。外经贸部部长助理安民和港方工商局局长周德熙分别发表讲话。

8日 国家主席江泽民在京会见乌兹别克斯坦共和国总统伊斯兰·卡里莫夫时说，中乌经贸合作潜力尚未完全挖掘，双方应寻找新的合作资源，采取有利于两国经贸合作的方式。

9日 朱镕基总理在京分别会见瑞士联邦委员兼公共经济部长帕斯卡尔·库什潘率领的瑞士政府和经济代表团和由澳门货币暨汇兑监理署行政委员会主席丁连星率领的澳门银行界代表团。

10日 中国国际贸易促进委员会与欧盟、欧洲商会共同在北京和成都举办“中国水星计划商会业务培训班”，其宗旨是为中国各有关商会提供了解和学习欧洲商会经验的机会，以促进中欧经贸合作，特别是中小企业的合作。

12日 全国人大委员会委员长李鹏在京会见法国布依格集团总裁米歇尔·德尔贝斯一行时指出，中法两国在经济领域有着良好合作关系，欢迎法国企业来华投资。

15日 外经贸部部长石广生与美国贸易代表巴尔舍夫斯基分别代表中美两国政府在京签署关于中国加入世界贸易组织的双边协议，该协议标志着中美就中国加入全球最大贸易组织的双边谈判正式结束，为中国“入世”迈出重要一步。

22日～12月4日 应马来西亚总理马哈蒂尔、菲律宾总统埃斯特拉达、新加坡总理吴作栋和越南总理潘文凯的邀请，国务院总理朱镕基对上述四国进行友好访问。

24日 朱镕基向马来西亚工商界发表讲话。28日 朱镕基出席在马尼拉举行的第三次东盟与中日韩领导人非正式会晤，会晤结束时发表《东亚合作联合声明》，对深化中国与东盟国家睦邻友好及加强东亚国家之间的互利合作具有重要意义。

23日 国家主席江泽民在京会见哈萨克斯坦共和国总统努尔苏丹·阿比舍维奇·纳孔尔巴耶夫时说，中哈两国应采取积极措施使两国经贸合作再上一个新台阶。

23日 国家出入境检验检疫局主办的亚欧会议贸易便利行动计划 SPS 研讨会在京举行，围绕“方便贸易往来”这一主旨就简化 SPS 程序及单证等问题进行积极探讨。来自18个国家的114名代表参加会议。

26日 石广生部长与加拿大国际贸易部长佩蒂格鲁在温哥华，代表两国政府签署中国与加拿大关于中国加入世界贸易组织的双边协议。加拿大是迄今为止第14个与中国结束世贸组织双边谈判的国家。同日 两位部长共同出席加拿大加中贸易理事会举办的第21届大型年会，石广生部长在讲话中高度评价中加经贸关系并鼓励加拿大企业家来华投资。

26日～27日 中国和阿尔巴尼亚政府经济贸易混合委员会在地拉那举行第二次会议，双方签定进一步推进双边经贸合作的会议纪要，并对今后的经贸合作进行具体探讨。

12 月

1日 由中国贸促会同伊朗驻华使馆联合主办的’99中国—伊朗经贸洽谈会在京举行。伊朗副总统穆罕默德·哈希米、中国国务委员吴仪、贸促会会长俞晓松、外经贸部副部长孙振宇出席会议。

2日 国家主席江泽民在京会见印尼总统阿卜杜勒—拉赫曼·瓦希德，双方一致同意建立和发展长期稳定的睦邻互信全面合作关系，把双边贸易、投资及科技合作推向更高水平。

3日 国务院总理朱镕基在越南主席府同越南政府总理潘文凯举行会谈时表示，中国愿继续为促进两国经贸合作的进一步发展作出积极努力。

3日 为期4天的世界贸易组织第三届部长会议在美国西雅图结束，本届会议未能就启动新一轮多边贸易谈判达成一致，与会者同意2000年1月在日内瓦继续进行有关新一轮谈判的磋商。中国对外贸易经济合作部部长石广生参会期间分别会见乌拉圭、巴基斯坦、俄罗斯、沙特阿拉伯等国的贸易部长及欧盟贸易委员帕斯卡尔·拉米。

6日 江泽民主席在京会见约旦国王阿卜杜拉·本·侯赛因时提出几点框架设想，其中包括加强两国经贸部门及企业家之间的联系与交流，探讨和建立多形式、多渠道的经贸合作关系。

9日 江泽民主席同俄罗斯总统叶利钦在京举行非正式会晤。两国元首高度评价双边友好合作关系的顺利发展，表示愿进一步加强经济、贸易领域的交流。

10日 中国、坦桑尼亚、赞比亚三国政府关于坦赞铁路技术合作的部长级会谈在京举行。石广生部长、赞比亚通讯交通部长恩康杜·罗和坦桑尼亚驻华使馆临时代办恩古马共同主持会谈，并签署关于中国政府向坦赞铁路提供专项贷款协定和坦赞铁路经济技术合作意向书。

10日 外经贸部首席谈判代表龙永图和英国国际发展部副部长在京签署《中英技术合作国有企业改革与发展》项目换文，并就共同关心的问题交换意见。

13日 外经贸部副部长孙振宇出席在上海召开的《科技兴贸与跨国经营——迎接新世纪上海外经贸发展战略研讨会》，并就当前我国外经贸形势及2000年工作展望作主题发言，强调要进一步完善投资环境，力争今年外经贸全面增长。

13日～17日 首届上海国际工业博览会在上海展览中心举行。工博会以电子信息、电气装备、生物医药、新材料等高新技术产业为主要内容，参观人数达22万人次，境外客商3000多人。产品、技术和产权三大类总成交25亿元人民币，达成成交意向超过20亿元人民币。

15日 石广生部长就《台湾同胞投资保护法实施细则》颁布发表谈话指出，《实施细则》是鼓励台湾同胞投资、保护台湾同胞投资合法权益的又一重要举措。

16日　朱镕基总理在京会见捷克总理米洛什·泽曼时表示，中国政府支持双方企业加强合作，双方应共同努力寻求两国经济互补之处，充分发挥合作潜力。

17日　中国和吉尔吉斯政府间经贸合作委员会第四次会议在京举行。外经贸部副部长张祥和吉外长伊马纳利耶夫共同主持会议。双方签署《中吉经贸合作委员会第四次会议纪要》。

20日　江泽民主席凌晨在澳门向全世界郑重宣告，中华人民共和国澳门特别行政区政府成立，全部由澳门人组成的澳门特别行政区政府宣誓就职。同日　澳门特别行政区第一届立法会举行全体会议，通过《回归法》，这是回归后特别立法会通过的第一部法律。

22日　全国外经贸工作会议在京隆重召开。国务委员吴仪在会议上强调指出，我国1999年的对外经济贸易工作在相当困难情况下，取得较好成绩。石广生部长主持开幕式，并作《抓住新机遇，迎接新挑战，开创2000年全国外经贸工作新局面》工作报告。

24日　中国和古巴结束关于中国加入WTO双边谈判。同日　中国和委内瑞拉结束关于中国加入WTO双边谈判。

27日　国务院副总理李岚清在京会见韩国财政经济部长官康奉均，就加强中韩两国在经济、贸易等领域的交流与合作交换意见。

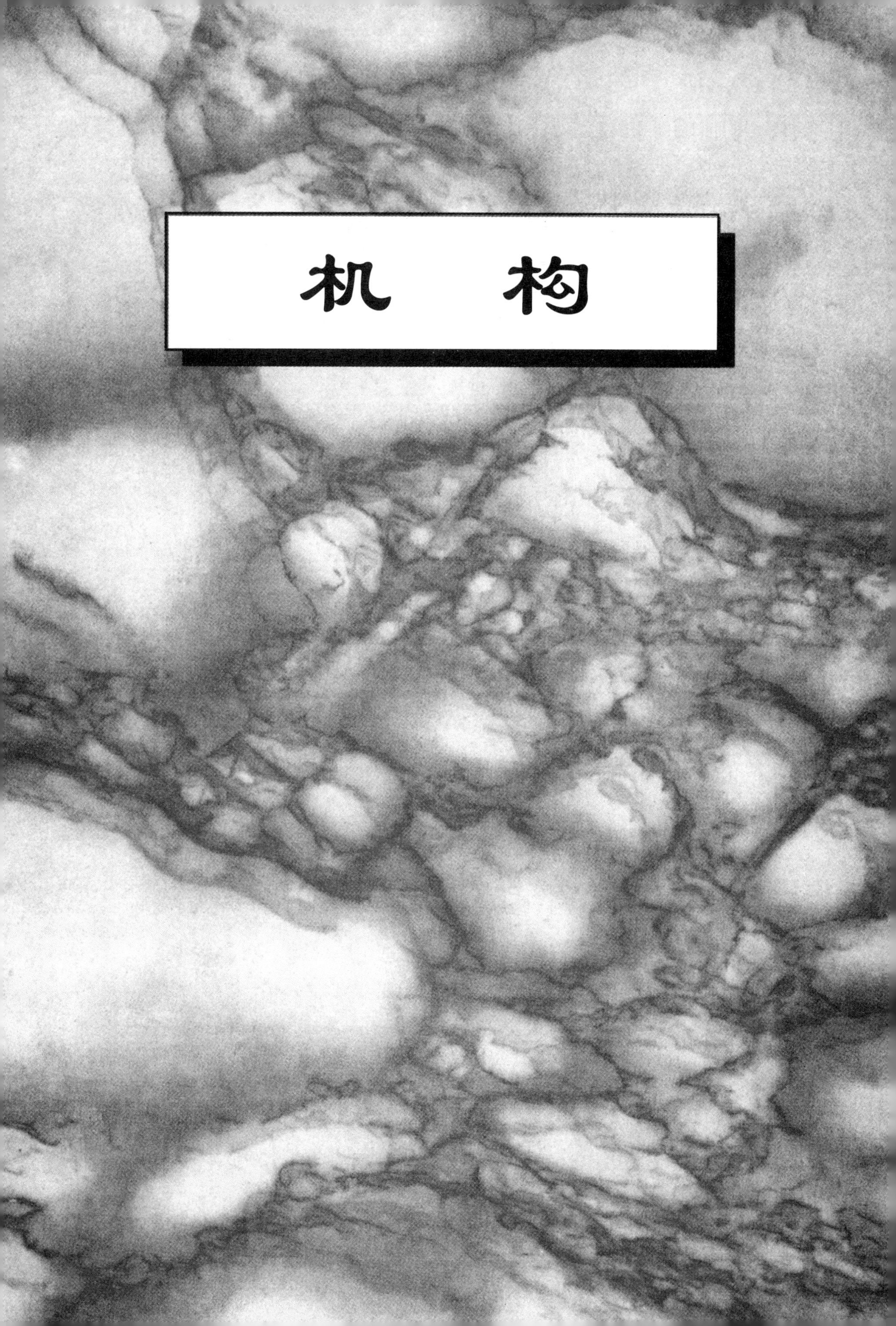

机　构

外 经 贸 部 机 关

外经贸部机关

地址：北京东长安街2号
邮政编码：100731
电话区号：010

办公厅

电话：65198340 65198313 65198318
传真：65198315

人事司

电话：65198515 65198941 65198550
传真：65198537

发展司

电话：65197495 65197492 65197456
传真：65197491

计财司

电话：65198616 65198676 65198457
传真：65198458

亚洲司

电话：65198726 65198716
传真：65198903

西亚非洲司

电话：65197748 65197220 65197750
传真：65197908

欧洲司

电话：65198632 65198685 65198622
传真：65198902

美大司

电话：65198821 65198820 65198860
传真：65198904

台港澳司

电话：65198628 65198630

国际司

电话：65197217 65197703 65197248
传真：65197903

贸易管理司

电话：65197430 65197405 65197435
传真：65197952

机电司

电话：65198776 65198790 65198797
传真：65198775

外资司

电话：65197303 65197304 65197331
传真：65197322

援外司

电话：65197531 65197558
传真：65197905

合作司

电话：65197163 65197173 65197196
传真：65197992

科技司

电话：65197372 65197355

传真：65197926

条法司

电话：65198725 65198733 65198723

传真：65198905

交际司

电话：65198204 65198203 65198230

传真：65198962

直属机关党委

电话：65197552 65197551 65197923

传真：65197582

监察局

电话：65198814 65198815

传真：65198911

老干部局

电话：65128927 65135533－530 65135533－230 65135533－579

行政事务管理局（机关服务中心）

电话：65197262

传真：65197271

审计署驻外经贸部审计局

电话：65198433 65198401 65198402

传真：65198483

外经贸部事业单位

许可证事务局

地址：台基厂头条二号

电话区号：010

电话：65225873 65225872

传真：65225874

邮政编码：100005

EDI 电子商务中心

地址：东长安街 2 号（东配楼）

电话区号：010

电话：65198171 65198185

传真：65129164

邮政编码：100731

研究院

地址：安外东后巷 28 号

电话区号：010

电话：64216661－1201 64245741

传真：64212175

邮政编码：100710

研究院商务信息部

地址：东长安街 2 号（东配楼）

电话区号：010

电话：65197349 65197345 65197350

传真：

邮政编码：100731

交流中心

地址：北三环中路 18 号

电话区号：010

电话：62013084

传真：62011328

邮政编码：100011

计算中心

地址：安外东后巷 28 号

电话区号：010

电话：64253866

传真：64211497

邮政编码：100710

亚太培训中心

地址：昌平县东三旗

电话区号：010
电话：61781188－6326、6518
传真：61784657
邮政编码：102209

国际商报

地址：方庄芳星园三区 14 楼
电话区号：010
电话：67629145
传真：67629153
邮政编码：100078

经贸大学

地址：朝阳区和平街北口惠新东街
电话区号：010
电话：64492107　64968039
传真：64968037
邮政编码：100013

管理干部学院

地址：昌平县东三旗
电话区号：010
电话：61781188－3132、3370
传真：61781033
邮政编码：102200

外经贸部商会、协会、学会

纺织商会

地址：潘家园大厦
电话区号：010
电话：67739258　67739291
传真：67739204
邮政编码：100021

轻工商会

地址：潘家园南里 12 号
电话区号：010
电话：67732707
传真：
邮政编码：100021

五矿化工商会

地址：崇文区永外桃园东里 15 号百万庄园
电话区号：010
电话：67249100　67214433－3415
传真：67249104
邮政编码：100037

食品土畜商会

地址：东城区西堂子胡同 21 号
电话区号：010
电话：65132569　65132370
传真：65139064
邮政编码：100006

机电商会

地址：潘家园南里 12 号
电话区号：010
电话：67735114　67735077
传真：67735350
邮政编码：100021

医保商会

地址：潘家园南里十二楼八层
电话区号：010
电话：67734761
传真：67734768
邮政编码：100021

承包商会

地址：安外东后巷 28 号
电话区号：010
电话：64211159
传真：64213959
邮政编码：100710

外资协会

地址：东安门大街 82 号
电话区号：010

电话：65131509
传真：65129390
邮政编码：100740

国际工程咨询协会
地址：安外东后巷 28 号
电话区号：010
电话：64245409
传真：64267562
邮政编码：100710

企管协会
地址：台基厂头条 10 号
电话区号：010
电话：65128960
传真：65128960
邮政编码：100005

贸易学会
地址：台基厂头条 10 号
电话区号：010
电话：65128257
传真：65128257
邮政编码：100005

会计学会
地址：广渠门夕照寺街 14 号富瑞苑公寓 2E
电话区号：010
电话：67165172
邮政编码：100061

合作学会
地址：安外东后巷 28 号
电话区号：010
电话：64239509
传真：64239509
邮政编码：100710

统计学会
地址：东城区王府井大街菜厂胡同 58 号
电话区号：010
电话：65239340
传真：65239338
邮政编码：100710

亚太经贸合作促进会
地址：国贸咨询信息大楼
电话区号：010
电话：65052255－1818
传真：65052255－1818
邮政编码：100020

国际民间组织合作促进会
地址：西城区北三环中路 18 号
电话区号：010
电话：62011830　62011832
传真：62011328
邮政编码：100011

外经贸部信息化领导小组办公室
地址：东长安街 2 号
电话区号：010
电话：65198082　65198083
传真：65198081
邮政编码：100731

外贸中心

国际贸易中心
地址：建国门外大街 1 号
电话区号：010
电话：65053231　65052288－8345
传真：65051002
邮政编码：100020

广州外贸中心
地址：广州市流花路 117 号
电话区号：020

电话：86678000－80011
传真：86666920
邮政编码：510014

福建外贸中心

地址：福州五四路外贸中心
电话区号：0591
电话：7533575　7536241
传真：7537173
邮政编码：350003

上海外贸中心

地址：上海世纪大道2号金贸大厦7楼
电话区号：021
电话：50472601
传真：50472608
邮政编码：

深圳外贸中心

地址：深圳市深南东路170号金山大厦26楼
电话区号：0755
电话：2073034－868
传真：2073442
邮政编码：518002

外经贸部各特派员办事处

广州特派员办事处

地址：广州市流花路117号
电话区号：020
电话：86677314
传真：86677314
邮政编码：510014

上海特派员办事处

地址：上海永福路1号
电话区号：021
电话：64327212
传真：64318707
邮政编码：200031

天津特派员办事处

地址：天津市和平区南京路59号
电话区号：022
电话：23307724
传真：23308071
邮政编码：300050

大连特派员办事处

地址：中山广场2号
电话区号：0411
电话：2630778
传真：2630213
邮政编码：116001

深圳特派员办事处

地址：深圳市红岭大厦5栋
电话区号：0755
电话：2243256
传真：2247369
邮政编码：518046

海南特派员办事处

地址：华海路安海大厦
电话区号：0898
电话：6776186
传真：6776957
邮政编码：570105

青岛特派员办事处

地址：青岛市燕儿岛路12号
电话区号：0532
电话：5734278
传真：5734682
邮政编码：266071

西安特派员办事处

地址：环城南路26号外贸大厦5楼
电话区号：029

电话：7234934
传真：7234933
邮政编码：710054

成都特派员办事处

地址：环路西三段抚琴西南街 18 号
电话区号：028
电话：7734181
传真：7781984
邮政编码：610031

武汉特派员办事处

地址：江汉北路 8 号
电话区号：027
电话：85774211
传真：85774298
邮政编码：430022

郑州特派员办事处

地址：郑州市文化路 115 号
电话区号：0371
电话：3943388－3204
传真：3942780
邮政编码：450003

福州特派员办事处

地址：福州市五四路 75 号
电话区号：0591
电话：7536473
传真：7536473
邮政编码：350001

南京特派员办事处

地址：南京中山东路 378 号
电话区号：025
电话：4402304
传真：4402934
邮政编码：210002

南宁特派员办事处

地址：南宁市圆湖南路 17 号
电话区号：0771
电话：5867858
传真：5867740
邮政编码：530022

杭州特派员办事处

地址：杭州延安路 464 号
电话区号：0571
电话：5177854
传真：5177853
邮政编码：310006

昆明特派员办事处

地址：昆明市关渡区关上关兴路 194 号万兴花园
电话区号：0871
电话：7181299
传真：7181396
邮政编码：650200

各省市、自治区外经贸厅（委）

北京市外经贸委

地址：东城区朝内大街 190 号
电话区号：010
电话：65251866　65248780
传真：65135946
邮政编码：100010

天津市外经贸委

地址：天津市和平区曲阜道 80 号
电话区号：022
电话：23304858
传真：23315231
邮政编码：300042

上海市外经贸委

地址：娄山关路 55 号
电话区号：021
电话：62752200

传真： 62751159
邮政编码： 200336

河北省外经贸厅
地址： 石家庄市和平西路 334 号
电话区号： 0311
电话： 7044842
传真： 7041570
邮政编码： 050071

山西省外经贸厅
地址： 太原市新建路 15 号
电话区号： 0351
电话： 4041722 4040120
传真： 4081004
邮政编码： 030002

内蒙古外经贸厅
地址： 呼和浩特市中山西路 138 号
电话区号： 0471
电话： 6967398
传真： 6962138
邮政编码： 010020

辽宁省外经贸厅
地址： 沈阳市北陵大街 45－1 号
电话区号： 024
电话： 86892462 86892844
传真： 86893858
邮政编码： 110032

大连市外经贸委
地址： 大连市黄河路 219 号
电话区号： 0411
电话： 3686665
传真： 3686426
邮政编码： 116011

吉林省外经贸厅
地址： 长春市人民大街 119 号
电话区号： 0431
电话： 5628077 5637881
传真： 5624772
邮政编码： 130021

黑龙江省外经贸厅
地址： 哈尔滨市动力区和平路 173 号
电话区号： 0451
电话： 2621345
传真： 2623585
邮政编码： 150040

哈尔滨市外经贸局
地址： 哈尔滨市道里区中地街 102 号
电话区号： 0451
电话： 4614368 4617832
传真： 4616661
邮政编码： 150010

江苏省外经贸委
地址： 南京市北京东路 29 号
电话区号： 025
电话： 7712600
传真： 7712072
邮政编码： 210008

浙江省外经贸厅
地址： 杭州市延安路 470 号
电话区号： 0571
电话： 5153292
传真： 5154139
邮政编码： 310006

宁波市外经贸委
地址： 宁波市灵桥路 190 号
电话区号： 0574
电话： 7310963
传真： 7328288
邮政编码： 315000

安徽省外经贸委
地址： 合肥市金寨路 389－399 号胜安大厦
电话区号： 0551
电话： 2831268
传真： 2831272
邮政编码： 230062

福建省外经贸委

地址：福州市六一北路92号
电话区号：0591
电话：7593604 7841917
传真：7856133
邮政编码：350013

厦门市贸易发展委员会

地址：厦门市湖里工业区信息大厦12层
电话区号：0592
电话：6021017
传真：6021901
邮政编码：361006

江西省外经贸厅

地址：南昌市站前路200号
电话区号：0791
电话：6227281
传真：6246306
邮政编码：330002

山东省外经贸委

地址：山东省济南市黑虎泉西路121号
电话区号：0531
电话：6915762
传真：6912793
邮政编码：250011

青岛市外经贸委

地址：青岛市香港中路6号青岛世界贸易中心
电话区号：0532
电话：5918109
传真：3836036
邮政编码：266071

河南省外经贸厅

地址：郑州市文化路115号
电话区号：0371
电话：3941359
传真：3945422
邮政编码：450003

湖北省外经贸厅

地址：武汉市汉口江汉北路8号
电话区号：027
电话：85774233
传真：85773668
邮政编码：430022

湖南省外经贸委

地址：湖南省长沙市五一中路80号
电话区号：0731
电话：2295145
传真：2295160
邮政编码：410001

广东省外经贸委

地址：广州市天河路351号
电话区号：020
电话：38802165
传真：38802219
邮政编码：510620

深圳市贸易发展局

地址：深圳市上步中路8号市府二办
电话区号：0755
电话：2240972
传真：2243803
邮政编码：518006

广西省外经贸厅

地址：南宁市七星路137号
电话区号：0771
电话：5311810
传真：5321237
邮政编码：530022

海南省外经贸厅

地址：海口市国贸大道18号
电话区号：0898
电话：6777795
传真：6773012
邮政编码：570125

四川省外经贸委

地址：成都市成华街4号
电话区号：028
电话：3394060
传真：3337610
邮政编码：610081

重庆市外经贸委

地址：重庆市江北区建新北路65号
电话区号：023
电话：67853525
传真：67853458
邮政编码：400020

贵州省外经贸厅

地址：贵州省贵阳市中华北路328号外贸中心5－7楼
电话区号：0851
电话：6822341
传真：6826509
邮政编码：550004

云南省外经贸厅

地址：云南省昆明市北京路175号
电话区号：0871
电话：3135001
传真：3123541
邮政编码：650011

西藏自治区外经贸厅

地址：西藏拉萨市北京中路184号
电话区号：0891
电话：6839337
传真：6835733
邮政编码：850000

陕西省外经贸厅

地址：西安市新城内　电话区号：029
电话：7291583
传真：7291618
邮政编码：710004

甘肃省外经贸厅

地址：兰州市定西路386号
电话区号：0931
电话：8619723
传真：8618083
邮政编码：730000

青海省外经贸厅

地址：青海西宁市西树林巷25号
电话区号：0971
电话：8174541
传真：8176805
邮政编码：810007

宁夏自治区外经贸厅

地址：宁夏银川市解放西街119号
电话区号：0951
电话：5044277
传真：5044239
邮政编码：750001

新疆自治区外经贸厅

地址：团结路11号
电话区号：0991
电话：2860255
传真：2860255
邮政编码：830001

新疆生产建设兵团外经贸局

地址：新疆乌鲁木齐市
电话区号：0991
电话：2832649
传真：22833981
邮政编码：830002

附　　录

第一部分

中国国民经济基本情况统计(一)

(1985 年—1999 年)

指　标	单　位	绝对数					1999 年为以下年份 %			
		1985	1990	1995	1998	1999	1985	1990	1995	1998
国内生产总值	亿元	8964	18548	58478	78345	82054	354.4	242.7	137.7	107.1
第一产业	亿元	2542	5017	11993	14552	14212	174.1	141.8	115.7	102.8
第二产业	亿元	3867	7717	28538	38619	40807	499.6	325.1	145.9	108.1
工业	亿元	3449	6858	24718	33388	35357	519.1	334.0	148.0	108.5
建筑业	亿元	418	859	3820	5231	5450	346.8	253.8	127.0	104.6
第三产业	亿元	2556	5814	17947	25174	27036	344.8	220.3	137.1	107.5
运输邮电业	亿元	407	1148	3055	4121	4460	404.2	252.8	149.3	109.3
商业	亿元	878	1420	4932	6579	6842	237.3	189.6	132.0	107.2
人均国内生产总值	元/人	853	1634	4854	6277	6546	297.0	219.8	132.3	106.1
固定资产投资										
全社会固定资产投资总额	亿元	2543.2	4517.0	20019.3	28406.2	29876.0	1174.7	661.4	149.2	105.2
基本建设投资	亿元	1074.4	1703.8	7403.6	11916.4	12618.7	1174.5	740.6	170.4	105.9
财政总收入	亿元	2004.8	2937.1	6242.2	9876.0	11377.0	567.5	387.4	182.3	115.2
财政总支出	亿元	2004.3	3083.6	6823.7	10798.2	13136.0	655.4	426.0	192.5	121.6
交通、邮电										
货物周转量	亿吨公里	18365	26207	35730	37841	40273	219.3	153.7	112.7	106.4
沿海主要港口货物吞吐量	万吨	31154	48321	80166	92237	105162	337.6	217.6	131.2	114.0
旅客周转量	亿人公里	4437	5628	9002	10559	11214	252.7	199.3	124.6	106.2
邮电业务总量	亿元	29.60	81.65	988.85	2431.21	3311.00	1036.7	4037.8	334.8	136.2
商业和物价										
社会消费品零售额	亿元	3801.4	7250.3	20620.0	29152.5	31134.7	819.0	429.4	151.0	106.8
年末城乡集市贸易点	个	61337	72579	82892	89177	88576	144.4	122.0	106.9	99.3
农产品收购价格总指数	上年=100	108.6	97.4	119.9	92.0	87.8				
商品零售物价指数	上年=100	108.8	102.1	114.8	97.4	97.0				
全国居民消费价格总指数	上年=100	109.3	103.1	117.1	99.2	98.6				

中国国民经济基本情况统计(二)
(1985年—1999年)

指标	单位	绝对数					1999年为以下年份%			
		1985	1990	1995	1998	1999	1985	1990	1995	1998
城市居民消费价格指数	上年=100	111.9	101.3	116.8	99.4	98.7				
农村居民消费价格指数	上年=100	107.6	104.5	117.5	99.0	98.5				
外贸、旅游										
进出口总额	亿美元	696.0	1154.4	2808.6	3240.5	3606.5	518.2	312.4	128.4	111.3
出口总额	亿美元	273.5	620.9	1487.8	1838.1	1949.3	712.7	313.9	131.0	106.0
进口总额	亿美元	422.5	533.5	1320.8	1402.4	1657.2	392.2	310.6	125.5	118.2
实际利用外资	亿美元	46.47	102.89	481.33	585.6	526.6	1133.2	511.8	109.4	89.9
对外借款	亿美元	26.88	65.34	103.27	110.00	102.12	379.9	156.3	98.9	92.8
外商直接投资及其他	亿美元	19.59	37.55	378.06	475.57	424.47	2166.8	1130.4	112.3	89.3
接待外来旅游人数	万人	1783.3	2746.2	4638.7	6347.8	7279.6	408.2	265.1	156.9	114.7
外国人	万人	137.0	174.7	588.7	710.8	843.2	615.5	482.7	143.2	118.6
港澳台同胞	万人	1637.8	2562.4	4038.4	5624.9	6425.6	392.3	250.8	159.1	114.2
旅游收入外汇	亿美元	12.5	22.2	87.3	126.0	141.0	1128.0	635.1	161.5	111.9
科学、教育、文化										
国家级重大科学技术成果	项	10476.0	26829.0	31099.0	28584.0	31060.0	296.5	115.8	99.9	108.7
国有企业事业单位专业技术人员	万人	781.7	1080.9	1913.4	2091.4	2143.1	274.2	198.3	112.0	102.5
在校学生：										
普通高等学校	万人	170.3	206.3	290.6	340.9	413.4	242.7	200.4	142.3	121.3
成人高等学校	万人	172.5	166.6	257.0	282.2	305.5	177.1	183.4	118.9	108.3
普通中学	万人	4706.0	4586.0	5371.0	6301.0	6771.3	143.9	147.7	126.1	107.5
中等专业学校	万人	157.1	224.4	372.2	498.1	515.5	328.1	229.7	138.5	103.5
成人中等学校	万人	547.0	1529.4	5646.3	6676.0	7503.9	1371.8	490.6	132.9	112.4
成人初等学校	万人	833.8	2282.1	778.3	538.6	536.8	64.4	23.5	69.0	99.7
小学	万人	13370.2	12241.4	13195.2	13953.8	13548.0	101.3	110.7	102.7	97.1
艺术表演团体	个	3317.0	2805.0	2682.0	2652.0	2614.0	78.8	93.2	97.5	98.6

中国国民经济基本情况统计(三)
(1985年—1999年)

指标	单位	绝对数					1999年为以下年份%			
		1985	1990	1995	1998	1999	1985	1990	1995	1998
文化馆	个	2965.0	2955.0	2886.0	2901.0	2899.0	97.8	98.1	100.5	99.9
公共图书馆	个	2344	2527	2615	2731	2769	118.1	109.6	105.9	101.4
广播电台	座	213	635	1202	298	299	140.4	47.1	24.9	100.3
电视台	座	202	509	837	347	353	174.8	69.4	42.2	101.7
出版报纸总印数	亿份	246.8	211.3	263.3	300.4	318.4	129.0	150.7	120.9	106.0
各类杂志出版	亿册	25.6	17.9	23.4	25.4	27.9	109.0	155.9	119.2	109.8
图书出版	亿册	66.7	56.4	63.2	72.4	73.2	109.7	129.8	115.8	101.1
卫生、体育										
医院病床	万张	222.9	262.4	283.6	291.4	292.9	131.4	111.6	103.3	100.5
专业卫生技术人员	万人	341.1	389.8	425.7	442.4	445.9	130.7	114.4	104.7	100.8
#医生	万人	141.3	176.3	191.8	200.0	204.5	144.7	116.0	106.6	102.3
护师、护士	万人	63.7	97.5	112.6	121.9	124.5	195.4	127.7	110.6	102.1
获得世界体育冠军	项	42	54	98	75	91	216.7	168.5	92.9	121.3
打破体育世界纪录	项	5	14	13	31	24	480.0	171.4	184.6	77.4
举办县以上运动会	万次	2.69	3.02	2.80	2.67	2.68	99.6	88.7	95.7	100.4
人民生活										
农民平均每人纯收入	元	397.6	686.3	1577.7	2162.0	2210.3	176.1	152.2	123.4	103.8
城市居民人均可支配收入	元	739.1	1510.2	4283.0	5425.1	5854.0	224.8	182.0	124.2	109.3
年末职工人数	万人	12358.0	14059.0	14908.0	12337.0	11773.0	95.3	83.7	79.0	95.4
职工工资总额	亿元	1382.8	2951.1	8100.0	9296.5	9875.5	202.7	157.3	110.7	107.6
职工平均工资	元	1148.0	2140.0	5500.0	7479	8346	206.4	183.3	137.8	113.1
年末城乡人民储蓄存款余额	亿元	1622.6	7119.8	29662.3	53407.5	59621.8	3674.5	837.4	201.0	111.6
城镇人均住房面积	平方米	5.2	6.7	8.1	9.3	9.8	188.5	146.3	121.0	105.4
农村人均住房面积	平方米	14.7	17.8	21.0	23.7	24.4	166.0	137.1	116.2	103.0
人口										

中国国民经济基本情况统计(四)
(1985年—1999年)

指标	单位	绝对数					1999年为以下年份%			
		1985	1990	1995	1998	1999	1985	1990	1995	1998
年末全国人口	万人	105851.00	114333.00	121121.00	124810.00	125909.00	118.90	110.0	104.0	100.9
年人口出生率	‰	21.04	21.06	17.12	16.03	15.23				
年人口死亡率	‰	6.78	6.67	6.57	6.50	6.46				
年人口自然增长率	‰	14.26	14.39	10.55	9.53	8.77				

注:1.表中的数字,均未包括香港、澳门特别行政区和台湾省。

2.本表价值指标绝对数按当年价格计算;国内生产总值、邮电业务总量、农民人均纯收入、城镇居民人均可支配收入、职工工资总额、职工平均工资发展速度均按可比价格计算。

3.国内生产总值是指物质生产部门和非物质生产部门的增加值之和,是一个国家(或地区)所有常住单位在核算期内生产活动的最终成果。

4.邮电业务总量1985年、1990年按1980年不变价格计算,1995年以后按1990年不变价格计算。

5.农村和城市居民人均收入,是根据家庭抽样调查得出的。职工工资总额包括发给职工的物价补贴。1998年以后职工人数为在岗职工。

6.表中的出口、进口总额系中国海关统计数字。

7.1998、1999年广播电台和电视台只包括省、地、市级数,不包括县级数。

资料来源:1986年—1999年《中国统计年鉴》、2000年《中国统计摘要》。

(国家统计局)

1986 年—1999 年中国长期与短期外债的结构与增长

项目/年度		1986	1987	1988	1989	1990	1991	1992	1993	1994	1995	1996	1997	1998	1999
外债余额(亿美元)		214.8	302.0	400.0	413.0	525.5	605.6	693.2	835.7	928.1	1065.9	1162.8	1309.7	1460.4	1518.3
中长期外债	余额(亿美元)	167.1	244.8	326.9	370.3	457.8	502.6	584.7	700.2	823.9	946.8	1021.7	1128.2	1287.0	1366.5
	比上年增长(%)	77.6	46.5	33.5	13.3	23.6	9.8	16.4	20.0	17.7	14.9	7.9	10.4	14.1	6.2
	占总余额的比例(%)	77.8	81.0	81.7	89.7	87.1	83.0	84.4	83.8	88.8	88.8	87.9	86.1	88.1	90.0
短期外债	余额(亿美元)	47.7	57.2	73.0	42.7	67.7	103.0	108.5	135.5	104.2	119.1	141.1	181.4	173.4	151.8
	比上年增长(%)	-25.7	19.9	27.8	-41.6	58.5	52.2	5.2	24.3	-23.1	14.3	18.4	28.6	-4.4	-12.5
	占总余额的比例(%)	22.2	19.0	18.3	10.3	12.9	17.0	15.6	16.2	11.2	11.2	12.1	13.9	11.9	10.0

（国家外汇管理局）

1986 年—1999 年中国外债流动与国民经济、外汇收入

项目/年度	1986	1987	1988	1989	1990	1991	1992	1993	1994	1995	1996	1997	1998	1999
外债流入（亿美元）	87.2	92.1	142.3	174.3	164.8	188.6	152.2	273.7	343.3	391.1	309.5	431.0	456.6	300.5
比上年增长（%）	4.7	5.6	54.5	22.5	-5.5	14.4	-19.3	79.8	25.4	13.9	-20.9	39.3	5.9	-34.2
外债流出（亿美元）	62.3	51.2	72.8	170.2	96.2	127.9	134.3	182.5	250.6	317.1	224.7	324.2	424.8	309.9
比上年增长（%）	641.7	-17.8	42.2	133.7	-43.5	33.0	5.0	35.9	37.3	26.5	-29.1	44.3	31.0	-27.0
外债净流入（亿美元）	24.9	40.9	69.5	4.1	68.6	60.7	17.9	91.2	92.7	74.0	84.8	106.8	31.8	-9.4
国内生产总值（亿元人民币）	10202.2	11962.5	14928.5	16909.2	18547.9	21617.8	26638.1	34634.4	46759.4	58478.1	67884.6	74772.4	79553.0	82054.0
外债流出/国内生产总值	2.1	1.6	1.8	3.8	2.5	3.1	2.8	3.0	4.6	4.5	2.8	3.6	4.4	3.1
外汇收入（亿美元）	297.8	391.7	459.1	478.2	573.7	659.0	788.2	865.6	1189.3	1472.4	1716.8	2072.5	2075.9	2189.0
偿债率（%）	15.4	9.0	6.5	8.3	8.7	8.5	7.1	10.2	9.1	7.6	6.0	7.3	10.9	11.5

注：1.从 1998 年开始，原使用的“国民生产总值”数据调整为“国内生产总值”数据，以前年份数据均按《中国统计提要 1998》中公布数据进行了调整。计算负债率时按当年年平均汇率折美元。

2.外债流出指当年发生的还本付息额。

3.从 1998 年开始，本报表中外汇收入指国际收支口径的货物和服务收入，以前年份数据均据此进行了调整。

（国家外汇管理局）

1986 年—1999 年中国外债与国民经济、外汇收入

项目/年度	1986	1987	1988	1989	1990	1991	1992	1993	1994	1995	1996	1997	1998	1999
外债余额（亿美元）	214.8	302.0	400.0	413.0	525.5	605.6	693.2	835.7	928.1	1065.9	1162.8	1309.6	1460.4	1518.3
比上年增长（%）	35.7	40.6	32.5	3.3	27.2	15.2	14.5	20.6	11.1	14.8	9.1	12.6	11.5	4.0
国内生产总值(亿元人民币)	10202.2	11962.5	14928.5	16909.2	18547.9	21617.8	26638.1	34634.4	46759.4	58478.1	67884.6	74772.4	79553.0	82054.0
比上年增长（%）	13.8	17.3	24.8	13.3	9.7	16.6	23.2	30.1	35.0	25.1	16.1	10.1	6.4	7.1
负债率(%)	7.3	9.4	10.0	9.2	13.5	14.9	14.4	13.9	17.1	15.2	14.2	14.5	15.2	15.3
外汇收入（亿美元）	297.8	391.7	459.1	478.2	573.7	659.0	788.2	865.6	1189.3	1472.4	1716.8	2072.5	2075.9	2189.0
比上年增长（%）	5.4	31.5	17.2	4.2	20.0	14.9	19.6	9.8	37.4	23.8	16.6	20.7	0.2	5.4
债务率(%)	72.1	77.1	87.1	86.4	91.6	91.9	87.9	96.5	78.0	72.4	67.7	63.2	70.4	69.4

注： 1.从 1998 年开始，原使用的“国民生产总值”数据调整为“国内生产总值”数据，以前年份数据均按《中国统计提要 1998》中公布数据进行了调整。计算负债率时按当年年平均汇率折美元。

2.第四行“比上年增长”是按可变价格计算。

3.从 1998 年开始，本报告中外汇收入指国际收支口径的货物和服务收入，以前年份数据均据此进行了调整。

（国家外汇管理局）

1999年末全国所欠债务简表

金额单位:万美元

债务人/债务类型	外国政府贷款	国际金融组织贷款	国外银行及其他金融机构贷款	买方信贷	向国外出口商,国外企业或私人借款	在华外资银行贷款	对外发行债券	延期付款	海外私人存款	国际金融租赁	补偿贸易中用现汇偿还的债务	合计
国务院有关部委	1720351.51	2445186.67	45889.70				513105.00	5189.91				4729722.79
国内银行	930779.81		821435.95	1216731.58	59788.07	9813.05	333612.97	64897.73	5841.07	117.00		3443017.23
非银行金融机构			307450.49	5911.32	57.02	75679.98	256294.00		749.17	1009.34		647151.32
租赁公司			104110.46	2460.00	2117.63	40750.13		4104.80		7717.69		161260.71
外商投资企业	3787.72	68687.13	1012766.21	146972.77	1934132.46	1363036.97	96952.30	77057.81		26077.31	188.73	4729659.41
国内企业	1032.60		143431.55	8855.06	27890.48	32521.16		53634.80		1192740.63	11185.27	1471291.55
其他			194.90		318.32					352.50		865.72
合计	2655951.64	2513873.80	2435279.26	1380930.73	2024303.98	1521801.29	1199964.27	204885.05	6590.24	1228014.47	11374.00	15182968.73

(国家外汇管理局)

1999 年中国外汇市场人民币对主要外币月平均汇率

外币单位	货币	月平均汇率												累计平均
		1	2	3	4	5	6	7	8	9	10	11	12	
100	美元	827.90	827.80	827.91	827.92	827.85	827.80	827.77	827.73	827.74	827.74	827.82	827.93	827.83
100	英镑	1366.17	1345.80	1342.70	1366.20	1377.18	1321.10	1304.40	1328.62	1343.73	1371.79	1341.69	1336.45	1345.49
100	加拿大元	544.99	552.60	545.50	545.01	566.05	563.90	556.45	554.38	545.01	560.38	564.18	562.45	555.07
100	瑞士法郎	597.85	580.33	564.74	597.86	549.30	538.97	534.91	548.24	597.86	555.83	532.67	523.28	560.15
100	瑞典克朗	105.89	104.22	101.57	105.89	98.04	97.50	98.08	100.09	105.89	101.66	99.13	97.58	101.30
100	挪威克朗	111.05	107.26	106.02	111.06	106.82	105.26	104.78	106.14	111.06	106.99	104.36	103.40	107.02
100	丹麦克朗	128.95	124.83	121.21	128.94	118.38	115.66	115.28	118.03	128.94	119.21	114.99	112.61	120.59
100	日元	7.3138	7.1788	6.9201	6.9070	6.7922	6.8432	6.8956	7.2815	7.7043	7.8000	7.8882	8.0684	7.2994
100	新加坡元	493.03	487.03	478.84	493.04	483.08	483.98	488.33	493.05	487.94	494.14	495.55	494.61	489.39
100	澳大利亚元	523.42	530.20	522.54	523.44	547.12	543.68	543.41	533.64	537.28	539.28	529.09	530.49	533.63
100	港币	106.82	106.82	106.82	106.82	106.75	106.69	106.63	106.58	106.55	106.51	106.51	106.49	106.67
100	欧元	959.44	927.82	901.18	959.46	879.76	859.61	858.15	876.83	869.20	886.33	885.10	837.90	889.23

（国家外汇管理局）

第二部分

世界部分国家和地区国内生产总值(一)

金额单位:亿美元

国别(地区) \ 金额 \ 年份	1985	1987	1988	1989	1990	1991	1992	1993	1994	1995	1996	1997	1998
美国	40387.0	45399.0	49004.0	52508.0	57438.0	59167.0	62444.0	65581.0	69470.0	72654.0	76616.0	81109.0	85107.0
德国	7419.3	12590.6	11763.2	13097.0	15036.2	17195.5	19693.9	19082.4	20460.3	24140.7	23524.7	21027.0	21336.6
日本	15981.0	28212.6	29513.6	27619.2	29700.9	34021.2	37194.2	42750.1	46889.7	51373.6	45951.6	41902.4	37981.7
英国	5161.8	7923.6	8530.5	8283.7	9835.8	10185.9	10573.9	9477.6	10247.5	11115.2	11589.2	13117.0	13874.3
法国	6216.2	9993.6	9465.4	10642.2	11954.3	12010.1	13222.3	12496.6	13310.0	15531.2	15543.7	14091.7	14517.7
沙特阿拉伯	861.3	735.5	761.4	830.0	1046.7	1180.4	1232.0	1185.2	1201.7	1278.1	1413.2	1464.9	1288.8
意大利	4829.3	8413.6	8361.2	9393.9	10939.8	11507.3	12191.7	9851.3	10163.1	10880.3	12136.9	11453.8	11718.7
加拿大	3420.3	4243.7	5080.2	5620.6	5738.0	5904.5	5709.6	5619.4	5620.3	5880.9	6116.0	6311.9	6037.7
荷兰	1534.6	2478.8	2287.6	2530.4	2835.4	2899.9	3219.2	3117.4	3342.9	3983.9	3925.5	3604.8	3783.8
比利时	941.4	1570.9	1489.9	1686.8	1937.5	1985.5	2248.5	2145.6	2327.2	2758.5	2690.7	2439.5	2497.0
瑞典	1137.9	1750.3	1810.1	1979.4	2297.6	2393.3	2475.6	1858.1	1984.3	2313.0	2517.4	2277.6	2464.9
瑞士	1098.0	1993.0	1784.6	1877.8	2284.0	2327.1	2434.9	2367.4	2613.9	3072.3	2959.5	2560.5	2621.1
印度	2155.5	2587.6	2647.5	2681.7	3059.5	2712.2	2723.7	2875.9	3308.0	3756.0	3978.9	4305.8	…
印度尼西亚	862.2	756.5	820.9	930.4	1061.4	1166.2	1391.2	1580.1	1768.9	2021.3	2273.7	2157.5	941.6
墨西哥	1275.0	874.7	1711.8	1922.1	2470.4	2905.3	3636.1	4032.0	4207.8	2861.7	3294.8	4014.6	4149.7
澳大利亚	1568.3	2044.4	2731.8	2833.1	2948.0	2966.7	2928.0	2979.6	3396.1	3645.1	4084.4	4087.3	3645.1
韩国	921.8	1415.3	1946.1	2194.9	2536.7	2941.8	3079.4	3457.2	4025.2	4892.6	5202.1	4764.9	3207.5
中国	2664.4	3038.6	3780.1	3388.3	3877.7	4060.9	4690.1	5987.7	5466.1	7113.2	8343.1	9177.2	9645.2
中国香港	334.4	475.9	552.8	629.7	726.2	833.4	1006.4	1159.6	1308.2	1392.2	1541.2	1711.4	1637.1
中国台湾	732.5	1159.0	1284.3	1539.7	1627.4	1917.4	2144.6	2234.5	2457.9	2549.9	2737.7	2505.5	2706.5
新加坡	176.9	202.5	248.5	294.6	374.5	435.7	496.8	576.2	698.4	836.8	915.1	959.4	844.5
西班牙	1829.5	3316.0	3539.8	4105.4	4919.6	5286.0	5773.1	4789.6	4838.2	5596.3	5822.1	5320.5	5532.1
巴西	2279.5	3030.8	3504.6	4821.7	4429.1	4045.0	4092.0	4405.3	5464.9	7039.1	7750.1	8015.9	7750.3

世界部分国家和地区国内生产总值(二)

金额单位:亿美元

国别(地区) \ 金额 年份	1985	1987	1988	1989	1990	1991	1992	1993	1994	1995	1996	1997	1998
挪威	659.7	900.9	887.8	939.4	1154.5	1177.6	1263.1	1119.8	1190.1	1426.7	1551.7	1505.7	1434.5
阿联酋	270.2	237.0	236.7	272.7	336.4	339.1	354.1	355.2	366.7	400.4	446.2	251.9	…
委内瑞拉	598.7	468.6	603.8	344.8	486.0	534.6	604.2	600.5	584.2	773.9	705.4	884.3	950.2
尼日利亚	723.6	262.9	271.3	293.8	324.3	327.0	317.8	315.9	414.4	…	…	…	…
奥地利	780.3	1316.8	1246.6	1415.9	1584.3	1650.0	1872.1	1827.1	1959.3	2310.0	2280.7	2060.3	2118.6
丹麦	685.8	1147.9	1065.0	1161.0	1291.2	1294.4	1471.0	1388.3	1518.2	1800.8	1836.5	1692.6	1740.9
芬兰	612.2	980.4	1041.8	1199.8	1348.1	1189.1	1064.4	863.2	998.2	1285.6	1279.2	1214.5	1265.1
马来西亚	319.6	319.4	334.6	379.5	427.7	481.4	583.1	641.8	725.0	873.1	991.7	978.8	…
波兰	706.6	536.9	589.5	822.1	589.8	764.8	843.6	860.0	985.3	1263.2	1429.7	1431.3	…
科威特	223.2	230.9	204.3	244.6	181.8	110.1	198.6	239.7	248.0	265.6	306.5	302.1	251.7
罗马尼亚	519.6	615.1	596.4	554.0	382.5	288.5	195.8	263.6	300.7	354.8	351.4	348.4	381.6

资料来源:国际货币基金组织《国际金融统计》(月报和年报)。
中国台湾省《统计月报》。
中国香港《香港统计月报》。

(对外贸易经济合作部国际贸易经济合作研究院)

世界主要国家(地区)外汇储备(一)
(期末数)

金额单位:亿美元

国别(地区) \ 年份	1988	1990	1992	1993	1994	1995	1996	1997	1998	1999
世界	**6650.60**	**8445.29**	**9257.70**	**10304.35**	**11843.09**	**13849.87**	**15532.79**	**16025.73**	**16293.29**	**16677.01** *
日本	905.14	694.87	618.88	887.20	1151.46	1724.43	2073.35	2078.66	2032.15	2777.08
德国	533.24	629.67	858.87	727.27	722.19	777.94	758.03	698.53	641.33	426.61
新加坡	168.61	275.35	396.61	480.66	578.90	683.49	764.91	708.83	744.18	737.30 *
美国	173.60	521.90	400.10	415.30	412.20	491.00	382.90	308.10	360.00	321.80
西班牙	354.01	493.89	441.76	397.98	401.82	324.91	558.79	660.23	524.90	306.22
英国	411.20	329.30	340.90	346.30	385.30	391.80	371.20	288.80	273.60	…
瑞士	240.45	292.21	324.40	316.50	335.54	346.85	367.75	368.99	383.46	341.76
荷兰	145.42	160.28	202.37	296.69	327.16	310.60	241.19	218.81	175.36	66.07
马来西亚	61.34	93.27	167.84	268.14	248.88	229.45	261.56	200.13	247.28	296.70
巴西	69.71	74.30	225.20	306.02	370.69	497.07	583.22	508.26	425.78	403.63 *
泰国	59.97	132.47	200.12	240.78	288.84	354.63	371.92	256.97	284.34	338.05
意大利	325.00	601.76	249.66	251.40	301.07	329.42	440.64	534.31	254.47	187.13
中国	175.48	285.94	194.43	211.99	516.20	735.79	1050.29	1398.90	1449.59	1537.70
中国香港	…	245.70	351.70	429.90	492.50	554.00	638.10	928.00	896.00	921.00 *
中国台湾	…	724.41	823.06	835.73	924.54	903.10	880.38	835.02	903.41	…
法国	223.59	340.67	243.84	200.08	235.20	231.42	231.20	270.97	387.53	339.33
加拿大	135.17	158.02	93.82	104.71	102.19	126.29	180.28	151.22	199.11	244.32
挪威	121.73	143.03	111.01	186.42	179.92	211.09	252.36	220.74	169.27	191.39
澳大利亚	129.89	156.05	105.36	104.70	107.06	113.40	139.67	160.99	141.33	204.60
韩国	123.40	144.59	166.40	197.04	250.32	319.28	332.37	197.10	519.63	737.00
沙特阿拉伯	112.19	85.82	45.61	56.82	58.88	71.01	52.95	59.44	60.14	…
丹麦	102.24	100.63	104.77	97.91	84.44	102.62	133.66	181.57	137.53	211.45
比利时	83.06	111.21	128.25	104.74	128.84	146.80	153.80	145.19	157.63	83.72

世界主要国家(地区)外汇储备(二)
(期末数)

金额单位:亿美元

国别(地区) \ 年份	1988	1990	1992	1993	1994	1995	1996	1997	1998	1999
瑞典	77.52	173.65	219.59	183.72	225.27	229.39	181.72	96.56	124.20	142.96 *
墨西哥	48.85	94.46	183.94	248.86	61.01	152.50	191.76	281.36	314.61	309.92
奥地利	67.11	87.54	115.06	138.66	160.08	178.67	218.61	186.05	299.18	137.64
芬兰	58.75	92.12	47.74	49.93	100.51	92.93	62.05	75.32	85.08	64.22
印度	41.48	12.05	54.61	98.07	193.86	174.67	197.42	243.24	269.58	313.17 *
印度尼西亚	49.48	73.53	101.81	109.88	118.20	133.06	178.20	160.88	224.01	…
葡萄牙	50.83	142.52	187.69	154.81	151.06	153.15	153.59	151.30	150.67	80.23
阿联酋	41.41	42.76	54.22	58.06	63.61	70.12	76.79	80.27	86.64	…
以色列	40.16	62.75	51.27	63.82	67.92	81.19	114.13	203.32	226.75	212.96 *
希腊	35.23	33.06	46.33	76.34	143.22	146.11	173.37	124.41	171.88	177.26
智利	31.16	60.68	91.67	96.39	130.87	141.37	147.81	169.91	150.49	139.77
哥伦比亚	30.94	40.49	72.36	72.85	74.53	77.24	91.83	89.79	75.23	…
委内瑞拉	29.75	83.11	92.88	85.31	73.93	56.88	111.24	140.00	116.12	117.08
新西兰	28.24	40.71	29.29	31.95	35.61	42.45	57.71	42.73	38.46	34.90 *
爱尔兰	47.25	48.49	30.80	55.79	57.45	81.78	77.15	60.20	86.22	48.68

注: * 仅 11 月份数字。

资料来源: 国际货币基金组织《国际金融统计》(月刊和年鉴)。

中国台湾《统计月报》。

(对外贸易经济合作部国际贸易经济合作研究院)

世界主要国家(地区)黄金储备(一)
(期末数)

单位:万盎司

国别(地区) \ 年份	1985	1989	1990	1991	1992	1993	1994	1995	1996	1997	1998	1999
世界	**95145**	**94104**	**93901**	**93801**	**92881**	**91950**	**91544**	**90616**	**90395**	**88669**	**96956**	**94506** *
美国	26265	26193	26191	26191	26184	26179	26173	26170	26166	26164	26161	26168 *
德国	9518	9518	9518	9518	9518	9518	9518	9518	9518	9518	11898	11152
瑞士	8328	8328	8328	8388	8328	8328	8328	8328	8328	8328	8328	8328
法国	8185	8185	8185	8185	8185	8185	8185	8185	8185	8189	10237	9724
意大利	6667	6667	6667	6667	6667	6667	6667	6667	6667	6667	8336	7883
荷兰	4394	4394	4394	4394	4394	3505	3477	3477	3477	2707	3383	3157
比利时	3418	3023	3023	3023	2504	2504	2504	2504	1532	1532	952	830
日本	2423	2423	2423	2423	2423	2423	2423	2423	2423	2423	2423	2423
奥地利	2114	2066	2039	2003	1993	1860	1834	1199	1075	787	964	1310
西班牙	1465	1572	1561	1562	1562	1562	1562	1563	1563	1563	1954	1683
印度	940	1045	1069	1128	1135	1146	1180	1278	1278	1274	1149	1150 *
委内瑞拉	1146	1146	1146	1146	1146	1146	1146	1146	1146	1146	976	976
黎巴嫩	922	922	922	922	922	922	922	922	922	922	922	922 *
澳大利亚	793	793	793	793	793	790	790	790	790	256	256	256
葡萄牙	2023	1605	1583	1587	1606	1606	1607	1607	1607	1607	2009	1951
英国	1903	1899	1894	1889	1861	1845	1844	1843	1843	1842	2300	…
加拿大	2011	1610	1476	1296	994	605	389	341	309	309	249	181
希腊	412	340	340	343	343	344	345	346	347	364	362	424
芬兰	191	200	200	200	200	200	200	160	160	160	200	158
丹麦	163	164	165	166	166	164	163	165	166	169	214	214
瑞典	607	607	607	607	607	607	607	470	470	472	472	596 *
沙特阿拉伯	460	460	460	460	460	460	460	460	460	460	460	460
南非	484	308	409	647	665	476	420	425	379	399	400	394

世界主要国家(地区)黄金储备(二)
(期末数)

单位:万盎司

国别(地区) \ 年份	1985	1989	1990	1991	1992	1993	1994	1995	1996	1997	1998	1999
土耳其	386	378	409	416	405	403	382	375	375	375	375	374
科威特	254	254	254	254	254	254	254	254	254	254	254	254
泰国	249	248	248	248	247	247	247	247	247	247	247	247
巴基斯坦	190	195	195	196	202	204	205	205	206	207	208	209 *
菲律宾	148	245	289	337	280	322	289	358	465	499	543	605 *
中国	1270	1270	1270	1270	1270	1270	1270	1270	1270	1270	1270	1270 *
印度尼西亚	310	310	310	311	310	310	310	310	310	310	310	310
马来西亚	234	237	235	235	239	239	239	239	239	235	235	118
阿根廷	437	437	423	412	437	437	437	437	437	36	36	34
巴西	310	298	457	202	223	293	371	458	369	303	460	433 *
智利	…	175	186	186	187	187	186	186	186	186	122	122
秘鲁	195	197	221	183	182	130	112	112	111	111	110	110
乌拉圭	262	261	240	226	203	170	170	172	174	176	178	…
罗马尼亚	382	217	221	225	231	237	263	270	282	302	322	331 *

注: * 仅 11 月份数字。

资料来源:国际货币基金组织《国际金融统计》(月报和年鉴)。

(对外贸易经济合作部国际贸易经济合作研究院)

世界部分国家(地

国别(地区) \ 金额 \ 年份	1990			1993			1994			1995		
	总额	出口	进口	总额	出口	进口	总额	出口	进口	总额	出口	进
世界	**69815.52**	**34250.43**	**35565.09**	**73751.63**	**36638.88**	**37112.75**	**84156.20**	**41889.11**	**42267.09**	**110112.24**	**49885.84**	**5022**
发达的市场经济国家	50287.14	24551.42	25735.72	51061.09	25666.55	25394.54	57643.54	28862.89	28780.65	68042.27	34178.87	3386.
发展中的市场经济国家	15859.33	7985.57	7873.76	20556.90	9932.18	10624.72	23565.43	11563.27	12002.16	28273.91	13858.68	1441
石油输出国组织	2863.01	1766.80	1096.21	3289.74	1895.85	1393.89	3192.89	1899.85	1293.04	3624.78	2097.23	1527
其他国家	3669.06	1713.45	1955.61	2133.65	1040.15	1093.50	2947.22	1462.94	1484.28	3796.05	1848.29	1947
美洲	**13623.68**	**6277.08**	**7346.60**	**15956.49**	**7143.93**	**8812.56**	**18011.34**	**7965.00**	**10046.34**	**20340.93**	**9215.71**	**1112**
美国	9105.79	3935.92	5169.87	10682.11	4647.73	6034.38	12018.42	5126.27	6892.15	13555.95	5847.43	7708
加拿大	2508.81	1276.34	1232.47	2842.21	1451.82	1390.39	3204.56	1653.80	1550.76	3602.57	1922.04	1680
巴西	539.38	314.14	225.24	662.95	385.55	277.40	795.42	435.45	359.97	1002.89	465.06	537.
阿根廷	164.29	123.53	40.76	299.02	131.18	167.84	371.86	156.59	215.27	410.89	209.67	201.
智利	160.51	83.73	76.78	203.24	91.99	111.25	234.29	116.04	118.25	320.37	161.37	159.
哥伦比亚	123.56	67.66	55.90	169.48	71.16	98.32	203.02	84.19	118.83	239.09	100.56	138.
墨西哥	582.78	271.31	311.47	798.11	301.88	496.23	955.12	345.32	609.80	930.33	470.56	459.
委内瑞拉	252.26	177.83	74.43	268.05	145.36	122.69	262.04	169.12	92.92	313.58	187.39	126.
秘鲁	67.01	32.31	34.70	83.74	35.15	48.59	112.46	45.55	66.91	147.99	55.75	92.
哥斯达黎加	34.38	14.48	19.90	61.40	26.25	35.15	66.58	28.69	37.89	74.89	34.53	40.
危地马拉	28.12	11.63	16.49	39.39	13.40	25.99	41.26	15.22	26.04	54.49	21.56	32.
古巴	116.55	49.10	67.45	32.65	12.75	19.90	34.40	13.85	20.55	44.25	16.00	28.
多米尼加	27.97	7.35	20.62	29.47	5.11	24.36	32.70	6.44	26.26	37.43	7.67	29.
牙买加	30.82	11.58	19.24	32.04	10.71	21.33	34.32	12.11	22.21	42.28	14.20	28.
特立尼达和多巴哥	30.69	19.60	11.09	31.25	16.62	14.63	29.96	18.66	11.30	41.70	24.56	17.
荷属安地列斯	39.31	17.90	21.41	32.30	12.83	19.47	31.34	13.76	17.58	33.63	15.22	18.
巴拿马	18.79	3.40	15.39	27.41	5.53	21.88	29.87	5.83	24.04	31.36	6.25	25.
萨尔瓦多	18.45	5.82	12.63	26.44	7.32	19.12	30.93	8.44	22.49	38.51	9.98	28.
乌拉圭	30.36	16.93	13.43	39.71	16.45	23.26	46.99	19.13	27.86	49.73	21.06	28.
厄瓜多尔	45.76	27.14	18.62	54.66	29.04	25.62	74.42	38.20	36.22	84.60	43.07	41.
洪都拉斯	17.66	8.31	9.35	19.44	8.14	11.30	18.98	8.42	10.56	22.80	10.61	12.
欧洲	**36273.22**	**17791.09**	**18482.13**	**32830.19**	**16620.49**	**16209.70**	**37766.50**	**19210.58**	**18555.92**	**45935.56**	**23463.01**	**2247**
德国 a	7549.90	4099.58	3450.32	7287.61	3826.31	3461.30	8138.21	4290.75	3847.46	9529.52	5083.98	4445
法国	4433.76	2101.69	2332.07	4069.81	2062.31	2007.50	4667.11	2360.72	2306.39	5643.15	2873.34	2769
英国	4098.76	1853.26	2245.50	3878.80	1815.59	2063.21	4301.81	2040.09	2261.72	5073.57	2420.36	2653
意大利	3523.66	1703.83	1819.83	3160.54	1677.46	1483.08	3606.10	1914.31	1691.79	4400.05	2339.80	2060
荷兰	2582.72	1317.87	1264.85	2638.69	1391.27	1247.42	2968.71	1555.54	1413.17	3731.49	1962.76	1768

品 贸 易 额 (一)

金额单位:亿美元

1996			1997			1998			1998 比 1997 增减%			1999 *		
额	出口	进口	总额	出口	进口	总额	出口	进口	总额	出口	进口	总额	出口	进口
59.84	**51787.73**	**52672.11**	**108388.42**	**53772.18**	**54616.24**	**107135.52**	**53242.72**	**53892.80**	**-1.2**	**-1.0**	**-1.3**	**114850.00**	**56100.00**	**58750.00**
91.59	35180.84	35210.75	72190.82	36102.32	36088.50	73094.05	36220.51	36873.54	1.3	0.3	2.2	56999.51*	27895.30*	29104.21*
18.94	14645.98	15272.96	31698.34	15585.40	16112.94	29623.30	14989.76	14633.54	-6.5	-3.8	-9.2	22617.91	11404.78	11213.13*
2.56	2442.60	1529.96	4253.00	2552.16	1700.84	4063.47	2413.33	1650.14	-4.5	-5.4	-3.0	3029.31*	1836.38*	1192.93*
9.30	1960.91	2188.39	4499.27	2084.47	2414.80	4418.18	2032.45	2385.73	-1.8	-2.5	-1.2	3009.12*	1422.88*	1586.24*
48.83	**9884.66**	**11864.17**	**24055.64**	**10790.02**	**13265.62**	**24327.70**	**10569.61**	**13758.09**	**1.1**	**-2.0**	**3.7**	**18855.69***	**8031.12***	**10824.57**
70.98	6250.73	8820.25	15877.15	6886.96	8990.19	16268.50	6824.97	9443.53	2.5	-0.9	5.0	17549.00	6950.00	10599.00
5.98	2016.36	1749.62	4104.08	2144.28	1959.80	4153.95	2143.35	2010.60	1.2	-0.0	2.6	4586.00	2384.00	2202.00
6.94	477.47	569.47	1179.97	529.90	650.07	1086.70	511.20	575.50	-7.9	-3.5	-11.5	998.00	480.00	518.00
5.73	238.11	237.62	568.20	263.70	304.50	566.29	252.27	314.02	-0.3	-4.3	3.1	488.00	233.00	255.00
1.76	153.53	178.23	363.25	166.63	196.62	336.09	148.30	187.79	-7.5	-11.0	-4.5	226.29*	114.21*	112.08*
2.71	105.87	136.84	269.00	115.22	153.78	254.87	108.52	146.35	-5.3	-5.8	-4.8	…	82.99*	…
2.51	590.72	611.79	1423.29	655.83	767.46	…	…	…	…	…	…	2849.00	1367.00	1482.00
8.68	230.54	98.14	356.40	210.67	145.73	…	156.82	…	…	-25.6	…	…	189.00	…
3.70	58.97	94.73	170.77	68.14	102.63	…	57.35	…	…	-15.8	…	…	…	…
.30	37.03	43.00	91.92	42.68	49.24	117.41	55.11	62.30	27.7	29.1	26.5	97.27*	49.76*	47.51*
.77	20.31	31.46	61.96	23.44	38.52	72.33	25.82	46.51	16.7	10.2	20.7	49.83*	18.64*	31.199*
.20	20.15	32.05	…	…	…	…	…	…	…	…	…	…	…	…
.03	8.17	36.86	57.03	8.82	48.21	56.92	7.95	48.97	-0.2	-9.9	1.6	…	…	…
.14	13.82	39.32	44.94	13.81	31.13	43.07	13.12	29.95	-4.2	-5.0	-3.8	…	…	…
.44	25.00	21.44	55.32	25.42	29.90	52.57	22.58	29.99	-5.0	-11.2	0.3	…	…	…
.88	12.69	25.19	35.71	14.88	20.83	…	…	…	…	…	…	…	…	…
.03	6.23	27.80	37.52	7.23	30.02	38.58	7.84	30.74	3.6	8.4	2.4	…	…	…
.95	10.24	26.71	43.32	13.59	29.73	43.75	12.63	31.12	1.0	-7.1	4.7	32.46*	8.93*	23.53*
.20	23.97	33.23	64.42	27.26	37.16	65.77	27.69	38,08	2.1	1.6	2.5	…	…	…
.35	49.00	39.35	102.19	52.64	49.55	97.79	42.03	55.76	-4.3	-20.2	12.5	…	…	…
.56	13.16	18.40	35.95	14.46	21.49	40.75	15.75	25.00	11.3	8.9	16.3	…	…	…
56.28	**24342.07**	**23314.21**	**48122.01**	**24526.35**	**23595.66**	**49722.30**	**25167.56**	**24554.74**	**3.3**	**2.6**	**4.1**	**38532.30***	**19381.60***	**19150.75***
0.38	5242.28	4588.10	9581.85	5125.03	4456.82	10147.70	5432.92	4714.78	5.9	6.0	5.8	10131.00	5405.00	4726.00
0.94	2886.58	2804.36	5601.40	2902.01	2699.39	5923.39	3054.92	2868.47	5.7	5.3	6.3	5851.00	2990.00	2861.00
5.41	2620.04	2875.37	5876.73	2810.82	3065.91	5858.82	2718.49	3140.33	-0.3	-3.3	2.4	5891.00	2684.00	3207.00
3.24	2503.55	2069.69	4464.45	2381.37	2083.08	4578.68	2421.47	2157.21	2.6	1.7	3.6	4468.00	2308.00	2160.00
0.62	1974.20	1806.42	3730.41	1949.09	1781.32	3890.96	2013.63	1877.33	4.3	3.3	5.5	3930.00	2041.00	1889.00

世界部分国家(地区

年份 金额 国别(地区)	1990			1993			1994			1995		
	总额	出口	进口	总额	出口	进口	总额	出口	进口	总额	出口	进口
比利时·卢森堡	2386.53	1183.28	1203.25	2317.72	1195.23	1122.49	2629.13	1372.76	1256.37	3247.29	1696.20	1551.
西班牙	1430.83	555.28	875.55	1408.39	610.84	797.55	1651.18	729.29	921.89	2043.60	910.43	1133.
瑞士	1334.84	637.93	696.91	1154.16	586.94	567.22	1303.23	662.38	640.85	1550.67	780.61	770.6
瑞典	1118.08	575.42	542.66	925.51	498.64	426.87	1130.84	613.52	517.32	1444.68	798.16	646.5
前苏联	2248.28	1041.77	1206.51	…	…	…	…	…	…	…	…	…
前苏联欧洲部分	…	…	…	958.54	552.93	405.61	1555.95	853.43	702.52	1971.37	1057.53	913.8
俄罗斯	…	…	…	771.05	442.97	328.06	1181.60	676.42	505.18	1420.53	811.37	609.1
丹麦	673.65	351.35	322.30	677.18	371.72	305.46	763.04	414.22	348.82	948.53	497.63	450.9
挪威	612.64	340.45	272.19	556.70	317.78	238.92	619.88	346.85	273.03	749.68	419.95	329.7
奥地利	902.30	411.38	490.92	888.16	402.00	486.16	1003.71	450.31	553.40	1239.33	575.95	663.3
芬兰	535.75	265.72	270.03	414.80	234.47	180.33	528.72	296.58	232.14	676.87	395.73	281.1
爱尔兰	444.29	237.47	206.82	508.16	290.22	217.94	600.65	341.55	259.10	777.06	446.38	330.6
葡萄牙	417.77	164.19	253.58	397.06	153.86	243.20	449.48	180.09	269.39	525.78	202.29	323.4
波兰	220.40	136.27	84.13	329.77	141.43	188.34	384.25	170.42	213.83	519.45	228.95	290.5
前捷克斯洛伐克	249.88	118.82	131.06	…	…	…	…	…	…	…	…	…
捷克共和国	…	…	…	290.68	144.66	146.02	337.34	162.34	175.00	469.92	216.86	253.0
斯洛伐克	…	…	…	118.42	54.82	63.60	133.10	66.95	66.15	173.83	85.96	87.8
匈牙利	182.68	95.97	86.71	214.09	88.88	125.21	250.72	106.89	143.83	274.81	124.35	150.4
罗马尼亚	156.18	57.75	98.43	114.14	48.92	65.22	132.60	61.51	71.09	181.88	79.10	102.7
南斯拉夫	332.02	143.12	188.90	…	…	…	…	…	…	…	…	…
希腊	278.86	81.06	197.80	307.84	87.77	220.07	308.81	93.92	214.89	364.79	109.70	255.0
保加利亚	265.17	134.28	130.89	84.92	37.27	47.65	81.92	39.96	41.96	110.07	53.52	56.5
冰岛	32.70	15.91	16.79	27.42	14.00	13.42	30.95	16.23	14.72	35.58	18.03	17.5
马尔他	30.91	11.30	19.61	35.29	13.55	21.74	40.13	15.72	24.41	48.55	19.13	29.4
非洲	**1971.53**	**1004.88**	**966.65**	**1778.48**	**865.58**	**912.90**	**1871.99**	**899.66**	**927.33**	**2223.29**	**1036.17**	**1187.**
南非	404.99	228.34	176.65	424.29	233.39	190.90	468.85	244.15	224.70	565.26	269.26	296.0
阿尔及利亚	222.49	126.75	95.74	180.00	102.30	77.70	182.50	88.80	93.70	204.90	102.40	102.5
埃及	217.40	49.57	167.83	104.66	22.52	82.14	136.93	34.75	102.18	152.10	34.50	117.6
利比亚	194.76	138.77	55.99	…	…	…	…	…	…	…	…	…
摩洛哥	111.90	42.65	69.25	105.90	34.28	71.62	111.93	40.05	71.88	169.06	68.83	100.2
突尼斯	90.40	35.27	55.13	100.16	38.02	62.14	112.38	46.57	65.81	133.78	54.75	79.0
喀麦隆	34.02	20.02	14.00	23.31	14.43	8.88	20.91	13.70	7.21	28.55	16.54	12.0
加蓬	31.35	22.13	9.22	32.17	23.00	9.17	31.06	23.48	7.58	35.93	27.12	8.81
尼日利亚	186.53	129.61	56.92	174.36	99.23	75.13	158.93	93.76	65.17	199.69	106.37	93.3

品贸易额(二)

金额单位:亿美元

1996			1997			1998			1998 比 1997 增减%			1999*		
额	出口	进口	总额	出口	进口	总额	出口	进口	总额	出口	进口	总额	出口	进口
86.58	1658.56	1528.02	3452.93	1788.10	1664.83	3398.71	1776.62	1622.09	-1.6	-0.6	-2.6	3535.00	1841.00	1694.00
37.96	1020.02	1217.94	2270.89	1043.68	1227.21	2423.84	1092.31	1331.53	6.7	4.7	8.5	2544.00	1094.00	1450.00
06.76	762.05	744.71	1435.81	725.06	710.75	1493.24	754.39	738.85	4.0	4.0	4.0	1607.00	806.00	801.00
17.17	848.60	668.57	1478.40	828.12	650.28	1531.59	847.39	684.20	3.6	2.3	5.2	1527.00	845.00	682.00
…	…	…	…	…	…	…	…	…	…	…	…	…	…	…
59.34	1168.84	990.50	2325.85	1191.89	1133.96	2000.03	1031.66	968.37	-14.0	-13.4	-14.6	1325.63*	719.08*	606.55*
13.88	891.10	622.78	1619.39	883.26	736.13	1330.92	741.57	589.35	-17.8	-16.0	-19.9	1154.00	743.00	411.00
5.36	501.01	444.35	917.64	477.20	440.44	926.70	473.43	453.27	1.0	-0.8	2.9	911.00	478.00	433.00
5.74	489.58	356.16	842.60	485.47	357.13	758.45	396.49	361.96	-10.0	-18.3	1.4	787.00	449.00	338.00
51.48	578.24	673.24	1233.82	584.80	649.02	1309.33	627.46	681.87	6.1	7.3	5.1	1298.00	620.00	678.00
7.00	384.35	292.65	691.04	393.18	297.86	752.64	429.63	323.01	8.9	9.3	8.4	…	415.00	…
5.70	486.70	359.00	926.82	534.49	392.33	1091.92	645.72	446.20	17.8	20.8	13.7	1152.00	696.00	456.00
9.31	238.23	341.08	572.22	233.99	338.23	612.64	242.18	370.46	7.1	3.5	9.5	644.00	268.00	376.00
5.77	244.40	371.37	680.59	257.51	423.08	736.85	271.91	464.94	8.3	5.6	9.9	…	…	448.00
…	…	…	…	…	…	…	…	…	…	…	…	…	…	…
1.62	201.60	290.02	499.39	227.51	271.89	552.08	264.07	288.01	10.6	16.1	5.9	557.00	268.00	289.00
9.55	88.31	111.24	185.20	82.51	102.69	273.91	107.20	130.71	47.9	29.9	27.3	…	…	…
5.03	126.47	158.56	392.65	186.13	206.52	485.51	229.55	255.96	23.6	23.3	23.9	523.00	246.00	277.00
5.20	80.85	114.35	197.11	84.31	112.80	201.21	83.00	118.21	2.1	-1.6	4.8	…	…	…
9.44	18.42	41.02	71.76	23.68	47.99	72.26	26.04	46.22	0.8	10.0	-3.7	…	…	…
8.78	94.80	273.98	363.74	86.56	277.18	…	…	…	…	…	…	…	…	…
8.48	48.33	50.15	105.45	53.22	52.23	92.81	42.98	49.83	-12.0	-19.02	-4.6	…	…	…
6.62	16.35	20.27	38.44	18.52	19.92	45.39	20.50	24.89	18.1	10.7	24.9	…	…	…
5.27	17.31	27.96	41.95	16.40	25.55	45.05	18.20	26.85	7.4	11.0	5.1	…	…	…
69.40	**1130.73**	**1138.67**	**2374.03**	**1153.62**	**1220.41**	**2314.74**	**1043.50**	**1271.24**	**-2.5**	**-9.5**	**4.2**	**1670.04***	**787.13***	**882.91***
2.50	281.45	291.05	619.03	299.64	319.39	536.73	253.96	282.77	-13.3	-15.2	-11.5	535.00	267.00	268.00
3.11	126.21	86.90	…	…	…	…	…	…	…	…	…	…	…	…
5.77	35.39	130.38	171.32	39.21	132.11	192.96	31.30	161.66	12.6	-20.2	22.4	…	…	162.00
…	…	…	146.29	90.36	55.93	118.23	61.31	56.92	-19.2	-32.1	1.8	…	…	…
5.85	68.81	97.04	165.59	70.33	95.26	175.43	72.67	102.76	5.9	3.3	7.9	…	…	…
2.17	55.17	77.00	134.73	55.59	79.14	140.88	57.50	83.38	4.6	3.4	5.4	…	…	…
9.95	17.69	12.26	32.18	18.60	13.58	…	…	…	…	…	…	…	…	…
.04	3.07	0.97	3.97	2.94	1.03	…	…	…	…	…	…	…	…	…
6.11	186.14	79.97	296.68	176.48	120.20	251.43	115.19	136.24	-15.3	-34.7	13.3	…	…	…

世界部分国家(地区

国别(地区) \ 金额 \ 年份	1990			1993			1994			1995		
	总额	出口	进口	总额	出口	进口	总额	出口	进口	总额	出口	进口
肯尼亚	31.55	10.31	21.24	30.71	12.97	17.74	36.55	15.65	20.90	48.96	18.90	30.0
毛里求斯	28.17	11.96	16.21	30.15	12.99	17.16	32.77	13.47	19.30	34.90	15.37	19.5
赞比亚	25.70	13.11	12.59	16.79	8.50	8.29	13.57	8.27	5.30	17.63	10.55	7.0
津巴布韦	35.79	17.29	18.50	33.82	15.65	18.17	41.22	18.81	22.41	47.75	21.14	26.6
刚果(金)	18.87	9.99	8.88	7.41	3.69	3.72	8.01	4.19	3.82	8.35	4.38	3.9
坦桑尼亚	16.95	3.31	13.64	19.48	4.50	14.98	20.23	5.19	15.04	23.64	6.85	16.7
马拉维	9.92	4.17	5.75	8.64	3.19	5.45	8.20	3.25	4.95	8.80	4.05	4.7
塞拉利昂	2.85	1.37	1.48	2.65	1.18	1.47	2.66	1.15	1.51	1.59	0.25	1.3
埃塞俄比亚	13.79	2.98	10.81	9.86	1.99	7.87	14.05	3.72	10.33	15.64	4.22	11.4
马达加斯加	9.70	3.19	6.51	7.29	2.61	4.68	8.22	3.75	4.47	9.13	3.70	5.4
亚洲	**16808.41**	**8676.39**	**8132.02**	**22012.18**	**11459.59**	**10552.59**	**25147.39**	**13200.61**	**11946.78**	**30075.59**	**15488.14**	**14587.**
日本	5230.71	2876.48	2354.23	6039.38	3622.86	2416.52	6723.16	3970.48	2752.68	7792.56	4432.65	3359.
中国香港	1646.50	821.60	824.90	2738.94	1352.44	1386.50	3132.40	1513.99	1618.41	3665.01	1737.50	1927.
中国	1154.36	620.91	533.45	1940.58	909.70	1030.88	2367.28	1210.47	1156.81	2779.10	1487.97	1291.
新加坡	1135.04	527.30	607.74	1592.37	740.08	852.29	1994.95	968.25	1026.70	2427.65	1182.63	1245.
韩国	1348.60	650.16	698.44	1660.36	822.36	838.00	1983.61	960.13	1023.48	2601.77	1250.58	1351.
中国台湾	1219.30	672.14	547.16	1621.52	850.91	770.61	1783.98	930.49	853.49	2152.09	1116.59	1035.
马来西亚	587.12	294.53	292.59	927.88	471.31	456.57	1183.36	587.55	595.81	1513.29	737.15	776.
印度尼西亚	475.12	256.75	218.37	651.51	368.23	283.28	720.38	400.55	319.83	860.47	454.17	406.
泰国	561.02	230.71	330.31	830.39	369.63	460.76	996.74	452.36	544.38	1267.70	561.91	705.
土耳其	352.61	129.59	223.02	447.73	153.45	294.28	413.76	181.06	232.70	573.46	216.37	357.
以色列	283.76	115.73	168.03	520.52	226.24	294.28	485.07	252.37	232.70	652.88	295.79	357.
菲律宾	211.03	80.68	130.41	298.43	110.93	187.54	155.68	133.04	22.64	203.36	175.02	28.3
印度	415.53	179.70	235.83	443.62	215.73	227.89	518.65	250.22	268.43	653.39	306.29	347.
科威特	108.79	69.56	39.23	172.86	102.44	70.42	179.08	112.28	66.80	205.77	127.85	77.9
巴基斯坦	129.65	55.89	73.76	161.89	66.88	95.01	162.54	73.65	88.89	194.53	79.92	114.
阿曼	81.83	55.08	26.81	94.12	52.98	41.14	94.60	55.45	39.15	103.16	60.68	42.4
巴林	74.73	37.61	37.12	75.81	37.23	38.58	73.65	36.17	37.48	78.29	41.13	37.1
叙利亚	66.12	42.12	24.00	72.86	31.46	41.40	85.14	30.47	54.67	82.72	35.36	47.0
斯里兰卡	46.02	19.13	26.89	68.44	28.51	39.93	79.76	32.09	47.67	91.05	37.98	53.0
前苏联亚洲部分	…	…	…	74.71	42.81	31.90	195.03	100.32	94.71	228.08	124.03	104.
孟加拉国	52.89	16.71	36.18	62.72	22.78	39.94	72.63	26.61	46.02	96.74	31.73	65.0
文莱	32.14	22.13	10.01	33.99	21.98	12.01	39.91	22.96	16.95	42.55	22.73	19.8
中国澳门	32.28	16.94	15.34	37.62	17.63	19.99	39.24	18.34	20.90	40.09	19.83	20.2

品贸易额(三)

金额单位:亿美元

1996			1997			1998			1998比1997 增减%			1999 *		
额	出口	进口	总额	出口	进口	总额	出口	进口	总额	出口	进口	总额	出口	进口
.16	20.67	29.49	53.50	20.54	32.96	52.01	20.07	31.94	-2.8	-2.3	-3.1	…	…	…
.29	17.51	22.78	38.61	16.30	22.31	39.17	17.34	21.83	1.5	6.4	-2.2	…	…	…
.96	10.52	8.44	17.32	9.14	8.18	…	…	…	…	…	…	…	…	…
.14	23.97	28.17	…	…	…	45.65	18.64	27.01	…	…	…	…	…	…
.16	5.92	4.24	…	…	…	…	…	…	…	…	…	…	…	…
.44	7.58	13.86	20.53	7.18	13.35	21.27	6.75	14.52	3.6	-6.0	8.8	15.24*	2.90*	12.34*
.04	4.81	6.23	13.26	5.40	7.86	12.21	5.54	6.67	-7.9	2.6	-15.1	…	…	…
.58	0.47	2.11	1.09	0.17	0.92	1.02	0.07	0.95	-6.4	-59.0	3.3	…	…	…
…	4.17	…	…	5.87	…	…	5.60	…	…	-4.6	…	…	…	…
.06	2.99	5.07	6.86	2.21	4.65	7.52	2.41	5.11	9.6	9.0	9.9	…	…	…
94.92	**15668.85**	**15426.07**	**32017.89**	**16421.63**	**15596.26**	**29191.77**	**15779.21**	**13412.56**	**-8.8**	**-3.9**	**-14.0**	**22383.41***	**12025.56***	**10357.85***
1.04	4109.28	3491.76	7598.80	4210.51	3388.29	6687.35	3881.17	2806.18	-12.0	-7.8	-17.2	7301.00	4194.00	3107.00
93.00	1807.50	1985.50	3966.73	1880.59	2086.14	3584.93	1739.90	1845.03	-9.6	-7.5	-11.6	3565.00	1748.00	1817.00
1.41	1511.97	1389.44	3250.66	1828.77	1421.89	3238.94	1835.89	1403.05	-0.4	0.4	-1.3	3606.00	1949.00	1657.00
53.56	1250.16	1313.40	2574.32	1249.90	1324.42	2146.33	1099.05	1047.28	-16.6	-12.1	-20.9	2256.00	1146.00	1110.00
0.54	1297.15	1503.39	2807.80	1361.64	1446.16	2255.95	1323.13	932.83	-19.7	-2.8	-35.5	2639.00	1442.00	1197.00
83.12	1159.42	1023.70	2365.06	1220.81	1144.25	2152.47	1105.82	1046.65	-9.0	-9.4	-8.5	2326.00	1216.00	1110.00
66.71	782.53	784.18	1577.71	787.41	790.30	1316.30	733.04	583.26	-16.6	-6.9	-26.2	1500.00	845.00	655.00
7.43	498.14	429.29	951.37	534.43	416.94	761.84	488.47	273.37	-19.9	-8.6	-34.4	724.00	485.00	239.00
78.58	555.28	723.30	1202.92	574.13	628.79	974.26	544.55	429.71	-19.0	-5.2	-31.7	1090.00	584.00	506.00
8.51	232.24	436.27	748.30	262.45	485.85	713.07	259.38	453.69	-4.7	-1.2	-6.6	654.00	262.00	392.00
2.30	206.10	316.20	532.84	225.02	307.82	523.35	229.93	293.42	-1.8	2.2	-4.7	585.00	253.00	332.00
4.54	20.41	34.13	63.71	25.09	38.62	59.29	27.78	31.51	-6.9	10.7	-18.4	676.00	350.00	326.00
0.51	331.07	379.44	757.20	345.62	411.58	764.21	336.56	427.65	0.9	-2.6	3.9	811.00	365.00	446.00
2.63	148.89	83.74	224.71	142.25	82.46	181.70	95.53	86.17	-19.1	-32.8	4.5	…	…	…
4.52	93.21	121.31	203.46	87.31	116.15	178.16	85.01	93.15	-12.4	-2.6	-19.8	…	…	…
9.24	73.46	45.78	126.56	76.30	50.26	…	…	56.82	…	…	13.1	…	…	…
9.73	47.00	42.73	84.10	43.84	40.26	67.32	32.69	34.63	-20.0	-25.4	-14.0	52.40*	28.36*	24.04*
3.79	39.99	53.80	79.44	39.16	40.28	67.85	28.90	38.95	-14.6	-26.2	-3.3	…	…	…
5.07	40.95	54.12	104.84	46.33	58.51	106.51	47.34	59.17	1.6	2.2	1.1	…	…	…
2.18	147.66	134.52	285.74	154.94	130.80	252.28	134.20	118.08	-11.7	-13.4	-9.7	165.99*	88.88*	77.11*
9.18	32.97	66.21	106.74	37.78	68.96	109.77	38.31	71.46	2.8	1.4	3.6	…	…	…
…	…	…	…	…	…	…	…	…	…	…	…	…	…	…
9.82	19.89	19.93	42.24	21.45	20.79	40.84	21.35	19.49	-3.3	-0.5	-6.3	…	…	…

世界部分国家(地[

国别(地区) \ 年份 / 金额	1990			1993			1994			1995		
	总额	出口	进口	总额	出口	进口	总额	出口	进口	总额	出口	进口
缅甸	5.95	3.25	2.70	14.00	5.86	8.14	16.70	7.92	8.78	21.86	8.51	13.3
尼伯尔	8.76	2.04	6.72	12.74	3.84	8.90	15.17	3.62	11.55	16.79	3.46	13.3
约旦	36.66	10.63	26.03	47.85	12.46	35.39	48.06	14.24	33.82	54.65	17.69	36.9
塞浦路斯	35.17	9.48	25.69	34.01	8.67	25.34	39.86	9.68	30.18	49.19	12.29	36.9
卡塔尔	52.24	35.29	16.95	50.72	31.81	18.91	…	…	19.27	…	…	33.9
沙特阿拉伯	684.86	444.17	240.69	705.93	423.95	281.98	659.52	426.14	233.38	781.31	500.40	280.
阿联酋	…	…	…	…	…	195.20	479.46	269.22	210.24	487.37	277.53	209.
大洋洲	**1049.66**	**501.00**	**548.66**	**1128.19**	**549.28**	**578.91**	**1295.14**	**613.25**	**681.89**	**1451.28**	**682.81**	**768.**
澳大利亚	817.84	397.60	420.24	882.61	427.04	455.57	1009.51	475.25	534.26	1134.14	530.97	603.
新西兰	188.95	93.94	95.01	201.78	105.42	96.36	240.98	121.85	119.13	276.04	136.45	139.
巴布亚新几内亚	23.69	11.77	11.92	38.83	25.84	12.99	41.51	26.30	15.21	41.06	26.54	14.5
斐济	12.52	4.98	7.54	11.69	4.49	7.20	13.79	5.50	8.29	14.86	6.19	8.6
新喀里多尼亚	13.32	4.49	8.83	12.17	3.59	8.58	12.42	3.66	8.76	14.27	5.15	9.1
美属萨摩亚	6.71	3.11	3.60	…	…	…	…	…	…	…	…	…
法属波利尼西亚	10.40	1.11	9.29	10.00	1.48	8.52	11.07	2.26	8.81	12.15	1.96	10.1
所罗门	1.65	0.70	0.95	2.32	1.31	1.01	2.84	1.42	1.42	3.22	1.68	1.5
瓦努阿图	1.15	0.19	0.96	1.02	0.23	0.79	1.12	0.25	0.87	1.23	0.28	0.9

注:a. 包括前民主德国数字。*1至9月数字。

资料来源:联合国《统计月报》,中国台湾省《统计月报》,世界贸易组织《新闻简报》。

品贸易额(四)

金额单位:亿美元

1996			1997			1998			1998比1997 增减%			1999*		
额	出口	进口	总额	出口	进口	总额	出口	进口	总额	出口	进口	总额	出口	进口
.99	7.44	13.55	29.03	8.66	20.37	10.66	37.33	26.67	28.6	23.1	30.9	…	…	…
.27	3.85	14.42	21.22	4.02	17.20	17.17	4.74	12.43	-19.1	17.9	-27.7	…	…	…
.10	18.17	42.93	59.38	18.36	41.02	56.35	17.99	38.36	-5.1	-2.0	-6.5	…	…	…
.66	13.87	39.79	47.99	11.04	36.95	47.49	10.62	36.87	-1.0	-3.8	-0.2	…	…	…
.20	37.52	28.69	…	…	33.22	…	…	…	…	…	…	…	…	…
4.97	607.29	277.68	911.23	623.81	287.42	…	…	…	…	…	…	805.00	505.00	300.00
7.23	280.85	226.38	625.65	396.13	229.52	749.24	426.74	322.50	19.8	7.7	40.5	584.00	295.00	289.00
93.75	**761.42**	**832.33**	**1613.74**	**780.58**	**833.16**	**1477.61**	**682.83**	**794.78**	**-8.4**	**-12.5**	**-4.6**	**1117.36***	**497.56***	**619.80***
57.28	603.00	654.28	1288.02	629.10	658.92	1205.30	559.00	646.30	-6.4	-11.1	-1.9	1251.00*	561.00*	690.00
0.87	143.62	147.25	287.22	142.03	145.19	245.66	120.71	124.95	-14.5	-15.0	-13.9	192.70*	92.88*	99.82*
2.56	25.15	17.41	38.41	21.45	16.96	30.04	17.72	12.32	-21.8	-17.4	-27.4	…	…	…
7.32	7.48	9.84	15.54	5.89	9.65	…	…	…	…	…	…	…	…	…
4.97	4.92	10.05	14.64	5.27	9.37	…	…	…	…	…	…	…	…	…
…	…	…	…	…	…	…	…	…	…	…	…			
2.80	2.54	10.26	11.69	2.24	9.45	…	…	…	…	…	…	…	…	…
.13	1.62	1.51	3.43	1.73	1.70	…	1.26	…	…	-27.2	…	…	…	…
.27	0.30	0.97	1.29	0.35	0.94	1.22	0.34	0.88	-5.4	-2.9	-6.4	…	…	…

(对外贸易经济合作部国际贸易经济合作研究院)

世界部分国家（地

国别(地区) \ 年份 金额	1985			1990			1994			1995		
	总额	出口	进口	总额	出口	进口	总额	出口	进口	总额	出口	进口
世界	**7825.00**	**3809.00**	**4016.00**	**16058.00**	**7888.00**	**8170.00**	**20696.00**	**10375.00**	**10321.00**	**23784.00**	**11881.00**	**11903**
北美	**1468.00**	**772.00**	**696.00**	**2808.00**	**1551.00**	**1257.00**	**3555.00**	**2038.00**	**1517.00**	**3848.00**	**2226.00**	**1622**
加拿大	210.93	86.97	123.96	458.30	183.51	274.79	552.98	232.10	320.88	584.10	254.25	329
美国	120.67	634.90	571.80	2349.60	1367.50	982.10	3001.50	1805.62	1195.88	3264.24	1971.60	1292
拉美	**400.00**	**179.00**	**221.00**	**634.00**	**291.00**	**343.00**	**930.00**	**412.00**	**518.00**	**985.00**	**445.00**	**540**
巴西	54.06	19.93	34.13	104.39	37.06	67.33	146.53	48.17	98.36	191.66	60.05	131.
阿根廷	36.16	15.99	20.17	51.40	22.64	28.76	101.45	32.80	68.65	106.16	37.05	69.
智利	16.55	6.56	9.99	37.68	17.85	19.83	56.32	27.64	28.68	65.54	31.26	34.
哥伦比亚	21.99	8.24	13.75	32.31	15.48	16.83	41.82	15.97	25.85	45.32	17.03	28.
墨西哥	97.80	44.36	53.44	172.85	72.22	100.63	224.66	100.75	123.91	186.06	95.85	90.
委内瑞拉	27.42	7.60	19.82	35.11	11.21	23.90	59.79	14.54	45.25	61.83	15.29	46.
秘鲁	14.77	6.26	8.51	17.85	7.15	10.70	24.35	9.51	14.84	28.43	10.43	18.
哥斯达黎加	5.34	2.59	2.75	11.23	5.83	5.40	20.09	11.63	8.46	22.04	12.71	9.
危地马拉	2.20	0.52	1.68	6.76	3.13	3.63	12.61	6.59	6.02	13.00	6.28	6.
多米尼加共和国	8.49	5.79	2.70	15.21	10.86	4.35	26.48	17.37	9.11	28.51	18.94	9.
牙买加	9.53	5.64	3.89	16.42	9.75	6.67	21.63	12.79	8.84	24.17	13.83	10.
特立尼达和多巴哥	9.57	2.45	7.12	7.82	3.22	4.60	7.41	3.17	4.24	5.54	3.31	2.
荷属安的列斯	11.10	6.63	4.47	16.40	11.30	5.10	20.47	13.82	6.65	23.75	16.56	7.
巴拿马	20.53	11.05	9.48	15.40	8.80	6.60	22.02	11.72	10.30	23.41	12.92	10.
萨尔瓦多	4.67	1.96	2.71	5.97	3.01	2.96	7.47	3.38	4.09	8.30	3.42	4.
乌拉圭	6.97	3.76	3.21	8.23	4.60	3.63	21.45	13.24	8.21	21.23	13.09	8.
厄瓜多尔	9.81	3.70	6.11	11.09	5.08	6.01	15.67	7.02	8.65	17.37	8.05	9.
洪都拉斯	2.81	0.90	1.91	3.34	1.21	2.13	5.11	2.07	3.04	5.47	2.21	3.
西欧	**3587.00**	**1936.00**	**1651.00**	**8133.00**	**4176.00**	**3957.00**	**9516.00**	**4942.00**	**4574.00**	**10965.00**	**5664.00**	**5301.**
奥地利	158.20	94.85	63.35	368.58	227.54	141.04	480.84	274.94	205.94	592.44	316.92	275.
比利时－卢森堡	191.81	95.21	96.60	489.88	246.90	242.98	689.42	353.92	335.50	661.30	336.19	325.
克罗地亚	…	…	…	…	…	…	40.81	28.57	12.24	38.61	24.51	14.
丹麦	100.98	53.92	47.06	228.37	127.31	101.06	255.75	135.78	119.97	291.16	151.71	139.
芬兰	52.07	23.77	28.30	119.94	45.62	74.32	126.25	56.79	69.46	169.62	74.73	94.
法国	597.37	347.19	250.18	1167.25	662.74	504.51	1308.65	746.88	561.77	1476.30	831.08	645.
德国	558.00	228.10	329.90	1308.10	516.00	792.10	1631.02	590.11	104.91	2004.90	751.82	1253.
希腊	38.48	25.67	12.81	92.70	65.14	27.56	125.62	91.42	34.20	135.31	95.28	40.

务贸易额(一)

金额单位:亿美元

1996			1997			1998			1998年比1997年增减%			1999		
额	出口	进口	总额	出口	进口	总额	出口	进口	总额	出口	进口	总额	出口	进口
50.00	**12708.00**	**12552.0**	**26171.00**	**131209.00**	**12962.00**	**26240.00**	**13178.00**	**13062.00**	**0.3**	**-0.2**	**0.8**	**26750.00**	**13400.00**	**13350.00**
59.00	**2442.00**	**1727.00**	**4541.00**	**2646.00**	**1895.00**	**4713.00**	**2702.00**	**2011.00**	**3.8**	**2.1**	**6.1**	…	…	…
36.66	285.17	351.49	663.90	298.07	365.83	655.30	302.81	352.49	-1.3	1.6	-3.6	695.00	324.00	371.00
32.84	2157.03	1375.81	3877.85	2348.33	1529.52	4057.84	2399.57	1658.27	4.6	2.2	8.4	4340.00	2517.00	1823.00
34.00	**468.00**	**566.00**	**1170.00**	**506.00**	**664.00**	**1221.00**	**530.00**	**691.00**	**4.4**	**4.7**	**4.1**	…	…	…
78.85	49.22	129.63	243.77	67.65	176.12	266.13	76.17	189.96	9.2	12.6	7.9	…	…	116.00
17.67	42.78	74.89	127.62	43.58	84.04	131.10	44.48	86.62	2.7	2.1	3.1	…	…	…
58.63	32.80	35.83	74.46	35.92	38.54	78.04	37.67	40.37	4.8	4.9	4.7	…	…	…
55.19	21.92	33.27	56.89	21.22	35.67	54.79	20.67	34.12	-3.7	-2.6	-4.3	…	…	…
96.61	106.93	99.68	230.26	112.14	118.12	245.56	119.37	126.19	6.6	6.4	6.8	253.00	116.00	137.00
50.73	14.48	46.25	65.03	12.90	52.13	59.98	12.48	47.50	-7.8	-3.3	-8.9	…	…	…
33.14	13.24	19.90	36.37	14.47	21.90	38.07	16.26	21.81	4.7	12.4	0.4	…	…	…
24.03	13.53	10.50	26.25	14.90	11.35	26.37	13.37	13.00	0.5	-10.3	14.5	…	…	…
1.71	5.33	6.38	11.69	5.42	6.27	13.40	5.81	7.59	14.6	7.2	21.1	…	…	…
31.78	20.78	11.00	35.33	23.73	11.60	36.85	24.03	12.82	4.3	12.6	10.5	…	…	…
24.45	13.72	10.73	25.97	14.42	11.55	…	…	…	…	…	…	…	…	…
5.60	3.73	1.87	6.83	4.64	2.19	…	…	…	…	…	…	…	…	…
21.69	14.23	7.46	21.13	14.22	6.91	22.18	14.56	7.62	5.0	2.4	10.3	…	…	…
23.20	13.32	9.88	26.69	14.38	12.31	27.27	15.70	11.57	2.2	9.2	-6.0	…	…	…
7.99	3.18	4.81	6.30	2.76	3.54	8.57	2.77	5.80	36.0	0.4	63.8	…	…	…
21.83	13.88	7.95	22.53	14.13	8.40	22.48	13.82	8.66	-0.2	2.2	3.1	…	…	…
7.08	8.07	9.01	17.78	6.89	10.89	18.30	6.68	11.62	2.9	-4.0	6.7	…	…	…
6.03	2.77	3.26	6.86	3.28	3.59	7.71	3.83	3.88	12.2	16.8	8.1	…	…	…
9.00	**5912.00**	**5507.00**	**11532.00**	**6013.00**	**5519.00**	**12288.00**	**6359.00**	**5929.00**	**6.6**	**5.8**	**7.4**	…	…	…
6.20	334.25	291.95	575.84	292.13	283.71	625.15	323.81	301.34	8.6	10.8	6.2	621.00	326.00	295.00
3.14	341.28	321.86	655.09	340.40	314.69	693.64	354.26	339.38	5.9	4.1	7.8	731.00	376.00	355.00
0.14	32.97	17.17	59.91	40.11	19.80	58.53	39.64	18.89	-2.3	-1.2	-4.6	…	…	…
9.83	163.41	146.42	277.71	140.44	137.27	301.69	148.23	153.46	8.6	5.5	11.8	322.00	160.00	162.00
2.48	75.65	86.83	152.77	70.97	81.80	147.92	67.62	80.30	-3.2	-4.7	-1.8	…	…	…
2.02	825.85	656.17	1422.86	802.69	620.17	1500.47	846.27	654.20	5.5	5.4	5.5	1685.00	793.00	592.00
0.69	787.97	1272.72	1983.21	766.00	1217.21	2039.42	789.03	1250.39	2.8	3.0	2.7	2040.00	768.00	1272.00
0.92	92.62	38.30	134.20	92.24	41.96	…	…	…	…	…	…	…	105.00	…

世界部分国家（地

国别(地区) \ 年份 金额	1985			1990			1994			1995		
	总额	出口	进口	总额	出口	进口	总额	出口	进口	总额	出口	进口
冰岛	6.63	3.11	3.52	9.67	4.27	5.40	10.96	5.29	5.67	12.16	5.86	6
爱尔兰	27.56	12.30	15.26	84.31	32.86	51.45	125.49	41.45	84.04	160.51	47.99	112
意大利	353.84	193.91	159.93	985.71	487.11	498.60	1012.45	531.70	480.75	1157.86	611.73	546
马尔他	4.72	2.61	2.11	12.20	7.21	4.99	16.43	9.75	6.68	18.50	10.60	7
荷兰	280.25	134.10	146.15	595.76	301.00	294.76	822.60	418.11	404.49	918.95	470.18	448
挪威	148.13	73.37	74.76	246.99	124.52	122.47	238.20	119.15	119.05	261.69	131.33	130
葡萄牙	30.83	18.95	11.88	88.27	50.54	37.73	119.56	67.01	52.55	145.00	81.61	63
斯洛文尼亚	…	…	…	…	…	…	29.14	18.02	11.12	33.88	20.12	13
西班牙	168.07	126.37	41.70	428.45	276.49	151.96	522.26	337.55	184.71	614.39	397.14	217
瑞典	125.74	59.55	66.19	304.11	134.52	169.59	279.77	133.83	145.94	324.48	153.36	171
瑞士	136.59	88.17	48.42	300.88	188.93	111.95	353.88	226.18	127.70	410.62	260.22	150
土耳其	40.59	28.35	12.24	106.76	78.82	27.94	141.41	107.23	34.18	191.29	144.75	46
英国	501.36	294.54	206.49	982.00	535.10	446.90	1181.43	647.02	534.41	1341.85	745.72	596
前南斯拉夫	66.66	32.36	34.30	213.86	63.74	150.12	…	…	…	…	…	…
中/东欧,波罗地海国家和独联体												
保加利亚	17.01	10.47	6.54	14.37	8.37	6.00	25.03	12.57	12.46	27.09	14.31	12
捷克共和国	…	…	…	…	…	…	98.05	51.20	46.85	114.98	66.38	48
匈牙利	12.95	6.16	6.79	49.40	26.76	22.64	59.21	30.46	28.75	77.66	42.10	35
波兰	39.50	21.04	18.46	60.47	32.00	28.47	104.01	66.55	37.46	176.45	106.37	70
罗马尼亚	12.70	7.46	5.24	13.97	6.10	7.87	21.89	10.23	11.66	32.77	14.76	18
俄罗斯	…	…	…	…	…	…	234.49	83.94	150.55	305.82	105.21	200
斯洛伐克共和国	…	…	…	…	…	…	37.70	22.21	15.49	41.78	23.78	18
乌克兰	…	…	…	…	…	…	42.85	27.47	15.38	41.80	28.46	13
非洲	**325.00**	**114.00**	**211.00**	**455.00**	**186.00**	**269.00**	**548.00**	**226.00**	**322.00**	**615.00**	**251.00**	**364**
南非	44.34	19.82	24.52	75.38	34.43	40.95	90.77	37.95	52.82	105.51	42.54	62
阿尔及利亚	29.43	5.10	24.33	16.35	4.79	11.56	…	…	…	…	…	…
埃及	57.73	29.18	28.53	81.38	48.12	33.26	130.75	76.93	53.82	127.73	82.62	45
利比亚	15.27	0.63	14.64	10.09	0.83	9.26	…	…	…	…	…	…
摩洛哥	13.94	9.15	4.79	28.11	18.71	9.40	30.85	18.77	12.08	33.70	20.20	13
突尼斯	13.32	8.84	4.48	22.56	15.74	6.82	33.72	21.74	11.98	36.46	24.01	12

务贸易额(二)

金额单位:亿美元

1996			1997			1998			1998年比1997年增减%			1999		
总额	出口	进口	总额	出口	进口	总额	出口	进口	总额	出口	进口	总额	出口	进口
13.67	6.41	7.26	15.00	7.13	7.87	17.78	8.26	9.52	18.5	15.8	21.0	…	…	…
89.78	55.62	134.16	210.52	60.20	150.32	268.79	68.63	200.16	27.7	14.0	33.2	…	…	235.00
19.43	649.13	570.30	1253.53	664.09	589.44	1295.08	666.21	628.87	3.3	0.3	6.7	1272.00	645.00	627.00
19.01	10.97	8.04	19.10	11.45	7.65	20.09	12.16	7.93	5.2	6.2	3.7	…	…	…
39.27	489.47	449.80	951.23	505.08	446.15	982.49	516.33	466.16	3.3	2.2	4.5	996.00	531.00	465.00
73.73	139.51	134.22	290.82	144.27	146.55	291.64	139.53	152.11	0.3	-3.3	3.8	291.00	137.00	154.00
41.03	78.76	62.27	135.89	75.33	60.56	152.20	85.12	67.08	12.0	13.0	10.8	…	…	…
35.26	21.17	14.09	34.71	20.32	14.39	35.65	20.45	15.20	2.7	0.6	5.6	…	…	…
79.67	439.06	240.61	678.34	435.70	242.64	762.24	487.29	274.95	12.4	11.8	13.3	850.00	541.00	309.00
53.20	166.69	186.51	369.31	175.05	194.26	397.05	178.85	218.20	7.5	2.2	12.3	408.00	180.00	228.00
19.54	262.59	156.95	402.17	256.56	145.61	431.52	270.76	160.76	7.3	5.5	10.4	429.00	272.00	157.00
89.27	128.95	60.32	272.78	191.93	80.85	326.02	231.61	94.41	19.5	20.7	16.8	…	160.00	…
56.17	808.13	648.04	1632.29	919.46	712.83	1793.40	1005.48	787.92	9.9	9.4	10.5	1828.00	1014.00	814.00
…	…	…	…	…	…	…	…	…	…	…	…	…	…	…
26.12	13.66	12.46	24.64	13.07	11.57	23.24	12.34	10.90	-5.7	-5.6	-5.8	…	…	…
42.69	80.71	61.98	123.38	70.33	53.05	126.86	72.70	54.16	2.8	3.4	2.1	…	…	…
83.90	49.44	34.46	84.59	48.25	36.34	90.42	48.70	41.72	6.9	0.9	14.8	…	…	…
61.00	97.86	63.14	146.50	89.69	56.81	160.03	89.19	70.84	9.2	-0.6	24.7	…	98.00	…
34.76	15.52	19.24	33.99	15.00	18.99	30.30	11.92	18.38	-10.9	-20.5	-3.2	…	…	…
16.07	129.46	186.61	330.02	141.56	188.46	290.26	129.40	160.86	-12.0	-8.6	-14.6	214.00	97.00	117.00
40.57	20.60	19.97	42.13	21.51	20.62	45.47	22.75	22.72	7.9	5.8	10.1	…	…	…
64.24	47.99	16.25	72.05	49.37	22.68	64.67	39.22	25.45	-10.2	-20.6	12.6	…	…	…
37.00	**273.00**	**364.00**	**655.00**	**27.50**	**380.00**	**648.00**	**267.00**	**381.00**	**-1.1**	**-2.9**	**0.3**	…	…	…
01.88	43.97	57.91	109.32	48.82	60.50	104.24	48.23	56.01	-4.6	-1.2	-7.4	…	…	…
…	…	…	…	…	…	…	…	…	…	…	…	…	…	…
37.88	90.79	47.09	149.09	90.96	58.13	137.27	78.45	58.82	-7.9	-13.8	1.2	…	…	…
…	…	…	…	…	…	…	…	…	…	…	…	…	…	…
37.34	24.33	13.01	34.70	22.03	12.67	39.14	24.99	14.15	12.8	13.4	11.7	…	…	…
36.58	25.27	11.31	35.84	25.18	10.66	38.15	26.62	11.53	6.4	5.7	8.2	…	…	…

世界部分国家（地[区]

国别(地区) \ 年份 金额	1985			1990			1994			1995		
	总额	出口	进口	总额	出口	进口	总额	出口	进口	总额	出口	进口
喀麦隆	13.38	4.57	8.81	13.87	3.69	10.18	7.86	3.09	4.77	7.27	2.42	4
加蓬	11.59	1.19	10.40	11.98	2.14	9.84	10.09	2.00	8.09	11.78	2.48	9
尼日利亚	19.24	3.16	16.08	28.66	9.65	19.01	33.52	3.71	29.81	50.06	6.08	43
肯尼亚	7.19	4.11	3.08	13.72	7.74	5.98	14.16	8.15	6.01	16.28	8.73	7
毛里求斯	2.45	1.17	1.28	8.85	4.78	4.07	11.55	6.29	5.26	14.03	7.73	6
赞比亚	3.06	0.57	2.49	4.65	0.95	3.70	…	…	…	…	…	…
津巴布韦	7.17	2.71	4.46	7.13	2.53	4.60	9.98	3.53	6.45	…	…	…
坦桑尼亚	3.15	1.06	2.09	4.19	1.31	2.88	8.50	4.11	4.39	12.95	5.66	7
马拉维	1.69	0.26	1.43	3.05	0.37	2.68	2.56	0.22	2.34	…	…	…
塞拉利昂	0.58	0.18	0.40	1.12	0.45	0.67	1.79	0.86	0.93	1.50	0.71	0
埃塞俄比亚	…	…	…	6.08	2.60	3.48	5.65	2.66	2.99	6.52	3.10	3
马达加斯加	1.78	0.50	1.28	3.01	1.29	1.72	4.32	1.83	2.49	4.96	2.19	2
中东												
巴林	13.59	8.75	4.84	15.25	8.74	6.51	15.67	8.20	7.47	14.63	6.85	7
塞浦路斯	8.99	6.04	2.95	24.23	17.60	6.63	32.45	23.98	8.47	37.68	26.84	10
伊朗	34.90	3.33	31.57	40.46	3.43	37.03	34.72	4.10	30.62	27.25	5.33	21
以色列	57.71	31.23	26.48	101.49	45.12	56.37	140.72	65.49	75.23	159.03	77.13	81
约旦	22.44	11.60	10.84	25.48	14.30	11.18	27.40	15.43	11.97	30.74	16.89	13
科威特	42.59	9.44	33.15	38.58	10.54	28.04	48.30	11.89	36.41	49.90	11.43	38
叙利亚	12.04	4.65	7.39	14.42	7.40	7.02	30.66	16.16	14.50	30.70	17.12	13
沙特阿拉伯	…	…	…	157.25	30.31	126.94	122.75	33.47	89.28	121.61	34.80	86
亚洲（包括大洋洲）	**1430.00**	**614.00**	**816.00**	**3119.00**	**1324.00**	**1795.00**	**4914.00**	**2209.00**	**2705.00**	**5895.00**	**2618.00**	**3277**
澳大利亚	114.67	40.56	74.11	229.56	97.79	131.77	288.31	137.67	150.64	324.32	157.41	166
孟加拉国	6.08	2.07	4.01	8.50	2.96	5.54	12.76	4.19	8.57	16.61	4.69	11
柬埔寨	…	…	…	…	…	…	1.77	0.45	1.32	2.84	1.03	1
中国	51.86	29.25	22.61	98.61	57.48	41.13	321.35	163.54	157.81	430.65	184.30	246
中国台湾	78.52	27.29	51.23	208.60	69.37	139.23	335.80	131.15	204.65	379.09	149.27	229
中国澳门	…	…	…	16.29	14.92	1.37	29.79	27.28	2.51	34.27	31.50	2
中国香港	124.25	77.31	46.94	291.46	181.28	110.18	497.84	311.42	186.42	551.34	343.38	207
斐济	3.47	2.31	1.16	6.16	3.77	2.39	8.33	4.89	3.44	8.95	5.24	3
印度	70.89	32.74	38.15	105.53	46.10	59.43	140.61	60.31	80.30	168.25	67.63	100
印度尼西亚	58.54	84.40	50.10	83.86	24.88	58.98	158.16	46.80	111.36	185.72	53.42	132

务贸易额(三)

金额单位:亿美元

1996			1997			1998			1998年比1997年增减%			1999		
额	出口	进口	总额	出口	进口	总额	出口	进口	总额	出口	进口	总额	出口	进口
…	…	…	…	…	…	…	…	…	…	…	…	…	…	…
…	…	…	…	…	…	…	…	…	…	…	…	…	…	…
52.74	7.33	45.41	54.80	7.86	46.94	…	…	…	…	…	…	…	…	
15.68	8.18	7.50	14.95	7.64	7.31	…	…	…	…	…	…	…	…	
16.21	9.55	6.66	15.83	9.11	6.72	16.85	9.68	7.17	6.4	6.3	6.7	…	…	…
…	…	…	…	…	…	…	…	…	…	…	…	…	…	…
…	…	…	…	…	…	…	…	…	…	…	…	…	…	…
14.85	6.02	8.83	11.66	4.60	7.06	…	…	…	…	…	…	…	…	…
…	…	…	…	…	…	…	…	…	…	…	…	…	…	…
…	…	…	…	…	…	…	…	…	…	…	…	…	…	…
6.52	3.21	3.31	6.97	3.18	3.79	7.53	3.48	4.05	8.0	9.4	6.9	…	…	…
5.33	2.53	2.80	…	…	…	…	…	…	…	…	…	…	…	…
14.71	6.68	8.03	14.28	6.39	7.89	15.09	7.69	7.40	5.7	20.3	-6.2	…	…	…
…	…	…	…	…	…	…	…	…	…	…	…	…	…	…
36.42	7.43	28.99	42.00	10.18	31.82	…	…	…	…	…	…	…	…	…
71.10	80.31	90.79	175.55	83.48	92.07	186.06	89.80	96.26	6.0	7.6	4.6	210.00	103.00	107.00
31.78	18.30	13.48	29.58	17.17	12.41	33.98	18.10	15.88	14.9	5.4	28.0	…	…	…
54.77	12.62	42.15	55.62	15.07	40.55	56.76	14.96	41.80	2.0	-0.7	3.1	…	…	…
29.59	15.81	13.78	26.68	13.66	13.02	28.48	15.51	12.97	6.7	13.5	-0.4	…	…	…
53.64	27.72	125.92	186.85	42.07	144.78	130.99	44.21	86.78	-29.9	5.1	-40.1	…	…	…
80.00	**2862.00**	**3518.00**	**6597.00**	**2994.00**	**3603.00**	**5753.00**	**2554.00**	**3199.00**	**-12.8**	**-14.7**	**-11.2**	…	…	…
63.14	181.17	181.97	368.09	183.79	184.30	327.37	159.71	167.66	-11.1	-13.1	-9.0	352.00	172.00	180.00
12.82	2.23	10.59	14.54	2.66	11.88	14.32	2.52	11.80	-1.5	-5.3	-0.7	…	…	…
3.61	1.52	2.09	3.32	1.50	1.82	2.84	0.99	1.85	-14.5	-3.4	-1.6	…	…	…
29.36	205.67	223.69	545.79	245.16	300.63	528.18	240.41	287.77	-3.2	-1.8	-4.3	587.00	266.00	321.00
99.04	161.54	237.50	411.33	170.21	241.12	399.59	166.38	233.21	-2.9	-2.3	-3.3	380.00	148.00	232.00
35.49	32.38	3.11	35.22	31.32	3.90	…	…	…	…	…	…	…	…	…
03.96	382.95	221.01	613.88	381.79	232.09	568.77	341.71	227.06	-7.3	-10.5	-2.2	578.00	354.00	224.00
9.64	5.77	3.87	9.96	6.12	3.84	…	…	…	…	…	…	…	…	…
81.79	71.79	110.00	212.03	89.26	122.77	252.59	110.67	141.92	19.1	24.0	15.6	305.00	132.00	173.00
12.39	64.62	147.77	230.06	67.92	162.14	159.36	43.40	115.96	-30.7	-36.1	-28.5	…	…	127.00

世界部分国家（地

国别(地区) \ 年份 金额	1985			1990			1994			1995		
	总额	出口	进口	总额	出口	进口	总额	出口	进口	总额	出口	进口
日本	552.30	205.20	347.10	1256.60	413.80	842.80	1622.25	567.76	1054.49	1855.14	639.66	1215
韩国	90.04	50.42	212.95	192.05	91.55	100.50	344.81	162.33	182.48	475.27	221.33	253
马来西亚	56.49	18.34	38.15	91.64	37.70	53.94	211.18	92.00	119.18	262.59	114.38	148
马尔代夫	0.84	0.61	0.23	1.56	1.19	0.37	2.57	1.95	0.62	3.05	2.30	0
蒙古	2.21	0.71	1.50	2.03	0.48	1.55	1.23	0.35	0.88	1.34	0.47	0
缅甸	1.38	0.63	0.75	1.66	0.94	0.72	3.74	2.56	1.18	5.80	3.50	2
尼泊尔	2.05	0.93	1.12	3.25	1.66	1.59	8.17	5.27	2.90	8.97	5.92	3
新西兰	31.36	14.24	17.12	56.66	24.15	32.51	76.33	35.99	40.34	90.00	44.00	46
巴基斯坦	17.47	7.40	10.07	30.67	12.13	18.54	36.14	14.39	21.75	38.50	14.27	24
巴布亚新几内亚	3.23	0.48	2.75	5.91	1.98	3.93	8.43	2.35	6.08	9.63	3.21	6
菲律宾	27.07	18.62	8.45	46.18	28.97	17.21	113.88	67.49	46.39	162.29	93.23	69
新加坡	81.10	45.98	35.12	212.98	127.19	85.79	367.39	229.39	138.00	473.66	297.24	176
斯里兰卡	6.73	2.34	4.39	10.45	4.25	6.20	17.49	7.29	10.20	19.69	8.00	11
泰国	36.40	18.97	17.43	124.51	62.91	61.60	266.56	114.25	152.31	332.53	146.52	186
瓦努阿图	0.56	0.36	0.20	0.80	0.56	0.24	1.03	0.70	0.33	1.10	0.75	0

注:①1985—1990年中期的数字是前联邦德国的数字。

②由于服务贸易数据的频繁修订,一些国家和地区的贸易值序列出现多处中断。

资料来源:世界贸易组织《年度报告》。

务贸易额（四）

金额单位：亿美元

1996			1997			1998			1998年比1997年增减%			1999		
总额	出口	进口	总额	出口	进口	总额	出口	进口	总额	出口	进口	总额	出口	进口
50.56	663.82	1286.74	1902.15	681.36	1220.79	1725.00	617.95	1107.05	-9.3	-9.3	-9.3	1737.00	598.00	1139.00
18.06	226.48	291.58	544.76	254.39	290.37	476.31	238.81	237.50	-12.6	-6.1	-18.2	517.00	250.00	267.00
14.85	143.45	171.40	322.31	148.68	173.63	230.43	106.90	123.53	-28.5	28.1	-28.9	238.00	108.00	130.00
3.63	2.86	0.77	3.94	3.08	0.86	…	106.90	…	…	…	…	…	…	…
1.51	0.43	1.08	1.51	0.50	1.01	2.14	0.75	1.39	41.7	50.0	37.0	…	…	…
7.06	4.17	2.89	9.37	5.08	4.29	9.58	5.29	4.29	2.2	4.1	0	…	…	…
9.14	6.79	2.35	10.11	7.95	2.16	6.22	4.33	1.89	-38.5	-45.5	-12.5	…	…	…
95.16	45.53	49.63	90.85	41.40	49.45	81.46	36.49	44.97	-10.3	-11.9	-9.1	…	…	…
44.46	15.42	29.04	38.82	14.65	24.17	35.45	14.16	21.29	-8.7	-3.3	-11.9	…	…	…
12.11	4.32	7.79	13.21	3.97	9.24	…	…	…	…	…	…	…	…	…
223.21	129.29	93.92	292.03	151.30	140.73	175.52	74.65	100.87	-39.9	-50.7	28.3	…	…	…
494.64	298.59	196.05	496.85	303.99	192.86	361.27	182.43	178.84	-27.3	-40.0	-7.3	422.00	229.00	193.00
19.14	7.41	11.73	21.21	8.50	12.71	22.13	8.88	13.25	4.3	4.5	4.2	…	…	…
360.17	167.04	193.13	327.45	156.19	171.26	249.83	130.85	118.98	-23.7	-16.2	-30.5	280.00	141.00	139.00
1.21	0.85	0.36	1.15	0.80	0.35	1.51	1.10	0.41	31.3	37.5	17.1	…	…	…

（对外贸易经济合作部国际贸易经济合作研究院）

发达国家官方发展援助协议额的财政条件 a(一)

国别	全部官方发展援助的赠与成分[b] 标准:86%		官方发展援助中赠与所占比重		官方发展援助贷款中的赠与成分	对最不发达国家官方发展援助中的赠与成分 c	对最不发达国家双边发展援助中的赠与成分
	1987－1988	1997－1998	双边援助	全部援助			
澳大利亚	100.0	100.0	100.0	100.0	－	100.0	100.0
奥地利	71.7	95.0	80.8	87.4	55.4	100.0	100.0
比利时	99.2	99.5	96.3	97.9	74.1	99.9	99.9
加拿大	99.6	99.9	99.8	99.9	89.2	100.0	100.0
丹　麦	99.5	100.0	100.0	100.0	－	100.0	100.0
芬　兰	97.7	99.8	98.0	98.9	43.9	99.7	99.5
法　国	86.5	92.2	77.2	80.3	53.7	98.8	98.2
德　国	88.8	96.0	77.2	86.1	71.0	100.0	100.0
爱尔兰	100.0	100.0	100.0	100.0	－	100.0	100.0
意大利	92.1	98.4	74.7	94.3	76.0	99.6	98.8
日　本	74.3	80.0	34.9	43.5	64.3	99.1	98.5
卢森堡	－	100.0	100.0	100.0	－	100.0	100.0
荷　兰	94.2	100.0	100.0	100.0	－	100.0	100.0
新西兰	100.0	100.0	100.0	100.0	－	100.0	100.0
挪　威	99.6	99.4	98.6	99.1	31.7	99.2	98.7
葡萄牙	－	97.5	65.1	87.2	58.8	97.6	96.7
西班牙	50.4	91.5	60.8	75.9	64.7	96.3	90.0
瑞　典	100.0	100.0	99.8	99.9	－	100.0	100.0
瑞　士	100.0	100.0	99.5	99.6	－	100.0	100.0
英　国	99.7	100.0	92.4	95.8	－	100.0	100.0
美　国	97.0	99.1	97.5	98.2	51.1	99.8	99.5
总　计	89.7	92.7	70.8	79.0	63.9	99.5	99.1

注:a)不包括债务重新安排。

b)官方发展援助占国民生产总值的比重明显低于经合组织发展援助委员会平均水平的国家,不能视为已达到发展援助委员会制订的有关援助条件的指标,1998年未达到的国家有意大利、葡萄牙和美国。

c)包括多边援助中的赠与成分。

资料来源:经济合作与发展组织《1999年发展合作评论》。

(对外贸易经济合作部国际贸易经济合作研究院)

发达国家官方发展援助协议额的财政条件(二)

国别	赠与在官方发展援助中所占比重		双边官方发展援助贷款							
			赠与成份 %		偿还期 (年)		宽限期 (年)		利率 %	
	1997	1998	1997	1998	1997	1998	1997	1998	1997	1998
澳大利亚	100.0	100.0	–	–	–	–	–	–	–	–
奥地利	89.8	85.4	53.0	57.1	22.9	27.8	7.5	10.9	2.7	2.9
比利时	97.7	98.1	69.3	79.6	20.8	29.2	10.5	10.2	0.9	0.4
加拿大	100.0	99.8	89.1	89.4	38.5	38.0	13.9	13.3	0.0	0.0
丹　麦	100.0	100.0	–	–	–	–	–	–	–	–
芬　兰	98.3	99.3	51.4	31.3	7.8	10.0	2.8	10.0	8.3	5.5
法　国	82.4	78.1	53.9	54.2	21.1	20.7	8.2	7.4	2.5	2.2
德　国	84.3	88.1	67.3	76.4	37.3	40.0	8.0	10.2	1.9	1.2
爱尔兰	100.0	100.0	–	–	–	–	–	–	–	–
意大利	85.7	99.1	75.9	76.7	27.3	31.1	12.1	13.1	1.0	1.0
日　本	45.0	41.8	60.8	67.7	29.0	31.2	9.4	9.6	2.4	1.8
卢森堡	100.0	100.0	–	–	–	–	–	–	–	–
荷　兰	100.0	100.0	–	–	–	–	–	–	–	–
新西兰	100.0	100.0	–	–	–	–	–	–	–	–
挪　威	98.8	99.5	31.7	31.7	8.5	9.1	3.8	2.8	2.3	2.2
葡萄牙	97.5	81.7	39.3	62.4	12.0	24.1	3.0	4.0	2.0	1.0
西班牙	82.4	71.0	60.5	66.6	21.0	26.2	9.5	9.2	1.7	1.1
瑞　典	100.0	99.8	–	–	–	–	–	–	–	–
瑞　士	99.4	100.0	–	–	–	–	–	–	–	–
英　国	95.9	95.8	–	–	–	–	–	–	–	–
美　国	98.1	98.2	50.9	50.6	27.6	26.7	5.4	5.4	3.2	3.2
总　计	**78.4**	**79.5**	**60.9**	**66.8**	**28.9**	**30.7**	**9.1**	**9.4**	**2.4**	**1.8**

注:不包括债务重新安排。

资料来源:经济合作与发展组织《1999 年发展合作评论》。

(对外贸易经济合作部国际贸易经济合作研究院)

世界商品贸易额及增长率＊(一)

年份	贸易额(亿美元)			增减率(％)		
	出口	进口	总额	出口	进口	总额
1950	554.00	580.00	1134.00	–	–	–
1955	843.00	892.00	1735.00	52.2	53.8	53.0
1960	1131.00	1194.00	2325.00	34.2	33.9	34.0
1961	1183.00	1245.00	2428.00	4.6	4.3	4.4
1962	1241.00	1321.00	2562.00	4.9	6.1	5.5
1963	1354.00	1435.00	2789.00	9.1	8.6	8.9
1964	1522.00	1610.00	3132.00	12.4	12.2	12.3
1965	1643.00	1743.00	3386.00	8.0	8.3	8.1
1966	1808.00	1921.00	3729.00	10.0	10.2	10.1
1967	1898.00	2015.00	3913.00	5.0	4.9	4.9
1968	2124.00	2248.00	4372.00	11.9	11.6	11.7
1969	2434.00	2565.00	4999.00	14.6	14.1	14.3
1970	3145.81	3289.21	6435.02	–	–	–
1971	3883.90	3663.84	7547.74	23.5	11.4	17.3
1972	4155.34	4340.21	8495.55	7.0	18.5	12.6
1973	5729.67	5999.35	11729.02	37.9	38.2	38.1
1974	8417.57	8607.16	17024.73	46.9	43.5	45.2
1975	8745.99	9045.12	17791.11	3.9	5.1	4.5
1976	9894.95	10135.73	20030.68	13.1	12.1	12.6
1977	11255.42	11605.20	22860.62	13.7	14.5	14.1
1978	12973.87	13471.30	26445.17	15.3	16.1	15.7
1979	16390.50	16868.07	33258.57	26.3	25.2	25.8
1980	19936.25	20474.25	40410.50	21.6	21.4	21.5
1981	19763.11	20360.88	40123.99	–0.9	–0.6	–0.7
1982	18575.50	19222.31	37797.81	–6.0	–5.6	–5.8
1983	18124.94	18718.42	36843.36	–2.4	–2.6	–2.5
1984	19093.15	19799.69	38892.84	5.4	5.8	5.6
1985	19300.05	20005.50	39305.55	1.1	1.0	1.1

世界商品贸易额及增长率*(二)

年份	贸易额(亿美元)			增减率(%)		
	出口	进口	总额	出口	进口	总额
1986	21280.93	21979.05	43259.98	10.3	9.9	10.1
1987	24908.05	25596.64	50504.69	17.0	16.5	16.7
1988	28253.38	29118.79	57372.17	13.4	13.8	13.6
1989	30213.46	31347.24	61560.70	6.9	7.7	7.3
1990	34250.43	35565.09	69815.52	13.4	13.5	13.4
1991	34299.09	35517.42	69816.51	0.1	−0.1	0.0
1992	36716.86	37709.59	74426.45	7.0	6.2	6.6
1993	36638.88	37112.75	73751.63	−0.2	−1.6	−0.9
1994	41889.11	42267.09	84156.20	14.3	13.9	14.1
1995	49885.84	50226.40	100112.24	19.1	18.8	19.0
1996	51787.73	52672.11	104459.84	3.8	4.9	4.3
1997	53772.18	54616.24	108388.42	3.8	3.7	3.8
1998	53242.72	53892.80	107135.52	−1.0	−1.3	−1.2
1999	56100.00	58750.00	114850.00	5.4	9.0	7.2

注: * 1970年以前不包括前中央计划经济国家。

资料来源:联合国《统计月报》,世界贸易组织《新闻简报》。

(对外贸易经济合作部国际贸易经济合作研究院)

世界服务贸易额及增长率

年份	贸易额(亿美元)			增减率(%)		
	出口	进口	总额	出口	进口	总额
1981	4130.00	4120.00	8250.00	–	–	–
1982	4050.00	4000.00	8050.00	−1.9	−2.9	−2.4
1983	3910.00	3840.00	7750.00	−3.5	−4.0	−3.7
1984	4030.00	3970.00	8000.00	3.1	3.4	3.2
1985	3809.00	4016.00	7825.00	−5.5	1.2	−2.2
1986	4496.00	4527.00	9023.00	18.0	12.7	15.3
1987	5328.00	5365.00	10693.00	18.5	18.5	18.5
1988	6001.00	6182.00	12183.00	12.6	15.2	13.9
1989	6581.00	6788.00	13369.00	9.7	9.8	9.7
1990	7832.00	8112.00	15944.00	19.0	19.5	19.3
1991	8269.00	8417.00	16686.00	5.6	3.8	4.7
1992	9231.00	9320.00	18551.00	11.6	10.7	11.2
1993	9421.00	9498.00	18919.00	2.1	1.9	2.0
1994	10375.00	10321.00	20696.00	10.1	8.7	9.4
1995	11881.00	11903.00	23784.00	14.5	15.3	14.9
1996	12708.00	12552.00	25260.00	7.0	5.5	6.2
1997	13209.00	12962.00	26171.00	3.9	3.3	3.6
1998	13178.00	13062.00	26240.00	−0.2	0.8	0.3
1999	13400.00	13350.00	26750.00	1.7	2.2	1.9

资料来源:世界贸易组织《年度报告》,《新闻简报》。

(对外贸易经济合作部国际贸易经济合作研究院)

1988年—1998年世界初级产品出口价格指数(一)

(1990=100)

项目 \ 年份	1988	1989	1991	1992	1993	1994	1995	1996	1997	1998
食品、饮料和烟草	110	109	99	98	97	111	118	125	122	106
食品	106	110	99	101	100	105	114	128	114	99
其中										
谷物	103	114	98	105	98	105	123	148	114	96
小麦	107	125	95	112	104	111	131	153	118	93
玉米	98	102	98	95	93	99	113	151	107	93
大米	105	112	109	99	88	100	119	125	112	113
油籽、油及油脂、油籽饼及粉	125	113	101	105	106	115	124	137	137	122
肉类	97	98	101	96	102	93	77	76	79	71
牛肉	98	100	104	96	102	91	74	70	72	67
羊肉	90	87	87	95	103	104	94	120	124	96
糖	89	96	89	83	88	99	108	101	95	81
香蕉	88	101	104	88	82	81	81	87	92	88
饮料	138	114	93	81	86	150	151	125	165	140
咖啡	159	126	94	73	83	180	184	139	192	150
可可豆	125	98	94	87	88	110	113	115	128	132
茶叶	88	99	91	98	91	90	81	87	117	117
烟草	93	98	106	101	80	88	78	90	104	98
农业原料	111	106	96	99	117	129	135	130	120	99
其中										
原木	111	107	105	117	155	157	148	151	141	121
棉花	77	92	93	70	70	97	119	98	96	79
羊毛	142	117	71	68	58	83	93	84	84	61
橡胶	137	112	96	100	96	130	183	162	118	84
皮革及革皮	95	98	86	82	87	94	96	95	96	83

1988年—1998年世界初级产品出口价格指数(二)

(1990=100)

项目 \ 年份	1988	1989	1991	1992	1993	1994	1995	1996	1997	1998
黄麻	91	91	90	68	66	72	90	111	74	63
剑麻	77	91	94	71	86	85	99	121	109	115
矿石及有色金属(不包括原油)	118	112	87	84	72	84	100	89	92	78
其中										
铜	98	107	88	86	72	87	110	86	86	62
铝	155	119	80	77	70	90	110	92	98	83
铁矿砂	77	86	108	103	91	83	88	93	93	96
锡	118	141	91	100	85	90	102	101	93	91
镍	155	150	92	79	60	71	93	85	78	52
锌	82	109	74	82	64	66	68	68	87	68
铅	81	83	69	67	50	68	78	96	77	65
磷酸盐石	103	105	103	98	83	90	99	113	114	117
以上总计	**109**	**107**	**94**	**94**	**96**	**109**	**118**	**117**	**113**	**96**
原油	**64**	**78**	**84**	**83**	**73**	**69**	**75**	**89**	**84**	**57**
初级产品总计	**88**	**94**	**90**	**91**	**90**	**98**	**106**	**109**	**105**	**86**

注:以美元计算的指数。

资料来源:世界贸易组织《年度报告》。

(对外贸易经济合作部国际贸易经济合作研究院)

1975 年—1998 年世界部分国家和地区工业制成品出口价格指数 a(一)

(1990 = 100)

国家(地区)	1975	1988	1990	1991	1992	1993	1994	1995	1996	1997	1998
世界总计 b	**48**	**93**	**100**	**100**	**103**	**99**	**101**	**110**	**106**	**98**	…
市场经济发达国家	46	92	100	100	103	97	99	110	106	98	95
美洲	47	96	100	102	100	99	99	100	100	100	96
加拿大	58	96	100	99	91	88	84	80	83	77	69
美国	45	95	100	102	103	103	104	107	106	108	108
欧洲	46	88	100	98	102	91	93	107	104	93	92
欧洲联盟	45	88	100	98	102	92	93	107	103	92	92
奥地利	52	95	100	95	99	91	90	104	94	77	68
比利时－卢森堡	50	89	100	97	99	90	93	110	105	96	94
丹麦	44	88	100	96	102	92	97	112	108	98	97
芬兰	42	85	100	95	90	74	83	105	99	89	88
法国	49	88	100	96	100	94	98	111	107	96	96
德国	47	89	100	98	103	93	94	108	101	87	89
希腊	58	86	100	95	94	81	82	88	84	…	…
爱尔兰	…	88	100	95	97	96	89	98	97	81	75
意大利	42	85	100	99	105	89	86	96	98	90	91
荷兰	48	88	100	96	102	92	92	109	102	…	…
葡萄牙	…	88	100	101	106	98	94	111	105	96	96
西班牙	…	83	100	95	109	85	86	99	99	88	86
瑞典	47	89	100	100	101	82	85	105	106	94	90
英国	38	91	100	101	102	98	103	114	113	113	112
欧洲自由贸易联盟	47	89	100	97	101	87	96	116	113	97	97
冰岛	38	99	100	88	86	76	80	114	106	101	89
挪威	51	96	100	95	92	80	82	102	96	88	85
瑞士	43	88	100	98	103	88	99	120	117	100	100
其他市场经济发达国家	50	101	100	107	113	120	129	138	128	121	108
澳大利亚	56	97	100	92	86	81	88	96	94	89	78

1975 年—1998 年世界部分国家和地区工业制成品出口价格指数 a(二)
(1990 = 100)

国家(地区)	1975	1988	1990	1991	1992	1993	1994	1995	1996	1997	1998
以色列	…	86	100	101	101	102	101	105	105	102	105
日本	48	102	100	108	115	124	134	144	133	126	112
新西兰	47	107	100	94	89	89	98	112	109	102	…
南非	…	89	100	96	101	100	101	123	107	…	…
发展中国家	55	97	100	100	103	104	104	111	105	99	…
中国香港	…	…	100	102	104	104	105	108	108	104	101
印度	…	…	100	80	92	89	88	86	69	84	…
韩国	…	…	100	101	106	109	98	102	86	85	…
巴基斯坦	…	…	100	98	101	98	107	125	123	129	128
新加坡	…	…	100	101	103	99	108	112	109	102	92
土耳其	…	…	100	98	100	95	90	106	97	89	84

注:a 用美元计价的出口单价指数。
b 不包括东欧国家和前苏联。
资料来源:联合国《统计月报》。

(对外贸易经济合作部国际贸易经济合作研究院)

发达国家向发展中国家和国际多边机构提供的官方发展援助(一)

净交付额,现值

国别	亿美元							占国民生产总值百分比						
	1982—1983平均	1987—1988平均	1994	1995	1996	1997	1998	1982—1983平均	1987—1988平均	1994	1995	1996	1997	1998
澳大利亚	8.18	8.64	10.91	11.94	10.74	10.61	9.60	0.53	0.40	0.34	0.36	0.28	0.28	0.27
奥地利	1.97	2.51	6.55	7.67	5.57	5.27	4.56	0.30	0.21	0.33	0.33	0.24	0.26	0.22
比利时	4.89	6.44	7.27	10.34	9.13	7.64	8.83	0.58	0.44	0.32	0.38	0.34	0.31	0.35
加拿大	13.13	21.16	22.50	20.67	17.95	20.45	16.91	0.43	0.48	0.43	0.38	0.32	0.34	0.29
丹麦	4.05	8.90	14.46	16.23	17.72	16.37	17.04	0.75	0.88	1.03	0.96	1.04	0.97	0.99
芬兰	1.49	5.20	2.90	3.88	4.08	3.79	3.96	0.30	0.55	0.31	0.32	0.34	0.33	0.32
法国	29.79	53.56	84.66	84.43	74.51	63.07	57.42	0.56	0.59	0.64	0.55	0.48	0.45	0.40
德国	31.64	45.61	68.18	75.24	76.01	58.57	55.81	0.48	0.39	0.33	0.31	0.32	0.28	0.26
爱尔兰	0.40	0.54	1.09	1.53	1.79	1.87	1.99	0.23	0.20	0.25	0.29	0.31	0.31	0.30
意大利	8.22	29.04	27.05	16.23	24.16	12.66	22.78	0.20	0.37	0.27	0.15	0.20	0.11	0.20
日本	33.92	82.38	132.39	144.89	94.39	93.58	106.40	0.30	0.31	0.29	0.28	0.20	0.22	0.28
卢森堡	0.04	0.16	0.59	0.65	0.82	0.95	1.12	0.09	0.19	0.40	0.36	0.44	0.55	0.65
荷兰	13.34	21.63	25.17	32.26	32.46	29.47	30.42	0.99	0.98	0.76	0.81	0.81	0.81	0.80
新西兰	0.63	0.95	1.10	1.23	1.22	1.54	1.30	0.28	0.27	0.24	0.23	0.21	0.26	0.27
挪威	5.71	9.38	11.37	12.44	13.11	13.06	13.21	1.06	1.11	1.05	0.87	0.85	0.86	0.91
葡萄牙	0.08	0.62	3.03	2.58	2.18	2.50	2.59	0.04	0.16	0.34	0.25	0.21	0.25	0.24
西班牙	1.53	2.40	13.05	13.48	12.51	12.34	13.76	0.09	0.08	0.28	0.24	0.22	0.24	0.24
瑞典	8.70	14.54	18.19	17.04	19.99	17.31	15.73	0.93	0.87	0.96	0.77	0.84	0.79	0.72

发达国家向发展中国家和国际多边机构提供的官方发展援助(二)

净交付额,现值

国别	亿美元							占国民生产总值百分比						
	1982－1983平均	1987－1988平均	1994	1995	1996	1997	1998	1982－1983平均	1987－1988平均	1994	1995	1996	1997	1998
瑞士	2.86	5.82	9.82	10.84	10.26	9.11	8.98	0.28	0.31	0.36	0.34	0.34	0.34	0.32
英国	17.05	22.58	31.97	32.02	31.99	34.33	38.64	0.36	0.30	0.31	0.29	0.27	0.26	0.27
美国	81.42	96.28	99.27	73.67	93.77	68.78	87.86	0.25	0.21	0.14	0.10	0.12	0.09	0.10
总计	**269.04**	**438.34**	**591.52**	**589.26**	**554.38**	**483.24**	**518.88**	**0.35**	**0.33**	**0.29**	**0.27**	**0.25**	**0.22**	**0.24**
其中：														
欧盟	123.18	213.74	304.16	313.58	312.93	266.12	274.62	0.45	0.44	0.42	0.38	0.37	0.33	0.33

资料来源:经济合作与发展组织《1999年发展合作评论》。

(对外贸易经济合作部国际贸易经济合作研究院)

发达国家双边援助的部门分布(一)

占双边援助协议额百分比

国别	社会与管理基础设施		经济基础设施		农业		工业与其他产业		物资援助和方案援助		紧急援助		其他		NGOs援助比重
	1977年至1978年	1997年至1998年	1977年至1978年	1997年至1998年	1977年至1978年	1997年至1998年	1977年至1978年	1997年至1998年	1977年至1978年	1997年至1998年	1977年至1978年	1997年至1998年	1977年至1978年	1997年至1998年	1997年至1998年
澳大利亚	10.5	60.0	9.8	7.9	6.3	7.3	4.1	0.6	59.0	8.8	0.2	6.7	10.0	8.7	0.0
奥地利	17.4	44.3	31.2	1.9	25.5	3.6	19.2	2.3	–	0.4	0.3	8.0	6.5	39.5	0.5
比利时	5.8	32.4	0.9	3.5	3.7	8.8	1.8	3.4	2.6	6.2	0.9	5.5	84.3	40.2	0.3
加拿大	10.2	24.8	27.6	7.1	13.2	4.8	8.9	4.1	14.7	9.4	0.4	12.4	25.0	37.4	7.7
丹麦	13.3	28.2	3.6	12.6	14.4	8.8	15.6	0.8	12.1	0.2	1.9	8.5	39.1	40.9	0.4
芬兰	9.4	35.4	32.2	5.2	18.9	10.7	16.7	3.4	4.4	0.1	1.2	13.1	17.2	32.2	0.7
法国	56.9	43.8	12.5	8.5	7.6	6.7	14.7	2.5	4.5	3.2	0.2	0.3	3.6	35.1	0.2
德国	23.0	39.3	24.8	16.2	11.0	8.2	19.7	2.2	4.5	2.1	0.4	4.0	16.5	28.1	–
爱尔兰	–	45.4	–	5.6	–	5.6	–	1.5	–	3.9	–	8.2	100.0	29.8	0.9
意大利	33.5	16.2	4.5	10.9	7.2	3.5	6.1	1.2	19.8	7.8	0.2	4.5	28.6	55.9	1.0
日本	6.6	20.2	40.5	41.4	11.2	10.3	13.6	3.7	0.9	5.9	0.2	0.8	26.9	17.7	3.0
卢森堡	–	60.2	–	2.1	–	8.6	–	5.1	–	1.4	–	13.0	–	9.7	0.8
荷兰	30.8	23.2	12.3	6.3	23.9	7.2	8.7	1.3	6.2	1.4	1.3	10.8	16.8	49.8	9.6
新西兰	34.1	51.9	18.9	4.8	18.4	4.1	7.3	2.8	18.6	–	0.3	4.6	2.3	31.8	3.4
挪威	21.1	29.7	28.5	10.8	27.7	2.9	6.7	2.1	–	0.3	7.9	29.4	8.1	24.7	–
葡萄牙	–	21.7	–	9.0	–	1.5	–	1.3	–	0.7	–	0.2	–	65.5	0.9

发达国家双边援助的部门分布(二)

占双边援助协议额百分比

国别	社会与管理基础设施		经济基础设施		农业		工业与其他产业		物资援助和方案援助		紧急援助		其他		NGOs援助比重
	1977年至1978年	1997年至1998年	1977年至1978年	1997年至1998年	1977年至1978年	1997年至1998年	1977年至1978年	1997年至1998年	1977年至1978年	1997年至1998年	1977年至1978年	1997年至1998年	1977年至1978年	1997年至1998年	1997年至1998年
西班牙	–	34.1	–	14.6	–	5.6	–	2.8	–	1.0	–	2.4	–	39.5	0.0
瑞典	20.0	33.8	4.5	12.7	8.5	7.7	16.4	1.4	1.6	2.7	1.5	19.7	47.6	21.9	6.6
瑞士	10.9	21.8	1.8	8.6	10.6	10.8	6.7	4.5	8.7	3.2	6.9	21.4	54.5	29.7	3.7
英国	15.8	27.1	11.1	10.3	8.3	7.3	21.4	3.0	3.4	6.2	0.3	7.4	39.7	38.7	2.6
美国	6.1	31.0	5.1	10.5	7.4	4.4	1.3	0.2	28.7	16.8	0.8	11.2	50.6	25.8	–
总计	**20.0**	**28.8**	**15.7**	**21.4**	**10.2**	**7.7**	**10.7**	**2.4**	**12.6**	**6.5**	**0.7**	**5.8**	**301**	**27.3**	**2.0**

注:按交付额统计。NGOs为非政府组织,最后一栏为“备注:通过NGOs提供官方发展援助的比重”。

资料来源:经济合作与发展组织《1999年发展合作评论》。

(对外贸易经济合作部国际贸易经济合作研究院)

非发展援助委员会国家提供的官方发展援助

净交付额　　单位:亿美元

国别(地区)	1994	1995	1996	1997	1998
OECD 非 DAC 成员国					
捷克共和国	0.25	…	…	…	0.16
爱沙尼亚	…	…	…	…	0.002
希腊	1.22	1.52	1.84	1.73	1.79
韩国	1.40	1.16	1.59	1.86	1.83
波兰	…	…	…	…	0.19
土耳其	0.58	1.07	0.88	1.06	…
阿拉伯国家					
科威特	5.55	3.84	4.26	3.73	2.78
沙特阿拉伯	3.17	1.92	3.27	2.35	2.88
阿拉伯联合酋长国	1.00	0.65	0.31	…	…
其他国家和地区					
中国台湾	0.79	0.92	0.89	0.65	0.27
总　　计	**13.96**	**11.08**	**13.04**	**11.37**	**9.90**
其中:双边援助					
OECD 非 DAC 成员国					
捷克共和国	0.21	…	…	…	0.06
爱沙尼亚	…	…	…	…	0.001
希腊	0.30	0.27	0.27	0.36	0.63
韩国	0.60	0.71	1.23	1.11	1.25
波兰	…	…	…	…	0.14
土耳其	0.20	0.84	0.56	0.43	…
阿拉伯国家					
科威特	4.94	3.57	3.77	3.55	2.47
沙特阿拉伯	1.76	1.34	1.77	0.79	1.23
阿拉伯联合酋长国	0.92	0.55	0.29	…	…
其他国家和地区					
中国台湾	0.71	0.78	0.89	0.65	0.27
总　　计	**9.65**	**8.07**	**8.79**	**6.89**	**6.05**

注:中国也提供援助,但未提供数据。

资料来源:经济合作与发展组织《1999 年发展合作评论》。

(对外贸易经济合作部国际贸易经济合作研究院)

国际直接投资流量

年份	发达国家		发展中国家		中东欧		所有国家	
	流进	流出	流进	流出	流进	流出	流进	流出
金额(单位:亿美元)								
1986—1991(年均)	1295.83	1691.55	290.90	113.31	6.58	0.25	1593.31	1805.10
1992	1202.94	1799.84	511.08	207.14	44.39	1.02	1758.41	2008.00
1993	1388.87	2058.10	725.28	349.29	61.43	1.61	2175.59	2409.00
1994	1415.03	2414.81	955.82	425.12	59.14	2.68	2429.99	2842.61
1995	2114.65	3064.65	1055.11	456.42	142.14	4.08	3311.89	3525.14
1996	1953.93	2834.76	1298.13	491.61	123.44	9.93	3375.50	3336.29
1997	2331.15	3592.36	1498.44	611.38	184.28	32.92	4004.86	4236.66
1998	4606.31	5946.99	1659.36	523.18	175.13	19.03	6438.79	6489.20
占世界比重(%)								
1986—1991(年均)	81.3	93.77	18.3	6.3	0.4	0.01	100	100
1992	68.5	89.6	29	10.3	2.5	0.1	100	100
1993	63.8	85.4	33.4	14.5	2.8	0.1	100	100
1994	58.2	85.0	39.3	15.0	2.4	0.1	100	100
1995	63.9	86.9	31.9	12.9	4.3	0.1	100	100
1996	57.9	85.1	38.5	14.8	3.7	0.2	100	100
1997	58.2	84.8	37.2	14.4	4.6	0.8	100	100
1998	71.5	91.6	25.8	8.1	2.7	0.3	100	100
增长率(%)								
1986—1991(年均)								
1992	−7.2	6.4	75.7	82.8	574.6	3.8	10.4	11.2
1993	15.5	14.3	41.9	68.6	38.4	57.8	23.7	20
1994	1.9	17.3	31.8	21.7	−3.7	66.5	11.7	18
1995	49.4	26.9	10.4	7.4	140.3	52.2	36.3	24
1996	−7.6	−7.5	23	7.7	−13.2	143.4	19	−5.4
1997	19.3	26.7	14.7	24.4	49.3	231.5	18.6	27
1998	97.5	65.5	10.7	−14.4	−5	−42.2	60.8	53.2

资料来源:联合国《1999年世界投资报告》。

(对外贸易经济合作部国际贸易经济合作研究院)

1998年世界最大100家国际工程设计咨询公司名录(一)

单位:百万美元

名次	公司名称	国别	国际市场营业额	% of total
1	福陆丹尼尔公司	美国	797	32
2	耐瑟咨询公司	荷兰	777	50
3	克劳格布朗路特公司	美国	704	39
4	贝克特尔集团	美国	688	36
5	SNC—拉瓦林国际公司	加拿大	619	38
6	ABB鲁姆斯环球公司	美国	605.8	46
7	福格勒公司	荷兰	599.2	47
8	福斯特惠勒公司	美国	501.1	35
9	雅可保利集团	芬兰	440	46
10	JGC公司	日本	362	45
11	ARCADIS公司	荷兰	357	39
12	AGRA公司	加拿大	339	32
13	达艾尔汉德莎咨询公司	埃及	306	50
14	菲利浦霍兹曼公司	德国	283	46
15	路易斯伯格集团	美国	274.7	46
16	帕森氏普林克赫夫公司	美国	271.4	27
17	雅可伯斯弗扎普公司	美国	262	19
18	雷神工程师和建设者公司	美国	259	28
19	EGIS集团	法国	258.9	36
20	NEDECO公司	荷兰	258	50
21	东洋工程公司	日本	252	46
22	四通韦博斯特	美国	246.6	37
23	阿夫阿路普合股公司	英国	238	36
24	布莱克维奇公司	美国	234	29
25	地球科技公司	美国	217	24
26	芒塞尔公司	英国	214.2	45
27	谟特麦克唐纳	英国	196.2	37
28	帕森氏公司	美国	189.6	17
29	西斯特拉公司	法国	157.3	47
30	太平洋咨询国际公司	日本	148	22
31	URS格雷纳乌德华德	美国	145.7	14
32	蒙特哥马利华特森公司	美国	145.7	26
33	海科路集团有限公司	英国	125.2	37
34	哥德联合公司	加拿大	122.7	38
35	大林工程公司	韩国	117.5	48
36	海德咨询集团公司	英国	111.1	33
37	日本科恩公司	日本	110.8	23

1998年世界最大100家国际工程设计咨询公司名录(二)

单位:百万美元

名次	公司名称	国别	国际市场营业额	% of total
38	特拉克特贝尔工程公司	比利时	110.6	23
39	ERM	美国	107.4	29
40	斯奈普罗盖蒂公司	意大利	105	29
41	劳吉伯集团	美国	104.8	25
42	戴姆斯默瑞集团	美国	103.7	13
43	伊莱克特洛威特工程服务公司	美国	101.7	42
44	WS爱特科斯公司	英国	101.3	14
45	斯科特威尔森公司	英国	101	35
46	COWI	丹麦	100.3	32
47	CH2M希尔公司	美国	98.8	11
48	哈兹联合公司	加拿大	98	40
49	三星工程公司	韩国	96.9	36
50	麦克德谟特国际公司	美国	96.9	36
51	TECHNIP集团	法国	89	37
52	卡尔博集团	丹麦	85.1	30
53	GTM集团	法国	78	35
54	霍赤蒂夫	德国	78	50
55	拉米耶国际公司	德国	75.1	27
56	HBG	荷兰	73	35
57	HASKONING	荷兰	71.2	30
58	中国化学工程公司	中国	70	38
59	斯堪的亚咨询国际公司	瑞典	69.4	32
60	哈泽工程公司	美国	66.1	34
61	萨根特朗迪 LLC	美国	64	19
62	BCEOM联合公司	法国	60.5	44
63	海耳姆斯公司	美国	60	17
64	凯普德累斯米奇公司	美国	60	15
65	现代工程公司	韩国	60	35
66	RAMBOLL集团	丹麦	58.5	23
67	劳克伍德绿色工程公司	美国	57.3	17
68	ICF恺撒国际公司	美国	57	8
69	LG工程公司	韩国	52.2	32
70	福特姆工程公司	芬兰	48	37
71	多奇咨询工程公司	德国	46.8	31
72	奈特皮索公司	英国	45.5	49
73	ENSR	美国	43	20
74	博恩斯R企业	美国	42.3	18

1998 年世界最大 100 家国际工程设计咨询公司名录(三)

单位:百万美元

名次	公 司 名 称	国 别	国际市场营业额	% of total
75	联合承包商国际公司	希腊	42.3	50
76	AHT 管理服务集团	德国	42.2	40
77	AMEC PLC	英国	42	9
78	霍尔麦斯纳沃公司	美国	40	21
79	泰克尼卡公司	西班牙	40	35
80	SK 工程建筑公司	韩国	39.1	27
81	管道工程公司	德国	38.5	26
82	联合咨询工程师	希腊	37.7	50
83	高夫恩泽公司	德国	37.1	37
84	斯坦泰克公司	加拿大	37	23
85	弗莱德瑞克 R 哈利斯公司	美国	36.7	17
86	菲科耐尔公司	德国	36	37
87	科坡罗公司	美国	34.1	25
88	KA 联合工程公司	黎巴嫩	34	45
89	RTKL 联合公司	美国	32	26
90	莫里森纳德森公司	美国	32	12
91	高点林德尔公司	英国	31.5	43
92	PCG	葡萄牙	31.2	39
93	斯哥德默尔	美国	31	26
94	戴兹默曼国际公司	美国	30.6	16
95	阿吉普兰公司	德国	30	21
96	雪山工程公司	澳大利亚	29.4	41
97	丹尼尔公司	美国	28	10
98	桑德韦尔国际公司	加拿大	27.9	36
99	阿克瑞斯国际公司	加拿大	26.3	36
100	公爵工程服务公司	美国	26.2	5

(对外贸易经济合作部国际贸易经济合作研究院)

1998 年国际 225 家最大承包公司营业额的市场分布

承包商国籍	公司数量	国外营业额		中　东		亚　洲		非　洲		欧　洲		美　国		加拿大		拉　美	
		亿美元	%	亿美元	%	亿美元	%	亿美元	%	亿美元	%	亿美元	%	亿美元	%	亿美元	%
美　国	64	282.46	24.3	48.96	34.3	76.01	22.5	19.71	5.8	70.66	23.0	NA	NA	22.4	0.75	44.72	42.2
加拿大	6	2.56	0.2	.0	.0	0.58	0.2	.0	.0	0.23	0.1	1.49	1.2	NA	NA	0.06	0.1
欧　洲	63	539.11	46.3	45.82	32.1	76.64	22.7	57.06	16.9	211.49	69.0	101.59	80.0	6.9	23.4	38.5	36.3
英　国	5	44.80	3.8	2.61	1.8	7.63	2.3	1.14	0.3	13.23	4.3	18.85	149	1.16	3.9	0.17	0.2
荷　兰	3	51.67	4.4	4.93	3.5	1.98	0.6	4.08	1.2	32.37	10.6	4.0	3.2	.0	.0	3.22	3.0
法　国	7	153.97	13.2	8.62	6.0	20.21	6.0	26.47	7.8	78.53	25.6	12.36	9.7	4.7	15.9	3.08	2.9
德　国	13	138.14	11.9	3.58	2.5	37.54	11.1	10.48	3.1	46.55	15.2	31.58	24.9	0.67	2.3	7.75	7.3
意大利	13	49.38	4.2	12.91	9.0	5.36	1.6	8.02	2.4	8.73	2.8	1.66	1.3	.0	.0	12.71	12.0
其　他	22	101.15	8.7	13.17	9.2	3.92	1.2	6.86	2.0	32.08	10.5	33.15	26.1	0.37	1.3	11.57	10.9
日　本	20	164.44	14.1	18.50	13.0	107.29	31.7	8.87	2.6	7.72	2.5	16.84	13.3	0.23	0.8	4.99	4.7
中　国	30	50.29	4.3	6.78	4.7	30.71	9.1	10.86	3.2	0.73	0.2	0.65	0.5	.0	.0	0.56	0.5
韩　国	11	47.00	4.0	9.21	6.4	28.69	8.5	2.29	0.7	1.87	0.6	0.36	0.3	.0	.0	4.58	4.3
所有其他	31	78.08	6.7	13.55	9.5	18.34	5.4	13.67	4.0	13.90	4.5	6.0	4.7	.0	0.7	12.61	11.9
全部公司	225	1163.94	100	142.83	100	338.26	100	112.46	100	306.59	100	126.93	100	29.54	100	106.0	100

资料来源：美国《工程新闻记录》1999 年 8 月 16 日。

（对外贸易经济合作部国际贸易经济合作研究院）

1998 年最大 200 家设计公司国际市场营业额

单位:亿美元,%

公司国别	公司数量	国际市场		中东		亚洲		非洲		欧洲		美国		加拿大		拉美	
		亿美元	%	亿美元	%	亿美元	%	亿美元	%	亿美元	%	亿美元	%	亿美元	%	亿美元	%
美国	80	73.59	43.4	7.27	42.8	21.7	43.4	3.60	25.7	28.5	52.3	NA	NA	2.63	89.4	9.62	59.8
加拿大	10	13.14	7.7	0.55	3.2	2.09	4.2	3.38	24.2	1.55	2.9	4.55	30.6	NA	NA	1.01	6.3
欧洲	74	62.49	36.8	4.62	27.2	16.0	31.9	4.31	30.8	23.5	43.1	8.93	60.1	0.26	8.8	3.69	22.9
英国	12	11.33	6.7	1.76	10.3	6.76	13.5	0.59	4.2	1.19	2.2	0.66	4.4	0.06	1.9	0.25	1.5
德国	16	7.59	4.5	0.36	2.1	1.79	3.5	0.89	6.4	1.39	2.6	2.25	15.1	0.02	0.7	0.93	5.8
法国	9	7.12	4.2	0.52	3.1	1.95	3.9	0.96	6.9	2.87	5.3	0.44	3.0	0.03	1.0	0.33	2.1
意大利	5	1.64	1.0	0.34	2.0	0.11	0.2	0.10	0.7	0.90	1.7	0.0	0.0	0.0	0.0	0.19	1.2
荷兰	10	21.94	12.9	0.93	5.5	3.77	7.5	0.88	6.3	10.6	19.4	5.01	33.7	0.06	1.9	0.71	4.4
其他	22	12.88	7.6	0.72	4.2	1.62	3.2	0.88	3.3	6.54	12.0	0.58	3.9	0.10	3.2	1.28	8.0
日本	13	9.93	5.9	1.52	8.9	6.08	12.1	1.39	9.9	0.26	0.5	0.17	1.2	0.01	0.3	0.51	3.2
其他	23	10.58	6.2	3.04	17.9	4.20	8.4	1.32	9.4	0.68	1.3	1.21	8.1	0.04	1.5	1.26	7.8
总计	200	169.72	100	17.0	100	50.1	100	14.0	100	54.4	100	14.9	100	2.94	100	16.1	100

资料来源:ENR,1999 年。

(对外贸易经济合作部国际贸易经济合作研究院)

1998年世界最大100家国际工程承包公司名录(一)

金额单位:亿美元

排名	公 司 名 称	国别(地区)	境外营业额	总营业额	新签合同额
1	贝克特尔集团	美国	60.22	97.71	125.13
2	福陆丹尼尔公司	美国	53.43	96.4	63.88
3	布依格公司	法国	52.80	125.2	135.43
4	斯勘斯卡公司	瑞士	48.25	69.39	100.82
5	克劳格布朗路特公司	美国	47.72	68.35	59.83
6	HBG	荷兰	35.40	46.97	47.93
7	GTM 集团	法国	34.38	74.30	76.52
8	SGE	法国	33.59	93.48	87.31
9	霍赤蒂夫	德国	33.12	69.14	69.55
10	菲利浦霍尔兹曼公司	德国	32.29	72.05	70.10
11	比尔芬格伯格建筑公司	德国	30.69	51.22	52.02
12	福斯特惠勒公司	美国	22.05	30.72	52.69
13	阿莫克公司	英国	21.80	53.50	46.60
14	JGC 公司	日本	20.54	24.66	27.84
15	泰克尼普集团	法国	19.43	20.04	23.00
16	千代田株式会社	日本	18.90	26.02	6.92
17	现代工程建设公司	韩国	18.47	41.69	40.67
18	大林组株式会社	日本	17.33	117.8	107.37
19	东洋工程公司	日本	16.82	19.73	10.06
20	西松建设株式会社	日本	16.43	58.29	45.17
21	鹿岛建设株式会社	日本	14.15	111.9	107.09
22	贝拉斯特奈德姆国际公司	荷兰	14.05	24.12	23.79
23	联合承包商国际公司	希腊	13.87	13.87	13.43
24	中国建筑工程总公司	中国	13.60	46.93	57.36
25	斯特拉巴格公司	德国	13.04	31.42	NA
26	欧德布莱克特公司	巴西	12.47	26.12	21.36
27	斯南普罗格蒂公司	意大利	12.40	18.85	NA
28	麦克德莫特国际公司	美国	12.19	20.68	16.82
29	德拉格多斯集团	西班牙	9.95	38.47	72.46
30	西松建设株式会社	日本	9.84	112.86	115.05
31	IMPREGILO 公司	意大利	9.66	19.92	NA
32	五洋建设株式会社	日本	9.64	44.71	41.12
33	沃尔特公司	德国	9.04	28.08	28.64
34	鲍佛贝蒂公司	英国	9.02	35.52	45.44
35	雷神工程建设者公司	美国	9.02	19.14	22.75
36	乔安诺帕拉斯克维德斯海外公司	塞浦路斯	8.29	8.29	9.83
37	PCL 建造商公司	美国	8.25	15.08	16.33

1998年世界最大100家国际工程承包公司名录(二)

金额单位:亿美元

排名	公司名称	国别(地区)	境外营业额	总营业额	新签合同额
38	泰勒伍德罗建筑公司	英国	8.20	20.55	NA
39	布莱克韦奇公司	美国	8.19	15.73	25.08
40	EIFFAGE公司	法国	8.13	59.85	NA
41	特克尼蒙特公司	意大利	7.36	8.36	6.87
42	泰琴特建筑集团	意大利	7.25	17.17	17.51
43	ABB鲁玛斯全球公司	美国	6.95	10.80	19.71
44	熊谷组株式会社	日本	6.19	76.76	75.03
45	穆雷罗伯特承包公司	南非	5.65	11.68	14.50
46	竹中工务店	日本	5.61	101.17	93.11
47	大成建设株式会社	日本	5.40	132.38	117.50
48	大林工程公司	韩国	5.33	5.94	6.81
49	帕森斯公司	美国	5.25	11.82	5.83
50	雅可伯斯弗扎普公司	美国	5.25	16.61	47.76
51	索勒唐希贝奇公司	法国	5.10	6.70	5.10
52	旭普林公司	德国	5.09	23.69	22.65
53	斯通韦伯斯特公司	美国	4.99	8.26	12.11
54	林德租赁地产服务公司	澳大利亚	4.96	15.96	16.10
55	SK工程建筑公司	韩国	4.89	13.00	9.09
56	芝加哥桥梁钢铁公司	美国	4.88	7.76	7.61
57	前田株式会社	日本	4.87	39.23	35.17
58	艾姆普勒萨斯ICA公司	墨西哥	4.84	13.86	10.57
59	中国石油工程建设(集团)公司	中国	4.83	6.09	5.60
60	三星工程公司	韩国	4.68	7.84	10.48
61	威斯弗雷塔格公司	德国	4.68	14.65	10.16
62	中国港湾建设(集团)总公司	中国	4.65	14.60	13.45
63	保罗建筑控股公司	中国香港	4.63	14.78	17.84
64	BESIX公司	比利时	4.58	7.30	8.75
65	阿斯塔尔蒂公司	意大利	4.56	9.19	8.07
66	蒂克霍夫威德曼公司	德国	4.43	23.55	21.38
67	莱顿控股有限公司	澳大利亚	4.41	19.11	20.74
68	弗莱彻建筑公司	新西兰	4.40	6.22	6.87
69	黑利特沃纳建筑公司	德国	4.20	20.01	22.12
70	间组株式会社	日本	4.08	43.72	37.51
71	NECSO公司	西班牙	4.00	24.96	17.76
72	恩卡建筑产业公司	土耳其	3.78	4.37	15.47
73	弗门多建筑承包公司	西班牙	3.67	38.65	71.15
74	大气社公司	日本	3.52	13.93	12.59

1998年世界最大100家国际工程承包公司名录(三)

金额单位:亿美元

排名	公司名称	国别(地区)	境外营业额	总营业额	新签合同额
75	安德拉德古铁雷斯建筑公司	巴西	3.40	11.08	12.49
76	科勒集团公司	英国	3.32	4.44	4.80
77	中国土木工程集团公司	中国	3.22	3.26	3.34
78	双龙工程建设公司	韩国	3.06	9.17	6.77
79	伊利斯顿建筑公司	美国	2.659	4.96	5.22
80	POSCO 工程建设公司	韩国	2.61	10.13	3.78
81	特克尼塔斯雷乌尼达斯公司	西班牙	2.51	2.71	2.97
82	莫里森纳德森公司	美国	2.49	16.31	40.21
83	雷英公司	英国	2.47	19.73	18.16
84	东亚建设株式会社	日本	2.44	21.35	25.94
85	泰克芬建筑安装公司	土耳其	2.43	4.18	4.08
86	近敦株式会社	日本	2.38	46.52	44.48
87	JDC 公司	日本	2.37	22.11	17.00
88	中国路桥公司	中国	2.36	8.98	12.83
89	RSEA 工程公司	中国台湾省	2.34	8.54	4.05
90	STFA 集团	土耳其	2.33	4.26	3.52
91	东急建筑株式会社	日本	2.33	35.38	26.10
92	YIT 公司	芬兰	2.30	13.60	NA
93	福特姆工程公司	芬兰	2.30	3.71	5.30
94	布菲特工业公司	墨西哥	2.25	5.61	7.82
95	大林工程公司	韩国	2.24	15.89	12.70
96	阿科海运公司	美国	2.23	4.18	4.41
97	荷利马装配集团公司	荷兰	2.22	3.99	3.61
98	现代工程公司	韩国	2.05	2.85	6.25
99	托尼构造公司	美国	2.05	14.92	16.38
100	中国东方电力公司	中国	2.03	2.87	0.36

(对外贸易经济合作部国际贸易经济合作研究院)

1998 年世界最大的 500 家企业（一）

位次 1998年	位次 1997年	公司名称	国别（地区）	收入 金额 百万美元	收入 比1997年变化（%）	利润 金额 百万美元	利润 位次	利润 比1997年变化（%）	资产 金额 百万美元	资产 位次	股东权益 金额 百万美元	股东权益 位次	雇员 人数	雇员 位次
1	1	通用汽车	美国	161315.0	(9.5)	2956.0	42	(55.9)	257389.0	48	14984.0	75	594000	4
2	17	戴姆勒－奔驰 1,2	德国	154615.0	116.1	5656.0	9	21.9	159738.0	74	35629.0	12	441502	6
3	2	福特汽车	美国	144416.0	(6.0)	22071.0	1	218.9	237545.0	53	23409.0	29	345175	8
4	8	沃尔－马特百货公司 3	美国	139208.0	16.7	4430.0	17	25.6	49271.0	162	21112.0	36	910000	2
5	3	三井物产 1,4	日本	109372.9	(23.3)	233.0	388	(13.3)	56264.2	146	5678.8	256	32961	342
6	6	伊藤忠商事 4	日本	108749.1	(14.1)	(266.7)	462	–	56846.9	143	2579.5	388	5775	480
7	4	三菱商事 1,4	日本	107184.4	(16.9)	244.0	328	(37.1)	74644.7	123	8016.7	178	36000	325
8	7	埃克森石油	美国	100697.0	(17.7)	6370.0	5	(24.7)	92630.0	109	43750.0	7	79000	164
9	12	通用电气	美国	100469.0	10.6	9296.0	2	13.3	355935.0	32	38880.0	11	293000	13
10	11	丰田汽车 4	日本	99740.1	4.8	2786.5	47	(24.7)	124562.2	90	52143.4	4	183879	40
11	5	荷兰皇家/壳牌	英/荷	93692.0	(26.9)	350.0	296	(95.5)	110068.0	98	54962.0	2	102000	115
12	9	丸红商事 4	日本	93568.6	(15.8)	(921.0)	481	(756.2)	54979.5	148	2989.0	368	65000	209
13	10	住友商事 1,4	日本	89020.7	–	(102.3)	444	–	45502.3	169	4809.6	293	30700	354
14	14	国际商用机器(IBM)	美国	81667.0	4.0	6328.0	6	3.9	86100.0	112	19433.0	43	291067	14
15	16	安盛	法国	78729.3	2.4	1702.4	85	25.5	451874.6	16	15894.7	67	87896	140
16	58	华旗集团 6	美国	76431.0	103.2	5807.0	8	87.1	668641.0	3	42708.0	8	170100	45
17	22	大众	德国	76306.6	16.8	1261.3	114	63.3	70458.7	125	10714.7	126	297916	12
18	15	日本电报电话 4	日本	76118.7	(1.1)	4715.1	14	99.7	147011.1	81	52464.1	3	224400	28
19	20	英国石油 7	英国	68304.0	(4.1)	3260.0	33	(19.4)	84500.0	116	41786.0	10	96650	128
20	13	日商岩井 4	日本	67741.7	(17.3)	(770.9)	479	(3215.0)	39327.8	193	1408.6	448	19461	406
21	19	日本生命保险公司 4	日本	66299.6	(7.1)	827.6	182	(60.9)	362808.5	31	8153.5	175	71015	186

1998 年世界最大的 500 家企业（二）

位次	位次	公司名称	国别（地区）	收入		利润			资产		股东权益		雇员	
1998年	1997年			金额 百万美元	比1997年变化（%）	金额 百万美元	位次	比1997年变化（%）	金额 百万美元	位次	金额 百万美元	位次	人数	位次
22	24	西门子 8	德国	66037.8	3.6	370.3	295	(74.1)	67024.0	130	17101.2	59	416000	7
23	28	联邦保险股份公司 9,10	德国	64874.7	–	2021.9	68	–	402411.4	23	26106.8	22	105676	110
24	21	日立 1,4	日本	62409.9	(9.0)	(2650.5)	490	(9457.5)	81698.4	118	24221.1	24	328351	10
25	27	美国邮政总局 G,8	美国	60072.0	3.2	550.0	242	(56.5)	54543.0	149	(810.0)	497	904636	3
26	23	松下电器 4	日本	59771.4	(7.0)	105.9	395	(86.1)	67022.6	131	29829.6	18	282153	17
27	29	菲利浦·莫利斯	美国	57813.0	3.0	5372.0	10	(14.9)	59920.0	137	16197.0	65	144000	59
28	57	荷兰国际集团	荷兰	56468.7	46.0	2909.7	44	38.3	463695.8	13	34140.8	15	82750	153
29	39	波音公司	美国	56154.0	22.6	1120.0	136	–	36672.0	199	12316.0	101	227000	26
30	32	美国电报电话	美国	53588.0	0.6	6398.0	4	37.9	59550.0	138	25522.0	23	107800	105
31	30	索尼 4	日本	53156.7	(3.4)	(1400.4)	102	(22.6)	53182.9	152	15397.2	71	177000	43
32	73	都市控股	德国	52126.4	59.0	326.1	302	2.1	22266.1	268	4230.8	314	181282	41
33	31	日产汽车 4	日本	51477.7	(3.7)	(216.8)	459	–	58405.0	140	10592.5	128	131260	70
34	33	菲亚特	意大利	50998.9	(3.0)	692.3	213	(51.2)	76256.6	121	15251.8	72	220549	30
35	163	美洲银行集团 11,12	美国	50777.0	133.6	5165.0	12	67.9	617679.0	5	45938.0	5	170975	44
36	36	雀巢	瑞士	49504.1	2.6	2960.7	41	7.2	41089.0	183	16761.5	62	231881	24
37	37	瑞士信贷银行	瑞士	49143.3	1.9	2116.9	62	673.5	474974.0	11	18809.3	47	62296	222
38	34	本田汽车 1,4	日本	48747.7	(0.3)	2386.5	55	12.4	42504.1	179	14892.2	77	112200	98
39	86	通用保险股份公司 13	意大利	48478.1	57.3	996.5	157	64.7	177946.6	69	7951.8	181	54598	250
40	26	美孚石油	美国	47678.0	(20.5)	1704.0	84	(47.9)	42754.0	178	18370.0	50	41500	303
41	47	惠普 14	美国	47061.0	9.7	2945.0	43	(5.6)	33673.0	211	16919.0	60	124600	77
42	51	德意志银行 10,15	德国	45165.0	10.7	1879.2	76	240.7	735808.2	1	20715.0	38	75306	174

1998 年世界最大的 500 家企业（三）

位次 1998年	位次 1997年	公司名称	国别（地区）	收入 金额 百万美元	收入 比1997年变化（%）	利润 金额 百万美元	利润 位次	利润 比1997年变化（%）	资产 金额 百万美元	资产 位次	股东权益 金额 百万美元	股东权益 位次	雇员 人数	雇员 位次
43	35	联合利华	英/荷	44908.0	(7.9)	3270.2	32	(40.1)	35807.0	203	5577.4	257	267000	20
44	42	州立农业保险	美国	44620.9	1.5	1319.7	109	(65.6)	111365.2	97	41793.9	9	76257	173
45	38	第一相互生命保险 4	日本	44485.6	(6.2)	557.2	241	(62.7)	252654.1	49	5332.7	272	63427	220
46	43	费巴集团 16	德国	43407.5	(1.1)	1330.1	107	(17.9)	50574.7	159	13818.2	88	116774	88
47	59	汇丰银行控股	英国	43338.3	15.6	4316.1	18	(21.5)	484735.4	10	27492.5	20	144521	57
48	41	东芝 4	日本	41470.9	(6.7)	(108.7)	446	(281.9)	50856.9	157	8868.0	162	198000	34
49	65	雷诺汽车	法国	41353.3	16.1	1499.8	95	61.3	44765.4	172	9229.6	155	138321	67
50	50	西尔斯·罗巴克	美国	41322.0	0.1	1048.0	146	(11.8)	37675.0	198	6066.0	240	324000	11
51	52	富士通 4	日本	41017.8	1.0	(106.7)	445	(334.4)	43163.4	175	9838	140	188000	39
52	46	东京电力 4	日本	39808.4	(7.4)	762.2	198	(30.9)	121641.7	92	13437	90	42170	298
53	56	德国电信 G	德国	39710.5	1.9	2494.2	52	30.9	93110.0	108	28534.0	19	195876	36
54	48	住友生命保险公司 4	日本	39535.4	(6.5)	962.6	164	(12.0)	205623.3	59	3883.3	333	66858	196
55	49	杜邦	美国	39130.0	(5.3)	4480.0	16	86.3	39724.0	190	14208.0	82	101000	117
56	116	苏黎士保险有限公司 10,17	瑞士	39115.0	47.8	802.0	189	(34.9)	214651.0	58	22994.0	32	68876	193
57	55	飞利普电气	荷兰	38455.6	(1.9)	6598.5	3	124.5	33055.4	216	16672.4	63	224573	27
58	189	CGU 18	英国	37588.5	91.9	825.4	183	35.5	176146.4	71	15039.9	74	52000	260
59	78	标致	法国	37539.8	17.3	538.8	243	–	40276.4	188	9982.5	137	156500	53
60	54	日本电气 1,4	日本	37234.6	(6.7)	(1235.7)	486	(467.3)	42017.0	181	7203.5	206	157773	52
61	64	宝洁 19	美国	37154.0	3.9	3780.0	22	10.7	30966.0	223	12236.0	104	110000	101
62	62	法国电气 G,20	法国	36672.9	–	264.1	321	–	113360.3	96	35220.1	14	116462	90

1998 年世界最大的 500 家企业（四）

位次	位次	公司名称	国别（地区）	收入		利润			资产		股东权益		雇员	
1998年	1997年			金额 百万美元	比1997年变化（%）	金额 百万美元	位次	比1997年变化（%）	金额 百万美元	位次	金额 百万美元	位次	人数	位次
63	53	莱茵集团 19	德国	36603.1	(9.0)	799.7	192	(1.8)	47383.6	165	5048.6	287	145467	55
64	94	教师保险和学院退休基金	美国	35889.1	1.23	840.4	180	(31.5)	249714.6	50	6323.2	235	5229	483
65	69	宝马汽车(BMW)	德国	35886.7	3.4	513.3	254	(28.6)	35978.4	202	7491.2	200	119913	83
66	44	埃尔夫·阿奎坦	法国	35864.0	(17.7)	600.8	231	(37.4)	43172.1	174	14378.9	81	85000	150
67	81	美林公司	美国	35853.0	13.0	1259.0	115	(33.9)	299804.0	38	10132.0	135	63800	218
68	131	慕尼黑再保险集团 21	德国	35464.5	–	489.0	263	–	130625.6	88	5428.9	267	27465	369
69	100	通用水管公司	法国	35292.3	23.3	1246.4	120	34.9	57513.3	142	9205.7	156	235610	23
70	75	苏黎士里昂自来水公司	法国	34873.5	6.9	1117.5	137	62.5	85112.9	115	10486.5	130	201000	32
71	60	美国万全人寿保险公司	美国	34427.0	(7.1)	1106.0	139	81.3	279422.0	43	20395.0	40	77806	168
72	97	荷兰银行	荷兰	34235.0	18.3	1992.6	70	0.9	507324.2	7	12589.5	98	105826	109
73	·	中国石化集团 G	中国	34025.2	29.2	194.2	354	(65.4)	51605.3	156	18686.2	48	1190000	1
74	104	普天寿公司	英国	33676.8	20.7	1458.6	99	6.4	197357.7	61	5406.0	271	22834	392
75	76	凯马特 3	美国	33674.0	4.6	568.0	237	90.6	14166.0	354	5979.0	244	278525	18
76	88	美国国际集团	美国	33296.0	9.1	3765.6	23	13.0	194398.0	62	27131.0	21	48000	279
77	70	农业信贷银行	法国	33022.4	(2.9)	2089.4	65	23.7	458688.8	15	24112.6	26	86100	145
78	61	国家碳化氢	意大利	32389.3	(12.4)	2593.7	50	(13.7)	48503.0	164	18956.3	46	78906	166
79	90	化学银行	美国	32379.0	6.6	3782.0	21	2.0	365875.0	29	23838.0	27	72683	180
80	227	抵押联合银行 10,22	德国	31816.2	88.4	2127.0	61	336.1	541031.8	6	13967.7	87	39447	311
81	40	德士古石油	美国	31707.0	(32.1)	578.0	236	(78.3)	28570.0	233	11833.0	113	24628	381
82	91	贝尔大西洋公司	美国	31565.9	4.5	2965.3	40	20.8	55143.9	147	13073.3	94	140439	63

1998 年世界最大的 500 家企业（五）

位次 1998年	位次 1997年	公司名称	国别（地区）	收入 金额 百万美元	收入 比1997年变化（%）	利润 金额 百万美元	利润 位次	利润 比1997年变化（%）	资产 金额 百万美元	资产 位次	股东权益 金额 百万美元	股东权益 位次	雇员 人数	雇员 位次
83	106	联邦国家抵押协会公司	美国	31498.0	13.4	3418.1	28	11.9	485013.8	9	15452.8	70	3800	489
84	143	福蒂斯公司 23,24	比/荷	31325.3	31.6	1521.0	91	47.2	396874.1	24	12150.1	106	59481	228
85	179	安龙天然气公司	美国	31260.0	54.2	703.0	212	569.5	29350.0	228	7048.0	214	17800	414
86	80	拜耳 10	德国	31197.2	(1.7)	1794.5	79	5.8	34352.5	208	14756.6	80	145100	56
87	132	康柏电脑	美国	31169.0	26.8	(2743.0)	492	(247.9)	23051.0	258	11351.0	119	80500	159
88	108	莫根－斯坦利集团 25	美国	31131.0	14.7	3276.0	31	26.7	317590.0	35	14119.0	84	49300	272
89	107	戴顿·赫德森 3	美国	30951.0	11.5	935.0	168	24.5	15666.0	333	5311.0	274	165750	49
90	45	东绵 4	日本	30934.9	(28.7)	21.5	426	–	18453.6	301	747.3	478	10409	461
91	67	东京－三菱公司 4	日本	30928.8	(11.0)	(679.8)	477	–	663627.8	4	23283.4	31	17878	413
92	83	阿西巴、勃朗、勃威力	瑞士	30872.2	(1.3)	1,305.0	112	128.1	32383.0	217	5959.0	245	199232	33
93	77	巴斯夫	德国	30731.6	(4.5)	1889.3	75	1.2	31355.2	222	15171.0	73	105945	108
94	87	J.C.佩尼公司 3	美国	30678.0	0.4	594.0	234	4.9	23638.0	254	7169.0	209	250000	22
95	96	家乐福公司	法国	30479.0	5.1	719.1	209	17.1	20410.1	282	4591.3	301	144142	58
96	136	家庭用具公司 3	美国	30219.0	25.1	1614.3	88	39.1	13465.0	336	8740.0	166	14000	64
97	117	朗讯科技 8	美国	30147.0	14.4	970.0	162	79.3	26720.0	241	5534.0	263	141600	61
98	99	兴业银行	法国	29762.1	3.6	750.7	202	(28.3)	450330.3	17	11939.3	111	58600	231
99	85	三菱电机 4	日本	29682.3	(4.1)	(348.5)	469	–	35365.4	204	4564.4	303	116479	89
100	93	摩托罗拉	美国	29398.0	(1.3)	(962.0)	482	(181.5)	28728.0	231	12222.0	105	133000	68
101	119	雷马克斯股份公司	荷兰	28871.0	11.4	596.5	232	24.6	13416.1	369	1823.1	425	162746	50
102	121	三星	韩国	28839.0	11.8	12.7	429	(19.0)	11186.1	398	1352.2	454	7400	475
103	71	鲜京公司	韩国	28808.9	(14.8)	50.2	415	(59.8)	28003.4	236	7565.1	197	24023	385

1998 年世界最大的 500 家企业（六）

位次	位次	公司名称	国别（地区）	收入		利润			资产		股东权益		雇员	
1998年	1997年			金额 百万美元	比1997年变化（%）	金额 百万美元	位次	比1997年变化（%）	金额 百万美元	位次	金额 百万美元	位次	人数	位次
104	128	SBC 电信公司	美国	28777.0	15.8	4023.0	20	172.9	45066.0	171	12780.0	97	129850	73
105	109	罗玻特－布施公司	德国	28610.3	5.9	445.6	275	(50.3)	21820.3	270	6788.7	223	189537	38
106	84	明治相互生命保险公司 4	日本	28476.1	(8.3)	234.8	335	(76.7)	146278.3	82	3303.7	352	37968	320
107	110	泰斯科 26	英国	28442.3	5.6	1004.5	153	21.5	13936.2	358	7012.2	217	131031	71
108	118	英国电信 4	英国	28323.7	7.7	4934.8	13	76.2	45136.4	170	24116.2	25	124700	76
109	114	克罗格 27	美国	28203.3	6.2	410.8	279	(0.2)	6700.1	449	(387.8)	495	140000	64
110	101	工业企业联合股份有限公司	德国	27921.6	(2.3)	660.8	225	33.3	34992.0	205	5030.5	288	85694	148
111	89	三菱汽车工业公司 4	日本	27480.4	(9.7)	44.3	417	–	25838.8	246	2985.6	369	26749	373
112	112	法国电信	法国	27408.7	2.1	2557.3	51	0.4	54197.1	150	19950.6	42	169099	48
113	234	瑞士银行公司	瑞士	27221.2	65.7	2090.6	64	–	687316.4	2	23538.6	28	48011	278
114	74	道达尔石油 28	法国	27058.8	(17.4)	985.6	159	(24.4)	27199.6	238	12147.8	107	57166	237
115	144	默克公司	美国	26898.2	13.8	5248.2	11	13.7	31853.4	218	12801.8	96	57300	236
116	63	雪佛龙	美国	26801.0	(26.3)	1976.0	71	(39.3)	36535.0	200	17671.0	53	39191	313
117	134	巴黎国民银行	法国	26786.6	10.1	1238.9	121	21.3	381405.7	28	11655.6	115	56286	240
118	137	沃尔沃	瑞典	26773.2	11.4	1086.1	141	(19.9)	25205.7	247	8391.3	169	70330	190
119	133	大都会人寿保险公司	美国	26735.0	9.7	1343.0	105	11.6	215346.0	57	14865.0	78	41700	301
120	111	日本兴业银行 4	日本	26495.8	(2.1)	(1418.2)	487	–	389783.0	26	13182.5	93	6024	479
121	125	英特尔公司	美国	26273.0	4.8	6068.0	7	(12.6)	31471.0	221	23377.0	30	64500	211
122	103	洛克希德·马丁公司	美国	26266.0	(6.4)	1001.0	155	(23.0)	28700.0	232	6137.0	238	170000	46

1998 年世界最大的 500 家企业（七）

位次 1998年	位次 1997年	公司名称	国别（地区）	收入 金额 百万美元	收入 比1997年变化（%）	利润 金额 百万美元	利润 位次	利润 比1997年变化（%）	资产 金额 百万美元	资产 位次	股东权益 金额 百万美元	股东权益 位次	雇员 人数	雇员 位次
123	124	意大利电信	意大利	26163.9	4.1	2,204.1	58	43.9	53094.1	153	19180.5	45	123966	79
124	127	全州保险公司	美国	25879.0	3.7	3294.0	30	6.1	87691.0	111	17240.0	57	53000	255
125	130	联合技术公司	美国	25715.0	4.1	1255.0	116	17.1	18375.0	303	4378.0	309	178800	42
126	66	委内瑞拉石油公司 G,1	委内瑞拉	25659.0	(26.6)	663.0	223	(86.1)	48816.0	163	31763.0	17	50821	263
127	323	第一银行 29	美国	25595.0	93.6	3108.0	35	138.0	261496.0	46	20560.0	39	91310	135
128	82	日棉实业 4	日本	25476.1	(18.8)	(170.3)	455	(512.2)	15936.1	330	1077.3	465	21621	398
129	146	通用电话电子	美国	25473.0	9.5	2172.0	59	(22.2)	43615.0	173	8766.0	165	120000	81
130	162	皇家太阳联合保险集团	英国	25435.8	16.4	757.5	199	(20.3)	107785.4	99	12094.8	108	44494	292
131	122	伊藤洋华堂 1,26	日本	25400.6	(0.8)	518.0	252	(10.2)	17402.1	312	8289.1	171	107066	107
132	141	J.圣斯伯雷公司 30	英国	25139.1	5.6	928.1	169	16.1	16222.8	326	7496.4	199	109245	103
133	178	巴西银行	巴西	25073.1	23.5	749.8	203	40.8	107227.3	101	5486.9	265	72350	182
134	92	赫司特	德国	24842.3	(17.3)	1077.2	143	39.0	33561.8	212	9966.0	139	96967	127
135	154	联合包裹运输公司	美国	24788.0	10.4	1741.0	82	91.5	17067.0	315	7173.0	208	333000	9
136	171	USX 公司	美国	24754.0	17.6	674.0	219	(31.8)	21133.0	273	6405.0	231	52279	259
137	156	劳埃德银行	英国	24514.2	9.9	3513.9	27	(8.1)	279529.1	42	12437.6	100	77196	169
138	152	塞夫韦商店	美国	24484.1	8.9	806.7	188	44.7	11389.6	396	3082.1	362	170000	46
139	135	蒂森－克虏伯 8,31	德国	24427.9	0.5	1066.7	144	(14.5)	17640.2	309	5120.6	284	116174	93
140	105	现代集团	韩国	24373.3	(12.4)	6.0	432	9.7	1012.1	500	238.2	491	660	500
141	160	价格成本公司 32	美国	24269.9	11.0	459.8	270	47.3	6259.8	455	2965.9	371	48825	274
142	129	CNP 保险公司	法国	24108.0	(2.8)	305.5	311	8.9	117981.6	93	3005.4	365	2506	495
143	138	康纳格拉 33	美国	23840.5	0.7	613.2	229	(0.3)	11702.8	389	2778.9	382	82629	154

1998 年世界最大的 500 家企业（八）

位次	位次	公司名称	国别（地区）	收入		利润			资产		股东权益		雇员	
1998年	1997年			金额 百万美元	比1997年变化（%）	金额 百万美元	位次	比1997年变化（%）	金额 百万美元	位次	金额 百万美元	位次	人数	位次
144	150	强生公司	美国	23657.0	4.5	3059.0	37	(7.4)	26211.0	243	13590.0	89	93100	131
145	79	阿尔卡特－阿尔斯通集团 34	法国	23640.7	(25.8)	2602.1	49	225.5	34801.9	207	11638.8	116	118272	86
146	120	大荣 26	日本	23573.5	(8.9)	(321.1)	467	(3334.8)	17039.8	317	572.5	482	10000	118
147	208	法国船坞公司集团	法国	23531.8	(1.3)	134.6	386	39.3	16144.9	328	3740.4	340	110000	101
148	159	爱立信	瑞典	23190.0	5.6	1639.7	87	4.9	20647.3	279	7781.7	185	103667	112
149	176	贝尔南方公司	美国	23123.0	12.5	3527.0	26	8.2	39410.0	192	16110.0	66	88450	139
150	153	沃尔特·迪斯尼公司 8	美国	22976.0	2.2	1850.0	77	(5.9)	41378.0	182	19388.9	44	117000	87
151	166	德累斯顿银行 10	德国	22779.5	–	1033.8	147	–	429170.7	18	12844.4	95	48950	273
152	123	三菱重工公司 4	日本	22784.5	(9.8)	141.5	382	(71.3)	40075.5	189	11291.5	120	65949	203
153	161	西德意志州银行 G	德国	22643.7	3.6	377.4	292	(5.7)	416093.0	20	8654.2	167	14072	440
154	155	里昂信贷银行 G	法国	22564.4	0.7	183.1	362	1.1	245256.8	51	5251.7	278	46371	285
155	95	百事可乐公司	美国	22348.0	(23.7)	1993.0	69	(7.0)	22660.0	264	6401.0	232	141000	62
156	191	三井相互生命保险公司 4	日本	22225.6	14.4	70.4	404	(86.5)	85868.2	113	847.2	474	22480	394
157	233	英格拉姆、麦罗克公司	美国	22034.0	32.9	245.2	327	26.6	6733.4	448	1399.3	451	14256	438
158	170	巴克莱银行	英国	21897.1	(3.6)	2212.7	57	19.5	365214.6	30	13183.0	92	80200	160
159	167	山多兹公司	瑞士	21873.8	1.8	4184.1	19	16.5	40283.9	187	22555.6	33	82449	155
160	·	中国工商银行	中国	21830.3	(13.8)	416.7	277	13.3	390915.7	25	22195.9	34	565619	5
161	197	普罗莫德工商	法国	21816.4	15.1	325.5	303	17.3	12310.0	385	2009.3	411	66233	200
162	158	意大利国家电力公司 G	意大利	21761.6	(1.9)	2466.5	54	26.5	56517.9	145	21743.2	35	84938	151

1998 年世界最大的 500 家企业(九)

位次 1998年	位次 1997年	公司名称	国别(地区)	收入 金额 百万美元	收入 比1997年变化(%)	利润 金额 百万美元	利润 位次	利润 比1997年变化(%)	资产 金额 百万美元	资产 位次	股东权益 金额 百万美元	股东权益 位次	雇员 人数	雇员 位次
163	169	国民西敏斯特银行	英国	21718.1	2.7	2680.2	48	143.5	309472.5	37	14144.8	83	64400	212
164	113	英美烟草工业公司 35	英国	21626.9	(19.3)	1055.9	145	(35.2)	12399.3	383	106.5	493	57884	233
165	148	佳能公司	日本	21616.2	(5.2)	838.0	181	(14.6)	24118.1	252	10177.7	133	79799	163
166	126	新日本制铁公司 4	日本	21587.8	(13.9)	89.8	400	85.4	37907.0	197	7420.1	202	85600	149
167	284	第一联合银行	美国	21543.0	50.3	2891.0	45	52.5	237363.0	54	17173.0	58	71486	183
168	183	西格纳	美国	21437.0	7.0	1292.0	113	19.0	114612.0	95	8277.0	172	49900	269
169	193	商业银行 10	德国	21216.9	10.9	991.3	158	37.4	383063.6	27	11812.9	114	32470	345
170	151	曼内斯曼公司	德国	21194.7	(6.0)	534.9	246	89.6	20372.2	283	6582.8	227	116247	92
171	173	中国银行 G	中国	21143.9	1.0	683.9	214	(39.3)	337929.1	33	17242.6	56	197547	35
172	198	卡特彼勒公司	美国	20977.0	10.8	1513.0	92	(9.1)	25128.0	249	5131.0	283	65824	204
173	172	住友银行 4	日本	20950.3	(0.3)	(4450.6)	498	–	464144.4	12	14835.4	79	14995	433
174	102	墨西哥石油 G	墨西哥	20891.1	(26.9)	(1108.2)	485	(210.5)	42782.3	177	17552.5	55	131433	69
175	174	麦克埃森公司 36,37	美国	20857.3	–	154.9	375	–	5607.5	465	1406.8	449	13700	445
176	229	普鲁伊萨格股份公司 8	德国	20810.8	23.8	276.4	318	28.1	9878.8	420	1538.1	437	66563	199
177	188	洛斯公司	美国	20713.0	5.4	464.8	267	(41.4)	70906.4	124	10201.2	132	34300	332
178	205	艾特纳人寿和意外事故保险公司	美国	20604.1	11.1	848.1	179	(5.9)	105148.1	102	11388.9	118	41100	305
179	437	富国银行 38	美国	20482.0	112.0	1950.0	72	44.3	202475.0	60	20759.0	37	92178	133
180	165	关西电力 4	日本	20317.9	(6.2)	410.7	280	(34.8)	60593.6	136	10669.4	127	26333	376
181	147	富士银行 4	日本	20109.7	(12.2)	(3301.7)	493	–	489128.7	8	18370.4	49	13976	442
182	209	施乐	美国	20019.0	10.2	395.0	287	(72.8)	30024.0	226	5544.0	261	92700	132

1998 年世界最大的 500 家企业（十）

位次 1998年	位次 1997年	公司名称	国别（地区）	收入 金额 百万美元	收入 比1997年变化（%）	利润 金额 百万美元	利润 位次	利润 比1997年变化（%）	资产 金额 百万美元	资产 位次	股东权益 金额 百万美元	股东权益 位次	雇员 人数	雇员 位次
183	185	塞拉里公司 19	美国	20011.0	1.4	(523.0)	472	(151.8)	10989.0	402	1816.0	426	140000	64
184	253	太平洋天然气和电力	美国	19942.0	29.5	719.0	210	0.4	33234.0	213	8066.0	177	23300	387
185	228	莱曼兄弟控股 25	美国	19894.0	17.8	736.0	206	13.8	154000.0	77	5413.0	270	8873	463
186	195	美国百货公司 3,39	美国	19866.7	3.8	233.7	336	(16.7)	8885.3	431	2699.2	385	121000	80
187	199	纽约人寿保险公司	美国	19848.9	5.0	752.9	201	15.7	90368.1	110	5575.5	258	7186	476
188	206	圣戈班化学公司	法国	19817.8	8.0	1219.9	124	26.5	26045.6	244	10297.0	131	114433	94
189	181	大都会饭店有限公司 19,40	英国	19808.1	–	1447.4	101	–	28790.3	230	7724.0	190	68445	194
190	203	哥伦比亚医药卫生	美国	19681.0	(5.5)	379.0	289	–	19429.0	292	7581.0	194	229500	25
191	301	雷锡昂	美国	19530.0	42.8	364.0	175	64.0	27939.0	237	10.856.3	124	108200	104
192	182	国际纸业	美国	19500.0	(3.0)	213.0	344	–	26356.0	242	8902.0	160	82000	156
193	239	西班牙电话公司 41	西班牙	19456.6	20.6	1456.8	100	12.2	58192.9	141	15851.5	68	101809	116
194	177	东日本铁路 4	日本	19430.0	(5.2)	171.6	367	(68.2)	61524.4	134	6474.8	229	87880	141
195	164	朝日相互生命保险公司 4	日本	19418.0	(10.4)	461.4	268	(20.0)	102812.3	106	1941.8	415	30480	356
196	204	美洲航空公司	美国	19205.0	3.4	1314.0	110	33.4	22303.0	267	6698.0	224	116300	91
197	194	吉之岛公司 42	日本	19171.3	0.1	140.9	383	52.7	13813.6	361	3002.7	366	44022	295
198	214	美国运输公司	美国	19132.0	7.7	2141.0	60	7.5	126933.0	89	9698.0	142	84732	152
199	149	三和银行 4	日本	18849.8	(17.3)	(3681.4)	495	–	425292.1	19	17579.8	54	13747	444
200	175	日本邮政局 G,43	日本	18849.2	(9.1)	161.3	372	(80.7)	75657.6	122	33621.8	16	141647	60
201	201	可口可乐公司	美国	18813.0	(0.3)	3533.0	25	(14.4)	19145.0	295	8403.0	168	29500	359

1998 年世界最大的 500 家企业（十一）

位次 1998 年	位次 1997 年	公司名称	国别（地区）	收入 金额 百万美元	收入 比 1997 年变化（%）	利润 金额 百万美元	利润 位次	利润 比 1997 年变化（%）	资产 金额 百万美元	资产 位次	股东权益 金额 百万美元	股东权益 位次	雇员 人数	雇员 位次
202	240	阿洪保险公司	荷兰	18726.9	16.7	1359.4	104	20.2	154042.1	76	9316.0	153	20723	402
203	139	BCE 公司	加拿大	18506.9	(22.8)	3099.5	36	–	20878.9	277	7776.2	187	58000	232
204	248	拉博银行	荷兰	18474.7	18.2	1020.0	149	4.4	293203.6	40	14110.7	85	45310	290
205	184	道氏化学	美国	18441.0	(7.9)	1310.0	111	(27.5)	23830.0	253	7429.0	201	39029	314
206	216	J.P.摩根公司	美国	18425.0	4.1	963.0	163	(34.3)	261067.0	47	11261.0	121	15674	431
207	142	三星电子	韩国	18394.2	(22.7)	(258.5)	461	–	20031.0	287	4143.8	319	62264	223
208	256	皮诺春天百货公司	法国	18364.6	20.2	564.7	239	15.5	14807.8	346	3623.1	344	80000	162
209	230	布里斯托－迈尔斯－施贵宝公司	美国	18283.6	9.5	3141.2	34	(2.0)	16272.5	324	7575.2	196	54700	248
210	363	戴尔计算机 3	美国	18243.0	48.0	1460.0	98	54.7	6877.0	446	2321.0	398	24400	383
211	265	桑坦德集团	西班牙	18168.4	22.1	951.8	166	26.0	182060.5	65	6011.5	242	71390	184
212	283	联邦家庭贷款抵押 44	美国	18048.0	25.3	1700.0	86	21.9	321421.0	34	10835.0	125	3200	491
213	157	工业复兴 G	意大利	17812.0	(19.9)	1831.7	78	(36.1)	66380.0	132	8169.5	174	112651	97
214	·	MCI WORLDCOM 45	美国	17678.0	140.5	(2669.0)	491	(795.7)	80193.0	119	44995.0	6	77000	171
215	237	公爵能源公司	美国	17610.0	8.0	1252.0	118	28.5	26806.0	240	8359.0	170	22000	396
216	·	北方电讯	加拿大	17575.0	–	(537.0)	473	–	19732.0	290	11565.0	117	75052	176
217	220	联合航空公司	美国	17561.0	1.1	821.0	185	(13.5)	18559.0	299	3281.0	353	95035	129
218	440	共和工业公司 46	美国	17487.3	69.7	449.5	261	13.6	13925.8	359	5424.2	268	47100	283
219	231	法国国营铁路公司 G	法国	17468.2	4.9	(51.5)	439	–	52537.4	154	4121.3	320	210437	31
220	222	瓦卢超级市场批发公司 26	美国	17420.5	1.3	191.3	357	(17.1)	4265.9	479	1305.6	455	50000	267

1998 年世界最大的 500 家企业（十二）

位次 1998年	位次 1997年	公司名称	国别（地区）	收入 金额 百万美元	收入 比1997年变化（%）	利润 金额 百万美元	利润 位次	利润 比1997年变化（%）	资产 金额 百万美元	资产 位次	股东权益 金额 百万美元	股东权益 位次	雇员 人数	雇员 位次
221	291	阿比国家公司	英国	17397.0	22.8	1753.6	80	12.3	295805.3	39	8996.7	158	27963	368
222	382	联合保健公司	美国	17355.0	47.2	(166.0)	454	(136.1)	9701.0	421	4038.0	324	30592	355
223	·	哈利伯顿公司	美国	17353.1	96.8	(14.7)	435	(103.2)	11112.0	399	4061.2	323	107800	105
224	115	兼松 4	日本	17198.6	(35.1)	(325.0)	468	–	10504.8	410	6.8	494	8142	468
225	241	亚美达科	美国	17154.0	7.2	3606.0	24	57.1	30299.0	224	10897.0	123	70525	188
226	219	布鲁肯希尔公司 33	澳大利亚	17148.0	2.2	(1024.8)	484	(418.1)	23224.1	256	7255.6	205	55000	246
227	266	斯普林德公司	美国	17134.3	15.2	414.5	278	(56.5)	33231.1	214	12448.3	99	64900	210
228	235	布依格公司	法国	17111.7	4.3	89.8	399	(30.5)	15120.3	339	1512.4	440	103350	114
229	212	桥石轮胎公司	日本	17107.0	(4.6)	800.2	191	147.3	17058.8	316	7017.2	215	97767	125
230	218	德意志巴恩公司 G	德国	17062.9	(2.9)	188.1	361	(17.6)	41053.6	184	9973.2	138	252468	21
231	225	纳比斯科控股公司 47	美国	17037.0	(0.1)	(577.0)	475	(251.4)	28892.0	229	8014.0	179	74000	178
232	334	罗奇控股公司 10	瑞士	17016.3	31.5	3030.4	39	–	40679.9	186	15772.8	69	66707	198
233	207	中部电力公司 4	日本	17015.1	(7.1)	321.9	305	(1.8)	52257.6	155	7890.8	182	20203	404
234	484	诺威奇联合公司	英国	16903.1	82.0	903.3	171	105.8	99577.4	107	9505.8	145	16500	422
235	257	电子数据系统公司	美国	16891.0	10.9	743.4	204	1.8	11526.1	393	5916.5	247	120000	81
236	345	布拉德斯科银行	巴西	16758.1	32.3	872.7	174	13.2	56735.5	144	5231.3	279	64226	213
237	168	樱花樱花 4	日本	16735.9	(21.4)	(3749.5)	496	–	413833.7	22	18359.2	51	16330	425
238	·	澳相互节检社	澳大利亚	16687.3	–	(413.4)	470	–	69234.6	126	5320.5	273	4991	485
239	215	东京海上火灾保险公司 4	日本	16630.3	(6.3)	243.7	329	(17.9)	47085.1	166	5754.7	253	14869	435

1998 年世界最大的 500 家企业（十三）

位次 1998年	位次 1997年	公司名称	国别（地区）	收入 金额 百万美元	收入 比1997年变化（%）	利润 金额 百万美元	利润 位次	利润 比1997年变化（%）	资产 金额 百万美元	资产 位次	股东权益 金额 百万美元	股东权益 位次	雇员 人数	雇员 位次
240	226	弗朗茨－哈尼尔股份有限公司	德国	16540.0	(2.2)	170.5	368	(4.0)	6878.2	445	1101.5	464	39410	312
241	267	瑞士再保险	瑞士	16416.7	10.6	1725.0	83	18.3	64283.9	133	9471.3	147	8770	464
242	259	巴黎巴银行	法国	16365.6	7.5	1114.3	138	(1.1)	311308.6	36	10510.7	129	21100	399
243	186	第一劝业银行 4	日本	16320.3	(17.2)	(3483.7)	494	－	463440.0	14	20289.2	41	16090	428
244	247	德国邮政总局 G	德国	16307.4	4.2	172.8	365	－	14858.1	344	3201.3	356	223863	29
245	140	俄罗斯天然气工业	俄罗斯	16220.1	(32.3)	(4023.8)	497	(202.2)	54079.5	151	35248.7	13	278400	19
246	297	阿－丹－米公司 19	美国	16108.6	16.3	403.6	282	7.0	13833.5	360	6504.9	228	23132	388
247	232	马自达汽车 4	日本	16093.4	(3.2)	302.8	312	－	12487.5	381	3190.7	357	31851	347
248	338	哈利法克斯住宅互助协会	英国	16061.1	25.4	1940.9	73	13.2	240555.7	52	11895.2	112	31442	352
249	200	安田相互人寿保险公司 4	日本	16054.6	(15.0)	682.9	215	(17.3)	82499.5	117	2067.7	408	22934	390
250	271	埃伯森 3,48	美国	16005.1	9.0	567.2	238	9.7	6234.0	456	2810.5	380	100000	118
251	415	卡迪纳尔保健品公司 19	美国	15918.1	18.5	247.1	326	33.8	3961.1	484	1625.2	430	11200	456
252	392	联邦快递公司 33	美国	15872.8	37.8	503.0	259	39.3	9686.1	423	3961.2	328	113000	96
253	246	三洋电器 3	美国	15833.0	1.1	662.0	224	23.5	13464.0	367	5709.0	255	118800	85
254	249	法国邮政总局 G	法国	15830.7	1.9	57.1	411	474.9	14446.7	351	1548.9	436	288015	15
255	330	卡西诺集团	法国	15741.2	20.5	239.5	331	25.5	9055.3	429	2344.0	395	63491	219
256	282	鲁尔煤矿	德国	15625.7	8.5	193.6	355	13.8	19617.6	291	1849.8	421	104330	111
257	224	莱普索尔	西班牙	15610.1	(8.6)	974.3	161	13.1	20175.6	285	7095.4	213	23762	386

1998 年世界最大的 500 家企业(十四)

位次 1998年	位次 1997年	公司名称	国别(地区)	收入 金额 百万美元	收入 比1997年变化(%)	利润 金额 百万美元	利润 位次	利润 比1997年变化(%)	资产 金额 百万美元	资产 位次	股东权益 金额 百万美元	股东权益 位次	雇员 人数	雇员 位次
258	·	INVENSYS 4,49	英国	15573.8	–	(173.7)	456	–	15746.6	331	12313.2	102	130626	72
259	211	巴西石油公司 G	巴西	15527.3	(14.0)	1196.9	125	(14.6)	33185.9	215	17987.6	52	38235	317
260	263	瑞士养老金和人寿保险公司	瑞士	15518.1	3.9	188.6	360	79.4	85543.1	114	5201.0	280	8616	466
261	311	美国铝公司 50	美国	15489.4	14.9	853.0	176	5.9	17462.5	311	6055.9	241	103500	113
262	210	帝国化学工业公司	英国	15391.4	(15.1)	319.9	306	(24.6)	15030.0	342	247.9	490	60600	226
263	281	西斯科 19	美国	15327.5	6.0	296.8	313	(1.9)	3780.2	486	1356.8	453	33400	337
264	314	沃尔格林公司 32	美国	15307.0	14.5	511.0	256	17.2	4902.0	473	2849.0	378	75000	177
265	328	CVS	美国	15273.6	16.7	396.4	286	951.5	6736.2	447	3110.6	361	97000	126
266	279	爱理德·西格诺	美国	15128.0	4.5	1331.0	106	13.8	15560.0	335	5297.0	276	70400	189
267	322	巴伐利亚州立银行	德国	15081.0	13.8	338.8	300	2.0	285333.3	41	7107.4	210	7425	474
268	254	弗莱明	美国	15069.3	(2.0)	(510.6)	471	(2110.8)	3491.0	488	570.0	483	38100	318
269	317	哈特福特集团	美国	15022.0	12.9	1015.0	150	(23.8)	150632.0	79	6423.0	230	22000	396
270	261	明尼苏达矿业制造公司	美国	15021.0	(0.3)	1175.0	128	(44.6)	14153.0	355	5963.0	246	73564	179
271	292	日本烟草 G,4	日本	15009.5	6.3	583.9	235	23.5	18815.8	297	11955.3	110	31000	353
272	·	FRED MEYER 3,51	美国	14878.8	171.5	(162.8)	453	(1445.9)	10151.2	415	2314.4	399	92000	134
273	276	标准人寿保险公司 52	英国	14830.9	2.1	N.A.		–	107712.9	100	N.A.		11016	458
274	268	丽都有限公司	瑞典	14776.7	(0.1)	499.8	260	984.8	10269.5	413	3018.4	363	99322	121
275	290	英国航空公司 4	英国	14748.3	3.9	340.8	299	(54.9)	20700.6	278	5415.7	269	64051	215
276	·	德克萨斯公用事业公司	美国	14736.0	85.5	740.0	205	12.0	39514.0	191	8246.0	173	22055	395
277	245	三洋电器 1,4	日本	14727.0	(6.1)	(202.5)	457	(301.8)	22479.7	265	5873.1	249	77071	170

1998 年世界最大的 500 家企业（十五）

位次 1998年	位次 1997年	公司名称	国别（地区）	收入 金额 百万美元	收入 比1997年变化（%）	利润 金额 百万美元	利润 位次	利润 比1997年变化（%）	资产 金额 百万美元	资产 位次	股东权益 金额 百万美元	股东权益 位次	雇员 人数	雇员 位次
278	287	印度石油 G,4	印度	14719.4	3.3	528.8	249	14.6	6229.8	457	2904.7	375	34100	334
279	252	罗纳－普朗克公司	法国	14714.4	(4.5)	874.2	173	–	28553.0	234	9498.3	146	65180	208
280	354	辉瑞有限公司	美国	14704.0	17.6	3351.0	29	51.4	18302.0	304	8810.0	164	46000	289
281	312	西北相互人寿保险公司	美国	14644.9	9.0	808.9	187	17.4	77995.7	120	4740.8	295	4117	488
282	318	时代－华纳	美国	14582.0	9.7	168.0	369	(31.7)	31640.0	220	8852.0	163	38100	318
283	449	诺基亚 10	芬兰	14542.9	43.5	1910.4	74	58.4	11782.9	388	5999.9	243	44543	291
284	400	微软公司 19	美国	14484.0	27.5	4490.0	15	30.0	22357.0	266	16627.0	64	27055	371
285	180	三星生命保险公司 4	韩国	14407.4	(28.9)	68.2	406	4.5	30228.8	225	489.8	485	8080	469
286	262	日理公司 26	日本	14402.2	(4.0)	(276.6)	463	(432.6)	15240.1	338	1928.9	417	41677	302
287	349	毕尔巴鄂－比斯开银行	西班牙	14387.4	14.3	1095.5	140	22.6	157328.8	75	7778.6	186	69999	191
288	260	达诺纳集团	法国	14384.0	(5.1)	665.1	221	5.9	17662.1	308	7648.1	192	78945	165
289	242	科尔斯－梅耶 53	澳大利亚	14350.4	(9.7)	249.2	325	(17.8)	4355.2	478	1600.9	431	154829	54
290	280	DELHAIZE “LE LION”	比利时	14329.4	(0.9)	162.4	370	17.8	5332.6	467	1070.1	466	118942	84
291	299	储蓄银行集团	法国	14324.0	4.1	401.3	284	15.9	237158.2	55	10049.6	136	38500	315
292	296	蒙特爱迪生	意大利	14312.0	3.0	377.5	291	(56.8)	19400.5	293	5086.2	286	28600	364
293	223	日本石油 4,54	日本	14290.7	(16.5)	76.1	403	(18.7)	24608.1	251	5541.6	262	10539	460
294	313	DYNEGY 55	美国	14258.0	6.6	108.4	393	–	5260.0	468	1128.0	461	2400	496
295	380	托尔尼奥保罗银行 56	意大利	14245.8	20.0	1012.8	152	928.5	185732.9	64	10171.1	134	24527	382
296	244	日本钢管 4	日本	14150.6	(10.2)	(849.3)	480	(830.2)	22723.5	261	2768.9	383	42000	300
297	304	德尔塔航空公司 19	美国	14138.0	4.0	1001.0	155	17.2	14603.0	350	4023.0	325	70846	187
298	217	斯塔特石油公司 G,10	挪威	14131.8	(19.8)	35.9	422	(94.1)	18621.2	298	5306.0	275	18133	412

1998年世界最大的500家企业（十六）

位次	位次	公司名称	国别（地区）	收入		利润			资产		股东权益		雇员	
1998年	1997年			金额 百万美元	比1997年变化（%）	金额 百万美元	位次	比1997年变化（%）	金额 百万美元	位次	金额 百万美元	位次	人数	位次
299	302	米其林	法国	13884.3	1.7	595.6	233	(10.5)	15070.6	340	4581.9	302	127241	74
300	264	大成 4	日本	13870.6	(7.0)	(44.4)	437	–	23185.2	257	2388.1	394	21091	400
301	435	伯克什·哈索维公司	美国	13832.0	32.6	2830.0	46	48.8	122237.0	91	57403.0	1	47566	281
302	316	曼柴油机有限公司 19	德国	13826.7	3.6	318.9	307	61.8	8366.8	432	2291.6	400	64054	214
303	339	迪尔公司 14	美国	13821.5	8.1	1021.4	148	6.4	18001.5	306	4079.8	322	37000	322
304	213	中国化工进出口总公司 G	中国	13793.3	(22.7)	67.6	407	5.9	4953.7	472	1040.1	468	8219	467
305	306	日本电装公司 4	日本	13760.1	1.3	461.3	269	(20.4)	16186.9	327	9466.0	148	72359	181
306	387	伯根·伯伦斯维格公司 8	美国	13720.0	17.7	3.1	433	(96.2)	3003.2	494	629.1	481	5400	482
307	274	夏普 4	日本	13656.0	(6.4)	36.2	421	(82.1)	17070.8	314	7973.1	180	48820	275
308	324	温–迪克西百货公司 19	美国	13617.5	3.0	198.6	352	(2.8)	3068.7	492	1368.9	452	98000	124
309	358	柏林银行 G	德国	13608.4	9.5	32.1	423	(80.2)	221632.3	56	4793.6	294	16673	420
310	362	阿克苏诺贝尔公司	荷兰	13607.1	10.4	664.3	222	(19.7)	14043.5	357	2136.5	406	85900	147
311	308	马克斯–斯番塞 4	英国	13605.2	0.5	615.6	228	(54.8)	12598.2	379	7883.6	184	51306	261
312	457	斯勘的亚集团	瑞典	13543.5	18.9	156.2	374	(64.9)	46202.1	168	1846.4	422	10185	462
313	365	加拿大帝国商业银行 14	加拿大	13536.1	10.1	721.8	208	(36.1)	181916.4	66	7198.3	207	47171	282
314	238	丰田同商公司 4	日本	13519.1	(17.0)	7.3	431	(86.5)	5980.2	460	1134.3	460	6420	478
315	337	加拿大皇家银行 14	加拿大	13506.7	5.4	1246.7	119	1.9	177371.5	70	7687.0	191	53468	254
316	286	福陆 14	美国	13504.8	(5.6)	235.5	334	61.1	5019.2	471	1525.6	439	56886	238
317	289	美国家庭用品公司	美国	13462.7	(5.2)	2474.3	53	21.1	21079.1	275	9614.8	144	52984	257

1998 年世界最大的 500 家企业（十七）

位次 1998年	位次 1997年	公司名称	国别（地区）	收入 金额 百万美元	收入 比1997年变化（%）	利润 金额 百万美元	利润 位次	利润 比1997年变化（%）	资产 金额 百万美元	资产 位次	股东权益 金额 百万美元	股东权益 位次	雇员 人数	雇员 位次
318	364	埃默森电器 8	美国	13447.2	9.3	1228.6	123	9.5	12659.8	377	5803.3	250	111800	99
319	372	伊塔乌投资银行	巴西	13415.9	11.4	404.2	281	(6.4)	42368.4	180	2469.9	392	52304	258
320	401	可口可乐企业	美国	13414.0	18.9	142.0	381	(17.0)	21132.0	274	2438.0	393	66199	201
321	344	五月百货公司 3	美国	13413.0	5.7	849.0	177	9.5	10553.0	406	3836.0	336	127000	75
322	269	伊斯曼柯达	美国	13406.0	(8.9)	1390.0	103	27770.0	14733.0	347	3988.0	327	86200	144
323	341	斯密克兰－比彻姆	英国	13395.8	4.9	1004.4	154	(43.2)	15001.7	343	2906.8	374	59500	227
324	236	LG 国际公司	韩国	13388.2	(18.2)	8.8	430	–	1371.6	499	219.9	492	2288	497
325	495	意大利信贷银行 57	意大利	13317.2	45.9	224.8	341	(20.4)	172035.3	72	7511.4	198	35600	328
326	329	葛兰素医药公司	英国	13231.7	1.2	3043.1	38	0.4	15550.7	336	4495.8	306	55273	245
327	327	乔治－太平洋	美国	13223.0	1.0	98.0	397	42.0	11538.0	392	3209.0	355	46500	284
328	192	大西洋富田公司	美国	13195.0	(31.5)	452.0	272	(74.5)	25199.0	248	7580.0	195	18400	409
329	385	自由相互保险公司	美国	13166.0	12.8	385.0	288	(26.1)	49317.0	161	6874.0	219	37000	322
330	393	无线电缆公司 4	英国	13141.9	14.3	1502.1	94	(29.0)	28227.6	235	7378.5	204	50671	265
331	347	全国保险企业公司	美国	13105.0	3.6	1195.7	126	48.4	104642.4	104	11061.0	122	32815	343
332	·	INTESA 银行 58	意大利	13067.8	–	650.3	226	–	179617.2	67	4966.2	291	35681	326
333	402	澳大利亚新闻公司 19	澳大利亚	12994.9	15.4	1153.5	132	104.7	33736.2	210	16813.6	61	33400	337
334	243	鹿岛建设 4	日本	12978.0	(17.8)	(1553.4)	488	–	20284.1	284	1474.1	444	13210	448
335	·	GROUPAMA 59	法国	12941.2	–	172.6	366	–	68888.0	127	5166.3	282	25700	380
336	305	挪威水电 G,1	挪威	12908.0	(6.5)	497.2	262	(32.4)	16271.8	325	6335.8	233	39552	310
337	315	汉沙集团 10	德国	12876.9	–	813.2	186	–	14433.8	352	3879.5	334	54867	247
338	277	日本通运 4	日本	12854.0	(11.4)	196.7	353	(10.7)	9692.5	422	2849.9	377	59475	229

1998 年世界最大的 500 家企业(十八)

位次	位次	公司名称	国别(地区)	收入		利润			资产		股东权益		雇员	
1998年	1997年			金额 百万美元	比1997年变化(%)	金额 百万美元	位次	比1997年变化(%)	金额 百万美元	位次	金额 百万美元	位次	人数	位次
339	320	艾奥瓦牛肉罐头公司	美国	12848.6	(3.1)	190.0	359	62.4	3008.1	493	1400.9	450	40000	309
340	·	达纳公司	美国	12838.7	46.4	534.1	248	44.7	10137.5	416	2939.2	373	86400	143
341	295	贝图斯曼公司 19	德国	12803.2	(8.6)	480.2	265	(3.8)	7629.1	439	2145.6	405	57807	234
342	381	奥雷阿尔公司	法国	12785.9	8.0	756.1	200	10.7	12374.5	384	5802.4	251	49665	270
343	356	澳大利亚国民银行 8	澳大利亚	12755.8	2.5	1325.6	108	(22.5)	149066.7	80	9333.8	152	46300	286
344	·	WASHINGTON MUTUAL	美国	12745.6	69.4	1486.9	97	208.6	165493.3	73	9344.4	151	27330	370
345	·	RITE AID 26	美国	12731.9	11.9	143.7	379	(54.6)	10421.7	411	2953.7	372	89900	136
346	·	废物处理公司 60	美国	12703.5	386.0	(770.7)	478	(388.6)	22715.2	262	4372.5	310	67676	195
347	442	泛加输油管道公司	加拿大	12690.7	23.4	291.2	316	(11.8)	16640.2	319	4710.0	296	5218	484
348	273	五十铃汽车公司 4	日本	12666.8	(13.6)	48.8	416	(0.8)	13739.3	363	1500.9	443	28508	365
349	303	太阳相互人寿保险公司 4	日本	12649.0	(7.0)	66.9	408	(46.7)	59111.5	139	1116.7	463	16261	426
350	325	固特异型轮胎橡胶公司	美国	12648.7	(3.8)	682.3	216	22.1	10589.3	408	3745.8	339	98265	123
351	399	强生控制器公司 8	美国	12586.8	10.5	337.7	301	17.1	7942.1	435	1941.4	416	89000	138
352	·	UTILICORP UNITED	美国	12563.4	40.7	132.2	388	8.3	5991.5	459	1446.3	446	4300	486
353	377	米格罗百货公司	瑞士	12557.7	5.6	275.3	319	43.7	10847.2	403	N.A.		76876	172
354	407	阿斯达集团 61	英国	12539.4	13.0	504.4	258	2.5	6444.3	451	3812.4	337	48072	277
355	·	ALSTOM 4,62	法国	12538.0	–	270.0	320	–	21233.0	272	1506.0	441	113707	951
356	285	清水建设 4	日本	12511.9	(12.6)	(994.7)	483	–	18487.4	300	1425.4	447	14969	434

1998 年世界最大的 500 家企业（十九）

位次 1998年	位次 1997年	公司名称	国别（地区）	收入 金额 百万美元	收入 比1997年变化（%）	利润 金额 百万美元	利润 位次	利润 比1997年变化（%）	资产 金额 百万美元	资产 位次	股东权益 金额 百万美元	股东权益 位次	雇员 人数	雇员 位次
357	275	农林中央银行 4	日本	12487.2	(14.4)	452.2	271	(58.6)	414618.9	21	14044.5	86	2858	493
358	379	雅培制药公司	美国	12477.8	5.0	2333.2	56	11.4	13216.2	372	5713.7	254	56236	241
359	360	奥托邮购两合公司 63	德国	12436.7	0.4	201.0	351	(20.4)	5147.2	470	973.3	470	58939	230
360	395	塞夫韦商店 4	英国	12425.1	8.4	402.3	283	1.7	7201.3	442	3427.1	349	55706	242
361	397	麦当劳	美国	12421.4	8.9	1550.1	89	(5.6)	19784.0	289	9464.7	149	284000	16
362	309	中国粮油食品进出口总公司 G	中国	12401.9	(8.3)	93.2	398	(15.5)	4770.0	474	1599.7	432	28000	367
363	336	英国煤气公司	英国	12399.7	(3.5)	147.5	378	–	6635.6	450	1450.9	445	16427	423
364	·	美国西部公司 64	美国	12378.0	–	1508.0	93	–	18407.0	302	755.0	476	54483	251
365	430	KINGFISHER 3	英国	12370.8	18.0	724.7	207	14.5	10075.4	417	3697.4	342	75264	175
366	·	TYCO INTERNATIONAL 1,8	美国	12311.3	–	1174.7	129	–	16526.6	320	6136.9	239	87000	142
367	351	金伯利－克拉克	美国	12297.8	(2.0)	1165.8	130	29.3	11510.3	394	3887.2	332	54700	248
368	388	拉格代尔集团	法国	12283.1	5.4	311.1	309	31.6	11457.9	395	2264.2	401	49961	268
369	335	日本航空公司 4	日本	12252.1	(4.9)	209.5	345	–	16511.3	321	1831.8	423	19455	407
370	448	LOW'S 3	美国	12244.9	20.8	482.4	264	34.9	6344.7	453	3136.0	359	65706	205
371	·	LEGAL & GENERAL	英国	12134.5	20.2	674.6	218	(16.3)	130762.1	87	4492.5	307	7899	472
372	390	亨克尔公司 10	德国	12127.8	4.8	373.5	293	(39.0)	10721.3	405	3018.2	364	56619	239
373	·	苏格兰皇家银行 8	英国	12103.7	29.2	1149.3	133	38.1	135411.3	84	5018.7	289	31680	350
374	310	维亚康田有限公司	美国	12096.1	(10.4)	(122.4)	448	(115.4)	23613.0	255	12000.0	109	80090	161
375	405	公众超级市场	美国	12067.1	7.5	378.3	290	6.7	3617.3	487	2327.6	396	81800	157

1998 年世界最大的 500 家企业（二十）

位次 1998年	位次 1997年	公司名称	国别（地区）	收入 金额 百万美元	收入 比1997年变化（%）	利润 金额 百万美元	利润 位次	利润 比1997年变化（%）	资产 金额 百万美元	资产 位次	股东权益 金额 百万美元	股东权益 位次	雇员 人数	雇员 位次
376	366	纽约银行家信托公司 65	美国	12048.0	(1.1)	(73.0)	442	(108.4)	133115.0	85	4696.0	297	20541	403
377	333	东北电力公司 4	日本	12041.8	(7.5)	294.5	314	(23.7)	34133.3	209	5564.7	260	16371	424
378	319	托斯科	美国	12021.5	(9.5)	106.2	394	(50.1)	5842.8	462	1913.0	418	26300	377
379	421	施伦伯格公司 1	美国	11997.3	11.6	1014.2	151	(21.7)	16077.9	329	8119.1	176	64000	216
380	340	电通公司	日本	11992.5	(6.1)	53.0	412	(28.3)	7538.5	440	2540.1	390	5553	481
381	418	金属股份公司 8	德国	11991.2	10.7	151.2	377	18.5	4143.7	480	449.4	484	26188	379
382	293	三菱化工 4	日本	11982.5	(15.1)	(215.3)	458	(571.5)	16771.4	318	3583.5	346	17576	415
383	419	汤普森－拉莫－伍尔德里奇公司	美国	11886.0	9.7	477.0	266	–	7169.0	443	1878.0	420	78000	167
384	378	TELSTRA G,19	澳大利亚	11865.4	(0.2)	2060.1	66	71.3	16390.1	322	6831.6	221	66760	197
385	357	伍尔沃特公司 19	澳大利亚	11851.6	(4.8)	191.7	356	(5.0)	2529.0	495	848.1	473	100000	118
386	251	菲利浦石油	美国	11845.0	(23.2)	237.0	333	(75.3)	14216.0	353	4219.0	315	17300	417
387	298	比利时石油金融 28	比利时	11793.8	(14.7)	508.1	257	(17.6)	11313.9	397	4674.7	298	14489	436
388	425	蒙特利尔银行 14	加拿大	11782.9	11.4	922.7	170	(2.9)	143882.2	83	6857.0	220	33400	337
389	376	英国航空航天公司	英国	11672.0	(2.0)	1147.0	134	334.9	15058.2	341	3361.1	351	47900	280
390	342	日本交通会社 4	日本	11633.6	(8.8)	22.4	425	(2.3)	3389.1	490	481.8	486	12227	452
391	386	大同人寿保险公司 4	日本	11562.2	(0.9)	346.9	297	(11.4)	46450.0	167	1195.0	457	22866	391
392	202	千代田相互人寿保险公司 4	日本	11560.5	(38.7)	154.3	376	19.1	39170.5	194	750.4	477	17066	418
393	492	达信公司	美国	11549.0	9.5	608.0	230	9.0	13721.0	364	2997.0	367	64000	216
394	·	TECH DATA 3	美国	11529.0	63.4	129.0	390	44.1	3842.1	485	967.7	471	8045	470

1998 年世界最大的 500 家企业（二十一）

位次 1998年	位次 1997年	公司名称	国别（地区）	收入 金额 百万美元	收入 比1997年变化（%）	利润 金额 百万美元	利润 位次	利润 比1997年变化（%）	资产 金额 百万美元	资产 位次	股东权益 金额 百万美元	股东权益 位次	雇员 人数	雇员 位次
395	478	ENTERGY	美国	11494.8	20.2	785.6	194	161.1	22848.0	260	7107.0	211	12757	450
396	·	RELIANT ENERGY 66	美国	11488.5	67.1	(141.1)	452	(133.5)	19138.5	296	4321.9	311	12916	449
397	·	STORA ENSO 10	芬兰	11447.8	103.1	208.5	347	86.9	18099.3	305	6216.1	237	40679	307
398	348	南方天然气公司	美国	11403.0	(9.6)	977.0	160	0.5	36192.0	201	9797.0	141	31848	348
399	368	铃木汽车公司 4	日本	11389.5	(6.1)	190.6	358	(22.4)	9556.2	426	3698.4	341	13896	443
400	404	富士摄影胶片公司 4	日本	11248.5	0.2	559.7	240	(22.7)	17894.6	307	12263.6	103	37551	321
401	408	安霍伊塞－布希公司	美国	11245.8	1.6	1233.3	122	5.5	12484.3	382	4216.0	316	24344	384
402	391	怡和有限公司	中国	11229.5	(2.5)	50.6	413	(84.4)	9565.3	424	2799.0	381	160000	51
403	·	阿尔贝德钢铁公司	卢森堡	11212.3	49.3	226.1	340	57.4	14091.0	356	2523.0	391	41215	304
404	410	美国“R”字玩具公司 3	美国	11200.0	1.5	(132.0)	449	(126.9)	7889.0	437	3624.0	343	94000	130
405	383	九州电力公司 4	日本	11188.7	(4.9)	202.1	350	(26.3)	34816.3	206	5569.9	259	14445	437
406	396	理光公司 1,4	日本	11156.1	(2.4)	239.8	330	(2.3)	13745.3	362	4115.6	321	65400	207
407	451	英国邮政总局 G,43	英国	11099.1	–	712.7	211	–	10018.1	418	N.A.		194000	37
408	·	克韦尔纳公司	挪威	11012.8	6.0	(219.7)	460	(226.6)	7132.6	444	1194.7	458	69100	192
409	367	皮西尼公司	法国	10937.3	(9.9)	346.2	298	11.4	10799.6	404	2982.0	370	33155	340
410	441	通用电气公司 4	英国	11902.0	5.9	1743.7	81	56.8	16300.2	323	9667.5	143	86000	146
411	477	新斯科舍银行 14	加拿大	10901.2	13.6	952.8	165	(13.6)	150991.3	78	6990.2	218	42046	299
412	·	拉发日耐火制品公司	法国	10899.5	51.2	518.6	251	24.4	14722.7	349	5284.3	277	66000	202
413	·	CIRCUIT CITY GROUP 26	美国	10804.4	21.8	142.9	380	37.0	3445.3	489	1905.1	419	54430	252
414	369	大林公司 4	日本	10795.0	(10.9)	69.6	405	(24.1)	17481.0	310	2614.5	387	12042	455

1998 年世界最大的 500 家企业（二十二）

位次 1998年	位次 1997年	公司名称	国别（地区）	收入 金额 百万美元	收入 比1997年变化（%）	利润 金额 百万美元	利润 位次	利润 比1997年变化（%）	资产 金额 百万美元	资产 位次	股东权益 金额 百万美元	股东权益 位次	雇员 人数	雇员 位次
415	406	惠好公司	美国	10766.0	(4.0)	294.0	315	(14.0)	12834.0	375	4526.0	305	35032	329
416	389	安田火灾海上保险公司 4	日本	10761.8	(7.5)	99.1	396	(14.6)	31758.5	219	2325.2	397	12115	454
417	350	西格拉姆公司 1,19	加拿大	10734.0	(14.5)	946.0	167	88.4	22179.0	269	9316.0	154	28900	362
418	479	麻省相互人寿保险公司	美国	10668.1	11.7	432.8	276	23.0	68166.0	128	3188.8	358	7885	473
419	361	北方炼铁联合公司	法国	10648.7	(13.7)	372.5	294	5.8	13113.1	374	4955.0	292	48456	276
420	423	富士重工业公司 4	日本	10581.3	(0.4)	263.7	322	5.4	8284.7	433	1690.5	427	19882	405
421	·	ADECCO	瑞士	10562.2	34.0	(134.5)	451	–	4081.9	482	1505.5	442	16000	429
422	411	太平洋联合公司	美国	10553.0	(4.2)	(633.0)	476	(246.5)	29374.0	227	7393.0	203	53000	255
423	374	住友金属工业银行 4	日本	10538.1	(12.0)	(543.5)	474	(1762.5)	22969.3	259	4240.5	313	51070	262
424	326	日本能源 4	日本	10446.3	(20.1)	138.2	384	(10.9)	13269.9	371	973.6	469	14084	439
425	437	法国天然气公司 G	法国	10400.8	0.6	536.2	245	71.2	20442.0	280	3133.0	360	31637	351
426	300	卡斯塔特	德国	10369.6	(24.4)	113.0	392	20.8	6428.0	452	1577.3	433	89399	137
427	398	英国钢铁公司 G	英国	10354.4	(9.2)	(134.0)	450	(136.1)	11575.5	390	7015.1	216	44200	293
428	·	惠尔普尔公司	美国	10322.0	19.8	325.0	304	–	7935.0	436	2001.0	412	61716	224
429	355	德意志合作银行	德国	10295.8	(17.3)	58.0	410	(68.7)	264005.5	45	4314.5	312	12466	451
430	455	乔治·威斯顿公司	加拿大	10292.2	2.4	521.1	250	195.7	5882.4	461	1555.2	435	124000	78
431	346	竹中公司	日本	10253.4	(19.0)	62.2	409	(51.5)	11567.4	391	2830.8	379	13342	447
432	·	美国通用保险公司	美国	10251.0	14.8	764.0	196	41.0	105107.0	103	8871.0	161	16100	427
433	370	东海银行 4	日本	10233.2	(15.5)	(2243.4)	489	(2031.6)	268822.7	44	13208.5	91	11094	457

1998 年世界最大的 500 家企业(二十三)

位次	位次	公司名称	国别(地区)	收入		利润			资产		股东权益		雇员	
1998年	1997年			金额 百万美元	比1997年变化(%)	金额 百万美元	位次	比1997年变化(%)	金额 百万美元	位次	金额 百万美元	位次	人数	位次
434	·	沃纳-兰伯特公司	美国	10213.7	24.9	1254.0	117	44.2	9230.6	428	3612.2	345	41000	306
435	353	神户钢铁公司 4	日本	10213.3	(18.3)	(304.1)	466	-	19168.0	294	2761.3	384	29572	358
436	487	爱迪生国际公司	美国	10208.0	10.5	668.0	220	(4.6)	24698.0	250	5099.0	285	18302	410
437	446	法国航空集团 G,43	法国	10185.7	-	314.4	308	-	11059.1	401	2547.9	389	55605	243
438	443	大西洋和太平洋茶叶公司 26	美国	10179.4	(0.8)	(67.2)	440	(206.5)	3141.7	491	837.3	475	54210	253
439	375	积水公司 3	日本	10160.3	(15.0)	176.6	363	(45.7)	13515.8	365	7103.1	212	17348	416
440	·	加拿大电力公司	加拿大	10148.6	63.1	283.1	317	18.4	38360.2	195	2047.4	409	23000	389
441	·	BEST BUY 26	美国	10077.9	20.6	224.4	342	137.6	2512.5	496	1064.1	467	33500	335
442	454	吉列公司	美国	10056.0	(0.1)	1081.0	142	(24.3)	11902.0	387	4543.0	304	43100	296
443	·	利利公司	美国	10051.3	18.0	2097.9	63	-	12595.5	380	4429.6	308	29800	357
444	294	韩国电力公司 G	韩国	10050.0	(27.0)	786.3	193	33.6	41034.3	185	14930.6	76	34753	330
445	427	住友电气工业公司 4	日本	10022.5	(5.1)	158.9	373	(41.1)	12618.5	378	4611.1	300	63177	221
446	414	朝日玻璃公司 4	日本	10021.6	(8.7)	39.9	418	(76.0)	15607.2	334	5170.5	281	44065	294
447	·	弗利特金融集团	美国	10002.0	23.6	1532.0	90	17.6	104382.0	105	9409.0	150	35612	327
448	462	意大利商业银行	意大利	9962.3	0.4	515.3	253	111.5	132423.0	86	5464.4	266	28618	363
449	416	大日本印刷公司 4	日本	9932.1	(8.8)	238.6	332	(48.2)	12202.6	386	7587.3	193	34276	333
450	424	CSX 公司	美国	9898.0	(6.8)	537.0	244	(32.8)	20427.0	281	5880.0	248	46147	288
451	·	TENET HEALTHGARE 33	美国	9895.0	13.9	261.0	323	-	12833.0	376	3558.0	347	99280	122
452	465	埃德卡中心有限公司	德国	9894.3	0.1	50.6	414	8.0	2504.3	497	383.5	488	723	499

1998 年世界最大的 500 家企业（二十四）

位次 1998年	位次 1997年	公司名称	国别（地区）	收入 金额 百万美元	收入 比1997年变化（%）	利润 金额 百万美元	利润 位次	利润 比1997年变化（%）	资产 金额 百万美元	资产 位次	股东权益 金额 百万美元	股东权益 位次	雇员 人数	雇员 位次
453	447	雪印业公司 4	日本	9886.6	(2.7)	24.1	424	(26.6)	4585.6	476	1180.4	459	15307	432
454	472	半岛－东方航空公司	英国	9798.6	1.1	450.8	273	(17.4)	10686.5	407	4971.2	290	57701	235
455	·	太阳微电子公司 19	美国	9790.8	13.9	762.9	197	0.1	5711.1	463	3513.6	348	26300	377
456	463	SEPI G	西班牙	9787.6	(1.3)	511.1	255	–	19955.1	288	6597.2	226	71233	185
457	·	胡曼纳公司	美国	9781.0	24.1	129.0	389	(25.4)	5217.0	469	1690.0	428	17000	419
458	476	DDI 4	日本	9752.5	1.6	133.5	387	97.2	13389.3	370	1952.1	414	3024	492
459	332	出光兴产石油公司 4	日本	9748.0	(25.1)	15.8	428	93.5	14727.6	348	683.9	479	4276	487
460	371	浦项综合制铁公司	韩国	9716.0	(19.6)	680.1	217	(11.2)	17119.2	313	6827.6	222	28485	366
461	436	中日本铁路公司 4	日本	9656.1	(7.3)	85.2	402	(68.0)	50603.7	158	3996.9	326	27000	372
462	432	凸片印刷公司 4	日本	9571.4	(8.5)	208.9	346	(45.9)	10700.2	406	5774.1	252	33464	336
463	490	耐克公司 33	美国	9553.1	4.0	399.6	285	(49.8)	5397.4	466	3261.6	354	22800	393
464	499	太平洋健康系统公司	美国	9521.5	6.0	202.4	349	–	4630.9	475	2238.1	402	8700	465
465	431	高岛屋百货公司 26	日本	9519.2	(9.0)	36.5	419	(46.1)	7219.1	441	1823.7	424	16506	421
466	468	法国宇航 G	法国	9509.6	(2.6)	175.8	364	(27.6)	15384.7	337	1123.0	462	36647	324
467	413	OJI 造纸公司 4	日本	9436.4	(14.1)	(97.0)	443	(208.3)	14835.9	345	3770.9	338	13563	446
468	456	西日本铁路公司 4	日本	9427.8	(5.8)	(70.5)	441	(143.4)	21733.9	271	2639.4	386	50800	264
469	426	川崎重工业公司 4	日本	9405.1	(11.0)	(48.0)	438	(131.7)	10172.6	414	1685.5	429	26486	374
470	270	LG 电子	韩国	9378.0	(36.2)	(113.8)	447	–	11085.6	400	952.6	472	60753	225
471	489	LIMITED G	美国	9346.9	1.7	2053.6	67	844.7	4549.7	477	2233.3	403	80650	158
472	471	国泰生命保险公司	中国台湾	9286.9	(4.2)	448.2	274	(30.3)	25970.3	245	1984.9	413	31781	349
473	·	FORTUM G	芬兰	9269.5	–	232.6	339	–	13125.1	373	4667.5	299	18201	411

1998 年世界最大的 500 家企业（二十五）

位次 1998年	位次 1997年	公司名称	国别（地区）	收入 金额 百万美元	收入 比1997年变化（%）	利润 金额 百万美元	利润 位次	利润 比1997年变化（%）	资产 金额 百万美元	资产 位次	股东权益 金额 百万美元	股东权益 位次	雇员 人数	雇员 位次
474	412	国家石油产品公司 G,4	马来西亚	9267.3	(15.7)	1491.3	96	(52.3)	20944.3	276	7761.4	189	20767	401
475	·	苏格兰 WIDOWS FUND	英国	9250.4	29.0	N.A.		–	49718.5	160	7883.7	183	2671	494
476	·	加拿大永明人寿保险公司	加拿大	9232.5	4.7	36.4	420	(90.1)	60779.3	135	3958.7	329	10700	459
477	352	共荣人寿保险公司 4	日本	9231.5	(26.4)	161.7	371	(21.2)	42922.3	176	654.3	480	15961	430
478	483	H.J.亨氏公司 61	美国	9209.3	(1.6)	801.6	190	165.5	8023.4	434	2216.5	404	40500	308
479	403	川铁公司 4	日本	9178.5	(18.3)	(6.8)	434	–	6320.9	454	334.9	489	3297	490
480	434	旭日化学工业公司 4	日本	9167.8	(12.2)	136.1	385	(19.7)	10007.1	419	3920.4	330	29263	360
481	·	重建信贷银行 G	德国	9153.2	4.2	256.9	324	(14.8)	189134.2	63	6335.6	234	1827	498
482	·	ASTRAZENECA 68	英国	9132.8	7.3	1183.4	127	(1.0)	9001.7	430	4183.0	317	34600	331
483	445	屈曼纸业公司	芬兰	9128.9	(6.0)	1123.3	135	39.4	13444.6	368	6236.1	236	32351	346
484	·	北德意志地方银行 G	德国	9125.7	10.0	203.7	348	25.3	178397.0	68	3857.1	335	7080	477
485	422	中国石油公司 G	中国台湾	9115.5	(15.0)	890.0	172	134.4	15689.2	332	8950.2	159	18684	408
486	·	ST. PAUL COS	美国	9108.4	46.5	89.3	401	(87.3)	38322.7	196	6636.4	225	14000	441
487	·	SPAR HANDELS	德国	9072.9	11.2	19.4	427	(33.7)	2264.8	498	400.20	487	32639	344
488	474	西屋电气公司	美国	9061.0	(5.9)	(21.0)	436	(103.8)	20139.0	286	9054.0	157	46189	287
489	·	科尔公司	美国	9059.4	23.4	115.5	391	(44.3)	5677.3	464	1300.0	456	65466	206
490	·	加普公司 3	美国	9054.5	39.1	824.5	184	54.4	3963.9	483	1573.7	434	111000	100
491	444	西北航空公司	美国	9044.8	(11.5)	(285.5)	465	(147.9)	10280.8	412	(476.7)	496	50565	266
492	·	大众商店有限公司 4	英国	9043.5	62.2	534.3	247	(25.9)	9332.8	427	3888.8	331	55575	244
493	·	多伦多自治领银行 14	加拿大	9018.1	18.2	766.2	195	(0.5)	117535.6	94	5515.7	264	29236	361

1998 年世界最大的 500 家企业（二十六）

位次	位次	公司名称	国别（地区）	收入		利润			资产		股东权益		雇员	
1998年	1997年			金额 百万美元	比1997年变化（%）	金额 百万美元	位次	比1997年变化（%）	金额 百万美元	位次	金额 百万美元	位次	人数	位次
494	·	OFFICE DEPOT	美国	8997.7	33.9	233.2	337	46.0	4113.0	481	2028.9	410	33000	341
495	497	高露洁	美国	8971.6	(0.9)	848.6	178	14.6	7685.2	438	2085.6	407	38300	316
496	·	北伯林顿 SANTA FE	美国	8941.0	6.3	1155.0	131	30.5	22690.0	263	7770.0	188	42900	297
497	493	德高沙公司 8,69	德国	8924.3	(2.4)	307.5	310	35.6	6036.6	458	1536.9	438	26364	375
498	481	三井不动产公司 4	日本	8920.5	(5.5)	(280.0)	464	–	27038.1	239	4158.9	318	12194	453
499	·	约翰·汉考克相互人寿保险	美国	8911.7	8.6	627.3	227	51.5	67079.4	129	3388.7	350	7959	471
500	492	诺思罗普·格鲁曼公司	美国	8902.0	(2.7)	214.0	343	(47.4)	9564.0	425	2878.0	376	49600	271
		总计		**11 463 407.9**		**440 271.5**			**38 989 284.0**		**4 233 812.4**		**39 685 624**	

定义及解释

收入额及利润额

本表中各公司均应公布其财务数字并向政府部门报告部分或全部数字。本表包括了填报 10K 表格的美国私营公司和合伙公司。收入额包括至统计之日止中断了的业务收入。商业银行和储蓄机构的收入额含利息收入和无息收入。保险公司的收入额含保险费及年金收入、投资收入和资本损益，但不包含保证金。收入额包括合并的子公司的数字，但营业额除外。

本表中的利润额均为税后利润，已经除去非常贷款或应付款，并减去因财务统计方法变化而引起的重复计算。括号中的数字为亏损数字。利润下降幅度超过 100%，反映了从 1997 年盈利转为 1998 年亏损。

统计中的财政年度，除特别指明外，均截至到 1999 年 3 月 31 日。公司的收入额和利润额均按公司财政年度内的官方平均汇率折算为美元（除特别指明外，截至到 1998 年 12 月 31 日）。

资产和股东权益

表中资产额为公司财政年度末的数字。股东权益为同一天的股本、实收资本和存留收益之和。未包括少数股权益。

公司的数字均按各公司的财政年度末的官方汇率折算为美元。

雇员人数

人数均按公司公布的年底实际人数或者全年平均人数统计。

脚　　注

E　已扣除营业税。

G　国营公司。

*　包括 10% 以上的中断了的业务的收入。

★　反映了至少 10% 的特别信贷。

1. 根据美国通用会计原则编制的数字。
2. 于 1998 年 11 月 12 日兼并克莱斯勒公司（1997 年排名：第 25 位）之后，由 Daimler-Benz 改为现名。
3. 财政年度截至到 1999 年 1 月 31 日。
4. 财政年度截至到 1999 年 3 月 31 日。
5. 仅含母公司。
6. 于 1998 年 10 月 8 日兼并花旗银行（1997 年排名：第 68 位）之后，由 Travelers Group 改为现名。
7. 于 1998 年 12 月 31 日兼并阿莫科公司（1997 年排名：第 72 位）之后，由 British Petroleum 改为现名。
8. 财政年度截至到 1998 年 9 月 30 日。
9. 于 1998 年 3 月 20 日兼并法国通用保险公司。
10. 根据国际会计标准编制的数字。
11. 于 1998 年 9 月 30 日兼并美洲银行（1997 年排名：第 145 位）之后，由 Nations Bank Corp. 改名为 Bank America Corp.。
12. 于 1999 年 4 月 28 日由 Bank America Corp. 改为现名。
13. 于 1998 年 5 月 29 日兼并亚琛和慕尼黑保险公司（1997 年排名：第 343 位）。
14. 财政年度截至到 1998 年 10 月 31 日。
15. 于 1999 年 6 月 4 日兼并 Bankers Trust（1998 年排名：第 376 位）。
16. 数字不包括 Degussa-Huls（1998 年排名：第 497 位），该公司于 1999 年 2 月 1 日被兼并。
17. 于 1998 年 9 月 7 日由苏黎士保险集团（1997 年排名：第 116 位）与英美烟草金融服务集团（1998 年排名：第 164 位）合并成立。
18. 于 1998 年 6 月 1 日兼并通用事故保险公司（1997 年排名：第 258 位）之后，由 Commercial Union 改为现名。
19. 财政年度截至到 1998 年 6 月 30 日。
20. 财政年度截至到 1997 年 12 月 31 日。
21. 财政年度截至日变更，从 6 月 30 日改为 12 月 31 日。
22. 于 1998 年 9 月 1 日与 Hypo-Bank（1997 年排名：第 288 位）

合并之后，由 Bayerische Vereinsbank 改名现名。
23. 于1998年6月兼并兴业银行（1997年排名：第439位）。
24. 根据1998年12月31日的汇率，由欧元折算的数字。
25. 财政年度截至到1998年11月30日。
26. 财政年度截至到1999年2月28日。
27. 于1999年5月27日兼并 Fred Meyer（1998年排名：第272位）。
28. 于1999年6月4日 Total 兼并 PetroFina（1998年排名：第387位）。并于1999年6月14日由 Total 改为现名。
29. 于1998年10月1日兼并芝加哥第一国民银行（1997年排名：第452位）之后，由 Banc One 改为现名。
30. 财政年度截至到1999年3月6日。
31. 数字不包括1998年10月1日兼并的福雷特·克鲁普公司（1997年排名：第278位）。于1999年3月17日由 Thyssen 改为现名。
32. 财政年度截至到1998年8月31日。
33. 财政年度截至到1998年3月31日。
34. 于1998年6月22日由 Alcatel Alshom 改为现名，并与 Alsthom（1998年排名：第355位）保持非联盟关系。
35. 于1998年6月7日由 BAT Industries 改为现名，其金融服务业务已并入 Zurich finacial Services（1998年排名：第56位）。
36. 于1999年1月13日兼并 HBOC 之后，由 McKesson 改为现名。
37. 财政年度截至到1998年3月31日。在发稿时，发现截至到1999年3月31日财政年度的数字不可比，原因是部分账目税收数字属前 HBOC 公司的。
38. 于1998年11月2日兼并 Wells Fargo & Co.（1997年排名：第475位）后，由 Norwest Corp. 改为现名。
39. 于1999年6月23日兼并 A1bertson's（1998年排名：第250位）。
40. 财政年度截至日由12月31日改为6月30日。
41. 于1998年3月17日由 Teleonica de Espana 改为现名。
42. 财政年度截至到1999年2月20日。
43. 财政年度截至到1998年3月31日。
44. 于1997年7月1日由 Federal Home Loan Mortagage Corp. 改为现名。
45. 于1998年9月14日兼并 MCI 通讯设备公司（1997年排名：第187位）之后，由 WorldCom 改为现名。
46. 于1999年4月6日由 Republic Industries 改为现名。
47. 于1999年6月15日由 RJR Nabisco Holdings Corp. 改为现名。
48. 于1999年6月23日被 American Stores（1998年排名：第186位）兼并，本项不含该公司数字。
49. 1999年2月4日由 Siebe 与 BTR（1997年排名：第321位）合并成立。
50. 于1999年1月1日由 Aluminum Co. of America 改为现名。
51. 于1999年5月27日被 Kroger（1998年排名：第109位）兼并。
52. 财政年度截至到1998年11月15日。
53. 财政年度截至到1998年7月31日。
54. 于1999年4月1日由 Nippon Oil Co. 改为现名。
55. 与1998年7月6日由 NGP Corp. 改为现名。
56. 于1998年11月1日由 Istituto Bancario San Paolo 改为现名。
57. 于1998年11月1日由 Gredito Italiano 改为现名。
58. 1998年1月2日由 Banco Ambrosiano 与卡普罗公司（1997年排名：第458位）合并成立。
59. 于1998年7月28日被 Acquired Gan（1997年排名：第98位）兼并。
60. 于1998年7月16日兼并废物管理公司（1997年排名：第85位）之后，由 USA Waste Services 改为现名。
61. 财政年度截至到1998年4月30日。
62. 于1998年6月22日由从前 Alcatel Alsthom 公司的一部分，成为今日的 Alcatel（1998年排名：第145位）独立公司。

63．财政年度截至到 1998 年 2 月 28 日。

64．于 1998 年 6 月 12 日从 US West 脱离，现名为 Media One Group（1997 年排名：第 255 位）。

65．于 1999 年 6 月 4 日被 Deutsche Bank（1998 年排名：第 42 位）兼并。

66．于 1999 年 5 月 5 日由 Houston Industrir 改为现名。

67．非联盟。

68．于 1999 年 4 月 6 日由 Zeneca 改为现名。

69．于 1999 年 2 月 1 日同 Huls 合并，成为 VEDA（1998 年排名：第 46 位）的子公司，并改为现名。

资料来源：美国《财富》杂志。

（对外贸易经济合作部国际贸易经济合作研究院）

1999年中国进出口额最大的500家企业（一）

对外贸易经济合作部二〇〇〇年七月三日公布

金额单位：万美元

名次	企业名称	进出口额	出口额	进口额
1	中国石化国际事业公司	493383	71128	422255
	中国国际石油化工联合有限责任公司	276384	20781	255603
	镇海炼油化工股份有限公司	26777	9854	16923
	中国石化国际事业茂名公司	23413	8506	14907
	中国金山联合贸易有限责任公司	16366	3077	13289
	仪征化纤集团公司	15894	20	15874
	仪征化纤股份有限公司	8012	13	7999
	中国石化国际事业上海公司	16660	7251	9408
	中国石化国际事业扬子公司	10444	2033	8411
	中国石化国际事业广州公司	10172	5759	4413
	中国石化国际事业金陵公司	9283	481	8802
2	中国化工进出口总公司	476596	144709	331887
	中化国际化肥贸易公司	111291	571	110720
	中化国际石油公司	57056	0	57056
	中化广东进出口公司	52114	4110	48004
	中化江苏进出口公司	31739	27320	4419
	中化国际股份责任有限公司	25489	11600	13889
	中化辽宁进出口公司	25174	24921	253
	中化浦东贸易有限公司	17956	1130	16826
	中化河北进出口公司	16863	15879	984
	中化上海进出口公司	16649	8277	8372
	中化宁波进出口公司	12530	10300	2230
	中化山东进出口集团公司	11059	7828	3231
	中化国际招标公司	10314	490	9824
	中化天津进出口公司	8972	8343	629
3	中国通用技术(集团)控股有限责任公司	287368	57056	230312
	中国技术进出口总公司	123730	19080	104650
	中技国际贸易公司	10687	692	9995
	中国机械进出口(集团)有限公司	80457	23603	56854
	中国运输机械进出口公司	11910	2566	9344
	中机国际招标公司	8065	20	8045
	中国仪器进出口总公司	67474	5899	61575
	中仪英斯泰克进出口公司	13178	1020	12158
	中仪英康进出口公司	12694	611	12083
	中仪设备进出口公司	10099	738	9361
	中国医药保健品进出口公司	13612	6993	6619
4	摩托罗拉(中国)电子有限公司	266475	98662	167813

1999年中国进出口额最大的500家企业（二）

金额单位：万美元

名次	企业名称	进出口额	出口额	进口额
5	东方国际(集团)有限公司	261030	177619	83411
	上海丝绸(集团)有限公司	82153	64059	18094
	上海市对外贸易有限公司	48585	10392	38193
	东方国际创业股份有限公司	41003	30569	10434
	东方国际集团上海市服装进出口公司	34915	26844	8071
	东方国际集团上海市针织品进出口公司	24512	22347	2165
	东方国际集团上海市家用纺织品进出口公司	22774	21525	1249
	东方国际集团上海市纺织品进出口有限公司	21677	19873	1804
	东方国际商业有限公司	7891	5508	2383
6	中国粮油食品进出口(集团)有限公司	255108	117287	137821
	中粮上海粮油进出口公司	29381	4216	25165
	中粮粮油饲料进出口公司	26102	18670	7432
	东海粮油公司	19728	0	19728
	中粮辽宁粮油进出口公司	13508	13177	331
	中粮黑龙江粮油食品进出口公司	11411	9431	1980
	中粮糖业杂品进出口公司	10856	4511	6345
	中粮山东粮油进出口公司	9916	9400	516
	中国玉米出口有限责任公司	9911	9911	0
	秦皇岛中粮进出口公司	8703	305	8398
7	中国电子进出口总公司	175979	86016	89963
	中国电子进出口广东公司	14865	9509	5356
	广东省惠州电子技术进出口公司	9794	6045	3749
	深圳中电投资股份有限公司	12138	8324	3814
	中国电子进出口彩虹公司	10656	6381	4275
	中国电子进出口吉林公司	9361	444	8917
	中国电子进出口宁波公司	8572	6655	1917
8	中国航空器材进出口总公司	164270	8444	155826
	中国航空器材进出口西南公司	36764	6319	30445
	中国航空器材进出口总公司西北公司	22161	61	22100
	中国航空器材北方公司	10342	975	9367
9	中国石油天然气集团公司	158406	75520	82886
	中国联合石油有限责任公司	95364	51243	44121
	大连中联油国际贸易有限公司	29647	29638	9
	中国石油技术开发公司	42994	16499	26495
	深圳石油技术开发进出口公司	7352	145	7207
10	中国航空技术进出口总公司	152848	67357	85491
	中国航空技术进出口北京公司	16760	14154	2606
	中航技国际工贸公司	8884	1533	7351
	中国航空技术进出口深圳公司	7722	3176	4546

1999年中国进出口额最大的500家企业（三）

金额单位：万美元

名次	企业名称	进出口额	出口额	进口额
11	中国五金矿产进出口总公司	147822	51789	96033
	五矿国际有色金属贸易公司	27186	17759	9427
	中国五矿石油器材贸易有限公司	18914	382	18532
	五矿贸易有限公司	15231	4505	10726
	五矿钢铁有限责任公司	9735	5	9730
	中国五金制品进出口公司	7635	7414	221
12	宝钢集团国际经济贸易总公司	128101	38208	89893
13	中国工艺品进出口总公司	123201	111998	11203
	中国抽纱上海进出口公司	13806	10555	3251
	中国珠宝首饰进出口公司	10631	10631	0
	中国抽纱汕头进出口公司	9119	9060	59
	中国工艺品深圳贸易中心	7579	7578	1
14	中国船舶工业贸易公司	121583	88982	32601
	中国船舶工业贸易公司	35201	28481	6720
	大连造船新厂	24290	20125	4165
	广船国际股份有限公司	14464	8874	5590
	大连造船厂	14366	10698	3668
	沪东船厂	7671	5379	2292
	广船国际集装箱厂	7443	5059	2384
15	希捷国际科技(无锡)有限公司	116311	62248	54063
16	中国机械装备(集团)公司	116002	76461	39541
	中国机械设备进出口总公司	79592	53347	26245
	中设江苏机械设备进出口集团公司	15081	4764	10317
	中国工程与农业机械进出口总公司	16845	14378	2467
	中国机械对外经济技术合作总公司	13197	8196	5001
17	中国煤炭工业进出口集团公司	110439	92178	18261
	中国煤炭工业秦皇岛进出口有限公司	33149	33149	0
	中国煤炭工业进出口集团日照有限公司	21441	21441	0
	中国煤炭工业进出口集团青岛有限公司	11077	11077	0
	中国煤炭工业进出口集团连云港公司	8316	8316	0
	天津中煤进出口有限公司	8079	8029	50
18	深圳希捷科技有限公司	108835	57986	50849
19	英特尔科技(中国)有限公司	108005	55609	52396
20	中国土产畜产进出口总公司	105482	62828	42654
	中国木材进出口公司	11463	1324	10139
	福建茶叶进出口有限责任公司	9077	8905	172
21	北京诺基亚移动通信有限公司	99133	15680	83453
22	中国国际海运集装箱(集团)股份有限公司	97551	60325	37226
	深圳南方中集集装箱制造有限公司	24576	15641	8935

1999年中国进出口额最大的500家企业（四）

金额单位：万美元

名次	企 业 名 称	进出口额	出口额	进口额
	新会中集集装箱有限公司	16922	11657	5256
	上海中集冷藏有限公司	16529	5786	10743
	南通中集顺达集装箱股份有限公司	15898	11977	3921
	上海中集远东集装箱有限公司	10901	8981	1920
23	中国北方工业公司	93951	70386	23565
	中国北方工业广州公司	15558	11694	3864
	中国北方工业深圳公司	8843	7405	1438
	中国北方工业北京公司	8587	1704	6883
24	中国铜铅锌集团公司	87802	54137	33665
	铜陵有色金属(集团)公司	35451	9700	25751
	铜陵金隆铜业公司	19770	6762	13008
	铜陵有色金属上海进出口有限公司	9111	496	8615
	株洲冶炼厂	14283	13813	470
	葫芦岛锌厂	12018	11469	549
25	浙江中大集团控股有限公司	84668	39500	45168
	浙江中大技术进出口集团有限公司	57933	13661	44272
	浙江中大集团股份有限公司	26735	25839	896
26	中国有色金属进出口总公司	83418	53450	29968
27	冠捷电子(福建)公司	80090	40586	39504
28	上海东方航空进出口公司	78340	16071	62269
29	中国烟草进出口总公司	74728	31171	43557
	中国烟草云南进出口公司	16242	7362	8880
	中国烟草上海进出口公司	9509	6897	2612
30	中国钢铁工贸集团公司	67217	37778	29439
31	深圳开发科技股份有限公司	65880	36524	29356
32	北京·松下电子部品有限公司	63753	22733	41020
33	爱普生技术(深圳)有限公司	62353	37751	24602
34	中谷粮油集团公司	60638	664	59974
	中国粮食贸易公司	9630	425	9205
35	中国海洋石油总公司	60568	39470	21098
	阿科(中国)公司	22452	21378	1074
	中国海洋石油渤油公司	7778	888	6890
36	中国第一汽车集团进出口公司	60525	5667	54858
	一汽大众汽车有限公司	39372	3337	36035
37	中国出口商品基地建设总公司	60505	38774	21731
38	友利电电子(深圳)有限公司	60499	33872	26627
39	中国包装进出口总公司	59929	30166	29763
	中国包装进出口广东公司	8278	1351	6927
40	中国电力技术进出口公司	58337	219	58118

1999年中国进出口额最大的500家企业（五）

金额单位：万美元

名次	企　业　名　称	进出口额	出口额	进口额
	阳城国际发电有限责任公司	29286	0	29286
	河北邯峰发电有限责任公司	18367	0	18367
41	广东核电合营有限公司	56693	54399	2294
42	江苏省海外企业集团有限公司	56111	21031	35080
43	中国纺织品进出口总公司	55797	45928	9869
	中纺棉花进出口公司	16004	15887	117
	中纺纱布进出口公司	7383	6927	456
	中纺化纤毛麻进出口公司	6996	6079	917
44	中国对外贸易运输(集团)总公司	55372	37831	17541
	中外运深圳公司	20186	20108	78
	镇江外运进出口公司	15365	12116	3249
	满洲里华运经济贸易公司	9403	636	8767
45	深圳海量存储设备有限公司	54530	25663	28867
46	联想进出口有限公司	54319	2485	51834
47	上海大众汽车有限公司	54282	324	53958
48	上海索广电子有限公司	52749	26953	25796
49	珠海振戎公司	51811	272	51539
50	南京爱立信通信有限公司	50484	8195	42289
51	才众电脑(深圳)有限公司	50142	26619	23523
52	中国国际信托投资公司	50134	24337	25797
	中信贸易公司	16181	6384	9797
53	江苏舜天国际集团有限公司	49682	38918	10764
	江苏舜天国际集团服装进出口股份有限公司	30019	24764	5255
	江苏舜天国际集团机械进出口股份有限公司	17570	12063	5507
54	唯冠科技(深圳)有限公司	49664	32073	17591
55	大连西太平洋石油化工有限公司	48883	15725	33158
56	万向集团公司	47726	3837	43889
57	北京爱立信移动通信有限公司	47627	6209	41418
58	厦门太古飞机工程有限公司	46501	20689	25812
59	仁宝电脑工业(中国)有限公司	46396	27264	19132
60	苏州明基电脑有限公司	45881	25362	20519
61	深圳长科国际电子有限公司	45431	23039	22392
62	中国化工建设总公司	45384	21789	23595
63	上海轻工国际(集团)有限公司	45293	30146	15147
	上海市五金矿产进出口公司	23902	11350	12552
	上海市轻工业品进出口公司	21394	18796	2598
	上海市轻工业品进出口有限公司	9341	8937	404
64	深圳三洋华强激光电子有限公司	45100	26277	18823
65	海福发展(深圳)有限公司	44973	4695	40278

1999 年中国进出口额最大的 500 家企业（六）

金额单位：万美元

名次	企 业 名 称	进出口额	出口额	进口额
66	中国深圳对外贸易(集团)公司	44411	28072	16339
67	飞利浦电子元件(上海)有限公司	44303	23720	20583
68	江苏国泰国际集团有限公司	44152	37755	6397
69	苏州飞利浦消费电子有限公司	43416	18901	24515
70	富金精密工业(深圳)有限公司	42941	28606	14335
71	中国原子能工业公司	42868	10697	32171
72	天津三星电机有限公司	42314	20900	21414
73	北方国际集团有限公司	41780	36860	4920
	北方国际集团天津纺织品进出口有限公司	9284	8650	634
	北方国际集团天津亿利达有限公司	8291	7504	787
	天津食品进出口股份有限公司	7603	7095	508
74	中国华源集团有限公司	39663	31187	8476
	上海华源进出口股份有限公司	7357	5270	2087
75	海尔集团	39129	11398	27731
76	中国长城工业总公司	38892	24298	14594
77	中国轻工业品进出口总公司	38865	19082	19783
	中国纸张纸浆进出口公司	7886	135	7751
78	江苏汇鸿国际集团有限公司	37818	34900	2918
	江苏汇鸿国际集团针棉织品进出口有限公司	16297	14588	1709
79	苏州罗技电子有限公司	36769	23127	13642
80	深圳市盐田国际集装箱码头有限公司	36720	31408	5312
81	夏普办公设备(常熟)有限公司	36399	25076	11323
82	浙江省丝绸进出口公司	35813	32091	3722
83	伟创力实业(深圳)有限公司	34960	18138	16822
84	厦门建发股份有限公司	34941	17231	17710
85	中国北方工业集团公司	34869	25139	9730
	山西柴油机厂	31851	23461	8390
86	三美电机有限公司	34642	18655	15987
87	广东省五金矿产进出口集团公司	34269	5608	28661
88	上海兰生(集团)有限公司	33779	28173	5606
	上海市医药保健品进出口公司	7648	6394	1254
89	浙江省土产畜产进出口公司	33656	30292	3364
90	新疆对外经济贸易(集团)有限责任公司	33056	28406	4650
91	广州轻出集团有限公司	32589	22569	10020
	广州五金矿产进出口公司	7623	3002	4621
92	上海西门子移动通信有限公司	32443	2023	30420
93	中国化工供销(集团)总公司	32410	1530	30880
94	苏州爱普生有限公司	32229	17930	14299
95	理光(深圳)工业发展有限公司	32225	24562	7663

1999年中国进出口额最大的500家企业（七）

金额单位：万美元

名次	企业名称	进出口额	出口额	进口额
96	山东省对外贸易集团有限公司	31120	12678	18442
	山东省对外贸易总公司	12125	3721	8404
97	三洋电机(蛇口)有限公司	30832	19278	11554
98	江苏省轻工业品进出口集团股份有限公司	30269	22897	7372
99	江苏省丝绸进出口集团股份有限公司	30176	27200	2976
100	重庆对外贸易进出口公司	29720	1055	28665
101	四川长虹电子集团公司	29389	404	28985
102	浙江东方集团股份有限公司	29300	22639	6661
103	日本电产(大连)有限公司	29291	17432	11859
104	厦门灿坤实业股份有限公司	29142	19535	9607
105	上海通用汽车有限公司	29077	13	29064
106	山东省机械进出口公司	28765	23809	4956
107	鑫茂科技(深圳)有限公司	28707	16369	12338
108	北京诺基亚航星通讯系统有限公司	28706	463	28243
109	丹东饭山显示器有限公司	28697	15969	12728
110	柯达(中国)股份有限公司	28501	4520	23981
111	深圳市物资集团公司	28200	24954	3246
112	上海新康电子有限公司	27975	15330	12645
113	广东省纺织品进出口(集团)公司	27909	24686	3223
114	嘉兴市进出口公司	27524	24614	2910
115	山东省服装进出口集团总公司	27422	20299	7123
116	上海服装(集团)有限公司	27392	18782	8610
117	苏州进出口(集团)有限公司	27303	23814	3489
118	浙江省粮油食品进出口股份有限公司	27273	23450	3823
119	中国邮电器材总公司	27022	864	26158
120	中国稀有稀土金属集团公司	27008	23019	3989
	宁夏有色金属冶炼厂	7653	5525	2128
	中国有色金属进出口株洲硬质合金公司	7410	5640	1770
121	葆祥国际服装中心	26656	26056	600
	葆祥河北进出口集团公司	24939	24390	549
122	中国远洋运输(集团)总公司	26526	3550	22976
	中远国际贸易公司	18069	1875	16194
123	大连东芝电视有限公司	26357	8961	17396
124	深圳乐意液体仓储有限公司	26356	10533	15823
125	南通市经济技术开发区总公司	26355	15652	10703
126	奥林巴斯(深圳)工业有限公司	26262	14976	11286
127	上海市工艺品进出口有限公司	25967	22433	3534
128	中国联合通信有限公司	25958	0	25958
	联通进出口有限公司	25958	0	25958

1999 年中国进出口额最大的 500 家企业（八）

金额单位：万美元

名次	企业名称	进出口额	出口额	进口额
129	江南造船(集团)有限责任公司	25854	15948	9906
130	深圳赛意法微电子有限公司	24980	14122	10858
131	中华映管(福州)有限公司	24795	8011	16784
132	西迪斯(天津)电子有限公司	24420	13805	10615
133	中国江苏国际经济技术合作公司	24397	20216	4181
134	华阳电业有限公司	24071	0	24071
135	中广核电进出口有限公司	24015		24015
136	福建省粮油食品进出口公司	23878	19203	4675
137	中国华录集团有限公司	23621	13777	9844
	中国华录·松下电子信息有限公司	23443	13721	9722
138	中国汽车工业进出口总公司	23537	11535	12002
139	中国水产(集团)总公司	23507	9660	13847
	中国乡镇企业总公司	8231	229	8002
140	福建厦门经贸集团有限公司	23364	21412	1952
141	宁波中海贸进出口有限公司	23355	19843	3512
142	国航集团进出口贸易公司	23053	7903	15150
143	华飞彩色显示系统有限公司	22999	3882	19117
144	茉织华实业(集团)有限公司	22993	13264	9729
145	深圳国际商业机器技术产品有限公司	22886	10266	12620
146	山东省纺织品进出口公司	22836	21167	1669
147	青岛三美电机有限公司	22760	13059	9701
148	中国(福建)对外贸易中心集团	22670	19624	3046
149	上海 JVC 电器有限公司	22424	13266	9158
150	中国工艺美术(集团)公司	22294	15417	6877
151	青岛泰光制鞋有限公司	22238	12617	9621
152	力捷电脑(中国)有限公司	22127	13709	8418
153	浙江省纺织品进出口公司	22108	20909	1199
154	凯远集团公司	22052	19793	2259
155	山东工艺品进出口(集团)股份有限公司	22039	15981	6058
156	广东省机械进出口(集团)公司	21786	5339	16447
	广东省机械进出口股份有限公司	10230	1315	8915
157	南京纺织品进出口股份有限公司	21740	19714	2026
158	厦门国贸集团股份有限公司	21582	13403	8179
159	飞利浦桑达消费通信(深圳)有限公司	21547	6179	15368
160	东风汽车公司	21525	2137	19388
	神龙汽车有限公司	10239	73	10166
161	中国远大集团公司	21378	11439	9939
	浙江远大进出口有限公司	13903	9308	4595
162	深圳市华为技术有限公司	21106	1337	19769

1999年中国进出口额最大的500家企业（九）

金额单位：万美元

名次	企 业 名 称	进出口额	出口额	进口额
163	辽宁成大股份有限公司	21025	16915	4110
164	广东省轻工业品进出口(集团)公司	21004	18098	2906
165	邯郸钢铁集团进出口有限公司	20950	4591	16359
166	上海美蓓亚精密机电有限公司	20922	15201	5721
167	中国港湾建设(集团)总公司	20766	13464	7302
	上海振华港口机械股份有限公司	13136	9754	3382
168	鞍钢集团国际经济贸易公司	20724	12202	8522
169	金朋(上海)有限公司	20348	13354	6994
170	中国交通进出口总公司	20240	7960	12280
171	天津外总集团有限公司	20232	11927	8305
172	福建太平洋电力有限公司	19994	0	19994
173	南太电子(深圳)有限公司	19964	9715	10249
174	上海申达股份有限公司	19930	17302	2628
175	上海新格有色金属有限公司	19921	7516	12405
176	天津阿尔卑斯电子有限公司	19904	12200	7704
177	上海惠普有限公司	19864	377	19487
178	中国丝绸进出口总公司	19803	17550	2253
179	广东格兰仕企业(集团)公司	19395	10610	8785
	顺德格兰仕电器厂有限公司	13804	8099	5705
180	武钢集团国际经济贸易总公司	19294	9544	9750
181	中国远东国际贸易总公司	19268	1190	18078
	中国远东深圳国际贸易公司	15480	306	15174
182	华科立资讯科技(深圳)有限公司	19192	10461	8731
183	常熟市对外贸易公司	19019	16561	2458
184	中国航天机电集团公司	18877	3296	15581
	沈阳航天三菱汽车发动机制造有限公司	10081	0	10081
185	上海新锐实业有限公司	18693	17457	1236
186	康佳集团股份有限公司	18553	5102	13451
187	广州纺织品进出口集团有限公司	18552	16272	2280
188	无锡夏普电子元器件有限公司	18517	10241	8276
189	哈尔滨双太电子实业有限公司	18400	9729	8671
190	中国华能国际经济贸易公司	18382	8822	9560
191	深圳华安液化石油气有限公司	18214	768	17446
192	中国恒天集团公司	18127	9071	9056
	中国纺织机械和技术进出口公司	10017	7611	2406
193	富士通将军(上海)有限公司	18098	10166	7932
194	江苏省纺织品进出口集团股份有限公司	18026	14829	3197
195	长城国际信息产品(深圳)有限公司	17956	8490	9466
196	惠普计算机产品(上海)有限公司	17866	9360	8506

1999年中国进出口额最大的500家企业（十）

金额单位：万美元

名次	企业名称	进出口额	出口额	进口额
197	江苏省技术进出口公司	17819	10457	7362
198	乐金电子(天津)电器有限公司	17648	6598	11050
199	吉粮集团进出口公司	17616	17616	0
200	安徽省技术进出口股份有限公司	17442	10590	6852
201	TCL集团有限公司	17417	290	17127
202	天津三星电子有限公司	17340	12488	4852
203	上海索广映像有限公司	17225	3038	14187
204	常州市对外贸易公司	17193	13536	3657
205	深圳赤湾港航股份有限公司	17165	6478	10687
206	上海大霸实业有限公司	17113	6909	10204
207	安徽省粮油食品进出口(集团)公司	17085	16397	688
208	上海机械进出口(集团)有限公司	17028	11096	5932
209	厦门进雄企业有限公司	16559	11202	5357
210	雅达电子有限公司	16527	8612	7915
211	宁波市慈溪进出口股份有限公司	16494	14457	2037
212	上海申信进出口公司	16472	579	15893
213	中国首钢国际贸易工程公司	16401	3085	13316
214	上海畜产(集团)有限公司	16281	11983	4298
215	大连日通外运货运公司	16201	14877	1324
216	温州市进出口公司	16116	11126	4990
217	深圳奥康德石油贸易集团公司	16101	10281	5820
218	上海华虹NEC电子有限公司	16085	3670	12415
219	金东纸业(江苏)有限公司	16021	536	15485
220	蛇口招商港务股份有限公司	15980	7146	8834
221	河北省五矿进出口公司	15975	7972	8003
222	天津雅马哈电子乐器有限公司	15921	9521	6400
223	万宝至马达大连有限公司	15835	10392	5443
224	宁波维科集团	15834	14565	1269
225	上海夏普电器有限公司	15817	9841	5976
226	江苏省工艺品进出口集团股份有限公司	15782	15412	370
227	浙江省畜产进出口公司	15733	15221	512
228	上海新联纺进出口公司	15631	14174	1457
229	宁波中华纸业有限公司	15589		15589
230	厦门华侨电子股份公司	15342	2624	12718
231	北京工艺进出口有限责任公司	15337	15067	270
232	东方科学仪器进出口集团公司	15150	2519	12631
233	广东省外贸开发公司	15107	2552	12555
234	深圳创维－RGB电子有限公司	14915	4805	10110
235	中国南光进出口总公司	14775	3697	11078

1999 年中国进出口额最大的 500 家企业（十一）

金额单位：万美元

名次	企 业 名 称	进出口额	出口额	进口额
236	青岛三湖制鞋有限公司	14671	8817	5854
237	保利科技有限公司	14666	10069	4597
238	诺基亚(苏州)有限公司	14661	5655	9006
239	中国土产畜产浙江茶叶进出口公司	14570	13262	1308
240	南通市对外贸易公司	14544	12147	2397
241	东芝大连有限公司	14509	8157	6352
242	三星电子(苏州)半导体有限公司	14458	12148	2310
243	浙江庆丰纺织印染有限公司	14415	7600	6815
244	上海贝尔电话设备制造有限公司	14414	98	14316
245	广东省土产进出口(集团)公司	14402	7030	7372
246	苏州富士胶片映像机器有限公司	14288	7338	6950
247	深圳经济特区发展(集团)公司	14287	5762	8525
248	深圳市南方航空器材有限公司	14272		14272
249	广州越秀企业(集团)公司	14201	8809	5392
250	新利实业(深圳)有限公司	14167	7131	7036
251	厦门建松电器有限公司	14149	8230	5919
252	大连阿尔派电子有限公司	14043	6643	7400
253	欧姆龙(大连)有限公司	14029	7986	6043
254	上海市食品进出口公司	13931	11412	2519
255	珠海格力集团公司	13898	6043	7855
	珠海格力电器股份有限公司	10849	5459	5390
256	北京市富亿通进出口有限责任公司	13890	13597	293
257	至卓飞高线路板(深圳)有限公司	13848	8996	4852
258	深圳赛格日立彩色显示器件有限公司	13784	2266	11518
259	辽宁时代服装进出口股份有限公司	13761	9772	3989
260	北京国际交换系统有限公司	13728	27	13701
261	攀钢集团国际经济贸易总公司	13696	12115	1581
262	宁波经济技术开发区进出口公司	13686	10827	2869
263	河北省纺织品进出口(集团)公司	13677	12274	1403
264	河北圣仑进出口集团公司	13669	12225	1444
265	连云港市对外贸易公司	13651	12917	734
266	宇达(中国)投资有限公司	13621	7564	6057
267	北京 JVC 电子产业有限公司	13621	8414	5207
268	绥芬河市金恒基工业原料有限公司	13618	0	13618
269	深圳市金森珠宝首饰有限公司	13525	7092	6433
270	福建三丰鞋业有限公司	13426	7497	5929
271	天津矢崎汽车配件有限公司	13408	7862	5546
272	富士康电脑接插件昆山有限公司	13400	8423	4977
273	福建天成集团	13375	12758	617

1999年中国进出口额最大的500家企业（十二）

金额单位：万美元

名次	企业名称	进出口额	出口额	进口额
274	无锡阿尔卑斯电子有限公司	13358	5962	7432
275	上海航空进出口有限公司	13283	1687	11596
276	深圳施乐高科技有限公司	13255	7757	5498
277	安徽省轻工进出口有限责任公司	13244	12262	982
278	山西煤炭进出口集团公司	13216	13216	0
279	翔鹭涤纶纺纤(厦门)有限公司	13113	217	12896
280	天津三星电子显示器有限公司	13106	5387	7719
281	福建省珠宝首饰进出口公司	13093	11941	1152
282	福建清禄鞋业有限公司	13072	8934	4138
283	上海汉森进出口有限公司	13030	11180	1850
284	天津星湖实业有限公司	12999	6845	6154
285	中国航天科技集团公司	12958	5232	7726
	申航进出口公司	7814	3809	4005
286	中国普天信息产业集团公司	12903	721	12182
	东方通信股份有限公司	8975	561	8414
287	五矿国际货运上海公司保税仓库	12877	66	12811
288	浙江省工艺品进出口公司	12871	12259	612
289	福建荔丰鞋业开发有限公司	12811	8171	4640
290	戴尔计算机(中国)有限公司	12770	4866	7904
291	新世纪国际租赁有限公司	12661	0	12661
292	首钢日电电子有限公司	12591	8217	4374
293	江西省粮油食品进出口公司	12539	12509	30
294	天津三星视界有限公司	12534	273	12261
295	四海电子(昆山)有限公司	12447	7757	4690
296	神华集团有限责任公司	12440	6097	6343
	神华国际贸易有限责任公司	12440	6097	6343
297	北京市服装进出口股份有限公司	12373	9564	2809
298	浙江省萧山市进出口公司	12332	11012	1320
299	安徽省服装进出口股份有限公司	12067	11400	667
300	中国医药集团总公司	11953	2730	9223
	中国医药对外贸易总公司	7150	2632	4518
301	上海上实国际贸易(集团)有限公司	11906	5785	6121
302	深圳创华合作有限公司	11901	6583	5318
303	江苏省粮油食品进出口集团股份有限公司	11900	11697	203
304	青岛世原鞋业有限公司	11885	6954	4931
305	上海阿法泰克电子有限公司	11819	4079	7740
306	中国轻工集团公司	11782	335	11447
307	宁波工艺品进出口公司	11727	10814	913
308	牧田(中国)有限公司	11703	7246	4457

1999年中国进出口额最大的500家企业（十三）

金额单位：万美元

名次	企业名称	进出口额	出口额	进口额
309	深圳市宝安外贸实业股份有限公司	11645	7980	3665
	广东省宝安纺织品进出口公司	8289	5791	2498
310	杭州市轻工工艺纺织品进出口公司	11602	10846	756
311	济南钢铁集团总公司	11580	6106	5474
312	上海轮胎橡胶(集团)股份有限公司	11563	8807	2756
313	远纺工业(上海)有限公司	11550	3393	8157
314	上海爱梯恩梯通信设备有限公司	11531	7036	4495
315	厦门 TDK 有限公司	11476	5227	6249
316	江苏省畜产进出口集团股份有限公司	11437	10072	1365
317	三协精机(福州)有限公司	11430	5821	5609
318	丰源制靴大连有限公司	11415	6480	4935
319	深圳成丰电子有限公司	11409	6279	5130
320	汕头海洋(集团)公司	11336	482	10854
321	安徽省合肥联合发电有限公司	11315	0	11315
322	上海美能达光学仪器有限公司	11305	6060	5245
323	上海永新彩色显象管有限公司	11275	943	10332
324	北京国际贸易公司	11241	1446	9795
325	青岛安普连接器有限公司	11203	6273	4930
326	山东省丝绸进出口公司	11123	9814	1309
327	旭电(苏州)科技有限公司	11107	3087	8020
328	广东风华高新科技集团有限公司	11105	8848	2257
	风华进出口公司	9255	7309	1946
329	斯大精密(大连)有限公司	11054	6256	4798
330	日立半导体(苏州)有限公司	11011	5374	5637
331	丹东阿尔派电子有限公司	10994	6413	4581
332	江苏新科电子集团有限公司	10909	652	10257
333	上海钟表进出口有限公司	10881	7113	3768
334	厦门富士电气化学有限公司	10779	6019	4760
335	上海市土产进出口公司	10758	6476	4282
336	中国纺织物资(集团)总公司	10735	775	9960
337	广东省工艺品进出口(集团)公司	10732	9982	750
338	上海科艺电子有限公司	10693	5935	4758
339	天津三星光电子有限公司	10681	6124	4557
340	福建协丰鞋业有限公司	10653	7112	3541
341	上海新发展进出口贸易实业有限公司	10650	522	10128
342	四川省丝绸进出口公司	10645	10530	115
343	佳能大连办公设备有限公司	10637	2258	8379
344	厦门正新橡胶工业有限公司	10562	5049	5513
345	浙江省医药保健品进出口公司	10523	8893	1630

1999年中国进出口额最大的500家企业（十四）

金额单位：万美元

名次	企业名称	进出口额	出口额	进口额
346	厦门松下音响有限公司	10508	6993	3515
347	上海市机械设备进出口有限公司	10475	6663	3812
348	深圳三星电管有限公司	10466	3484	6982
349	浙江省国兴进出口公司	10424	6849	3575
350	厦门象屿集团有限公司	10386	3182	7204
351	飞利浦照明电子(上海)有限公司	10337	6374	3963
352	青岛大明皮革有限公司	10229	4771	5458
353	中国对外贸易开发总公司	10222	3521	6701
354	鸿城电子(上海)有限公司	10209	5875	4334
355	深圳市美芝工业公司	10145	4972	5173
356	青岛益佳集团	10115	8801	1314
357	英迈国际贸易(上海)有限公司	10050	2253	7797
358	杜邦中国集团有限公司	10032	5032	5000
359	福建省五金矿产进出口公司	10028	9100	928
360	上海对外经济贸易实业有限公司	9997	7215	2782
361	湖南三力通信经贸公司	9959	0	9959
362	上海乐金广电电子有限公司	9949	5595	4354
363	湖南省粮油食品进出口集团有限公司	9896	9853	43
364	温州经济技术开发区经济技术开发总公司	9823	4405	5418
365	福建省轻工业品进出口集团公司	9817	8913	904
366	青岛昌新鞋业有限公司	9817	5629	4188
367	中基宁波对外贸易有限责任公司	9682	6779	2903
368	上海派克电气有限公司	9654	5238	4416
369	天津市机械进出口集团有限公司	9541	7681	1860
370	青岛朗讯科技通讯设备服务有限公司	9541	164	9377
371	镇江奇美化工有限公司	9536	160	9376
372	上海大霸电子有限公司	9487	6192	3295
373	吉林德大有限公司	9486	5424	4062
374	四川省机械设备进出口公司	9440	394	9046
375	三菱四通集成电路有限公司	9414	3126	6288
376	山东省五金矿产进出口公司	9392	6742	2650
377	宁波市鄞县对外贸易有限责任公司	9343	8954	389
378	武汉市机械设备进出口公司	9340	4236	5104
379	苏州工业园区亚太纸品有限公司	9280	1929	7351
380	中国新兴(集团)总公司	9263	5050	4213
381	天津服装进出口公司	9254	7499	1755
382	上海理光传真机有限公司	9249	5960	3289
383	安徽省化工进出口股份有限公司	9241	7073	2168
384	青岛马士基集装箱工业有限公司	9197	2567	6630

1999年中国进出口额最大的500家企业（十五）

金额单位：万美元

名次	企业名称	进出口额	出口额	进口额
385	广西广达进出口集团公司	9171	8045	1126
386	陕西省机械设备进出口公司	9143	7880	1263
387	捷安特(中国)有限公司	9107	7102	2005
388	北京松下通信设备有限公司	9091	2194	6897
389	广西凭祥市进出口贸易公司	9087	8226	861
390	山东威海进出口集团有限公司	9026	6799	2227
391	中国石化国际事业大连公司	9022	5953	3069
392	湖北美岛服装有限公司	9009	4984	4025
393	上海汽车进出口公司	9008	4702	4306
394	广州市对外贸易总公司	8995	3196	5799
395	惠浦贸易(上海)有限公司	8971	19	8952
396	深圳王利电机有限公司	8967	5640	3327
397	浙江省化工进出口公司	8957	8283	674
398	上海进道集装箱有限公司	8934	4859	4075
399	长营电器(深圳)有限公司	8904	5386	3518
400	福建顺大运动用品有限公司	8895	6466	2429
401	扬州通运集装箱有限公司	8853	7226	1627
402	深圳先进微电子科技有限公司	8819	4376	4443
403	宁波宁兴集团公司	8718	7258	1460
404	北京富亿通达经贸有限责任公司	8696	7841	855
405	百得(苏州)电动工具有限公司	8690	5836	2854
406	辽宁佳益实业发展有限公司	8669	7463	1206
	辽宁省五矿进出口公司	8549	7343	1206
407	万威电讯(深圳)有限公司	8590	5089	3501
408	苏州日本电波工业有限公司	8581	4695	3886
409	大连松下通信工业有限公司	8550	4619	3931
410	上海太平国际货柜有限公司	8538	6752	1786
411	安徽省芜湖市进出口公司	8535	6547	1988
412	苏州精达集团公司	8515	4586	3929
413	安徽佳通轮胎有限公司	8493	4400	4093
414	辽宁省轻工业品进出口公司	8493	7472	1021
415	南京机械五金矿产医药保健品进出口股份有限公司	8484	7523	961
416	上海宝丽来影像有限公司	8483	4558	3925
417	英业达集团(上海)电子技术有限公司	8468	5110	3358
418	中国铝业集团公司	8466	6401	2065
419	中国航空工业第二集团公司	8451	1689	6762
420	新马制衣(深圳)有限公司	8437	4569	3868
421	天津汽车工业进出口公司	8426	1857	6569
422	罗姆电子大连有限公司	8399	4368	4031

1999年中国进出口额最大的500家企业（十六）

金额单位：万美元

名次	企业名称	进出口额	出口额	进口额
423	中商企业集团公司	8360	3409	4951
424	中国成套设备进出口(集团)总公司	8348	5237	3111
425	温州市鹿城对外贸易公司	8343	5458	2885
426	广东省食品进出口集团公司	8305	7904	401
427	辽宁华曦集团公司	8296	6497	1799
428	上海华申进出口有限公司	8295	7526	769
429	广州对外经济发展总公司	8291	4542	3749
430	乐山－菲尼克斯半导体有限公司	8270	3642	4628
431	北京市五金矿产进出口公司	8261	7434	827
432	浙江省轻工业品进出口公司	8217	7322	895
433	乐金曙光电子有限公司	8212	2339	5873
434	天津畜产进出口集团有限公司	8187	6592	1595
435	柯达电子(上海)有限公司	8183	5657	2526
436	莱芜钢铁集团有限公司	8142	6475	1667
437	美利达自行车(中国)有限公司	8127	5273	2854
438	上海三菱电梯有限公司	8099	468	7631
439	中国富利进出口集团公司	8094	2793	5301
440	深圳石川电子有限公司	8082	4889	3193
441	中国农垦(集团)总公司	8052	2370	5682
	中国农垦进出口公司	8052	2370	5682
442	深圳南天油粕工业有限公司	8041	2	8039
443	上海海外公司	8026	5883	2143
444	中国宁波国际合作(集团)有限责任公司	8005	4512	3493
445	烟台土畜产进出口集团有限公司	8001	4885	3116
446	云南冶金集团进出口有限公司	7979	7475	504
447	北京市京工服装进出口有限公司	7926	6938	988
448	上海东洋电装有限公司	7912	4865	3047
449	马钢国际经济贸易公司	7908	3019	4889
450	西安杨森制药有限公司	7902	371	7531
451	山东省食品进出口公司	7769	6178	1591
452	宝吉工艺品(深圳)有限公司	7750	4642	3108
453	长飞光纤光缆有限公司	7745	2982	4763
454	山东省畜产进出口公司	7743	6166	1577
455	河南省服装进出口公司	7716	5777	1939
456	深圳粤海电讯有限公司	7716	4463	3253
457	鸿兴印刷(深圳)有限公司	7684	2327	5357
458	深圳以莱特凉宇空调有限公司	7675	5304	2371
459	天津松下电子部品有限公司	7673	3515	4158
460	上海电视电子进出口公司	7642	4673	2969

1999年中国进出口额最大的500家企业（十七）

金额单位：万美元

名次	企 业 名 称	进出口额	出口额	进口额
461	淮阴市对外贸易公司	7620	6937	683
462	青岛纺织品联合进出口公司	7597	6636	961
463	上海先锋电声器材有限公司	7572	4450	3122
464	威海纺织集团进出口有限责任公司	7474	5324	2150
465	浙江省五金矿产进出口公司	7471	4866	2605
466	辽宁省对外贸易总公司	7434	3725	3709
467	东芝复印机(深圳)有限公司	7418	5101	2317
468	合肥日立挖掘机有限公司	7397	1	7396
469	中贸船舶进出口公司	7388	6540	848
470	北京东方冠捷电子有限公司	7381	3770	3611
471	上海先进半导体制造有限公司	7353	5526	1827
472	吴江市外贸集团公司	7344	6587	757
473	广州畜产进出口公司	7331	6090	1241
474	苏州工业园区华能阿莫科清洁能源有限公司	7309	0	7309
475	新疆农垦进出口股份有限公司	7283	7250	33
476	浙江桐乡外贸集团股份有限公司	7282	6579	703
477	上海浦东新区进出口公司	7268	2222	5046
478	宁波海田国际贸易有限公司	7238	6305	933
479	河北省进出口公司	7234	3238	3996
480	张家港浦项不锈钢有限公司	7231	0	7231
481	东北制药总厂进出口公司	7203	6144	1059
482	重庆长安汽车进出口公司	7183	29	7154
483	广西粮油食品进出口公司	7181	7050	131
484	安徽进出口股份有限公司	7178	4646	2532
485	辽宁省纺织品进出口公司	7177	6273	904
486	正新橡胶(中国)有限公司	7175	4113	3062
487	山东省医药保健品进出口公司	7168	5260	1908
488	福建华星石化有限公司	7159	0	7159
489	三九企业集团	7153	1062	6091
490	浙江省机械设备进出口公司	7139	6325	814
491	宁波市纺织品进出口公司	7077	6818	259
492	天津富士光机有限公司	7072	3734	3338
493	河北省食品进出口(集团)公司	7046	6653	393
494	华北制药集团有限责任公司	7040	6523	517
495	耐克(苏州)体育用品有限公司	7035	4543	2492
496	四川省东方电力设备联合公司	7006	4839	2167
497	福建省土产畜产进出口公司	7000	5568	1432
498	绥芬河市对外贸易公司	6994	6994	0
499	沪士电子昆山有限公司	6993	4407	2586
500	宏碁电脑(深圳)有限公司	6981	3918	3063

1999年中国出口额最大的200家企业（一）

对外贸易经济合作部二〇〇〇年七月三日公布

金额单位：万美元

序号	企业名称	出口额
1	东方国际(集团)有限公司	177619
2	中国化工进出口总公司	144709
3	中国粮油食品进出口(集团)有限公司	117287
4	中国工艺品进出口总公司	111998
5	摩托罗拉(中国)电子有限公司	98662
6	中国煤炭工业进出口集团公司	92178
7	中国船舶工业贸易公司	88982
8	中国电子进出口总公司	86016
9	中国机械装备(集团)公司	76461
10	中国石油天然气集团公司	75520
11	中国石化国际事业公司	71128
12	中国北方工业公司	70386
13	中国航空技术进出口总公司	67357
14	中国土产畜产进出口总公司	62828
15	希捷国际科技(无锡)有限公司	62248
16	中国国际海运集装箱(集团)股份有限公司	60325
17	深圳希捷科技有限公司	57986
18	中国通用技术(集团)控股有限责任公司	57056
19	英特尔科技(中国)有限公司	56009
20	广东核电合营有限公司	54399
21	中国铜铅锌集团公司	54137
22	中国有色金属进出口总公司	53450
23	中国五金矿产进出口总公司	51789
24	中国纺织品进出口总公司	45928
25	冠捷电子(福建)公司	40586
26	浙江中大集团控股有限公司	39500
27	中国海洋石油总公司	39470
28	江苏舜天国际集团有限公司	38918
29	中国出口商品基地建设总公司	38774
30	宝钢集团国际经济贸易总公司	38208
31	中国对外贸易运输(集团)总公司	37831
32	中国钢铁工贸集团公司	37778
33	江苏国泰国际集团有限公司	37755
34	爱普生技术(深圳)有限公司	37751
35	北方国际集团有限公司	36860
36	深圳开发科技股份有限公司	36524
37	江苏汇鸿国际集团有限公司	34900
38	友利电电子(深圳)有限公司	33872
39	浙江省丝绸进出口公司	32091
40	唯冠科技(深圳)有限公司	32073
41	盐田国际集装箱码头有限公司	31408
42	中国华源集团有限公司	31187
43	中国烟草进出口总公司	31171
44	浙江省土产畜产进出口公司	30292
45	中国包装进出口总公司	30166
46	上海轻工国际(集团)有限公司	30146
47	富金精密工业(深圳)有限公司	28606
48	新疆对外经济贸易(集团)有限责任公司	28406
49	上海兰生(集团)有限公司	28173
50	中国深圳对外贸易(集团)公司	28072
51	仁宝电脑工业(中国)有限公司	27264
52	江苏省丝绸进出口集团股份有限公司	27200
53	上海索广电子有限公司	26953
54	才众电脑(深圳)有限公司	26619
55	深圳三洋华强激光电子有限公司	26277
56	葆祥国际服装中心	26056
57	深圳海量存储设备有限公司	25663
58	苏州明基电脑有限公司	25362
59	中国北方工业集团公司	25139
60	夏普办公设备(常熟)有限公司	25076
61	深圳市物资集团公司	24954
62	广东省纺织品进出口(集团)公司	24686
63	嘉兴市进出口公司	24614
64	理光(深圳)工业发展有限公司	24562
65	中国国际信托投资公司	24337
66	中国长城工业总公司	24298
67	苏州进出口(集团)有限公司	23814
68	山东省机械进出口公司	23809
69	飞利浦电子元件(上海)有限公司	23720
70	浙江省粮油食品进出口股份有限公司	23450

1999年中国出口额最大的200家企业（二）

金额单位：万美元

序号	企业名称	出口额	序号	企业名称	出口额
71	苏州罗技电子有限公司	23127	109	常熟市对外贸易公司	16561
72	深圳长科国际电子有限公司	23039	110	安徽省粮油食品进出口(集团)公司	16397
73	中国稀有稀土金属集团公司	23019	111	鑫茂科技(深圳)有限公司	16369
74	江苏省轻工业品进出口集团股份有限公司	22897	112	广州纺织品进出口集团有限公司	16272
			113	上海东方航空进出口公司	16071
75	北京·松下电子部品有限公司	22733	114	山东工艺品进出口(集团)股份有限公司	15981
76	浙江东方集团股份有限公司	22639			
77	广州轻工业品进出口(集团)公司	22569	115	丹东饭山显示器有限公司	15969
78	上海市工艺品进出口有限公司	22433	116	江南造船(集团)有限责任公司	15948
79	中国化工建设总公司	21789	117	大连西太平洋石油化工有限公司	15725
80	福建厦门经贸集团有限公司	21412	118	北京诺基亚移动通信有限公司	15680
81	山东省纺织品进出口公司	21167	119	南通市经济技术开发区总公司	15652
82	江苏省海外企业集团有限公司	21031	120	中国工艺美术(集团)公司	15417
83	浙江省纺织品进出口公司	20909	121	江苏省工艺品进出口集团股份有限公司	15412
84	天津三星电机有限公司	20900			
85	厦门太古飞机工程有限公司	20689	122	上海新康电子有限公司	15330
86	山东省服装进出口集团总公司	20299	123	浙江省畜产进出口公司	15221
87	中国江苏国际经济技术合作公司	20216	124	上海美蓓亚精密机电有限公司	15201
88	宁波中海贸进出口有限公司	19843	125	北京工艺进出口有限责任公司	15067
89	凯远集团公司	19793	126	奥林巴斯(深圳)工业有限公司	14976
90	南京纺织品进出口股份有限公司	19714	127	大连日通外运货运公司	14877
91	中国(福建)对外贸易中心集团	19624	128	江苏省纺织品进出口集团股份有限公司	14829
92	厦门灿坤实业股份有限公司	19535			
93	三洋电机(蛇口)有限公司	19278	129	宁波维科集团	14565
94	福建省粮油食品进出口公司	19203	130	宁波市慈溪进出口股份有限公司	14457
95	中国轻工业品进出口总公司	19082	131	上海新联纺进出口公司	14174
96	苏州飞利浦消费电子有限公司	18901	132	深圳赛意法微电子有限公司	14122
97	上海服装(集团)有限公司	18782	133	西迪斯(天津)电子有限公司	13805
98	三美电机有限公司	18655	134	中国华录集团有限公司	13777
99	伟创力实业(深圳)有限公司	18138	135	力捷电脑(中国)有限公司	13709
100	广东省轻工业品进出口(集团)公司	18098	136	北京市富亿通进出口有限责任公司	13597
101	苏州爱普生有限公司	17930	137	常州市对外贸易公司	13536
102	吉粮集团进出口公司	17616	138	中国港湾建设(集团)总公司	13464
103	中国丝绸进出口总公司	17550	139	厦门国贸集团股份有限公司	13403
104	上海新锐实业有限公司	17457	140	金朋(上海)有限公司	13354
105	日本电产(大连)有限公司	17432	141	上海JVC电器有限公司	13266
106	上海申达股份有限公司	17302	142	茉织华实业(集团)有限公司	13264
107	厦门建发股份有限公司	17231	143	中国土产畜产浙江茶叶进出口公司	13262
108	辽宁成大股份有限公司	16915	144	山西煤炭进出口集团公司	13216

1999年中国出口额最大的200家企业（三）

金额单位：万美元

序号	企业名称	出口额	序号	企业名称	出口额
145	青岛三美电机有限公司	13059	173	上海机械进出口(集团)有限公司	11096
146	连云港市对外贸易公司	12917	174	浙江省萧山市进出口公司	11012
147	福建天成集团	12758	175	杭州市轻工工艺纺织品进出口公司	10846
148	山东省对外贸易集团有限公司	12678	176	宁波经济技术开发区进出口公司	10827
149	青岛泰光制鞋有限公司	12617	177	宁波工艺品进出口公司	10814
150	江西省粮油食品进出口公司	12509	178	中国原子能工业公司	10697
151	天津三星电子有限公司	12488	179	广东格兰仕企业(集团)公司	10610
152	河北省纺织品进出口(集团)公司	12274	180	安徽省技术进出口股份有限公司	10590
153	安徽省轻工进出口有限责任公司	12262	181	深圳乐意液体仓储有限公司	10533
154	浙江省工艺品进出口公司	12259	182	四川省丝绸进出口公司	10530
155	河北圣仑进出口集团公司	12225	183	华科立资讯科技(深圳)有限公司	10461
156	鞍钢集团国际经济贸易公司	12202	184	江苏省技术进出口公司	10457
157	天津阿尔卑斯电子有限公司	12200	185	万宝至马达大连有限公司	10392
158	三星电子(苏州)半导体有限公司	12148	186	深圳奥康德石油贸易集团公司	10281
159	南通市对外贸易公司	12147	187	深圳国际商业机器技术产品有限公司	10266
160	攀钢集团国际经济贸易总公司	12115	188	无锡夏普电子元器件有限公司	10241
161	上海畜产(集团)有限公司	11983	189	富士通将军(上海)有限公司	10166
162	福建省珠宝首饰进出口公司	11941	190	江苏省畜产进出口集团股份有限公司	10072
163	天津外总集团有限公司	11927	191	保利科技有限公司	10069
164	江苏省粮油食品进出口集团股份有限公司	11697	192	广东省工艺品进出口(集团)公司	9982
			193	湖南省粮油食品进出口集团有限公司	9853
165	中国汽车工业进出口总公司	11535	194	上海夏普电器有限公司	9841
166	中国远大集团公司	11439	195	山东省丝绸进出口公司	9814
167	上海市食品进出口公司	11412	196	辽宁时代服装进出口股份有限公司	9772
168	安徽省服装进出口股份有限公司	11400	197	哈尔滨双太电子实业有限公司	9729
169	海尔集团	11398	198	南太电子(深圳)有限公司	9715
170	厦门进雄企业有限公司	11202	199	中国水产(集团)总公司	9660
171	上海汉森进出口有限公司	11180	200	北京市服装进出口股份有限公司	9564
172	温州市进出口公司	11126			

对外贸易经济合作部主要出版物

1. 中国对外经济贸易年鉴

《中国对外经济贸易年鉴》是一部以编年体详细记述中国对外经济贸易发展情况的政府出版物；

《中国对外经济贸易年鉴》由对外贸易经济合作部主持编纂，编委会主任、副主任分别由外经贸部部长和海关总署署长担任；

《中国对外经济贸易年鉴》创刊于1984年，每年用中、英两种文字分册出版，面向国内外公开发行；

《中国对外经济贸易年鉴》分设“法规”“统计”“地方经贸”“国别经贸”“机构”“大事记”等九个栏目，内容全面、系统、资料翔实，是我国对外经济贸易领域唯一一部专业性年鉴；

《中国对外经济贸易年鉴》是海内外各界人士了解、研究中国对外经济贸易的权威性工具书和史料性参考书。

通讯地址：北京市安定门外东后巷28号外经贸部《中国对外经济贸易年鉴》编辑部

邮编：100710

电话：(010) 64246856、64216661-1101

传真：(010) 64212175、64246856

2. 国际商报

《国际商报》是对外贸易经济合作部的机关报，是我国对外经贸领域权威性和综合性的报纸，也是海外发行量最大的中国五大财经报纸之一。由邓小平同志亲自题写报头。1985年4月1日正式出版，每周七刊。《国际商报》的宗旨是“让世界了解中国，让中国了解世界”。其主要内容是：宣传对外开放的方针政策，独家刊载对外贸易经济合作部发布的政策法规，公布配额招标公告和结果，以舆论指导全国对外经贸工作；报道国际经贸动态、市场行情、国际经贸热点新闻，发表权威言论，展望发展趋势：传播贸易机会、商品供求、国际招标、技术转让、劳务合作等最新信息，为进出口贸易、利用外资、引进技术提供咨询服务；解释对外经贸政策，普及国际经贸知识。介绍中外名牌产品和国内外经贸企业。

社址：北京方庄路芳星园三区14号楼

邮编：100078

电话：67628822、67629580

传真：67629153、67626875

3. 国际经贸消息

《国际经贸消息》是由外经贸部主管、外经贸部国际贸易经济合作研究院主办的涉外经济类专业报纸，创刊于1958年1月7日，是中国经济领域历史最悠久的权威性中央级产业报。现为对开四版，每周一、二、三、四、五、六出版，每年不定期出版三十多期彩色国别/地区市场专刊。及时全面报道世界经济贸易领域重大事件，动态跟踪国际市场行情变化是该报的主要特色。每日刊登国际市场200余种商品价格和大量准确实用的贸易机会是该报的独家信息。报道中国外经贸政策法规和各地外经贸事业的发展成就，是该报的重要内容。该报的主要版块有：要闻版、世界经济版、理论实务版、综合信息版、中国外经贸版、商务周刊、物流周刊以及按商品和服务类别划分的市场导刊——包括粮油食品土畜、纺织品服装、轻工电子医保、机电汽车、五矿化工、交通运输等。《国际经贸消息》是各界读者了解包括中国在内的各国（地区）外经贸政策法规、洞悉世界经济、把握国际市场行情的公认的主要媒体之一。该报的主要读者分布在各国驻华及中国驻外使领馆商务机构、外国公司驻华机构、专业外贸公司、工贸公司、边贸公司、三资企业、海关、商检、各级政府及大专院校和科研院所等。

社址：北京安定门外东后巷28号

邮编：100710

电话：64248987

传真：64211398

网址：http：//www.itn.com.cn
e-mail：itna @ public.bta.net.cn
邮发代号：1—35
国外代号：D796

社址：中国北京安定门外东后巷28号
邮编：100710
电话：(010) 64241425、64241423
传真：(010) 64212149
E-mail：intertrade@netchina.com.cn

4. 中华人民共和国对外贸易经济合作部文告

《中华人民共和国对外贸易经济合作部文告》是1993年根据国务院办公厅的通知精神和我国在对外谈判中的承诺，经国家新闻出版署批准，由外经贸部办公厅编辑出版的政府出版物，是外经贸部指定的刊载发生法律效力的对外经济贸易文件的公开出版物。

自1999年7月1日起，外经贸部将主要以《文告》形式及时、统一对外公布有关法律、法规和规章，刊登《文告》后不再另行发文。《文告》刊载的有关文件与红头文件具有同等法律效力，其他报刊转载或有关部门发的对外经贸法律、法规和规章性文件，如与《文告》有出入时，一律以《文告》为准。

《中华人民共和国对外贸易经济合作部文告》为周刊，向国内外发行，国内统一刊号：CN11—3214/D。
通讯地址：北京市东长安街2号
邮政编码：100731

5. 国际贸易

《国际贸易》杂志（中文版）于1982年创刊，系中国对外贸易经济合作部主管的第一本国内外公开发行的国际经济贸易专业刊物，被“WTO”、联合国国际贸易中心图书馆、国际货币基金、世界银行、美国国会图书馆等国际组织及知名机构所订阅和收藏，是国内外经贸界公认的中国经济贸易期刊中权威专业杂志。

杂志宗旨：阐述中国改革开放政策，促进国际经济贸易发展。

栏目设置：封面文章、中国贸易、贸易关系、国际商务、市场、投资、金融、法律。

读者结构：中央及地方政府经济主管决策官员；国有外贸进出口公司、工商企业、中外合资企业经理；各国驻华商务机构代表及主管；大专院校师生及研究人员等。

6. 国际经济合作

《国际经济合作》杂志集新闻、理论、实务于一体，报导国际经贸重大动态介绍对外经贸实务知识，推荐兴办“三资”企业的经验，提供合资合作机会，传递经贸政策法规信息，特别是在跨国经营、国际发展与合作、产业发展政策等领域具有权威性和指导性。《国际经济合作》杂志，每月20日在北京用中文出版，附有英文提要。杂志在国内外公开发行10年来，已经成为中国对外经济贸易的重要刊物，拥有包括从中央政府决策者到基层企业经营管理人员在内的庞大的读者群。与此同时，《国际经济合作》杂志还通过举办展览会、讲习班，为中外客商提供各种相关的服务。
地址：北京安定门外东后巷28号
邮编：100710
电话：(8610) 64211078
传真：(8610) 64212175

7. 中华人民共和国对外贸易经济合作部新闻公报

《新闻公报》系中国外经贸部官方权威刊物，主要介绍中国对外经贸行业当前的发展现状、发展动向以及对外经贸正在和将要采取的政策措施、管理办法和法规条例等，还将对国外所关注的一些问题作解释说明，并附有中国进出口商品构成表，中国进出口主要国别（地区）情况表以及中国利用外资统计表等。可供各级对外经贸行政管理部门、进出口企业的领导、外事人员和业务人员在对外经贸与涉外活动中掌握使用。也是世界各国经贸界了解中国对外经贸发展的窗口。

本刊全年12期，月初出版，中英文对照。由中国对外经济贸易出版社在国内外全权发行。
地址：北京市安定门外东后巷28号
邮政编码：100710
发行部电话：64215625　64226011

编辑部电话：64218072

8. 商业周刊/中文版（月刊）（Business Week/China）

《商业周刊/中文版》（原《国际商业与管理》）创刊于1986年，由中国对外经济贸易出版社与美国麦格劳·希尔公司（McGraw—Hill Inc.）合作出版。

《商业周刊/中文版》内容全部选译自美国Business Week（《商业周刊》）文章，旨在传播介绍世界经贸、金融、科技和新兴产业、企业管理经验等权威信息。它特别有助于决策者掌握和提高企业管理水平，是经贸人士、企业管理人员和从事经济研究的师生学者不可多得的参考读物。本刊采用进口高级铜版纸彩印，图文并茂，装帧精美。

地址：北京市安定门外东后巷28号
邮编：100710
发行部电话：64215625　64226011
编辑部电话：64218072
传真：64219392

9. 中国经贸画报

《中国经贸画报》系外经贸部主管、外经贸企业协会主办，国内外公开发行的经贸类综合性月刊，于1996年正式出版。

《中国经贸画报》立足企业、服务企业，向国内外经贸界、企业提供中外最新权威性经济贸易信息，是国际贸易和经济技术合作交流的重要媒体和信息桥梁。主要读者对象为：海内外经贸界、企业界人士、政府经济贸易部门，企业经营管理部门，商务商情部门以及媒体工作人员，高等院校师生和有关科研人员。

该刊采用大16开本，图文并茂，彩色精印。可发布国内、外商来华广告。国内统一刊号：CN11—3592/F，自办发行。国际标准刊号：ISSN1006－9380，由中国国际图书贸易总公司发行，发行代号1350M。

社址：中国北京东城区台基厂头条10号
邮编：100005
综合业务部电话（兼传真）：65270698
广告、发行部电话（兼传真）：65141428
编辑部电话（兼传真）：65240877
E－mail：jingmao@public.bta.net.cn

10. 国际贸易问题

《国际贸易问题》杂志是对外贸易经济合作部主管、对外经济贸易大学主办的国际经济贸易类刊物，创刊于1975年。读者对象主要是外经贸主管部门和业务部门的决策人员、外商投资企业的管理人员、国际经贸理论的研究人员以及高等院校师生。主要栏目有经贸论坛、部长及省市长专访、省市外经贸委主任专稿、海外来稿、世贸组织、国际商务研究、世界市场透视、国际投资与跨国经营、国际服务贸易、国际金融、国际经济法、企业家论坛、电子商务、环境与贸易、台港澳等。本刊选题密切结合当前国内外的热点问题，题材新颖，有较高的学术水平。

本刊为月刊，每月6日出版，刊号CN11－1692F，邮发代号2－847。

地址：北京市朝阳区惠新东街对外经济贸易大学106信箱
邮编：100029
电话：64492401，64492402

第一届（1998/99年度）全国外经贸研究成果奖获奖名单

著作奖

奖项	获奖者	成果
一等奖	张　祥（主编）	《知识经济与国际经济贸易》
二等奖	（空缺）	
三等奖	（按姓氏笔划排列）	
	王志乐	《日本企业在中国的投资》
	巴曙松、邢毓静、邵长毅	《中国外汇市场运行研究》
	陈文敬、默瑞·吉布斯、唐小兵、赵玉敏主编	《多边贸易体系与“入世”：中国面对的贸易壁垒》
	沈根荣	《绿色营销管理》

论文奖

奖项	获奖者	成果
一等奖	王洛林、裴长洪、徐　鸣	《国有企业利用外商投资的认识与政策建议》
二等奖	（按姓氏笔划排列）	
	江小涓	《利用外资与经济增长方式的转变》
	张小济	《开拓加工贸易中间投入品市场》
	陈家勤、贾　康、江旭东、翟　凡、程　永	《我国外贸对经济增长的贡献与外贸扶持政策调整的基本取向》
	薛　宏（执笔）、王成安、曹运池、叶继奖、尹集庆、麦沛然、肖明湘	《我国援外规模、布局和结构问题研究》
三等奖	（按姓氏笔划排列）	
	田维明、何秀荣、王秀清、肖海峰、李伟克、介跃建	《中国农产品贸易政策选择》
	张玉卿、徐进亮	《如何有效提高我国加工贸易水平》
	张应文	《引导民营经济走向外向型发展道路》
	沈四宝	《把握大同和小异——涉外经济合同适用新合同法的基本原则》
	李邦君	《上海国有外贸企业与“三资”企业出口贸易比较研究》
	李善同、翟　凡、王　直、徐　林	《中国加入世界贸易组织对世界经济及其自身的影响》
	杜公朴、孙福庆、桑　琦、赵抗美	《扩大工程承包业务，带动商品出口发展》
	谷克鉴	《HBS推断的验证与拓展：中国国民部门与外资部门出口波动差异的实证分析》
	贾金思	《优化结构：步入成熟债务国后我国利用外商直接投资的战略取向》
	高建华、康玉燕、万正华、王小健、赵君琦	《制定政府采购用的原产地规则在我国的现实意义和作用》

鼓 励 奖

(按姓氏笔划排列)

王玉海	《当代西方“新贸易理论”评析》
王凤鸣	《创新托管 搞活兼并 重组外贸无形资产》
卢先堃	《加强协调指导 建立预警机制——关于应对欧盟反倾销工作的思考和建议》
刘汉波	《中远集团海外发展战略和策略研究》
刘 亚、黄开忠	《银贸债务问题探析》
张向晨、孙 亮	《论发展中国家参加多边贸易体制的得与失》
张瑞昆	《论云南边贸政策》
张建民	《中国专业服务贸易的对外开放和适度保护》
闵 森	《中国境外投资企业规避投资政治险的对策》
杨圣明、赵 瑾	《论我国外资中介组织创新》
金柏松	《关于建立亚洲货币体系的几点思考》
傅慧芬	《关系营销与竞争优势》

广　告　索　引

宁波市对外经济贸易合作委员会

Ningbo Foreign Trade & Economic Cooperation Commission

宁波位于中国大陆海岸线中段，是我国东南沿海重要的港口城市，也是长江三角洲南翼经济中心。全市辖3县、3市、5区，总面积9365平方公里，人口538万。1999年全市国内生产总值1070亿元，进出口贸易额50.09亿美元，财政收入104亿元，全市已形成以石油及精细化工、电力为主体，电子、冶金、建材、轻纺、食品、医药等协调发展的工业体系。宁波以深水良港著称。宁波港拥有大中小泊位60余座，1999年货物吞吐量9660万吨，位居中国3大港口之一，也是全球10个能接卸30万吨级货轮的深水港之一；集装箱干线连接亚欧美各大港口，集装箱吞吐量已突破60万标箱。新的千年，宁波将与世界各国共同合作，在港口建设、经济发展取得更快更大的进展。

Located in the middle of China's coastline, Ningbo is an important port city on the southeast coastline and the economic center of the south flank of the Yangtze River delta. The Municipality governs 3 counties, 3 cities and 5 districts with a total area of 9365 square kilometers and a population of 5.38 million. Its GDP in 1999 hit RMB107 million, 50.09 billion U.S.Dollars for its import & export trade volume, RMB 10.4 billion for its financial revenue, an industrial set-up has taken shape with petrochemical, refined chemical and power as it mainstay and machinery, electronics, metallurgical, building material, light industry, textile, food and pharmaceutical developed in harmony. Ningbo is known for its deep-water port. With more than 60 berths of all sizes and a throughput of 96.6 million tons of cargo in 1999, Ningbo Port stands the third among the largest ports in mainland China and finds its membership of the 10 deep-water ports around the world capable of berthing 300,000-tonnage cargo ships. The container handling capacity of the port topped 600,000 TEU with its container lines connecting large ports of Asla, Europe and America. In the new kiloyear, Ningbo is going to cooperate with the countries of all over the world to make larger and more repid progress on port construction and economic development.

地址：宁波市灵桥路190号
Add：190, Lingqiao Road, Ningbo
电话（Tel）：0574-7328188（总机，Switchboard） 传真（Fax）：0574-7328288
E-mail：nftec@ec.com.cn

吉林德大有限公司

Jilin De Da Company Limited

吉林德大有限公司董事长 / 总裁：王秀林
Chairman of The Board / President:Wang Xiulin

吉林德大有限公司位于吉林省德惠市，创立于1989年5月，是吉林省松辽禽业联营公司与泰国正大集团合资经营的肉鸡“一条龙”企业，公司是集种禽、繁育、肉鸡饲养、饲料加工、肉食加工、油脂加工于一体，多种优势集于一身的多元化经济实体。

企业实行“公司加农户”的组织模式和贸工农一体化、产加销“一条龙”的经营方式。主要产品有鸡雏、各种饲料、色拉油、高蛋白豆粕、冻分割鸡肉、烧烤熟食、火腿肠等，年产鸡肉11万吨。产品远销日本、南非、中东、欧洲等十几个国家和地区，国内市场已覆盖了29个省、市、自治区。年销售收入25亿元人民币、出口创汇6000万美元。公司经过十年的经营，不但取得了较好的企业效益，而且还取得了广泛的社会效益。

Jilin De Da Company Limited Brief Introduction

Jilin De Da Company Limited is a coordinated Sino- foreign joint Ventures between jilin Provincial Songliao Poultry Cooperative Company and Chia Tai Group of Thailand

founded in May 1989,located in Dehui city, Jilin Provine,P.R. China, with broiler raising, feed milling ,

meat processing and oil processing to be onelt is an economic entity with multi-coordinated businesses and various.

Jilin De Da Co.Ltd. carries out the pattern of "company plus farmers"and the managing mode of a vertical integration of "production plus sales".De Da major Productions include Day-old -chicken various feeds, salad oil, high protein soybean meal°¢various cutting chickens and ham etc.sausage ect.It annually prodluces 110, 000 tons of chicken De Da Brand products have been exported to more than ten countries and areas such as Japan,South Africa, Middle East and Europe etc.and have been sold to 29 proinences, cities and autonomous regions in China and the annual sale income is 2,50 million yuan, the annual expoort income is 60 million yuan the operation of the past ten years,the Jilin De Da has achieved not only a better profit,but also a wide spread social benefits.

饲料二厂
Feed Mill II

灌装车间 Filling Oil Workshop

油脂厂全景 Exterior View of Oil Plant

优良种鸡
Good Breeders

优选鸡雏 Day-oid-chicken chosen

公司地址：吉林省德惠市(邮编：130300)
Address: Dehui City, Jilin Province,P.R.C.
Post code:130300
电话：0431-7201001 Telephone: 0431-7201001
传真 0431-7201017 E-mail: DHWY@yeah.net
董事长 总裁：王秀林
Chairman of the Board/President: Wang Xiulin

肉食加工厂全貌 Exterior View of Meat Processing Plant

分割车间 Cutting Room

汇鸿国际集团有限公司

江苏汇鸿国际集团成立于1996年12月18日，是由原江苏省针棉织品进出口集团公司为骨干，联合原江苏省土产进出口集团股份有限公司、江苏省医药保健品进出口集团公司组建的大型外贸集团企业，是江苏省省级重点企业集团之一。

江苏汇鸿国际集团核心企业——江苏汇鸿国际集团有限公司主营对外贸易、实施项目投资、资本运作、房地产开发、物业管理、国内贸易及其它服务性贸易。集团公司拥有全资或控股的生产及贸易型企业20多家，其中有7家从事进出口业务的专业外贸子公司，并在美国、日本、德国、英国、俄罗斯、罗马尼亚、中国香港等国家和地区设立了10家海外机构。

江苏汇鸿国际集团有限公司拥有雄厚的实力，净资产总额逾4亿多元。1998年进出口总额达3.42亿美元，其中出口3.26亿美元，位居全省前茅，在经贸部发表的中国进出口总额最大的500家企业中，98年名列第51位。

汇鸿国际集团遵循现代企业管理原则，运用社会主义市场经济营销策略，坚持以资产为核心，效益为中心，经营与管理并重，努力实现自我积累，向着国际化、综合化目标迈进。

Jiangsu High Hope International Group was founded on December 18th, 1996. As one of the pivotal group enterprises in Jiangsu Province, it is a large foreign trade group enterprise incorporated from the former Jiangsu Knitwear and Home-textiles Import & Export Group corporation, its mainstay, in combination with the former Jiangsu Native Produce Import and Export Group Corporation and the former Jiangsu Medicines and Health Products Import and Export Group Corporation.

Jiangsu Hign Hope International Group Corporation Limited, the core enterprise of Jiangsu High Hope International Group, mainly deals in foreign trade, project investment, capital operation, real estate development and management, domestic trade and trade of services. The Group Corporation owns over 20 full capital or share holding manufacturing or trading enterprises, among which 7 professional foreign trade subsidiary companies specialize in import and export business. It has also set up 10 overseas branch offices in USA, Japan, Germany, UK, Russia, Romania and the Hong Kong Administrative District.

High Hope International Group Corporation Limited bases its solid economic strength on a net asset of over four hundred million Yuan. The total Import and export business in 1998 accumulated to 342 million US dollars. An export quantity of 324 million US dollars won the Group Corporation its third place position in the province and enabled it to be one of the 500 enterprises with the greatest sum of import and export in China.

High Hope International Group Corporation Limited follows the principles of modern enterprise management and applies marketing strategy of socialist market economy, holding capital as its core and profitability its goal. With simultaneous focus on both development and management, the Corporation endeavors to achieve self-accumulation on its way to globalization and diversification.

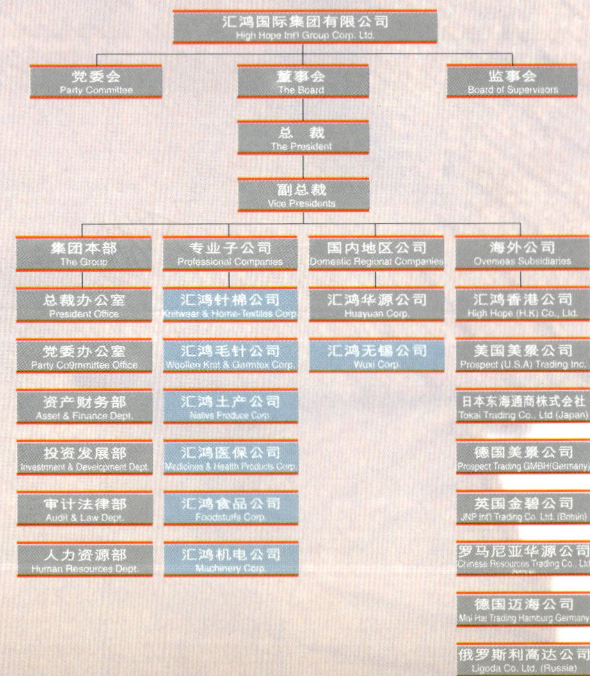

上海轻工国际（集团）有限公司

SHANGHAI LIGHT INDUSTRIAL INTERNATIONAL (GROUP) CORP., LTD.

上海轻工国际（集团）有限公司是一家以经营轻工业品出口为主业的大型国有外贸企业，它的前身为1954年成立的上海市轻工业品进出口公司。近半个世纪以来，凭借着优质的产品、优良的服务和灵活多样的贸易方式，公司规模得到迅速发展。目前已拥有16家子分公司经营40个大类、400多个品种和10000多种规模的进出口业务。本公司在全球已建立了一个可信赖的国际营销网络，有160多个国家和地区的6000家客商与我们有着贸易往来。

集团在经贸部发表的中国进出口总额最大的500家企业中，98年名列第50位，并在1999年上海外贸专业公司中率先通过ISO9000质量体系认证，这将为海内外客商提供更优惠的产品和服务。

董事长：马家骏

Shanghai Light Industrial International (Group) Corp., Ltd. former "Shanghai Light Industrial Products Import & Export Corporation" is one of the largest state-owner foreign trade enterprise founded in 1954. Over the last half century, the corporation has been rapid developed, relying on its superior quality of commodities, satisfying service and flexible trade method. Subordinated to our group, There are 16 importing and exporting subsidary companies dealing in 40 categories over 400 kinds and more than ten thousand specifications of light industrial products. A credible international sales network has been set up and we have over 6000 regular clients from over 160 countries and regions worldwide.

In 1998, the group is listed as the 50th among the top 500 foreign trade corporations of China and in 1999, the group is the leading one in the local foreign trade enterprise obtaining ISO9000 certificated, which is to be another strength to ensure both quality goods and perfect service.

马家骏董事长（左）接受中国进出口商品质量认证中心授予我公司ISO9002质量体系认证证书

地址：上海市四平路198号
Add：198, SiPing Road, Shanghai, China
邮编 (Post Code)：200086
电话 (Tel)：0086-21-65081688
传真 (Fax)：0086-21-65082388
网址 (Web site)：http ://www.shanghailight.com.cn
E-mail：sligroup@guomai.sh.cn

中国南京国际经济技术合作有限责任公司

中国南京国际经济技术合作有限责任公司是经国家外经贸部授权，南京市人民政府批准设立的大型外经企业。公司由外经窗口企业与大型建筑企业联合组建，国家建设部设点企业、上市公司中国广厦集团控股，实行经营实体与资本市场结合，按现代企业制度规范运作。

中国南京国际经济技术合作有限责任公司具有对外工程承包，劳务合作，进出口贸易等经营权，业务范围主要包括：承包各类国外工程，承担我国对外经济援助项目，向境外派遣劳务人员，在海外举办各类企业，进出口贸易，房地产投资、开发，商品房销售、租赁，国内工业与民用建筑等。

截止一九九九年底，公司先后在二十几个国家和地区成功实施了五十多个国际招标项目，向中东、东南亚地区派了大量劳务人员，在科威特，乌干达，纳米比亚等国家设立了办事处和分公司，在国际市场赢得了较高的地位和良好商誉。

中国南京国际经济技术合作有限责任公司愿与各界朋友开展全方位的真诚合作。

China Nanjing International Limited (hereinafter referred to as CNI) is a large-scale foreign economic enterprise licensed by the Ministry of Foreign Trade and Economic Cooperation of the People's Republic of China and approved by the People's government of Nanjing Municipality. Combining business entity with capital market, CNI, joint venture of foreign economic etnteprise and listing company China Guangsha Group, which is also a pilot company of State Construction Ministry and holds shares of CNI, will carry out its business in accordance with contemporary enterprise system.

CNI has been authorized to undertake foreign project contracting, labor service cooperation and import and export trade etc. The main business includes contracting foreign projects, implementing foreign economic aid program assigned by the Chinese Government, dispatching labors abroad, establishing enterprise abroad, import and export trade, real estate investment and development, sale and leasing of commercial residential buildings, domestic industrial and civilian construction, etc.

Till now, CNI has successfully undertaken more than 50 projects through international bidding in about 20 countries and regions, and has dispatched large quantities and all kinds of labors to the Middle-east and Southeast Asia, Africa, Europe and America. Simultaneously, CNI has respectively established branch companies and offices in Kuwait, Uganda and Namibia, etc., becoming an influential company with good reputation internationally.

CNI sincerely wishes to cooperate with all partners in various fields.

法定代表人：刘佑成（董事长）

地址：中国南京市中山路129号中南国际大厦24-25楼　邮编（Post Code）：210005

电话（Tel）：0086-25-4729240, 4718814

传真（Fax）：0086-25-4710661

电子邮箱（E-mail）：cni.ltd@jlonline.com

广东省清远化工机械医药保健品进出口公司

Qingyuan Chemical Industry, Machinery, Medicing, Pharmaceutical and Health Products Import and Export of Guangdong

广东省清远化工机械医药保健品进出口公司是1988年4月12日经广东省外经贸委批准，国家外经贸部审定的专业进出口公司。主营化工原料产品、机械设备、电子电器、仪器、仪表、运输工具、中西药材及原料、保健品、五金矿产、轻工业品、服装、纺织品等进出口业务。

十多年来，我公司的进出口贸易得到迅速扩大和发展，从成立初期年进出口贸易额五十多万美元发展到现在的年进出口贸易额六千多万美元。在经贸部发表的中国进出口总额最大的500家企业中，97年名列第274位。我公司在对外贸易经营过程中将“质量保证、信誉至上”作为企业的一贯原则。同时，我公司连年被市政府评为“重合同、守信用”企业，还被评为省、市外经贸系统先进企业。

公司奉行诚实、守信的原则，同国内外客商开展商贸合作。

法人代表、总经理：潘小勇

Qingyuan Chemicals Machinery Medicines and Health Products I/E Co. of Guangdong is a professional import and export company apprvoed by the Ministry of Foreign Trade and Economic Co-operation and was founded on April 12, 1988, mainly engaging in import and export of chemicals, raw material, machinery equipment, electronic and electric appliances, instrument, apparatus, transportation vehicles, Chinese and western medicine and raw material, health products, metals and mineral, light industrial products, garments and textiles, etc.

Since the past more than 10 years our company's import and export value has been fast increased and developed. The total import and export value of our company inereases from the foundation's more than U.S. dollars fifty thousand a year, to nowadays more than U.S. dollars sixty million a year. In 1997 the total import and export value of our company ranks 274 among the top 500 foreign trade companies of China. We keep always the "Guarantee quality and quantity, credit and reputation be the first" as our consistent principle during our foreign trade and business. For many years on end, our company has been appraised as the enterprise of "Laying Stress on Contracts and Keeping their Promise" by Municipal Government, and as the outstanding unit in the departments of the province and the city's foreign economic and trading organization.

Our company will always be honest and keep its word in the commercial cooperation with domestic and overseas customers.

公司办公大楼

法人代表：潘小勇

Legal Representative：Pan XiaoYong

地址：广东省清远市新城五号区17幢2楼

Add：2/F 17 Building, District 5, New City, QingYuan, Guangdong Province

邮编（Post Code）：511515

电话（Tel）：0763-3365750　传真（Fax）：0763-3365650

科教兴院　走向世界

——迈向新世纪的北京市建筑设计研究院

北京市建筑设计研究院成立于1949年10月1日，是一家以设计大型综合民用建筑为主并享有对外经营权的设计、科研单位。1998年12月正式通过ISO9001质量体系认证。其代表作品有：人民大会堂、民族文化宫、北京饭店、国家奥林匹克体育中心及亚运村、国际金融中心、首都机场新航站楼等，并与境外建筑事务所合作设计了长富宫中心、中国工商银行总行、东方广场、恒基中心等一批较有影响的建筑。

北京市建筑设计研究院从50年代就开始援外工程设计，积累了丰富的设计经验，已建成和在建的援外项目有数十项，如摩洛哥体育中心、突尼斯青年之家、扎伊尔人民宫、加蓬议会大厦、多哥洛美体育场、马达加斯加塔那那利佛体育馆、孟加拉国际会议中心等。

北京市建筑设计研究院以科教兴院为方针，以追求高品质的建筑设计为目标，愿竭诚为海内外客户提供优良的设计与服务。

Beijing Institute of Architectural Design and Research was set up on October 1st, 1949. It is a big comprehensive design and research unit socializing in civil architecture and having the right to do business in foreign countries. It was listed as the No.1 civil architectural design unit of "the top one hundred comprehensive strong geological survey and design units of China" in the evaluation in 1992 made by the Ministry of Construction and the State Statistics Bureau. The Institute was formally given certification of ISO9001, Representative works include the Great Hall of People, Minzo Cultural Palace. Beijing Hotel, the National Olympic Sports Center and village, International Finance Center, New Terminal Building of the Capital Airport, and other prominent buildings like Changfugong Center, Industry and Commerce Bank of China, Oriental Plaza, Hengji Center in cooperation with foreign architectural firms.

The Institute has undertaken designs of foreign aid projects since 50s and gained rich design experiences. Dozens of foreign aid projects have been completed or are under way. Among them are Morocco Sports Center, Tunisia Youth Center, Zaire People's Palace, Gabon Parliament Building, Togo Lome Stadium, Madagascar Tananarive Gymnasium and Bangladesh International Convention Center.

The Institute follows the principle of vitalizing the Institute with science and education, pursue high quality architectural designs and sincerely provides excellent services for home and foreign customers.

单位：北京市建筑设计研究院
BEIJING INSTITUTE OF ARCHITECTURAL DESIGN & RESEARCH. (BIAD)
地址：北京市西城区南礼士路62号
邮编 (Post Code)：100045
Add：No. 62 Nanlishi Road, Western District Beijing, China
电话 (Tel)：010-68011155
传真 (Fax)：010-68034041
网址 (Web)：http ://www.biad.com.cn
E-mail：biad@mx.cei.gov.cn

中国航空器材进出口总公司

CHINA AVIATION SUPPLIES IMPORT & EXPORT CORPORATION

中国航空器材进出口总公司是专门从事民用航空产品进出口业务的贸易公司。经营的范围有民用飞机、发动机及其零备件，机场设备和各种安全保障设施，民用航空相关的各种工业产品和原材料，并办理产品的租赁、送修、寄售、展览、表演、咨询、人员培训，以及合资经营、合作生产、加工装配业务。年进出口总额20多亿美元。

公司在全国各地及国外有关地区设有分支机构，与众多的国家和地区的厂商保持着广泛的业务联系和密切的合作关系。自一九八零年以来，先后进口了各种民用飞机500多架，以及大量的通信、导航、空中交通管制、气象测报、特种车辆等安全保障和机场配套设施。出口额也有较大幅度的增长。在经贸部发表的中国进出口额最大的500家企业中，96年名列第12位，97年名列第5位，98年名列第13位，99年名列第5位。除各类航空产品不断出口到有关的国家和地区外，非航空产品的出口近年来也有一定的发展，公司出口的家用电器、服装等，国外客商有较高的评价。同时，公司还与国内有关单位合作，为国外多家飞机和发动机生产厂家转包生产零部件，并开发研制国内急需的航空产品。

公司与波音和空中客车公司合作，相继在北京首都机场建立了大型零备件供应服务中心，与GE、罗罗、普惠等航空发动机生产厂家以及其它有关生产厂家也合作开展了零备件寄售业务，实行不间断服务，保障供应。从而有效地改进了产品的售后服务工作，同时对保证航空公司的飞机安全正常飞行，也起到了积极的作用。

公司还与空中客车公司合作，在北京首都机场建立了飞行模拟机培训中心，为航空公司飞行人员和乘务人员的培训提供了良好的条件。

总经理：白志坚

CHINA AVIATION SUPPLIES IMPORT & EXPORT CORPORATION (CASC) is a trading company specializing in the import and export of the civil aviation products, with an annual turnover of more than 2 billion dollars. Its business scope covers commerical aircraft, engines and spare parts, ground support equipment and facilities as well as the civil aviation related raw materials and their products. It is also engaged in leasing, repair, consignment, exhibition, demo flights, consulting, personnel training, joint ventures, industrial cooperation, manufacturing and assembling.

With a network of branches and representative offices at home and abroad, CASC maintains a wide and cooperative business relationship with suppliers in many countries and regions. Since 1980 when it was established, CASC has imported more than 500 commercial aircraft and wide range of ground support equipment, including communications, navigation aids, ATC systems, weather observation and forecast systems and special vehicles etc. In addition, a big increase has been made in its export business. While continuing to export aviation prdoucts abroad, other products such as home electrical appliances and garments are also well received by overseas customers. CASC has been actively involved not only in the industrial cooperation with leading aircraft and engine manufacturers through offset programs, but also in research and development of the aviation equipment badly needed by the domestic market.

In cooperation with Airbus, Boeing, GE, R.R and PWA, CASC has established spares support service centers and bonded warehouses at the Beijing Capital Airport. By providing the clock round services, these centers and stores have helped to improve the after sale product support, and have played a very important role in respect of flight safety and regularity.

A training center equipped with flight simulators has been jointly established by CASC and Airbus Industrie, which provides excellent training facilities both for pilots and flight attendants.

中国国际贸易中心 中国与世界相汇之地

China World Trade Center Where China Meets The World

在浩瀚精彩的千年皇城，你可以体味到至远的古老与至新的现代，依稀的城郭与清晰的楼宇交织着万众长久的瞩目。都城，一段挥之不去的情节中，又续写着另一座理想之城一中国国际贸易中心的城中故事。

由古老的京城深入，叩开未来时代的城门。中国国际贸易中心豁然展现：国际甲级写字楼支持商业发展，现代展览中心透视当代前沿风采，星级酒店带来尊贵级至善享受，国际公寓演绎温馨家居内涵，购物商场时尚潮流全面登陆，东西方千种佳肴美馔任君浅呷品啖，国际会议中心汇集各国精英畅所言论，娱乐设施丰富齐全，更有室内水冰场独树一帜、情趣盎然。

城中之城，万千包容。您所探寻与期待的未来体验就在中国国际贸易中心……

Beijing,a city built on the past, is now taking its rightful place as a city of the future. A place where ancient city walls rub shoulders with sparkling new office towers. And in amongst this perfect mix of the old and the new ,towers the China World Trade Center,a proud testament to Beijing's progress.

Within its shimmering walls, spacious offices are equipped with intelligent equipment systems to help ensure the efficiency of your business.A modern exhibition center and luxury hotels are on hand to provide every facility for modern commerce. Our international apartments boast amenities of the very highest global standards.Inside our luxury shopping mall you'll find elements of taste and style from across the globe. A galaxy of restaurants provides every imaginable cuisine from the four cormers of the world.

Unlock the secrets of Beijing's modern age, discover the future at China World Trade Center,a veritable city within a city.

中国国际贸易中心 中国北京建国门外大街一号 邮编 100004 电话 (8610)65052288 网址 http: // www.cwtc.com

China World Trade Center NO.1 JianGuoMenWai Avenue Beijing 100004,China TEL: (8610)65052288 http://www.cwtc.com

中国安徽国际经济技术合作公司

China Anhui Corporation for International Techno-Economic Cooperation

法人代表：董苏皖
Chairman of the Broad,
General Manager:
Mr. Dong Suwan

中国安徽国际经济技术合作公司于1982年经国务院批准成立，直属安徽省政府领导的国有大型外经贸企业。

公司本着平等互利的原则，采取灵活多样的经营方式，主营国际承包工程、外派劳务及商品进出口贸易。兼营房地产开发及工程监理、设计、咨询等，在国内外先后承建了60多项大中型工程，并向世界80多个国家派出大批工程管理专家及劳务人员，与各国政府、企业进行广泛的经济技术合作。

公司正着手建立现代企业制度，逐步朝国际化、集团化目标迈进。

China Anhui Corporation for International Techno-Economic Cooperation (CAITEC)a large state-owned enterprise,was founded in Dec, 1982, under the approval of the State Council of China and led directly by people's government of Anhui Province, which mainly deals with contracting overseas engineering projects and providing labor service besides running real estate and providing design, supervision and consultant for engineering projects.

CAITEC is engaged in various forms of international economic and technical cooperation and trade with foreign governments,enterprises following the principle of equal ity and mutual benefit and adopting the flexible operating means.CAITEC has unde rtaken over 60 large and medium engineering projects at home and abroad and dispatched a large number of management experts for engineering and skilled works for more than 80 countries.

CAITEC is seeking to establish the modern enterprise mode and striding forward as an internationalized and group formated enterprise.

地址：安徽合肥市琥珀山庄绿岛大厦北座
邮编：230061
电话：0551-2840979 2843049 2840975
传真：0551-2840990 2840991
电子信箱：caiteczb@mail.hf.ah.cn

Address: North block,Ludao Building, Huposhanzhuang, Hefei, Anhui, P.R. China
Zpi Code: 230061
Tel: 0551-2840979 2843049 2840975
Fax: 0551-2840990 2840991
E-mail: caiteczb@mail.hf.ah.cn

鞍山市对外建筑工程承包（集团）公司

ANSHAN OVERSEAS CONSTRUCTION CONTRACTING GROUP CORPORATION

鞍山市对外建筑工程承包(集团)公司是经中华人民共和国外经贸部和建设部批准的具有外经权的国家施工总承包一级企业，注册资金1.68亿元人民币。集团公司下设20个企、事业单位，有国家授予专业技术职称的人员1387名。在勘察设计方面，有国家一级资质的鞍山建筑设计院，在建筑施工方面，有以5个国家一级施工企业为代表的15家建筑施工、装饰装修企业，具有机电安装、建筑构配件生产、机械制造等综合承包能力。目前，集团公司为扩大国际经济合作领域广交天下朋友而努力，相继在莫桑比克、澳大利亚、德国建立了分公司，并与南非、泰国、菲律宾、柬埔寨、俄罗斯、冰岛、日本等国家的合作伙伴建立了友好合作关系。集团公司愿为国际经济的持续发展奉献自己的力量。

地址：中国·辽宁·鞍山市铁东区爱民街1号
Address：No. 1, Aimin Street Tiedong District Anshan, Liaoning Province, P.R.China
电话 (Tel)：0086-412-2244432
传真 (Fax)：0086-412-2244238
网址 (web address)：http://www.waijian.com
E-mail：aswj@waijian.com

Anshan Municipal overseas Constructional Project Contracting Corp. (Group) is both a 1st class state major contractor for constructional projects, approved by the Ministry of Construction of the People's Republic of China, and a company with the right to do business overseas, approved by the Ministry of foreign Trade and Economic Cooperation of the People's Republic of China. The registered bankroll is 168 million of Renminbi Yuan. Under this company there are 20 businesses and institutions and staffed with 1387 persons entitled by the state with technical professional titles. In the prospecting and design it has Anshan Construction Design and Research Institute with 1st state qualifications and quality. In the building constructional work it has 15 constructing and decorational design and embellishment firms, including 5 1st-class state constructing firms, with comprehensive capacity to contract projects such as erection of mechanical and electric equipment, and manufacture of constructional structural members and constructional machinery and others.

Today, this group company is working hard for broadening the field for international cooperation and making friends extensively in the world. The corporation has set up branch corporations in, Mozambique, Australia, and Germany. Similarly, establishing the relationship of friendly cooperation with the international partners in some country of South Africa, Thailand, the Philippines and the Cambodia, the Confederation of Russia, Iceland and Japan thus. This group company is willing to commit itself to the permanent development in the international economy with great efforts.

中国云南国际经济技术合作公司

中国云南国际经济技术合作公司于1984年6月12日经外经贸部批准成立，是云南省政府直接领导的大型外经贸企业。近年来先后跻身于我国大型服务行业之列和大型外经企业之列。

公司的经营范围：对外承包工程、对外劳务合作、执行中国政府下达的援外任务、开展国际贸易、在国内外兴办独资或合资企业。

十六年来，我公司先后在40个国家实施了140余个 承包工程、劳务合作等项目，均取得了圆满成功。

Set up on June 12, 1984 with approval from the State Council, China Yunnan Corporation for International Techno-Economic Cooperation, is a large foreign trade enterprise affiliated directly to Yunnan Provincial People's govemment. In recent years, the corporation has maintained its position in China's top 500 service enterprises and top 50 enterprises engaged in foreign trade and economic cooperation.

The business scope of this corporation covers contracting of overseas engineering projects, launching of labour cooperation projects with foreign countries, fulfilling foreign aid tasks assigned by the Central Government, handling of imports and exports, and running of exclusively-funded or joint ventures at home or in foreign countries.

In the past 16 years, this corporation has successfully executed over 140 projects in 40 countries, such as contracting of overseas engineering projects, launching of labour cooperation projects, etc.

公司总部地址：中国·云南·昆明市春城路202号　邮编 (Postcode)：650041
Head office：No.202 Chun Cheng Road, Kunming, China
电话 (Tel)：0086-871-3545885, 3554520　传真 (Fax)：0086-871-3547663
电子信箱 (E-mail)：yietc@public.km.yn.cn

抚顺对外建设经济合作（集团）股份有限公司

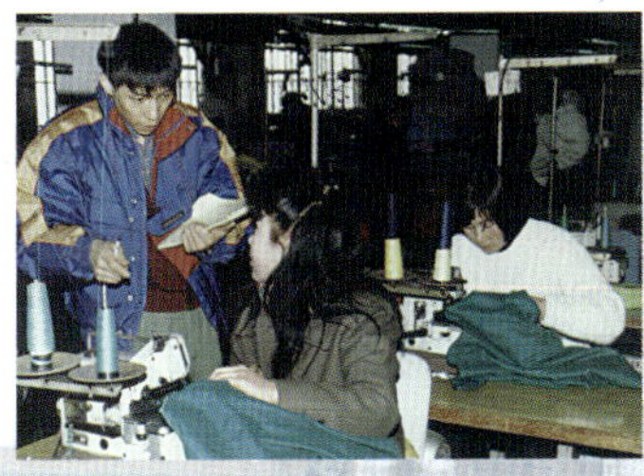

本公司是经国家外经贸部批准具有国际工程承包、劳务合作及对外贸易资格的大型企业。自一九八二年成立以来，承接实施了境内外工业、民用、城市供排水、道路、桥梁、机场、码头等建设工程，先后与20多个国家开展了经济技术及贸易合作，向30多个国家和地区派出各类劳务人员2.6万余人次，建立了较高信誉。

本公司将本着"平等互利、共同发展"和"守约、保持、薄利、重义"的原则，更多地结交海内外朋友，并与其进行广泛合作。

Fushun International Construction And Economic Cooperation (Group) Co., Ltd. (FICC) is a comprehensive enterprise for foreign economic & trade business and capable for undertaking all sorts of projects both at home and abroad---factories, bridges, airports, seaports, industrial & domestic structures and rehabilitation works. Since its founding in 1982, it has conducted technical and trade cooperation with more than 20 companies from different countries, sent about 26,000 workers to more than 30 countries and established good reputation.

On the principle of "equality and mutual benefit, common development, abiding by contracts, assuring quality, small profits and valuing the sense of obligation", FICC will associate with domestic and overseas friends and conduct business with them.

地址：中国抚顺市凤翔路41号
Add：41, Fengxiang Rd, Fushun. P.R. China
邮编（Post Code）：113008　　电话（Tel）：0086-413-2423784　　传真（Fax）：0086-413-2427012

中国广东对外劳务经济合作公司

中国广东对外劳务经济合作公司于一九七九年成立。业务包括对外劳务合作、为外国及港澳台企业提供雇员、进出口贸易、对外承包工程等。成立至今已向世界73个国家和地区派送各行业各类劳务人员十几万人，向外国、港澳台在粤企业提供众多外企雇员和综合性服务。

一九九九年，公司的外派劳务和外企服务业务继续稳步发展，业绩继续居全国同行前列。

Founded in 1979, CHINA GUANGDONG CORPORATION FOR FOREIGN LABOUR & ECONOMIC COOPERATION, mainly engages in the international labour service cooperation, supplying staff members, for representative offices run by Taiwan, Hongkong, Macau and foreign countries, and import/export trading, foreign project contracting, etc. Since its establishment, the Corp. has already sent more than 100,000 labours and professionals of all kinds of trades to 73 countries and regions, and provided thousands of employees with various services to the foreign enterprises in Guangdong. It has been listed by the State Authority according to its ourstanding achievement among "the top 500 Service Enterprises in China", "the top 100 Enterprises in Contracting and Foreign Labour Service", and "the top 200 Transnational Enterprises."

In 1999, the Corp. remain in top rank of the trade with stead development in the field of international labour service cooperation and providing service for foreign enterprises in Guangdong.

公司地址：广东省广州市麓景路7号东四楼　　邮编：510091
Add：No. 7 East Building lujing Road, GuangZhong City, GuangDong Province, China　　Post Code：510091
电话（Tel）：020-83573888　　传真（Fax）：020-83573575

内蒙古进出口贸易公司

内蒙古进出口贸易公司成立于1980年是经国家对外经济贸易部和内蒙古人民政府批准成立的经贸实体。

本公司目前主要经营：自营和代理除国家组织统一联合经营的16种出口商品和国家实行核定公司经营的14种进口商品以外的商品及技术的进出口业务。开展“三来一补”进料加工业务。经营对销贸易和转口贸易。经国家财政部批准，享有500万美元以下外国政府贷款项目采购资格。本公司在满洲里设有分公司。具有边境小额贸易经营权。

Approved by the Government of Inner Mongolia and the Ministry of Foreign Economic Relations & Trade of P.R.C., the Import & Export Trading Corp. of inner Mongolia Autonomous Region (IMIECO) was established in 1980.

IMIECO deals in all kinds of import and export business for commodity and technology that have got state permits. We undertake processing with materials and samples supplied, assmbling with component parts supplied, compensation trade, counter trade and entrepot trade. Approved by the Ministry of Finance, IMIECO is qualified for a loan of less than $5 million from foreign governments for purchases. IMIECO has its branch office in Manzhouli. IMIECO also has managerial authority for frontier trade.

IMIECO is willing to cooperate with customers from all circles in the world on the basis of mutual benefit.

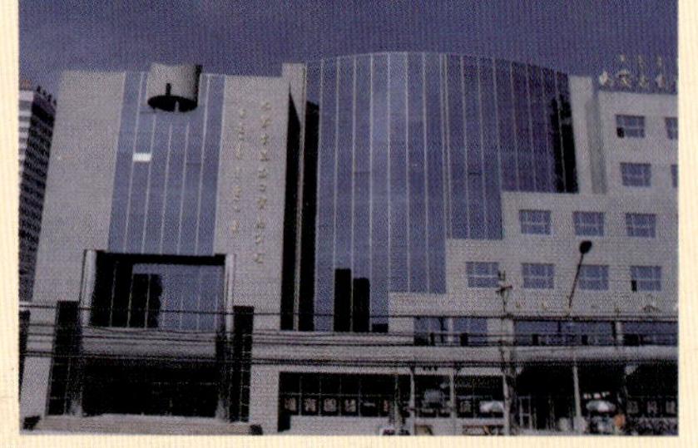

地址：中国呼和浩特公园西路26号　　邮编（Post Code）：010020
Add：26, Gong Yuan Road W. Huhhot, China
电话（Tel）：0471-6937613　　传真（Fax）：0471-6966824
E-mail：imieco@sina.com

陕西省畜产进出口公司

总经理：胡少华

陕西省畜产进出口公司是国有对外贸易企业。创建于五十年代初，从事畜产品经营已有近五十年的历史，已经同世界上30多个国家和地区的商家建立了良好的贸易关系。公司地处畜牧业、矿产、土特产等自然资源丰富，高等院校较多，科技实力雄厚的陕西省。当前适逢西部大开发的历史机遇，必将为开展各类贸易提供优越条件和广阔的发展空间。

公司主要经营羊绒、羊毛及其绒毛制品类；裘、革皮及其制品类；地毯类；羽绒及其制品类；猪鬃及其制品类；细尾毛类；肠衣及肥饲料类；粮油食品类；医药保健品类；纺织轻工类；土特产品类；工艺品类；五金矿产、有色金属类；机电产品类；化工产品类等进出口业务和来料加工业务。

公司现有员工80名，设三个经营部，三个下属企业，二个境外企业，一个中外合资企业。公司坚持“质量为本，信誉至上，平等互利，优质服务”的经营宗旨，采取灵活多样的贸易形式。

竭诚欢迎海内外朋友，洽谈业务，共谋发展。

As a State-Owned Professional Foreign Trade Company founed in earlier 1950's, China Shaanxi Animal By-Products I/E Corp. has engaged in animal by-products for about 50 years. From the frist beginning till now, the company has already established the trade relationship with nearly 30 countries and regions. Locating in Shaanxi Province, where are spread all over higher institutions being vast in scientific knowledge ability, and with abundant natural resource of animal husbandry, minerals local and special products, China Shaanxi animal by-products I/E Corp. Must be undoubtedly provided with fourable conditions and broad prospects for the purpose of the various trade promotions by the historical chance of large scale development in the western area.

We are mainly importing and exporting the products such as cashmere, leather, carpet, down, fur skin and their by-products. We're also handling brush, cercus, bristles, casing for sausages, animal feedstuffs and furtilizers, medical helth care products, grain and oil products, textile, hardware and chemicals, nonferrous metal, mechanical and electrical products.

Now in the company, there are total 80 staff members and also three management department, three owned enterprises, two abroad branchs and one joint venture as well. Holding on the principle: "Quality first superior reputation and mutual peace and profit", the company will make all kind of business in flexble measures.

Sincerely cooperation and developing with the friends all over the world.

地址：西安市莲湖路37号　邮编（Post Code）：710003
电话（Tel）：0086-029-7333641
传真（Fax）：0086-029-7315332
网址（Web site）：http ://www.sxabc.com
E-mail：sabc@pudlic.xasn.cn

攀钢集团国际经济贸易总公司

Pangang Group International Economic & Trading Corporation

攀钢集团国际经济贸易总公司位于四川省攀枝花市大渡口，成立于1988年，现有员工125人，是中国钢铁钒钛生产基地－攀枝花钢铁（集团）公司经营对外贸易与国际经济合作的专业公司。公司主要经营钢轨、热轧板（卷）、冷轧板（卷）、钢管、钢球、板坯、方圆钢、五氧化二钒、钒铁、钛白粉、钛精矿等钢铁钒钛产品及生产技术的出口，冶金生产设备、备品备件、原辅材料、先进技术的进口，以及国际工程承包、对外招商引资与劳务输出。主要出口市场是东亚、东南亚、南亚、北美、欧盟等地区的数十个国家和地区。

Pangang Group International Economic & Trading Corporation, located in Dadukou, Panzhihua city, Sichuan province, is a specialized corporation of Pangang Group-China's iron & steel, vanadium & titanium processing base, engaging in foreign trade and international economic cooperation. The corporation's business scope lies: export of steel , vanadium & titanium products and its technology, including hot rolling plate(coil), cold rolling plate(coil), iron and steel finishing processing products, vanadium pentoxide, Ferro-vanadium, titanium dioxide, titanium concentrate etc.; import of equipment, spare parts, raw material and advanced technology for processing of steel, vanadium & titanium products; contacting of international projects and the labor export. The main markets of export are East Asia , Southeast Asia, South Asia, North America and EU etc.

总经理：张祖生
地址：四川省攀枝花市大渡口55号
邮政编码：617067
总经理电话：(0812) 2248893
传真：(0812) 2224083
公司成立日期：1988.1 职工人数：125
电传：611519 MIECP CN
业务电话：钢铁产品 (0812) 2236135
钒钛产品 (0812) 2236133
设备和备件进口 (0812) 2236126

General Manager : Zhang Zusheng
Vice Genertal Manager : YangJie
Add : 55.Dadukou, Panzhihua, Sichuan
Zip : 617067
Tel. of G. M. : 2248893 Fax : (0812) 2224083
Date of Set-up : Jan. 1988 Staff : 125
Telex : 611519 MIECP CN
Tel. Of Business for steel products : 2236135
for vanadium products : 2236133
for equipment and spare parts import : 2236126

攀钢集团国际经济贸易总公司历年出口创汇图

年份	1988年	1989年	1990年	1991年	1992年	1993年	1994年	1995年	1996年	1997年	1998年	1999年
	110	362	3715	5060	7235	10073	12088	14248	14113	16008	[illegible]	[illegible]

东莞福安纺织印染有限公司

Dongguan Fuan Textiles Limited is a joint venture formed between H.K. and Chinese enterprises with total investment at HK$650 million.. Its principle activities include yarn dying, knitting, fabric dying and fabric finishing. Its products are exported and well received by customers all over the world.

东莞福安纺织印染有限公司是粤港合资企业。主要生产经营优质筒子色纱、针织布及染整布，总投资额达六亿五千万港元，产品外销世界各地，在国际上享有颇高的声誉。

地址：广东省东莞市长安镇霄边大道福安纺织城
Add : Dongguan Fuan Textiles Complex, Chang An Town
电话 (Tel) : 0769-5532318 传真 (Fax) : 0769-5532005
邮编 (Post Code) : 523840

北京市针棉织品进出口集团公司

BEIJING KNITWEAR IMP. & EXP. GROUP CORP.

北京市针棉织品进出口集团公司，正式成立于1993年11月19日，其前身为北京市针棉织品进出口公司，该公司是我国首批获准经营针棉织品进出口业务的专业外贸公司之一，已有30多年的外贸经营史，是经营棉针织品、毛针织品、家用纺织品、梭织服装、轻工产品和纺织原料、辅料以及机器设备和包装物料等大宗商品的进出口企业，并拥有国内注册有效商标42枚，国外和地区注册有效商标8枚。目前集团公司的产品已经遍布世界各地。

“雪莲”牌羊绒衫是我集团公司传统出口的名牌产品，它注册于1964年，早在1981年就荣获国家金质奖，为使雪莲产品更好地走入国际市场，我集团公司先后在香港、马德里协定国、日本、美国对该商标进行了注册。雪莲商标的产品系选用优质的中国山羊绒作原料制成，具有色泽鲜艳、手感柔滑、穿着舒适及品质优良、做工精细、款式新颖等特点。

“White Birch”牌商标是使用在毛针织服装上的商标，它注册于1985年，该商标的产品是各种精纺、精纺的毛针织品、毛针织时装，其原料有驼羊毛、马海毛、纯羊毛、羊仔毛、雪兰毛等，具有穿着轻盈、舒适、美观、雅致、保暖性强等特点。

“费神点”牌商标是近几年我集团公司新注册的商标，它使用在棉针织服装上，“费神点”牌商标的产品是各种纱支、面料制成的园领衫、T恤衫、运动套装以及各种针织服装，其特点为款式多样，品种繁多、配色和谐、品质优良。

“STAR”牌商标是使用在毛巾类中的商标，它注册于1984年，“STAR”牌商标的产品是由单纱、双纱、螺旋等质地的各种漂白、素色、印花、绣花、提花、彩条、彩格、缎档、产品制成，该商标的产品特点柔软、蓬松、舒适，既可用于餐前餐后，也适用于劳动、旅游等。

总经理：戴秀芳
副总经理：胡明智、宋红英
副总经理：郭世明（兼针织品分公司经理）
副总经理：赵俊波（兼毛针织品分公司经理）
总经理助理：张九常（兼家用纺织品分公司经理）

地址：北京市朝阳区和平里小黄庄北街2号
Add：No.2 Xiaohuangzhuang Beijie Hepingli, Chaoyang District, Beijing, China
电话（Tel）：84281610　传真（Fax）：84281896
E-mail：knit@public.bta.net.cn　Web Site：http ://www.knitgroup.com

Inaugurated on November 19, 1993, the Beijing Knitwear Imp. & Exp. Group Corp.(BKGC), whose predecessor was the Beijing Knitwear Imp. & Exp. Corp., is China's first professional foreign trade company ratified for managing knitgoods import and export business. It has a history of foreign trade management for over three decades and one of China's top 500 enterprises in terms of import and export volumes, an enterprise importirting and exporting large quantities of such commodities as cotton knitwear, sweaters, home textiles, shuttle-knit dresses, light industrial products, textile raw and auxiliary materials, machinery and packaging materials, boasting 42 effective licensed trademarks at home and eight others abroad or on a regional basis. Now our products have gained access into all corners of the world.

Beijing cashmere sweaters under the registered brandname Snow-Lotus are our famous traditional export commodities. It was licensed in 1964. Products of the trademark had scored the State Gold Summit Prize as far back as 1981. In 1992 and 1995 the trademark was twice appraised as one of Beijint's famous trademarks. In order to promote its sales on the international market, we licensed the trademark in Hongkong, the Madrid Agreement countries, Japan and the United States. The products series of the Snow-Lotus Brand Trademark are all made of refined Chinese goat wool as raw material and are brightly colored, soft and smooth to feel, and comfortable to wear. They are of excellence in quality, exquisite workmanship and new style.

Licensed in 1985, the White Birch Brand Trademark is employed for woolen knitwear suits. Products under the trademark include delicately and coarsely-spun and-weaved woolen knitwear, with raw materials ranging from camel hair, mohair, pure wool, lamb wool to snowy orchid hair. They are light and warm, comfortable and beautiful looking, graceful.

Employed on cotton fabrics dresses, the Faistniss Brand Trademark is a newly-licensed trademark of our group company. Products under that trademark range from round-collar shirts, T-shirts, sports suits and a variety of knitwear dresses and knitwear fashions. They are of many styles and specifications, well-matched in colors, super excellence in quality.

Licensed in 1984, the Star Brand Trademark is employed on towels, whichmade of single-thread, double-yarn or spiral quality bleached, plain colored, printed, embroidered, broche, color-striped, color-latticed satins and brocades. Products under that trademark are soft, puffy and comfortable. They can be used befroe or after meals, or during labor, tourism, sports events and leisure hours.

Gereral Manager: Dai Xiufang
Deputy General Manager: Hu Mingzhi, Song Hongying
Deputy General Manager: Guo Shiming (also in charge of cotton knitwear i/e branch)
Deputy General Manager: Zhao Junbo (also in charge of woolen knitwear i/e branch)
Assistant to Gereral Manager: Zhang Jiuchang (also in charge of home textile i/b branch)

中国西安国际经济技术贸易公司

CHINA XI'AN INTERNATIONAL ECONOMIC TECHNICAL TRADE CORP.

中国西安国际经济技术贸易公司是1985年经国家外经贸部批准成立的具有对外承包工程、劳务合作及进出口贸易经营权限的外经公司。注册资金5300万人民币。1994年以来，在对外工程承包和劳务合作方面取得了较大的成绩。公司连续三年被省、市政府评为外经先进企业。

在西部大开发的今天，我们将充分利用西安及陕西人才资源优势大力开展对外劳务合作及工程承包，努力扩大进出口业务。在我国即将加入世界贸易组织的大环境下，我们致力于自身的发展，提高参与国际经济大环境的竞争意识，树立“以质量（工作质量）求生存，以信誉求发展”的经营思想，恳诚与国内外朋友共同合作，共同发展。

China xi'an International Economic Technical Trade Corp was established in 1985 with the approval of the Ministry of Foreign Economic Relation and Trade of the P.R.C. It is a corperation of foreign economic relation entitled to contracting foreign engineerings, labour cooperation and the import and export business with registered capital RMB 53,000,000.

Since 1994, it has achieved great progress in contracting foreign engineerings and labour cooperation. Our Corp was elected an advanced enterprise by the provincial and municipal governments in three consecutive years.

Today in developing the West, we will develop, with every endeavour, foreign cooperation of labour, contracting of engineerings and increase greatly the exporting business by making full use of the talent advantages in Xi'an in Shanxi Province.

Under the situation of our country's entering soon into WTO, we shall devote ourselves to self-development to raise our competition conciousness under international economic circumstances and forster the idea of running business "striving for existing by good work and for developing by prestige". We sincerely hope to cooperate with foreign friends for joint development.

公司地址：中国西安市东大街118号
Add：118Dong Da Jie Xi'an China
电话（Tel）：0086-29-7427426, 7422668
传真（Fax）：0086-29-7420734
邮编（Post Code）：710001

中华映管（福州）有限公司

CHUNGHWA PICTURE TUBES (FUZHOU) LTD.

中华映管（福州）有限公司位于福州市经济技术开发区快安延伸区，是专门从事单、彩显示管及电子枪零组件生产和销售的高新技术电子视讯企业。公司于1994年元月由台湾总公司（中华映管股份有限公司）投资设立。总投资额6亿美元，占地面积为492亩，现有员工约5000人，各期工程完成后员工总数约达8000人，年产值约12亿美元。

公司成立伊始，即秉承了华映总公司“正诚勤俭”之经营理念，发扬“创造革新、追求完美、团结合作”之企业精神，以满足客户要求为宗旨，加强新产品之研究开发，进入全方位视讯多媒体产品领域，确保品质零缺点，提高生产力，实现“世界的华映，贡献全球化”的伟大经营目标。

Chunghwa Picture Tubes (Fuzhou) Ltd. (CPTF), Located in the extended area of Kuaian District, Fuzhou Economic and Technological Development Zone, is a high-tech electronic enterprise, specialized in producing and marketing monochrome/color Cathode Ray Tube (CRT) and Electron Gun Parts.

CPTF was set up in January 1994, with total investment of 600 million US Dollars by its headquarters, Chunghwa Picture Tubes Ltd., Taiwan. It occupies 328,164 square meters with 5,000 employees. 8,000 employees andthe total annual revenue 1.2 billion US Dollars are expected when all projects are fulfilled.

Since it commenced, CPTF has carried forward the managerial philosophy of "HONESTY, INTEGRITY, INDUSTRY AND FRUALITY", developed the enterprise's spirit of "CREATION, PERFECTION, TEAMWORK" set up the mission of "meet the expectation of customers". The company has strengthened in R&D of new products to access the integrated multimedia field, maintained zero-defect quality standard, improved productivity hereby to achieve our managerial goal "Globalized CPT, of the world and for the world".

地址：福州马尾经济技术开发区快安延伸区兴业路1号　邮编（P.C）：350015
Add：Kuaian extend area. Fuzhou economic technology development zone.P.R.C.
电话（Tel）：0591-3971357　传真（Fax）：0591-3970489　网址（Web Site）：www.cptf.com.cn

重庆茧丝绸集团有限公司

CHONGQING SILK GROUP CORP., LTD.

重庆茧丝绸集团有限公司是1997年9月重庆市人民政府根据国务院国办发［1996］49号通知要求，批准成立的省级茧丝绸贸工农一体化的国有独资大型企业集团。具有经营职能和政府赋予的行业管理职能，主营丝、绸、绢、服装产品出口和统一负责组织重庆市茧丝绸的生产、经营和管理。现有资产7400万元，负债2133万元，资产负债率28.82%。经中华人民共和国对外贸易经济合作部［2000］外经贸发展审函字第1380号文批准，进出口经营范围扩大为：自营和代理各类商品及技术的进出口业务；经营进料加工和“三来一补”业务；经营转口贸易和对销贸易。公司的蚕丝类产品、丝绸面料、服装及制成品货源稳定，与国内外客户贸易信誉正在逐步增强。本着“诚实信用，互惠互利”的原则，我们愿与各商家真诚合作，共谋发展。

As per writ No.guo ban fa [1996] 49 of State Council and approved by Chongqing People Government, Chongqing Silk Group Corp., was fonded in Sep., 1997 as state-owned large scale group enterprise of provincial level which units silk trade, industry and agriculture. With the operation function and administrative function granted by the government, it deals in exportation of silk materials, fabrics, spun products, garments and it administrates the city's silk production, operation and management in united way. Today the corp., possesses RMB 74 million yuan of assets and RMB 21.33 million yuan of liabilities and its liability-assets rate is 28.82%. Approved by the writ No. [2000] wai jing mao fazhan shen han zi 1380 of MOFTEC, the corporation's foreign trade business scope was expanded as: direct and cooperative import and export assortment of products and technology; processing with imported or customer supplied materials, samples assembling with customer's parts and compensation trade; transfer and barter trade. The corporation has stable supply channal of mulberry raw silk products, silk fabrics, garments and other ready made products and is strengthening its relationship with domestic and overseas clients. On the principle of "Honesty, Faith and Mutual Benifit", the corporation is seeking sincere cooperation with clients for together development.

法人代表：薛建农

地址：中国重庆江北区建新北路72号　邮编：400020

电话：(023) 67850151　传真：(023) 67851666

宁波经济技术开发区进出口公司

宁波经济技术开发区进出口公司，是宁波经济技术开发区内享有进出口权的综合性外贸公司，在经贸部发表的中国进出口总额最大的500家企业中，98年名列第246位，99年名列第262位。

公司设有9个业务部门和四个职能部门，拥有六家下属生产企业，并经外经贸部批准投资成立了中外合资宁波志晓国际货运服务有限公司。

公司主要经营纺织品、服装、机电、化工、粮油食品、土畜产品、王金矿产、医疗器械、电子器件与设备等商品的进出口业务和国际货运业务。同时兴办中外合资、合作项目，承办技术设备引进业务。

公司本着锐意创新，竭诚合作，互惠互利的精神，愿与国内外工商界建立广泛友好的业务联系，并向您提供优秀的服务。

我们将继续采取灵活多样的贸易方式，守信用、讲诚意、重友谊。我们热忱希望与世界各地更多的朋友们在平等互利的基础上发展多种形式的贸易和建立更广泛的经贸合作关系，为繁荣世界经济作出贡献。

NingBo Economic & Technical Development Zone Import & Export Corporation is a comprehensive trading company, which has been one of the top 500 I/E corporation of China for four consecutive years.

We consist of nine depts and hold six manufacturers. Approved by the ministry of foreign trade & economic cooperation, we established a JV, Ningbo Zhishao international forwarding co., Ltd.

We main cover textiles, garments, machinery, chemical, foodstuffs, native products & animal by-products, metals & mineral, electronic components & equipment, medical instruments and international transportation. We also deal sino-foreign co-investment, cooperation and introduction of advanced technology and equipment from abroad.

We rely our development of exclusive and friendly business relation with commercial circle domestic and overseas on our company spirit-active trial, sincere cooperation and mutual benefit, to provide you best service you can hope.

You are always welcome to us.

地址：宁波长春路35号银河大厦7-8楼　Add：7-8/F Galaxy tower No.35 Changchun Road Ningbo P.R.China

电话（Tel）：0574-7304387, 7322412, 7300325　传真（Fax）：0574-7295204, 7328092

总经理：陈伟明　General Manager：Cheng Weiming　副总经理：郁善鸣　Vice General Manager：Yu Shanming

阅历岁月长卷，凝固时光短暂